Small Business Management

Launching and Growing
Entrepreneurial Ventures

Justin G. Longenecker
Baylor University

Carlos W. Moore
Baylor University

J. William Petty
Baylor University

Leslie E. Palich
Baylor University

14e

SOUTH-WESTERN
CENGAGE Learning

Australia • Brazil • Canada • Mexico • Singapore • Spain • United Kingdom • United States

SOUTH-WESTERN
CENGAGE Learning

Small Business Management: Launching and Growing Entrepreneurial Ventures, 14e
Justin G. Longenecker, Carlos W. Moore, J. William Petty, Leslie E. Palich

VP/Editorial Director:
Jack W. Calhoun

Editor-in-Chief:
Melissa Acuna

Senior Acquisitions Editor:
Michele Rhoades

Senior Developmental Editor:
Susanna C. Smart

Editorial Assistant:
Ruth Belanger

Senior Marketing Manager:
Clint Kernen/Kimberly Kanakes

Senior Marketing Communications Manager:
Jim Overly

Content Project Manager:
Jacquelyn K Featherly

Technology Project Manager:
Kristen Meere

Senior Manufacturing Coordinator:
Doug Wilke

Production House/Compositor:
Lifland et al., Bookmakers/
ICC Macmillan Inc.

Copyeditor:
Jeanne Yost

Printer:
Transcontinental
Beauceville, Quebec

Senior Art Director:
Tippy McIntosh

Cover and Internal Designer:
Grannan Graphic Design Ltd.

Cover Images:
PhotoAlto Agency/Getty Images;
Youngblood's Books

Photography Manager:
John Hill

Photo Researcher:
Rose Alcorn

Library of Congress Control Number:
2007938373

For more information about our
products, contact us at:

Cengage Learning
Customer & Sales Support

1-800-354-9706

South-Western
5191 Natorp Boulevard
Mason, OH 45040
USA

In Remembrance

Justin G. Longenecker
Professor Emeritus of Management
Hankamer School of Business
Baylor University
May 4, 1917–September 14, 2005

Carlos W. Moore
Edwin Streetman Professor of Marketing
Hankamer School of Business
Baylor University
February 3, 1943–May 27, 2007

It is with deep sadness that we inform you of the deaths of our two co-authors and dear friends. We cannot put into words the loss we feel. Their deaths cannot be measured by their absence in revising this book. They were not only our colleagues, but also our confidants and mentors. They were tremendous role models for us and for literally thousands of individuals who knew and loved them. In this book, we encourage you to consider the legacy you will leave at the end of your entrepreneurial journey. Justin and Carlos left a legacy that few can ever dream of leaving. They will be missed for many years to come.

In working with Justin and Carlos for over a decade, we have developed a shared vision about the book. So, while the specific responsibilities have changed for this edition, the dream of helping others become entrepreneurs lives on. Be assured that we will continue to build on the great legacy of this textbook. Justin and Carlos would be disappointed with anything less, and we are not about to let them down.

Brief Contents

Contents

Part 2

Part 3

Developing the New Venture Business Plan   149

Part 5

Managing Growth in the Small Business 471

Part 6

Understanding What the Numbers Mean 571

Preface

Welcome to the 14th edition of *Small Business Management: Launching and Growing Entrepreneurial Ventures*! Textbooks rarely survive in the marketplace for more than five or six editions—much less 14—but this one has. This edition of the book represents more than four decades of writing about small business. Why has this book not only survived but been a market leader for so long? We believe there is one reason—*commitment*! Although the author team has changed some over the years, there has been one constant: We have always measured our success by the effectiveness of our presentation to you, the reader. And though you may not have selected this textbook yourself, we consider you to be our customer nonetheless. We make every effort to be sensitive to the student's learning needs. In fact, we have taken your point of view into consideration when writing each chapter and have gone to great lengths to make the material informative, as well as easy to understand and interesting to read.

In writing *Small Business Management,* we celebrate the initiative of small business owners everywhere; they are our heroes. And among them is Sharonda Youngblood, whose new business is featured on the cover of the book.

As a mother of three and a teacher of information literacy at Sullivan University in Louisville, Kentucky, Youngblood became concerned about challenges her students were facing, including the rising costs of textbooks. Thinking "There must be a better way," she arrived at the concept of a community-friendly bookstore, Youngblood's Books, where customers would have the option to trade in previously read books for store credit. Although she thought she had a great idea, Youngblood wisely did extensive research and visited bookstores in other areas of the state. She said, "I was putting my own money into the venture, and I wanted to make certain that I was not doing something I would regret. Some of the bookstore owners were so encouraging and gave me some great ideas. I even bought some of their inventory." Youngblood's Books has relocated from its original site to a new and larger building, but still maintains its inviting, community-centered atmosphere.

Small Business Management is a tribute to all the Sharonda Youngbloods of the world, entrepreneurs who want to build something of meaning. We believe passionately that this book can make a truly significant contribution to the work and lives of entrepreneurs, and we commit to giving you our best.

Follow Your Dreams

Entrepreneurs need to dream BIG dreams—to see opportunities where others see only failures. Did you know that Benjamin Franklin was admonished to stop experimenting with electricity? It's true! Trying to improve on the reliable and perfectly functional oil lamp was considered an absurd waste of time. And even Thomas Edison, a shrewd entrepreneur in his own right, tried to discourage his friend Henry Ford from working on his daring idea of building a motorcar. Convinced the idea was worthless, Edison advised Ford to give up this wild fancy and work for him instead. Ford, however, remained steadfast and tirelessly pursued his dream. Progress was slow. Although his first attempt produced a vehicle without a reverse gear, Ford knew he could make it happen—and, of course, he did. People like Franklin and Ford dreamed big dreams and dared to do great things, and now we all benefit from their achievements. Can you imagine a world without electric lights and automobiles? The contributions of these two entrepreneurs have been immeasurable!

This book lays out, in step-by-step fashion, the knowledge and insights needed to lead and manage a small business. Simultaneously, it focuses on a much broader concern: the pursuit of entrepreneurial dreams. Entrepreneurs build businesses to fulfill dreams—for themselves, for their families, for their employees, and for their communities. When we write about small companies, therefore, we are writing about individuals whose business lives have had an impact on a wide range of people.

The aim of the 14th edition of *Small Business Management* is to provide instruction and guidance that will greatly improve your odds of success as you take your own entrepreneurial journey. It is our hope that the information we present in this book—and in the tools and ancillaries that accompany it—will support the varied goals of those seeking independent business careers, either directly or indirectly through the wise counsel of the instructor who has selected this book.

There has never been a more exciting time to be an entrepreneur! If you are committed strongly enough to your dream, in one creative way or another you will overcome all of the obstacles that lie ahead. New ventures can create tremendous personal value for both entrepreneurs and the investors who back them with time and money. New ventures can also protect and improve quality of life by creating jobs and providing new products and services to those who value them.

Our best wishes to you for a challenging and successful learning experience!

What's New?

A central purpose of this revision of *Small Business Management* is to present current, relevant content in unique and interesting ways. When we started writing, we found many innovative ideas, trends, companies, and people to write about.

With an abundance of real-world examples to keep both first-time readers and readers of earlier editions totally engaged, this edition of *Small Business Management* offers plenty that's new.

> **How They See It: Getting Started**
>
> Sara Blakely
>
> Getting started is the toughest part. I always tell aspiring entrepreneurs who have a business idea to keep their idea to themselves in the beginning. I didn't tell anyone my idea for footless pantyhose, not even friends or family. Everyone knew I was working on an invention, but they didn't know what it was until I had already invested a year of my time.
>
> This is important because so many people stop dead in their tracks because someone, out of love, brings up 50 things for them to worry about. The minute you put your idea out there, you're forced to justify it. A year after working on my prototype for SPANX footless pantyhose, I told everyone my idea and was met with a lot of questions and skepticism. People asked, "Is that really such a good idea? The big guys will just knock you off." If I hadn't already invested a year, I might not have started SPANX.

■ We are excited about a new feature that we believe you will enjoy immensely. In our work over the years, we have come to know many entrepreneurs who, we believe, represent the best of what entrepreneurship is about. We wanted you to have the benefit of sharing some of their life experiences. So, we formed a group of entrepreneurs of the type you would want to go to when you needed advice. We call them our "go-to team." We draw on their experiences to complement what we present in the chapters. You will be hearing from your teacher (if you are enrolled in a course) and the authors of this text, but you will also learn from the wisdom and seasoned insights of these talented individuals who have spent many years in the entrepreneurial arena. Their comments will appear in the How They See It boxes throughout the book.

■ Numerous updated Living the Dream features capture entrepreneurs in action as they face the challenges of small business and entrepreneurship. To add depth to these features and ensure accuracy, the authors corresponded or had personal conversations with many of the entrepreneurs profiled.

video case 10

■ Thirteen new video-enriched cases are available with the 14th edition of *Small Business Management*. These new cases, which draw on the resources of the popular PBS television series *Small Business School*, bring together high-interest video segments and in-text case material. Case instruction, augmented by video filmed on location in such diverse businesses as Mo's Chowder, Le Travel Store, and Biolife LLC, makes studying effective small business management all the more interesting.

■ Chapter 6 offers an expanded presentation of how to write a business plan. In addition to describing how to write a plan, we provide more insight into the purposes of a business plan and how to determine the type and amount of planning that make sense for you as an entrepreneur.

- Understanding and using financial information is frequently difficult for small business owners and students alike. Some of our readers are uncomfortable with the topic or feel intimidated by it. However, given their importance in managing a business, financial statements can be ignored only at your own peril. Accordingly, we give careful attention to the matter, always striving to make the issues in finance more understandable, even intuitive.

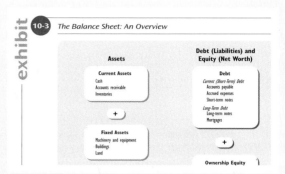

Achieving Your Best

Small Business Management is organized to help students and future entrepreneurs achieve success in whatever field they choose. The wide spectrum of content, applications, cases, graphics, stories, and other details offered in *Small Business Management* has assisted many small business entrepreneurs in making their dreams come true. With a focus on learning, our features emphasize hands-on activities that capture student interest and guarantee practical knowledge.

- ***Unique Spotlight Features.*** The chapter-opening In the Spotlight and In the Video Spotlight features profile an amazing collection of business owners, whose unique insights into how to start, run, and grow a business will help readers identify and explore the full range of issues facing today's business owners. Ten spotlights are video-enriched, because nothing helps students master the lessons of small business and entrepreneurship as much as seeing them put into practice.

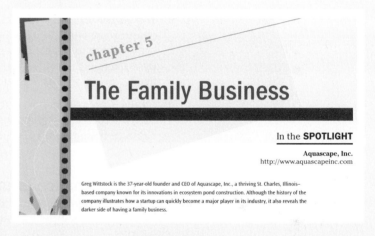

- ***Unique Support for Building a Business Plan.*** The material in Part 3, "Developing the New Venture Business Plan," is integral to learning how to develop workable plans. Closely aligned with the approaches to planning that we present in the textbook are additional business plan templates found at Small Business Management Online (http://sbmonline.swlearning.com), which can be accessed by registering the pincode that accompanies this text.

- ***Integrated Learning System.*** Our integrated learning system uses each chapter's learning objectives to give structure and coherence to the text content, study aids, and instructor's ancillaries, all of which are keyed to these objectives. The numbered objectives are introduced in the Looking Ahead section, and each is concisely addressed in the Looking Back section at the end of each chapter.

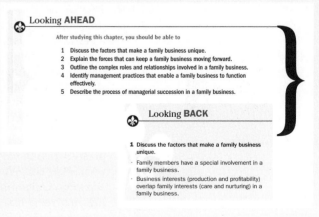

The integrated learning system also simplifies lecture and test preparation. The lecture notes in the *Instructor's Manual* are grouped by learning objective and identify the PowerPoint slides that relate to each objective. Questions in the *Test Bank* are grouped by objective as well. A correlation table at the beginning of each *Test Bank* chapter permits selection of questions that cover all objectives or that emphasize objectives considered most important.

Living the Dream   entrepreneurial challenges

Incubating a Cure for Hospital Infections

MedMined is in the business of saving lives as well as saving money for hospitals and insurance companies. By using data mining and artificial intelligence models to identify the sources of infections, it helps hospitals reduce hospital-acquired infections in patients. The company's products and services are saving, on average, about five people each week. That's a big relief for anyone who has ever been in the hospital.

The National Business Incubating Association (NBIA) awarded MedMined its Outstanding Incubator Client Award in 2002 and its Outstanding Incubator Graduate Award in 2005. MedMined's sales grew from $5,000 in 2000 to $1.2 million in 2003 [the year it "graduated" from the Office for the Advancement of Developing Industries (OADI) technology center] and $3.3 million in 2004. That's over 600-percent growth in five years. The OADI technology center incubator contributed to this growth by developing a training program for MedMined's sales force and coaching the MedMined team on how to create an effective fund-raising presentation that led to $2 million in initial venture capital funding in 2001.

MedMined outgrew the incubator and now leases the entire floor of an office building in Birmingham, Alabama. Its staff expanded from three employees in 2000 to 45 in 2005. Being an incubator client provided

■ **Living the Dream.** Practical examples from the world of small business and entrepreneurship carry both instructional and inspirational value. Living the Dream boxes appear at critical junctures throughout the chapters, refueling and refreshing chapter concepts with documented experiences of practicing entrepreneurs.

■ **Exploring the Web Exercises.** Structured Internet exercises appear at the end of every chapter. Designed to familiarize students with the best online resources for small businesses, these exercises direct students to specific websites, prompting them to perform targeted searches, analyze the effectiveness of what they find, and theorize about what could be done better. The future of technology in small businesses is wide open; these exercises go a long way toward ensuring that students will be informed about the trends to watch. A list of useful URLs, which can be found on the website for this book at academic.cengage.com/management/longenecker, provides a helpful compilation of the most informative websites for small businesses and entrepreneurs.

■ **You Make the Call Exercises.** You Make the Call situations at the end of each chapter are very popular with both students and instructors because they present realistic business situations that require examining key operating decisions. By taking on the role of a small business owner in these exercises, students get a head start in addressing the concerns of small businesses.

■ **Cases.** Cases—many new to this edition, including 13 new video cases—are available for each chapter, providing opportunities for students to apply chapter concepts to realistic entrepreneurial situations.

Updated and Enhanced Supplements

All resources and ancillaries that accompany *Small Business Management,* 14th edition, have been created to support a variety of teaching methods, learning styles, and classroom situations.

■ **Instructor's Manual.** Lecture notes in the *Instructor's Manual* are grouped by learning objective and tied to PowerPoint slides that relate to each objective. The manual also contains sources of audio/video and other instructional materials, answers to the Discussion Questions, comments on You Make the Call situations, and teaching notes for the cases. This edition's *Instructor's Manual* has been revised by James A. Roberts of Baylor University. It is available on the text's website at academic.cengage.com/management/longenecker and on the Instructor's Resource CD-ROM.

■ **Test Bank.** The *Test Bank* also has been revised by James A. Roberts of Baylor University. Questions in the *Test Bank* are grouped by learning objectives and include true/false, multiple-choice, and discussion questions. A correlation table at the beginning of each *Test Bank* chapter helps instructors select questions that cover all objectives or that emphasize objectives most important to the instructor's specific course. The *Test Bank,* in Word, is available on the text's website at academic.cengage.com/management/longenecker and on the Instructor's Resource CD-ROM.

■ **ExamView® Testing Software.** ExamView contains all of the questions in the printed *Test Bank.* This program is easy-to-use test-creation software compatible with Microsoft Windows. Instructors can add or edit questions, instructions, and answers. Questions may be selected randomly, by number, or through previewing on screen. Instructors can also create quizzes online over the Internet, a local area network (LAN), or a wide area network (WAN).

- **_PowerPoint® for Instructors._** A complete PowerPoint package is available as a lecture presentation aid. Computer-driven projection makes it easy to use these colorful images to add emphasis and interest to lectures. The PowerPoint slides, prepared by Charlie Cook of the University of West Alabama, are available both on the Instructor's Resource CD-ROM and on the password-protected instructor's website.

- **_Instructor's Resource CD-ROM._** Instructors can get quick access to all of these ancillaries from the easy-to-use Instructor's Resource CD-ROM (IRCD), which lets the user electronically review, edit, and copy what's needed. The CD contains the _Instructor's Manual,_ the _Test Bank_ in Microsoft Word and in ExamView, PowerPoint slides, and exercises to accompany the optional Small Business and Entrepreneurship Resource Center package.

- **_Small Business School Videos._** Available in DVD format, selections from the popular television series Small Business School on PBS stations let you in on some very big ideas at work in a variety of innovative small businesses. The small businesses covered include Joseph's Lite Cookies, Rodgers

Chevrolet, Nicole Miller, eHarmony, and Modern Postcard, among many others. These videos bring the real world into the classroom, allowing students to learn from the experts.

- **_NEW! Small Business and Entrepreneurship Resource Center._** New to this edition is the Small Business and Entrepreneurship Resource Center (SBERC) from Gale. This optional package gives students access to 900,000 published, full-text articles directly related to small business management. These articles are easily searchable by business topic, business type, and commonly asked how-to questions. This powerful resource also includes access to hundreds of sample business plans and the legal forms necessary to start a new venture in every state. Powered by InfoTrac, the how-to section provides direct access to popular topics and to answers to questions students frequently ask about starting and running a small business. SBERC student exercises to accompany the text can be found on the student website at http://sbmonline.swlearning.com.

- **_NEW! Small Business Management Online (http://sbmonline. swlearning.com)._** SBM Online provides students with a robust array of learning tools to enrich their course experience. SBM Online is packaged with every new text and includes access to the Small Business School videos, business plan templates, exercises to accompany the optional Small Business and Entrepreneurship Resource Center, and helpful interactive quizzes and e-lectures.

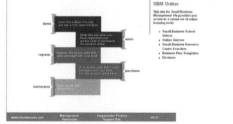

- **_WebTutor™ on Blackboard or WebCT._** This dynamic technology tool complements _Small Business Management_ by providing interactive reinforcement that helps students fully grasp key concepts. WebTutor's online teaching and learning environment brings together content management, assessment, communication, collaboration opportunities, quizzes, tutorials, and other opportunities for the interactive instruction that makes the world of small business come alive.

Optional Course Add-On

- **_BizPlanBuilder® Express: A Guide to Creating a Business Plan with BizPlanBuilder by Jian and Kapron._** Now students can learn how to use the award-winning, best-selling, professional software _BizPlanBuilder_ 8.1 to create a business plan. This optional workbook/CD-ROM package provides all the essentials for creating winning business plans, from the latest *BizPlanBuilder* software to step-by-step instructions for preparing each section of a plan. Ready-to-customize samples, advice, a detailed marketing analysis with links to demographic and marketing tools, and helpful financial tools make it easy to create a solid plan. Hands-on exercises and activities throughout the workbook ensure that students fully understand how to maximize *BizPlanBuilder's* dynamic tools.

Bundle this text with *BizPlanBuilder® Express* for a package that will help students get a head start on their path to business success. Contact your South-Western representative or visit academic.cengage.com/management for more information.

Special Thanks and Acknowledgments

There are numerous individuals to whom we owe a debt of gratitude for their assistance in making this project a reality. In particular, we thank our friends at South-Western. We are especially indebted to Michele Rhoades and Susan Smart, and to Jeanne Yost of Lifland et al., Bookmakers. They are all true professionals!

A talented team of writers contributed an outstanding set of ancillary materials. Special thanks go to Dr. James A. Roberts, the W. A. Mays Professor of Entrepreneurship at Baylor University, for his preparation of the *Instructor's Manual* and *Test Bank,* and to Benjapon Jivasantikarn for providing her business plan, which appears in Appendix A. We are grateful as well to Charlie Cook of the University of West Alabama, who created the PowerPoint images, and to Mary Abrahams, Peggy Davies, and Joy Winand, all at Baylor University. And we offer a special word of appreciation for the understanding and support of our wives—Donna and Dianna—during this process.

For their useful suggestions and thoughtful comments, which helped to shape this edition, we are grateful to the following reviewers and to many others who, for reasons of privacy, chose to remain anonymous:

Dr. Jeffrey Alstete
Iona College

David Ambrosini
Cabrillo College

Chandler Atkins
Adirondack Community College

Lee Baldwin
University of Mary Hardin-Baylor

Francis B. Ballard
Florida Community College

Hilton Barrett
Elizabeth City State University

Bill Bauer
Carroll College–Waukesha

Verona K. Beguin
Black Hills State University

Narendra C. Bhandari
Pace University

Greg Bier
Stephens College

Karen Bishop
University of Louisville

Ross Blankenship
State Fair Community College

John Boos
Ohio Wesleyan University

Marvin Borgelt
University of Mary

Don B. Bradley III
University of Central Arkansas

Steven Bradley
Austin Community College

Margaret Britt
Eastern Nazarene College

Mark Brosthoff
Indiana University

Penelope Stohn Brouwer
Mount Ida College

Rochelle R. Brunson
Alvin Community College

Kevin Chen
County College of Morris

Felipe Chia
Harrisburg Area Community College

Mike Cicero
Highline Community College

Edward G. Cole
St. Mary's University

Michael D. Cook
Hocking College

Roy A. Cook
Fort Lewis College

George R. Corbett
St. Thomas Aquinas College

Karen Cranford
Catawba College

George W. Crawford
Clayton College & State University

Bruce Davis
Weber State University

Terri Davis
Howard College

Bill Demory
Central Arizona College

Michael Deneen
Baker College

Sharon Dexler
Southeast Community College

Warren Dorau
Nicolet College

Max E. Douglas
Indiana State University

Bonnie Ann Dowd
Palomar College

Michael Drafke
College of Dupage

Franklin J. Elliot
Dine College

Franceen Fallett
Ventura College

R. Brian Fink
Danville Area Community College

Dennette Foy
Edison College

David W. Frantz
Purdue University

Janice S. Gates
Western Illinois University

Armand Gilinsky, Jr.
Sonoma State University

Darryl Goodman
Trident Technical College

William Grace
Missouri Valley College

William W. Graff
Maharishi University of Management

Mark Hagenbuch
University of North Carolina–Greensboro

James R. Hindman
Northeastern University
Suffolk University

Betty Hoge
Limestone College

Eddie Hufft
Alcorn State University

Sherrie Human
Xavier University

Ralph Jagodka
Mt. San Antonio College

Larry K. Johansen
Park University
Indiana Wesleyan University

Michael Judge
Hudson Valley Community College

Mary Beth Klinger
College of Southern Maryland

Charles W. Kulmann
Columbia College of Missouri

Rosemary Lafragola
University of Texas–El Paso

William Laing
Anderson College

Ann Langlois
Palm Beach Atlantic University

Rob K. Larson
Mayville State University

David E. Laurel
South Texas Community College

Les Ledger
Central Texas College

Michael G. Levas
Carroll College

Richard M. Lewis
Lansing Community College

Thomas W. Lloyd
Westmoreland County Community College

Elaine Madden
Anne Arundel Community College

Kristina Mazurak
Albertson College

James J. Mazza
Middlesex Community College

Lisa McConnell
Oklahoma State University–Oklahoma City

Angela Mitchell
Wilmington College

Frank Mitchell
Limestone College

Douglas Moesel
University of Missouri–Columbia

Michael K. Mulford
Des Moines Area Community College

Bernice M. Murphy
University of Maine–Machias

Eugene Muscat
University of San Francisco

John J. Nader
Grand Valley State University

Charles "Randy" Nichols
Sullivan University

Robert D. Nixon
University of Louisville

Marcella M. Norwood
University of Houston

Donalus A. Okhomina, Sr.
Jackson State University

Rosa L. Okpara
Albany State University

Timothy O'Leary
Mount Wachusett Community College

Pamela Onedeck
University of Pittsburgh–Greensburg

Claire Phillips
North Harris College

Dean Pielstick
Northern Arizona University

Mark S. Poulos
St. Edward's University

Julia Truitt Poynter
Transylvania University

Fred Pragasam
University of North Florida

Mary Ellen Rosetti
Hudson Valley Community College

Jaclyn Rundle
Central College

John K. Sands
Western Washington University

Craig Sarine
Lee University

Duane Schecter
Muskegon Community College

Matthew Semadeni
Texas A&M University

Marjorie Shapiro
Myers University

Sherry L. Shuler
American River College

Cindy Simerly
Lakeland Community College

James Sisk
Gaston College

Victoria L. Sitter
Milligan College

Bernard Skown
Stevens Institute of Technology

Kristin L. H. Slyter
Valley City State University

William E. Smith
Ferris State University

Bill Snider
Cuesta College

Roger Stanford
Chippewa Valley Technical College

Phil Stetz
Stephen F. Austin State University

Peter L. Stone
Spartanburg Technical College

James Swenson
Minnesota State University–Moorhead

Ruth Tarver
West Hills Community College

Darrell Thompson
Mountain View College

Melodie M. Toby
Kean University

Charles N. Toftoy
George Washington University

Charles Torti
Schreiner University

Gerald R. Turner
Limestone College

Barry L. Van Hook
Arizona State University

Brian Wahl
North Shore Community College

Mike Wakefield
University of Southern California

Charles F. Warren
Salem State College

Janet Wayne
Baker College

Nat B. White, Jr.
South Piedmont Community College

Jim Whitlock
Brenau University

Ira Wilsker
Lamar Institute of Technology

Note to Instructors   As a final word of appreciation, we express our sincere thanks to the many instructors who use our text in both academic and professional settings. Based on years of teaching and listening to other teachers and students, *Small Business Management* has been designed to meet the needs of its readers. And we continue to listen and make changes in the text. Please write or call us to offer suggestions to help us make the book even better for future readers. Contact Bill Petty at 254-710-2260 or bill_petty@baylor.edu or Les Palich at 254-710-6194 or les_palich@baylor.edu. Let us hear from you.

About the Authors

JUSTIN G. LONGENECKER   Justin G. Longenecker's authorship of *Small Business Management* began with the first edition of this book. He authored a number of books and numerous articles in such journals as *Journal of Small Business Management, Academy of Management Review, Business Horizons*, and *Journal of Business Ethics*. He was active in several professional organizations and served as president of the International Council for Small Business. Dr. Longenecker grew up in a family business. After attending Central Christian College of Kansas for two years, he went on to earn his B.A. in political science from Seattle Pacific University, his M.B.A. from Ohio State University, and his Ph.D. from the University of Washington. He taught at Baylor University, where he was Emeritus Chavanne Professor of Christian Ethics in Business until his death in 2005.

CARLOS W. MOORE   Carlos W. Moore was the Edwin W. Streetman Professor of Marketing at Baylor University, where he was an instructor for more than 35 years. He was honored as a Distinguished Professor by the Hankamer School of Business, where he taught both graduate and undergraduate courses in Marketing Research and Consumer Behavior. Dr. Moore authored articles in such journals as *Journal of Small Business Management, Journal of Business Ethics, Organizational Dynamics, Accounting Horizons,* and *Journal of Accountancy*. His authorship of this textbook began with its sixth edition. Dr. Moore received an associate arts degree from Navarro Junior College in Corsicana, Texas, where he was later named Ex-Student of the Year. He earned a B.B.A. degree from The University of Texas at Austin with a major in accounting, an M.B.A. from Baylor University, and a Ph.D. from Texas A&M University. Besides fulfilling his academic commitments, Dr. Moore served as co-owner of a small ranch and a partner in a small business consulting firm until his death in 2007.

J. WILLIAM PETTY   J. William Petty is Professor of Finance and the W. W. Caruth Chairholder in Entrepreneurship at Baylor University. He holds a Ph.D. and an M.B.A. from The University of Texas at Austin and a B.S. from Abilene Christian University. He has taught at Virginia Tech University and Texas Tech University and served as dean of the business school at Abilene Christian University. He taught entrepreneurship and small business courses in China, the Ukraine, Kazakhstan, Indonesia, Thailand, and Russia. He has been designated a Master Teacher at Baylor. His research interests include acquisitions of privately held companies, shareholder value–based management, the financing of small and entrepreneurial firms, and exit strategies for privately held firms. He has served as co-editor for the *Journal of Financial Research* and as editor of the *Journal of Entrepreneurial and Small Business Finance*. He has published articles in a number of finance journals and is the co-author of two leading corporate finance textbooks—*Financial Management* and *Foundations of Finance*. Dr. Petty has worked as a consultant for oil and gas firms and consumer product companies. He also served as a subject matter expert on a best-practices study by the American Productivity and Quality Center on the topic of shareholder value–based management. He was a member of a research team sponsored by the Australian Department of Industry to study the feasibility of establishing a public equity market for small and medium-sized enterprises in Australia. Finally, he serves as the audit chair for a publicly traded energy firm.

LESLIE E. PALICH   Leslie E. Palich is Associate Professor of Management and Entrepreneurship and the Ben H. Williams Professor of Entrepreneurship at Baylor University, where he teaches courses in small business management, international entrepreneurship, strategic management, and international management to undergraduate and graduate students in the Hankamer School of Business. He is also Associate Director of the Entrepreneurship Studies program at Baylor. He holds a Ph.D. and an M.B.A. from Arizona State University and a B.A. from Manhattan Christian College. His research has been published in the *Academy of*

Management Review, Strategic Management Journal, Journal of Business Venturing, Journal of International Business Studies, Journal of Management, Journal of Organizational Behavior, Journal of Small Business Management, and several other periodicals. He has taught entrepreneurship and strategic management in a number of overseas settings, including Cuba, France, the Netherlands, the United Kingdom, and the Dominican Republic. His interest in entrepreneurial opportunity and small business management dates back to his grade school years, when he set up a produce sales business to experiment with small business ownership. That early experience became a springboard for a number of other enterprises. Since that time, he has owned and operated domestic ventures in agribusiness, automobile sales, real estate development, and educational services, as well as an international import business.

## chapter 1

The Entrepreneurial Life

In the **VIDEO SPOTLIGHT**

Bridgecreek
http://www.bridgecreek.com

When Frank Jao left Communist Vietnam with his wife and headed for Camp Pendleton, California, it was not the first time he had struck out on his own. In fact, Jao had left home when he was 11 years old. Although still in school, he supported himself by working six hours a day delivering papers, and after two short years, the newspaper distributor assigned Jao the distribution routes for the entire city of Da Nang. He had six employees by the time he was 13 years old.

The lessons Jao learned from his family, his newspaper business, and his independent life in Vietnam provided the drive and persistence that helped him develop Bridgecreek, a unique Vietnamese cultural center in Southern California. What started as a single-building shopping center is now a commercial campus of 3,500 Vietnamese-owned businesses and home to the largest Vietnamese population outside of Vietnam. A simple mall has become a city in its own right and was given the name "Little Saigon" by the governor of California. (You may already be familiar with Little Saigon: Its gates were featured in the movie *The Fast and the Furious*.)

The drivers of Frank Jao's success are similar to those driving millions of entrepreneurs across the country: the desire to be independent, to create, and to prosper. Watch this video spotlight to see how the persistence and resourcefulness of one entrepreneur can fuel the success and vitality of an entire community.

Video material provided by Hattie Bryant, Producer of Small Business School, the series on PBS Stations, Worldnet, and the Web at http://www.smallbusinessschool.org.

SmallBusiness**School** ▣
the Series on PBS stations and the Web

Looking AHEAD

After studying this chapter, you should be able to

1 Discuss the availability of entrepreneurial opportunities and give examples of successful businesses started by entrepreneurs.
2 Explain the nature of entrepreneurship and how it is related to small business.
3 Identify some motivators or rewards of entrepreneurial careers.
4 Describe the various types of entrepreneurs and entrepreneurial ventures.
5 Identify five potential advantages of small entrepreneurial firms.
6 Discuss factors related to readiness for entrepreneurship and getting started in an entrepreneurial career.
7 Explain the concept of an entrepreneurial legacy and the challenges involved in crafting a worthy legacy.

Would you like to become an entrepreneur, to start and operate a small business of your own? If so, you are not alone. Today, some 40 percent of adults say they would like to launch their own company, to call their own shots—and many are doing just that. According to the Small Business Administration, 600,000 businesses are started each year in the United States alone.[1] That's more than one new company launched every minute! If you dream of owning your own business one day, the time to start preparing is now.

An entrepreneurial fever is also sweeping the nation's campuses, as students take classes to learn how to launch, finance, and run their own companies. John Fernandes, president and CEO of AACSB International (the organization that accredits business schools around the world), puts it this way, "Entrepreneurship will continue to grow and mature into a distinct management discipline. . . . Elements of entrepreneurship will emerge as *essential* to any business education."[2] In other words, in today's world your business courses, whatever your particular specialty or major, had best include the study of entrepreneurship. Business students, along with engineers, teachers, artists, pharmacists, lawyers, nurses, and many others, are hearing the call to own their own businesses. You are living in a world of entrepreneurial opportunity, one that is an immensely more hospitable place for entrepreneurs than it was 20 years ago!

You are about to embark on a course of study that will prove invaluable if you elect to pursue a career in entrepreneurship or small business—or even if you don't. An entrepreneurial career can provide an exciting life and substantial personal rewards, while also contributing to the welfare of society. As a general rule, when you talk to entrepreneurs about what they are currently doing and what their plans are for the future, you can feel their excitement and anticipation—it can be contagious!

Taking a small business or entrepreneurship class is not likely to turn a student who lacks basic business intuition into an opportunity-spotting, money-making genius. Yet there is considerable evidence suggesting that such classes can facilitate the learning curve for those who have the "right stuff." These classes teach many of the basic skills, such as understanding financial statements, writing a business plan, and learning how to impose structure and deadlines on dreams that you might never achieve otherwise. Consider Megan Wettach, who during high school opened a store to sell prom dresses in her hometown of Mount Pleasant, Iowa. After taking a class in entrepreneurship at the University of Iowa, she began designing her own gowns and secured a $150,000 line of credit with a bank in Cedar Rapids. She then signed a contract with an apparel maker in China and negotiated a deal to sell her dresses in WordStar. "My professors opened my eyes to the idea that I can be bigger than a little dress store in Iowa," Wettach says. "I can be a global force in fashion."[3]

1 Discuss the availability of entrepreneurial opportunities and give examples of successful businesses started by entrepreneurs.

Having worked for over three decades with both entrepreneurs and students who aspire to own businesses, we have designed this book to prepare you for the life of an entrepreneur. You are in for an exciting adventure!

Entrepreneurial Opportunities

Entrepreneurial opportunities exist for those who can produce enough products or services desired by customers to make the enterprise economically attractive. A promising entrepreneurial opportunity is more than just an interesting idea. It involves a product or service that is so attractive to customers that they are willing to pay their hard-earned money for it. In other words, an entrepreneur must find a way to create value for customers.

entrepreneurial opportunity
An economically attractive and timely opportunity that creates value for interested buyers or end users

Our working definition of **entrepreneurial opportunity**, as an economically attractive and timely opportunity that creates value for interested buyers or end users, distinguishes between opportunities and ideas. It is important to note, however, that a given opportunity will not be equally attractive to everyone. Because of differences in experiences and perspectives, one person may see an opportunity where others do not. But, in any case, a true opportunity exists only for the entrepreneur who has the interest, resources, and capabilities required to succeed.

Entrepreneurial opportunities exist today in a business world that differs markedly from the business world of yesterday. Let's look at three successful entrepreneurial ventures started by some present-day entrepreneurs.

Three Success Stories

LATEMODEL RESTORATION SUPPLY (WACO, TX) At the early age of 6 years, Shannon Guderian fell in love with his uncle's Ford Mustang. When he turned 15, his mother bought him his very own 1965 Mustang. Before he acquired his driver's license, Guderian would sneak out at night to listen to the V8 engine. For him, Mustangs were a lifestyle, representing image and freedom.

Guderian began his career in the automotive world straight out of high school, working for a Mustang parts company. At age 26, seeing the need for parts for late-model cars, Guderian quit his job and pursued his dream. With only $7,000 in his pocket from selling his car, and without any business experience, he started calling on everyone he knew in the industry, asking for advice. He explains, "My goal was to create credibility within the industry."

Starting with 17 part numbers from one vendor and a $20,000 bank loan to help finance his small inventory, Guderian originally located his business in a 650-square-foot "hole in the wall." Today, the business is in a 27,000-square-foot building with a showroom where he displays Mustangs. His annual sales have now reached over $10 million.

Guderian is proud of his accomplishments, but he is not patting himself on the back. Crediting God and friends for his success, Guderian says, "This is not something I could have created on my own. . . . Twenty-three of the 35 people who work for the business now own Mustangs. A lot of these people I knew before they had driver's licenses. They are an important part of my foundation."

When asked what he wished he had known at the beginning, Guderian replies, "I wish I had known the importance of leveraging my assets to acquire financing. If I had worked my business off the cash-only basis over the years, I would not be number one today."

Guderian is characterized by passion for his work and passion for people, explaining "People do business with people, not companies. So I view employees and vendors as gold, and I treat them as such."[4]

SPANX (ATLANTA, GEORGIA)   Many entrepreneurs have said that the place to find your "idea" is at a party. Listen to determine what people want or are complaining about, and then find a way to fix it. Sara Blakely did exactly that, and the problem she found was visible underwear lines, which are not only unfashionable but also uncomfortable. In 1998, Blakely cut the feet off her pantyhose to look fashionable in her cream-color pants, and her idea was born. With a lot of hard work and persistence, Blakely embarked on her journey to create a multi-million-dollar patented pantyhose product that is practical and comfortable.

"Working as a sales trainer by day and performing stand-up comedy at night, I didn't know the first thing about the pantyhose industry (except I dreaded wearing most pantyhose)," Blakely reflected. With no business background, she saved on costs by writing the patent herself and trademarked the term SPANX®.

In 2000, Blakely took a week off and drove to visit different manufacturers in North Carolina. Each one turned her "crazy" idea down. Two weeks later, a mill owner called and offered to make her product. He had two daughters who didn't think it was a crazy idea at all. Perfecting the prototype took a year because of Blakely's obsession with comfort.

After Blakely flew to Dallas to demonstrate her product, Neiman Marcus agreed to test SPANX in several stores. Saks, Nordstrom, and other retailers soon followed. With no money to advertise, Blakely went store to store, doing rallies and in-store demonstrations to spread the word. She also called news stations, magazines, and newspapers to generate interest in doing a story on her product. SPANX has been featured on *The Oprah Winfrey Show, The View, The Today Show, Good Morning America, American Inventor,* and countless news channels, as well as in the pages of *Forbes, Fortune, People, Entrepreneur, InStyle, Vogue, Glamour, Essence, Self, New York Times,* and *USA Today.*

Blakely stresses to the consumer that this product is made for women by women. This marketing strategy led Sara Blakely to be named the 2002 "Entrepreneur of the Year in the Southeast Region" by Ernst and Young. By 2007, SPANX was up to 55 employees and had launched more than 100 new products for women.

For Sara Blakely, wanting to look good at a party paid off.[5]

MP4 SOLUTIONS (SAN ANTONIO, TX)   Trey Moore and Cameron Powell, M.D., met after Moore observed Powell regularly checking his PDA during church services. As a software developer, Moore was always interested in how people use their devices and how they could be improved, so he followed Powell out of church, introduced himself, and began asking questions. He quickly learned that Powell was an obstetrician who was using his PDA to communicate with nurses about the condition of his patients and that he needed a better way to do it. "If I could see this real-time tracing of the baby's heart and the mom's contractions and all the data from labor and delivery when I'm not there, that would be huge, because you can't do that right now," Powell said.

Over the next several years, the men gave their time and energy to developing the software for wireless devices to transmit charts and data directly from the hospital to the physician. Once the applications of the product were in place, the company they named MP4 Solutions still needed FDA approval and a reseller for support. Consent from the FDA took only six months, which Moore and Powell said is "unheard of." But finding a company to lend financial and technological support did not come so easily.

They were able to arrange a meeting with a representative from General Electric, but received no news from GE for several months after the meeting. During that time, the men courted other companies, but with little response. Eventually, MP4 Solutions formed an exclusive partnership with GE. The relationship added the benefit of the GE name, marketing, installation, and support for the product, now called Airstrip OB.

"[Airstrip OB is] not just a convenience thing; it's for critical decisions that need to be made," said Moore (in photo). The technology also lends itself to other medical applications and to anything that requires historical and live graph data for analysis.

Airstrip OB has already taken off, and the men are hard at work developing similar products and software. Moore said the next likely product from MP4 Solutions, other than the next version of AirStrip OB, is software that will give cardiologists nearly live access to electrocardiograms and patient monitors from their handheld communications devices. He also sees possibilities in nearly every medical specialty and for any professionals who need to review live wave pattern logs, such as geologists who are monitoring oil wells.

Both men have found a way to use their education and experience to create something completely new and are excited about where they have been and where they are going.[6]

Evidence of Opportunities

In a private enterprise system, any individual is free to enter into business for himself or herself. In the previous three examples, we have described very different people who took that step—a young man who did not attend college but had an obsession with Ford Mustangs, a woman who saw a need for comfortable pantyhose, and a computer software developer who partnered with a doctor to develop a device that allows obstetricians to better meet the needs of expectant mothers. In contrast to many others who have tried and failed, these individuals have achieved remarkable success.

At any given time, many potentially profitable business opportunities exist. But these opportunities must be recognized and grasped by individuals with abilities and desire strong enough to assure success. The startups just presented were quite successful; they were chosen to show the diverse, impressive opportunities that exist. Many individuals achieve success on a more modest level in business endeavors far different from those described here. Others fail, but a failure in business is not a failure in life. Many learn from the experience and go on to start a successful business.

Entrepreneurship and Small Business

2 Explain the nature of entrepreneurship and how it is related to small business.

Thus far, we have discussed entrepreneurship and small business opportunities in a very general way. However, it is important to note that, despite many similarities, the terms *entrepreneur* and *small business manager* are not synonymous. Some entrepreneurial endeavors, for example, begin as small businesses but quickly grow into large businesses. They may still be entrepreneurial. We need, then, to clarify the meanings of these terms.

Who Are the Entrepreneurs?

Entrepreneurs are frequently thought to be individuals who discover market needs and launch new firms to meet those needs. They are risk takers who provide an impetus for change, innovation, and progress in economic life. (In contrast, salaried employees receive some specified compensation and do not assume ownership risks.)

entrepreneur
A person who starts or owns and operates an enterprise

For our purposes, we consider all active owner-managers to be **entrepreneurs**. We do not limit the term *entrepreneur* to only founders of business firms; we also apply the term to second-generation operators of family-owned firms, franchisees, and owner-managers who have bought out the founders of existing firms. Our definition, however, does exclude salaried managers of larger corporations, even those sometimes described as entrepreneurial because of their flair for innovation and willingness to accept risk.

exhibit

1-1   *The Independent Entrepreneur*

Source: By permission of John L. Hart FLP and Creators Syndicate, Inc.

To get an idea of the unlimited potential of entrepreneurial ventures, think of the achievements of entrepreneurs such as Sergey Brin and Larry Page, the founders of Google. If success is having your firm's name become a verb in languages around the world, then these two individuals can without question claim success. Google has clearly been a phenomenal success, with a total stock value of over $140 billion at the end of 2006. But while few of us can relate to Brin and Page's level of success, their experience teaches us that we will never know what is possible until we try.

What Is Small Business?

What does it mean to talk about "small business"? A neighborhood restaurant or bakery is clearly a small business, and Toyota is obviously not. But among small businesses, there is great diversity in size.

Being labeled a "small business" may convey the impression that the business is unimportant. That impression, however, would be totally incorrect. The significance of small business in today's society is clearly expressed in this excerpt from *Business Week:*

> *Small businesses produce 14 times as many patents per employee as large companies do, and they are twice as likely to turn those inventions into successes, according to a Congressional report. They account for half of the private gross domestic product, create more than 60% of net new jobs each year, and pay 44.3% of the private payroll.*[7]

Let's hear it for the "little guys"!

There have been many efforts to define the term *small business,* using such criteria as number of employees, sales volume, and value of assets. There is no generally accepted or universally agreed-on definition. Size standards are basically arbitrary, adopted to serve a particular purpose. For example, legislators sometimes exclude firms with fewer than 10 or 15 employees from certain regulations, so as to avoid imposing a financial burden on the owner of a very small business.

In this book, primary attention is given to businesses that meet the following criteria:

1. Financing for the business is supplied by one individual or only a few individuals.
2. Except for its marketing function, the business's operations are geographically localized.
3. Compared to the biggest firms in the industry, the business is small.
4. The number of employees in the business is fewer than 100.

Living the Dream
entrepreneurial challenges

In the Pink

Wanting to make "a major difference for women in the workplace," Genevieve Bos and Cynthia Good, who worked in publishing in Atlanta, Georgia, believed they could find a market for a magazine aimed at helping professional women excel.

In 2002, after deciding women were underserved by business and personal finance magazines, Bos, 41, and Good, 46, created a magazine prototype with $50,000 from family and friends. They called the magazine *Pink*, to suggest that women can be both powerful and feminine.

It wasn't the best time for an entrepreneurial venture in the magazine industry. An ad recession was under way, and *Working Women* magazine had gone out of business in 2001, after a 25-year run. But assertiveness helped. Bos and Good relentlessly pushed for meetings with acquaintances and friends of friends at big companies in Atlanta, including Coca-Cola and Home Depot.

With $300,000 coaxed from advertisers over a one-year period, the first 98-page issue was produced in mid-2005. Appropriately, the cover story was about women on Madison Avenue.

Pink has since published 12 issues, covering such topics as starting a business and pushing for a pay raise. With $5 million in income from ads, conferences, and syndication (Forbes.com runs *Pink* articles), they claim a pretax margin (net income ÷ sales) of 16 percent.

Source: Helen Coster, "In the Pink," *Forbes*, March 12, 2007, p. 81. Reprinted by permission of *Forbes* Magazine © 2007, Forbes Media LLC.

http://www.pinkmagazine.com

Obviously, some small firms fail to meet all of these standards. For example, a small executive search firm—a firm that helps corporate clients recruit managers from other organizations—may operate in many sections of the country and thereby fail to meet the second criterion. Nevertheless, the discussion of management concepts in this book is aimed primarily at the type of firm that fits the general pattern outlined by these criteria.

Thus, small businesses include tiny one-person firms—the kind you may decide to start. They also include small firms that have up to 100 employees. In most cases, however, they are drastically different in their structure and operations from the huge corporations that are generally featured in the business media.

The Payoff of Entrepreneurship

> **3** Identify some motivators or rewards of entrepreneurial careers.

What might cause you to consider running your own business? Clearly, different individuals have varied reasons and motivations for wanting to own their own business. In one study, researchers identified 38 different reasons for self-employment.[8] But we suggest a primary reason for becoming an entrepreneur and owning your own business: *to make the world a better place*. John Doerr, one of the most famous venture capitalists of all time, inspired the phrase *make meaning*.[9] Your first goal should be to create a product or service that makes the world a better place. Your company should be about something

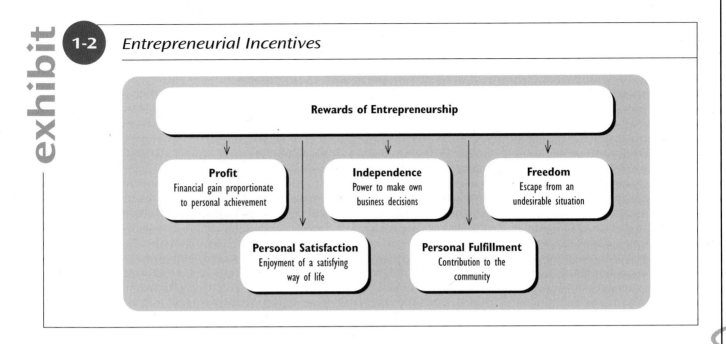

exhibit **1-2** *Entrepreneurial Incentives*

Rewards of Entrepreneurship

Profit
Financial gain proportionate
to personal achievement

Independence
Power to make own
business decisions

Freedom
Escape from an
undesirable situation

Personal Satisfaction
Enjoyment of a satisfying
way of life

Personal Fulfillment
Contribution to the
community

more significant than yourself. Then, when the days get long or you become discouraged, you will have a sense that what you are doing is significant and well worth the effort.

While we believe the first reason for becoming an entrepreneur is to "make meaning," many things make being an entrepreneur attractive. Although any attempt to identify all the various attractions will be at best incomplete, Exhibit 1-2 summarizes some of the reasons frequently cited by individuals for becoming entrepreneurs. We will discuss each in turn.

Make Money (Profit)

Like any other job or career, entrepreneurship provides for one's financial needs. Starting one's own business is a way to earn money. Indeed, some entrepreneurs earn lots of money. In *The Millionaire Next Door,* Stanley and Danko conclude that self-employed people are four times more likely to be millionaires than are those who work for others.[10]

How much money should an entrepreneur expect in return for starting and running a business? Certainly, some profit is necessary for a firm's survival. Some entrepreneurs work hard just to have adequate profits to survive, while others receive a modest income for their time and investment. From an economic perspective, however, the financial return of a business should compensate its owner not only for his or her investment of personal time (in the form of a salary equivalent), but also for any personal money invested in the business (in the form of dividends and increased value of the firm). That is, entrepreneurs should seek a financial return that will compensate them for the time and money they invest and also reward them well for the risks and initiative they take in operating their own businesses.

A significant number of entrepreneurs are, no doubt, highly motivated by the prospect of profits. They have heard the stories about young people who launched dot-com companies and quickly became multimillionaires. While some entrepreneurs do become rich quickly, the majority do not. Instead, the goal should be to get rich *slowly.* Wealth will come, provided the business is economically viable and the owner has the patience and determination to make it happen.

Be Your Own Boss (Independence)

Freedom to operate independently is another reward of entrepreneurship. Its importance is evidenced by the results of one survey of small business owners, in which 38 percent of those who had left jobs at other companies said that their main reason for leaving was that they wanted to be their own boss.[11] Like these entrepreneurs, many people have a strong desire to make their own decisions, take risks, and reap the rewards. Being one's own boss can be an attractive ideal.

The smallest businesses (i.e., part-time businesses and one-person firms), of which there are millions in the United States, probably offer the greatest flexibility to entrepreneurs. Some of these businesses can even hang a "Gone Fishing" (or the equivalent) sign on the door when the entrepreneur feels the urge to engage in nonbusiness activities.

Obviously, most entrepreneurs don't carry their quest for flexibility to such lengths. But entrepreneurs, in general, appreciate the independence inherent in their chosen careers. They can do things their own way, reap their own profits, and set their own schedules. For instance, Karen Taylor started her own public relations firm, Southwest Ink, after working in advertising and public relations much of her career. "I may work more hours some weeks, but they're my hours," says Taylor.[12]

Of course, independence does not guarantee an easy life. Most entrepreneurs work very hard for long hours. They must remember that the customer is, ultimately, the boss. But they do have the satisfaction of making their own decisions within the constraints imposed by economic and other environmental factors, including undesirable working conditions.

Escape a Bad Situation (Freedom)

People sometimes use entrepreneurship as an escape hatch, to free themselves from an undesirable situation. Some may wish to leave an unpleasant job situation, while others may seek change out of necessity. Diane D'Agostino-Smith provides one such an example. D'Agostino-Smith was putting in 15-hour days as an oil company executive's assistant. "My work had taken over my life," she said. "I felt like I couldn't even take the 30-minute exercise break my doctor had recommended." When her health began to slip, she knew she had to get out. After returning to school, she set up a life-coaching practice to help others choose new careers. She runs her business out of her home and values working her own hours. "I took a difficult situation and changed it into something positive for myself and others," she said. "I'm proud of that."[13]

reluctant entrepreneur
A person who becomes an entrepreneur as a result of some severe hardship

Other individuals become entrepreneurs after being laid off by an employer. Unemployed personnel with experience in professional, managerial, technical, and even relatively unskilled positions often contemplate the possibility of venturing out on their own. Individuals who have entered business ownership as a result of financial hardship or other severe negative conditions have been described as **reluctant entrepreneurs**.[14]

refugee
A person who becomes an entrepreneur to escape an undesirable situation

Individuals may also flee the bureaucratic environment of a corporation that seems stifling or oppressive to them. "Dilbert," a cartoon strip that appears in many U.S. newspapers, highlights the worst features of such organizations. Entrepreneurship often provides an attractive alternative for individuals fleeing from such undesirable situations (sometimes called **refugees**). Take Bob and Cathy Dammeyer, for example. Having become weary of all the travel and meetings associated with their corporate jobs, as well as the politics and bureaucracy, they went into business for themselves, selling Swirl frozen-drink distributorships. Three years later, the Dammeyers' company, Culpepper Sales, does several million dollars in business annually. "It's rejuvenated us," Cathy said. "We don't worry about corporate minutiae anymore. We only have to satisfy ourselves."[15]

Enjoy a Satisfying Life (Personal Satisfaction)

Entrepreneurs frequently speak of the satisfaction they experience in their own businesses; some even refer to their work as fun. Rick Davis, founder and CEO of DAVACO, says, "There is nothing else I would rather do. I love the challenges, working with others to see our dreams come true, and making a difference in the community. It is fun."[16]

Part of their enjoyment may derive from their independence, but some of it reflects an owner's personal gratification from working with the firm's products and services. Bill Thomas, who bought his first pair of khaki pants at an army surplus store in 1984, sensed a business opportunity when that pair of deep-pocketed World War II uniform pants wore out and he couldn't find another like it. In 1990, he founded Bill's Khakis, which by 2005 had sales of $9.5 million. Why did he start the business? In his words,

I felt like I had such a great opportunity to start a business, and it was thanks in part to the generation I was trying to celebrate—my father's generation. Just to have the right to start this—the freedom—and to live in a country where I could have this opportunity was something I did not take for granted. I was not as concerned about making a living in the beginning, but just to see the idea live and breathe.[17]

Most small business owners report satisfaction in their careers. In a poll conducted by the National Federation of Independent Business, small employers rated the level of their personal satisfaction on average as 8 on a scale of 1 (extremely dissatisfied) to 10 (extremely satisfied).[18] A majority (51 percent) also indicated that they spend most of their time doing what they like to do best.

The reward, then, may derive from a pleasurable activity, from enjoyable associations, from respect in the community, or from some other aspect of the business. For many

Living the Dream   entrepreneurial challenges

Courtesy of South Texas College

Thinking Entrepreneurially Works for Any Kind of Startup

In 1994, Shirley Reed arrived in McAllen, Texas, a city located 510 miles southeast of Chihuahua, Mexico, in a region of the Rio Grande Valley beset by poverty, unemployment, and some of the lowest education rates in the country. Her assignment was to build South Texas College (STC). As a first-time president with trustees who were new to the job as well, Reed faced several challenges: no bank account, no professors, no computers, and no students. However, Reed and the trustees shared a surplus of ambition.

"We were starting from scratch," recalls Gary Gurwitz, one of the original trustees appointed by then-governor Ann Richards. "I had more books in my house than we had at the college." Undaunted, Reed predicted that the institution would serve 20,000 students within 20 years. "I was on a mission. I was going to get it done no matter what," says Reed.

Initially, the college held classes in any unoccupied space administrators could find, including church basements, police stations, a converted laundromat, and vacant buildings. Reed bought up surplus portable buildings that had been used as food-stamp distribution centers. "The joke at the time was that I would go to garage sales and buy the garages," she says.

In recent years, South Texas College has been one of the nation's fastest-growing community colleges, with 90 degree programs and 16 new structures in 16 months. Today it serves some 18,000 students at three campuses and is one of three community colleges in Texas to offer 4-year degrees.

The college has been a transformative force for Starr County, Texas, whose unemployment rate has declined from 40 percent to about 13 percent since the college opened. In Hidalgo, unemployment has fallen from 24 percent to 7 percent. The consensus in this corner of the state is that Reed and South Texas College have been critical factors in the region's rising economic fortunes.

What Reed did was nothing more or less than an entrepreneurial venture. Reed likens the creation of a college to the launch of a company. "It's just like starting a business," she says. "Where are we going to locate? How do we market it? How do we price the product?" It was a startup and required the same knowledge, skills, and passion needed for starting a for-profit venture. Entrepreneurship is a way of thinking and seeing the world. It is about making the world a better place.

Source: John Pulley, "Rising Stars: Right Person, Right Time," UniversityBusiness.com, November 2006, http://www.universitybusiness.com/viewarticle.aspx?articleid=618, accessed January 15, 2007.

http://www.southtexascollege.edu

entrepreneurs, the life satisfaction they receive is much more important than money or independence.

CONTRIBUTE TO THE COMMUNITY (PERSONAL FULFILLMENT)   Some people are drawn to entrepreneurship by their desire to do good, to make some positive contribution to their communities. In many cases, this impulse is merely one element in a mix of motivations. In some endeavors, however, it is a particularly strong force behind the thinking of the entrepreneur.

Trey Moore and Cameron Powell (one of the "three success stories" described at the beginning of the chapter) provide a great example of entrepreneurs who want to make a difference in the lives of pregnant women and their babies. As you will recall, their product, Airstrip OB, allows obstetricians to track a mother's labor contractions and her baby's heart rate without having to be at the hospital. If proved effective, it will no doubt reduce the risk during a woman's labor.

The Many Varieties of Entrepreneurship

Entrepreneurship is marked by diversity—that is, there is great variety both in the people and in the firms termed *entrepreneurial*. As a potential entrepreneur, you can be encouraged by this diversity; you do not need to fit some narrow stereotype.

Founder Entrepreneurs versus Other Business Owners and Franchisees

Generally considered to be "pure" entrepreneurs, **founders** may be inventors who initiate businesses on the basis of new or improved products or services. They may also be artisans who develop skills and then start their own firms. Or they may be enterprising individuals, often with marketing backgrounds, who draw on the ideas of others in starting new firms. Whether acting as individuals or as part of a group, founders bring firms into existence by surveying the market, raising funds, and arranging for the necessary facilities. The process of starting an entirely new business is discussed in detail in Chapter 3.

At some point after a new firm is established, it may be purchased or taken over by a second-generation family member or another entrepreneur who acts as administrator of the business. These "second-stage" entrepreneurs do not necessarily differ greatly from founding entrepreneurs in the way they manage their businesses. Sometimes, their well-established small firms grow rapidly, and their orientation may be more akin to that of a founder than to that of a manager. Nevertheless, it is helpful to distinguish between entrepreneurs who found or substantially change firms (the "movers and shakers") and those who direct the continuing operations of established firms.

Another category of entrepreneurs comprises franchisees. **Franchisees** differ from other business owners in the degree of their independence. Because of the constraints and guidance provided by contractual relationships with franchising organizations, franchisees function as limited entrepreneurs. Chapter 4 presents more information about franchisees.

High-Potential Ventures versus Attractive Small Firms and Microbusinesses

Small businesses differ drastically in their growth potential. Amar V. Bhide, who studied the nature of entrepreneurial businesses, distinguished between promising startups and marginal startups.[19] According to Bhide, promising startups are those with the potential for attaining significant size and profitability, while marginal startups lack such prospects.

The few businesses that have such glowing prospects for growth are called **high-potential ventures**, or **gazelles**. Even within this group, there is variation in styles of operation and approaches to growth. Some are high-tech startups—the kind that once made

---

4 Describe the various types of entrepreneurs and entrepreneurial ventures.

founder
An entrepreneur who brings a new firm into existence

franchisee
An entrepreneur whose power is limited by a contractual relationship with a franchising organization

high-potential venture (gazelle)
A small firm that has great prospects for growth

Silicon Valley in California famous. The success stories often feature a technology wizard with a bright idea, backed by venture capitalists eager to underwrite the next Microsoft. When such companies prosper, they usually grow at blinding speed and make their founders wealthy by being sold or going public.

In contrast to such high-potential ventures, **attractive small firms** offer substantial financial rewards for their owners. Income from these entrepreneurial ventures may easily range from $100,000 to $500,000 or more annually. They represent a strong segment of small businesses—solid, healthy firms that can provide rewarding careers.

The least profitable types of firms, including many service firms such as dry cleaners, beauty shops, and appliance repair shops, provide only very modest returns to their owners. They are called **microbusinesses**, and their distinguishing feature is their limited ability to generate significant profits. Entrepreneurs who devote personal effort to such ventures receive a profit that does little more than compensate them for their time. Many businesses of this type are also called **lifestyle businesses** because they permit an owner to follow a desired pattern of living, even though they provide only modest returns. Businesses of this type do not attract investors.

attractive small firm
A small firm that provides substantial profits to its owner

microbusiness
A small firm that provides minimal profits to its owner

lifestyle business
A microbusiness that permits the owner to follow a desired pattern of living

Artisan versus Opportunistic Entrepreneurs

Because of their varied backgrounds, entrepreneurs display differences in the degrees of professionalism and in the management styles they bring to their businesses. The ways in which they analyze problems and approach decision making may differ radically. Norman R. Smith has suggested two basic entrepreneurial patterns, exemplified by artisan (or craftsman) entrepreneurs and opportunistic entrepreneurs.[20]

According to Smith, the education of the **artisan entrepreneur** is limited to technical training. Such entrepreneurs have technical job experience, but they typically lack good communication skills and managerial training. Artisan entrepreneurs' approach to business decision making is often characterized by the following features:

artisan entrepreneur
A person with primarily technical skills and little business knowledge who starts a business

- They are paternalistic—they guide their businesses much as they might guide their own families.

- They are reluctant to delegate authority.

- They use few (usually only one or two) capital sources to create their firms.

- They define marketing strategy in terms of the traditional components of price, quality, and company reputation.

- Their sales efforts are primarily personal.

- Their time orientation is short, with little planning for future growth or change.

A mechanic who starts an independent garage, a beautician who operates a beauty shop, or a painter who opens a studio is an example of an artisan entrepreneur.

In contrast to the artisan entrepreneur, an **opportunistic entrepreneur** is one who has supplemented his or her technical education by studying such nontechnical subjects as economics, law, or history. Opportunistic entrepreneurs generally avoid paternalism, delegate authority as necessary for growth, employ various marketing strategies and types of sales efforts, obtain original capitalization from more than two sources, and plan for future growth. An example of an opportunistic entrepreneur is a small building contractor and developer who adopts a relatively sophisticated approach to management, including careful record keeping and budgeting, precise bidding, and systematic marketing research.

opportunistic entrepreneur
A person with both sophisticated managerial skills and technical knowledge who starts a business

Smith's description of entrepreneurial styles illustrates two extremes: At one end is a craftsperson in an entrepreneurial position, and at the other end is a well-educated and experienced manager. The former "flies by the seat of the pants," and the latter uses systematic management procedures and something resembling a scientific approach. In practice, of course, the distribution of entrepreneurial styles is less polarized than that suggested by Smith's model, with entrepreneurs scattered along a continuum of managerial sophistication. This book is intended to help you move toward the opportunistic and away from the artisan end of the continuum.

Living the Dream   entrepreneurial challenges

The Guitar Man

Sherwood T. "Woody" Phifer, who builds handcrafted guitars, exemplifies the artisan entrepreneur. His business success rests on his extraordinary skill in building outstanding electric and acoustic guitars. His clientele includes such musicians as Ronnie Jordan, Mos Def, Will Lee, Ron Carter, Stanley Clark, Wyclef Jean, and George Benson. They obviously agree with Phifer's personally crafted slogan: "If you don't have a Woody, you just have a guitar."

Although Phifer began as a mathematics and physics major in college, his love of the guitar led him in a different direction—first to playing the guitar and then to working at repairing and restoring them. All of his instruments are made of wood and incorporate his own designs of bridge, tailpiece systems, and internal structures. According to Phifer, "Woodys" stand alone in the industry. As a talented artisan in a business of his own—Phifer Designs and Concepts—he is also a successful lifestyle entrepreneur.

Sources: Sonia Alleyne, "Guitar Man," *Black Enterprise,* Vol. 33, No. 9 (April 2003), p. 64; and a personal visit with Woody Phifer, January 2007.

http://www.phiferdesigns.com

Women Entrepreneurs

Although entrepreneurship and business in general have been male dominated for decades, the scene is rapidly changing. Between 1997 and 2006, growth in the number of women-owned firms was nearly twice that of all U.S. firms (42.3 percent vs. 23.3 percent). As of 2006, there were an estimated 7.7 million women-owned firms, accounting for 30 percent of all businesses in the United States. In 2006, women-owned firms in the United States generated $1.1 trillion in annual sales and employed 7.2 million people nationwide.[21] While revenues generated by companies owned by women are still small relative to those of businesses owned by men, women-owned businesses make a significant contribution to the U.S. economy.

The largest share of women-owned firms is in the service sector. More than two-thirds of women-owned firms provide services. An additional 14 percent are in retail trade, and 8 percent are in real estate sales, rental, and leasing. From 1997 to 2006, the greatest growth among women-owned firms was found in the following sectors:

- Wholesale trade (283 percent growth)

- Healthcare and social assistance services (130 percent growth)

- Arts, entertainment, and recreation services (116 percent growth)

- Professional, scientific, and technical services (83 percent growth).

Some women are starting firms in nontraditional industries, with ambitious plans for growth and profit. Faced with losing the family farm, Elaine J. Martin started her Nampa, Idaho–based highway construction project company, MarCon Inc., in 1985.[22] To help her get started, Martin's mother put up a $25,000 certificate of deposit as collateral so that she could borrow $25,000. At the time, Martin had no construction background.

While looking for construction work, she heard about the Idaho Department of Transportation's highway fencing needs. Since she had been raised on a farm and knew how to build fence, she started bidding for highway work. To improve her chances, she went to the state library to study fencing and highway management. She eventually modified the business by getting into guardrail construction. Today, Martin runs a $6-million business in a male-dominated industry. In 2002, she was named the Idaho Small Business Person of the Year.

Female entrepreneurs obviously face problems common to all entrepreneurs. However, they must also contend with difficulties associated with their newness in entrepreneurial roles. Lack of access to credit has been a common problem for women who enter business. This is a troublesome area for most small business owners, but women often carry the added burden of discrimination.

Another barrier for some women is the limited opportunity they find for business relationships with others in similar positions. It takes time and effort to gain full acceptance and to develop informal relationships with others in local, male-dominated business and professional groups.

These conditions have improved in recent years, as women have assumed strong entrepreneurial roles. In a panel discussion of the issue, some women entrepreneurs emphasized the improved business climate:[23]

> *Cristi Cristich, founder of Cristek Interconnects, Inc.* (a maker of connectors and cabling for medical and military applications in Anaheim, California): "Access to capital and the acceptance of women in the workplace and as business owners has improved dramatically over the past 15 years."

> *Shari L. Parrack, president of Texas Motor Transportation Consultants* (a professional registration, tax, and title service company in Houston, Texas): "In 2003, I find that being female does nothing but help me to grow my business. What was once a negative has become a positive."

> *Terrie Jones, CEO and owner of AGSI* (a provider of Internet technology resource solutions in Atlanta, Georgia): "In 22 years, I've seen the business world evolve tremendously. . . . In the same way businessmen helped their 'fraternity brothers' in the past, they are more willing to help women today."

Women are definitely making inroads into the entrepreneurial world, and the trend will only accelerate in the future.

Entrepreneurial Teams

Our discussion thus far has focused on entrepreneurs who function as individuals, each with his or her own firm. And this is usually the case. However, entrepreneurial teams are becoming increasingly common, particularly in ventures of any substantial size. An **entrepreneurial team** consists of two or more individuals who combine their efforts to function in the capacity of entrepreneurs. In this way, the talents, skills, and resources of two or more entrepreneurs can be concentrated on one endeavor. This very important form of entrepreneurship is discussed at greater length in Chapter 8.

entrepreneurial team
Two or more people who work together as entrepreneurs on one endeavor

The Winning Hand of Entrepreneurship

{ 5 Identify five potential advantages of small entrepreneurial firms.

Small entrepreneurial firms need not be weaklings. Indeed, a look at the structure of the U.S. business community reveals small, entrepreneurial businesses to be a robust part of the total economy. How is it that small and entrepreneurial firms can hold their own and often gain an edge over successful, more powerful businesses? The answer lies in the ability of new and smaller firms to exploit opportunities.

In this section, we will take a look at some ways in which new firms can gain a competitive edge. In Chapter 3, we'll discuss specific strategies for exploiting these potential advantages and capturing the business opportunities they make possible.

Customer Focus

Business opportunities exist for those who can produce products and services desired by customers. If a business can make its product or service "cheaper, faster, and better," then its prospects will be bright.

Good customer service can be provided by a business of any size, of course. However, small firms have a greater potential than larger businesses do for achieving this goal. If properly managed, small entrepreneurial firms have the advantage of being able to serve customers directly and effectively, without struggling through layers of bureaucracy or breaking corporate policies that tend to stifle employee initiative. In many cases, customers are personally acquainted with the entrepreneur and other key people in the small business.

The first step toward creating customer satisfaction and getting customer loyalty is to earn it. One entrepreneur who has used his entrepreneurial aptitude in a number of business ventures has described the powerful potential of this process as follows: "Running your own business is easy, not hard! I don't mean the work itself is easy. You do need to work hard. But you can easily be successful. Just do for the customer what you say you are going to do, and do it every time."[24]

Not all small firms manage to excel in customer service, but many realize their potential for doing so. Having a smaller number of customers and a close relationship with those customers makes customer service a powerful tool for entrepreneurial businesses. For further discussion of this subject, see Chapter 13.

Quality Performance

There is no reason that a small business needs to take a back seat in achieving quality in operations. In service businesses, quality performance is closely linked to customer service. Think of your favorite restaurant, for example. What distinguishes it from other dining places? It may be the atmosphere, the freshness and taste of the food, or the attentiveness of servers who are quickly aware of your needs and who promptly refill your beverage glass or coffee cup. These elements of dining quality can be found in a very small restaurant. In fact, the owner of a small establishment can insist on high levels of quality without experiencing the frustration of a large-company CEO who may have to push a quality philosophy through many layers of bureaucracy.

Many small firms excel in performing quality work, whether it is in auto repair, hair styling, financial audits, candy production, computer services, or clothing retailing. In quality management, entrepreneurial firms have a tool that enables them to compete effectively, not only with their peers but also with large corporations.

Integrity and Responsibility

The future is particularly bright for firms that add to excellent product quality and good customer service a solid reputation for honesty and dependability. Customers respond to evidence of integrity because they are aware of ethical issues. Experience has taught them that advertising claims are sometimes not accurate, that the fine print in contracts is sometimes detrimental to their best interests, and that businesses sometimes fail to stand behind their work.

Jeffry Timmons and Stephen Spinelli recently conducted a study of 128 presidents/founders who were attending a management program at Harvard Business School. They were asked to identify the most critical concepts, skills, and know-how for success at their companies.[25] Interestingly, 72 percent of the respondents stated that the single most important factor in long-term success was high ethical standards. Consistently operating with integrity can set a small business apart as being trustworthy at a time when stories of corporate greed and corruption abound. Chapter 2 discusses the critical importance of integrity and its role in entrepreneurship.

Living the Dream   focus on the customer

A Customer-Oriented Body Shop

One small firm that excels in keeping a focus on the customer is Auto Body World of Phoenix, Arizona, the state's oldest and largest independent collision repair company. The business strives to make customers happy with its service. Its focus is epitomized in the slogan "Same Family, Same Quality, Same Integrity."

A recent customer reported her satisfaction with a simple bumper repair at Auto Body World: "After I had my bumper repaired, they detailed the car completely and called me on the phone later that night. They asked about my experience with the work, the workers, the rental car, the insurance company—in short, to see if I was a 'delighted customer'!"

A family business, Auto Body World was started by Warren Fait and is now run by his son, David. David Fait has taken top honors as the Greater Phoenix Chamber of Commerce's Small Business Person of the Year, and the company has won a Better Business Bureau ethics award and a national award as the "Collision Business of the Year." The trophy inscription attests to the firm's excellent customer service and quality performance: "The collision business that set a standard by which all others will be measured." Fait has said, "Our success has been, and will be, driven by our customers." Reflecting its success is the fact that the firm has expanded and now operates in seven locations in the Phoenix area.

Sources: http://www.autobodyworld.com, accessed April 21, 2004; Angela Gabriel, "Top Business Person: It Was Fait," *Business Journal of Phoenix,* June 28, 1999; and personal interview with Auto Body World customer Emily Kaufmann, January 2007.

http://www.autobodyworld.com

Innovation

How the world is changing! Can you believe that when Bill Clinton was elected president, hardly anyone—with the exception of some people in the government and academia—had e-mail? In his book *The World Is Flat,* Thomas Friedman describes the convergence of 10 forces that have "flattened" the world.[26] Friedman's contention that the world is flat means that anything can now be done from anywhere in the world. Individuals, not governments or large corporations, are driving the globalization that we are experiencing all around us, Friedman says. Innovation, both in products or services and in ways to be more competitive, is within the reach of the small business entrepreneur in ways that were not thought possible a few years ago.

New product innovation has often come from the world of small business. Most of the radical inventions of the last century, such as the computer and the pacemaker, came from small companies, not large ones. And this will not change.

Research departments of big businesses tend to emphasize the improvement of existing products. Creative ideas may be sidetracked because they are not related to existing products or because they are unusual. Preoccupation with an existing product can obscure the value of a new idea. Scott Anthony, co-author of *Seeing What's Next,* says, "The thing that's so tricky is that everything an established company is trained to do—watch your markets carefully, listen to your best customers, innovate to meet their needs—oftentimes causes them to miss some of these disruptive transformation trends."[27] For instance, Apple Computer controls 80 percent of the MP3 player market today, whereas Sony, which had strong CD player sales in the 1990s, holds only a miniscule amount of the MP3 market.

The bureaucracy within larger firms can also cause the delay or even the death of new ideas. Most large companies insist on a lengthy process of approving new ideas. That's not the case at some smaller companies. For instance, Raving Brands, an Atlanta-based fast-casual restaurant franchisor, goes from finished concept to store opening in about a year, compared to two or even more years for most franchisors.[28] Being smaller clearly has advantages when it comes to innovation. Luda Kopeikina is president of the Equinox Corporation, a firm that advises companies on innovation processes. In her words, "Entrepreneurs excel at creating new ideas, and that's a big advantage. Very rarely do you see large companies good at innovation, creating ideas and ramping them up. That, by its nature, creates opportunity for small companies."[29]

The Internet has evened the global playing field, allowing small companies to connect with individuals anywhere in the world in the blink of an eye. Sophisticated computer software, once accessible only to large businesses, is now available at prices small companies can afford.

Offshoring is another phenomenon of recent years that has allowed small companies to be competitive. In a *Business Week* cover story on outsourcing, Pete Engardio, Michael Arndt, and Dean Foust observe, "Creative new companies can exploit the possibilities of offshoring even faster than established players." The authors offer Crimson Consulting Group as a good example. The firm, with only 14 full-time employees, provides global market research on everything from routers to software. It farms out the research to 5,000 independent experts all around the world. Crimson's CEO, Gleen Gow, comments, "This allows a small firm like us to compete with McKinsey and Bain [two of the world's largest consulting firms] on a very global basis with very low costs."[30]

The bottom line: Smaller firms have no reason to despair about not being competitive in an innovative world. They often lead in developing new and different products and services, and they are frequently an equal beneficiary of new technologies with large companies.

Special Niche

If a small business can find a special niche of some type, it may compete with great strength in that area. The niche might consist of a uniquely specialized service or product, or it might be a focus on serving a particular geographical area.

By finding a special niche, a small business may avoid intense competition from large corporations. Lowe's Supermarkets of Littlefield, Texas, provides an example of a family business that followed this path to business success.[31] In 1964, Roger Lowe, Sr., and his father purchased a small supermarket in Olton, Texas. The family business shifted to the next generation in 1973, when Roger Lowe, Jr., joined the firm as vice president and CEO following the death of his grandfather. The business gradually expanded to 58 stores by adding supermarkets, mostly in small rural towns of West Texas and New Mexico. In many towns, Lowe's faces no local competitor. In the few locations where it competes head to head with large chains like Wal-Mart, Lowe's Supermarket distinguishes itself by offering product selections carefully tailored to the unique local and ethnic tastes of the neighborhood population.

Getting Started

6 Discuss factors related to readiness for entrepreneurship and getting started in an entrepreneurial career.

Starting any type of business career is exciting. Launching one's own business, however, can be absolutely breathtaking because of the extreme risk and great potential in such a venture. Let's think for a moment about some special concerns of individuals who are ready to get their feet wet in entrepreneurial waters.

Age and Entrepreneurial Opportunity

One practical question is, What is the right age to become an entrepreneur? As you might guess, there is no single answer to this question. Most businesses require some background knowledge. In addition, most prospective entrepreneurs must first build their financial resources in order to make the necessary initial investments. A certain amount of time is usually required, therefore, to gain education, experience, and financial resources. Some find it helpful to work for a large company to gain experience and then start their own business. For example, Jody Hall worked for Starbucks for 12 years before starting Vérité Coffee in 2003. During her time at Starbucks, she had the opportunity to observe Howard Schultz, Starbucks' founder. Hall, who worked her way up to the position of Starbucks' head of promotions and events for new stores, explained, "I learned a lot about the coffeehouse experience through [Schultz] and his vision."[32]

Though there are no hard-and-fast rules concerning the right age for starting a business, some age deterrents do exist. Young people are often discouraged from entering entrepreneurial careers by inadequacies in their preparation and resources. Older people develop family, financial, and job commitments that make entrepreneurship seem too risky; they may have acquired interests in retirement programs or achieved promotions to positions of greater responsibility and higher salaries.

The ideal time for entrepreneurship, then, appears to lie somewhere between the late 20s and the early 40s, when there is a balance between preparatory experiences on the one hand and family obligations on the other. As Tyler Self, co-founder of Vision Research Organization, says, it is about the tradeoff between confidence (usually characterized by youth) and wisdom (usually based on years of experience).[33]

Research conducted by Paul Reynolds shows that the highest percentage of startups is in the 25- to 35-year age group.[34] Obviously, there are exceptions to this generalization: Some teenagers, such as Caroline Gray, start their own firms. At the age of 13, Gray already was a serial entrepreneur, having started four businesses. In her words,

> *Now all of my friends want to start their own businesses too, because it is so much cooler than bagging groceries or cleaning tables at a restaurant. Plus, you make lots more money! Last summer, among all my businesses, I made about $800. Being an entrepreneur is a perfect equation: Fun plus money plus happy customers equals a great job.*[35]

An increasing number of 50- and 60-year-olds today walk away from successful careers in big business when they become excited by the prospects of entrepreneurship and doing something on their own. Retirees who opt to start new careers as entrepreneurs often view retirement as an opportunity to pursue interests they never before had time for. More than the money, their new businesses offer them a chance to work on something they really want and love to do. For instance, after a 30-year career as a magazine editor, Richard Busch decided to quit his job to pursue his passion for pottery.

In his early 50s, Busch had started asking himself what his life would be when his magazine career ended and what it was that he really wanted to do in the years to come. Describing that stage in his life, Busch says, "The more I thought about it, the more I felt like I'd really like to be a potter. . . . I set a timetable, which had me retire early, in my mid-late 50s. Then, as luck would have it, they offered me an early out, at age 56." As a result, Glenfiddich Farm Pottery was born.[36]

Characteristics of Successful Entrepreneurs

What kinds of people become successful entrepreneurs? As already mentioned, no well-defined entrepreneurial profile exists; individual entrepreneurs differ greatly from each other. Knowing this should encourage you if you wish to start your own business: You do not need to fit some prescribed stereotype.

Some qualities, however, are common among entrepreneurs and probably contribute to their success. One of these characteristics is a strong commitment to or passion for the business. It is an attitude that results in tenacity in the face of difficulty and a willingness to work hard. Entrepreneurs do not give up easily.

Such individuals are typically confident of their ability to meet the challenges confronting them. This factor of self-confidence was described by psychologist J. B. Rotter as an **internal locus of control**—a feeling that success depends on one's own efforts.[37] In contrast, an **external locus of control** reflects an attitude of dependence on luck or fate for success.

internal locus of control
A belief that one's success depends on one's own efforts

external locus of control
A belief that one's life is controlled more by luck or fate than by one's own efforts

Living the Dream   entrepreneurial challenges

© Switchpod

Reading, Writing, Running a Company

In June 2005, two 17-year-olds, living 1,440 miles apart, got to talking about podcasts on an Internet message board. Within the month, Weina Scott (from Miami, Florida) and Jake Fisher (from Rochester, Minnesota) had co-founded Switchpod, a computer Web company.

Scott already had a Web design business, which she had started at age 13. Fisher, says, "I wanted to get into a business at the beginning of some new technology bubble."

Switchpod's basic podcasting package, which covers hosted space on its servers, costs as much as $30 a month, but the package is free to customers who take out an advertisement on its site. By the time Switchpod's product had generated 800,000 downloads, Scott and Fisher had been contacted by a company named Wizzard Software. The Pittsburgh-based business, which makes speech-recognition and text-to-speech technology, was looking to add podcasting to its product mix.

Wizzard Software CEO Chris Spencer, 37, remembers that it took him a while to realize that he was negotiating with high school students. Scott and Fisher met face to face for the first time at Spencer's home in Fort Lauderdale, where their parents had brought them to sign the paperwork transferring ownership of Switchpod to Wizzard in an all-stock transaction worth $200,000. The sale provides the enterprising teens with annual salaries of $40,000 for a 20-hour work week; however, the contract acknowledges that their schoolwork comes before business.

Source: Patrick J. Sauer, "A Portfolio of Young Business Owners," *Inc.,* February 2007, p. 24. Copyright 2007 by Mansueto Ventures LLC. Reproduced with permission of Mansueto Ventures LLC in the format Textbook via Copyright Clearance Center.

http://www.switchpod.com

Entrepreneurs are often portrayed as risk takers. Certainly, they do assume risk. By investing their own money, they assume financial risk. If they leave secure jobs, they risk their careers. The stress and time required to start and run a business may place their families at risk. Even though entrepreneurs assume risk, they are what we might term moderate risk takers—accepting risks over which they have some control—rather than extreme risk takers, who accept outcomes depending purely on chance.

Timmons and Spinelli have summarized research on entrepreneurial characteristics.[38] They group what they describe as "desirable and acquirable attitudes and behaviors" into the following six categories:

1. *Commitment and determination.* Such entrepreneurs are tenacious, decisive, and persistent in problem solving.

2. *Leadership.* Such entrepreneurs are self-starters and team builders and focus on honesty in their business relationships.

3. *Opportunity obsession.* Such entrepreneurs are aware of market and customer needs.

4. *Tolerance of risk, ambiguity, and uncertainty.* Such entrepreneurs are risk takers, risk minimizers, and uncertainty tolerators.

5. *Creativity, self-reliance, and adaptability.* Such entrepreneurs are open-minded, flexible, uncomfortable with the status quo, and quick learners.

6. *Motivation to excel.* Such entrepreneurs are goal oriented and aware of their weaknesses and strengths.

Taking the Plunge

In starting a business, there comes a point at which the entrepreneur must "take the plunge." It may be scary because of the risks, but entrepreneurship is not for the faint of heart.[39] For many people, the right time for beginning a business is hastened by some special circumstance, described as a **precipitating event**. The individual may be fired, for example, or discover an unusual opportunity with strong potential.

Criticizing management has the potential for creating change—especially in the life of the critic! Consequently, it can lead to a precipitating event. Dave and Annette King, a husband-and-wife team, were avid weekend players of slow-pitch softball. While playing in a tournament in a small Colorado town, they made critical comments about the poor management of the event. The event manager asked them to leave and told them that if they thought they could do it better, they should try it. This was their precipitating event. The Kings' response was to do just that by creating Triple Crown Sports, and today they profitably run approximately 400 events a year in softball, baseball, soccer, and basketball.[40]

It is difficult to say what proportion of new entrepreneurs make their move because of some particular event. Whether propelled by a precipitating event or not, those who decide on entrepreneurship must eventually summon their courage and take the plunge.

> **precipitating event**
> An event, such as losing a job, that moves an individual to become an entrepreneur

Finding "Go-To" Persons

Although there are many different types of entrepreneurs, most have one thing in common—they found mentors along the way.

As you begin and continue on the entrepreneurial journey, you can make no better decision than to find mentors. Mentors are individuals to whom you can go for advice and counsel—people who are pulling for you, wanting you to succeed, and supporting your efforts. They are people who can teach you what to do and how to do it and, most importantly, encourage you on those days when you want to throw in the towel and apply for a job at a coffee shop. These individuals can help you avoid mistakes and be there to give you the benefit of their years of experience.

Although we can emphasize the importance of good mentors, only you can develop these vital relationships. We can, however, provide you with insights from individuals who have traveled where you want to go. We have created what we call a "go-to" team whose experience-based knowledge will be showcased in the How They See It feature, which you will find throughout this textbook. You will be reading about not only our perspective, as co-authors of this text, but also that of individuals who have spent even more time in the entrepreneurial arena. Their wisdom and knowledge will prove invaluable to you.

Growing and Managing the Business

An airplane pilot not only controls the plane during takeoff but also flies it and lands it. Similarly, entrepreneurs not only launch firms but also "fly" them; that is, they manage their firm's subsequent operation. In this book, you will find a discussion of the entire entrepreneurial process. It begins in the remainder of Part 1 (Chapter 2) with a discussion of the fundamental values of the firm. This discussion is followed in Parts 2 and 3 with a look at a firm's basic strategy, the various types of entrepreneurial ventures, and the initial planning that is required for business startups. Parts 4 through 6 deal with the marketing and management of a growing business, including its human resources, operations, and finances.

How They See It: The Go-To Team

Below are the entrepreneurs whose advice on starting and running a small business will appear in this feature throughout this text. Their perspectives are based on years of experience. Pay attention to them!

Sara Blakely

- Started SPANX, a leader in the shapewear revolution, with $5,000 in savings and had grown the company to $150 million in retail sales in 2006
- Launched The Sara Blakely Foundation, which is dedicated to supporting and empowering women around the world
- Launched ASSETS by Sara Blakely, a brand exclusive to Target
- Named Ernst & Young's Southeast Regional Entrepreneur of the Year
- Named Georgia's Woman of the Year

Rick Davis

- Formed his first company, Rick Davis Properties, at the age of 25
- Instrumental in start-up of First Interstate National Bank in Dallas, Texas
- Owner and CEO of DAVACO, the nation's number one turn-key retail service provider and technology leader, with double-digit annual growth
- Inducted into the 2006 Retail Construction Hall of Fame
- Finalist for the Ernst & Young Entrepreneur of the Year award in 2000 and 2006
- Member of the Salvation Army's Dallas/Fort Worth Metro-plex Advisory Board

Denny Fulk

- President of Fulk Equipment Company, Inc., a provider of storage and distribution systems to multinational companies
- Managing Partner for Hunters Row Properties, an industrial park real estate project
- Began second career as Director of Business Strategies for Keyway Associates in 2000, focusing on sharing principles of free enterprise system and modeling ethical business leadership for Asian businesspersons
- Chairman of the Board of Trustees at Milligan College

- Only American trustee of the Springdale College Charitable Trust for Educational and Training Development in Birmingham, England

Cecilia Levine

- President of MFI International Mfg., LLC, a provider of manufacturing, warehousing, distribution, and consulting services, with locations in Mexico and the United States
- Member of the President's Export Council
- Founder, Director, and President of the US/Mexico Strategic Alliance
- Founding member of the Midland, Texas, Hispanic Chamber of Commerce
- Small Business Association's 2007 Exporter of the Year
- USHCC Regional and National Hispanic Business Woman of the Year

Sally Lifland

- Started out her professional career working for a year in Paris, France, for Videocolor, an affiliate of RCA
- Gained experience in the publishing world first in a small packaging firm (Service to Publishers) and then in two large publishing houses (Allyn & Bacon and Bobbs-Merrill)
- With partner, founded a freelance production company in 1979, which handles complete production services (editing, proofreading, etc.) on approximately 25 college textbooks per year
- President of the Williamsport, Pennsylvania, chapter of the National Organization for Women
- Founding member and President of the Board of Directors of the Transitional Living Center, a community corrections facility for female offenders

Trey Moore

- Developed rate competitive analysis applications for USAA's actuary department
- Founder of S3 Software LLC, a provider of consulting services to companies seeking expertise in object-oriented design patterns
- Pioneered high-speed barcode scanning applications for wireless handheld scanners in the food industry

- Developed AirStrip OB with GE Healthcare, a medical software application that allows obstetricians to view critical real-time fetal and maternal vital signs on their PDAs

Scott J. Salmans

- Business development officer and events producer for the Greater Waco Chamber of Commerce

- President of WRS Group Ltd., the largest provider of supplemental teaching aids for health educators operating under the brand names of HealthEdco, Childbirth Graphics, and Special/Health Impressions

- Founder of SIS Family Enterprises, an umbrella entity for real estate and other small business ventures

- Chairman of the capital campaign for the New Life Children's Home in Guatemala

- Member of Baylor Development Council

John (Johnny) Stites, II

- CEO of J&S Construction Company, Inc., a small family-owned company

- Recognized by the Tennessee Center for Performance Excellence for his strategic approach to building a business and focus on risk reduction in the construction industry

- Trustee for the College of Business at Tennessee Technological University

- Trustee for Abilene Christian University

- Member of the President's Advisory Council of American Buildings Company

- State board member of the Associated General Contractors of Tennessee

Winston Wolfe

- Worked for seven years at Great Southern Corporation, selling and marketing its line of sunglasses

- Founder of Olympic Optical, a provider of industrial safety sunglasses to the shooting sports industry

- Licensed the names Remington, Smith & Wesson, and Zebco

- Owner-manager of Sherwood, a 500-acre rural property near Memphis

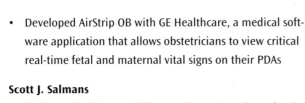

Living the Dream   entrepreneurial challenges

Don't Go It Alone—Find Mentors

Luke Eddins is grateful for the time he spent with his mentor at a former job before founding Luke Hits, an online company that helps unsigned bands get their songs on movie and TV soundtracks. As an avid musician, Eddins wanted to combine his two loves, music and business, but knew that he needed to develop the business skills necessary for success.

Eddins's mentor wasn't actually in the music industry—Eddins was working in the gem industry under the supervision of Sam Gadodia, a Harvard MBA. There, he learned everything he could about business simply by spending time near his mentor.

Working inside Gadodia's office proved invaluable: "I was able to overhear all the [goings-on]," says Eddins. "I could learn his approach, his tactics, his strategies." Eddins likens the experience to taking a very real-world business course. "You have to act like a sponge," says Eddins.

But it wasn't just observing Gadodia that helped Eddins. Even after the two no longer worked together, Eddins would seek his mentor's input on startup issues like how to approach a particular client or pitch a certain proposal. Although he hasn't had much contact with his mentor since Gadodia moved to India six months ago, the lessons Eddins learned are still fresh in his mind.

Source: Nichole L. Torres, "Why Mentors Rock—and How They Can Help You Grow Your Business," *Entrepreneur's Start-Ups* magazine, August 2002, pp. 46, 47, http://www.entrepreneur.com/ startingabusiness/startupbasics/findinghelp/article541623.html, accessed December 14, 2006.

http://www.lukehits.com

7 Explain the concept of an entrepreneurial legacy and the challenges involved in crafting a worthy legacy.

Success in Business and Success in Life

So far, we have discussed entrepreneurship and small business from a number of angles. As you contemplate such a career, we now urge you to broaden your perspective and to think about some of the values and intangibles that are part of the entrepreneurial life.

Looking Back at an Entrepreneurial Career

When an entrepreneur makes that final exit from the entrepreneurial stage, his or her business achievements become history. Reflecting on their lives and businesses at that point in their journeys, numerous entrepreneurs have come face to face with such questions as these: Was it a good trip? What kind of meaning does it hold for me now? Can I feel good about it? What are my disappointments? How did I make a difference? Such questions lead entrepreneurs to reassess their values, priorities, and commitments. By anticipating these questions, an entrepreneur can identify his or her most basic concerns early in the journey. Without such reflection, the entrepreneurial journey and its ending may prove disappointing.

Evaluating Accomplishments

Assessment of entrepreneurial performance requires establishing criteria. Obviously, no one standard can be applied. For example, a person who measures everything by the dollar sign would determine the degree of an entrepreneur's success by the size of his or her bank account.

The exiting entrepreneur will, at some point, think about achievements in terms of personal values and goals, rather than textbook criteria, popular culture, or financial rules of thumb. In all likelihood, a number of basic considerations will be relevant to the entrepreneur's sense of satisfaction.

In looking ahead to this time of looking back, one naturally thinks in terms of a legacy. A *legacy* consists of those things passed on or left behind. In a narrow sense, it describes material possessions bequeathed to one's heirs. In a broader sense, it refers to everything that one leaves behind—material items, good or bad family relationships, a record of integrity or avarice, a history of exploitation or contribution. An **entrepreneurial legacy** includes both tangible items and intangible qualities passed on not only to heirs but also to the broader society. One can appreciate, then, the seriousness with which the entrepreneur needs to consider the kind of legacy he or she is building.

entrepreneurial legacy
Material assets and intangible qualities passed on to both heirs and society

Winning the Wrong Game

It is easy for entrepreneurs to get caught up in an activity trap, working harder and harder to keep up with the busy pace of life. Ultimately, such entrepreneurs may find their business accomplishments overshadowed by the neglect or sacrifice of something more important to them. It's possible to score points in the wrong game or win battles in the wrong war.

This type of entrepreneurial error produces a disappointing legacy, a sense that one's professional achievements are to some extent inadequate. Consider what happens, for example, when the legitimate goal of earning money becomes a consuming passion. The CEO of a former *Inc.* 500 company has critiqued the entrepreneurial experience in this way:

> *I believe that when our companies fail to satisfy our fundamental need to contribute to the community and instead exist predominantly to fill a bank account, then we lose our souls. Life is short. No one's gravestone reads, "He made a lot of money." Making a difference in your own life, your employees' lives, and your customers' lives is the real payoff.*[41]

Ed Bonneau revolutionized the distribution of sunglasses in the United States and eventually dominated that market with his highly successful business. While growing the firm, Bonneau purchased Pennsylvania Optical (with its patents and contracts with Wal-Mart and Kmart) and industry giant Foster Grant (with its patents and manufacturing divisions).

Then, Bonneau sold the business and walked away from it all. Reflecting on the transaction, he said, "It was hard for me to figure out what to do with all this money." From a business standpoint, his was a huge entrepreneurial success story. However, in a comment on how he'd like to be remembered, Bonneau downplayed his financial wealth:

> *I would hope that they knew something else besides that I once ran the biggest sunglass company in the world. That's not the number one thing that I'd want to be known for. It's okay, but I'd much rather have that final assessment made by my kids and have them say, "He was a terrific dad." I never wanted to sacrifice my family or my church for my business.*[42]

And Bonneau's advice to younger entrepreneurs follows a similar theme:

> *Take God and your family with you when you go into business, and keep that balance in your life. Because when you get to be 60 years old and you look back over your life, if all you have is the biggest sunglass company in the world and a pot full of money in the bank . . . it won't be enough. Your life is going to be hollow, and you can't go back and redo it.*[43]

Entrepreneurs typically work—indeed, often must work—long hours, especially in the beginning. Sometimes, however, the obsession with work and the long hours become too extreme. Based on interviews with repeat entrepreneurs, Ilan Mochari summarized their reports of early mistakes: "If they had it to do all over again, most of the group would have spent more time away from their first companies, hanging with the family, schmoozing up other CEOs, and pondering the long-term picture."[44]

An excessive focus on money or work, then, can twist the entrepreneurial process. The outcome appears less satisfying and somehow less rewarding when the time for exit arrives.

How They See It: On Mentoring

Sara Blakely

I read Sir Richard Branson's book *Losing My Virginity* right out of college and was inspired by his maverick approach to business. In 2004, I jumped at the chance to meet him by becoming a cast member on his reality show, *The Rebel Billionaire*. Branson traveled with us around the world, giving me the opportunity to talk with him about SPANX, his experience with Virgin, and his global nonprofit work. I was really interested in learning how to set up a nonprofit foundation, because this had been a dream of mine since I was a young girl. I wanted to find a way to empower women who do not have the same opportunities that we do in America. At the conclusion of the show came a completely unexpected twist: Branson handed me a check for $750,000—his paycheck for the show—for me to start my own foundation to help women! Branson has since been an amazing mentor and even came to Atlanta to help me launch The Sara Blakely Foundation.

Oprah is another mentor of mine whom I've been lucky enough to meet. Her dedication to paying it forward and helping others to achieve success is a huge inspiration to me.

Rick Davis

My number one mentor and the person who has had the biggest influence on my professional career was my father, Charles "Skip" Davis. While both my father and my mother served as role models in many areas throughout my life, it was my father who nurtured my entrepreneurial spirit. He led by example through his own professional accomplishments and supported me—financially, emotionally, and spiritually.

Like my father, I served as a fireman, and, like him, I chose to take advantage of my "off-days" to venture into other business opportunities. He delved into plumbing and eventually started his own insurance company, while my interest was in real estate and construction.

Like many young men with an entrepreneurial spirit, I had a vision, but I didn't have the capital to make it all happen. Without my dad to co-sign my first $4,500 loan, I could not have financed my first HUD renovation project. In effect, his signature launched my career. Later, as I set my sights on multi-family apartment complexes, my dad was there to co-sign for me again. Obviously, this was a significant investment that could have resulted in financial ruin. Fortunately, that particular project turned a profit for both of us. His ongoing guidance and leadership throughout that project, as well as his support, demonstrated incredible faith in my abilities. This blend of risk taking, hard work, and trust ultimately gave me the confidence I needed to be successful.

My dad taught me values and skills that make for both an entrepreneur and a great person; do what you say you are going to do, never settle for anything less than the best, and learn from your mistakes and your triumphs.

Denny Fulk

My first position as a co-op student at the University of Cincinnati College of Business Administration was with an Indianapolis-based publishing company. Howard W. Sams & Company, Inc., and all its subsidiaries were later acquired by ITT, the aggressive conglomerate of the 1960s.

I served as the eyes, ears, and feet for the chairman and CEO, Howard Sams, by traveling all over North America and Europe, establishing research projects for new products to serve the electronics and then-infant computer industry. We later expanded into textbook publishing, including legal and medical books, through acquisitions. After each trip, I would review my detailed reports personally with Mr. Sams in his office. My findings influenced him, other members of top management, and those on the company's board of directors to invest capital in new products as well as complete acquisitions of companies and private vocational education schools.

In spite of working many hours, Mr. Sams always had time to talk and share his vision for the company with those of us who were younger. During the summer, he would host cookouts at his very lovely home for those of us who were new college graduates and the summer interns. The exchange of ideas between the younger generation and the more mature members of management provided an excellent basis for building professional and social relationships that have existed to this day. It firmly planted in my mind the need to always be open to accepting new ideas while respecting the value of experience and judgment from seasoned individuals in an organization.

Cecilia Levine

Mentors are people who positively impact our lives without looking back to see what they have done for us and without being aware of what they were doing. For me, they are not only my mentors in business but also in life as a whole.

My father, Juan Ochoa Reynoso, first became an entrepreneur at eight years of age. Affected by the Mexican Revolution, he found himself without anything to eat and with no father, a mother who could not support him, and two brothers. To support himself and his family, he would pedal the sewing machine for ladies who sewed at home; at the same time, he used his roller skates to get to his day job as an office boy. There were many opportunities for him to make a living in ways that were not proper or ethical, but he chose the right path, which was working hard and with honesty. He would always ask to learn more on the job; he learned English to serve the owner of the company that he worked for. He learned everything on the job until he owned his own company, with not only one location but with sites throughout Mexico and Colombia; he also sold cotton in the U.S. What I learned from him was work with integrity. Nothing bad happens if you overwork, are fair, and are kind to the people that work for you.

Emma Wilson de Bunsow, my grandmother, was another mentor for me as a businessperson. First, she was a designer in the U.S.; later, she was a hotel owner who ran several ranches and had over 50 rental homes. Integrity, hard work, vision, and creativity were some of the most important things that I learned from her. There was nothing that she faced that was out of the question to do, especially as a woman with great strength and incredible grace.

When I went into business myself, she always encouraged me to do things and let me know that I could do it. Her support was very important because I believed in her; if she told me so, I could do it. The way she treated the people that worked for her was very important because she was an inspiration to them. She taught others to do things that they would have never done if it wasn't for her direction and support. It was as if she were the most talented lady in the world, and she always was trying to pass on what she knew. She always expected people to perform to the best of their abilities, and she pulled out the talents in people.

Scott Salmans

My mentors have served throughout my life without holding the title or direct knowledge that I viewed them as such. In college and since then, Richard C. Scott, then dean of the business school at Baylor, would invite me in and just ask me questions about what I was doing and how my life was going. He would always talk about "business" or schooling efforts, but never failed to ask me about my family and their well-being as well. I learned the most from him by watching or listening to his reactions—some verbal and others with knowing looks or body language—to my answers, statements, choices, and plans. He was very encouraging to me as a student and often gave me the confidence to step out and do more than I thought I was capable of. He helped me keep perspective later in life, as I faced many difficulties in business and family matters. Finally, he helped me realize that I could do more than one thing well, as he always had many balls in the air, including serving as the vice president of development of Baylor University, operating small businesses in other states, serving on corporate boards of directors, and so many other roles.

Later in life, Stanley Strum has been a mentor to me by listening as an honest sounding board more than in any other way. The value of the hours he gave me as he listened to me in times of trouble can never be repaid. His ability to understand the importance of proximity and "being there" as a key to success prompted him to keep me close by his side as a resource as he served out his year as the chief volunteer officer of the Chamber of Commerce. He returned the favor by introducing me as a member to the Young Presidents' Organization later in my life. This introduction has been extremely important in my continuing education process and for contacts who have been enormously valuable to my business and family endeavors.

John Stites

One of the first and most influential mentors of my life was my grandfather, Wesley P. Flatt, Sr. "Big Wes," as we affectionately called him, was the youngest of 12 brothers who grew up in poverty on a hillside farm in Tennessee. Unlike his brothers,

he left Flynn's Creek, Tennessee, and became a teacher and lawyer.

By his words and actions, my grandfather taught me the value of history. When I was in high school, he took me to museums and explained how events in history had affected his life and the country he lived in. He demonstrated in his life the importance and the necessity of men standing tall when others were reluctant or afraid.

Big Wes never sought the favor of men in lieu of doing the right thing for the moment. He lived his life not worrying about earning money and taught us to freely give to others our time and money.

Although my parents were extremely positive influences in my life, I could see even there the influences of Big Wes. I thank God for men like him and miss him often.

Winston Wolfe

I did not have a mentor with whom I could confer during the development of my business. I did, however, have a person whose help and encouragement was a great inspiration. That person was my uncle, Tom Little.

My uncle retired from the Navy and started a moving and storage business. When I discussed with him my desire to start my own business, he asked me if I needed any money. I remember dressing up in my best suit, flying up to Virginia to meet with him, and getting a $10,000 loan, along with much encouragement. The confidence he had in me was an extra incentive to make the business work. I repaid the loan in less than a year.

Crafting a Worthy Legacy

In entrepreneurial terms, what constitutes a worthy legacy? One issue is the nature of the endeavor itself. A business that operates within the law, provides jobs, and serves the public provides a good foundation for a satisfying entrepreneurial experience. Although a business that peddles pornography on the Internet might make a lot of money for its owner, most Americans would dismiss it as an unworthy enterprise because of its harmful, destructive character.

Within many individuals is a streak of nobility that gives them a genuine concern for the well-being of others. Their positive attitudes propel them toward endeavors of practical service to society.

Bernard Rapaport, a highly successful, principled, and generous entrepreneur, has stressed the importance of the means one takes to achieve a given end. "Whatever it is you want to achieve," he said, "*how* you achieve it is more important than *if* you achieve it." At 90 years of age, reflecting on life and legacy, he said, "What do I want to do? I want to save the world."[45]

Such idealism can guide an entrepreneur into many endeavors that are useful to our economic system. In fact, some entrepreneurial ventures are specifically designed to meet the particular needs of society. J. O. Stewart, a successful entrepreneur, has in his later years launched a firm whose primary objective is to provide good, low-cost housing to families who cannot otherwise afford it. His motivation for this venture is personal concern for the needs of low-income families.

For most entrepreneurs looking back on their careers, satisfaction requires that their businesses have been constructive or positive in their impact—at the least, their effect should have been benign, causing no harm to the social order. In most cases, entrepreneurial businesses make positive contributions by providing jobs and services. A few make even greater contributions by addressing special needs in society.

The criteria by which one evaluates entrepreneurship must be personal. Stephen R. Covey suggests that the most effective way "to begin with the end in mind" is to develop a personal mission statement or philosophy or creed.[46] Though individuals will have different mission statements because their goals and values will differ, widely shared values will underlie many of their judgments.

Beginning with the End in Mind

An entrepreneur builds a business, a life, and a legacy day by day, starting with the initial launch and proceeding through the months and years of operation that follow. A person exiting an entrepreneurial venture has completed the business part of his or her legacy—it must be constructed during the life of the business itself.

Therefore, as Covey would say, an entrepreneur needs to "begin with the end in mind" and to keep that end in mind while making the innumerable operating decisions that follow. By selecting the proper values and wisely balancing their application, an entrepreneur can make a satisfying exit, leaving a positive and substantial legacy to heirs, employees, the community, and the broader society.

It is the authors' deepest hope that your journey as an entrepreneur will be a richly rewarding experience, not only financially, but also, more importantly, in the things that matter most in life. Above all, we hope that your legacy will bring satisfaction to you and enhance the important relationships in your life. Go for it!

Looking BACK

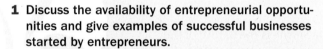

1 Discuss the availability of entrepreneurial opportunities and give examples of successful businesses started by entrepreneurs.

- An entrepreneurial opportunity is a desirable and timely innovation that creates value for interested buyers and end users.

- Exciting entrepreneurial opportunities exist for those who recognize them. However, a true opportunity exists only for those who have the interest, resources, and capabilities required to succeed.

- Latemodel Restoration Supply, SPANX, and MP4 Solutions are examples of highly successful businesses started by entrepreneurs.

2 Explain the nature of entrepreneurship and how it is related to small business.

- Entrepreneurs are individuals who discover market needs and launch new firms to meet those needs.

- Owner-managers who buy out founders of existing firms, franchisees, and second-generation operators of family firms may also be considered entrepreneurs.

- Definitions of small business are arbitrary, but this book focuses on firms of fewer than 100 employees that have mostly localized operations and are financed by a small number of individuals.

- Most entrepreneurial firms are small when they begin, but a few grow (some very quickly) into large businesses.

3 Identify some motivators or rewards of entrepreneurial careers.

- Researchers have identified up to 38 different reasons for self-employment.

- Entrepreneurial motivators or rewards include profit, independence, freedom (escaping from a bad situation), personal satisfaction, and personal fulfillment (contributing to one's community).

4 **Describe the various types of entrepreneurs and entrepreneurial ventures.**

- Founders of firms are "pure" entrepreneurs, but those who acquire established businesses and franchisees may also be considered entrepreneurs.

- A few entrepreneurs start high-potential ventures (gazelles); other entrepreneurs operate attractive small firms and microbusinesses.

- Based on their backgrounds and management styles, entrepreneurs may be characterized as artisan entrepreneurs or opportunistic entrepreneurs.

- The number of women entrepreneurs is growing rapidly, and they are entering many nontraditional fields.

- Entrepreneurial teams consist of two or more individuals who combine their efforts to function as entrepreneurs.

5 **Identify five potential advantages of small entrepreneurial firms.**

- Entrepreneurial managers have an opportunity to know their customers well and to focus on meeting their needs.

- By emphasizing quality in products and services, small firms can build a competitive advantage.

- Independent business owners can build an internal culture based on integrity and responsibility in relationships both inside and outside the firm; such a culture helps strengthen the firm's position in a competitive environment.

- Many small firms and individual operators have demonstrated a superior talent for finding innovative products and developing better ways of doing business.

- Small firms that find a special niche of some type can gain an advantage in the marketplace.

6 **Discuss factors related to readiness for entrepreneurship and getting started in an entrepreneurial career.**

- The period between the late 20s and early 40s appears to be when a person's education, work experience, family situation, and financial resources are most likely to enable him or her to become an entrepreneur.

- There is no well-defined entrepreneurial profile, but many entrepreneurs have such helpful characteristics as a passion for their business, strong self-confidence, and a willingness to assume moderate risks.

- Successful entrepreneurs are also thought to possess leadership skills, a strong focus on opportunities, creativity and adaptability, and motivation to excel.

- Entry into entrepreneurial careers is often triggered by a precipitating event, such as losing a job.

- Entrepreneurs can make no better decision than to develop relationships with mentors who can provide advice and counsel.

- Once a business is launched, the entrepreneur must manage growth of the business and issues related to its ongoing operation.

7 **Explain the concept of an entrepreneurial legacy and the challenges involved in crafting a worthy legacy.**

- An entrepreneur's legacy includes not only money and material possessions but also nonmaterial things such as personal relationships and values.

- Part of the legacy is the contribution of the business to the community.

- A worthy legacy includes a good balance of values and principles important to the entrepreneur. Errors in choosing or applying goals and values can create a defective legacy.

- Building a legacy is an ongoing process that begins at the launch of the firm and continues throughout its operating life.

Key TERMS

entrepreneurial opportunity, p. 4

entrepreneur, p. 6

reluctant entrepreneur, p. 10

refugee, p. 10

founder, p. 12

franchisee, p. 12

high-potential venture (gazelle), p. 12

attractive small firm, p. 13

microbusiness, p. 13

lifestyle business, p. 13

artisan entrepreneur, p. 13

opportunistic entrepreneur, p. 13

entrepreneurial team, p. 15

internal locus of control, p. 19

external locus of control, p. 19

precipitating event, p. 21

entrepreneurial legacy, p. 24

Discussion QUESTIONS

1. The outstanding success stories discussed at the beginning of the chapter are exceptions to the rule. What, then, is their significance in illustrating entrepreneurial opportunity? Are these stories misleading?

2. What is meant by the term *entrepreneur*?

3. Consider an entrepreneur you know personally. What was the most significant reason for his or her deciding to follow an independent business career? If you don't already know the reason, discuss it with that person.

4. The motivators/rewards of profit, independence, and personal satisfaction are three reasons individuals enter entrepreneurial careers. What problems might be anticipated if an entrepreneur were to become obsessed with one of these rewards—for example, if she or he had an excessive desire to accumulate wealth, operate independently, or achieve a particular lifestyle?

5. Distinguish between an artisan entrepreneur and an opportunistic entrepreneur.

6. What is the advantage of using an entrepreneurial team?

7. Explain how customer focus and innovation can be special strengths of small businesses.

8. Why is the period from the late 20s to the early 40s considered to be the best time in life to become an entrepreneur?

9. Explain the concept of an entrepreneurial legacy.

10. Explain the following statement: "One can climb the ladder to success only to discover it is leaning against the wrong wall."

You Make the CALL

SITUATION 1

In the following statement, a business owner attempts to explain and justify his preference for slow growth in his business.

I limit my growth pace and make every effort to service my present customers in the manner they deserve. I have some peer pressure to do otherwise by following the advice of experts—that is, to take on partners and debt to facilitate rapid growth in sales and market share. When tempted by such thoughts, I think about what I might gain. Perhaps I could make more money, but I would also expect a lot more problems. Also, I think it might interfere somewhat with my family relationships, which are very important to me.

Question 1 Should this venture be regarded as entrepreneurial? Is the owner a true entrepreneur?

Question 2 Do you agree with the philosophy expressed here? Is the owner really doing what is best for his family?

Question 3 What kinds of problems is this owner trying to avoid?

SITUATION 2

Nineteen-year-old Kiersten Berger, now in her second year at a local community college, has begun to think about starting her own business. She has taken piano lessons since she was seven years old and is regarded as a very good pianist. The thought has occurred to her that she could establish a piano studio and offer lessons to children, young people, and even adults. The prospect sounds more attractive than looking for a salaried job when she graduates in a few months.

Question 1 If Kiersten Berger opens a piano studio, will she be an entrepreneur?

Question 2 Which type of reward(s) will be greatest in this venture?

Question 3 Even though she is an artisan, she will need to make decisions of a business nature. What decisions or evaluations may be especially difficult for her?

SITUATION 3

Dover Sporting Goods Store occupies an unimpressive retail location in a small city in northern Illinois. Started in

1935, it is now operated by Duane Dover—a third-generation member of the founding family. He works long hours trying to earn a reasonable profit in the old downtown area.

Dover's immediate concern is an announcement that Wal-Mart is considering opening a store at the southern edge of town. As Dover reacts to this announcement, he is overwhelmed by a sense of injustice. Why should a family business that has served the community honestly and well for 60 years have to fend off a large corporation that would take big profits out of the community and give very little in return? Surely, he reasons, the

law must offer some kind of protection against big business predators of this kind. Dover also wonders whether small stores such as his have ever been successful in competing against business giants like Wal-Mart.

Question 1 Is Dover's feeling of unfairness justified? Is his business entitled to some type of legal protection against moves of this type?

Question 2 How should Dover plan to compete against Wal-Mart, if and when this becomes necessary?

Experiential EXERCISES

1. Analyze your own education and experience as qualifications for entrepreneurship. Identify your greatest strengths and weaknesses.

2. Explain your own interest in each type of entrepreneurial reward. Point out which type of incentive is most significant for you personally and tell why.

3. Interview someone who has started a business, being sure to ask for information regarding the entrepreneur's background and age at the time

the business was started. In your report of the interview, indicate whether the entrepreneur was in any sense a refugee, and show how the timing of her or his startup relates to the ideal time for startup explained in this chapter.

4. Interview a woman entrepreneur about what problems, if any, she has encountered in her business because she is a woman.

Exploring the WEB

1. In addition to the Small Business Administration website, which you can find at **http://www.sba.gov**, numerous other websites and online resources are available to assist entrepreneurs and small business owners. Using your favorite search engine, locate five sites that you think are particularly interesting and valuable. In your opinion, what makes them stand out?

2. This chapter highlights Latemodel Restoration Supply, SPANX, and MP4 Solutions as examples of entrepreneurial success. Using the Internet as a research tool, choose two or three other examples of businesses started by entrepreneurs, either thriving or struggling ones. Then explain why you chose these businesses, and identify what type of entrepreneurial venture each is.

Case 1

Boston Duck Tours (p. 620)
Tiring of work in investment banking, this entrepreneur left salaried employment, withstood the skepticism of others, and built an unusual but highly successful tourism business.

Alternative Cases for Chapter 1:
Case 9, Le Travel Store, p. 638
Case 14, Country Supply, p. 648
Case 19, Gibson Mortuary, p. 658

## chapter 2

Entrepreneurial Integrity and Ethics

A Gateway to Small Business Opportunity

In the VIDEO SPOTLIGHT

Joseph's Lite Cookies
http://www.josephslitecookies.com

When growing a company to annual revenues of $100 million and hundreds of employees, the founder is sure to face any number of ethical dilemmas. In today's world, staying true to your convictions and acting with integrity seem to present a significant number of challenges. For Joseph Semprevivo, however, honesty and integrity have been key elements in building a successful company. Not only is Semprevivo committed to being socially responsible regarding the quality of the cookies his company sells; he is also committed to his employees, his customers, and his community.

When he was 12 years old, Semprevivo, a diabetic, developed a sugar-free ice cream that he sold in his parents' restaurant and in 197 grocery stores throughout New Mexico. Three years later, he asked his parents to develop a recipe for a sugar-free cookie. Joseph's Lite Cookies was born out of his desire to share that sugar-free treat with other diabetics, and this eagerness to share has shaped his company's culture.

Interdependence, reliability, and honesty characterize working relationships at the company, which has grown to have annual sales topping $100 million, dozens of products (not just cookies), and a presence in over 37 countries and 125,000 stores worldwide. Watch this video spotlight to see how integrity can create a strong foundation for growth.

Video material provided by Hattie Bryant, Producer of Small Business School, the series on PBS Stations, Worldnet, and the Web at http://www.smallbusinessschool.org.

Small**Business**School ▣
the Series on PBS stations and the Web

After studying this chapter, you should be able to

1 Define integrity and understand its importance to small businesses.
2 Explain how integrity applies to various stakeholder groups, including owners, customers, employees, the community, and the government.
3 Identify challenges to integrity that arise in small businesses and explain the benefits of integrity to small firms.
4 Explain the impact of the Internet and globalization on the integrity of small businesses.
5 Describe practical approaches for building a business with integrity.
6 Describe social entrepreneurship and the costs and opportunities of environmentalism to small businesses.

When you consider the way business is presented in the media and entertainment, the picture is not a pretty one (think Hollywood productions such as *Wall Street, Erin Brockovich,* or even *Fun with Dick and Jane*). In fact, the image is quite negative. Ironically, this window into marketplace misconduct is sometimes self-focused. Mel Brooks's clever movie *The Producers,* adapted into a Tony-winning stage musical and then remade as a movie in 2005, captures the thought processes of a businessman who drifts away from appropriate ethical moorings. Brooks tells the story of Max Bialystock, a Broadway producer whose string of hits and good fortune has played out. When his accountant, Leo Bloom, arrives to audit his books, it becomes clear that the former entertainment heavy hitter is now on the verge of financial disaster—that is, until Bloom stumbles upon a surefire solution. His recipe for success is simple: Raise a million dollars from unwitting investors, produce a flop so bad that it closes on opening night, pay off the modest initial costs of the play, and escape to Brazil with the remaining cash.

Bialystock and Bloom's scheme is hatched from pure desperation (see Exhibit 2-1), but the circumstances are not at all unique—decision makers sometimes respond to pressure to perform by compromising their principles, which explains why reports of corporate scandals continue to surface in the news. Corporations are run by people, after all, and it is reasonable to assume that some will give in to temptation as they make decisions for their companies. However, being aware of human frailties doesn't ease the shock of discovering that yet another corporation that enjoyed the public's trust has been compromised in a big way. In this chapter, we discuss the personal integrity of the entrepreneur, which is the foundation of ethical behavior in small business, and provide insights that lead to the honorable management of enterprises.

Integrity and Entrepreneurship

1 Define integrity and understand its importance to small businesses.

Stories in the news media concerning insider trading, fraud, and bribery usually involve large corporations. However, in the less-publicized day-to-day activities of small businesses, decision makers regularly face ethical dilemmas and temptations to compromise principles for the sake of business or personal advantage. This strikes at the heart of integrity.

2-1   *Dialogue from* The Producers

Bloom: You raised two thousand more than you needed to produce your last play.

Bialystock: So what? What did it get me? I'm wearing a cardboard belt.

Bloom: Ahhhhhh! But that's where you made your error. You didn't go all the way. You see, if you were really a bold criminal, you could have raised a million.

Bialystock: But the play only cost $60,000 to produce.

Bloom: Exactly, and how long did it run?

Bialystock: One night.

Bloom: See? You could have raised a million dollars, put on a sixty thousand dollar flop and kept the rest.

Bialystock: But what if the play was a hit?

Bloom: Oh, you'd go to jail. If the play were a hit, you'd have to pay off the backers, and with so many backers there could never be enough profits to go around, get it?

Bialystock: Aha, aha, aha, aha, aha, aha!! So, in order for the scheme to work, we'd have to find a sure fire flop.

Bloom: What scheme?

Bialystock: What scheme? Your scheme, you bloody little genius.

Bloom: Oh, no. No. No. I meant no scheme. I merely posed a little, academic accounting theory. It's just a thought.

Bialystock: Bloom, worlds are turned on such thoughts! . . . Don't you see, Bloom? Darling, Bloom, glorious Bloom, it's so simple. Step one: We find the worst play in the world—a sure flop. Step two: I raise a million dollars—there's a lot of little old ladies in this world. Step three: You go back to work on the books. Phoney lists of backers—one for the government, one for us. You can do it, Bloom, you're a wizard. Step four: We open on Broadway and before you can say "step five" we close on Broadway. Step six: We take our million dollars and fly to Rio de Janeiro.

.
.
.

Bloom: But if we're caught, we'll go to prison.

Bialystock: You think you're not in prison now? Living in a grey little room. Going to a grey little job. Leading a grey little life.

Bloom: You're right. You're absolutely right. I'm a nothing. I spend my life counting other people's money—people I'm smarter than, better than. Where's my share? Where's Leo Bloom's share? I want, I want, I want, I want everything I've ever seen in the movies! . . . Hey, we're going up.

Bialystock: You bet your boots, Leo. It's Bialystock and Bloom—on the rise. Upward and onward. Say you'll join me. Nothing can stop us.

Bloom: I'll do it! By God, I'll do it!

What Is Integrity?

The seeds of corporate misdeeds are sown when individuals compromise their personal integrity—that is, they do not do what they believe to be right and proper, nor do they respond to what Max DePree, chairman emeritus of Herman Miller, Inc., calls "a fine sense of one's obligations."[1] Reflecting personal integrity, the hallmarks of business integrity include such values as honesty, reliability, and fairness. Some acts, such as cheating on taxes, clearly violate this standard, while others are more subtle but just as inappropriate. For example, one entrepreneur who owned a flooring sales business often sold sheets of linoleum at first-quality prices, even though they were graded as "seconds" by the factory. To hide his deception, he developed an ink roller that changed the factory stamp from "SECONDS" to read "SECONDS TO NONE!" Those who caught the inaccuracy probably figured it was a typo and gave it no more thought, but unsuspecting customers were paying for first-quality flooring, only to receive imperfect goods. By anyone's measure, this shady business practice reveals a lack of integrity on the part of the entrepreneur.

As discussed in Chapter 1, the entrepreneurial experience is far more fulfilling when the entrepreneur understands that the core purpose of the business is to create value for interested customers. This perspective makes clear that relationships are critical and integrity is essential to success. Money is important, but it cannot be the only goal of interest. In fact, excessive focus on financial gain can quickly lead to distortions in business behavior; it certainly is the root cause of many ethical failings. In other words, integrity is as much about *what to do* as it is *who to be*.

Lapses in integrity, once discovered, quickly make the headlines when they involve large, high-profile corporations, but the problem does not end there. Small business owners and managers confront situations every day that require them to make ethical decisions. They must decide which course of action will preserve the integrity of the company and safeguard its reputation, a decision that can be especially difficult when doing the right thing runs counter to the immediate financial interests of the business.

integrity
An uncompromising adherence to doing what is right and proper

---

How They See It: Doing the Right Thing

Scott Salmans

It's said that your people are your most valuable assets, but how should you deal with them when they become more of a liability than an asset to your company through no fault of their own? A successful business associate of mine found himself confronted with a difficult situation that, in turn, taught me the right way to handle a similar situation a few years later.

My friend was looking to replace himself as CEO with a high-caliber individual, as he considered taking a back seat and eventually retiring. He worked hard to find the best person for the job. After months of searching and evaluation, he chose a top-notch performer to take the role. Only a few months after he took the job, the highly paid executive developed a degenerative health condition that made it impossible for him to do the work my friend had hired him to do. In spite of the unfulfilled purpose, my friend paid the CEO for years and kept him on in an alternative capacity as long as it was physically possible.

A few years later, a key employee of mine developed a debilitating illness that was devastating to a new line of business we were creating at the time. The timing was critical and cost our company a great deal of money, but our team rallied, and the product was eventually completed and launched. Then came the ethical question, "How long do you keep this person on as a significant economic drain on the company?" I recalled my friend's situation, and it emboldened my decision to do the "right thing," at least for our situation. The employee remains a part of our team to this day, and we hope to see success with the product line and this individual for years to come.

Fortunately, many small firms strive to achieve the highest standards of honesty, fairness, and respect in their business relationships. Although unethical practices receive extensive attention in the news media, the majority of entrepreneurs and other business leaders are people of principle whose integrity regulates their quest for profits.

Doing the Right Thing

ethical issues
Questions of right and wrong

It is probably evident by now that the notion of integrity is closely tied to **ethical issues**, which involve questions of right and wrong. Such questions go far beyond what is legal or illegal. Entrepreneurs must often make decisions regarding what is honest, fair, and respectful.

Individuals who face ethical issues are sometimes tempted to place self-interest and personal financial gain ahead of the reasonable and legitimate interests of others. Self-interest is a valid force in human life, but it can, when left unchecked, lead to behavior that is unfair or harmful to others. For example, one company ordered several thousand dollars of goods from its suppliers just as it was filing for bankruptcy, knowing that it would probably not have to pay for the merchandise because of this legal protection. To act with integrity, an individual must consider the welfare of others.

In the short run, honesty does not always pay—in fact, doing the right thing can be downright costly. But most people who show integrity in their business lives do not weigh the economic benefits before deciding how honest and forthright they can afford to be. Instead, they live by the highest of standards simply because it's the right thing to do.

A Framework for Integrity

2 Explain how integrity applies to various stakeholder groups, including owners, customers, employees, the community, and the government.

In order to pinpoint the types of ethical issues that are most troublesome for small companies, small business owners nationwide were asked the following question: "What is the most difficult ethical issue that you have faced in your work?" As might be expected, the question yielded a wide variety of responses, which have been grouped into the categories shown in Exhibit 2-2.

These responses provide a general idea of the kinds of issues that challenge the integrity of small business owners. As you can see in the exhibit, the issues mentioned most often are related to customers and competitors. However, the second most common category is concerned with the way a company treats its employees, including decisions about layoffs, workplace discrimination, and fairness in promotions. The fact that this set of issues received almost as many responses as the first should not be surprising, given the challenges of the current economic climate. In fact, this category was near the bottom of the list when entrepreneurs responded to the same survey six years earlier.[2] Times have changed.

The third category is related to the obligations of employees to their employers, focusing on the actions of personnel that may not align with the best interests of their companies. In fourth place are management processes and relationships. Management relationship issues can be especially disturbing because they reflect the moral fiber or culture of the firm, including weaknesses in managerial actions and commitments.

The results of this survey reveal that entrepreneurs must consider the interests of a number of groups when making decisions—owners (or stockholders), customers, employees, the community, and the government. The individuals in these groups are sometimes referred to as stakeholders, indicating that they have a stake in the operation of the business. In essence, **stakeholders** are those who either can affect the performance of the company or are affected by it.

stakeholders
Individuals who either can affect or are affected by the performance of the company

Because the interests of various stakeholder groups are different, they sometimes conflict; thus, decisions can be very difficult to make. And since there is often no obviously right or wrong position to take, managing the process can be extremely complicated.

One executive observed that running a business is sometimes like juggling (see Exhibit 2-3). In his words, "I am given four balls to balance: the customers', the employees', the community's, and the stockholders', by which I mean profit. It's never made clear

exhibit

2-2   *Difficult Ethical Issues Facing Small Firms*

ETHICAL ISSUES	NUMBER OF RESPONDENTS	SAMPLE RESPONSES
Relationships with customers, clients, and competitors (relationships with outside parties in the marketplace)	111	"Avoiding conflicts of interest when representing clients in the same field" "Putting old parts in a new device and selling it as new" "Lying to customers about test results"
Human resource decisions (decisions relating to employment and promotion)	106	"Whether to lay off workers who [are] surplus to our needs and would have a problem finding work or to deeply cut executive pay and perks" "Sexual harassment" "Attempting to rate employees based on performance and not on personality"
Employee obligations to employer (employee responsibilities and actions that in some way conflict with the best interests of the employer)	90	"Receiving kickbacks by awarding overpriced contracts or taking gratuities to give a subcontractor the contract" "Theft of corporate assets" "Getting people to do a full day's work"
Management processes and relationships (superior–subordinate relationships)	63	"Reporting to an unethical person" "Having to back up the owner/CEO's lies about business capability in order to win over an account and then lie more to complete the job" "Being asked by my superiors to do something that I know is not good for the company or its employees"
Governmental obligations and relationships (compliance with governmental requirements and reporting to government agencies)	40	"Having to deal with so-called anti-discrimination laws which in fact force me to discriminate" "Bending state regulations" "Employing people who may not be legal [citizens] to work"
Relationships with suppliers (practices and deceptions that tend to defraud suppliers)	25	"Vendors want a second chance to bid if their bid is out of line" "Software copyright issues" "The ordering of supplies when cash flows are low and bankruptcy may be coming"
Environmental and social responsibilities (business obligations to the environment and society)	20	"Whether to pay to have chemicals disposed of or just throw them in a dumpster" "Environmental safety versus cost to prevent accidents" "Environmental aspects of manufacturing"

Source: Leslie E. Palich, Justin G. Longenecker, Carlos W. Moore, and J. William Petty, "Integrity and Small Business: A Framework and Empirical Analysis," proceedings of the forty-ninth World Conference of the International Council for Small Business, Johannesburg, South Africa, June 2004.

exhibit 2-3

Juggling the Interests of Stakeholder Groups and the Government

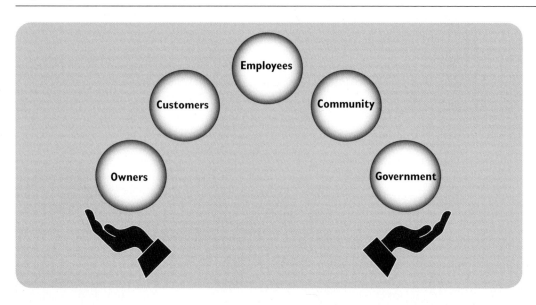

to me how I am to keep them all going, but I know for certain that there is one that I'd better not drop, and that's profit."[3]

As if the business juggler's job were not already difficult enough, we must add one more ball to the mix—government. Wandering beyond the limits of the law can quickly land a company in hot water, and there is no more certain way to compromise its integrity and its reputation. However, the concerns of all of these groups are fundamental to the management of the business. If neglected, any one group can use its influence to negatively affect the performance of the company.

Promoting the Owners' Interests

The Nobel Prize–winning economist Milton Friedman outlined the responsibilities of businesses to society in very focused terms: "There is only one social responsibility of business—to use its resources and engage in activities designed to increase its profits so long as it stays within the rules of the game, which is to say, engages in open and free competition without deception or fraud."[4]

Friedman argued that businesses should be expected simply to earn profits honestly; any other use of the firm's resources is justified only if it enhances the firm's value. Though we believe there is adequate room for entrepreneurs to adopt a broader view of their social responsibilities, it is undeniable that an owner has a clear and legitimate right to benefit from the financial performance of the company.

Many businesses, even small ones, have more than one owner. When this is the case, high standards of integrity require an honest attempt to promote the interests of all the owners, which include a commitment to financial performance and protection of the firm's reputation. But this does not always happen, as Jeff Dennis found out the hard way. In 1989, he and three co-founders started a financial investment company called Ashton-Royce Capital Corporation. But when the venture started to take off, two of the partners decided to "check out" and spend a good part of their time in California in semiretirement. This left the two remaining co-founders with more of the day-to-day work of the business and a growing resentment about the unfairness of the situation. In time, the conflict led to the dissolution of what had been a very profitable business.[5] Though entrepreneurs should be able to make their own decisions about personal matters, such as where they live, they have an obligation to make decisions that protect the investment that others have in the company. Integrity demands it!

In many small businesses, a number of people own a small part of the enterprise but have no direct involvement in its operation. When this is the case, questions concerning proper conduct can show up in a number of areas. For example, entrepreneurs sometimes face ethical issues when reporting financial information. They must decide the extent to which they will be honest and candid. Because a firm has considerable discretion in reporting performance results, financial reports can sometimes be misleading without technically being illegal. But providing misleading financial information could easily persuade the other owners to make poor decisions regarding their investment in the company. Furthermore, outsiders such as bankers, investors, and suppliers depend on a firm's financial reports to be accurate. It is always best to err on the side of honest disclosures that do not tend to mislead; this protects the reputation of the firm, and it is simply the right thing to do.

Respecting Customers

What do you call a business without customers? *Bankrupt!* Customers are obviously one of the most important stakeholder groups that a company must please. The fact that they are central to the purpose of any business has implications for integrity. Entrepreneurs who take customers seriously and care about them as individuals are apt to have more of them. And those they have are likely to return again and again because of that attitude.

Marc Katz sets an example as an entrepreneur with an appropriate view of customers. After joining with a partner to buy a building in which many other restaurants had failed, Katz began offering the first complete and authentic deli menu in Austin, Texas. Katz Deli thrives because customers love the high-quality food and Marc and his staff love the customers. Katz treats his guests as valued friends and family, making people feel as if they were visiting his home, where he had prepared a party for them. His driving motivation is not profit, though the deli is an undeniable success. Rather, it is his desire to provide a quality dining experience, marked by a genuine attitude of service.[6]

Katz Deli illustrates how a business can capitalize on integrity by treating customers with respect and building strong relationships with them. But entrepreneurs are often tempted to take advantage of customers or to be less than honest with them. When making marketing decisions, a business owner is confronted with a variety of ethical questions. For example, advertising content must sell the product or service but also tell "the truth, the whole truth, and nothing but the truth." Salespeople must walk a fine line between persuasion and deception. In some businesses, a salesperson might obtain contracts more easily by offering improper inducements to buyers or by joining with competitors to rig bids. This is clearly illegal, but it does happen.

Criticisms of unethical conduct in direct selling (that is, face-to-face selling) focus on such practices as pyramid schemes, bait-and-switch selling, and front-loading, in which new sales representatives are required to purchase large inventories, which they then must try to sell. In general, these practices are evidence of a simple lack of regard for the customer.

Making a completely safe product and avoiding all errors in service are almost impossible goals to reach. But when a company delivers an excellent product with excellent service, customer satisfaction is sure to follow. Mike Jacobs, owner of two Wetzel's Pretzels franchises in California, believes his success has come from building employee teams that make things happen. With virtually no turnover since launching his businesses, Jacobs has communicated to his employees how important they are and how their performance impacts the business. In fact, their service orientation currently generates well over $1.1 million in annual sales.[7] This suggests that a company's response to its customers will often be determined by its employees.

Valuing Employees

The level of integrity in a firm is reflected in the amount of respect given to employees. Through management decisions, an owner affects employees' personal and family lives. Issues of fairness, honesty, and impartiality are inherent in decisions and practices regarding hiring, promotions, salary increases, dismissals, layoffs, and work assignments. Employees are also concerned about privacy, safety, and health issues, and these should not be ignored.

In communicating with employees, an owner may be truthful and fair, vague, misleading, or totally dishonest. Some entrepreneurs treat outsiders with great courtesy but

Living the Dream entrepreneurship and integrity

Ethics Training Is Good ... and Good for Business

EntreQuest is a Baltimore-based sales training and development firm that offers its client companies the tools and principles they need to grow and prosper. The company was founded in 2000 by Jason Pappas and Joe Mechlinski (now CEO and president of the young venture, respectively). The two experienced some pretty rough times when they were trying to get their startup off the ground. In fact, they ran into serious trouble with their very first customer—their *only* client at the time.

When they learned that the customer was planning to back out of its contract with EntreQuest, Pappas and Mechlinski had to think fast and seriously about how they would handle the problem. In situations such as this, where a contract is about to be violated and the life of a new venture threatened, it is easy for entrepreneurs to panic and strike back, almost by reflex. For example, Pappas and Mechlinski knew they could sue, but that would be ugly and expensive, and they really didn't want to destroy the other business. There had to be another way.

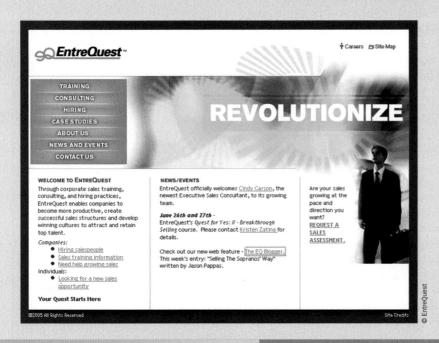

Using insights from ethics training in college, Mechlinski decided to take a few steps back mentally and look at the situation from all sides. After giving it some thought, he realized it was time to give the relationship another chance. After meeting with the client for a few hours, they were able to hammer out a new agreement, one that actually made EntreQuest more money, as it turned out. More important, though, the solution made sense for both sides. No lawsuit, no bad press, no loss of business—for either party.

The moral of the story? There is a creative alternative that will solve nearly every business problem, but finding it usually takes time and energy. And good ethics training can help to lead the way.

Sources: "EntreQuest Is a Different Kind of Company," http://www.entrequest.com/company.html, accessed September 9, 2006; and Nichole L. Torres, "Ethically Speaking," *Entrepreneur*, Vol. 33, No. 12 (December 2005), p. 142.

http://www.entrequest.com

display demeaning behavior or attitudes toward subordinates, whom they regard as mere pawns in the game of business. Showing proper appreciation for subordinates as human beings and as valuable members of the team is an essential ingredient of managerial integrity. It is also wise, since employees are a firm's most important resource.

The enormous value of thoughtful treatment of employees is evident at companies like PaeTec Communications, a privately held communications solutions provider located outside Rochester, New York. Founded in 1998, the firm has expanded rapidly and today employs more than 1,000 people. The venture's revenue growth has been nothing short of extraordinary, averaging more than 250 percent per year between 2000 and 2002; revenue crossed the $500 million mark in 2005. How could PaeTec go from startup

Living the Dream   entrepreneurship and integrity

Clean and Green

© Organic Bouquet, Inc.

Americans buy four billion flowers each year, about 78 percent of which are imported (mostly from Latin America). The flowers look beautiful, but the picture is actually not quite so rosy. The problem? The U.S. government requires that all imported flowers be free of pests, and that simple regulation has set off the heavy use of harsh pesticides—the only surefire way to prevent a shipment from being rejected at customs. Few people think about the drawbacks of the practice, but that is beginning to change.

Gerald Prolman, founder of OrganicBouquet.com, set out to reshape the industry by growing and marketing pesticide-free flowers—hopefully at a profit. His concern for the environment was serious, but he was even more troubled about the Latin American workers who harvested the flowers and prepared them for shipment. They were exposed to elevated levels of toxic chemicals in greenhouses and other enclosed areas. Indirectly, these workers were Prolman's employees, so he wanted to offer them better work conditions. He found he could protect the workers and the environment only by going organic. However, when OrganicBouquet.com was launched in 2001, no grower could supply the company's unique needs. To prime the supply pipeline, he had to persuade growers to shift their practices over to organic standards.

Some made the switch, and today Prolman purchases from growers in five countries. Though he pays a premium for certified-organic bouquets, he is still able to price his product at or below the level of his competitors by holding the line on marketing costs. For example, he partners with non-profits and markets to their members through the organizations' e-mails and newsletters. In return, these charities receive a percentage of sales on select bouquets. The model seems to be working. Prolman estimates annual sales to be around $5 million.

Sources: Joel Millman, "Flower Seller Hopes to Ride Organic Boom," *Wall Street Journal*, August 16, 2005, p. B7; April Y. Pennington, "In Full Bloom," *Entrepreneur*, Vol. 34, No. 5 (May 2006), p. 34; Bonnie Miller Rubin, "Valentine Roses, Candy Go PC," http://www.organicbouquet.com/i_193/press/20060213-ChicagoTribune.html, accessed July 18, 2007; personal communication with Gerald Prolman, April 25, 2007; and Amy Stewart, "Pick Your Poison," *New York Times*, May 14, 2006, Section 4, p. 13.

http://www.organicbouquet.com

to major player in so short a period of time? These results can be credited largely to a corporate culture that sincerely values its employees: "Everything at PaeTec revolves around respect for the employee. The word *customer* may be a little more prominent in the mission statement, but PaeTec puts employees first—and then watches them voluntarily put customers before themselves."[8] By doing things like treating one another as equals (regardless of position), faithfully recognizing achievement, emphasizing open communication between departments and between individuals, and honoring family life, PaeTec has shown what can be achieved when companies place employees first.

Small businesses do not always show the level of respect for employees that PaeTec expresses. And, unfortunately, lapses in integrity can sometimes be passed down from superiors to subordinates. Employees of small firms can face pressure from various sources to act in ways that conflict with their own sense of what is right and wrong. For example, a salesperson may feel pressured to compromise personal ethical standards in order to make a sale. Or an office employee may feel pressured by her or his boss to act unethically, perhaps by destroying documents or misrepresenting sales data. Such situations are guaranteed to produce an organizational culture that fails to promote integrity.

Fortunately, most employees of small firms do not face such pressures, as was discovered by a research team at Baylor University. In their nationwide survey of individuals holding managerial and professional positions in small firms, respondents reported feeling the following degrees of pressure to act unethically:[9]

No pressure   72.3%
Slight pressure   24.1%
Extreme pressure   3.6%

While it is encouraging to note that nearly three-fourths of the respondents reported an absence of pressure to compromise personal standards, the fact that more than one-fourth of the respondents experienced either slight or extreme pressure is disturbing. The strictness of a person's standards of integrity is related to that individual's perception of pressure to act unethically. A person with low ethical standards would probably encounter few situations that violated his or her standards; however, a person with high ethical standards would find more situations that violated personal norms. The ideal is to develop a business environment in which the best ethical practices are consistently and uniformly encouraged.

In some cases, employees may engage in unethical behavior at their employer's expense. They may fail in their ethical obligation to do "an honest day's work." Loafing on the job, working too slowly, and taking unjustified sick leave are all examples of such failure.

Other unethical behaviors are more flagrant. Some employees have feigned injuries and drawn fraudulent workers' compensation checks, thereby inflating their employer's insurance costs. Employee theft and embezzlement cost employers millions of dollars each year. Items stolen from employers include merchandise, tools, and equipment. In the case of embezzlement, of course, an employee steals money from the firm. This type of unethical behavior is extremely serious and clearly can cost the company a lot of money!

Social Responsibility and Small Business

To most people, an ethical business is one that not only treats customers and employees honestly but also acts as a good citizen in its community. These broader obligations of citizenship are called **social responsibilities.**

social responsibilities
Ethical obligations to customers, employees, and the community

Some regard social responsibility as a price of freedom to operate independently in a free economy. They believe that the public has certain social expectations regarding business behavior, not all of which are required by law. Accordingly, they regard some socially responsible expenditures as proper, even when they are costly.

To varying degrees, companies have increasingly been accepting responsibility to the communities where they do business. Their contribution starts with creating jobs and adding to local tax revenues, but many entrepreneurs feel a duty to give back even more to the community in return for the local support they enjoy—and they usually benefit from increased goodwill as a result. It is important to recognize that opinions differ as to the extent to which businesses are obligated to engage in socially desirable activities, and the response of small businesses to those obligations also varies. Some emphasize environmentalism, minority contracting, or regional economic development, while others focus their attention on volunteerism, philanthropy, or even day care for employees' dependents. Still others give only minimal attention to peripheral social issues.

EXAMPLES OF CITIZENSHIP IN THE COMMUNITY   Craig Hall wrote a book called *The Responsible Entrepreneur* to encourage others to be more generous and appreciate how fulfilling this can be. And it's more than just talk. His Dallas, Texas, company—Hall Financial Group—donates 5 percent of its income to charity, and any employee can take off up to 40 hours a year to work with charitable organizations. Hall firmly believes that his company gets generous returns on this investment. He observes, "In my experience, good things happen to good companies. Better employees and more customers gravitate toward you, and you establish loyalty."[10]

Formulas for community contributions vary, however. Marc Benioff founded Salesforce. com in 1999 to offer online customer relationship management services, and his privately

Living the Dream　entrepreneurship and integrity

Skills-Based Volunteering—Help That Is Right on the Beat

Fluid is an original music, sound design, and visual effects studio located in New York City. It was started in 1998 when two composers, David Shapiro and Andrew Sherman, decided to join their talents and resources with those of designer and flame artist Alex Frowein to open a creative studio. The result has been a combination of original music scoring/sound design and design/visual effects services that is far from traditional, and demand has taken off.

Today, the company has more than 20 employees, a growing list of very high-profile clients (eBay, FedEx, and Sony, among others), and more than $6 million in annual revenues. But the company also does a great deal of pro bono work—that is, service to the community free of charge. Many small businesses encourage their employees to make a difference in the community by donating their time to worthwhile causes like Habitat for Humanity, hunger relief services, or student mentoring programs, and some even give employees time off from work to make this possible. But companies like Fluid are taking a different approach. They want more than just good PR from employee contributions of time and talent—they want maximum impact, which happens best when specific job skills are put to use.

This trend toward "skills-based volunteering" is growing rapidly; in fact, recent research shows that around 40 percent of volunteers look for opportunities to put their specific skill sets to use. For Fluid, this emphasis has led to some interesting and high-impact projects. For example, the company produced a post-9/11 public service announcement for the New York City mayor's office and worked on ads for the Alzheimer Foundation, projects that tapped into the specific skill sets Fluid employees had to offer.

The bottom line: Nonprofit organizations receive services for free that they would otherwise not be able to afford, and Fluid employees give back to their community by doing what they love to do. Now they are all making beautiful music together.

Sources: "Fluid Expands, Launches Fluid Editorial," Prosound News, April 11, 2006, http://www.prosoundnews.com/article_3523.shtml, accessed November 1, 2006; Chris Penttila, "Got Skills?" *Entrepreneur*, Vol. 34, No. 9 (September 2006), pp. 100–101; and personal conversation with David Shapiro, February 13, 2007.

http://www.fluidny.com

held company has been very successful. In *Compassionate Capitalism,* a book he coauthored in 2004, Benioff argues that corporate philanthropy, done well, allows employees to find fulfillment in their own workplace. But he also takes a deep interest in community needs. For example, he advocates the "One Percent Model," whereby 1 percent of Salesforce.com's profits, 1 percent of its equity, and 1 percent of employee hours are given back to the communities the company serves. In his book, he describes similar projects at several other firms, highlighting the practical advantages and returns from such programs.[11]

Smaller businesses can demonstrate a sense of social responsibility in special ways. Steve Fuller, owner of a plumbing company in Chula Vista, California, with a total staff of five people, took steps to meet the needs of the homebound elderly in his community. The company's plumbers were sent out to repair toilets and faucets, unclog stoppages, and fix water system leaks for low-income seniors and disabled people. Fuller's attitude is illustrated by this comment: "I like to think I owe a little bit back to the community that has supported us for 40 years. . . . That's why I think we can contribute our services to people in need."[12]

VARYING VIEWS ON SOCIAL RESPONSIBILITY   How do small business owners compare with big business CEOs in their view of social responsibility? The evidence is limited, but entrepreneurs who head small, growth-oriented companies seem to be more narrowly focused on profits and are, therefore, less socially sensitive than CEOs of large corporations. A study that compared small business entrepreneurs with large business CEOs concluded the following: "The entrepreneurial CEOs were found to be more economically driven and less socially oriented than their large-firm counterparts. Apparently, [corporate social responsibility] is a luxury many small growth firms believe they cannot afford. Survival may be the first priority."[13]

In defense of small firm owners, we have to note that they are usually spending their own money rather than corporate funds. It is easier to be generous when spending someone else's money. Furthermore, small business philanthropy often takes the form of personal contributions by business owners.

Entrepreneurs must reconcile their social obligations with the need to earn profits. Earning a profit is absolutely essential. Without profits, a firm will not long be in a position to recognize its social responsibilities. And meeting the expectations of society can be expensive. For example, small firms must sometimes purchase new equipment or make costly changes in operations in order to protect the environment, and auto repair shops incur additional costs when they dispose of hazardous waste, such as used oil and filters. It is evident that acting in the public interest often requires spending money, which reduces profits. There are limits to what particular businesses can afford.

Fortunately, many types of socially responsible actions can be consistent with a firm's long-term profit objective. Some degree of goodwill is earned by socially responsible behavior. A firm that consistently fulfills its social obligations makes itself a desirable member of the community and may attract customers because of that image. Conversely, a firm that refuses its social responsibilities may find itself the target of restrictive legislation and discover that its customers and employees lack loyalty to the business. Researchers Melissa Baucus and David Baucus of Utah State University compared the long-term performance of 67 corporations convicted of corporate wrongdoing with the performance of 188 other firms.[14] They found that the law-abiding firms experienced significantly higher returns on assets and on sales. To some extent, therefore, socially responsible practices may have a positive impact on profits.

A 2004 study conducted by Cone, Inc., a Boston-based strategic marketing firm, found that 8 out of 10 Americans claim corporate support of causes earns their trust in that firm, a 21 percent increase over 1997. Eighty-six percent of respondents said they are very or somewhat likely to switch brands based on corporate citizenship commitments. Carol Cone, CEO of the research firm, concludes, "It's clear from our research that the public wants to know . . . what a company is doing in the community—good and bad."[15] Small businesses seem to be responding to this message. A recent National Federation of Independent Business study found that 91 percent of small businesses made contributions to their communities, through volunteering, in-kind contributions, and/or direct cash donations. The same study reported 74 percent of all small business owners volunteered for community and charitable activities, and the average commitment was just over 12 hours per month (which translates to 18 working days per year).[16] Overall, the evidence on performance impact is far from certain, but it suggests that commitment to the community may very well be good for business.

Governmental Laws and Regulations

Government at all levels serves a purpose, though there is room to debate whether it has too much power or too little. It intervenes directly in the economy when it establishes laws to ensure healthy competition. But its reach extends into other business matters as well—workplace safety, equal employment opportunities, fair pay, clean air, and safe products, to name a few. Entrepreneurs must comply with government laws and regulations if they are to maintain integrity—and avoid spending time behind bars.

One glaring example of unethical behavior by small firm management is fraudulent reporting of income and expenses for income tax purposes. This conduct includes *skimming*—that is, concealing some income—as well as improperly claiming personal expenses as business expenses. We do not mean to imply that all or even most small firms engage in such practices. However, tax evasion does occur within small firms, and the practice is widespread enough to be recognized as a general problem.

The Internal Revenue Service regularly uncovers cases of income tax fraud. For example, the John E. Long family, the largest promoter of country folk art shows in the nation, was forced to pay millions in back taxes, and four members of the family were given prison terms for tax law violations.[17] The Longs did not record the cash they collected for admission to their shows. Instead, they deposited into corporate accounts only checks received from such sources as booth rentals and magazine sales. Unfortunately for the Longs, the IRS discovered 2,000 unreported deposits that members of the family made into 37 different accounts. The Longs had reported that their business was losing money when, in fact, it was doing very well.

The IRS finds many violations like the Longs' every year. However, tax avoidance can be much less flagrant, though nonetheless illegal, and entrepreneurs sometimes come up short on their tax commitments because of casual accounting systems, single-minded focus on their product or service, or both. One student entrepreneur confesses that he had a close brush with the law because he and his friends were creating clothing in his dorm room and selling it on his campus, but the company did not legally exist and he was not keeping track of sales and expenses because he didn't take seriously the obligations and advantages of keeping good records. He explains what he was thinking:

> *At that time I refused to accept the responsibilities of accounting and the work it would take to follow through to make things sound. It's amazing how when things are going well, it is much easier to ignore the little formalities and nagging issues. It's almost as if you believe that as small as you are, you are above the legalities, requirements, and responsibilities of starting a business. I found myself with my ambition to be an entrepreneur outweighing my commitment to actually following through with the state and federal requirements.[18]*

Eventually, the "tax man" came calling. This young entrepreneur learned from his close encounter with the IRS that accurate record keeping and legal formalities are necessary to ethical practice and, just as important, to peace of mind.

How They See It: An Ethical Dilemma

John Stites

A recent ethical dilemma I had to face involved a lot of money. I believe most every ethical dilemma is somehow wrapped up in how we value money and what priority it takes in our lives.

I was told by my accountant that I could save over $65,000 in franchise and excise taxes properly due to the state. He assured me it was definitely owed, and if I didn't pay the tax and the government discovered it, they would surely pursue me for the taxes and the penalties resulting from the failure to pay. However, he suggested I could put the return in my desk drawer, because it was very unlikely the state would ever know about the tax being due, since the company was new and the state would have no record of tax being due on a new company.

I had used this man for many years as my accountant, and he was very aware of our mission statement and values. I did not believe that losing my integrity in the eyes of this man was worth the money I would be saving. The realization of the good I could do with the money did not escape my mind, but I resolved I could not bless anyone with money that I had stolen from someone else, even if it was the government. After all, a gift that cost me nothing, because I stole it from someone else, is not my gift at all. My decision was made even harder knowing how poorly the government spends its money.

Finally, my faith demanded that I "do the right thing." Incidentally, shortly after paying the taxes due, I rented a 32,200-square-foot building for 10 years for $115,500 annually. I had been trying to rent that building for over two years.

3 Identify challenges to integrity that arise in small businesses and explain the benefits of integrity to small firms.

The Challenges and Benefits of Acting Ethically

When it comes to integrity and entrepreneurial ventures, it is important to recognize that the news is not all good: Small companies face unique challenges to integrity. At the same time, the news can be very positive: The benefits of integrity are real and can offer small businesses a distinct advantage in the marketplace.

The Vulnerability of Small Companies

Walking the straight and narrow may be more difficult and costly on Main Street than it is on Wall Street. That is, small, privately held firms that are not part of the corporate world epitomized by Wall Street may face greater pressures than large businesses do to act unethically. Indeed, because small firms are at a disadvantage relative to larger competitors with superior resources, entrepreneurs may find it easier to rationalize inappropriate gift giving or bribery as a way of offsetting what seems to be an unfair competitive disadvantage and securing a level playing field. And isn't a "little white lie" justified when the life and future of the company are at risk? It's easy to cave in to the pressure when your back is against the wall.

When small business owners create false impressions to make their companies look good, are they being dishonest or simply resourceful? While there is nothing wrong with setting up an 800 number or establishing a Web presence to gain scale advantages to compete better against larger competitors, pretending to be something he or she is not is less than forthright and can lead the entrepreneur into what is, at the very least, a gray area. When one entrepreneur launched his own fund-raising business in 1996 in South Carolina, he had only a few local projects to work on. Profits were slim, but that didn't stop him from telling everyone that business was great. To add to the charade, he set up an 800 number and launched a website to create an image of greater scale.[19] In a similar way, when another small business owner was just starting a trucking company in Michigan, she sometimes used the phone in "creative ways" to shade customer impressions about the business. For example, "she pretended to transfer customers to different lines and used phoney voices to make the company seem bigger."[20] The drive and ingenuity of these entrepreneurs is certainly impressive, but their behavior raises questions about ethical standards. Such moves may save companies, but how would customers feel if they knew they were being manipulated?

The temptation for small business owners to compromise ethical standards as they strive to earn profits is suggested in the results of a study of entrepreneurial ethics conducted by a team of researchers from Baylor University (including the authors).[21] In this research, small business owners' views about various ethical issues were compared with responses of managers who did not own businesses. Participants were presented with 16 situations (or vignettes), each describing a business decision with ethical overtones. They were asked to rate the degree to which they found each action compatible with their personal ethical views.

For the most part, the participants in this study, including small business owners, expressed a moral stance; that is, they condemned decisions that were ethically questionable as well as those that were clearly illegal. For all situations, the average response of entrepreneurs and others indicated some degree of disapproval. For 11 of the 16 vignettes, the responses of small business owners did not differ much from those of others. However, in five situations, entrepreneurs appeared significantly less disapproving of questionable conduct than the other respondents.[22] Three of these situations involved an opportunity to gain financially by cutting corners or underreporting income. For example, owners were less severe in their condemnation of obtaining copyrighted computer software from a friend or using production processes that exceed pollution controls in order to increase profits.

Obviously, a special temptation exists for entrepreneurs who are strongly driven to earn profits, but these findings must be kept in perspective. Even though small business owners appeared less moral than the other respondents in their reactions to five ethical issues, no significant differences surfaced in the majority of scenarios tested, and other recent research indicates that ethical standards of entrepreneurs are, in fact, *rising* over time.[23] In the original study, the majority of the entrepreneurs were actually *more* moral in their responses to two other issues that had no immediate impact on profit.[24] One of these issues involved an engineer's decision to keep quiet about a safety hazard that his employer had declined to correct.

Evidence shows, then, that most entrepreneurs exercise great integrity, but some are particularly vulnerable with regard to ethical issues that directly affect profits. While business pressures do not justify unethical behavior, they help explain the context in which the decisions are made. Decision making about ethical issues often calls for difficult choices on the part of the entrepreneur.

The Integrity Edge

The price of integrity is high, but the potential payoff is incalculable. For example, it is impossible to compute the value of a clear conscience. The entrepreneur who makes honorable decisions, even when it comes to the smallest of details, can take satisfaction in knowing that he or she did the right thing, even if things do not turn out as planned.

But integrity yields other important benefits as well. In their book *Becoming a Person of Influence,* John Maxwell and Jim Dornan conclude that integrity is crucial to business success. They cite notable research to make their point: A recent survey of 1,300 senior executives showed that 71 percent considered integrity to be the personal quality that is most necessary to success in business.[25] Though an entrepreneur may lack personal integrity and still achieve financial success, he or she must often swim against a very swift current to do so.

In a study of 207 American firms, John Kotter and James Heskett, professors at the Harvard Business School, found that the more a company focuses on the needs of shareholders alone, the lower its performance. Kotter and Heskett concluded that firms perform better when their cultures emphasize the interests of *all* stakeholders—customers, employees, stockholders, and the community. Over the 11-year period of the study, those companies that looked beyond the income statement "increased revenues by an average of 682 percent versus 166 percent for those companies that didn't, expanded their work forces by 282 percent versus 36 percent, grew their stock prices by 901 percent versus 74 percent, and improved their net incomes by 756 percent versus 1 percent."[26] While these results are impressive, they do not *guarantee* that doing the right thing will lead to positive results for a company. However, these findings suggest that exhibiting integrity in business does not rule out financial success—in fact, doing the right thing may actually boost the company's performance.

Perhaps the greatest benefit of integrity in business is the *trust* it generates. Trust results only when the stated values of a company and its behavior in the marketplace match. When a small business owner looks to the needs of others and follows through on her or his promises, stakeholders notice. Customers buy more of what a firm sells when they realize that the company is doing its best to make sure that its products are of high quality and its customer service is excellent. Employees are much more likely to "go the extra mile" for a small company when it is clear that they are more than simply replaceable parts in an impersonal machine.

And members of the community also respond positively to business integrity. When they are convinced that a firm is living up to its commitments to protect the environment and pay its fair share of taxes, their support can keep the company going even if it falls on hard times. It all comes down to trust. If they conclude that the business is simply taking advantage of them, then all bets are off. There is no substitute for trust, and there is little hope for trust without integrity.

Integrity in an Expanding Economy

{ 4 Explain the impact of the Internet and globalization on the integrity of small businesses.

For the entrepreneur with integrity, decisions are often complicated by developments in the world economy. Businesses that operate across national boundaries must consider the ethical standards that exist in other cultures, which often differ from those of their own country. And firms using the Internet face a host of ethical issues that have arisen in the online-marketplace. As small firms move toward international commerce and harness the power of the Internet to launch and sustain their enterprises, these issues become all the more important.

Integrity and the Internet

It is not surprising that issues of honesty, deception, and fraud have affected Internet-based businesses, just as they have traditional commerce. It simply follows from the fact that those who buy and sell on the Internet are the same people who participate in all other forms of the marketplace. One quickly encounters questions of right and wrong in business relationships in every venue.

One issue of great concern to Internet users is personal privacy. Businesses and consumers often disagree about how private the identity of visitors to websites should be. For example, businesses can use cookies to collect data on patterns of usage related to a particular Internet address. In this way, a business may create a detailed profile of customers, which it may then sell to other parties for profit. Internet businesses—and even many of their customers—see the collection of personal information as helpful. A bookseller might, for example, welcome a customer back by name and tell him or her about a special book similar to those the customer ordered previously.

The extent to which an employer may monitor an employee's Internet activity is also hotly debated. According to a survey conducted by the Society of Financial Service, 44 percent of workers surveyed considered it seriously unethical for employers to monitor employee e-mail.[27] In their opinion, such a practice constitutes snooping and an invasion of privacy. Employers, however, are concerned that employees may be wasting time dealing with personal e-mail, shopping online, and surfing the Internet. And it appears there is reason for concern. In 2006, *Inc.* magazine reviewed research indicating that accessing the Internet at work for personal reasons is escalating rapidly.

In 2005, American workers spent the equivalent of 2.3 million years' worth of 40-hour workweeks reading nonwork-related blogs while at work, according to a study by Advertising Age *magazine. And that's just blogs. Millions more work years were spent shopping online, checking eBay listings, cruising social networks, looking for vacation deals, Googling old flames, and, of course, ogling porn. A 2005 survey by America Online and Salary.com concluded that employers spend nearly $760 billion a year paying employees to goof off on the Web.[28]*

While the author concluded that this Internet activity is not all bad (for example, an employee who spends time on the Internet can spot emerging trends and bring that insight to his or her work), it still hinders productivity in the workplace, and that makes it a concern for the employer. According to a 2005 study of employers conducted by the American Management Association and the ePolicy Institute, more than 75 percent of all businesses monitor employee Web use, 65 percent use software to block access to inappropriate websites, and 36 percent track what employees pull up on their screens and type on their keyboards.[29]

Many businesses, including giants like IBM and AT&T, have created the position of chief privacy officer to deal with privacy issues.[30] And a number of firms have developed privacy policies—they either will not share personal data or will not share it if the customer requests privacy. These policies are usually spelled out on a firm's website.

Widespread use of the Internet has also focused attention on the issue of **intellectual property**. Traditionally, protection has been granted to original intellectual creations—whether inventions, literary works, or artistic products such as music—in the form of patents and copyrights. The law allows originators of such intellectual property to require compensation for its use. However, the Internet has made it easy for millions of users to copy intellectual property free of charge.

intellectual property
Original intellectual creations, including inventions, literary creations, and works of art, that are protected by patents or copyrights

In the virtual world, journalists, photographers, filmmakers, authors, and musicians are referred to as content providers, a phrase that neatly sums up two problems: first, the [tradable] nature of this "content," and second, the dicey question of who pays these artists if everything they create can be reproduced free on the Net a hundred million times.[31]

Protection of intellectual property is a political as well as an ethical issue. Recent congressional hearings, lawsuits, and proposed legislation suggest that additions or changes to current laws are likely, and international enforcement is a major problem. As use of the Internet continues to grow and practices like online selling and file sharing are made easier, it is safe to assume that property rights will become more difficult to protect.

Content providers and other intellectual property owners will have to take increasingly stronger measures to guard what is legally theirs.

International Issues of Integrity

Every country faces questionable business behavior within its borders, but some must deal with very serious forms of illegal business activity. In 2006, Italian police raided a Chinese-owned counterfeiting factory in the Tuscan town of Prato and confiscated more than 650,000 fake Gucci and Louis Vuitton handbags and accessories. Many such factories are setting up shop in Tuscany to be close to European consumers and to be able to add a "Made in Italy" label to their goods.[32]

In extreme cases, criminal gangs engage in business operations that might better be characterized as evil, rather than unethical. For example, Italian authorities recently conducted raids in 28 cities, breaking up a criminal network of some 200 members in China, Russia, and Italy.[33] These gangs brought Chinese immigrants to Italy and forced them to work 12 to 16 hours a day in textile, apparel, shoe, and leather factories for little or no pay. Other raids have discovered children as young as 11 years old laboring under sweatshop conditions. It is likely that isolated instances of extreme criminal behavior also occur in the United States. In addition, some U.S. companies have exploited labor in countries with weak labor laws in order to procure products at low costs. Acts of this kind should be condemned and targeted by law enforcement agencies.

Of more widespread concern in the area of global business ethics is the following question: Does a payment to a customs employee or to a well-connected, helpful individual in another country constitute a tip, extortion, a consulting fee, or a bribe? The answer may depend on the size of the payment and also on the individual's country of origin. Cultures differ in what they condone as ethical and condemn as unethical.

In operating abroad, U.S. businesspeople encounter ethical issues that are clouded by cultural differences. Frequently, they simply apply U.S. standards to the situation. In some cases, however, this approach has been criticized for resulting in **ethical imperialism**, an arrogant attempt to impose U.S. standards on other societies. Some guidance is provided by restrictions specified in the Foreign Corrupt Practices Act, which makes it illegal for U.S. businesses to use bribery in their dealings anywhere in the world. (Some allowance is made for small "grease payments," which are payments offered to speed up a legitimate process.) Regardless of local practices, U.S. firms must comply with these laws, although "gray areas" exist, in which there are no obvious answers.

ethical imperialism
The belief that the ethical standards of one's own country can be applied universally

Another viewpoint is embodied in the saying "When in Rome, do as the Romans do." This philosophy, which might be termed **ethical relativism**, is troublesome, as it implies that anything goes if the local culture accepts it. Nicholas G. Moore, recently retired global chairman of PricewaterhouseCoopers, distinguished between business activities that reflect simple cultural differences and those, such as bribery, that are clearly unethical:

ethical relativism
The belief that ethical standards are subject to local interpretation

> [T]he gray areas are tougher to deal with. Think about the issues we deal with here in the United States, and then transplant them to foreign soil. Issues like diversity, the environment, child labor. We are much more sensitive to these issues. Still, the answers are very, very gray. And if they're gray here, they are really murky overseas. They require clear thinking and organizational support.[34]

To define its ethical landscape and work out its position on difficult issues, a small business must consider the nuances of its particular international environment. Training is also needed to ensure that each employee understands the firm's commitment to integrity.

Building a Business with Integrity

{ **5** Describe practical approaches for building a business with integrity.

The goal of an entrepreneur with integrity is to have a business that operates honorably in all areas. This goal is not reached automatically, however. To build a business with integrity, management must provide the leadership, culture, and instruction that support appropriate patterns of thought and behavior.

A Strong Foundation

underlying values
Unarticulated ethical beliefs that provide a foundation for ethical behavior in a firm

The business practices that a firm's leaders or employees view as right or wrong reflect their **underlying values**. An individual's beliefs affect what that person does on the job and how she or he acts toward customers and others. Of course, people sometimes engage in verbal posturing, speaking more ethically than they act. Thus, actual behavior provides the best clues to a person's underlying system of basic values. Behavior may reflect the level of a person's commitment to honesty, respect, and truthfulness—that is, to integrity in all of its dimensions.

Strongly held values sometimes require tough choices. The most ethical and the most economical actions may differ, since taking the "right" course of action can be expensive. In such cases, an entrepreneur who has strong, widely recognized moral values will still do the right thing simply because it is the right thing to do.

Values that serve as a foundation for integrity in business are based on personal views of the role of humankind in the universe. Such values, therefore, are part of basic philosophical and/or religious convictions.[35] In the United States, Judeo-Christian values have traditionally served as the general body of beliefs underlying business behavior, although there are plenty of examples of honorable behavior based on principles derived from other religions. Since religious and/or philosophical values are reflected in the business practices of firms of all sizes, a leader's personal commitment to certain basic values is an important determinant of a small firm's commitment to business integrity.

A long-time observer of high-tech startups has commented on the significance of an entrepreneur's personal values:

> *I can tell you, even with the smallest high-technology companies, the product had to be good, the market had to be good, the people had to be good. But the one thing that was checked out most extensively by venture capitalists was the integrity of the management team. And if integrity wasn't there, it didn't matter how good the product was, how good the market was—they weren't funded.*[36]

Entrepreneurs who are deeply committed to underlying values of integrity operate their businesses in ways that reflect their personal interpretation of those values. After spending several years shuttling gamblers from Richmond, Virginia, to Atlantic City, New Jersey, bus driver Tom Winston became convinced that he should no longer take poor people to gamble away what little money they had. So he resigned and started his own company, Universal Tours, which avoids the lucrative casino runs.[37] Another business that places the entrepreneur's personal values above dollars is Ukrop's Super Markets, a Richmond, Virginia–area supermarket chain that does not sell alcohol, closes every Sunday, and donates 10 percent of its profits to charity. More than once, *Fortune* magazine has named Ukrop's to its list of the best 100 companies to work for. Ninety percent of its employees say they are proud of the company's involvement in the community.[38]

It seems apparent that a deep commitment to basic values affects behavior in the marketplace and gives rise to business principles that are widely appreciated and admired. Without a strong commitment to integrity on the part of small business leadership, ethical standards can easily be compromised.

Leading with Integrity

Entrepreneurs who care about ethical performance in their firms can use their influence as leaders and owners to urge and even insist that all those in their firms act with honesty and integrity in all their dealings. Ethical values are established by leaders in all organizations, and those at lower levels take their cues regarding proper behavior from the statements and conduct of top-level management.

In a small organization, the influence of a leader is more pronounced than it is in a large corporation, where leadership can become diffused. This fact is recognized by J. C. Huizenga, who in 1995 started a public school management company called Heritage Academies, which was ranked as one of the fastest-growing U.S. companies by *Inc.* magazine.

> *The executive of a small company must often face moral challenges more directly, because he or she has more direct contact with customers, suppliers, and employees than an*

executive in a large corporation who may have a management team to deliberate with. The consequences of his or her choices often affect the business more significantly because of the size of the issue relative to the size of the company.[39]

In a large corporation, the chief executive has to exercise great care to make sure that her or his basic ethical principles are shared by those in the various divisions and subsidiaries. Some corporate CEOs have professed great shock on discovering behavior at lower levels that conflicted sharply with their own espoused principles.

The opportunity for establishing high standards of integrity is more apparent in small firms than in large ones. For example, an entrepreneur who believes strongly in honesty and truthfulness can insist that those principles be followed throughout the organization. In effect, the founder or head of a small business can say, "My personal integrity is on the line, and I want you to do it this way." Such statements are easily understood. And such a leader becomes even more effective when he or she backs up such statements with appropriate behavior. In fact, a leader's behavior has much greater influence on employees than his or her stated philosophy does. Everyone is watching what he or she does, and this conduct establishes the culture of the company—what is allowed or encouraged and what is prohibited.

In summary, the personal integrity of the founder or owner is the key to a firm's ethical performance. The dominant role of this one person (or the leadership team) gives him or her (or the team) a powerful voice in the ethical performance of the small firm, for good or for ill. Think about it: Employees owe their position to the founder or owner, so that person wields profound influence deriving from his or her unique position in the organization.

A Supportive Organizational Culture

Integrity in a business requires a supportive organizational culture. Ideally, every manager and employee should instinctively resolve every ethical issue by simply doing the "right" thing. An ethical culture requires an environment in which employees at every level are confident that the firm is fully committed to honorable conduct. To a considerable degree, strong leadership helps build this understanding. As a small business grows, however, personal interactions between the owner and employees occur less often, creating a need to articulate and reinforce principles of integrity in ways that supplement the personal example of the entrepreneur. A good place to start is to establish an ethics policy for the company.

In their highly influential book *The Power of Ethical Management,* Kenneth Blanchard and Norman Vincent Peale offer insights to guide the development of an ethics policy. They suggest that the policy be based on the following five fundamental principles:[40]

- **Purpose.** The vision for the company and your core values will guide business conduct.

- **Pride.** When employees take pride in their work and their company, they are much more likely to be ethical in their dealings.

- **Patience.** If you push too hard for short-term results, sooner or later acting unethically will seem to be the only way to achieve the outcomes you seek.

- **Persistence.** Stand by your word, as it is the foundation of trust. If you are not committed to an ethical framework, your integrity is at risk, as is the reputation of the company.

- **Perspective.** Stopping from time to time to reflect on where your business is going, why it is going that way, and how you plan to get there will allow you to be more confident that you are on the right track now and will continue to be in the future.

To define ethical behavior in the company more specifically, the owner-manager of a small firm should formulate a **code of ethics** (sometimes called a *code of values*) similar to that of most large corporations. Exhibit 2-4 offers an example of such a code. A survey of MBA students employed by small and medium-size companies revealed that codes of ethics shape and improve conduct in their organizations in a number of ways: by defining

code of ethics
Official standards of employee behavior formulated by a firm

exhibit

2-4   *The Ethical Code of The Dwyer Group*

CODE OF VALUES

We believe . . .

. . . in superior service to our customers, to our community, and to each other as members of The Dwyer Group family.

. . . in counting our blessings every day in every way.

. . . success is the result of clear, cooperative, positive thinking.

. . . that loyalty adds meaning to our lives.

. . . management should seek out and recognize what people are doing right, and treat every associate with respect.

. . . challenges should be used as learning experiences.

. . . our Creator put us on this earth to succeed. We will accept our daily successes humbly, knowing that a higher power is guiding us.

. . . in the untapped potential of every human being. Every person we help achieve their potential fulfills our mission.

. . . we must re-earn our positions every day in every way.

. . . in building our country through the free enterprise system. We demonstrate this belief by continually attracting strong people in The Dwyer Group.

We live our Code of Values by . . .

INTEGRITY

. . . making only agreements we are willing, able and intend to keep.

. . . communicating any potentially broken agreements at the first appropriate opportunity to all parties concerned.

. . . looking to the system for correction and proposing all possible solutions if something is not working.

. . . operating in a responsible manner: "above the line."

. . . communicating honestly and with purpose.

. . . asking clarifying questions if we disagree or do not understand.

. . . never saying anything about anyone that we would not say to him or her.

RESPECT

. . . treating others as we would like to be treated.

. . . listening with the intent to understand what is being said and acknowledging that what is said is important to the speaker.

. . . responding in a timely fashion.

. . . speaking calmly, and respectfully, without profanity or sarcasm.

. . . acknowledging everyone as right from their own perspective.

CUSTOMER FOCUS

. . . continuously striving to maximize internal and external customer loyalty.

. . . making our best effort to understand and appreciate the customer's needs in every situation.

HAVING FUN IN THE PROCESS!

Source: Reprinted with permission of The Dwyer Group, Waco, Texas.

---

behavioral expectations, by communicating that those expectations apply to employees at all levels in the business, by helping employees convey the company's standards for conduct to suppliers and customers, by serving as a tool for handling peer pressure, and by providing a formal channel for communicating with superiors without fear of reprisal.[41] In other words, a code of ethics identifies conduct that is ethical and appropriate, but it is also a practical tool that can encourage and protect ethical behavior.

A well-written code expresses the principles to be followed by employees of the firm and gives examples of these principles in action. A code of ethics might, for example, prohibit acceptance of gifts or favors from suppliers but point out standard business courtesies, such as free lunches, that might be accepted without violating the policy.[42] If a code of ethics is to be effective, employees must be aware of its nature and convinced of its importance. At the very least, each employee should read and sign it. As a firm grows larger, employees will need training to ensure that the code is well understood and taken seriously. It is also imperative that management operate in a manner consistent with its own principles and deal decisively with any infractions.

At a minimum, a code of ethics should establish a foundation for business conduct. With training and consistent management, a firm can then develop the level of under-standing employees need to act in the spirit of the code in situations not covered by spe-cific rules. Entrepreneurs further reinforce ethical culture in the business when they hire and promote ethical people, recognize and correct behavior that is unethical, and lead by example in business dealings, while encouraging all employees to do the same.

An Ethical Decision-Making Process

Ethical decision making often is not a very clear-cut process. In fact, even after much thought and soul searching, the appropriate course of action may still not be apparent in some business situations. The Ethics Resource Center in Washington, D.C., offers a decision-making process that may help with challenging dilemmas. We have adapted their simple six-step decision-making process here to help small business owners see the issues more clearly and make better, more ethical decisions.[43]

Step 1: Define the problem.   How you define the problem is important because this will guide where you look for solutions. For example, in the case of a student who is consistently late for class, is the problem that he is not managing his time well, the professor in the prior class consistently lets him out late, or he is coming from a classroom that is on the other side of a very large campus? If the student is careless with his time, a penalty for tardiness may correct the problem, but this solution will change nothing if one of the other causes is at work. Looking for the root of the problem is the best place to start in your search for a solution to a challenging ethical problem, whether it is a customer who is slow to settle his accounts or an overseas client who wants to give you a "tip" to overlook a questionable practice.

Step 2: Identify alternative solutions to the problem.   It's tempting to go with the obvious solution or the one that has been used in the past, but this is often not the best answer—even if it is ethical. Be open-minded, and consider creative alternatives. Many times, an innovative solution is available that is consistent with your personal ethics, protects the interests of other parties, and offers superior outcomes. Seeking advice from trusted friends and advisors who have faced similar situations can spur your thinking and lead to options that you might otherwise overlook.

Step 3: Evaluate the identified alternatives.   Rotary Club International, a worldwide organization of business and professional leaders, has set a high standard for business conduct. It calls on its members to ask the following four questions when they prepare to make a decision about the things they think, say, or do:[44]

1. Is it the TRUTH?

2. Is it FAIR to all concerned?

3. Will it build GOODWILL and BETTER FRIENDSHIPS?

4. Will it be BENEFICIAL to all concerned?

Taking a similar approach, you might ask yourself, "How would I feel if my decision were reported in the daily newspaper?" Or, the question can be even more personal: "How well could I explain this decision to my mother or children?" The answer could help to steer you away from unethical behavior.

Perhaps the most widely recommended principle for ethical behavior is sim-ply to follow the Golden Rule: "Treat others as you would want to be treated." This simple rule is embraced, in one form or another, by most of the world's religions and philosophies.[45] You may think of it as a basic teaching of Christianity, but its influence is very far reaching. For example, the influential philosopher Immanuel Kant presented the so-called categorical imperative, a sophisticated way of asking, "How would it be if everyone decided to do what you intend to do?"[46] Asking questions like these can be a very practical way for an entrepreneur to evaluate ethical decisions and guard her or his integrity.

No matter what approach you take, evaluating alternatives requires time and patience. And to make the exercise even more challenging, personal perceptions and biases are likely to cloud the way you see solutions. Therefore, it is important to separate what you *think* is the case from what you *know* to be true. It often helps to write down your thoughts about alternatives so that you can keep track of your concerns as well as important facts and details. You might list the ethical pros and cons of each alternative or identify the impact of each option on every person or company that will be affected. Another possibility is to rank all potential options based on their overall merits and then narrow the list to the two or three best solutions so that you can consider these further. This will allow you to organize your thoughts and make a better selection.

Step 4: Make the decision.   The next step is to choose the "best" ethical response, based on your evaluation of all possible alternatives. On the surface, this sounds easy enough, but unfortunately no single option will completely solve the problem in most cases; in fact, you may not even be able to identify an obvious winner. No matter how you go about making the decision, keep your vision and core values firmly in mind—this is essential to making solid decisions that do not compromise your ethical standards.

Step 5: Implement the decision.   This may seem like a "no-brainer," but entrepreneurs sometimes put off responding to ethical challenges because the solution is not apparent or because any response will be bad news for someone involved. But putting off the decision may allow a small problem to grow into a major crisis. Even if the decision is not pressing, delaying your response will cause you to spend more time thinking about the dilemma when other important matters deserve your attention.

Step 6: Evaluate the decision.   The goal of making a decision is to resolve an ethical dilemma. So, how has your response panned out? Has the situation improved, gotten worse, or stayed about the same? Has the solution created ethical issues of its own? Has information come to light indicating that your decision was not the most ethical course of action? Everyone makes mistakes. You may very well need to reopen the matter to make things right. But remember, if your decision was based on the best of intentions and information available at the time, you can wade back into the waters of ethical turmoil with a clear conscience, and there is no substitute for that.

Social Entrepreneurship: A Fast-Emerging Trend

6 Describe social entrepreneurship and the costs and opportunities of environmentalism to small businesses.

social entrepreneurship
Entrepreneurial activity whose goal is to find innovative solutions to social needs, problems, and opportunities

The social issues affecting businesses are numerous and diverse. Businesses are expected— at different times and by various groups—to help solve social problems related to education, crime, poverty, and the environment. In fact, these expectations are converging into a form of venturing called **social entrepreneurship**, which is rapidly gaining momentum. Though the term has been defined in different ways, Harvard researchers suggest that *social entrepreneurship* refers to "entrepreneurial activity with an embedded social purpose."[47] In other words, a social entrepreneur is one who comes up with innovative solutions to society's most pressing needs, problems, and opportunities.

Becoming a social entrepreneur usually does not mean that one is no longer concerned with making money—making money is just one of an expanded set of goals. In fact, the outcomes of interest are sometimes referred to as the "triple bottom line" because they focus on people, profits, and the planet. Profits are essential because, as you already know, no enterprise can exist for long without them. But social enterpreneurs believe ventures should also be concerned with people and the environment. To get a feel for the wide range of enterprises that fall under the social entrepreneurship umbrella, consider the following cases:

- Alicia Polak enjoyed some nice perks as a Wall Street investment banker, but she had studied in South Africa as an MBA student and could not get the country out of her mind. To create jobs in the poor townships outside Capetown, she started Khayelitsha Cookie Co. By 2006, two years after launch, the company was providing employment for 10 women and was poised to move beyond the South African market to sell cookies and brownies in the United States.[48]

- Windows of Opportunity is a for-profit business that has already replaced energy-wasting, lead-painted windows in 700 houses in the inner city. Since children can be poisoned when they eat lead paint, the safety benefits are clear. The windows installed to date will also save families more than $350,000 in energy costs.[49]

- In 1998, Ross Evans and Kipchoge Spencer, both in their mid-20s, started a company called Xtracycle. Today, their primary product is a bicycle accessory called the FreeRadical Kit, which features modular racks and accessories that permit riders to carry as much as 200 extra pounds (allowing them, for example, to carry groceries in Nicaragua or deliver smoothies in China). Despite sales in the mid-six figures, Evans identifies the ultimate goal of the company as going beyond making money: "Our passion and mission is to get more people riding bikes, because they're going to be happier, healthier and more in touch with their neighbors, community and environment."[50]

These entrepreneurs clearly do not fit the money-obsessed stereotype that some associate with business owners. They are hoping to do more than make a profit, but they are doing well financially, too.

The Burden of Environmentalism

The triple bottom line formula specifically mentions the planet. In recent decades, deterioration of the environment has become a matter of widespread concern. Today, **environmentalism**, the effort to protect and preserve the environment, directly affects most businesses. Releasing industrial waste into streams, contaminants into the air, and noise into neighborhoods is no longer acceptable.

environmentalism
The effort to protect and preserve the environment

The interests of small business owners and environmentalists are not necessarily—or uniformly—in conflict. Some business leaders, including many in small companies, have consistently worked and acted for the cause of conservation. For example, many small firms have modernized their equipment and changed their procedures to reduce air and water pollution. Others have taken steps to landscape and otherwise improve the appearance of plant facilities. Some small businesses have actually been in a position to benefit from the growing emphasis on the environment. For example, firms whose products do not harm the environment are generally preferred by customers over competitors whose products pollute. And some small firms actually build their business on planet-saving services. Small auto repair shops, for example, service pollution-control devices on automobiles.

Other small firms, however, are adversely affected by new laws passed to protect the environment. Businesses such as fast lube and oil change centers, medical waste disposal operations, self-service car washes, and asbestos removal services have been especially hard hit by expanding environmental regulations. The costs can be punishing. In fact, many companies in these industries and others have closed because of the financial burden of environmental controls. Small companies that enjoy favorable market conditions can often pass higher environmental costs on to their customers, but these can easily sink a small, marginal firm with obsolete equipment and not enough resources to upgrade.

Regardless of the financial impact, it is critical to follow the environmental regulations that apply to your business; to ignore this responsibility is to violate the law. The authors of *Greening Your Business: A Primer for Smaller Companies* caution small firms to comply with regulations at all levels (federal, state, and local), but their overall message is actually very upbeat: "There are dozens of ways companies of all sizes can reduce their environmental footprints, save money, earn consumer trust and stakeholder confidence, comply with government regulations, be ready to snag new market opportunities, and boost efficiency and productivity."[51]

Win-win solutions are possible. Compliance may actually lead to additional benefits, such as a reduction in governmental paperwork for companies that can show they are in line with regulations. And assistance is available. The Small Business Administration is prepared to lead you through the sometimes choppy waters of environmental law, and the U.S. Environmental Protection Agency (EPA) offers the Small Business Gateway, an Internet portal that will connect you to information, technical assistance, and solutions to challenges related to the environment. For example, the EPA provides online access to a guide called *Managing Your Hazardous Waste: A Guide for Small Businesses,* which makes compliance much easier to manage.[52] Taking advantage of resources such as these can help you avoid the potentially terrible consequences of noncompliance.

The Potential of Environmentalism

Although it adds to the cost of doing business for some small companies, environmental concern opens up great opportunities for others. In fact, many startups have come to life precisely because of "the greening of business," and the "green" (money, that is) has definitely started to flow into these new ventures.

The possibilities are endless. For example, in August of 2003, four entrepreneurs in Denver launched Revolution Cleaners, which its founders claim is the only dry cleaner in Colorado to use an alternative cleaning solvent that does not cause cancer. To enhance the company's planet-friendly image, the team runs its delivery trucks on biodiesel fuel, buys only laundry bags and uniforms that are 100 percent hemp (the farming of which is much kinder to the environment than that of cotton), and uses renewable materials in building out its stores. Rusty Perry, one of the co-founders, describes the motivation behind the company: "There's a chance to clean up a really dirty industry and do the right thing, and we think doing the right thing is good business." And it may also be the right way to make money—company sales were around $900,000 in 2005.[53]

Marty Metro started a company in 2003 called BoomerangBoxes.com, which recycles used boxes. This would not seem to be the most fascinating of businesses, but you might be more interested if you knew the company had sales of more than $750,000 and gross margins north of 75 percent.[54] Or, consider Lars Hundley, who launched CleanAirGardening.com in 1998 to sell environmentally friendly gardening products like reel mowers, the kind that have no engine and therefore create no emissions. An initial investment of $700 has turned into an enterprise with projected annual sales of around $1 million.[55] Not bad! If cell phones are more in line with your interests, that industry presents its own planet-saving opportunities. Inform Inc., a research firm in New York City, estimated that of the 128 million cell phones that are thrown out each year, only 5 percent are recycled. Those that end up in landfills leak toxins such as lead and beryllium into the ground. That's where companies like Florida-based GRC Wireless come in. GRC buys used cell phones for $1 per pound and then refurbishes them or harvests precious metals from them. Because cell phone purchases continue to increase, the company's annual revenues have been on a tear. In fact, they have been doubling in recent years and now exceed $4 million.[56]

Recent reports indicate that investor dollars have started to flow into ventures based on technologies that are labeled "green," "clean," "sustainable," or "environmental."[57] Many of these businesses are focused on sophisticated technologies that run well beyond the reach of the typical small business. However, some opportunities in this category are accessible to small companies. James Poss founded Seahorse Power Company in 2003 to develop, manufacture, and sell innovative energy-efficient products. The company's flagship product is the BigBelly Cordless Compaction System, which is a trash can like no other. Boxy and green, this innovative product looks more like a mailbox with no legs than a garbage can. But what a difference! When the can is filled with refuse, a solar-powered motor kicks on and compresses the trash to one-eighth of its original size. This cuts trash collection requirements by 70 percent, reducing the number of garbage trucks on the road, cutting down on traffic congestion, and decreasing the estimated 1 billion gallons of diesel fuel that the trucks burn each year. The formula makes sense, and a number of U.S. cities have bought in. Planned innovations will only make the value proposition more attractive—these include adding a separate bin for recyclables and attaching a wireless device that will signal workers when the bin needs to be emptied.[58] This is one recent startup that may cash in big on rising fuel costs.

Here's a technology that's even more down to earth. TerraCycle was started in 2001 when two Princeton University students were inspired by a box of worms to change the way business is done—to be financially successful while being socially and ecologically responsible. From their dorm room, Tom Szaky and Jon Beyer developed the premise behind their novel idea: Take waste, use earthworms to process it, and turn the output into a useful product. Though the plan was simple enough in concept, the two entrepreneurs had to innovate their way around a number of obstacles in order to turn it into reality. But what they came up with may very well be the world's first commercial product made entirely from garbage. At TerraCycle, millions of earthworms feast on organic garbage, and their waste is turned into a "vermicompost tea," which is a rich fertilizer. The fertilizer is loaded into recycled soda bottles, and the bottles are capped with spray tops that have been thrown out by other manufacturers. The bottles are even shipped in misprinted boxes rejected by large companies. It all sounds terribly unattractive, but the co-founders don't see it that way. Sales to big retailers like Wal-Mart and Home Depot pushed demand to around 2 million bottles in 2006, and the pace of growth has been doubling each year.[59] For TerraCycle, being good to the environment is also good for business.

For some, the ultimate goal is to save the planet, but more companies are likely to join the environmental movement as it actually generates value for shareholders. According to Stuart L. Hart, a professor of strategy at the University of North Carolina, the movement will provide huge opportunities for companies with "moxie" and creativity, as long as they can execute the plan.[60] This sounds like prime territory for small entrepreneurial companies, given their flexibility and innovative thinking. Entrepreneurs may be able to do well *and* do good—guarding the environment and their integrity at the same time.

 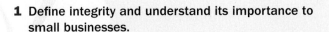

Looking **BACK**

1 Define integrity and understand its importance to small businesses.

- Integrity is an uncompromising adherence to doing what is right and proper.
- Integrity is as much about what the entrepreneur *should do* as it is about what he or she *should be*.
- Closely tied to integrity are ethical issues, which go beyond what is legal or illegal to include more general questions of right and wrong.

2 Explain how integrity applies to various stakeholder groups, including owners, customers, employees, the community, and the government.

- The most troublesome ethical issues for small businesses involve relationships with customers and competitors, human resource decisions, and employees' obligations to their employers.
- When they make business decisions, entrepreneurs must consider the interests of all stakeholder groups, in particular those of owners, customers, employees, the community, and the government.
- Research shows that about one-fourth of the employees in small businesses experience some degree of pressure to act unethically in their jobs.

- Most people consider an ethical business to be one that acts as a good citizen in its community.
- Entrepreneurs must obey governmental laws and follow governmental regulations if they want to maintain their integrity and avoid jail time.

3 Identify challenges to integrity that arise in small businesses and explain the benefits of integrity to small firms.

- The limited resources of small firms make them especially vulnerable to allowing or engaging in unethical practices.
- Research suggests that most entrepreneurs exercise great integrity, but some are likely to cut ethical corners when it comes to issues that directly affect profits.
- Exhibiting integrity in business may actually boost a firm's performance.
- The greatest benefit of integrity is the trust it generates.

4 Explain the impact of the Internet and globalization on the integrity of small businesses.

- Use of the Internet has highlighted ethical issues such as invasion of privacy and threats to intellectual property rights.

- Cultural differences complicate decision making for small firms operating in the global marketplace.

5 Describe practical approaches for building a business with integrity.

- The underlying values of business leaders and the behavioral examples of those leaders are powerful forces that affect ethical performance.
- An organizational culture that supports integrity is key to achieving appropriate behavior among a firm's employees.
- Small firms should develop codes of ethics to provide guidance for their employees.
- Following an ethical decision-making process can help entrepreneurs protect their integrity and that of their business.

6 Describe social entrepreneurship and the costs and opportunities of environmentalism to small businesses.

- Social entrepreneurship (entrepreneurship with an embedded social purpose) is a fast-emerging trend.
- Many small businesses help protect the environment, and some contribute positively by providing environmental services.
- Some small firms, such as fast lube and oil change centers, are adversely affected by costly environmental regulations.
- Small companies are sometimes launched precisely to take advantage of opportunities created by environmental concerns.
- Creating environmentally friendly products requires creativity and flexibility, areas in which small businesses tend to excel.

Key **TERMS**

integrity, p. 35
ethical issues, p. 36
stakeholders, p. 36
social responsibilities, p. 42

intellectual property, p. 48
ethical imperialism, p. 49
ethical relativism, p. 49
underlying values, p. 50

code of ethics, p. 51
social entrepreneurship, p. 54
environmentalism, p. 55

Discussion **QUESTIONS**

1. The owner of a small business felt an obligation to pay $15,000 to a subcontractor, even though, because of an oversight, the subcontractor had never submitted a bill. Can willingness to pay under these circumstances be reconciled with the profit goal of a business in a free enterprise system?

2. Give an example of an unethical business practice that you have personally encountered.

3. Based on your experience as an employee, customer, or observer of a particular small business, how would you rate its ethical performance? On what evidence or clues do you base your opinion?

4. Give some examples of the practical application of a firm's basic commitment to supporting the family life of its employees.

5. What is skimming? How do you think owners of small firms might attempt to rationalize such a practice?

6. What are some of the advantages of conducting business with integrity? Some people say they have no responsibility beyond maximizing the value of the firm in financial terms. Can this position be defended? If so, how?

7. Explain the connection between underlying values and integrity in business behavior.

8. Why might small business CEOs focus more attention on profit and less on social goals than large business CEOs do?

9. Give some examples of expenditures required on the part of small business firms to protect the environment.

10. Should all firms use biodegradable packaging? Would your answer be the same if you knew that using such packaging added 25 percent to the price of a product?

You Make the CALL

SITUATION 1

Sally started her consulting business a year ago and has been doing very well. About a month ago, she decided she needed to hire someone to help her since she was getting busier and busier. After interviewing several candidates, she decided to hire the best one of the group, Mary. She called Mary on Monday to tell her she had gotten the job. They both agreed that she would start the following Monday and that Mary could come in and fill out all the hiring paperwork at that time.

On Tuesday of the same week, a friend of Sally's called her to say that she had found the perfect person for Sally. Sally explained that she had already hired someone, but the friend insisted. "Just meet this girl. Who knows, maybe you might want to hire her in the future!"

Rather reluctantly, Sally consented. "Alright, if she can come in tomorrow, I'll meet with her, but that's all."

"Oh, I'm so glad. I just know you're going to like her!" Sally's friend exclaimed.

And Sally did like her. She liked her a lot. Sally had met with Julie on Wednesday morning. She was everything that Sally had been looking for and more. In terms of experience, Julie far surpassed any of the candidates Sally had previously interviewed, including Mary. On top of that, she was willing to bring in clients of her own which would only increase business. All in all, Sally knew this was a win-win situation. But what about Mary? She had already given her word to Mary that she could start work on Monday.

Source: http://www.sba.gov/managing/leadership/ethics.html, accessed October 11, 2006.

Question 1 What decision on Sally's part would contribute most to the success of her business?

Question 2 What ethical reasoning would support hiring Mary?

Question 3 What ethical reasoning would support hiring Julie?

SITUATION 2

Software piracy is a serious problem in Ukraine. While the latest version of Microsoft's Windows normally sells for more than $100 when purchased through a legitimate vendor, the same package can be picked up on the black market in Kiev for around $2, and it is usually bundled with additional software as a bonus! Brad, a project manager working in the Ukrainian office of an American consulting services firm, ponders the question of whether or not to buy 325 copies of pirated software through a local source for $1.85 per copy, versus purchasing these through an authorized vendor. The cost saving from this one decision would be nearly $32,000, and Brad knows that annual bonuses are tied to any cost savings. To complicate matters further, Brad's office is up against strong rivals in the same market, and they usually purchase pirated software to control costs. The competition is so fierce and margins are so thin that Brad's company is thinking about pulling out of the market. Having to pay full price for legitimate software might be "the straw that breaks the camel's back"—that is, it might be all it takes to convince management in the United States to close the office down. The move to Ukraine was hard on Brad's wife and their twin daughters. After 14 months of settling in, they are finally getting comfortable with their new life in Kiev. Brad really doesn't want to move them again, at least not now. And furthermore, it is well known that social standards in Ukraine do not emphasize proprietary property rights anyway. Microsoft is so big that one lost order would hardly be noticed, and Microsoft won't even get the order if the company decides to close the Kiev office down.

Question 1 Is the project manager acting with integrity if he purchases unauthorized copies of the software on the black market?

Question 2 What might be the long-term effects of deciding to buy the pirated software? Of insisting on buying only legitimate copies of the software?

Question 3 What are the important questions to ask in a situation like this? Follow the ethical decision-making process outlined in the chapter. Does it work in this scenario?

Question 4 What course of action do you recommend? Why?

SITUATION 3

Skylar is a self-employed commercial artist who reports taxable income of $7,000 to the IRS. Actually, her income is considerably higher, but much of it takes the form of cash for small projects and thus is easy to conceal. Skylar considers herself part of the "underground economy" and defends her behavior as a tactic that allows her small business to survive. If the business were to fail, she argues, the government would receive even less tax revenue, so what difference does it make?

Question 1 Is the need to survive a reasonable defense for the practice described here?

Question 2 If the practice of concealing income is widespread, as implied by the phrase "underground economy," is it really wrong?

Experiential EXERCISES

1. Examine a recent business periodical, and report briefly on some lapse in integrity that is in the news. Could this type of problem occur in a small business? Explain.

2. Employees sometimes take sick leave when they are merely tired, and students sometimes miss class for the same reason. Separate into groups of four or five, and prepare a statement on the nature of the ethical issue (if any) in these practices.

3. Visit or telephone the nearest Better Business Bureau office to research the types of inappropriate business practices it has uncovered in the community and the ways in which it is attempting to support practices that reflect integrity. Report briefly on your findings.

4. Interview an entrepreneur or a small business manager to discover how environmentalism affects her or his firm.

Exploring the WEB

1. Go to **http://www.sba.gov** and select "Small Business Planner." Then click on "Lead" under "Manage Your Business," and scroll down to "Business Ethics."

   a. After reading the short article on business ethics that you'll find there, take the accompanying quiz regarding your honesty and sincerity level.

   b. Write a short paragraph about how you scored.

2. Many companies have codes of conduct or ethical business policies that stress the importance of ethical behavior in the workplace. Casual-dining operator Brinker International is an example of a large organization that has created a detailed ethics policy. Go to Brinker International's website at **http://www.brinker.com/corp_gov/ethical_business_policy.asp** and review its ethical business policy. What aspects of Brinker's policy would you implement in your small business?

3. *Business Ethics* magazine annually recognizes socially responsible companies with an award. Go to **http://www.business-ethics.com/awardspastwinners** and read about past winners. What ideas or lessons would you take from the winners to implement in your business?

Video Case 2

Joseph's Lite Cookies (p. 622)
This case explores some of the ways in which an entrepreneur can build a business on a foundation of honesty and integrity as expressed by a strong commitment to employees, customers, and the community.

Alternative Cases for Chapter 2:
Case 13, Rodgers Chevrolet, p. 646
Case 14, Country Supply, p. 648

chapter 3

Getting Started

In the **VIDEO SPOTLIGHT**

Cybex/Avocent
http://www.avocent.com

Remigius Shatas likes to say that when he caught the bug of ambition, the only cure was success. Shatas, as he likes to be called, is the founder of Cybex (now called Avocent), a firm whose products allow companies to remotely control their computer servers from as far away as 25,000 miles from the desks of the people using them. What drove Shatas to start the business, however, was not an obsessive need to manage office space. It was the epiphany that a tremendous opportunity existed to create a business where people would enjoy coming to work each day. So he struck out on his own, with organizational culture as his differentiating factor.

Positive work environments alone do not make a company successful, of course; a firm needs to have products that meet the needs of its market better than those of its competitors. While installing computers for Marshall Space Flight Center, Shatas had trouble getting all the computer equipment to fit on each desk without breaking or in any way harming the cabling for the peripherals. Facing this problem on a daily basis prepared his mind to think creatively about solving it. He developed the core Cybex remote systems for a particular customer—himself. But Shatas astutely recognized that the result of his weekend tinkering was more than a neat project. It was a solution to a problem that no other company had figured out, an idea around which Remigius Shatas has built an extremely successful enterprise.

Video material provided by Hattie Bryant, Producer of Small Business School, the series on PBS Stations, Worldnet, and the Web at http://www.smallbusinessschool.org.

Small**BusinessSchool** ▫
the Series on PBS stations and the Web

Part 2

Starting from Scratch or Joining an Existing Business

Looking AHEAD

After studying this chapter, you should be able to

1 Identify several factors that determine whether an idea for a new venture is a good investment opportunity.
2 Give several reasons for starting a new business from scratch rather than buying a franchise or an existing business.
3 Distinguish among the different types and sources of startup ideas.
4 Describe external and internal analyses that might shape new venture opportunities.
5 Explain broad-based strategy options and focus strategies.

It was just a 1985 Volvo with a lot of miles and an odd yellow paint job, but John was thrilled with his first car and grateful to his parents for the surprise gift. With 163,000 miles of "character" behind it, his new ride was pretty worn out, but John was sure his banana-colored European classic was unusual enough to turn heads the next day at his high school. Or was it? On the short drive to class the next morning, he passed two other Volvos just like his—same model, nearly the same color. What was going on? Only two explanations were possible. Either more of these cars had mysteriously appeared overnight, or John just hadn't noticed them in the past. Of course, there was no magic involved. The only thing that had changed was John's level of awareness of yellow Volvos. The fact that he could now spot one at a moment's glance is evidence that people can learn to sharpen their ability to recognize specific features of the world around them that they overlooked in the past—such as potential new business ideas. The identification of potential new products or services that may lead to promising businesses is so central to the entrepreneurial process that it has its own name: **opportunity recognition**.

Business opportunities are like air—they are always around, even though you may not realize it. What sets entrepreneurs apart from everyone else is their ability to see the potential businesses that others overlook and then take the bold steps necessary to get them up and running. How do they do it? These entrepreneurs have uncommon observational skills and the motivation to act on what they see. In some cases, the identification of a new business opportunity may be the result of an active search for possibilities or insights derived from personal experience or work background. In other cases, the search for opportunities may be a less deliberate and more automatic process.[1] Israel Kirzner, a well-known economist, proposed that entrepreneurs have a unique capability, which he called **entrepreneurial alertness**. According to this view, entrepreneurs are not actually the source of innovative ideas; rather, they are simply "alert to the opportunities that exist *already* and are waiting to be noticed."[2] When these opportunities are aligned with an entrepreneur's knowledge and aspirations, they are even more likely to be spotted.

While a discussion of the finer points of the entrepreneurial alertness concept is beyond the scope of this textbook, it is important to understand that thinking about the world around you and being aware of conditions that might lead to new business opportunities can really pay off.[3] Try it and see what opportunities become apparent to you. Over the next week or so, instead of just passing through life and enjoying the experience, take note of trends, changes, or situations that might support a new business. You will probably be surprised at how many potential opportunities you can identify. If you continue this rather deliberate search, over time you may find that it becomes more of a habit and mostly automatic. And all it will cost you is a little time and mental effort.

opportunity recognition
Identification of potential new products or services that may lead to promising businesses

entrepreneurial alertness
Readiness to act on existing, but unnoticed, business opportunities

Perhaps you already have a business idea in mind that you would like to pursue. With good planning and the right strategy, you may soon be well on your way to becoming a successful entrepreneur. On the other hand, maybe you have a passionate desire to start your own company but are not sure you have come up with the right business idea to get you there. Or maybe you have an *idea* in mind but are not sure if it is a good business *opportunity*. No matter which group you fall into, this chapter will help to get you started on the right foot, with the right idea and the right strategy.

In Chapters 1 and 2, we talked about the mindset and lifestyle of the entrepreneur and the importance of integrity in the enterprise. Now, in Part 2, we will focus on topics that will help the individual entrepreneur decide what kind of startup is best for him or her.

In this chapter, we will describe opportunity recognition and strategy setting for startups—businesses that did not exist before entrepreneurs created them. In later chapters, we will go beyond a discussion of businesses "started from scratch" and consider business opportunities that already exist, including purchasing a franchise or buying out a business (Chapter 4) and joining a family business (Chapter 5).

Identifying Startup Ideas

1 Identify several factors that determine whether an idea for a new venture is a good investment opportunity.

It is critical to determine whether an idea for a new business actually represents a good opportunity. Many people have ideas about new products or services that seem like winners—but just because something is a good idea does not mean it is a good opportunity, as you will see. In fact, those who become infatuated with an idea sometimes underestimate the difficulty of tapping into market interest in that idea or building the company required to capture it.

To qualify as a good investment opportunity, a product or service must meet a real market need, such as a problem for which the entrepreneur offers a sensible solution. If consumers are convinced that the benefits of a product or service are worth the price they will have to pay to get it, they will likely want to buy it—assuming they know about it and can afford it. All of these factors are critical. Amar Bhide, an entrepreneurship expert and professor at Columbia University, put it this way: "Startups with products that do not serve clear and important needs cannot expect to be 'discovered' by enough customers to make a difference."[4]

Many popular frameworks highlight important factors to consider when deciding whether a new business idea can lead to a promising business opportunity. Some of the more important features of these approaches follow.

- *Market factors.* The product or service must meet a clearly defined market need; furthermore, the timing must be right. Even when the concept is good, success requires a window of opportunity that remains open long enough for an entrepreneur to take advantage of it. If the window closes before the enterprise can get established, it is unlikely to survive for long.

- *Competitive advantage.* In practical terms, a **competitive advantage** exists when a firm offers a product or service that customers perceive to be superior to those offered by competitors. It follows that the business must be able to achieve an edge that can withstand challenges from rival businesses. Many startups fail because entrepreneurs do not understand the nature and importance of a competitive advantage.

competitive advantage
A benefit that exists when a firm has a product or service that is seen by its target market as better than those of competitors

- *Economics.* The venture needs to be financially rewarding, allowing for significant profit and growth potential. Its profit potential must be sufficient to allow for errors and mistakes and still offer acceptable economic benefits. At a minimum, the enterprise must offer a reasonable path to profitability—no business can operate for long when it is losing money. And without adequate growth, the business will not be able to provide sufficient returns to attract investors, if they are ever needed.

- *Management capability.* The fit between entrepreneur and opportunity must be good. In other words, a business idea is an opportunity only for the entrepreneur who has the appropriate experience, skills, and access to the resources necessary for the venture's launch and growth. For example, offering suborbital space tourism services is out of reach for most entrepreneurs, but not for Sir Richard Branson, an extraordinary and very well-funded British entrepreneur who has set up Virgin Galactic, with plans to offer space flights to the general public before the end of the decade.[5] Launching the world's first "spaceline" is a challenging but promising business opportunity for Branson, but it is at best a dream for nearly every other entrepreneur.

■ *Fatal flaws.* There must be no fatal flaw in the venture—that is, no circumstance or development that could, in and of itself, make the business unsuccessful. John Osher, serial innovator and entrepreneur, estimates that nine out of ten entrepreneurs fail because their business concept is deficient. In his words, "They want to be in business so much that they often don't do the work they need to do ahead of time, so everything they do is doomed. They can be very talented, do everything else right, and fail because they have ideas that are flawed."[6] It is important to look (honestly) for potential weaknesses in your own startup ideas. No matter how awesome the startup concept may seem to be, moving forward is pointless if it uses a manufacturing process that is patent protected, requires startup capital that cannot be raised, ignores environmental regulations, or is unsound in some other way.

Exhibit 3-1 presents these five evaluation criteria more fully. Above all, beware of thinking that an idea is a "natural" and cannot miss. The market can deal harshly with those who have not done their homework. However, for those who succeed in identifying a meaningful opportunity, the rewards can be sizable. Thus, it is the *market* that ultimately determines whether an idea has potential as an opportunity.

Creating a New Business from Scratch

Several motivations may lead you to start a business from scratch rather than pursuing other alternatives, such as buying a franchise or an existing business or joining a family business. They include the following:

1. Having a personal desire to develop the commercial market for a recently invented or newly developed product or service

2. Hoping to tap into unique resources that are available, such as an ideal location, new equipment technologies, or exceptional employees, suppliers, and bankers

3. Avoiding undesirable features of existing companies, including unfavorable cultures, policies, procedures, and legal commitments

4. Wanting the challenge of succeeding (or failing) on your own

Assuming you have sound reasons for considering a startup, you should still address several basic questions before making the commitment:

■ What are some other types of startup ideas you might consider?

■ What are some sources for additional new business ideas?

■ How can you identify a genuine opportunity that creates value, for both the customer *and* the company's owner(s)?

■ How should you refine your business idea?

■ What could you do to increase the odds of success in your business?

■ What competitive advantage could your business have over its rivals?

The entrepreneur's ability to carefully and honestly examine questions such as these will determine the direction she or he will follow. We will examine the issues raised by these questions in the remainder of this chapter.

> 2 Give several reasons for starting a new business from scratch rather than buying a franchise or an existing business.

exhibit

3-1   *Selected Evaluation Criteria for a Startup*

ATTRACTIVENESS

Criterion	Favorable	Unfavorable
Market Factors		
Need for the product	Well identified	Unfocused
Customers	Reachable; receptive	Unreachable; strong loyalty to competitor's product or service
Value created for customers	Significant	Not significant
Market structure	Emerging industry; not highly competitive	Mature or declining industry; highly concentrated competition
Market growth rate	Growing by at least 15% a year	Growing by less than 10% a year
Competitive Advantage		
Control over prices, costs, and distribution	Moderate to strong	Weak to nonexistent
Barriers to entry:		
Proprietary information or regulatory protection	Have or can develop	Not possible
Response/lead time advantage	Competition slow, nonresponsive	Unable to gain an edge
Legal/contractual advantage	Proprietary or exclusive	Nonexistent
Contacts and networks	Well developed; accessible	Poorly developed; limited
Economics		
Return on investment	25% or more; sustainable	Less than 15%; unpredictable
Investment requirements	Small to moderate; easily financed	Large; difficult to finance
Time required to break even or to reach positive cash flows	Under 2 years	More than 4 years
Management Capability	Management team with diverse skills and relevant experience	Solo entrepreneur with no related experience
Fatal Flaws	None	One or more

Source: Adapted from Jeffrey A. Timmons and Stephen Spinelli, *New Venture Creation: Entrepreneurship for the 21st Century* (Boston: McGraw-Hill Irwin, 2007), pp. 128–129.

How They See It: Getting Started

Sara Blakely

Getting started is the toughest part. I always tell aspiring entrepreneurs who have a business idea to keep their idea to themselves in the beginning. I didn't tell anyone my idea for footless pantyhose, not even friends or family. Everyone knew I was working on an invention, but they didn't know what it was until I had already invested a year of my time.

This is important because so many people stop dead in their tracks because someone, out of love, brings up 50 things for them to worry about. The minute you put your idea out there, you're forced to justify it. A year after working on my prototype for SPANX footless pantyhose, I told everyone my idea and was met with a lot of questions and skepticism. People asked, "Is that really such a good idea? The big guys will just knock you off." If I hadn't already invested a year, I might not have started SPANX.

Finding Startup Ideas

Business ideas are not all equal, and they originate from many different sources. By recognizing the nature and origin of startup ideas, the entrepreneur can broaden the range of new ideas available for his or her consideration.

> **3** Distinguish among the different types and sources of startup ideas.

Types of Startup Ideas

Exhibit 3-2 shows the three basic types of ideas that develop into startups: ideas to enter new markets, ideas based on new technologies, and ideas to offer new benefits.

Many startups develop from what we will call **Type A ideas**—those concerned with providing customers with a product or service that does not exist in a particular market but that exists somewhere else. Randall Rothenberg, an author and the director of intellectual capital at consulting powerhouse Booz Allen Hamilton, says that this type of startup idea may have the greatest potential: "There's ample evidence that some of the biggest businesses are built by taking existing ideas and applying them in a new context."[7]

Many small businesses are built on this platform. Filmmaker Christian D'Andrea was making a documentary on Special Forces when he saw a soldier chomping down an energy bar issued by the United States military, which had been developed specifically to

Type A ideas
Startup ideas centered around providing customers with an existing product not available in their market

exhibit

3-2   *Types of Ideas That Develop into Startups*

Type A Ideas	Type B Ideas	Type C Ideas
New Market	New Technology	New Benefit
Example: Targeting the "New Age" beverage market by selling soft drinks with nutritional value	Example: Using high-tech computers to develop a simulated helicopter ride	Example: Developing a personal misting device to keep workers cool

provide the extra boost those in uniform need on the battlefield. D'Andrea recognized an opportunity to take the product, which civilians couldn't buy, to a whole new market. He and his brother, Mark, signed a deal in 2004 giving them license to use the science behind the product, and they used it to create the Hoorah! Bar, a pick-me-up snack that today sells in thousands of stores and online outlets. Business is good, and growing; in fact, their Los Angeles–based startup, D'Andrea Brothers LLC, recently expanded its product line to include an energy drink based on the same formulation. With sales poised to cross the $1 million mark, it is clear that tapping "military intelligence" to take an existing product to the civilian market can yield impressive results.[8]

Type B ideas
Startup ideas, involving new technology, centered around providing customers with a new product

Some startups are based on **Type B ideas**, which involve new or relatively new technology. This type of startup can be high risk because there is usually no model of success to follow, but it can also have tremendous potential. In 1998, Richard Mayer and Malcolm Currie launched Currie Technologies, a Van Nuys, California, venture that produces electric bicycles and scooters. Within five years, the company was employing 40 people and had revenues of $10 million,[9] but that was only the beginning. With the spike in fuel prices and escalating concerns about global warming, the company's products make more sense than ever. Perhaps one of Currie's executives best captured the essence of the business: "Clean, green and no gasoline!"[10]

Type C ideas
Startup ideas centered around providing customers with an improved product

Type C ideas, those based on offering customers benefits from new and improved ways of performing old functions, probably account for the largest number of startups. In fact, most new ventures, especially in the service industry, are founded on "me, too" strategies—they set themselves apart through features such as superior service or lower prices. Laurie Johnson's effort to redefine the common crutch fits into the Type C category. As founder of LemonAid Crutches, Johnson found a way to take some of the sting out of having to be on crutches after an injury. Her designer crutches were born of experience. While Johnson was recovering from a broken leg sustained in a small-plane crash that took the lives of her husband and two-year-old son, her sister tried to cheer her up some by spraypainting her crutches and trimming the handles in fabric. Her response? "I sat there thinking, 'Oh my gosh, this is so silly, but they make me feel better!'" Deciding to turn life's lemons into lemonade (hence the name of the company), Johnson decided to run with the concept and help other crutch users feel better, too. In mid-2005, she launched her venture to sell a variety of fashionably functional crutches, with prices ranging from $140 to $175 a pair. With expected annual sales of $150,000, Johnson's startup will soon be on a solid footing.[11]

Sources of Startup Ideas

At this point, you may be saying, "I want to start a new business but still haven't come up with a startup idea that sounds like a good investment opportunity." There are a number of sources you can turn to for inspiration. And if one source fails to lead you to the idea of your dreams, keep looking! Inspiration can come from many different places.

Several studies have identified sources of ideas for small business startups. Exhibit 3-3 shows the results of one such study by the National Federation of Independent Business (NFIB), which found that prior work experience accounted for 45 percent of new ideas. This finding is consistent with another national study of entrepreneurs, the Panel Study of Entrepreneurial Dynamics (PSED). The PSED data also show that entrepreneurs most often consider work experience in a particular industry or market to be the source of their startup ideas.[12] However, there are other important sources. As shown in the exhibit, the NFIB study found that personal interests and hobbies represented 16 percent of the total, and chance happenings accounted for 11 percent. Ideas for a startup can come from virtually anywhere, but we will focus on four possible sources: personal experience, hobbies, accidental discovery, and deliberate search.

PERSONAL EXPERIENCE   The primary source of startup ideas is personal experience, either at work or at home. Knowledge gleaned from a present or former job often allows a person to see possibilities for modifying an existing product, improving a service, or duplicating a business concept in a different location. Or personal contacts may open up conversations with suppliers who are interested in working with you or customers who have needs that are not currently being met. These insights may lead you to an opportunity with tremendous potential.

exhibit 3-3   *Sources of Startup Ideas*

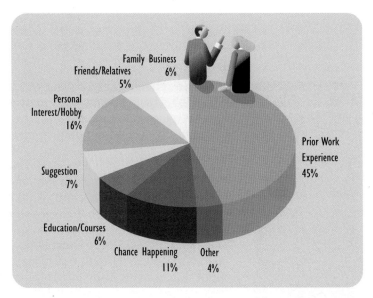

Source: Data developed and provided by the National Federation of Independent Business and sponsored by the American Express Travel Related Services Company, Inc.

Ken and Jennifer Miller started their outdoor-clothing company, Thousand Mile, based on Ken's personal experience as a lifeguard in Carlsbad, California. The faded swimming trunks of fellow lifeguards inspired Ken and his wife-to-be, Jennifer, to buy $166 of material and make 30 pairs of trunks. When the trunks quickly sold to Ken's co-workers, the couple knew their business idea was an attractive startup opportunity. After several years of development, they now have a complete line of mail-order outdoor wear.[13] Clearly, work experience played a role in the launching of this business, as did close interactions with customers who recognized that Thousand Mile provided a product they could really use.

HOBBIES AND PERSONAL INTERESTS   Sometimes hobbies grow beyond being leisure activities to become businesses. For instance, people who love skiing might start a ski equipment rental business as a way to make income from an activity that they enjoy, and those who love books might explore concepts that lead to new bookstore businesses. Hobbies and personal interests certainly add passion to the startup process.

Kevin Rose was only in his mid-20s when he launched Digg.com in 2004 with two of his buddies, Owen Byrne and Jay Adelson, but his company is off to a fast start. The former Unix administrator and TechTV personality found inspiration for his company in Slashdot, the wildly popular, community-driven tech news website. Rose described himself as "a big fan" of Slashdot, but he concluded that the website was missing out by restricting the participation of users. He believed that the user community should have complete control of content. This concept that led to the launch of Digg: "a site where users could submit stories that fall into a general queue, and if they were popular enough—if they got enough 'diggs' [user endorsements]—they would be promoted to the home page for everyone to see." Now, a hot story can be promoted at Internet speed and picked up by heavy hitters like Yahoo! and Google. This "democratic approach to the news" is becoming quite popular, and fast! The thought of generating revenue from advertising is a no-brainer, and plans for expanding the range of features on the site will only enhance the financial performance of the business, which is already a profitable operation with more than 180,000 registered users.[14] Clearly, Rose's experience shows that a hobby can be financially rewarding.

ACCIDENTAL DISCOVERY   Another source of new startup ideas—accidental discovery— involves something called **serendipity**, or a gift for making desirable discoveries by accident.

serendipity
A gift for making desirable discoveries by accident

Living the Dream   putting technology to work

So You Think You Have a Great Business Idea? In Your Dreams!

You have probably heard about Monster Worldwide, the Massachusetts-based job search engine, but you are more likely to know the company by its Web address: Monster.com. The central thrust of the now-monstrous enterprise is spelled out on the firm's webpage:

> *Life is too short not to enjoy what you do every day. At Monster our goal is to help you make the most of the 80 or 90 years you have on this planet by connecting you to the real world opportunities that can help you achieve your goals and realize your dreams.*

That last word—*dreams*—was literally the source of the idea for Monster.com. It's been more than a decade now, but when company founder Jeff Taylor awoke at 4:30 one morning after an interesting dream, he had a feeling he was on to something. The dream was not all that clear—a flurry of graphics and a text-oriented bulletin board—but it meant something to Taylor. He jotted down a few notes on a pad near his bed and headed for a coffee shop to pull together his thoughts. Five hours later, he had the sketch of an incredible business idea, and many lives have been changed by the service that evolved from that idea.

Taylor sums up the importance of responding to inspiration for business ideas, no matter what the source: "It would have been pretty easy to have rolled over and gone [back] to sleep, and that would have been a multibillion-dollar opportunity I would have let go by."

Maybe we should all take our dreams a little more seriously. . . .

Sources: Geoff Williams, "In Your Dreams," *Entrepreneur*, Vol. 33, No. 6 (June 2005), p. 36; http://www.monster.com, accessed December 7, 2006; and personal communication with Hilary Blowers, public relations representative for Monster.com, February 12, 2007.

http://www.monster.com

Of course, awareness obviously plays a role here, but anyone may stumble across a useful idea in the course of day-to-day living.

This is exactly what happened to Tia Wou, founder of Tote Le Monde, a handbag manufacturer in New York City. Wou had traveled to Bolivia for her friend's wedding in 1989 and loved the rich fabrics she saw in the marketplace.

> *Wou, who was working in fashion at the time, got a creative spark from that trip. A few years later, she traveled to Japan and was on the hunt for the perfect handbag. Not finding what she wanted, Wou recalled the beautiful fabrics in Bolivia. That's when it hit her: she could design handbags like the ones she was looking for in Japan, using the materials she'd seen in Bolivia, and sell them in America.*[15]

Launched in 1994, Tote le Monde produces lifestyle brands, selling handbags, housewares, travel pieces, and personal accessories featuring the company's stylish, environmentally friendly materials. And the entrepreneurial spirit of the business is alive and well, as is Tote le Monde's original mission: "To create innovation where function finds form."[16]

Or consider the invention of the pocket protector (called a "nerd pack" in some circles) by electrical engineer Gerson Strassberg in 1952. "It happened by accident," Strassberg says.

I was just starting up my company, and we were making the clear plastic covers that cover bankbooks. At that time, ballpoint pens were prone to leaking. One day I cut one side of the plastic longer than the other. The phone rang, so I stuck the plastic in my pocket and thought "Wow, this might make a great product."[17]

Sales for the pocket protector peaked in the late 1960s, but Strassberg still sells close to 30,000 of his nifty "fashion accessories" each year, which now retail at around $1 apiece.[18]

DELIBERATE SEARCH Startup possibilities may also emerge from an entrepreneur's deliberate search for new ideas. In fact, this kind of exploration may be especially useful because it stimulates a readiness of mind, which motivates prospective entrepreneurs to be more receptive to new ideas from any source. A deliberate search often involves looking for change-based opportunities, but it may take a number of other paths.

An Eye on Change   Change is one of the most important sources of ideas for entrepreneurs. Whereas large firms prefer things to remain the same, entrepreneurs are much more likely to recognize change as an opportunity and to have the creativity and flexibility to adjust to it. Business guru Peter Drucker believed entrepreneurs should consider seven sources of opportunity as they prepare to launch or grow their enterprises.[19] These change-based sources of opportunity are outlined in Exhibit 3-4.

3-4   *Change-Based Sources of Entrepreneurial Opportunities*

Change Factor *Industry Factors*	Definition	Illustration
The unexpected	Unanticipated events lead to either enterprise success or failure.	Pet pharmaceuticals have been very successful, with more than 30% of dogs and cats now taking medication.
The incongruous	What is expected is out of line with what will work.	Low-fat ice cream was developed for those trying to lose weight.
Process needs	Current technology is insufficient to address an emerging challenge.	Carmakers offer gas-electric hybrid cars to deal with rising energy costs.
Structural change	Changes in technology, markets, etc., alter industry dynamics.	Growth in the use of the Internet for e-commerce has been dramatic.
Human and Economic Factors		
Demographics	Shifts in population size, age structure, ethnicity, and income distribution impact product demand.	Many baby boomers are still in their prime income-earning years and are saving for retirement, promoting an increase in the need for financial planning.
Changes in perception	Perceptual variations determine product demand.	Perceived security threats have led to development of gated communities.
New knowledge	Learning opens the door to new product opportunities with commercial potential.	Increased knowledge of the Internet has fueled the growth of online investment firms.

Drucker suggested that innovation is "the means by which the entrepreneur either creates new wealth-producing resources or endows existing resources with enhanced potential for creating wealth."[20] In other words, entrepreneurship harnesses the power of creativity to provide innovative products and services. Since change inspires innovation, recognizing shifts in the factors described in Exhibit 3-4 can expand the range of entrepreneurial opportunities.

Other Idea Leads   If analyzing emerging changes does not reveal the specific entrepreneurial opportunity that is right for you, other sources of leads are available. The following have been useful to many entrepreneurs:

- Tapping personal contacts with potential customers and suppliers, professors, patent attorneys, former or current employees or co-workers, venture capitalists, and chambers of commerce

- Visiting trade shows, production facilities, universities, and research institutes

- Observing trends related to material limitations and energy shortages, emerging technologies, recreation, fads, pollution problems, personal security, and social movements

- Reading trade publications, bankruptcy announcements, Commerce Department publications, and business classifieds

Inc., Entrepreneur, My Business, and other periodicals are excellent sources of startup ideas, as they provide articles on the creativity of entrepreneurs and various business opportunities. Visiting the library and even looking through the Yellow Pages in other cities can spark new ideas as well. Traveling to other cities to visit entrepreneurs in your field of interest can also be extremely helpful. Of course, the Internet provides an unlimited amount of information regarding the startup process and even specific opportunities.

Applying Innovative Thinking to Business Ideas

A creative person can find useful ideas in many different places. It is important to commit to a lifestyle of creative thinking so that everyday thoughts can work in your favor. Although the following suggestions are designed to help guide your search for that one great idea for a startup, they can also help keep an existing business fresh, alive, and moving forward.

1. *When it comes to ideas, borrow heavily from existing products and services or other industries.* "Good artists borrow; great artists steal," said Pablo Picasso or T. S. Eliot or Salvador Dali—no one seems to know for sure. This principle launched Apple Computer on the road to greatness when its founder Steve Jobs identified technologies that Xerox had developed but was not using. It can work for you, too, within the limits of the law and ethical conduct. Explore ideas and practices that you come across, and think deeply about how you might put them to work in launching a startup or accelerating the growth of an existing business. Research shows that this is a powerful starting place for innovation.

2. *Combine two businesses into one to create a market opening.* Aimie's Dinner and Movie is just what you would guess: a restaurant and movie theater in one. This revolutionary concept is exceptionally practical for patrons. How many times have you rushed through dinner to get to the theater, only to find that the movie you wanted to see was already sold out? That won't happen at this Glens Falls, New York, startup. After a leisurely dinner, when the lights begin to dim, sit back in cushioned comfort and enjoy the show.[21] The restaurant business is often ruthless, and the theater industry is even more competitive, but bringing the two together puts Aimie's in a unique position.

   At some point, it may make sense to start (or buy) more than one business (although not necessarily merging their operations as closely as Aimie's Dinner and Movie), a strategy known as *diversification*. To see how this can work to your advantage, consider the outdoor lighting company that Derek Norwood and his father have owned for more than a decade. Their business had done pretty well over the years, but they found that the severe weather in Chicago (where they are located) typically hit their winter revenues hard. Norwood found a bright solution to the problem: He launched a new company that offers holiday lighting supplies. Now the revenue lag has disappeared, and since many of Norwood's outdoor lighting customers are buying holiday lighting from him as well, cross-selling advantages are also helping to boost the bottom line. Experts warn, however, that becoming too diversified can sometimes cause an entrepreneur to lose focus, which can drag down performance on all fronts.[22] It clearly pays to think through the pros and cons very carefully.

3. *Begin with a problem in mind.* Bankable business ideas usually address problems that people have. Think about a significant problem, disect it, chart it out on a sheet of paper, roll it over and over in your mind, and consider possible solutions. Sometimes amazing business ideas will come quickly to mind. For example, so many migratory birds were passing through Texas cities—settling on trees and buildings, becoming a nuisance, and making an incredible mess—that they spawned their own pest-control industry. Numerous small companies started up to address this particular problem, using flashing lights, explosions, and even falcons to drive the winged menaces from urban areas. And though the problem is obviously a seasonal one, their services are very much in demand.[23]

4. *Recognize a hot trend and ride the wave. Fads* can lead to serious, though sometimes short-lived, money-making opportunities (ever hear of the Pet Rock?), but *trends* provide a much stronger foundation for businesses because they are connected to a larger change in society. Even more powerful is the product or service that builds on three or four trends as they come together. For example, one entrepreneurship expert observed that the iPod's outrageous success is the result of multiple merging trends: the desire for increased mobility, instant gratification, and customization, all melded together with the natural pull toward fashion.[24]

But what if the wave has already crashed on the shore? Look for countertrends—every trend has one. For example, even as wireless technologies extend the reach of communication, people pay more to travel to destinations beyond the reach of their BlackBerries. Interesting, isn't it? To identify a countertrend, make it a habit to ask those who resist a trend (like the coffee drinker who refuses to go to Starbucks) what products or services would appeal to them, and then see what possibilities come to mind.[25] Try to set aside your preconceived notions of what "ought to be" and get into the minds of those who resist the flow. If you use the trend as your starting point, you will know better where to look for the countertrend, and that's where you can get ahead of the game.

How They See It: Build on Your Strengths

Trey Moore

My partner, Dr. Cameron Powell, and I met in church, where I noticed him using his PDA to respond to on-call text messages. I approached him and asked what type of things he would like to do with his PDA that he could not currently do. His initial answer was what eventually became our first product—AirStrip OB, which allows obstetricians to view fetal heart tracings and maternal contraction patterns on their PDA anywhere they have a cell-phone connection. Even though we met at Starbucks shortly after that first meeting and

kicked around many different medical-related ideas for software PDA applications, after much thought and prayer we finally arrived back at his original idea.

One of the primary reasons that we chose to pursue this idea is because it capitalized on both of our strengths. He was a young, fresh-out-of-residency OB who also was a master salesman, and I had a unique technical background in creating high-speed scanning applications for PDAs in the food industry. The alignment of our backgrounds and expertise with the niche that our product addresses has culminated in a focus strategy that has allowed us to succeed in the market with no competitors to date.

5. *Study an existing product or service and explore ways to improve its function.* Products or services that work can be improved so that they work even better. TissueKups is a tissue dispenser shaped so that it fits perfectly in a car cup holder. Lorraine Santoli came up with the seed of the idea in her car after struggling with a tissue box that kept sliding away from her. She knew there had to be a solution, and there was. The company was launched online in 2003 and reached sales of around $3 million within two years.[26] The simplicity of the product may be its best feature.

6. *Think of possibilities that would streamline a customer's activities.* Many people are busy, so they look for firms that can bear some of the burdens of life for them. That's what keeps businesses like dry cleaner and grocery delivery services going. Take some time to ponder the day-to-day experience of people in the market segment you would like to serve. What activities would they gladly off-load onto a startup that could make life more manageable for them?

7. *Consider ways to adapt a product or service to meet customer needs in a different way.* Darren Hitz realized that bachelor parties could be about more than just serious drinking and exotic dancers. That's when he came up with the idea to launch Adventure Bachelor Party, a company that brings thrills to bachelor parties by taking guys on packaged adventures like whitewater rafting trips. The startup has only been around since 2004, but Hitz already offers over 20 adventures, including cattle herding in Texas and fishing off the California coast. He also provides trips for bachelorette parties. Annual sales exceed $300,000, but just as important, Hitz is having a good time doing what he does. In his words, "I enjoy being able to provide a service where everyone has a great time and is happy."[27]

8. *Imagine how the market for a product or service could be expanded.* Jane Silber's 9-year-old daughter had a weight problem, and Silber found that few gyms allow children to use their facilities. Matching this information with the trend toward increased childhood obesity (up 300 percent since 1980), Silber realized that she had identified a wonderful business opportunity. In August of 2006, she opened Generation Now Fitness in Chatsworth, California, to expand the reach of fitness services to tweens and teens.[28] Though this story is focused on one industry, the principle will apply to any market that may be of interest to you.

9. *Keep an eye on new technologies.* New technologies often open up potential for startups, but only those who take note of the possibilities can reap the rewards. Read widely, talk to industry experts, consult government offices that promote new technologies, go to a nearby research university and visit with faculty who work at the cutting edge of their fields—there are so many sources of insight! Regardless of where you look, be sure to research innovations that have commercial value, particularly for new ventures.

    Chris Savarese is an avid golfer who wanted to find a way to use new technology to track golf balls hacked off into the rough and high brush. He searched a patent library (a good place to start) and found several possible approaches, but the answer to his question came from a trip to a department store. He noticed the security tags that stores attach to apparel items and other goods and figured they might work for his golf ball concept. Sure enough, they did! The radio frequency identification (RFID) technology that keeps track of an item's location (for example, a sweater that a shoplifter might like to walk away with) can also be used as a homing device in golf balls, allowing them to be detected from as far away as 100 feet. Savarese's company, RadarGolf, now packages a dozen radio-tagged balls with a locator to find them for $250, and the market really likes his innovation. His business is growing 30 percent a year, with revenues about to hit the $1 million mark.[29] New technology was clearly the key that got the ball rolling for Savarese, and it could be for you, too!

If you follow the suggestions provided here, you just might hit paydirt with your own new venture. However, these suggestions represent only a few of the possibilities. We encourage you to seek and size up new venture ideas *in whatever circumstances you find yourself.* Then, by considering a number of internal and external factors, you should be able to bring together the pieces of the opportunity puzzle.

Living the Dream   putting technology to work

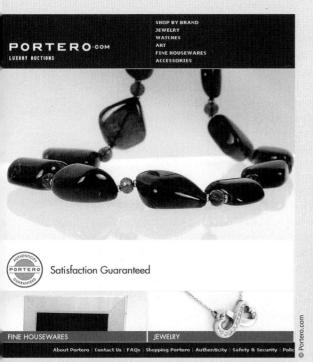

A Three-Word Revolution: "Buy It Used"

Daniel Nissanoff, author of the book *FutureShop,* describes how eBay and other auction services are turning the world of business upside-down. By his report, "Sixty million dollars in Rolex watches traded on eBay last year, and Rolex didn't get a dime for that." What does this mean? Out with the old (approach) and in with the new (way of doing business). Whereas the old standards of consumer culture socialized us to prefer to buy new products and keep them for a lifetime, the new eBay mindset says, "Used is fine, and I can sell it when I am done with it." This opens the door to innovative business ideas that simply would not have worked under the old way of doing business.

Nissanoff himself is tapping into new opportunities created by the growing popularity of online exchanges and auctions. In 2004, he co-founded Portero.com, an online resale company that deals in high-end jewelry, watches, fine housewares, collectibles, fashion accessories, and other luxury items. Nissanoff believes that people are starting to ask questions that few had thought to ask before. For example, you may choose the brand of shoes you purchase based, in good part, on the eBay value you expect it to have a year from now (when you anticipate selling the shoes). This new mindset could change the calculus of nearly all buying decisions, and savvy companies, like Portero, are positioning themselves to be leaders of that parade. At the very least, the surge in online sales and auction activity could give you and your startup a great medium through which to reach a worldwide market. And it's only a few mouse clicks away!

Sources: Max Chafkin, "Three Scary Words: 'Buy It Used,'" *Inc.*, Vol. 28, No. 9 (September 2006), pp. 29–31; http://www.portero.com/about_portero.html, accessed December 7, 2006; April Y. Pennington, "Bid on It," *Entrepreneur,* Vol. 34, No. 5 (May 2006), p. 20; Daniel Nissanoff, "The eBay Economy," http://www.washingtonpost.com/wp-dyn/content/discussion/2006/01/10/DI2006011000714.html, accessed January 26, 2006; and "FutureShop," http://www.auctionculture.com, accessed December 7, 2006.

http://www.portero.com

Using Internal and External Analyses to Evaluate an Opportunity

> **4** Describe external and internal analyses that might shape new venture opportunities.

In his book *Making Sense of Strategy,* Tony Manning points out that there are two general approaches to evaluating business opportunities: inside-out and outside-in. In other words, entrepreneurs can evaluate their own capabilities and then look at new products or services they might be able to offer to the market (inside-out), or they can first look for needs in the marketplace and then relate those opportunities to their own capabilities (outside-in).[30] Of course, there is yet another approach—both inside-out *and* outside-in. This is the path that we recommend and that we will discuss in greater detail later in this section.

It is important to understand the finer points of the two basic methods, since they can reveal business ideas that may otherwise be overlooked. In addition, the perspective that an entrepreneur gains through these analyses can help identify opportunities with potential from among the many business ideas that are sure to surface.

Remember, an opportunity is not just an idea. A business opportunity must grow from an idea with the potential to develop into an enterprise that has a reasonable chance to succeed. This means that all of the pieces of the puzzle must come together, and in the right order. For example, the entrepreneur must have a serious interest in the new venture idea, as well as the resources and capabilities to start and operate it. The rest of this section contains suggestions for evaluating internal and external factors that may influence the potential of a startup opportunity.

Outside-In Analysis

According to recent research, entrepreneurs are more successful when they study context in order to identify business ideas and determine which of these are most likely to lead to success.[31] This outside-in analysis should consider the general environment, or big picture, and the industry setting in which the venture might do business. It should also factor in the competitive environment that is likely to have an impact. The **general environment** is made up of very broad factors that influence all—or at least most—businesses in a society. In comparison, the **industry environment** is defined more narrowly as the factors that directly impact a given firm and all of its competitors. Even more specifically, the **competitive environment** focuses on the strength, position, and likely moves and countermoves of competitors in an industry.

general environment
The broad environment, encompassing factors that influence most businesses in a society

industry environment
The combined forces that directly impact a given firm and its competitors

competitive environment
The environment that focuses on the strength, position, and likely moves and countermoves of competitors in an industry.

THE GENERAL ENVIRONMENT   The general environment has a number of important segments, as shown in Exhibit 3-5. Forces in the *macroeconomic segment* include changes in the rate of inflation, interest rates, and even currency exchange rates, all of which promote or discourage business growth. The *sociocultural segment* represents societal trends that may affect consumer demand, opening up new markets and forcing others into decline. In the *political/legal segment,* changes in tax law and government regulation (such as safety rules) may pose a threat to businesses or devastate an inventive business concept. The *global segment* reflects international developments that create new opportunities to expand markets, outsource, and invest abroad. As people and markets around the world become increasingly connected, the impact of the global segment on small business opportunities is increasing.

The *technological segment* is perhaps most important to small businesses, since developments in this segment spawn—or wipe out—many new ventures. One new technology that is making life interesting for many entrepreneurs is satellite-based cameras and the aerial imaging services they provide. At one time considered the stuff of military intelligence gathering and James Bond–like spy thrillers, the ready (and free!) availability of this technology through services like Google Earth and Windows Live Local is changing the opportunity landscape for anyone with the vision to use it. For example, Jay Saber, founder of RoofAds in Redwood City, California, noticed a surge of interest in his rooftop advertising business when companies realized that a logo or message painted on the top of their buildings could be seen by anyone with a computer and an Internet connection, not just the occasional helicopter passenger.[32]

exhibit 3-5   *Segments of the General Environment*

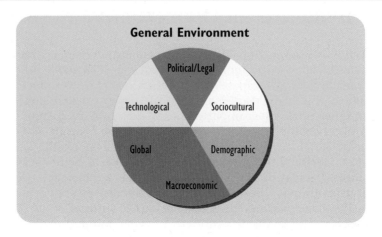

But it's not just advertising that will notice the impact—this new technology promises to revolutionize a host of other industries as well. For example, real estate marketing is feeling the heat from Zillow.com, a website that allows a user to type in the address of a house and pull up a satellite photo of it, along with its price and that of neighboring properties. You can ask for a "bird's-eye view" of the property and even obtain additional details, such as the original selling price and annual property taxes.[33] And this is just the beginning. As the technology develops further, the business landscape will again be reformed, and the rules will change.

With features like population size, age structure, ethnic mix, and wage distribution, the *demographic segment* plays an import role in shaping opportunities for startups. Many entrepreneurs, for example, are looking at aging baby boomers (the 78 million Americans born between 1946 and 1964) and seeing dollar signs. Given their $2 trillion in annual spending power and willing self-indulgence, the focus on this segment may really pay off. Jeff Taylor, 45-year-old founder of Monster.com, is launching a new website called Eons.com, which is something like a MySpace for the 50-plus crowd. He is betting that advertisers that work hard to link their brand image with younger consumers will still be willing to buy ad space on his site because its audience is self-selecting—that is, only older buyers will go to Eons.com.[34] And, there is no limit to the products and services that can be targeted to this age group. Cell phones with larger keys that can easily be seen in dim lighting, health clubs that cater to those with more gray hair and less revealing apparel, and magazines that focus on health issues in the retirement years are all business ideas that have emerged with demographic trends in mind.

Some people believe that evaluation of the general environment is appropriate only for large firms that have a corporate staff to manage the process, but small businesses can also benefit from such analysis. For example, entrepreneurs have taken note of the fact that many people struggle with their weight; in fact, government statistics show that the problem is big and getting bigger. Today, more than 60 million Americans qualify as obese, up from 23 million in 1980, and projections indicate that this number will rise by another 28 million by 2013.[35] What's happening? Experts say this development is largely the predictable result of a kind of unholy alliance of three societal trends—bigger portions of cheaper, fattier foods; an increase in dual-income households, which leads people to choose eating out over home-cooked meals; and a shift away from active urban living and toward couch-potato lifestyles in the suburbs.[36] Entrepreneurs have realized that a multitude of business opportunities can be launched based on this trend toward obesity, from weight-loss services to products that help heavier people live more comfortably with their condition. Among the many businesses that have been launched as a result of reading the numbers and seeing the shift are startups offering airline seatbelt extenders, plus-size fashion items, and oversized furniture. In other words, entrepreneurs have already proven that it can pay handsomely to look very carefully at trends in the general environment.

THE INDUSTRY ENVIRONMENT   An entrepreneur is even more directly affected by the startup's industry than by the general environment. In his classic book *Competitive Advantage,* Michael Porter lists five factors that determine the nature and degree of competition in an industry:[37]

- *New competitors.* How easy is it for new competitors to enter the industry?

- *Substitute products/services.* Can customers turn to other products or services to replace those that the industry offers?

- *Rivalry.* How intense is the rivalry among existing competitors in the industry?

- *Suppliers.* Are industry suppliers so powerful that they will demand high prices for inputs, thereby increasing the company's costs and reducing its profits?

- *Buyers.* Are industry customers so powerful that they will force companies to charge low prices, thereby reducing profits?

Exhibit 3-6 shows these five factors as weights that offset the potential attractiveness and profitability of a target industry. It illustrates how profits in an industry tend to be

exhibit

3-6   *Major Factors Offsetting Market Attractiveness*

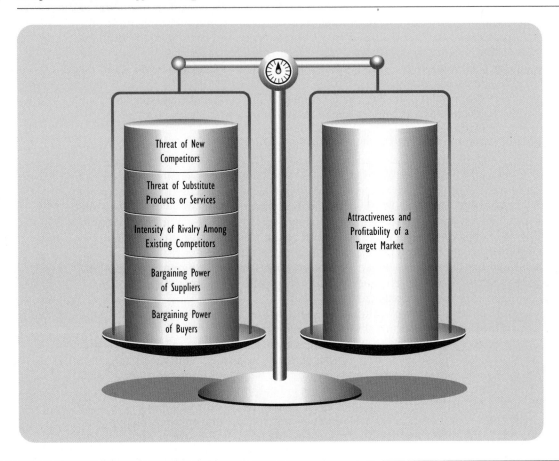

Threat of New Competitors

Threat of Substitute Products or Services

Intensity of Rivalry Among Existing Competitors

Bargaining Power of Suppliers

Bargaining Power of Buyers

Attractiveness and Profitability of a Target Market

inversely related to the strength of these factors—that is, strong factors yield weak profits, whereas weak factors yield strong profits.

Entrepreneurs who understand industry influences can better assess market opportunities and guard against threats to their ventures. Obviously, the forces dominating an industry depend on its unique circumstances; the entrepreneur must recognize and understand these forces to position the venture in a way that makes the most of what the industry offers. In other words, analyzing Porter's five industry factors will provide a good overview of the competitive landscape.

Bill Waugh, founder of the restaurant chain Taco Bueno, helped develop the concept of Mexican fast-food restaurants in the 1960s, but only after he had extensively researched the fast-food industry in general and Mexican food in particular did he decide to launch his business. Based on what he learned, he wanted to acquire a franchise from El Chico, a national chain of Mexican restaurants, but he was turned down as a prospective franchisee. Not to be denied, Waugh decided that the research he had done provided a foundation for starting his own Mexican food restaurant. Eighty-four restaurants later, he sold his business to Unigate, Ltd., a London-based company, for $32 million. Then, in the late 1980s, Waugh began the research process again, looking for his next venture. This time, he developed a concept for a new fast-food restaurant that sells hamburgers, which he named Burger Street. It is family owned and not franchised. By 2006, as a result of thorough research, he had 21 successful restaurants in operation in Texas and Oklahoma.[38]

THE COMPETITIVE ENVIRONMENT   Within any given industry, it is important to determine the strength, position, and likely responses of rival businesses. In fact, experts insist such analyses are critical to effective business plans. William A. Sahlman of

Harvard University contends that every business plan should answer several questions about the competition:[39]

- Who are the new venture's current competitors?

- What resources do they control?

- What are their strengths and weaknesses?

- How will they respond to the new venture's decision to enter the industry?

- How can the new venture respond?

- Who else might be able to observe and exploit the same opportunity?

- Are there ways to co-opt potential or actual competitors by forming alliances?

This analysis helps an entrepreneur to evaluate the nature and extent of the competition and to fine-tune future plans. It can also help to identify business opportunities based on the competitive situation.

Big Dog Motorcycles knows the value of understanding the competition when crafting a strategy. In the heavyweight segment of motorcycle manufacturing, Harley-Davidson is the undisputed champion. However, there was a time when demand for its cruisers out-stripped Harley's capacity to produce, leading to high dealer markups and two-year delays in the delivery of some models. That's when Big Dog Motorcycles entered the picture. Sheldon Coleman launched this startup in 1994 to respond to excess demand for Harleys, and it had more than $400,000 in sales the first year. Given untapped market potential, Big Dog focuses on providing highly customized cruisers at a premium price. As for the effectiveness of the strategy, the results speak for themselves. The company announced the manufacture of its 20,000th motorcycle in May of 2006. With 300 employees, Big Dog is outgrowing its identity as a small business, but it provides inspiration to other companies that are just getting off the ground.[40] And the success of Big Dog Motorcycles proves the value of knowing the weaknesses of competitors and recognizing business opportunities.

Strategy expert Gary Hamel recommends that entrepreneurs take one more step when analyzing the industry—identifying the thinking that shapes competitor behavior.[41] For example, most people assume that poor consumers in underdeveloped countries around the world do not appreciate high-end consumer products and could not afford them if they did. This view of the consumer can be excessively limiting. The shampoo market in India, for example, is actually as large as the U.S. market. And entrepreneurial luxury hair care product makers have penetrated nearly 90 percent of the market in India, many by selling shampoo in a single-use sachet that nearly anyone can afford. Relaxing the old assumption made a new business opportunity seem possible—and it turned out to be very profitable.[42] This case shows that such insights, when combined with awareness of changes in the general environment (including new technologies with market potential, lifestyle trends that call for new products or services, and political decisions that open foreign markets), can shed light on a path that leads to competitive advantage.[43]

Inside-Out Analysis

Identifying opportunities in the external environment is definitely worth the effort, but business concepts make sense only if they fit well with the internal potentials of the business. In other words, the entrepreneur's understanding of potential business opportunities should be combined with insights into what the entrepreneur and the startup are able to do. It should be noted that these concepts apply to existing businesses as well as startups.

RESOURCES AND CAPABILITIES   In order to assess the internal potentials of a business, the entrepreneur must understand the difference between resources and capabilities. **Resources** are those basic inputs that a firm uses in its business, including cash for investment, useful technologies, access to equipment, and capable employees. Companies have both tangible and intangible resources. **Tangible resources** are visible and easy to measure. An office building, computer equipment, and cash reserves are all tangible resources. These are very different from **intangible resources**, which are invisible and

resources
The basic inputs that a firm uses to conduct its business

tangible resources
Those organizational resources that are visible and easy to measure

intangible resources
Those organizational resources that are invisible and difficult to assess

difficult to assess. Intangible assets include intellectual property rights such as patents and copyrights, as well as an established brand and firm reputation.

The terms are often used interchangeably, but resources technically are not the same as capabilities. Whereas resources are singular in nature, **capabilities** are best viewed as the integration of various resources in a way that boosts the firm's competitive advantage. Like a keyboard, which is of no practical value until it is integrated into a system of computer components, resources cannot provide competitive advantage until they are bundled into some useful configuration.

capabilities
The integration of various organizational resources that are deployed together to the firm's advantage

core competencies
Those resources and capabilities that provide a firm with a competitive advantage over its rivals

CORE COMPETENCIES   Once entrepreneurs have an accurate view of their resources and capabilities, they are ready to identify core competencies. **Core competencies** are those resources and capabilities that provide an enterprise with a competitive advantage over its rivals. To illustrate, Starbucks is known for its wide selection of gourmet coffees, but that is not its only edge in the marketplace. In fact, many of its competitors—large and small—also provide high-quality coffee products. So why has the company been so successful? Most observers believe that it is the premium product, combined with the special "Starbucks experience," that has allowed the coffee icon to grow from a single store in the mid-1980s to nearly 12,500 retail locations around the world today.[44] Core competencies emerge when a company learns over time to use its resources and capabilities in unique ways that reflect the "personality" of the enterprise. Entrepreneurs who can identify core competencies and apply them effectively are in the best position to help their ventures achieve a competitive advantage and superior performance.

Integrating Internal and External Analyses

SWOT analysis
A type of assessment that provides a concise overview of a firm's strategic situation

A solid foundation for competitive advantage requires a match between the strengths and weaknesses of a business and current opportunities and threats. This integration is best revealed through **SWOT** (standing for *S*trengths, *W*eaknesses, *O*pportunities, and *T*hreats) **analysis**, which provides a simple overview of a venture's strategic situation. Exhibit 3-7 lists a number of factors that can be strengths, weaknesses, opportunities, and threats; however, these are merely representative of the countless possibilities that may exist.

exhibit

3-7   *Examples of SWOT Factors*

	POSITIVE FACTORS	NEGATIVE FACTORS
INTERNAL FACTORS	**Strengths** • Important core competencies • Financial strengths • Innovative capacity • Skilled or experienced management • Well-planned strategy • Effective entry wedge • Protection from competitive threats • Positive reputation in the marketplace • Proprietary technology	**Weaknesses** • Inadequate financial resources • Poorly planned strategy • Lack of management skills or experience • Inadequate innovation • Negative reputation in the marketplace • Inadequate facilities • Distribution problems • Inadequate marketing skills • Production inefficiencies
EXTERNAL FACTORS	**Opportunities** • Untapped market potential • New product or geographic market • Favorable shift in industry dynamics • Potential for market growth • Emerging technologies • Changes allowing foreign market entry • Deregulation • Increasing market fragmentation	**Threats** • New competitors • Rising demands of buyers or suppliers • Sales shifting to substitute products • Increased government regulation • Adverse shifts in the business cycle • Slowed market growth • Changing customer preferences • Adverse demographic shifts

In practice, a SWOT analysis provides a snapshot view of a company's current situation. This is unfortunate, since businesses perform better when they see their strategic setting as being in continuous motion. That is, companies perform better when they look forward, using their current capabilities to position their enterprises for business opportunities to come. In short, the high-performing companies of the future will be those that improve on today's capabilities to meet the challenges of tomorrow.

Outside-in and inside-out approaches come together in the SWOT analysis to help an entrepreneur identify opportunities that match the venture. The entrepreneur can then determine the *best* opportunity by asking a few additional questions:

- Will the opportunity selected lead to others in the future?

- Will the opportunity help to build skills that open the door to new opportunities in the future?

- Will pursuit of the opportunity be likely to lead to competitive response by potential rivals?

Obviously, the most promising opportunities are those that lead to others (offering value and profitability over the long run), promote the development of additional skills that equip the venture to pursue new prospects, and yet do not provoke competitors to strike back.

Hugh Kenneth Holyoak has learned how one business can lead to another and how new skills can open the floodgates of opportunity. Holyoak, owner of Ken's Hatchery and Fish Farms, two commercial lakes, and a wild-pig hunting business, has introduced a number of fishy innovations over the years, including Ken's Floating Raceway Fish Factory, the Scale-O-Matic Electric Fish Scaler, the E-Z Floating Fish Cage, and his own hybrid fish called the Georgia Giant. Noting that rising demand and disappearing wetlands have created a serious shortage of free-range frogs for dining and dissecting, he set his sights on the frog-farming business, offering an indoor frog-raising system that can grow up to 1,500 baby frogs on a mere 12 square feet of floor space. Future prospects are bright indeed, given current demand. And because most frog farms are located in low-wage countries and use labor-intensive methods, competitive retaliation is unlikely.[45] By setting his sights on frog farming, Holyoak found a way to match external developments (rising demand for frogs) with internal capabilities (fish-raising know-how). With virtually no competition at the moment, related opportunities are sure to open up, and the skills Holyoak learns from frog farming are likely to benefit his fish-related operations as well.

Like most successful entrepreneurs, Holyoak discovered areas of business opportunity that tap into emerging potentials in the external environment, but he moved in the direction of those that match his personal capabilities and the strengths of his current businesses. As shown in Exhibit 3-8, this is an entrepreneur's "opportunity sweet spot."

3-8   *The Opportunity "Sweet Spot"*

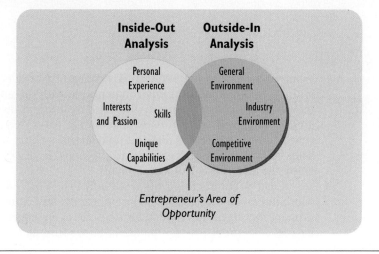

Living the Dream   entrepreneurial challenges

When a Side Business Hits the Skids, It Might Be Time to "Bag It"

Mark Talucci and Todd Elliot are, respectively, CEO and president of THE SAK, a highly successful wholesaler of handbags that they founded in 1989. The company's forte is fabricating high-quality handbags from distinctive, richly textured (original) textiles. The success of the enterprise speaks for itself—THE SAK handbag, sold in more than 1,800 department stores and 600 boutiques across the United States and in 22 international markets, has evolved into a lifestyle brand. The firm's growth has been extraordinary, but the road to the top has included a few bumps along the way.

In 1999, after 10 very successful years in the handbag business, Talucci and Elliot decided it was time to expand their product line. Their success had proven that they knew more than a thing or two about handbags, so why not use those capabilities to sell additional products like footwear, belts, and jewelry? As Talucci describes it, "The math looked good on paper, so we played spin the wheel of growth and got a little crazy." Unfortunately, these new business opportunities did not tap into the set of core competencies that played so well in the handbag industry, and sales began to slide. The entrepreneurial duo concluded it was time to reconsider their expansion plan. "We decided to focus on what we *should* be doing, not what we *could* be doing," said Talucci. "We're great at handbags. We should be making handbags." Once Talucci and Elliot were able to realign the strengths and weaknesses of the company with the opportunities and threats in the environment, they were off and running again. In fact, sales hit the $50 million mark in 2005!

So what's the secret to success? For THE SAK, it's in the bag!

Sources: Andrea Poe, "Want It All?" *Entrepreneur*, Vol. 34, No. 7 (July 2006), p. 89; and "Heritage," http://www.thesak.com/about/?display=heritage, accessed December 7, 2006.

Mona wanted to be sure *everything matched* her magnificent new bag.

THE SAK

Artwork by Bbiana Tanen

© Stefan Hagen/THE SAK/PRNewsFoto

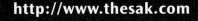

http://www.thesak.com

When potentials in the external environment (revealed through analysis of the general, industry, and competitive environments) fit with the unique capabilities and core competencies of the entrepreneur (highlighted by internal assessment), the odds of success are greatly improved. Therefore, we encourage you to be observant and systematic in your search for opportunities and to think carefully about how these fit your background and skills as well as your interests and passions. If you do so, you are much more likely to enjoy the adventure. Not a bad payoff!

Clearly, conducting outside-in and inside-out analyses and integrating the results will build a solid foundation for competitive advantage. With that foundation, the entrepreneur can begin to create a strategy for achieving superior financial performance (see Exhibit 3-9), and it's to that subject that we turn next.

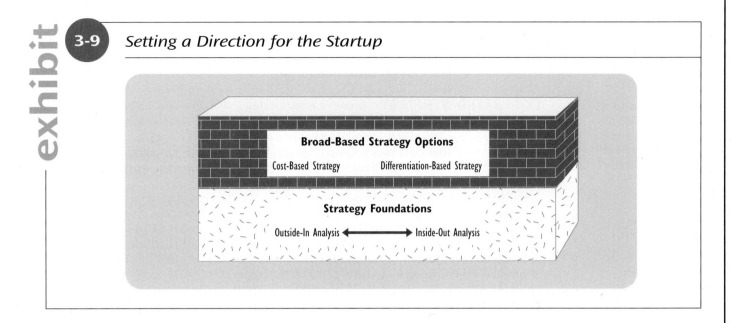

exhibit

3-9 *Setting a Direction for the Startup*

Broad-Based Strategy Options

Cost-Based Strategy   Differentiation-Based Strategy

Strategy Foundations

Outside-In Analysis ⟷ Inside-Out Analysis

Selecting Strategies That Capture Opportunities

{ 5 Explain broad-based strategy options and focus strategies.

A **strategy** is, in essence, a plan of action for coordinating the resources and commitments of a business to boost its performance. Strategy selections should be guided by the firm's situation, rather than past choices, the latest industry fad, or whatever "feels" right at the moment. Choosing a strategy that makes sense for a particular entrepreneur and his or her startup is a critical first step toward superior performance. But keeping an eye on strategy options can also guide established companies toward success.

strategy
A plan of action that coordinates the resources and commitments of an organization to achieve superior performance

Broad-Based Strategy Options

Firms competing in the same industry can adopt very different strategies. Consider two lobster restaurants located on an island in the middle of Maine's Casco Bay, each competing directly with the other for nearly 50 years: Estes Lobster House and Cook's Lobster House. The two restaurants are close to each other and even share the same picture-perfect view, but they are miles apart in competitive approach.

Cook's is using marketing savvy and its notoriety from an appearance in a Visa credit-card commercial (because "they don't take American Express") to go upscale—expanding the menu, upgrading the décor, and raising prices to match. According to Curtis Parent, the current owner of Cook's, the goal is to attract a different crowd—a more sophisticated clientele from Boston and New York, who are willing to pay $20.95 for a $1\frac{1}{4}$-pound lobster with baked potato and salad. Business has increased more than 10 percent a year, so the strategy seems to be working.

Estes's owner, Larry Croker, decided to take a different strategy, emphasizing low prices and paying close attention to costs. A one-pound boiled lobster in a paper tray costs $10.95, which Croker believes is about right. In his words, "People are looking for big portions and little prices." To hold the line on costs, Croker cut the menu in half and converted the operation to a counter-service system, which can function with only seven employees (down from 30 previously). He also takes competitive bids from suppliers for his paper needs, has set up a bulk deal for soft drinks, and relies on a local supplier for lobsters. The restaurant is popular, especially with local diners who think it offers better value for the money.

Though the restaurants differ in size, both strategies are working. During the summer months, Estes sells 4,000 pounds of lobster a week—about the same volume as Cook's. However, Estes is open less than half of the year, whereas Cook's is closed only from New Year's Day to Valentine's Day. Because of the shorter season and lower prices at Estes, this cost-based competitor grosses less than $1 million in revenue each year—well below the $2.5 million in annual revenue that Cook's takes in. But the lean cost structure at Estes makes it a successful business, while leaving room for the success of its upscale counterpart, Cook's.[46] The experiences of these two businesses illustrate how a competitive position can be guided by broad-based strategy options—creating an advantage related to cost or offering a differentiated product or service.

cost-based strategy
A plan of action that requires a firm to be the lowest-cost producer within its market

COST-BASED STRATEGY   A cost-based strategy, like the one Estes Lobster House uses, requires a firm to be the lowest-cost producer within the market. The sources of cost advantages are varied, ranging from low-cost labor to efficiency in operations. Many people assume that cost-based strategies will not work for small companies, and this is often true.[47] However, cost-advantage factors are so numerous and varied that, in some cases, small businesses may be able to use them with great success.

Steve Shore and Barry Prevor are old friends. They are also co-founders of a very successful casual apparel business, Steve and Barry's University Sportswear in Port Washington, New York, where they have priced every item under $10 and lean heavily on word-of-mouth promotion (they do no advertising). They got their start in business as teenagers, making T-shirts and selling them at flea markets. In 1985, as university seniors, Shore and Prevor opened a store to serve the apparel needs of budget-minded college students. They were hitting the books, all right, but it was as much about manufacturing processes as anything, and the goal was to undercut prices at the campus bookstore. Therefore, cost was critical.

> Budget consciousness is "deeply ingrained within the company," says Prevor. "We only ship merchandise in full truckloads. We'll make a product's garment labels for the whole year and work with manufacturers to produce items in the off-season to have level production throughout the year—the lowest-cost way to do things." Adds Shore, "We've been very successful in terms of giving people great clothing and great prices."[48]

Successful indeed! This business is no longer a typical T-shirt shop startup. In 1998, with seven campus stores in operation, Shore and Prevor opened their first mall store, and that has been their focus ever since. In 2006, with approximately 200 stores, they began diversifying, moving away from campus apparel and toward casual clothing for the entire family. They even sell under their own Steve and Barry private label now. But for these two entrepreneurs, the focus is still on cost—just as it has been from the beginning.[49]

differentiation-based strategy
A plan of action designed to provide a product or service with unique attributes that are valued by consumers

DIFFERENTIATION-BASED STRATEGY   The second general option for building a competitive advantage is creating a differentiation-based strategy, an approach that emphasizes the uniqueness of a firm's product or service (in terms of some feature other than cost). A firm that can create and sustain an attractive differentiation strategy is likely to be a successful performer in the marketplace. For the strategy to be effective, the consumer must be convinced of the uniqueness and value of the product or service—whether real or perceived. A wide variety of operational and marketing tactics, ranging from design to promotion, can lead to product or service differentiation.

Inventor Adam H. Oreck is convinced that his innovative footwear is the best in the world. Everyone has shoes, but Oreck believes that more people need to have "The World's Greatest Fitting Shoe"—the product he invented in 1984. His company, Tucson-based UFIT, Inc., offers shoes that combine stylish design with a patented lacing system that "pulls the arch of the foot up and wraps comfortably around the side of the foot [so that it] cradles the foot in the shoe." The result is a lacing system that wraps the foot so as to provide the best support possible without putting pressure on the top of the foot. The design is certainly eye-catching. According to the company's website, several major footwear companies have attempted to copy the UFIT concept, but none has come close to duplicating its comfort-creating technology. It seems there is no substitute for Oreck's design; the product stands apart from standard models of footwear.[50]

Focus Strategies

If one firm controlled the only known water supply in the world, its sales volume would be huge. This business would not be concerned about differences in personal preferences concerning taste, appearance, or temperature. It would consider its customers to be one market. As long as the water product was wet, it would satisfy everyone. However, if someone else discovered a second water supply, the first company's view of the market would change. The first business might discover that sales were drying up and take measures to modify its strategy. The level of rivalry would likely rise as competitors struggled for position in the industry.

If the potential for water sales were enormous, small businesses would eventually become interested in entering the market. However, given their limited resources and lack of experience, these companies would be more likely to succeed if they avoided head-to-head competition with industry giants and sought a protected market segment instead. In other words, they could be competitive if they implemented a **focus strategy**, adapting their efforts to concentrate on the needs of a specific niche within the market. To get started, these businesses might focus their resources on a fragment of the market that was small enough to escape the interest of major players (for example, filtered water delivered to individual homes) or perhaps take a completely new approach to permit access without immediate competitive response (for example, filling market gaps resulting from supply shortages).

Focus strategies represent a strategic approach in which entrepreneurs try to shield themselves from market forces, such as competitors, by targeting a specific market segment (sometimes called a *market niche*). The strategy can be implemented through any element of the marketing mix—price, product design, service, packaging, and so on. A focus strategy is particularly attractive to a small firm that is trying to escape direct competition with industry giants while building a competitive advantage. And by focusing on a specialized market, some small businesses develop unique expertise that leads to higher levels of value and service for customers, which is great for business. In fact, this advantage prompted superstar marketing expert Philip Kotler to declare, "There are riches in niches."[51]

The two broad options discussed earlier—a cost-based strategy and a differentiation-based strategy—can also be used when focusing on a niche market. Although few entrepreneurs adopt a cost-based focus strategy, it does happen. For example, outlets with names like The Watermarket Store, Drinking Water Depot, and H2O2Go have opened over the years, using an efficient purification system to offer high-quality, good-tasting drinking water to price-sensitive customers at a fraction of the price charged by competitors. These small businesses are clearly following a cost-based focus strategy.

Contrast this approach with the differentiation-based focus strategy that 28-year-old Ali Raissi-Dehkordy of London adopted for his startup, SavRow Bespoke Technology. It seems everyone has a computer these days, but how many of them are like the ones Raissi-Dehkordy sells? He launched the company because he "was tired of the Dell postpurchase anticlimax. You'd buy it, you'd get the new computer smell, and it was a little bit faster—but not really cool." SavRow products appeal to those who want to buy a functional machine that is also a work of art. And the models the company offers leave quite an impression! For example, the Grand Prix racetrack–inspired "Monza" laptop averages $3,000 and features a red casing accented with a green, white, and red racing stripe. The company also sells an iridescent model named after the British-made TVR sports car; the paint job alone will set you back a hefty $1,000, and other finishes cost even more. SavRow has sold a hand-stitched leather model for $13,000 and a gold-plated desktop computer for $36,000. As you might expect, these ultra-luxury computers appeal to a very limited market, but SavRow generates a spreadsheet-revving $4 million a year on sales of a mere 400 units.[52] Offering a highly differentiated product that sells for a premium price requires intense customer service, including one-on-one technical support and even house calls. But the strategy is clearly paying off in SavRow's case.

ADVANTAGES AND DISADVANTAGES OF FOCUS STRATEGIES   Focus strategies can be effective in both domestic and international markets. More than a decade ago, noted author John Naisbitt predicted that the future would see a huge global economy with smaller and smaller market niches. He further suggested that success in those niches would depend on speed to market and innovation, both of which typically are strengths of the small firm.[53] Recent evidence shows that Naisbitt's predictions are coming true, which suggests that small firms will likely see rich opportunities in the future, at home and abroad.

New ventures often fail because of poor market positioning or lack of a perceived advantage in the minds of customers in their target market. To minimize the chance of failure, an entrepreneur should consider the benefits of exploiting gaps in a market rather

focus strategy
A plan of action that isolates an enterprise from competitors and other market forces by targeting a restricted market segment

than going head to head with the competition. Focus strategies can be implemented in any of the following ways:

- Restricting focus to a single subset of customers
- Emphasizing a single product or service
- Limiting the market to a single geographical region
- Concentrating on superiority of the product or service

Many entrepreneurs have focused on market niches, and their creative efforts illustrate just how well these strategies can work. Historic Newspapers, Ltd., a British company, buys vintage newspapers from libraries as they convert their collections to

Living the Dream   entrepreneurial challenges

A Part-Time Focus Strategy, but a Full-Time Challenge

When an entrepreneur launches a new company, many times she or he has to wrestle with whether to give up an existing job and jump full-time into the startup or hold onto the job while getting a part-time business going on the side. There are advantages and drawbacks to both approaches, of course, but research shows most entrepreneurs prefer to launch a part-time enterprise and keep the income flowing until they can afford to make a complete transition to the new business.

That's the way it worked for Brian Eddy and Chad Ronnebaum back in 1999. Both in their mid-20s at the time, these long-time friends decided to hold onto their successful careers *and* launch Q3 Innovations, a product design, development, and distribution company that creates personal safety and monitoring devices. In line with their niche strategy, they came up with some unique and very interesting products to sell. Their AlcoHAWK® Series is a line of handheld breath alcohol screeners for personal or professional use. The ThermoHAWK™ Series pen-sized thermometers feature patent-pending technology that allows a user to determine the surface temperature of almost any object without actually touching it. And the UV HAWK™ measures the intensity of ultraviolet light, making it easier to know when your skin has had enough exposure to the sun.

The strategy at Q3 Innovations has been clear, but the pace has been grueling. Eddy figures that he and Ronnebaum were booking 90- to 100-hour work weeks during the company's six-year startup phase (only about half of those at their regular jobs), so the part-time business wasn't always so part-time. They always knew what they were doing for the weekend, and the task took up most of their evenings, too!

Q3 Innovations has grown enough that Eddy recently left his career to tend to the company's affairs full-time. Ronnebaum still works full-time in the pharmaceutical industry, but that really may be only a matter of . . . time.

Sources: Nichole L. Torres, "Weekenders," *Entrepreneur*, Vol. 33, No. 8 (August 2005), p. 80; "About Q3 Innovations," http://www.q3i.com/aboutus.htm, accessed June 13, 2007; and personal conversation with Chad Ronnebaum, February 7, 2007.

http://www.q3i.com

digital and microfilm formats, and then the company sells them to individuals who want a souvenir to mark a specific date, such as a birthday or an anniversary. Today, the company has over four million newspapers dating as far back as the 1780s, and business has been good. Historic Newspapers has more than 40 employees in the United States and Scotland and generates about $3 million a year from shipping old papers to interested customers in a vinyl portfolio with a certificate of authenticity. Their bestsellers usually cost around $40.[54]

In 1976, Timothy Hughes founded a similar company in Williamsport, Pennsylvania, that follows a somewhat different strategy, focusing on newspapers that are collectible because they carry reports about historic events. This approach seems to be working, too. A recent report put annual sales for Timothy Hughes Rare & Early Newspapers at $680,000. Hughes himself is less involved with the company these days, after selling 85 percent of the business for $2.4 million in 2002, but he remains connected as a consultant and still owns a significant portion of the enterprise.[55]

These companies and their competitors are trying to keep up with demand, but they all face the same problem—dwindling stocks of old newspapers. This is where creativity enters the picture. A number of these companies are adding reproductions to their offerings, even though customers prefer the real thing and the printing costs and royalties for reproductions cut into profits. Stephen A. Goldman Historic Newspapers in Parkton, Maryland, licenses images from old newspapers to television shows and co-publishes books that feature newspaper front pages on certain themes, such as baseball or the Civil War. The company reports rising revenues.[56] Yesterday's news is worth something after all, but it takes creativity to make the most of this market niche.

By selecting a particular focus strategy, an entrepreneur decides on the basic direction of the business. Such a choice affects the very nature of the business and is thus referred to as a **strategic decision**. A firm's overall strategy is formulated, therefore, as its leader decides how the firm will relate to its environment—particularly to the customers and competitors in that environment. One small business analyst expresses a word of caution about selecting a niche market:

> *Ventures that seek to capture a market niche, not transform or create an industry, don't need extraordinary ideas. Some ingenuity is necessary to design a product that will draw customers away from mainstream offerings and overcome the cost penalty of serving a small market. But features that are too novel can be a hindrance; a niche market will rarely justify the investment required to educate customers and distributors about the benefits of a radically new product.*[57]

Selection of a very specialized market is, of course, not the only possible strategy for a small firm. But focus strategies are very popular because they allow a small firm to operate in the gap that exists between larger competitors. If a small firm chooses to compete head to head with other companies, particularly large corporations, it must be prepared to distinguish itself in some way—for example, by attention to detail, highly personal service, or speed of service—in order to make itself a viable competitor.

Consider the extraordinary customer service of Zane's Cycles in Branford, Connecticut. Chris Zane borrowed money from his parents to start his bicycle shop in 1981 at the ripe age of 16. Since the launch, he has considered numerous modern business ideas to give his entrepreneurial venture the edge it needs to survive in the competitive world of bicycle dealerships. He has examined the merits of continuous learning, the benefits of surprise from guerrilla marketing, and the advantages of image branding. But the fast-wheeling entrepreneur has determined that "doing anything to attract and keep customers" will continue to be the mainspring that drives the success of Zane's Cycles. Zane gains and holds customers' loyalty by developing a personal relationship with them and by providing extraordinary product assurances.

> *Of course, everyone says they offer superior customer service, including extended guarantees of one time period or another. In his business, the norm among all his competitors was to offer a thirty-day guarantee on routine parts and service. Zane decided to jump up his guarantee to one year. It took his competitors two years to realize they were losing market share to Zane's Cycles, due to this indirect approach on "the flank" of the mainstream way of competing.*

strategic decision
A decision regarding the direction a firm will take in relating to its customers and competitors

Competitors finally caught on and eventually matched Zane's one-year guarantee. Unfortunately for them, Zane immediately doubled his guarantee to two years. When competitors tried to play catch-up and followed him again, he went to a five-year guarantee. In the end, Zane offered a lifetime guarantee. Competitors thought that at last this was as far as he could go, but it wasn't. Those competitors that could, reluctantly extended to a lifetime guarantee. However, even that wasn't the ultimate. Zane soon extended his lifetime guarantee to everything in his store! By then, he had plenty of additional cycling products to offer. By taking an indirect approach, Zane had found a way to compete at which his competitors were always behind, and at which he had the advantage, even though his competition in some areas was far stronger and more powerful. As a result of his indirect strategy, Zane grew pretty powerful himself; soon he was the number-one bicycle retailer in size for his geographic area.[58]

Zane has been growing his business at 25 percent a year and now sells about 2,500 bikes annually from his 7,500-square-foot store. His advantage begins with a unique point of view. As Zane puts it, "The attitude [must change] from 'The customer is inconveniencing you and preventing you from doing your job' to 'The customer *is* your job.'"[59]

MAINTAINING THE POTENTIAL OF FOCUS STRATEGIES   Firms that adopt a focus strategy tread a narrow line between maintaining a protected market and attracting competition. If their ventures are profitable, entrepreneurs must be prepared to face competition. In his classic book *Competitive Advantage,* Michael Porter cautions that a segmented market can erode under any of the following four conditions:[60]

1. The focus strategy is imitated.

2. The target segment becomes structurally unattractive because the structure erodes or because demand simply disappears.

3. The target segment's differences from other segments narrow.

4. New firms subsegment the industry.

The experience of Minnetonka, a small firm widely recognized as the first to introduce liquid hand soap, provides an example of how a focus strategy can be imitated. The huge success of its brand, Softsoap, quickly attracted the attention of several giants in the industry, including Procter & Gamble. Minnetonka's competitive advantage was soon washed away. Some analysts believe this happened because the company focused too much on the advantages of liquid soap in general and not enough on the particular benefits of Softsoap.

It should be clear that focus strategies do not guarantee a sustainable advantage. Small firms can boost their success, however, by developing and extending their competitive strengths. Good strategic planning can help point the way through these challenging situations.

Putting It All Together

If you have come up with a business idea you are excited about, you have taken the first step toward an adventure into entrepreneurship. Performing an outside-in analysis will show you the really big picture (the general environment) and provide an overview of the industry and the competition. An inside-out analysis will help you match your personal strengths and capabilities to the external environment. If a SWOT analysis suggests there is a fit between opportunities and threats in the external environment and the strengths and weaknesses of your planned enterprise, you can conclude that your *idea* is likely to be a promising business *opportunity.* Going one step further, you can use the strategy framework provided in this chapter to set a general direction for the venture—low cost or differentiation—and to learn how to find and maintain a market niche for your startup. You have come a long way!

But you may not be interested in starting a business from scratch. Is there room left in the entrepreneurial game for you? Absolutely! Chapters 4 and 5 will give you a closer look at franchise and buyout opportunities and help you figure out whether you want to join a family-owned business. These are all forms of entrepreneurship.

And what's the next step in moving toward the launch of the business of your dreams? A business plan! Chapters 6 through 12 will show you how to sort out the specifics of your business opportunity, from start to finish. After showing the importance of the business plan and providing a model to get you started (Chapter 6), the rest of Part 3 will help you plan for marketing (Chapter 7), organization (Chapter 8), location and physical facilities (Chapter 9), and financial requirements (Chapters 10 and 11). Looking down the road a bit, Chapter 12 even shows you how to plan for the eventual harvest of your venture. Let's continue the journey!

Looking BACK

1 Identify several factors that determine whether an idea for a new venture is a good investment opportunity.

- To represent a good investment opportunity, a product or service must meet a real market need with respect to benefits offered and price.

- The fundamental requirements for a good business idea relate to market factors, competitive advantage, economics, management capability, and fatal flaws.

2 Give several reasons for starting a new business from scratch rather than buying a franchise or an existing business.

- Some entrepreneurs start businesses from scratch when they want to market a new product or service.

- Other entrepreneurs hope to tap into unique resources.

- Another reason that entrepreneurs start a new business from scratch is that they want to avoid undesirable features of existing companies.

- Still other entrepreneurs want the challenge of succeeding (or failing) on their own.

3 Distinguish among the different types and sources of startup ideas.

- Type A startup ideas are concerned with products or services that exist but are not present in all markets.

- Type B ideas involve new or relatively new technology.

- Type C ideas are based on new and improved ways of performing old functions.

- Sources of startup ideas include personal experience, hobbies and personal interests, accidental discovery, and a deliberate search process.

- Business ideas can also be spurred by innovative thinking that can result from the following: borrowing ideas from existing products and services or other industries, combining businesses to create a market opening, focusing on a problem, responding to a trend, improving an existing product or service, making customers' lives easier, meeting customer needs in a new way, expanding the market for a product or service, or tapping into new technologies.

4 Describe external and internal analyses that might shape new venture opportunities.

- Outside-in analysis considers the external environment, including the general, industry, and competitive environments.

- The major segments of the general environment are the macroeconomic, sociocultural, political/legal, global, technological, and demographic segments.

- The major forces that determine the level of competition within the industry environment are the threat of new competitors, the threat of substitute products or services, the intensity of rivalry among existing competitors, the bargaining power of suppliers, and the bargaining power of buyers.

- Opportunities arise for small businesses that are alert to changes in the general, industry, and competitive environments.

- Inside-out analysis helps the entrepreneur to understand the internal potentials of the business.

- Tangible resources are visible and easy to measure, whereas intangible resources are invisible and difficult to quantify.

- Capabilities represent the integration of several resources in a way that boosts the firm's competitive advantage.

- Core competencies are those resources and capabilities that can be leveraged to enable a firm to do something that its rivals cannot do.
- A SWOT analysis provides an overview of a firm's strengths and weaknesses, as well as opportunities for and threats to the organization.

5 Explain broad-based strategy options and focus strategies.

- A competitive advantage can be created using broad-based strategy options—cost-based or differentiation-based strategies.
- A cost-based strategy requires the firm to become the lowest-cost producer within the market.
- Product differentiation is frequently used as a means of achieving superior performance.

- Focusing on a specific market segment is a strategy that small firms often use successfully.
- A focus strategy may involve restricting focus to a single subset of customers, emphasizing a single product or service, limiting the market to a single geographical region, or concentrating on product/service superiority.
- The basic direction of the business is chosen when the entrepreneur makes a strategic decision and selects a particular focus strategy.
- The benefits of a focus strategy can diminish when the strategy is imitated, the segment becomes unattractive or demand dwindles, the segment loses its uniqueness, or new firms subsegment the industry.

Key TERMS

opportunity recognition, p. 63
entrepreneurial alertness, p. 63
competitive advantage, p. 64
Type A ideas, p. 67
Type B ideas, p. 68
Type C ideas, p. 68
serendipity, p. 69

general environment, p. 76
industry environment, p. 76
competitive environment, p. 76
resources, p. 79
tangible resources, p. 79
intangible resources, p. 79
capabilities, p. 80

core competencies, p. 80
SWOT analysis, p. 80
strategy, p. 83
cost-based strategy, p. 84
differentiation-based strategy, p. 84
focus strategy, p. 85
strategic decision, p. 87

Discussion QUESTIONS

1. What is the difference between a good idea and a good opportunity?

2. Why might an entrepreneur prefer to launch an entirely new venture rather than buy an existing firm?

3. What are the three basic types of startup ideas? What are the most common sources of inspiration for startup ideas?

4. List the six segments of the general environment. Give a hypothetical example of a way in which each segment might affect a small business.

5. What are the primary factors shaping competition in an industry, according to Porter's model? In your opinion, which of these factors will have the greatest impact on industry prices and profits?

6. How are capabilities related to tangible and intangible resources? How are these related to core competencies?

7. What is SWOT analysis? How can SWOT analysis help the entrepreneur match opportunities in the external environment with organizational capabilities?

8. What are the two basic strategy options for creating a competitive advantage?

9. Explain what is meant by the term *focus strategy*.

10. What are the advantages and disadvantages of a focus strategy? What must an entrepreneur know and do to maintain the potential of a focus strategy?

You Make the CALL

SITUATION 1

Marty Lane worked for a card company specializing in invitations and announcements. Every day for 25 years, he went to an office, sat at a desk, and took orders over the phone. He hated it. He was bored out of his mind. He didn't know what to do.

So he began skimming the business opportunities section of the Sunday *New York Times.* He wasn't sure what he was looking for. At almost 50 years of age, he had few business skills. Accounting was a foreign language to him. He figured that if he ever bought a business, it would have to be one that didn't require much specialized knowledge—something that would be relatively easy to manage. He considered a franchise, but he found that the good ones were very expensive. Then he came across an Italian-bread route for sale. He thought "How difficult could it be to run a delivery route?" He called the phone number in the ad and spoke with the business broker who was handling the sale.

It turned out that the route was in Queens, New York, not far from where Lane and his wife, Annabelle, lived. It was a one-person operation. The individual who owned it had had the route for 20 years and took home about $65,000 a year. He wanted $200,000 for the business, but he was willing to help finance the deal. If Lane would put $60,000 down, he could pay the balance over five years at 10 percent interest, or about $35,000 a year. That would leave Lane with an annual income of $30,000 until the debt was paid. Combined with Annabelle's salary, it would be enough to make ends meet. If he worked hard, moreover, he could expect his sales, and his income, to grow by 10 to 15 percent a year.

It seemed perfect. Lane went to meet with the owner and returned sounding even more enthusiastic. "This is a can't-miss deal," he told his wife. "The guy has signed contracts with all the places he delivers to, and none of them is more than 25 miles from here. I could do the entire route in seven hours."

However, Annabelle wasn't buying. "You're not quitting your job until you talk to an expert," she said. Lane agreed to meet with a broker.

On the date of the meeting, Lane brought all his paperwork along. He laid out the terms of the deal in great detail. "What do you think?" he asked.

The broker said, "Tell me something, Marty. Do you like this business?"

He shrugged. "I can't really say. I haven't tried it yet."

"What's involved in it besides picking up the bread and delivering it to the stores?"

"I'm not sure," he said. "Whatever it is, it can't be that complicated."

"What happens if the truck breaks down?"

"I don't know," he said. "I guess I'll just work it out."

After asking Lane a series of questions along those lines, the broker finally said, "Listen, Marty. You want to know if this deal makes sense from a financial standpoint. That's easy to check. The guy has an income tax return, and his sales are verifiable. This isn't a cash business, after all. He sells to delis and supermarkets. They pay by check. We can go over his expense figures and make sure they're realistic, but my guess is that the deal is OK. If you're asking me whether I could negotiate him down a little, the answer is probably yes."

Lane turned to his wife: "See, I told you he'd approve."

The broker said, "I didn't approve anything. Only you can do that, and you're not ready to."

"What do you mean?" he asked.

"You haven't done your homework," the broker said. "You don't know what you're actually going to do in this business, and you don't know if you'll be happy doing it."

"How am I going to find that out?" Lane asked.

Question 1 How would you suggest that Lane find out if he would be happy in this business?

Question 2 Would you recommend that Lane buy the business, given the asking price and terms of the deal?

Question 3 Is Lane relying too much on nonquantitative factors?

SITUATION 2

Amy Wright is the owner of Fit Wright Shoes, a manufacturer of footwear located in Alice, Texas. Her company has pledged that all customers will have a lifetime replacement guarantee on all footwear bought from the company. This guarantee applies to the entire shoe, even though another company makes parts of the product.

Question 1 Do you think a lifetime guarantee is too generous for this kind of product? Why or why not?

Question 2 What impact will this policy have on quality standards in the company? Be specific.

Question 3 What alternative customer service policies would you suggest?

SITUATION 3

Jay Sorenson of Portland, Oregon, created a product called the Java Jacket, which is a patented honey-combed insulating sleeve that slides over a paper cup containing a hot beverage to make it comfortable to hold. Having introduced the new product to the market, Sorenson already has cut deals with coffeehouses, specialty stores, and convenience stores nationwide. He started the business with $15,000 in 1993, but Java Jacket has grown tremendously since then. In fact, the company has already sold more than one billion cup sleeves! Sorenson is now in a position where he would like to continue expanding his business, but he is concerned that large and established competitors could introduce their own variations of the same product.

Sources: Don Debelak, "Send in the Clones," *Entrepreneur,* September 2003, pp. 128–132; and "About Java Jacket," http://www.javajacket.com/company. php, accessed December 6, 2006.

Question 1 Will the market for Sorenson's product continue to grow in the years ahead?

Question 2 If he is successful, what sources of competition should he expect?

Question 3 What steps would you recommend that he take to protect his company from the onslaught of competition that is likely to come?

Experiential **EXERCISES**

1. Select a product that is manufactured by a small business, and look for the likely drivers of its attributes in the dynamics of the general and/or industry environments.

2. Examine a recent issue of a business publication, and describe the type of target market strategy you believe the magazine uses.

3. Visit a local small retailer, and ask the manager to describe the firm's customer service policies.

4. Working in small groups, write a brief but specific description of the best target market for a new product that is familiar to most of the class. A member of each group should read the group's market profile to the class.

5. Interview the owner of a local small business about the venture's performance outcomes. Find out what results were achieved, and then systematically explore how those performance outcomes have been reinvested in the business. For example, if the venture has yielded considerable customer loyalty, examine how that commitment has been leveraged for future results.

6. On the website of a small business, identify the factors in the external (general, industry, and competitive) environment and the internal (organizational) environment around which the business seems to have been built. Does it appear to you that the firm is more sensitive to internal or external factors? Given your knowledge of the firm's business, is that good or bad?

7. The Electric Transportation Company sells electrically powered bicycles, like the ETC Express. Review the information found at http://store. nycewheels.com/etc.html. Using the terminology introduced in this chapter, identify the specific type of strategy the Electric Transportation Company is using as it expands its business.

Exploring the **WEB**

1. Reread what this chapter has to say about the external and internal analyses that might help you evaluate a new venture opportunity. To assess the impact of these factors on your business idea, go to the website of Bplans. com (**http://www.bplans.com/st/#**), and click on the link to Success Potential Quiz. The quiz will appear in another window.

   a. Take the quiz, and print out your score.

   b. What does your score imply for the future of your business?

2. It's never too early to start thinking about where you will get the funding to start your business. Go to **http://www.myownbusiness.org/s7**, and read the information about business financing on the Session 7 page.

    a. Where do you think you might find funding for your business idea?

    b. Name three other funding sources for a startup business not touched on by the My Own Business writers.

3. The editors of *Inc.* publish a series of "How-To" guides on the magazine's website at **http://www. inc.com** to help business owners start, run, and grow successful businesses. Go to the "How-To" guide on finance and capital at **http://www.inc. com/guides/finance/20797.html**.

    a. From among those listed on this website, read at least five articles on raising startup capital.

    b. Write a brief description of the information in the articles you selected, and summarize the best of the tips for raising startup capital.

4. Familiarize yourself with the resources provided by QuickMBA that can help a business owner "make sense of strategy." Go to **http://www. quickmba.com/strategy/**.

    a. Click on the PEST Analysis link and read about the PEST framework.

    b. Follow the SWOT Analysis link and use the information you find there to create a SWOT analysis for your small business or a small business that you're familiar with.

Case 3

Biolife LLC (p. 624)
This case describes the experiences of two research scientists who discovered a new product and then launched a startup to take their innovative product to the market.

Alternative Cases for Chapter 3:
Case 1, Boston Duck Tours, p. 620
Case 7, eHarmony, p. 633
Case 14, Country Supply, p. 648
Case 15, Nicole Miller Inc., p. 650

## chapter 4

Franchises and Buyouts

Firehouse Subs: A Blazing Success Story!

In the **SPOTLIGHT**

http://www.firehousesubs.com

Risk is nothing new for Firehouse Subs (FHS) founders (and brothers) Robin and Chris Sorensen. The Sorensen family has more than 200 years of experience fighting fires; their father retired from firefighting after 43 years. Robin and Chris, who worked as firefighters for the Jacksonville, Florida, Fire Department for a combined 14 years, also share a passion for cooking.

As frequent cooks for their firefighting brethren, they received as many compliments for their cooking as they did for their firefighting prowess. After much deliberation, they decided to leave the fire department and open their first FHS restaurant in 1994. However, they did not leave the firehouse completely behind. FHS restaurants are well decorated with a firehouse motif, including tables that are spotted like a Dalmatian, walls that are red and white with black chair rails, and brick pillars. Black and white pictures of firefighters and fire trucks, along with firefighter hats and fire hose signs complete the firehouse theme. And it doesn't stop with the decorations. The most popular menu item is the cleverly named "Hook & Ladder" sub.

With 33 company restaurants and more than 250 franchised units, FHS is making good progress toward its goal of being one of the top five "sub" chains in the nation. The bulk of the company's growth comes from franchising. However, the brothers and their management team are careful to screen potential franchisees and will not sacrifice quality to achieve their expansion goals. FHS has a lengthy approval process for prospective franchisees, and training is extensive.

Despite the success of FHS, the brothers have not forgotten their roots. Supporting public safety organizations, like fire and police, is the focus of their Firehouse Subs Public Safety Foundation, created in 2005, and recent television ads for FHS have used real firefighters to convey safety messages. These ads are more oriented to public service than to selling the FHS brand. The chain does not offer coupons and only recently began limited advertising.

The brothers' story, their connection with firefighters, and, of course, great subs have made the FHS chain a blazing success.

Source: http://www.firehousesubs.com, accessed January 5, 2007.

© Firehouse Restaurant Group

After studying this chapter, you should be able to

1 Identify the major pros and cons of franchising.
2 Explain franchising options and the structure of the industry.
3 Describe the process for evaluating a franchise opportunity.
4 List four reasons for buying an existing business and describe the process of evaluating a business.

Chapter 3 examined how entrepreneurs take their ideas, develop them into opportunities, and pursue their entrepreneurial dreams by starting a business from scratch. This chapter considers franchises and buyouts—startup options involving existing businesses.

The Pros and Cons of Franchising

1 Identify the major pros and cons of franchising.

"Look before you leap" is an old adage that should be heeded by entrepreneurs considering franchising. Entrepreneurs should not let their enthusiasm blind them to the realities of franchising, both good and bad. Weighing the purchase of a franchise against alternative paths to starting a business is an important task, which requires careful consideration of many factors. Exhibit 4-1 illustrates the major advantages and disadvantages of franchising.

exhibit 4-1 *Major Pluses and Minuses in the Franchising Calculation*

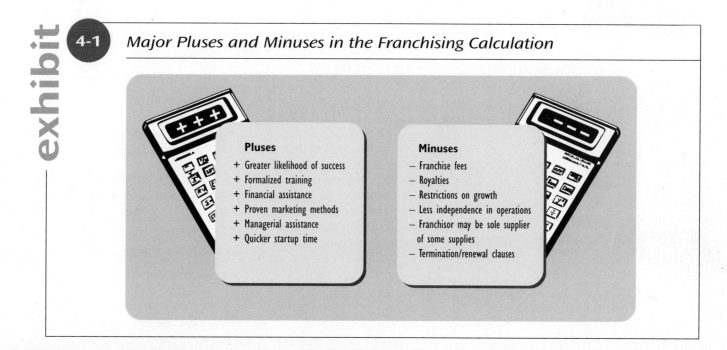

Pluses
+ Greater likelihood of success
+ Formalized training
+ Financial assistance
+ Proven marketing methods
+ Managerial assistance
+ Quicker startup time

Minuses
− Franchise fees
− Royalties
− Restrictions on growth
− Less independence in operations
− Franchisor may be sole supplier of some supplies
− Termination/renewal clauses

Given the different personal goals and circumstances of individuals, franchising will not be the ideal choice for all prospective entrepreneurs. However, many people find a franchise to be the best alternative for owning a business. When you are evaluating future entrepreneurial opportunities, carefully weigh the pros and cons of franchising presented in this chapter.

In this book, we use a broad definition of franchising to encompass the term's diversity. **Franchising** is a marketing system revolving around a two-party legal agreement whereby one party (the **franchisee**) is granted the privilege to sell a product or service and conduct business as an individual owner but is required to operate according to methods and terms specified by the other party (the **franchisor**). For example, Subway (the franchisor) franchises quick-service, fast-food outlets to local owners (franchisees).

Advantages of Franchising

Buying a franchise can be attractive for a variety of reasons. The greatest overall advantage by far is the probability of success. Franchisors offer a business model with proven success. Business data on failures of franchises are difficult to find and evaluate. Nevertheless, the success rate for franchises seems to be much higher than that for nonfranchised businesses. One explanation for the lower failure rate is that most franchisors are highly selective when granting franchises. Many potential franchisees who qualify financially are still rejected.

There are three additional, and more specific, reasons why a franchise opportunity is appealing. A franchise is typically attractive because it offers training, financial assistance, and operating benefits that are not readily available to the entrepreneur starting a business from scratch. Naturally, different franchises vary in the depth of support they provide for each of these forms of assistance. For example, McDonald's offers excellent training but no financing.

TRAINING   The training received from franchisors is invaluable to many small entrepreneurs because it compensates for weaknesses in their managerial skills. Training by the franchisor often begins with an initial period of a few days or a few weeks at a central training school or another established location and then continues at a franchise site. McDonald's is widely recognized for its off-site franchisee training effort at Hamburger University.

The training by Kwik Kopy Printing, another famous franchisor, is very extensive, covering the technical aspects of running a printing business as well as the standard topics of accounting, computer purchasing and use, and leadership. Its training facility, located in the picturesque city of Northwest Forest, a few miles from Houston, Texas, looks like an amusement park, with a full-size replica of the Alamo. However, franchise trainees quickly realize that the three-week training program is very demanding. Classes start at 7:00 A.M. and conclude at 6:00 P.M., Monday through Friday, and they continue for a half-day on Saturday.

Express Personnel Services (EPS) is also a strong believer in initial training for prospective franchisees. Consider this description of EPS's new franchisee training system:

> *Franchisees and their staff attend this intensive three-week start-up training. Our curriculum involves three levels of learning. Cursory learning provides an overview of materials. Working knowledge provides thorough understanding without performing tasks and the competency level involves performing the task, through role plays to enhance understanding and retention of knowledge.*
>
> *The first two weeks of learning are held at Express Personnel's international headquarters in Oklahoma City. This allows the students an opportunity to learn and practice the key functions they will be performing within their offices. The students will be involved in various role-play scenarios, group exercises and classroom discussions to learn the three pillars of our business:*
>
> - *Sales*
> - *Recruiting*
> - *Service*
>
> *The first two weeks of training focus on Inside Sales, Outside Sales and Business Management.*
> *   Week three is actual on the job training, which allows the new franchisee to perform the major business functions in an Express University certified extension office. These offices are model offices that provide an avenue for the new franchisee to truly acquire live experience prior to their opening week.*[1]

franchising
A marketing system involving a legal agreement, whereby the franchisee conducts business according to terms specified by the franchisor

franchisee
An entrepreneur whose power is limited by a contractual relationship with a franchisor

franchisor
The party in a franchise contract that specifies the methods to be followed and the terms to be met by the other party

Naturally, the nature of both the product and the business affect the amount and type of training needed by the franchisee. In most cases, training constitutes an important advantage of the franchising system, as it permits individuals who have had little training or education to start and succeed in businesses of their own.

Subsequent training and guidance may involve refresher courses and/or visits by a company representative to the franchisee's location from time to time. The franchisee may also receive manuals and other printed materials that provide guidance in operating the business. Although the franchisor normally places considerable emphasis on observing strict controls, much of the continuing training goes far beyond the application of controls. In particular cases, however, it may be difficult to distinguish between guidance and control.

Although many franchising systems have developed excellent training programs, be aware that this is by no means universal. Some unscrupulous promoters falsely promise extensive training and then leave the entrepreneur to run his or her own business with little or no guidance.

Living the Dream   entrepreneurial challenges

Got Junk?

The brightly painted truck reads "1-800-GOT-JUNK?" and serves as a rolling advertisement. Robert Burns, who formerly did fundraising and development for the Boy Scouts of America, purchased the Louisville territory of the relatively new franchise.

Burns had known for some time that he wanted to own a business, but he didn't know what business. After deciding that a franchise would be his best bet, he began looking into available franchise opportunities and discovered 1-800-GOT-JUNK? Burns carefully researched the company and its reputation before making the purchase. He also attended a seminar entitled "Owning Your Own Business," sponsored by the Louisville SCORE chapter. The seminar provided him with helpful information in the early phases of becoming a business owner.

The company hauls "junk" from both homes and businesses. Prices are based on volume: from one-eighth of the space in a truck to the whole truck. Anything that is still usable or can be recycled does not go to waste. All usable items are delivered to Goodwill or the Salvation Army; recyclables go to recycling centers; everything else goes to the landfill. The company does not pick up paints, chemicals, or hazardous materials.

Burns began the business with one truck and has since added a second. His entry costs into the business included a franchise fee, the price of a truck, and various other startup costs. Financing was done through Stock Yards Bank with an SBA-guaranteed loan.

1-800-GOT-JUNK? is growing, and Burns is working hard to develop a solid base of commercial customers. Even though it's hard work, Burns is enjoying himself. He says, "Since I left my job at the Boy Scouts, I don't feel like I have gone to work a single day. Building this business is like playing a game, and I am playing to win."

Sources: http://www.sba.gov/ky/kysuccess.html, August 2003; personal communication with Robert Burns, April 2004; and http://www.1800gotjunk.com, January 20, 2007.

http://www.1800gotjunk.com

FINANCIAL ASSISTANCE   The costs of starting an independent business are often high, and the typical entrepreneur's sources of capital are quite limited. The entrepreneur's standing as a prospective borrower is weakest at this point. By teaming up with a franchising organization, the aspiring franchisee may enhance her or his likelihood of obtaining financial assistance.

If the franchising organization considers the applicant to be a suitable prospect with a high probability of success, it frequently extends a helping hand financially. The franchisee is seldom required to pay upfront the complete cost of establishing the business. In addition, the beginning franchisee is normally given a payment schedule that can be met through successful operation. For example, in the early days of the Jiffy Lube franchise, the franchisor would loan the franchisee funds to purchase the real estate for a store. Also, the franchisor may permit the franchisee to delay payments for products or supplies obtained from the parent organization, thus increasing the franchisee's working capital.

Association with a well-established franchisor may also improve a new franchisee's credit standing with a bank. The reputation of the franchising organization and the managerial and financial controls that it provides serve to recommend the new franchisee to a banker. Also, the franchisor will frequently cosign a note with a local bank, thus guaranteeing the franchisee's loan.

The U.S. Small Business Administration (SBA) has introduced the Franchise Registry (http://www.franchiseregistry.com), which greatly expedites loan processing for small business franchisees. The Registry "enables lenders and SBA local offices to verify a franchise system's lending eligibility through the Internet. This reduces red tape, time, and cost for all concerned."[2] Listing on this registry means that the SBA has found that the particular franchise agreement does not impose unacceptable control provisions on the franchisee. Therefore, loan applications for registered franchises can be reviewed and processed more quickly.

Living the Dream   focus on the customer

Courtesy of Culver Franchising System, Inc.

Are You Ready to Work?

Craig and Lea Culver are particular about who buys their franchises and how their fast-food franchisees treat customers. When first developing the concept for Culver's back in 1984, the Culver family focused on treating customers right, and they still do. They now have over 350 restaurants nationwide.

The Culvers have been very careful in their selection of franchisees. Candidates must show a net worth of $500,000. "I won't even interview them if the right numbers aren't on the application," says Thomas Wakefield, who helps line up potential franchisees. And even if a franchisee can borrow the necessary capital, he or she must first complete a 60-hour evaluation. Once the paperwork for the chosen site has been submitted, the franchisee must attend a 16-week training program, including working in the classroom and on the job at a family-owned Culver's and assisting with two new restaurant openings. Ongoing training happens at the restaurant, off-site seminars, and an annual convention, as well as in Culver's Learning Support Center.

Most franchises are profitable in two years. "I want to create millionaires," says Craig Culver.

Sources: Erin Killian, "Butter 'Em Up," *Forbes*, Vol. 171, No. 12 (June 9, 2003), pp. 175–176; http://www.culvers.com/AboutCulvers/History.aspx, June 19, 2007; "28th Annual Franchise 500," *Entrepreneur*, January 2007, p. 194; and personal communication with Barbara Behling, director of Culver's public relations, May 2004.

http://www.culvers.com

OPERATING BENEFITS   Most franchised products and services are widely known and accepted. For example, consumers will readily buy Baskin-Robbins ice cream or use PIP Printing services because they are aware of the reputation these businesses have. Travelers will recognize a restaurant or a motel because of its name or type of roof or some other feature such as the "Golden Arches" of McDonald's. They may turn into a Denny's restaurant or a Holiday Inn because of their previous experiences with the chain and their knowledge that they can depend on the food and service these outlets provide. Thus, franchising offers both a proven line of business and product/service identification.

An entrepreneur who enters into a franchising agreement acquires the right to use the franchisor's nationally advertised trademark or brand name. This serves to identify the local enterprise with the widely recognized product or service. Of course, the value of product identification depends on the type of product or service and the extent to which it has been promoted. In any case, the franchisor must maintain the value of its name by continued advertising and promotion.

In addition to a proven line of business and readily identifiable products or services, franchisors offer well-developed and thoroughly tested methods of marketing and management. The manuals and procedures supplied to franchisees enable them to function more efficiently from the start. This is one reason why franchisors insist on the observance of high quality methods of operation and performance. If one franchise were allowed to operate at a substandard level, it could easily destroy customers' confidence in the entire system.

The existence of proven products and methods, however, does not guarantee that a franchise will succeed. For example, a location that the franchisor's marketing research shows to be satisfactory may turn out to be inferior. Or the franchisee may lack ambition or perseverance. But the fact that a franchisor has a record of successful operation proves that the system can work, because it has worked elsewhere.

Limitations of Franchising

Franchising is like a coin—it has two sides. We have presented the positive side of franchising, but it is important that you also learn about its negative side. Four shortcomings, in particular, permeate the franchise form of business: (1) the costs associated with the franchise, (2) the operating restrictions that can be a part of the franchise agreement, (3) the loss of entrepreneurial independence, and (4) a lack of franchisor support.

FRANCHISE COSTS   Generally speaking, higher costs characterize the better known and more successful franchises. Franchise costs have several components, all of which need to be recognized and considered.

1. *Initial franchise fee.* The total cost of a franchise begins with an initial franchise fee, which may range from several hundred to many thousands of dollars. The initial fee for a Wing Zone, a takeout/delivery restaurant, is $20,000–$25,000; McDonald's initial fee is $45,000.

2. *Investment costs.* Significant costs may be involved in renting or building an outlet and stocking it with inventory and other equipment. Also, certain insurance premiums, legal fees, and other startup expenses must be paid. It is often recommended that funds be available to cover personal expenses and emergencies for at least six months. A reputable franchisor will always provide a detailed estimate of investment costs; Exhibit 4-2 shows the information provided by Wing Zone. Curves for Women, a women's workout facility, charges between $30,000 and $40,000 for a franchise, workout equipment included. The total net worth requirement for a KFC restaurant exceeds $1,000,000—the prospective franchisee must have cash and other personal assets worth this amount.

3. *Royalty payments.* A common practice is for the franchisor to receive continuing royalty payments, calculated as a percentage of the franchisee's gross income. McAlister's Deli, for example, charges a 5 percent royalty fee. McDonald's currently charges a "service fee" of 4 percent of monthly sales plus the greater of (a) a monthly base rent or (b) a percentage rent based on monthly sales.

exhibit

4-2   *An Estimate of Investment Costs by Wing Zone*

	Low	High
Franchise fee	$ 20,000	$ 25,000
Leasehold improvements	50,000	80,000
Equipment (excludes sales tax)	48,000	53,000
Signs	6,000	8,000
Computer P.O.S. system	18,000	18,000
Office equipment/phone system	3,000	3,500
Drop safe and lock	1,000	1,500
Digital security system	0	3,000
Initial inventory	4,000	4,000
Start-up marketing	3,000	3,000
Grand-opening fund	5,000	5,000
Insurance (down payment)	3,000	3,500
Initial training expenses	2,000	3,000
Uniforms	1,000	1,000
Utility deposits	1,000	2,500
Architectural plans	5,000	8,000
Real estate cost	4,000	7,000
Working capital	15,000	20,000
Total Investment	**$189,000**	**$249,000**

Source: http://www.wingzone.com, accessed August 7, 2007.

4. *Advertising costs.* Many franchisors require that franchisees contribute to an advertising fund to promote the franchise. These fees are generally 1 to 2 percent of sales or even more.

If entrepreneurs could generate the same level of sales by setting up an independent business, they would save the franchise fee and some of the other costs. However, if the franchisor provides the benefits previously described, the money franchisees pay for their relationship with the franchisor may prove to be a very good investment.

RESTRICTIONS ON BUSINESS OPERATIONS   Franchisors, understandably concerned about the image of their businesses, make every effort to control how franchisees conduct certain aspects of the franchise business. Thus, the franchisee is restricted in her or his ability to use personal business judgment. The following types of control are frequently exercised by a franchisor:

- Restricting sales territories

- Requiring site approval for the retail outlet and imposing requirements regarding outlet appearance

- Restricting goods and services offered for sale

- Restricting advertising and hours of operation

LOSS OF INDEPENDENCE   Frequently, individuals leave salaried employment for entrepreneurship because they dislike working under the direct supervision and control of others. But when they enter into a franchise relationship, such individuals may find that a different pattern of supervision has taken over. The franchisee surrenders a considerable amount of independence in signing a franchise agreement.

Even though the franchisor's influence on business operations may be helpful in ensuring success, the level of control exerted may be unpleasant to an entrepreneur who cherishes independence. In addition, some franchise contracts go to extremes, covering unimportant details or specifying practices that are more helpful to others in the chain than to the local operation. For example, a food franchise may be prevented from selling a nonapproved product in a local market.

Also, entrepreneurs should recognize that they can lose the right to a franchise if they do not abide by performance standards or fail to pay royalties. Additionally, there is no guarantee that a franchise will be renewed beyond the contracted time, which is typically 15 to 20 years.

LACK OF FRANCHISOR SUPPORT   Just like a marriage, a franchisor/franchisee relationship can experience stress, which may lead to a breakup. Perceived lack of franchisor support sometimes creates disputes, especially when the franchisee believes the franchisor is not honoring its commitments.

Disputes may revolve around a lack of continued training, poor promotional support, or other issues. Once a communication breakdown occurs between the two parties, the well-being of the franchise is in jeopardy. Entrepreneurs who are considering purchasing a franchise should recognize this inherent disadvantage of franchising.

Franchising Options and the Structure of the Franchising Industry

2 Explain franchising options and the structure of the industry.

The term *franchising* was derived from a French word meaning "freedom" or "exemption from duties." In business, franchising describes a unique type of business option that offers entrepreneurs the possibility of reducing the overall risk associated with buying an independent business or starting a business from scratch. The franchise arrangement allows new business operators to benefit from the accumulated business experience of all members of the franchise system.

Franchising Options

The potential value of any franchising arrangement is defined by the rights contained in a legal agreement known as the **franchise contract**; the rights it conveys are called the **franchise**. The extent and importance of these rights may be quite varied. When the main benefit the franchisee receives is the privilege of using a widely recognized product name, the arrangement between the franchisor (supplier) and the franchisee (buyer) is called **product and trade name franchising**. Automobile tire outlets carrying the Goodyear brand name and soft drink bottlers distributing Dr Pepper are both engaged in this type of franchising.

Alternatively, entrepreneurs who receive an entire marketing and management system are participating in a broader type of arrangement referred to as **business format franchising**. Fast-food outlets (e.g., Burger King), hotels and motels (e.g., Radisson), and business services (e.g., Mail Boxes Etc.) typically engage in this type of franchising. The volume of sales and the number of franchise units associated with business format franchising have increased steadily over the years.

A **master licensee** is a firm or individual having a continuing contractual relationship with a franchisor to sell its franchises. This independent company or businessperson is a type of middleman or sales agent. Master licensees are responsible for finding new franchisees within a specified territory. Sometimes, they even provide support services such as training and warehousing, which are more traditionally provided by the franchisor. Also gaining widespread usage is **multiple-unit ownership**, in which a single franchisee owns more than one unit of the franchised business. Some of these franchisees are **area developers**—individuals or firms that obtain the legal right to open several outlets in a given area.

Piggyback franchising refers to the operation of a retail franchise within the physical facilities of a host store. Examples of piggyback franchising include a cookie franchise doing business inside an Arby's fast-food outlet and a Krispy Kreme donut franchise

franchise contract
The legal agreement between franchisor and franchisee

franchise
The privileges conveyed in a franchise contract

product and trade name franchising
A franchise agreement granting the right to use a widely recognized product or name

business format franchising
A franchise arrangement whereby the franchisee obtains an entire marketing system geared to entrepreneurs

master licensee
An independent firm or individual acting as a sales agent with the responsibility for finding new franchisees within a specified territory

multiple-unit ownership
Holding by a single franchisee of more than one franchise from the same company

exhibit

4-3   *The Structure of Franchising*

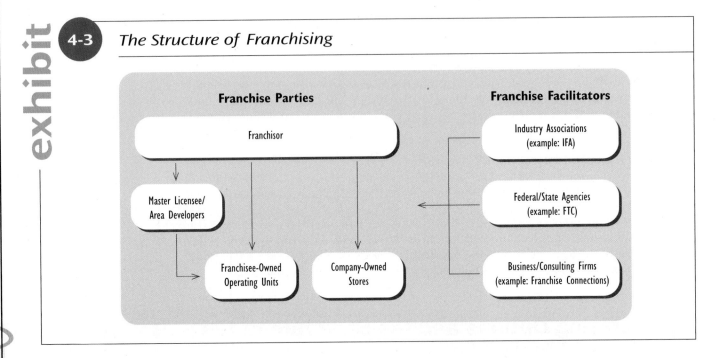

Franchise Parties

Franchisor

Master Licensee/
Area Developers

Franchisee-Owned
Operating Units

Company-Owned
Stores

Franchise Facilitators

Industry Associations
(example: IFA)

Federal/State Agencies
(example: FTC)

Business/Consulting Firms
(example: Franchise Connections)

area developers
Individuals or firms that obtain the legal right to open several franchised outlets in a given area

piggyback franchising
The operation of a retail franchise within the physical facilities of a host store

operating within a Wal-Mart store. A new trend in piggyback franchising is locating walk-in health clinics in Wal-Marts, Target stores, drugstores, and other retail outlets. This form of franchising benefits both parties. The host store is able to add a new product line, and the franchisee obtains a location near prospective customers.

The Structure of the Franchising Industry

Franchisors and franchisees are the two main parties in the franchise industry. A franchisor may be a manufacturer or another channel member (a wholesaler or retailer) that has an attractive business concept worthy of duplication. As shown in Exhibit 4-3, a franchise can be sold by the franchisor directly to individual franchisees or marketed through master licensees or area developers. Most franchisors also own one or more outlets that are not franchised. These outlets are referred to as company-owned stores.

In addition to these parties, the franchising industry contains other important groups called *facilitators*. Facilitators include industry associations, governmental agencies, and private businesses.

The International Franchise Association (http://www.franchise.org), or IFA, is an industry association that serves franchise members by attempting to safeguard and enhance the business and regulatory environment of the industry. It has over 30,000 members—franchisors, franchisees, and suppliers—that operate in more than 100 countries. Nevertheless, the IFA is highly selective, and not all companies applying for membership are accepted. Referring to itself as "The Voice of Franchising," the IFA sponsors legal and government affairs conferences, franchise management workshops, seminars on franchisor/franchisee relations, and trade shows. The IFA also champions the causes of minority business groups. For example, the Women's Franchise Committee (WFC), formed in 1996, provides leadership conferences, mentoring programs, a network of professionals, and other services for women franchisees.

Numerous federal and state agencies are involved in the franchise industry. Agencies such as the Federal Trade Commission (http://www.ftc.gov), or FTC, provide information on franchise opportunities and enforce franchising laws and regulations. Presale franchise disclosure practices are subject to special scrutiny by these agencies.

A third category of facilitators includes private businesses providing franchise information and consulting services to franchisors and franchisees. For example, Franchise Connections (http://www.franchiseconnections.com) and The Franchise Company (http://www.thefranchisecompany.com) are two businesses that assist with franchising evaluation and offer development services.

Evaluating Franchise Opportunities

{ 3 Describe the process for evaluating a franchise opportunity.

After making a decision to pursue a franchising opportunity, the prospective franchisee must identify a franchise candidate and investigate it completely. As we discuss the investigation process, we will continue to use examples involving Wing Zone, a takeout/delivery restaurant franchise featuring buffalo wings.

Selecting a Franchise

With the growth of franchising over the years, the task of selecting an appropriate franchise has become easier. Personal observation frequently sparks interest, or awareness may begin with exposure to an advertisement in a newspaper or magazine or on the Internet. The headlines of these advertisements usually highlight the financial and personal rewards sought by the entrepreneur. *Inc., Entrepreneur,* and the *Wall Street Journal* are three examples of publications that include advertisements of franchisors.

Investigating the Potential Franchise

The nature of the commitment required in franchising justifies careful investigation of the situation. Launching a franchised business typically requires a substantial financial investment, usually many thousands of dollars. Furthermore, the business relationship generally continues over a period of years.

The evaluation process is a two-way effort. The franchisor wishes to investigate the franchisee, and the franchisee obviously wishes to evaluate the franchisor and the type of opportunity being offered. Time is required for this kind of analysis. You should be skeptical of a franchisor who pressures you to sign a contract without time for proper investigation.

What should be the prospective entrepreneur's first step in evaluating a franchising opportunity? What sources of information are available? Do government agencies provide

---

How They See It: Buying a Franchise

Scott Salmans

You can definitely learn the most from your mistakes. One of mine was when I purchased a franchise from a reputable and successful franchisor in a related field.

This franchisor had been very good in low-end food stores and several high-end restaurants. They thought they would try their hand at mid-level fast service with better-quality foods than the fast food available in the market. The problem was that experience at both ends of the food service spectrum did not serve them well in the untried market of high-quality food with the low-price expectations of fast-food service establishments. The entire business, from corporate on down, failed. Where I fault myself is not listening to my inner voice when I felt the franchisor was not prepared for our meetings prior to contract signing. They and we were relying too much on the idea that past success was an indicator of future success, even if all the food costs and other key matters had not been completely refined.

When it comes to franchises, the buyer should beware. Oftentimes, the promise of dollar signs and seeming ease of process can lead us to overlook our own better judgments. Franchise salesmen can hang their hats on the legal requirement that in some states they are not allowed to state the financial status of existing stores because conditions will vary from location to location. This is true, but in some ways it serves to create a mysterious upside to whatever the franchisor is selling. This is not to say that franchises are not good business ventures; but it is important to do more homework than just work with the selling agent of the business in question.

information on franchising? Basically, three sources of information should be tapped: (1) independent, third-party sources, (2) the franchisors themselves, and (3) existing and previous franchisees.

INDEPENDENT, THIRD-PARTY SOURCES OF INFORMATION State and federal agencies are valuable sources of franchising information. Since most states require registration of franchises, a prospective franchisee should not overlook state offices as a source of assistance. The Federal Trade Commission publishes the *Franchise Opportunities Handbook,* which is a useful directory of hundreds of franchisors. Also, a comprehensive listing of franchisors can be found in the *Franchise Opportunities Guide,* which is published by the International Franchise Association. Exhibit 4-4 displays selected listings

exhibit

4-4   *Profiles from the Franchise Opportunities Guide (2005)*

FIREHOUSE SUBS
Firehouse Restaurant Group
(904) 886-8300
(904) 886-2111 FAX
3410 Kori Road, Jacksonville, FL 32257
Email: sjoost@firehousesubs.com
Internet: http://www.firehousesubs.com
Full Member

TYPE OF BUSINESS: In 1994, Firehouse Subs was founded by brothers Robin and Chris Sorensen, members of the Jacksonville, Florida fire department. As the frequent cooks for their stationhouse, they quickly gained a reputation for fighting hunger with the same success (and passion!) that they fought fires. After countless compliments at their first location, the brothers decided to take their culinary talents to a larger audience. They created a unique sandwich restaurant concept that specializes in hot, large-portion submarine sandwiches, served in a dining environment filled with authentic firefighting memorabilia. The brothers then developed a business model that will grow Firehouse Subs by using a two-tiered system of Area Representatives and Franchises.

HISTORY: 127 franchised units; 29 company-owned units; in business since 1994; franchising since 1995.

CASH INVESTMENT: $136,300-$280,475 startup cash; $136,300-$280,475 total investment required.

TRAINING/SUPPORT: The Firehouse Subs Training Program lasts for approximately 6–8 weeks. The first 4–6 weeks takes place in a certified Firehouse Subs' Training Restaurant. After the initial in-store Training is complete, the Trainee travels to Jacksonville, Florida for an intensive 2-week Training and Certification course. Several days of hands-on evaluations take place in a live setting in a Firehouse Restaurant, and an exam is given at the end of the 2-week Training course. Those that pass the hands-on skills assessment and make 90 or higher are certified and given and official Firehouse Subs' diploma. All General Managers, Franchisees and Area Representatives must complete this intensive training process.

CONTACT: Stephen Joost, Partner/Chief Financial Officer

WING ZONE
Wing Zone Franchise Corp.
(877) 333-946 Ext. 16
(404) 875-5045 Ext. 16
(404) 521-4310 FAX
900 Circle 75 Parkway, Suite 930, Atlanta, GA 30339
Email: stan@wingzone.com
Internet: http://www.wingzone.com
Full Member

TYPE OF BUSINESS: A unique new franchise that specializes in take-out and delivery of 25 flavors of fresh buffalo wings, grilled sandwiches, salads, and appetizers. We are known for serving only the freshest buffalo wings, as well as our 25 top quality sauces. Our take-out and delivery concept offers an alternative to the never-ending pizza delivery. Our low overhead and specialized food concept makes our offering very attractive.

HISTORY: 58 franchised units; 2 company-owned units; in business since 1991; franchising since 1999.

CASH INVESTMENT: $60,000-$75,000 start-up cash; $144,500-$224,500 total investment required. Minimum net worth of $150,000. Wing Zone assists in locating third party financing.

TRAINING/SUPPORT: Complete start-up and ongoing assistance, including site selection, lease negotiation, restaurant design and construction advice. Eleven days of pre-opening training in Atlanta. Ten days of on-site training at your location.

QUALIFICATIONS: Prior restaurant experience not required. Marketing and/or people oriented past experience is very helpful. This is a 'keep it simple' business concept.

CONTACT: Stan Friedman, Executive Vice President & Partner; Clint Lee, Franchise Development

MAUI WOWI FRESH HAWAIIAN BLENDS
Maui Wowi Franchising, Inc.
(888) 862-8555
(303) 781-7800
(303) 781-2438 FAX
5445 DTC Parkway, Suite 1050, Greenwood Village, CO 80111
Email: mauiifa@franchisehub.com
Internet: http://www.mauiwowi.com
Full Member

TYPE OF BUSINESS: The largest Hawaiian Coffee/Smoothie franchise in the United States, Maui Wowi is ranked #1 in the Juice Bar category of *Entrepreneur* 500 (2005) with over 310 locations.

HISTORY: 360 franchised units; in business since 1983; franchising since 1997.

CASH INVESTMENT: $65,000-$200,000 startup cash; $65,000-$400,000 total investment required. Third party financing available on equipment.

TRAINING/SUPPORT: Maui Wowi provides 4 days of training in Colorado and ongoing 24/7 support.

QUALIFICATIONS: Ability to follow a proven system. Ability to project a positive and constructive attitude. Desire to commit to accomplishing articulated goals. Liquidity of $40,000 and Net Worth of $250,000.

CONTACT: Kera Vo, Franchise Development Marketing Manager; Mike Edwards, Vice President, Franchise Development

CULVER'S
Culver Franchising System, Inc.
(608) 643-7980
(608) 643-7982 FAX
540 Water Street, Prairie du Sac, WI 53578
Email: franchise@culvers.com
Internet: http://www.culvers.com
Full Member

TYPE OF BUSINESS: Culver's is famous for their cooked to order ButterBurgers and premium frozen custard. A quick service restaurant serving a great variety of sandwiches, salads, dinners, frozen custard desserts, beverages and other menu items.

HISTORY: 264 franchised units; 5 company-owned units; in business since 1984; franchising since 1987.

CASH INVESTMENT: $250,000-$400,000 startup cash; $354,250-$2,898,250 total investment required.

TRAINING/SUPPORT: All operating franchisees complete an intense 16-week training program. The cost of this training is included in the initial franchise fee. Franchisees pay their own costs for transportation, lodging and meals. All training takes place in Wisconsin in one of our family-owned restaurants and at our Culver's Support Center in Prairie du Sac, Wisconsin.

QUALIFICATIONS: You will need $250,000 to $400,000 in liquid assets to qualify. Liquid assets do not include real estate (including home), automobiles, personal effects, or borrowed funds. Applicant will be the owner/operator maintaining a minimum of 50 percent ownership in the operating business entity and involved full-time in the day-to-day operations of the restaurant. Successfully completes a one week 60-hour evaluation program in Prairie du Sac, Wisconsin.

CONTACT: Gary Rudsinski, Franchise Development Manager

Source: International Franchise Association, 2005, http://www.franchise.org, August 2, 2007.

from the online guide. Note the entries for Wing Zone and Firehouse Subs, featured in the opening Spotlight for this chapter.

Business publications are also excellent sources of franchisor ratings. *Fortune, Entrepreneur,* and the *Wall Street Journal,* to name a few, can be found in most libraries, and all have websites with archives. The *Entrepreneur* magazine website contains a profile

Living the Dream   entrepreneurial challenges

Get into the Wing Zone

As college students at the University of Florida in 1991, Matt Friedman and Adam Scott were disappointed to discover that the only food delivered late at night was pizza. Nothing against pizza, but they—and many of their fellow students—couldn't live on pizza alone; they needed buffalo wings, grilled sandwiches, burgers, chicken fingers, salads, and more, delivered day and night.

So the two budding entrepreneurs commandeered their fraternity's kitchen and soon had perfected their special sauces (25 flavors) and techniques for preparing chicken wings. With a $500 investment for a phone line and printed flyers, they were in business. Their idea was an instant hit, and the first Wing Zone storefront opened near the University of Florida three weeks later. The duo opened six stores, and in 1999 they began franchising their concept.

Currently, there are 58 Wing Zone franchises located across the United States, and Wing Zone has been named to *Inc.* magazine's 500 fastest-growing private companies in the country. *Success* magazine ranks the company in the top 25 restaurant franchises.

Source: http://www.wingzone.com, accessed January 5, 2007

http://www.wingzone.com

of the top-20 fastest-growing franchises in 2007 (see Exhibit 4-5). The rankings are based on the number of franchise units added in 2006.

A search of the Web uncovered numerous articles describing the Wing Zone restaurant franchise—one of the fastest-growing franchises in recent years. Frequently, such articles provide information not available from the franchisor or from government agencies. They often give an extensive profile of franchise problems and strategy changes within a company. Third-party coverage helps in evaluating the credibility of information provided directly by the franchisor. The Internet search also revealed that Wing Zone is listed in the Small Business Administration's Franchise Registry, discussed earlier in this chapter.

In recent years, franchise consultants have appeared in the marketplace to assist individuals seeking franchise opportunities. Some consulting firms, such as FranCorp, present seminars on choosing the right franchise. Of course, the prospective franchisee needs to be careful to select a reputable consultant. And since franchise consultants are not necessarily attorneys, an experienced franchise attorney should evaluate all legal documents.

exhibit

4-5   Entrepreneur's *2007 Fastest-Growing Franchises Rankings (Top 20)*

Rank	Franchise	Where Based	Contact Information	Description	# of Franchises Added, 2006
1	Subway	Milford, CT	(800)888-4848 www.subway.com	Submarine sandwiches & salads	1,690
2	Jan-Pro Franchising Int'l. Inc.	Little River, SC	(800)668-1001 www.jan-pro.com	Commercial cleaning	1,265
3	Dunkin' Donuts	Randolph, MA	(800)777-9983 www.dunkindonuts.com	Donuts & baked goods	682
4	Coverall Cleaning Concepts	Boca Raton, FL	(800)537-3371 www.coverall.com	Commercial cleaning	595
5	Jazzercise	Carlsbad, CA	(760)476-1750 www.jazzercise.com	Dance/exercise	536
6	Jackson Hewitt Tax Service	Parsippany, NJ	(800)475-2904 www.jacksonhewitt.com	Tax preparation services	508
7	RE/MAX Int'l. Inc.	Englewood, CO	(800)525-7452 www.remax.com	Real estate	425
8	CleanNet USA Inc.	Columbia, MD	(800)735-8838 www.cleannetusa.com	Commercial cleaning	405
9	Bonus Building Care	Indianola, OK	(918)823-4990 www.bonusbuldingcare.com	Commercial cleaning	281
10	Jani-King	Addison, TX	(800)552-5264 www.janiking.com	Commercial cleaning	280
11	Liberty Tax Service	Virginia Beach, VA	(800)790-3863 www.libertytax.com	Tax preparation services	279
12	Cold Stone Creamery	Scottsdale, AZ	(480)362-4800 www.coldstonecreamery.com	Ice cream, frozen yogurt, Italian sorbet	244
13	Cartridge World	Emeryville, CA	(510)594-9000 www.cartridgeworldusa.com	Toner replacement services	227
14	Coffee News	Bangor, ME	(207)941-0860 www.coffeenewsusa.com	Advertising services-publishing	202
15 (tie)	Budget Blinds, Inc.	Orange, CA	(800)420-5374 www.budgetblinds.com	Windows and floors	198
15 (tie)	Edible Arrangements	Hamden, CT	(888)727-4258 www.ediblearrangements.com	Food-design business	198
17	Brooke Franchise Corp.	Overland Park, KS	(800)642-1872 www.brookefranchise.com	Miscellaneous financial services	195
18	Choice Hotels International	Silver Spring, MD	(866)560-9871 www.choicehotelsfranchise.com	Hotels and motels	190
19	The UPS Store/Mail Boxes Etc.	San Diego, CA	(877)623-7253 www.theupsstore.com	Postal/business/communications services	181
20	Century 21 Real Estate LLC	Parsippany, NJ	(800)221-5737 www.century21.com	Real estate	175

Source: "28th Annual Franchise 500," *Entrepreneur*, January 2007, p. 255. Reprinted with permission from *Entrepreneur* Magazine, January 2007, http://www.entrepreneur.com.

THE FRANCHISOR AS A SOURCE OF INFORMATION   Obviously, the franchisor being evaluated is a primary source of information. However, information provided by a franchisor must be viewed in light of its purpose—to promote the franchise.

One way to obtain information about franchisors is to communicate directly with them. For example, when we decided to investigate the franchise Wing Zone, we first accessed its home page. We requested information, and within a few days we received a packet containing an attractive brochure and various marketing materials. The brochure included such information as startup costs and franchisees' testimonials.

It is important for potential franchisees to remember that many of the financial figures provided in the franchisor's information packet are only estimates. While profit claims are becoming more common, reputable franchisors are careful not to misrepresent what a franchisee can expect to attain in terms of sales, gross income, and profits. The importance of earnings to a prospective franchisee makes the subject of profit claims a particularly sensitive one.

After an entrepreneur has expressed further interest in a franchise by completing the application form and the franchisor has tentatively qualified the potential franchisee, a meeting is usually arranged to discuss the disclosure document. A **disclosure document** is a detailed statement of such information as the franchisor's finances, experience, size, and involvement in litigation. The document must inform potential franchisees of any restrictions, costs, and provisions for renewal or cancellation of the franchise. Important considerations related to this document are examined more fully later in this chapter.

disclosure document
A detailed statement provided to a prospective franchisee, containing such information as the franchisor's finances, experience, size, and involvement in litigation

EXISTING AND PREVIOUS FRANCHISEES AS SOURCES OF INFORMATION   There may be no better source of franchise facts than existing franchisees. Sometimes, however, the distant location of other franchisees precludes a visit to their place of business. In that case, a simple telephone call can elicit that person's viewpoint. If possible, talk also with franchisees who have left the business; they can offer valuable insights into their decision to give up the franchise.

Finding Global Franchising Opportunities

A great opportunity continues to exist for small business firms in the United States to franchise internationally. Traditionally, U.S. franchisors did most of their international franchising in Canada because of that country's proximity and language similarity. This, however, has changed. A combination of events, including the structuring of the European Union (EU) and the passage of the North American Free Trade Agreement (NAFTA), have opened other foreign markets to U.S. franchisors.[3]

Although the appeal of foreign markets is substantial, the task of franchising abroad is not easy. The challenges of international franchising are described on the website of Gaebler Ventures in the following way:

> International franchising is more risky than domestic franchising, but there's a world of opportunity out there. Whether you are a franchisor or a franchisee, international franchising could put you on track to achieve your business and personal goals beyond your wildest dreams. But, be sure you understand some of the differences between international franchising and domestic franchising. . . . Unlike domestic franchising, international franchising requires an added level of expertise, primarily around issues involved with doing business in an unfamiliar cultural context.
>
> The good news is that the challenges of international franchising are not insurmountable. Regardless of whether you are a current business owner exploring the possibility of franchising your company internationally or a potential new business owner interested in opening a franchise abroad, you can take advantage of opportunities in international franchising by addressing a few issues upfront.[4]

Many sources of international franchising information are available to entrepreneurs. Many U.S. government publications are helpful, as is the information on several websites, such as that of the *International Herald-Tribune*. Also, individual foreign countries may host websites that contain useful information about franchising opportunities in that country; the British Franchising Association's site at http://british-franchise.org is one example.

Considering Legal Issues in Franchising

THE FRANCHISE CONTRACT The basic features of the relationship between the franchisor and the franchisee are embodied in the franchise contract. This contract is typically a complex document, running to many pages. Because of its importance as the legal basis for the franchised business, the franchise contract should never be signed by the franchisee without legal counsel. In fact, reputable franchisors insist that the franchisee have legal counsel before signing the agreement. An attorney may anticipate trouble spots and note any objectionable features of the contract.

In addition to consulting an attorney, a prospective franchisee should use as many other sources of help as practical. In particular, he or she should discuss the franchise proposal with a banker, going over it in as much detail as possible. The prospective franchisee should also obtain the services of a professional accounting firm in examining the franchisor's statements of projected sales, operating expenses, and net income. An accountant can help in evaluating the quality of these estimates and in identifying projections that may be unlikely to be realized.

One of the most important features of the franchise contract is the provision relating to termination and transfer of the franchise. Some franchisors have been accused of devising agreements that permit arbitrary cancellation of the franchise relationship. Of course, it is reasonable for the franchisor to have legal protection in the event that a franchisee fails to obtain an appropriate level of operation or to maintain satisfactory quality standards. However, the prospective franchisee should be wary of contract provisions that contain overly strict cancellation policies. Similarly, the rights of the franchisee to sell the business to a third party should be clearly stipulated. A franchisor who can restrict the sale of the business to a third party could potentially assume ownership of the business at an unreasonably low price. The right of the franchisee to renew the contract after the business has been built up to a successful operating level should also be clearly stated in the contract.

FRANCHISE DISCLOSURE REQUIREMENTS The offer and sale of a franchise are regulated by both state and federal laws. At the federal level, the minimum disclosure standards are specified by Rule 436 of the Federal Trade Commission (FTC). The rule, formally entitled "Disclosure Requirements and Prohibitions Concerning Franchising and Business Opportunity Ventures," went into effect in October of 1979. A guide to the rule can be found on the Federal Trade Commission's website at http://www.ftc.gov/bcp/franchise/netrule.htm. Addresses of the state offices administering franchise disclosure laws can be found at http://www.ftc.gov/bcp/franchise/netdiscl.htm.

A document called the **Uniform Franchise Offering Circular (UFOC)** provides the accepted format for satisfying the franchise disclosure requirements of the FTC. The original UFOC format was amended in April 1993 by its creator, the North American Securities Administrators Association (NASAA). Effective January 1, 1996, all franchisors using the UFOC disclosure format were obliged to abide by the new amendments.

The UFOC disclosure must include information on a variety of items, including litigation and bankruptcy history, investment requirements, and conditions that would affect renewal, termination, or sale of the franchise. Most franchise experts recommend that a franchisee's attorney and accountant review the document.

Another option for the entrepreneur seeking to make his or her dream a reality is buying an existing business. In the next section, we discuss some of the issues facing the individual who chooses this alternative.

Uniform Franchise Offering Circular (UFOC)
A document accepted by the Federal Trade Commission as satisfying its franchise disclosure requirements

Buying an Existing Business

For would-be entrepreneurs, one alternative to starting from scratch or buying a franchise is to buy an established business. The decision to purchase an existing business should be made only after careful consideration of the advantages and disadvantages.

4 List four reasons for buying an existing business and describe the process of evaluating a business.

Reasons for Buying an Existing Business

The reasons for buying an existing business can be condensed into the following four general categories:

1. To reduce some of the uncertainties and unknowns that must be faced in starting a business from the ground up

2. To acquire a business with ongoing operations and established relationships with customers and suppliers

3. To obtain an established business at a price below what it would cost to start a new business or to buy a franchise

4. To begin a business more quickly than by starting from scratch

Let's examine each of these reasons in more detail.

REDUCTION OF UNCERTAINTIES   A successful business has already demonstrated its ability to attract customers, manage costs, and make a profit. Although future operations may be different, the firm's past record shows what it can do under actual market conditions. For example, just the fact that the location must be satisfactory eliminates one major uncertainty. Although traffic counts are useful in assessing the value of a potential location, the acid test comes when a business opens its doors at that location. This test has already been met in the case of an existing firm. The results are available in the form of sales and profit data. Noncompete agreements are needed, however, to discourage the seller from starting a new company that will compete directly with the one being sold.

ACQUISITION OF ONGOING OPERATIONS AND RELATIONSHIPS   The buyer of an existing business typically acquires its personnel, inventories, physical facilities, established banking connections, and ongoing relationships with trade suppliers and customers. Extensive time and effort would be required to build these elements from scratch. Of course, the advantage derived from buying an established firm's assets depends on the nature of the assets. For example, a firm's skilled, experienced employees constitute a valuable asset only if they will continue to work for the new owner. The physical facilities must not be obsolete, and the firm's relationships with banks, suppliers, and customers must be healthy. In any case, new agreements will probably have to be negotiated with current vendors and leaseholders.

A new business owner who fails to carefully consider the nature of the assets may face some unpleasant surprises. Consider the experience of Norman Savage. Shortly after buying a small mortgage company in Fort Wayne, Indiana, Savage learned that the seller had given some employees 20 percent pay increases after the deal was made, effectively buying for himself credit for being a generous boss and leaving the cost of that generosity for Savage to pay. In addition, some of the firm's business licenses were about to expire, and Savage had difficulty locating the necessary documents to renew them. To top it off, one of the office computers needed to be replaced.[5]

On the other hand, Thomas J. Cerri encountered no such problems when he bought Mill Valley Lumber Company in Mill Valley, California. He recalls, "When we took over, eight key employees stayed on with us, and it really made all the difference." The sales staff had nearly 100 years of experience among them and "seemed to be friends with everyone in the area." With a well-connected sales staff and other key employees staying on the job, Mill Valley Lumber continued to enjoy a close relationship with its customers, despite the invasion of giant competitors like Home Depot.[6]

A BARGAIN PRICE   If the seller is more eager to sell than the buyer is to buy, an existing business may be available at what seems to be a low price. Whether it is actually a good buy, however, must be determined by the prospective new owner. Several factors could make a "bargain price" anything but a bargain. For example, the business may be losing money, the neighborhood location may be deteriorating, or the seller may intend to open a competing business nearby. On the other hand, if research indicates that the business indeed is a bargain, purchasing it is likely to turn out to be a wise investment.

A QUICK START   Most entrepreneurs are eager to "get going" in their new business and may not be comfortable waiting the months and years sometimes required to launch a business from scratch. Buying an existing business may be an excellent way to begin operations much more quickly.

Finding a Business to Buy

Sometimes, in the course of day-to-day living and working, a would-be buyer comes across an opportunity to buy an existing business. For example, a sales representative for a manufacturer or a wholesaler may be offered an opportunity to buy a customer's retail business. In other cases, the prospective buyer needs to search for a business to buy.

Sources of leads about businesses available for purchase include suppliers, distributors, trade associations, and even bankers. Realtors—particularly those who specialize in the sale of business firms and business properties—can also provide leads. In addition, there are specialized brokers, called **matchmakers**, that handle all the arrangements for closing a buyout. A large number of matchmakers, such as Certified Business Brokers (http://www.certifiedbb.com) in Houston, Texas, deal with mergers and acquisitions of small and mid-sized companies in the United States. Entrepreneurs need to be wary of potential conflicts of interest with matchmakers, however. For example, if matchmakers are paid only if a buy–sell transaction occurs, they may be tempted to do whatever it takes to close the deal, even if doing so is detrimental to the buyer.

matchmakers
Specialized brokers that bring together buyers and sellers of businesses

Investigating and Evaluating Available Businesses

Regardless of the source of the lead, a business opportunity requires careful evaluation—what some call **due diligence**. As a preliminary step, the buyer needs to acquire background information about the business, some of which can be obtained through personal observation or discussion with the seller. Talking with other informed parties, such as suppliers, bankers, employees, and customers of the business, is also important.

due diligence
The exercise of reasonable care in the evaluation of a business opportunity

Living the Dream   entrepreneurial challenges

Do Your Homework

Buying an existing business is often the fastest way to become a business owner and has advantages over starting your own company. However, you must do your homework before buying a business. This homework is called due diligence. Cut corners on due diligence and you may be purchasing someone else's headache.

Mark Forst and his father, Mel, are happy that they took the time for due diligence when they were looking to purchase instead of build a business. After weeks of searching, they discovered a Fort Lauderdale, Florida, business called Rip's Uniforms, which specialized in outfitting postal workers. The asking price was $100,000. After much due diligence, which included industry research, interviewing the owner of Rip's and postal workers themselves, and carefully scrutinizing the company's balance sheet and income statement, Mark determined that Rip's had more debt and less inventory than the seller had realized. With this important discovery, Mark and his father were able to purchase Rip's, later renamed A.M.E.'s Uniforms, Inc., for only $10,000.

When you're buying a business, it's important to sweat the details—just ask Mark and Mel Forst.

Source: Dimitra Kessenides, "Getting Started: Buyer Beware," *Inc.,* Vol. 26, No. 13 (December 2004), pp. 48–50.

http://www.amesuniforms.com

RELYING ON PROFESSIONALS   Although some aspects of due diligence require personal checking, a buyer can also seek the help of outside experts. The two most valuable sources of outside assistance are accountants and lawyers. It is also wise to seek out others who have acquired a business, in order to learn from their experience. Their perspective will be different from that of a consultant, and it will bring some balance to the counsel received.

The time and money spent on securing professional help in investigating a business can pay big dividends, especially when the buyer is inexperienced. However, the final consequences of a business purchase, good and bad, are borne by the buyer, and thus the prospective buyer should never leave the final decision to the experts. For one thing, it is a mistake to assume that professionals' help is either unbiased or infallible, particularly when their fees may be greater if the business is acquired. Prospective buyers should seek advice and counsel, but they must make the final decision themselves, as it is too important to entrust to someone else.

FINDING OUT WHY THE BUSINESS IS FOR SALE   The seller's *real* reasons for selling may or may not be the *stated* ones. When a business is for sale, always question the owner's reasons for selling. There is a real possibility that the firm is not doing well or that underlying problems exist that will affect its future performance. The buyer must be wary, therefore, of taking the seller's explanations at face value. Here are some of the most common reasons that owners offer their businesses for sale:

- Old age or illness
- Desire to relocate to a different part of the country
- Decision to accept a position with another company
- Unprofitability of the business
- Loss of an exclusive sales franchise
- Maturing of the industry and lack of growth potential

A prospective buyer cannot be certain that the seller-owner will be honest in presenting all the facts about the business, especially concerning financial matters. Too frequently, sellers have "cooked the books" or taken unreported cash out of the business. The only way for the buyer to avoid an unpleasant surprise later is to do his or her best to determine whether the seller is an ethical person. The following story highlights the importance of investigating the honesty of people selling a business:

An employee at a private equity firm (a company that buys or invests in other companies) was responsible for expansion into Eastern Europe. He discovered an opportunity to invest in a manufacturing company that had been formerly owned by the government and recently privatized. The chief executive officer of this company was likable and highly competent. However, as the negotiations carried on for months, it was discovered that the CEO had been convicted of embezzling money from his former employer and had ties to organized crime. In light of this discovery, negotiations with the CEO were terminated immediately.[7]

The important lesson in this story is that background checks on key personnel should be the first action performed when conducting due diligence.[8]

EXAMINING THE FINANCIAL DATA   The first stage in evaluating the financial health of a firm is to review the financial statements and tax returns for the past five years or for as many years as they are available. (*If these statements are not available, think twice before buying the business.*) This first stage helps determine whether the buyer and the seller are in the same ballpark. If so, the parties move on to the second stage (discussed in the next section)—valuing the firm.

To determine the history of the business and the direction in which it is moving, the buyer must examine financial data pertaining to the company's operation. If financial statements are available for the past five years, the buyer can use these to get some idea of trends for the business. As an ethical matter, the prospective buyer is obligated to show the financial statements to others—such as a potential lender or legal advisor—only on a need-to-know basis. To do otherwise is a violation of trust and confidentiality.

The buyer should recognize that financial statements can be misleading and may require normalizing to yield a realistic picture of the business. For example, business owners sometimes understate business income in an effort to minimize taxable income. On the other hand, expenses for such entries as employee training and advertising may be reduced to abnormally low levels in an effort to make the income look good in the hope of selling the business.

Other financial entries that may need adjustment include personal expenses and wage or salary payments. For example, costs related to personal use of business vehicles frequently appear as a business expense. Family members may receive excessive compensation or none at all. All entries must be examined to ensure that they relate to the business and are appropriate.

The buyer should also scrutinize the seller's balance sheet to see whether asset book values are realistic. Property often appreciates in value after it is recorded on the books. In contrast, physical facilities, inventory, and receivables may decline in value, so their actual worth is less than their accounting book value. Although these changes in value are generally not reflected in the accountant's records, they should be considered by the prospective buyer.

Valuing the Business

Once the initial investigation and evaluation have been completed, the buyer must arrive at a fair value for the firm. Valuing a business is not easy or exact, even in the best of circumstances. Despite the fact that buyers prefer audited financial statements, many firms operate without them. In valuing such firms, the buyer will have to rely on federal tax returns and state sales tax statements. It may also be helpful to scrutinize invoices and receipts—of both customers and suppliers—as well as the firm's bank statements.

Although numerous techniques are used for valuing a company, they are typically derivations of three basic approaches: (1) asset-based valuation, (2) market-comparable valuation, and (3) cash flow–based valuation. These techniques are examined in detail in Appendix B.

Nonquantitative Factors in Valuing a Business

When applying the quantitative techniques discussed in Appendix B, you must consider a number of factors to evaluate an existing business. These factors include the following:

- *Competition.* The prospective buyer should look into the extent, intensity, and location of competing businesses. In particular, the buyer should check to see whether the business in question is gaining or losing in its race with competitors. Additionally, new competitors to the marketplace (e.g., Wal-Mart) may dramatically change an existing firm's likelihood of success. Past performance is no guarantee of future performance.

- *Market.* The ability of the market to support all competing business units, including the one to be purchased, should be determined. This requires marketing research, study of census data, and personal, on-the-spot observation at each competitor's place of business.

- *Future community development.* Examples of future developments in the community that could have an indirect impact on a business include a change in zoning ordinances already enacted but not yet in effect, a change from a two-way traffic flow to a one-way traffic flow, and the widening of a road or construction of an overpass.

- *Legal commitments.* Legal commitments may include contingent liabilities, unsettled lawsuits, delinquent tax payments, missed payrolls, overdue rent or installment payments, and mortgages of record against any of the real property acquired.

■ *Union contracts.* The prospective buyer should determine what type of labor agreement, if any, is in force, as well as the quality of the firm's employee relations. Private conversations with key employees and rank-and-file workers can be helpful in determining their job satisfaction and the company's likelihood of success.

■ *Buildings.* The quality of the buildings housing the business should be checked, with particular attention paid to any fire hazards. In addition, the buyer should determine whether there are any restrictions on access to the buildings.

■ *Product prices.* The prospective owner should compare the prices of the seller's products with those listed in manufacturers' or wholesalers' catalogs and also with the prices of competing products in the locality. This is necessary to ensure full and fair pricing of goods whose sales are reported on the seller's financial statements.

Negotiating and Closing the Deal

The purchase price of a business is determined by negotiation between buyer and seller. Although the calculated value may not be the price eventually paid for the business, it gives the buyer an estimated value to use when negotiating price. Typically, the buyer tries to purchase the firm for something less than the full estimated value; of course, the seller tries to get more than that value.

In some cases, the buyer may have the option of purchasing the assets only, rather than the business as a whole. When a business is purchased as a total entity, the buyer takes control of the assets but also assumes any outstanding debt, including any hidden or unknown liabilities. Even if the financial records are audited, such debts may not surface. If the buyer instead purchases only the assets, then the seller is responsible for settling any outstanding debts previously incurred. An indemnification clause in the sales contract may serve a similar function, protecting the buyer from liability for unreported debt.

An important part of the negotiation process is the terms of purchase. In many cases, the buyer is unable to pay the full price in cash and must seek extended terms. At the same time, the seller may be concerned about taxes on the profit from the sale. Terms may become more attractive to the buyer and the seller as the amount of the down payment is reduced and/or the length of the repayment period is extended. Like a purchase of real estate, the purchase of a business is closed at a specific time. A title company or an attorney usually handles the closing. Preferably, the closing occurs under the direction of an independent third party. If the seller's attorney is the closing agent, the buyer should exercise caution—a buyer should never go through a closing without the aid of an experienced attorney who represents only the buyer.

A number of important documents are completed during the closing. These include a bill of sale, certifications as to taxing and other government regulations, and agreements pertaining to future payments and related guarantees to the seller. The buyer should apply for new federal and state tax identification numbers to avoid being held responsible for past obligations associated with the old numbers.

Looking **BACK**

1 Identify the major pros and cons of franchising.

· Franchising is a formalized arrangement that describes a certain way of operating a small business.

· The overall advantage of franchising is its high rate of success.

· A franchise may be favored over other alternatives because it offers training, financial assistance, and operating benefits.

· The major limitations of franchising are its costs, restrictions on business operations, loss of entrepreneurial independence, and potential lack of franchisor support.

2 Explain franchising options and the structure of the industry.

- The main parties in the franchising system are the franchisor and the franchisee.
- The potential value of any franchising arrangement is determined by the rights contained in the franchise contract.
- In product and trade name franchising, the main benefit the franchisee receives is the privilege of using a widely recognized product name.
- In business format franchising, entrepreneurs receive an entire marketing and management system.
- A master licensee is a firm or individual having a continuing contractual relationship with a franchisor to sell its franchises.
- Multiple-unit ownership, in which a single franchisee owns more than one unit of a franchised business, is becoming widely used.
- Some single franchisees are area developers, individuals or firms that obtain the legal right to open several outlets in a given area.
- Piggyback franchising is the operation of a retail franchise within the physical facilities of a host store.
- Facilitating groups include industry associations, government agencies, and private businesses.

3 Describe the process for evaluating a franchise opportunity.

- The substantial investment required by most franchisors justifies careful investigation by a potential franchisee.
- Independent third parties, such as state and federal government agencies, the International Franchise Association, and business publications, can be valuable sources of franchise information.
- The most logical source of the greatest amount of information about a franchise is the franchisor.

- Existing and previous franchisees are good sources of information for evaluating a franchise.
- Sources of international franchising information include government publications and websites hosted by individual foreign countries.
- A franchise contract is a complex document and should be evaluated by a franchise attorney.
- An important feature of the franchise contract is the provision relating to termination and transfer of the franchise.
- Franchise disclosure requirements are specified by FTC Rule 436.
- The Uniform Franchise Offering Circular (UFOC) provides the accepted format for satisfying the franchise disclosure requirements of the FTC.

4 List four reasons for buying an existing business and describe the process of evaluating a business.

- Buying an existing firm can reduce uncertainties.
- In acquiring an existing firm, the entrepreneur can take advantage of the firm's ongoing operations and established relationships.
- An existing business may be available at a bargain price.
- The entrepreneur may be in a hurry to get the business going.
- Investigating a business requires due diligence.
- A buyer should seek the help of outside experts, the two most valuable sources of outside assistance being accountants and lawyers.
- The buyer needs to investigate why the seller is offering the business for sale.
- The financial data related to the business should always be examined.
- Nonquantitative information about the business for sale should also be used in determining its value.

Key TERMS

Discussion QUESTIONS

1. What makes franchising different from other forms of business? Be specific.

2. What is the difference between product and trade name franchising and business format franchising? Which one accounts for the majority of franchising activity?

3. Identify and describe the parties in the franchising system.

4. Discuss the advantages and limitations of franchising from the viewpoints of the potential franchisee and the potential franchisor.

5. Should franchise information provided by a franchisor be discounted? Why or why not?

6. Do you believe that the Uniform Franchise Offering Circular is useful for franchise evaluation? Defend your position.

7. Evaluate loss of control as a disadvantage of franchising from the franchisor's perspective.

8. What are possible reasons for buying an existing company versus starting a new business from scratch?

9. What are some common reasons that owners offer their businesses for sale? Which of these reasons might a buyer consider to be negative?

10. What are some of the nonquantitative factors in valuing a business?

You Make the CALL

SITUATION 1

Ethan Moore is a college student in Phoenix, Arizona, currently enrolled as an entrepreneurship major at a local university. Moore's home is in Chandler, a nearby city, where he is considering purchasing a franchise. The franchise, which caught his interest while he was on a shopping trip to the Tucson Mall, is operated by an Idaho-based gumball company named Gumball Gourmet.

Moore talked to the owner of the franchise at the Tucson Mall while he was stocking the kiosk, which is set up in three tiers with 47 gumball machines and a money changer. The owner mentioned in their brief conversation that this particular kiosk had sold 12,000 gumballs in the last 30-day period.

From information he found at the Gumball Gourmet website, Moore determined that franchises are available with as little as a $17,200 investment.

Source: http://www.gumballgourmet.com, accessed January 25, 2007.

Question 1 What other Internet sites might provide helpful information to Moore as he tries to learn more about this franchise?

Question 2 What other questions should Moore have asked the Tucson franchisee?

Question 3 What information might a Uniform Franchise Offering Circular from Gumball Gourmet provide?

SITUATION 2

Scott Prewitt, his brother Steven Prewitt, and his brother-in-law Tony Mansoor have no experience in the restaurant business. But one of their goals is to start their own business and move their families from Jackson, Mississippi, to the mountains of western North Carolina. They are considering buying a Back Yard Burgers franchise.

As of July 2007, there were 183 Back Yard Burgers restaurants, operating in 20 states. The franchise, with headquarters in Memphis, Tennessee, specializes in charbroiled, freshly prepared food. The company began franchising in 1988 and currently has only U.S. franchises. Back Yard Burgers, Inc., started as a double drive-through restaurant, but most new franchises include a full dining room, self-service beverages, and a single drive-through window.

The Prewitt family is concerned about their inexperience and the harsh weather in the snowy mountains of North Carolina.

Sources: http://www.backyardburger.com, accessed July 18, 2007; and Tracy Stapp, "Never Say Die," *Entrepreneur,* December 2002, p. 130.

Question 1 How concerned do you think this family should be about their inexperience? Why?

Question 2 Will the proposed location in the mountains be a potential problem for this type of restaurant? Why or why not?

SITUATION 3

Todd Finkle, a college professor at a major university in the midwestern United States, is passionate about fly-fishing, which he learned as a child from his father. So his interest was piqued when he heard that his favorite fly-fishing rod manufacturer, Thomas and Thomas, was for sale. Founded in 1969 and well known among fly-fishing aficionados, Thomas and Thomas has a solid reputation, good products, and a loyal customer base.

Source: Dimitra Kessenides, "Getting Started: Buyer Beware," *Inc.*, Vol. 26, No. 13 (December 2004), pp. 48–50.

Question 1 What benefits could Finkle expect if he bought Thomas and Thomas rather than starting his own fly-fishing business?

Question 2 What sources of information about Thomas and Thomas should he use in evaluating the company for possible purchase?

Question 3 What nonquantitative factors should he use in placing a value on Thomas and Thomas?

SITUATION 4

Growth prospects have never been brighter for this 22-year-old manufacturer of custom-designed sky-lights, which has grown to more than $2 million in annual sales by letting light into homes, museums, symphony halls, upscale commercial buildings, and more. The California company ended last year with its strongest sales quarter since its current owners bought the business in 1995. Some 60 percent of its revenues come from jobs within California, where construction has remained steady throughout the economic downturn. Furthermore, the energy crisis has driven up demand for skylights, which pay for themselves in energy savings.

The manufacturer's state-of-the-art products also protect furniture and carpeting against fading from sunlight. The owners of the business are selling because they intend to move overseas. Their 22 staffers, including two installation crews and four sales and marketing professionals, appear willing to stay and help a new owner "illuminate" a variety of new growth opportunities.

The asking price is $675,000, with 60 percent down. The owners will consider financing a portion of the deal.

Source: Based on Jill Andresky Frazer, "A Blue-Sky Deal," *Inc.*, Vol. 24, No. 7 (July 2002), p. 40.

Question 1 Should a prospective buyer of this firm investigate other possible reasons why the owners might want to sell? Why or why not?

Question 2 What sales and revenue numbers are needed to evaluate the asking price?

Question 3 What nonquantitative factors might have an impact on the fairness of the asking price?

Experiential **EXERCISES**

1. Interview a local owner-manager of a widely recognized retail franchise, such as McDonald's. Ask him or her to explain the process of obtaining the franchise and what he or she considers to be the advantages of buying a franchise over starting a business from scratch.

2. Find a franchise advertisement in a recent issue of a business magazine. Research the franchise, and report back to the class with your findings.

3. As a class, consider the potential for locating a hypothetical new fast-food restaurant next to your campus. (Be as specific about the assumed location as you can.) Divide into two groups—one that supports buying a franchised operation and one that favors starting an independent, nonfranchised business. Plan a debate on the merits of each operation for the next class meeting.

4. Consult the Yellow Pages of your local telephone directory for the name of a business broker. Interview the broker and report to the class on how she or he values businesses.

5. In a business publication, such as *Inc.*, locate a listing or information about a business for sale. In class, discuss what information is needed to place a value on the business.

Exploring the WEB

1. FranChoice's website is dedicated to helping people find best-fit franchise opportunities. Go to **http://www.franchoice.com/selftest.cfm** and take FranChoice's Franchise Aptitude self-test.

   a. Which of the listed characteristics stand out in your mind as most important for a successful franchise operator to have? Briefly explain your choice(s).

   b. Reread the chapter-opening Spotlight on brothers Robin and Chris Sorensen of FHS. Of the characteristics listed on the self-test, which reflect the Sorensens' strongest aptitudes? Explain.

2. Everyone has heard about McDonald's Hamburger University, but many franchisors offer similar training and lifelong learning programs where franchisees come together to learn about quality, service, and value. Go to *Entrepreneur* magazine's website at **http://www.entrepreneur. com** to learn more about the training programs of top franchisors.

   a. Select "Franchises & Opportunities," and then follow the link to "Franchise 500ᴿ". Learn about the training programs of five different franchises by selecting the "Training & Support" tab on the franchises you select. Write a short summary of the differences and similarities among the programs.

   b. This chapter points out that higher costs generally characterize the more successful franchises. These costs include the initial franchise fee, investment costs, royalty payments, and advertising costs. Compare and contrast the costs and fees of the same five franchises you used in part a, and briefly summarize why you think the costs and fees vary.

3. Return to *Entrepreneur's* website to examine the top global franchises indexed at the site. Go to **http://www.entrepreneur.com/topglobal/index. html** to link directly to the list of top global franchises for 2007.

   a. Imagine that you were interested in opening a franchise outside of the United States. Decide in what country or region you would like to locate a business, and then find five franchises that are actively seeking franchisees in that country or region.

   b. Select the one of those five franchises that you think represents the best opportunity, and explain why.

4. Buying an existing business is challenging and requires careful evaluation of potential opportunities. Online resources can be helpful in finding a business to buy and assessing its value.

   a. Using the Web, find five online resources dedicated to helping people who want to buy a business.

   b. Which of the five resources would you recommend to a friend who wanted to purchase a business? Why?

Video Case **4**

Mo's Chowder (p. 626)
This case describes the experience of one entrepreneur who bought and transformed a simple family-owned diner into a successful, growing culinary destination.

Alternative Case for Chapter 4:
Case 8, Silver Zephyr Restaurant, p. 635

## chapter 5

The Family Business

In the SPOTLIGHT

Aquascape, Inc.
http://www.aquascapeinc.com

Greg Wittstock is the 37-year-old founder and CEO of Aquascape, Inc., a thriving St. Charles, Illinois–based company known for its innovations in ecosystem pond construction. Although the history of the company illustrates how a startup can quickly become a major player in its industry, it also reveals the darker side of having a family business.

Wittstock started his company to design and sell pond-building supplies, both to do-it-yourselfers and to professionals. His approach was working—sales in 1995 were a solid $800,000.

A few months after Wittstock started his business, his father, Gary, left his own engineering consulting firm to work with his son. But conflicts between father and son soon arose. Gary's attention to detail seriously cramped Greg's more creative entrepreneurial style, and before long the two were battling for control of the company. Over time, these problems took their toll on life beyond the business. In fact, Gary and his wife, Lauri (Greg's mother), divorced as a result of the conflict.

Distraught over the divorce, Gary withdrew from the day-to-day operations of the business and eventually sold his share of the company to Greg. In 1997, Gary started a new company, located only 20 miles from Aquascape. The rivalry continued, with father and son as direct competitors in the marketplace. The bitterness between Gary and Greg spilled over to affect relationships with members of the extended family; starting a competing business in essence cut off Gary's relationship with his two young grandsons. As Greg recalls, "It was hard for us to have a normal family life after dad left [Aquascape]."

Fortunately, the story has a happy ending. After repairing his relationship with his father, Greg bought the elder Wittstock's company in February of 2006 and later hired his father to work (once again) at Aquascape. Reflecting on his renewed relationship with Greg and his sons, Gary is happy to say, "I can finally go fishing with the boys whenever we want." Things are going very well now, but the Wittstocks' struggles show just how complicated life can be in a family business.

Sources: http://www.aquascapeinc.com/about_us/about-pond-guy.php, accessed May 9, 2007; http://www.aquascapeinc.com/first_look.html, accessed March 10, 2004; Bo Burlingham, "Building a Marketing Juggernaut," *Inc.,* Vol. 25, No. 11 (November 2003), pp. 58–73; Darren Dahl, "Pond Guy Reunion," *Inc.,* Vol. 28, No. 6 (June 2006), p. 24; and Jim Ritter, "Rising Popularity of Backyard Ponds Ripples Through Suburbs," *Chicago Sun-Times,* July 21, 2003, p. 5.

After studying this chapter, you should be able to

1 Discuss the factors that make a family business unique.
2 Explain the forces that can keep a family business moving forward.
3 Outline the complex roles and relationships involved in a family business.
4 Identify management practices that enable a family business to function effectively.
5 Describe the process of managerial succession in a family business.

When you hear the word *entrepreneur,* what comes to mind? Most people imagine a hard-driving individual who comes up with a new product or service and shapes it into an amazing enterprise. What they associate with the process includes high energy, scrappy resourcefulness, very long workdays (and even long nights), and perhaps a few tears. This is the scenario outlined in Chapter 3. In Chapter 4, we painted a somewhat different picture, pointing out that many entrepreneurs do not start companies "from scratch," preferring instead to become their own boss through the purchase of either a franchise or an existing company. While these represent lower-risk opportunities, in many cases they still offer great financial potential.

Entrepreneurial life goes beyond startups, buyouts, and franchises. Some people get into business by joining an enterprise started by parents, grandparents, or other relatives. Startups catch more headlines and generate greater flash and excitement, but don't be deceived: Family businesses are vital to the American economy! More than one-third of the 500 largest corporations in the United States and nearly 80 percent of its small businesses are family owned or controlled.[1] Perhaps even more surprising, family-controlled companies outperform their rivals on a wide range of performance measures, and by a good margin.[2] Family businesses enjoy an apparent edge in the marketplace.

For some people, joining the family business is a "no brainer," especially if they have been groomed for a position in the firm and look forward to its challenges. Others see a job in the family firm as merely one possibility among many career options to be considered during or after their college years. In any case, the family business offers another doorway to entrepreneurship for those whose families have their own firms. Ideally, the decision to join the family business should be based on an understanding of the unique dynamics of such an enterprise. This chapter examines the distinctive features that characterize the entrepreneurial alternative known as the family business.

The Family Business: A Unique Institution

1 Discuss the factors that make a family business unique.

A family business is like a double-edged sword—it cuts both ways, with unique advantages and potentially frustrating disadvantages.[3] Many advantages arise from the exceptional commitment to the enterprise of family employees, who recognize that the firm's performance has a profound effect on the family, financially and otherwise. On the downside, family businesses sometimes experience severe complications, such as business conflicts that cross over to create problems in the entrepreneur's personal life, and vice versa. There is no question that family firms differ from other types of small businesses in many ways. For example, decision making in a family business is typically more complex since it involves a mixture of family and business values and interests. This section discusses some characteristics of this unique institution.

What Is a Family Business?

We define a **family business** as a company that two or more members of the same family own or operate together or in succession.[4] The nature and extent of family members' involvement vary. In a number of firms, some family members work part-time. In a small restaurant, for example, one spouse may serve as host and manager, the other may keep the books, and the children may work in the kitchen or as servers. A recent National Federation of Independent Business (NFIB) study found that the family members most frequently involved in family businesses in the United States are spouses, siblings, children, and parents. In-laws participate in some cases, but this is far less common, and the involvement of other relatives, such as aunts, uncles, and cousins, is even more unusual.[5]

When it comes to transferring firm leadership across generations, families that manage to do so successfully are beating the odds. The NFIB study reports that although 48 percent of American family business owners would like to see a family member eventually take over operation of their venture, only 13 percent of respondents believed this was "very likely" and another 22 percent thought it was "likely."[6] Research has shown that, in fact, around 30 percent of family businesses survive into the second generation, and less than 16 percent make it to the third.[7] We will discuss later the conflicts and challenges that often disrupt the transfer of the family business.

Now for the good news. As already noted, family considerations may continue to be important, even in large corporations. In companies such as Wal-Mart, Levi Strauss, Ford Motor Company, and Marriott Corporation, the founding family is still involved to some extent in the ownership and operation of the business. In contrast to these extraordinary success stories, most family businesses are small. But small does not mean insignificant. Recent estimates suggest that the 24 million family firms nationwide generate two-thirds of the business revenue in the United States and employ 62 percent of its workforce.[8] Clearly, these companies are vital to the U.S. economy.

Family and Business Overlap

Any family business is composed of both a family and a business. Although the family and the business are separate institutions—each with its own members, goals, and values—they overlap in the family firm. For many people, these two overlapping institutions represent the most important areas of their lives.

Families and businesses exist for fundamentally different reasons. The family's primary function is the care and nurturing of family members, while the business is concerned with the production and distribution of goods and/or services. The family's goals include the personal development of each member (sometimes with scant concern for limitations in abilities) and the creation of equal opportunities and rewards for each member; the business's goals are profitability and survival.

Individuals involved, directly or indirectly, in a family business have interests and perspectives that differ according to their particular situations. The model in Exhibit 5-1 shows the ways in which individuals may be involved—as members of the family, employees of the business, individuals with a vested interest in the business, and various combinations of these—and the configuration of roles can affect the way they think about the enterprise. For example, a family member who works in the firm but has no personal or ownership interest (segment a) might favor more generous employment and advancement opportunities for family members than, say, a family member who owns part of the business but works elsewhere (segment b) or an employee with neither family nor ownership interest (segment c).

Competing interests can complicate the management process, creating tension and sometimes leading to conflict. Relationships among family members in a business are

exhibit

5-1   *Competing Interests in the Family Business*

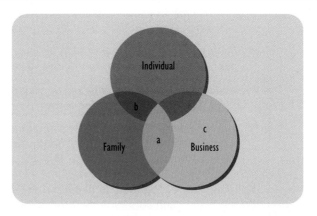

Source: Adapted from Tim Barnett and Franz W. Kellermanns, "Are We Family and Are We Treated as Family? Nonfamily Employees' Perceptions of Justice in the Family Firm," *Entrepreneurship Theory and Practice,* Vol. 30, No. 6 (November 2006), pp. 837–854.

more sensitive than relationships among unrelated employees. For example, disciplining an employee who consistently arrives late is much more problematic if he or she is also a family member. Or, consider a performance review session between a parent-boss and a child-subordinate. Even with nonfamily employees, performance reviews are potential minefields. The existence of a family relationship adds emotional overtones that vastly complicate the review process. As successful entrepreneur and author Lowell J. Spirer observes, no one wants his or her tombstone to read: "Here lies a parent or spouse who fired his own flesh and blood without just cause."[9]

Competition Between Business and Family

Which comes first, the family or the business? In theory, at least, most people opt for the family. Few business owners would knowingly allow the business to destroy their family. In practice, however, the resolution of such tensions becomes difficult. For example, despite being motivated by a sense of family responsibility, a parent may nevertheless become so absorbed in the business that he or she spends insufficient time with the children.

In most cases, families are accustomed to making minor sacrifices for the good of the business. In many family enterprises, the long hours needed in the business can sometimes mean missing dinner with the family or skipping a Little League baseball game. Families usually tolerate some inconveniences and disruptions to family life. Occasionally, however, the clash of business interests and family interests is so persistent or so severe that entrepreneurs must decide which comes first. Even when the stakes are high, some choose business over family. Others declare that their highest loyalty belongs to the family but deny it with their behavior.

When Heather Blease started Envisionet in Brunswick, Maine, to provide technical support and customer service for clients' websites, she still found time for her sons. She attended their sporting events and volunteered at kindergarten. But when the business grew to 1,000 employees and $12 million in revenues, it became more difficult for Blease to squeeze in family time. The business seemed to dominate every facet of her life. Blease tried to reserve evenings and weekends for her kids, but this was a struggle. She was asked a heart-breaking question by her seven-year-old son: "Mommy, do you love your company more than me?" Of course, Blease wished the question hadn't even needed to be asked. (Envisionet was later sold to Microdyne Outsourcing.)[10]

There is a lot of talk these days about balancing the needs of work and family, but the various reactions of entrepreneurs to this issue highlight how challenging it can be to sort it all out. Business owners have offered the following views about the conflicting priorities of work and personal life:[11]

- *I don't think* workaholic *is a bad word. Professional dancers aren't expected to have a balanced life. I'm not sure why entrepreneurs are.*

- *I enjoy the rush of working long hours . . . [but] I've become consumed by the business. . . . I have to make family time a priority.*

- *And even while I'm singing to [my young children] in the bathtub, in the back of my mind, I'm grinding on stuff at work.*

- *You can't regain your children's childhood; no amount of professional success can compensate for the loss of that family time. At the end of the day, if you aren't a success at home as well, [success at work] probably won't count for much.*

Keeping this all together is like a daring trapeze act—that is, balance can make all the difference between successfully moving forward and tumbling to a tragic end. If a family business is to survive, its interests cannot be unduly compromised to satisfy family wishes. To grow, family firms must recognize that professional management is sometimes needed and that family interests must often be secondary. This fact is not lost on Ingvar Kamprad, founder of Ikea, a large family business based in Sweden.

Kamprad started Ikea to sell good furniture at reasonable prices to middle-class families. The business has since grown to be the world's biggest furniture retailer, with nearly 250 stores in 35 countries, but it is still a family business. Although Kamprad's personal fortune is estimated at an eye-popping $32 billion, he retains a simple lifestyle, traveling economy class, taking the subway to work, and driving an old 1993 Volvo station wagon. One of Kamprad's three sons—Peter, Jonas, or Matthias—would seem the logical choice to succeed him, as each has worked for Ikea. But according to company insiders, it is not apparent that any of Kamprad's sons is being groomed to replace him.[12] Ikea has been so successful and grown so large that any new leader would need to be a person of truly exceptional management skills, which may leave all family members out of the running. Clearly, business interests may trump family interests when it comes to leadership succession at a family firm like Ikea.

The upshot of the story is that family members can contribute to the success of a family business, but membership in the family does not automatically endow them with the abilities needed for key positions. The health and survival of a family business require proper attention to both business and family interests, as well as a proper balancing of those interests. Otherwise, in the long run at least, results will be unsatisfactory for both. Decisions on the advancement of individual family members should be made carefully, based on leadership ability and after consultation with the firm's board of directors and/ or other knowledgeable outside observers. Such decisions should be made in advance (and revised if necessary) rather than postponed until an emergency requires the hurried appointment of a new manager.

Advantages of a Family Business

Problems with family firms can easily blind young people to the unique advantages that come with participating in the business. The benefits associated with family involvement should be recognized and discussed when recruiting younger members to work in the family firm.

One primary benefit derives from the strength of family relationships. Family members have a unique motivation because the firm is a family firm. Business success is also family success. Studies have shown that family CEOs possess greater internal motivation than do nonfamily CEOs and have less need to receive additional incentives through compensation.[13] CEOs and other family members are drawn to the business because of family ties, and they tend to stick with the business through thick and thin. A downturn in business fortunes might cause nonfamily employees to seek greener employment pastures elsewhere, but a son or daughter may be reluctant to leave. The family name, its welfare, and possibly its fortune are at stake. In addition, a person's reputation in the family and in the business community may hinge on whether she or he can continue the business that Mom or Grandfather built.

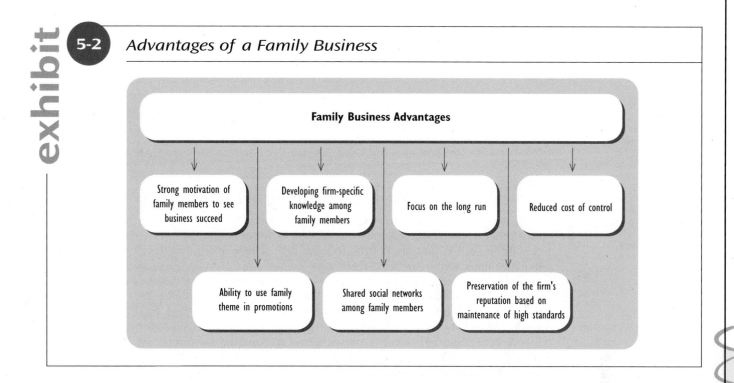

exhibit 5-2 *Advantages of a Family Business*

Family Business Advantages

- Strong motivation of family members to see business succeed
- Developing firm-specific knowledge among family members
- Focus on the long run
- Reduced cost of control

- Ability to use family theme in promotions
- Shared social networks among family members
- Preservation of the firm's reputation based on maintenance of high standards

Family members may also sacrifice income to keep a business going. Rather than draw large salaries or high dividends, they are likely to permit resources to remain in the business in order to meet current needs. Many families have postponed the purchase of a new car or new furniture long enough to let a business get started or to get through a period of financial stress, thereby greatly increasing the company's chances of survival.

Businesses that are family owned often highlight this feature in their promotional materials to set themselves apart from competitors. For example, a phrase such as "A Family Serving Families" is often placed on signage, websites, and promotional literature where potential customers can't miss it. This is a "high-touch" message, one that resonates with customers who don't want to be treated as "just another number"; as a result, the theme is especially effective for companies that offer highly customized products or very personal services, such as investment planning, chiropractic care, funeral services, and fine dining. Such promotional efforts attempt to convey the fact that family-owned firms have a strong commitment to the business, high ethical standards, and a personal commitment to serving their customers and the local community.

Other features of family involvement in a firm can also contribute to superior business performance. From their study of resource management in family businesses, business professors David Sirmon and Michael Hitt identified the following features of these firms as offering unique advantages (see also Exhibit 5-2):[14]

1. *Firm-specific knowledge.* Family businesses often compete using firm-specific knowledge that is best shared and further developed by individuals who care deeply about the business and who trust one another. These companies are in a unique position to pass this knowledge along from generation to generation, sharpening the edge of that advantage over time.

2. *Shared social networks.* Family members bring valuable social capital to the business when they share their networks with younger members of the family and thus help to ensure the firm's future performance.

3. *A focus on the long run.* Most family managers tend to take a long-range perspective of the business, in part because they view it as an asset that must be maintained for the sake of future generations.

4. *Preservation of the firm's reputation.* Because they have a stake in preserving the family's reputation, members of the family are likely to maintain high standards when it comes to honesty in business dealings, such as offering quality and value to the consumer.

5. *Reduced cost of control.* Because key employees in a family business are related and trust one another, the firm can spend less on systems designed to reduce theft and to monitor employees' work habits.

Family Business Momentum

2 Explain the forces that can keep a family business moving forward.

organizational culture
Patterns of behaviors and beliefs that characterize a particular firm

Like other organizations, family businesses develop particular ways of doing things and certain priorities that are unique to each firm. These special patterns of behaviors and beliefs comprise the firm's **organizational culture**. As new employees and family members enter the business, they pick up these unique viewpoints and ways of operating, which create staying power for the company. The culture of the family firm can be a strategic resource that promotes learning, risk taking, and innovation. In fact, family business expert John L. Ward has conducted research that suggests family businesses have an advantage precisely because of their cultures, which tend to emphasize important values like mutual respect, integrity, the wise use of resources, personal responsibility, and "fun" (enthusiasm, adventure, celebration, etc.) in the family business experience.[15]

The Founder's Imprint on the Family Business Culture

Research indicates that founders leave a deep impression on the family businesses they launch.[16] And the distinctive values that motivate and guide an entrepreneur in the founding of a company may help to create a competitive advantage for the new business. For example, the founder may cater to customer needs in a special way and emphasize customer service as a guiding principle for the company. The new firm may go far beyond normal industry practices in making sure customers are satisfied, even if it means working overtime or making deliveries on a weekend or at odd hours. Those who work in such an enterprise quickly learn that customers must always be handled with special care.

In a family business, the founder's core values may become part of both the business culture and the family code—that is, "the things we believe as a family." This is certainly the case with Truett Cathy, the well-known founder of Chick-fil-A, Inc. Dan Cathy, the founder's son, president, and chief operating officer of the company, describes the legacy of his father:

> *My dad's determination and industry knowledge combined with his endless dedication to his faith and moral values continue to inspire our business goals and our daily excitement. He started a legacy that we are proud to continue, and we will always insist that the Chick-fil-A business reflect the spirit of Dad's first sixty years of service-oriented attitude, a giving and caring heart, and savvy business-oriented philosophies.[17]*

Truett Cathy is a very determined man with a lot to show for his commitment to his business—today, the company has more than 1,300 restaurants throughout the United States.[18] But Dan Cathy's comments indicate that his father's attitude and style will not fade from the family firm's culture anytime soon. Family members and others in the company learn what's important to the business and absorb the traditions of the firm simply by functioning as part of the organization.

Of course, there is always a darker possibility—that of a founder's *negative* imprint on the organizational culture. Successful business founders may develop an unhealthy narcissism, or exaggerated sense of self-importance. Such individuals occasionally develop a craving for attention, a fixation with success and public recognition, and a lack of empathy for others. Unfortunately, these attitudes can harm the business by creating a general feeling of superiority and a sense of complacency. While contributions of founders deserve proper acknowledgment, any negative legacy must be avoided.

The Commitment of Family Members

The culture of a particular firm includes numerous distinctive beliefs and behaviors, which help to keep the business moving forward according to the vision of the founder. But sooner or later, the reins of leadership will have to be turned over to a new generation. The continuity of the business will depend, in large part, on next-generation family members and their level of commitment to the business. Recent research suggests that family members coming into a business do so for a variety of reasons, and these reasons shape the strength and nature of their commitment to the company.

The competing interests model pictured in Exhibit 5-1 is often used to summarize the complexities of dealing with the family firm's interactive components: the business, the family, and the individual. The model is usually applied to founders, since they have an obvious interest in the business, which puts them in the sometimes difficult position of having to balance this interest, their personal aspirations, and the needs of the family. However, if they choose to pursue a career in the business, next-generation family members must deal with some of these same challenges, and their commitment to the company will likely determine the value of their contribution to the business, the financial benefits they bring to the family, and their personal satisfaction with work-related roles.

To explore the connection between commitment and family business involvement, two family business experts from Canada studied the research on family enterprises. They found the following four bases of commitment among successors in family businesses: emotional attachment, a sense of obligation, cost considerations, and personal need.[19] In all cases, the outcome was the same—members of the family were persuaded to join the business—but the reasons for joining were very different.

DESIRE-BASED COMMITMENT   When family members join a firm based on a deep-seated, gut-level attraction to the business, it is probably because they believe in and accept the purpose of the enterprise and want to contribute to it. Typically, their personal identity is closely tied to the business, and they believe they have the ability to contribute something to it. In short, these individuals join the company because they genuinely *want to*. This was clearly the situation for Tim, a young next-generation family member:

> We have an item that we manufacture from scratch, we warehouse it, we wholesale it, and we retail it. I see the business from every angle and I'm involved in it from every angle. It's kind of neat to be able to do that. . . . I love being a part of the family business.

desire-based commitment Commitment based on a belief in the purpose of a business and a desire to contribute to it

OBLIGATION-BASED COMMITMENT   Obligation-based commitment is what drives individuals who feel that they really *ought to* pursue a career in the family business. Often, the goal is to do what the parent/founder wants, even if that career path is not what the family member had in mind. In many cases, guilt is the primary motivator, as was the case with Polly, who "answered the call" to join the family business:

> [My father] said that the most important thing right now for you as a Stillman is to be visible here because your sister is out. . . . We need another family member here. And so with that kind of plea I had no choice in my mind. I couldn't let the family down. So I dropped everything I was doing and . . . went the next day and started working.

obligation-based commitment Commitment that results from a sense of duty or expectation

COST-BASED COMMITMENT   If a family member concludes that there is too much to lose by turning away from a career opportunity within the family business, then his or her decision to join is based on a calculation, not a sense of obligation or emotional identification. Often, this *have to* response is motivated by the perception that the opportunity for gain is too great to pass up or that the value of the business will fall if somebody doesn't step in to take care of it. In other words, joining the business may be the best way to benefit from what the family firm has to offer or to protect the investment value of what is likely to be inherited in the future. Rob recognized this when he looked more closely at a business that his wife's family owned:

> At that point we really didn't know what [my wife's] involvement was from a share-holder's standpoint. And what we found out was she was heavily involved to the point

cost-based commitment Commitment based on the belief that the opportunity for gain from joining a business is too great to pass up

where it dwarfed what we were doing personally and all of a sudden it did change our
perspective. . . . It sort of changed our outlook on [the business] . . . and that is when
we decided we cannot pass this up.

need-based
commitment
Commitment based on an
individual's self-doubt and
belief that he or she lacks
career options outside the
current business

NEED-BASED COMMITMENT   When family members join the business because of
self-doubt or a concern that they might not be able to reach significant career success
on their own, their commitment to the family enterprise is based on perceived necessity. That is, they *need to* join the business because they lack options for career success
outside of it. This reasoning is common among young heirs who leapfrog over nonfamily
employees into coveted positions, the demands of which exceed their knowledge and
experience. They often feel guilty for their privileged status and are left to wonder if they
"have what it takes" to succeed on their own. Ted was 33 years old when he was tapped to
run his family's 900-employee business. His self-doubt rings loudly in his reflections:

> *I always am a little bit concerned about whether I would have been able to have suc-*
> *ceeded and achieved outside of the family's environment. . . . That's always something*
> *that I think most people in family businesses think about. Whether they believe they*
> *would have been as successful outside.*

Why Should Anyone Care About Commitment?

Research shows any form of commitment is better than no commitment at all; however,
next-generation family members motivated by desire-based commitment are most likely
to pursue long-term careers with the family business. Their deep-seated connection with
the enterprise and its alignment with their career interests make for a successful match.
And since knowledge and insight passed down from one generation to the next is an advantage that is unique to family businesses, keeping family members in the enterprise can
pay in more ways than one.[20]

But commitment is about more than just staying with the company—it also affects
what a person does while he or she is on the job. For example, research suggests that
people with higher levels of desire- and obligation-based commitment are more likely
to support efforts to promote change, which are common in small businesses and very
important to their performance and survival. Cost-based commitment may motivate a
person to go "beyond the call of duty" to protect or extend his or her financial interests
in the company. Obligation-based commitment provides no such motivation, as family
members may see their participation in the company as a birthright that provides great
job security. However, those with a deep-seated sense of identity with the enterprise
(desire-based commitment) are the most likely to work hard, because of their passion
for the business. Family members who are committed mostly out of need are often in
a perpetual state of self-doubt and lack the confidence to excel; this problem is compounded if they are promoted only because of their last name and honestly lack the
capabilities to do the job.

These observations suggest that the type of commitment a person has can significantly impact job performance. Exhibit 5-3 illustrates the forms of commitment and their
implications for family businesses.

Breaking with the Past

Over time, the sure foundation of the family business—right down to its leadership—has
to adjust to a changing environment. But the process of adjustment is almost certain to
be complicated by, and interwoven with, changes in the dominant approach of the family
business. To appreciate this point, think about the patriarchal culture that is quite common in the early days of a family business. That cultural emphasis may lose its usefulness
as business conditions change. For example, as a family business grows, it requires a
greater measure of professional expertise. The firm may then be pressured to break from
the paternalistic mold, which gives first priority to family authority and less attention to
professional abilities. Likewise, the aging of the founder and the maturation of the founder's children tend to weaken the patriarchal family culture with its one dominant source
of authority—a parent who "always knows best."

5-3   *Commitment to the Family Business*

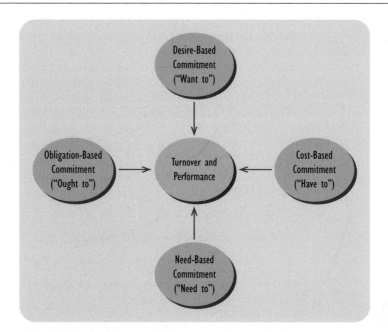

Source: Based on Pramodita Sharma and P. Gregory Irving, "Four Bases of Family Business Successor Commitment: Antecedents and Consequences," *Entrepreneurship Theory and Practice,* Vol. 29, No. 1 (January 2005), pp. 13–33.

While the values of the founder and the continuity of the culture may give the family firm an edge in the marketplace, these features can also be the ball and chain that keeps it tethered to the past, preventing it from moving forward. As disturbing as it may be, change—at some level—will eventually be necessary. In some cases, a change in leadership may play a role in introducing or bringing about a break with traditional methods of operation. That is, a successor may act as a change agent, as when a founder's son or daughter with a business degree or technical training moves into a leadership position and replaces outdated managerial practices with a more up-to-date professional approach or introduces cutting-edge technology in the company's processes. The topic of leadership succession will be considered in greater detail later in the chapter.

As you can see, growth of the business and changes in leadership over time will make some cultural adjustments necessary. However, certain values are timeless and should never be altered—the commitment to honesty in dealing with customers and suppliers, for example. While some traditions may embody inefficient business practices and require alteration, others underlie the competitive strength and integrity of the firm.

Family Roles and Relationships

3 Outline the complex roles and relationships involved in a family business.

The overlapping of two institutions—a family and a business—makes the family firm incredibly difficult to manage. "Family business," says the wife of one family business owner, "is an oxymoron. The hope of building something for your kids and passing on traditions is usually thwarted by dynamics within the family."[21] This dim view of the family enterprise is not shared by everyone; however, significant conflicts can result when family roles and business interests collide. Anticipating these challenges and planning for them can really pay off. This section examines a few of the many possible family roles and relationships that contribute to this managerial complexity.

Mom or Dad, the Founder

A common figure in family businesses is the man or woman who founded the firm and plans to pass it on to a son or a daughter. In most cases, the business and the family have grown simultaneously. Some founders achieve a delicate balance between their business and family responsibilities. Others must diligently plan time for weekend activities and vacations with the children.

Entrepreneurs who have children typically think in terms of passing the business on to the next generation. Parental concerns associated with this process include the following:

- Does my child possess the temperament and ability necessary for business leadership?

- How can I, the founder, motivate my child to take an interest in the business?

- What type of education and experience will be most helpful in preparing my child for leadership?

- What timetable should I follow in employing and promoting my child?

- How can I avoid favoritism in managing and developing my child?

- Is sibling rivalry likely to be a problem, and can it be avoided?

- How can I prevent the business relationship from damaging or destroying the parent–child relationship?

Of all the relationships in a family business, the parent–child relationship has been recognized for generations as the most troublesome. In recent years, the problems inherent in this relationship have been addressed by counselors, seminars, and books too numerous to count. In spite of all this attention, however, the parent–child relationship continues to perplex many families involved in family businesses.

Husband–Wife Teams

Some family businesses are owned and managed by husband–wife teams. Their roles vary depending on their backgrounds and expertise. In some cases, the husband serves as general manager and the wife runs the office. In others, the wife functions as operations manager and the husband keeps the books. Whatever the arrangement, both individuals are an integral part of the business.

One potential advantage of the husband–wife team is the opportunity to work with someone you really trust and to share more of your lives together. For some couples, however, the benefits can be overshadowed by problems related to the business. Differences of opinion about business matters can carry over into family life. And the energy of both parties may be so spent by working long hours in a struggling company that little zest remains for a strong family life.

Many couples have had to set boundaries and develop routines to cope with the demands of everyday life (like raising children) and still have sufficient time for the business. Rio Miura and Scott Lowe have two businesses—San Francisco–based David Rio Coffee & Tea Inc. and Soma Beverage Company LLC—and two young children—Luke and Kira. Tending both fronts makes for a demanding lifestyle, but this husband–wife team has developed several strategies for managing their time. For example, they want to give the kids their full attention when they pick them up at 5 p.m., so they have agreed to put aside all talk of business until 9 p.m., when Luke and Kira are finally in bed. Then they "flip the switch" and go back to talking about business again, with discussions of strategy and decision making going on until the wee hours of the morning in some cases. While Miura and Lowe feel that they're stretched pretty thin, this approach has allowed them to juggle the heavy demands of family and business and make it all work.[22]

Sons and Daughters

Should sons and daughters be groomed for the family business, or should they pursue careers of their own choosing? In the entrepreneurial family, the natural tendency is to think in terms of a family business career and to push a child, either openly or subtly, in that

Living the Dream   entrepreneurial challenges

© My Flat in London

A Marriage That Is Always in Fashion

It is often said that marriage is hard work. And starting a business has a way of pushing you to the limit. So, what happens when you put these two together—that is, when a husband and wife start a business together? Well, it can work for better . . . or for worse.

Todd and Jan Haedrich are married, but they are also co-founders of My Flat in London (MFIL), a high-fashion design company that manufactures and sells handbags, accessories, apparel items, body lotions, and other products to style-conscious buyers. The company gets its name from Jan's many years of designing in the capitals of Europe, but its roots are actually more than a little American. After being stopped repeatedly on the streets of New York and Boston to be asked where she had bought her handbag, Jan realized that she might have a potential business opportunity on her hands (or on her shoulder). You see, she had designed the bag herself. That public response led to the 2002 launch of MFIL in Boston, though the company was later relocated to Frenchtown, New Jersey.

Key to the success of the business is that the Haedrichs share the same vision for the company: to create a brand that epitomizes the luxury lifestyle. Apparently, their efforts are hitting the mark. "Distinctive and high quality," says the *Financial Times* of MFIL, "the company has quickly carved out a covetable niche in the competitive and fickle fashion world." Today, the company's products are available in more than 450 specialty stores worldwide, including prestige outlets such as Nordstrom and Fred Segal. Not bad!

To be successful on all fronts, couples in business need to be on the same page regarding the goals of the business, but it is also important that they recognize the skill sets each person brings to the enterprise and carve out distinct roles to match. For the Haedrichs, the distinction is quite clear. Jan brings design genius to MFIL; as president of the company, Todd tends to the business side of the venture, including overseeing manufacturing in Asia, keeping the books, and selecting software applications for the company. Having set roles based on the strengths of each spouse is good for business, but it also tends to promote mutual respect, which supports the marriage. Of course, it helps that both Todd and Jan "could definitely see themselves working together all the time." Togetherness supports the health and growth of a marriage relationship, but it is also unavoidable in a business partnership.

Sources: http://myflatinlondon.com, accessed January 2, 2007; Annie Counsell "Scalability Is in the Bag," *Financial Times*, March 9, 2005, p. 6; and Nichole L. Torres, "For Better or Worse," *Entrepreneur*, Vol. 33, No. 10 (October 2005), pp. 104–109.

http://www.myflatinlondon.com

direction. Little thought may be given to the underlying issues, including the child's talent, aptitude, and temperament. The child may be "a chip off the old block" in many ways but may also be an individual with unique abilities and aspirations. He or she may prefer music or medicine to the world of business and may fit the business mold very poorly. It is also possible that the abilities of the son or daughter may simply be insufficient for a leadership role. Or, a child's talents may be underestimated by parents merely because there has been little opportunity for the child to develop or demonstrate those talents.

Another issue is personal freedom. Today's society values the right of the individual to choose his or her own career and way of life. If this value is embraced by a son or daughter, that child must be granted the freedom to select a career of his or her own choosing. It's best not to force the issue, because you may be swimming against a strong current of personal interest. Sue Birley, professor of entrepreneurship and director of the Entrepreneurship Centre at Imperial College in London, surveyed 412 children of business owner-managers to see if they planned to enter the family business in the future. Eighty percent of those who were not already working in the business did not intend to join it. And of those who intended to enter the business at some point, 70 percent planned to work somewhere else first.[23]

A son or daughter may feel a need to go outside the family business, for a time at least, to prove that he or she can make it without help from the family. To build self-esteem, he or she may wish to operate independently of the family. Entering the family business immediately after graduation from high school or college may seem stifling, as the child continues to "feel like a little kid with Dad telling me what to do."

Sometimes it is the parent who tells a child that the family business is not for her or him. Michelle Rousseff Kemp has owned or helped launch more than one venture of note, but she has refused to let any of her three grown kids—Jonathan, Katrina, and Natalie—join the family firm. She lays out her reasoning very clearly: "If children go into the business from the get-go, they don't appreciate what they have, and they don't take risks. I don't believe in nepotism. It doesn't create the hunger; it stifles the discovery." Apparently, her logic is sound. Jonathan and Katrina have founded successful companies of their own, and even Natalie has gotten into the startup game.[24] And, who knows? Perhaps some day, one of the kids will be battle-tested and prepared to come back and take the lead of the family business started by Kemp and her husband.

Kemp's attitude is not exactly the norm, though. Many family businesses have been launched with the hope from day 1 that one of the kids would take it over when the time was right. And if the family business is profitable, this can provide substantial rewards. A son or daughter may be well advised to give serious consideration to accepting such an opportunity. But if the business relationship is to be satisfactory, family pressure must be minimized. Both parties must recognize the choice is a business decision as well as a family decision—and a decision that may be reversed, if things do not go well.

Sibling Cooperation, Sibling Rivalry

In families with a number of children, two or more may become involved in the family business. This depends, of course, on the interests of the individual children. In some cases, parents feel fortunate if even one child elects to stay with the family firm. Nevertheless, it is not unusual for siblings to take positions within the firm. Even those who do not work in the business may be more than casual observers on the sidelines because of their stake as heirs or partial owners.

At best, siblings work as a smoothly functioning team, each contributing services according to his or her respective abilities. Just as families can experience excellent cooperation and unity in their relationships with one another, some family businesses benefit from effective collaboration among brothers and sisters.

However, just as there are sometimes squabbles within a family, there can also be sibling rivalry within a family business. Business issues tend to generate competition, and this affects family, as well as nonfamily, members. Siblings, for example, may disagree about business policy or about their respective roles in the business. And, in some cases, the conflicts can spiral seriously out of control.

Rivalry is a problem between William and David Koh, two brothers who are caught up in a nasty "bean curd war" in Singapore. The family's history in the bean curd business (selling a sort of tofu custard and syrup dessert) goes back to the 1960s, when the Kohs' parents first started selling the sticky delight from a pushcart. The product developed a strong following, and the family business soon became an established and popular enterprise. Sometime after their father died in 1986, their mother turned the ownership of the family store, Rochor Original Beancurd, over to William and his wife. At that point, William, who was the older

Living the Dream   entrepreneurial challenges

Having Babies Gives Birth to a Business

© Barry Austin/Digital Vision/Getty Images

Family businesses tend to follow a classic story line: Father starts business, son gets into the business, son gets more involved in the business, father retires and gives control of the business to the son. And then the story repeats for the next generation when a grandson enters the picture.

But what happens when a mother and daughter go into business together? To warp the stereotype a bit further, consider a case in which the daughter started a business and the mother joined her in it. When Emily Cohen started a maternity-clothing boutique called Bella Belli in downtown Birmingham, Michigan, she asked her mother, Annie, to be her partner in the business. (To be precise, Emily owns the store, but she still considers her mother to be a partner in the business.)

It all began in 2003, when Emily found herself in the midst of a baby boom of sorts. That is, many of her friends were getting pregnant, and they all complained about the same problem: a lack of stylish and trendy maternity clothing in their area. Recognizing a business opportunity, Emily talked to her mother, who had experience as a retail shop owner, and together they started Bella Belli Maternity. The store offers "everything you need to celebrate your pregnancy so you don't have to sacrifice your style," including designer label clothing for expectant mothers (from the traditional to more funky lines of apparel), baby gifts, diaper bags, skin care products, and informational books for mothers-to-be.

But how do Annie and Emily get along in business? Mother–daughter relationships can be more nuanced and loaded than those between father and son. Emily and Annie say the association is intense at times, but the two-generation combo is working. This may be due in part to the fact that they each have carved out distinct duties that suit them—Annie takes care of advertising and graphics and runs errands, while Emily handles the finances and almost everything else. But mother–daughter roles sometimes die hard. For example, Annie can't help sweeping up and cleaning mirrors all the time. "She still wants to be my mother, even if we're in business," Emily says.

Annie is trying to adjust, though. She makes it a point to back off and let Emily solve problems on her own. She also tries not to ask too many questions or be too bossy—a challenge for any parent. All those years of raising children are hard to shake, but learning to change for the good of the relationship is also good for business—and in this case, good for well-dressed mothers-to-be in Birmingham, Michigan.

Sources: http://www.bellabellimaternity.com, accessed January 2, 2007; Juddith Harris Solomon, "Joint Ventures: Mothers and Daughters Create Local Dynasties," *Signature*, April-May 2005, pp. 46–47; and Hillary Stout, "When Mom Is a Business Partner," *Wall Street Journal*, June 29, 2005, p. D5.

http://www.bellabellimaternity.com

son, quickly asserted control and edged David out of the business. So David decided there was only one thing to do: open up another bean curd shop right next door to the original location. The two are now competing head to head (and door to door) on the same street in Singapore. Despite being next-door business neighbors, the brothers have not spoken to each other for years, and hopes of a reconciliation are nowhere in sight.[25] As you can see, the family business can do serious damage to the business family.

In-Laws In and Out of the Business

As sons and daughters marry, daughters-in-law and sons-in-law become significant actors in the family business drama. Some in-laws become directly involved by accepting positions in the family firm. If a son or daughter is also employed in the firm, rivalry and conflict may develop. For example, family members may disagree about how rewards for performance should compare for an in-law and a son or daughter.

For a time, effective collaboration may be achieved by assigning family members to different branches or roles within the company. But competition for leadership positions eventually will force decisions that distinguish among children and in-laws employed in the business. Being fair and maintaining family loyalty become more difficult as the number of family employees increases.

Sons-in-law and daughters-in-law who are on the sidelines are also participants with an important stake in the business, and their influence on the business and the family can be considerable. They are keenly interested in family business issues that impact their spouses, but, unfortunately, their perspective is typically distorted because they often hear only half of the story when it comes to work-related situations. One highly regarded family business consultant put it this way:

> How many times do brothers and sisters in business together go rushing home or make a phone call home and say, "Dear, I just wanted to let you know that we are so lucky to be in partnership with my brother." Or, "We wouldn't be anywhere near as successful as we are without my sister's leadership skills." I don't think that conversation happens very often.[26]

When family frustrations come up at work, spouses tend to hear all about it at home, often just before the couple goes to bed. The family member vents, then feels better, and goes to sleep. The spouse, on the other hand, is just hearing about the situation and spends the rest of the night worried, angry, or both. Then, when the two siblings sort everything out at the office the next morning and get back to the challenging, satisfying work at hand, neither even thinks about phoning the spouse to let him or her know that the problem was just a silly little matter and that everything is fine. Spouses tend to hear only one side of the story—the bad side—and it shades their view of the business. So, the criticism they receive for having a bad attitude about the family and its enterprise is often undeserved.[27]

When in-laws are employed in the family business, a different set of dynamics can emerge. In some cases, the connections with in-laws can get very complicated. In 2000, Michael Kalinsky cofounded Empyrean Management Group, a recruiting and staffing company. His father-in-law, Bruce Kenworthy, offered to bankroll the startup with $100,000 of his own money . . . but only if his son, David, could be vice president and a minority shareholder. Kalinsky agreed to the terms, accepted the money, and launched the company. A few years later, however, he discovered that David was neglecting a critical client and had openly criticized Kalinsky and his leadership in front of employees. After thinking about the potential for family fallout, he decided to fire David, which led to a whole new set of problems. After a difficult legal battle, Kalinsky was forced to buy out Bruce's and David's shares of ownership in the company and to pay back the $100,000 he owed Bruce. Empyrean continues to operate, but Kalinsky and David have not spoken since the settlement. David has since opened his own business and wooed away Empyrean's biggest (by far) client. Bruce Kenworthy has concluded that Kalinsky and David will never speak to each other again. "[That] is sad for me," he laments. "It would have been nice if the family and the business had been able to stay together."[28]

The Entrepreneur's Spouse

One of the most critical roles in the family business is that of the entrepreneur's spouse. Traditionally, this role has been fulfilled by the male entrepreneur's wife and the mother of his children. However, more women are becoming entrepreneurs, and many husbands have now assumed the role of entrepreneur's spouse.

How They See It: An "Out-law's" Perspective

Scott Salmans

As the son-in-law of the founder of our family business, I often found myself at odds with the family due to one major factor: the lack of quality communication. I say "quality communication" because efforts were made to talk about succession planning and the roles to be played, but many times legal matters were not understood and alternative agendas blocked what was actually being heard.

Ultimately, the plan was completed, and we were able to buy the company outright and go back to having nice holiday gatherings, but it was not accomplished without a great deal of pain. My mistake may have been in allowing the communication to go through the founder instead of insisting on meetings with all parties concerned, with full disclosure of the plans and the true history of the situation.

If you are ever confronted with the impasses that can occur in family business planning, I recommend using a family business counselor, who can help you traverse the path of dealing with both business and family issues that impact the future of any family business. I also strongly recommend that decisions be made and policies implemented toward a clear plan of succession and who may or may not benefit from future actions and how. Leaving the big questions unanswered only leads to greater frustration and poor decisions that usually benefit the government more than anyone.

In order for the spouse to play a supporting role in the entrepreneur's career, there must be effective communication between the spouse and the entrepreneur. The spouse needs to hear what's going on in the business; otherwise, she or he may begin to feel detached and respond by competing with the business for attention. The spouse can offer understanding and act as a sounding board for the entrepreneur only if the couple communicates on matters of obvious importance to them, both as individuals and as a family.

It is easy for the spouse to function as worrier for the family business. This is particularly true if there is insufficient communication about business matters. One small business owner correctly observed that the spouse of an entrepreneur is stepping into a crazy adventure, but with limited input or control over the decisions and risks that the whole family then takes on. His wife described the situation in her own way:

> Being the spouse of an entrepreneur can be the ultimate in risk-taking ventures. When you decide, with or without your spouse's consent, to start a business of your own, you thrust the spouse into the front car of what can be a wild roller-coaster ride. . . . [And] although your spouse has little control over your business, she suffers all of the consequences of ill-advised decision making. "Honey, I lost our fortune. Time to sell the house!" is an experience I know all too well. There's also constant uncertainty. What kind of year will we have? Can we pay our bills? How about retirement?[29]

No wonder so many spouses are worriers!

But the spouse takes on other roles as well. As a parent, he or she helps prepare the children for possible careers in the family business. The spouse may also serve as a mediator in business relationships between the entrepreneur and the children. One wife's comments to her husband, John, and son Terry illustrate the nature of this function:

- "John, don't you think that Terry may have worked long enough as a stockperson in the warehouse?"

- "Terry, your father is going to be very disappointed if you don't come back to the business after your graduation."

- "John, do you really think it is fair to move Stanley into that new office? After all, Terry is older and has been working a year longer."

- "Terry, what did you say to your father today that upset him?"

Ideally, the entrepreneur and his or her spouse form a team committed to the success of both the family and the family business. Such teamwork does not occur automatically—it requires a collaborative effort by both parties to the marriage.

Professional Management of the Family Firm

4 Identify management practices that enable a family business to function effectively.

"It used to be that there were professional businesses and there were family businesses," according to John L. Ward, but this is certainly less true today.[30] Facing global competition and rapidly changing markets, family businesses have to look carefully at family members who want a leadership position in the enterprise and determine whether they are up to the task. The complex relationships in family firms require the oversight of competent and professional management, whether from within or outside the family.

The Need for Good Management

Good management is necessary for the success of any business, and the family firm is no exception. Significant deviations, for family reasons, from what would be considered good management practices only serve to weaken the firm. Compromising in this way runs counter to the interests of both the firm and the family.

Family business experts and practitioners have proposed a number of "best practices" for family enterprises. Each family and each family business is different, so what is actually "best" will depend on the individual situation; nonetheless, the best practices listed below have helped many family businesses design effective management systems:

- Promote learning to stimulate new thinking and fresh strategic insights.
- Solicit ample input from outsiders to keep things in perspective.
- Establish channels for constructive communication, and use them often.
- Build a culture that accepts continuous change.
- Promote family members only according to their skill levels.
- Attract and retain excellent nonfamily managers.
- Ensure fair compensation for all employees, including those outside the family.
- Establish a solid leadership succession plan.
- Exploit the unique advantages of family ownership.

The family firm is a business—a competitive business. Observing these and other practices of good management will help the business thrive and permit the family to function as a family. Disregarding them will pose a threat to the business and impose strains on family relationships.

Nonfamily Employees in a Family Firm

Those employees who are not family members are still affected by family considerations. In some cases, their opportunities for promotion are lessened by the presence of family members who seem to have the inside track. Few parents will promote an outsider over a competent daughter or son who is being groomed for future leadership, and this is understandable. But this limits the potential for advancement of nonfamily employees, which may lead them to become frustrated and to feel cheated.

Consider the case of a young business executive who worked for a family business that operated a chain of restaurants. When hired, he had negotiated a contract that gave him a specified percentage of the business based on performance. Under this arrangement, he was doing extremely well financially—until the owner called on him to say "I am here to buy you out." When the young man asked why, the owner replied, "You are doing too well, and your last name is not the same as mine!"

The extent of limitations on nonfamily employees depends on the number of family members active in the business and the number of managerial or professional positions in the business to which nonfamily employees might aspire. It also depends on the extent to which the owner demands competence in management and maintains an atmosphere of fairness in supervision. To avoid future problems, the owner should make clear, when hiring nonfamily employees, the extent of opportunities available and identify the positions, if any, that are reserved for family members.

Those outside the family may also be caught in the crossfire between family members who are competing with each other. It is difficult for outsiders to maintain strict neutrality in family feuds. If a nonfamily employee is perceived as siding with one of those involved in the feud, he or she may lose the support of other family members. Hard-working employees often feel that they deserve hazard pay for working in a firm plagued by family conflict.

Family Retreats

Some families hold retreats in order to review family business concerns. A **family retreat** is a meeting of family members (including in-laws), usually held at a remote location, to discuss family business matters. In most cases, the atmosphere is informal to encourage family members to communicate freely and discuss their concerns about the business in an environment that does not feel adversarial. The retreat is not so much an *event* as it is the *beginning of a process* of connecting family members. It presents an opportunity to celebrate the founders and their sacrifices, as well as highlight the legacy they wanted to pass down to future generations of the family.

family retreat
A gathering of family members, usually at a remote location, to discuss family business matters

The prospect of sitting down together to discuss family business matters may seem threatening to some family members. As a result, some families avoid extensive communication, fearing it will stir up trouble. They assume that making decisions quietly or secretly will preserve harmony. Unfortunately, this approach often glosses over serious differences that become increasingly troublesome. Family retreats are designed to open lines of communication and to bring about understanding and agreement on family business issues.

Initiating discussion can be difficult, so family leaders often invite an outside expert or facilitator to lead early sessions. The facilitator can help develop an agenda and establish ground rules for discussion. While chairing early sessions, the moderator can establish a positive tone that emphasizes family achievements and encourages rational consideration of sensitive issues. If family members can develop an atmosphere of neutrality, however, they may be able to chair the sessions without using an outsider.

To ensure the success of a family business retreat, Steven White, CEO of a family business consulting firm, suggests that these guidelines be followed:[31]

1. *Set a time and place.* The retreat should be held at a convenient time and in a central location so that everyone can be involved.

2. *Distribute an agenda prior to meeting.* An agenda helps participants organize their thoughts about the issues that are to be discussed.

3. *Plan a schedule in advance.* Details for sessions should be planned ahead of the retreat. Sufficient blocks of time should be provided to deal with important matters and room left in the schedule for refreshment breaks. It's a good idea to set aside one evening for the family to get together and do something fun as a group.

4. *Give everyone a chance to participate.* In sessions, family members should be honest, and they should not interrupt one another. The conversation may be allowed to wander a bit, if this is therapeutic, but the focus should stay on the business.

5. *Keep it professional.* The conversation may become emotional when sensitive topics are discussed, but it should never be allowed to become personal or to spiral out of control. Everyone should leave the retreat feeling good about what was accomplished.

But the talk at family retreats is not always about business. After a retreat, families often speak of the joy of sharing family values and stories of past family experiences. Thus, retreats can strengthen the family as well as the company.

Family Councils

family council
An organized group of family members who gather periodically to discuss family-related business issues

A family retreat could pave the way for creation of a **family council**, in which family members meet to discuss values, policies, and direction for the future. A family council functions as the organizational and strategic planning arm of a family. It provides a forum for the ongoing process of listening to the ideas of all members and discovering what they believe in and want from the business. A family council formalizes the participation of the family in the business to a greater extent than does the family retreat. It can also be a focal point for planning the future of individual family members, the family as a whole, and the business, as well as how each relates to the others.

A council should be a formal organization that holds regular meetings, keeps minutes, and makes suggestions to the firm's board of directors. Experts recommend that it be open to all interested family members and spouses of all generations. During the first several meetings, an acceptable mission statement is usually generated, as well as a family creed.

Family businesses that have such councils find them useful for developing family harmony. The meetings are often fun and informative and may include speakers who discuss items of interest. Time is often set aside for sharing achievements, milestones, and family history. The younger generation is encouraged to participate because much of the process is designed to increase their understanding of family traditions and business interests and to prepare them for working effectively in the business.

As with family retreats, an outside facilitator may be useful in getting a council organized and helping with initial meetings. After that, the organization and leadership of meetings can rotate among family members.

Family Business Constitutions

family business constitution
A statement of principles intended to guide a family firm through times of crisis and change

Some experts suggest that families write a **family business constitution**, which is a statement of principles intended to guide a family firm through times of crisis and change, including the succession process. While this is not a legally binding document, it nonetheless helps to preserve the intentions of the founder(s) and ensure that the business survives periods of change largely intact. When a transfer between generations occurs and there is no guiding document, issues such as ownership, performance, and compensation can become flash points for conflict.[32]

When Randall Clifford's father died in 1994, the ownership and control of Ventura Transfer Co., the oldest trucking company in California, were suddenly called into question. Clifford's stepmother sued him and his three brothers for an interest in the business. Then, to make matters worse, the four Clifford brothers began to struggle among themselves for control of the company. After a drawn-out legal battle, the sons decided to enlist the help of a consultant to draft a family business constitution. The resulting document helped the family sort out many of the issues that had plagued the transition process.

A family business constitution cannot foresee every eventuality, but that is not a problem since a family business constitution is a "living, breathing document" that can be amended as needed.[33] The important point is that this document can smooth any transitions—such as a change in leadership, the subject of the next section.

The Process of Leadership Succession

5 Describe the process of managerial succession in a family business.

The task of preparing family members for careers and, ultimately, leadership within the business is difficult and sometimes frustrating. Professional and managerial requirements tend to become intertwined with family feelings and interests, so the transfer of leadership can quickly run into trouble. And to make the succession process even more challenging, nobody wants to talk about it, for a variety of reasons.

> *The spouse doesn't want to talk about succession because he or she has to face changes at home. The patriarch or the matriarch doesn't want to talk about succession because what are they going to do after retirement? . . . The next generation doesn't want to bring it up. It's inappropriate and painful; it brings on all sorts of very difficult feelings.*[34]

Because everyone is so uncomfortable with the subject, plans for succession often are not well developed or at least are poorly communicated. At a major family business conference at Northwestern University in Chicago, potential leadership successors were asked if they knew the rules and plans for succession at their family firm, and 60 percent said they did not.[35] In other words, a majority of those who may be stepping into the primary role of responsibility for the family business in the future are not really certain they are solidly on that track. This could lead to some very uncomfortable times ahead if things do not turn out as expected, and the health and prosperity of both the family business and the business family could well hang in the balance.

Available Family Talent

A stream can rise no higher than its source, and the family firm can be no more brilliant than its leader. The business is dependent, therefore, on the quality of leadership talent provided. If the available talent is not sufficient, the owner must bring in outside leadership or supplement family talent to avoid a decline under the leadership of second- or third-generation family members.

The question of competency is both a critical and a delicate issue. With experience, individuals can improve their abilities; younger people should not be judged too harshly early on. Furthermore, potential successors may be held back by the reluctance of a parent-owner to delegate realistically to them.

In some cases, a younger family member's skills may actually help to rescue the company, especially when a family business becomes mired in the past and fails to keep up with changing technology and emerging markets. In 1983, Tom Jennison opened Jennison Manufacturing Corporation, a gritty, small tool-and-die operation in Carnegie, Pennsylvania, a now-faded steel town. Its basic, simple products included parts for gas masks and injection molds for making plumbing mechanisms. As Tom began to computerize the business in 1988, he ran into major problems and called on his son Mike, a junior at Penn State University. Mike came home to help his father get the system working smoothly and then joined the firm after graduation. Using his education and knowledge of technology, Mike developed a whole new line of products that led Tom and Mike, together, to plan a business expansion that would triple the number of people employed by the firm. For Jennison Manufacturing, the process of transferring leadership to a second generation has involved not only training a potential successor but also moving into new areas of technology and new markets.[36]

In any case, a family firm need not accept the existing level of family talent as an unchangeable given. Instead, the business may offer various types of development programs to teach younger family members and thereby improve their skills. Some businesses include mentoring as a part of such programs. **Mentoring** is the process by which a more experienced person guides and supports the work, progress, and professional relationships of a new or less-experienced employee. In the family business, mentor and protégé have the opportunity to navigate and explore family as well as business-related roles and responsibilities.[37]

mentoring
Guiding and supporting the work and development of a new or less-experienced organization member

Perhaps the fairest and most practical approach is to recognize the right of family members to prove themselves. A period of development and testing may occur either in the family business or, preferably, in another organization. If children show themselves to be capable, they earn the right to increased leadership responsibility. If potential successors are found, through a process of fair assessment, to have inadequate leadership abilities, preservation of the family business and the welfare of family members demand that they be passed over for promotion. The appointment of competent outsiders to these jobs, if necessary, increases the value of the firm for all family members who have an ownership interest in it.

Living the Dream   entrepreneurial challenges

An Entrepreneur with a Special Place for Mom in His Heart and Business

Jay Oxenhorn co-founded Hot Headz of America LLC, a Philadelphia-based manufacturer and distributor of herbal products for health and wellness that "help [customers] get through the days, weeks, and months of today's stressful world." The company sells products such as Nature's Way aromatherapy herbal packs, to ease aches and pains; fleece-covered, herb-filled Cozy Line blankets and slippers, to soothe and comfort; Cool Downz bandanas, with special crystals that provide relief from warm afternoons; and Hot Wavez gloves and hoods made of Wind-Tec fabric, to protect wearers from cold temperatures and biting breezes. The company has pretty much everything covered—sometimes literally!

Hot Headz has 10 employees, one of whom is Oxenhorn's mother. He spells out his reasons for hiring her: "She's in her 70s and basically needed to get away from my dad all day, and the income helps her. So she's my order-entry and retail order–taking person on the phone." Putting her on the payroll has had an upside and a downside. Oxenhorn says his mother is the most trustworthy person in the office, but she really can't work all that hard, so she taps out a little early, especially during the busy season. Still, hiring a parent is like contributing to her or his retirement plan, which can be a big help when the golden years last longer than the gold.

Family business experts caution that observing a few simple guidelines can make hiring parents work out more smoothly. For example, it's best to place them in roles that fit their skills and expertise. Letting them try something new can prove disastrous, leaving other employees frustrated, too. Though it may seem impersonal, it is best to treat parents like other employees, providing a real job description and paying a fair wage so that other workers won't feel slighted. Despite the entrepreneur's best intentions, having a parent on the payroll may be confusing for other employees. Is the parent in charge? How do you correct parents when they make a mistake? Do they deserve special status in the workplace? Small business owners can ease this confusion by clearly communicating expectations.

Even though an entrepreneur may make every effort to treat a parent like any other employee, it doesn't make sense to pretend he or she is just another worker. It's best to acknowledge the problems, recognizing that having a parent in the business can nonetheless be a good thing. As Oxenhorn says, "You get to see them a lot more, which is great."

Sources: http://www.hotheadz.net, accessed January 3, 2007; and Mark Hendricks, "Parent Trap?" *Entrepreneur*, Vol. 33, No. 3 (March 2005), pp. 96–98.

http://www.hotheadz.net

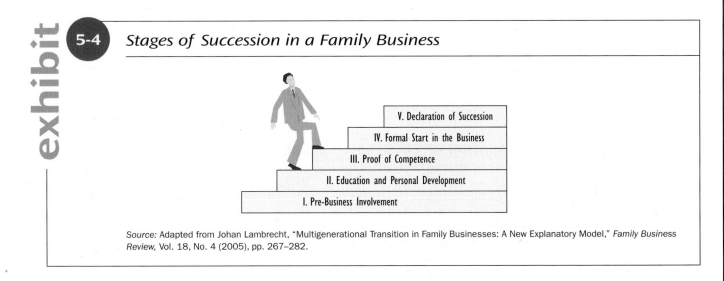

5-4 *Stages of Succession in a Family Business*

V. Declaration of Succession
IV. Formal Start in the Business
III. Proof of Competence
II. Education and Personal Development
I. Pre-Business Involvement

Source: Adapted from Johan Lambrecht, "Multigenerational Transition in Family Businesses: A New Explanatory Model," *Family Business Review,* Vol. 18, No. 4 (2005), pp. 267–282.

Stages in the Process of Succession

Sons or daughters do not typically assume leadership of a family firm at a particular moment in time. Instead, a long, drawn-out process of preparation and transition is customary—a process that extends over years and often decades. The succession process in family businesses has been described in terms of stages, or "stepping stones," that lead, in time, to the transfer of leadership to the next generation.[38] Exhibit 5-4 outlines this process as a series of **stages in succession**.

PRE-BUSINESS STAGE   In Stage I, a potential successor becomes acquainted with the business as a part of growing up. The young child accompanies a parent to the office, store, or warehouse or plays with equipment related to the business. This early stage does not entail any formal planning to prepare the child for entering the business. It simply forms a foundation for the more deliberate stages of the process that occur in later years. In the latter phases of this stage, the child is introduced to people associated with the firm and, in time, begins to work part-time in various functional areas to get a feel for the business.

EDUCATION AND PERSONAL DEVELOPMENT STAGE   Stage II usually begins when the potential successor goes off to study at a college or university, which is often viewed as a time to "grow up" (the family's perspective) in an environment that facilitates intellectual growth, personal maturity, and network development. This stage provides an opportunity to chart one's own course, but with an eye on the family business and its needs. For example, a business owner who sells pollution control equipment may convince his son or daughter to major in environmental science. Of course, the emphasis placed on a formal education varies with the business. In some cases, the family may not feel that formal studies are necessary; in other cases, earning a diploma is a condition for a career in the business.

PROOF OF COMPETENCE STAGE   One of the difficulties future successors are likely to face when joining a family business is the perception that they are not up to the task, that they have their position only because they are family. Thinking back to his early days with the company owned by his family, Austin Ramirez recalls, "I had the same name as my dad, [so] I was always concerned that there was this presumption that I was not competent unless proved otherwise."[39] No doubt, that thought crossed the minds of some employees, too, underscoring the importance of Stage III, establishing competence. One way to do this is for a son or daughter to prove he or she can do the job somewhere else first. Often, mom or dad will push a potential successor to take a position in another company before returning to the family firm, hoping that the independent achievements of the son or daughter will speak for themselves and establish his or her credibility.

FORMAL START IN THE BUSINESS STAGE   Stage IV starts when a son or daughter comes to work at the family business full-time, beginning on a lower wrung of the

stages in succession
Phases in the process of transferring leadership of a family business from parent to child

corporate ladder. It is common practice for family members to start out by working in various departments in the firm to prove themselves, to win the confidence of employees, and to learn about the business from all perspectives. Handling potential successors wisely involves giving them reasonable freedom to "try their wings," learn from their own mistakes, and gravitate toward business functions that play to their personal strengths and natural capabilities. At this point, succession is not a sure bet, but it is a likely scenario.

DECLARATION OF SUCCESSION STAGE   In Stage V, the son or daughter is named president or general manager of the business and presumably exercises overall direction, although a parent usually is still in the background. The successor has not necessarily mastered the complexities of the role, and the predecessor may be reluctant to give up decision making completely, but all the pieces are now in place. At this stage, it is important to establish a written plan so that there is no doubt about the soon-to-be predecessor's wishes, which could otherwise be questioned in the event of an untimely death or resignation. Establishing the plan in writing will help to minimize political positioning by others who aspire to take the lead, wrangling that can be emotionally explosive and counterproductive to the work of the firm.

Reluctant Parents and Ambitious Children

When the founder of a business is preparing her or his child to take over the firm, the founder's attachment to the business must not be underestimated. Not only is a father, for example, tied to the firm financially—it is probably his primary, if not his only, major investment—but he is also tied to it emotionally. The business is his "baby," and he is understandably reluctant to entrust its future to one whom he sees as immature and unproven. Unfortunately, parents often tend to see their sons and daughters through the lens of their childhood years, even decades after their adolescence.

The child may be ambitious, well educated, and insightful regarding the business. His or her tendency to push ahead—to try something new—often conflicts with the father's caution. As a result, the child may see the father as excessively conservative, stubborn, and unwilling to change.

At the root of many such difficulties is a lack of understanding between parent and child. They work together without a map showing where they are going. Children in the business, and also their spouses, may have expectations about progress that, in terms of the founder's thinking, are totally unrealistic. The successor can easily become hypersensitive to such problems and deal with them in ways that harm the parent–child relationship and actually hinder the progress of the business. But the situation is far from hopeless. In many cases, these problems can be avoided or defused if communication channels are open and all parties come to a better understanding of the development process and how it is to unfold.

Transfer of Ownership

A final and often complex step in the traditional succession process in the family firm is the **transfer of ownership**. Questions of inheritance affect not only the leadership successor but also other family members having no involvement in the business. In distributing their estate, parent-owners typically wish to treat all their children fairly, both those involved in the business and those on the outside.

One of the most difficult decisions is determining the future ownership of the business. If there are several children, should they all receive equal shares? On the surface, this seems to be the fairest approach. However, such an arrangement may play havoc with the future functioning of the business. Suppose each of five children receives a 20-percent ownership share, even though only one of them is active in the business. The child active in the business—the leadership successor—becomes a minority stockholder completely at the mercy of relatives on the outside.

A parent might attempt to resolve such a dilemma by changing the ownership structure of the firm. Those children active in the firm's management, for example, might be given common (voting) stock and others given preferred (nonvoting) stock. However, this is still troublesome because of the relative weaknesses of various ownership securities.

transfer of ownership
Passing ownership of a family business to the next generation

How They See It: Plan Early

John Stites

The typical family business seldom matures beyond the second generation. There are many reasons for this, but perhaps the primary reason is that family issues override good business practices. The best of intentions will not prevent this occurrence; only well-thought-out planning and the persistent execution of that plan will ensure success for subsequent generations.

The most important aspect of planning is the timing. Only the planning done early will be effective. By early, I mean planning done before it is applicable to any specific individual. When individuals become subject to any planning scheme, it makes business decisions and planning subject to personalities rather than business wisdom. An example of this was when our partners agreed to a buy-sell agreement. A part of the agreement required the buyout of any partner upon the disability of that partner. The decision was made to fund the disability of the partner with insurance. Ten years later, one of the partners became disabled, and because the decision about what would be done had been made before it applied to a specific individual, the transition occurred seamlessly and without disruption to the continuity or harmony of the family unit. Had the decision been delayed, every nuance of the transaction and every dollar of valuation would have been subject to scrutiny and second-guessing. The decisions on how to value the company, how the buyout would occur, and how the disabled partner would be provided for were all made before they specifically applied to any individual partner. Therefore, no one could reasonably claim the decisions were made to benefit one partner over another.

Tax considerations are relevant, and they tend to favor gradual transfer of ownership to all heirs. As noted, however, transfer of equal ownership shares to all heirs may be inconsistent with the future efficient operation of the business. Tax advantages should not be allowed to blind one to possible adverse effects on management.

Ideally, the founder has been able to arrange his or her personal holdings to create wealth outside the business as well as within it. In that case, he or she may bequeath comparable shares to all heirs while allowing business control to remain with the child or children active in the business. Planning and discussing the transfer of ownership is not easy, but it is recommended. Over a period of time, the owner must reflect seriously on family talents and interests as they relate to the future of the firm. The plan for transfer of ownership can then be firmed up and modified as necessary when it is discussed with the children or other potential heirs. In discussing exit strategies in Chapter 12, we explain a variety of possible financial arrangements for the transfer of ownership.

Looking BACK

1 Discuss the factors that make a family business unique.

- Family members have a special involvement in a family business.
- Business interests (production and profitability) overlap family interests (care and nurturing) in a family business.

- Entrepreneurs face difficult choices in reconciling the competing demands of business and family, and maintaining an appropriate balance between the two is difficult.
- The advantages of a family business include the strong commitment of family members to the success of the firm, the ability to use a family theme

in advertising, the development of firm-specific knowledge, the sharing of social networks among family members, a focus on long-term goals, an emphasis on the firm's reputation, and reduced cost of control.

2 Explain the forces that can keep a family business moving forward.

- Special patterns of beliefs and behaviors constitute the organizational culture of a family business.
- The founder often leaves a deep imprint on the culture of a family firm.
- Family members may be committed to the family business for different reasons (desire, sense of obligation, calculated costs, and personal needs), and these reasons will likely determine the nature and strength of that commitment.
- Sometimes it is important to change the direction or practices of the family business so that it can keep up with emerging realities, and this often occurs as leadership passes from one generation to the next.

3 Outline the complex family roles and relationships involved in a family business.

- A primary and sensitive relationship is that between founder and son or daughter.
- Some couples in business together find their marriage relationship strengthened, while others find it weakened.
- Sons, daughters, in-laws, and other relatives may either cooperate or squabble with each other as they work together in a family business.
- In-laws play a crucial role in the family business, either as direct participants or as sideline observers.
- The role of the founder's spouse is especially important, as he or she often serves as a mediator in family disputes and helps prepare the children for possible careers in the family business.

4 Identify management practices that enable a family business to function effectively.

- Good management practices are as important as good family relationships in the successful functioning of a family business.
- Family members, as well as all other employees, should be treated fairly and consistently, in accordance with their abilities and performance.
- Following best practices can help family firms design effective management systems.
- Motivation of nonfamily employees can be enhanced by open communication and fairness.
- Family retreats bring all family members together to discuss business and family matters.
- Family councils provide a formal framework for the family's ongoing discussion of family and business issues.
- Family business constitutions can guide a company through times of crisis or change.

5 Describe the process of managerial succession in a family business.

- The quality of leadership talent available in the family determines the extent to which outside managers are needed.
- Succession is a long-term process starting early in the successor's life.
- The succession process begins with the pre-business stage and includes introductions to people associated with the company and part-time jobs in the firm. Later stages involve education and personal development, proof of competence, a formal start in the business, and a declaration of succession.
- Tension often arises between the founder and the potential successor as the latter gains experience.
- Transfer of ownership involves issues of fairness, taxes, and managerial control.
- Discussing and planning the transfer of ownership is sometimes difficult but usually desirable.

Key **TERMS**

Discussion **QUESTIONS**

1. How are family businesses and other types of small businesses both similar and different? Explain what makes a business a family business.

2. Suppose that you, as founder of a business, have a sales manager position open. You realize that sales may suffer somewhat if you promote your son from sales representative to sales manager. However, you would like to see your son make some progress and earn a higher salary to support his wife and young daughter. How would you go about making this decision? Would you promote your son?

3. What benefits result from family involvement in a business?

4. What are the bases of commitment to the family firm, and what do these have to do with the strength of that commitment?

5. With a college-level business degree in hand, you are headed for a job in the family business. As a result of your education, you have become aware of some outdated business practices in the family firm. In spite of them, the business is showing a good return on investment. Should you "rock the boat"? How should you proceed in correcting what you see as obsolete approaches?

6. Describe a founder–son or founder–daughter relationship in a family business with which you are familiar. What strengths or weaknesses are evident in that business relationship?

7. Should a son or daughter feel an obligation to carry on a family business? What is the source of such a feeling?

8. Assume that you are an ambitious, nonfamily manager in a family firm and that one of your peers is the son or daughter of the founder. What, if anything, would keep you interested in pursuing a career with this company?

9. Identify and describe the stages outlined in the model of succession shown in Exhibit 5-4.

10. In making decisions about transferring ownership of a family business from one generation to another, how much emphasis should be placed on estate tax laws and other concerns that go beyond the family? Why?

You Make the **CALL**

SITUATION 1

Though they are brothers, you might not know it by watching them interact. Even a simple "Good morning" at the start of a workday seems to be more than anyone can manage. No one is happy to be at the office.

The three Patton brothers—John, Richard, and Bill—have been in business together for 25 years, running the janitorial services company that was started by their father. Most of the years were happy ones, but the good times have now faded into distant memory. What could have gone so wrong?

The conflict started when the founder's grandchildren got involved in the business. Today, John's oldest son manages the employees who work with residential accounts, Richard's daughter does most of the bookkeeping, and Bill's son is an outside salesperson for the company. Despite differences in their personal goals and interests, and even in their long-term vision for the company, the cousins get along very well.

But the Patton brothers disagree about who should lead the company in the future. As the oldest brother with the most experience in the business, John believes his son is best positioned to take over the reins of the company when the time comes, but Richard and Bill realize that this means opportunities for their kids will be limited. Bill is convinced that his son shows more managerial promise than his nephew, and Richard believes that his daughter is underpaid and underappreciated, even though she is "obviously" the financial mind behind the machine. This is no small matter to the Patton brothers. Early on, the arguments became so heated that the brothers nearly came to blows.

Today, the disagreements are mostly unspoken. Though the business is in no immediate danger of failing, it has not been doing all that well during the last 18 months or so. More importantly, the Patton brothers need to make some major decisions that will position the company for the future, but these are being neglected as the brothers continue their war of silence.

Under the circumstances, progress is impossible. What can be done to get this family business back on track?

Question 1 Why do you think the cousins get along better than their fathers do?

Question 2 How might this conflict over the future leadership of the firm be resolved?

SITUATION 2

Harrison Stevens, second-generation president of a family-owned heating and air conditioning business, is concerned about his 19-year-old son, Barry, who works as a full-time employee in the firm. Although Barry made it through high school, he has not distinguished himself as a student or shown interest in further education. He is somewhat indifferent in his attitude toward his work, although he does reasonably—or at least minimally—satisfactory work. His father sees Barry as immature and more interested in riding motorcycles than in building a business.

Stevens wants to provide his son with an opportunity for personal development. In his mind, the process should begin with learning to work hard. If Barry likes the work and shows promise, he might eventually be groomed to take over the business. His father also holds out faint hope that hard work might eventually inspire him to get a college education.

In trying to achieve these goals, Stevens senses two problems. The first problem is that Barry obviously lacks motivation. The second problem relates to his supervision. Supervisors seemed reluctant to demand much from Barry. They may be afraid that being too hard on the son might antagonize the boss, so they often allow Barry to get by with marginal performance.

Question 1 In view of Barry's shortcomings, should Harrison Stevens seriously consider him as a potential successor?

Question 2 How could Barry be motivated? Can Stevens do anything more to improve the situation, or does the responsibility lie with Barry?

Question 3 How could the quality of Barry's supervision be improved to make his work experience more productive?

SITUATION 3

Siblings Rob, 37, and Julie, 36, work in their family's $15 million medical products firm. Both are capable leaders and have experienced success in their respective areas of responsibility. Compared to Julie, Rob is more introverted, more thorough in his planning, and much better with detail and follow through. In contrast, Julie is more creative, more extroverted, and stronger in interpersonal skills. Since childhood, they have been rather competitive in their relationships. Their 62-year-old father is contemplating retirement and considering the possibility of co-leadership, with each child eventually holding a 50-percent ownership interest in the company.

Question 1 If you were to choose one leader for the firm, based on the brief description above, which sibling would you recommend? Why?

Question 2 What are the strengths and/or weaknesses of the co-leadership idea? Would you favor it or reject it?

Question 3 How could the father secure practical advice to help with this decision?

Experiential EXERCISES

1. Interview a college student who has grown up in a family business about the ways he or she has been trained or educated, both formally and informally, for entry into the business. Prepare a brief report, relating your findings to the stages of succession shown in Exhibit 5-4.

2. Interview another college student who has grown up in a family business about parental attitudes toward his or her possible entry into the business. Submit a one-page report describing the extent of

    pressure on the student to enter the family business and the direct or indirect ways in which family expectations have been communicated.

3. Identify a family business and prepare a brief report on its history, including its founding, family involvement, and any leadership changes that have occurred.

4. Read and report on a biography or autobiography about a family in business or on a nonfictional book about a family business.

Exploring the **WEB**

1. This chapter discusses the process of succession in a family business. Now go to **http://www. gofso.com/Premium/BS/fg/fg-succession.html** to find an online resource on planning for succession. What suggestions do you find on this website?

Case **5**

The Brown Family Business (p. 628)
This case presents the philosophy, criteria, and procedures adopted by one family to regulate work opportunities for family members in the family business.

Alternative Cases for Chapter 5
Case 18, Douglas Electrical Supply, Inc., p. 656

Case 19, Gibson Mortuary, p. 658

Part 3

Developing the New Venture Business Plan

## chapter 6

The Business Plan

Visualizing the Dream

In the **SPOTLIGHT**

Luxe Jewels
http://www.luxejewels.com

An entrepreneur's first presentation of a business plan to investors can be a lesson in humility. That's what Jessica Herrin learned as a business school student who was trying to start an online wedding registry during the dot-com boom.

Her lack of experience in the wedding industry almost ended her plans for the startup before she began. Herrin's intent was to sell products directly to consumers and also through retailers. But, of course, retailers are not interested in supporting their competitors. Herrin was able to obtain financing only when she revised her business plan and used a retailer-only distribution system.

Herrin's experience is not uncommon. Such errors in business plans can doom a business with investors. But Herrin learned her lesson well.

In 2004, Herrin was able to quickly raise the $350,000 that her current business, Luxe Jewels, needed to get off the ground. This time, the 34-year-old Burlingame, California, entrepreneur went to a retailer to learn about the custom jewelry industry before she even began to solicit investors.

Luxe Jewels currently has $1.2 million in sales and 10 employees. Clearly, a good business plan can make all the difference.

Source: Mark Henricks, "Build a Better Business Plan," *Entrepreneur's StartUps,* February 2007, p. 85.

© Luxe Jewels

Looking **AHEAD**

You're excited about an idea for a new business. But when you mention it to a business friend, she says, "You'll need to prepare a business plan." While the business idea sounds great, sitting down and writing some cold, formal document is not exactly your notion of fun, and you wonder if it is really necessary. After all, you know an entrepreneur who started and successfully grew a company based on an idea developed on the back of a napkin over dinner at a local restaurant. And isn't it true that the founders of such notable companies as Microsoft, Dell Computers, *Rolling Stone* magazine, and Calvin Klein all started their businesses without business plans?[1]

An Overview of the Business Plan

To answer the question of whether or not you should write a business plan, you'll need to first understand its purpose and objectives. We'll help you examine the considerations in making a decision about whether to write a business plan for your venture. Then we'll look at the two basic forms a plan might take.

The Purpose of a Business Plan

There is no one correct formula for a business plan. After all, no one plan will work in all situations. But, in general, a **business plan** is a document that outlines the basic idea underlying a business and describes related startup considerations. A business plan is an entrepreneur's game plan; it crystallizes the dreams and hopes that motivate an entrepreneur to take the startup plunge. The business plan should lay out your basic idea for the venture and include descriptions of where you are now, where you want to go, and how you intend to get there.

David Gumpert, who for years headed up the MIT Enterprise Forum,[2] offers a concise and practical definition of a business plan, focusing on how it should lead to action: "It's a document that convincingly demonstrates that your business can sell enough of its product or service to make a satisfactory profit and to be attractive to potential backers."[3] For Gumpert, the business plan is essentially a selling document used to convince key individuals, both inside and outside the firm, that the venture has real potential. Equally important, it is an opportunity to convince yourself, the entrepreneur, that what appears to be a good idea is also a good investment opportunity, both economically and in terms of your personal goals.

The issue of your personal goals deserves careful thought: *If the business does not align with your personal goals, you are not likely to succeed and you certainly will not enjoy*

business plan
A document that presents the basic idea for the venture and includes descriptions of where you are now, where you want to go, and how you intend to get there

6-1   *Users of Business Plans*

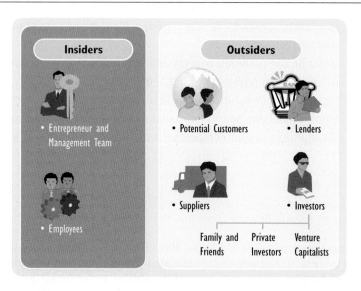

the journey. So, be sure to think about your personal aspirations and the personal costs of starting a business before becoming immersed in the business opportunity itself.

For the entrepreneur starting a new venture, a business plan has three basic objectives:

1. To identify the nature and the context of the business opportunity—that is, why does such an opportunity exist?

2. To present the approach the entrepreneur plans to use to exploit the opportunity

3. To recognize factors that will determine whether the venture will be successful

Stated differently, a business plan is used to provide a statement of goals and strategies for use by company *insiders* and to aid in the development of relationships with *outsiders* (investors and others) who could help the company achieve its goals. Exhibit 6-1 provides an overview of those who might have an interest in a business plan for a new venture. The first group consists of the internal users of the plan: the entrepreneur and the new firm's management and employees. The second group consists of outsiders who are critical to the firm's success: its prospective customers, suppliers, lenders, and investors.

Do You Really Need a Business Plan?

2 Give the rationale for writing (or not writing) a business plan when starting a new venture.

The justification often used for *not* writing a business plan goes something like this: "Companies that start up based on business plans are no more successful than those that do not." It is true that studies attempting to measure the success of entrepreneurs with business plans against the success of those without have produced mixed results. Some findings suggest a relationship; others find none.[4]

Given what we know about Apple, Calvin Klein, and other businesses started without business plans, clearly having a business plan is not a prerequisite for success. *This simply tells us that the business plan is not the business.* It may well be that some entrepreneurs spend untold hours writing a 60-page business plan with another 50 pages of appendixes but never follow the plan. In such cases, we can say confidently that writing the plan was a waste of time. What matters is not writing a plan, but implementing it. If the plan is not going to lead to action, there is no need to bother to write it. Only if you *execute* the business plan does it have a good chance of making a difference. Thomas Stemberg, the founder of Staples who later became a venture capitalist, says it well:

In my experience, entrepreneurs often confuse envisioning what a business will be with laying the foundation for what it could be. So they dream big dreams and construct detailed

business plans, which is fine. But it's nowhere near as important as putting in place as early as humanly possible the people and systems that will carry them through their journey, no matter what unexpected directions, changing markets or technology force them to take.

To me, business plans are interesting chiefly as indications of how an entrepreneur thinks. Here at Highland Capital Partners, the venture capital firm I'm part of now, we spend most of our time talking about what really matters: management and markets. If you have the right management team and an exciting market, the rest will take care of itself.[5]

An entrepreneur must also find the right balance between planning and adaptability. No matter how well your plan has been thought out, events will occur that were not expected. One of the key attributes of a successful entrepreneur is adaptability, regardless of what the business plan says to do. So, if you have to choose between action and planning, go for action.

Vinay Gupta of Ann Arbor, Michigan, spent six months attending conferences, meeting with consultants, and writing a 60-page business plan before launching an outsourcing consulting firm for mid-sized businesses in 2004. But soon after he started the business, it became clear that far fewer mid-sized firms actually sought outsourcing help than his research had suggested. He scrapped his original idea and developed outsourcing-management software geared toward companies with annual revenues of more than $1 million. While the planning had helped Gupta learn about the industry, it hadn't pointed out the fundamental flaw in his original idea.[6]

The benefits of a business plan also depend on the individual circumstances surrounding the startup. Consider the following:

1. For some startups, the environment is too turbulent for extensive planning to be beneficial. Entrepreneurs in new fields may find that there is not enough information to allow them to write a comprehensive plan. As already noted, an entrepreneur's ability to adapt may be more important than a careful plan for the future. Having an excessively detailed plan can even be a problem if investors become so focused on "the plan" that they insist that the entrepreneur not vary from it.

2. Planning may also pose a problem when the timing of the opportunity is a critical factor. In some cases, becoming operational as quickly as possible may have to take priority over in-depth planning, but be careful not to use timing as an easy excuse not to write a business plan.

3. A business may be so constrained by a shortage of capital that planning is not an option. In his study of *Inc.* 500 companies (firms identified by *Inc.* magazine as the fastest-growing firms in the United States), Amar Bhide concluded that a lack of planning may make sense for some companies: "Capital-constrained entrepreneurs cannot afford to do much prior analysis and research. The limited profit potential and high uncertainty of the opportunity they usually pursue also make the benefits low compared to the costs."[7]

Though writing a business plan offers no guarantee of success, most entrepreneurs need the discipline that comes with the process. Activity started without adequate preparation tends to be haphazard. In the words of Thomas Carlyle, the Scottish mathematician and writer, "Nothing is more terrible than activity without insight." This is particularly true of such a complex process as initiating a new business. Although planning is a mental process, it should go beyond the realm of speculation. Thinking about a proposed new business must become more thorough for rough ideas to come together. A written plan helps to ensure systematic, complete coverage of the important factors to be considered in starting a new business. Frank Moyes, a successful entrepreneur who has for many years taught courses on writing business plans at the University of Colorado, offers the following observations:

Perhaps the most important reason to write a business plan is that it requires you to engage in a rigorous, thoughtful and often painful process that is essential before you start a venture. It requires you to answer hard questions about your venture. Why is there a need for your product/service? Who is your target market? How is your product/service different than your competitor's? What is your competitive advantage? How profitable is the business and what are the cash flows? How should you fund the business?[8]

So the business plan becomes a model that helps the entrepreneur and the management team focus on important issues and activities for the new venture. Furthermore, it helps the entrepreneur communicate his or her vision to current—and prospective—employees of the firm. After all, entrepreneurs who are building good companies seldom, if ever, work alone.

The business plan also matters to outsiders. Although typically thought to be the primary risk takers in a startup, the entrepreneur and the management team are by no means the only risk takers. To make the company successful, the entrepreneur must convince outsiders—prospective customers, suppliers, lenders, and investors—to become linked with the firm. Why should they do business with your startup, rather than with an established firm? They need evidence that you will be around in the future. As Amar Bhide explains, "Some entrepreneurs may have an innate capability to outperform their rivals, acquire managerial skills, and thus build a flourishing business. But it is difficult for customers (and others) to identify founders with these innate capabilities."[9]

By enhancing the firm's credibility, the business plan serves as an effective selling tool with prospective customers and suppliers, as well as investors. For example, a well-prepared business plan can be helpful in gaining a supplier's trust and securing favorable credit terms. Likewise, a plan can improve sales prospects by convincing prospective customers that the new firm is likely to be around for a long time to service a product or to continue as a procurement source.

Finally, the entrepreneur may face the task of raising money to supplement personal savings. This requires an effective presentation to bankers, individual investors, or, on rare occasions, venture capitalists. Approach almost any investor for money today and the first thing she or he will ask is "Where is your business plan?"

As discussed earlier, a business plan is not a prerequisite for entrepreneurial success. A plan may not be needed in certain situations, especially if you want only to build a very small company and have no plans for significant growth. But we encourage you to dream and hope for more. Ewing Marion Kauffman, who founded Marion Labs with $5,000 and later sold it for $6 billion, once said, "You should not choose to build a common company. It's your right to be uncommon if you can. You seek opportunity to compete, to take calculated risks, to dream, to build; yes, even to fail and succeed."[10] And Peter Drucker wrote, "Even if you are starting your business on a kitchen table, you must have a vision of becoming a world leader in your field, or you will probably never be successful."[11] Granted, you may have no interest in building a company that is a world leader in its field, but neither should you dream too small.

How They See It: Getting Started

Denny Fulk

Within three years after I began my career with a mid-sized company in Indiana, the company was sold to a much larger corporation, based in New York City. Fortunately, it was not a sudden event, so I had time to think and plan the necessary action steps that were the basis of starting my own business.

One insightful bit of advice that I received was "If you are the person who is actually responsible for generating an income stream with real profit for another company, you most likely have the ability to do it for yourself, even on a smaller scale, if necessary." I had confidence that I had indeed been responsible for a profit center of the business. Therefore, the Monday after leaving my position, I began to operate my own company, Fulk Equipment, in a field that was non-competitive with my former employer.

Making the necessary preparations while maintaining good business ethics is essential for success. Equally important is your own work ethic, along with generating that same entrepreneurial spirit in any staff who may be working with you. I believe your probability of success is higher if the business you choose is directly tied to your sales and marketing abilities. Manufacturing, engineering, and construction companies require a longer start-up time and considerably more initial capital. And a sound business plan, developed with good counsel, is essential in every situation because it forces you and those who advise you to think through the many opportunities available to you, as well as obstacles to your future success.

How Much Planning?

We would submit that for most entrepreneurs, the issue is not *whether* to prepare a business plan but *how* to engage in effective planning, given the situation. As we have already observed, different situations lead to different needs and, thus, to different levels of planning.

The issue, then, goes beyond answering the question "Do I plan?" It is more about deciding how much to plan. In starting a business, an entrepreneur has to make some tradeoffs, as preparing a plan requires time and money, two resources that are always in short supply. At the extremes, an entrepreneur has two basic choices when it comes to writing a business plan: the dehydrated plan or the comprehensive plan.[12]

THE DEHYDRATED PLAN   As noted earlier, extensive planning may be of limited value when there is a great amount of uncertainty in the environment or when timing is a critical factor in capturing an opportunity. A **dehydrated plan** is a short form of a business plan, presenting only the most important issues and projections for the business. Focusing heavily on market issues, such as pricing, competition, and distribution channels, the dehydrated plan provides little in the way of supporting information.

This type of plan will often be adequate for seeking outside financing from banks, especially if it includes past and projected financial results. In fact, it is so rare for an entrepreneur to provide any form of a plan when requesting a loan that a brief dehydrated plan will probably make a favorable impression on a banker. Furthermore, a dehydrated plan may be helpful in trying to gauge investor interest, to see if writing a full-length plan would be worth the time and effort.

THE COMPREHENSIVE PLAN   When entrepreneurs and investors speak of a business plan, they are usually referring to a **comprehensive plan**, a full business plan that provides

> **dehydrated plan**
> A short form of a business plan that presents only the most important issues and projections for the business
>
> **comprehensive plan**
> A full business plan that provides an in-depth analysis of the critical factors that will determine a firm's success or failure, along with all the underlying assumptions

Living the Dream   entrepreneurial challenges

© SmartONE/Getty Images

Will Your Plan Win a Prize?

The stakes in business plan competitions can be hundreds of thousands of dollars, and even taking third place looks great on a résumé. Winners often get a big payoff. Just ask Matt Ferris, president of SignalONE Safety, which developed a smoke alarm that gives escape instructions in a parent's voice. His startup, originally called KidSmart Corporation, raised more than $100,000 in winnings from several venture competitions, including the Moot Corp. Competition in Austin, Texas, where the team won first prize.

Some competitions backed by venture capitalists, such as the Carrot Capital VentureBowl in New York, provide upwards of $750,000 in equity funding to first-place finishers. Those sponsored by business schools offer between a few thousand dollars and $100,000 in equity or cash. In addition, students get valuable advice from successful entrepreneurs, a chance to hone presentation skills, and mentoring from professors and venture capitalists.

The founders of many startups have benefited from the connections they made through venture competitions. Indeed, feedback from experts might be the best reason to enter. "There are few other avenues I can think of where you are going to get such candid and sincerely helpful feedback from a wide array of professionals who know what they are talking about," says Chad Sorenson, who has an MBA from the University of Wisconsin at Madison. His company won about $45,000 in several competitions, based on a plan to develop a device to help farmers monitor the machinery that applies fertilizer.

Source: Jennifer Merritt, "Will Your Plan Win a Prize?" *Business Week,* March 15, 2004, pp. 108–110.

http://www.signalonesafety.com

an in-depth analysis of the critical factors that will determine a firm's success or failure, along with all the underlying assumptions. Such a plan is beneficial when describing a new opportunity (startup), facing significant change in the business or the external environment (changing demographics, new legislation, or developing industry trends), explaining a complex business situation, etc. In the remainder of this chapter and in the following chapters, we will be discussing the comprehensive business plan.

3 Describe the preferred content and format for a business plan.

Preparing a Business Plan

Two issues are of primary concern in the actual writing of a business plan: the content and format of the plan and the effectiveness of the written presentation.

The Content and Format of a Business Plan

In considering the content of a business plan, think first and foremost about the opportunity. Strategies and financial plans should come later. In the evaluation of an opportunity, give thorough consideration to the following basic and interdependent factors. Decisions about these factors will, in turn, help determine the content of a business plan for a startup.

- *The entrepreneurial team.* Nothing is more important than the people who are starting and managing the venture—specifically, their qualifications and the depth and breadth of experience they bring to the venture.

- *The opportunity.* A profile is needed of the business itself—what it will sell, to whom it will sell, and how rapidly it can grow. The industry and market outlook should include an assessment of everything that can go wrong or right, with a discussion of how the entrepreneurial team could respond to the various challenges.

- *The resources.* The critical resources for an entrepreneurial venture include not just money, but also the human assets (suppliers, accountants, lawyers, investors, etc.) and hard assets (accounts receivable, inventories, etc.). The entrepreneurial approach to resources is "doing the most with the least." The entrepreneur should think of ways to work with minimal resources and focus on "minimizing and controlling" rather than on "maximizing and owning."

- *The financing structure.* How a firm's financing is structured (debt versus equity) and how the ownership percentage is shared by the founders and investors have a significant impact on an entrepreneur's incentive to work hard. The goal is to find a win-win deal.

- *The big picture.* The *context* (or external factors) of an opportunity includes the regulatory environment, interest rates, demographic trends, inflation, and other factors that inevitably change but cannot be controlled by the entrepreneur.

While the issues listed above are important on their own as a foundation for an effective business plan, there must also be a good fit among all the factors. As shown in Exhibit 6-2, a good plan pulls together the right entrepreneurial team, the right opportunity, the right resources, the right financing structure, and the right context. There will always be uncertainties and ambiguities; the unanticipated is bound to happen. But by addressing all these interdependent factors, you can be sure that you have made an attempt to deal with the important issues.

There is no single format to be followed in writing a business plan. A plan for a retail store, restaurant, or wholesaling business will, by necessity, be moderately different in terms of topics, order of presentation, and what is emphasized. However, investors want to see a format that is familiar to them. Thus, you do not want to write a business plan that is fundamentally different from what they are accustomed to seeing. Deviating materially from this format would be a mistake.

Exhibit 6-3 summarizes the major sections common to most business plans, providing a bird's-eye view of what's included. We will now briefly consider each of these sections.[13] Chapters 7 through 12 take an in-depth look at each section of the business plan.

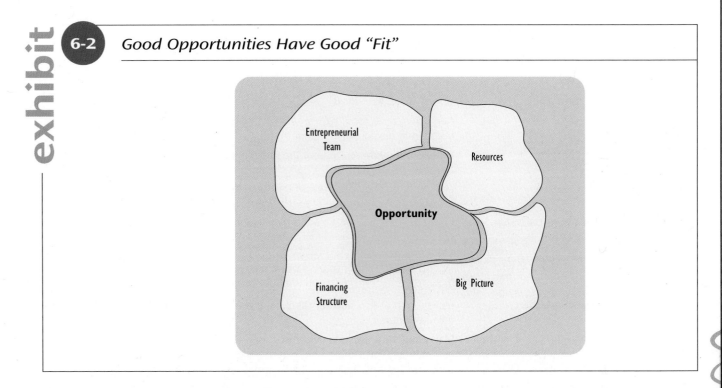

6-2 *Good Opportunities Have Good "Fit"*

COVER PAGE   The cover page should contain the following information:

- Company name, address, phone number, fax number, and website

- Tagline and company logo

- Name of contact person (preferably the president) with mailing address, phone number, fax number, and e-mail address

- Date on which the business plan was prepared

- If the plan is being given to investors, a disclaimer that the plan is being provided on a confidential basis to qualified investors only and is not to be reproduced without permission

- Number of the copy (to help keep track of how many copies are outstanding)

TABLE OF CONTENTS   The table of contents provides a sequential listing of the sections of the plan, with page numbers. This allows the reader to spot-read the plan (a common practice) rather than reading it from front to back. Exhibit 6-4 presents the table of contents for the business plan for Benjapon's, a Thai restaurant located in Boston. (While the table of contents for Benjapon's business plan does not follow exactly the format presented in Exhibit 6-3, note that it has much of the same content and follows a similar order.)

EXECUTIVE SUMMARY   The executive summary is often thought to be the most important section of the business plan. If you don't catch the readers' attention in the executive summary, most likely they will not continue reading. At the very outset, it must convey a clear and concise picture of the proposed venture and, at the same time, create a sense of excitement regarding its prospects. This means that it must be written—and, if necessary, rewritten—to achieve clarity and create interest. Even though the executive summary comes at the beginning of the business plan, it provides an overview of the whole plan and should be written last. In no more than three (preferably two) pages, the executive summary should include the following subsections:

- A description of the opportunity

- An explanation of the business concept

executive summary
A section of the business plan that conveys a clear and concise overall picture of the proposed venture

exhibit

6-3   *Abbreviated Business Plan Outline*

Section Heading	Information Provided
Cover Page	Company name, logo, tagline, contact information, copy number, date prepared, and disclaimer (if needed)
Table of Contents	Listing of the key sections of the business plan and where they can be found in the document
Executive Summary	One- to three-page overview of the significant points from each section, intended to motivate the reader to continue reading
Industry, Target Customer, and Competitor Analysis	Key characteristics of the industry (including the different segments), your potential customers, and the niche where you plan to compete
Company Description	Company objectives, the nature of the business, its primary product/service, its current status (startup, buyout, or expansion) and history (if applicable), and the legal form of organization
Product/Service Plan	Explanation of why people will buy the product or service, based on its unique features
Marketing Plan	Marketing strategy, including the methods of identifying and attracting customers, selling approach, type of sales force, distribution channels, types of sales promotions and advertising, and credit and pricing policies
Operations and Development Plan	Operating or manufacturing methods, facilities (location, space, and equipment), quality-control methods, procedures to control inventory and operations, sources of supply, and purchasing procedures
Management Team	Description of the management team, outside investors and/or directors, and plans for recruiting and training employees
Critical Risks	Any known risks inherent in the venture
Offering	How much capital the entrepreneur needs and how the money will be used (used to attract investors)
Financial Plan	Historical financial statements for the last three to five years or as available; and pro forma financial statements for three to five years, including income statements, balance sheets, cash flow statements, and cash budgets
Appendix of Supporting Documents	Various supplementary materials and attachments to expand the reader's understanding of the plan

- An industry overview

- The target market

- The competitive advantage you hope to achieve in the market

- The economics of the opportunity

- The management team

- The amount and purpose of the money being requested (the "offering") if you are seeking financing

Depending on the situation and the preference of the entrepreneur, the executive summary may be in the form of a synopsis or a narrative.

Synopsis   The synopsis is the more straightforward of the two summary formats. A synopsis briefly covers all aspects of the business plan, giving each topic relatively equal treatment. It relates, in abbreviated fashion, the conclusions of each section of the completed business plan. Although it is easy to prepare, the synopsis can be rather dry reading for the prospective investor.

exhibit

6-4   *Benjapon's Table of Contents*

Narrative   Because the narrative tells a story, it can convey greater excitement than the synopsis. However, composing an effective narrative requires a gifted writer who can communicate the necessary information and generate enthusiasm without crossing the line into hyperbole. A narrative is more appropriate for businesses that are breaking new ground, with a new product, a new market, or a new operational techniques. It is also a better format for ventures that have one dominant advantage, such as holding an important patent or being run by a well-known entrepreneur. Finally, the narrative works well for companies with interesting or impressive backgrounds or histories.[14]

Benjapon's again provides us with an example, as Exhibit 6-5 shows the executive summary for the business.

INDUSTRY, TARGET CUSTOMER, AND COMPETITOR ANALYSIS   The primary purpose of this section is to present the opportunity and demonstrate why there is a significant market to be served. You should describe the broader industry in which you will be competing, including industry size, growth rate, major trends, and major players. You should next identify the different segments of the industry and finally describe in detail the niche in which you plan to participate. It is tempting to begin describing your own company at this point. Instead, you should provide the context of the opportunity and demonstrate that a market segment is being underserved. There will be an opportunity later to introduce your product and/or service.

exhibit

6-5   *Benjapon's Executive Summary*

1.1 The Opportunity
1)   Thai food is one of the fastest growing food trends in the U.S. and is rapidly moving into the mainstream[1].
2)   Americans are leading a busier lifestyle and thus rely more on meals outside the home. Restaurants account for 46% of total food dollars spent[2], up from 44.6% in 1990 and 26.3% in 1960[3]. By 2010, 53% of food dollars will be spent on away-from-home sources[4].
3)   Americans are demanding better quality food and are willing to pay for that quality. As a result, fast food establishments have recently added premium items to their menus. For example, Arby's has a line of "Market Fresh" items[5]; Carl's Jr. offers "The Six Dollar Burger."[6]

The fast casual segment emerged to meet the demands for better-quality foods at a slightly higher price than that of fast food. Despite the immense popularity of Asian food, and Thai food in particular, the fast casual segment is dominated by cafes/bakeries (Panera Bread, Au Bon Pain) and Mexican food restaurants (Chipotle Grill, Baja Fresh, Qdoba). In recent years, however, Asian fast casual players have begun to emerge in various regions in the U.S. Such players include Mama Fu's, Nothing but Noodles, and Pei Wei Asian Diner, but are still considered regional competitors.

Therefore, customers are limited in choices:
- Thai food patrons are currently limited to full-service restaurant options, requiring more time and money than fast food or fast casual options.
- Busy consumers are currently limited to hamburgers, sandwiches, pizzas, and Mexican food, when it comes to fast-serve options.

1.2 The Company
- Benjapon's is a fast-casual restaurant serving fresh Thai food, fast, at affordable prices, in a fun and friendly atmosphere. We will open two company locations, with future plans to grow through franchising.
- The restaurant will be counter-order and table-service with an average ticket price of $8.50. Store hours are from 11am–10pm, seven days a week. We expect 40% of our business to come from take-out orders.

[1]Packaged Facts, Marketresearch.com, 2003.
[2]"Restaurant Industry Report", The Freedonia Group, Inc., 2003.
[3]"Restaurant Industry Report", Standard and Poor's, 2003.
[4]National Restaurant Association.
[5]Arby's website: www.arbys.com.
[6]Carl's Jr. website: www.carlsjr.com.

- The company will offer Thai culture and food "information fun facts" on the menu, on the packaging, and as part of the restaurant décor to enhance the overall experience.
- Our target customers are urban, 18–35 year-old college students and young working professionals.
- The size of the restaurant will be approximately 1,500 square feet with 50 seats. The first location will be selected from one of the bustling neighborhood squares in the cities of Somerville or Cambridge, Massachusetts, due to proximity to the target market.

1.3 The Growth Plan

Our plan is to grow via franchising after opening two company-owned stores. We plan to first saturate the Greater Boston Area, and move towards national expansion via Area Development Agreements. According to our calculations, the city of Boston can support three to five stores, while the Greater Boston Area can support twenty stores.

1.4 The Team

Management Team:

Benjapon Jivasantikarn, Founder and Owner—Six years of experience in finance and business incentives at KPMG, a Big Four professional services firm. MBA, Magna Cum Laude, from Babson College. Douglass Foundation Graduate Business Plan Competition Finalist. Sorensen Award for Entrepreneurial and Academic Excellence.
Zack Noonprasith, General Manager—Six years experience in financial services. Five years experience in restaurant management.
Supranee Siriaphanot, Chef—Over 15 years experience as Thai restaurant owner and chef in the U.S.

Board of Advisors:

Rick Hagelstein—Lifelong successful entrepreneur. Founder and CEO of The Windham Group, a marketing, manufacturing, food, property and hotel development company in Thailand and Asia Pacific. The Minor Food Group is the Thai franchisee of Burger King, Swensen's, Dairy Queen, and Sizzler, and a franchisor of The Pizza Company, which owns 75% of the pizza market in Thailand.
Steve Sabre—Co-founder of a large franchise operation and expert in entrepreneurship.
Hull Martin—Former venture capitalist in the restaurant industry and current advisor to start-up ventures.

1.5 The Financials

We estimate an initial required investment of $550,000. The following are our summary financials for a five-year forecast period.

	Year 1	Year 2	Year 3	Year 4	Year 5
Summary Financials ($)					
# Company-Owned Stores	1	1	2	2	2
# Franchises Sold	—	—	—	3	13
# Franchises in Operation	—	—	—	—	3
Revenue	691,200	881,280	1,977,592	2,253,516	2,784,853
Gross Profit	451,080	601,749	1,380,195	1,595,422	2,059,897
Operating Profit	(110,145)	74,104	129,202	340,453	474,007
Oper. Profit before Depreciation	(72,526)	111,723	204,440	407,358	540,912
Net Earnings	(116,145)	68,104	90,257	198,512	280,084
Cash	137,284	249,977	211,881	862,845	1,202,743
Total Equity	299,321	367,425	457,683	1,056,195	1,336,279
Total Debt	50,000	50,000	90,000	80,000	60,000
Growth					
Revenue Growth Rate—CAGR:		28%	124%	14%	24%
Profitability					
Gross Profit %	65.3%	68.3%	69.8%	70.8%	74.0%
EBIT %	–15.9%	8.4%	6.5%	15.1%	17.0%
EBITDA %	–10.5%	12.7%	10.3%	18.1%	19.4%
Net Earnings %	–16.8%	7.7%	4.6%	8.8%	10.1%
Returns					
Return on Assets	–29.1%	14.1%	13.4%	15.5%	17.8%
Return on Equity	–38.8%	18.5%	19.7%	18.8%	21.0%
Return on Capital (LT Debt + Equity)	–33.2%	16.3%	16.5%	17.5%	20.1%

Next, describe your target customers in terms of demographics and psychological variables, such as their values, their attitudes, and even their fears. The more clearly you can identify your customer, the more likely it is that you will provide a product/service that is actually in demand. Finally, knowing what the customer looks like and wants serves as the basis for understanding who your competitors are. Analyze competitors in terms of product or service attributes that they are or are not providing.

COMPANY DESCRIPTION   This section gives a brief description of the firm. If the business is already in existence, its history is included. The company description informs the reader of the type of business being proposed, the firm's objectives, where the firm is located, and whether it will serve a local or international market. In many cases, legal issues—especially those concerning the firm's form of organization—are addressed in this section of the plan. (Legal issues regarding the form of organization are discussed at length in Chapter 8.) In writing this section, the entrepreneur should answer the following questions:

- When and where is the business to be started?
- What is the history of the company?
- What are the firm's objectives?
- What changes have been made in structure and/or ownership?
- In what stage of development is the firm—for example, seed stage or full product line?
- What has been achieved to date?
- What is the firm's distinctive competence?
- What are the basic nature and activity of the business?
- What is its primary product or service?
- What customers will be served?
- What is the firm's form of organization—sole proprietorship, partnership, limited liability company, or corporation?
- What are the current and projected economic states of the industry?
- Does the firm intend to sell to another company or an investment group, does it plan to be a publicly traded company, or do the owners want to transfer ownership to the next generation of the family?

product/service plan
A section of the business plan that describes the product and/or service to be provided and explains its merits

PRODUCT/SERVICE PLAN   The product/service plan describes the products and/or services to be offered to the firm's customers. Now is the time to make a convincing presentation of your competitive advantage. Based on your earlier description of the industry and the major players, explain how your product/service fills a gap in the market or how your product/service is "better, cheaper, and/or faster" than what is currently available. In the case of a physical product, try to provide a working model or prototype. Investors will naturally show the greatest interest in products that have been developed, tested, and found to be functional. Any innovative features should be identified and any patent protection explained. (Chapter 14 discusses this topic more fully.) Also, your growth strategy for the product/service should be explained in this section, as growth is a primary determinant of a firm's value. If relevant, describe secondary target markets the firm will pursue.

marketing plan
A section of the business plan that describes the user benefits of the product or service and the type of market that exists

MARKETING PLAN   The marketing plan describes how the firm will reach and service customers within a given market. In other words, how will you entice customers to make the change to your product/service and to continue using it? This section should present the marketing strategy, including the methods of identifying and attracting customers; pricing strategies, selling approach, type of sales force, distribution channels; types of sales promotions and advertising; and credit and pricing policies. Based on the foregoing strategies, sales forecasts will need to be developed. Finally, in terms of servicing the customer, this section should describe any warranties, as well as planned product updates. (Chapter 7 provides in-depth coverage of the marketing plan.)

OPERATIONS AND DEVELOPMENT PLAN   The **operations and development plan** offers information on how the product will be produced and/or the service provided. Here, you will explain how the operations will contribute to the firm's competitive advantage—that is, how operations will create value for the customer. This section discusses such items as location and facilities: how much space the business will need and what type of equipment it will require. In today's age, it is important to describe the choice between building and outsourcing in order to minimize costs. Remember, however, never to plan on outsourcing a part of operations that contributes to your competitive advantage. (These aspects of the operations and development plan are discussed at length in Chapter 9.) The operating plan should also explain the firm's proposed approach to assuring quality, controlling inventory, and using subcontractors or obtaining raw materials. (See Chapter 20 for further discussion of these issues.)

> **operations and development plan**
> A section of the business plan that offers information on how a product will be produced or a service provided, including descriptions of the new firm's facilities, labor, raw materials, and processing requirements

MANAGEMENT TEAM   Prospective investors look for well-managed companies. Of all the factors they consider, the quality of the **management team** is paramount; it may even be more important than the nature of the product/service. Investors frequently say that they would rather have an "A" management team and a "B" product or service than a "B" team and an "A" product. Unfortunately, an entrepreneur's ability to conceive an idea for a new venture is no guarantee of her or his managerial ability. The management team section, therefore, must detail the proposed firm's organizational structure and the backgrounds of those who will fill its key positions.

Ideally, a well-balanced management team—one that includes financial and marketing expertise as well as production experience and innovative talent—is in place. Managerial experience in related enterprises and in other startup situations is particularly valuable in the eyes of prospective investors. (The factors involved in preparing the management team section are discussed in detail in Chapter 8.)

> **management team**
> A section of the business plan that describes a new firm's organizational structure and the backgrounds of its key players

CRITICAL RISKS   The business plan is intended to tell a story of success, but there are always risks associated with starting a new venture. Thus, the plan would be incomplete if it did not identify the risks inherent in the venture. The **critical risks** section identifies the potential pitfalls that may be encountered by an investor. Frequent risks include a lack of market acceptance (customers don't buy the product as anticipated), competitor response, longer time and higher expenses than expected to start and grow the business, inadequate financing, and government regulations.

> **critical risks**
> A section of the business plan that identifies the potential risks that may be encountered by an investor

OFFERING   If the entrepreneur is seeking capital from investors, an **offering** should be included in the plan to indicate clearly how much money is needed and when. It is helpful to convey this information in a *sources and uses table* that indicates the type of financing being requested (debt or equity) and how the funds will be used. For example, for a firm needing $500,000, including the founder's investment, the sources and uses table for the first year might appear as follows:

> **offering**
> A section of the business plan that indicates to an investor how much money is needed and when, and how the money will be used

and Financial plan

Sources:	
Bank debt	$100,000
Equity:	
New investors	300,000
Founders	100,000
Total sources	$500,000

Uses:	
Product development	$125,000
Personnel costs	75,000
Working capital:	
Cash	20,000
Accounts receivable	100,000
Inventory	80,000
Machinery	100,000
Total uses	$500,000

If equity is being requested, the entrepreneur will need to decide how much ownership of the business she or he is willing to give up—not an easy task in most cases. Typically, the amount of money being raised should carry the firm for 12 to 18 months—enough time to reach some milestones. Then, if all goes well, it will be easier and less costly to raise more money later. (These issues will be discussed in greater detail in Chapters 10 and 11.)

financial plan
A section of the business plan that projects the company's financial position based on well-substantiated assumptions and explains how the figures have been determined

pro forma statements
Projections of a company's financial statements for up to five years, including balance sheets, income statements, and statements of cash flows, as well as cash budgets

FINANCIAL PLAN   The financial plan presents financial forecasts in the form of pro forma statements. In the words of Paul Gompers, a Harvard professor,

One of the major benefits of creating a business plan is that it forces entrepreneurs to confront their company's finances squarely. That's because a business plan isn't complete until entrepreneurs can demonstrate that all the wonderful plans concerning strategy, markets, products, and sales will actually come together to create a business that will be self-sustaining over the short term and profitable over the long term.[15]

Pro forma statements, which are projections of the company's financial statements, are presented for up to five years. The forecasts include balance sheets, income statements, and statements of cash flows on an annual basis for three to five years, as well as cash budgets on a monthly basis for the first year and on a quarterly basis for the second and third years. It is vital that the financial projections be supported by well-substantiated assumptions and explanations of how the figures have been determined.

While all the financial statements are important, statements of cash flows deserve special attention, because a business can be profitable but fail if it does not produce positive cash flows. A statement of cash flows identifies the sources of cash—how much will be generated from operations and how much will be raised from investors. It also shows how much money will be devoted to investments in such areas as inventories and equipment. The statement of cash flows should clearly indicate how much cash is needed from prospective investors and for what purpose. (The preparation of pro forma statements and the process of raising needed capital are discussed in Chapters 10 and 11. Chapter 12 presents ways that an investor—and the entrepreneur—can cash out, or exit, the business investment.)

APPENDIX OF SUPPORTING DOCUMENTS   The appendix should contain various supplementary materials and attachments to expand the reader's understanding of the plan. These supporting documents include any items referenced in the text of the business plan, such as the résumés of the key investors and owners/managers; photographs of products, facilities, and buildings; professional references; marketing research studies; pertinent published research; and signed contracts of sale.

The fact that it appears at the end of the plan does not mean that the appendix is of secondary importance. First, the reader needs to understand the assumptions underlying the premises set forth in the plan. Also, nothing is more important to a prospective investor than the qualifications of the management team. Thus, the presentation of the management team's résumés is no small matter, and each résumé should be carefully prepared.

Each chapter in this part of the book (Chapters 6 through 12) ends with a special set of exercises to take you through the process of writing a business plan. These exercise sets consist of questions to be thoughtfully considered and answered. They are entitled "The Business Plan: Laying the Foundation," because they deal with issues that are important to starting a new venture and provide guidelines for preparing the different sections of a business plan.

Making an Effective Written Presentation

4 Offer practical advice on writing a business plan.

When it comes to making an effective presentation, we should emphasize again that the quality of a business plan ultimately depends on the quality of the underlying business opportunity. We repeat, the plan is not the business. A poorly conceived new venture idea cannot be rescued by a good presentation. But, on the other hand, a good concept may be destroyed by a presentation that fails to communicate effectively.

Entrepreneurs tend to fall prey to a number of mistakes when preparing a business plan. It is absolutely essential that you avoid these mistakes if you want readers to give your business plan serious consideration. Below are recommendations that will help you avoid some of the common mistakes.[16]

INSIST ON CONFIDENTIALITY Prominently indicate that all information in the plan is proprietary and confidential. Number every copy of the plan, and account for each outstanding copy by requiring all recipients of the plan to acknowledge receipt in writing. When a startup is based on proprietary technology, be cautious about divulging certain information—the details of a technological design, for example, or the highly sensitive specifics of a marketing strategy—even to a prospective investor. But, while you should be cautious about releasing proprietary information, you should not be overly worried about someone taking your idea and "beating you to the punch." If that happens, it may suggest that you were the wrong person to start the business.

USE GOOD GRAMMAR Nothing turns off a reader faster than a poorly written business plan. Find a good editor, and then review, review, review.

LIMIT THE PRESENTATION TO A REASONABLE LENGTH The goal is not to write a long business plan, but to write a good business plan. People who read business plans appreciate brevity and view it as an indication of your ability to identify and describe in an organized way the important factors that will determine the success of your business. In all sections of your plan, especially the executive summary, get to the point quickly.

GO FOR AN ATTRACTIVE, PROFESSIONAL APPEARANCE To add interest and aid readers' comprehension, make liberal but effective use of visual aids, such as graphs, exhibits, and tabular summaries. The plan should be in a three-ring loose-leaf binder to facilitate future revisions, however—not bound like a book and printed on shiny paper with flashy images and graphs.

PROVIDE SOLID EVIDENCE FOR ANY CLAIMS Too often, entrepreneurs make broad statements without good, solid data to support them. Factual support must be supplied for any claims or assurances made. When promising to provide superior service or explaining the attractiveness of the market, for example, include strong supporting evidence. In short, the plan must be believable.

DESCRIBE THE PRODUCT IN LAY TERMS Present your product/service in simple, understandable terms, and avoid the temptation to use too much industry jargon. Answer the question "Why would anyone want to buy our product or service?"

EMPHASIZE THE QUALIFICATIONS OF THE MANAGEMENT TEAM Typically, investors first look at the management team—especially in terms of relevant experience—and only then assess the product/service. Without the right people in management, investors seldom will have an interest.

ANALYZE THE MARKET THOROUGHLY Everyone has competitors. Saying "We have no competition" is almost certain to make readers skeptical. You must show in your plan where your business will fit in the market and what your competitors' strengths and weaknesses are. If possible, include estimates of their market shares and profit levels.

INCLUDE FINANCIAL STATEMENTS THAT ARE NEITHER OVERLY DETAILED NOR INCOMPLETE Entrepreneurs tend to err either by providing incomplete financial statements or by including page after page of monotonous financial data. They also fall prey to being overly optimistic, even to the point of wishful thinking, which gives investors the impression that they have no idea what it takes to run a company. In terms of completeness, you should provide an exhaustive list of the assumptions that underlie the financial information. Most importantly, make sure that the numbers make sense.

DON'T HIDE WEAKNESSES—IDENTIFY POTENTIAL FATAL FLAWS One difficult aspect of writing a business plan is effectively dealing with problems or weaknesses—and every business has them. An entrepreneur, wanting to make a good impression, may become so infatuated with an opportunity that he or she cannot see potential fatal flaws.

For instance, an entrepreneur might fail to ask, "What is the possible impact of new technology, e-commerce, or changes in consumer demand on the proposed venture?" And ignoring or glossing over a negative issue when trying to raise capital can prove damaging, even fatal. If there are weaknesses in the plan, the investors will find them. At that point, an investor's question will be "What else haven't you told me?" The best way to properly handle weaknesses is to be open and straightforward and to have an action plan that effectively addresses the problem. To put it another way, *integrity matters.*

The guidelines above are designed to help you avoid features that are not acceptable to frequent readers of business plans. Otherwise, the plan will detract from the

Living the Dream   entrepreneurial challenges

© Aroma Kitchen & Winebar. Courtesy of Workhouse Publicity.

Dealing with Startup Change

Imagine you are building a sandwich restaurant, are knee-deep into construction, and suddenly you realize that you have to make a big change in your business plan in order to succeed.

That's exactly where husband-and-wife team Alexandra Degiorgio and Vito Polosa found themselves in mid-2004. Their original plan to open a sandwich bar in their New York City locale was abruptly stopped as continued market research revealed that their area's demographic wouldn't likely support such a restaurant. "[Locally], the median age was about 30, income was high, and the [residents] were highly educated," says Degiorgio. "There's a lot of competition to have something unique." Degiorgio, 39, and Polosa, 33, felt changing the plan midcourse was the right decision. Their solution was to create Aroma Kitchen & Winebar, a gourmet Italian restaurant, instead.

Watching for that wind of change is incredibly important to any startup. "Entrepreneurs need to understand what's happening in the market at large," says David Zahn, president of StartUpBuilder.com, a subscription-based website that connects startups with business experts.

If you discover a need to change something small or large about your business plan, don't panic. Give yourself more time to get started, like Degiorgio and Polosa, who delayed the grand opening in order to complete the construction of their full kitchen and dining room.

Notes Zahn, "[Some] entrepreneurs throw the baby out with the bath water and say, 'We have to chuck the whole idea.' Not necessarily. Reflect on the original [idea] that caused you to have passion for this enterprise. Perhaps with some modification, the basic premise [can be] very similar."

Degiorgio and Polosa's revised plan kept the idea of a small, intimate eatery, but changing their specialty enabled them to serve their elite clientele and bring in annual sales of nearly $700,000.

Remember that your business plan is a living thing—if you need to make a change, be agile enough to do it. Run through all the ifs, backups, contingencies and disaster scenarios you can. Says Zahn, "Don't become too wedded to your initial plan. Running a business is going to demand flexibility."

Source: Nichole L. Torres, "Dealing with Startup Change," *Entrepreneur,* Vol. 34, No. 10 (October 2006), http://www.entrepreneur.com/startingabusiness/startupbasics/article167848.html, accessed February 15, 2007.

http://www.aromanyc.com

opportunity itself, and you may lose the chance to capture a good opportunity. Ideally, have experienced entrepreneurs give their perspectives on the business concept and the effectiveness of the business plan presentation. They know the minefields to avoid.

Presenting the Business Plan to Investors

5 Explain what investors look for in a business plan.

Many small firms do not seek outside capital, except in the form of small loans. But where there is a substantial need for outside capital, both investors and lenders use the business plan to understand the new venture, the type of product or service it will offer, the nature of the market, and the qualifications of the entrepreneur and the management team. In today's world, a sophisticated investor will rarely consider investing in a new business before he or she has reviewed a properly prepared business plan.

The significance of the business plan in dealing with investors is aptly expressed by Mark Stevens, an advisor to small businesses:

> *If you are inclined to view the business plan as just another piece of useless paperwork, it's time for an attitude change. When you are starting out, investors will justifiably want to know a lot about you and your qualifications for running a business and will want to see a step-by-step plan for how you intend to make it a success.* [17]

If you are preparing a business plan in order to seek significant outside capital, you must understand the investor's basic perspective and see the world as the investor sees it—that is, you must think as the investor thinks. However, most entrepreneurs perceive a new venture very differently than an investor does. The entrepreneur characteristically focuses on the positive potential of the startup—what will happen if everything goes right. The prospective investor, on the other hand, plays the role of the skeptic, thinking more about what could go wrong. One investor in small firms, Daniel Lubin, admits, "The first thing I look for is a lie or bad information—a reason to throw it out." [18] An entrepreneur's failure to appreciate this difference in perspectives almost ensures rejection by investors.

At the most basic level, a prospective investor has a single goal: to maximize potential return on an investment through cash flows that will be received, while minimizing risk exposure. Even investors in startups, such as venture capitalists, who are thought to be risk takers, want to minimize their risk. Like any informed investor, they look for ways to shift risk to others, usually to the entrepreneur.

Given the fundamentally different perspectives of the investor and the entrepreneur, the important question becomes "How do I write a business plan that will capture a prospective investor's interest?" There is no easy answer, but two facts are relevant: Investors have a short attention span, and certain features attract investors, while others repel them.

The Investor's Short Attention Span

Kenneth Blanchard and Spencer Johnson wrote a popular book about being a one-minute manager—a manager who practices principles that can be applied quickly and produce great results. [19] Investors in startup and early-stage companies are, in a sense, one-minute investors. Because they receive many business plans, they cannot read them all in any detailed fashion. Tim Smith, a former officer of the Capital Southwest Corporation, a Dallas-based venture capital firm, observed, "We receive some 300 or more plans per year but invest only in three or four firms in any given year. Thus, we simply do not have the luxury to analyze each opportunity thoroughly." [20] At the annual Rice University business plan competition in Houston, Texas, competing teams from different universities have only 15 minutes to present their business venture. In the 2007 competition, the winner walked away with $175,000. Not bad for a 15-minute presentation! Of course, there is more involved than just the presentation, but the point is that you should be able to present your concept concisely and effectively.

An example of an investor's short attention span was witnessed by one of the authors when he delivered an entrepreneur's business plan to a prospective investor with whom he had a personal relationship. The plan was well written, clearly identifying a need. While the investor was courteous and listened carefully, he made a decision not to consider the opportunity in a matter of five minutes. A quick read of the executive summary did not spark his interest, and the discussion quickly changed to other matters. We may be overstating the case when we refer to investors in startups and early-stage firms as one-minute investors, but even five minutes is not much time to work with.

Business Plan Features That Attract or Repel Investors

In order to raise capital from outside investors, the business plan must speak the investors' language. The entrepreneur must know what is important and what is not important to investors and how to present the business idea or concept in a way that is meaningful

exhibit

6-6   *A Glossary of Business Plan Terms*

What They Say . . .	**. . . and What They Really Mean**
We conservatively project . . .	We read a book that said we had to be a $50 million company in five years, and we reverse-engineered the numbers.
We took our best guess and divided by 2.	We accidentally divided by 0.5.
We project a 10% margin.	We did not modify any of the assumptions in the business plan template that we downloaded from the Internet.
The project is 98% complete.	To complete the remaining 2% will take as long as it took to create the initial 98% but will cost twice as much.
Our business model is proven . . .	if you take the evidence from the past week for the best of our 50 locations and extrapolate it for all the others.
We have a six-month lead.	We tried not to find out how many other people have a six-month lead.
We only need a 10% market share.	So do the other 50 entrants getting funded.
Customers are clamoring for our product.	We have not yet asked them to pay for it. Also, all of our current customers are relatives.
We are the low-cost producer.	We have not produced anything yet, but we are confident that we will be able to.
We have no competition.	Only IBM, Microsoft, Netscape, and Sun have announced plans to enter the business.
Our management team has a great deal of experience . . .	consuming the product or service.
A select group of investors is considering the plan.	We mailed a copy of the plan to everyone in Pratt's Guide.
We seek a value-added investor.	We are looking for a passive, dumb-as-rocks investor.
If you invest on our terms, you will earn a 68% rate of return.	If everything that could ever conceivably go right does go right, you might get your money back.

Source: William A. Sahlman, "How to Write a Great Business Plan," *Harvard Business Review,* July-August 1997, p. 106.

to them. Otherwise, the entrepreneur will immediately lose credibility—and a potential source of financing.

For one thing, investors are more *market-oriented* than *product-oriented,* realizing that most patented inventions never earn a dime for the inventors. The essence of the entrepreneurial process is to identify new products or services that meet an identifiable customer need. Thus, it is essential for the entrepreneur to appreciate investors' concerns about the target customers' response to a new product or service.

Like any readers of a business plan, investors require that the plan be credible. On several occasions, the authors have had the opportunity to watch entrepreneurs present business plans to prospective investors. More than once, an entrepreneur has presented financial projections that were extremely optimistic—beyond being believable. The opportunity would still have been attractive with more conservative projections. But instead of adjusting the forecasts to make them more credible to the investors, the entrepreneur continued to argue that the numbers were already "conservative." It's no surprise that investors declined to invest in these deals.

Bill Sahlman at the Harvard Business School has seen a lot of business plans in his time and has heard most of the "lines" used by entrepreneurs when presenting to investors. With tongue only a little in cheek, Sahlman tells how investors interpret an entrepreneur's language in his "Glossary of Business Plan Terms" (see Exhibit 6-6). In writing and presenting a business plan, you may want to keep in mind how skeptical your audience is likely to be. As Sahlman illustrates, a presentation that is not believable to investors is a deal killer.

Investors are quickly disillusioned by plans that contain page after page of detailed computer-generated financial projections, suggesting—intentionally or unintentionally—that the entrepreneur can predict with great accuracy what will happen. The experienced investor knows this isn't the case.

Finally, it should be understood that the business plan is not a legal document for actually raising needed capital. When it comes time to solicit investment, a **prospectus**, or **offering memorandum**, must be used. This document contains all the information necessary to satisfy federal and state requirements for warning potential investors about the possible risks of the investment. But because the prospectus alone is not an effective marketing document with which to sell a concept, an entrepreneur must first use the business plan to create interest in the startup. He or she should then follow up with a formal offering memorandum to those investors who seem genuinely interested.

prospectus (offering memorandum)
A document that contains all the information necessary to satisfy federal and state requirements for warning potential investors about the possible risks of the investment

Resources for Business Plan Preparation

When writing a business plan, it is important to know what works and what does not work. There are many books, websites, and computer software packages that you can use to guide you step by step through the preparation of a business plan. [21] (A listing of some of these resources appears at the end of this chapter.) Such resources can be invaluable. In general, however, you should resist the temptation to adapt an existing business plan for your own use. Changing the numbers and some of the verbiage of another firm's business plan is simply not effective.

6 Identify available sources of assistance in preparing a business plan.

Computer-Aided Business Planning

The use of a computer greatly facilitates preparation of a business plan. Its word-processing capabilities, for example, can speed up the writing of the narrative sections of the report. Computer spreadsheets are likewise helpful for preparing the financial statements needed in the plan.

A number of business plan software packages have been designed to help an entrepreneur think through the important issues in starting a new company and organize his or her thoughts to create an effective presentation. However, these software packages are not capable of producing a unique plan and thus may limit an entrepreneur's creativity and flexibility. Remember, there is no simple procedure for writing a business plan—no "formula for success"—despite what software advertisements may claim. If you recognize their limitations, however, you can use business plan software packages to facilitate the process.

Professional Assistance in Business Planning

As already discussed, company founders are most notably doers—and evidence suggests that they had better be, if the venture is to be successful. But most entrepreneurs lack the breadth of experience and know-how, as well as the inclination, needed for planning.

An entrepreneur who is not able to answer the tough questions about the business may need a business planning advisor—someone accustomed to working with small companies, startups, and owners who lack financial management experience. Such advisors include accountants, marketing specialists, attorneys (preferably with an entrepreneurial mindset), incubator organizations, small business development corporations (SBDCs), and regional and local economic development offices.

An investment banker or financial intermediary can draw up a business plan as part of a firm's overall fundraising efforts. However, as explained by Jill Andresky Fraser, "His strategy will cost you—you may pay an hourly fee as well as a contingency percentage based on the amount raised or even an equity stake. However, a well-chosen intermediary will have contacts you lack, and may even help you reformulate your business plan entirely."[22]

The Small Business Administration (SBA) and the Service Corps of Retired Executives (SCORE) can also be helpful. Both organizations have programs to introduce business owners to volunteer experts who will advise them.

Another source of assistance is the FastTrac Entrepreneurial Training Program sponsored by the Kauffman Center for Entrepreneurial Leadership in Kansas City, Missouri. Located in universities, chambers of commerce, and SBDCs across the country, the FastTrac program teaches the basics of product development, concept recognition, financing strategies, and marketing research, while helping entrepreneurs create a written business plan in small, well-organized increments.

Securing help in business plan preparation does not relieve the entrepreneur of the responsibility for being the primary planner. Her or his ideas remain essential to producing a plan that is realistic and believable.

Keeping the Right Perspective

7 Maintain the proper perspective when writing a business plan.

To summarize, we contend that the business plan has an important place in starting and growing a business. As suggested in the chapter, writing an effective plan is important both for internal purposes and for telling the firm's story to outsiders who can contribute to the firm's success. But good judgment should be used in deciding if and how much to plan, given the circumstances. No single answer can be applied to all situations. Furthermore, it is important to avoid the misconception, held by too many entrepreneurs, that a good business plan will ensure success. The business plan, no matter how beneficial, is not the business. Building

---

How They See It: Stay Focused

Winston Wolfe

If someone asked me what I felt is the single most important personality trait for an entrepreneur, I would say it's the ability to stay focused.

First of all, you must stay focused on the goals you have for your company. Don't lose sight of the vision you have in your business plan. Keep in mind that you can't be everything to everybody. If you try, you'll likely end up being nothing to everybody.

I have always been amazed at how easy it is for the original focus of a meeting to go astray. If you are meeting with three or four of your key employees, keep the focus of the discussion going in the proper direction. Solve the problem, and don't get distracted. And, in the process, you'll teach your employees the value of staying focused.

Being intense and focused will not only help you solve problems—it will make you a more effective leader.

a good business involves much more. A good business plan leads to a successful company only when it is effectively executed by the entrepreneur and the management team.

Writing a business plan should be thought of as an ongoing process and not as the means to an end. In fact, when it comes to writing a plan, the process is just as important as the final outcome, which some entrepreneurs have difficulty accepting, given their orientation to "bottom line" results. But this point deserves to be repeated: *Writing a business plan is primarily an ongoing process and only secondarily the means to an outcome. The process is just as important as—if not more so than—the finished product.*

While your plan will represent your vision and goals for the firm, it will rarely reflect what actually happens. With a startup, too many unexpected events can affect the final outcome. Thus, a business plan is in large part an opportunity for an entrepreneur and management team to think about the potential key drivers of a venture's success or failure. Anticipating different scenarios and the ensuing consequences can significantly enhance an entrepreneur's adaptability—an essential quality for an entrepreneur, when so much is uncertain.

Now that you are aware of the role of the business plan in a new venture, you are ready for Chapters 7 through 12, which will closely examine each of the plan's components.

 ## Looking BACK

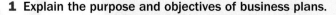

1 Explain the purpose and objectives of business plans.

- A business plan is a document that sets out the basic idea underlying a business and describes related startup considerations. It should describe where the entrepreneur is presently, indicate where she or he wants to go, and outline how she or he proposes to get there.

- A business plan has three basic objectives: (1) to identify the nature and the context of a business opportunity, (2) to present the approach the entrepreneur plans to take to exploit the opportunity, and (3) to recognize factors that will determine whether the venture will be successful.

2 Give the rationale for writing (or not writing) a business plan when starting a new venture.

- Studies attempting to test whether entrepreneurs who have business plans do better than those who don't have produced mixed results. Some findings suggest a relationship; others do not.

- What ultimately matters is not writing a plan, but implementing it. The goal is to execute the plan.

- An entrepreneur must find the right balance between planning and adaptability.

- The benefits of a business plan depend on the individual circumstances surrounding a startup.

- Most entrepreneurs need the discipline that comes with writing a business plan. A written plan helps to ensure systematic, complete coverage of the important factors to be considered in starting a new business.

- A business plan helps an entrepreneur communicate his or her vision to current—and prospective—employees of the firm.

- By enhancing the firm's credibility, a business plan serves as an effective selling tool with prospective customers and suppliers, as well as investors.

- A dehydrated plan is a short form of a business plan that presents only the most important issues and projections for the business.

- A comprehensive plan is beneficial when (1) describing a new opportunity (startup), (2) facing significant change in the business or the external environment (changing demographics, new legislation, or developing industry trends), or (3) explaining a complex business situation.

3 Describe the preferred content and format for a business plan.

- The entrepreneurial team, the opportunity, the resources, the financing structure, and the "big picture" are all interdependent factors that should be given consideration when thinking about the content of a business plan.

- Key sections of a business plan are the (1) cover page, (2) table of contents, (3) executive summary, (4) industry, target customer, and competitor analysis, (5) company description, (6) product/service plan, (7) marketing plan, (8) operations and development plan, (9) management team, (10) critical risks, (11) offering, (12) financial plan, and (13) appendix of supporting documents.

4 Offer practical advice on writing a business plan.

- Insist on confidentiality.
- Use good grammar.
- Keep the presentation to a reasonable length.
- Go for an attractive, professional appearance.
- Provide solid evidence for any claims.
- Describe the product in lay terms.
- Emphasize the quality of the management team.
- Analyze the market thoroughly.
- Include financial statements that are neither overly detailed nor incomplete.
- Don't hide weaknesses; try to identify potential fatal flaws.

5 Explain what investors look for in a business plan.

- When writing the business plan, remember that (1) investors have a short attention span and (2) certain features appeal to investors, while others are distinctly unappealing.
- In seeking financing, an entrepreneur must first use the business plan to create interest in the startup and then follow up with a formal offering memorandum to solicit investment from those investors who seem genuinely interested.

6 Identify available sources of assistance in preparing a business plan.

- A variety of books, websites, and computer software packages are available to assist in the preparation of a business plan.
- Professionals with planning expertise, such as attorneys, accountants, and marketing specialists, can provide useful suggestions and assistance in the preparation of a business plan.
- The Small Business Administration (SBA), the Service Corps of Retired Executives (SCORE), and the FastTrac Entrepreneurial Training Program can also be helpful.

7 Maintain the proper perspective when writing a business plan.

- Despite the potential benefits of a well-drafted plan, good judgment should be used in deciding how much to plan in view of the specific circumstances.
- The business plan, no matter how beneficial, is not the business. A good business plan leads to a successful company only when it is effectively executed by the entrepreneur and the management team.
- A business plan can be viewed as an opportunity for the entrepreneur and the management team to think about the potential key drivers of a venture's success or failure.

Key TERMS

business plan, p. 151
dehydrated plan, p. 155
comprehensive plan, p. 155
executive summary, p. 157
product/service plan, p. 162

marketing plan, p. 162
operations and development plan, p. 163
management team, p. 163
critical risks, p. 163

offering, p. 163
financial plan, p. 164
pro forma statements, p. 164
prospectus (offering memorandum), p. 169

Discussion QUESTIONS

1. Describe what entrepreneurs mean when they talk about a business plan.

2. When should you write a business plan? When might it not be necessary or even advisable to write a plan?

3. Explain the two types of business plans. In what situation(s) would you use each type of plan?

4. How might a business plan be helpful to individuals outside the firm?

5. Why is the executive summary so important?

6. How might an entrepreneur's perspective differ from that of an investor in terms of the business plan?

7. Describe the major sections to be included in a business plan.

8. If the income statement of a financial plan shows that the business will be profitable, why is there a need for a statement of cash flows?

9. Describe common mistakes that entrepreneurs make in writing a business plan.

10. Discuss whether a sophisticated investor would really make a decision based on a five-minute review of a business plan.

11. Investors are said to be more market-oriented than product-oriented. What does this mean? What is the logic behind this orientation?

12. What advantages are realized by using a computer in preparing the narrative sections of a business plan? In preparing the financial plan?

You Make the CALL

SITUATION 1

When they created Round Table Group (RTG) Inc., Russ Rosenstein and Robert Hull envisioned a company offering one-stop shopping for intellectual expertise. They wanted to help businesspeople, management consultants, and litigation attorneys get answers to important questions from top-notch thinkers anywhere in the world through the Internet.

RTG's plan was to have a kind of SWAT team of professors who would answer questions based on their expertise. A team might consist of one or two professors, who would communicate with the client via e-mail, phone, or videoconferencing on projects that might involve a few hours or a few weeks of input. In the traditional management-consulting model, work on a project often lasts as long as a couple of years, and the team consists of a group of junior analysts, managers, and partners.

RTG assembled a database made up mainly of 3,000 university professors available to consult on an as-needed basis. The firm's fixed costs would be low because the professors would be paid only when they did billable work. But an unexpected wrinkle soon emerged. RTG's customers wanted RTG to start acting more like a traditional consulting firm. Business executives wanted face-to-face contact with the professors giving the information. They also wanted number crunching and follow-up analysis. And they wanted current, customized research.

That has left RTG at a crossroads. Should it try to become a more traditional management-consulting firm or continue to pursue its original mission of providing advice through Internet content and virtual links?

Taking the first path would mean providing support to clients, adding infrastructure and formalizing its operation by dividing it into distinct specialties. That would have the downside of making RTG's competitive point of differentiation murky. But the second path would risk putting off clients who say they want more.

Source: Elena De Lisser, "A Plan May Look Good, but Watch Out for the Real World," Startup Journal, August 24, 1999, *The Wall Street Journal Online,* http://www.startupjournal.com/howto/management/199908240948-lisser.html, accessed January 15, 2007.

Question 1 What is the basic problem that Rosenstein and Hull need to resolve?

Question 2 What are the advantages and disadvantages of the proposed online consulting and the traditional approach to consulting?

Question 3 What do you think Rosenstein and Hull should do?

SITUATION 2

A young journalist is contemplating launching a new magazine that will feature wildlife, plant life, and nature around the world. The prospective entrepreneur intends for each issue to contain several feature articles—about the dangers and benefits of forest fires, the features of Rocky Mountain National Park, wildflowers found at high altitudes, and the danger of acid rain, for example. The magazine will make extensive use of color photographs, and its articles will be technically accurate and interestingly written. Unlike *National Geographic,* the proposed publication will avoid articles dealing with the general culture and confine itself to topics closely related to the natural world. Suppose you are a prospective investor examining a business plan prepared by this journalist.

Question 1 What are the most urgent questions you would want the marketing plan to answer?

Question 2 What details would you look for in the management plan?

Question 3 Do you think this entrepreneur would need to raise closer to $1 million or $10 million in startup capital? Why?

Question 4 At first glance, would you consider the opportunity potentially attractive? Why or why not?

SITUATION 3

John Martin and John Rose decided to start a new business to manufacture noncarbonated soft drinks. They believed that their location in East Texas, close to high-quality water, would give them a competitive edge. Although Martin and Rose had never worked together, Martin had 17 years of experience in the soft drink industry. Rose had recently sold his firm and had funds to help finance the venture; however, the partners needed to raise additional money from outside investors. Both men were excited about the opportunity and spent almost 18 months developing their business plan. The first paragraph of their executive summary reflected their excitement:

> The "New Age" beverage market is the result of a spectacular boom in demand for drinks with nutritional value from environmentally safe ingredients and waters that come from deep, clear springs free of chemicals and pollutants. Argon Beverage Corporation will produce and market a full line of sparkling fruit drinks, flavored waters, and sports drinks that are of the highest quality and purity. These drinks have the same delicious taste appeal as soft drinks while using the most healthful fruit juices, natural sugars, and the purest spring water, the hallmark of the "New Age" drink market.

With the help of a well-developed plan, the two men were successful in raising the necessary capital to begin their business. They leased facilities and started production. However, after almost two years, the plan's goals were not being met. There were cost overruns, and profits were not nearly up to expectations.

Question 1 What problems might have contributed to the firm's poor performance?

Question 2 Although several problems were encountered in implementing the business plan, the primary reason for the low profits turned out to be embezzlement. Martin was diverting company resources for personal use, even using some of the construction materials purchased by the company to build his own house. What could Rose have done to avoid this situation? What are his options after the fact?

Experiential EXERCISES

1. Appendix A provides the complete business plan for Benjapon's, a Thai restaurant in Boston. Based on your reading of this chapter, write a one-page report on what you like about the plan and what you do not like.

2. A former chef wants to start a business to supply temporary kitchen help (such as chefs, sauce cooks, bakers, and meat cutters) to restaurants in need of staff during busy periods. Prepare a one-page report explaining which section or sections of the business plan would be most crucial to this new business and why.

3. Suppose that you wish to start a tutoring service for college students in elementary accounting courses. List the benefits you would realize from preparing a written business plan.

4. Interview a person who has started a business within the past five years. Prepare a report describing the extent to which the entrepreneur engaged in preliminary planning and his or her views about the value of business plans.

Exploring the WEB

1. As you might imagine, the Web is full of resources that can help you develop a business plan. One such business plan site is the Entrepreneur's Center at The Beehive.

   a. Go to The Beehive website at **http://www.thebeehive.org** and click on "Starting and Owning a Business" to get to the Entrepreneur's center. Then click on "Start Your Business," and follow the "Build a Business Plan" link. Before you can create a mini-plan, you'll need to register (it's free).

   b. Create a plan, print it out, and evaluate it.

2. This chapter highlights several organizations—SBDC, SBA, and SCORE—that can be extremely helpful during the planning phase of starting your own business.

a. At The Beehive's Entrepreneur's Center, follow the link to locate the offices of these organizations and others in your area that might be helpful to you.

b. Many of these local organizations have their own websites that provide details on the services, workshops, and opportunities they

sponsor. Check out several of these sites. Which interest you most? Briefly explain why.

3. Many software packages designed to assist in the writing of a business plan can be demo'd online. Use the Web to try out two different software applications. Which do you prefer? Why?

Case 6

Adgrove.com, Inc. (p. 630)
This case presents the executive summary of a business plan.

Alternative Cases for Chapter 6:

Case 7, eHarmony, p. 633

Case 8, Silver Zephyr Restaurant, p. 635

The Business Plan

Laying the Foundation

Part 3 (Chapters 6 through 12) deals with issues that are important in starting a new venture. This chapter presented an overview of the business plan and its preparation. Chapters 7 through 12 focus on major segments of the business plan, such as the marketing plan, the organizational and development plan, the location plan, the financial plan, and the exit plan. After you have carefully studied these chapters, you will have the knowledge you need to prepare a business plan.

Since applying what you study facilitates learning, we have included, at the end of each chapter in Part 3, a list of important questions that need to be addressed in preparing a particular segment of a business plan. In this chapter, we also include lists of books, websites, and software packages useful for preparing business plans.

Company Description Questions

Now that you have learned the main concepts of business plan preparation, you can begin the process of creating a business plan by writing a general company description. In thinking about the key issues in starting a new business, respond to the following questions:

1. When and where is the business to start?
2. What is the history of the company?
3. What are the company's objectives?
4. What changes have been made in structure and/or ownership?
5. In what stage of development is the company?
6. What has been achieved to date?
7. What is the company's distinctive competence?
8. What are the basic nature and activity of the business?
9. What is its primary product or service?
10. What customers will be served?
11. What is the company's form of organization?
12. What are the current and projected economic states of the industry?
13. Does the company intend to become a publicly traded company or an acquisition candidate, or do the owners want to transfer ownership to the next generation of the family?

Books on Preparing Business Plans

Abrams, Rhonda M. M., *Successful Business Plan: Secrets and Strategies* (Atlanta, GA: Rhonda, Inc., 2003).

Bangs, David H., *Business Plans Made Easy,* 3rd ed. (*Entrepreneur Made Easy* Series, 2005).

Bangs, David H., *The Business Planning Guide: Creating a Winning Plan for Success,* 9th ed. (New York: Kaplan Professional Company, 2002).

Burke, Franklin, Jill E. Kapron, and JIAN Tools for Sale, Inc., *BizPlanBuilder Express: A Guide to Creating a Business Plan with BizPlanBuilder,* 2nd ed. (Mason, OH: South-Western, 2007).

Bygrave, William D., and Andrew Zacharakis (eds.), *The Portable MBA in Entrepreneurship,* 3rd ed. (New York: John Wiley & Sons, 2003).

Deloitte & Touche, LLP, *Writing an Effective Business Plan* (New York: Author, 2003).

Gumpert, David E., *How to Really Create a Successful Business Plan,* 4th ed. (Needham, MA: Lauson Publishing, 2003).

Harvard Business Review, *Harvard Business Review on Entrepreneurship* (Boston: Harvard Business Review Press, 1999).

Henricks, Mark, *Business Plans Made Easy* (Newburgh, NY: Entrepreneur Press, 1999).

Kawasaki, Guy, *The Art of the Start: The Time-Tested, Battle-Hardened Guide for Anyone Starting Anything* (New York: Portfolio, 2004).

King, Jan B., *Business Plans to Game Plans: A Practical System for Turning Strategies into Action,* rev. ed. (Hoboken, NJ: John Wiley & Sons, 2004).

Mancuso, Joseph R., *How to Write a Winning Business Plan* (New York: Simon & Schuster, 2006).

Patsula, Peter J., and William Nowik (eds.), *Successful Business Planning in 30 Days: A Step-by-Step Guide for Writing a Business Plan and Starting Your Own Business,* 2nd ed. (Singapore: Patsula Media, 2002).

Peterson, Steven D., and Peter E. Jaret, *Business Plans Kit for Dummies* (Indianapolis, IN: For Dummies, 2005).

Pinson, Linda, *Anatomy of a Business Plan: A Step-by-Step Guide to Building a Business and Securing Your Company's Future* (Chicago: Enterprise/Dearborn, 2004.)

Pinson, Linda, and Jerry Jinnett, *Anatomy of a Business Plan,* 5th ed. (Chicago: Enterprise/Dearborn, 2001).

Rich, Stanley R., and David E. Gumpert, *Business Plans That Win $$$: Lessons from the MIT Enterprise Forum* (New York: HarperCollins, 1987).

Rogoff, Edward, *Bankable Business Plans* (Mason, OH: South-Western, 2003).

Sutton, Garrett, and Robert T. Kiyosaki, *The ABC's of Writing Winning Business Plans: How to Prepare a Business Plan That Others Will Want to Read—and Invest In* (New York: Rich Dad's Advisors, 2005).

Tiffany, Paul, and Steven Peterson, *Business Plans for Dummies,* 2nd ed. (Indianapolis, IN: For Dummies, 2004).

Timmons, Jeffrey A., Andrew Zacharakis, and Stephen Spinelli, *Business Plans That Work* (New York: McGraw Hill, 2004).

Tooch, David, *Building a Business Plan,* 2nd ed. (Upper Saddle River, NJ: Prentice Hall, 2004).

Articles on Preparing Business Plans

Delmar, Frederic, and Scott Shane, "Does Business Planning Facilitate the Development of New Ventures?," *Strategic Management Journal,* December 2003, pp. 1165–1185.

Hormozi, Amir M., et al., "Business Plans for New or Small Businesses: Paving the Way to Success," *Management Decision,* Vol. 40, Nos. 7 and 8 (2002), pp. 755–763.

Karlsson, Thomas, Benson Honig, and Wilfrid Laurrier, "Business Planning Practices in New Ventures: An Institutional Perspective," paper presented at the Babson Conference, April 2007.

Lange, Julian E., et al., "Pre-Startup Formal Business Plans and Post-Startup Performance: A Study of 116 New Ventures," forthcoming in *Venture Capital Journal.*

Perry, Stephen C., "The Relationship Between Written Business Plans and the Failure of Small Business in the U.S.," *Journal of Small Business Management,* Vol. 39, No. 2 (2001), pp. 201–208.

Rich, Stanley R., and David E. Gumpert, "How to Write a Winning Business Plan," *Harvard Business Review,* Vol. 63, No. 3 (May-June 1985), pp. 156–166.

Sahlman, William A., "How to Write a Great Business Plan," *Harvard Business Review,* Vol. 75, No. 4 (July-August 1997), pp. 114–121.

Schilit, W. K., "How to Write a Winning Business Plan," *Business Horizons,* Vol. 30, No. 5 (1987), pp. 13–22.

Shane, Scott, and Frederick Delmar, "Planning for the Market: Business Planning Before Marketing and the Continuation of Organizing Efforts," *Journal of Business Venturing,* Vol. 19 (2004), pp. 767–785.

Online Resources for Preparing Business Plans

BPlans.com, Inc., *BPlans.com: The Business Planning Experts,* http://www.bplans.com. Designed for self-preparers by PaloAlto Software; provides advice, sample plans, and links to many consultants.

Business Confidant, Inc., *Business Confidant: Your Business Planning Specialist,* http://businessconfidant.com. Provides strategic thinking, technical writing, and financial analytical skills needed to produce professional, investor-ready business plans.

Business PlanWare, *Business Plan Software,* http://www.planware.org. Features financial projection and cash flow forecasting software, business plan freeware, white papers, and other tools and resources; based in Ireland.

Business Tools and Advice, *Business Week,* http://allbusiness.businessweek.com/3473091-1.html#2976247. Provides guidelines and examples for writing business plans.

Dow Jones & Company, *Startup Journal: The Wall Street Journal Center for Entrepreneurs,* http://www.startupjournal.com. Features a miniplan business assumptions test, sample business plans, and calculators for startup costs and cash flow, as well as articles on starting a business.

Entrepreneur.com, Inc., *Entrepreneur.com: Solutions for Growing Businesses,* http://www.entrepreneur.com. Has a site search engine through which you can find articles and tips by entering keywords such as *business plan writing*.

Good-to-Go Business Plans Inc., *Good-to-Go Business Plans: Plans for Every Business,* http://www.goodtogobusinessplans.com. Provides a range of services, including business-specific templates in predrafted language and other tools and forms.

One Economy Corporation, *Entrepreneur's Center,* http://www.thebeehive.org. Serves as a clearinghouse for weblinks to business-planning articles.

Small Business Administration, *Small Business Administration: Your Small Business Resource,* http://www.sba.gov. The federal government's online business planning and finance resource center classroom and library.

SmartOnline, http://smallbusiness.smartonline.com. Builds a business plan around simple questions posed to the user one by one, with explanations and examples; uses a wizard-driven approach; also integrates forms for incorporation and loan applications from the Small Business Administration.

The Small Business Administration funds programs designed to help entrepreneurs. One of these programs, the Service Corps of Retired Executives (SCORE), has a gallery of detailed downloadable templates for business plans and financial statements on its website (http://www.score.org), under "business toolbox."

Bank websites are another source for business-planning tools and advice. For example, Bank of America has a downloadable outline and business-planning guide at http://www.bankofamerica.com/smallbusiness/resourcecenter/index.cfm?template=rc_startingyourbusiness&context=rc_businessplan

Software for Preparing Business Plans

JIAN, Inc., *BizPlan*Builder *2007,* http://www.jian.com. A suite of business planning software and other business tools.

PaloAlto Software, *Business Plan Pro 2007,* http://www.paloalto.com. Business plan–creating software featuring over 400 sample business plans.

Smart Online, Inc., *Smart Business Plan Deluxe,* http://www.smartonline.com. Software suite that features the "Smart Wizard," which guides users through the creation of a tailored business plan; includes a "Financial Advisor," which helps to find ways to fund businesses.

## chapter 7

The Marketing Plan

In the **VIDEO SPOTLIGHT**

eHarmony
http://www.eharmony.com

When Dr. Neil Clark Warren wrote *Finding the Love of Your Life* in 1993, it was a resounding success. He was invited to appear on numerous talk shows, including *Oprah*. After two years of speaking engagements, he joined with Greg Forgatch to launch a company to offer seminars based on the book. It was Forgatch who convinced Clark Warren to use his decades of research on marital relationships as the foundation for an Internet-based dating service. In August 2000, eHarmony was born.

Today, eHarmony is one of the best-known Internet-based companies in any industry. How the company grew to become a multibillion-dollar enterprise in a few short years is a testament to its marketing plan. Not only did the founders and management have a good understanding of the external environment in which they were trying to launch this new venture, but they also understood their target market and the unique benefits eHarmony could provide the people in that market. As a result, eHarmony was able to create a meaningful marketing mix, with a core product that is more than just a dating service. The company uses a 436-question survey and a set of complex mathematical formulas to create a personality profile based on a client's core values and disposition. What this means is that the criteria used for matchmaking are no longer arbitrary and superficial (e.g., a friend of a friend has a single friend who would be "great" for you, or "if you like running, you'll like this guy"). That distinction shows that eHarmony's customer orientation is driving the company's multibillion-dollar success.

Video material provided by Hattie Bryant, Producer of Small Business School, the series on PBS Stations, Worldnet, and the Web at http://www.smallbusinessschool.org.

SmallBusinessSchool
the Series on PBS stations and the Web

Looking **AHEAD**

After studying this chapter, you should be able to

1 Describe small business marketing.
2 Identify the components of a formal marketing plan.
3 Discuss the nature of the marketing research process.
4 Define market segmentation and its related strategies.
5 Explain the different methods of forecasting sales.

Unfortunately, some entrepreneurs ignore marketing in the early stages of planning new ventures. They concentrate on the cart and neglect the horse—emphasizing the idea behind the product or service while overlooking the marketing activities that will carry the idea to customers. Consider the following conversation between an aspiring entrepreneur and a marketing consultant:

> *Marketing Consultant:* May I see your marketing plan?
> *Entrepreneur:* You could if I had one, but I don't. It's a great concept, and I just know people will want to buy it.
> *Marketing Consultant:* How do you know that these people will be so eager to buy? Is this what your consumer research indicates?
> *Entrepreneur:* I don't have any research . . . but my friends tell me it's a fantastic idea that will sell like hotcakes.

Such optimism is commendable, but infatuation with an idea can have devastating consequences if the entrepreneur doesn't understand how to transfer the idea into a product or service that customers will purchase.

In Chapter 6, we discussed the importance of a business plan for both the entrepreneur and potential investors. In this chapter, we will look at the nature of marketing and the marketing plan. Then, in Chapters 8 through 12, we'll consider the other major components of a business plan. Although our presentation will not cover the specific elements of all plans, the features we will discuss are important components of any well-written plan.

It is appropriate first to answer a few basic questions about marketing:

■ How can marketing be defined?

■ What are the components of an effective marketing philosophy?

■ What does a consumer orientation imply about the business?

What Is Small Business Marketing?

1 Describe small business marketing.

small business marketing
Business activities that direct the creation, development, and delivery of a bundle of satisfaction from the creator to the targeted user and that satisfy the targeted user

Marketing means different things to different people. Some entrepreneurs view marketing as simply selling a product or service. Others see marketing as those activities directing the flow of goods and services from producer to consumer or user. In reality, small business marketing is much broader. It consists of many activities, some of which occur even before a product is produced and made ready for distribution and sale.

We begin with a comprehensive definition of small business marketing in order to convey its true scope to entrepreneurs. **Small business marketing** consists of those business activities that direct the creation, development, and delivery of a *bundle of satisfaction* from the creator to the targeted user and that satisfy the targeted user. Notice how this definition emphasizes the concept of a bundle of satisfaction—a core product and or service plus all its important extras. It may be helpful to view a product/service as having three levels: core product/service, actual product/service, and augmented product/service (see Exhibit 7-1). The core product/service is the fundamental benefit or solution sought by customers. The actual product/service is the basic physical product/service that delivers those benefits. The augmented product/service is the basic product/service plus extra or unsolicited benefits to the consumer that may prompt a purchase. In the case of television, for example, the core product is entertainment and/or information (the news); the actual product is the physical television set. The augmented product might include the ability to vote on acts that appear on *American Idol* or the ability to watch a live sports event.

Ultimately, a business provides satisfaction to its customers, not merely the tangible product or intangible service that is the focus of the exchange. Consider Blue Nile Incorporated, which sells engagement rings and other jewelry on its website. Although jewelry is its core product, the bundle of satisfaction the firm provides includes more than jewelry. In keeping with the company's strong commitment to helping customers make the right purchase, Blue Nile's website provides a great deal of extra information. This assistance, along with competitive prices and free shipping, is part of the bundle of satisfaction offered. And it appears to be working well. The average value of an order generated on Blue Nile's website is $1,000, which is very high for this type of business.[1]

exhibit

7-1 *The Three Levels of a Product/Service*

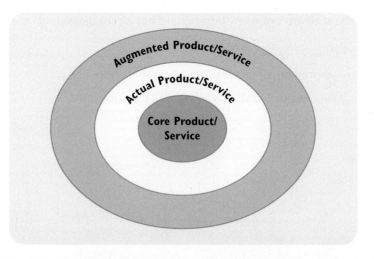

Marketing Philosophies Make a Difference

Just as an individual's personal philosophy influences the strategy he or she uses to achieve personal goals, a firm's marketing philosophy determines how its marketing activities are developed, reflected in the marketing plan, and used to achieve business goals. Three different marketing perspectives that permeate small businesses are the production-oriented, sales-oriented, and consumer-oriented philosophies.

A *production-oriented philosophy* emphasizes the product as the single most important part of the business. The firm concentrates resources on developing the product or service in the most efficient manner, even if promotion, distribution, and other marketing activities are slighted. On the other hand, a *sales-oriented philosophy* deemphasizes production efficiencies and customer preferences in favor of a focus on sales. Achieving sales goals becomes the firm's highest priority. In contrast, a firm adopting a *consumer-oriented philosophy* believes that everything, including production and sales, centers around the consumer and his or her needs. The result: All marketing efforts begin and end with the consumer.

A Consumer Orientation—the Right Choice

Over the years, both large and small businesses have gradually shifted their marketing emphasis from production to sales and, more recently, to consumers. Adhering to this marketing concept is essential to marketing success. The marketing concept is a two-stage process that underlies all marketing efforts: identifying customer needs and satisfying those needs. This simple observation—that a company must first identify needs and then satisfy those needs—is easy to understand but difficult to implement, given the competitive nature of most markets. Still, for a company to be successful, it is essential that a product and/or service meet a real need in the marketplace. *We strongly recommend that all new businesses begin with a consumer orientation, as this philosophy is most consistent with long-term success.* Remember, customer satisfaction is not a means to achieving a goal—it *is* the goal!

Why have some small firms failed to adopt a consumer orientation when the benefits seem so obvious? The answer lies in three key factors. First, the state of competition always affects a firm's marketing orientation. If there is little or no competition and if demand exceeds supply, a firm is tempted to emphasize production. This is usually a short-term situation, however, and so the approach often leads to disaster in due time.

Second, an entrepreneur may have strong production skills but be weak in marketing ability. Naturally, such owners will concentrate on production considerations.

Third, some entrepreneurs are simply too focused on the present. They expect the firm's marketing efforts to reap immediate dividends and, consequently, favor a sales-oriented philosophy. However, putting too much emphasis on selling merchandise often creates customer dissatisfaction, especially if high-pressure selling is used with little regard for customers' needs.

Both production- and sales-oriented philosophies may generate short-run success. However, a consumer orientation not only recognizes production efficiency goals and professional selling but also adds concern for customer satisfaction. In effect, a firm that adopts a consumer orientation incorporates the best of each marketing philosophy.

Once a small firm makes a commitment to a customer orientation, it is ready to develop the marketing strategy to support this goal. Marketing activities include taking the steps necessary to locate and describe potential customers—a process called **market analysis**. Marketing activities also encompass the development of a marketing mix. Product/service, pricing, promotion, and distribution activities combine to form the **marketing mix**. Marketing research, market segmentation, and sales forecasting are additional key activities underlying market analysis and development of a marketing mix.

Exhibit 7-2 depicts the major components of the marketing plan and the marketing activities required to generate the information needed for the plan—marketing research, market segmentation, and sales forecasting. In the remainder of the chapter, we will take a more in-depth look at these plan components and marketing activities.

market analysis
The process of locating and describing potential customers

marketing mix
The combination of product, pricing, promotion, and distribution activities

7-2   *The Marketing Plan and Supporting Marketing Activities*

The Formal Marketing Plan

> **2** Identify the components of a formal marketing plan.

After the entrepreneur's idea has been examined and judged to be a viable opportunity, he or she is ready to prepare the formal marketing plan. Each business venture is different; therefore, each marketing plan is unique. An entrepreneur should not feel it necessary to develop a cloned version of a plan created by someone else—even the one suggested by the authors of this textbook. Nevertheless, most marketing plans should cover market analysis, the competition, and marketing strategy.

We have provided several excerpts from actual marketing plans to show the flavor of certain sections. The following discussion is not intended to be complete or comprehensive. A more detailed treatment of marketing activities and strategies for both new and established small businesses is provided in Part 4, in Chapters 13 through 17. Much of this later material will also be helpful for writing the actual marketing plan.

Market Analysis

customer profile
A description of potential customers in a target market

In the market analysis section of the marketing plan, the entrepreneur describes the target market. This description of potential customers is commonly called a **customer profile**. Marketing research information, compiled from both secondary and primary data, can be used to construct this profile. A detailed discussion of the major benefits to customers provided by the new product or service should also be included in this section of the plan. Obviously, these benefits must be reasonable and consistent with statements in the product/service section of the plan.

Review the following excerpt from the "Market Needs" section of the marketing plan of Adorable Pet Photography, a home-based business located in Atlanta, Georgia.

> *Pets have always been an important part of the American family. However, as the American culture has changed in the last two decades, an even more prominent role for the pet has emerged. In today's mobile society, people often lose touch with their community, friends, and family, so they draw closer to their pets. As more people put off having children until later in life, pets are increasingly lapping up the luxuries that had once been reserved for*

human housemates. Making pets into family members is typical of an economy driven by middle-aged professionals with two-income households and fewer, if any, children. These "baby boomers" are now hitting the peak years of 35 to 65. In some cases, the pet allevi- ates the Empty Nest Syndrome for older married couples. Their animals are not just pets but companions, and many consider their pets as their children. Society is getting better educated and more accepting of pets across the board, and there is existing research that proves pets are a benefit to one's health. . . . People are now treating their pets as children, a pampering not seen 20 years ago.[2]

If an entrepreneur envisions several target markets, each segment must have a corresponding customer profile. Likewise, different target markets may call for an equal number of related marketing strategies. Typically, however, a new venture will initially concentrate on a select few target markets—or even just one.

Another major component of market analysis is the actual sales forecast. It is usu- ally desirable to include three sales forecasts covering the "most likely," "pessimistic," and "optimistic" scenarios. These scenarios provide investors and the entrepreneur with different numbers on which to base their decisions.

As we point out later in this chapter, forecasting sales for a new venture is extremely difficult. While it will be necessary to make assumptions during forecasting, they should be minimized. The forecasting method should be described and backed up by data wherever feasible.

The Competition

Frequently, entrepreneurs ignore the reality of competition for their new ventures, believing that the marketplace contains no close substitutes or that their success will not attract other entrepreneurs. This is simply not realistic.

Existing competitors should be studied carefully, and their key management personnel profiled. A brief discussion of competitors' overall strengths and weaknesses should be a part of the competition section of the plan. Also, related products currently being marketed or tested by competitors should be noted. An assessment should be made of the likelihood that any of these firms will enter the entrepreneur's target market. A SWOT analysis is always a good idea. As we discussed in Chapter 3, SWOT stands for strengths, weaknesses, oppor- tunities, and threats. It is important that your company have a clear understanding of what it does well (strengths), what it doesn't do so well (weaknesses), available market opportuni- ties, and threats from competitors as well as from changes in the company's operating envi- ronment (social, technological, economic, political, and other environmental variables).

Consider the following excerpt from the competition section of a marketing plan for the startup Yes, We Do Windows:

> *At this time there are 5 window cleaning services and 10 housecleaning services listed in my area Yellow Pages.*
> *Taking the time to make phone calls to these competitors made me feel even better about my idea for a business. Many of these firms did not return calls, did not seem interested, and were unable to provide phone bids.*
> *I can see two "musts" for the business: (a) my bids must be firm, and (b) my phone skills must be customer-oriented. If I can't answer the phone, I must find a phone person who fulfills these two musts. The image we're presenting here is "We aim to please. We're interested in servicing your home."[3]*

Many competitors can be monitored by visiting their websites. Todd Stoner, owner of Waco, Texas–based Disciplined Investors, an investment advisement firm, uses several search engines to keep tabs on his competition. "I am always curious to see what other investment firms in and around Waco are up to," Stoner says. "I can see which firms are growing and what types of products and services they offer."[4]

Marketing Strategy

A well-prepared market analysis and a discussion of the competition are important to the formal marketing plan. But the information on marketing strategy forms the most detailed section of the marketing plan and, in many respects, is subject to the closest scrutiny from potential investors. Such a strategy plots the course of the marketing actions that will make or break the entrepreneur's vision.

The following excerpt describes the marketing strategy of Fantastic Florals, a startup that imports handmade florals from Indonesia:

> *Fantastic Florals, Inc. has a variety of silk flowers and products from which to choose. During the first two years, the product line will include tulips and roses; two kinds of flower arrangements; silk scarf and silk hair assessories; and seasonal bouquets. . . . FFI sets standard prices for each product line. These prices are not expected to experience significant change over the next three years. Tulips and roses—$2.25; arranged flower 1—$18.99; arranged flower 2—$39.99; silk scarf—$15.99; other hair accessories—$9.99; and other/seasonal bouquet—$59.99. These prices exhibit quality products at reasonable costs to consumers. . . . The goal of FFI is to promote its products as fine collectibles for the collector or the gift-buyer. This will be done through promotions, direct-mail advertisements, appearances in related catalogs, and publicity events. . . . Products will be distributed through the retail store in Anytown Third Street Market or be pre-orders until FFI is able to further expand. Sales is one area that needs to be developed in order to better serve the consumer and meet objectives.[5]*

Four areas of marketing strategy should be addressed: (1) product decisions that will transform the basic product or service idea into a bundle of satisfaction, (2) distribution activities regarding the delivery of the product to customers, (3) pricing decisions that will set an acceptable exchange value on the total product or service, and (4) promotion activities that will communicate the necessary information to target markets.

Obviously, the nature of a new venture has a direct bearing on the emphasis given to each of these areas. For example, a service business will not have the same distribution problems as a product business, and the promotional challenges facing a new retail store will be quite different from those faced by a new manufacturer. Despite these differences, we can offer a generalized format for presenting marketing strategy in a business plan.

THE PRODUCT AND/OR SERVICE SECTION   The product and/or service section of the marketing plan includes the name of the product and/or service and the name of the business and why they were selected. Any legal protection that has been obtained for the names should be described. It is also important to explain the logic behind the name selection. An entrepreneur's family name, if used for certain products or services, may make a positive contribution to sales. In other situations, a descriptive name that suggests a benefit of the product may be more desirable. A good name is simple, memorable, and descriptive of the benefit provided by the product or service. Whatever the logic behind the choice of names, the selection should be defended and the names registered with the appropriate agencies to provide protection.

Sometimes, names selected for a business and a product/service may be challenged many years later, particularly if they haven't been registered. This is what Richard Hagelberg learned when he received a certified letter from the United States Olympic Committee in March 2000, saying Hagelberg had two years to change the name of his small playground equipment manufacturing business in Gary, Indiana, or else he would be sued. The company had been founded back in 1982 with the name Olympic Recreation. After much thought, Hagelberg decided to switch rather than fight. "We consulted our lawyer and were very careful to choose a name that wasn't trademarked," he said. He finally settled on Kidstuff Playsystems.[6]

Other components of the total product, such as the packaging, should be presented via drawings. Sometimes, it may be desirable to use professional packaging consultants to develop these drawings. Customer service plans such as warranties and repair policies also need to be discussed in this section. These elements of the marketing strategy should be tied directly to customer satisfaction. (Chapter 13 further examines the importance of creating and maintaining good customer relationships.)

THE DISTRIBUTION SECTION   Quite often, new ventures will use established intermediaries to handle the distribution of their product. This distribution strategy expedites the process and reduces the investment necessary for start up. How those intermediaries will be persuaded to carry the new product should be explained in the distribution section of the marketing plan. Any intention the new business may have to license its product or service should also be covered in this section.

How They See It: Choosing a Product Name

Trey Moore

Because the Internet is often the very first place (and sometimes the only place) that a potential customer checks out your product, we decided from the beginning that we would not pick a product name unless we could obtain the corresponding domain name, specifically the .com version.

So while we had many great product name ideas, we immediately tested their availability using http://www.register.com, and that helped us to quickly narrow down our possible choices. Our criteria were that the name needed to be related to the product, yet common enough so that it could be easily remembered.

We ended up going with the overall product suite name of "AirStrip" because it conveyed the concept of the waveform "strips" (i.e., fetal strips) being transferred over the "air." Since airstrip.com was not available, we decided to register the domain names that corresponded to each specific product within the overall suite. So, for AirStrip OB, we registered http://www.airstripob.com; for AirStrip Cardio, we registered http://www.airstripcardio.com; and likewise for the other product lines.

This approach is a little bit unusual in that our domain name is for our product, not our company name. However, we felt our product name was so "catchy" that we were better off building brand recognition for our product name than for our company name. While our company name is MP4 Solutions, we registered the domain name http://www.airstriptech.com to serve as the umbrella for all of our products. Our http://www.mp4solutions.com domain name just redirects to http://www.airstriptech.com.

Some new retail ventures require fixed locations; others need mobile stores. The layouts and configurations of retail outlets should be explained here.

When a new firm's method of product delivery is exporting, the distribution section must discuss the relevant laws and regulations governing that activity. Knowledge of exchange rates between currencies and distribution options must be reflected in the material included in this section. (Distribution concepts are explained in detail in Chapter 14, and exporting is discussed in Chapter 17.)

THE PRICING SECTION At a minimum, the price of a product and/or service must cover the costs of bringing it to customers. Therefore, the pricing section must include a schedule of both production and marketing costs. Break-even computations should be included for alternative prices. Naturally, forecasting methods used for analysis in this section should be consistent with those used in preparing the market analysis section. However, setting a price based exclusively on break-even analysis is not advisable, as it ignores other aspects of pricing. If the entrepreneur has found a truly unique niche, she or he may be able to charge a premium price—at least in the short run.

Competitors should be studied to learn what they are charging. To break into a market an entrepreneur will usually have to price a new product or service within a reasonable range of the competition. (Chapter 15 examines break-even analysis and pricing strategy in more depth.)

THE PROMOTION SECTION The promotion section of the marketing plan should describe the entrepreneur's approach to creating customer awareness of the product and/or service and motivating customers to buy. Among the many promotional options available to the entrepreneur are personal selling (that is, direct person-to-person selling) and advertising.

If personal selling is appropriate, the section should outline how many salespeople will be employed and how they will be compensated. The proposed system for training the sales force should be mentioned. If advertising is to be used, a list of the specific media to be employed should be included and advertising themes should be described. Often, it is advisable to seek the services of a small advertising agency. In this case, the name and credentials of the agency should be provided. A brief mention of successful campaigns supervised by the agency can add to the appeal of this section of the marketing plan. (Personal selling and advertising are discussed more extensively in Chapter 16.)

Living the Dream   entrepreneurial experiences

© Lisa Carpenter/Lisa Carpenter Photography

Distressed Jeans Artist

You might still have a pair in your closet: jeans that appear to have survived a natural disaster, a painting job, and a skateboarding accident. Artist Lincoln Mayne charges from $350 to $1,000 per pair to work jeans over, to give them a "rawer" appeal.

Mayne first got this business idea when people stopped him on the street to ask about the distressed jeans he was wearing. His response was, "Bring me your old jeans, and I'll do something with them." (You can try to make your own pair of distressed jeans by reading articles on the subject at http://www.wikihow.com.)

Trained as an artist and sculptor, Mayne uses grinders, sanders, and drills to achieve the desired look. He starts by nailing the jeans to boards (this is not for the squeamish) and using his tools to break them down. Then, he begins to create his masterpiece, with the jeans as his canvas. He uses his own fabrics for patches, so every pair of jeans that Mayne works on is unique.

According to Mayne, "[Jeans are] one of the rare items of clothing that gets better with time." Let's just hope the market for distressed jeans doesn't fade away.

Sources: Jia Lynn Yang, "Distressed Jeans Artist" *Fortune,* December 12, 2005, p. 44; and http://www.wikihow.com, accessed December 8, 2006.

http://www.lincolnmayne.com

Marketing Research for the New Venture

3 Discuss the nature of the marketing research process.

A marketing plan can be based on intuition alone, or intuition can be supplemented by sound market information. *In every case, it is advisable to write the marketing plan only after collecting and evaluating marketing research data.* A marketing plan based on research will undoubtedly be stronger than a plan without such a foundation.

The Nature of Marketing Research

marketing research
The gathering, processing, interpreting, and reporting of market information

Marketing research may be defined as the gathering, processing, interpreting, and reporting of marketing information. It is all about finding out what you want to know. A small business typically conducts less marketing research than does a big business, partly because of the expense involved but also because the entrepreneur often does not understand the basic research process. Therefore, our discussion of marketing research focuses on the more widely used and practical techniques that entrepreneurs can employ as they analyze potential target markets and make preparations to develop their marketing plans.

Although a small business can conduct marketing research without the assistance of an expert, the cost of hiring such help is often money well spent, as the expert's advice may help increase revenues or cut costs. Marketing researchers are trained, experienced professionals, and prices for their research services typically reflect this. For example, focus groups run from $3,000 to $10,000 each, and a telephone survey may range anywhere from $5,000 to $25,000 or more, depending on the number of interviews and the length of the questionnaire. However, companies such as SurveySite, Inc. (http://www.surveysite.com) are now reducing overall research costs by taking advantage of the Internet to offer Web-based surveys and online focus groups.

Before committing to research, an entrepreneur should always estimate the projected costs of marketing research and compare them with the benefits expected. Such analysis is never exact, but it will help the entrepreneur decide what research should be conducted.

Steps in the Marketing Research Process

The typical steps in the marketing research process are (1) identifying the informational need, (2) searching for secondary data, (3) collecting primary data, and (4) interpreting the data gathered.

STEP ONE: IDENTIFYING THE INFORMATIONAL NEED   The first step in marketing research is to identify and define the informational need. Although this step seems almost too obvious to mention, the fact is that entrepreneurs sometimes commission surveys without pinpointing the specific information needed. Obviously, a broad statement such as "Our need is to know if the venture will be successful" will do little to guide the research process, but even a more specific goal can easily miss the mark. For example, an entrepreneur thinking about a location for a restaurant may decide to conduct a survey to ascertain customers' menu preferences and reasons for eating out when, in fact, what he or she needs to know most is how often residents of the target area eat out and how far they are willing to drive to eat in a restaurant.

Once a venture's informational needs have been defined correctly, research can be designed to concentrate on those specific needs. Later in this chapter, you will see a survey questionnaire developed for a car-wash owner who wanted to assess customer satisfaction. This entrepreneur identified a clear informational need: Determine the level of customers' satisfaction with the car-cleaning experience at his business.

STEP TWO: SEARCHING FOR SECONDARY DATA   Information that has already been compiled is known as **secondary data**. Generally, collecting secondary data is less expensive than gathering new, or primary, data. Therefore, after defining their informational needs, entrepreneurs should exhaust available sources of secondary data before going further into the research process. It may be possible to base much of the marketing plan for the new venture solely on secondary data. A massive amount of information is available in libraries throughout the United States and on the Internet.

secondary data
Market information that has been previously compiled

As you already know, the Internet is a rich source of secondary data. Information that once took days and even weeks to obtain is now often only a click away. Software programs and hundreds of websites (many offering free information) can help an entrepreneur research customers for her or his product and/or service. Don't make the mistake, however, of thinking that the Internet is the *only* source of secondary data or even the most reliable source. Like all repositories of information, it is most helpful when used in tandem with other sources. And one must be very careful to verify the accuracy of all secondary data gathered from the Internet and other sources.

A particularly helpful source of secondary data for the small firm is the Small Business Administration (http://www.sba.gov), or SBA. This agency publishes extensive bibliographies on many topics, including marketing research.

Unfortunately, the use of secondary data has several drawbacks. One is that the data may be outdated. Another is that the units of measure in the secondary data may not fit the current problem. For example, a firm's market might consist of individuals with incomes between $20,000 and $25,000, while secondary data may report only the number of individuals with incomes between $15,000 and $50,000.

Finally, the question of credibility is always present. Some sources of secondary data are less trustworthy than others. Mere publication of data does not in itself make the data valid and reliable. It is advisable to compare several different sources to see whether they are reporting similar data. Professional research specialists can also help assess the credibility of secondary sources.

primary data
New market information that is gathered by the firm conducting the research

STEP THREE: COLLECTING PRIMARY DATA   If the secondary data are insufficient, a search for new information, or **primary data**, is the next step. Observational methods and questioning methods are two techniques used in accumulating primary data. Observational methods avoid interpersonal contact between respondents and the researcher, while questioning methods involve some type of interaction with respondents.

Observational Methods   Observation is probably the oldest form of research in existence. Indeed, learning by observing is quite common. It is hardly surprising that observation can provide useful information for small businesses. A simple but effective form of observation research is mystery shopping. Mystery shoppers gather observational data about a store (yours or a competitor's) by looking at how items are displayed, in-store advertising, and other aspects of the store. Mystery shopping can also be used to test employee product knowledge, sales techniques, and more. The results of such activities are used to make important changes in store design and merchandising as well as reward good employees.[7]

When Scott Semel and Reed Chase wanted to learn more about their competitors and customers after buying a candy-importing company, Cody Kramer Imports, in Orangeburg, New York, what did they do? They attended several major industry trade shows and checked out competitors' booths. They also wandered the aisles of candy retailers, observing whatever they could about candy-buying customers.[8]

Observational methods can be inexpensive. Furthermore, they avoid the potential bias that can result from a respondent's contact with an interviewer during questioning. Observation—for example, counting customers going into a store—can be conducted by a person or by mechanical devices, such as hidden video cameras. The cost of mechanical observation devices is rapidly declining, bringing them within the budget of many small businesses.

Questioning Methods   Surveys and experimentation are both questioning methods that involve contact with respondents. Surveys can be conducted by mail, telephone, the Web, or personal interview. Mail surveys are often used when target respondents are widely dispersed; however, they usually yield low response rates—only a small percentage of the surveys sent out are typically returned. Telephone surveys and personal interview surveys achieve higher response rates. But personal interviews are very expensive, and individuals are often reluctant to grant such interviews if they think a sales pitch is coming. Some marketing researchers, such as i.think inc., offer firms a new way to survey customers—through an online questionnaire. Although some websites claim that online surveys have better response rates than do paper surveys, Internet surveying is still relatively new and data on response rates are questionable.

A questionnaire is the basic instrument guiding the researcher who is administering the survey and the respondent who is taking it. A questionnaire should be developed carefully and pre-tested before it is used in the market. Here are several considerations to keep in mind when designing and testing a questionnaire:

- Ask questions that relate to the issue under consideration. An interesting question may not be relevant. A good test of relevance is to assume an answer to each question and then ask yourself how you would use that information.

- Select the form of question that is most appropriate for the subject and the conditions of the survey. Open-ended and multiple-choice questions are two popular forms.

- Carefully consider the order of the questions. Asking questions in the wrong sequence can produce biased answers to later questions.

- Ask the more sensitive questions near the end of the questionnaire. Age and income, for example, are usually sensitive topics.

- Carefully select the words in each question. They should be as simple, clear, and objective as possible.

- Pre-test the questionnaire by administering it to a small sample of respondents who are representative of the group to be surveyed.

Exhibit 7-3 shows a questionnaire developed for a car-wash owner. This survey illustrates how the considerations above can be incorporated into a questionnaire. Note

exhibit **7-3**   *Small Business Survey Questionnaire*

PLEASE—WE NEED YOUR HELP!

You're The Boss. All of us here at Genie Car Wash have just one purpose . . . *TO PLEASE YOU!*

Date_____ Time of Visit _____

How are we doing?

	Yes	No		
1. Personnel–courteous and helpful?				
Service writer	☐	☐		
Vacuum attendants	☐	☐		
Cashier	☐	☐		
Final finish & inspection	☐	☐		
Management	☐	☐		

2. Do you feel the time it took to wash your car was . . .				
Right amount of time	☐			
Too much time	☐			
Not enough time	☐			

	Excel	Good	Avg	Poor
3. How do you judge the appearance of the personnel?	☐	☐	☐	☐
4. Please rate the quality of workmanship of the interior of your car.				
Inside vacuum	☐	☐	☐	☐
Dashboard	☐	☐	☐	☐
Doorjambs	☐	☐	☐	☐
Ash trays	☐	☐	☐	☐
Windows	☐	☐	☐	☐
Console	☐	☐	☐	☐
5. Please rate the quality of workmanship of the exterior of your car.				
Tires and wheels	☐	☐	☐	☐
Bumpers and chrome	☐	☐	☐	☐
Body of car	☐	☐	☐	☐
Grill	☐	☐	☐	☐
6. Please rate the overall appearance of our facility.				
Outside building & grounds	☐	☐	☐	☐
Inside building	☐	☐	☐	☐
Rest rooms	☐	☐	☐	☐
7. Please rate your overall impression of the experience you had while at Genie Car Wash.	☐	☐	☐	☐

It is important that we clean your car to your satisfaction. Additional comments will be appreciated.

_____

_____

_____

OPTIONAL

Your Name _____

Address _____

City _____ State _____ Zip _____

Thank you!

the use of both multiple-choice and open-ended questions. As it turned out, the additional comments were particularly useful to this firm.

STEP FOUR: INTERPRETING THE DATA GATHERED   After the necessary data have been gathered, they must be transformed into usable information. Without interpretation, large quantities of data are only isolated facts. Methods of summarizing and simplifying information for users include tables, charts, and other graphics. Descriptive statistics (for example, the average response) are most helpful during this step in the research procedure. Inexpensive personal computer software, such as Excel, is now available to perform statistical calculations and generate report-quality graphics.

It is important to remember that *formal* marketing research is not always necessary. The entrepreneur's first decision should be whether to conduct primary research at all. It may be best not to conduct formal research in the following situations: [9]

1. Your company doesn't have the resources to conduct the research properly or to implement any findings generated from the proposed research.

2. The opportunity for a new business or product introduction has passed. If you've been beaten to the punch, it may be wise to wait and see how the early entrant to the market fares.

3. A decision to move forward has already been made. There's no need to spend good money on a decision that has already been made.

4. You can't decide what information is needed. If you don't know where you are going, any road will get you there.

5. The needed information already exists (that is, secondary information is available).

6. The cost of conducting the research outweighs the potential benefits.

Isabella Trebond suggests several ways entrepreneurs can do their own research with very little money. First, read everything you can—newspaper and magazine articles, as well as any information that can be acquired from industry trade associations. Usually, membership in a trade association gives you access, for a nominal fee, to research the association conducts in your business sector. Second, you will be amazed at the specific information and sources that can be located on the Web. Existing research should always be reviewed—it's quick, cheap, and easy to access. Third, check out your competition. This can involve a search of their websites as well as a drive-by and/or walk-through of their businesses. Finally, you can always enlist students from local colleges to help stretch your limited research budget.[10]

As important as marketing research is, it should never be allowed to suppress entrepreneurial enthusiasm or be used as a substitute for a hands-on feel for the target market. It should be viewed as a supplement to, not a replacement for, intuitive judgment and cautious experimentation in launching new products and services. Ultimately, the marketing plan should reflect the entrepreneur's belief about the best marketing strategy for her or his firm.

Understanding Potential Target Markets

4 Define market segmentation and its related strategies.

market
A group of customers or potential customers who have purchasing power and unsatisfied needs

To prepare the market analysis section of the marketing plan, an entrepreneur needs a proper understanding of the term *market,* which means different things to different people. It may refer to a physical location where buying and selling take place ("They went to the market"), or it may be used to describe selling efforts ("We must market this product aggressively"). Still another meaning is the one we emphasize in this chapter: A **market** is a group of customers or potential customers who have purchasing power and unsatisfied needs. Note carefully the three ingredients in this definition of a market.

1. A market must have buying units, or *customers.* These units may be individuals or business entities. Thus, a market is more than a geographic area; it must contain potential customers.

2. Customers in a market must have *purchasing power.* Assessing the level of purchasing power in a potential market is very important. Customers who have unsatisfied needs but who lack money and/or credit do not constitute a viable market because they have nothing to offer in exchange for a product or service. In such a situation, no transactions can occur.

3. A market must contain buying units with *unsatisfied needs.* Consumers, for instance, will not buy unless they are motivated to do so—and motivation can occur only when a customer recognizes his or her unsatisfied needs. It would be extremely difficult, for example, to sell luxury urban apartments to desert nomads!

In light of our definition of a market, determining market potential is the process of locating and investigating buying units that have both purchasing power and needs that can be satisfied with the product or service that is being offered.

Market Segmentation and Its Variables

In Chapter 3, cost- and differentiation-based strategies were applied to marketplaces that were relatively homogeneous, or uniform, in nature. As discussed, these strategies can also be used to focus on a limited market within an industry. In his book *Competitive Advantage,* Michael Porter refers to this type of competitive strategy—in which cost- and differentiation-based advantages are achieved within narrow market segments—as a *focus strategy.*[11]

A focus strategy depends on market segmentation and becomes a consideration in competitive markets. Formally defined, **market segmentation** is the process of dividing the total market for a product or service into groups with similar needs, such that each group is likely to respond favorably to a specific marketing strategy. Developments in the cell phone industry provide a good example of real-world market segmentation. Initially, cell phone service providers aimed at a broad market and practiced very little market segmentation. But as competition developed, they began to focus on market segments, such as small businesses, families, younger customers, and customers who want to send text messages and photographs.

In order to divide the total market into appropriate segments, an entrepreneur must consider **segmentation variables,** which are parameters that identify the particular dimensions that distinguish one form of market behavior from another. Two broad sets of segmentation variables that represent major dimensions of a market are benefit variables and demographic variables.

BENEFIT VARIABLES   The definition of a market highlights the unsatisfied needs of customers. **Benefit variables** are related to customer needs since they are used to identify segments of a market based on the benefits sought by customers. For example, the toothpaste market has several benefit segments. The principal benefit to parents might be cavity prevention for their young children, while the principal benefit to teenagers might be fresh breath. Toothpaste is the product in both cases, but it has two different market segments.

DEMOGRAPHIC VARIABLES   Benefit variables alone are insufficient for market analysis; it is impossible to implement forecasting and marketing strategy without defining the market further. Therefore, small businesses commonly use demographic variables as part of market segmentation. Recall the definition of a market—customers with purchasing power and unsatisfied needs. **Demographic variables** refer to certain characteristics that describe customers and their purchasing power. Typical demographic variables are age, marital status, gender, occupation, and income.

market segmentation
The division of a market into several smaller groups with similar needs

segmentation variables
The parameters used to distinguish one form of market behavior from another

benefit variables
Specific characteristics that distinguish market segments according to the benefits sought by customers

demographic variables
Specific characteristics that describe customers and their purchasing power

Marketing Strategies Based on Segmentation Considerations

There are several types of strategies based on market segmentation efforts. The three types discussed here are the unsegmented approach, the multisegment approach, and the single-segment approach. These strategies can best be illustrated by using an example— a hypothetical small firm called the Community Writing Company.

THE UNSEGMENTED STRATEGY   When a business defines the total market as its target, it is following an **unsegmented strategy** (also known as **mass marketing**). This strategy can sometimes be successful, but it assumes that all customers desire the same basic benefit from the product or service. This may hold true for water but certainly does not hold true for shoes, which satisfy numerous needs through a wide range of styles, prices, colors, and sizes. With an unsegmented strategy, a firm develops a single marketing mix—one combination of product, price, promotion, and distribution. Its competitive advantage must be derived from either a cost- or a differentiation-based advantage. The unsegmented strategy of the Community Writing Company is shown in Exhibit 7-4. The Community Writing Company's product is a mechanical pencil that is sold at the single unit price of $3.49 and is promoted through one medium and an extensive distribution plan. Even with an unsegmented strategy, some segmenting must occur. Note in Exhibit 7-4 that the market does not include everyone in the universe—just those who might use writing instruments.

THE MULTISEGMENT STRATEGY   With a view of the market that recognizes individual segments with different preferences, a firm is in a better position to tailor marketing mixes to various segments. If a firm determines that two or more market segments have

unsegmented strategy (mass marketing)
A strategy that defines the total market as the target market

exhibit   **7-4**   *An Unsegmented Market Strategy*

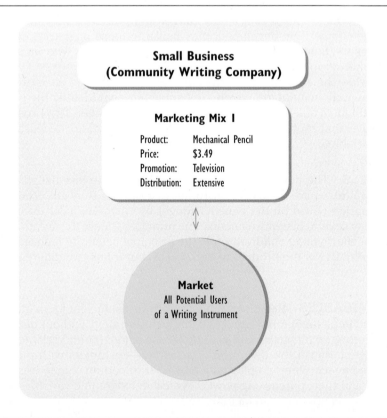

exhibit

7-5   *A Multisegment Market Strategy*

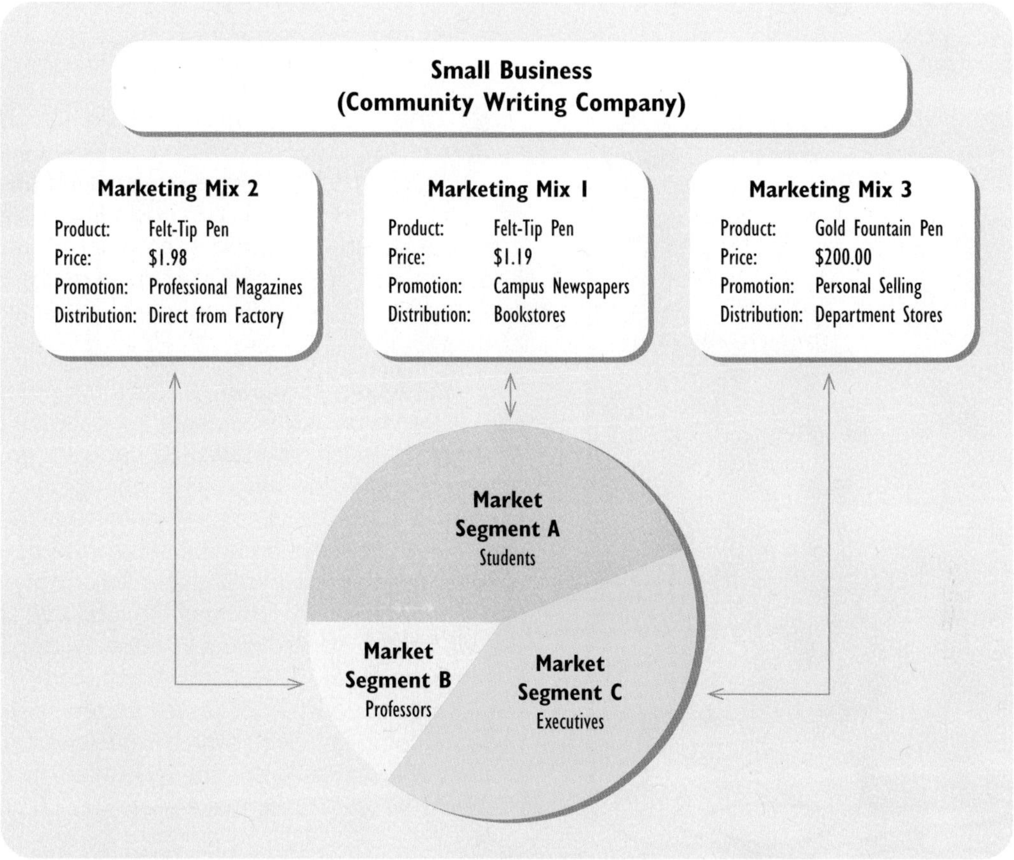

Small Business (Community Writing Company)

Marketing Mix 2
Product: Felt-Tip Pen
Price: $1.98
Promotion: Professional Magazines
Distribution: Direct from Factory

Marketing Mix 1
Product: Felt-Tip Pen
Price: $1.19
Promotion: Campus Newspapers
Distribution: Bookstores

Marketing Mix 3
Product: Gold Fountain Pen
Price: $200.00
Promotion: Personal Selling
Distribution: Department Stores

Market Segment A Students

Market Segment B Professors

Market Segment C Executives

the potential to be profitable and then develops a unique marketing mix for each segment, it is following a **multisegment** strategy.

Let's assume that the Community Writing Company has recognized three separate market segments: students, professors, and executives. Following the multisegment approach, the company develops a competitive advantage with three marketing mixes, based on differences in pricing, promotion, distribution, or the product itself, as shown in Exhibit 7-5. Marketing Mix 1 consists of selling felt-tip pens to students through college bookstores at the lower-than-normal price of $1.19 and supporting this effort with a promotional campaign in campus newspapers. With Marketing Mix 2, the company markets the same pen to universities for use by professors. Professional magazines are the promotional medium used in this mix, distribution is direct from the factory, and the product price is $1.98. Finally, Marketing Mix 3, which is aimed at corporate executives, consists of selling a gold fountain pen, priced at $200.00, only in exclusive department stores and promoting it by personal selling. Note the distinct differences in these three marketing mixes. Obviously, many other segments exist for a simple product such as a pen. Entrepreneur Patrick H. Pinkston, for example, serves a very unique target segment with limited-edition pens made of diamond, gold, and platinum that he sells for an average price of $45,000.[12] Small businesses tend to resist early on the use of the multisegment strategy because of the risk of spreading their limited resources too thinly among several marketing efforts.

multisegment strategy
A strategy that recognizes different preferences of individual market segments and develops a unique marketing mix for each

THE SINGLE-SEGMENT STRATEGY When a firm recognizes that several distinct market segments exist but chooses to concentrate on reaching only one segment, it

Living the Dream   entrepreneurial challenges

A Battery of Setbacks

U.S. Air Force photo/Staff Sgt. Stacy Fowler

Tom Hauke and a friend, Earl Martin, created McDowell Research, a Waco, Texas–based technology company. They say that everything is big in Texas, and that's the way the story goes for this Lone Star startup. After its modest launch in 1992, the company began to expand—and quickly. By 2005, McDowell Research was growing at an eye-popping 375 percent per year, generating $23 million in annual sales and employing 100 people.

The track record of McDowell Research proves that a startup can be tremendously successful by following a single-segment strategy: focusing its marketing energies on a single market and having a narrow range of technologies. The strategy is no secret—the company website explains that McDowell Research was founded to develop and manufacture power solutions and accessories to support military communications. The founders had a definite vision: "To bring the best possible technology to the warfighter." One customer—the United States military—buys nearly all of the company's products, which include battery chargers, power supplies, amplified speaker units, and integrated communication systems designed to withstand harsh combat conditions. According to Hauke, "If a soldier can survive in it, we're going to make sure our equipment will, too."

The company's strategy has been so good and its performance so impressive that McDowell Research was named to the prestigious *Inc.* 500 list in 2005. It was acquired in 2006 by Ultralife Batteries Inc. (http://www.ultralifebatteries.com) and is now an operating unit of Ultralife Batteries, along with its UK and China units. It seems that McDowell Research's single-segment market focus will live on!

Sources: "McDowell Research—Corporate Overview," http://www.mcdowellresearch.com/company.php?ID=4, accessed August 6, 2007; PennWell Publishing, "Ultralife Batteries Completes Acquisition of McDowell Research," http://mae.pennnet.com/articles/article_display.cfm?article_id=259624, accessed June 18, 2007; and *Inc.* 500, "McDowell Research," (2005) http://www.inc.com/resources/inc500/2005/profiles/357.html, accessed August 4, 2007.

http://www.mcdowellresearch.com

single-segment strategy
A strategy that recognizes the existence of several distinct market segments but focuses on only the most profitable segment

is following a **single-segment strategy**. The segment selected is the one that promises to offer the greatest profitability. Once again, a competitive advantage is achieved through a cost- or differentiation-based strategy. In Exhibit 7-6, the Community Writing Company decides to pursue a single-segment approach and selects the student market segment.

The single-segment approach is probably the wisest strategy for small businesses to use during initial marketing efforts. It allows a small firm to specialize and make better use of its limited resources. Then, once its reputation has been established, the firm will find it easier to enter new markets.

exhibit

7-6   *A Single-Segment Market Strategy*

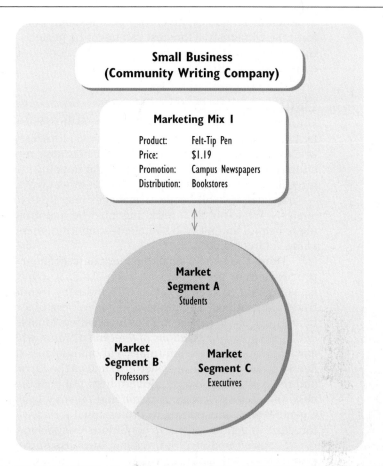

Estimating Market Potential

{ 5 Explain the different methods of forecasting sales.

A small business can be successful only if an adequate market exists for its product or service. The sales forecast is the typical indicator of market adequacy. Forecasting is particularly important prior to writing the marketing plan. An entrepreneur who enters the marketplace without a forecast is much like an enthusiastic swimmer who leaves the diving board without checking the depth of the water. Many types of information from numerous sources are required to determine market potential. This section examines the forecasting process.

The Sales Forecast

Formally defined, a **sales forecast** is an estimate of how much of a product or service can be sold within a given market in a defined time period. The forecast can be stated in terms of dollars and/or units.

sales forecast
A prediction of how much of a product or service will be purchased within a market during a specified time period

Because a sales forecast revolves around a specific target market, the market should be defined as precisely as possible. The market description forms the forecasting boundary. If the market for electric razors is described as "men," the sales forecast will be extremely large. A more precise definition, such as "men between the ages of 15 and 25 who are dissatisfied with nonelectric shavers," will result in a smaller but possibly more useful forecast.

It is also important to note that a sales forecast implies a specified time period. One sales forecast may cover a year or less, while another may extend over several years. Both short-term and long-term forecasts are needed for a well-constructed business plan.

A sales forecast is an essential component of the business plan because it is critical to assessing the feasibility of a new venture. If the market is insufficient, the business is destined for failure. A sales forecast is also useful in other areas of business planning. Production schedules, inventory policies, and personnel decisions all start with a sales forecast. Obviously, a forecast can never be perfect, and entrepreneurs should remember that a forecast can be wrong in either direction—underestimating potential sales or over-estimating potential sales.

Limitations to Forecasting

For a number of practical reasons, forecasting is used less frequently by small firms than by large firms. First, for any new business, forecasting circumstances are unique. Entrepreneurial inexperience, coupled with a new idea, represents the most difficult forecasting situation, as illustrated in Exhibit 7-7. An ongoing business that requires only an updated forecast for its existing product is in the most favorable forecasting position.

Second, a small business manager may be unfamiliar with methods of quantitative analysis. While not all forecasting must be quantitatively oriented—qualitative forecasting is helpful and may be sufficient—quantitative methods have repeatedly proven their value in forecasting.

Third, the typical small business entrepreneur lacks familiarity with the forecasting process and/or personnel with such skills. To overcome these deficiencies, some small firms attempt to keep in touch with industry trends through contacts with appropriate trade associations. The professional members of a trade association staff are frequently better qualified to engage in sales forecasting. Most libraries have a copy of *National Trade and Professional Associations of the United States,* which lists these groups. Entrepreneurs can also obtain current information about business trends by regularly reading trade publications and economic newsletters such as the *Kiplinger Washington Letter, BusinessWeek,* and the *Wall Street Journal.* Government publications, such as the *Survey of Current Business,* the *Federal Reserve Bulletin,* and *Monthly Labor Review,* may also be of interest in a general way. Subscribing to professional forecasting services is another way to obtain forecasts of general business conditions or specific forecasts for given industries.

Despite the difficulties, a small business entrepreneur should not neglect the forecasting task. Instead, he or she should remember how important the sales outlook in the business plan is to obtaining financing. The statement "We can sell as many as we can produce" does not satisfy the information requirements of potential investors.

exhibit 7-7 *Dimensions of Forecasting Difficulty*

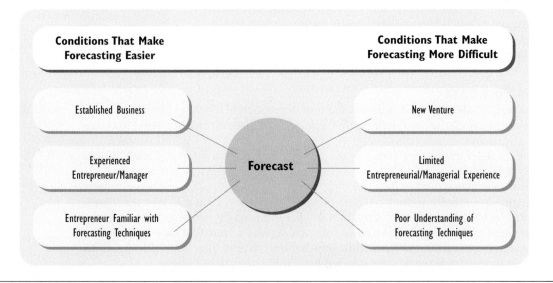

Conditions That Make Forecasting Easier		Conditions That Make Forecasting More Difficult
Established Business		New Venture
Experienced Entrepreneur/Manager	Forecast	Limited Entrepreneurial/Managerial Experience
Entrepreneur Familiar with Forecasting Techniques		Poor Understanding of Forecasting Techniques

The Forecasting Process

Estimating market demand with a sales forecast is a multistep process. Typically, the sales forecast is a composite of several individual forecasts, so the process involves merging these individual forecasts properly.

The forecasting process can be characterized by two important dimensions: the point at which the process is started and the nature of the predicting variable. Depending on the starting point, the process may be designated as a *breakdown process* or a *buildup process.* The nature of the predicting variable determines whether the forecasting is direct or indirect.

THE STARTING POINT In the breakdown process, sometimes called the chain-ratio method, the forecaster begins with a variable that has a very large scope and systematically works down to the sales forecast. This method is frequently used for consumer products forecasting. The initial variable might be a population figure for the target market. Through the use of percentages, an appropriate link is built to generate the sales forecast. For example, consider the market segment identified by the hypothetical Community Writing Company. Assume that the target market is older students (25 years of age or over), seeking convenience and erasability in their writing instrument. Assume further that the initial geographic target is the state of Idaho. Exhibit 7-8 outlines the breakdown process. The more links in the forecasting chain, the greater the potential for error.

In contrast to the breakdown process, the buildup process calls for identifying all potential buyers in a target market's submarkets and then adding up the estimated demand. For example, a local dry-cleaning firm forecasting demand for cleaning high school letter jackets might estimate its market share within each area school as

breakdown process (chain-ratio method)
A forecasting method that begins with a larger-scope variable and works down to the sales forecast

buildup process
A forecasting method in which all potential buyers in the various submarkets are identified and then the estimated demand is added up

---

exhibit 7-8   *Sales Forecasting with the Breakdown Method*

Linking Variable	Source	Estimating Value	Market Potential*
1. Idaho state population	U.S. census of population		1,429,096
2. State population in target age category	*Sales & Marketing Management Survey of Buying Power*	12%	171,492
3. Target age enrolled in colleges and universities	Idaho Department of Education	30%	51,448
4. Target age college students preferring convenience over price	Student survey in a marketing research class	50%	25,724
5. Convenience-oriented students likely to purchase new felt-tip pen within next month	Personal telephone interview by entrepreneur	75%	19,293
6. People who say they are likely to purchase who actually buy	Article in *Journal of Consumer Research*	35%	6,753
7. Average number of pens bought per year	Personal experience of entrepreneur	4	27,012

↑
SALES FORECAST FOR IDAHO

*Figures in this column, for variables in rows 2–7, are derived by multiplying the percentage or number in the Estimating Value column by the amount on the previous line of the Market Potential column.

20 percent. Then, by determining the number of high school students obtaining a letter jacket at each school—perhaps from school yearbooks—an analyst could estimate the total demand.

The buildup process is especially helpful for industrial goods forecasting. To estimate potential, forecasters often use data from the Census of Manufacturers by the U.S. Department of Commerce. The information can be broken down according to the North American Industry Classification System (NAICS), which classifies businesses by type of industry. Once the code for a group of potential industrial customers has been identified, the forecaster can obtain information on the number of establishments and their geographic location, number of employees, and annual sales. A sales forecast can be constructed by summing this information for several relevant codes.

direct forecasting
A forecasting method in which sales is the estimated variable

indirect forecasting
A forecasting method in which variables related to sales are used to project future sales

THE PREDICTING VARIABLE   In **direct forecasting**, which is the simplest form of forecasting, sales is the forecasted variable. Many times, however, sales cannot be predicted directly and other variables must be used. **Indirect forecasting** takes place when surrogate variables are used to project the sales forecast. For example, if a firm lacks information about industry sales of baby cribs but has data on births, the strong correlation between the two variables allows planners to use the figures for births to help forecast industry sales for baby cribs.

We hope that the marketing research, market segmentation, and forecasting tools presented in this chapter will help you create an excellent marketing plan, one that is well tailored to meet the needs of your business.

Looking **BACK**

1 Describe small business marketing.

- The product and/or service as a bundle of satisfaction has three levels: (1) Core product/service, (2) actual product/service, and (3) augmented product/service.
- Three distinct marketing philosophies are the production-, sales-, and consumer-oriented philosophies.
- A small business should adopt a consumer orientation to marketing, as that philosophy is most consistent with long-term success.
- Small business marketing consists of numerous activities, including market analysis and determining the marketing mix.

2 Identify the components of a formal marketing plan.

- The formal marketing plan should include sections on market analysis, the competition, and marketing strategy.

- The market analysis should include a customer profile.
- A SWOT analysis is helpful in assessing the competition.
- Four areas of marketing strategy that should be discussed in the marketing plan are (1) decisions affecting the total product and/or service, (2) distribution activities, (3) pricing decisions, and (4) promotion activities.

3 Discuss the nature of the marketing research process.

- Marketing research involves the gathering, processing, interpreting, and reporting of marketing information.
- The cost of marketing research should be evaluated against its benefits.
- The steps in marketing research are identifying the informational need, searching for secondary data, collecting primary data, and interpreting the data gathered.

4 Define market segmentation and its related strategies.

- A focus strategy relies on market segmentation, which is the process of dividing the total market for a product and/or service into groups with similar needs, each of which is likely to respond favorably to a specific marketing strategy.

- Broad segmentation variables that represent major dimensions of a market are benefit variables and demographic variables.

- Three types of market segmentation strategies are (1) the unsegmented approach, (2) the multisegment approach, and (3) the single-segment approach.

- The unsegmented strategy—when a business defines the total market as its target—is also known as mass marketing.

- A firm that determines that two or more market segments have the potential to be profitable and then develops a unique marketing mix for each segment is following a multisegment strategy.

- A firm that follows a single-segment strategy recognizes that several distinct market segments exist but chooses to concentrate on reaching only one segment.

5 Explain the different methods of forecasting sales.

- A sales forecast is an estimation of how much of a product or service will be purchased within a market during a defined time period.

- The forecasting process may be either a breakdown or a buildup process and may be either direct or indirect, depending on the predicting variable.

Key TERMS

small business marketing, p. 182

market analysis, p. 183

marketing mix, p. 183

customer profile, p. 184

marketing research, p. 188

secondary data, p. 189

primary data, p. 190

market, p. 192

market segmentation, p. 193

segmentation variables, p. 193

benefit variables, p. 193

demographic variables, p. 193

unsegmented strategy (mass marketing), p. 194

multisegment strategy, p. 195

single-segment strategy, p. 196

sales forecast, p. 197

breakdown process (chain-ratio method), p. 199

buildup process, p. 199

direct forecasting, p. 200

indirect forecasting, p. 200

Discussion QUESTIONS

1. What is the scope of small business marketing? Has it always been as broad as it is now? Why or why not?

2. How do the three marketing philosophies differ? Select a product and discuss marketing tactics that could be used to implement each philosophy.

3. What are the obstacles to adopting a consumer orientation in a small firm?

4. Briefly describe each of the components of a formal marketing plan.

5. What are the steps in the marketing research process?

6. What are the major considerations in designing a questionnaire?

7. Briefly explain the three components of the definition of a market, as presented in this chapter.

8. What types of variables are used for market segmentation? Would a small firm use the same variables as a large business? Why or why not?

9. Explain the difference between a multisegment strategy and a single-segment strategy. Which one is more likely to be appealing to a small firm? Why?

10. Explain why forecasting is used more widely by large firms than by small ones.

You Make the CALL

SITUATION 1

In 1998, Rosie Herman was in debt up to her ears. Years of fertility treatments had left her owing $75,000. She needed money but did not want to leave her young twins while she worked. So she turned to what she knew best. Herman had been a manicurist for 20 years and put this experience to use. She focused her attention on creating a body-care product. Mixing a combination of oils, sea salts, and other organic products, she came up with what she thought was a winning product. She was the guinea pig (what we refer to as a *test market*) for her product and found that the lotion she had created was perfect for treating her own skin, which had become dry and cracked from exposure to chemicals and water in her career as a manicurist.

Source: Sara Wilson, "Skin Deep," *Entrepreneur,* January 2005, p. 21.

Question 1 What type of research could Herman do to estimate the demand for her skin-care product?

Question 2 How might she raise the funds to start up her small business?

Question 3 How could a marketing plan help Herman be more successful as her company grows?

SITUATION 2

Alibek Iskakov has opened a small café named Oasis in Kokshetau, a city in Kazakhstan. In order to get primary data on the market for his café, he conducted a survey of 100 people—45 men and 55 women. Forty-eight respondents were between 18 and 24 years old, 38 were between 25 and 50 years old, and 14 were over 50 years old. The survey asked the following questions:

1. How often do you visit restaurants?
2. What is your favorite restaurant in Kokshetau? Why?
3. What is the most important factor for you in choosing a restaurant?
4. Would a small, neat café with traditional food appeal to you?
   a. (If no) Why not?
   b. (If yes) When would you patronize it?
5. How much are you willing to pay for dinner?

Question 1 What are the strengths and weaknesses of the sample used in this survey?

Question 2 Evaluate the questions used in the survey.

SITUATION 3

Mary Wilson is a 31-year-old wife and mother who wants to start her own company. She has no previous business experience but has an idea for marketing an animal-grooming service, with an approach similar to that used for pizza delivery. When a customer calls, Wilson will arrive in a van in less than 30 minutes and will provide the grooming service. Many of her friends think the idea has promise but dismiss her efforts to seriously discuss the venture. However, Wilson is not discouraged; she plans to purchase the van and the necessary grooming equipment.

Question 1 What target market or markets can you identify for Wilson? How could she forecast sales for her service in each market?

Question 2 What advantage does her business have over existing grooming businesses?

Question 3 What business name and promotional strategy would you suggest that Wilson use?

SITUATION 4

Watch your older relatives the next time you go out to eat. Do they have trouble seeing the menu well enough to read it? Chandler Powell did, and he had no luck finding a lighted magnifying glass to correct the situation.

When the 21-year-old college student attended a musical (at a poorly lit theater) and had a tough time reading the program, he again thought that a lighted magnifying glass was just what he needed. Eventually, he located several types online, but none proved entirely satisfactory. He decided that he had identified a marketing opportunity. He set his sights on the U.S. symphony market because it attracts older people who would likely benefit from such a product. But first, he needed a product.

Source: Sarah E. Needleman, "Selling Your Product to an Exclusive Club," *Startup Journal,* WSJ.com, accessed May 18, 2006.

Question 1 Where might Powell go to have a prototype of his product built?

Question 2 Where should Powell seek advice about how to market his product?

Question 3 What other markets might be right for a lighted magnifying glass?

Experiential EXERCISES

1. Interview a local small business manager about what she or he believes is the marketing philosophy followed by the business.

2. Assume you are planning to market a new facial tissue. Write a detailed customer profile, and explain how you would develop the sales forecast for this product.

3. Interview a local small business owner to determine the type of marketing research, if any, he or she has used.

4. Visit a local small retailer and observe its marketing efforts—for example, salesperson style, store atmosphere, and warranty policies. Report your observations to the class, and make recommendations for improving these efforts to increase customer satisfaction.

Exploring the WEB

1. About.com is a large and complex site offering advice and information on a wide range of topics. Its marketing advice and information pages are viewable at **http://marketing.about. com.** Under "Topics," click on "Small Business Marketing," and then select "Market Segmentation for the Small Business." Compare and contrast the sources listed. Then identify the best tips for using market segmentation strategies.

2. Go to the Small Business Administration's website at **http://www.sba.gov.** Select "Plan Your Business" under the site's "Small Business Planner."

a. Click on the "Write a Business Plan" link. The links you find there will provide you with valuable information on how to write a business plan and on sample plans.

b. Next click on "Finding a Niche." Based on your business idea, what might be the most promising niche for you?

c. Now, click on the "Sample Business Plans" link under the "Write a Business Plan" pulldown. After looking at several plans, where in the plans are marketing strategies and target markets (niches) discussed?

Case 7

eHarmony (p. 633)
This case illustrates the use of a marketing plan, from conception to implementation, in the development and ultimate success of one of the most highly recognized online dating services.

Alternative Cases for Chapter 7:
Case 1, Boston Duck Tours, p. 620
Case 13, Rodgers Chevrolet, p. 646

The Business Plan

Laying the Foundation

As part of laying the foundation for your own business plan, respond to the following questions regarding the marketing plan, marketing research, market segmentation, and sales forecasting.

Marketing Plan Questions

1. Who is your competition?
2. Have you conducted a SWOT analysis?
3. What is the customer profile for your product and/or service?
4. How will you identify prospective customers?
5. What geographic area will you serve?
6. What are the distinguishing characteristics of your product and/or service?
7. What steps have already been taken to develop your product and/or service?
8. What do you plan to name your product and/or service?
9. Will there be a warranty?
10. How will you set the price for your product and/or service?
11. What type of distribution plan will you use?
12. Will you export to other countries?
13. What type of selling effort will you use?
14. What special selling skills will be required?
15. What types of advertising and sales promotion will you use?
16. Can you use public relations and publicity to promote your company and product/service?

Marketing Research Questions

1. What types of research should be conducted to collect the information you need?
2. How much will this research cost?
3. What sources of secondary data will address your informational needs?
4. What sources of relevant data are available in your local library?
5. What sources of outside professional assistance would you consider using to help with marketing research?
6. Is there information available on the Internet that might be helpful?
7. What research questions do you need answers to?

Market Segmentation Questions

1. Will you focus on a limited market within the industry?
2. What segmentation variables will you use to define your target market?
3. If you determine that several distinct market segments exist, will you concentrate on just one segment?

Forecasting Questions

1. How do you plan to forecast sales for your product and/or service?
2. What sources of forecasting assistance have you consulted?
3. What sales forecasting techniques are most appropriate to your needs?
4. What is the sales forecast for your product and/or service?
5. How reliable is your sales forecast?

## chapter 8

The Organizational Plan

Teams, Legal Forms, and Strategic Alliances

In the VIDEO SPOTLIGHT

Biosite, Inc.
http://www.biosite.com

Few entrepreneurs imagine going public when they initially structure their business. Most small businesses start out as simple proprietorships, with a single owner (the founder). For the three founders of Biosite, Inc., however, things were a bit different. The company they worked for had been acquired, and the new owner, pharmaceutical giant Eli Lilly, was not interested in letting Kim Blickenstaff, Dr. Ken Buechler, and Dr. Gunars Valkirs set up their own internal company to develop unique medical testing technologies. So these three scientists decided to start their own company.

From the start, the success of Biosite has hinged on the overlapping strengths of its founders, the commitment they have to one another, their recognition that the structure of the business should be formalized, and their ability to bring all these elements to bear on the development of extremely innovative medical technologies. The result has been a highly creative biotechnology company, built on a strong business foundation.

How a company is structured can significantly affect the business activities of the founders. Before going public, the three founders of Biosite were creative, nimble, and focused on science. Once they changed the company structure by recreating it as a public corporation, however, almost half of their time was immediately relegated to investor relations. Watch this video spotlight to see how a strong team can propel great ideas, even when the structure of the business changes.

Video material provided by Hattie Bryant, Producer of Small Business School, the series on PBS Stations, Worldnet, and the Web at http://www.smallbusinessschool.org.

 SmallBusinessSchool
the Series on PBS stations and the Web

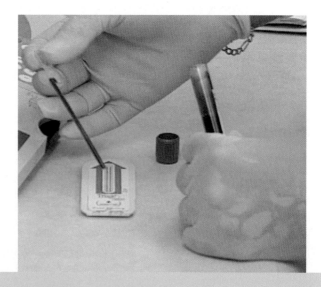

After studying this chapter, you should be able to

1 Describe the characteristics and value of a strong management team.
2 Explain the common legal forms of organization used by small businesses.
3 Identify factors to consider in choosing among the primary legal forms of organization, including tax consequences.
4 Describe the unique features and restrictions of five specialized organizational forms.
5 Explain the nature of strategic alliances and their uses in small businesses.
6 Describe the effective use of boards of directors and advisory councils.

One of the most enduring myths in American business is that of the lone entrepreneur who defies the odds by taking a creative business idea and turning it into reality by sheer force of will and personality. It makes a great story, but is that how it usually happens?

One small business writer has expressed doubt about the storyline: "There is no question that small companies are almost always driven, at least at the outset, by the passion of a single risk-taking individual. But the myth of the solo flier, however romantic, obscures something crucial: Business success depends on collaboration."[1] In many cases, collaboration begins almost from the start, when two or more individuals come together as a team to launch a new enterprise.

To be sure, there are still plenty of solo entrepreneurs starting new businesses,[2] but evidence is mounting to show that team-founded ventures tend to outperform ventures with a single founder.[3]

In all but the simplest businesses, the entrepreneur's personal talents are more likely to lead to success when they are supplemented with the energy, insights, and contributions of other individuals. The prospects for any venture are most promising when a firm's leadership is composed of competent, resourceful, and tenacious individuals. So, in most cases it is very helpful for an entrepreneur to identify and attract a strong management team. A business plan that provides for strong leadership is appealing to both potential investors and prospective managerial personnel. Clearly, the management team can have a profound impact on the performance of the venture, and founders have much greater control over this factor than they do over others, including market conditions and competitor reactions.[4]

Whether potential investors and prospective managerial personnel have the opportunity to also become partial owners of the company depends on the ownership structure selected by the entrepreneur—that is, the legal form of organization. The direction of the business will be strongly affected by whether the entrepreneur chooses to go with a sole proprietorship, a partnership, a corporation, or one of various other forms. We will discuss legal forms of organization in greater depth later in this chapter.

A new business rarely has the financial resources to incorporate within the organization all the leadership and managerial personnel it could use. One way to deal with this limitation is to build alliances; another is to take advantage of the expertise of outside directors. Strategic alliances are becoming increasingly important to small businesses, as are active, objective boards of directors.

Wise decisions regarding the management team, the form of organization, strategic alliances, and the board of directors can greatly enhance the performance of a company. On the other hand, even *brilliant* ideas can be doomed if the enterprise is not connected to the human resources it needs or fails to use them effectively. The tired old slogan "Our People Make the Difference" can be true, but only if those people are carefully selected, well organized, and effectively led.

Building a Management Team

1 Describe the characteristics and value of a strong management team.

management team
Managers and other key persons who give a company its general direction

If a firm is extremely small, the founder will probably be the key manager and perhaps the only manager. In most firms, however, others share leadership roles with the owner or owners, which creates opportunities to leverage their combined networks and resources for the good of the company. In general, the management team consists of individuals with supervisory responsibilities, as well as nonsupervisory personnel who play key roles in the business.[5] For example, members of the management team might include a financial manager who supervises a small office staff and another person who directs the marketing effort.

If you should find that you don't have your "dream team" in place, understand that the team arrangement does not have to be permanent. Though it can be difficult to do, sometimes you have to respectfully and appropriately let individuals go when they cannot or will not effectively support the business; new members can be added to the team as the need arises.[6]

Strong management can make the best of a good business idea by securing the resources needed to make it work. Of course, even a highly competent management team cannot rescue a firm that is based on a weak business concept or that lacks adequate resources. The importance of strong management to startups is evident in the attitudes of prospective investors, who consider the quality of a new venture's management to be the single most important factor in decisions to invest or take a pass. One entrepreneurship expert sums up popular opinion this way: "If there is one issue on which the majority of theorists and practitioners agree, it is that a high-quality management team is a key ingredient in the success of many high-growth ventures . . . and most of the reasons for failure may be traced to specific flaws in the venture team."[7]

As indicated earlier, a management team often can bring greater strength to a venture than an individual entrepreneur can. One reason for this is that a team can provide a diversity of talent to meet various managerial needs, which can be especially helpful to startups built on new technologies that must manage a broad range of factors. In addition, a team can provide greater assurance of continuity, since the departure of one member of a team is less devastating to a business than the departure of a sole entrepreneur.

The competence required in a management team depends on the type of business and the nature of its operations.[8] For example, a software development firm and a restaurant call for very different types of business experience. Whatever the business, a small firm needs managers with an appropriate combination of educational background and experience. In evaluating the qualifications of an applicant for a key position, an entrepreneur needs to know whether she or he has experience in a related type of business, as a manager or as an entrepreneur.

Achieving Balance

Not all members of a management team need competence in all areas—the key is balance. If one member has expertise in finance, another should have an adequate marketing background. And there should be someone who can supervise employees effectively.[9] This diversity in perspectives and work styles is what enables the completion of complex tasks, but it can also lead to serious conflict, which can squeeze all the energy and enthusiasm out of a venture.[10]

Even when entrepreneurs recognize the need for team members with varying expertise, they frequently seek to replicate their own personalities and management styles. Interpersonal compatibility and cooperation between team members are necessary for effective collaboration, and cohesive teams tend to perform better.[11] However, experience suggests that a functionally diverse and balanced team will be more likely to cover all the bases, giving the company a competitive edge.

The goal in planning the company's leadership, then, should be to produce a management team that will be able to give competent direction to the new firm. The team

Living the Dream   entrepreneurial challenges

Three Men and a Restaurant

© Timothy D. Sofranko/Colgate University

Chris Nordsiek, Preston Burnes, and Matt Brown are college buddies (from Colgate University), but they also worked together as an entrepreneurial team to launch a quick-serve Mexican restaurant called Chilly Willy's. The business idea was cooked up by the trio so that they could participate in a business plan competition as sophomores. According to Burnes, their early surveys of students showed that the Colgate crowd "really wanted Mexican food and a late-night diner," and the early success of the business proved their research was accurate.

Although a good idea and a little seed money (each received $4,000 for winning a business plan competition) were important factors, the human element was critical. The founders of Chilly Willy's each have different strengths and skills, and the balanced perspective they provided *as a team* served the startup well. By focusing on the quality of the food and emphasizing customer service, they generated a lot of repeat business—enough to keep 25 part-time employees busy and generate $100,000 in sales during their first year of business. That's a lot of burritos!

The trio clearly worked well as a team. They attributed this to having known each other as fraternity brothers for a year before starting the business, which made them confident that they could work together and cover one another's weaknesses. While some entrepreneurship experts are not enthusiastic about friends starting a business, others recognize that the "personal chemistry" among friends can translate into business success, especially if their strengths and insights as individuals are complementary. This seems to have been the case for this student startup.

The three friends recently closed Chilly Willy's to move on to other career opportunities, but their positive experiences from working together highlight the advantages of starting a business as part of an entrepreneurial team.

Sources: Charlie Melichar, "New Eatery Gives Colgate Juniors Taste of Entrepreneurship," Colgate University News, May 3, 2005, http://www.colgate.edu/printerfriendly.aspx?tabid=731&pgID=6014&nwID=3729, accessed January 1, 2007; Nichole L. Torres, "Buddy System," *Entrepreneur*, Vol. 33, No. 10 (October 2005), p. 118; and personal correspondence with Tim O'Keefe, director of Web content, Colgate University, June 7, 2007.

should be balanced in terms of covering the various functional areas and offering the right combination of education and experience. It may comprise both insiders and outside specialists. For example, a small firm may benefit by developing working relationships with such external organizations as a commercial bank, a law firm, and an accounting firm. A number of outside sources of managerial assistance are identified and discussed in Chapter 18. The role of an active board of directors in providing counsel and guidance to the management team is discussed later in this chapter.

Expanding Social Networks

Sometimes it's not *what* you know but *who* you know that matters. The management team can not only help the venture obtain investment and technology resources, but also, and perhaps most important, connect the enterprise with a social network that can provide access to a wide range of resources beyond the reach of individual team members. A

social network
An interconnected system comprising relationships with other people

social network is the web of relationships that a person has with other people, including roommates or other acquaintances from college, former employees and business associates, contacts through community organizations like the Rotary Club, and friends from church or synagogue. But it doesn't end there. A friend from college may not have what you need, but she may know someone who does. It is often said that business is all about relationships—a principle that is certainly not lost on successful entrepreneurs. And the power of social networks is expanded tremendously as well-connected people are added to the management team.

What does an entrepreneur need from his or her network? That all depends on the situation. Howard Aldrich and Nancy Carter, two highly regarded experts on management teams and social networks, analyzed Panel Study of Entrepreneurial Dynamics (PSED) data and found that nearly half of those who are starting businesses use their networks to access information or get advice. About one-fourth use their networks to gain introductions to other people, while a much smaller percentage use connections to obtain money, business services, physical facilities and equipment, help with personal needs, and other forms of assistance.[12] Clearly, a healthy system of personal relationships can help a small business access the resources it needs to get established and grow.

Beyond providing access to resources, social networks can be especially helpful in establishing legitimacy and jump-starting sales. New ventures and small businesses often find it difficult to "get the business ball rolling" because potential customers simply don't know them well enough. Reputable firms may hesitate to do business with a company that doesn't have an established track record for reliable delivery or quality products or services. But acquiring one or more high-profile customers may persuade others to give a relatively unknown company a shot at their business, too. For an entrepreneur, having a healthy social network and a management team with helpful connections can be critical in establishing a solid reputation.

social capital
The advantage created by an individual's connections in a social network

An active and robust network is necessary for building **social capital**, which we define as the advantage created by an individual's connections within a network of social relationships. But this advantage doesn't develop overnight or by accident. It takes years to build social capital, and the building blocks are well known—being reliable as a friend, being fair in your dealings, being true to your word.

reciprocation
A powerful social rule based on an obligation to repay in kind what another has done for or provided to us

The principle of reciprocation can be extremely helpful in adding to whatever social capital you already have. In his popular book on influence, Robert Cialdini defines **reciprocation** as a subtle but powerful obligation, deeply embedded in every society, to repay in kind what another person has done for us or provided to us.[13] In simple terms, people naturally feel that they should return favors. You can easily prime the pump of social capital by being the first to lend a hand and then watch those you assist come to your rescue when you run up against a challenge and ask for help. You don't have to fake it; just slow down a bit, and take a genuine interest in the needs of your friends and acquaintances. And helping others doesn't have to be costly; in today's information economy, passing along an important bit of knowledge or insight can be as good as gold! So, think ahead, and reach out to help where you can. Your social capital is sure to increase, binding friends and acquaintances to you and providing a solid foundation for building a business.

Specifying Structure

Once members of the management team have been selected, an entrepreneur must design an internal management structure that defines relationships among all members of the organization. Relationships among the various positions—such as advertising manager, marketing director, financial officer, and human resource manager—should be determined. Although these relationships need not be worked out in great detail, planning should be sufficient to ensure orderly operations and avoid an overlapping of responsibilities that invites conflict.

The management plan should be drawn up in a way that provides for business growth. Any unfilled positions should be specified, and job descriptions should spell out the duties of and necessary qualifications for such positions. Methods for selecting key employees should be explained. Compensation arrangements, including bonuses or other incentive plans for key organization members, should be carefully considered and specified in the plan.

Choosing a Legal Form of Organization

In launching a new business, an entrepreneur must choose a form of legal organization, which will determine who the actual owners of the business are. The most basic options are the sole proprietorship, partnership, and C corporation. More specialized forms of organization exist, but many small businesses find one of the common forms suitable for their needs. After outlining the primary options, we will look first at some criteria for choosing among them and then at five specialized forms that offer their own unique features and advantages. Exhibit 8-1 shows the various basic forms of organization. (The S corporation option, presented in the exhibit, is one of the specialized forms of organization that will be described later in this chapter.)

2 Explain the common legal forms of organization used by small businesses.

The Sole Proprietorship Option

A **sole proprietorship**, the most basic business form, is a company owned by one person. An individual proprietor has title to all business assets and is subject to the claims of creditors. He or she receives all of the firm's profits but must also assume all losses, bear all risks, and pay all debts. Although this form is often most appropriate only for a new small business, forming a sole proprietorship is the simplest and cheapest way to start operation. Most states do not even require such companies to have a business license. Because of the ease of startup, the vast majority of small businesses (nearly 70 percent) adopt this legal structure (see Exhibit 8-2).

sole proprietorship
A business owned by one person, who bears unlimited liability for the enterprise

exhibit

8-1   *Basic Forms of Legal Organization for Small Businesses*

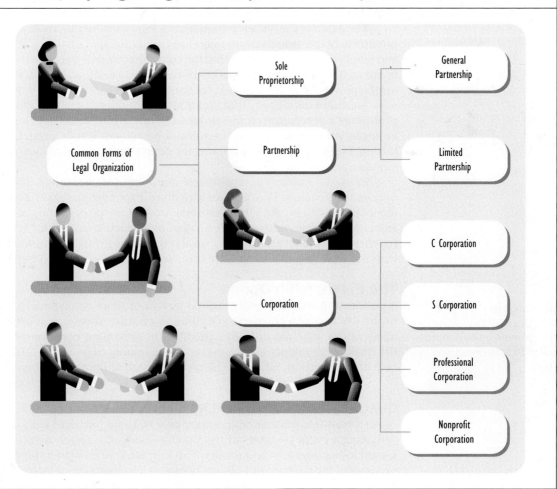

8-2   Percentage of Small Businesses by Legal Form of Organization

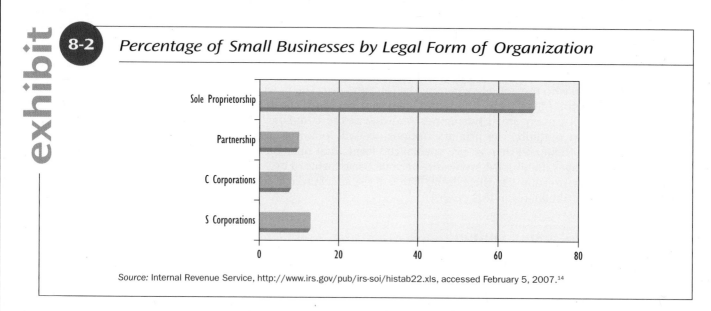

Source: Internal Revenue Service, http://www.irs.gov/pub/irs-soi/histab22.xls, accessed February 5, 2007.[14]

unlimited liability
Liability on the part of an owner that extends beyond the owner's investment in the business

In a sole proprietorship, an owner is free from interference by partners, shareholders, and directors. However, a sole proprietorship lacks some of the advantages of other legal forms. For example, there are no limits on the owner's personal liability—that is, the owner of the business has **unlimited liability,** and thus his or her personal assets can be taken by business creditors if the enterprise fails. For this reason, the sole proprietorship form is usually the practical choice only for very small businesses. In addition, sole proprietors are not employees of the business and cannot receive the advantage of many tax-free fringe benefits, such as insurance and hospitalization plans, which are often provided by corporations for their employees.

The death of the owner terminates the legal existence of a sole proprietorship. Thus, the possibility of the owner's death may cloud relationships between a business and its creditors and employees. It is important that the owner have a will, because the assets of the business minus its liabilities will belong to her or his heirs. In a will, a sole proprietor can give an executor the power to run the business for the heirs until they can take it over or it can be sold.

Another contingency that must be provided for is the possible incapacity of the sole proprietor. For example, if she or he were badly hurt in an accident and hospitalized for an extended period, the business could be ruined. A sole proprietor can guard against this contingency by giving a competent person legal power of attorney to carry on in such circumstances.

In some cases, circumstances argue against selecting the sole proprietorship option. If the nature of a business involves exposure to legal liability—for example, the manufacture of a potentially hazardous product or the operation of a child-care facility—a legal form that provides greater protection against personal liability is likely to be a better choice. For most companies, however, various forms of insurance are available to deal with the risks of a sole proprietorship, as well as those related to partnerships.[15]

The Partnership Option

partnership
A legal entity formed by two or more co-owners to carry on a business for profit

A **partnership** is a legal entity formed by two or more co-owners to operate a business for profit. Because of a partnership's voluntary nature, owners can set it up quickly, avoiding many of the legal requirements involved in creating a corporation. A partnership pools the managerial talents and capital of those joining together as business partners. As in a sole proprietorship, however, the owners share unlimited liability.

QUALIFICATIONS OF PARTNERS   Any person capable of contracting may legally become a business partner. Individuals may become partners without contributing capital or having a claim to assets at the time of dissolution; such persons are partners only in regard to management and profits. The formation of a partnership involves consideration not only of legal issues but also of personal and managerial factors. A strong partnership requires partners who are honest, healthy, capable, and compatible.

exhibit

8-3   *The Advantages and Disadvantages of Partnerships*

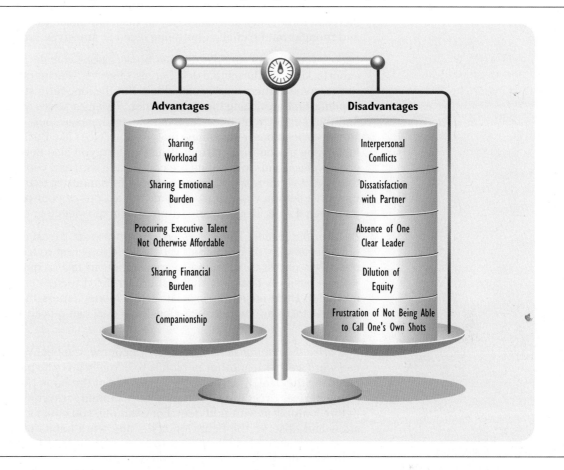

Advantages	Disadvantages
Sharing Workload	Interpersonal Conflicts
Sharing Emotional Burden	Dissatisfaction with Partner
Procuring Executive Talent Not Otherwise Affordable	Absence of One Clear Leader
Sharing Financial Burden	Dilution of Equity
Companionship	Frustration of Not Being Able to Call One's Own Shots

Operating a business as a partnership has benefits, but it is also fraught with potential problems. Most experts discourage the use of partnerships as a way to run a business, even though there are good and bad qualities associated with this form of organization (see Exhibit 8-3). The benefits of partnerships include the ability to share the workload as well as the emotional and financial burdens of the enterprise and to buy management talent that might otherwise break the budget. And it should not be overlooked that partners can add companionship to life in a small business.

However, many believe the personal conflicts common in partnerships more than offset the benefits, and partners often fall short of one another's expectations. Of course, decision making is more complicated in partnerships because leadership is shared, and owners must also share their equity position in the business, which naturally dilutes the control of each partner. While some of the difficulties of partnerships are financial in nature, most are relational—for example, coping with a partner's dishonesty or dealing with differing priorities. Partnerships clearly have both disturbing and redeeming qualities, so the issue is not black and white. The important point is that *a partnership should be formed only if it appears to be the best option when all features of the enterprise are taken into consideration.*

Many entrepreneurs have learned about partnerships the hard way—from "the school of hard knocks." Based on the experiences of those who have seen firsthand the extraordinary ups and debilitating downs of partnerships, the following suggestions may help entrepreneurs make the most of this form of organization.

- *Capitalize on the unique advantages of a partnership.* It is important to recognize the advantages of partnerships and to build on the synergies that can result from them. For example, Brian Miller, co-owner of the marketing firm MillerWhite, LLC, in Terre Haute, Indiana, was grateful that his partner could "keep the ship sailing" while he was out of work for seven months having treatments for leukemia.[16] Even when partners are devoting full time to the business, working together can increase the quality and efficiency of decision making by focusing more energy and thought on the challenges being faced at any given time.

- *Choose your partner carefully.* In their book *Lessons from the Edge,* entrepreneurship experts Jana Matthews and Jeff Dennis observe, "Partnerships are just like marriages; some of them work, some don't. But the long-term success of a partnership depends first on picking the right partner."[17] Many sources are available to help you find that perfect someone—for example, trade magazines, client contacts, professional associations, even online matching services like BusinessPartners.com. But identifying a promising partner is just a start; you also need to be sure that your goals, values, and work habits are compatible with and your skills complementary to those of your prospective partner before committing to the deal. Above all, team up with a person you can trust, since the actions of your partner can legally bind you, even if a decision is made without your knowledge or consent.[18]

- *Be open, but cautious, about partnerships with friends.* If trust is critical to the success of a partnership, then wouldn't it be best to look first to friends as potential partners? Not necessarily. Valued relationships can take a quick turn for the worse when a business deal gets rocky, and a Dr. Jekyl friend can sometimes transform into a Mr. Hyde business associate when money enters the picture. And remember, the stakes are high: a minor business deal can quickly ruin a very important friendship.[19]

- *Test-drive the relationship, if possible.* Of course, the best way to determine if you can work well with another person is to actually give the partnership a try before finalizing the deal. Karen Cheney, co-author of the book *How to Start a Successful Home Business,* recommends trying more limited forms of business collaboration before jumping in with both feet. For example, you could share a booth at a trade show and observe the behavior, style, and work habits of the person you hope to team up with. This allows you to assess his or her strengths and weaknesses before committing to a long-term relationship.[20]

- *Create a combined vision for the business.* It's important that partners be "on the same page" when it comes to forming the business concept they hope to develop together. This takes time, patience, and a lot of conversation. Hal Scogin, owner of a multimedia design company in Olympia, Washington, discovered just how challenging the process can be. He had hopes of creating a company with two partners, but it soon became obvious that they did not see the business in the same way. Scogin thought the venture was a multimedia design company,

How They See It: Finding the Right Partner

Sally Lifland

If you can find the right partner, forming a partnership can be just the right way to take advantage of two different people's skill sets without establishing an arbitrary hierarchy or getting mired in legal paperwork.

Since I love to travel and am outgoing, I do most of our customer relations work—making sales calls on publishers, negotiating working relationships,

attending meetings, participating in seminars, and tending to the occasional crisis. But because I love to travel, I also take a lot of vacations, and I would never be able to do that if I didn't have a partner who was quietly and very competently working away in the office day in and day out (including many Saturdays), making sure the projects get done.

In 28 years, we have never had a decision that we were not able to make by consensus.

but his partners considered it to be a technology company. Needless to say, the partnership did not last long.[21] Some of the specific matters you should discuss before joining forces include the expectations of all partners (contributions of time, money, expertise, etc.), planned division of work, anticipated vacation time, and the division of profits and losses.

■ *Prepare for the worst.* Keep in mind that more than half of all partnerships fail. That is why most experts recommend having an exit strategy for the partnership from the beginning. What looks like a good business arrangement at the outset can quickly fall apart when market conditions shift, a partner becomes involved in another business venture, or personal circumstances change. For example, the birth of a child, a sudden divorce, or the unexpected death of a spouse can alter everything. If it becomes necessary, exiting a partnership is far more difficult when plans for such an unfortunate outcome were not considered early on.

Failure to take concerns like these into account can derail efforts to build an effective working relationship or doom an otherwise workable partnership to an unnecessary or painful demise.

RIGHTS AND DUTIES OF PARTNERS   An oral partnership agreement is legal and binding, but memory is always less than perfect. In his book *Legal Guide for Starting and Running a Small Business,* author and practicing business attorney Fred Steingold strongly recommends that partners sign a written **partnership agreement** to avoid problems later on.[22] This document, which explicitly delineates the partners' rights and duties, should be drawn up before the venture is launched. Though the partners may choose to have an attorney draw up the agreement in order to ensure that all important features are included, many other sources of assistance (such as online resources) also are available to guide you through this process. For example, a Google search on "partnership agreements" will pull up a number of helpful resources.

partnership agreement
A document that states explicitly the rights and duties of partners

Unless the articles of the partnership agreement specify otherwise, a partner is generally recognized as having certain implicit rights. For example, partners share profits or losses equally, unless they have agreed to a different ratio.

In a partnership, each party has **agency power**, which means that a business decision by one partner binds all members of the firm, even if the other partners were not consulted in advance or didn't approve the agreement or contract. And as with a sole proprietorship, the scale of personal liability of the partners can be terrifying. The assets of the business are at risk, of course, but so are the personal assets of the partners, including their homes, cars, and bank accounts. Good faith, together with reasonable care in the exercise of managerial duties, is required of all partners in the business. Since the partnership relationship is fiduciary in character, a partner cannot compete in another business and remain a partner. Nor can a partner use business information solely for personal gain.

agency power
The ability of any one partner to legally bind the other partners

HELP FOR AILING PARTNERSHIPS   All partnerships experience stress, and many do not survive the challenge. According to Dr. David Gage, a psychologist, business mediation expert, and principal of BMC Associates in Washington, D.C., the "divorce rate" of business partnerships is, unfortunately, very high. Often, the problems that lead to conflict stem from turf battles over control.[23]

Complications can arise even if partners have been careful to match their expectations at the start of the partnership and the business arrangement has been formalized through a partnership agreement. When problems emerge and trust begins to break down, partners should move quickly to try to resolve underlying issues. If they cannot do so, they should consider hiring a business mediator. Working with a business mediator can be expensive, but the dissolution of the partnership is likely to be far more costly.

TERMINATION OF A PARTNERSHIP   Death, incapacity, or withdrawal of a partner ends a partnership and requires liquidation or reorganization of the business. Liquidation often results in substantial losses to all partners, but it may be legally necessary, because a partnership represents a close personal relationship of the parties that cannot be maintained against the desire of any one of them.

When one partner dies, loss due to liquidation may be avoided if the partnership agreement stipulates that surviving partners can continue the business after buying the decedent's interest. This option can be facilitated by having each partner carry life insurance that names the other partners as beneficiaries.

Partnerships sometimes have immediate concerns to address when a partner decides to leave the business, especially if the departure was unexpected. In 1999, Aaron Keller, Brian Aducci, and a third partner started a marketing and design firm in Minneapolis called Capsule. Eighteen months later, when their partner decided to leave the business and start a competing company (taking several employees and clients with him), Keller and Aducci knew they would have to move quickly to avoid serious losses. Lea A. Strickland, small business expert and author of *Out of the Cubicle and Into Business,* analyzed their situation and offered the following emergency prescription: First, cut off the departing partner's access to bank accounts, physical facilities, and company assets to avoid loss or damage to equipment critical to the business. Then quickly assess that partner's role in the enterprise and take steps to fill his shoes, to get the business back to normal as soon as possible. Once these very pressing matters are under control, sort out any legal issues that remain, such as abiding by any exit agreements that may have been signed. With time, and a lot of hard work, Keller and Aducci were able to regain their footing, but the experience helped them to understand just how fragile a partnership can be—and how important it is to have a rapid response plan when things go wrong.[24]

The C Corporation Option

corporation
A business organization that exists as a legal entity and provides limited liability to its owners

In 1819, Chief Justice John Marshall of the United States Supreme Court defined a **corporation** as "an artificial being, invisible, intangible, and existing only in contemplation of the law." With these words, the Supreme Court recognized the corporation as a **legal entity**, meaning that it can file suit and be sued, hold and sell property, and engage in business operations that are stipulated in the corporate charter. In other words, a corporation is a separate entity from the individuals who own it. The ordinary corporation—often called a **C corporation** to distinguish it from more specialized forms—is discussed in this section.

legal entity
A business organization that is recognized by the law as having a separate legal existence

A corporation is chartered under state laws. The length of its life is independent of its owners' (stockholders') lives. The corporation, *not* its owners, is liable for the debts of the business. Directors and officers represent the corporation as its agents and can enter into agreements on its behalf.

C corporation
An ordinary corporation, taxed by the federal government as a separate legal entity

THE CORPORATE CHARTER   To form a corporation, one or more persons must apply to the secretary of state (at the state level) for permission to incorporate. After preliminary steps—including payment of an incorporation fee—have been completed, the written application (which should be prepared by an attorney) is approved by the secretary of state and becomes the **corporate charter**. This document—sometimes called *articles of incorporation* or *certificate of incorporation*—shows that the corporation exists.

corporate charter
A document that establishes a corporation's existence

A corporation's charter should be brief, in accord with state law, and broad in its statement of the firm's powers. Details should be left to the *corporate bylaws,* which outline the basic rules for ongoing formalities and decisions of corporate life, including the size of the board of directors, the duties and responsibilities of directors and officers, the scheduling of regular meetings of the directors and shareholders, the means of calling for a special meeting of these groups, procedures for exercising voting rights, and restrictions on the transfer of corporate stock.

stock certificate
A document specifying the number of shares owned by a stockholder

RIGHTS AND STATUS OF STOCKHOLDERS   Ownership in a corporation is evidenced by **stock certificates**, each of which stipulates the number of shares owned by a stockholder. An ownership interest does not confer a legal right to act for the firm or to share in its management. It does, however, provide the stockholder with the right to receive dividends in proportion to stockholdings—but only when the dividends are properly declared by the firm. Ownership of stock typically carries a **pre-emptive right**, or the right to buy new shares, in proportion to the number of shares already owned, before new stock is offered for public sale.

pre-emptive right
The right of stockholders to buy new shares of stock before they are offered to the public

Living the Dream   entrepreneurial challenges

Pals in Partnership

© Ken Reagan/Feature Photo Service/NewsCom

Penn and Teller are in the business of entertainment. The comedy-magic duo has been at it for 30 years, with projects ranging from stage to television to best-selling books. You can find them in Las Vegas, where they appear on stage nightly, or you might see them on DVD or hear them on the radio. The partners started performing together in 1975 and decided to incorporate in the early 1990s. Today, they bring in $10 million to $12 million a year. How do they do it? By refusing to compromise and by challenging each other's ideas until they find something they both like.

The strength of their friendship is a sign that partnerships work best when you go into business with someone you know, right? Not necessarily! Brad Powell, a 35-year-old software business owner in Vienna, Virginia, entered into a partnership with a longtime friend, but the business fizzled in only seven years. When Powell resigned because of disagreements over how to manage the business, not only did he lose a business—he also lost a friend. "From a legal perspective, the separation was fairly easy," says Powell, "but it was emotionally draining, and it brought me down for months on end."

Powell has since formed another partnership with another friend, but this time they are doing things very differently. Planning is the key. For example, the new partners have run through all kinds of potential scenarios so that they will know what to expect no matter what comes their way. They have signed a buy-sell agreement to nail down what will happen if one of them leaves the business, and they have assigned roles to prevent conflict. There's still no guarantee that the friendship will survive a difficult business breakup, but they've increased its chances.

Forming a partnership with a friend seems to make so much sense—you know each other, trust has already been established, and you feel good about going the extra mile for a person you care about. But those qualities can be the very factors that doom the business—and the friendship. When it comes to due diligence, who feels comfortable doing a background check on a friend? Perhaps more devastating, how many businesses continue because of friendship when the smart thing to do would be to close down? The problem seems to be stickier when friendship is the glue that holds a business together—and unlike with Penn and Teller, there may be no comic relief in sight.

Sources: "Penn & Teller/Biography," http://www.pennandteller.com/03/coolstuff/bio.html, accessed February 5, 2007; Patrick J. Sauer, ". . . Work with a Partner (Year After Year After Year)," *Inc.*, Vol. 26, No. 1 (October 2004), pp. 88–89; Nichole L. Torres, "Pairing Up," *Entrepreneur*, Vol. 33, No. 9 (September 2005), p. 99; and Kelly Spors, "Small Talk," *Wall Street Journal*, April 4, 2006, p. A16.

http://www.pennandteller.com

The legal status of stockholders is fundamental, of course, but it may be overemphasized. In many small corporations, the owners typically serve both as directors and as managing officers. The person who owns most or all of the stock can control a business as effectively as if it were a sole proprietorship. Thus, this form of organization works well for individual- and family-owned businesses, where maintaining control of the firm is important.

LIMITED LIABILITY OF STOCKHOLDERS   For most stockholders, their limited liability is a major advantage of the corporate form of organization. Their financial liability is limited to the amount of money they invest in the business. Creditors cannot require them to sell personal assets to pay corporation debts. However, small corporations are often in a somewhat shaky financial condition during their early years of operation. As a result, a bank that makes a loan to a small firm may insist that the owners assume personal liability for the firm's debts by signing the promissory notes not only as representatives of the firm but personally as well. If the corporation is unable to repay the loan, the banker can then look to the owners' personal assets to recover the amount of the loan. In this case, the corporate advantage of limited liability is lost.

Why would owners agree to personally guarantee a firm's debt? Simply put, they may have no choice if they want the money. Most bankers are not willing to loan money to an entrepreneur who is not prepared to put his or her own personal assets at risk.

DEATH OR WITHDRAWAL OF STOCKHOLDERS   Unlike a partnership interest, ownership in a corporation is readily transferable. Exchange of shares of stock is sufficient to convey an ownership interest to a different individual.

Stock of large corporations is exchanged continually without noticeable effect on the operation of the business. For a small firm, however, a change of owners, though legally similar, can involve numerous complications. For example, finding a buyer for the stock of a small firm may prove difficult. Also, a minority stockholder in a small firm is vulnerable. If two of three equal shareholders in a small business sold their stock to an outsider, the remaining shareholder would then be at the mercy of that outsider.

The death of a majority stockholder can have unfortunate repercussions in a small firm. An heir, the executor, or a purchaser of the stock might well insist on direct control, with possible adverse effects for other stockholders. To prevent problems of this nature, legal arrangements should be made at the outset to provide for management continuity by surviving stockholders and fair treatment of a stockholder's heirs. As in the case of a partnership, taking out life insurance ahead of time can ensure the ability to buy out a deceased stockholder's interest.

exhibit

8-4   *Comparison of Basic Legal Forms of Organization*

Form of Organization	Initial Organizational Requirements and Costs	Liability of Owners	Continuity of Business
Sole proprietorship	Minimum requirements; generally no registration or filing fee	Unlimited liability	Dissolved upon proprietor's death
General partnership	Minimum requirements; generally no registration or filing fee; written partnership agreement not legally required but strongly suggested	Unlimited liability	Unless partnership agreement specifies differently, dissolved upon withdrawal or death of partner
C corporation	Most expensive and greatest requirements; filing fees; compliance with state regulations for corporations	Liability limited to investment in company	Continuity of business unaffected by shareholder withdrawal or death
Form of organization preferred	Proprietorship or partnership	C corporation	C corporation

MAINTAINING CORPORATE STATUS   Establishing a corporation is one thing; keeping that status is another. Certain steps must be taken if the corporation is to retain its status as a separate entity. For example, the corporation must hold annual meetings of both the shareholders and the board of directors, keep minutes to document the major decisions of shareholders and directors, maintain bank accounts that are separate from owners' bank accounts, and file a separate income tax return for the business.

Criteria for Choosing an Organizational Form

Choosing a legal form for a new business deserves careful attention because of the various, sometimes conflicting features of each organizational option. Depending on the particular circumstances of a specific business, the tax advantages of one form, for example, may offset the limited-liability advantages of another form. Some tradeoffs may be necessary. Ideally, an experienced attorney should be consulted for guidance in selecting the most appropriate form of organization.

Some entrepreneurship experts insist that the two most basic forms of business— sole proprietorship and partnership—should *never* be adopted. While these forms clearly have drawbacks, they are workable. As illustrated in Exhibit 8-2, the IRS projected that nearly 70 percent of all new businesses in 2007 would be formed as sole proprietorships; 10 percent would be set up as partnerships, and 21 percent would be established as corporations (8 percent as C corporations and 13 percent as S corporations).[25]

Exhibit 8-4 summarizes the main considerations in selecting one of the three primary forms of ownership. A description of each factor follows.

INITIAL ORGANIZATIONAL REQUIREMENTS AND COSTS   Organizational requirements and costs increase as the formality of the organization increases. That is, a sole proprietorship is typically less complex and less expensive to form than a partnership, and a partnership is less complex and less expensive to form than a corporation. In view of the relatively modest costs, however, this consideration is of minimal importance in the long run.

> 3 Identify factors to consider in choosing among the primary legal forms of organization, including tax consequences.

Transferability of Ownership	Management Control	Attractiveness for Raising Capital	Income Taxes
May transfer ownership of company name and assets	Absolute management freedom	Limited to proprietor's personal capital	Income from the business is taxed as personal income to the proprietor
Requires the consent of all partners	Majority vote of partners required for control	Limited to partners' ability and desire to contribute capital	Income from the business is taxed as personal income to the partners
Easily transferred by transferring shares of stock	Shareholders have final control, but usually board of directors controls company policies	Usually the most attractive form for raising capital	The C corporation is taxed on its income and the stockholder is taxed if and when dividends are received
Depends on the circumstances	Depends on the circumstances	C corporation	Depends on the circumstances

LIABILITY OF OWNERS   A sole proprietorship and a partnership have the inherent disadvantage of unlimited liability for the owners. With these forms of organization, there is no distinction between the firm's assets and the owners' personal assets. In contrast, setting up a corporation limits the owners' liability to their investment in the business. Liability risks are among the most important factors to consider when selecting an organizational form.

Choosing a form of organization merely for the sake of simplicity can sometimes cost an entrepreneur dearly—and more than just money! Against the advice of his attorney, Max Baer decided to operate his production studio in Memphis, Tennessee, as a sole proprietorship, to make startup easier. Things were going well until he was sued by a former employee. That's when the folly of Baer's decision became evident. The litigation went on for nearly a year. During that agonizing period, Baer was tormented by the possibility of losing all of his personal assets, including his house, his boat, and his savings account. Fortunately, the suit was settled for a modest sum, but Baer learned his lesson. He decided to convert his business to a corporation and enjoy the peace of mind that comes with limited liability.[26]

CONTINUITY OF BUSINESS   A sole proprietorship is immediately dissolved on the owner's death. Likewise, a partnership is terminated on the death or withdrawal of a partner, unless the partnership agreement states otherwise. A corporation, on the other hand, offers continuity. The status of an individual investor does not affect the corporation's existence.

TRANSFERABILITY OF OWNERSHIP   Ownership is transferred most easily in the corporation. The ability to transfer ownership, however, is intrinsically neither good nor bad. Its desirability depends largely on the owners' preferences. In certain businesses, owners may want the option of evaluating any prospective new investors. In other circumstances, unrestricted transferability may be preferred.

MANAGEMENT CONTROL   A sole proprietor has absolute control of the firm. Control within a partnership is normally based on the majority vote—an increase in the number of partners reduces each partner's voice in management. Within a corporation, control has two dimensions: (1) the formal control vested in the stockholders who own the majority of the voting common shares and (2) the functional control exercised by the corporate officers in conducting daily operations. In a small corporation, these two forms of control usually rest with the same individuals.

ATTRACTIVENESS FOR RAISING CAPITAL   A corporation has a distinct advantage when raising new equity capital, due to the ease of transferring ownership through the sale of common shares and the flexibility in distributing the shares. In contrast, the unlimited liability of a sole proprietorship and a partnership discourages new investors.

INCOME TAXES   Income taxes frequently have a major effect on an owner's selection of a form of organization. To understand the federal income tax system, you must consider the following twofold question: Who is responsible for paying taxes, and how is tax liability determined? The three major forms of organization are taxed in different ways.

Sole Proprietorship   Self-employed individuals who operate a business as a sole proprietorship report income from the business on their individual federal income tax returns. They are then taxed at the rates set by law for individuals. For tax year 2007, IRS tax rates for a married couple reporting their income jointly were as follows:

Range of Taxable Income	Tax Rate
$0–$15,650	10%
$15,651–$63,700	15%
$63,701–$128,500	25%
$128,501–$195,850	28%
$195,851–$349,700	33%
Over $349,700	35%

As an example, assume that a sole proprietor, who is married and files a joint return with her spouse, has taxable income of $150,000 from a business. The taxes owed on this income would be $30,992.50, computed as follows:

Income	× Tax Rate	=	Taxes
First $ 15,650	10%		$ 1,565.00
Next $ 48,050	15%		$ 7,207.50
Next $ 64,800	25%		$16,200.00
Next $ 21,500	28%		$ 6,020.00
Total $150,000			$30,992.50

Partnership   A partnership reports the income it earns to the Internal Revenue Service, but the partnership itself does not pay any taxes. The income is allocated to the partners according to their agreement. The partners each report their own shares of the partnership income on their personal tax returns and pay any taxes owed.

C Corporation   The C corporation, as a separate legal entity, reports its income and pays any taxes related to these profits. The owners (stockholders) of the corporation need only report on their personal tax returns any amounts paid to them by the corporation in the form of dividends. For tax year 2007, IRS corporate tax rates were as follows:

Range of Taxable Income	Tax Rate
$0–$50,000	15%
$50,001–$75,000	25%
$75,001–$100,000	34%
$100,001–$335,000	39%
$335,001–$10,000,000	34%
$10,000,001–$15,000,000	35%
$15,000,001–$18,333,333	38%
Over $18,333,333	35%

Thus, the tax liability of the K&C Corporation, with $150,000 in taxable income, would be $41,750, calculated as follows:

Income	× Tax Rate	=	Taxes
First $ 50,000	15%		$ 7,500
Next $ 25,000	25%		$ 6,250
Next $ 25,000	34%		$ 8,500
Next $ 50,000	39%		$19,500
Total $150,000			$41,750

If the K&C Corporation paid a dividend to its owners in the amount of $40,000, the owners would need to report this dividend income when computing their personal income taxes. Thus, the $40,000 would be taxed twice, first as part of the corporation's income and then as part of the owners' personal income. However, taxes on most dividends have recently been reduced to 5 percent for taxpayers in the 10- and 15-percent tax brackets and to 15 percent for taxpayers in higher tax brackets.

An owner who decides to organize a C corporation would do well to consider issuing Section 1244 stock. Then, in the case of business failure, the owner could realize a tax savings that would not be allowed with regular stock. For tax purposes, **ordinary income** is income earned in the everyday course of business. Salary is considered ordinary income. **Capital gains and losses** are financial gains and losses incurred from the sale of property that is not a part of a firm's regular business operations, such as gains or losses from the sale of common stock. Typically, capital losses may be deducted only from capital gains, not from ordinary income. However, holding stock issued pursuant to Section 1244 of the Internal Revenue Code—**Section 1244 stock**—somewhat protects the stockholder in case of corporate failure. If such stock becomes worthless, the loss (up to $100,000 on a joint tax return) may be treated as an *ordinary* tax-deductible loss.

ordinary income
Income earned in the ordinary course of business, including any salary

capital gains and losses
Gains and losses incurred from sales of property that is not a part of the firm's regular business operations

Section 1244 stock
Stock that offers some tax benefit to the stockholder in the case of corporate failure

Specialized Forms of Organization

4 Describe the unique features and restrictions of five specialized organizational forms.

The majority of new and small businesses use one of the three major organizational forms just described—the sole proprietorship, partnership, or C corporation. However, other specialized types of organizations are also used by small firms. Five of these specialized forms merit further consideration below: the limited partnership, the S corporation, the limited liability company, the professional corporation, and the nonprofit corporation.

limited partnership
A partnership with at least one general partner and one or more limited partners

general partner
A partner in a limited partnership who has unlimited personal liability

limited partner
A partner in a limited partnership who is not active in its management and has limited personal liability

S corporation (Subchapter S corporation)
A type of corporation that offers limited liability to its owners but is taxed by the federal government as a partnership

THE LIMITED PARTNERSHIP   The limited partnership is a special form of partnership involving at least one general partner and one or more limited partners. The general partner remains personally liable for the debts of the business; limited partners have limited personal liability as long as they do not take an active role in the management of the partnership. In other words, limited partners risk only the capital they invest in the business. An individual with substantial personal wealth can, therefore, invest money in a limited partnership without exposing his or her personal assets to liability claims that might arise through activities of the business. If a limited partner becomes active in management, however, his or her limited liability is lost. To form a limited partnership, partners must file a certificate of limited partnership with the proper state office, as state law governs this form of organization.

THE S CORPORATION   The designation S corporation, or Subchapter S corporation, is derived from Subchapter S of the Internal Revenue Code, which permits a business to retain the limited-liability feature of a C corporation while being taxed as a partnership. To obtain S corporation status, a corporation must meet certain requirements, including the following:

- No more than 100 stockholders are allowed.[27]
- All stockholders must be individuals or certain qualifying estates and trusts.[28]
- Only one class of stock can be outstanding.
- Fiscally, the corporation must operate on a calendar year basis.
- Nonresident alien stockholders are not permitted.

A restriction preventing S corporations from owning other corporations, including C corporations, has recently been removed, resulting in tax advantages for some small firms. Whereas in the past different businesses had to be legally separate, individual subsidiaries now may consolidate under one S corporation and submit one tax return.[29] However, combining two businesses under one legal entity can create problems. For example, liability is shared, so if one business gets sued or is bogged down in debt, the other will be exposed to that legal or financial risk. And combined businesses are more difficult to market and sell because potential buyers find it hard to distinguish between the two and determine their individual values.[30]

An S corporation does not pay corporate income taxes and instead passes taxable income or losses on to the stockholders. This allows stockholders to receive dividends from the corporation without double taxation on the corporation's profit (once through a corporate tax and again through a personal tax). A competent tax attorney should be consulted before S status is elected, as tax law changes have considerable effect on the S corporation arrangement.

limited liability company
A form of organization in which owners have limited liability but pay personal income taxes on business profits

THE LIMITED LIABILITY COMPANY   The limited liability company is a relatively new form of organization. It has grown in popularity because it offers the simplicity of a sole proprietorship and the liability protection of a corporation. A limited liability company can have an unlimited number of owners (even a single owner), and these may include non–U.S. citizens. This form differs from the C corporation in that it avoids double taxation. Limited liability companies do not pay tax on corporate income but simply pass that income on to their owners, who pay taxes on it as part of their personal income taxes.

The major advantage of the limited liability company over the partnership form is the liability protection it affords. While general partners are exposed to personal liability, owners in a limited liability company are, as the name implies, protected with respect to their personal assets.

According to many attorneys, the limited liability company is usually the best choice for new businesses. It has the same ability as the S corporation to pass taxable income on to shareholders, and compared to an S corporation, the limited liability company is easier to set up, is more flexible, and offers some significant tax advantages.[31] But a limited liability company isn't always the best way to go. For example, under the following conditions, it would be better to use a C corporation:

- You want to provide extensive fringe benefits to owners or employees. The C corporation can deduct these benefits, and they are not treated as taxable income to the employees.

- You want to offer stock options to employees. Since limited liability companies do not have stock, they cannot offer such incentives.

- You hope to go public or sell out at some time in the future. A C corporation can go public or sell out to another corporation in a tax-free, stock-for-stock exchange.

- You plan to convert to a C corporation eventually. You cannot change from a passthrough entity like a limited liability company without paying additional taxes.

THE PROFESSIONAL CORPORATION   Have you noticed the initials PC or PA as part of the corporate name on the letterhead or signage of your doctor, dentist, or attorney? These letters indicate that the practice is set up as a **professional corporation** in order to offer professional services. Though its meaning varies from state to state, the term *professional* usually applies to those individuals whose professions require that they obtain a license before they can practice, including doctors, chiropractors, lawyers, accountants, engineers, architects, and other highly trained people. But unlike other liability-shielding organizational forms, the professional corporation does not protect a practitioner from his or her own negligence or malpractice; rather, it shields one owner from the liability of other owners in the practice. In some states, a different business structure called a limited liability partnership can serve the same purpose and may have additional advantages. Obviously, the professional corporation applies to a fairly narrow range of enterprises, but it is usually the best option for businesses that fall into that category. In fact, many state laws require this form of organization before a practice can operate.

> **professional corporation**
> A form of corporation that shields owners from liability and is set up for individuals in certain professional practices

THE NONPROFIT CORPORATION   For some ventures, the most practical form of organization is the **nonprofit corporation**. Most elect to become 501(c)(3) organizations, which are created to serve civic, educational, charitable, or religious purposes. To qualify for 501(c)(3) status, the money-raising concern, fund, or foundation must be a corporation; the IRS will not grant this option to an individual or partnership. In the application process, the officers need to submit articles of organization that spell out and limit the range of activities of the enterprise—for a tax exemption to be granted, the organization must pass the **organizational test** ("IRS-speak" for verification that the organization is staying true to the articles filed). A nonprofit corporation must establish a board of directors or trustees to oversee its operations, and if it should dissolve, it is required to transfer its assets to another nonprofit corporation.

> **nonprofit corporation**
> A form of corporation for enterprises established to serve civic, educational, charitable, or religious purposes but not for generation of profits

> **organizational test**
> Verification of whether a nonprofit organization is staying true to its stated purpose

Though social entrepreneurs certainly do not have to charter their enterprises as nonprofit corporations, they often choose this option. Matthew Gutschick and Ben Whiting, both 2006 graduates of Wake Forest University, started a social enterprise called MagicMouth Productions, to teach theater and magic to young people and offer opportunities for them to perform. As Gutschick recalls, when they selected a business structure, the two "decided to go nonprofit because it gave us a larger measure of credibility and authenticity."[32] In other words, choosing to structure an organization as a nonprofit corporation can be a way to reinforce the message and work of the organization.

5 Explain the nature
of strategic alliances
and their uses in
small businesses.

strategic alliance
An organizational
relationship that links
two or more independent
business entities in a
common endeavor

Forming Strategic Alliances

A **strategic alliance** is an organizational relationship that links two or more independent business entities in some common endeavor. Without affecting the independent legal status of the participating business partners, it provides a way for companies to improve their individual effectiveness by sharing certain resources. And these alliances can take many forms, from informal information exchanges to formal equity or contract-based relationships and everything in between. According to a recent study by the National Federation of Independent Business, some types of alliances that are most popular with small businesses include licensing contracts, working with long-term outside contractors, entering production agreements, and distribution-focused deals (see Exhibit 8-5).[33]

Strategic alliances are more important to small businesses today than ever before, and an increasing number of entrepreneurs are finding creative ways to use these cooperative strategies to their advantage. In fact, statistics show that nearly two-thirds of small businesses use alliances, and three-fourths of these companies report having positive experiences with them.[34] Given the escalating pace of competition and the rising cost of developing essential capabilities, alliances provide a way for small companies to access another firm's world-class resources so that they can compete to win. Since a competitive advantage often goes to the entrepreneur who is quick to exploit it, many small business owners see strategic alliances as an essential part of their plan for growth. Cooperative strategies represent one way to keep up with the accelerating pace of change in today's business environment. (See Chapter 17 for a discussion of strategic alliances as a strategy option for global enterprises.)

Strategic Alliances with Large Companies

Large corporations create strategic alliances not only with other large corporations but also with small businesses. Typically, these alliances are formed to join the complementary skills and expertise of the partnered firms, in order to promote the competitive edge of both (or all) parties. For example, large manufacturers sometimes team up with innovative small manufacturers in product development efforts, and giant retailers form alliances with smaller suppliers to work hand in hand to achieve specific quality requirements and meet demanding delivery schedules.

exhibit **8-5**   *Most Popular Small Business Alliances by Type*

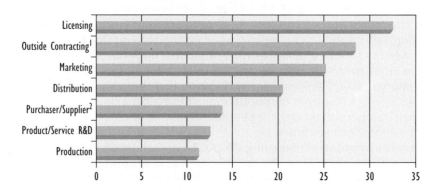

[1]These alliances include only relationships that are long-term in nature.
[2]These alliances include agreements relating to programs, such as just-in-time supply or total quality management, that are relatively long-term in nature.

Source: William J. Dennis, Jr. (ed.), "Strategic Alliances," *National Small Business Poll,* Vol. 4, No. 4 (Washington, DC: NFIB Research Foundation, 2004), pp. 1–8.

How They See It: Forming a Strategic Alliance

Trey Moore

When we set out to create AirStrip OB, we decided to have a simple and keen focus on delivering patient information to a PDA phone. We wanted to bring our product to market as soon as possible, so it was not feasible to try to address the entire hospital solution, which involved getting the data into a database to begin with. As a result, MP4 Solutions' business model from the outset was to partner with one or more companies.

We ended up striking an exclusive reseller's agreement with GE Healthcare to interface with their Centricity Perinatal (CPN) System, which is the software that collects patient information in labor and delivery. We chose GE Healthcare for several reasons, including its having a larger install base by a wide margin than any other competitors and its being part of one of the largest firms in the world, with a very large advertising budget that we could directly benefit from. Also, GE Healthcare had a well-trained, experienced sales force that already had close communication and long-standing relationships with their assigned customers.

The partnership, in which GE Healthcare sells, distributes, installs, and supports our product, allows our company to focus on our expertise, which is creating software. It thereby allows us to continuously improve the product through new versions. Furthermore, we have been able to bring the product to market very rapidly at a fraction of the cost that we would have had to bear if we had not partnered. It is truly a win-win situation.

Combining the speed, flexibility, and creative energy of a small business with the industry experience, production capabilities, and market reach of a large corporation can be a winning strategy. In some cases, merging efforts can open up a whole new line of business. Mary Boone Wellington is CEO of M.B. Wellington in Nashua, New Hampshire. After patenting a creative process to color-laminate plastic sheets that can be used to form translucent blocks, Wellington found a number of architects who wanted to use her innovation in their projects. The opportunity quickly lost its luster, however, because of the high material costs and the time-consuming manufacturing process involved. The picture looked bleak. But then Arkema, the Philadelphia-based manufacturer of Plexiglass, learned about Wellington's process and was so impressed with it that the company agreed to make the raw material Wellington needed, using her innovative color palettes. With its bulk, experience, and advanced production capabilities, Arkema was able to cut Wellington's manufacturing costs substantially, making the new business financially feasible and opening the door to still other business possibilities. A well-placed strategic alliance can truly make things happen![35]

Alliances with large firms can give a tremendous boost to the business of a small company, but some small businesses are discovering that bigger isn't always better. The advantages offered by the financial depth and expansive market reach of large firms must be weighed against potentially serious bureaucratic complications. Janice Bryant Howroyd, chairman and CEO of ACT-1 Group, a small staffing company based in Torrance, California, jumped at the chance to work with a multinational firm in the same industry. In the rush to tie up an important deal, she did not examine the contract closely enough, and her company ended up paying a hefty price. One year after the contract ended, the multinational firm still owed ACT-1 Group $1.2 million. And one invoice discrepancy held up payments to ACT-1, choking its cash flow and forcing the company to close a regional office. The company still has not recovered $300,000 that it is owed.[36] Clearly, there is a potential downside to being so dependent on a single relationship, but this early misstep did not keep Howroyd down for long. A recent press release reports that ACT-1 now ranks nationally as one of the top 15 staffing companies and is the largest woman-owned staffing agency in the United States.[37]

Strategic Alliances with Small Companies

Small businesses can also form strategic alliances with other small firms in ways that enhance mutual competitive strength. Recent statistics suggest that about half of all small businesses maintain one or more strategic alliances with companies that are smaller or equal in size, especially when it comes to outside contractors, licensing partners, import/export operations, marketing agreements, and shared manufacturing.[38] When *Inc.* researchers asked dozens of entrepreneurs which alliance partners

Living the Dream   putting technology to work

Kosher.com and Amazon.com: A Marriage Made in Heaven

Benson Altman is the founder, CEO, and president of Kosher.com, an Internet-based enterprise that sells food items that "adhere to the strictest rabbinical supervision guidelines" and nonfood items of interest to Jewish customers. The focus is on helping buyers find what they need at good prices, with quality service that keeps them coming back for more. The emphasis on customer service fits well with the company's new relationship with Amazon.com—a strategic alliance that makes it possible for Altman to sell more than 20,000 kosher products, from canned fish to cosmetics, from all over the world.

To do business with Kosher.com, buyers need look no further than Amazon. com's catalogue, where the niche retailer's products can be easily purchased. Kosher.com handles the shipment of products to customers, but Amazon.com takes care of everything else, including customer support and billing. Altman predicts that the relationship will boost his revenues by 10 to 20 percent (on $2 million in annual sales), and it certainly presents an opportunity to reach a broader market.

Is there a downside to the relationship? Definitely. Joining forces with Amazon.com is not cheap. It cost Kosher.com about $25,000 to integrate operations with the online giant, and the expansion required Altman to hire four additional employees just to keep up with the increase in orders. And Kosher.com has to pay Amazon.com a commission on each sale, which can really add up. Then there are inventory worries. Don't even think about this option if you can't fill the flood of orders that are almost certain to come in. Finally, it often takes a serious technology upgrade to make the transition. According to Altman, "The back-end system required to deal with Amazon.com is extremely complex and not for the faint of heart." In other words, going in this direction requires a substantial commitment to changes that are not easy to pull off.

Altman knows that the alliance will cease to work if Kosher.com ever fails to be a competent, professional shop. In his words, "Your packages have to be on time, your orders have to be correct, and your customer service has to be great." Amazon.com cannot afford to risk its image by associating with businesses that come up short. If too many customers complain, plan to be dropped from the Amazon family. You may still get to do business with Amazon.com, but only as a buyer with a valid credit card.

Sources: http://www.kosher.com, accessed February 5, 2007; and Melissa Campanelli, "Taking Off," *Entrepreneur,* Vol. 34, No. 5 (May 2006), pp. 42–43. Reprinted by permission from Entrepreneur Magazine, http://www.entrepreneur.com

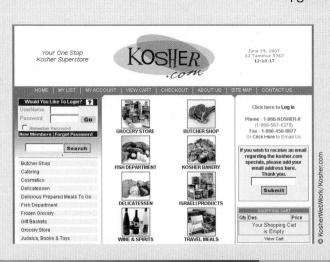

had really performed for them, they were surprised to learn that the most enthusiastic anecdotes were about other small companies. They were more flexible, dedicated, creative, and understanding of the specific needs of small business—apparently, it takes one to know one!

The Center for Systems Management (CSM), a small Vienna, Virginia–based consulting and training company, found that it was in over its head when it accepted a contract from NASA to develop coursework that would help with problems in the space shuttle program. CSM had been given just 45 days to produce a slick video for an internal marketing campaign. This was a huge opportunity, one that could boost the small company's image and generate business in a whole new category of work, but a botched job would probably damage its relationship with NASA for good. Rather than attempting to go it alone, CSM contracted the job out to Technovative Marketing, a seven-person business in Peapack, New Jersey. Within a few days, Harriet Donnelly, Technovative's president, was on the job, and she personally worked on the video and stayed with the project, even attending all meetings with NASA as if she were the chief marketing officer of CSM. As far as Donnelly was concerned, she was part of the CSM team. In the end, the video project was a huge success. CSM has been hired to do more internal marketing campaign work for NASA as a result—and, of course, Donnelly has been asked to help.[39] What a surprise!

Strategic alliances hold great promise for small entrepreneurial businesses. By combining resources with carefully selected partners, small firms can increase their competitive strength and reach goals that would otherwise be too costly or too difficult for them to accomplish on their own.

Setting Up and Maintaining Successful Strategic Alliances

Although an appropriate strategic alliance may be essential to business growth, finding a suitable partner can be challenging. Some small business owners have given up in frustration after months—even years—of trying to establish such connections. But persistent entrepreneurs are always finding ways to bridge the gap.

Launched in 1999, Staffcentrix is an Internet outsourcing company based in Woodstock, Connecticut. Despite having only $10,000 in first-year sales, the company was able to form alliances with Microsoft, the United Nations, and Waterside Productions. How did co-founders Christine Durst and Michael Haaren pull it off? First, they identified potential e-mail contacts by scouring the websites of prospective partners and taking note of anyone associated with projects parallel to Staffcentrix's interests. Using this information, they created a "contact profile," which detailed each contact's personal involvement with these projects. Then Durst and Haaren sent personal e-mail messages to these contacts, promoting an alliance with Staffcentrix. Within months, the company was up and running with big-name partners.[40]

For help in making essential linkages, especially with large corporations, many entrepreneurs consult strategic alliance matchmakers. These brokers provide two basic services. First, they maintain a wealth of contacts with decision makers at corporations that have the resources small companies need to fill in the gaps in their operations. Second, they help entrepreneurs fine-tune their alliance proposals to ensure that corporate insiders take them seriously.

A product manager at Microsoft once estimated that he received hundreds of partnership requests each month. He followed a simple rule when determining which companies would get the nod to work with the software giant: Without a compelling business plan, there would be no access to his developers and their time.[41] In other words, Microsoft needed to know why it should be willing to invest its resources before even considering such a partnership. But this does not mean that Microsoft (and other large corporations) are slow to consider alliances with small companies. Microsoft's IP Ventures division, for example, is set up specifically to license intellectual property that the firm cannot or does not want to use. But the aspiring partner must be able to present a compelling case before Microsoft will sign on.[42]

Strategic alliances often are not easy to set up, and they can be difficult to maintain. Although many small businesses report that they are happy with the results of their strategic alliances,[43] a number of alliances run into trouble and, in time, fail. Fortunately, when setting up alliances, entrepreneurs can take the following steps to improve their chances of success:

- Establish a healthy network of contacts. These people can lead you to still other contacts, and eventually to the one you need. Industry analysts, executive recruiters, public relations agencies, business reporters, and even the government can provide important leads.

- Identify and contact individuals within a firm who are likely to return your call. "Dialing high" (calling contacts at the vice presidential level or higher) works in small- or medium-sized firms, but in large firms you may need to call managers or other mid-level employees to get a response.

- Do your homework, and you will win points just for being prepared. You should be able to clearly outline the partner's potential financial benefits from the alliance. If possible, show that your firm can deliver value to the alliance across several fronts.

- Learn to speak and understand the "language" of your partner. You will not pick up on subtle messages in conversations with partners unless you know how they communicate, and this can eventually make or break the alliance.

- Continue to monitor the progress of the alliance to ensure that goals and expectations are being met, and make changes as they become necessary. Remember, alliances are not supposed to last forever.

The goal is to form strategic alliances that are beneficial to all partners and to manage these alliances effectively. In their book *Everyone Is a Customer,* Jeffrey Shuman, Janice Twombly, and David Rottenberg point out that a key to successful strategic alliances is understanding the true nature of the relationship: "Relationships are advertised as being between companies, whereas in reality relationships are built between people. And that's a very important distinction."[44]

Making the Most of a Board of Directors

6 Describe the effective use of boards of directors and advisory councils.

board of directors
The governing body of a corporation, elected by the stockholders

In entrepreneurial firms, the **board of directors** tends to be small (usually five or fewer members) and serves as the governing body for corporate activity. In concept, the stockholders elect the board, which in turn chooses the firm's officers, who manage the enterprise. The directors also set or approve management policies, consider reports on operating results from the officers, and declare dividends (if any).

All too often, the majority stockholder in a small corporation (usually the entrepreneur) appoints a board of directors only to fulfill a legal requirement or as mere window dressing for investors. Such owners make little or no use of directors in managing their companies. In fact, the entrepreneur may actively resist efforts of these directors to provide managerial assistance. When appointing a board of directors, such an entrepreneur tends to select personal friends, relatives, or businesspersons who are too busy to analyze the firm's circumstances and are not inclined to argue. Entrepreneurs who take a more constructive approach find an active board to be both practical and beneficial, especially when the members are informed, skeptical, and independent.

Making use of boards of directors is becoming increasingly attractive for a number of reasons. The growing complexity of small businesses, arising in part from globalization and technological developments, makes the expertise of well-chosen directors especially valuable. In a family business, outsiders can play a unique role in helping evaluate family talent and mediate differences among family members.

Contributions of Directors

Small businesses stand to gain significantly from a strong board of directors, especially when its members help the entrepreneur look beyond the next few months to make important, long-term strategic decisions. According to Pat Gross, a director at three public companies, "The ultimate value of a director is [in his or her ability] to step back and see the forest for the trees."[45]

A well-selected board of directors can also bring supplementary knowledge and broad experience to corporate management. By virtue of their backgrounds, directors can fill gaps in the knowledge of a management team. The board should meet regularly to provide maximum assistance to the chief executive. In board meetings, ideas should be debated, strategies determined, and the pros and cons of policies explored. In this way, the chief executive is informed by the unique perspectives of all the board members. Their combined knowledge makes possible more intelligent decisions on issues crucial to the firm.

By utilizing the experience of a board of directors, the chief executive of a small corporation is in no way giving up active control of its operations. Instead, by consulting with and seeking the advice of the board's members, he or she is simply drawing on a larger pool of business knowledge. A group will typically make better decisions than will a single individual working in isolation.

An active board of directors serves management in several important ways: by reviewing major policy decisions, by advising on external business conditions and on proper reaction to the business cycle, by providing informal advice from time to time on specific problems that arise, and by offering access to important personal contacts. With a strong board, a small firm may gain greater credibility with the public, as well as with the business and financial communities.

Selection of Directors

Many resources are available to an entrepreneur who is attempting to assemble a cooperative and experienced group of directors. The firm's attorney, banker, accountant, other business executives, and local management consultants might all be considered as potential directors, but such individuals lack the independence needed to critically review an entrepreneur's plans. Also, the owner is already paying for their expertise. For this reason, the owner needs to consider the value of an outside board—one with members whose income does not depend on the firm. The National Association of Corporate Directors surveyed the directors of nearly 100 boards of entrepreneurial firms and found that, on average, 28 percent were independent outside directors. This number is increasing—which is good—but the study also reports that private company boards tend to have only half as many independent members as their public counterparts.[46]

Objectivity is a particularly valuable contribution of outside directors. They can look at issues more dispassionately than can insiders who are involved in daily decision making. Outside directors, for example, are freer to evaluate and to question a firm's ethical standards. Some operating executives, without the scrutiny of outside directors, may rationalize unethical or illegal behavior as being in the best interest of the company.

In a family business, an outside board can help mediate and resolve issues related to leadership succession, in addition to providing more general direction. As outsiders, they bring to the business a measure of detachment from potentially explosive emotional differences.

Working with outside board members is not always easy. Dennis Gertmenian is the founder, chairman, and CEO of Ready Pac Produce, Inc., an Irwindale, California–based produce-packaging company. Long ago, Gertmenian established a board of directors to provide diverse solutions to challenges the company faces. As it turns out, board members have had a profound impact on Gertmenian's decision making, most notably by persuading him to back out of a plan to provide jobs in an economically depressed area and by encouraging him to take a hit on his personal real-estate portfolio. But the tough decisions the board has advised him to make have ultimately improved the business. Gertmenian reflects, "I wasn't taking the time to formally structure some of the areas of my company that needed attention from a long-term point of view, such as: What are we doing with our banking relationship a year from now? What is our strategic plan? I had a plan, but it was in my mind, not written down."[47] CEOs can spend as much as 20 percent of their time on board-related activities, but the time commitment is worth the cost if the directors are doing their jobs well.

The nature and needs of a business will help determine the qualifications required in its directors. For example, a firm that faces a marketing problem may benefit greatly from the counsel of a board member with a marketing background. Business prominence in the community is not essential, although it may help give the company credibility and enable it to attract other well-qualified directors. Having a "fat" Rolodex can only be helpful, as directors with influential business contacts can contribute greatly to the company's performance.

After deciding on the qualifications to look for, a business owner must seek suitable candidates as board members. Effective directors will be honest and accountable, offer valuable insights based on business experience, and enhance the company's credibility with its stakeholders (especially customers and suppliers). Suggestions for such candidates may be obtained from the firm's accountant, attorney, banker, and other associates in the business community. Owners or managers of other, noncompeting small companies, as well as second- and third-level executives in large companies, are often willing to accept such positions. Before offering candidates positions on the board, however, a business owner would be wise to do some discreet background checking.

Compensation of Directors

The compensation paid to board members varies greatly, and some small firms pay no fees at all. If compensation is provided, it is usually offered in the form of an annual retainer, board meeting fees, and pay for committee work. (Directors may serve on committees that oversee executive compensation, audit the company's financial reports, and perform other critical functions.) One study found that entrepreneurial firms pay, on average, over $12,500 in total annual compensation for directors of private companies and almost $26,000 for public firm directors.[48] Some small businesses also offer each board member a small percentage of the company's stock or profits (typically one-half of 1 percent) for their participation,[49] but keep in mind that some directors may serve for free because of their interest in seeing a new or small business prosper.

The relatively modest compensation offered for the services of well-qualified directors suggests that financial compensation is not their primary motivation for serving on a board. Reasonable compensation is appropriate, however, if directors are making important contributions to the firm's operations.

An Alternative: An Advisory Council

In recent years, increased attention has been directed to the legal responsibilities of directors. Because outside directors may be held responsible for illegal company actions, even though they are not directly involved in wrongdoing, some individuals are reluctant to accept directorships. Thus, some small companies use an **advisory council** as an alternative to a board of directors. Qualified outsiders are asked to serve on a council as advisors to the company. This group then functions in much the same way as a board of directors does, except that its actions are only advisory in nature.

The legal liability of members of an advisory council is not completely clear. However, limiting their compensation and power is thought to lighten, if not eliminate, the personal liability of members.[50] Since it is advisory in nature, the council also may pose less of a threat to the owner and possibly work more cooperatively than a conventional board.

Without a doubt, a well-selected advisory board or board of directors can do a great deal for a small company, but this is only one part of an effective organizational plan. The success of any business depends on the quality of its people, who must also be well organized and skillfully led. That's why having a balanced entrepreneurial team, selecting an organizational form with care, and joining advantageous strategic alliances are all so important. This chapter has touched on each of these topics to help you think through key factors involved in a solid organizational plan that will give your business a good running start and help to ensure its long-term success.

advisory council
A group that functions like a board of directors but acts only in an advisory capacity

Looking BACK

1 **Describe the characteristics and value of a strong management team.**

· A strong management team nurtures a good business idea and helps provide the necessary resources to make it succeed.

· The skills of management team members should complement each other, forming an optimal combination of education and experience.

· A small firm can enhance its management by drawing on the expertise of outside specialists.

· Building social capital through networking and goodwill is extremely helpful in developing a small business.

· An entrepreneur should create a management structure that defines relationships among all members of the organization.

2 **Explain the common legal forms of organization used by small businesses.**

· The most basic legal forms of organization used by small businesses are the sole proprietorship, partnership, and C corporation.

· In a sole proprietorship, the owner receives all profits and bears all losses. The principal disadvantage of this form is the owner's unlimited liability.

· In a partnership, which should be established on the basis of a written partnership agreement, success depends on the partners' ability to build an effective working relationship.

· C corporations are particularly attractive because of their limited-liability feature. The fact that ownership is easily transferable makes them well suited for combining the capital of numerous owners.

3 **Identify factors to consider in choosing among the primary legal forms of organization, including tax consequences.**

· Currently, nearly 70 percent of all new businesses are organized as sole proprietorships, 10 percent are set up as partnerships, and 21 percent are established as corporations.

· The key factors in the choice among different legal forms of organization are initial organizational requirements and costs, liability of the owners, continuity of the business, transferability of ownership, management control, attractiveness for raising capital, and income taxes.

· Self-employed individuals who operate businesses as sole proprietorships report income from the businesses on their individual tax returns.

· A partnership reports the income it earns to the Internal Revenue Service, but the partnership itself does not pay income taxes. The income is allocated to the owners according to their partnership agreement.

· A C corporation reports its income and pays any taxes due on this corporate income. Individual stockholders must also pay personal income taxes on dividends paid to them by a corporation.

· Holding Section 1244 stock helps to protect the stockholder in case of corporate failure. If such stock becomes worthless, the loss (up to $100,000) may be treated as an ordinary tax-deductible loss.

4 **Describe the unique features and restrictions of five specialized organizational forms.**

· In a limited partnership, general partners have unlimited liability, while limited partners have only limited liability as long as they are not active in the firm's management.

· S corporations, also called Subchapter S corporations, enjoy a special tax status that permits them to avoid the corporate tax but requires individual stockholders to pay personal taxes on their proportionate shares of the business profits.

· In limited liability companies, individual owners have the advantage of limited liability but pay only personal income taxes on the firm's earnings.

· Professional corporations are set up for those who offer professional services (usually those that require a license), to protect them from the liability of other owners in the practice.

· Some enterprises (especially those with a social focus) benefit from greater credibility and authenticity when they organize as a nonprofit corporation, such as a 501(c)(3) organization.

5 **Explain the nature of strategic alliances and their uses in small businesses.**

· Strategic alliances allow business firms to combine their resources without compromising their independent legal status.

· Strategic alliances may be formed by two or more independent businesses to achieve some common purpose. For example, a large corporation and a small business or two or more small businesses may collaborate on a joint project.

· Strategic alliance matchmakers can help small businesses find suitable alliance partners.

- Entrepreneurs can improve their chances of creating and maintaining a successful alliance by establishing productive connections, identifying the best person to contact, being prepared to confirm the long-term benefits of the alliance, learning to speak the partner's "language," and monitoring the progress of the alliance.

6 Describe the effective use of boards of directors and advisory councils.

- Boards of directors can assist small corporations by offering counsel and assistance to their chief executives.

- To be most effective, a board of directors should include properly qualified, independent outsiders.

- One alternative to an active board of directors is an advisory council, whose members are not personally liable for the company's actions.

Key TERMS

management team, p. 208

social network, p. 210

social capital, p. 210

reciprocation, p. 210

sole proprietorship, p. 211

unlimited liability, p. 212

partnership, p. 212

partnership agreement, p. 215

agency power, p. 215

corporation, p. 216

legal entity, p. 216

C corporation, p. 216

corporate charter, p. 216

stock certificate, p. 216

pre-emptive right, p. 216

ordinary income, p. 221

capital gains and losses, p. 221

Section 1244 stock, p. 221

limited partnership, p. 222

general partner, p. 222

limited partner, p. 222

S corporation (Subchapter S corporation), p. 222

limited liability company, p. 222

professional corporation, p. 223

nonprofit corporation, p. 223

organizational test, p. 223

strategic alliance, p. 224

board of directors, p. 228

advisory council, p. 230

Discussion QUESTIONS

1. Why would investors tend to favor a new business led by a management team over one headed by a lone entrepreneur? Is this preference justified?

2. Discuss the merits of the three major legal forms of organization.

3. Does the concept of limited liability apply to a sole proprietorship? Why or why not?

4. Suppose a partnership is set up and operated without a formal partnership agreement. What problems might arise? Explain.

5. Evaluate the three major forms of organization in terms of management control by the owner and sharing of the firm's profits.

6. What is an S corporation, and what is its principal advantage?

7. Why are strategic alliances important for many small businesses? What steps can an entrepreneur take to create strategic alliances and to prevent their failure?

8. How might a board of directors be of value to management in a small corporation? What qualifications are essential for a director? Is ownership of stock in the firm a prerequisite for being a director?

9. What may account for the failure of most small companies to use boards of directors as more than "rubber stamps"? What impact is this likely to have on the business?

10. How do advisory councils differ from boards of directors? Which would you recommend to a small company owner? Why?

You Make the CALL

SITUATION 1

Ted Green and Mark Stroder became close friends as 16-year-olds when both worked part-time for Green's dad in his automotive parts store. After high school, Green went to college, while Stroder joined the National Guard Reserve and devoted his weekends to auto racing. Green continued his association with the automotive parts store by buying and managing two of his father's stores.

In 2005, Green conceived the idea of starting a new business that would rebuild automobile starters, and he asked Stroder to be his partner in the venture. Originally, Stroder was somewhat concerned about working with Green because their personalities are so different. Green has been described as outgoing and enthusiastic, while Stroder is reserved and skeptical. However, Stroder is now out of work, and so he has agreed to the offer. They will set up a small shop behind one of Green's automotive parts stores. Stroder will do all the work; Green will supply the cash.

The "partners" have agreed to name the business STARTOVER, and now they need to decide on a legal form of organization.

Question 1 How relevant are the individual personalities to the success of this entrepreneurial team? Do you think Green and Stroder have a chance to survive their "partnership"? Why or why not?

Question 2 Do you consider it an advantage or a disadvantage that the members of this team are the same a

Question 3 Which legal form of organization would propose for STARTOVER? Why?

Question 4 If Stroder and Green decided to incorporate, would STARTOVER qualify as an S corporation? so, would you recommend this option? Why or why n

SITUATION 2

Matthew Freeman started a business in 2001 to provide corporate training in project management. He initially organized his business as a sole proprietorship. Until 2007, he did most of his work on a contract basis for Corporation Education Services (CES). Under the terms of his contract, Freeman was responsible for teaching 3- to 5-day courses to corporate clients—primarily *Fortune* 1000 companies. He was compensated according to a negotiated daily rate, and expenses incurred during a course (hotels, meals, transportation, etc.) were reimbursed by CES. Although some expenses were not reimbursed by CES (such as those for computers

and office supplies), Freeman's costs usually amounted to less than 1 percent of his revenues.

In 2007, Freeman increasingly found himself working directly with corporate clients rather than contracting with CES. Over the years, he had considered incorporating but had assumed the costs and inconveniences of this option would outweigh the benefits. However, some of his new clients said that they would prefer to contract with a corporation rather than with an individual. And Freeman sometimes wondered about potential liability problems. On the one hand, he didn't have the same liability issues as some other businesses—he worked out of his home, clients never visited his home office, all courses were conducted in hotels or corporate facilities, and his business involved only services. But he wasn't sure what would happen if a client were dissatisfied with the content and outcomes of his instruction. Finally, he wondered whether there would be tax advantages to incorporating.

Question 1 What are the advantages and disadvantages of running the business as a sole proprietorship? As a corporation?

Question 2 If Freeman decided to incorporate his business, which types of corporations could he form? Which type would you recommend? Why?

SITUATION 3

distributor of welding materials had of most small firms, treating the merely a legal necessity. Comers and a retired steel company was not a working board. But the ally with traditional management able.

seminar, the majority owner decided that a board might be useful for more than legal or cosmetic purposes. Thus, he invited two outsiders—both division heads of larger corporations—to join the board. This brought the membership of the board to five. The majority owner believed the new members would be helpful in opening up the business to new ideas.

Question 1 Can two outside members on a board of five make any real difference in the way the board operates?

Question 2 Evaluate the owner's choices for board members.

Question 3 What will determine the usefulness or effectiveness of this board? Do you predict that it will be useful? Why or why not?

Experiential **EXERCISES**

1. Prepare a one-page résumé of your personal qualifications to launch a software instruction business at your college or university. Then write a critique that might be prepared by an investor, evaluating your strengths and weaknesses as shown on the résumé.

2. Interview an attorney whose clients include small businesses. Inquire about the legal considerations involved in choosing the form of organization for a new business. Report your findings to the class.

3. Interview the partners of a local business. Inquire about the factors they considered when drawing up their partnership agreement. Report your findings to the class.

4. Discuss with a corporate director, attorney, banker, or business owner the contributions of directors to small firms. Prepare a brief report on your findings. If you discover a particularly well-informed individual, suggest that person to your instructor as a possible guest speaker.

Exploring the **WEB**

1. Go to the Small Business Administration's website at **http://www.sba.gov/aboutsba/index.html.** Select the Small Business Planner tab, click on "Start Your Business," and then "Choose a Structure." This site can help you determine what form of business ownership is right for you.

   a. Read about the different structures, and write a brief report on which structure might be best for the kind of business you wish to start and why you think it's best.

   b. What are the long-term implications of the business form you have under consideration?

2. Read Ed Rigsbee's article, "10 Tips for Creating Strong Ties," at **http://www.allbusiness.com/ business-planning/business-development-strategic-alliances/825795-1.html.** Ed Rigsbee is the president of Rigsbee Research and maintains a website at **http://www.rigsbee.com** on the topics of partnering and alliances. Compare Rigsbee's 10 tips with the recommendations given in this chapter to help entrepreneurs improve their chances of success when setting up and maintaining strategic alliances. How are they similar? Different?

Video Case **8**

Silver Zephyr Restaurant (p. 635)
This case presents issues that relate to choosing a legal form of organization.

Alternative Cases for Chapter 8:

Case 1, Boston Duck Tours, p. 620

Case 17, Sunny Designs, Inc., p. 654

Case 18, Douglas Electrical Supply, Inc., p. 656

The Business Plan

Laying the Foundation

As part of laying the foundation to prepare your own business plan, respond to the following questions regarding your management team, legal form of organization, strategic alliances, and board of directors.

1. Who are the members of your management team? What skills, education, and experience do they bring to the team?
2. What other key managers do you plan to recruit?
3. Do you plan to use consultants? If so, describe their qualifications.
4. What are your plans for future employee recruitment?
5. What will be the compensation and benefit plans for managers and other employees?
6. What style of management will be used? What will be the decision-making process in the company? What mechanisms are in place for effective communication between managers and employees? If possible, present a simple organization chart.
7. How will personnel be motivated? How will creativity be encouraged? How will commitment and loyalty be developed?
8. What employee retention and training programs will be adopted? Who will be responsible for job descriptions and employee evaluations?
9. Who will have an ownership interest in the business?
10. Will the business function as a sole proprietorship, partnership, or corporation? If a corporation, will it be a C corporation, an S corporation, a limited liability company, a professional corporation, or a nonprofit corporation?
11. What are the liability implications of this form of organization?
12. What are the tax advantages and disadvantages of this form of organization?
13. If a corporation, where will the corporation be chartered and when will it be incorporated?
14. What attorney or legal firm has been selected to represent the firm? What type of relationship exists with the firm's attorney or law firm?
15. What legal issues are presently or potentially significant?
16. What licenses and/or permits may be required?
17. What strategic alliances are in place, and what others do you plan to establish in the future? Describe the forms and nature of these alliances. What are the responsibilities of and benefits to the parties involved? What are the exit strategies?
18. Who are the directors of the company? What are their qualifications? How will they be compensated?

## chapter 9

The Location Plan

In the SPOTLIGHT

An eBay Success Story
eBay user ID: powerwheelerchris

An entrepreneur has several options when deciding where to locate his or her business: (1) in a brick-and-mortar building, (2) at home, (3) on the Web, or (4) in some combination of these places. The Internet has radically transformed how business is conducted; it is now the location of choice for many entrepreneurs. The online auction site eBay is a shining example of what's possible on the Internet.

Founded in 1995, eBay has approximately 1.3 million sellers who use it as either a primary or a secondary source of income, and it claims 212 million registered users worldwide. eBay success stories are now part of entrepreneurial folklore; the auction site may even be a life saver.

In 2002, Chris Mitchell checked into the hospital for what he thought would be a three- to five-day stay to fix a problem with his heart. He had been selling items on eBay from his home in Modesto, California, for about a year and a half, and he even kept his listings on eBay running as he headed for the hospital. Little did he know that he would have a stroke and be in the hospital for a month and a half. The stroke kept Mitchell off eBay for about three months, but there was no way he was giving it up for good. "I was not going to let this stroke win. I was going to beat it and get back to as much of a normal life as I had before," explains Mitchell.

eBay helped Mitchell get through some tough times. It took him nearly a year to get back to his old eBay form after the stroke. "It makes me feel like a productive member of society," Mitchell says. Although confined to a wheelchair, he does almost everything for himself concerning his eBay business.

Mitchell went on to become an eBay Trader Assistant, teaching a hands-on course on eBay at Modesto Junior College. His eBay classes were so popular that extra sections had to be added to accommodate demand. In the summer of 2006, he moved to Webb City, Missouri, where he still works from home selling on eBay. And he is now an eBay Education Specialist, doing consulting work for local and regional eBay members.

Mitchell's eBay success story is an inspiring one and proof that you can't keep a true entrepreneur down for long.

Sources: April Y. Pennington, "Overcoming Tough Times with eBay," *Entrepreneur,* August 29, 2005, http://www.entrepreneur.com/ebusiness/ebay/enter/ebaysuccessstories/article79534.html, accessed July 15, 2007; and Perri Capell, "How to Make Money on eBay," *Wall Street Journal,* December 18, 2006, p. R5.

Looking AHEAD

After studying this chapter, you should be able to

1 Describe the five key factors in locating a brick-and-mortar startup.
2 Discuss the challenges of designing and equipping a physical facility.
3 Understand both the attraction and the challenges of creating a home-based startup.
4 Understand the potential benefits of locating a startup on the Internet.

The entrepreneur who decides to purchase a franchise or an existing business usually receives considerable location guidance from the franchisor or members of the existing firm. But for the entrepreneur who chooses to start a venture from scratch, the location decision is very time consuming. Regardless of how the decision is made, all location intentions should be described in the business plan.

Locating the Brick-and-Mortar Startup

In many cases, the choice of a location is a one-time decision. However, an entrepreneur may later consider relocating the business to reduce operating costs or gain other advantages. For example, Mitchell Greif, CEO of Coast Converters, relocated his plastic bag manufacturing plant to Las Vegas, Nevada, because of the high taxes and pricey real estate in his hometown of Los Angeles.[1] Also, as a business grows, it is sometimes desirable to expand operations to other locations to be closer to customers.[2]

> 1 Describe the five key factors in locating a brick-and-mortar startup.

In this chapter, we discuss three primary options for the initial location decision—a traditional physical building, the entrepreneur's home, and a website on the Internet. Although we recognize that the Internet can be an integral part of operations for both a traditional and a home-based business, we treat e-commerce ventures in a separate category because of the Internet's significance as a sole sales outlet for these small businesses. Exhibit 9-1 depicts the three location options.

The Importance of the Location Decision

The importance of the initial decision as to where to locate a traditional physical building—a **brick-and-mortar store**—is underscored by both the high cost of such a store and the hassle of pulling up stakes and moving an established business. Also, if the site is particularly poor, the business may never become successful, even with adequate financing and superior managerial ability. The importance of location is so clearly recognized by national chains that they spend thousands of dollars investigating sites before establishing new stores.

brick-and-mortar store
The traditional physical store from which businesses have historically operated

The choice of a good location is much more vital to some businesses than to others. For example, the site chosen for a dress shop can make or break the business because it must be convenient for customers. In contrast, the physical location of the office of a painting contractor is of less importance, since customers do not need frequent access to

9-1 *Location Options for the Startup*

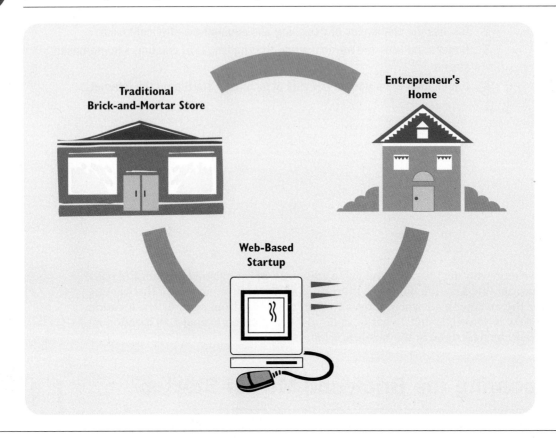

the facility. Even painting contractors, however, may suffer if their business site is poorly chosen. For example, some communities are more willing or able than others to invest resources to keep property in good condition, thereby providing greater opportunities for painting jobs.

Key Factors in Selecting a Good Location

Five key factors, shown in Exhibit 9-2, guide the location selection process: customer accessibility, business environment conditions, availability of resources, the entrepreneur's personal preference, and site availability and costs. Other factors relevant to location include neighbor mix (who's next door?), security and safety (how safe is the neighborhood?), services (is there municipal trash pickup?), past tenants' fate (what happened to them?), and the life-cycle stage of the area (is the site in the embryonic, mature, or declining stage?).[3]

In a particular situation, one factor may carry more weight than others. However, each of the five key factors should always have some influence on the final location decision.

CUSTOMER ACCESSIBILITY Customer accessibility is generally an important consideration in selecting a location. Retail outlets and service firms are typical examples of businesses that must be located so as to make access convenient for target customers. Rarely will customers be willing to regularly travel long distances to shop. That's why Glenn Campbell and Scott Molander decided to sell hats in high-traffic areas. Each store, located in a shopping mall or airport, offers a vast assortment of officially licensed baseball-style hats. The first store was opened in 1995, and in five years the company, Hat World Corporation, had grown to 157 stores. By 2003, it had purchased several competitors; in 2007, it reported operating more than 600 stores in 46 states.[4]

exhibit

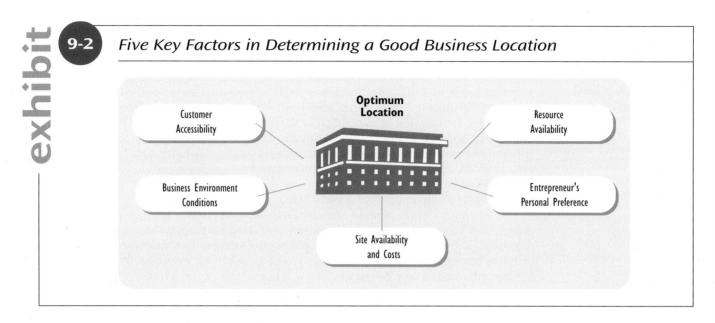

9-2 *Five Key Factors in Determining a Good Business Location*

Many products, such as snack foods and gasoline, are convenience goods, which require a retail location close to target customers; otherwise, consumers will substitute competitive brands when a need arises. Services such as tire repair and hair styling also require a location readily accessible to customers.

Choosing the best location for a retail store used to be a hit-or-miss proposition. The recent emergence of site-selection software has removed much of the guesswork from finding a good location. Its popularity has taken off as the software has become more sophisticated and user-friendly. Site-selection software programs can now give users access to demographic information such as age, income, and race for specific neighborhoods, as well as information on other businesses located nearby, climate, traffic flow, and more.

Carvel Ice Cream, a 71-year-old chain of ice-cream shops, knows the importance of being easily accessible to customers. Carvel hired MapInfo, a site-selection software maker, to identify good locations for Carvel Ice Cream shops. Carvel is visiting each of the 127 sites identified by MapInfo and hopes to line up franchisees for most of the locations, believing that, with the use of site-selection software, "there's less risk of a meltdown."[5]

Customer accessibility is also vital in industries in which the cost of shipping the finished product is high relative to the product's value. For example, packaged ice and soft drinks must be produced near consuming markets, because transporting these products can be an expensive process.

Convenient access for customers is one reason small businesses have successfully created such a strong presence on the Internet. With the appropriate computer connection, customers can access a small business's home page from anywhere in the world. (Locating a startup on the Internet is discussed later in this chapter.)

BUSINESS ENVIRONMENT CONDITIONS A startup business is affected in a number of ways by the environment in which it operates. Environmental conditions can hinder or promote success. Weather is one important environmental factor that influences the location decision, as well as the demand for many products such as air conditioners and outdoor swimming pools. Environmental issues are particularly important to entrepreneur Tsering Gyalzen, who is planning to build a cybercafé, containing eight laptop computers and solar-powered generators, at the 17,400-foot-high base camp of Mount Everest. He will be forced to construct a temporary structure because the base camp sits on a glacier that moves several inches each day.[6]

Competition, legal requirements, and tax structure are a few of the other critical environmental factors. Every entrepreneur seeks profits; therefore, all factors affecting the financial picture are of great concern. State and local governments can help or hinder a new business by forgiving or levying taxes. Considerable variation exists across the United States in state corporate income taxes, with only a few states having no such tax. One state with an advantageous tax policy is Wyoming, whose website proudly states,

enterprise zones
State-designated areas
that are established to
bring jobs to economically
deprived regions through
regulatory and tax
incentives

"The state of Wyoming does not levy a personal or corporate income tax. Further, there is no legislative plan to implement any of these types of taxes".[7] Obviously, the best time to evaluate environmental conditions is prior to making a location commitment.

Many states offer location incentives. One popular strategy is to establish **enterprise zones** in order to bring jobs to economically deprived areas. Sponsored by local city/county governments, these zones lure businesses by offering regulatory and tax relief. In exchange for locating or expanding in these areas, eligible business firms receive total exemption from the property taxes normally assessed on a new plant and equipment for three to five years. Oregon had 49 enterprise zones as of January 2005.[8] Enterprise zones are not a cure-all. Locating in an enterprise zone will not solve problems created by poor management or make up for an ill-conceived idea. However, enterprise zones can be used as a catalyst to help jump-start a small firm.

While most efforts of state and city governments are designed to support startups, most cities have regulations that restrict new business operations under certain circumstances. For example, cities have zoning ordinances that may limit the operations of home-based businesses. Limitations typically relate to vehicular traffic and parking, signage, nonrelated employees working in a home, the use of a home more as a business than as a residence, the sale of retail goods to the public, and the storage of hazardous materials and work-related equipment.[9]

AVAILABILITY OF RESOURCES   The availability of resources associated with producing a product and operating a business should also be considered in selecting a location. Raw materials, labor supply, and transportation are some of the factors that have a bearing on location. Nearness to raw materials and suitability of labor supply are particularly critical considerations in the location of a manufacturing business.

Nearness to Raw Materials   If required raw materials are not abundantly available in all areas, a region in which these materials abound offers special location advantages. For a business dependent on bulky or heavy raw materials that lose much of their bulk or weight in the manufacturing process, proximity to these materials is a powerful force driving the location decision. A sawmill is an example of a business that must stay close to its raw materials in order to operate economically.

Suitability of Labor Supply   A manufacturer's labor requirements depend on the nature of its production process. Availability of workers, wage rates, labor productivity, and a history of peaceful relations with employees are all particularly important considerations for labor-intensive firms. In some cases, the need for semiskilled or unskilled labor justifies locating in an area with surplus labor. In other cases, firms find it desirable to seek a pool of highly skilled labor.

Availability of Transportation   Access to good transportation is important to almost all firms. For example, good highways and bus systems provide customers with convenient access to retail stores. For small manufacturers, quality transportation is especially vital. They must carefully evaluate all the trucking routes that support their transportation needs, considering the costs of both transporting supplies to the manufacturing location and shipping the finished product to customers. It is critical that they know whether these costs will allow their product to be competitively priced.

PERSONAL PREFERENCE OF THE ENTREPRENEUR   As a practical matter, many entrepreneurs tend to discount customer accessibility, business environment conditions, and resource availability and consider only their personal preference in locating a business. Often, their personal preference is to stay in their home community; the possibility of locating elsewhere never enters their mind. Just because an individual has always lived in a particular town, however, does not automatically make the town a satisfactory business location!

On the other hand, locating a business in one's home community is not necessarily illogical. In fact, it offers certain advantages. From a personal standpoint, the entrepreneur generally appreciates and feels comfortable with the atmosphere of the home community, whether it is a small town or a large city. From a practical business standpoint, the entrepreneur can more easily establish credit. Hometown bankers can be dealt with more confidently, and other businesspersons may be of great service in helping evaluate a given opportunity. If local residents are potential customers, the prospective entrepreneur probably has a better idea of their tastes and preferences than an outsider would. Relatives and friends may be the entrepreneur's first customers and may help advertise his or her products or services.

Sometimes entrepreneurs choose a location offering unique lifestyle advantages. Entrepreneur Pete Nelson has a home office 10 feet off the ground, in a stand of 70-year-old Douglas fir trees in Fall City, Washington, where he operates TreeHouse Workshop (THW), a general contracting business. THW has built treehouses across the country, and its team of skilled carpenters will travel just about anywhere to fulfill a customer's request. Nelson and his wife, Judy, enjoy the outdoor location of their home-based business, where they are "face-to-beak with woodpeckers and wrens" on the other side of their office window.[10]

Personal preference, however, should not be allowed to take priority over obvious location weaknesses.

SITE AVAILABILITY AND COSTS

Once an entrepreneur has settled on a certain area of the country, a specific site must still be chosen. The availability of potential sites and the costs associated with obtaining them must be investigated.

Site Availability

After evaluating a site for his new business, one entrepreneur is said to have exclaimed, "It must be a good site—I know of four businesses that have been there in the last two years!" Fortunately, such a misguided approach to site evaluation is not typical of entrepreneurs, many of whom recognize the value of seeking professional assistance in determining site availability and appropriateness. Local realtors can serve as a good source of insight.

If an entrepreneur's top choices are unavailable, other options must be considered. One choice is shared facilities. In recent years, business incubators have sprung up in all areas of the country. A **business incubator** is a facility that rents space to new businesses or to people wishing to start businesses. Incubators are often located in recycled buildings, such as abandoned warehouses or schools. They serve fledgling businesses by making space available, offering management advice, and providing clerical assistance, all of which help lower operating costs. An incubator tenant can be fully operational the day after moving in, without buying phones, renting a copier, or hiring office employees.

business incubator
A facility that provides shared space, services, and management assistance to new businesses

The purpose of business incubators is to see new businesses hatch, grow, and leave the incubator. Most incubators—though not all—have some type of government or university sponsorship and are motivated by a desire to stimulate economic development. Although the building space provided by incubators is significant, their greatest contribution is the business expertise and management assistance they provide.

Site Costs

Ultimately, the site selection process must depend on evaluation of relevant costs. Unfortunately, an entrepreneur is frequently unable to afford the "best" site. The costs involved in building on a new site may be prohibitive, or the purchase price of an existing structure may exceed the entrepreneur's budget.

Assuming that a suitable building is available, the entrepreneur must decide whether to lease or buy. Although ownership confers greater freedom in the modification and use of a building, the advantages of leasing usually outweigh these benefits. We recommend that most new firms lease for two reasons:

1. A large cash outlay is avoided. This is important for a new small firm, which typically lacks adequate financial resources.

2. Risk is reduced by avoiding substantial investment and by postponing commitments for space until the success of the business is assured and the nature of building requirements is better known.

When entering into a leasing agreement, the entrepreneur should check the landlord's insurance policies to be sure there is proper coverage for various types of risks. If not, the lessee should seek coverage under his or her own policy. It is important to have the terms

Living the Dream
entrepreneurial challenges

© Fabian Bimmer/Associated Press

Staying Home

James Dyson's experience provides a good example of the kind of dilemma that may confront entrepreneurs when circumstances—such as profit—conflict with a decision to locate their business in their home community.

Dyson, 60, smiles when he talks about bringing his neon-colored, warhead-shaped, English-made vacuum cleaners to America. His upright, bagless, vacuum cleaner is the result of 15 years of innovation and failed proto-types. By creating a technology of spinning air in a plastic cone to achieve a superior cleaning action, Dyson has dominated his niche in the European market and more recently carved a big slice out of the U.S. market.

From the start, Dyson's production facilities were located in his home community of Malmesbury, England. For years, his firm was the town's largest employer at the Tetbury Hill site. "I live here, this is my home, and it is the home of everybody here at Dyson," he said. "We love being here; we're a big employer and, I hope, a big contributor to the community."

Nevertheless, in 2002 Dyson moved the manufacture of his upright vacuum to the Far East—Malaysia—where labor costs are much cheaper. The move resulted in a loss of 800 jobs in a town with only 4,500 residents. Even former Prime Minister Tony Blair said he was "deeply disappointed" by the decision.

Four years later, however, Dyson said the move helped double the firm's business and allowed it to employ almost as many employees in Britain as it had prior to the move. And wages are higher, because the jobs remaining in Malmesbury are primarily in research and development. So, according to Dyson, his products are still "British-engineered."

Sources: Zareer Masan, *New Statesman,* August 14, 2006, p. 14; Joshua Levine, "Carpet Diem," *Forbes,* Vol. 170, No. 8 (October 14, 2002), pp. 206–207; "Dyson Plant Shuts Up Shop," http://news.bbc.co.uk/1/hi/england/2282809.stm, accessed April 8, 2004; and "Blair 'Disappointed' over Dyson's Jobs," http://news.bbc.co.uk/1/hi/england/1805050.stm, accessed April 8, 2004.

http://www.dyson.com

of the leasing agreement reviewed by an attorney. Sometimes, an attorney can arrange for special clauses to be added to a lease, such as an escape clause that allows the lessee to exit the agreement under certain conditions. And an attorney can ensure that an entrepreneur will not be unduly exposed to liability for damages caused by the gross negligence of others. Consider the experience of one firm that wished to rent 300 square feet of storage space in a large complex of offices and shops. On the sixth page of the landlord's standard lease, the firm's lawyer found language that could have made the firm responsible for the entire 30,000-square-foot complex if it burned down, regardless of blame!

Designing and Equipping the Physical Facilities

> 2 Discuss the challenges of designing and equipping a physical facility.

A location plan should describe the physical space in which the business will be housed and include an explanation of equipment needs. Although the plan may call for a new building or an existing structure, ordinarily a new business occupies an existing building, with minor or major remodeling.

Living the Dream   entrepreneurial challenges

Incubating a Cure for Hospital Infections

MedMined is in the business of saving lives as well as saving money for hospitals and insurance companies. By using data mining and artificial intelligence models to identify the sources of infections, it helps hospitals reduce hospital-acquired infections in patients. The company's products and services are saving, on average, about five people each week. That's a big relief for anyone who has ever been in the hospital.

The National Business Incubating Association (NBIA) awarded MedMined its Outstanding Incubator Client Award in 2002 and its Outstanding Incubator Graduate Award in 2005. MedMined's sales grew from $5,000 in 2000 to $1.2 million in 2003 [the year it "graduated" from the Office for the Advancement of Developing Industries (OADI) technology center] and $3.3 million in 2004. That's over 600-percent growth in five years. The OADI technology center incubator contributed to this growth by developing a training program for MedMined's sales force and coaching the MedMined team on how to create an effective fund-raising presentation that led to $2 million in initial venture capital funding in 2001.

MedMined outgrew the incubator and now leases the entire floor of an office building in Birmingham, Alabama. Its staff expanded from three employees in 2000 to 45 in 2005. According to MedMined founder Stephen Brossette, being an incubator client provided the stamp of approval the company needed to woo clients—MedMined's experience is a shining example of the valuable role an incubator can play in the life of a young company.

Source: http://www.nbia.org/awards_showcase/2005/graduate.php, accessed December 2006.

http://www.medmined.com

Challenges in Designing the Physical Facilities

When specifying building requirements, the entrepreneur must avoid committing to a space that is too large or too luxurious. At the same time, the space should not be too small or too austere for efficient operation. Buildings do not produce profits directly; they merely house the operations and personnel that do so. Therefore, the ideal building is practical, not pretentious.

The general suitability of a building for a given type of business operation depends on the functional requirements of the business. For example, a restaurant should ideally be on one level. Other important factors are the age and condition of the building, fire hazards, heating and air conditioning, lighting and restroom facilities, and entrances and exits. Obviously, these factors are weighted differently for a factory operation than for a wholesale or retail operation. But in any case, the comfort, convenience, and safety of the business's employees and customers must not be overlooked.

Challenges in Equipping the Physical Facilities

The final step in arranging for physical facilities is the purchase or lease of equipment and tools. A survey conducted by the National Federation of Independent Business (NFIB) found that, overwhelmingly, owners of small businesses would rather own their equipment than lease it (see Exhibit 9-3). The majority believe that, in the long run, it is cheaper to buy than to lease. Having the flexibility to use the equipment as they wish and to keep it until it is no longer needed are also important reasons small business owners prefer to own rather than lease.[11]

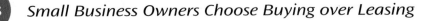

exhibit

9-3   *Small Business Owners Choose Buying over Leasing*

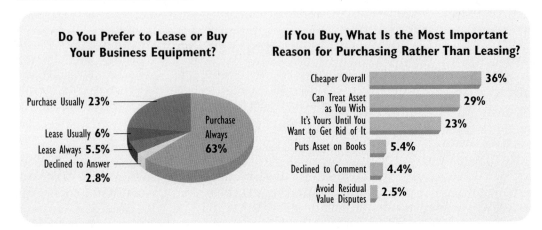

Do You Prefer to Lease or Buy Your Business Equipment?

Purchase Usually **23%**
Lease Usually **6%**
Lease Always **5.5%**
Declined to Answer **2.8%**
Purchase Always **63%**

If You Buy, What Is the Most Important Reason for Purchasing Rather Than Leasing?

Cheaper Overall — **36%**
Can Treat Asset as You Wish — **29%**
It's Yours Until You Want to Get Rid of It — **23%**
Puts Asset on Books — **5.4%**
Declined to Comment — **4.4%**
Avoid Residual Value Disputes — **2.5%**

Source: Richard Breeden, "Small Businesses Favor Buying over Leasing," *Wall Street Journal,* February 24, 2004, p. B11. Copyright 2004 by Dow Jones & Company, Inc. Reproduced with permission of Dow Jones & Company, Inc. in the format Textbook via Copyright Clearance Center.

The types of equipment and tools required obviously depend on the nature of the business. Even within the three areas discussed here—manufacturing, retailing, and office equipment—there is great variation in the need for tools and equipment.

MANUFACTURING EQUIPMENT   Machines used in a factory may be either general purpose or special purpose.

general-purpose equipment
Machines that serve many functions in the production process

General-Purpose Equipment   General-purpose equipment requires a minimal investment and is easily adapted to varied types of operations. Small machine shops and cabinet shops, for example, utilize this type of equipment. General-purpose equipment for metalworking includes lathes, drill presses, and milling machines. In a woodworking plant, general-purpose machines include ripsaws, planing mills, and lathes. In each case, jigs, fixtures, and other tooling items set up on the basic machinery can be changed so that two or more shop operations can be accomplished using the same piece of equipment. General-purpose equipment contributes important flexibility in industries in which products are so new that the technology is not yet well developed or there are frequent design changes.

special-purpose equipment
Machines designed to serve specialized functions in the production process

Special-Purpose Equipment   Special-purpose equipment can reduce costs in industries in which the technology is fully established and capacity operation is more or less ensured by high sales volume. Bottling machines and automobile assembly-line machinery are examples of special-purpose equipment used in factories. A milking machine in a dairy is an example of special-purpose equipment used by small firms. A small firm cannot, however, use special-purpose equipment economically unless it makes a standardized product on a fairly large scale. Using special-purpose machines with specialized tooling results in greater output per machine-hour of operation. The labor cost per unit of product is, therefore, lower. However, the initial cost of such equipment is much higher, and it has little or no resale value because of its highly specialized function.

RETAIL STORE EQUIPMENT   Small retailers need merchandise display racks or counters, storage racks, shelving, mirrors, seats for customers, customer pushcarts, cash registers, and other items to facilitate selling. Such equipment may be costly, but it is usually less expensive than that necessary for a factory operation.

If a store is intended to serve a high-income market, its fixtures should display the elegance and style expected by such customers. For example, polished mahogany showcases with bronze fittings lend a richness to the atmosphere. Indirect lighting, thick rugs, and big easy chairs also contribute to an air of luxury. In contrast, a store that caters to lower-income customers should concentrate on simplicity, as luxurious fixtures create an atmosphere inconsistent with low prices.

OFFICE EQUIPMENT   Obviously, every business office needs furniture, storage cabinets, and other such items. The more challenging task is selecting office equipment—computers, fax machines, copiers, printers, and telephone systems—that reflects the latest advances in technology applicable to a particular business.

The location plan should list the major pieces of equipment needed to furnish a business office. Careful selection of equipment helps a business operate efficiently. Also, by identifying major equipment needs in this section of the business plan, the entrepreneur can ensure that the financial section of the plan includes funds for their purchase.

Building Image

All new ventures, whether they are retailers, wholesalers, manufacturers, or service businesses, should be concerned with projecting the appropriate image to customers and the public at large. The appearance of the workplace should create a favorable impression about the quality of a firm's product or service and, generally, about the way the business is operated. For a small firm, it is important to use the physical facilities to convey the image of a stable, professional company.

Locating the Startup in the Entrepreneur's Home

{ 3 Understand both the attraction and the challenges of creating a home-based startup.

home-based business
A business that maintains its primary facility in the residence of its owner

Rather than lease or buy a commercial site, many entrepreneurs elect to use their basement, garage, or spare room for their business operation, creating a **home-based business**. In the past, a home location for a business was regarded as second-rate. But times have changed, and home-based entrepreneurs no longer feel embarrassed about their location. The home office, once simply a stage in the growth of many businesses, is a viable permanent option for some. At present, many entrepreneurs have no plans to ever move out of the home.

The Attraction of Home-Based Businesses

Why do many entrepreneurs find operating a business at home so attractive? Although motivations vary (see Exhibit 9-4), the main attractions of a home-based business relate to financial and family lifestyle considerations.

exhibit 9-4   *Entrepreneurs' Reasons for Operating a Home-Based Business*

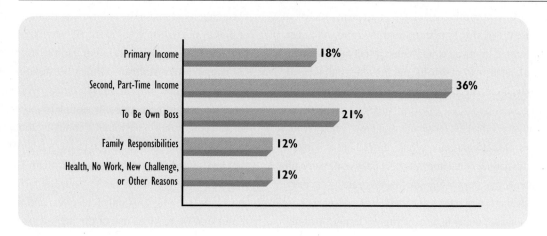

Reason	Percentage
Primary Income	18%
Second, Part-Time Income	36%
To Be Own Boss	21%
Family Responsibilities	12%
Health, No Work, New Challenge, or Other Reasons	12%

Sources: Joanne Pratt, "Home-Based Business: The Hidden Economy," *The Small Business Advocate,* Vol. 19, No. 2 (Spring 2000), p. 6; and http://www.perfectsystem.co.uk, accessed June 20, 2007.

FINANCIAL CONSIDERATIONS   Like most business ventures, a home-based business has an important goal—earning money—and locating at home helps increase profits by reducing costs. This was the motivation of Bianca Wright, who does freelance writing for magazines. She needed a computer, office supplies, and an Internet connection for her home-based business venture. Since she already owned a computer, her startup costs were only about $150.[12]

With the ups and downs of the advertising industry, Donavan Andrews, 31, and Stephen Smyk, 35, thought it would be best to start their fledgling advertising agency in their home. "We . . . built the business slowly and were conservative until we got to the point where we had excess capital," says Andrews. This conservative approach worked well; Andrews and Smyk moved into office space only four months after they started the business and now have offices in Binghamton, New York, and New York City.[13]

Receiving full compensation for her work was Rose Anne Raphael's motivation for starting a home-based business. Her boyfriend noticed that her employer was billing clients more than seven times as much as Raphael was earning. "I was getting paid $17 an hour and the company was billing clients at $125 an hour for my work. . . . That's when I thought I had the opportunity to become self-employed," says Raphael. She's been running a public-relations firm out of a one-bedroom apartment in Berkeley, California, ever since.[14]

FAMILY LIFESTYLE CONSIDERATIONS   Many young entrepreneurs remain in a family business because of close family ties. Similarly, entrepreneurs who locate business operations in the home are frequently motivated by the desire to spend more time with family members. Consider the following examples.

Joyce Thomas, 47, owns Chino Hills, California–based Medical Reimbursement Specialists (MRS), a Medicare-compliance company. MRS started out handling electronic claims for local physicians. After two years, Thomas decided to use her experience to train other women to process claims from their homes. She helped start 500 affiliate businesses across the country and won contracts with hospitals nationwide. What does she

---

How They See It: Our Virtual Location

Trey Moore

Our company is completely "virtual," with every employee working out of his or her home office. This has worked to our advantage in numerous ways, including significant savings in not having to supply office space and equipment. And when you add up the driving time saved over the course of a year, it is much more than you would think. If half of that time is spent working instead of driving and the other half is spent with family, then it becomes a win-win for the employer and employee.

Another advantage is fewer interruptions. A common question I get is "How do you work with the distractions at home?" (such as kids getting home from school). I have worked in both environments, and I can assure you that there are just as many, if not many more, distractions at a traditional work environment. Personally, I prefer to be "interrupted" by my 2-year-old's hugs. New cutting-edge collaboration software, coupled with

high-speed Internet access (DSL/cable modem), has been a key factor in our virtual company's success.

While the concept of working out of a home office is becoming more and more acceptable, there is still a lot of bias in the industry. For example, when GE Healthcare contacted us to perform its initial audit in order to approve our company as a strategic partner, the auditor refused to perform the audit until we moved into a "real" office, stating that "you cannot have a quality system in a home office." So, as a compromise, we found a company that allowed us to use as our new computer server room a very tiny room that had served as a storage closet for them. The auditor had scheduled an hour and a half to "tour the facilities." Needless to say, the tour took only 5 seconds, and we are proud to report that we received one of the highest scores ever given by this auditor.

like most about being her own boss: "I can set my own hours and decide if I want to do something or not," Thomas explains. Thomas initially went into the business so that she could work from home and take care of her three children. Although she does travel about two weeks each month giving seminars, she appreciates being at home the rest of the time. "I do the Little League thing, keep up with my two boys. . . . I'm also a grandmother, so I do a little of that role when I'm home," she adds. Thomas states that she couldn't do what she does without the help of her husband: "It has to be a partnership." Her mother, too, plays an important role; she calls Thomas every night when she's on the road and even travels with her on occasion.[15]

Marisa Shipman, 31, owner of Shipman Associates, the manufacturer of the Balm line of cosmetics, has run her business from her home since 2001. "I love working from home," says Shipman. Her home, however, has had to change several times to accommodate her growing business with sales of over $2 million. Shipman Associates is a true family affair; despite being spread across the country, her family helps run the business. Her dad, who is in Greenwich, Connecticut, and a sister in Philadelphia both work out of their homes to help grow the business. Shipman thinks that a home is a great place to start a business: "If you have something you think could work, do it on a small scale and see."[16]

The Challenges of Home-Based Businesses

Just as most businesses located at commercial sites have their problems, home-based businesses face special challenges attributable to their location. We will briefly examine two of these challenges—business image and legal considerations. Another major challenge—family and business conflicts—was discussed in Chapter 5.

BUSINESS IMAGE   Maintaining an image of professionalism when working at home is a major challenge for home-based entrepreneurs. Allowing young children to answer the telephone, for example, may undermine a professional image. Likewise, a baby crying or a dog barking in the background during a phone call can be distracting to a client.

If clients or salespeople visit the home-based business, it is critical that a professional office area be maintained. Space limitations sometimes make this difficult. For example, when you own a home-based business, house guests can create a real problem. Unless you want Aunt Sophie wandering into a client meeting in her swim suit or your nephew Johnnie playing his electric guitar during a work call, ground rules need to be set for house guests. These rules should be clearly spelled out in advance of the visit to avoid any major disruptions to your business.[17]

LEGAL CONSIDERATIONS   Some local laws pose a problem for home-based businesses. Zoning ordinances, for example, regulate the types of enterprises permitted in various geographical areas. Some cities outlaw any type of home-based business within city limits.

Many zoning laws, dating as far back as the 1930s, have never been updated. The intent of such laws is to protect a neighborhood's residential quality by preventing commercial signs and parking problems. The neighborhood you live in may have a homeowners' association that can limit your ability to run a home-based business (see Exhibit 9-5). Some entrepreneurs first become aware of these zoning laws when neighbors initiate zoning enforcement action. Consider "good neighbor" Lauren Januz of Libertyville Township, Illinois.

zoning ordinances
Local laws regulating land use

> One of Januz's neighbors was running a landscaping and tree-service business out of his home. He erected a large fence to obscure the view of his heavy equipment which was fine with the subdivision's other residents, but he had 10 to 15 workers parking their cars on the street every day. "This is an area of $300,000 homes, and a lot of the cars were really wrecks," explains Januz. Although several neighbors approached the offending property owner, he made no attempt to correct the problem, and a complaint was finally filed with the Lake County Building and Zoning Department. He ended up selling the property and relocating the business.[18]

exhibit **9-5**   *The Challenges of Home-Based Businesses*

There are also tax issues related to a home-based business. Generally, a separate space must be clearly devoted to business activities in order for the entrepreneur to claim a tax deduction. A certified public accountant can be helpful in explaining these tax regulations.

Insurance considerations may also affect a home-based business. An entrepreneur's homeowner's policy is not likely to cover business activities, liabilities, and equipment.

Technology and Home-Based Businesses

Advancements in business-application technology are a major catalyst in the rapid growth of home-based businesses. Personal computers, fax machines, voice mail, and e-mail are among the technological tools that help the home-based business compete effectively with commercial-site businesses. Such technology makes it possible to operate many types of businesses almost anywhere.

One important technological tool available to home-based businesses is the Internet. Millions of small firms—many of them based at home—are using websites to sell products and services. Virtually every product sold in traditional retail outlets is now sold over the Internet. In the next section, we will examine the potential of the Internet as a place to host a new business.

Locating the Startup on the Internet

4 Understand the potential benefits of locating a startup on the Internet.

We currently live in a digital economy fueled by the tremendous growth of the Internet. Access to the Internet continues to transform the way we live and the way business is conducted. It is important for aspiring entrepreneurs to learn as much as they can about cyberspace because there's opportunity online.

What is the Internet, and how does it support e-commerce? What benefits does e-commerce offer the startup? What business models reflect an e-commerce strategy? These are the primary questions we address in this section of the chapter. We hope that our discussion will help you understand both the opportunities and the limitations associated with today's digital economy. Additional e-commerce topics are discussed in other chapters.

What Is E-Commerce?

e-commerce
The paperless exchange of business information via the Internet

What does the term *e-commerce* really describe? **E-commerce** means electronic commerce, or the paperless exchange of business information via the Internet. It is an alternative means of conducting business transactions that traditionally have been carried out by telephone, by mail, or face to face in brick-and-mortar stores. Internet businesses continue to grow in number, despite a crash in Web-based stocks in 2000 and 2002.

Although the Internet, like the telephone, is basically a tool that parties use to communicate with each other, it is a communication medium unlike any previously available to companies. A Web location reshapes the way small firms conduct business, while also providing an alternative to the brick-and-mortar store.

Benefits of E-Commerce to Startups

Electronic commerce benefits a startup in a number of ways. Basically, it offers the new firm the opportunity to compete with bigger businesses on a more level playing field. Limited resources frequently restrict the ability of small firms to reach beyond local markets. Confined to their brick-and-mortar world, small firms typically serve a restricted geographic area. But the Internet blurs geographic boundaries. E-commerce allows any business access to customers almost anywhere. The Internet is proving to be a great equalizer, giving small firms a presence comparable to that of the giants in the marketplace. For example, Jill-Anne Partain operates her handbag manufacturing business in Lexington, Virginia—a favorable production site—and then uses the Web to sell her upscale products for as much as $550 each. Partain employs no sales or marketing staff, relying on one-to-one relationships created with her customers through the Internet. Her company, Pilgrim Designs, was named one of the top 30 "style-packed" websites by *Harper's Bazaar* magazine.[19]

An e-commerce operation can help the startup with early cash flow problems by compressing the sales cycle—that is, reducing the time between receiving an order and converting the sale to cash. E-commerce systems can be designed to generate an order, authorize a credit card purchase, and contact a supplier and shipper in a matter of minutes, all without human assistance. The shorter cycle translates into quicker payments from customers and improved cash flows to the business.

E-commerce also enables small firms to build on one of their greatest strengths—customer relationships. The Internet has brought new life and technology to bear on the old-fashioned notion of customer service. **Electronic Customer Relationship Marketing (eCRM)** is an electronically based system that emphasizes customer relationships. At the heart of eCRM is a customer-centric data warehouse. A typical eCRM system allows an e-commerce firm to integrate data from websites, call centers, sales force reports, and other customer contact points, with the goal of building customer loyalty. There are, of course, innumerable other benefits that small firms can reap from e-commerce; space does not allow us to discuss them all here.

E-commerce has several limitations that also need to be considered when you are deciding where to locate and how to operate your business. These potential limitations fall into two categories: technical limitations and non-technical limitations. *Technical limitations* include the cost of developing and maintaining a website, insufficient telecommunications bandwidth, constantly changing software, the need to integrate digital and non-digital sales and production information, and access limitations of dial-up, cable, and wireless, as well as the fact that not all of your potential customers will have Internet access. *Non-technical limitations* include customer concern over privacy issues, the security and privacy of your Web operations, customers' inability to touch products, employees' lack of technical knowledge, and the challenges of dealing with global cultures and languages.[20]

E-Commerce Business Models

The dictionary defines an opportunity as a "combination of circumstances favorable for a chance to advance oneself." Thus, it is logical to study the circumstances surrounding e-commerce in order to uncover the opportunities the Internet offers as a startup location. Let's begin by examining some existing e-commerce business models.

The term **business model** describes a group of shared characteristics, behaviors, and goals that a firm follows in a particular business situation. Online business firms differ in their decisions concerning which customers to serve, how best to become profitable, and what to include on their websites. Exhibit 9-6 shows some possible alternatives for business models. None of these models can currently be considered dominant, and some Internet businesses cannot be described by any single model. The real world of e-commerce contains endless combinations of business models. However, it is important to keep in mind that a poorly devised business model can be a major factor in business failure.

Electronic Customer Relationship Marketing (eCRM)
An electronically based system that emphasizes customer relationships

business model
A group of shared characteristics, behaviors, and goals that a firm follows in a particular business situation

exhibit

9-6   *E-Commerce Business Models*

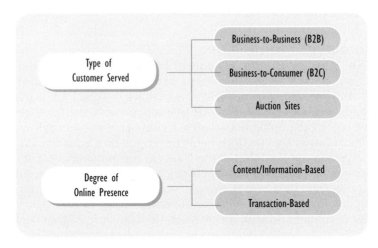

TYPE OF CUSTOMERS SERVED   Marketing theory classifies traditional brick-and-mortar firms as manufacturers, wholesalers, or retailers, depending on the customers they serve. E-commerce businesses also are commonly distinguished according to customer focus. There are three major categories of e-commerce business models: business-to-business (B2B), business-to-consumer (B2C), and auction sites. In this section, we examine some strategies used by e-commerce firms within these three categories.

business-to-business (B2B) model
A business model based on selling to business customers electronically

Business-to-Business Models   The dollar amounts generated by firms using a **business-to-business (B2B) model** (selling to business customers) are significantly greater than those for firms with a business-to-consumer (B2C) model (selling to final consumers). Because B2B success stories generally receive less publicity than B2C ventures do, the potential of a B2B opportunity may be overlooked. Aspiring entrepreneurs should be sure to consider the B2B model.

All B2B firms do not look alike. One form of B2B strategy emphasizes sales transactions. By using online capabilities, a B2B firm can achieve greater efficiency in its selling and buying. International Business Machines (IBM) is a good example. By dealing directly with its corporate customers online, it is able to build its computer systems and related products to meet the specific needs of its customers. As much as IBM relies on the Internet to deliver its business solution, it also has an extensive sales force and consulting services to deliver value to its many customers worldwide.

As B2B e-commerce models continue to develop and evolve, new versions will emerge. The wise entrepreneur will continue to monitor these changes to learn where opportunities lie.

business-to-consumer (B2C) model
A business model based on selling to final customers electronically

Business-to-Consumer Models   In contrast to a B2B model, a **business-to-consumer (B2C) model** has final consumers as customers. In the traditional retail setting, customers generally approach a business location (a brick-and-mortar store) with the intent of shopping or purchasing. Alternatively, customers might purchase via telephone or mail order, using a printed catalog. The B2C model introduces another alternative for consumers—buying online.

Amazon.com represents the classic B2C firm, which is directly focused on individual final consumers. B2C ventures are extremely diverse in the products they sell, with offerings ranging from clothing to pet items, computer software, toys, and groceries. The B2C model offers three main advantages over brick-and-mortar retailing: speed of access, speed of transaction, and round-the-clock access to products and services, often referred to as **24/7 e-tailing**.

24/7 e-tailing
Electronic retailing providing round-the-clock access to products and services

exhibit **9-7**

Selling Your Item on eBay

Step 1:   Register as an eBay member, then click the "Sell" link at the top of any page.
Step 2:   Gather information and digital pictures for your item description.
Step 3:   Write your title and item description.
Step 4:   Pre-pack your item to determine its shipping weight (but don't seal it yet).
Step 5:   Choose the methods of payment you will accept; PayPal is the fastest and safest.

Source: http://www.eBayuniversity.com, accessed December 20, 2006.

It is true that many final consumers avoid online shopping for several reasons, the primary ones being reluctance to send credit card data electronically and to purchase a product without first seeing it. However, B2C e-commerce businesses have many advantages, including the ability to quickly change merchandise mixes and prices, as well as the appearance of their "store" (their website). Traditional merchants located in brick-and-mortar stores find such changes very costly and time-consuming.

Auction Site Models   Some entrepreneurs sell their wares over the Internet without either a website or a storefront, by means of e-commerce sites based on the auction site model. Internet **auction sites** are Web-based businesses offering participants—final consumers and businesses—the ability to list products for bidding by potential buyers. Revenues to the auction site are derived from listing fees and commissions on sales.

Online auctions have become one of the real success stories on the Web. And, as you might have guessed, eBay, founded in 1995 by computer programmer Pierre Omidyar, is the 900-pound gorilla of auction sites. "I got it on eBay" is quickly becoming part of our collective vocabulary. You can buy or sell nearly anything on eBay—and it is incredibly easy. eBay consultants abound; for a fee, they will coach you on how to be a successful seller. Or you can "attend" eBay University to learn the ins and outs of operating an eBay business. Exhibit 9-7 provides a simple five-step procedure for selling items on eBay.

As easy as it is to sell a few items on eBay, it is a very different matter to actually make money as an ongoing business on the site. As in the more conventional forms of retailing, a well-thought-out business plan is helpful in turning your business idea (or hobby) into a money-making proposition. Here are a few statistics about eBay that you might find interesting:[21]

auction sites
Web-based businesses offering participants the ability to list products for bidding

1.   There are 212 million registered eBay users worldwide.

2.   Roughly $1,590 worth of goods are sold on eBay every second.

3.   eBay has approximately 1.3 million sellers around the world.

4.   At any given time, 105 million items are listed on eBay.

5.   Six million new items are listed every day.

6.   There are 254,000 online stores worldwide selling on eBay.

7.   eBay has 45,000 categories of merchandise.

As mentioned earlier, eBay generates much of its revenue through listing fees and advertising. To continue its rapid growth, eBay is expanding its services and entering new markets across the globe—most recently, in China, India, South Korea, Spain, Switzerland, and Taiwan—through new sites, acquisitions, and co-ventures. Overall, eBay does business in more than 20 countries. PayPal, eBay's global payments platform, has nearly 100 million accounts. No longer the only show in town, however, eBay faces marketing competition from the likes of Amazon.com and smaller competitors such as Overstock.com. Exhibit 9-8 contains a list of the top ten auction sites. How many have you visited?

exhibit

9-8 *Top 10 Online Auction Sites*

1. eBay
2. Ubid
3. Bidz.com
4. Yahoo auctions
5. MSN auctions
6. Amazon.com
7. Auctionweiser
8. Auction Addict
9. Auction-warehouse
10. Auctonet.com

Source: http://www.auctions.nettop20.com, accessed December 2006.

In mid-2006, eBay took the bold step of opening eBay Express, a site dedicated to selling new merchandise at set prices. This site allows eBay to target consumers who are looking for bargains and don't like the auction format. Pierre Omidyar, eBay chairman and founder, owns approximately 14 percent of the online behemoth.[22]

DEGREE OF ONLINE PRESENCE A second broad way of categorizing e-commerce models relates to the firm's intended level of online presence. The role of a website can range from merely offering content and information to enabling complex business transactions.

content/information-based model

A business model in which the website provides information but not the ability to buy or sell products and services

Content/Information-Based Model In a content/information-based model of e-commerce, a website provides access but not the ability to buy or sell products and services. During the early days of e-commerce, the *content model* was the model of choice. For example, America Online (AOL) began with this model. Originally, revenue for AOL came from fees paid by users for the privilege of connecting and gaining access to its content. Today, many content models are still found, mostly in countries where Internet usage by small firms is less developed.

A slight variation of the content model is the *information-based model*. A website built on this model contains information about the business, its products, and other related matters but doesn't charge for its use. It is typically just a complement to an existing brick-and-mortar store. Many small businesses use this model for their online operations. Your dentist or plumber may have a website that simply describes the services offered but requires a phone call to set up an appointment.

transaction-based model

A business model in which the website provides a mechanism for buying or selling products or services

Transaction-Based Model In a transaction-based model of e-commerce, a website provides a mechanism for buying or selling products or services. The transaction-based model, which is at the very heart of e-commerce, calls for websites to be online stores where visitors go to shop, click, and buy.

Many Internet ventures sell a single product or service. For example, Huber and Jane Wilkinson, based in Waco, Texas, market their reading comprehension program, Ideachain, through their MindPrime, Inc. website. Similarly, Phil Rockell and his wife, Stephanie, of Helotes, Texas, sell hillbilly teeth pacifiers only from their website. Other ventures are direct extensions of a brick-and-mortar store, creating a click-and-mortar strategy. For example, if you were interested in purchasing a new printer, you might research options on Office Depot's website and then choose to either buy your selection online or drive to the neighborhood Office Depot store and pick up the printer there. Gradually, a small firm can add to and improve its website store until all of its products are available online.

Clearly, the location decision is complicated, but it is vital to a successful venture. Take your time, do your research, and make a wise choice.

Living the Dream   utilizing the internet

© 2007 Pluck

Student Entrepreneur Turns to Blogging

One of the newest Internet crazes is blogging, or Web logging—that is, creating an online venue to chronicle your thoughts. Bloggers produce online journals to trade comments with friends and readers. Small firms have found blogs easy to use and thus an attractive platform from which to promote a sale on an overstocked item or give an employee special recognition.

Adam Weinroth used his winter break from the University of Texas in 2001 to build his initial version of the Easyjournal website, designed to attract novice bloggers. Weinroth built his site on a shoestring budget of less than $10,000. Easyjournal now has over 125,000 registered members and offers both a free account and a paid account with additional features. These features include a public comment board and journal templates, as well as other services. The site also brings in revenue from advertising.

In February of 2005, a completely redesigned blogging system was introduced on Easyjournal.com, along with a new logo and Web design. Users now have more control over the look and behavior of their blogs. Easyjournal was acquired in 2005 by Pluck, a company focused on social media software solutions. And Weinroth is still with the company as Director of Product Marketing for Pluck.

A new twist to the blogging phenomenon is its use by businesses as a forum for discussing important topics. It provides an easy way to maintain an ongoing dialogue between the company and its many constituents. Time will tell whether blogging will run its course or become a useful form of expression and dialogue for individuals and businesses alike.

Sources: Personal correspondence with Adam Weinroth, August 6, 2007; http://www.easyjournal.com/about.html, accessed December 18, 2006; Kirk Ladendorf, "Blogging It Through," *Waco Tribune-Herald,* August 14, 2003, p. 4B; and "Ease into Business Blogging," *MyBusiness,* October-November 2004, p. 24.

http://www.easyjournal.com

Looking BACK

1 Describe the five key factors in locating a brick-and-mortar startup.

- Customer accessibility is a key factor in the location decision of retail and service businesses.

- Climate, competition, legal requirements, and the tax structure are types of environmental factors affecting the location decision.

- Availability of resources such as raw materials, labor supply, and transportation is important to location decisions.

- The entrepreneur's personal preference is a practical consideration in selecting a location.

- An appropriate site must be available and priced within the entrepreneur's budget.

2 **Discuss the challenges of designing and equipping a physical facility.**

· The ideal building is practical, not pretentious.

· The general suitability of a building depends on the functional requirements of the business.

· The comfort, convenience, and safety of the business's employees and customers must not be overlooked.

· Most small manufacturing firms must use general-purpose equipment, although some can use special-purpose equipment for standardized operations.

· The cost of special-purpose equipment is high, and it has little or no resale value because of its highly specialized function.

· Small retailers must have merchandise display racks and counters, mirrors, and other equipment that facilitates selling.

· Display counters and other retailing equipment should create an atmosphere appropriate for customers in the retailer's target market.

· Entrepreneurs must select office equipment that reflects the latest advances in technology applicable to a particular business.

3 **Understand both the attraction and the challenges of creating a home-based startup.**

· Home-based businesses are started to both make money and incorporate family lifestyle considerations.

· Operating a business at home can pose challenges, particularly in the areas of business image and legal considerations.

· Technology, especially the Web, has helped entrepreneurs start home-based businesses.

4 **Understand the potential benefits of locating a startup on the Internet.**

· E-commerce offers small firms the opportunity to compete with bigger companies on a more level playing field.

· Internet operations can help small firms with cash flow problems by compressing sales cycles.

· E-commerce enables small firms to build stronger customer relationships.

· New versions of the business-to-business (B2B) model continue to develop and evolve.

· The three main advantages of online business-to-consumer (B2C) firms are speed of access, speed of transaction, and continuous access to products and services, often referred to as 24/7 e-tailing.

· Auction sites are online firms that bring buyers and sellers together.

· The role of a website can range from merely offering content and information to permitting the buying and selling of products and services online.

Key TERMS

brick-and-mortar store, p. 237
enterprise zones, p. 240
business incubator, p. 241
general-purpose equipment, p. 244
special-purpose equipment, p. 244
home-based business, p. 245
zoning ordinances, p. 247

e-commerce, p. 248
Electronic Customer Relationship Marketing (eCRM), p. 249
business model, p. 249
business-to-business (B2B) model, p. 250
business-to-consumer (B2C) model, p. 250

24/7 e-tailing, p. 250
auction sites, p. 251
content/information-based model, p. 252
transaction-based model, p. 252

Discussion QUESTIONS

1. What are the key attributes of a good business location? Which of these would probably be most important for a retail location? Why?

2. What is the special appeal of an enterprise zone to an entrepreneur seeking the best site for his or her business?

3. Which resource factors might be most vital to a new manufacturing venture that produces residential home furniture? Why?

4. Is the hometown of the business owner likely to be a good location? Is it logical for an owner to allow personal preferences to influence a decision about business location? Explain your answers.

5. Discuss the conditions under which a new small manufacturer should buy (a) general-purpose equipment and (b) special-purpose equipment.

6. Under what conditions would it be most appropriate for a new firm to buy rather than lease a building for the business?

7. What factors should an entrepreneur evaluate when considering a home-based business? Be specific.

8. Discuss how zoning and tax laws might impact the decision to start a home-based business.

9. Discuss the two different ways of categorizing business models used for e-commerce.

10. Contrast B2B and B2C businesses. Identify some of the reasons final consumers give for not using online shopping.

You Make the CALL

SITUATION 1

Entrepreneurs Alan Stein, 52, and his wife, Nancy Virts, 47, had a decision to make. Located just outside of Washington, D.C., their six-year-old company, Tanglewood Conservatories, was growing rapidly. The need for a larger space was pressing, as the current facility was just 4,000 square feet.

They knew the move was risky. But encouragement from the Economic Development Commission in Caroline County, Maryland, in the form of tax breaks and financial assistance, along with a readily available workforce, convinced the couple to build a new facility in rural Denton, Maryland.

Since the move, company sales have tripled. And the new facility has grown from 10,000 square feet to 40,000 square feet.

Source: Andrea C. Poe, "Head for the Hills," *Entrepreneur,* December 2006, p. 101.

Question 1 How important was the location decision for these two entrepreneurs? Why?

Question 2 What types of permits and zoning ordinances did they need to consider before deciding to relocate?

Question 3 Is a presence on the Internet helpful for a business like Tanglewood Conservatories?

SITUATION 2

Is it possible to build a $1.2-million business in a town with only 650 residents? Duane Ruh did. Ruh, 49, cofounded and is now sole owner of Little Log Company,

which manufactures log birdhouses and feeders in Sargent, Nebraska. Ruh believes it is all about treating your employees right. His 32 employees enjoy flexible schedules and ample personal time.

Ruh's love for his employees and loyalty to the town of Sargent (where he employs 5 percent of the population) has paid off. Clients include 65 U.S. colleges, John Deere, and *National Geographic Magazine.* Failure isn't an option for Ruh and his employees. Ruh says, "I think if you really love something, you can't fail at it."

Source: Michelle Prather, "Talk of the Town," *Entrepreneur,* February 2003. http://www.entrepreneur.com/magazine.entrepreneur/2003/february/58828. html, accessed June 12, 2007.

Question 1 What impact, if any, do you think that Internet-based businesses have had on Ruh's business?

Question 2 In what way(s) could he use e-commerce to grow his business?

Question 3 How much presence on the Web, if any, do you think Ruh should consider?

Question 4 What do you think will happen to this firm if it ignores the Internet?

SITUATION 3

A business incubator rents space to a number of small firms that are just beginning operations or are fairly new. In addition to supplying space, the incubator provides a receptionist, computer, conference room, fax machine, and copy machine. It also offers management counseling and assists new businesses in getting reduced advertising rates and reduced legal fees. One client of the incubator is a jewelry repair, cleaning, and remounting service that does work on a contract basis for pawn shops and jewelry stores. Another is a home health-care company that employs a staff of nurses to visit the homes of elderly people who need daily care but who cannot afford or are not yet ready to go to a nursing home.

Question 1 Evaluate each of the services offered by the incubator in terms of its usefulness to these two businesses. Which of the two businesses seems to be a better fit for the incubator? Why?

Question 2 If rental costs for incubator space were similar to rental costs for space outside the incubator, would the benefits of the services offered seem to favor location in the incubator? Why or why not?

SITUATION 4

Entrepreneur Karen Moore wants to start a catering and decorating business to bring in money to help support her two young children. Moore is a single parent; she works in the banking industry but has always had the desire to start a business. She enjoys decorating for friends' parties and is frequently told, "You should do this professionally. You have such good taste, and you are so nice to people."

Moore has decided to take this advice but is unsure whether she should locate in a commercial site or in her home, which is in rural central Texas. She is leaning toward locating at home because she wants more time with her children. However, she is concerned that the home-based location is too far away from the city, where most of her potential customers live.

Initially, her services would include planning wedding receptions and other special events, designing flower arrangements, decorating the sites, and even cooking and serving meals.

Question 1 What do you see as potential problems with locating Moore's new business at home?

Question 2 What do you see as the major benefits for Moore of a home-based business?

Question 3 How could Moore use technology to help her operate a home-based business?

Experiential **EXERCISES**

1. Search for articles in business periodicals that provide rankings of states or cities as business sites. Report on your findings.

2. Identify and evaluate a local site that is now vacant because of a business closure. Point out the strengths and weaknesses of that location for the former business, and comment on the part location may have played in the closure.

3. Interview a small business owner concerning the strengths and weaknesses of his or her business's location. Prepare a brief report summarizing your findings.

4. Interview the owner of a local small business that you believe might benefit from e-commerce. Prepare a report on the e-commerce strategy being pursued or the reasons this particular business is not involved in e-commerce.

5. Contact the Chamber of Commerce office in your local area and ask what e-commerce assistance it provides to small firms. Report on your findings.

Exploring the **WEB**

1. Go to **http://www.business.gov**, and choose "Start a Home-Based Business." Select "Starting a Home-based Business—Is It Right for You?" Are there questions and issues noted that you had not considered and that might affect your location decision? Can you think of questions not addressed on this website?

2. Visit the Free Advice website at **http://www. freeadvice.com**, and under Law and Legal Advice, select "Business Law," then choose "Starting a Business."
   a. Read the questions related to home-based businesses. Before you look at the answers, consider how you would respond.
   b. Now click on "General Questions." Find the four questions and/or topics that will most affect a location decision for your business. In what ways could these affect your decision?

Video Case 9

Le Travel Store (p. 638)
This case study illustrates the importance of location to a business and demonstrates how desired growth, along with the maturing of the business, can alter the optimal location, requiring relocation for continued desired growth.

Alternative Cases for Chapter 9:

Case 14, Country Supply, p. 648

Case 16, Glidden Point Oyster Company, A.G.A. Correa & Son, Hardy Boat Cruises, Maine Gold, p. 652

Case 17, Sunny Designs, Inc., p. 654

The Business Plan

Laying the Foundation

As part of laying the foundation for preparing your own business plan, respond to the following questions regarding location.

Brick-and-Mortar Startup Location Questions
1. How important are your personal reasons for choosing a location?
2. What business environment factors will influence your location decision?
3. What resources are most critical to your location decision?
4. How important is customer accessibility to your location decision?
5. What special resources do you need?
6. How will the formal site evaluation be conducted?
7. What laws and tax policies of state and local governments have been considered?
8. What is the cost of the proposed site?
9. Is an enterprise zone available in the area where you want to locate?

Physical Facility Questions
1. What are the major considerations in choosing between a new and an existing building?
2. What is the possibility of leasing a building or equipment?
3. How feasible is it to locate in a business incubator?
4. What is the major objective of your building design?
5. What types of equipment do you need for your business?

Home-Based Startup Location Questions
1. Will a home-based business be a possibility for you?
2. What are the advantages and disadvantages of a home-based business?
3. Have you given consideration to family lifestyle issues?
4. Will your home project the appropriate image for the business?
5. What zoning ordinances, if any, regulate the type of home-based business you want to start?

Internet Startup Questions
1. What type of customers will be served by the Internet startup?
2. What degree of online presence will you strive for?

## chapter 10

The Financial Plan

Projecting Financial Requirements

In the **SPOTLIGHT**

Planning for Growth
http://www.builtny.com

Managing rapid growth can become an entrepreneur's worst nightmare. Unhappy customers and employees, a lack of cash, and the inability to fill orders can overwhelm a small business owner.

Entrepreneurs rarely prepare for the challenges that growth brings, according to Jeff DeGraff, an associate professor of management education at the Ross School of Business at the University of Michigan: "They're too busy working in the business to work on the business." But taking the time to plan for growth, especially when it's unexpected, can keep your business on track.

In 2003, Carter Weiss, Aaron Lown, and John Roscoe Swartz started BuiltNY, a supplier of innovative wine totes and other accessories. In the first six months, the company had sales of $600,000 and even turned a profit, which is rare for most startups. By 2006, sales were $13 million; in 2007, it expected $20 million in sales. Managing this kind of growth is extremely difficult and can be a downfall for many companies.

Weiss says that they followed three rules: "Go sell it, make it, and figure out how to pay for it." Sounds simple, but Weiss warns, "It is not. You have to match expectations with sufficient financing, so we decided not to maximize sales, nor to focus solely on long-term profits. Instead, we traded some of both to have some short-term profits, too, which allowed us to attract bank financing. As a profitable firm with bank financing, we could then approach venture capitalists for expansion financing on better terms." He continues, "You have to decide what you want from the business and then know what it will take financially to make it happen. And above all, make sure you never run out of cash."

Plans for growth, which may be part of the original business plan or added at a later date, are essential if you want to keep your entrepreneurial dream alive.

Sources: Lena Basha, "Growth Gone Wild," *MyBusiness,* February-March 2007, pp. 36–41; and personal interview with Carter Weiss, July 11, 2007.

After studying this chapter, you should be able to

1   Describe the purpose and content of the income statement, the balance sheet, and the cash flow statement.
2   Forecast a new venture's profitability.
3   Determine asset requirements, evaluate financial sources, and estimate cash flows for a new venture.
4   Explain the importance of using good judgment when making projections.

A good idea may or may not be a good investment opportunity. As we discussed in Chapter 3, a good investment opportunity requires a product or service that meets a definite customer need and creates a sustainable competitive advantage. To be attractive, an opportunity must generate strong profits relative to the required amount of investment.

Therefore, projections of a venture's profits, its asset and financing requirements, and its cash flows are essential in determining whether a venture is economically feasible. In order to make such financial projections, an entrepreneur must have a good understanding of financial statements.

Understanding Financial Statements

The goal in this chapter is not to make you an accountant, but to help you understand the consequences of your decisions; otherwise, you can seriously jeopardize your business! A survey of entrepreneurs who had recently started new businesses indicated that many of the respondents felt inadequate in terms of the financial skills needed for managing their new businesses. Understandably, they considered marketing, acquiring sales, and getting the work done to maintain viability at startup as more important than their finances. In other words, these entrepreneurs were in survival mode.

> *It would seem that these owner-managers, while they might have the ability to read and understand fundamental financial statements, do not have the ability to make informed judgments and to make effective decisions regarding the use and management of money.... Indeed, all the elements of entrepreneurship are important, [but] leaving accounting and financial literacy on the fringes of attention may be an impediment to further business opportunity.* [1]

In the sections that follow, you will learn how to construct **financial statements**, also called **accounting statements**. Three basic financial statements provide important information about a firm's performance and resources: the income statement, the balance sheet, and the cash flow statement. Only with this essential information can you assess a firm's potential. Let's begin with a discussion of the income statement.

1   Describe the purpose and content of the income statement, the balance sheet, and the cash flow statement.

financial statements (accounting statements) Reports of a firm's financial performance and resources, including an income statement, a balance sheet, and a cash flow statement

How They See It: Better Know Your Numbers

Johnny Stites

When you start and run your own business, it no longer matters whether you were a marketing, management, finance, or any other specific major. As an entrepreneur, you have to know how a business operates, which requires more than having knowledge in a specific academic field.

So whatever your major, you had best know the basics of accounting and finance. You do not need to be an accountant, but you had better be able to read and understand financial statements. Sure, you can hire an accountant, but if you do not understand what the numbers are telling you, you are in big trouble.

The construction industry is one of the riskiest industries you can enter, second only to the restaurant industry. For years, we would bid a job based on our best understanding of the costs that would be incurred. Then we would have to wait until the completion of the job to see if we made or lost money—not exactly an ideal situation to be in. Today, we have the ability to know how we are doing in terms of profits and costs on a daily basis. Not having accurate and timely accounting information would be deadly. We simply could not exist in such a competitive industry, and certainly not profitably, without understanding where we are financially.

The Income Statement

income statement (profit and loss statement)
A financial report showing the profit or loss from a firm's operations over a given period of time

An **income statement**, or **profit and loss statement**, indicates the amount of profits generated by a firm over a given time period, usually monthly or yearly. In its most basic form, the income statement may be represented by the following equation:

$$\text{Sales (revenue)} - \text{Expenses} = \text{Profits}$$

Before trying to understand an income statement for a company, think on a personal level. Suppose you bought a 1964 Ford Thunderbird for $35,000. To purchase the car, you used $20,000 in savings and borrowed $15,000 from the local bank. While the car is a lot of fun to drive and a great topic of conversation with friends, you nonetheless decide to sell it. You advertise in the local newspaper and in two car magazines over three months until someone offers you $45,000 for the car, which you accept. The cost of advertising the car came to $300, and you paid $1,200 in interest on the bank loan. Let's determine your profits (income) from the sale of the car:

1. Your *gross profit* (profit before expenses), the sales price less the cost of the car, is $10,000—that is, $45,000 − $35,000.

2. From the $10,000 gross profit you received, you paid $300 in advertising expenses and $1,200 in interest expense to finance the purchase of the car, resulting in a profit after expenses of $8,500.

3. At the end of the year, your accountant tells you that you will have to pay income tax on the gain at a rate of 15 percent. Ouch, that hurts!

We can summarize the transaction as follows:

Selling price of the car		$45,000
Cost of the car		(35,000)
Profit before expenses		$10,000
Advertising expenses	($ 300)	
Interest expense	(1,200)	
Total expenses		($ 1,500)
Profit before taxes		$ 8,500
Income taxes (15% of $8,500 profits)		1,275
Net profits after all expenses		$ 7,225

We have just constructed an income statement very similar to that of a company. Of course, the terminology in a company's income statement will be a little different—for

exhibit

10-1 *The Income Statement: An Overview*

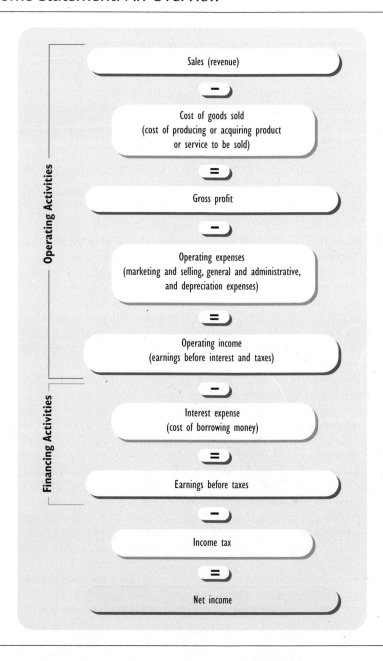

example, the term *sales* or *revenue* will replace "selling price of the car," and *cost of goods sold* will replace "cost of the car." Also, companies sell many units of their products or services, not just one, and companies have more varied types of expenses, such as employee salaries and depreciation expense on equipment and buildings. But if you understand an income statement for selling one unit of a product, such as a car, you should have no difficulty understanding a more comprehensive income statement for a business, like that shown in Exhibit 10-1.

To this point, you have learned how to measure a firm's profits. You begin with sales or revenue (such as the selling price of the car), from which you subtract the **cost of goods sold** (the cost of producing or acquiring the product or service, such as the cost of the car) to compute the firm's **gross profit**. Next, **operating expenses**, consisting of marketing and selling expenses, general and administrative expenses, and

cost of goods sold
The cost of producing or acquiring goods or services to be sold by a firm

gross profit
Sales less the cost of goods sold

operating expenses
Costs related to marketing and selling a firm's product or service, general and administrative expenses, and depreciation

operating income
Earnings or profits after operating expenses but before interest and taxes are paid

depreciation expense, are deducted to determine **operating income** (also called *earnings before interest and taxes*).

Operating income shows the consequences of management's decisions about the *operations* of the business, which involve the processes of buying and selling the firm's products or services. More specifically, the operating income of a firm includes the results of the following activities:

1. The pricing decisions for the product or service and the number of units sold (*selling price per unit × units sold = total sales*)

2. The cost of producing or acquiring the goods or service to be sold (*cost of one unit × units sold = cost of goods sold*)

3. The expenses incurred in selling and marketing the firm's product or service

4. The firm's overhead expenses (*general and administrative expenses and depreciation expenses*)

Note that no interest expense (the cost of using debt financing) has been subtracted to determine operating income.

financing costs
The amount of interest owed to lenders on borrowed money

Given the firm's earnings before interest and taxes (operating profit), we next deduct its **financing costs**—the firm's interest expense on its debt—to find **earnings before taxes**—a company's taxable income. A firm's income taxes are calculated by multiplying earnings before taxes by the applicable tax rate. For instance, if a firm had earnings before taxes of $100,000 and its tax rate was 28 percent, then it would owe $28,000 in taxes ($0.28 × \$100,000 = \$28,000$). *A word about taxes:* When entrepreneurs sell their products or services on a cash-only basis, some may be tempted *not* to report all income for tax purposes. Such a decision is neither legal nor ethical. Our advice: *Don't even think about not reporting taxable income.*

earnings before taxes
Earnings or profits after operating expenses and interest expenses but before taxes

net income available to owners (net income)
Income that may be distributed to the owners or reinvested in the company

The number resulting when taxes are subtracted from earnings is the **net income available to owners** (usually called **net income**), which represents income that may be reinvested in the firm or distributed to its owners—provided, of course, the cash is available to do so. As you will come to understand, *a positive net income on an income statement does not necessarily mean that a firm has generated positive cash flows.*

Exhibit 10-2 shows the 2007 income statement for Trimble & Associates Leasing, Inc., an equipment leasing company. The company had sales of $850,000 for the 12-month period ending December 31, 2007. The cost of goods sold was $550,000, resulting in a gross profit of $300,000. The company had $200,000 in operating expenses, which included marketing expenses, general and administrative expenses, and **depreciation expense** (the cost of the firm's fixed assets allocated over their useful life). After total operating expenses were subtracted, the company's operating income (earnings before interest and taxes) amounted to $100,000. To this point, we have calculated profits based only on expenses related to the firm's operating activities. We have thus far excluded interest expense, which is a result of the firm's financing decisions—something we will consider shortly. Therefore, the figure for operating income represents the income that Trimble & Associates would generate if it had no debt.

depreciation expense
Costs related to a fixed asset, such as a building or equipment, allocated over its useful life

The figure for operating income is important to the owners because it best measures a company's profitability on its investments (total assets or total debt and equity), before any money is distributed to investors and creditors. As a result, it is a good measure of the economic attractiveness of a business opportunity. For example, assume that a firm's total assets are $100,000 (financed with $40,000 in debt and $60,000 in equity) and that operating income and net income are $15,000 and $10,000, respectively. Thus, the firm's management used $100,000 of investment (from both debt and ownership equity) to generate $15,000 in operating profits, for a 15 percent return on assets ($15,000 \div \$100,000 = 0.15 = 15\%$). The net income, on the other hand, is the income that remains for the owners after paying interest and taxes and *does not* measure the return on the firm's total assets.

Trimble & Associates' interest expense of $20,000 (the expense it incurred from using debt financing) is then deducted from operating income to arrive at the company's earnings (profits) before taxes of $80,000. If we assume a 25 percent tax rate, the

Test Your Understanding

...ome Statement

...ct an income statement, using the following information. What are
...'s gross profit, operating income, and net income? Which expense
...*cash* expense? (Check your solution to this problem with the answer
...on page 269.)

...expense	$ 10,000
...goods sold	160,000
...ng expenses	70,000
...strative expenses	50,000
	400,000
...vidends	5,000
...tax	20,000
...ation expense	20,000

this decision based on profitability or for some other (possibly hidden) reason?"

For example, when you hear an executive justifying a decision based on its supposed impact on market share, he's really saying "I want to look good versus the competition, but it's a lot easier to give our products away than have to sell them at a profitable price."

Here's what happens when market share becomes your mantra. The sales force gets the okay to start selling on price. Your salespeople cut prices in order to generate volume. The volume comes and the company ramps up quickly to meet the new demand. That ramp up always drives costs up.

This happens to company after company despite how illogical it sounds. You have to battle it by sticking to your guns. You have to be maniacal in your focus on profitability.[2]

Living the Dream   entrepreneurial challenges

Everyone's a CFO

At a monthly staff meeting, Maria Mantz nibbled her pen top and shuffled the spreadsheets in her lap, anxiously awaiting her turn at the podium. Mantz had good reason to be nervous. She had worked at Development Counsellors International (DCI)—a New York City public relations firm that represents dozens of cities, states, and countries—for only five months. And she was just 23. But she was about to present the monthly financial report for the company.

Mantz's anxiety seemed to abate as she stood before about 30 of her colleagues and began. "Several accounts had quite an increase in May," she said, asking her audience to refer to the revenue table in their handouts. She gestured to a large flip board. "Does anyone know what the five clients listed on this page have in common?" she asked. "They're all performance-based accounts," yelled out account exec Malcolm Griffiths, referring to clients whose fees are based on results. "Right," Mantz replied, handing him a gift card for Cosi, a nearby sandwich shop. "In fact, 20% of our billings for May came from performance-based accounts. Is this a good thing or a bad thing?"

Andrew Levine, DCI's president, wants each of DCI's employees—from receptionists to tech support staffers—to become financially savvy. So each month, a different staffer is appointed CFO for a day, responsible for leading DCI's monthly finance meeting. The CFO of the day goes through a breakdown of the company's sales and expenses for the previous month, pointing out irregularities and trends, taking questions from staffers, and sparking conversations about everything from cost-cutting to contract negotiations. At the end of the report, the acting CFO unveils the bottom line and reveals if the company met its profit goal for the month. Each

exhibit 10-2 *Income Statement for Trimble & Associates Leasing, Inc., for t Ending December 31, 2007*

Sales		$850,000
Cost of goods sold		550,000
Gross profit on sales		$300,000
Operating expenses:		
Marketing expenses	$90,000	
General and administrative expenses	80,000	
Depreciation expense	30,000	
Total operating expenses		$200,000
Operating income		$100,000
Interest expense		20,000
Earnings before taxes		$ 80,000
Income tax (25%)		20,000
Net income		$ 60,000
Net income		$ 60,000
Dividends paid		15,000
Change in retained earnings		$ 45,000

company will have to pay $20,000 in income taxes ($80,000 × 0.25), leaving a net income of $60,000. The net income of $60,000 represents the "bottom line" of the income statement. This amount is the profit that was earned for the firm's owners on their investment. However, as shown at the bottom of Exhibit 10-2, dividends in the amount of $15,000 were paid to Trimble's stockholders (owners); the remaining $45,000 ($60,000 net income less $15,000 in dividends) was retained by the firm—an amount you will see later in the balance sheet. *Dividends paid to a firm's owners, unlike interest expense, are not considered an expense in the income statement.* Instead, they are viewed as a distribution to the owners.

In summary, the income statement answers the question "How profitable is the business?" In providing the answer, the income statement reports financial information related to five broad areas of business activity:

1. Sales (revenue)

2. Cost of producing or acquiring the goods or services

3. Operating expenses

4. Financing costs

5. Tax payments

Being able to measure profitability, as explained above, isn't enough; you must also have the discipline to impose profitability on your decision making. Philip Campbell, a CPA, a consultant, and the author of *Never Run Out of Cash: The 10 Cash Flow Rules You Can't Afford to Ignore,* offers this advice:

> *If you ask a business owner whether he runs his company to make money, the answer will always be "Yes." The reality is, he doesn't.... More often than not, you hear words like "brand," "market share," or "shelf space." When you hear those words, you can be sure that you've just found an opportunity to make some money.*
>
> *Why? Because those words always are used to justify unprofitable decisions. They are big red flags that you are not making decisions based on a common-sense approach to profitability. When you hear those words, ask yourself this simple question, "Are we making*

time DCI's accumulated profit hits another $100,000 increment during the course of the year, 30% is distributed among employees along with their next paychecks.

Levine wanted to try out a more open management style, so he added a financial segment to DCI's monthly staff meetings. But employees seemed bored. During one staff meeting, he asked his employees how to calculate a profit. Only one employee, receptionist Sergio Barrios, knew the answer. "It was mind-boggling," Levine says.

Then Barrios's knack for figures gave Levine an idea: What if he required employees to present the financial reports themselves? They'd have to learn at least the basics, he reasoned. So for the next staff meeting, Levine appointed his receptionist CFO of the day—and was pleased to see the reactions in the room during the presentation. Unlike Levine, Barrios was new to accounting and explained things in a way that any layperson could understand. "They figured, 'Gosh, if our receptionist can get this, so can I,'" Levine says.

Since then, the approach has helped transform the most unlikely staffers into finance whizzes. At first Mantz, who recently graduated from Penn State with a degree in advertising and public relations, dreaded the idea of being CFO. "The first time I saw the numbers, it was a little nerve-wracking," Mantz says. But after several months of seeing her colleagues make sense of complex financial details, she began to see that it wasn't as hard as it looked. By the time she was selected to be CFO in June, she was ready.

As far as Mantz is concerned, it was worth the extra effort and nerves. "I'm a new, young employee," she says. "And I'm being trained not only as a PR executive but also as a business executive."

http://www.dc-intl.com

The Balance Sheet

While an income statement reports the results of business operations over a period of time, a **balance sheet** provides a snapshot of a business's financial position at a *specific point in time.* Thus, a balance sheet captures the cumulative effects of all earlier financial decisions. At a given point in time, the balance sheet shows the assets a firm owns, the liabilities (or debt) outstanding or owed, and the amount the owners have invested in the business (ownership equity). In its simplest form, a balance sheet follows this formula:

balance sheet
A financial report showing a firm's assets, liabilities, and ownership equity at a specific point in time

$$\text{Total assets} = \text{Debt} + \text{Ownership equity}$$

Before looking at a firm's balance sheet, let's return to your purchase of the Ford Thunderbird, described on page 262. Before buying the car, you had a savings account of $20,000 at the college credit union. If, before deciding whether to loan you money to buy the car, the banker had asked you to prepare a personal balance sheet *showing your net worth,* that statement would have looked like this:

Assets:		**Net Worth:**	
Savings account	$20,000	Personal net worth	$20,000

After buying the car, your balance sheet would be as follows:

Assets:		Debt and Net Worth:	
1964 Ford	$35,000	Bank debt	$15,000
		Net worth (equity in the car)	20,000
Total assets	$35,000	Total debt and net worth	$35,000

A company's balance sheet and an individual's balance sheet both show net worth, or what is called *equity* in the business. There will be more complexity in a firm's balance sheet, but the basic principle is the same: Total assets equal debt plus net worth (equity). Keep that in mind as you study a balance sheet, and it will make more sense.

Exhibit 10-3 illustrates the elements in the balance sheet of a typical firm. Each of the three main components of the balance sheet—assets, debt, and ownership equity—is discussed in the following sections.

current assets (gross working capital)
Assets that can be converted into cash within a company's operating cycle

ASSETS   A company's assets, shown on the left side of Exhibit 10-3, fall into three categories: (1) current assets, (2) fixed assets, and (3) other assets.

Current assets, or **gross working capital,** include those assets that are relatively liquid—that is, assets that can be converted into cash within the firm's normal

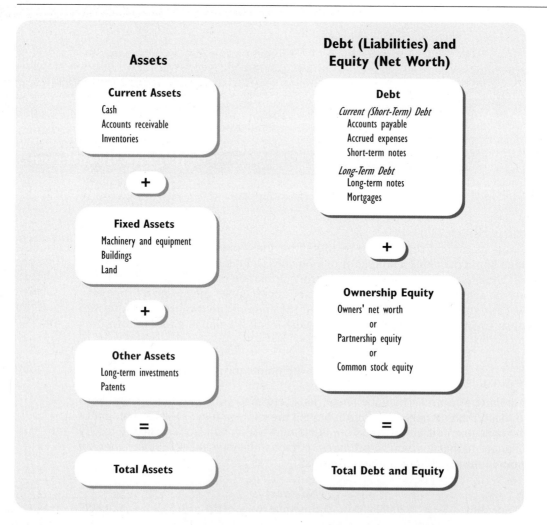

exhibit **10-3**   *The Balance Sheet: An Overview*

Assets

Current Assets
Cash
Accounts receivable
Inventories

+

Fixed Assets
Machinery and equipment
Buildings
Land

+

Other Assets
Long-term investments
Patents

=

Total Assets

Debt (Liabilities) and Equity (Net Worth)

Debt
Current (Short-Term) Debt
Accounts payable
Accrued expenses
Short-term notes

Long-Term Debt
Long-term notes
Mortgages

+

Ownership Equity
Owners' net worth
or
Partnership equity
or
Common stock equity

=

Total Debt and Equity

operating cycle. Current assets primarily include cash, accounts receivable, and inventories. Ineffective management of current assets is a prime cause of financial problems in small companies. (We will discuss this issue more thoroughly in Chapter 22.)

- *Cash.* Every firm must have cash for current business operations. A reservoir of cash is needed to compensate for the uncertainty of the cash flows into a business (cash receipts) and out of a business (cash expenditures). Thus, the size of a firm's cash reservoir should be determined not only by the volume of its sales, but also by the predictability of cash receipts and cash payments.

- *Accounts receivable.* The firm's **accounts receivable** consist of payments due from its customers for previous credit sales. Accounts receivable can become a significant asset for firms that sell on a credit basis.

- *Inventories.* The raw materials and products held by the firm for eventual sale constitute **inventory**. Although their relative importance differs from one type of business to another, inventories often account for a major part of a firm's working capital. Seasonality of sales and production levels affect the size of inventories. Retail stores, for example, may find it desirable to carry a larger-than-normal inventory during the pre-Christmas season.

Fixed assets are the more permanent assets in a business. They may include machinery and equipment, buildings, and land. Some businesses are more capital-intensive than others—for example, a motel is more capital-intensive than a gift store—and, therefore, it will have more fixed assets.

Most fixed assets are also **depreciable assets**, as their value declines, or depreciates, over time. Although the depreciation expense for a given year is shown as an expense on the income statement, the balance sheet reports the cumulative depreciation, taken over the life of the asset. For instance, assume that a truck purchased for $20,000 is being depreciated in equal amounts (straight-line depreciation) over four years. The depreciation expense for each year would be $5,000 ($20,000 ÷ 4 years = $5,000). When the firm buys the truck, the original cost of $20,000 is shown on the balance sheet as a **gross fixed asset**. Each year, the cumulative depreciation expense, or what is called **accumulated depreciation**, is subtracted from the original cost to yield the **net fixed asset**. For this example, the balance sheet at the end of each year would appear as follows:

	Year 1	Year 2	Year 3	Year 4
Gross fixed asset	$20,000	$20,000	$20,000	$20,000
Accumulated depreciation	5,000	10,000	15,000	20,000
Net fixed asset	$15,000	$10,000	$ 5,000	$ 0

The third category, **other assets**, includes such intangible assets as patents, copyrights, and goodwill. For a startup company, organizational costs—costs incurred in organizing and promoting the business—may also be included in this category.

How Did You Do?

Understanding the Income Statement

On page 266, you were asked to develop an income statement based on the information provided. Your results should be as follows:

Sales	$400,000
Cost of goods sold	160,000
Gross profit	$240,000
Operating expenses:	
Marketing expenses	$ 70,000
Administrative expenses	50,000
Depreciation expense	20,000
Total operating expenses	$140,000
Operating income	$100,000
Interest expense	10,000
Earnings before taxes	$ 90,000
Income tax	20,000
Net income	$ 70,000

Note: The stock dividends are not shown as an expense in the income statement but will appear as a reduction in retained earnings in the balance sheet.

---

accounts receivable
The amount of credit extended to customers that is currently outstanding

inventory
A firm's raw materials and products held in anticipation of eventual sale

fixed assets
Relatively permanent assets intended for use in the business, such as plant and equipment

depreciable assets
Assets whose value declines, or depreciates, over time

gross fixed assets
Original cost of depreciable assets before any depreciation expense has been taken

accumulated depreciation
Total depreciation expense taken over the assets' life

net fixed assets
Gross fixed assets less accumulated depreciation

other assets
Assets other than current assets and fixed assets, such as patents, copyrights, and goodwill

DEBT AND EQUITY The right side of the balance sheet in Exhibit 10-3, showing debt and equity, indicates how a firm is financing its assets. Financing comes from two main sources: debt (liabilities) and ownership equity. Debt is money that has been borrowed and must be repaid by some predetermined date. Ownership equity, on the other hand, represents the owners' investment in the company—money they have personally put into the firm without any specific date for repayment. Owners recover their investment by withdrawing money from the firm in the form of dividends or by selling their interest in the firm.

Debt is financing provided by a creditor. As shown in Exhibit 10-3, it is divided into (1) current, or short-term, debt and (2) long-term debt. **Current debt**, or **short-term liabilities**, includes borrowed money that must be repaid within the next 12 months. Sources of current debt may be classified as follows:

- Accounts payable represent the credit extended by suppliers to a firm when it purchases inventories. The purchasing firm usually is given 30 or 60 days to pay for the inventory. This form of credit is also called **trade credit**.

- Accrued expenses are expenses that have been incurred but not yet paid. For example, employees may have performed work for which they will not be paid until the following week or month. Accrued taxes are taxes that are owed but have not yet been paid.

- Short-term notes represent cash amounts borrowed from a bank or other lending source for 12 months or less. Short-term notes are a primary source of financing for most small businesses, as these businesses have access to fewer sources of long-term capital than do their larger counterparts.

Long-term debt includes loans from banks or other sources that lend money for longer than 12 months. When a firm borrows money for five years to buy equipment, it signs an agreement—a long-term note—promising to repay the money in five years. When a firm borrows money for 30 years to purchase real estate, such as a warehouse or office building, the real estate usually stands as collateral for the long-term loan, which is called a **mortgage**. If the borrower is unable to repay the loan, the lender can take the real estate in settlement.

Ownership equity is money that the owners invest in a business. Note that they are *residual owners* of the business; that is, if the company is liquidated, creditors are always paid before the owners are paid.

The amount of ownership equity in a business is equal to (1) the total amount of the owners' investments in the business plus (2) the cumulative profits (net of any losses) since the firm's beginning less any dividends paid to the owners. The second item (profits less dividends) is frequently called **retained earnings**—because these earnings have been reinvested in the business instead of being distributed to the owners. Thus, the basic formula for ownership equity is as follows:

$$\text{Ownership equity} = \text{Owners' investment} + \overbrace{\text{Cumulative profits} - \text{Cumulative dividends paid to owners}}^{\textbf{Earnings retained within the business}}$$

Exhibit 10-4 presents balance sheets for Trimble & Associates for December 31, 2006, and December 31, 2007, along with the dollar changes in the balance sheets from 2006 to 2007. By referring to the columns representing the two balance sheets, we can see the financial position of the firm at the beginning *and* at the end of 2007.

The 2006 and 2007 balance sheets for Trimble & Associates show that the firm began 2007 (ended 2006) with $800,000 in total assets and ended 2007 with total assets of $920,000. We can also see how much has been invested in current assets (cash, accounts receivable, and inventories) and in fixed assets.

We next observe how much debt and equity were used to finance the assets. Debt represents approximately one-third of the total financing and equity about two-thirds. On December 31, 2007, total debt was $300,000, relative to $920,000 in total debt and equity (and total assets), or almost 33 percent. Stated differently, the firm's assets were financed

debt
Business financing provided by creditors

current debt (short-term liabilities)
Borrowed money that must be repaid within 12 months

accounts payable (trade credit)
Outstanding credit payable to suppliers

accrued expenses
Short-term liabilities that have been incurred but not paid

short-term notes
Cash amounts borrowed from a bank or other lending sources that must be repaid within a short period of time

long-term debt
Loans from banks or other sources with repayment terms of more than 12 months

mortgage
A long-term loan from a creditor for which real estate is pledged as collateral

ownership equity
Owners' investments in a company, plus profits retained in the firm

retained earnings
Profits less withdrawals (dividends) over the life of the business

exhibit

10-4   Balance Sheets for Trimble & Associates Leasing, Inc., for December 31, 2006 and 2007

	2006	2007	Changes
Assets			
Current assets:			
Cash	$ 45,000	$ 50,000	$ 5,000
Accounts receivable	75,000	80,000	5,000
Inventories	180,000	220,000	40,000
Total current assets	$300,000	$350,000	$ 50,000
Fixed assets:			
Gross fixed assets	$860,000	$960,000	$100,000
Accumulated depreciation	(360,000)	(390,000)	(30,000)
Net fixed assets	$500,000	$570,000	$ 70,000
TOTAL ASSETS	$800,000	$920,000	$120,000
Debt (Liabilities) and Equity			
Current liabilities:			
Accounts payable	$ 15,000	$ 20,000	$ 5,000
Short-term notes	60,000	80,000	20,000
Total current liabilities (debt)	$ 75,000	$100,000	$ 25,000
Long-term debt	150,000	200,000	50,000
Total debt	$225,000	$300,000	$ 75,000
Common stockholders' equity:			
Common stock	$300,000	$300,000	$ 0
Retained earnings	275,000	320,000	45,000
Total common stockholders' equity	$575,000	$620,000	$ 45,000
TOTAL DEBT AND EQUITY	$800,000	$920,000	$120,000

approximately 33 percent by debt and 67 percent by equity. Also, about half of the equity came from investments made by the owners (common stock), and the other half came from reinvesting profits in the business (retained earnings). Referring back to the income statement in Exhibit 10-2, note that the $45,000 increase in retained earnings, shown in the Changes column in Exhibit 10-4, is the firm's net income for the year less the dividends paid to the owners.

In summary, financing for a new business derives from two sources: debt and ownership equity. Debt is money borrowed from financial institutions, suppliers, and other lenders. Ownership equity represents the owners' investment in the company, either through cash invested in the firm or through profits retained in the business (shown as retained earnings on the balance sheet).

Thus far, we have discussed the income statement and the balance sheet as separate reports. But they actually complement each other to give an overall picture of the firm's financial situation. Because the balance sheet is a snapshot of a firm's financial condition at a point in time and the income statement reports results over a given period, both are required to determine a firm's financial position.

Test Your Understanding

The Balance Sheet

Construct a balance sheet, using the following information. What are the firm's current assets, net fixed assets, total assets, current liabilities, long-term debt, total ownership equity, and total debt and equity? (Check your solution to this problem with the answer shown on page 273.)

Gross fixed assets	$ 75,000
Cash	10,000
Other assets	15,000
Accounts payable	40,000
Retained earnings	15,000
Accumulated depreciation	20,000
Accounts receivable	50,000
Long-term note	5,000
Mortgage	20,000
Common stock	100,000
Inventories	70,000
Short-term notes	20,000

10-5   *The Fit of the Income Statement and Balance Sheet*

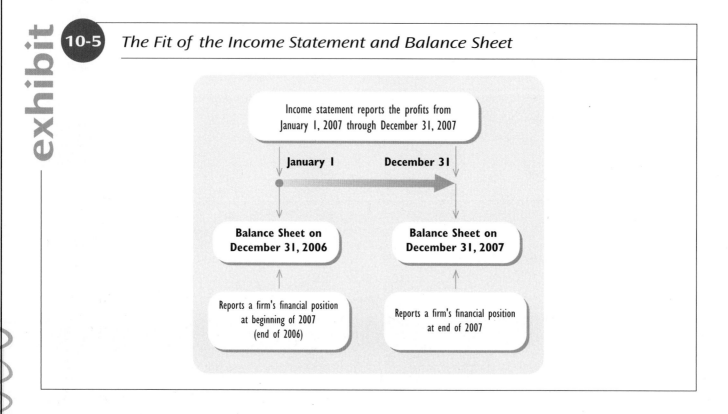

Exhibit 10-5 shows how the income statement and the balance sheet fit together. To understand how a firm performed during 2007, you must know the firm's financial position at the beginning of 2007 (balance sheet on December 31, 2006), its financial performance during the year (income statement for 2007), and its financial position at the end of the year (balance sheet on December 31, 2007). As you will soon see, all three statements are needed to measure Trimble & Associates' cash flows for 2007.

The Cash Flow Statement

If you spend time with an entrepreneur, eventually you are likely to hear the phrase "CASH IS KING!" (We capitalize the saying because it is always said with passion.) Cash flow problems are a constant concern of small business owners. Even a "successful" company may encounter problems with cash flows. For this reason, the ability to understand a cash flow statement is *extremely* important. A **cash flow statement** shows the sources of a firm's cash and its uses of the cash. In other words, it answers the questions "Where did the cash come from?" and "Where did the cash go?"

An entrepreneur once told us how intimidated she felt when her accountant presented the firm's monthly financial reports and how difficult she found it to understand cash flows. Our advice was to get a new accountant—one who would explain the statements carefully—and also to spend the time necessary to gain a solid understanding of the financial statements and the firm's cash flows.

It's important to understand that the profits shown on a company's income statement are not the same as its cash flows, although both are measures of a firm's performance. Many entrepreneurs have been deceived by a good-looking income statement, only to discover that their companies were running out of cash. Effectively managing cash flows is essential. To do so, the small business owner must understand the sources and uses of the firm's cash. In the words of author Jan Norman, "Even profitable companies can go broke. That's a difficult truth for start-up business owners to swallow. But the sooner you learn that when you're out of cash, you're out of business, the better your chances for survival will be."[3]

cash flow statement
A financial report showing a firm's sources and uses of cash

PROFITS VERSUS CASH FLOWS An income statement is not a measure of cash flows because it is calculated on an *accrual* basis rather than a *cash* basis. This is an important point to understand. In **accrual-basis accounting**, income is recorded when it is earned—whether or not the income has been received in cash—and expenses are recorded when they are incurred—even if money has not actually been paid out. In **cash-basis accounting**, income is reported when cash is received and expenses are recorded when they are paid.

For a number of reasons, profits based on an accrual accounting system will differ from the firm's cash flows, such as:

1. Sales reported in an income statement include both *cash* sales and *credit* sales. Thus, total sales do not correspond to the actual cash collected.

2. Some inventory purchases are financed by credit, so inventory purchases do not exactly equal cash spent for inventories.

3. The depreciation expense shown in the income statement is a noncash expense. It reflects the costs associated with using an asset that benefits the firm's operations over a period of more than one year, such as a piece of equipment used over five years.

4. Frequently, not all of the income tax shown in the income statement is paid in the period reported. Instead, some tax expense may be accrued as taxes payable and paid in later periods.

How Did You Do?

Understanding the Balance Sheet?

On page 271, you were asked to develop a balance sheet based on the financial data provided. Your results should be as follows:

Assets

Cash	$ 10,000
Accounts receivable	50,000
Inventories	70,000
Total current assets	$130,000
Gross fixed assets	$ 75,000
Accumulated depreciation	(20,000)
Net fixed assets	$ 55,000
Other assets	15,000
TOTAL ASSETS	$200,000

Debt and Equity

Accounts payable	$ 40,000
Short-term notes	20,000
Total current debt	$ 60,000
Long-term note	5,000
Mortgage	20,000
Total long-term debt	$ 25,000
Total debt	$ 85,000
Common stock	$100,000
Retained earnings	15,000
Total ownership equity	$115,000
TOTAL DEBT AND EQUITY	$200,000

MEASURING A FIRM'S CASH FLOWS As discussed earlier, the cash flow statement measures a firm's cash inflows and outflows. Exhibit 10-6 presents this statement for Trimble & Associates for the year ending December 31, 2007. It shows that the data required for computing a firm's cash flows come from both the income statement and the balance sheets. Also, we can see that there are three main sections of the statement:[4]

1. Cash flows from operations (operating activities)

2. Cash flows related to the investment in or sale of assets (investment activities)

3. Cash flows related to financing the firm (financing activities)

We will now consider each of the three parts of the cash flow statement.

Operating Activities The first part of a cash flow statement reflects cash flows from operations. **Cash flows from operations** are the net cash flows generated from a firm's normal day-to-day business activities—purchasing inventories on credit, selling on credit, paying for the inventories, and finally collecting on the sales made on credit.

accrual-basis accounting
A method of accounting that matches revenues when they are earned against the expenses associated with those revenues, no matter when they are paid

cash-basis accounting
A method of accounting that reports transactions only when cash is received or a payment is made

cash flows from operations
Net cash flows generated from operating a business, calculated by adding depreciation back to operating income, deducting income taxes, and factoring in any changes in net working capital

As shown in Exhibit 10-6, Trimble & Associates' cash flows from operations are computed as follows:

> *Step 1:* Based on the income statement for Trimble & Associates (see Exhibit 10-2), we begin with Trimble's operating income (earnings before interest and taxes) of $100,000; add back $30,000 in depreciation expense, since it is not a cash expense; and subtract $20,000 in income tax to get the after-tax cash flow, or what we call **adjusted income**, which in this case is a cash inflow of $110,000.

adjusted income
After-tax cash flow

net working capital
Money invested in current assets, other than cash, less accounts payable and accruals

> *Step 2:* Subtract Trimble & Associates' $40,000 increase in **net working capital**— money invested in current assets (except for cash) less accounts payable and accruals. Looking at Trimble's balance sheets in Exhibit 10-4, we see that accounts receivable and inventories increased by $45,000 (a use of cash) and that accounts payable increased by $5,000 (a source of cash).

The $110,000 in cash inflow (step 1) less the $40,000 addition to net working capital (step 2) results in cash flows from operations of $70,000.

What Should You Do?

Your brother-in-law has asked you to help him finance what he considers to be a "great opportunity." He plans to sell a new brand of European clothing that is becoming popular in the United States. He thinks that a location close to the nearby university, from which you both graduated, would be ideal. He estimates that the financing could come mostly from a bank loan and credit from suppliers. However, together you would need to put in $5,000; he'd invest $3,000, leaving you to invest the remaining $2,000.

It's not that you don't trust him, but you have decided to undertake your own investigation into the opportunity. After considerable effort, you have developed what you think are realistic estimates of the potential profitability for the venture. You have also estimated how much money it would take to start the business.

There's a slight problem, however: Your six-month-old puppy tore up your worksheets. After putting the dog in the backyard, you pick up the pieces and begin reconstructing your work. The remnants of your hard work are as follows:

Advertising expense $16,000	
Inventories $14,000	
Interest expense $1,000	
Cash needed in the business $6,000	
Equipment $10,000	Sales $75,000
Cost of goods sold $40,000	Rent $4,000
Accounts payable $6,000	Office overhead $14,000
Depreciation expense $10,000	
90-day bank loan $10,000	

As you let the dog back into the house, you try to remember how all the pieces fit together. Once you have organized the information, what will you conclude about your brother-in-law's "great opportunity"?

What you will study in this chapter will help you decide if your sister married an entrepreneur in the rough or if he should keep his day job and forget about becoming a business owner. So, read on to see if you should join him as a partner in the business.

Investment Activities   When equipment or some other depreciable asset is purchased or sold, cash flows occur that are not shown in the income statement. Trimble & Associates spent $100,000 on new plant and equipment, based on the change in gross fixed assets from $860,000 to $960,000 (see Exhibit 10-4). This $100,000 expenditure is shown in the second section of the cash flow statement.

Financing Activities   The third section of the cash flow statement presents the cash inflows and outflows resulting from financing activities. These activities include (1) paying dividends and interest expense; (2) increasing or decreasing short-term and long-term debt, which means borrowing more money (an increase in debt) or paying off debt (a decrease in debt); and (3) issuing stock (source of cash) or repurchasing stock (use of cash). Trimble paid $35,000 in interest and dividends but borrowed an additional $70,000, resulting in a net cash inflow of $35,000 from financing activities.

To summarize, Trimble & Associates generated $70,000 in cash flows from operations, invested $100,000 in plant and equipment, and received $35,000 net from financing activities, for a net increase in cash of $5,000. This can be verified from the balance sheets (see Exhibit 10-4), which show that Trimble's cash increased $5,000 during 2007 (from $45,000 to $50,000).

Interpreting the Cash Flow Statement

As already noted, the three basic categories of activities related to a firm's cash flows are operating activities, investment activities, and financing activities. When

exhibit 10-6

Cash Flow Statement for Trimble & Associates Leasing, Inc., for the Year Ending December 31, 2007

Operating activities:		
Operating income	$100,000	
Plus depreciation	30,000	
Less income taxes	(20,000)	
Adjusted income		$110,000
Less increase in accounts receivable	($ 5,000)	
Less increase in inventories	(40,000)	
Plus increase in accounts payable	5,000	
Change in net working capital		($ 40,000)
CASH FLOWS FROM OPERATIONS		$ 70,000
Investment activities:		
Less increase in gross fixed assets		($100,000)
Financing activities:		
Less interest expense	($ 20,000)	
Less dividends paid	(15,000)	
Plus increase in short-term notes	20,000	
Plus increase in long-term debt	50,000	
TOTAL FINANCING ACTIVITIES		$ 35,000
Increase in cash		$ 5,000

Living the Dream   entrepreneurial challenges

Collect Early and Pay Later

Judy DeLello, founder of Informed Systems, Inc., launched her company in 1990 without having to borrow to do so. How did she do it? Following the lead of the magazine industry, where customers pay for their subscriptions in advance, the Bluebell, Pennsylvania, technology firm decided to offer its customers a chance to buy consulting hours in advance of service. The savings for the customer can be as much as 20 percent off Informed's $175 per hour rate on a purchase of 100 hours.

But customers like prepaying for Informed's guidance on installing and using Microsoft's management software, Dynamic GP, for other reasons, too. "If Informed's rates go up, I've already locked in a lower price," says Marie Gunning, a controller for PSC Info Group, which manages collection letters and claim forms for hospitals. Informed's monthly statement, which shows services used over the past three to nine months, also is a useful tool for analysis of spending and future consulting needs.

Asking for payment before performing the work has also supported expansion of the firm. It now has about $1.5 million in revenue and eight employees. To encourage more customers to prepay, DeLello has eliminated travel charges on bulk purchases and offers discounts on other products the company sells.

Source: Ellyn Spragins, "Pay It Forward," *Fortune Small Business*, February 2006, pp. 51–52.

http://isisupport.com

exhibit

Cash Flow Patterns

	CASH FLOW RELATED TO		
Cash Flow Pattern	Operations	Investments	Financing
1	+	−	+
2	+	−	−
3	−	+	+
4	−	−	+

thinking about the basic nature of a firm's cash flows, consider the following four cash flow patterns presented in Exhibit 10-7.

Pattern 1. A firm has positive cash flows from operations, negative investment cash flows, and positive cash flows from financing. This company (like Trimble & Associates) is using its cash flows from operations and new financing to expand the firm's operations.

Pattern 2. Cash flow pattern 2 depicts a firm that is using positive cash flows from operations to expand the business, pay down debt, and/or pay its owners.

Pattern 3. Cash flow pattern 3 describes a company that is encountering negative cash flows from operations, which are being covered by selling assets and by borrowing or acquiring more equity financing.

Pattern 4. A firm with cash flow pattern 4 has negative cash flows from operations and is growing the company's fixed assets through increased financing. This pattern might describe a startup business that has yet to break even, is investing in assets to produce future cash flows, and is having to raise capital to make that happen. Or it may simply be a loser that is surviving by selling off assets and borrowing money.

Other cash flow patterns exist, but the four patterns just described are sufficient to illustrate how to interpret a company's cash flow statement. Now that you have an understanding of a firm's financial statements, we'll discuss how to develop pro forma financial statements, an important part of any business plan.

We believe some of the best learning occurs when a student teaches another student. So, to help you understand the basics of financial statements, we asked two students to explain them. You can stream their presentation by going to academic. cengage.com/ management/ longenecker.

2 Forecast a new venture's profitability.

pro forma financial statements
Statements that project a firm's financial performance and condition

Financial Forecasting

Using the basic financial information discussed so far in this chapter, an owner-manager can develop **pro forma financial statements**, or projected financial statements. The necessity of financial forecasting is described quite aptly by small business consultant Paul A. Broni:

It doesn't matter whether you're applying for your first bank loan or your fifth, or whether you're seeking venture capital or debt financing. Sooner or later, you'll have to prepare a set of financial projections. Lenders will look for a strong likelihood of repayment; investors will calculate what they think is the value of your company.[5]

The purpose of pro forma financial statements is to answer three questions:

1. How profitable can the firm be expected to be, given the projected sales levels and the expected sales–expense relationships?

2. How much and what type of financing (debt or equity) will be used?

3. Will the firm have adequate cash flows? If so, how will they be used; if not, where will the additional cash come from?

Preparing historical financial statements, such as income statements, balance sheets, and cash flow statements, is not a difficult task; accountants have perfected that process. Projecting the financials for a new company is another matter, however, and presents a real challenge. However, it is not hopeless, as explained by Rhonda Abrams, a business plan consultant:

> One of the biggest challenges for a new company doing a business plan is figuring out the financial statements. If you have an existing business, you have a pretty good sense of how much things will cost, how much staff you'll need, and the sales you're likely to make. But when you're just starting out, these things seem a complete mystery.
>
> They're not. At least not entirely. Every decision you make when planning your business has a number attached: If you choose to exhibit at a trade show, there's a cost associated with that; if you choose to locate your business in one town versus another, there's a cost associated with that.
>
> How do you do this homework? The best place to start is by speaking with others in your industry, attending trade shows, and contacting your industry association. Another excellent source is the RMA Annual Statement Studies, which look at actual financial statements of companies in certain industries.[6]

An entrepreneur can get into trouble not only when sales are inadequate but also when the firm is experiencing high growth in sales. James Wong, the co-founder and CEO of Avidian Technologies, should know: His firm grew at 400 percent annually in both 2004 and 2005. As a result, he vigilantly watches cash flows and bottom-line profits. "I've learned that profitability takes conscious effort," he says. "If you just keep growing for growth's sake, you won't be nearly as profitable." Wong never ships a product until payment is received and never lets net profits fall below 15 percent of sales. Consequently, the firm has grown with no significant debt and no outside investors—a feat seldom accomplished by entrepreneurs whose firms are growing rapidly.[7]

Let's take a look at the process for projecting a firm's profitability, financing requirements, and cash flows.

How They See It: Know Where You Stand

Winston Wolfe

Knowing where you are sounds a bit silly, but when it comes to the first few years of a new business, it is very important, and many times it is neglected. Let me give some examples.

First of all, I believe it is important for a new business to produce a profit and loss statement every month. If the business involves distribution, this would include a physical inventory. Don't fool yourself by carrying unsaleable inventory at cost. The same applies to other assets that may have decreased in value.

Know where you are in your market. Have you found your niche? Are your products or services being offered where they are most viable?

Take the time to find out where you stand in your relationship with your customers, your vendors, and your employees. The biggest challenge for an entrepreneur is being effective in solving problems in these areas. But if you don't know about a problem, you can't solve it.

Take the time to know where you are. If you don't know where you are, you can't know where you're going.

Forecasting Profitability

Profits reward an owner for investing in a company and constitute a primary source of financing for future growth. Therefore, it is critical for an entrepreneur to understand the factors that drive profits. A firm's net income is dependent on five variables:

1. *Amount of sales.* The dollar amount of sales equals the price of the product or service times the number of units sold or the amount of service rendered.

2. *Cost of goods sold.* Cost of goods sold is the cost of producing or purchasing the firm's products or services. These costs can be either *fixed* (those that do not vary with a change in sales volume) or *variable* (those that change proportionally with sales).

3. *Operating expenses.* These expenses relate to marketing and distributing the product, general and administrative expenses, and depreciation expenses. As with cost of goods sold, operating expenses can be fixed or variable in nature.

4. *Interest expense.* An entrepreneur who borrows money agrees to pay interest on the loan principal. For example, a loan of $25,000 for a full year at a 12 percent interest rate results in an interest expense of $3,000 for the year (0.12 × $25,000).

5. *Taxes.* A firm's income taxes are figured as a percentage of taxable income (earnings before taxes).

Let's consider a hypothetical example that demonstrates how to estimate a new venture's profits. Assume that Kate Lynn is planning to start a new business called C&G Products, Inc., which will do wood trim work for luxury homes. A newly developed lathe will allow the firm to be responsive to varying design specifications in a very economical manner. Based on a study of potential market demand and expected costs-to-sales relationships, Lynn has made the following estimates for the first two years of operations:

1. *Amount of sales.* Lynn expects to sell the firm's product for $125 per unit, with total sales for the first year projected at 2,000 units, or $125 × 2,000 = $250,000, and total sales for the second year projected at 3,200 units, or $125 × 3,200 = $400,000.

2. *Cost of goods sold.* The fixed cost of goods sold (including production costs and employee salaries) is expected to amount to $100,000 per year, while the variable costs of production will be around 20 percent of dollar sales.

3. *Operating expenses.* The firm's fixed operating expenses (marketing expenses, general and administrative expenses) are estimated at $46,000 per year. In addition, depreciation will be $4,000 annually. The variable operating expenses will be approximately 30 percent of dollar sales.

4. *Interest expense.* Based on the anticipated amount of money to be borrowed and the corresponding interest rate, Lynn expects interest expense to be $8,000 in the first year, increasing to $12,000 in the second year.

5. *Taxes.* Income taxes will be 25 percent of earnings before taxes (taxable income).

Given the above estimates, we can forecast C&G's net income as shown in the pro forma statement in Exhibit 10-8. We first enter our assumptions on an Excel spreadsheet (rows 1–10). Then, in rows 13–28, we see the two years of pro forma income statements (columns B and C) and the equations used to compute the numbers (columns D and E).

The computations in Exhibit 10-8 indicate that C&G Products, Inc., will have a $33,000 loss in its first year, followed by a positive net income of $28,500 in its second year. A startup typically experiences losses for a period of time, frequently as long as two or three years.[8] In a real-world situation, an entrepreneur should project the profits of a new company three to five years into the future, as opposed to the two-year projection shown for C&G Products, Inc.

Let's now shift our attention from forecasting profits to estimating asset and financing requirements.

exhibit 10-8

Pro Forma Income Statements for C&G Products, Inc.

	A	B	C	D	E
1	INCOME STATEMENT ASSUMPTIONS				
2	Year 1 projected units of sales	2,000			
3	Year 2 projected units of sales	3,200			
4	Selling price	$ 125			
5	Fixed cost of goods sold	$100,000			
6	Fixed operating expenses	$ 46,000		Equations based on assumptions	
7	Depreciation expense	$ 4,000			
8	Variable cost of goods sold	20%			
9	Variable operating expenses	30%			
10	Income tax rate	25%			
11				Equations for	
12		Year 1	Year 2	Year 1	Year 2
13	Sales	$250,000	$400,000	=B2*B4	=B3*B4
14	Cost of goods sold				
15	Fixed cost of goods sold	$100,000	$100,000	=B5	=B5
16	Variable cost of goods sold (20% of sales)	$ 50,000	$ 80,000	=B8*B13	=B8*C13
17	Total cost of goods sold	$150,000	$180,000	=B15+B16	=C15+C16
18	Gross profits	$100,000	$220,000	=B13−B17	=C13−C17
19	Operating expenses				
20	Fixed operating expenses	$ 46,000	$ 46,000	=B6	=B6
21	Depreciation expense	$ 4,000	$ 4,000	=B7	=B7
22	Variable operating expenses (30% of sales)	$ 75,000	$120,000	=B13*B9	=C13*B9
23	Total operating expenses	$125,000	$170,000	=B20+B21+B22	=C20+C21+C22
24	Operating income	($ 25,000)	$ 50,000	=B18−B23	=C18−C23
25	Interest expense	$ 8,000	$ 12,000	Given	Given
26	Earnings before taxes	($ 33,000)	$ 38,000	=B24−B25	=C24−C25
27	Taxes (25% of earnings before taxes)	0	$ 9,500	0	=C26*B10
28	Net income	($ 33,000)	$ 28,500	=B26−B27	=C26−C27

Forecasting Asset and Financing Requirements and Cash Flows

The amount and types of assets required for a new venture will vary, depending on the nature of the business. High-technology businesses—such as computer manufacturers, designers of semiconductor chips, and gene-splicing companies—often require millions of dollars in investment. Most service businesses, on the other hand, require minimal initial capital. For example, IRM Corporation, a Dallas-based information technology firm serving the consumer packaged goods industry, has little in the way of assets. The firm leases its office space and has no inventory. Its only asset of any significance is accounts receivable.

3 Determine asset requirements, evaluate financial sources, and estimate cash flows for a new venture.

. . . and What About Your Brother-in-Law?

With an understanding of the income statement and balance sheet, let's return to your brother-in-law's proposition that you join him as a partner in the clothing business. You have reconstructed the following income statement and balance sheet from the fragments of your dog-chewed papers.

Projected Income Statement

Sales	$75,000
Cost of goods sold	40,000
Gross profit	$35,000
Operating expenses:	
Office overhead	$14,000
Advertising expense	16,000
Rent	4,000
Depreciation expense	10,000
Total operating expenses	$44,000
Operating income	($ 9,000)
Interest expense	1,000
Earnings before taxes	($10,000)
Income tax	0
Net income	($10,000)

Projected Balance Sheet

Cash	$ 6,000
Inventories	14,000
Current assets	$20,000
Equipment	10,000
Total assets needed	$30,000
Accounts payable	$ 6,000
90-day bank loan	10,000
Total current debt	$16,000
Brother-in-law's investment	$ 3,000
Your investment	2,000
Total ownership equity	$ 5,000
Debt and equity	$21,000
Additional financing needed	$ 9,000
Total debt and equity needed	$30,000

So, based on your estimates, the venture can be expected to incur a loss of $10,000. Furthermore, the balance sheet suggests that the business will need $30,000 for investments in assets. Adding debt financing of $16,000 to the $3,000 from your brother-in-law and $2,000 from you gives $21,000—not the needed $30,000. The business will need an additional $9,000 (that is, $9,000 will be required for total debt and equity to equal total assets). Maybe, just maybe, this is not quite the opportunity your brother-in-law perceives it to be. At the very least, he needs to do a better job of understanding what will be required.

bootstrapping

Minimizing a firm's investments

Most firms of any size need both working capital (cash, accounts receivable, inventories, etc.) and fixed assets (equipment and buildings). For instance, a food store requires operating cash, inventories, and possibly limited accounts receivable. In addition, the owner will have to acquire cash registers, shopping carts, shelving, office equipment, and a building. The need to invest in assets results in a corresponding need for financing.

In many small firms, owners have a tendency to underestimate the amount of capital the business requires. Consequently, the financing they get may be inadequate. Without the money to invest in assets, they try to do without anything that is not absolutely essential and try to spend less money on those essential items. When Dan Cassidy started Baha's Fajita Bar, his goal was to raise $100,000 in capital; however, he opened the restaurant when he had raised only $70,000. As it turned out, Cassidy did not have enough money to operate the business successfully. In six months, he ran out of cash and had to close the business.

Trying to minimize the firm's investment is actually the best way to proceed—*if not carried to an extreme.* However, small problems can become large ones when adequate resources are not available to support the business. Clearly, the goal of the entrepreneur is to "minimize and control," rather than "maximize and own," resources. To the greatest extent possible, the entrepreneur should use other people's resources—for instance, leasing equipment rather than buying, negotiating with suppliers to provide inventory "just in time" to minimize the investment in inventories, and arranging to collect money owed the firm before having to pay the firm's bills. This is called **bootstrapping**, and it's the most common way entrepreneurs accomplish more with less. When Cecilia Levine, a member of our go-to team and the owner of MFI, a manufacturing firm, had the opportunity to get a contract to make clothing for a *Fortune* 500 company, she became a master of bootstrapping.

I never expected the fast growth and demand that my services would have. To finance the growth, debt financing would have been helpful, but it was not an option. The definition of credit in the dictionary reads, "The ability of a customer to obtain goods or services before payment, based on the trust that payment is going to be made in the future." What it does not say is that for a banker, trust means having collateral, and without collateral you don't get credit. But I still had children to feed and the desire to succeed so I looked for another form of financing—BOOTSTRAPPING.

I had a major customer who believed in me, and who had the equipment I needed. He sold me the equipment and then would reduce his weekly payment of my invoices by an amount to cover the cost of the equipment. Also, the customer paid me each Friday for what we produced and shipped that week. Everyone who worked for me understood that if we didn't perform and finish the needed production for the week, we didn't get paid by our customer. When I received the payment from the customer, I was then able to pay my employees. We were a team, and we understood the meaning of cash flow. Therefore, we performed.[9]

A limited amount of working capital makes forecasting all the more important, as there is much less slack in the system when surprises occur. Moreover, the uncertainties surrounding an entirely new venture make estimating asset and financing requirements difficult. Even for an established business, forecasts are never exact. Therefore, when seeking financing, an entrepreneur must be able to give informed answers about the firm's needs. His or her ability to answer questions regarding the amount of money needed, the purposes for which it will be used, and when and how the lender or creditor will be paid back is vital. Only careful analysis can provide answers to these questions.

To gather needed information, an entrepreneur may use a double-barreled approach to project asset requirements by using industry standard ratios to estimate dollar amounts and cross-checking those dollar amounts by applying break-even analysis and searching for relevant information from a variety of sources. Robert Morris Associates, Dun & Bradstreet, banks, trade associations, and similar organizations compile industry standard ratios for many types of businesses. If standard ratios cannot be found, then common sense and educated guesswork must be used to estimate asset requirements.

The analysis of capital requirements should also take into consideration the owner's personal financial situation, especially if no other income is available to make ends meet. Whether or not the owner's personal living expenses during the initial period of operation are part of the business's capitalization, they must be considered in the financial plan. Inadequate provision for personal expenses will inevitably lead to a diversion of business assets and a departure from the plan. Therefore, failing to incorporate these expenses into the financial plan as a cash outflow raises a red flag to any prospective investor.

In fact, a real danger exists that an entrepreneur will neglect personal finances later as well. As a firm grows, an increasing percentage of the owner's net worth is tied up in the firm. One survey of entrepreneurs found that, on average, 53 percent of business owners' wealth was invested in their businesses. Another survey by Financial Services Inc., of Columbus, Ohio, discovered that 63 percent of small business owners did not think they had planned adequately for their company's future or for their personal financial health.[10] SBA director Hector Barreto explains it well:

Small-business people don't know what they don't know when it comes to financial planning. They're busy building the business, and they don't start asking questions until a need or problem comes up. Entrepreneurs are doing a disservice to their businesses when they ignore even the most basic financial planning. The process isn't as time-consuming or as expensive as you might think."[11]

The key to effectively forecasting financing requirements is first to understand the relationship between a firm's projected sales and its assets. A firm's sales are the primary force driving future asset needs. Exhibit 10-9 depicts this relationship, which can be expressed as follows: *The greater a firm's sales, the greater the asset requirements will be and, in turn, the greater the need for financing.*

DETERMINING ASSET REQUIREMENTS Since asset needs tend to increase as sales increase, a firm's asset requirements are often estimated as a percentage of sales. Therefore, if future sales have been projected, a ratio of assets to sales can be used to estimate asset requirements. Suppose, for example, that a firm's sales are expected to be $1 million. If assets in the firm's particular industry tend to run about 50 percent of sales, the firm's asset requirements would be estimated to be $0.50 \times \$1,000,000 = \$500,000$.

Although the assets-to-sales relationship varies over time and with individual firms, it tends to be relatively constant within an industry. For example, assets as a percentage of sales average 20 percent for grocery stores, compared with 65 percent for oil and gas companies. This method of estimating asset requirements is called the **percentage-of-sales technique**. It can also be used to project figures for individual assets, such as accounts receivable and inventories.

percentage-of-sales technique
A method of forecasting asset investments and financing requirements

To illustrate the percentage-of-sales technique, let's return to Exhibit 10-8, which shows the pro forma income statements developed for C&G Products, Inc. We'll now consider what Kate Lynn needs in terms of assets to support the firm's activities.

10-9 Assets-to-Sales Financing Relationships

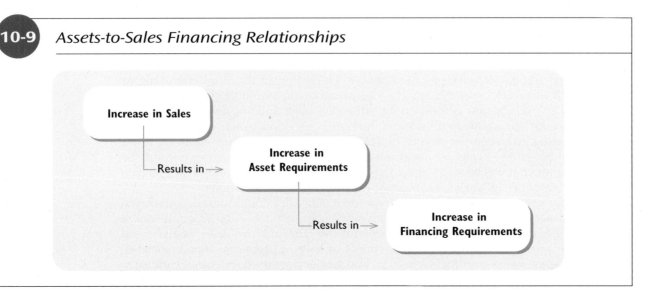

In financial forecasting, it is best to begin with projected sales, which Lynn expects to be $250,000 and $400,000 in years 1 and 2, respectively (see Exhibit 10-8). After considerable investigation into the opportunity, Lynn estimated the firm's current asset requirements (cash, accounts receivable, and inventories) as a percentage of sales:

Assets	Percentage of Sales
Cash	5%
Accounts receivable	10%
Inventories	25%

Lynn will need equipment, at a cost of $10,000. Also, she has found a building suitable for a manufacturing facility for $40,000. Combined, these items total gross fixed assets of $50,000. Given the anticipated sales and the assets-to-sales relationships, she was able to forecast the asset requirements for her venture as follows. If

		Year 1	Year 2
Sales		$250,000	$400,000

then

Assets	Assumptions	Year 1	Year 2
Cash	5% of sales	$ 12,500	$ 20,000
Accounts receivable	10% of sales	25,000	40,000
Inventories	25% of sales	62,500	100,000
Total current assets		$100,000	$160,000
Gross fixed assets	Equipment and building costs	$ 50,000	$ 50,000
Accumulated depreciation	$4,000 annually	(4,000)	(8,000)
Net fixed assets		$ 46,000	$ 42,000
TOTAL ASSETS		$146,000	$202,000

Thus, Lynn expects to need $146,000 in assets by the end of the first year and $202,000 by the conclusion of the second year. Although the figures used to obtain these estimates are only rough approximations, the estimates should be relatively close if Lynn has identified the assets-to-sales relationships correctly and if sales materialize as expected. Let's now consider the corresponding financing requirements.

DETERMINING FINANCING REQUIREMENTS There must be a corresponding dollar of financing for every dollar of assets. To effectively forecast a company's financing needs, an entrepreneur must understand certain basic principles that govern the financing of firms, which can be stated as follows:

1. The more assets a firm needs, the greater the firm's financial requirements. Thus, a firm experiencing rapid sales growth has greater asset requirements and, consequently,

greater pressure to find financing—and that pressure can be unbearable if not managed carefully.

2. A firm should finance its growth in such a way as to maintain proper liquidity. **Liquidity** measures the degree to which a firm has current assets available to meet maturing short-term debt. The need for adequate liquidity in small firms deserves special emphasis. A common weakness in small business financing is a disproportionately small investment in liquid assets. Too much money is tied up in assets that are difficult to convert to cash. A conventional measurement of liquidity is the **current ratio**, which compares a firm's current assets to its current liabilities.

$$\text{Current ratio} = \frac{\text{Current assets}}{\text{Current liabilities}}$$

To ensure payment of short-term debts as they come due, an entrepreneur should, as a general rule, maintain a current ratio of at least 2—that is, have current assets equal to twice current liabilities.

3. The amount of total debt that can be used in financing a business is limited by the amount of funds provided by the owners. A bank will not provide all the financing for a firm; owners must put some of their own money into the venture. Thus, a business plan should specify that at least half of the firm's financing will come from the owners and the rest will come from debt. In other words, management should limit the firm's **debt ratio**, which expresses debt as a percentage of total assets.[12]

$$\text{Debt ratio} = \frac{\text{Total debt}}{\text{Total assets}}$$

4. Some types of short-term debt—specifically, accounts payable and accrued operating expenses—maintain a relatively constant relationship with sales; that is, they rise or fall spontaneously as a firm's sales increase or decrease. Such **spontaneous financing** grows as a natural consequence of increases in the firm's sales. For instance, a rise in sales requires more inventories, causing accounts payable to increase when a firm purchases inventory on credit. If sales increase by $1, accounts payable might increase by $.15 or, in other words, 15 percent of sales. This type of financing is significant for most smaller companies. The rest of debt financing must come from loans by banks and other lending sources.

5. There are two sources of equity: external and internal. Initially, the equity in a company comes from the investment the owners make in the firm. These funds represent **external equity**. Once the company is in operation, additional equity may come from profits that are retained within the company rather than being distributed to the owners, or *retained earnings*. These funds are also called **internal equity**. For the typical small firm, internal equity is the primary source of capital for financing growth. (Be careful not to think of retained profits as a big cash resource. As already noted, a firm may have significant earnings but no cash to reinvest. This problem will be discussed further in Chapters 22 and 23.)

In summary,

$$
\begin{array}{l}
\text{Total asset} \\
\text{requirements}
\end{array}
=
\begin{array}{l}
\text{Total sources} \\
\text{of financing}
\end{array}
=
\begin{array}{l}
\text{Spontaneous} \\
\text{financing}
\end{array}
+
\begin{array}{l}
\text{Profits} \\
\text{retained} \\
\text{within the} \\
\text{business}
\end{array}
+
\begin{array}{l}
\text{External} \\
\text{sources of} \\
\text{debt}
\end{array}
+
\begin{array}{l}
\text{External} \\
\text{sources of} \\
\text{equity}
\end{array}
$$

This equation captures the essence of forecasting financial requirements. The entrepreneur who thoroughly understands these relationships should be able to accurately forecast his or her firm's financial requirements.

Recall that for C&G Products, Inc., Kate Lynn projected asset requirements of $146,000 and $202,000 for years 1 and 2, respectively. Lynn next made estimates of the financing requirements based on the following facts and assumptions:

1. Lynn negotiated with a supplier to receive 30 days' credit on inventory purchases, which means that accounts payable will average about 8 percent of sales.[13]

---

liquidity
The degree to which a firm has working capital available to meet maturing debt obligations

current ratio
A measure of a company's relative liquidity, determined by dividing current assets by current liabilities

debt ratio
A measure of the fraction of a firm's assets that are financed by debt, determined by dividing total debt by total assets

spontaneous financing
Short-term debts, such as accounts payable, that automatically increase in proportion to a firm's sales

external equity
Capital that comes from the owners' investment in a firm

internal equity
Capital that comes from retaining profits within a firm

2. Accrued expenses, such as wages owed but not yet paid, are expected to run approximately 4 percent of annual sales.

3. Lynn plans to invest $110,000 of her personal savings to provide the needed equity for the business. She will receive common stock for her investment.

4. The bank has agreed to provide a short-term line of credit of $25,000 to C&G Products, which means that the firm can borrow up to $25,000 as the need arises.

5. The bank has also agreed to help finance the purchase of a building for manufacturing and warehousing the firm's product. Of the $40,000 needed, the bank will lend the firm $35,000, with the building serving as collateral for the loan. The loan will be repaid in equal principal payments of $3,500 plus interest on the remaining note balance each year.

6. As part of the loan agreement, the bank has imposed two restrictions: (1) The firm's current ratio (current assets ÷ current liabilities) must stay at 2.0 or above, and (2) no more than 50 percent of the firm's financing may come from debt, either short term or long term (that is, total debt should be no more than 50 percent of total assets). Failure to comply with either of these conditions will cause the bank loans to come due immediately.

With this information, we can estimate the initial sources of financing for C&G Products as follows. If

	Year 1	Year 2
Sales	$250,000	$400,000

then

Sources of Financing	Assumptions	Year 1	Year 2
Accounts payable	8% of sales	$ 20,000	$ 32,000
Accrued expenses	4% of sales	$ 10,000	16,000
Mortgage	$35,000 − $3,500 annual payments	$ 31,500	$ 28,000
Common stock	Founder's investment	$110,000	$110,000

Any remaining financing up to $25,000 can come from the bank line of credit. If the line of credit is inadequate to meet the firm's needs, Lynn will have to put more equity into the business.

Based on the information above, Lynn can now develop the complete pro forma balance sheets for C&G Products, Inc. Exhibit 10-10 shows the assumptions made, the equations underlying the numbers, and the actual balance sheets, as developed in an Excel spreadsheet.

Several points about the projected balance sheets presented in Exhibit 10-10 need to be clarified:

1. Total assets and total sources of financing (debt and equity) must always balance. Note that C&G Products' asset requirements of $146,000 for the first year and $202,000 for the second year are the same as the firm's debt and equity totals.

2. To bring sources of financing into balance with total assets, C&G Products will need to borrow on the company's $25,000 short-term line of credit. Only $7,500 of the $25,000 line of credit is needed to bring the total debt and equity to $146,000 in the first year, but this increases to $20,500 to complete the $202,000 total financing at the end of the second year.

3. Based on Lynn's projections, the firm should be able to satisfy the bank's loan restrictions, maintaining both a current ratio of 2.0 or more and a debt ratio of less than 50 percent. The computations are as follows:

Ratio	Computation	Year 1	Year 2
Current ratio =	$\dfrac{\text{Current assets}}{\text{Current liabilities}}$	$\dfrac{\$100,000}{\$37,500} = 2.67$	$\dfrac{\$160,000}{\$68,500} = 2.34$

and

$$\text{Debt ratio} \quad = \quad \frac{\text{Total debt}}{\text{Total assets}} \quad \frac{\$69,000}{\$146,000} = 0.47, \text{ or } 47\% \quad \frac{\$96,500}{\$202,000} = 0.48, \text{ or } 48\%$$

DETERMINING CASH FLOWS   Given the pro forma income statements and balance sheets for C&G Products, Inc., we can now develop cash flow statements as well. The complete cash flow statements are presented in Appendix 10B. The following summary shows the primary sources and uses of the firm's cash flows:

Cash Flows	Year 1	Year 2
Cash flows from operations	($ 78,500)	$10,000
Investment activities	($ 50,000)	0
Financing activities	$141,000	($ 2,500)
Increase (decrease) in cash	$ 12,500	$ 7,500

Clearly, the first year will be critical for C&G Products, given the negative cash flows from operations and investment activities. The large financing requirements will most likely present a serious challenge to the new venture. In the second year, however, cash flows should not be as great a problem—not unless Lynn has been overly optimistic about being able to turn the cash flows from operations around and about not needing to make any significant capital investments.

The importance of carefully monitoring a new company's cash flows cannot be over-emphasized. The calculation of the cash flows for C&G Products, Inc., demonstrates that income statements and balance sheets do not provide the entrepreneur with adequate information about a firm's cash flows. Taking your eye off your firm's cash flows could be a fatal mistake and is certainly one to be avoided.

Good Forecasting Requires Good Judgment

The forecasting process requires an entrepreneur to exercise good judgment in planning, particularly when the planning is providing the basis for raising capital. The overall approach to forecasting is straightforward—entrepreneurs make assumptions and, based on these assumptions, determine financing requirements. But entrepreneurs may be tempted to overstate their expectations in order to acquire much-needed financing. Here are some practical suggestions about making financial forecasts.[14]

1. *Develop realistic sales projections.* Entrepreneurs often think they can accomplish more than they actually are able to, especially when it comes to forecasting future sales. When graphed, their sales projections for a new venture often resemble a hockey stick—the sales numbers are flat or rise slightly at first (like the blade of a hockey stick) and then soar upward like a hockey stick's handle. Such projections are always suspect—only the most astonishing changes in a business or market can justify such a sudden, rocketlike performance.

2. *Build projections from clear assumptions about marketing and pricing plans.* Don't be vague, and don't guess. Spell out the kinds of marketing you plan to do—for example, state specifically how many customers you expect to attract. Paul A. Broni offers this advice:

   When putting together your income statement, revenues should show more than just the projected sales figure for each year. You should also show how many units you plan to sell, as well as the mix of revenue (assuming that you have more than one product or service). If you have a service business, you may also want to show

4 Explain the importance of using good judgment when making projections.

exhibit

10-10 Projected Balance Sheets for C&G Products, Inc.

	A	B	C	D	E
1	ASSUMPTIONS				
2	Year 1 projected sales	$250,000			
3	Year 2 projected sales	$400,000			
4	Cash/sales	5%			
5	Accounts receivable/sales	10%		Equations based on assumptions	
6	Inventories/sales	25%			
7	Accounts payable/sales	8%			
8	Accrued expenses/sales	4%			
9	Cost of equipment	$ 10,000			
10	Building cost	$ 40,000			
11				Equations for	
12	ASSETS	Year 1	Year 2	Year 1	Year 2
13	Cash	$ 12,500	$ 20,000	=B2*B4	=B3*B4
14	Accounts receivable	25,000	40,000	=B2*B5	=B3*B5
15	Inventories	62,500	100,000	=B2*B6	=B3*B6
16	Total current assets	$100,000	$160,000	=B13+B14+B15	=C13+C14+C15
17	Gross fixed assets	$ 50,000	$ 50,000	Given	Given
18	Accumulated depreciation	($ 4,000)	($ 8,000)	Given	Given
19	Net fixed assets	46,000	42,000	=B17+B18	=C17+C18
20	Total assets	$146,000	$202,000	=B16+B19	=C16+C19
21					
22	DEBT AND EQUITY				
23	Accounts payable	$ 20,000	$ 32,000	=B2*B7	=B3*B7
24	Accrued expenses	10,000	16,000	=B2*B8	=B3*B8
25	Short-term line of credit	7,500	20,500	Required financing	Required financing
26	Total current liabilities	$ 37,500	$ 68,500	=B23+B24+B25	=C23+C24+C25
27	Mortgage	31,500	28,000	Original loan of $35,000 − annual payment $3,500	Year 1 balance of $31,500 − annual payment of $3,500
28	Total debt	$ 69,000	$ 96,500	=B26+B27	=C26+C27
29	Equity				
30	Owner's investment	$110,000	$110,000	Given	Given
31	Retained earnings	(33,000)	(4,500)	Year 1 loss	Year 1 loss + year 2 profit
32	Total equity	$ 77,000	$105,500	=B30+B31	C30+C31
33	Total debt and equity	$146,000	$202,000	=B28+B32	=C28+C32
34					
35	Current ratio (current assets ÷ current liabilities)	2.67	2.34	=B16/B26	=C16/C26
36	Debt ratio (total debt ÷ total assets)	47%	48%	=B28/B20	=C28/C20

how many customers or clients you will have each year. Investors will look at that number to determine whether it's realistic for you to sell to that many customers. For example, if your plan is to go from 12 customers in the first year to 36 customers in the second, can the sales team you've built accomplish that goal? What about marketing and advertising? Does your budget account for the money you'll need to spend to support such an effort?[15]

3. *Do not use unrealistic profit margins.* Projections are immediately suspect if profit margins (profits ÷ sales) or expenses are significantly higher or lower than the average figures reported by firms in the industry with similar revenues and numbers of employees. In general, a new business should not expect to exceed the industry average in profit margins. Entrepreneurs frequently assume that as their company grows it will achieve economies of scale, and gross and operating profit margins will improve. In fact, as the business grows and increases its fixed costs, its operating profit margins are likely to suffer in the short run. If you insist in your projections that the economies can be achieved quickly, you will need to explain your position.

4. *Don't limit your projections to an income statement.* Entrepreneurs frequently resist providing a balance sheet and cash flow statement. They feel comfortable projecting sales and profits but do not like having to commit to assumptions about the sources and uses of capital needed to grow the business. Investors, however, want to see those assumptions in print, and they are particularly interested in the firm's cash flows—and you should be as well.

5. *Provide monthly data for the upcoming year and annual data for succeeding years.* Many entrepreneurs prepare projections using only monthly data or only annual data for an entire three- or five-year period. Given the difficulty in forecasting accurately beyond a year, monthly data for the later years are not particularly believable. From year two on, annual projections are adequate.

6. *Avoid providing too much financial information.* Computer spreadsheets are extremely valuable in making projections and showing how different assumptions affect the firm's financials. But do not be tempted to overuse this tool. Instead, limit your projections to two scenarios: the most likely scenario (base case) and the break-even scenario. The base case should show what you realistically expect the business to do; the break-even case should show what level of sales is required to break even.

7. *Be certain that the numbers reconcile—and not by simply plugging in a figure.* All too often, entrepreneurs plug a figure into equity to make things work out. While everyone makes mistakes, that's one you want to avoid because it can result in a loss of credibility.

8. *Follow the plan.* After you have prepared the pro forma financial statements, check them against actual results at least once a month, and modify your projections as needed.

These suggestions, if followed, will help you avoid the old problem of overpromising and underdelivering. Given the nature of starting a business, entrepreneurs at times simply have to have faith that they will be able to deliver on what they promise, even though it may not be clear exactly how this will be accomplished. Risk is part of the equation, and often things will not go as planned. But integrity requires you to honor your commitments, and that cannot be done if you have made unrealistic projections about what you can accomplish.

The information provided in this chapter on financial planning for a new company will serve as a foundation for the examination of an entrepreneur's search for specific sources of financing in Chapter 11.

Looking BACK

1 Describe the purpose and content of the income statement, the balance sheet, and the cash flow statement.

- An income statement presents the financial results of a firm's operations over a given time period in selling its products or services, in producing or acquiring the goods or services, in running the firm, in financing the firm, and in paying taxes.

- A balance sheet provides a snapshot of a firm's financial position at a specific point in time, showing the amount of assets the firm owns, the amount of outstanding debt, and the amount of ownership equity.

- The income statement cannot measure a firm's cash flows, as it is calculated on an accrual basis rather than on a cash basis.

- Measuring cash flows involves calculating a firm's after-tax cash flows from operations and then subtracting any investments and adding any additional financing received.

2 Forecast a new venture's profitability.

- The purpose of pro forma financial statements is to determine (1) future profitability based on projected sales levels, (2) how much and what type of financing will be used, and (3) whether the firm will have adequate cash flows.

- A firm's net income is dependent on (1) amount of sales, (2) cost of goods sold and operating expenses, (3) interest expense, and (4) taxes.

- Estimates of fixed operating expenses and variable operating expenses, based on the projected level of sales, are deducted from gross sales profits to obtain a forecasted operating profit.

3 Determine asset requirements, evaluate financial sources, and estimate cash flows for a new venture.

- Funding for a new venture should cover its asset requirements and also the personal living expenses of the owner.

- A direct relationship exists between sales growth and asset needs: As sales increase, more assets are required. For every dollar of assets needed, there must be a corresponding dollar of financing.

- The two basic types of capital used in financing a company are debt financing and ownership equity.

- A firm's cash flows involve three activities: operations, investments, and financing.

4 Explain the importance of using good judgment when making projections.

- It is important to develop realistic sales projections and profit margins to establish your credibility with investors.

- Be clear about the assumptions on which you are basing your projections, and provide data to support those assumptions.

- Although risk is always involved in starting a new business, integrity requires that you honor your commitments.

Key TERMS

financial statements (accounting statements), p. 261

income statement (profit and loss statement), p. 262

cost of goods sold, p. 263

gross profit, p. 263

operating expenses, p. 263

operating income, p. 264

financing costs, p. 264

earnings before taxes, p. 264

net income available to owners (net income), p. 264

depreciation expense, p. 264

balance sheet, p. 267

current assets (gross working capital), p. 268

accounts receivable, p. 269

inventory, p. 269

fixed assets, p. 269

depreciable assets, p. 269

gross fixed assets, p. 269

accumulated depreciation, p. 269

net fixed assets, p. 269

other assets, p. 269

debt, p. 270

current debt (short-term liabilities), p. 270

accounts payable (trade credit), p. 270

accrued expenses, p. 270

Discussion **QUESTIONS**

1. What is the relationship between an income statement and a balance sheet?

2. Explain the purposes of the income statement and balance sheet.

3. Distinguish among (a) gross profit, (b) operating income (earnings before interest and taxes), and (c) net income available to owners.

4. Why aren't a firm's cash flows equal to its profit?

5. Describe the three major components of a cash flow statement.

6. Interpret a firm's cash flow statement that shows negative cash flows from operations, negative cash flows from investments, and positive cash flows from financing.

7. What determines a company's profitability?

8. Describe the process for estimating the amount of assets required for a new venture.

9. Distinguish between ownership equity and debt.

10. How are a startup's financial requirements estimated?

You Make the **CALL**

SITUATION 1

The Donahoo Furniture Sales Company was formed on December 31, 2007, with $1,000,000 in equity plus $500,000 in long-term debt. On January 1, 2008, all of the firm's capital was held in cash. The following transactions occurred during January 2008.

- January 2: Donahoo purchased $1,000,000 worth of furniture for resale. It paid $500,000 in cash and financed the balance using trade credit that required payment in 60 days.

- January 3: Donahoo sold $250,000 worth of furniture that it had paid $200,000 to acquire. The entire sale was on credit terms of net 90 days.

- January 15: Donahoo purchased more furniture for $200,000. This time, it used trade credit for the entire amount of the purchase, with credit terms of net 60 days.

- January 31: Donahoo sold $500,000 worth of furniture, for which it had paid $400,000. The furniture was sold for 10 percent cash down, with the remainder payable in 90 days. In addition, the firm paid a cash dividend of $100,000 to its stockholders and paid off $250,000 of its long-term debt.

Question 1 What did Donahoo's balance sheet look like at the outset of the firm's life?

Question 2 What did the firm's balance sheet look like after each transaction?

Question 3 Ignoring taxes, determine how much income Donahoo earned during January. Prepare an income statement for the month. Recognize an interest expense of 1 percent for the month (12 percent annually) on the $500,000 long-term debt, which has not been paid but is owed.

Question 4 What was Donahoo's cash flow for the month of January?

SITUATION 2

At the beginning of 2007, Mary Abrahams purchased a small business, the Turpen Company, whose income statement and balance sheets are shown below.

Income Statement for the Turpen Company for 2007

Sales revenue		$175,000
Cost of goods sold		105,000
Gross profit		$ 70,000
Operating expenses:		
Depreciation	$ 5,000	
Administrative expenses	20,000	
Selling expenses	26,000	
Total operating expenses		$ 51,000
Operating income		$ 19,000
Interest expense		3,000
Earnings before taxes		$ 16,000
Taxes		8,000
Net income		$ 8,000

Balance Sheets for the Turpen Company for 2006 and 2007

	2006	2007
Assets		
Current assets:		
Cash	$ 8,000	$ 10,000
Accounts receivable	15,000	20,000
Inventories	22,000	25,000
Total current assets	$45,000	$ 55,000
Fixed assets:		
Gross fixed assets	$50,000	$ 55,000
Accumulated depreciation	(15,000)	(20,000)
Net fixed assets	$35,000	$ 35,000
Other assets	12,000	10,000
TOTAL ASSETS	$92,000	$100,000
Debt (Liabilities) and Equity		
Current debt:		
Accounts payable	$10,000	$ 12,000
Accruals	7,000	8,000
Short-term notes	5,000	5,000
Total current debt	$22,000	$ 25,000
Long-term debt	15,000	15,000
Total debt	$37,000	$ 40,000
Equity	$55,000	$ 60,000
TOTAL DEBT AND EQUITY	$92,000	$100,000

The firm has been profitable, but Abrahams has been disappointed by the lack of cash flows. She had hoped to have about $10,000 a year available for personal living expenses. However, there never seems to be much cash available for purposes other than business needs. Abrahams has asked you to examine the financial statements and explain why, although they show profits, she does not have any discretionary cash for personal needs. She observed, "I thought that I could take the profits and add depreciation to find out how much cash I was generating. However, that doesn't seem to be the case. What's happening?"

Question 1 Given the information provided by the financial statements, what would you tell Abrahams? (As part of your answer, calculate the firm's cash flows.)

Question 2 How would you describe the cash flow pattern for the Turpen Company?

SITUATION 3

C&G Products, Inc., used as an example in this chapter, is an actual firm (although some of the facts were changed to maintain confidentiality). Kate Lynn bought the firm from its founding owners and moved its operations to her hometown. Although she has estimated the firm's asset needs and financing requirements, she cannot be certain that these projections will be realized. The figures merely represent the most likely case. Lynn also made some projections that she considers to be the worst-case and best-case sales and profit figures. If things do not go well, the firm might have sales of only $200,000 in its first year. However, if the potential of the business is realized, Lynn believes that sales could be as high as $325,000. If she needs any additional financing beyond the existing line of credit, she could conceivably borrow another $5,000 in short-term debt from the bank by pledging some personal investments. Any additional financing would need to come from Lynn herself, thereby increasing her equity stake in the business.

Source: Personal conversation with Kate Lynn. (Numbers are hypothetical.)

Question If all of C&G Products' other relationships hold, how will Lynn's worst-case and best-case projections affect the income statement and balance sheet in the first year?

Experiential EXERCISES

1. Interview an owner of a small firm about the financial statements she or he uses. Ask the owner how important financial data are to her or his decision making.

2. Acquire a small firm's financial statements. Review the statements and describe the firm's financial position. Find out if the owner agrees with your conclusions.

3. Dun & Bradstreet and Robert Morris Associates compile financial information about many companies. They provide, among other information, income statements and balance sheets for an average firm in an industry. Go to a library, look up financial information on two industries of your choice, and compute the following data for each industry:

    a. The percentages of assets in (1) current assets and (2) fixed assets (plant and equipment)

    b. The percentages of financing from (1) spontaneous financing and (2) internal equity

    c. The cost of goods sold and the operating expenses as percentages of sales

    d. The total assets as a percentage of sales

Given your findings, how would you summarize the differences between the two industries?

4. Obtain the business plan of a firm that is three to five years old. Compare the techniques used in the plan to forecast the firm's profits and financing requirements with those presented in this chapter. If actual data are available, compare the financial forecasts with the eventual outcome. What accounts for the differences?

Exploring the WEB

1. Bplans.com is owned and maintained by PaloAlto Software, Inc., as a free resource for entrepreneurs. Find the Planning Solutions portion of the Bplans.com site by going to **http://bplans.com/ contentkit**. Choose the "Interactive Calculators" link.

    a. Link to the "Starting Costs Calculator," and run through the exercise to determine the startup costs for your new business. Once you have computed your starting costs, print the page. To print, right click and then choose Print from the popup menu.

    b. Return to the Interactive Calculators page and click on "Cash Flow Calculator." What happens when you change the calculator's variables?

2. For some first-hand experience with debt ratios, go to **http://www.anz.com**, the site of the Australian and New Zealand Banking Group.

Choose the "Business" tab; then select "Business Toolkit," "Benchmark Your Business," and "Debt Ratio" from the menus on the left. Read the site's content about debt ratios and, if possible, use the simple calculator to determine your business's debt ratio.

    a. What are the advantages and disadvantages of a high debt ratio (greater than 0.50)?

    b. Why is the debt ratio useful as a business benchmark?

3. Visit the CCH Business Owner's Toolkit at **http:// www.toolkit.cch.com** to get an overview of what the site offers. CCH is a leading provider of business and tax information. Read more about financing basics at **http://toolkit.cch.com/text/ P10_2000.asp**. What figures are needed to calculate the debt-to-equity ratio?

Video Case 10

Understanding Financial Statements, Part 1 (p. 640)

This case explains the value of understanding financial statements to the small business owner and the importance of their proper interpretation in order to understand and project the firm's financial position.

Alternative Cases for Chapter 10:

Case 6, AdGrove.com, Inc., p. 630

Case 8, Silver Zephyr Restaurant, p. 635

Case 23, Understanding Financial Statements, Part 2, p. 667

The Business Plan

Laying the Foundation

As part of laying the foundation to prepare your own business plan, you will need to develop the following:

1. Historical financial statements (if applicable) and five years of pro forma financial statements, including balance sheets, income statements, and statements of cash flows.
2. Monthly cash budgets for the first year and quarterly cash budgets for the second year. (See Chapter 22 for an explanation of cash budgets.)
3. Profit and cash flow break-even analysis. (See Chapter 15 for an explanation of break-even analysis.)
4. Financial resources required now and in the future, with details on the intended use of funds being requested.
5. Underlying assumptions for all pro forma statements.
6. Current and planned investments by the owners and other investors.

Appendix 10A:
Computing Cash Flows for Trimble & Associates Leasing, Inc.

In Chapter 10, we presented the cash flow statement, giving the highlights and describing how it can be interpreted. We refrained from showing the details of the computations, realizing that for most people these details are not essential to understanding the statement. But cash flows are such a critical issue for entrepreneurs that we have provided this appendix to ensure a greater understanding for anyone with the desire to know more.

The Process and Data

We must re-emphasize that *the profits shown on a company's income statement are not the same as its cash flows.* To compute a firm's cash flows, we begin with selected information from the income statement and then make adjustments based on changes in the balance sheets from the end of the prior year to the end of the current year. We will illustrate this process by returning to our example of Trimble & Associates Leasing, Inc.

Exhibit A10-1 incorporates Trimble & Associates' 2007 income statement (from Exhibit 10-2) and the changes in the balance sheets from December 31, 2006, to December

exhibit

A10-1 *Income Statement and Balance Sheet Changes for Trimble & Associates Leasing, Inc., for the Year Ending December 31, 2007*

Income Statement		
Sales		$850,000
Cost of goods sold		550,000
Gross profit on sales		$300,000
Operating expenses:		
Marketing expenses	$90,000	
General and administrative expenses	80,000	
Depreciation expense	30,000	
Total operating expenses		$200,000
Operating income		$100,000
Interest expense		20,000
Earnings before taxes		$ 80,000
Income tax (25%)		20,000
Net income		$ 60,000
Net income		$ 60,000
Dividends paid		15,000
Change in retained earnings		$ 45,000
Balance Sheet Changes: Dec. 31, 2006 to Dec. 31, 2007		
Cash		$ 5,000
Accounts receivable		5,000
Inventories		40,000
Gross plant and equipment		100,000
Accounts payable		$ 5,000
Short-term notes		20,000
Long-term debt		50,000
Common stock		0

31, 2007 (from Exhibit 10-4). The information from the income statement needed for computing cash flows is in bold print. Also, to simplify the data from the balance sheets, we have done the following:

1. Eliminated all the totals (for example, *total current assets*)

2. Shown only the change in *gross fixed assets* and not in *accumulated depreciation* or *net fixed assets,* because these are affected by the firm's depreciation expense, a noncash expense

3. Disregarded the change in *retained earnings,* which is already recognized through the inclusion of the firm's income and dividend payments in the cash flow statement

All remaining changes directly affect a firm's cash flows and must be considered.

Components of the Cash Flow Statement

As explained in Chapter 10, there are three components of a cash flow statement:

1. *Cash flows from operations,* consisting of the cash generated from the firm's normal day-to-day business activities

2. *Investment in long-term assets,* such as purchasing or selling fixed assets

3. *Financing activities,* including paying dividends and interest expense, increasing or decreasing short-term or long-term debt, and issuing or repurchasing stock

---

exhibit **A10-2**   *Cash Flow Statement for Trimble & Associates Leasing, Inc., for the Year Ending December 31, 2007*

Operating activities:		
Operating income	$100,000	
Depreciation	30,000	
Income taxes	(20,000)	
Adjusted income		$110,000
Increase in accounts receivable (cash outflow)	($ 5,000)	
Increase in inventories (cash outflow)	(40,000)	
Increase in accounts payable (cash inflow)	5,000	
Change in net cash flow for working capital		($ 40,000)
CASH FLOWS FROM OPERATIONS		$ 70,000
Investment activities:		
Increase in gross fixed assets (cash outflow)		($100,000)
Financing activities:		
Interest expense	($ 20,000)	
Dividends	(15,000)	
Increase in short-term notes	20,000	
Increase in long-term debt	50,000	
TOTAL FINANCING ACTIVITIES		$ 35,000
Increase in cash		$ 5,000

Let's examine the computation of each of the above components in turn.

OPERATING ACTIVITIES A firm's *cash flows* from operations consist of two elements: (1) after-tax profits adjusted for any noncash expenses, such as depreciation, and (2) changes in the company's working capital.

We start with operating income (earnings before interest and taxes). Then we (1) add back depreciation expense, since it is not a cash expense even though it is shown as an expense in the income statement, and (2) subtract income taxes to get the cash flow on an after-tax basis, or adjusted income. For Trimble & Associates, we have the following:

Operating income	$100,000
Depreciation	30,000
Income taxes	(20,000)
Adjusted income	$110,000

Next, we factor in the change in net working capital, which is not reported in the income statement. Net working capital is the current assets (accounts receivable and inventories) less short-term debt (accounts payable and accruals) that are part of the firm's operating cycle. An increase in net working capital is subtracted because it is a *cash outflow,* and a decrease in net working capital is added because it is a *cash inflow.* For Trimble & Associates, the changes in net working capital are as follows:

	Changes
Increase in accounts receivable (cash outflow)	($ 5,000)
Increase in inventories (cash outflow)	(40,000)
Increase in accounts payable (cash inflow)	5,000
Net cash flow for working capital	($40,000)

So, cash flows from operations may be calculated as follows:

Operating activities:		
Operating income	$100,000	
Depreciation	30,000	
Income taxes	(20,000)	
Adjusted income		$110,000
Increase in accounts receivable (cash outflow)	($ 5,000)	
Increase in inventories (cash outflow)	(40,000)	
Increase in accounts payable (cash inflow)	5,000	
Change in net working capital		($ 40,000)
Cash flows from operations		$ 70,000

INVESTMENT ACTIVITIES As already noted, *depreciation expense is not a cash flow.* This entry in the income statement is the accountant's effort to allocate the cost of an asset over its useful life. However, when equipment or some other depreciable asset is purchased or sold, cash flows occur that are not shown in the income statement. Trimble & Associates spent $100,000 on new plant and equipment, as reflected in the change in gross fixed assets. (See the balance sheet shown in Exhibit 10-4.)

FINANCING ACTIVITIES The third section of the cash flow statement presents the cash inflows and outflows resulting from financing activities, including (1) paying dividends and interest expense, (2) increasing or decreasing short-term or long-term debt, and (3) issuing stock or repurchasing stock.

As shown in Exhibit A10-1, Trimble & Associates paid $20,000 in interest and $15,000 in dividends, but borrowed an additional $70,000 in debt ($20,000 in short-term notes and $50,000 in long-term notes), resulting in a net cash inflow of $35,000 from financing activities. Exhibit A10-2 shows Trimble & Associates' cash flow statement for the year ending December 31, 2007.

Appendix 10B:
Cash Flow Statements for C&G Products, Inc.

	Year 1	Year 2
Operating activities:		
Operating income	($ 25,000)	$50,000
Depreciation	4,000	4,000
Taxes	0	(9,500)
Adjusted income	($ 21,000)	$44,500
Increase in accounts receivable (cash outflow)	($ 25,000)	($15,000)
Increase in inventories (cash outflow)	(62,500)	(37,500)
Increase in accounts payable (cash inflow)	20,000	12,000
Increase in accruals (cash inflow)	10,000	6,000
Net cash flow for working capital	($ 57,500)	($34,500)
Cash flows from operations	**($ 78,500)**	**$ 10,000**
Investment activities:		
Increase in gross fixed assets (cash outflow)	($ 50,000)	$ 0
Cash flows from investments	**($ 50,000)**	**$ 0**
Financing activities:		
Interest expense	($ 8,000)	($12,000)
Increase in short-term line of credit	7,500	13,000
Increase in mortgage	31,500	(3,500)
Increase in stock	110,000	$ 0
Cash flows from financing	**$ 141,000**	**($ 2,500)**
Increase (decrease) in cash	$ 12,500	$ 7,500

## chapter 11

A Firm's Sources of Financing

In the SPOTLIGHT

Vizio, Inc.
http://www.vizio.com

Starting a business requires capital, and as most aspiring entrepreneurs aren't independently wealthy, the question arises: "How am I going to fund my venture?" William Wang was 26 when he began asking himself that question. He wanted to build a better computer monitor than an IBM standard, and that was going to take a significant investment. Wang cobbled together $350,000 by borrowing money from his parents, himself, an Asian investor—and from his boss. Within six years, his company, MAG Innovision, was grossing $600 million annually. Two years later, the company was overspending, the market had shifted, and Wang ended up selling MAG Innovision to its manufacturing vendor.

Wang's vision, however, didn't dry up; it became the plan for Vizio, a company that sells flat-screen televisions at low prices and with exceptional customer support. Again, Wang's business plan required significant investment, and again, he put together a modest financing package to get it off the ground. The second time around, Wang still relied on family and friends for support, but he also mortgaged his house. His seed money for Vizio totaled $600,000. Later in the growth of the business, he brought in outside investors, but Wang is still the majority shareholder in what is now a company with over $2 billion in revenue.

Source: William Wang, "Talk About New Beginnings: How I Did It," *Inc.,* June 2007, pp. 106–107.

Courtesy of http://www.vizio.com

After studying this chapter, you should be able to

1 Describe how the nature of a firm affects its financing sources.
2 Evaluate the choice between debt financing and equity financing.
3 Identify the typical sources of financing used at the outset of a new venture.
4 Discuss the basic process for acquiring and structuring a bank loan.
5 Explain how business relationships can be used to finance a small firm.
6 Describe the two types of private equity investors that offer financing to small firms.
7 Distinguish among the different government loan programs available to small companies.
8 Explain when large companies and public stock offerings can be sources of financing.

Chapter 10 addressed two questions: (1) *How much* financing is needed? and (2) *What types* of financing are available? Three basic types of financing were identified:

1. *Profit retention,* or internal financing, where the firm finances its growth through cash flows from operations, rather than distributing the cash to the owners in the form of dividends.

2. *Spontaneous financing,* such as accounts payable, which increases automatically with increases in sales. For instance, as a firm's sales grow, it purchases more inventories and suppliers extend the firm more credit, which increases accounts payable.

3. *External financing,* which comes from outside lenders and investors. Lenders (such as bankers) and investors (such as common stockholders, partners, or sole proprietors) provide equity financing.

This chapter discusses sources of spontaneous and external financing for small firms. But first we consider *how* a company should be financed. An understanding of this core issue is critical to identifying appropriate sources of financing.

The Nature of a Firm and Its Financing Sources

Four basic factors determine how a firm is financed: (1) the firm's economic potential, (2) the size and maturity of the company, (3) the nature of its assets, and (4) the personal preferences of the owners with respect to the tradeoffs between debt and equity.

> 1 Describe how the nature of a firm affects its financing sources.

A Firm's Economic Potential
A firm with potential for high growth and large profits has many more possible sources of financing than does a firm that provides a good lifestyle for the owner but little in the way of attractive returns to investors. Only those firms providing rates of return that exceed the investor's required rate of return create value for the investor. In fact, most investors in startup companies limit their investment to firms that offer potentially high returns within a 5- to 10-year period. Clearly, a company that provides a comfortable lifestyle for its owner but insufficient profits to attract outside investors will find its options for alternative sources of financing limited.

Company Size and Maturity

The size and maturity of a company have a direct bearing on the types of financing available. In a survey of small business finance, the Small Business Administration found a positive relationship between the use of bank debt and firm size. Larger and older firms have access to bank credit that simply is not available to younger and smaller companies. The survey also found that smaller firms rely more on personal loans and credit cards for financing.[1] In the early years of a business, most entrepreneurs bootstrap their financing—that is, they depend on their own initiative to come up with the necessary capital. Only after the business has an established track record will most bankers and other financial institutions be interested in providing financing.

Even venture capitalists limit how much they will invest in startup companies. Many equity investors believe that the additional risk associated with startups is too great relative to the returns they can expect to receive. On average, about three-fourths of a venture capitalist's investments are in later-stage businesses; only a few venture capitalists focus heavily on startups. Similarly, bankers demand evidence that the business will be able to repay a loan—and that evidence usually must be based on what the firm has done in the past and not what the owner says it will achieve in the future. So, a firm's life cycle position is a critical factor in raising capital.

Types of Assets

In Chapter 3, we mentioned two types of assets: tangible and intangible. A banker specifically considers these two types of assets when evaluating a loan. Tangible assets, which can be seen and touched, include inventories, equipment, and buildings. The cost of these assets appears on the firm's balance sheet, which the banker receives as part of the firm's financial statements. Tangible assets serve as great collateral when a firm is requesting a bank loan. On the other hand, intangible assets, such as goodwill or past investments in research and development, have little value as collateral. As a result, companies with substantial tangible assets have a much easier time borrowing money than do companies with intangible assets.

Owner Preferences for Debt or Equity

The owner of a company faces the question "Should I finance with debt or equity or some mix of the two?" The answer depends, in part, on his or her personal preference. The ultimate choice between debt and equity involves certain tradeoffs, which will be explained in the following section.

2 Evaluate the choice between debt financing and equity financing.

Debt or Equity Financing?

Most providers of financial capital specialize in *either* debt *or* equity financing. Furthermore, the choice between debt and equity financing must be made early in a firm's life cycle and may have long-term financial consequences. To make an informed decision, a small business owner needs to recognize and understand the tradeoffs between debt and equity with regard to potential profitability, financial risk, and voting control. The tradeoffs are presented graphically in Exhibit 11-1. Let's consider each of these tradeoffs in turn.

Potential Profitability

Anyone who owns a business wants it to be profitable. Of course, profits can be measured as a dollar amount, such as $500,000; however, the really important question is how much profit the business makes relative to the size of the investment. In other words, the owner is primarily interested in the rate of return on the investment. Making $500,000 in profits may sound great, but not if the owner must invest $50 million to earn it. It would be better to purchase a certificate of deposit that earned, say, 3 percent or even 2 percent; any rate over 1 percent would provide income greater than $500,000.

To see how the choice between debt and equity affects potential profitability, consider the Levine Company, a new firm that's still in the process of raising needed capital.

- The owners have already invested $100,000 of their own money in the new business. To complete the financing, they need another $100,000.

- Levine is considering one of two options for raising the additional $100,000: (1) investors who would provide $100,000 for a 30 percent share of the firm's outstanding stock or (2) a bank that would lend the money at an interest rate of 8 percent, so the interest expense each year would be $8,000 ($0.08 \times \$100,000$).

- The firm's operating income (earnings before interest and taxes) is expected to be $28,000, determined as follows:

Sales	$150,000
Cost of goods sold	80,000
Gross profit	$ 70,000
Operating expenses	42,000
Operating income (earnings before interest and taxes)	$ 28,000

- With the additional $100,000 in financing, the firm's total assets would be $200,000 ($100,000 original equity plus $100,000 in additional financing).

- Based on the projected operating income of $28,000 and assets of $200,000, the firm expects to earn $0.14 for each $1 of assets invested ($28,000 income ÷ $200,000 assets). In other words, there will be a 14 percent **return on assets**, which is the rate of return earned on a firm's total assets invested.

$$\text{Return on assets} = \frac{\text{Operating income}}{\text{Total assets}}$$

return on assets
Rate of return earned on a firm's total assets invested, computed as operating income divided by total assets

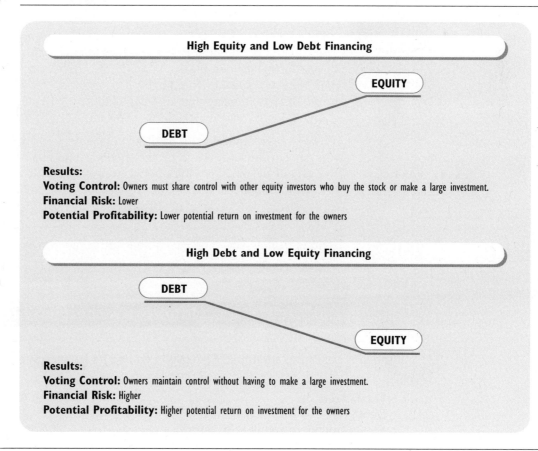

exhibit 11-1 *Tradeoffs Between Debt and Equity*

High Equity and Low Debt Financing

EQUITY

DEBT

Results:
Voting Control: Owners must share control with other equity investors who buy the stock or make a large investment.
Financial Risk: Lower
Potential Profitability: Lower potential return on investment for the owners

High Debt and Low Equity Financing

DEBT

EQUITY

Results:
Voting Control: Owners maintain control without having to make a large investment.
Financial Risk: Higher
Potential Profitability: Higher potential return on investment for the owners

Living the Dream   entrepreneurial challenges

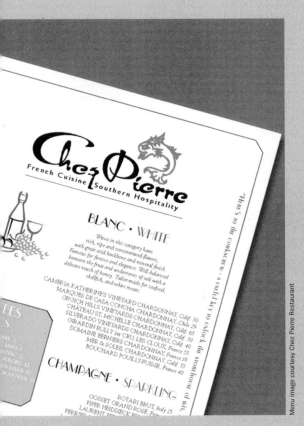

Managing Your Debt

Only a short time after husband-and-wife entrepreneurs Karen Cooley and Eric Favier bought a friend's restaurant in 1991, they had their first taste of success. Sales at their Tallahassee, Florida, restaurant, Chez Pierre, more than doubled in response to savvy marketing and expanded kitchen hours. But after five successful years at the location, the federal government acquired the restaurant's property to expand a nearby courthouse.

So the couple took another leap of faith, buying and renovating a commercial building for $1.2 million to house the restaurant. It marked a major entrepreneurial milestone for Cooley and Favier, who had previously leased restaurant space from the original Chez Pierre owners. Not only did they now own their own building, but they were also knee-deep in debt because of the purchase. "It was really challenging, and we weren't sure where to go next [or] what to do," says Cooley.

For help managing the debt and charting a new course for the business, the couple turned to The Jim Moran Institute for Global Entrepreneurship at Florida State University. Among other things, they were advised to intensify marketing and build up sales to help offset the loan payments. Eventually, sales more than doubled, to nearly $2 million annually, in response to their strong marketing efforts. "We had many sleepless nights," Cooley says of their decision. "But it has turned out to be absolutely the right thing to do. We have so many different avenues for growing our business right now."

Cooley and Favier, both 50, are now gearing up for another round of financing to further boost sales. And they plan to build an outdoor dining area that will include a wood-burning pizza oven and a seafood bar. "If you're going to take on more debt," Cooley says, "it not only has to generate enough in sales and profitability to take care of the debt service, but [also] put money back in the coffers."

"None of us has a crystal ball," she explains. "You're always trying to find that balance between having a successful business that is growing organically and knowing when it's time to go beyond that and put in more investment for infrastructure or new facilities. It's tough to do."

Indeed, taking on the right amount of debt can mean the difference between a business struggling to survive and one that can respond nimbly to changing economic or market conditions. A number of circumstances may justify acquiring debt.

Source: Crystal Detamore-Rodman, "Cutting Back," *Entrepreneur*, December 2006, pp. 75–78.

http://www.chezpierre.com

If the firm raises the additional $100,000 in equity, its balance sheet will appear as follows:

Total assets	$200,000
Debt	$ 0
Equity (founders and new investors)	200,000
Total debt and equity	$200,000

But if the firm instead borrows $100,000, the balance sheet will look like this:

Total assets	$200,000
Debt (8% interest rate)	$100,000
Equity (founders)	100,000
Total debt and equity	$200,000

If we assume no taxes (just to keep matters simple), we can use the above information to project the firm's net income when the additional $100,000 is financed by either equity or debt:

	Equity	**Debt**	
Operating income	$28,000	$28,000	
Interest expense	0	(8,000)	(0.08 × $100,000)
Net income	$28,000	$20,000	

From these computations, we can see that net income is greater if the firm finances with equity ($28,000 net income) than with debt ($20,000 net income). But the owners would have to invest *twice* as much money ($200,000 rather than $100,000) to avoid the $8,000 interest expense and get the higher net income.

Should owners always finance with equity to get higher net income? Not necessarily. The return on the owners' investment, or **return on equity**, is a better measure of performance than the absolute dollar amount of net income. We measure the owners' return on equity as follows:

return on equity
Rate of return earned on the owners' equity investment, computed as net income divided by owners' equity investment

$$\text{Return on equity} = \frac{\text{Net income}}{\text{Owners' equity investment}}$$

So when the firm uses *all* equity financing, the return on equity is 14 percent, computed as follows:

$$\text{Return on equity} = \frac{\text{Net income}}{\text{Owners' equity investment}}$$

$$= \frac{\$28,000}{\$200,000} = 0.14, \text{ or } 14\%$$

But if the additional financing comes from debt, leading to interest expense of $8,000 and equity investment of only $100,000, the rate of return on equity is 20 percent, calculated as follows:

$$\text{Return on equity} = \frac{\text{Net income}}{\text{Owners' equity investment}}$$

$$= \frac{\$20,000}{\$100,000} = 0.20, \text{ or } 20\%$$

Thus, Levine's return on equity is higher if half the firm's financing comes from equity and half from debt. By using only equity, Levine's owners will earn $0.14 for every $1 of equity invested; by using debt, they will earn $0.20 for every $1 of equity invested. So, in terms of a rate of return on their investment, Levine's owners get a better return by borrowing money at 8 percent interest than by using equity financing. That makes sense, because the firm is earning 14 percent on its assets but only paying creditors at an 8 percent rate. Levine's owners benefit from the difference. These relationships are shown in Exhibit 11-2.

As a general rule, *as long as a firm's rate of return on its assets (operating income ÷ total assets) is greater than the cost of the debt (interest rate), the owners' rate of return on equity will increase as the firm uses more debt.*

Financial Risk

If debt is so beneficial in terms of producing a higher rate of return for the owners, why shouldn't Levine's owners use as much debt as possible—even 100 percent debt—if they can? Then the rate of return on the owners' equity investment would be even higher—unlimited, in fact, if the owners did not have to invest any money.

exhibit 11-2 *Debt Versus Equity at the Levine Company*

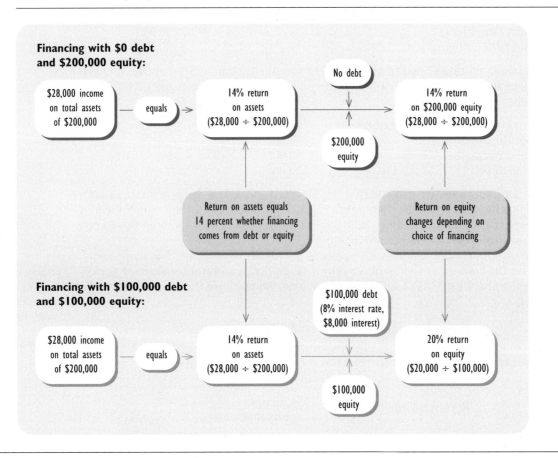

Financing with $0 debt and $200,000 equity:

$28,000 income on total assets of $200,000 — equals → 14% return on assets ($28,000 ÷ $200,000)

No debt

$200,000 equity

14% return on $200,000 equity ($28,000 ÷ $200,000)

Return on assets equals 14 percent whether financing comes from debt or equity

Return on equity changes depending on choice of financing

Financing with $100,000 debt and $100,000 equity:

$28,000 income on total assets of $200,000 — equals → 14% return on assets ($28,000 ÷ $200,000)

$100,000 debt (8% interest rate, $8,000 interest)

$100,000 equity

20% return on equity ($20,000 ÷ $100,000)

That's the good news. The bad news: *Debt is risky.* If the firm fails to earn profits, creditors will still insist on having their money repaid. Debt demands its pound of flesh from the owners regardless of the firm's performance. In an extreme case, creditors can force a firm into bankruptcy if it fails to honor its financial obligations.

Equity, on the other hand, is less demanding. If a firm does not reach its goal for profits, an equity investor must accept the disappointing results and hope for better results next year. Equity investors cannot demand more than what is earned.

Another way to view the negative side of debt is to contemplate what happens to the return on equity if a business has a bad year. Suppose that instead of earning 14 percent on its assets, or $28,000 in operating profits, the Levine Company earns a mere $2,000, or only 1 percent on its assets of $200,000. The return on equity would again depend on whether the firm used debt or equity to finance the second $100,000 investment in the company. The results would be as follows:

	Equity	**Debt**	
Operating income	$2,000	$2,000	
Interest expense	0	(8,000)	(0.08 × $100,000)
Net income	$2,000	($6,000)	

If the added financing came in the form of equity, the return on equity would be a disappointing 1 percent:

$$\text{Return on equity} = \frac{\text{Net income}}{\text{Owners' equity investment}}$$

$$= \frac{\$2,000}{\$200,000} = 0.01, \text{ or } 1\%$$

But if debt were used, the return on equity would be a painful negative 6 percent:

$$\text{Return on equity} = \frac{\text{Net income}}{\text{Owners' equity investment}}$$

$$= \frac{-\$6,000}{\$100,000} = -0.06, \text{ or } -6\%$$

If only 1 percent is earned on the assets, the owners would be better off if they financed solely with equity. Thus, debt is a double-edged sword—it cuts both ways. If debt financing is used and things go well, they will go *very* well for the owners; but if things go badly, they will go *very* badly. In short, debt financing makes business more risky.

Voting Control

The third issue in choosing between debt and equity is the degree of control retained by owners. Raising new capital through equity financing would mean giving up a part of the firm's ownership, and most owners of small firms resist giving up control to outsiders. They do not want to be accountable in any way to minority owners, much less take the chance of possibly losing control of the business.

Out of an aversion to losing control, many small business owners choose to finance with debt rather than with equity. They realize that debt increases risk, but it also permits them to retain full ownership of the firm.

With an understanding of the basic tradeoffs to be considered when choosing between debt and equity, we can now look at specific sources of financing. Where do small business owners go to find the money to finance their companies?

Sources of Financing

When initially financing a small business, an entrepreneur will typically rely on personal savings and then seek financing from family and friends. If these sources are inadequate, the entrepreneur may then turn to more formal channels of financing, such as banks and outside investors.

Exhibit 11-3 gives an overview of the sources of financing of smaller companies. As indicated, some sources of financing—such as banks, business suppliers, asset-based

> 3 Identify the typical sources of financing used at the outset of a new venture.

exhibit

11-3 Sources of Funds

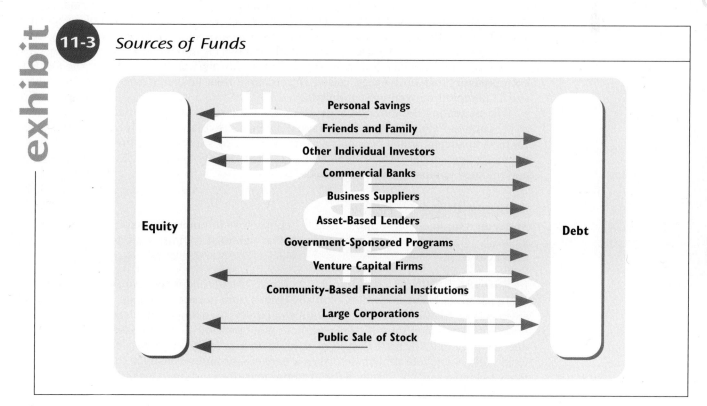

exhibit

11-4   *Startup Financing for* Inc. *500 Companies in 2003*

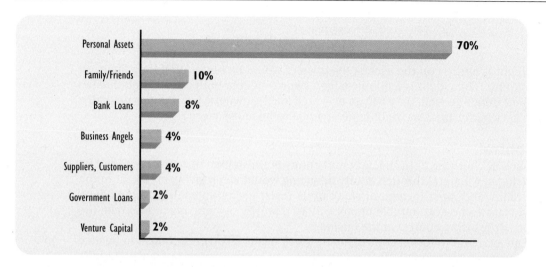

Personal Assets	**70%**
Family/Friends	**10%**
Bank Loans	**8%**
Business Angels	**4%**
Suppliers, Customers	**4%**
Government Loans	**2%**
Venture Capital	**2%**

Source: Mike Hofman, "The Big Picture," *Inc.,* Vol. 25, No. 12 (October 2003), p. 87. Copyright 2003 by Mansueto Ventures LLC. Reproduced with permission of Mansueto Ventures LLC in the format Textbook via Copyright Clearance Center.

lenders, and the government—are essentially limited to providing debt financing. Equity financing for most entrepreneurs comes from personal savings and, in rare instances, from selling stock to the public. Other sources—including friends and family, other individual investors, venture capitalists, and large corporations—may provide either debt or equity financing, depending on the situation. Keep in mind that the use of these and other sources of funds is not limited to a startup's initial financing. Such sources may also be used to finance a firm's day-to-day operations and business expansions.

To gain insight into how startups are financed, consider the responses given by owners of *Inc.* 500 firms—the 500 fastest-growing privately held firms in the United States—when they were asked about the financing sources they used to start their firms; the results are shown in Exhibit 11-4. Even for these high-growth firms, 70 percent of the startup financing came from the founders' personal savings, with another 10 percent coming from friends and family and 8 percent from bank loans. The remaining sources of financing were relatively insignificant in starting the firms. However, within five years, the *Inc.* 500 entrepreneurs had, on average, raised 17 percent of their financing from private investors and 12 percent from venture capitalists.[2]

In presenting the different sources of financing for smaller companies, we will look at (1) sources "close to home"—personal savings, friends and family, and credit cards; (2) bank financing, which becomes a primary financing source as the firm grows; (3) business suppliers and asset-based lenders; (4) private equity investors; (5) the government; and (6) large companies and stock sales.

Sources Close to Home

The search for financial support usually begins close to home. The aspiring entrepreneur basically has three sources of early financing: personal savings, friends and family, and credit cards.

PERSONAL SAVINGS   It is imperative for an entrepreneur to have some personal investment in the business, which typically comes from personal savings. Indeed, personal savings is by far the most common source of equity financing used in starting a new business. With few exceptions, the entrepreneur must provide an equity base. A new business needs equity to allow for a margin of error. In its first few years, a firm can ill afford large fixed outlays for debt repayment. Also, a banker—or anyone else for that matter—is unlikely to loan a venture money if the entrepreneur does not have his or her own money at risk, which is sometimes referred to as "having skin in the game."

A problem for many people who want to start a business is that they lack sufficient personal savings for this purpose. It can be very discouraging when the banker asks, "How much will you be investing in the business?" or "What do you have for collateral to secure the bank loan you want?" There is no easy solution to this problem, which is faced by an untold number of entrepreneurs. Nonetheless, many individuals who lacked personal savings for a startup have found a way to accomplish their goal of owning their own company. In most cases, it required creativity and some risk taking—as well as sometimes finding a partner who could provide the financing or friends and relatives who were willing to help.

FRIENDS AND FAMILY   Personal savings is the *primary* source of financing for most small business startups, with friends and family following in a distant second place. Exhibit 11-5 shows that friends, close family, and other relatives provide almost 80 percent of startup capital from personal sources beyond the entrepreneur's personal savings.

Entrepreneurs who acquire financing from friends and family are putting more than just their financial futures on the line—they're putting important personal relationships in jeopardy, too. "It's the highest risk money you'll ever get," says David Deeds, professor of entrepreneurship at Case Western Reserve University in Cleveland. "The venture may succeed or fail, but either way, you still have to go to Thanksgiving dinner."

At times, loans from friends or relatives may be the only available source of new financing. Such loans can often be obtained quickly, as this type of financing is based more on personal relationships than on financial analyses. However, friends and relatives who provide business loans sometimes feel that they have the right to offer suggestions concerning the management of the business. Also, hard business times may strain the relationship. But if relatives and friends are the only available source of financing, the entrepreneur has no alternative. To minimize the chance of damaging important personal relationships, the entrepreneur should plan to repay such loans as soon as possible. In addition, any agreements made should be put in writing, as memories tend to become fuzzy over time. It is best to clarify expectations up front, rather than be disappointed or angry later.

exhibit 11-5   *Sources of Personal Capital for Small Firms*

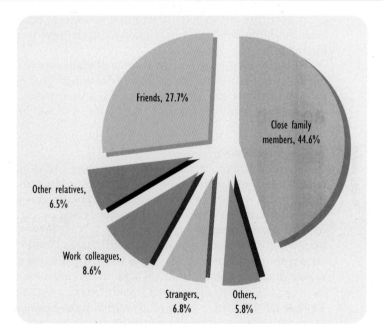

Source: Republished with permission of Dow Jones Inc. from Staff, "Entrepreneurship Monitor 2002," *Wall Street Journal,* August 26, 2003, p. B8; permission conveyed through Copyright Clearance Center, Inc.

The best advice comes from James Hutcheson, president of Regeneration Partners, a Dallas-based consulting group that specializes in family-owned businesses:

> *Entrepreneurs [should] approach their relatives only after they have secured investments or loans from unbiased outside sources.* "*Go and get matching funds,*" *he says.* "*If you need $25,000, then first get $12,500 from others before asking your family for the rest. If you can't do it that way—and if you don't have your own skin in the game—then you need to think twice about why you're asking someone you love to give you money. I believe you should get others to back the idea as well, so a parent or relative doesn't feel as though the money is a gift but rather a worthwhile investment. It puts a higher level of accountability into the entire process.*"[3]

So, use friends and family only as a last resort. But do it if necessary—and carefully and meticulously clarify expectations.

CREDIT CARDS   With unsolicited offers of a "free" credit card arriving in the mail all the time, credit cards have become readily available to almost anyone who is willing to apply. Using credit cards to help finance a small business has become increasingly common among entrepreneurs. It has been estimated that approximately half of all entrepreneurs use credit cards at one time or another to finance a startup or business expansion.

For someone who cannot acquire more traditional financing, such as a bank loan, credit card financing may be an option—not a great option, but a necessary one. The interest costs can become overwhelming over time, especially because of the tendency to borrow beyond the ability to repay. So it is essential that an entrepreneur using credit card financing be extremely self-disciplined to avoid becoming over-extended.

Why use credit cards? Along with being perhaps the only option open to the entrepreneur, credit cards have the advantage of speed. A lender at a bank has to be convinced of the merits of the business opportunity, and that involves extensive preparation. Credit-card financing, on the other hand, requires no justification of the use of the money.

Speed was certainly the main appeal of credit-card financing for Kelli Greene, who used 10 credit cards plus her savings to launch Pacific Data Designs in 1994. Greene had a day job and spent all of her downtime developing the software that would eventually become the company's hallmark product. "I had no time to talk to a bank, and I didn't want to make the effort of writing a plan," she says. The credit cards, which together accounted for about $50,000 in cash advances, funded Pacific's first 20 months. After that the company generated enough cash flow from its operations to avoid further financing.[4]

Clearly, credit cards provide an important source of financing for many entrepreneurs, particularly early in the game. But the eventual goal is to use credit cards as a method of payment and not as a source of credit. In other words, the sooner you can pay your credit card balance in full each month, the sooner you will be growing a viable business.

Bank Financing

4   Discuss the basic process for acquiring and structuring a bank loan.

Commercial banks are the primary providers of debt capital to small companies. However, banks tend to limit their lending to providing for the working-capital needs of *established* firms, specifically for financing accounts receivable and inventory. Quite simply, they want firms with proven track records and preferably plenty of collateral in the form of hard assets. Bankers are reluctant to loan money to finance losses, R&D expenses, marketing campaigns, and other "soft" assets. Such expenditures should be financed by equity sources. Nevertheless, it is wise to cultivate a relationship with a banker sooner rather than later, and well in advance of making a loan request.

TYPES OF LOANS   Bankers primarily make business loans in one of three forms: lines of credit, term loans, and mortgages.

line of credit
An informal agreement between a borrower and a bank as to the maximum amount of funds the bank will provide at any one time

Lines of Credit   A **line of credit** is an informal agreement or understanding between the borrower and the bank as to the maximum amount of credit the bank will provide

Living the Dream   entrepreneurial challenges

Plastic Can Be Very Expensive

Americans are often said to be addicted to plastic, and that's especially true of entrepreneurs. But convenience aside, financing with credit cards can be risky. It's easy to get in over your head—just ask Matt Jung and Chip George.

In 1995, as undergraduates at Michigan's Hope College, the pair founded Comfort Research, a Grand Rapids manufacturer of funky, beanbag-like chairs. "We had no assets," says Jung. "We were taking anything we could get." For the most part, that meant credit cards. Demand for their products soared, and with little cash on hand, the pair used credit for everything from buying equipment and raw materials to travel expenses and daily operating costs. "We tried not to look at the rates," says Jung.

Despite their efforts to make the minimum monthly payments, after six years of operation they found they owed about $17,000 at an excruciating 23 percent interest rate. "You can play the balance transfer game, and we were able to do it a couple of times," Jung says. "But it got to the point that a lot of credit card companies wouldn't let us take advantage of those lower rates anymore." Comfort Research grew rapidly, with $2 million in annual revenue by 2002. But it still took Jung three years to pay off his debts, which included several thousand dollars in interest alone.

These days, Jung—who now taps a line of bank credit when he needs funding—pays off his credit cards at the end of each month. "It's a very expensive way to borrow money," he says of credit cards. "I think they should be a last resort."

Source: Bobbie Gossage, "Charging Ahead," *Inc.,* January 2004, p. 42.

http://www.comfortresearch.com

the borrower at any one time. Under this type of agreement, the bank has no legal obligation to provide the stated capital. (A similar arrangement that *does* legally commit the bank is a **revolving credit agreement**.) The entrepreneur should arrange for a line of credit in advance of an actual need because banks extend credit only in situations about which they are well informed. Attempts to obtain a loan on a spur-of-the-moment basis are generally ineffective.

revolving credit agreement
A legal commitment by a bank to lend up to a maximum amount

Term Loans   Under certain circumstances, banks will loan money on a 5- to 10-year term. Such **term loans** are generally used to finance equipment with a useful life corresponding to the loan's term. Since the economic benefits of investing in such equipment extend beyond a single year, banks can be persuaded to lend on terms that more closely match the cash flows to be received from the investment. For example, if equipment has a useful life of seven years, it might be possible to repay the money needed to purchase the equipment over, say, five years. It would be a mistake for a firm to borrow money for a short term, such as six months, when the money is to be used to buy equipment that is expected to last for seven years. *Failure to match the loan's payment terms with the expected cash inflows from the investment is a frequent cause of financial problems for small firms.* The importance of synchronizing cash inflows with cash outflows when structuring the terms of a loan cannot be overemphasized.

term loan
Money loaned for a 5- to 10-year term, corresponding to the length of time the investment will bring in profits

chattel mortgage
A loan for which items of inventory or other movable property serve as collateral

real estate mortgage
A long-term loan with real property held as collateral

Mortgages   Mortgages, which represent a long-term source of debt capital, can be one of two types: chattel mortgages and real estate mortgages. A **chattel mortgage** is a loan for which certain items of inventory or other movable property serve as collateral. The borrower retains title to the inventory but cannot sell it without the banker's consent. A **real estate mortgage** is a loan for which real property, such as land or a building, provides the collateral. Typically, these mortgages extend over 25 or 30 years.

UNDERSTANDING A BANKER'S PERSPECTIVE   To be effective in acquiring a loan, an entrepreneur needs to understand a banker's perspective about making loans. All bankers have two fundamental concerns when they make a loan: (1) how much income the loan will provide the bank, both in interest income and in other forms of income such as fees, and (2) the likelihood that the borrower will default on the loan. A banker is not rewarded adequately to assume large amounts of risk and will, therefore, design loan agreements so as to reduce the risk to the bank.

In making a loan decision, a banker always considers the "five C's of credit": (1) the borrower's *character,* (2) the borrower's *capacity* to repay the loan, (3) the *capital* being invested in the venture by the borrower, (4) the *conditions* of the industry and economy, and (5) the *collateral* available to secure the loan. These issues are readily apparent in the six questions that Jack Griggs, a banker and long-time lender to small businesses, wants answered before he will make a loan:[5]

1. Do the purpose and amount of the loan make sense, both for the bank and for the borrower?

2. Does the borrower have strong character and reasonable ability?

3. Does the loan have a certain primary source of repayment?

4. Does the loan have a certain secondary source of repayment?

5. Can the loan be priced profitably for the customer and for the bank, and are this loan and the relationship good for both the customer and the bank?

6. Can the loan be properly structured and documented?

Obtaining a bank loan requires cultivation of a banker and personal selling. Although a banker's review of a loan request certainly includes analysis of economic and financial considerations, this analysis is best complemented by a personal relationship between the banker and the entrepreneur. This is not to say that a banker would allow personal feelings to override the facts provided by a careful loan analysis. But, after all, a banker's decision as to whether to make a loan is driven in part by the banker's confidence in the entrepreneur as a person and a professional. Intuition and subjective opinion based on past experience often play a role here.

When seeking a loan, an entrepreneur will be required to provide certain information in support of the loan request. Failure to provide such information in an effective manner will almost certainly result in rejection by the banker. Thus, the goal is not merely to present the needed information, but to make an *effective* presentation. Providing inaccurate information or not being able to justify assumptions made in forecasting financial results is sure to make the banker question the entrepreneur's business acumen.

A well-prepared written presentation—something like a shortened version of a business plan—is helpful, if not necessary. Capturing the firm's history and future in writing suggests that the entrepreneur has given thought to where the firm has been and where it is going. As part of the presentation, the banker will want to know early on the answers to the following questions:

■ How much money is needed?

■ What is the venture going to do with the money?

■ When is the money needed?

■ When and how will the money be paid back?

Furthermore, a banker will want, if at all possible, to see the following detailed financial information:

- Three years of the firm's historical financial statements, if available, including balance sheets, income statements, and cash flow statements

- The firm's pro forma financial statements (balance sheets, income statements, and cash flow statements), in which the timing and amounts of the debt repayment are included as part of the forecasts

- Personal financial statements showing the borrower's net worth (net worth = assets − debt) and estimated annual income. A banker simply will not make a loan without knowing the personal financial strength of the borrower. After all, in the world of small business, the owner *is* the business.

SELECTING A BANKER   The wide variety of services provided by banks makes choosing a bank a critical decision. For a typical small firm, the provision of checking-account facilities and the extension of short-term (and possibly long-term) loans are the two most important services of a bank. Normally, loans are negotiated with the same bank in which the firm maintains its checking account. In addition, the firm may use the bank's safe-deposit vault or its services in collecting notes or securing credit information. An experienced banker can also provide management advice, particularly in financial matters, to a new entrepreneur.

The location factor limits the range of possible choices of banks. For convenience in making deposits and conferring about loans and other matters, a bank should be located in the same general vicinity as the firm. All banks are interested in their home communities and, therefore, tend to be sympathetic to the needs of local business firms. Except in very small communities, two or more local banks are usually available, thus permitting some freedom of choice.

Banks' lending policies are not uniform. Some bankers are extremely conservative, while others are more willing to accept some risks. If a small firm's loan application is neither obviously strong nor patently weak, its prospects for approval depend heavily on the bank's approach to small business accounts. Differences in willingness to lend have been clearly established by research studies, as well as by the practical experience of many business borrowers.

NEGOTIATING THE LOAN   In negotiating a bank loan, the owner must consider the terms that will accompany the loan. Four key terms are included in all loan agreements: the interest rate, the loan maturity date, the repayment schedule, and the loan covenants.

Interest Rate   The interest rate charged by banks is usually stated in terms of either the prime rate or the LIBOR. The **prime rate** is the rate of interest charged by banks on loans to their most creditworthy customers. The **LIBOR (London InterBank Offered Rate)** is the interest rate that London-based banks charge other banks in London, which is considerably lower than the prime rate. This rate is published each day in the *Wall Street Journal*.

If a banker quotes a rate of "prime plus 3" and the prime rate is 5 percent, the interest rate for the loan will be 8 percent. If, alternatively, the bank is willing to loan at "LIBOR plus 4" when the LIBOR is at 3 percent, then the loan rate will be 7 percent. Typically, the interest will be lower if the loan rate is tied to the LIBOR than if it is based on the prime rate. The use of the LIBOR as a base rate for determining the interest rate for a business loan developed in the late 1990s, as banks began competing more aggressively for loans.

The interest rate can be a floating rate that varies over the loan's life—that is, as the prime rate or LIBOR changes, the interest rate on the loan changes—or it can be fixed for the duration of the loan. An entrepreneur known to the authors was recently given an option to pay interest on a new loan at LIBOR plus 2, in which case the interest rate would change (float) each month as the LIBOR changed, or a fixed rate of 6 percent. At the time, the LIBOR was 3 percent. So the entrepreneur had the option of paying an interest rate of 5 percent, which could increase if the LIBOR increased, or a constant rate of 6 percent for the duration of the loan.

Although a small firm should always seek a competitive interest rate, concern about the interest rate should not override consideration of the loan's maturity date, its repayment schedule, and any loan covenants.

prime rate
The interest rate charged by commercial banks on loans to their most creditworthy customers

LIBOR (London InterBank Offered Rate)
The interest rate charged by London banks on loans to other London banks

Living the Dream   entrepreneurial challenges

© Don Farrall/Photodisc/Getty Images

Financing with Wiggle Room

In June 2005, entrepreneur Megan Decker received a business offer that was just too good to pass up: the chance to purchase her much larger competitor. Financing, however, could be tricky for the company, a supplier of traffic control equipment for work-zone projects. Because her business was so seasonal, cash flow didn't follow the same steady pattern that most finance payments must. Decker therefore hoped for some flexibility in the financing arrangements for the multimillion-dollar deal.

"I need a lot of operating capital in the spring to get off the ground because, at that point, I'm getting employees back from being laid off for the winter months. I have pretty high startup costs with my labor and equipment purchases to perform these jobs in the summer," explains Decker, 28, president and founder of $9.5-million Mega Rentals, Inc. in Madison, Wisconsin.

While her spring startup costs are high, the bulk of her payments don't usually trickle in until late fall. Decker thought it was a lot to ask of a lender to structure loan payments around that cash-flow schedule. Much to her surprise, however, locally based First Business Bank agreed to tailor a loan payback schedule that closely matched her company's seasonal cash-flow cycle. "They addressed the fact that I have seasonality [in] my cash receipts by tailoring my revolving loan so that I'm paying the larger principal payments in November, which is when I will actually have the money," Decker explains.

"It's a tremendous advantage for me as far as my cash flow is concerned," she adds. "They took a long look at my business and understood what I was attempting to do with this acquisition, and why it made sense for my business to pursue the purchase of this other company."

Though Decker insists she would have found a way to fund the acquisition even without the flexible financing, she admits it would have required a stressful balancing act. "Instead of worrying about the things I need to do on a day-to-day basis to be successful," she says, "I would have been much more concerned with being able to work around an already established structure of financing that I didn't have as much input in."

Source: Crystal Detamore-Rodman, "Financing with Wiggle Room," *Entrepreneur,* January 2006, pp. 55–58.

http://www.megarentals.com

Loan Maturity Date   As already noted, a loan's term should coincide with the use of the money—short-term needs require short-term financing, while long-term needs demand long-term financing. For example, since a line of credit is intended to help a firm with only its short-term needs, it is generally limited to one year. Some banks require that a firm "clean up" a line of credit one month each year. Because such a loan can be outstanding for only 11 months, the borrower can use the money to finance seasonal needs but cannot use it to provide permanent increases in working capital, such as accounts receivable and inventories.

Repayment Schedule   With a term loan, the loan is set to be repaid over 5 to 10 years, depending on the type of assets used for collateral. However, the banker may have the option of imposing a **balloon payment**—a very large payment that the borrower is required to make at a specified point about halfway through the term over which the payments were calculated, repaying the rest of the loan in full. For instance, assume that you borrow $50,000 at an interest rate of 6 percent. If the loan were to be repaid in equal monthly payments over seven years, the amount of each payment would be $730.[6] However, if the lender has the option of imposing a balloon payment whereby the rest of the loan comes due in full in three years rather than seven years, the lender can reassess the quality of the loan and decide whether to collect the balance or to renew the loan.

Loan Covenants   In addition to setting the interest rate and specifying when and how the loan is to be repaid, a bank normally imposes other restrictions, such as loan covenants, on the borrower. **Loan covenants** require certain activities (positive covenants) and limit other activities (negative covenants) of the borrower to increase the chance that the borrower will be able to repay the loan. Some types of loan covenants a borrower might encounter include the following:

1. A bank will usually require that the business provide financial statements on a monthly basis or, at the very least, quarterly.

2. As a way to restrict a firm's management from siphoning cash out of the business, the bank may limit managers' salaries. It also may prohibit any personal loans from the business to the owners.

3. A bank may put limits on various financial ratios to make certain that a firm can handle its loan payments. For example, to ensure sufficient liquidity, the bank may require that the firm's current assets be at least twice its current liabilities (that is, current assets ÷ current liabilities must be equal to or greater than 2). Or the bank might limit the amount of debt the firm can borrow in the future, as measured by the ratio of total debt to the firm's total assets (total debt ÷ total assets).[7]

4. The borrower will normally be required to personally guarantee the firm's loan. A banker wants the right to use both the firm's assets and the owner's personal assets as collateral. If a business is structured as a corporation, the owner and the corporation are separate legal entities and the owner can escape personal liability for the firm's debts—that is, the owner has **limited liability**. However, most banks are not willing to lend money to any small business without the owner's personal guarantee as well. That's what Stephen Satterwhite, founder of Entelligence, a provider of e-business solutions, discovered when he sought financing for the firm. A banker offered to extend a $150,000 line of credit but required that the loan be secured not only by the company's assets but also by the personal assets of Satterwhite and those of an Entelligence investor and board member.[8]

When Bill Bailey, owner of Cherokee Communications, a pay-phone company located in Jacksonville, Texas, borrowed money, the loan was made on certain conditions— conditions that were intended to protect the banker. If Cherokee violated these loan covenants, the loan would become due immediately—or Bailey would have to get the banker's blessing to continue operations without repaying the loan at the time. Some of the loan covenants were as follows:[9]

■ Bailey, as the owner, was required to personally guarantee the loan.

■ The firm had to provide monthly financial statements to the bank within 30 days of the month's end.

■ There were to be no dividend payments to the owners.

■ Bailey could not change the fundamental nature of the business.

■ Without prior agreement, there could be no additional liens on equipment by other lenders.

■ Debt could not exceed a specified amount, nor could it be greater than a specified percentage of the firm's total assets.

balloon payment
A very large payment that the borrower may be required to make at a specified point about halfway through the term over which the payments were calculated, repaying the rest of the loan in full

loan covenants
Bank-imposed restrictions on a borrower that enhance the chances of timely repayment

limited liability
The restriction of an owner's legal financial responsibilities to the amount invested in the business

- Without prior approval, no assets could be sold and no acquisitions or mergers with other firms could take place.

- The proceeds of the loan could not be used for any other purpose than that designated by the bank.

- There was a limit on the amount of capital expenditures the firm could make.

- Executive compensation could not exceed a specified amount.

- The firm's net worth could not fall below a specified amount.

It is imperative that you pay close attention to the loan covenants being imposed by a banker. Ask for a list of the covenants before the closing date, and make certain that you can live with the terms. If you have an existing company, determine whether you could have complied with the covenants, especially key ratios, if the loan had been in place during the recent past. Then, if necessary, negotiate with your banker and suggest more realistic covenants. Bankers will negotiate, although they may sometimes try to convince you otherwise.

Even firms with straightforward financing needs should bear in mind that a variety of factors determine the cost of a loan, not just the interest rates and the fees a lender charges for reviewing and preparing documents.

Business Suppliers and Asset-Based Lenders

Companies that have business dealings with a new firm are possible sources of funds for financing inventories and equipment. Both wholesalers and equipment manufacturers/suppliers can provide trade credit (accounts payable) or equipment loans and leases.

ACCOUNTS PAYABLE (TRADE CREDIT)   Credit extended by suppliers is very important to a startup. In fact, trade (or mercantile) credit is the source of short-term funds most widely used by small firms. **Accounts payable (trade credit)** are of short duration—30 days is the customary credit period. Most commonly, this type of credit involves an unsecured, open-book account. The supplier (seller) sends merchandise to the purchasing firm; the buyer then sets up an account payable for the amount of the purchase.

The amount of trade credit available to a new company depends on the type of business and the supplier's confidence in the firm. For example, wholesale distributors of sunglasses—a very seasonal product line—often provide trade credit to retailers by granting extended payment terms on sales made at the start of a season. The sunglass retailers, in turn, sell to their customers during the season and make the bulk of their payments to the wholesalers after they have sold and collected the cash for the sunglasses. Thus, the retailer obtains cash from sales before paying the supplier. More often, however, a firm has to pay its suppliers prior to receiving cash from its customers. In fact, this can be a serious problem for many small firms, particularly those that sell to large companies. (This issue will be addressed in a discussion of asset management in Chapter 22.)

EQUIPMENT LOANS AND LEASES   Some small businesses, such as restaurants, use equipment that is purchased on an installment basis through an **equipment loan**. A down payment of 25 to 35 percent is usually required, and the contract period normally runs from three to five years. The equipment manufacturer or supplier typically extends credit on the basis of a conditional sales contract (or mortgage) on the equipment. During the loan period, the equipment cannot serve as collateral for another loan.

Instead of borrowing money from suppliers to purchase equipment, an increasing number of small businesses are beginning to lease equipment, especially computers, photocopiers, and fax machines. Leases typically run for 36 to 60 months and cover 100 percent of the cost of the asset being leased, with a fixed rate of interest included in the lease payments. However, manufacturers of computers and industrial machinery, working hand in hand with banks or financing companies, are generally receptive to tailoring lease packages to the particular needs of customers.

It has been estimated that 80 percent of all firms lease some or all of their business equipment. Three reasons are commonly given for the increasing popularity of leasing: (1) the firm's cash remains free for other purposes, (2) available lines of credit (a form of

---

5 Explain how business relationships can be used to finance a small firm.

accounts payable (trade credit)
Financing provided by a supplier of inventory to a given company

equipment loan
An installment loan from a seller of machinery used by a business

bank loan discussed earlier in this chapter) can be used for other purposes, and (3) leasing provides a hedge against equipment obsolescence.

While leasing is certainly an option to be considered for financing the acquisition of needed equipment, an entrepreneur should not simply assume that leasing is always the right decision. A business owner can make a good choice only after carefully comparing the interest charged on a loan to the implied interest cost of a lease, calculating the tax consequences of leasing versus borrowing, and examining the significance of the obsolescence factor. Also, the owner must be careful about contracting for so much equipment that it becomes difficult to meet installment or lease payments.

ASSET-BASED LENDING   As its name implies, an **asset-based loan** is a line of credit secured primarily by assets, such as receivables, inventory, or both. The lender cushions its risk by advancing only a percentage of the value of a firm's assets—generally, 65 to 85 percent against receivables and up to 55 percent against inventory. Also, assets such as equipment (if not leased) and real estate can be used as collateral for an asset-based loan. Asset-based lending is a viable option for young, growing businesses caught in a cash flow bind.

Of the several categories of asset-based lending, the most frequently used is factoring. **Factoring** is an option that makes cash available to a business before accounts receivable payments are received from customers. Under this option, a factor (an entity often owned by a bank holding company) purchases the accounts receivable, advancing to the business from 70 to 90 percent of the amount of an invoice. The factor, however, has the option of refusing to advance cash on any invoice considered questionable. The factor charges a servicing fee, usually 2 percent of the value of the receivables, and an interest charge on the money advanced prior to collection of the receivables. The interest charge may range from 2 to 3 percent above the prime rate.

asset-based loan
A line of credit secured by working-capital assets

factoring
Obtaining cash by selling accounts receivable to another firm

Private Equity Investors

Over the past decade, private equity markets have been the fastest growing source of financing for entrepreneurial ventures that have potential for becoming significant businesses. For an entrepreneur, these sources fall into two categories: business angels and venture capitalists.

6 Describe the two types of private equity investors that offer financing to small firms.

BUSINESS ANGELS   Business angels are private individuals who invest in early-stage companies.[10] They are the oldest and largest source of early-stage equity capital for entrepreneurs. The term *angel* originated in the early 1900s, referring to investors on Broadway who made risky investments to support theatrical productions.[11] This type of financing has come to be known as **informal venture capital** because no established marketplace exists in which business angels regularly invest.

The majority of these individuals are self-made millionaires who have substantial business and entrepreneurial experience. A few of the better-recognized business angels are Ken Oshman, founder of Rolm Corporation; Paul Allen, co-founder of Microsoft Corporation; and Warren Musser, founder of Safeguard Scientifics. These three individuals alone have helped finance a large group of new companies. But even more important are the untold millions of private investors across the country who, without fanfare, invest billions in new companies each year. In 2004, for example, there were several million angels who invested a total of $22.5 billion.[12]

Business angels generally make investments that are relatively small—over 80 percent of business angels invest in startup firms with fewer than 20 employees. They invest locally, usually no more than 50 miles from their homes. Some limit their investments to industries in which they have had experience, while others invest in a wide variety of business sectors. For instance, Terry Stevens, a successful entrepreneur turned business angel, has invested in restaurants, a sporting goods firm, a title company, and a specialty advertising firm.

Along with providing needed money, private investors frequently contribute know-how to new businesses. Because many of these individuals invest only in the types of businesses in which they have had experience, they can be very demanding. Also, they base their investment decision primarily on the potential risk and return of the investment, rather than on their personal relationship with the entrepreneur, unlike friends

business angels
Private individuals who invest in others' entrepreneurial ventures

informal venture capital
Funds provided by wealthy private individuals (business angels) to high-risk ventures

and family. Thus, the entrepreneur must be careful in structuring the terms of any such investors' involvement.

The traditional way to find informal investors is through contacts with business associates, accountants, and lawyers. Other entrepreneurs are also a primary source of help in identifying prospective investors. In addition, there are now a large number of formal angel networks and angel alliances. Many of these groups hold "speed-pitching" lunches, which combine aspects of a power lunch and a speed-dating get-together.[13] Central Texas Angel Network is an example of such a group; it is described on its website as follows:

The Central Texas Angel Network (CTAN) is a not-for-profit corporation dedicated to providing quality early-stage investment opportunities for accredited Central Texas angel investors, and to assisting, educating and connecting early stage growth companies in Central Texas with information and advisors for the purpose of raising money and assisting in their growth.... CTAN will measure its success by the quality of deal flow, amount of dollars invested, number of companies funded and, of course, ROI [return on investment] for members.[14]

Any entrepreneur who is serious about raising money from a business angel should first go to the website for the Angel Capital Association at http://www.angelcapitalassociation.org.

Listening to the sage advice of Brock Blake and Tad Bryant, two venture capitalists, can also save you some heartache when trying to raise angel money. Consider their suggestions:[15]

- Find something you're passionate about.

- Sell yourself as an entrepreneur. Angel investors are investing in you and the team, rather than just the idea.

- Prove your concept or ideas through sales. Entrepreneurs often have great ideas, but they have no paying customers. Most investors like to see that ideas are selling, which reduces the risk of an angel investment.

- Pitch to everyone. Get out of the office and constantly sell your idea.

- Assemble a strong team around your business idea.

- Fully develop a business plan, with an appealing executive summary of one to two pages.

- Develop a strong and convincing 20-minute PowerPoint presentation that can be used with venture capitalists, angel investors, and investment bankers.

- Develop a defensible competitive advantage over the competition.

- Develop a three- to five-year financial projection, a valuation of the firm, and the return to investors.

formal venture capitalists
Individuals who form limited partnerships for the purpose of raising venture capital from large institutional investors

VENTURE CAPITAL FIRMS In addition to business angels who provide *informal* venture capital, small businesses also may seek out **formal venture capitalists**, groups of individuals who form limited partnerships for the purpose of raising capital from large institutional investors, such as pension plans and university endowments. Within the group, a venture capitalist serves as the general partner, with other investors constituting the limited partners. As limited partners, such investors have the benefit of limited liability.

The venture capitalist raises a predetermined amount of money, called a *fund*. Once the money has been committed by the investors, the venture capitalist screens and evaluates investment opportunities in high-potential startups and existing firms. For example, the Sevin Rosen Funds in Dallas, Texas, raised $600 million for the Sevin Rosen Fund VIII. The money was then used to invest in a portfolio of companies.

For the investment, the venture capitalist receives the right to own a percentage of the entrepreneur's business. Reaching agreement on the exact percentage of ownership often involves considerable negotiation. The primary issues are the firm's expected profits in future years and the venture capitalist's required rate of return. Once an investment has been made, the venture capitalist carefully monitors the company, usually through a representative who serves on the firm's board.

Living the Dream   entrepreneurial challenges

Raising Angel Money Is Seldom Easy

© Grace Restaurant. Courtesy of JS² Communications

Entrepreneurs say wooing prospective angels can require a lot of hard work, time, and costs—with no guarantees. Neal Fraser, chef and co-owner of Grace restaurant in Los Angeles, met with some of his early investor prospects at the then-vacant space where his restaurant now operates. In addition to making restaurant visits, he spent $1,500 to host several dinner parties for potential investors. When none of them yielded start-up funds, he got discouraged.

"When I started, I didn't think I could pull it off. The economy was really flat, and getting people to invest in the restaurant was really hard," says Fraser, 36. "It was like asking people to invest in building igloos in the Caribbean."

But he was persistent. When it came to courting investors, he adopted an "any means necessary" policy—any means short of being rude. Shortly after 9/11, Fraser sent copies of his business plan to 300 friends and restaurateurs, offering them shares in the restaurant for $25,000. Some agreed to make smaller investments, which he accepted. Others said they were interested but didn't follow through. Of some dawdlers, Fraser asked a one-third down payment to determine their actual level of interest. He kept others abreast of the fund-raising developments through a stream of e-mails and meetings, letting them know the final deadline for getting on board was running short.

Ultimately, he raised $950,000 from three partners and 26 limited investors over three years. And when the restaurant doors opened to the public in 2003, not every angel who had promised money was yet on board. A few stragglers were writing checks while the wine was being poured. Ultimately, celebrities, restaurateurs, friends, family, and others outside the food and dining industry were among the early investors for the restaurant, which now brings in about $2.5 million in annual revenue. Fraser declines to release information about the investors' profits.

Source: Aja Carmichael, "The Money Game; In Search of an Angel," *Wall Street Journal,* January 30, 2006, p. R4.

http://www.gracerestaurant.com

Most often, investments by venture capitalists take the form of convertible debt or convertible preferred stock. In this way, venture capitalists ensure themselves senior claim over the owners and other equity investors in the event the firm is liquidated, but they can convert to stock and participate in the increased value of the business if it is successful. These investors generally try to limit the length of their investment to between 5 and 7 years, though it is frequently closer to 10 years before they are able to cash out.

Although venture capital as a source of financing receives significant coverage in the business media, *few small companies, especially startups, ever receive this kind of funding.* No more than 1 or 2 percent of the business plans received by any venture capitalist are eventually funded—not exactly an encouraging statistic. Failure to receive funding from a venture capitalist, however, does not indicate that the venture lacks potential. Often, the venture is simply not a good fit for the investor. So, before trying to compete for venture capital financing, an entrepreneur should assess whether the firm and the management team are a good fit for a particular investor.

The Government

Several government programs provide financing to small businesses. Over the past decade, federal and state governments have allocated increasing, but still limited, amounts of money to financing new businesses. Local governments have likewise increased their involvement in providing financial support to startups in their areas. Though funds are available, they are not always easy to acquire. Time and patience on the part of the entrepreneur are required. Let's take a look at some of the more familiar government loan programs offered by various agencies.

THE SMALL BUSINESS ADMINISTRATION   The federal government has a long history of helping new businesses get started, primarily through the programs and agencies of the Small Business Administration (SBA). For the most part, the SBA does not loan money, but rather serves as a guarantor of loans made by financial institutions. The five primary SBA programs are the 7(a) Loan Guaranty Program, the Certified Development Company (CDC) 504 Loan Program, the 7(m) Microloan Program, small business investment companies (SBICs), and the Small Business Innovative Research (SBIR) Program.

7(a) Loan Guaranty Program
Loan program that helps small companies obtain financing through a guaranty provided by the SBA

The 7(a) Loan Guaranty Program   The **7(a) Loan Guaranty Program** serves as the SBA's primary business loan program to help qualified small businesses obtain financing when they might not be eligible for business loans through normal lending channels. Guaranty loans are made by private lenders, usually commercial banks, and may be for as much as $750,000. The SBA guarantees 90 percent of loans not exceeding $155,000. For loans exceeding $155,000, the guaranty percentage is 85 percent. To obtain a guaranty loan, a small business must submit a loan application to a lender, such as a bank. After an initial review, the lender forwards the application to the SBA. Once the loan has been approved by the SBA, the lender disburses the funds. The loan proceeds can be used for working capital, machinery and equipment, furniture and fixtures, land and building, leasehold improvements, and debt refinancing (under special conditions). Loan maturity is up to 10 years for working capital and generally up to 25 years for fixed assets.

Certified Development Company (CDC) 504 Loan Program
SBA loan program that provides long-term financing for small businesses to acquire real estate or machinery and equipment

The Certified Development Company (CDC) 504 Loan Program   The **Certified Development Company (CDC) 504 Loan Program** provides long-term, fixed-rate financing to small businesses to acquire real estate or machinery and equipment for expansion or modernization. The lender in this instance is a certified development company, which is financed by the SBA. The borrower must provide 10 percent of the cost of the property, with the remaining amount coming from a bank and a certified development company funded by the SBA.

7(m) Microloan Program
SBA loan program that provides short-term loans of up to $35,000 to small businesses and not-for-profit child-care centers

The 7(m) Microloan Program   The **7(m) Microloan Program** grants short-term loans of up to $35,000 to small businesses and not-for-profit child-care centers for working capital or the purchase of inventory, supplies, furniture, fixtures, and machinery and equipment. The SBA makes or guarantees a loan to an intermediary, which in turn makes the microloan to the applicant. As an added benefit, the lender provides business training and support programs to its microloan borrowers.

small business investment companies (SBICs)
Privately owned banks, regulated by the Small Business Administration, that provide long-term loans and/or equity capital to small businesses

Small Business Investment Companies   **Small business investment companies** (SBICs) are privately owned banks that provide long-term loans and/or equity capital to small businesses. SBICs are licensed and regulated by the SBA, from which they frequently obtain a substantial part of their capital at attractive rates of interest. SBICs invest in businesses with fewer than 500 employees, a net worth of no more than $18 million, and after-tax income not exceeding $6 million during the two most recent years.

Small Business Innovative Research (SBIR) program
A government program that helps to finance companies that plan to transform laboratory research into marketable products

The Small Business Innovative Research (SBIR) Program   The **Small Business Innovative Research (SBIR) program** helps finance small firms that plan to transform laboratory research into marketable products. Eligibility for the program is based less on the potential profitability of a venture than on the likelihood that the firm will provide a product of interest to a particular federal agency.

STATE AND LOCAL GOVERNMENT ASSISTANCE　　State and local governments have become more active in financing new businesses. The nature of the financing varies, but each program is generally geared to augment other sources of funding. Several examples of such programs follow:

1. The city government of Des Moines, Iowa, established the Golden Circle Loan Guarantee Fund to guarantee bank loans of up to $250,000 to small companies.

2. Rhode Island offers financing programs tied to job growth.

3. The New Jersey Economic Development Authority makes loans to business owners at the U.S. Treasury rate, significantly lower than interest rates typically charged at banks.

4. The Colorado Housing and Finance Authority makes loans for equipment and real estate with down payments as low as 15 percent and up to 20 years to repay the loan.

Most of these loans are made in conjunction with a bank, which enables the bank to take on riskier loans for entrepreneurs who might not qualify for traditional financing. "And some loans have a lower down payment requirement," explains Donna Holmes, director of the Penn State Small Business Development Center in University Park. "The bank may do 50 percent, the state program another 40 percent, and the borrower only has to come up with 10 percent; with a straight bank loan, the bank might be looking for 20 percent or 25 percent."[16]

While such government programs may be attractive to an entrepreneur, they are frequently designed to enhance specific industries or to facilitate certain community goals. Consequently, you need to determine that a program is in sync with your specific business objectives.

COMMUNITY-BASED FINANCIAL INSTITUTIONS　　Community-based financial institutions are lenders that serve low-income communities and receive funds from federal, state, and private sources. They are increasingly becoming a source of financing for small companies that otherwise would have little or no access to startup funding. Typically, community-based lenders provide capital to businesses that are unable to attract outside investors but do have the potential to make modest profits, serve the community, and create jobs. An example of a community-based financial institution is the Delaware Valley Reinvestment Fund, which provides financing for small companies in Philadelphia's inner-city area.

community-based financial institution
A lender that uses funds from federal, state, and private sources to provide financing to small businesses in low-income communities

Where Else to Look

The sources of financing that have been described thus far represent the primary avenues for obtaining money for small firms. The remaining sources are generally of less importance but should not be ignored by an entrepreneur in search of financing.

{ 8 Explain when large companies and public stock offerings can be sources of financing.

LARGE CORPORATIONS　　Large corporations at times make funds available for investment in smaller firms when it is in their self-interest to maintain a close relationship with such a firm. Larger firms are now becoming even more involved in providing financing and technical assistance to smaller businesses. For instance, some large high-tech firms prefer to invest in smaller firms that are conducting research of interest, rather than conduct the research themselves.

Coca-Cola is a good example of a large corporation that invests in smaller firms. The purpose of the investments is to develop technologies that would benefit operations such as bottling and distribution. Coca-Cola also hopes to profit when the companies go public. The program—involving a wholly owned subsidiary called Fizzion—is part of a push to make Coca-Cola more innovative. By involving employees in startups, the company can give managers "a real sense for what it's like to move against deadlines of time and money," says Fizzion CEO Chris Lowe. Although large companies also face those issues, they're "not of the same character or ilk" as in a startup, Lowe says.[17]

STOCK SALES　　Another way to obtain capital is by selling stock to outside individual investors through either private placement or public sale. Finding outside stockholders can be difficult when a new firm is not known and has no ready market for its securities, however. In most cases, a business must have a history of profitability before its stock can be sold successfully.

Whether it is best to raise outside equity financing depends on the firm's long-range prospects. If there is opportunity for substantial expansion on a continuing basis and if other sources are inadequate, the owner may logically decide to bring in other owners. Owning part of a larger business may be more profitable than owning all of a smaller business.

private placement
The sale of a firm's capital stock to selected individuals

Private Placement   One way to sell common stock is through private placement, in which the firm's stock is sold to selected individuals—usually the firm's employees, the owner's acquaintances, members of the local community, customers, and suppliers. When a stock sale is restricted to private placement, an entrepreneur can avoid many of the demanding requirements of the securities laws.

initial public offering (IPO)
The issuance of stock that is to be traded in public financial markets

Public Sale   When small firms—typically, *larger* small firms—make their stock available to the general public, this is called going public, or making an initial public offering (IPO). The reason often cited for a public sale is the need for additional working capital.

In undertaking a public sale of its stock, a small firm subjects itself to greater governmental regulation, which escalated dramatically following the rash of corporate scandals in publicly owned companies such as Enron, Tyco, and WorldCom. In response to corporate malfeasance in recent years, the U.S. Congress passed legislation, including the Sarbanes-Oxley Act, to monitor public companies more carefully. This has resulted in a significant increase in the cost of being a publicly traded company—especially for small firms. Also, publicly traded firms are required to report their financial results quarterly in 10Q reports and annually in 10K reports to the Securities and Exchange Commission (SEC). The SEC carefully scrutinizes these reports before they can be made available to the public. At times, the SEC requirements can be very burdensome.

Common stock may also be sold to underwriters, which guarantee the sale of securities. Compensation and fees paid to underwriters typically make the sale of securities in this manner expensive. Fees frequently range from 20 to 25 percent of the value of the total stock issue—or even higher. The reason for the high costs is, of course, the elements of uncertainty and risk associated with public offerings of the stock of small, relatively unknown firms.

We have now completed our discussion of what an entrepreneur needs to understand when seeking financing for a company, in terms of both how to think about financing a business (Chapter 10) and the different sources of financing typically used by small firms (Chapter 11). We hope that our detailed explanations will help you avoid mistakes commonly made by entrepreneurs when trying to get financing to grow a business.

Looking BACK

1 Describe how the nature of a firm affects its financing sources.

- There are four basic factors that determine how a firm is financed: (1) the firm's economic potential, (2) the size and maturity of the company, (3) the nature of the firm's assets, and (4) the personal preference of the owners as they consider the tradeoffs between debt and equity.

- An entrepreneurial firm that has high growth potential has many more possible sources of financing

than does a firm that provides a good lifestyle for the owner but little in the way of attractive returns to investors.

- The size and maturity of a company have a direct bearing on the types of financing that are available.

- Tangible assets serve as great collateral when a business is requesting a bank loan; intangible assets have little value as collateral.

2 Evaluate the choice between debt financing and equity financing.

- Choosing between debt and equity financing involves tradeoffs with regard to potential profitability, financial risk, and voting control.

- Borrowing money rather than issuing common stock (ownership equity) creates the potential for higher rates of return to the owners and allows the owners to retain voting control of the company, but it also exposes the owners to greater financial risk.

- Issuing common stock rather than borrowing money results in lower potential rates of return to the owners and the loss of some voting control, but it does reduce their financial risk.

3 Identify the typical sources of financing used at the outset of a new venture.

- The aspiring entrepreneur basically has three sources of early financing: (1) personal savings, (2) friends and family, and (3) credit cards.

- Personal savings is the primary source of equity financing used in starting a new business; a banker or other lender is unlikely to loan a venture money if the entrepreneur does not have his or her own money at risk.

- Loans from friends and family may be the only available source of financing and are often easy and fast to obtain, though such borrowing can place the entrepreneur's most important personal relationships in jeopardy.

- Credit card financing provides easily accessible financing, but with high interest costs that may become overwhelming at times.

- Only if these sources are inadequate will the entrepreneur turn to more formal channels of financing, such as banks and outside investors.

4 Discuss the basic process for acquiring and structuring a bank loan.

- Bankers primarily make business loans in one of three forms: lines of credit, term loans, and mortgages.

- In making a loan decision, a banker always considers the "five C's of credit": (1) the borrower's *character,* (2) the borrower's *capacity* to repay the loan, (3) the *capital* being invested in the venture by the borrower, (4) the *conditions* of the industry and economy, and (5) the *collateral* available to secure the loan.

- Obtaining a bank loan requires cultivating a relationship with a banker and personal selling, including a presentation that addresses (1) how much money is needed, (2) what the venture is going to do with the money, (3) when the money is needed, and (4) when and how the money will be paid back.

- Other detailed financial information might be requested, including three years of the firm's historical financial statements, the firm's pro forma financial statements, and personal financial statements showing the borrower's net worth and estimated annual income.

- An entrepreneur should carefully evaluate available banks before choosing one, basing the decision on factors such as the bank's location, the extent of services provided, and the bank's lending policies.

- In negotiating a bank loan, the owner must consider the accompanying terms, which typically include the interest rate, the loan maturity date, the repayment schedule, and the loan covenants.

5 Explain how business relationships can be used to finance a small firm.

- Business suppliers can offer trade credit (accounts payable), which is the source of short-term funds most widely used by small firms.

- Suppliers also offer equipment loans and leases, which allow small businesses to use equipment purchased on an installment basis.

- Asset-based lending is financing secured by working-capital assets, such as accounts receivable and inventory.

6 Describe the two types of private equity investors that offer financing to small firms.

- Business angels are private individuals, generally having moderate to significant business experience, who invest in others' entrepreneurial ventures.

- Formal venture capitalists are groups of individuals who form limited partnerships for the purpose of raising capital from large institutional investors, such as pension plans and university endowments.

7 Distinguish among the different government loan programs available to small companies.

- The federal government helps new businesses get started through the programs and agencies of the Small Business Administration (SBA), which include the 7(a) Loan Guaranty Program, the Certified Development Company (CDC) 504 Loan Program, the 7(m) Microloan Program, small business investment companies (SBICs), and the Small Business Innovative Research (SBIR) Program.

- State and local governments finance new businesses in varying manners, though programs are generally geared to augmenting other sources of funding.

- Community-based financial institutions are lenders that use funds from federal, state, and private sources to serve low-income communities and small companies that otherwise would have little or no access to startup funding.

8 Explain when large companies and public stock offerings can be sources of financing.

- Large companies may finance smaller businesses when it is in their self-interest to have a close relationship with the smaller company.
- Stock sales, in the form of either private placements or public sales, may provide a few high-potential ventures with equity capital.

Key TERMS

return on assets, p. 302

return on equity, p. 303

line of credit, p. 308

revolving credit agreement, p. 309

term loan, p. 309

chattel mortgage, p. 310

real estate mortgage, p. 310

prime rate, p. 311

LIBOR (London InterBank Offered Rate), p. 311

balloon payment, p. 313

loan covenants, p. 313

limited liability, p. 313

accounts payable (trade credit), p. 314

equipment loan, p. 314

asset-based loan, p. 315

factoring, p. 315

business angels, p. 315

informal venture capital, p. 315

formal venture capitalists, p. 316

7(a) Loan Guaranty Program, p. 318

Certified Development Company (CDC) 504 Loan Program, p. 318

7(m) Microloan Program, p. 318

small business investment companies (SBICs), p. 318

Small Business Innovative Research (SBIR) Program, p. 318

community-based financial institution, p. 319

private placement, p. 320

initial public offering (IPO), p. 320

Discussion QUESTIONS

1. How does the nature of a business affect its sources of financing?

2. How is debt different from equity?

3. Explain the three tradeoffs that guide the choice between debt financing and equity financing.

4. Assume that you are starting a business for the first time. What do you believe are the greatest personal obstacles to obtaining funds for the new venture? Why?

5. If you were starting a new business, where would you start looking for capital?

6. Explain how trade credit and equipment loans can provide initial capital funding.

7. a. Describe the different types of loans made by a commercial bank.

   b. What does a banker need to know in order to decide whether to make a loan?

8. Distinguish between informal venture capital and formal venture capital.

9. In what ways does the federal government help with initial financing for small businesses?

10. What advice would you give an entrepreneur who was trying to finance a startup?

You Make the CALL

SITUATION 1

David Bernstein needs help financing his Lodi, New Jersey–based Access Direct Inc., a six-year-old $3.5 million company. "We're ready to get to the next level," says Bernstein, "but we're not sure which way to go." Access Direct spruces up and then sells used computer equipment for corporations; it is looking for up to $2 million in order to expand. "Venture capitalists, individual investors, or banks," says Bernstein, who owns the company with four partners, "we've thought about them all."

Question 1 What is your impression of Bernstein's perspective on raising capital to "get to the next level"?

Question 2 What advice would you offer Bernstein as to both appropriate and inappropriate sources of financing in his situation?

SITUATION 2

Carter Dalton is well on his way to starting a new venture—Max, Inc. He has projected a need for $350,000 in initial capital. He plans to invest $150,000 himself and either borrow the additional $200,000 or find a partner who will buy stock in the company. If Dalton borrows the money, the interest rate will be 6 percent. If, on the other hand, another equity investor is found, he expects to have to give up 60 percent of the company's stock. Dalton has forecasted earnings of about 16 percent in operating income on the firm's total assets.

Question 1 Compare the two financing options in terms of projected return on the owner's equity investment. Ignore any effect from income taxes.

Question 2 What if Dalton is wrong and the company earns only 4 percent in operating income on total assets?

Question 3 What should Dalton consider in choosing a source of financing?

SITUATION 3

Steve Mack is the president of Griggs Products, a metal stamper based in San Antonio, Texas. Mack has a long-term relationship with his banker. But recently his firm ran into financial difficulty, and the bank is demanding that Mack personally guarantee 100 percent of the company's loans. Mack would prefer not to do so, but isn't sure that he has a choice.

Question 1 Should Mack be surprised by the bank's demand for a personal guarantee? Why or why not?

Question 2 What would you advise Mack to do?

Experiential EXERCISES

1. Interview a local small business owner to determine how funds were obtained to start the business. Be sure you phrase questions so that they are not overly personal, and do not ask for specific dollar amounts. Write a brief report on your findings.

2. Interview a local banker about lending policies for small business loans. Ask the banker to comment on the importance of a business plan to the bank's decision to loan money to a small business. Write a brief report on your findings.

3. Review recent issues of *Entrepreneur* or *Inc.*, and report to the class on the financing arrangements of firms featured in these magazines.

4. Interview a stockbroker or investment analyst on his or her views regarding the sale of common stock by a small business. Write a brief report on your findings.

Exploring the WEB

1. As noted in this chapter, several government loan programs provide financing to small businesses. To find out more about the loan programs of the Small Business Administration, one of the more familiar sources of government loans, go to the SBA website at **http://www.sba.gov**. Choose "Small Business Planner," then "Finance Start-Up." Scroll down to find "Loan and Funding Information."

   a. What standard loan programs does the SBA offer?

   b. Search the SBA site further to determine what special-purpose loans the SBA offers and what each loan's purpose is.

2. Go to the CCH's Business Owner's Toolkit at **http://www.toolkit.com/small_business_guide/ sbg.aspx?nid=P10_2000**, and find content related to the basics of debt versus equity financing. What are the most common options for small business equity financing?

3. Although initial public offerings (IPOs) may not be in the cards for many small businesses, some larger small businesses may make their stock available to the general public. To learn more about IPO's, visit the following website: **http:// www.entrepreneur.com/growyourbusiness/ howtoguides/article81394.html**. Explain the basic steps in a typical timetable for an initial public offering, as described on this website.

Video Case 11

My Own Money (p. 642)
This case discusses the types of funding used by many entrepreneurs when starting a business; it specifically looks at the use of personal funding and borrowed funding and their use in bootstrap financing.

Alternative Cases for Chapter 11:
Case 4, Mo's Chowder, p. 626

Case 8, Silver Zephyr Restaurant, p. 635

Case 23, Understanding Financial Statements, Part 2, p. 667

The Business Plan

Laying the Foundation

As part of laying the foundation for your own business plan, respond to the following questions regarding the financing of your venture:

1. What is the total financing required to start the business?
2. How much money do you plan to invest in the venture? What is the source of this money?
3. Will you need financing beyond what you personally plan to invest?
4. If additional financing is needed for the startup, how will you raise it? How will the financing be structured—debt or equity? What will the terms be for the investors?
5. According to your pro forma financial statements, will there be a need for additional financing within the first five years of the firm's life? If so, where will it come from?
6. How and when will you arrange for investors to cash out of their investment?

## chapter 12

The Harvest Plan

In the **SPOTLIGHT**

Letting Go Is Never Easy

When Jay Butera told his accountant that he wanted to sell his business, the accountant was not surprised.

"You can sell," my accountant told me, "but I doubt you can walk away for long. Guys like you can't stop. You sell everything, lie on the beach for a year, then get so bored you jump right back in with another business. I see it all the time."

I didn't believe a word of it. I was different. Boredom a problem? Boredom sounded wonderful! "Trust me," I told him. "I can quit anytime."

"Spoken like a true addict," he said.

In the summer of 2003, I sold the company to a group of individual investors and signed papers that would, I thought, change my life. I had no regrets when I walked away. For the first time in decades I felt peace.

Just to be certain that I was really free, after the deal closed I drove 100 miles to the beach, walked to the end of the jetty, and hurled my cell phone into the Atlantic Ocean with a vengeance that twisted my shoulder. It was glorious. I made plans to stay at the shore and do absolutely nothing.

Peace, however, proved fleeting. "Is this all we're doing today?" I began to think. Envy followed, as I thought about new owners running my company. Would they do it better than I had? All this after just a few days in the sand.

Now here's the really sick part: A week later, on a beautiful morning with my wife and kids on the beach, I slipped away, found an Internet café, jumped online for a few hours, and started a new company.

The business plan flowed way too easily, as if my subconscious mind had been developing it all along. Dr. Jekyll was kicking back, but Mr. Hyde was planning the next product launch. I couldn't bring myself to tell my wife what I'd done, but that night she remarked that I looked happier.

So here I stand, at the beginning of the entrepreneurial circle, starting my second lap. I am loving it and cursing it daily. I guess it's just what I do. You can't change who you are just by signing a few documents. And, yes, I did buy another cell phone.

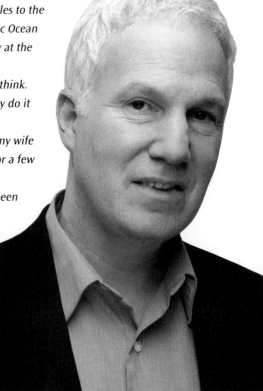

Photo by Henrik Olund/www.henrikolund.com

Source: Jay Butera, "Addicted to Startups," *Fortune Small Business,* October 2006, p. 101.

Looking AHEAD

After studying this chapter, you should be able to

1 Explain the importance of having a harvest, or exit, plan.
2 Describe the options available for harvesting.
3 Explain the issues in valuing a firm that is being harvested and deciding on the method of payment.
4 Provide advice on developing an effective harvest plan.

In previous chapters, we have talked about recognizing business opportunities and developing strategies for capturing these opportunities. Such activities represent the cornerstone for everything a company does. But that's not the end of the story. Experience suggests that an entrepreneur developing a company strategy should think about more than just starting (founding or acquiring) and growing a business; the entrepreneurial process is not complete until the owners and any other investors have exited the venture and captured the value created by the business. This final—but extremely important—phase can be enhanced through an effective harvest, or exit, plan. In other words, the goal is to create value during the entrepreneurial journey by making a difference and *to finish well!*

The Importance of the Harvest

1 Explain the importance of having a harvest, or exit, plan.

In recent times, there have been an unprecedented number of opportunities for entrepreneurs to sell their firms. Today, there are record numbers of investors who are actively buying firms in the same industry and then consolidating them into a single, larger company. Also, many entrepreneurs are transferring ownership to the next generation of family members who have an interest in the business.

George Walper at Chicago-based Spectrem Group, which publishes the *Affluent Market Insights* report, says that more than 20 percent of the total assets held by affluent individuals are in their privately held businesses. "And we are beginning to see a number of them sell," Walper says. In fact, the report has found that on any given day 1.7 million small businesses are for sale in the United States.[1]

Most entrepreneurs do not like to think about the harvest, even though few events in the life of an entrepreneur, and of the firm itself, are more significant. Consequently, the decision to harvest is frequently the result of an unexpected event, possibly a crisis, rather than a well-conceived strategy.

Harvesting—or **exiting**, as it is frequently called—is the method entrepreneurs and investors use to get out of a business and, ideally, reap the value of their investment in the firm. Many entrepreneurs successfully grow their businesses but fail to develop effective harvest plans. As a result, they are unable to capture the full value of the business they have worked so hard to create.

harvesting (exiting)
The process used by entrepreneurs and investors to reap the value of a business when they leave it

An entrepreneur needs to understand that harvesting encompasses more than merely selling and leaving a business; it involves capturing value (cash flows), reducing risk, and creating future options—the reason we prefer the term *harvest* over *exit*. In addition, there are personal, nonfinancial considerations for the entrepreneur. An owner may receive a lot of money for the firm but still be disappointed with the harvest if he or she is not prepared for a change in lifestyle. Thus, carefully designing an intentional exit strategy is as essential to an entrepreneur's personal success as it is to his or her financial success.

The word *success* has different meanings for different people. In this chapter, we offer suggestions for achieving a "successful" harvest. It is a mistake to define success only in terms of the harvest; there should also be success in the entrepreneurial journey. So, throughout the chapter, we encourage you to think about what *success* means to you. Arriving at the end of the journey only to discover that your ladder was leaning against the wrong wall is one of life's tragedies.

The harvest is vitally important to a firm's investors as well as to its founder. Investors who provide high-risk capital—particularly angels and venture capitalists—generally insist on a well-thought-out harvest strategy. They realize that it is easy to put money into a business, but difficult to get it out. As a result, a firm's appeal to investors is driven, in part, by the availability of harvest options. If investors are not convinced that opportunities will exist for harvesting their investment, there will most likely be no investment.

Methods of Harvesting a Business

2 Describe the options available for harvesting.

The four basic ways to harvest an investment in a privately owned company are (1) selling the firm, (2) releasing the firm's cash flows to its owners, (3) offering stock to the public through an initial public offering (IPO), and (4) issuing a private placement of the stock. These options are shown graphically in Exhibit 12-1.

Selling the Firm
In any harvest strategy, the financial questions associated with the sale of a firm include how to value the firm and how to structure the sale. Most frequently, an entrepreneur's motivation for selling a company relates to retirement and estate planning and a desire to diversify her or his portfolio of investments.

exhibit

12-1 *Methods for Harvesting a Business*

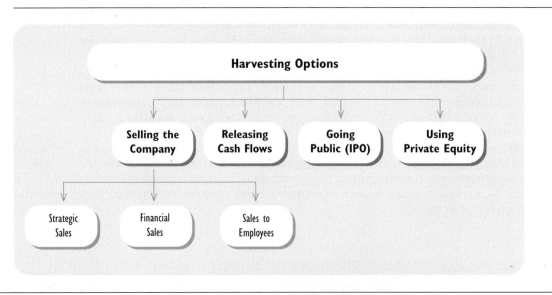

How They See It: Selling a Business

Scott Salmans

While you may be an expert at running your business, it is highly unlikely this also makes you an expert at selling a business. I highly recommend finding a reputable partner with the right expertise to assist in selling your business.

Although it is true that most investment bankers and business brokers don't provide their services for free, you will more than recoup their fee in the final selling price of the company if they do their job in positioning your enterprise to appeal to the most suitable candidates for purchasing your valuable asset. I receive more business sales inquiry letters than any other solicitation from "business brokers" with "partners" interested in buying my business. My experience proved successful in seeking out my own investment banker through a series of interviews of companies referred to me by trusted advisors that had nothing to gain, no matter which firm I selected.

Remember, the fee is negotiable. Don't pay too much cash up front, as it is likely that this could be the amount you pay if things go awry. Look for a match with bankers or brokers that specialize in industries and businesses of certain sizes. Be sure to find the match, or you may end up paying much too much for a service you could have done better without.

Sale transactions can, for all practical purposes, be reduced to three types, based on the motives of the buyers: sales to strategic buyers, sales to financial buyers, and sales to employees. A strategic buyer looks for synergies that can be gained by combining two or more firms, a financial buyer is more often interested in the firm as a stand-alone business, and an employee buyer is primarily concerned about preserving employment and participating in the success of the business. Let's consider each type of transaction in more detail.

SALES TO STRATEGIC BUYERS　From a seller's perspective, the key point to remember about a sale to a strategic buyer is that the value such buyers place on a business depends on the synergies they think they can create by combining the acquired firm with complementary businesses. Since the value of a business to a buyer is derived from both its stand-alone characteristics and its synergies, strategic buyers often will pay a higher price than will financial buyers, who value the business only as a stand-alone entity. Thus, in strategic acquisitions, the critical issue is the degree of strategic fit between the firm to be harvested and the potential buyer's other business interests. If the prospective buyer is a current rival and if the acquisition would provide long-term, sustainable competitive advantages (such as lower cost of production or superior product quality), the buyer may be willing to pay a premium for the company.

SALES TO FINANCIAL BUYERS　Unlike strategic buyers, buyers in financial acquisitions look primarily to a firm's stand-alone, cash-generating potential as its source of value. Often, the value a financial buyer hopes to tap depends on stimulating future sales growth, reducing costs, or both. This fact has an important implication for the owner of the business being purchased. The buyer often will make changes in the firm's operations that translate into greater pressures on the firm's personnel, resulting in layoffs that the current owner might find objectionable. As a result, financial acquisitions are not popular among many small business owners.

In earlier years, the **leveraged buyout (LBO)**, a financial acquisition involving a very high level of debt financing, became synonymous with the **bust-up LBO**, in which the new owners pay the debt down rapidly by selling off the acquired firm's assets. Frequently, acquisitions were financed with $9 in debt for every $1 in equity—thus the name *leveraged* buyout.

For example, Robert Hall, the former owner of Visador Corporation, sold his firm to a financial buyer for $67 million. The buyer financed the purchase as a leveraged buyout,

leveraged buyout (LBO)
A purchase heavily financed with debt, where the future cash flow of the target company is expected to be sufficient to meet debt repayments

bust-up LBO
A leveraged buyout involving the purchase of a company with the intent of selling off its assets

incurring lots of debt to finance the purchase. The firm's total assets and debt and equity (to the nearest million) before and after the sale were as follows:

	Before the Sale	After the Sale
Total assets	$18,000,000	$67,000,000
Total debt	$ 5,000,000	$60,000,000
Equity	13,000,000	7,000,000
Total debt and equity	$18,000,000	$67,000,000

Visador's before-sale and after-sale numbers differ in two important respects. First, the total assets (and total debt and equity) increased from $18 million to $67 million. In other words, the founders of Visador had invested just over $18 million in the firm during their years of ownership, up to the point of the acquisition. However, the buyer was willing to pay $67 million for the business.

Second, before the sale, the assets were financed with 28 percent debt ($5 million total debt ÷ $18 million total assets) compared to 90 percent debt ($60 million total debt ÷ $67 million total assets) after the sale. Consequently, the firm was exposed to significantly more financial risk. If sales decrease, the company may not be able to service its debt. This is typical for bust-up leveraged buyouts.[2]

More recently, the bust-up LBO has been replaced by the build-up LBO. As the name suggests, the **build-up LBO** involves pulling together a group of smaller firms to create a larger enterprise that might eventually be taken public via an initial public offering. Large private investors have successfully refined the build-up LBO and today are tapping into public capital markets at unprecedented levels.

The process begins with the acquisition of a company, which then acquires a number of smaller businesses that in some way complement it. These subsequent acquisitions may expand capacity in related or completely different businesses. The newly formed combination is operated privately for five years or so in order to establish a successful track record, and then it is taken public. These acquisitions continue to rely heavily on debt financing, but to a lesser extent than bust-up LBOs.

Build-up LBOs have occurred in a number of industries where smaller companies frequently operate, such as funeral services and automobile dealerships. Such LBOs frequently include the firm's top management as significant shareholders in the acquired firm—in which case the arrangement is referred to as a **management buyout (MBO)**. An MBO can contribute significantly to a firm's operating performance by increasing management's focus and intensity. Thus, an MBO is a potentially viable means of transferring ownership of both large and small businesses. In many entrepreneurial businesses, managers have a strong incentive to become owners but lack the financial capacity to acquire the firm. An MBO can solve this problem through the use of debt financing, which is often underwritten in part by the firm's owner.

SALES TO EMPLOYEES   Established by Congress in 1974, **employee stock ownership plans (ESOPs)** have gradually been embraced by more than 10,000 companies. Once established, an ESOP uses employees' retirement contributions to buy company stock from the owner and holds it in trust; over time, the stock is distributed to employees' retirement plans. In a **leveraged ESOP**, the stock is purchased with borrowed money. For ESOPs to work, businesses need to be profitable and have good cash flows; otherwise, they will be unable to make the necessary payments to the ESOP trust. Publicly traded firms rarely have ESOPs; these are primarily the domain of private companies.[3]

It is common for an owner to start an ESOP by selling only a portion of the company. But even if the owner sells all of his or her stock, he or she can still retain control of the business. And an ESOP creates significant tax advantages for the seller. For instance, if the entrepreneur sells at least 30 percent of the company, capital gains taxes can be deferred, in some cases indefinitely.

One motivation for selling to employees is to create an incentive for them to work harder—by giving them a piece of the profits. However, employee ownership is not a panacea. Although advocates maintain that employee ownership improves motivation, leading to greater effort and reduced waste, the value of increased employee effort resulting from improved motivation varies significantly from firm to firm. Selling all or part of a firm

build-up LBO
A leveraged buyout involving the purchase of a group of similar companies with the intent of making the firms into one larger company

management buyout (MBO)
A leveraged buyout in which the firm's top managers become significant shareholders in the acquired firm

employee stock ownership plan (ESOP)
A method by which a firm is sold either in part or in total to its employees

leveraged ESOP
An employee stock ownership plan that is financed with borrowed money

Living the Dream   entrepreneurship and integrity

© Lon C. Diehl/PhotoEdit Inc.

The Ultimate Employee Buy-In

Tom Schramski, a dark-haired, round-faced 53-year-old, is a psychologist turned businessman who lives in Tucson, Arizona. The son of a Minnesota gas station owner, he fled as a young man to the sunny Southwest after "one too many subzero mornings" manning his father's pumps. There, he earned his college degree and a doctorate in psychology, figuring he would set up a practice.

But the entrepreneurial itch was strong, and in 1980 he learned that the state of Arizona was beginning to contract out the care of people with developmental disabilities and mental illness, a clientele Schramski knew something about. Over the next 15 years, Community Psychology & Education Services [CPES], as the business was then known, grew into a healthy operation, with $5.5 million in annual revenue.

By the mid-1990s, though, Schramski was in his early 40s; he was ready to begin thinking about liquidity and an eventual exit strategy. He talked to a couple of potential strategic buyers of CPES. They were interested, even eager. He realized he could walk away with a multimillion-dollar check.

But something didn't sit right, and he found himself lying awake at night. Those buyers, he knew, would consolidate facilities. They would slap their own company's name on the office door, if they even kept the office open. Undoubtedly, they would lay off many of CPES's employees. "My perspective on it was, how would I feel about it when I was 80 years old and looking back?" he says now. "I had employees who had been with me 10 years or more. I couldn't have looked them in the face."

So Schramski began casting about for an alternative, and in the process discovered ESOPs. After considerable research, he decided an ESOP was best for him and his company, and in 1995 he began selling the business to his employees in stages. By 1998 he had sold all his shares. In 2004 he gave up CEO duties completely.

Was it the right choice? On the one hand, Schramski paid a considerable price for his decision. As required by law, CPES's valuation for the ESOP sale was determined by an independent appraiser, who put it at $2.5 million. Schramski believes he could have sold the company to a strategic buyer for $3.5 million—though, of course, he wouldn't have received the same tax breaks, which were worth between $200,000 and $300,000.

On the other hand, his employees kept their jobs, and CPES—now known as Community Provider of Enrichment Services—can no longer be considered a small company. The company grew from $5 million in revenue in 1995 to $25 million in 2004; the payroll has swelled from 250 to 775.

Source: John Case, "The Ultimate Employee Buy-in," *Inc.,* December 2005, pp. 108–109. Copyright 2005 by Mansueto Ventures LLC. Reproduced with permission of Mansueto Ventures LLC in the format Textbook via Copyright Clearance Center.

to employees works only if the company's employees have an owner's mentality—that is, they do not think in "9-to-5" terms. An ESOP may provide a way for the owner to sell the business, but if the employees lack the required mind-set, it will not serve the business well in the future. Daniel Brogan, CEO of Earl Walls Associates, an employee-owned design and engineering firm in San Diego, explains, "You have to implement [an ESOP] early enough. . . . The staff has to be mentally prepared to take over and run a company. And you have to continue hiring people who share an ownership mind-set."[4]

Releasing the Firm's Cash Flows

The second harvest strategy involves the orderly withdrawal of the owners' investment in the form of the firm's cash flows. The withdrawal process could be immediate if the owners simply sold off the assets of the firm and ceased business operations. However, for a value-creating firm—one that earns attractive rates of return for its investors—this does not make economic sense. The mere fact that a firm is earning high rates of return on its assets indicates that the business is worth more as a going concern than a dead one. Thus, shutting down the company is not an economically rational option. Instead, the owners might simply stop growing the business; by doing so, they increase the cash flows that can be returned to the investors.

In a firm's early years, all its cash is usually devoted to growing the business. Thus, the firm's cash flow during this period is zero—or, more likely, negative—requiring its owners to seek outside cash to finance future growth. As the firm matures and opportunities to grow the business decline, sizable cash flows frequently become available to its owners. Rather than reinvest all the cash in the firm, the owners can begin to withdraw the cash, thus harvesting their investment. If they decide to adopt this approach, only the amount of cash necessary to maintain current markets is retained and reinvested; there is little, if any, effort to grow the present markets or expand into new markets.

Harvesting by withdrawing a firm's cash from the business has two important advantages: The owners can retain control of the firm while they harvest their investment, and they do not have to seek out a buyer or incur the expenses associated with consummating a sale. There are disadvantages, however. Reducing reinvestment when the firm faces valuable growth opportunities results in lost value creation and could leave a firm unable to sustain its competitive advantage. The end result may be an unintended reduction in harvestable value, below the potential value of the firm as a long-term going concern. Also, there may be tax disadvantages to an orderly liquidation, compared with other harvest methods. For example, if a firm simply distributes the cash as dividends, the income may be taxed both as corporate income and as personal dividend income to the stockholders. (Of course, this would not be a problem for a sole proprietorship, partnership, limited liability company, or S corporation.)

Finally, for the entrepreneur who is simply tired of day-to-day operations, siphoning off the cash flows over time may require too much patience. Unless other people in the firm are qualified to manage it, this strategy may be destined to fail.

Going Public

initial public offering (IPO)
The first sale of shares of a company's stock to the public

The third method of harvesting a firm is going public. Many entrepreneurs consider the prospect of an **initial public offering (IPO)** as the "holy grail" of their career, as firms involved in an IPO are generally star performers. However, most entrepreneurs do not really understand the IPO process, especially when it comes to how going public relates to the harvest and the actual process by which a firm goes public.

THE IPO AS A HARVEST STRATEGY   An IPO occurs when a company offers its stock to the general public, rather than limiting its sale to founders, friends and family, and other private investors. The purpose of this process, described below, is to create a ready market for buying and selling the stock. Before the stock is traded publicly, there is no marketplace where the shares can be easily bought and sold, and thus it is difficult to know what the stock is worth.

IPOs have a number of benefits, including the following:

1. An IPO is one way to signal to investors that a firm is a quality business and will likely perform well in the future.[5]

2. A firm whose stock is traded publicly has access to more investors when it needs to raise capital to grow the business.

3. Being publicly traded helps create ongoing interest in the company and its continued development.

4. Publicly traded stock is more attractive to key personnel whose incentive pay includes the firm's stock.

While there are several reasons for going public, the primary reason is to raise capital. In 80 percent of the cases, money raised from selling a firm's stock to the public is used for expansion, paying down debt, and increasing the firm's liquidity (cash). The other 20 percent of public offerings result from the entrepreneurs' desire to sell their stock.[6]

Having their firm's stock traded in a public market gives entrepreneurs a ready means of selling stock, providing a way for them to harvest their investment *eventually*. We say "eventually" because founders are not allowed to sell their shares when the firm first goes public. However, over time entrepreneurs can and do sell their shares as a way to cash out of their companies. Thus, while IPOs are not primarily a way for entrepreneurs to cash out, going public does provide owners with increased liquidity—which facilitates their eventual exit.

THE IPO PROCESS   The basic steps in the IPO process are as follows:

Step 1. The firm's owners decide to go public.

Step 2. If it has not already done so, the firm must have its financial statements for the past three years audited by a certified public accountant.

Step 3. An investment banker is selected to guide management in the IPO process.

Step 4. An S-1 Registration Statement is filed with the Securities Exchange Commission (SEC), which requires about one month to review it.

Step 5. Management responds to comments by the SEC and issues a Red Herring/Prospectus, describing the firm and the offering.

Step 6. Management spends the next 10 to 15 days on the road, presenting the firm to potential investors.

Step 7. On the day before the offering is released to the public, the actual offering price is set. Based on the demand for the offering, the shares are priced to create active trading of the stock.

Step 8. Months of work come to fruition in a single event—offering the stock to the public and seeing how it is received.

The IPO process may be one of the most exhilarating—but frustrating and exhausting—experiences of an entrepreneur's life. It is difficult to say when the best time is for a company to go public. Nor is it easy to know the conditions that make going public better than other means of exiting a firm.[7] We are aware that entrepreneurs frequently do not like being exposed to the variability of public capital markets and to the prying questions of public-market investors. To many, the costs of the IPO process seem exorbitant. Also, they find themselves being misunderstood and having little influence on the decisions being made. As a consequence, they are frequently disillusioned with investment bankers and wonder where they lost control of the process.

To understand an IPO, you must consider the shift in power that occurs during the process. When the chain of events begins, the firm's managers are in control. They dictate whether or not to go public and who the investment banker will be. After the prospectus has been prepared and the road show is under way, however, the firm's managers, including the entrepreneur, are no longer the primary decision makers. The investment banker is now in control. Finally, the marketplace, in concert with the investment banker, begins to take over. Ultimately, it is the market that dictates the final outcome.

In addition to being prepared for the shift in control, it is important that the entrepreneur understand the investment banker's motivations in the IPO process. Who is the investment banker's primary customer? Clearly, the issuing firm is compensating the underwriter for its services through the fees paid and participation in the offering. But helping a firm with an IPO usually is not as profitable for the investment banker as are other activities, such as involvement in corporate acquisitions. And the investment banker is also selling the securities to the customers on the other side of the trade. These are the people who will continue to do business with the investment banker in the future. Thus, the investment banker is somewhat conflicted as to who is the "customer."

An entrepreneur must also consider more than just the costs of the IPO; he or she must think hard about the costs of running a publicly traded company. As you might expect, operating a publicly traded firm is more expensive than operating a private company. A publicly traded company has significant ongoing costs associated with reporting its financial results to investors and to the SEC. These costs were significantly increased in 2001 when, in response to corporate scandals such as those at Enron and WorldCom, the U.S. Congress passed the Sarbanes-Oxley Act. The act places a much greater burden on companies to have good corporate governance and accounting practices and controls that will prevent such egregious offenses by managers. While much good has come from Sarbanes-Oxley, the costs to a small firm are disproportionate and are no small consideration in the decision as to whether or not to go public.

So, although many entrepreneurs seek to take their firms public through an IPO, this strategy is appropriate for only a limited number of firms. And even for this small group, an IPO is more a means of raising growth capital than an effective harvest strategy.

Using Private Equity

private equity
Money provided by venture capitalists or private investors

The fourth method of harvesting is the use of private equity. **Private equity** is money provided by venture capitalists or private investors. The private investors are usually small groups of individuals who act together to invest in companies.

Private equity investors offer two key advantages that public investors do not: immediacy and flexibility. With private equity, an entrepreneur can sell most of her or his stock immediately, an option not available when a company is taken public. Also, private equity investors can be more flexible in structuring their investment to meet the entrepreneur's needs.

Although the situation is complicated by the different needs of each generation, private equity is particularly effective for family-owned businesses that need to transfer ownership to the next generation. In the transfer of ownership between generations, there must be a tradeoff among three important goals: (1) liquidity for the selling family members, (2) continued financing for company growth, and (3) the desire of the buying generation to maintain control of the firm. Thus, the older generation wants to get cash out of the business, while the younger generation wants to retain the cash needed to finance the firm's growth and yet not lose ownership control.

Recognizing a need for creativity, some investment groups have developed financing approaches that more fully satisfy the needs of exiting family owners whose firms have significant growth potential. One such approach is the Private IPO, a trademarked process designed for mature, successful family businesses.[8]

To understand the Private IPO, consider the following example. Assume that a company could be sold for $20 million through a leveraged buyout (LBO), which would most likely be financed through 80 percent debt and 20 percent equity. Many entrepreneurs would find such an arrangement intolerable, even though they would have cashed out. They simply would not want their company subjected to such a high-leverage transaction. Also, with an LBO the family generally loses control of the business. As an alternative to an LBO, the entrepreneur might consider a Private IPO, which provides less cash but allows the family to retain control. The firm just described would be sold for $18 million—10 percent less than the LBO price. The seller would receive $15 million in cash, as opposed to the full $18 million. But instead of relinquishing all or most of their ownership, the family owners would receive 51 percent of the equity in exchange for the $3 million retained in the company. The remaining $15 million of the purchase price would be financed from two sources: $7 million in senior debt and $8 million from the private investor, consisting of $4 million in preferred stock and $4 million in common stock. The

Living the Dream

entrepreneurial challenges

Off-the-Grid IPOs

In some respects, it wasn't such a terrible problem for Martin Lightsey to have: The value of Specialty Blades, Inc., had increased so much since he founded the medical and industrial blade manufacturer in 1985 that some of the company's 11 shareholders, including Lightsey's two daughters, wanted to cash in some of their earnings. In 12 years, the median $42,000 investment in the business, based in Staunton, Virginia, had soared to a value of more than $350,000. The problem was, Lightsey didn't have enough cash to fund the buyouts.

Lightsey briefly toyed with the idea of going public, which would allow his investors to buy and sell shares as they pleased. He called Gordon Smith, a securities lawyer at Richmond law firm McGuire Woods, who told him that the legal and accounting fees related to being a publicly held company would amount to roughly a half million dollars every year, overwhelming for a business booking $6 million in annual sales.

Lightsey asked Smith about a privately held community bank in Staunton that seemed to be trading its shares. Smith explained that the bank was taking advantage of a little-known Securities and Exchange Commission exemption called an intrastate offering, which allowed it to sell stock to Virginia residents without registering with the SEC. It seemed like a perfect solution for Specialty Blades: Lightsey could cash out the company's current investors by selling their stock to a new group of shareholders and avoid the hassle and expense of an IPO. At the same time, he could spread out ownership to a larger, more diverse pool of investors. "The public model is just more stable," Lightsey says.

Lightsey spent the next few months researching intrastate offerings before deciding to take the plunge. Lightsey began working with Bruce Campbell, then executive vice president of Richmond-based brokerage firm Scott & Stringfellow and a Specialty Blades board member who owned several thousand shares of the company. Campbell and some fellow board members estimated a value for the company's stock, based on factors such as cash flow and earnings, and began contacting clients to gauge their interest.

A few months later, Lightsey held a gathering at Specialty Blades' facility for 40 potential investors. Lightsey cautiously launched into his dog-and-pony show, highlighting the company's history and growth strategy. A few weeks later, investors purchased a total of 30,000 shares at $20 per share, which represented 6 percent of the company. All of the shares that were sold belonged to Lightsey's daughters. The offering cost Specialty Blades about $15,000, a small fraction of the price of an IPO. The firm regularly updates the stock price, which was recently $124 per share.

http://www.specialtyblades.com

preferred stock would provide an annual dividend, while the common stock would give the new investor 49 percent of the firm's ownership (see Exhibit 12-2).

The differences between the two capital structures are clear. The debt ratio is much lower in the Private IPO than in the LBO, allowing for a lower interest rate on the debt and

exhibit 12-2 *Private Equity Financing*

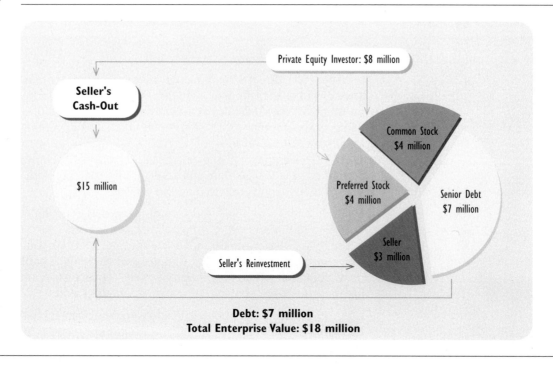

permitting the firm's cash flows to be used to grow the firm, rather than pay down debt. This arrangement allows the senior generation of owners to cash out, while the next generation retains control and the cash to grow the firm—a win-win situation. The younger generation also has the potential to realize significant economic gains if the firm performs well.

Firm Valuation and the Harvest

3 Explain the issues in valuing a firm that is being harvested and deciding on the method of payment.

As a firm moves toward the harvest, two issues are of primary importance: the harvest value (what the firm is worth) and the method of payment.

The Harvest Value

Valuing a company may be necessary on numerous occasions during the life of the business—but it is never more important than at the time of the exit. Owners can harvest only what they have created. Value is created when a firm's return on invested capital is greater than the investors' **opportunity cost of funds**, which is the rate of return that could be earned on an investment of similar risk.

opportunity cost of funds
The rate of return that could be earned on another investment of similar risk

Growing a venture to the point of diminishing returns and then selling it to others who can carry it to the next level is a proven way to create value. How this incremental value is shared between the old and the new owners depends largely on the relative strengths of each party in the negotiations—that is, who wants the deal the most or who has the best negotiating skills.

Business valuation is part science and part art, so there is no precise formula for determining the price of a private company. Rather, the price is determined by a sometimes intricate process of negotiation between buyer and seller. Much is left to the negotiating skills of the respective parties. But one thing is certain: There must be a willing buyer. It doesn't matter what a firm's owner believes the business is worth; it is worth only what someone who has the cash is prepared to pay.

The specific approaches to and methods for valuing a company are described in Appendix B at the end of the book. As described in the appendix, buyers and sellers frequently

Living the Dream   entrepreneurial challenges

Success Means Independence

Lurita Doan wasn't considered successful at her old job. A computer programmer for a large federal contractor, Doan couldn't help thinking outside the box—and that wasn't a good thing. When she went to her managers 13 years ago with an idea to customize software for their clients, they basically told her to go back to her cubicle and be quiet.

Devastated and a little angry, Doan quit her job a few weeks later and started her own company, New Technology Management, Inc., an IT company that specializes in border security and systems integration.

"Success is being my own boss and having it done my way," says Doan. "I'm really hard-headed. I know what is right. I have a way of doing things that adheres to excellence."

Though her hard work produces a comfortable salary, Doan says she is happy driving a Saturn—because independence is what drives her to work each morning. "The most amazing part of owning a business is that it's up to me to make it work. I can do what I want, and I don't have to check with anyone," Doan says.

Source: Rex Hammock and Shannon Scully, "Success: What's Your Definition?" *MyBusiness,* December/January 2004, http://www.mybusinessmag.com/fullstory.php3?sid=903, accessed May 2004.

http://www.ntmi.com

base the harvest value of a firm on a multiple of earnings. For instance, a company might be valued at five times its earnings. (Entrepreneur Robert Hall sold his firms for a multiple of earnings; his experience provides the basis for the example used in Appendix B.)

The Method of Payment

The actual value of the firm is only one issue; another is the method of payment. When selling a company, an entrepreneur has three basic choices: sell the firm's assets, sell its stock, or, if the buyer is another company, merge with the buyer (combine the two companies into one firm). The exiting entrepreneur may prefer to sell the firm's stock so that the gain on the sale will be a capital gain, resulting in lower taxes.[9] The buyer, on the other hand, may prefer to purchase the firm's assets rather than buy the company's stock. Buying the assets relieves the buyer of responsibility for any liabilities, known or unknown.

Harvesting owners can be paid in cash or in stock of the acquiring firm, with cash generally being preferred over stock. Entrepreneurs who accept stock in payment are frequently disappointed, as they are unable to affect the value of the stock once they have sold the firm. Only an entrepreneur who has great faith in the acquiring firm's stock should accept it in payment, and even then he or she is taking a big chance by not being well diversified. Having such a large investment in only one stock is risky, to say the least.

From an investor's viewpoint, cash is best—except for the tax consequences. As one investor advised, "Start with cash and work down from there." However, venture capitalists may not have a preference between stock and cash if their limited partners—frequently pension funds—have no preference, as long as the sale of the stock is not restricted in any way.

How They See It: Begin with the End in Mind

John Stites

When I started my business, I was focused on making money and being successful. I had been taught in business school the fundamentals of being in business. I visited other successful individuals and companies to see what I could replicate in my business to ensure its success. I went right to work and worked hard for 10 years. I did not take the time to sit down and envision what I wanted my business to look like in the future. I did not take the time to set a mission statement and establish that mission in the day-to-day operations of the business. I worked hard, but not smart.

After 10 years of mediocre success, I stepped back and looked at what I was doing and how it was impacting people—people inside my company and people outside my company. What I saw I didn't like. I saw a company finally making money, but not positively influencing lives.

I have determined that if, at the end of my tenure in our family business, I have not inspired individuals to be better spouses, better parents, and better citizens, then I have lost the greatest opportunity to increase the value of the company. A company that doesn't change lives in a positive way and just gives money to employees and provides services to customers is not one to be valued very highly.

---

4 Provide advice on developing an effective harvest plan.

Developing an Effective Harvest Plan

We have discussed why planning for the harvest is important, despite the tendency of many entrepreneurs to ignore it until some crisis or unanticipated event comes along. We have also described the methods for exiting. However, there is still a lot that can be said about developing a harvest plan. In the sections that follow, we provide suggestions on crafting an effective exit strategy.[10]

Manage for the Harvest

Entrepreneurs frequently do not appreciate the difficulty of harvesting a company. One investor commented that exiting a business is "like brain surgery—it's done a lot, but there are a lot of things that can go wrong." Harvesting, whether through a sale or a stock offering, takes a lot of time and energy on the part of the firm's management team and can be very distracting from day-to-day affairs. The result is often a loss of managerial focus and momentum, leading to poor performance.

Uncertainties accompanying an impending sale often lower employee morale. The stress can affect the whole organization, as employees become anxious about the prospect of a new owner. Lynn Baker, at Sutter Hill Ventures, offers this advice: "Don't start running the company for the liquidity event. Run the business for the long haul." Jim Porter, at CCI Triad, describes the situation in Silicon Valley in the 1990s, where some owners carried the practice to an extreme:

> Some people don't think in terms of long-term value as much as short-term returns. This carries over into developing an IPO exit strategy. I see a growing number of people who are already planning their next company before they are finished with the first company. They are looking to exit the first one, get the money out and start the second one, get the money out, and pyramid their return. In a hot market, you can do that and get away with it. They are professional company starters.

So, while an entrepreneur should not be caught unaware, there is also the risk of becoming so attentive to "playing the harvest game" that one forgets to keep first things first.

Investors are always concerned about how to exit, and entrepreneurs need to have a similar mind-set. Peter Hermann, general partner at Heritage Partners, a private equity investment group, notes, "People generally stumble into the exit and don't plan for it."

However, for Hermann, "The exit strategy begins when the money goes in." Similarly, Gordon Baty, at Zero Stage Capital, Inc., enters each investment with a clear understanding of its investment horizon and harvest plan. In his words, "We plan for an acquisition and hope for an IPO." Jack Kearney, at Dain Rauscher Inc., indicates that an exit strategy should be anticipated in advance, unless "the entrepreneur expects to die in the CEO chair. . . . The worst of all worlds is to realize, for health or other reasons, that you have to sell the company right now." Jim Knister, at the Donnelly Corporation, advises entrepreneurs to start thinking two or three years ahead about how they are going to exit so that they can correctly position their companies.

This type of advice is particularly important when the entrepreneur is planning an IPO. Running a public company requires information disclosures to stockholders that are not required of a privately held firm. Specifically, this means (1) maintaining an accounting process that cleanly separates the business from the entrepreneur's personal life, (2) selecting a strong board of directors that can and will offer valuable business advice, and (3) managing the firm so as to produce a successful track record of performance.

Having a harvest plan in place is also very important because the window of opportunity can open and close quickly. Remember that the opportunity to exit is triggered by the arrival of a willing and able buyer, not just an interested seller. For an IPO, a hot market may offer a very attractive opportunity, and a seller must be ready to move when the opportunity arises.

In summary, an entrepreneur should be sure to anticipate the harvest. In the words of Ed Cherney, an entrepreneur who has sold two companies, "Don't wait to put your package together until something dramatic happens. Begin thinking about the exit strategy and start going through the motions, so that if something major happens, you will have time to think through your options."

Expect Conflict—Emotional and Cultural

Having bought other companies does not prepare entrepreneurs for the sale of their own company. Entrepreneurs who have been involved in the acquisition of other firms are still ill-prepared for the stress associated with selling their own businesses. Jim Porter, who has been involved in a number of acquisitions, says, "It's definitely a lot more fun to buy something than it is to be bought." One very real difference between selling and buying comes from the entrepreneur's personal ties to the business that he or she helped create. A buyer can be quite unemotional and detached, while a seller is likely to be much more concerned about nonfinancial considerations.

For this reason and many others, entrepreneurs frequently do not make good employees. The very qualities that made them successful entrepreneurs can make it difficult for them to work under a new owner. In fact, an entrepreneur who plans to stay with the firm after a sale can become disillusioned quickly and end up leaving prematurely.

Lynn Baker observes, "There is a danger of culture conflict between the acquiring versus the acquired firm's management. The odds are overwhelming that somebody who's been an entrepreneur is not going to be happy in a corporate culture." When Ed Bonneau sold his wholesale sunglass distribution firm, he was retained as a consultant, but the buyer never sought his advice. Bonneau recalled that he "could not imagine that someone could or would buy a company and not operate it. The people who bought the firm had no operations expertise or experience whatsoever and, in fact, didn't care that much about it."

These conflicts occur to varying degrees whenever an entrepreneur remains with the company after the sale. Although the nature of the conflict varies, the intensity of the feelings does not. An entrepreneur who stays with the company should expect culture conflict and be pleasantly surprised if it does not occur.

Get Good Advice

Entrepreneurs learn to operate their businesses through experience gained in repeated day-to-day activities. However, they may engage in a harvest transaction only once in a lifetime. "It's an emotional roller-coaster ride," says Ben Buettell, who frequently represents sellers of small and mid-sized companies.[11] Thus, entrepreneurs have a real need for good advice, both from experienced professionals and from those who have personally been through a harvest. In seeking advice, be aware that the experts who helped you build and grow your business may not be the best ones to use when it's time to sell the company, as they may not have the experience needed in that area. So, choose your advisors carefully.

Bill Dedmon, at Southwest Securities, advises, "Don't try to do it alone, because it's a demanding process that can distract you from your business." Jack Furst, at HM Capital, a private equity investor, believes that advisors can give entrepreneurs a reality check. He contends that, without independent advice, entrepreneurs frequently fall prey to thinking they want to sell unconditionally, when in fact they really want to sell only if an unrealistically high price is offered.

Professional advice is vital, but entrepreneurs stress the importance of talking to other entrepreneurs who have sold a firm or taken it public. No one can better describe what to expect—both in events and in emotions—than someone who has had the experience. This perspective nicely complements that of the professional advisor.

Perhaps the greatest misconception among entrepreneurs is that an IPO is the end of the line. They often feel that taking their firm public through an IPO means they have "made it." The fact is that going public is but one transition in the life of a firm. Many entrepreneurs are surprised to learn that a public offering is just the beginning, not an end.

An entrepreneur will not be able to cash out for some time after the completion of the IPO. In a sense, investors in the new stock offering have chosen to back the entrepreneur as the driving force behind the company—that is, they have invested in the entrepreneur, not the firm. While the daily stock price quotes will let the management team keep score, the business will have to reach another plateau before the founder can think about placing it in the hands of a new team and going fishing. Ed Bonneau talks of being surprised in this matter:

> The question of an IPO was put to me a number of times over the years. I had some investment bankers come and look at our company to talk about going public; they said, "Yeah, you can go public." Then they asked me why I wanted to go public. I said, "For one thing, I want some money out of the company. I have every dime I've got stuck in here." They responded that I couldn't do that. I asked what they meant. They responded, "Getting money out [is] not the purpose of going public."

Lynn Baker describes the typical entrepreneur's thinking about an IPO as "the *Bride Magazine* syndrome":

> The entrepreneur is like the bride-to-be who becomes fixated on the events of the wedding day without thinking clearly about the years of being married that will follow. Life as head of a public corporation is very different from life at the helm of a private firm. Major investors will be calling every day expecting answers—sometimes with off-the-wall questions.

Under these circumstances, getting good advice is a must.

Understand What Motivates You

For an entrepreneur, harvesting a business that has been an integral part of life for a long period of time can be a very emotional experience. When an entrepreneur has invested a substantial part of his or her working life in growing a business, a real sense of loss may accompany the harvest. Walking away from employees, clients, and one's identity as a small business owner may not be the wonderful ride into the sunset that was expected.

Thus, entrepreneurs should think very carefully about their motives for exiting and what they plan to do after the harvest. Frequently, entrepreneurs have great expectations about what life is going to be like with a lot of liquidity, something many of them have never known. The harvest does provide the long-sought liquidity, but some entrepreneurs find managing money—in contrast to operating their own company—less rewarding than they had expected.

Entrepreneurs may also become disillusioned when they come to understand more fully how their sense of personal identity was intertwined with their business. While Jim Porter understands that a primary purpose of exiting is to make money, watching a number of owners cash out has led him to conclude that the money is not a very satisfying aspect of the event:

> *The bottom line is that you need more than money to sustain life and feel worthwhile. I see people who broke everything to make their money. They were willing to sacrifice their wives, their family, and their own sense of values to make money. I remember one person who was flying high, did his IPO, and went straight out and bought a flaming red Ferrari. He raced it down the street, hit a telephone pole, and died the day his IPO money came down. You see these guys...go crazy. They went out and bought houses in Hawaii, houses in Tahoe, new cars, and got things they didn't need.*

Peter Hermann believes that "seller's remorse" is definitely a major issue for a number of entrepreneurs. His advice is "Search your soul and make a list of what you want to achieve with the exit. Is it dollars, health of the company, your management team or an heir apparent taking over?" The answers to these and similar questions determine to a significant extent whether the exit will prove successful in all dimensions of an entrepreneur's life. There can be conflicting emotions, such as those expressed by Bill Bailey, founder of the Cherokee Corporation:

> *There is a period in your life when you get up in age and you begin thinking more about your family. For me, it became important for the first time in my life to have money available to do some long-range personal planning for myself, and for my family. But if there is any one thing to be understood when you are selling a business or anything else, it is the excitement of the journey and the enjoyment for doing what you're doing that matters.*

Entrepreneurs are also well advised to be aware of potential problems that may arise after the exit. There are stories about people selling a firm or going public and then losing everything. Ed Cherney says, "It is more difficult to handle success than it is to handle struggling. People forget what got them the success—the work ethic, the commitment to family, whatever characteristics work for an entrepreneur. Once the money starts rolling in, . . . people forget and begin having problems."

And for the entrepreneur who believes that it will be easy to adapt to change after the harvest, even possibly to start another company, William Unger, at the Mayfield Fund, quotes from Machiavelli's *The Prince:* "It should be remembered that nothing is more difficult than to establish a new order of things."

What's Next?

Entrepreneurs by their very nature are purpose-driven people. So, after the exit, an entrepreneur who has been driven to build a profitable business will need something larger than the individual to bring meaning to her or his life.

Many entrepreneurs have a sense of gratitude for the benefits they have received from living in a capitalist system. As a result, they want to give back, both with their time and with their money. The good news is that there is no limit to the number of worthy charitable causes, including universities, churches, and civic organizations. And it may be that, when all is said and done, the call to help others with a new venture may be too strong for an individual with an entrepreneurial mind-set to resist. But whatever you decide to do, do it with passion and let your life benefit others in the process.

Looking BACK

1 Explain the importance of having a harvest, or exit, plan.

- Harvesting, or exiting, is the means entrepreneurs and investors use to get out of a business and, ideally, reap the value of their investment in the firm.

- Harvesting is about more than merely selling and leaving a business. It involves capturing value (cash flows), reducing risk, and creating future options.

- A firm's accessibility to investors is driven by the availability of harvest options.

2 Describe the options available for harvesting.

- There are four basic ways to harvest an investment in a privately owned company: (1) selling the firm, (2) releasing the firm's cash flows to its owners, (3) offering stock to the public through an IPO, and (4) issuing a private placement of the stock.

- In a sale to a strategic buyer, the value placed on a business depends on the synergies that the buyer believes can be created.

- Financial buyers look primarily to a firm's stand-alone, cash-generating potential as the source of its value.

- In leveraged buyouts (LBOs), high levels of debt financing are used to acquire firms.

- With bust-up LBOs, the assets are then sold to repay the debt.

- With build-up LBOs, a number of related businesses are acquired, which may eventually be taken public via an initial public offering (IPO).

- A management buyout (MBO) is an LBO in which management is part of the group buying the company.

- In an employee stock ownership plan (ESOP), employees' retirement contributions are used to purchase shares in the company.

- The orderly withdrawal of an owner's investment in the form of the firm's cash flows is one method of harvesting a firm.

- An initial public offering (IPO) is used primarily as a way to raise additional equity capital to finance company growth, and only secondarily as a way to harvest the owner's investment.

- Private equity is a form of outside financing that can allow the original owners to cash out.

- Trying to finance liquidity and growth while retaining control is perhaps the most difficult task facing family firms.

3 Explain the issues in valuing a firm that is being harvested and deciding on the method of payment.

- Value is created when a firm's return on invested capital is greater than the investors' opportunity cost of funds.

- A firm will have greater value in the hands of new owners if the new owners can create more value than the current owners can.

- Often, buyers and sellers base the harvest value of a firm on a multiple of its earnings.

- Cash is generally preferred over stock and other forms of payment by those selling a firm.

4 Provide advice on developing an effective harvest plan.

- Investors are always concerned about exit strategy.

- Entrepreneurs who plan to stay with a business after a sale can become disillusioned quickly and end up leaving prematurely.

- Entrepreneurs frequently do not appreciate the difficulty of selling or exiting a company. Having bought other companies does not prepare entrepreneurs for the sale of their own firm.

- Entrepreneurs have a real need for good advice, both from experienced professionals and from those who have personally been through a harvest.

- Going public is not the end; it's only a transition in the life of a firm.

Key TERMS

harvesting (exiting), p. 327

leveraged buyout (LBO), p. 329

bust-up LBO, p. 329

build-up LBO, p. 330

management buyout (MBO), p. 330

employee stock ownership plan (ESOP), p. 330

leveraged ESOP, p. 330

initial public offering (IPO), p. 332

private equity, p. 334

opportunity cost of funds, p. 336

Discussion QUESTIONS

1. Explain what is meant by the term *harvesting*. What is involved in harvesting an investment in a privately held firm?

2. Why should an owner of a company plan for eventually harvesting his or her company?

3. Contrast a sale to a strategic buyer with one to a financial buyer.

4. Explain the term *leveraged buyout*. How is a leveraged buyout different from a management buyout?

5. Distinguish between bust-up LBOs and build-up LBOs.

6. What is the primary purpose of an initial public offering (IPO)? How does an IPO relate to a harvest?

7. Why might an entrepreneur find going public a frustrating process?

8. What determines whether a firm has value to a prospective purchaser?

9. What problems can occur when an entrepreneur sells a firm but continues in the management of the company?

10. How may harvesting a firm affect an entrepreneur's personal identity?

You Make the CALL

SITUATION 1

Bill and Francis Waugh founded Casa Bonita. They started with a single fast-food Mexican restaurant in Abilene, Texas. At the time, they both worked seven days a week. From that small beginning, they expanded to 84 profitable restaurants located in Texas, Oklahoma, Arkansas, and Colorado. Over the years, other restaurant owners expressed an interest in buying the firm; however, the Waughs were not interested in selling. Then an English firm, Unigate Limited, offered them $32 million for the business and said Bill could remain the firm's CEO. The Waughs were attracted by the idea of having $32 million in liquid assets. They flew to London to close the deal. On the flight home, however, Bill began having doubts about their decision to sell the business. He thought, "We spent 15 years of our lives getting the business where we wanted it, and we've lost it." After their plane landed in New York, they spent the night and then flew back to London the next day. They offered the buyers $1 million to cancel the contract, but Unigate's management declined the offer. The Waughs flew home disappointed.

Question 1 How could the Waughs be disappointed with $32 million?

Question 2 What should the Waughs have done to avoid this situation?

Question 3 What advice would you offer Bill about continuing to work for the business under the new owners?

SITUATION 2

Ed and Barbara Bonneau started their wholesale sunglass distribution firm 30 years ago with $1,000 of their own money and $5,000 borrowed from a country banker in Ed's hometown. The firm grew quickly, selling sunglasses and reading glasses to such companies as Wal-Mart, Eckerd Drugs, and Phar-Mor. In addition, the Bonneaus enjoyed using the company to do good things. For example, they had a company chaplain, who was available when employees were having family problems, such as a death in the family.

Although the company had done well, the market had matured recently and profit margins narrowed significantly. Wal-Mart, for example, was insisting on better terms, which meant significantly lower prof the Bonneaus. Previously, Ed had set the pric he needed to make a good return on his i Now, the buyers had consolidated, an power. Ed didn't enjoy running the as he had in the past, and he pleasure in other activities: on a local hospital boar church activities.

Just as Ed and the company, t who wanted to u buy up several sun the Bonneaus sold th addition, Ed received a consultant to the buyer. A

who was part of the company's management team, was named the new chief operating officer.

Question 1 Do you agree with the Bonneaus' decision to sell? Why or why not?

Question 2 Why did the buyers retain Ed as a consultant? (In answering this question, you might consider the quote by Bonneau in the chapter.)

Question 3 Do you see any problem with having the Bonneaus' son-in-law become the new chief operating officer?

SITUATION 3

At age 63, Michael Lipper sold his firm to Reuters. His assessment of the sale follows:

> One of the reasons we sold our business to Reuters was because we knew we probably couldn't manage the technology of the future by ourselves. Any entrepreneur who builds a business for as long as I have would be dishonest if he did not suffer a certain sadness [from selling]. If [Reuters] makes a wonderful success

out of this, there may be some ego pain. If they muck it up, they've damaged our name and hurt our people.

Lois Silverman co-founded CRA Managed Care (now known as Concentra Managed Care). When the firm went public in 1995, Silverman's stake was over $10 million. After taking Concentra public, Silverman gave up all involvement in day-to-day operations. Along with 12 other successful businesswomen, she formed the not-for-profit Commonwealth Institute, to help women entrepreneurs set up boards and secure capital. She also became involved with a newspaper called *Women's Business*. She later told this story:

> The other day a man said to me on a golf course, "I hope I hit this ball, because since I've left my business, I don't know what to do with myself." And I said to myself, "I'm so lucky."

Question 1 Compare the people in the above true stories in terms of their feelings about exiting their firms.

Question 2 What might explain the difference between those who have positive feelings about cashing out and those who do not?

Experiential **EXERCISES**

1. Check your local newspaper for a week or so to find a privately held company that has been sold recently. Try to determine the motivation for the sale. Did it have anything to do with the prior owners' desire to cash out of the business? If so, try to find out what happened.

2. Ask a local family business owner about future plans to harvest the business. Has the owner ever been involved in a harvest? If so, ask the owner to describe what happened and how it all worked out, as well as what she or he learned

from the experience. If not, ask whether the owner is aware of any company whose owners cashed out. Visit that company owner to inquire about the exit event.

3. Visit a local CPA to learn about his or her involvement in helping entrepreneurs cash out of companies.

4. Search a business magazine to identify a firm that has successfully completed an initial public offering (IPO). See what you can find out about the event on the Internet.

Exploring the **WEB**

d out more about harvest and exit strate-
small firms, go to the U.S. Chamber of
ce website at **http://www.uschamber.**
hoose "Finance" from the Toolkits and
ed help on. . ." dropdown box, select

"Getting Out of Your Business." What exit routes should you consider, according to the Chamber, when you own a small business?

2. Valuing a business is a topic covered extensively at the CCH's Business Owner Toolkit website,

which you may have visited before in earlier Web exercises. Drill a bit deeper into the site by keying in this URL on firm valuation: **http://www. toolkit.com/text/small_business_guide/sbg. aspx?nid=P11_2200.**

   a. Explain the role of a business appraiser.

   b. When setting a price for a small business, what must one consider?

3. Go to BizPlanIt's website at **http://www.bizplanit. com**. Choose "Free Business Planning Resources," "Virtual BizPlan," "Exit Strategy," and then "Exit Strategy Business Plan Basics."

   a. What are some common mistakes related to exit strategy and how might they be avoided?

   b. What are the most common exit strategies and what are the advantages and disadvantages of each?

   c. Which exit strategy is the most likely option for your proposed small business?

4. Go to **http://www.inc.com/articles/1999/11/ 15743.html** for explanations of SEC rules and regulations governing exemptions for small firms going public.

Case **12**

Tires Plus (p. 644)

This case discusses the process and options to be considered by an entrepreneur who is exiting a business.

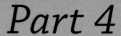

Part 4

Focusing on the Customer: Marketing Growth Strategies

## chapter 13

Building Customer Relationships

In the VIDEO SPOTLIGHT

Rodgers Chevrolet

http://www.rodgerschevrolet.com

The average business keeps only 70 to 90 percent of its customers each year. Even though this seems like a decent retention rate, consider that it costs nearly five times as much to acquire a new customer as it does to keep an existing one.[1] What's worse is that new customers buy only 20 percent as much as existing customers. The cost of replacing existing customers is so high that if a company could increase customer retention by a minimal 5 to 10 percent per year, profits would nearly double.[2] If keeping customers is this critical, how can a company do it effectively?

The first step in developing a lasting relationship with a customer is to put the customer at the center of the company. Pamela Rodgers understands this: Knowing, serving, and delighting her customers are the foundation of her successful dealership, Rodgers Chevrolet. Even though 75 percent of the company's revenue comes from car purchases, service is what sustains the company. Buying a car is exhilarating; having a car repaired is annoying. Rodgers Chevrolet has transformed the unpleasant aspects of car ownership (annual service, repairs, recalls) through a strong company culture focused on responsiveness, empathy, and reliability. Watch this video spotlight to see how serving the customer can be the lifeblood of this—and any—organization.

Video material provided by Hattie Bryant, Producer of Small Business School, the series on PBS Stations, Worldnet, and the Web at http://www.smallbusinessschool.org.

SmallBusinessSchool

the Series on PBS stations and the Web

Looking **AHEAD**

After studying this chapter, you should be able to

1 Define customer relationship management (CRM) and explain its importance to a small firm.

2 Discuss the significance of providing extraordinary customer service.

3 Illustrate how technology, such as the Internet, can improve customer relationships.

4 Describe the techniques for creating a customer profile.

5 Explain how consumers are decision makers and why this is important to understanding customer relationships.

6 Describe certain psychological influences on consumer behavior.

7 Describe certain sociological influences on consumer behavior.

Always remember that the customer (consumer) is the heartbeat of every firm. A better understanding of consumers and the transactional relationships a firm has with them will lead to a healthier small business.

Chapter 13 is the first in a sequence of chapters comprising Part 4, Focusing on the Customer: Marketing Growth Strategies. It examines customer relationship management (CRM) and argues that CRM is a key factor in small business survival and growth. Chapter 13 also discusses the importance of building a behavioral profile of customers. Chapters 14 through 17 discuss additional marketing topics essential to growth, based on the all-important customer focus developed in this chapter.

What Is Customer Relationship Management?

> 1 Define customer relationship management (CRM) and explain its importance to a small firm.

Customer relationship management (CRM) means different things to different firms. To some, it is symbolized by simple smiles or comments such as "thank you" and "come again" communicated by employees to customers who have just made a purchase. For others, CRM embodies a much broader marketing effort, leading to nothing short of complete customization of products and/or services to fit individual customer needs. The goals of a CRM program for most small companies fall somewhere between these two perspectives.

Regardless of the level of a firm's commitment to customer relationship management, the central message of every CRM program is "Court customers for more than a one-time sale." A firm that strongly commits to this idea will appreciate the many benefits a CRM program can offer.

Formally defined, **customer relationship management (CRM)** is a "company-wide business strategy designed to optimize profitability and customer satisfaction by focusing on highly defined and precise customer groups."[3] In a way, CRM is a mind-set—the implementation of customer-centric strategies, which put customers first so that the firm can succeed. CRM involves treating customers the way the entrepreneur would want to be treated if he or she were a customer—the business version of the Golden Rule.

The central theme of CRM isn't new. For decades, entrepreneurs have recognized the importance of treating customers well; "the customer is king" is an old adage. What is new is giving this idea a name and using technology to implement many of its techniques. Modern CRM focuses on (1) customers rather than products; (2) changes in company

customer relationship management (CRM)
A company-wide business strategy designed to optimize profitability and customer satisfaction by focusing on highly defined and precise customer groups

processes, systems, and culture; and (3) all channels and media involved in the marketing effort, from the Internet to field sales.

The forerunners of many modern CRM techniques were developed in the 1960s by marketers like Sears and various book clubs. They simply stored information about their customers in computers for reasons other than invoicing. Their goal was to learn who their customers were, what they wanted, and what sort of interests they had. Then along came marketers with ideas about the potential benefits of adopting a customer orientation, followed by the rise of the Internet.

It should be noted that CRM, in its purest form, has nothing to do with technology, although Internet technology has definitely been a major force in CRM's development. Just as putting on the latest $300 pair of technologically designed basketball shoes doesn't make the wearer a WNBA or NBA player, buying or developing CRM computer software does not, in itself, lead to higher customer retention. But it can help if it is used properly. (The role of technology in CRM is discussed later in this chapter.) Most importantly, there must be company-wide commitment to the concept if CRM is to be productive.

The Importance of CRM to the Small Firm

As depicted in Exhibit 13-1, a firm's next sale comes from one of two sources—a current customer or a new customer. Obviously, both current and potential customers are valued by a small firm, but sometimes current customers are taken for granted and ignored. While marketing efforts devoted to bringing new customers into the fold are obviously important, keeping existing customers happy should be an even higher priority. A CRM program addresses this priority. Some firms, however, appear not to recognize this simple truth, and this results in different levels of CRM initiatives. One interesting study of CRM involvement among family and nonfamily firms concluded that nonfamily businesses are ahead of family-owned companies with respect to starting and completing CRM initiatives."[4]

Brian Vellmure of Initium Technology, a provider of CRM solutions to small firms, has identified five economic benefits of maintaining relationships with current customers:[5]

1. Acquisition costs for new customers are huge.

2. Long-time customers spend more money than new ones.

3. Happy customers refer their friends and colleagues.

4. Order-processing costs are higher for new customers.

5. Old customers will pay more for products.

13-1   *Sources of the Next Sale*

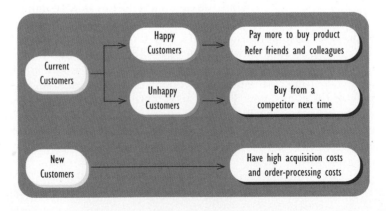

exhibit

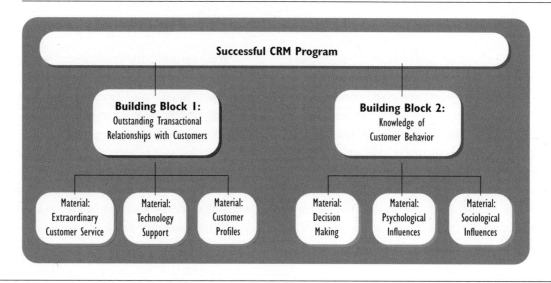

13-2   *Essential Materials of a Successful CRM Program*

Successful CRM Program

Building Block 1:
Outstanding Transactional
Relationships with Customers

Building Block 2:
Knowledge of
Customer Behavior

Material:
Extraordinary
Customer Service

Material:
Technology
Support

Material:
Customer
Profiles

Material:
Decision
Making

Material:
Psychological
Influences

Material:
Sociological
Influences

Essential Materials for a CRM Program

When you build something—a house, for example—you have a plan (a blueprint) that lists appropriate materials or component parts. Likewise, assembling a CRM program requires a plan so that the entrepreneur knows what people, processes, and so on (parts) she or he needs—and there are many parts in a successful CRM program. In the remainder of this chapter, we consider two vital building blocks of any CRM program: (1) outstanding relationships with customers and (2) knowledge of consumer behavior. These blocks may be constructed with a variety of "materials," as depicted in Exhibit 13-2. In the sections that follow, we examine those materials we believe to be tremendously important in constructing these two building blocks.

Creating Positive Transactional Relationships Through Extraordinary Service

To be successful in the long run, small firms need to concentrate on building positive transactional relationships with customers. A transactional relationship is an association between a business and a customer that relates to a purchase or a business deal. Consumers who have positive interactions with a business usually become loyal customers. Three basic beliefs underlie our emphasis on providing exceptional customer service:

1. Small businesses possess greater potential for providing superior customer service than do large firms.

2. Superior customer service leads to customer satisfaction.

3. Customer satisfaction results in a positive transactional relationship.

As these beliefs suggest, failure to emphasize customer service jeopardizes any effort to attain a positive customer relationship. "My message to small companies is that big companies are coming after you with better customer service, so you'd better be paying attention," says Edward Reilly, president and CEO of the American Management Association.[6]

> 2 Discuss the significance of providing extraordinary customer service.

transactional relationship
An association between a business and a customer that relates to a purchase or a business deal

How They See It: Maintaining Customer Relationships

Denny Fulk

No matter what type of business you operate, building and maintaining customer relationships is essential to its success. A friend of mine who operates a very successful e-commerce–based business responds regularly to his customers' questions, even if he is traveling outside of the United States. Since many of his customers are located in other parts of the world, customer inquiries arrive and are answered from several different time zones. His response mentions that he is traveling and is sending the e-mail from the city where he is located on that particular day. His staff is required to respond to all customer phone calls and e-mail within 24 hours.

If you operate a business, no matter how small or large, customers like to feel there is a person who really cares about their needs. Whether the information shared is by telephone or e-mail, promptness and a personal approach are keys to the customer's having a good feeling about your company. Regardless of whether your business is a startup or a very established company, a customer who receives a prompt, accurate, and understanding response will be very likely to continue doing business with your company. In the business-to-business setting, when I am dealing with a busy purchasing person or project manager, I like to say, "My job is to make your job easier."

Components of Customer Satisfaction

A number of factors under a firm's control contribute to customer satisfaction. One classic article identifies the following four elements as keys to customer satisfaction:[7]

1. Providing the most basic benefits of the product and/or service—the elements that customers expect all competitors to deliver

2. Offering general support services, such as customer assistance

3. Setting up a system to counteract any bad experiences customers may experience

4. Delivering extraordinary services that excel in meeting customers' preferences and make the product and/or service seem customized

Small firms are in a unique position to offer extraordinary service. Relationship marketing advocate Patrick Daly, who oversees a customer relations program for a company in Redwood City, California, suggests the following ways to provide extraordinary service:[8]

- *Naming names. In today's detached, "just give me your account number" world, nothing is more well received than individual, personalized attention. Even though you may already be courteous and friendly to customers, greeting them by name is valued 10 times more on the "worthy of loyalty" scale.*

- *Custom care. Customers pretty much know what they do and don't want from your company. If you remember what they want on an individual basis—even if it's something as simple as knowing a dry cleaning customer likes light starch in his collars—then you have mastered one of the key elements of a strong loyalty program.*

- *Keeping in touch. You can't communicate enough on a me-to-you basis with your customers. And don't just connect to make a pitch. Clip out a newspaper or magazine article that pertains to a customer's business and send it to him or her with a note saying "FYI—thought you'd be interested." When customers know that you're taking time to think about them, they don't forget it.*

- *"Boo-boo research." Part of any customer loyalty program is taking the time to reach out to lost customers to learn why they went elsewhere. In many cases, just contacting them and showing them that you really care about getting their business will win them back—along with their contribution to your profits.*

Living the Dream   putting technology to work

Photo by Scott Stewart/Scott Stewart Photography

Put Me on Hold Please

No one likes being put on hold, but entrepreneur and veteran radio talk show host Perry Wright knows how to keep you entertained while you wait. Known as the On-Hold Guy, Wright sells, through his website, software containing one-liners, odd facts, and puns to play for waiting customers.

"While I was doing radio, I spent a lot of time on the phone and on hold, listening to sterile, irritating messages," he says. "I thought there had to be a better way, an off-the-wall approach."

Automated phone systems can save on costs but frustrate callers. According to Wright's website, "70% of business phone callers are put on hold, . . . almost 60% of these callers hang up, and 30% will not call back . . . ever!" Wright's software randomly plays his messages, with the goal of putting customers in a good mood before they are connected to salespeople. One caller's comment was "Put me back on hold, QUICK; I want to hear the rest."

To hear a sample of the On-Hold Guy's product, go to http://www.onholdguy.com/demos.htm.

Sources: Bill Hudgins, "Hold Please," *MyBusiness*, April/May 2005, p. 50; and http://www.onholdguy.com, accessed March 1, 2007.

http://www.onholdguy.com

Providing exceptional customer service will give small firms a competitive edge, regardless of the nature of the business. Small firms must realize that it costs far more to replace a customer than to keep one. Offering top-notch customer service is something they can do better than large firms can.

Evaluating a Firm's Customer Service Health

Establishing an effective customer service program begins with determining the firm's "customer service quotient," which indicates how well the firm is currently providing service to its customers. Then strategies can be developed to improve the effectiveness of customer service efforts. Exhibit 13-3 shows some popular approaches to creating customer service strategies; it also provides space for evaluating how well your small firm is currently performing in each area and what it can do to improve its customer service.

How good or bad is the quality of customer service among both large and small firms? One extensive survey of consumers, reported in *USAToday,* described the situation this way:[9]

- *On the phone.* Some 80% of the nation's companies still haven't figured out how to do a decent job getting customers the assistance they need, says Jon Anaton, who oversees Purdue University's Center for Customer-Driven Quality and is research director at the consulting firm BenchmarkPortal.

- *Online.* Some 35% of all email inquiries to companies don't get a response within seven days, according to industry estimates. And about 25% never get a response at all, Forrester [Research] estimates.

exhibit

13-3   *Customer Service Strategies*

Which of the following can be used to support your marketing objectives?	For each strategy, comment below on: 1. How well your company is doing. 2. Improvements to pursue further.
Provide an exceptional experience throughout every transaction by ensuring that customers are acknowledged, appreciated, and find it easy to do business with you. Note that this requires you to (1) make a list of the typical chain of contacts between you and your customers—from when they first see your advertisement until you send them a customer survey after the sale and (2) evaluate your company's performance on each contact point.	
Provide sales materials that are clear and easy to understand, including website, marketing materials, retail displays, and sales conversations.	
Respond promptly to customers' requests and concerns by acting with urgency and responsibility in customer inquiries, transactions, and complaints. Have a service recovery plan in place.	
Listen to customers and respond accordingly by soliciting feedback, encouraging interaction, staying engaged throughout transactions, and taking the appropriate action necessary to please the customer.	
Stand behind products/services by providing guarantees and warranties and ensuring customers that you deliver on your promises. Also, create products and deliver services that exceed expectations.	
Treat customers as family members and best friends by valuing them the same way you honor those you care most about.	
Stay in the hearts and minds of customers by not taking customers for granted and finding ways to let them know you hold their best interests.	
Other initiatives? List them here.	

Source: "Exceptional Customer Experiences," *FastTrac,* Ewing Marion Kauffman Foundation, 2006.

- ***In "IVR" hell.*** To save on labor costs, many of America's largest companies have installed software that the industry calls Interactive Voice Response (IVR) systems. Yet more than 90% of financial service consumers say they don't like these systems, Forrester reports.

- *In a rage.* Nearly one in three customers say they have raised their voices at customer service reps and nearly one in 10 say they have cursed at them over the past year, according to a national phone survey by Customer Care Measurement & Consulting.

- *In response.* Two-thirds of the estimated 800,000 consumer complaints that have been passed along over the past three years to PlanetFeedback.com's trouble shooting Web site share the same theme: not getting a response from a company, says Sue MacDonald, marketing director.

Although customer service issues may be identified through a formal review process within the small firm, they often surface via customer complaints in the course of normal daily business operations. (Later in this chapter, we will show how complaint activity is part of the overall consumer behavior process.) Every firm strives to eliminate customer complaints. When they occur, however, they should be analyzed carefully to uncover possible weaknesses in product quality and/or customer service.

What is the special significance of customer complaints to small businesses? It is that small firms are *potentially* in a much better position than are big businesses to respond to such complaints and, thereby, to achieve customer satisfaction. Why? Because most problems are solvable by simply dealing with issues as they arise, thus giving customers more attention and respect. And showing respect is often easier for a small firm, because it has fewer employees and can give each of them the authority to act in customers' best interests. In contrast, a large business often assigns that responsibility to a single manager, who does not have daily contact with customers.

What do consumers do when they are displeased? As Exhibit 13-4 shows, consumers have several options for dealing with their dissatisfaction, and most of these options threaten repeat sales. Only one—a private complaint to the offending business—is desirable to the business. Customers' multiple complaint options emphasize the importance of quality customer service, both before and after a sale.

Managers can also learn about customer service concerns through personal observation and other research techniques. By talking directly to customers or by playing the customer's role anonymously—for example, by making a telephone call to one's own business—a manager can evaluate service quality. Some restaurants and motels invite feedback on customer service by providing comment cards to customers.

Consider the efforts of Jason Belkin, owner of Hampton Coffee Company, with two coffee-house locations in New Jersey. Belkin had always used a mystery shopper service to evaluate customer experiences but decided to turn to comment cards for the information he wanted, offering a free cup of coffee or tea to customers who fill out a card. Since he implemented the new approach, Belkin's business has increased, despite competition

---

How They See It: The CRM Advantage

John Stites

The advantage that a small firm has over a larger firm in customer relationship management is that the owner of the company is closer to the customers and more likely to get accurate feedback, unfiltered by layers of management. Unfortunately, the small business owner's time is often taken up with the urgent happenings in the company and customer relationship management may be neglected.

Most small business owners don't have the luxury of not being involved in customer relations, because an owner of a firm with only 100 customers must value those customers far more than the owner of a larger firm with 1,000 customers. The loss of one customer has a far greater impact on the smaller firm. However, a larger firm has more resources to address its customer relationship issues and can spread the cost of CRM over a greater customer base.

exhibit

13-4   *Consumer Options for Dealing with Product or Service Dissatisfaction*

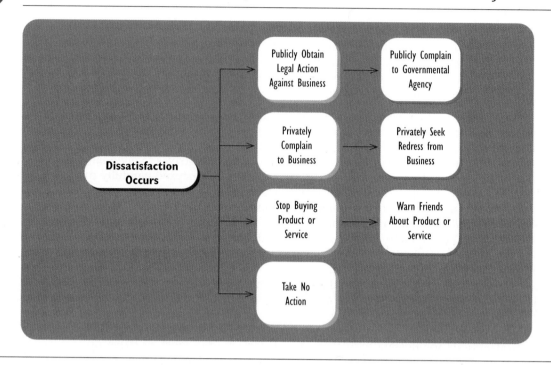

from new stores opened by Starbucks nearby.[10] Belkin attributes this success partly to effectively using the information collected on the comment cards.

Whatever method is used, evaluating customer service is critical for any business. Reflect on the success that Sewell Village Cadillac had after developing customer service tactics. This car dealership in Dallas, Texas, is famous for customer service. Its owner, Carl Sewell, started the customer service focus in 1967 when Sewell Village was in third place among three Dallas Cadillac dealers. He realized that most people didn't like doing business with car dealers. Therefore, he simply began asking customers what they didn't like about car dealers. Three major areas of dissatisfaction were identified—service hours, being without a car during service, and poor or incorrect repairs. By responding to these concerns—for example, by scheduling more service hours—Sewell Village Cadillac improved its customer satisfaction image.

Although many types of customer service cost very little, there are definite costs associated with superior customer service before, during, and after a sale. These costs can be reflected in the price of a product or service, or they can sometimes be recouped separately, based on the amount of service requested—through extended product warranties, for example. Most customers are willing to pay a premium for good service.

Using Technology to Support Customer Relationship Management

3 Illustrate how technology, such as the Internet, can improve customer relationships.

Long-term transactional relationships with customers are fostered by good information. A logical time to gather such data is during direct customer contacts, such as when a product is being sold. Customers may be contacted in many ways, including phone calls, letters, faxes, personal interactions, and e-mail. The ability to enjoy one-on-one contact with customers has always been a competitive advantage for small firms. Numerous software

How They See It: CRM in a Service-Oriented Business

Rick Davis

DAVACO is a service-oriented business, so we differentiate our company by the people we employ and the elements that make them more effective and productive at their jobs. Technology plays a very important role in making that happen. By utilizing a proprietary collection of technological components, DAVACO can provide operational efficiencies, increased visibility, and speed to market for a client list that represents the who's who of national retail brands.

For example, we use technology to manage our resources and skill sets internally, so that we can be assured that the right individuals and teams are always assigned to each job.

DAVACO equips its corporate and field employees with mobile technology, like pocket PCs, laptops, cell phones, BlackBerries, and digital cameras, which allows our clients to receive real-time updates. DAVACO also utilizes client-specific, Web-based portals that provide a centralized location for clients to view their store data, with 24-hour access to information, schedules, and customized reporting.

DAVACO has made it a priority to research, finance, and implement the best technology solutions that provide real business results and efficiencies for everyday operations. The firm's management team has made a conscientious decision to continuously reinvest profits in the company in order to better support our clients—because, in the end, happy clients are what makes our business a success.

packages containing word-processing, spreadsheet, and database tools are also available to assist in supporting customer contacts.

CRM software programs are designed to help companies gather all customer contact information into a single data management program. Web-based marketers, in particular, are attracted to CRM technology. Online shoppers expect excellent customer service, which is supported by such CRM tools as live chat. Overall, customer-service experts report positive perceptions by consumers of most company websites.[11]

Deciding which marketing activity should get initial CRM support is not always easy. However, the sales department is a popular place to start, because sales endeavors generate the greatest amount of customer contact. CRM focuses on such sales activities as accurate and prompt order filling, follow-up contacts to ensure customer satisfaction, and providing a user-friendly call center to handle all inquiries, including complaints.

Chris McCann, president of 1-800-flowers.com, seems to be ahead of the competition when it comes to incorporating technology into his business. By 1992, in the early days of the Internet, 1-800-flowers.com already had an online presence; by the late 1990s, it had a full-fledged e-commerce operation. Now McCann is using SAS CRM software to build close relationships with customers. He notes, "Everybody's available 24/7. The foundations of our early success have become a commodity. In order to retain our competitive advantage, we have to migrate toward becoming a customer-intimate company."[12]

Using a product called Enterprise Miner, McCann's business sifts through data looking for patterns that can be used to increase response rates of site visitors and tag the most profitable customers. For example, consider a customer who shops only once a year to purchase, say, roses on Valentine's Day; chances are that such a customer wouldn't appreciate repetitive marketing contacts. But another customer whose history shows purchases for occasions throughout the year might be responsive to more frequent contact and special offers. The SAS CRM software makes it possible to e-mail selected customers once a month to remind them of upcoming dates that the customers have pre-registered, thereby increasing the chance that they will make a purchase.

Having ample support resources for CRM information technology can be a concern for a small firm. This concern has led some entrepreneurs to outsource certain applications. For example, hosted call centers, which handle e-mail and Web communications for clients, may be more cost effective than comparable in-house centers, a crucial consideration for many cash-strapped small firms. In addition to cost, lack of in-house expertise is a major justification for using these outside services.

Living the Dream   putting technology to work

Courtesy of California Tortilla

Customers Love Taco Talk

The Internet provides small firms with the ability to distribute information about their products and services and sell them online. It can also be an effective tool for maintaining ongoing communication with customers, thereby cultivating positive customer motivations for the next purchase— that is, reasons to buy again.

Pam Felix started her quick-service Mexican restaurant California Tortilla in Bethesda, Maryland, in 1995. She launched a company website in 2000, with the primary goal of building an e-mail list to improve communication with customers. Since then, she has used the website to communicate the theme of "having fun."

Consider these observations of differences between how men and women act, which were posted on the site's "Taco Talk" page in January 2007, in celebration of Valentine's Day.

- A man will wait to see how much he spills on himself before he decides if he needs a napkin.

- A woman will rarely stand up in the middle of the restaurant and rub her belly when she's done with her burrito.

- A man will never ask another man if he can have a bite of his burrito.

- Men (and I) think it's perfectly acceptable to go to California Tortilla on a first date.

"I'm not sure I had any expectations [for the Internet]," says Felix. "But since I put out a goofy, monthly newsletter that most people seem to like, I thought at the very least I could keep conveying that goofy mom-and-pop feel via the Internet." And it has all worked well to help her build favorable relationships with customers. "People feel like they have a personal connection with us—and that's something the big chains are never going to have with their customers," Felix believes.

The Internet also provides feedback, identifying the restaurant's strengths and weaknesses. Plus, Felix says, "I get a lot of funny/strange e-mails that I get to use in the newsletter. . . . I ran out of things to say about burritos about 6 years ago."

Sources: Sharon Fling, "California Tortilla Customers Love Taco Talk," http://www.geolocal.com/public, May 27, 2004; and http://www.californiatortilla.com, accessed March 1, 2007.

http://www.californiatortilla.com

Building Customer Profiles for a CRM Program

4 Describe the techniques for creating a customer profile.

Most entrepreneurs say that the best way to stay in touch with customers and to identify their needs is to talk to them. Such conversations lead to a detailed understanding of who that customer really is and thus offer insights from which to build a **customer profile**, a collection of information about a customer, including demographic data, attitudes, preferences, and other behavioral characteristics, as defined by CRM goals. In a very small business, the customer profiles maintained in the entrepreneur's head often constitute the firm's CRM "database." At some point in a firm's growth, however, it becomes impossible for the entrepreneur to continue to develop profiles using this method alone. It is then time to turn to formal, computer-based databases.

customer profile
A collection of information about a customer, including demographic data, attitudes, preferences, and other behavioral characteristics, as defined by CRM goals

Customer profiles are essential to a successful CRM program, as they represent building material for the required knowledge of customers. Customer contact data, from sources such as warranty cards and accounting records, can be used to develop a profile. For Web-based ventures, current information can be collected at the point of contact, as customers order online.

What types of information should be included in a customer profile? Four major categories of information have been identified:[13]

- *Transactions.* A complete purchase history with accompanying details (price paid; SKU, which identifies the product puchased; delivery date).

- *Customer contacts.* Sales calls and service requests, including all customer- and company-initiated contacts.

- *Descriptive information.* Background information used for market segmentation and other data analysis purposes.

- *Responses to marketing stimuli.* Information on whether or not the customer responded to a direct marketing initiative, a sales contact, and/or any other direct contact.

Formal interviews with customers provide another way to gather profile information. These interviews can be oral, or they can take the form of a questionnaire. Consider, for example, Rejuvenation Lamp and Fixture Company, in Portland, Oregon, which sells reproduction light fixtures mainly through catalogs and its website. Its system for understanding its customers includes a questionnaire.

> *In every box of lights that is shipped, the company includes a questionnaire with a return stamp. The questionnaire is humorous and fun to fill out. It not only collects information about the purchases, it asks [customers] what products they might want that Rejuvenation doesn't carry. The "how can we help you?" message, combined with the prepaid return and humorous presentation, earns Rejuvenation thousands of responses each month.[14]*

Entrepreneur Mac McConnell conducts surveys of walk-in customers at his Artful Framer Gallery in Plantation, Florida. Based on the results of one recent survey, which consisted of a simple one-page questionnaire, he reworked his business to better satisfy customers' desires. The survey showed that quality was first priority for customers and price was last. McConnell dropped the low-end line and made higher-priced museum framing his specialty.[15]

Customer profiles primarily reflect demographic variables such as age, gender, and marital status, but they can also include behavioral, psychological, and sociological information. Understanding the aspects of consumer behavior presented in the following sections can help entrepreneurs create customer profiles that go beyond demographics. Some entrepreneurs might even want to consider taking a course to broaden their knowledge of consumer behavior concepts; such courses are commonly offered at local colleges. Exhibit 13-5 presents a simple model of consumer behavior structured around three interrelated aspects: the decision-making process, psychological influences, and sociological influences.

exhibit

13-5 *Simplified Model of Consumer Behavior*

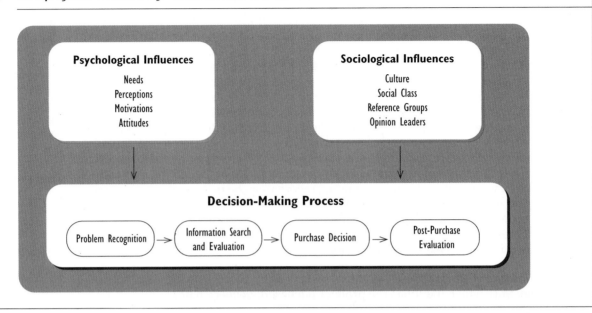

Psychological Influences

Needs
Perceptions
Motivations
Attitudes

Sociological Influences

Culture
Social Class
Reference Groups
Opinion Leaders

Decision-Making Process

Problem Recognition → Information Search and Evaluation → Purchase Decision → Post-Purchase Evaluation

Customers as Decision Makers

5 Explain how consumers are decision makers and why this is important to understanding customer relationships.

According to the model of consumer behavior shown in Exhibit 13-5, consumer decision making comprises four stages:

Stage 1: Problem recognition

Stage 2: Information search and evaluation

Stage 3: The purchase decision

Stage 4: Post-purchase evaluation

We'll use this widely accepted model to examine decision making among small business customers.

Problem Recognition

Problem recognition (stage 1) occurs when a consumer realizes that her or his current state of affairs differs significantly from some ideal state. Some problems are routine conditions of depletion, such as a lack of food when lunchtime arrives. Other problems arise less frequently and may evolve slowly. Recognition of the need to replace the family dining table, for example, may take years to develop.

A consumer must recognize a problem before purchase behavior can begin. Thus, the problem-recognition stage cannot be overlooked. Many small firms develop their product strategy as if consumers were in the later stages of the decision-making process, when in reality they have not yet recognized a problem!

Many factors influence consumers' recognition of a problem—either by changing the actual state of affairs or by affecting the desired state. Here are a few examples:

- A change in financial status (a job promotion with a salary increase)

- A change in household characteristics (the birth of a baby)

- Normal depletion (using up the last tube of toothpaste)

- Product or service performance (breakdown of the DVD player)

- Past decisions (poor repair service on a car)

- The availability of products (introduction of a new product)

An entrepreneur must understand the problem-recognition stage in order to decide on the appropriate marketing strategy to use. In some situations, a small business owner needs to *influence* problem recognition. In other situations, she or he may simply be able to *react* to problem recognition by consumers.

Information Search and Evaluation

The second stage in consumer decision making involves consumers' collection and evaluation of appropriate information from both internal and external sources. The consumer's principal objective is to establish evaluative criteria—the features or characteristics of the product or service that the consumer will use to compare brands.

Small business owners should understand which evaluative criteria consumers use to formulate their evoked set. An evoked set is a group of brands that a consumer is both aware of and willing to consider as a solution to a purchase problem. Thus, the initial challenge for a new firm is to gain *market awareness* for its product or service. Only then will the brand have the opportunity to become part of consumers' evoked sets.

evaluative criteria
The features or characteristics of a product or service that customers use to compare brands

evoked set
A group of brands that a consumer is both aware of and willing to consider as a solution to a purchase problem

Purchase Decision

Once consumers have evaluated brands in their evoked set and made their choice, they must still decide how and where to make the purchase (stage 3). A substantial volume of retail sales now comes from nonstore settings such as catalogs, TV shopping channels, and the Internet. These outlets have created a complex and challenging environment in which to develop marketing strategy. Consumers attribute many different advantages and disadvantages to various shopping outlets, making it difficult for the small firm to devise a single correct strategy. Sometimes, however, simple recognition of the factors can be helpful.

Of course, not every purchase decision is planned prior to entering a store or looking at a mail-order catalog. Studies show that most types of purchases from traditional retail outlets are not intended prior to the customers' entering the store. This fact places tremendous importance on such features as store layout, sales personnel, and point-of-purchase displays.[16]

Post-Purchase Evaluation

The consumer decision-making process does not end with a purchase. Small firms that desire repeat purchases from customers (and they all should) need to understand post-purchase behavior (stage 4). Exhibit 13-6 illustrates several consumer activities that occur

exhibit

13-6   *Post-Purchase Activities of Consumers*

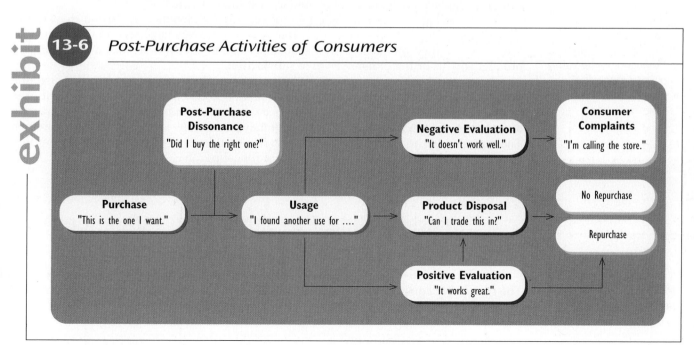

Living the Dream entrepreneurial challenges

© Kelly Cline./iStockphoto International

The Twenty-Foot Rule

At The Angus Barn in Raleigh, North Carolina, owner Van Eure empowers her employees to ensure customer satisfaction. Diners at the Raleigh landmark do not have to look for a manager when they have a complaint.

Eure, who took over the management of the restaurant after the death of her father in 1988, encourages employees to use the "twenty-foot rule"—that is, any restaurant employee within 20 feet of a problem, challenge, or opportunity should get involved in making sure that all customers leave completely satisfied. For example, waiters can provide dessert to a diner free of charge or accommodate a customer's needs by altering the seating chart. This rule reflects Eure's belief that employees are better able than managers (who often must juggle many projects at once) to see all sides of an issue.

The Angus Barn experiences very low turnover among its 220 employees. Each year, Eure hosts an employee banquet, where she presents numerous awards. She believes that her approach to resolving customer concerns underlies the satisfaction quotient of both her customers and her employees.

Sources: Laurie Zuckerman, "Picture Perfect," *MyBusiness,* April-May 2005, p. 12; and http://www. angusbarn.com, accessed March 3, 2007.

http://www.angusbarn.com

cognitive dissonance
The anxiety that occurs when a customer has second thoughts immediately following a purchase

during post-purchase evaluation. Two of these activities—post-purchase dissonance and complaint behavior—are directly related to customer satisfaction.

Post-purchase dissonance is a type of **cognitive dissonance**, a tension that occurs immediately following a purchase decision when consumers have second thoughts as to the wisdom of their purchase. This dissonance can influence how a consumer evaluates a product and his or her ultimate level of satisfaction.

Some purchases are never used, but most are. During and after product use, the product and the purchase process are evaluated. A consumer who is unhappy with the product or process may complain. This is an important opportunity for a business to make things right. A well-handled complaint may prevent the loss of a valuable customer. The outcome of the post-purchase process is a final level of customer satisfaction that affects customer loyalty and the likelihood of repeat purchases and product usage. It can also lead to brand switching and discontinuing use of the product category.

Understanding Psychological Influences on Customers

6 Describe certain psychological influences on consumer behavior.

The next major component of the consumer behavior model, as presented in Exhibit 13-5, is psychological influences. The four psychological influences that have the greatest relevance to small businesses are needs, perceptions, motivations, and attitudes.

Needs

Needs are often described as the starting point for all behavior. Without needs, there would be no behavior. Although consumer needs are innumerable, they can be identified as falling into four categories—physiological, social, psychological, and spiritual.

Consumers' needs are never completely satisfied, thereby ensuring the continued existence of business. One of the more complex characteristics of needs is the way in which they function together in generating behavior. In other words, various needs operate simultaneously, making it difficult to determine which need is being satisfied by a specific product or service. Nevertheless, careful assessment of the needs–behavior connection can be very helpful in developing marketing strategy. Different purchases of the same product satisfy different needs. For example, consumers purchase food products in supermarkets to satisfy physiological needs. But they also purchase food in status restaurants to satisfy their social and/or psychological needs. Also, certain foods are demanded by specific market segments to satisfy those consumers' religious, or spiritual, needs. A needs-based strategy would result in a different marketing approach in each of these situations.

needs
The starting point for all behavior

Perceptions

A second psychological factor, **perception**, encompasses those individual processes that ultimately give meaning to the stimuli consumers encounter. When this meaning is severely distorted or entirely blocked, consumer perception can cloud a small firm's marketing effort and make it ineffective. For example, a retailer may mark its fashion clothing "on sale" to communicate a price reduction from usual levels, but customers' perceptions may be that "these clothes are out of style."

Perception is a two-sided coin. It depends on the characteristics of both the stimulus and the perceiver. Consumers attempt to manage huge quantities of incoming stimuli through **perceptual categorization**, a process by which things that are similar are perceived as belonging together. Therefore, if a small business wishes to position its product alongside an existing brand and have it accepted as comparable, the marketing mix should reflect an awareness of perceptual categorization. Similar quality can be communicated through similar prices or through a package design with a color scheme similar to that of an existing brand. These techniques will help a consumer fit the new product into the desired product category.

Small firms that use an existing brand name for a new product are relying on perceptual categorization to pre-sell the new product. If, on the other hand, the new product is physically different or of a different quality, a brand name should be selected to create a distinctive perceptual categorization by the consumer.

If a consumer has strong brand loyalty to a product, it is difficult for other brands to penetrate his or her perceptual barriers. That individual is likely to have distorted images of competing brands because of a pre-existing attitude. Consumers' perceptions thus present a unique communication challenge.

perception
The individual processes that give meaning to the stimuli confronting consumers

perceptual categorization
The process of grouping similar things so as to manage huge quantities of incoming stimuli

Motivations

Unsatisfied needs create tension within an individual. When this tension reaches a certain level, the individual becomes uncomfortable and is motivated to reduce the tension.

Everyone is familiar with hunger pains, which are manifestations of the tension created by an unsatisfied physiological need. What directs a person to obtain food so that the hunger pains can be relieved? The answer is motivation. **Motivations** are goal-directed forces that organize and give direction to tension caused by unsatisfied needs. Marketers cannot create needs, but they can offer unique motivations to consumers. If an acceptable reason for purchasing a product or service is provided, it will probably be internalized by the consumer as a motivating force. The key for the marketer is to determine which motivations the consumer will perceive as acceptable in a given situation. The answer is found through an analysis of other consumer behavior variables.

Like physiological needs, the other three classes of needs—social, psychological, and spiritual—can be similarly connected to behavior through motivations. For example, when incomplete satisfaction of a person's social needs is creating tension, a firm may

motivations
Forces that organize and give direction to the tension caused by unsatisfied needs

show how its product can fulfill those social needs by providing acceptable motivations to that person. A campus clothing store might promote styles that communicate that the college student wearing those clothes has obtained membership in a group such as a fraternity or sorority.

Understanding motivations is not easy. Several motivations may be present in any situation, and they are often subconscious. However, they must be investigated in order for the marketing effort to be successful.

Attitudes

attitude
An enduring opinion based on knowledge, feeling, and behavioral tendency

Like the other psychological variables, attitudes cannot be observed, but everyone has them. Do attitudes imply knowledge? Do they imply feelings of good or bad, favorable or unfavorable? Does an attitude have a direct impact on behavior? The answer to each of these questions is a resounding yes. An **attitude** is an enduring opinion, based on a combination of knowledge, feeling, and behavioral tendency.

An attitude may act as an obstacle or a catalyst in bringing a customer to a product. For example, consumers with the belief that a local, family-run grocery store has higher prices than a national supermarket chain may avoid the local store. Armed with an understanding of the structure of a particular attitude, a marketer can approach the consumer more intelligently.

Understanding Sociological Influences on Customers

7 Describe certain sociological influences on consumer behavior.

Sociological influences, as shown in Exhibit 13-5, comprise the last component of the consumer behavior model. Among these influences are culture, social class, reference groups, and opinion leaders. Note that each of these sociological influences represents a different degree of group aggregation: Culture involves large masses of people, social classes and reference groups are smaller groups of people, and opinion leaders are single individuals who exert influence.

Culture

culture
Behavioral patterns and values that characterize a group of consumers in a target market

In marketing, **culture** refers to the behavioral patterns and values that characterize a group of customers in a target market. These patterns and beliefs have a tremendous impact on the purchase and use of products. Marketing managers often overlook the cultural variable because its influences are so subtly embedded within a society. Culture is somewhat like air; you do not think about its function until you are in water over your head! International marketers who have experienced more than one culture can readily attest to the impact of cultural influence.

The prescriptive nature of culture should concern the entrepreneur. Cultural norms create a range of product-related acceptable behaviors that influence what consumers buy. However, because culture does change by adapting slowly to new situations, what works well as a marketing strategy today may not work a few years from now.

An investigation of culture within a narrower boundary—defined by age, religious preference, ethnic orientation, or geographical location—is called *subcultural analysis*. Here, too, unique patterns of behavior and social relationships must concern the marketing manager. For example, the needs and motivations of the youth subculture are far different from those of the senior citizen subculture, and certain food preferences are unique to particular ethnic cultures. Small business managers who familiarize themselves with cultures and subcultures are able to create better marketing mixes.

social classes
Divisions within a society having different levels of social prestige

Social Class

Another sociological factor affecting consumer behavior is social class. **Social classes** are divisions within a society having different levels of social prestige. The social class system has important implications for marketing. Different lifestyles correlate with different levels of social prestige, and certain products often become symbols of a type of lifestyle.

For some products such as grocery staples, social class analysis will probably not be very useful. For others such as home furnishings, such analysis may help explain variations in shopping and communication patterns.

Unlike a caste system, a social class system provides for upward mobility. The social status of parents does not permanently fix the social class of their child. Occupation is probably the single most important determinant of social class. Other determinants used in social class research include possessions, source of income, and education.

Reference Groups

Technically, social class could be considered a reference group. However, marketers are generally more concerned with small groups such as families, work groups, neighborhood groups, or recreational groups. **Reference groups** are those smaller groups that an individual allows to influence his or her behavior.

reference groups
Groups that an individual allows to influence his or her behavior

The existence of group influence is well established. The challenge to the marketer is to understand why this influence occurs and how it can be used to promote the sale of a product. Individuals tend to accept group influence because of the benefits they perceive as resulting from it. These perceived benefits give the influencers various kinds of power. Five widely recognized forms of power, all of which are available to the marketer, are reward, coercive, referent, expert, and legitimate power.

Reward power and coercive power relate to a group's ability to give and to withhold rewards. Rewards may be material or psychological. Recognition and praise are typical psychological rewards. A Pampered Chef party is a good example of a marketing technique that takes advantage of reward power and coercive power. The ever-present possibility of pleasing or displeasing the hostess-friend tends to encourage the guests to buy.

Referent power and expert power involve neither rewards nor punishments. They exist because an individual attaches great importance to being like the group or perceives the group as being knowledgeable. Referent power influences consumers to conform to a group's behavior and to choose products selected by the group's members. Children will often be affected by referent power, so marketers can create a desire for products by using cleverly designed advertisements or packages. And a person perceived as an expert can be an effective spokesperson for a host of products.

Legitimate power involves the sanctioning of what an individual ought to do. We are most familiar with legitimate power at the cultural level, where it is evident in the prescriptive nature of culture, but it can also be used in smaller groups. Social marketing efforts are an attempt to encourage a certain behavior (e.g., wear your seat belt, don't drink and drive) as the right thing to do.

Opinion Leaders

According to widely accepted communication principles, consumers receive a significant amount of information through individuals called **opinion leaders**, who are group members playing a key communications role.

opinion leader
A group member who plays a key communications role

Generally speaking, opinion leaders are knowledgeable, visible, and exposed to the mass media. A small business firm can enhance its own image by identifying with such leaders. For example, a farm-supply dealer may promote its products in an agricultural community by holding demonstrations of these products on the farms of outstanding local farmers, who are the community's opinion leaders. Similarly, department stores may use attractive students as models when showing campus fashions.

Customer relationship management (CRM) is at the heart of any successful business. A satisfied customer is likely to be a repeat customer who will tell others about your company. Effectively managing customer relationships requires a thorough knowledge of the components of customer satisfaction, developing customer profiles, handling complaints, and understanding the customer decision-making process. The more small business owners know about their customers, the better job they can do in meeting the needs of those customers. Customer satisfaction is truly the key to small business success.

How They See It: Company Growth and CRM

Rick Davis

Since 1990, DAVACO's approach to customer relationships has been based on a simple corporate philosophy of exemplary service for national retail brands. Over the years, we've grown our revenue, our client base, and our number of employees, but customer service has remained the essence of our business operations. Our number one priority is servicing our clients' evolving needs at the retail level, and that's an unwavering commitment that won't be compromised by the size of DAVACO.

That being said, the fundamental components of our customer service program are some of those same relationship management approaches that are classically associated with smaller businesses. We continue to apply the same service philosophy that was established when the company was started, and that continues to be a key differentiator in the marketplace. DAVACO is a unique and emerging retail services company that offers clients a single point of contact, encourages open communication that fosters innovation, provides an accessible and experienced management team, and employs

great people that deliver customized services and quality execution.

At the same time, DAVACO has also developed a strong infrastructure that supports customer service initiatives that keep pace with larger businesses, especially as it relates to technology, innovation, nationwide reach, best practices, and extensive industry expertise. Because the company has been very strategic in assembling an experienced management team and developing a multi-year strategic plan to manage impressive annual growth, DAVACO has been able to provide the same exemplary service to our clients that they have always relied on.

In addition, our customer relationship management is driven by our employees and their commitment to excellence known as The DAVACO Way. This is a philosophy that defines who we are as a company and sets the standard of performance for all employees. The DAVACO Way places quality, professionalism, and teamwork above all else.

Looking BACK

1 Define customer relationship management (CRM) and explain its importance to a small firm.

- Customer relationship management (CRM) encompasses the strategies used by companies to manage their relationships with customers, including the capture, storage, and analysis of consumer information.
- The central message of every CRM program is "Court customers for more than a one-time sale."
- CRM is primarily a mind-set—the implementation of customer-centric strategies, which put customers first so that the firm can increase profits.
- A CRM program recognizes the importance of keeping current customers satisfied to ensure their

loyalty, given the high costs associated with attracting a new customer.

- Constructing a CRM program requires a plan so that the entrepreneur will know what people, processes, and so on he or she needs.
- Two vital building blocks of any CRM program are outstanding transactional relationships with customers and knowledge of consumer behavior.

2 Discuss the significance of providing extraordinary customer service.

- To be successful in the long run, small firms must provide outstanding service in order to develop and maintain loyal customers, as it costs far more to replace a customer than to keep one.

- Extraordinary service is the factor that small firms are in a unique position to offer.

- Providing exceptional customer service can give small firms a competitive edge, regardless of the nature of the business.

- Establishing an effective customer service program begins with determining the firm's "customer service quotient," which indicates how well the firm is currently providing service to its customers.

- The way customer service problems are most commonly recognized is through customer complaints.

- Managers can also learn about customer service problems through personal observation and other research techniques.

- Although many types of customer service cost very little, there are definite costs associated with superior levels of customer service.

3 Illustrate how technology, such as the Internet, can improve customer relationships.

- Long-term transactional relationships are built with information gathered from positive customer contacts.

- CRM technology helps companies gather all customer contact information into a single data management program.

- Web-based marketers, in particular, are attracted to CRM technology.

- CRM focuses on such sales functions as accurate and prompt order filling, follow-up contacts to ensure customer satisfaction, and the use of a user-friendly call center to handle all inquiries, including complaints.

- Having ample support resources for CRM information technology can be a concern for a small firm, and this concern has led some entrepreneurs to outsource certain applications.

- Hosted call centers require lower deployment costs than do comparable in-house centers, a crucial consideration for many cash-strapped small firms.

4 Describe the techniques for creating a customer profile.

- In a very small business, customer profiles are developed in the entrepreneur's head during conversations with customers.

- Customer profiles are essential to a successful CRM program, as they represent building material for the required knowledge of customers.

- Four categories of customer profile information are transactions, customer contacts, descriptive information, and responses to marketing stimuli.

- Formal interviews with customers provide another way to gather customer profile information.

5 Explain how consumers are decision makers and why this is important to understanding customer relationships.

- Consumer decision making involves four stages that are closely tied to ultimate customer satisfaction.

- Problem recognition (stage 1) occurs when a consumer realizes that her or his current state of affairs differs significantly from some ideal state.

- Stage 2 in consumer decision making involves consumers' collection and evaluation of appropriate information from both internal and external sources.

- Once consumers have evaluated brands in their evoked set and made their choice, they must still decide how and where to make the purchase (stage 3).

- Post-purchase evaluation (stage 4) may lead to cognitive dissonance, negatively influencing customer satisfaction with the product or service.

6 Describe certain psychological influences on consumer behavior.

- The four psychological influences that have the greatest relevance to small businesses are needs, perceptions, motivations, and attitudes.

- Needs are often described as the starting point for all behavior.

- Perception encompasses those individual processes that ultimately give meaning to the stimuli confronting consumers.

- Motivations are goal-directed forces that organize and give direction to tension caused by unsatisfied needs.

- An attitude is an enduring opinion, based on a combination of knowledge, feeling, and behavioral tendency.

7 Describe certain sociological influences on consumer behavior.

- Among the sociological influences are culture, social class, reference groups, and opinion leaders.

- In marketing, *culture* refers to the behavioral patterns and values that characterize a group of customers in a target market.

- Social classes are divisions within a society having different levels of social prestige.

- Reference groups are those smaller groups that an individual allows to influence his or her behavior.

- According to widely accepted communication principles, consumers receive a significant amount of information through opinion leaders, who are group members playing a key communications role.

Key TERMS

customer relationship management (CRM), p. 349

transactional relationship, p. 351

customer profile, p. 359

evaluative criteria, p. 361

evoked set, p. 361

cognitive dissonance, p. 362

needs, p. 363

perception, p. 363

perceptual categorization, p. 363

motivations, p. 363

attitude, p. 364

culture, p. 364

social classes, p. 364

reference groups, p. 365

opinion leader, p. 365

Discussion QUESTIONS

1. Define customer relationship management. What is meant by the statement "CRM is primarily a mind-set"?

2. Does CRM put more emphasis on current or potential customers? Why?

3. What are the two essential building blocks of a successful CRM program? What "materials" are used to construct these building blocks?

4. Why is a small firm potentially in a better position to achieve customer satisfaction than is a big business?

5. Discuss how technology supports customer relationship management.

6. What types of information should be part of a customer profile?

7. What techniques or sources of information can be used to develop a customer profile?

8. Briefly describe the four stages of the consumer decision-making process. Why is the first stage so vital to consumer behavior?

9. List the four psychological influences on consumers that were discussed in this chapter. What is their relevance to consumer behavior?

10. List the four sociological influences on consumers that were discussed in this chapter. What is their relevance to consumer behavior?

You Make the CALL

SITUATION 1

Jeremy Shepherd is the founder of PearlParadise.com, in Santa Monica, California. His jewelry business recognizes the importance of ensuring that customers keep coming back.

However, Shepherd is uncertain as to which customer retention techniques he should use to develop a strong foundation for repeat business. PearlParadise.com's website has the software capabilities to support customer interaction.

Sources: Melissa Campanelli, "Happy Returns," http://www.entrepreneur.com/mag/article/0,1539,312420,00.htm, January 2004; and http://www.pearlparadise.com, accessed July 11, 2007.

Question 1 What customer loyalty techniques would you recommend to Shepherd?

Question 2 What information would be appropriate to collect about customers in a database?

Question 3 What specific computer-based communication could be used to achieve Shepherd's goal?

SITUATION 2

Paul Layer is the owner of Aspen Funeral Alternatives in Albuquerque, New Mexico. Aspen is located in a converted restaurant with fluorescent lights, and its chapel has chairs, not pews. "It looks more like your insurance company or local business office, rather than a funeral home," Layer says.

Aspen has adopted a strategy of discounted prices for funeral products and services. Its website promotes low-cost alternatives with no fancy facilities, no limousines, and no hearses. A general price list, covering Aspen's professional services, use of its facilities, and caskets, is posted on the site.

Sources: Lorrie Grant, "Funeral Stores Sell Inevitable in Style," *USAToday,* May 30, 2001, p. 3B; and http://www.aspenfuneral.com, June 8, 2004.

Question 1 What psychological concepts of consumer behavior are relevant to marketing this service? Be specific.

Question 2 How can the stages of consumer decision making be applied to a person's decision to use a particular funeral home?

Question 3 What types of CRM techniques could be used by this type of business?

SITUATION 3

In the late 1990s, entrepreneur Neil Peterson was traveling in Europe when he observed what to him was a new way to own a car. It was called car sharing. Under this concept, the customer doesn't buy a car outright but uses the vehicle as a person would a timeshare property. The concept isn't totally new to the United States but has only caught on in a few places.

Peterson has big plans. He wants to bring the car-sharing concept to large U.S. cities. His research, based on American Automobile Association data, shows that the average cost of owning or leasing a new car, including insurance, is around $625 a month. He believes the average car-sharing member will pay only $100 a month.

Source: Kortney Stringer, "How Do You Change Consumer Behavior?" http://www.entrepreneur.com/Your_Business/YB_PrintArticle/0,2361,310457,00.html, June 7, 2004.

Question 1 What sociological issues may have an impact on the success of this venture?

Question 2 In which consumer decision-making stage do you believe Peterson's potential customers will be located? Why?

Experiential EXERCISES

1. For several days, make notes on your own shopping experiences. Summarize what you consider to be the best customer service you receive.

2. Interview a local entrepreneur about her or his company's consumer service efforts. Summarize your findings.

3. Interview a local entrepreneur about what types of customer complaints the business receives. Also ask how he or she deals with different complaints. Report your findings to the class.

4. Consider your most recent meaningful purchase. Compare the decision-making process you used to the four stages of decision making presented in this chapter. Report your conclusions.

Exploring the WEB

1. Visit the SBA Web site at **http://www.sba.gov**. Click on "Small Business Planner"; then under "Manage Your Business," click on "Market and Price," and then select "Customer Service." What are the "Five Rules of Customer Care" that one can follow to help keep customers happy?

Video Case 13

Rodgers Chevrolet (p. 646)
This case illustrates how one entrepreneur utilized customer service management to build a strong customer base, focusing not only on the customer but also on employee satisfaction.

Alternative Case for Chapter 13
Case 15, Nicole Miller Inc., p. 650

chapter 14

Product and Supply Chain Management

Country Supply
http://www.horse.com

Raising horses is an expensive undertaking, and not just for those who race thoroughbreds. A modest estimate of the cost of horse ownership is $6,000 a year, which includes only sheltering, feeding, grooming, and shoeing the animal. Then there are veterinary bills, toys, tack, riding gear for the owner, and so forth. The final expenditures can soar much higher, depending on where you live and how many horses you own. Still, there are over 30 million horse lovers in the United States, who dote on the 11 million horses in the country. Roughly 4 million households spend a combined total of $25 billion on goods and services for their horses!

Scott Mooney, founder of Country Supply, built his company to serve horse lovers. When he was in high school, he started selling horse equipment out of his barn in Ottumwa, Iowa (population 24,998). Despite his local success, Mooney realized that to grow the business, he was going to have to get more exposure for his products. He decided to transform Country Supply into a catalog company, which now serves roughly 450,000 customers and generates $17 million in annual revenue.

How was Mooney able to go from selling equine products in Ottumwa to selling equipment, tack, and supplies across the United States? He did it by creating a lean distribution network that keeps costs down, profits healthy, and customers coming back for more. Watch this spotlight to see how an effective distribution strategy can drive success.

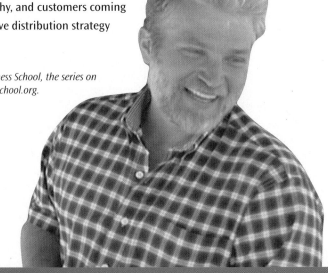

Video material provided by Hattie Bryant, Producer of Small Business School, the series on PBS Stations, Worldnet, and the Web at http://www.smallbusinessschool.org.

Small**BusinessSchool**
the Series on PBS stations and the Web

1   Explain the challenges associated with growth in a small firm.
2   Explain the role of innovation in a firm's growth.
3   Identify stages in the product life cycle and the new product development process.
4   Describe the building of a firm's total product.
5   Explain product strategy and the alternatives available to small businesses.
6   Describe the legal environment affecting product decisions.
7   Explain the importance of supply chain management.
8   Specify the major considerations in structuring a distribution channel.

In Chapter 13, you learned that entrepreneurs need to make a strong commitment to customer relationship management (CRM). Furthermore, you learned that marketing programs must reflect consumer behavior concepts if CRM efforts are to sustain the firm's competitive advantage. In this chapter, we address product and supply chain management decisions, which together have a significant impact on the total bundle of satisfaction targeted to customers.

To Grow or Not to Grow

1 Explain the challenges associated with growth in a small firm.

Once a new venture has been launched, the newly created firm settles into day-to-day operations. Its marketing plan reflects current goals as well as any thoughts of expansion or growth, which will impact marketing activities.

Entrepreneurs differ in their desire for growth. Some want to grow rapidly, while others prefer a modest growth rate. Many prefer not to grow at all—maintaining the status quo is challenge enough, and this becomes the driving force behind their marketing decisions. Despite this attitude, growth sometimes happens unexpectedly. The entrepreneur is then forced to concentrate all efforts on meeting demand. Consider the case of an entrepreneur named Jerry. When he showed a new line of flannel nightgowns to a large chain-store buyer, the buyer immediately ordered 500 of the gowns, with delivery expected in five days! Jerry accepted the order even though he had material on hand for only 50 gowns. He emptied his bank account to purchase the necessary material and frantically begged former college classmates to join him in cutting and sewing the gowns. After several sleepless nights, he fulfilled the order.[1] The lesson: Growing quickly can be a stressful proposition.

For many small firms, however, growth is an expected and achievable goal. In some cases, fast growth is part of the initial business plan. Karen McMasters launched her first online company, a baby products business, in February 2000. Today, Barebabies.com has six full-time employees and is thriving, with an average of 350 orders in a typical week. In 2003, she started AllCola.com, a website where Coca-Cola memorabilia is sold. And in 2004, she started a third online company to sell different lines of baby items. She is excited about all three ventures, because she had always wanted growth. McMasters recommends planning to start multiple companies; that way, "you know what steps need to be taken and in what order."[2]

Successful growth seldom occurs on its own. Many factors—including financing—must be considered and managed carefully. When a firm experiences rapid growth in sales volume, the firm's income statements will generally reflect growing profits. However, rapid growth in sales and profits may be hazardous to the firm's cash flows. A "growth trap" can occur, because growth tends to demand additional cash more rapidly than such cash is generated in the form of additional profits.

Inventory, for example, must be expanded as sales volume increases; additional dollars must be expended for merchandise or raw materials to accommodate the higher level of sales. Similarly, accounts receivable must be expanded proportionally to meet the increased sales volume. Obviously, a growing, profitable business can quickly find itself in a financial bind—growing profitably while its bank accounts dwindle.

The growth problem is particularly acute for small firms. Quite simply, increasing sales by 100 percent is easier for a small firm than for a *Fortune* 500 firm. And doubling sales volume makes a firm a much different business. This fact, combined with difficulty in obtaining external funding, may have detrimental effects if cash is not managed carefully. In short, a high-growth firm's need for additional financing may exceed its available resources, even though the firm is profitable. Without additional resources, the firm's cash balances may decline sharply, leaving it in a precarious financial position.

Growth also places huge demands on a small firm's personnel and the management style of its owners. When Cody Kramer Imports, a Blauvelt, New York, candy distributor, saw private-label orders triple from the same period the year before, its six-person staff was too small to handle the growth. Owners Scott Semel and Reed Chase quickly hired a production supervisor to coordinate shipments, but it "was hard for us to let go for a long, long time— probably to the detriment of the company," explains Semel.[3] High demand for products can stretch a firm's staff too thin and result in burnout, apathy, and poor overall performance.

Despite these and other challenges, the entrepreneurial spirit continues to carry small firms forward in pursuit of growth. Business expansion can occur in many ways. One path to growth is paved by innovation.

Innovation: A Path to Growth

2 Explain the role of innovation in a firm's growth.

From a menu of growth options, enterpreneurs generally choose the one they believe will lead to the most favorable outcomes, such as superior profitability, increased market share, and improved customer satisfaction. These are some "fruits" of competitive advantage, and they all contribute to the value of the firm.

Competitive Advantage and Innovation

Well-known economist Joseph Schumpeter viewed entrepreneurship as "creative destruction"—that is, making improvements to existing products, manufacturing methods, organizational processes, and other such factors to create new business opportunities. In his view, the spirit of innovation permeates any entrepreneurial enterprise.

As indicated in Chapter 1, entrepreneurs often simply see a different and better way of doing things. Studies have shown that small entrepreneurial firms produce twice as many innovations per employee as large firms, and these innovations account for half of all those created and an amazing 95 percent of all *radical* innovations.[4] It could be said that innovation provides the soil in which startups' competitive advantage can take root and grow, taking on a life of its own. Some of the most widely recognized examples of small firm innovation are soft contact lenses, the Zipper, safety razors, overnight national delivery, and air conditioning.

There is a certain glamour associated with innovation, but creating and then perfecting new products or services is often difficult. Consider a new technology designed to scan a person's body and determine his or her exact dimensions. Developed and marketed by [TC]² of Cary, North Carolina, it has been used by big-name players like Levi Strauss to provide jeans with a custom fit and footwear giant Nike to promise perfect-fitting shoes. The technology offers conveniences for both stores and customers—it makes dressing rooms obsolete, it ensures a better fit and thus fewer returns, and it even stores scanned measurements for future use. But when Rebecca Quick, a reporter for the *Wall Street Journal,* used an [TC]² scanner (a virtual dressing room) to try on clothes, she found that the software misread her dimensions and fashioned an exaggerated "pear shaped" figure for the reporter. This produced a shocking image that did not exactly promote a sale and certainly provided a less-than-perfect fit.[5] That's one way to eliminate repeat business!

Needless to say, the risk of failure increases when innovation is the goal. With this in mind, we offer a few "rules of thumb" that may help to reduce that risk somewhat.

- *Base innovative efforts on your experience.* Innovative efforts are more likely to succeed when you know something about the product or service technology. Entrepreneur Donna Boone, who swam competitively for her Ashburn, Virginia, high school, used her swimming experience to successfully open four indoor swim schools throughout the Washington, D.C., area, all within five years. Her Potomac Swim School is in its second year and doing "swimmingly."[6]

- *Focus on products or services that have been largely overlooked.* You are more likely to strike "pay dirt" in a vein that has not already been fully mined and in which competitors are few. Inventors and entrepreneurs Ron L. Wilson II and Brian LeGette, co-founders of the firm 180s LLC in Baltimore, Maryland, put a new twist on the familiar earmuff. Their ear warmers fit around the back of the neck and don't mess up the hair. So far, 4.5 million have been sold in 42 countries.[7]

- *Be sure there is a market for the product or service you are hoping to create.* This business fundamental is as applicable to innovation in startups as it is to innovation in existing businesses. For example, people who want help losing weight are everywhere. So if William Longley, founder of Scientific Intake in Atlanta, Georgia, can reach the target market for his invention, he should do well. Longley's firm produces a retainer-like device, called the DDS System, that specially trained dentists fit into the top of a person's mouth. The $500 device slows down eating, which translates into less food consumption and, theoretically, weight loss.[8]

- *Pursue innovation that customers will perceive as adding value to their lives.* It is not enough to create a product or service that you believe in; people become customers when *they* conclude that it will provide value they cannot find elsewhere. Entrepreneur Sharon Bennett followed this risk-reduction recommendation; her creation is based on concern for the welfare of pets. To give owners a more humane way to control their dogs when tugging on the leash, she developed a head collar, which she markets under the EasyWalker name.[9]

- *Focus on new ideas that will lead to more than one product or service.* Success with an initial product or service is critical, of course, but investment in innovation packs even more of a punch when it also leads to other innovative products or services. The experience of scientist James A. Patterson provides a good example of this strategy. His discovery, a topical brown powder that stops bleeding when sprinkled on minor cuts and scrapes, is named QR, short for "quick relief." His Sarasota, Florida, company Biolife LLC, which he began with a partner, has already added new products such as SportsQR, NosebleedQR, and Kid'sQR, as well as products for the hospital market.[10]

- *Raise sufficient capital to launch the new product or service.* It is easy to underestimate the cost of bringing an innovation successfully to market. Many small firms run short of cash before they are able to do so. Be prepared to look for new sources of capital along the way. Steve Dunn recognized the importance of obtaining sufficient funding to extend his new line of baby products in a competitive market, especially after previous successes had resulted in outside venture capitalists knocking at his door. Founded in 1991, Munchkin, Inc., has created products that "transform the ordinary to a new level of innovation and creativity." Located in Van Nuys, California, the company is the top seller of baby utensils at Wal-Mart.[11]

Small companies that are "one-hit wonders" may find that the ride comes to an abrupt and unpleasant ending. While one innovation can provide a launch pad for a new and interesting business, continued innovation is critical to sustaining competitive advantage in the years to follow.

Sustainability and Innovation

How can a company sustain its competitive advantage? Various strategies can help. For example, some entrepreneurs with sophisticated technology obtain patents, and this is often a wise thing to do. Others try to operate "below the radar screen" of competitors, but the effort to avoid attracting attention limits their growth. Some businesses find protection through contracts. In 1970, Doyle Owens started a company called Unclaimed Baggage, which sells luggage that is left at airports. In 1996, Owens sold the business to his son, Bryan, who has since expanded it by an amazing 400 percent. The business

exhibit

14-1   *The Competitive Advantage Life Cycle*

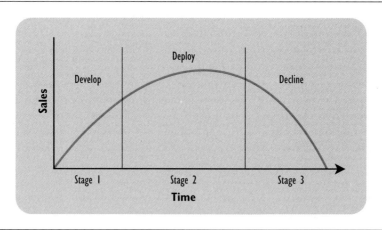

sustainable competitive advantage (SCA)
A value-creating position that is likely to endure over time

concept is simple—so how has Unclaimed Baggage been able to dominate the niche without contest? The answer is that the company has long-term contracts with major airports around the world, thereby blocking other companies from getting into the game.[12]

A business can take steps to slow down threats from competitors, but no competitive advantage lasts forever. Research has emphasized the importance of **sustainable competitive advantage (SCA)**, a value-creating position that is likely to endure over time. To incorporate sustainability into strategy, the entrepreneur should use the unique capabilities of the firm in a way that competitors will find difficult to imitate. Sooner or later, however, rivals will discover a way to copy any value-creating strategy. Therefore, it is also important to think of new ways to reinvest performance outcomes (financial returns, customer goodwill, etc.) so that the basis of competitive advantage can be renewed over the long run.[13]

Competitive advantage tends to follow a fairly consistent pattern. Building a competitive advantage requires resource commitments that lead to a performance payoff. However, returns from that competitive advantage will always diminish over time.

Exhibit 14-1 illustrates the competitive advantage life cycle, which has three stages: develop, deploy, and decline. Simply put, a firm must invest resources to *develop* a competitive advantage, which it can later *deploy* to boost its performance. But that position will eventually *decline* as rival firms build these advantages into their own strategies.

In order to maintain performance over time, firms must produce a continuous stream of competitive advantages to keep performance from falling off. However, tomorrow's performance can be maintained only if it is supported by today's surplus resources. In other words, a firm must launch a new competitive advantage *before* the current strategy has run its course (see Exhibit 14-2). And that is what many small companies are doing. Entrepreneurs are more likely to maintain venture performance if they keep an eye on the future. Introducing a new product or service, however, can be a tricky proposition. It can be expensive and time-consuming to introduce a new product or service, and failure rates can be high—on average, one-third of all new products fail, and in some industries, the failure rate can be much higher.[14]

Etrema Products, Inc., is a high-technology startup in Ames, Iowa, that is acutely aware of the need to continually refresh its competitive advantage. The company found a way to use Terfenol-D, a rare earth alloy, to create a product called Whispering Windows, which is a pair of chrome disks that can turn any window, wall, or conference table into an audio speaker. Though the disks cost a pricey $1,500 a pair, market interest is significant—and growing. The 40-employee company has a lock on the market for now, since no one else in the United States knows how to manufacture the product affordably. However, Etrema executives predict that they have only a few more years before competitors find a way to make Terfenol-D more cheaply (three Chinese companies already make pirated versions) or to replace it with something that works even better. Thinking ahead, Etrema scientists are scrambling to discover new applications (for example, would Terfenol-D work in hearing aids?) and to develop a successor to the alloy. And employees of the company

exhibit

14-2 *Sustaining Competitive Advantage*

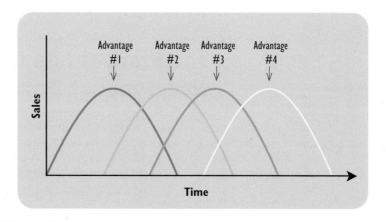

Living the Dream

utilizing the internet

Making a Sweet Connection

A small firm can try to extend the unique capabilities that constitute its competitive advantage to other value-creating ventures. One New York City–based retailer of candies and related items is giving it a try.

In October 2001, Dylan Lauren—daughter of well-known designer Ralph Lauren—founded Dylan's Candy Bar, which claims to offer the widest assortment of novelty candy in the world. The flagship store on the Upper East Side of Manhattan offers a "traditional 'sweets' store by creating a unique and completely unmatched shopping experience in a visually awe-inspiring environment." Store fixtures resemble candy, and the store stocks more than 5,000 varieties of candy.

Recently, Lauren took the business online, offering 85-plus products, including apparel, candy baskets, and candy spa items like candles and soap. The online approach is to use an "mmm-commerce" wireless campaign, which allows site visitors to send wireless phone users coupons redeemable for candy and merchandise in her five brick-and-mortar stores now located in New York, Texas, and Florida.

Music is one of the attractions of the website. Visitors, for a small fee, can download ring tones to their cell phones, including such songs as "Lollipop, Lollipop" and "I Want Candy." Users can also contact friends using the site's free text-messaging service. The ring tones and SMS messages are a very effective marketing tool as they drive traffic, not only back to the website, but directly into the stores.

Sources: http://www.dylanscandybar.com, accessed January 10, 2007; Beth Cox, "mmm-commerce—How Sweet Can It Be?" http://ecommerce.internet.com/news, April 25, 2004; and April Y. Pennington, "Eye Candy," *Entrepreneur,* April 2004, p. 168.

http://www.dylanscandybar.com

often make what they call "missionary calls" to find partners who would be willing to work with Etrema in creating new applications for the product, such as the dry razor they talked about developing with Remington.[15] The moral of the story is clear: Competitive advantage is sustainable only for those companies that are already planning for the future.

The Product Life Cycle and New Product Development

Our discussion of growth and innovation illustrated how entrepreneurial firms can be part of the development of new products for the marketplace. At this point, we will focus our discussion more narrowly, to answer two additional questions: What creates the need for innovation in a specific business? and How can innovation be managed? We will examine these questions by looking at the product life cycle concept and a four-stage approach to new product development.

The Product Life Cycle

product life cycle
A detailed picture of what happens to a specific product's sales and profits over time

An important concept underlying sound product strategy is the product life cycle, which allows us to visualize the sales and profits of a product from the time it is introduced until it is no longer on the market. The **product life cycle** provides a detailed picture of what happens to an *individual* product's or service's sales and profits; it has a shape similar to that of the competitive advantage life cycle, depicted in Exhibit 14-1 on page 374. Progressing along the product life cycle (sales) curve in Exhibit 14-3, we can see that the initial stages are characterized by a slow and, ideally, upward movement. The stay at the top is exciting but relatively brief. Then, suddenly, the decline begins, and downward movement can be rapid. Also, note the shape of the typical profit curve in Exhibit 14-3. The introductory stage is dominated by losses, with profits peaking in the growth stage.

The product life cycle concept is important to the small business owner for three reasons. First, it helps the entrepreneur to understand that promotion, pricing, and distribution policies should all be adjusted to reflect a product's position on the curve. Second, it highlights the importance of rejuvenating product lines, whenever possible, before they die. Third, it is a continuing reminder that the natural life cycle of a product follows the classic normal curve and, therefore that innovation is necessary for a firm's survival. Good business practice entails beginning a new curve before the existing curve of the product life cycle peaks.

exhibit

14-3 *The Product Life Cycle*

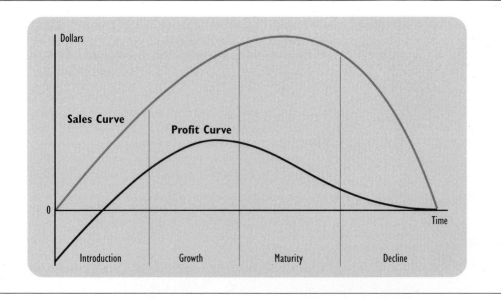

The New Product Development Process

A major responsibility of the entrepreneur is to find, evaluate, and introduce new products. This responsibility requires that the entrepreneur establish a process for developing new products. In big businesses, committees or entire departments are created for that purpose. Even in small firms, however, new product development needs to be a formalized process.

Entrepreneurs tend to treat new product development as a mountainous task—and it usually is. Many find that the four-stage, structured approach, described below, is the best way to tackle new product development.

IDEA ACCUMULATION The first stage of the new product development process—idea accumulation—involves increasing the pool of ideas under consideration. New products start with ideas, and these ideas have varied origins. The many possible sources include the following:

- Sales, engineering, or other personnel within the firm

- Government-owned patents, which are generally available on a royalty-free basis

- Privately owned patents listed by the U.S. Patent Office

- Other small companies that may be available for acquisition or merger

- Competitors' products and advertising

- Requests and suggestions from customers

- Brainstorming

- Marketing research (primary and secondary)

BUSINESS ANALYSIS Business analysis is the second stage in new product development. Every new product idea must be carefully studied in relation to several financial considerations. Costs and revenues are estimated and analyzed with techniques such as break-even analysis. Any idea failing to show that it can be profitable is discarded during the business analysis stage. Four key factors need to be considered in conducting a business analysis:

1. *The product's relationship to the existing product line.* Some firms intentionally add very different products to their product mix. However, in most cases, any product item or product line added should be consistent with—or somehow related to—the existing product mix. For example, a new product may be designed to fill a gap in a firm's product line or in the range of prices of the products it currently sells. If the product is completely new, it should have at least a family relationship to existing products. Otherwise, the new product may call for drastic and costly changes in manufacturing methods, distribution channels, type of promotion, and/or sales strategy.

2. *Cost of development and introduction.* One problem in adding new products is the cost of their development and introduction. Considerable capital outlays may be necessary, including expenditures for design and development, marketing research to establish sales potential, advertising and sales promotion, patents, and additional equipment. One to three years may pass before profits are realized on the sale of a new product.

3. *Available personnel and facilities.* Obviously, having adequate skilled personnel and production equipment is preferable to having to add employees and buy equipment. Thus, introducing new products is typically more appealing if the personnel and the required equipment are already available.

4. *Competition and market acceptance.* Still another factor to be considered in a business analysis is the potential competition facing a proposed product in its target market. Competition must not be too severe. Some studies, for example, suggest that a new product can be introduced successfully only if 5 percent of the total market can be secured. The ideal solution, of course, is to offer a product that is sufficiently different from existing products or that is in a cost and price bracket where it avoids direct competition.

DEVELOPMENT OF THE PRODUCT   The next stage of new product development entails sketching out the plan for branding, packaging, and other supporting efforts, such as pricing and promotion. An actual prototype may be needed at this stage. After these components have been evaluated, the new product idea may be judged a misfit and discarded or passed on to the next stage for further consideration.

PRODUCT TESTING   The last step in the product development process is product testing. The physical product should be proven acceptable through testing. While the product can be evaluated in a laboratory setting, a limited test of market reaction should also be conducted.[16]

Building the Total Product

A major responsibility of marketing is to transform a basic product concept into a total product. Even when an idea for a unique new pen has been developed into physical reality in the form of the basic product, it is still not ready for the marketplace. The total product offering must be more than the materials molded into the shape of the new pen. To be marketable, the basic product must be named, have a package, perhaps have a warranty, and be supported by other product features. Let's examine a few of the components of a total product offering.

Branding

An essential element of a total product offering is a brand. A **brand** is a means of identifying the product—verbally and/or symbolically. Small firms are involved in "branding," whether they realize it or not. An entrepreneur may neither know nor care, but his or her company has a brand identity. Exhibit 14-4 depicts the components of a firm's brand identity. The intangible **brand image** component—people's overall perception of a brand—may be even more important to acceptance of a firm's bundle of satisfaction than the tangible brand mark and brand name elements. For example, prior to 2003, Martha Stewart had arguably one of the strongest brand images in the marketplace. However, her personal legal troubles tarnished the Martha Stewart brand and even resulted in a temporary suspension of her popular home design/cooking show on national television. More recently, though, the Martha Stewart brand has recovered much of its former glory in the marketplace.

---

4 Describe the building of a firm's total product.

brand
A verbal and/or symbolic means of identifying a product

brand image
People's overall perception of a brand

---

exhibit

14-4   *Components of a Brand Identity*

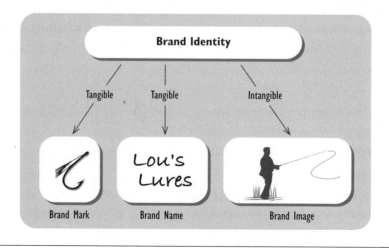

The tangible components of brand identity are brand names and brand marks. A **brand name** is a brand that can be spoken—like the name Dell. A **brand mark** is a brand that *cannot* be verbalized—like the golden arches of McDonald's.

Since a product's brand name is so important to the image of the business and its products, careful attention should be given to the selection of a name. In general, five rules apply in naming a product:

1. *Select a name that is easy to pronounce and remember.* You want customers to remember your product. Help them do so with a name that can be spoken easily— for example, TWO MEN & A TRUCK (a moving service) or Water Water Everywhere (a lawn irrigation business). Before choosing to use your own family name to identify a product, evaluate it carefully to ensure its acceptability.

2. *Choose a descriptive name.* A name that is suggestive of the major benefit of the product can be extremely helpful. As a name for a sign shop, Sign Language correctly suggests a desirable benefit. Blind Doctor is a creative name for a window blind repair business. The Happy Company is a great name for a small firm producing bath toys for young children. However, Rocky Road would be a poor name for a business selling mattresses!

3. *Use a name that is eligible for legal protection.* Be careful to select a name that can be defended successfully. Do not risk litigation by copying someone else's brand name. A new soft drink named Doc Pepper would likely be contested by the Dr Pepper company.

4. *Select a name with promotional possibilities.* Exceedingly long names are not, for example, compatible with good copy design on billboards, where space is at a premium. A competitor of the McDonald's hamburger chain is called Bob's, a name that will easily fit on any billboard. Radar Ball is a good name for a golf ball implanted with a homing chip that sends a signal to a hand-held device, allowing the ball to be found when it is lost.

5. *Select a name that can be used on several product lines of a similar nature.* Customer goodwill is often lost when a name doesn't fit a new line. The name Just Brakes is excellent for an auto service shop that repairs brakes—unless the shop plans to expand later into muffler repair and other car repair services.

How They See It: Intellectual Property

Winston Wolfe

I have frequently told my attorney friends that if I were a lawyer, I would be in the field of intellectual property. It is a fascinating subject and can be critical for a new business.

It almost goes without saying that any entrepreneur should be respectful of the patents and trademarks, etc. of others. You should likewise demand that others respect your intellectual property.

If your business is based on a product or process that is unique, pursue a patent as quickly as possible! Keep in mind that protecting intellectual property rights can make or break a business. It is suggested that you work with an attorney whose specialty is intellectual property.

You should strongly consider licensing a brand name if you have a product for which there is an appropriate available name. It can't be emphasized too strongly that the name must be appropriate for the product and the market. Smith and Wesson, for example, is a great brand name for shooting glasses, but not for baby diapers.

Licensing the right name can be magic. It can separate you from the crowd and give you a great sales advantage. It can also allow you greater profit margins, since most consumers are willing to pay more for a brand name they know. Be prepared for scrutiny from the licensor company. Part of being a successful entrepreneur is having a good basic understanding of the laws governing intellectual property and the opportunities that are offered.

A brand mark also has tremendous value. The Nike swoosh and the Chevy badge are marks widely associated with their owners. A small firm's special "signature," or logo, should symbolize positive images of the firm and its products. And if you don't get it right initially, consider a new design. This is what Penny Pritzker did a few years after launching the Parking Spot, an off-airport parking service, in 1998. The original logo on the company's shuttle buses and other sites reflected a "ho-hum image." In 2000, the Parking Spot unveiled a new design sporting "black spots of different sizes dancing against a vibrant yellow background."[17] The company now operates 11 sites in 6 cities.

Another example of a successful logo change is provided by the privately held shoe manufacturer White Mountain Footwear, based in Lisbon, New Hampshire. Its black-and-white logo in block lettering was judged to be dated and unrepresentative of the fashion-forward image it was marketing. A new logo was designed—a stylized W that reflects the letter M, "like a mountain's mirror image in a lake."[18](Take a look at the logo on the company's website at http://www.whitemt.com.) According to Elinor Selame, president of BrandEquity, who designed the logo, "The logo can be your company's hardest-working employee."[19]

Michael Bierut, a partner at the design firm Pentagram, offers the following tips about logo design:[20]

1. *Be simple.* Some of the best logos are the simplest. Target has made a red circle with a red dot in the middle seem the very essence of affordable, hip practicality. H&R Block uses a green square in association with its name. Simple things are easy to remember and tend not to become outdated quickly.

2. *Leave it open to interpretation.* Don't try to design a logo that will explain at a glance the complete nature of your company. A logo that raises a question and is open to interpretation is better than one that attempts to offer all the answers.

3. *Be relentlessly consistent.* Companies with strong graphic identities have built those identities through years of use. Pick a typeface. Pick a color. Use them over and over again, on everything. Before long, you'll find yourself with an identifiable look and feel. That's more valuable than a logo, and anyone can afford it.

4. *Don't be embarrassed about design.* Things like logos and colors are considered "cosmetic," and businesspeople sometimes avoid focusing on them. But most design-driven companies got to be that way thanks to a highly placed advocate, such as Thomas Watson at IBM or Steve Jobs at Apple. For a design program to work, it needs to be seen to be championed by important people.

5. *Get good advice.* You can go pretty far with common sense. But sooner or later, you'll need to hire a professional graphic designer. The website of the American Institute of Graphic Arts (http://www.aiga.org), the largest professional organization for graphic designers, offers information about how to find and work with experienced professionals.

6. *Don't expect miracles.* Your company's image is the sum total of many factors. Make sure that your company looks, sounds, and feels smart in every way, every time it goes out in public. That is actually much better than a logo.

trademark
A legal term identifying a firm's exclusive right to use a brand

service mark
A brand that a company has the exclusive right to use to identify a service

Trademark and **service mark** are legal terms indicating the exclusive right to use a brand. Once an entrepreneur has found a name or symbol that is unique, easy to remember, and related to the product or service, an attorney who specializes in trademarks and service marks should be hired to run a name or symbol search and then to register the trade name or symbol. The protection of trademarks is discussed later in this chapter.

Packaging

Packaging is another important part of the total product offering. In addition to protecting the basic product, packaging is a significant tool for increasing the value of the total product.

Living the Dream   entrepreneurial challenges

Girl Power

Courtesy, B*tween Productions

Being a kid has never been easy. The new millennium, however, is proving to be particularly challenging for girls between the ages of 8 and 13, who make up a market known as the "tweens." Addie Swartz, founder of B*tween Productions, refers to girls at this stage as "between toys and boys." Swartz is convinced that there is room for a cool but wholesome lifestyle brand targeted at the 10 million girls who fall into this tween category. In a youth culture dominated by young actors and singers who regularly check in and out of rehab, there clearly is a need for more wholesome role models.

With the help of a talented executive team, Swartz launched B*tween Productions in 2002. She decided to start with a series of books about girls like her daughter Aliza and her friends. "I wanted to use the media to empower girls in a positive way," says Swartz.

After several brainstorming sessions, Swartz and her team came up with the composites for the characters in her books and decided the setting would be the real-life town of Brookline, Massachusetts. The characters would be known as the Beacon Street Girls. Swartz financed the development of her new company with $50,000 from the sale of her first company. She knew, however, that she would have to sell more than just books to attract investors. So she paired the books with products that appear in the books—backpacks and pillows. "They wouldn't have invested in a book," says Swartz. "It was about building a brand that can be leveraged aggressively."

The Beacon Street Girls books and merchandise are currently in approximately 70 independent shops across the country. The books and merchandise are selling well, with sales around $1 million in 2005. Money, however, isn't the sole driving force behind the Beacon Street Girls. Swartz explains, "Girls are losing their childhoods so fast. I want to give them a world that's cool and fun and meaningful."

Source: Nadine Heintz, "Hands On Case Study," *Inc.*, Vol. 27, No. 3 (March 2005), pp. 44–46. Copyright 2005 by Mansueto Ventures LLC. Reproduced with permission of Mansueto Ventures LLC in the format Textbook via Copyright Clearance Center.

http://www.beaconstreetgirls.com

Consider for a moment some of the products you purchase. How many do you buy mainly because of a preference for package design and/or color? Innovative packaging is frequently the deciding factor for consumers. If products are otherwise similar to competitive products, their packaging may create the distinctive impression that makes the sale. For example, biodegradable packaging materials may distinguish a product from its competition. The original L'eggs packaging design—the shape of an egg containing ladies' stockings—is an example of creative packaging that sells well.

Labeling

Another part of the total product is its label. Labeling serves several important purposes for manufacturers, which apply most labels. One purpose is to display the brand, particularly when branding the basic product would be undesirable. For example, a furniture brand is typically shown on a label and not on the basic product. On some products, brand visibility is highly desirable; Louis Vuitton handbags would probably not sell as well if the name label were only inside the purse.

A label is also an important informative tool for consumers. It often includes information on product care and use and may even provide instructions on how to dispose of the product.

Laws concerning labeling requirements should be reviewed carefully. Be innovative in your labeling information, and consider including information that goes beyond the specified minimum legal requirements.

Making Warranties

warranty
A promise that a product will perform at a certain level or meet certain standards

A **warranty** is simply a promise, written or unwritten, that a product will do certain things or meet certain standards. All sellers make an implied warranty that the seller's title to the product is good. A merchant seller, who deals in goods of a particular kind, makes the additional implied warranty that those goods are fit for the ordinary purposes for which they are sold. A written warranty on a product is not always necessary. In fact, many firms operate without written warranties, believing that a written warranty will serve only to confuse customers or make them suspicious.

Warranties are important for products that are innovative, relatively expensive, purchased infrequently, relatively complex to repair, and positioned as high-quality goods. A business should consider the following factors in rating the merits of a proposed warranty policy:

- Cost
- Service capability
- Competitive practices
- Customer perceptions
- Legal implications

Product Strategy

product strategy
The way the product component of the marketing mix is used to achieve a firm's objectives

product item
The lowest common denominator in the product mix—the individual item

product line
The sum of related individual product items

product mix
The collection of a firm's total product lines

product mix consistency
The similarity of product lines in a product mix

Product strategy includes decisions related to the product mix. It covers choices involving branding, packaging, labeling, and other elements comprising the core component of the bundle of satisfaction, whether product or service.

Specifically, **product strategy** describes the manner in which the product component of the marketing mix is used to achieve the objectives of a firm. A **product item** is the lowest common denominator in a product mix. It is the individual item, such as one brand of bar soap. A **product line** is the sum of the related individual product items. The relationship is usually defined generically. Two brands of bar soap are two product items in one product line. A **product mix** is the collection of product lines within a firm's ownership and control. A firm's product mix might consist of a line of bar soaps and a line of shoe polishes. **Product mix consistency** refers to the closeness, or similarity, of the product lines. The more items in a product line, the greater its depth. The more product lines in a product mix, the greater its breadth. Exhibit 14-5 shows the product lines and product mix of the firm 180s LLC, mentioned on page 373.

Product Marketing versus Service Marketing

Traditionally, marketers have used the word *product* as a generic term describing both goods and services. However, whether goods marketing and services marketing strategies are the same is questionable. As shown in Exhibit 14-6, certain characteristics—tangibility, amount of time separating production and consumption, standardization, and perishability—lead to a number of differences between the two strategies. Based on these characteristics, for example, the marketing of a pencil fits the pure goods end of the scale and the marketing of a haircut fits the pure services end. The major implication of this distinction is that marketing services presents unique challenges that are not faced in product strategy development.

exhibit

14-5   *Product Lines and Product Mix for 180s LLC*

		BREADTH OF THE PRODUCT MIX			
		Ear Warmers	Eye Wear	Gloves	Training Apparel
DEPTH OF THE PRODUCT LINES	**Training**	3 styles		4 styles	• Zone base shirt • Zone base pant • Quantum jacket • Catalyst shirt
	Snow Sport	1 style		7 styles	
	Multisport	• Tec fleece • Tec fleece w/headphones • Tec fleece kids	• Dovetail • Mortise • Integral • Festo	1 style	
	Casual	9 styles		6 styles	

Source: http://www.180s.com, accessed January 23, 2007.

Although we recognize the benefit of examining the marketing of services as a unique form, space limitations require that it be subsumed under the umbrella category of product marketing. Therefore, from this point on, a **product** will be considered to include the total bundle of satisfaction offered to customers in an exchange transaction—whether it be a service, a good, or a combination of the two. In addition to the physical product or core service, a product also includes complementary components, such as packaging or a warranty. Of course, the physical product or core service is usually the most important element in the total bundle of satisfaction. But sometimes that main element is perceived by customers to be similar for a variety of products. In that case, complementary components become the most important features of the product. For example, a particular brand of cake mix may be preferred by consumers not because it is a better mix, but because of the unique toll-free telephone number on the package that can be called for baking hints. Or a certain dry cleaner may be chosen over others because it treats customers with respect, not because it cleans clothes exceptionally well.

product
A total bundle of satisfaction—including a service, a good, or both—offered to consumers in an exchange transaction

14-6   *Services Marketing versus Goods Marketing*

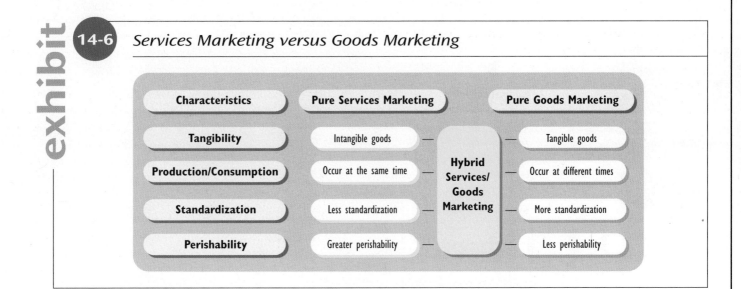

Characteristics	Pure Services Marketing	Hybrid Services/Goods Marketing	Pure Goods Marketing
Tangibility	Intangible goods	—	Tangible goods
Production/Consumption	Occur at the same time	—	Occur at different times
Standardization	Less standardization	—	More standardization
Perishability	Greater perishability	—	Less perishability

Product Strategy Options

Failure to clearly understand product strategy options will lead to ineffectiveness and conflict in the marketing effort. The major product strategy alternatives of a small business can be condensed into six categories, based on the nature of the firm's product offering and the number of target markets:

1. One product/one market

2. One product/multiple markets

3. Modified product/one market

4. Modified product/multiple markets

5. Multiple products/one market

6. Multiple products/multiple markets

Each alternative represents a distinct strategy, although two or more of these strategies can be pursued concurrently. A small firm, however, will usually pursue the alternatives in the order listed. Also, keep in mind that once any product strategy has been implemented, sales can be increased through certain additional growth tactics. For example, within any market, a small firm can try to increase sales of an existing product by doing any or all of the following:

- Convincing nonusers in the targeted market to become customers

- Persuading current customers to use more of the product

- Alerting current customers to new uses for the product

Living the Dream   entrepreneurial challenges

Taking on Goliath

Founded in 1871, Paige's Music is a mom-and-pop store based in Indianapolis. Its history shows that small businesses can survive and prosper despite the seeming invincibility (greater brand recognition, more cash to spend on marketing, etc.) of corporate giants. It's all in what strategies businesses use to approach their markets.

Paige's Music sells musical instruments to student musicians and school bands and orchestras. Despite competition from national chains and less expensive instruments made in China, the company's revenue for 2005 was $10 million and has grown 8 to 10 percent annually over the past few years. The firm's strategy has been to operate out of one facility in Indianapolis.

Mark Goff, who joined Paige's Music in 1985 as a salesman and purchased the company several years ago, calls the company's distribution system a "hub and spoke" system. With all 50 employees doing sales, order processing, accounting, and instrument repair at one location, the company is able to stay focused on its core customers: the 400 school bands and orchestras and 36,000 student musicians in Indiana.

Keeping it simple has allowed this David to take on the Goliaths of the business world.

Source: Edward Iwata, "Companies Can Grow in Goliath's Shadow," November 19, 2006, http://www.usatoday.com/money/smallbusiness/2006-11-17-goliaths_x.htm.

http://www.paigesmusic.com

When small firms add products to their product mix, they generally select related products. But there are, of course, strategies that involve unrelated products. For example, a local dealer selling Italian sewing machines might add a line of microwave ovens, a generically unrelated product. A product strategy that includes a new product quite different from existing products can be very risky. However, this strategy is occasionally used by small businesses, especially when the new product fits existing distribution and sales systems or requires similar marketing knowledge.

Adding a new unrelated product to the product mix to target a new market is an even higher-risk strategy, as a business is attempting to market an unfamiliar product in an unfamiliar market. However, if well planned, this approach can offer significant advantages. One electrical equipment service business recently added a private employment agency. If successful, this product strategy could provide a hedge against volatile shifts in market demand. A business that sells both snowshoes and suntan lotion expects that demand will be high in one market or the other at all times, evening out the sales curve and maintaining a steady cash flow throughout the year.

The Legal Environment

Strategic decisions about growth, innovation, product development, and the total product offering are always made within the guidelines and constraints of the legal environment of the marketplace. Let's examine a few of the laws by which the government protects both the rights of consumers and the marketing assets of firms.

> 6 Describe the legal environment affecting product decisions.

CONSUMER PROTECTION   Federal regulations on such subjects as labeling and product safety have important implications for product strategy. The Nutrition Labeling and Education Act of 1990 requires that every food product covered by the law have a standard nutrition label, listing the amounts of calories, fat, salt, and nutrients. The law also addresses the accuracy of advertising claims such as "low salt" and "fiber prevents cancer." Some experts estimate labeling costs at thousands of dollars per product.

To protect the public against unreasonable risk of injury, the federal government enacted the Consumer Product Safety Act of 1972. This act created the Consumer Product Safety Commission to set safety standards for toys and other consumer products and to ban goods that are exceptionally hazardous.

PROTECTION OF MARKETING ASSETS   Exhibit 14-7 shows the four primary means firms can use to protect certain marketing assets. The examples shown are representative of trademarks, patents, copyrights, and trade dress.

Trademarks   Trademark protection is important to a manufacturer or merchant. In some cases, a color or scent can be part of a trademark. Small manufacturers, in particular, often find it desirable to feature an identifying trademark in advertising.

Since names that refer to products are often registered trademarks, potential names should be investigated carefully to ensure that they are not already in use. Given the complexity of this task, many entrepreneurs seek the advice of an attorney experienced in trademark search and registration. An entrepreneur can conduct a trademark search personally, however, by using the Trademark Search Library of the U.S. Patent and Trademark Office (PTO) in Arlington, Virginia. A trademark search can also be done on the Internet by going to http://www.uspto.gov.

Common law recognizes a property right in the ownership of trademarks. However, reliance on common-law rights is not always adequate. For example, Microsoft Corporation, the major supplier of personal computer software, claimed it had common-law rights to the trademark *Windows* because of the enormous industry recognition of the product. Nevertheless, when Microsoft filed a trademark application in 1990 seeking to gain exclusive rights to the name *Windows,* the U.S. Patent and Trademark Office rejected the bid, claiming that the word was a generic term and, therefore, in the public domain.

Registration of trademarks is permitted under the federal Lanham Trademark Act, making protection easier if infringement is encountered. The act was revised in 1989 and now allows trademark rights to begin with merely an "intent to use," along with the filing of an application and payment of fees. Prior to this revision, a firm had to have already used the mark on goods shipped or sold. A trademark registered after

exhibit

14-7 *Protecting Marketing Assets*

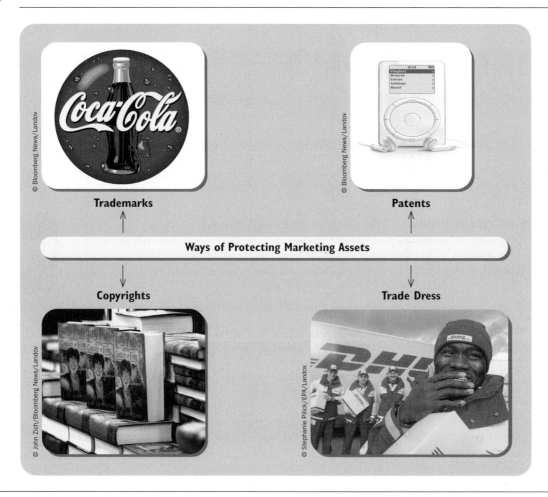

Trademarks

Patents

Ways of Protecting Marketing Assets

Copyrights

Trade Dress

---

patent
The registered, exclusive right of an inventor to make, use, or sell an invention

utility patent
Registered protection for a new process or a product's function

design patent
Registered protection for the appearance of a product and its inseparable parts

plant patent
Registered protection for any distinct, new variety of living plant

November 16, 1989, remains effective for 10 years and may be renewed for additional 10-year periods. Application to the U.S. Patent and Trademark Office for such registration can be made online.

A small business must use a trademark properly in order to protect it. Two rules can help. The first rule is to make every effort to see that the trade name is not carelessly used as a generic name. For example, the Xerox company never wants people to say that they are "xeroxing" something when they are using one of its competitors' copiers. The second rule is to inform the public that your trademark is a trademark by labeling it with the symbol ™. If the trademark is registered, the symbol ® or the phrase "Registered in the U.S. Patent and Trademark Office" should be used.

Patents A patent is the registered, exclusive right of an inventor to make, use, or sell an invention. The two primary types of patents are utility patents and design patents. A **utility patent** covers a new process or protects the function of a product. A **design patent** covers the appearance of a product and everything that is an inseparable part of the product. Utility patents are granted for a period of 20 years, while design patents are effective for 14 years. Patent law also provides for **plant patents**, which cover any distinct, new variety of living plants.

Items that may be patented include machines and products, improvements on machines and products, and original designs. Some small manufacturers have patented items that constitute the major part of their product line. Indeed, businesses such as Polaroid and IBM can trace their origins to a patented invention. Small business owners preparing a patent application often retain a patent attorney to act for them. A patent search can be conducted on the Internet.

Lawsuits concerning patent infringements are costly and should be avoided, if possible. Coming up with the money and legal talent to enforce this legal right is one of the major problems associated with patent protection in small businesses. Monetary damages and injunctions are available, however, if an infringement can be proved.

Copyrights   A **copyright** is the exclusive right of a creator (author, composer, designer, or artist) to reproduce, publish, perform, display, or sell work that is the product of that person's intelligence and skill. Works created on or after January 1, 1978, receive copyright protection for the duration of the creator's life plus 70 years. A "work made for hire" (work created by an employee for an employer) is protected for 95 years from its publication or 120 years from its creation, whichever is shorter. Copyrights are registered in the U.S. Copyright Office of the Library of Congress, whose website (http://www.copyright.gov) provides an enormous amount of useful material about copyrights.

> **copyright**
> The exclusive right of a creator to reproduce, publish, perform, display, or sell his or her own works

Under the Copyright Act of 1976, copyrightable works are automatically protected from the moment of their creation. However, any work distributed to the public should contain a copyright notice. This notice consists of three elements (which can be found on the copyright page in the front of this textbook):

1. The symbol ©

2. The year the work was published

3. The copyright owner's name

The law provides that copyrighted work may not be reproduced by another person without authorization. Even photocopying of such work is prohibited, although an individual may copy a limited amount of material for such purposes as research, criticism, comment, and scholarship. A copyright holder can sue a violator for damages.

Trade Dress   A small business may also possess a valuable intangible asset called trade dress. **Trade dress** describes those elements of a firm's distinctive operating image not specifically protected under a trademark, patent, or copyright. Trade dress is the "look" that a firm creates to establish its marketing advantage. For example, if the employees of a pizza retailer dress as prison guards and prisoners, a "jailhouse" image could become uniquely associated with this business and, over time, become its trade dress. Although there are currently no statutes covering trade dress, the courts are beginning to recognize the value of this asset.

> **trade dress**
> Elements of a firm's distinctive image not protected by a trademark, patent, or copyright

Having discussed the importance of effective management of a company's product, we will now focus on establishing a system to develop and distribute a company's product to its customers.

Supply Chain Management

> { 7 Explain the importance of supply chain management.

Supply chain management is a system of management that integrates and coordinates the ways in which a firm finds the raw materials and necessary components to produce a product or service, builds the actual product or service, and then delivers it to customers. Recent attention directed toward supply chain management has motivated attempts by both small and large firms to create a more competitive, customer-driven supply system. In other words, effective supply chain management can potentially lower the costs of inventory, transportation, warehousing, and packaging while increasing customer satisfaction.

> **supply chain management**
> A system of management that integrates and coordinates the means by which a firm creates or develops a product or service and delivers it to customers

The Internet and available software are major drivers of current developments in supply chain management. Pre-Internet, communication between parties in the supply chain was slow or nonexistent. But the Internet, with its simple, universally accepted communication standards, has brought suppliers and customers together in a way never before thought possible.

A comprehensive discussion of supply chain management is beyond the scope of this book. However, we will look briefly at the functions of intermediaries, the various distribution channels that comprise a supply chain, and the basics of logistics. Entrepreneurs often regard distribution as the least glamorous marketing activity. Nevertheless, an

distribution
Physically moving products and establishing intermediary relationships to support such movement

physical distribution (logistics)
The activities of distribution involved in the physical relocation of products

channel of distribution
The system of relationships established to guide the movement of a product

merchant middlemen
Intermediaries that take title to the goods they distribute

agents/brokers
Intermediaries that do not take title to the goods they distribute

8 Specify the major considerations in structuring a distribution channel.

direct channel
A distribution system without intermediaries

indirect channel
A distribution system with one or more intermediaries

dual distribution
A distribution system that involves more than one channel

effective distribution system is just as important as a unique package, a clever name, or a creative promotional campaign. Thus, a small business owner should understand the basic principles of distribution, which apply to both domestic and international distribution activities.

In marketing, **distribution** encompasses both the physical movement of products and the establishment of intermediary (middleman) relationships to achieve product movement. The activities involved in physically moving a product are called **physical distribution (logistics)**; the system of relationships established to guide the movement of a product is called the **channel of distribution**.

Distribution is essential for both tangible and intangible goods. Since distribution activities are more visible for tangible goods (products), our discussion will focus primarily on products. Most intangible goods (services) are delivered directly to the user. An income tax preparer and a barber, for example, serve clients directly. However, marketing a person's labor can involve channel intermediaries. An employment agency, for example, provides an employer with temporary personnel.

Intermediaries

Intermediaries can often perform marketing functions better than the producer of a product can. A producer can perform its own distribution functions—including delivery—if the geographic area of the market is small, customers' needs are specialized, and risk levels are low, as they might be for a producer of doughnuts. However, intermediaries generally provide more efficient means of distribution if customers are widely dispersed or if special packaging and storage are needed. Many types of small firms, such as retail stores, function as intermediaries.

Some intermediaries, called **merchant middlemen**, take title to the goods they distribute, thereby helping a firm to share or totally shift business risk. Other intermediaries, such as **agents** and **brokers**, do not take title to goods and, therefore, assume less market risk than do merchant middlemen.

Channels of Distribution

A channel of distribution can be either direct or indirect. In a **direct channel**, there are no intermediaries—the product goes directly from producer to user. An **indirect channel** of distribution has one or more intermediaries between producer and user.

Exhibit 14-8 depicts the various options available for structuring a channel of distribution. E-commerce (online merchandising) and mail-order marketing are direct channel systems for distributing consumer goods. Amazon.com is an example of an online merchandiser that uses a direct channel to final consumers. The systems shown on the right-hand side of Exhibit 14-8 are indirect channels involving one, two, or three levels of intermediaries. As a final consumer, you are naturally familiar with retailers. Industrial purchasers are equally familiar with industrial distributors. Channels with two or three stages of intermediaries are probably the ones most typically used by small firms producing products with geographically large markets. It is important to note that a small firm may use more than one channel of distribution—a practice called **dual distribution**.

Firms that successfully employ a single distribution channel may switch to dual distribution if they find that an additional channel will improve overall profitability. For example, the Boston Book Company, in business since 1979 in downtown Boston, Massachusetts, now also maintains a website where books can be purchased online.

A logical starting point in structuring a distribution system is to observe systems used by competing businesses. Such an analysis should reveal some practical alternatives, which can then be evaluated. The three main considerations in evaluating a channel of distribution are costs, coverage, and control.

COSTS   The absence of intermediaries does not make a direct channel inherently less expensive than an indirect channel. The least expensive channel may be indirect. For example, a firm producing handmade dolls need not purchase trucks and warehouses to distribute its product directly to customers but can instead rely on established intermediaries that own such facilities. Small firms should look at distribution costs as an investment—spending money in order to make money. They should ask themselves

exhibit

14-8   *Alternative Channels of Distribution*

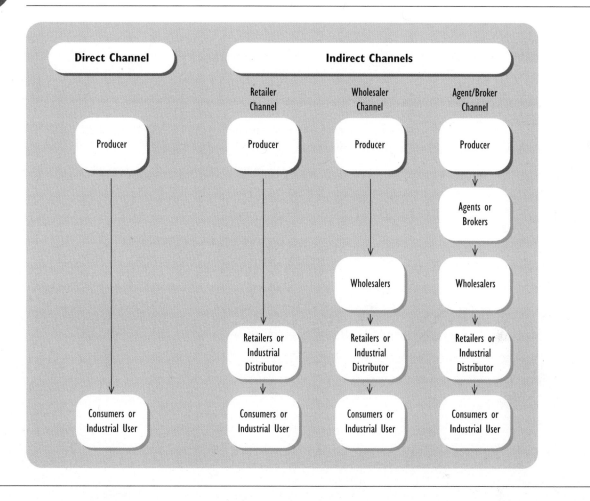

whether the amount of money they "invest" in intermediaries (by selling the product to them at a reduced price) would still get the job done if they used direct distribution.

COVERAGE   Small firms can often use indirect channels of distribution to increase market coverage. Suppose a small manufacturer's internal sales force can make 10 contacts a week with final users of the firm's product. Creating an indirect channel with 10 industrial distributors, each making 10 contacts a week, could expose the product to 100 final users a week.

CONTROL   A direct channel of distribution is sometimes preferable because it provides more control. Intermediaries may not market a product as desired. An entrepreneur must carefully select intermediaries that provide the desired support.

A small business that chooses to use intermediaries to help distribute and market its product must be sure that the intermediaries have a good understanding of how the product is best used and why it's better than competitors' offerings. Additionally, if a wholesaler carries competing products, an entrepreneur must be sure that her or his product gets its fair share of marketing efforts. Distributors must know what makes the product special and how best to market it. Sloppy marketing efforts and insufficient product knowledge by intermediaries can undermine the success of even the best product.

The Scope of Physical Distribution

In addition to the intermediary relationships that make up a channel, there must also be a system of physical distribution. The main component of physical distribution is transportation. Additional components include storage, materials handling, delivery terms, and

Living the Dream   entrepreneurial challenges

Boosting a Small Player's Sales

Entrepreneur Matt Jarman is a small player in a large field. But partnering with RCA has landed his parental control software in DVD players that are on the shelves of Wal-Mart (and available for puchase online at Wal-Mart's website). This channel of distribution will most certainly boost ClearPlay sales dramatically.

Founded by Jarman and his brother Lee, the 11-employee Utah-based company produces filtering software on a programmable chip that allows the DVD user to choose content options via an on-screen menu. The filters—for violence, sex, nudity, and language—give instructions to the DVD player to skip over or mute objectionable content previously identified and labeled by ClearPlay movie professionals. The DVD player comes preloaded with ClearPlay filters for 100 movies. Additional filters can be downloaded by subscribers to a personal computer and then burned onto a blank CD for transfer to the DVD player's memory.

Wal-Mart spokeswoman Karen Burke says the store's strategy of carrying DVD players with filtering software (and not carrying any music CDs that have parental advisory labels) is "based on what we think our customers want." And a recent federal court ruling that led to the closing of DVD-editing companies has left ClearPlay as the only option available for families wanting the ability to filter out objectionable content from the movies they watch.

Jarman says ClearPlay doesn't have a religious agenda, but, according to the ClearPlay website, it "feels good knowing that you can watch great Hollywood movies without having to worry about the profanity, nudity and gory violence."

Sources: http://www.clearplay.com, accessed January 10, 2007; "ClearPlay to Clean Up Hollywood," http://www.cbsnews.com/stories, May 5, 2004; Mike Snider, "Hollywood Riled Up over ClearPlay," *USA Today,* May 6, 2004, p. 12D; and http://www.Wal-Mart.com/catalog/product, May 5, 2004.

http://www.clearplay.com

inventory management. The following sections briefly examine all of these topics except inventory management, which is discussed in Chapter 20.

TRANSPORTATION   The major decision regarding physical transportation of a product is which method to use. Available modes of transportation are traditionally classified as airplanes, trucks, railroads, pipelines, and waterways. Each mode has unique advantages and disadvantages. The choice of a specific mode of transportation is based on several criteria: relative cost, transit time, reliability, capability, accessibility, and traceability.

Transportation intermediaries are legally classified as common carriers, contract carriers, and private carriers. **Common carriers,** which are available for hire to the general public, and **contract carriers,** which engage in individual contracts with shippers, are subject to regulation by federal and/or state agencies. Lines of transport owned by the shippers are called **private carriers.**

STORAGE   Lack of space is a common problem for small businesses. When a channel system uses merchant middlemen or wholesalers, title to the goods is transferred, as is responsibility for the storage function. On other occasions, the small business must plan for its own warehousing. If a firm is too small to own a private warehouse, it can rent space

common carriers
Transportation intermediaries available for hire to the general public

contract carriers
Transportation intermediaries that contract with individual shippers

private carriers
Lines of transport owned by the shippers

in a public warehouse. If storage requirements are simple and do not involve much special handling equipment, a public warehouse can provide economical storage.

MATERIALS HANDLING   A damaged product in the right place at the right time is worth little. Therefore, a physical distribution system must arrange for suitable materials-handling methods and equipment. Forklifts, as well as special containers and packaging, are part of a materials-handling system.

DELIVERY TERMS   A small but important part of a physical distribution system is the delivery terms, specifying which party is responsible for several aspects of the distribution:

- Paying the freight costs
- Selecting the carriers
- Bearing the risk of damage in transit
- Selecting the modes of transport

The simplest delivery term and the one most advantageous to a small business as seller is F.O.B. (free on board) origin, freight collect. This shifts all the responsibility for freight costs to the buyer. Title to the goods and risk of loss also pass to the buyer at the time the goods are shipped.

Logistics companies specialize in transportation and distribution services, providing trucking, packaging, and warehousing services for small and medium-sized companies with limited in-house staff. Many small businesses believe that using these third-party logistics firms is more cost effective than carrying out the same functions in-house. For example, Premier Inc., of Greenwich, Connecticut, uses a firm named APL Logistics to handle packaging and shipping of its health and beauty-aid products. Products produced in plants around the country go to the APL warehouse in Dallas, Texas, and are then shipped to distribution outlets nationwide.

Innovation is the key to competitive advantage and small business success. Effective management of your company's products requires attention to both maintaining existing products and developing new products. Like people, products pass through life cycle stages and face different obstacles at each stage. A successful entrepreneur must have a carefully planned product strategy. Managing your supply chain requires planning how and from where you will get the components for your products and how you will deliver the finished product to your customers. Various channels of distribution exist to deliver your product to your customers, but the advantages and disadvantages of each must be considered carefully.

Looking BACK

1 Explain the challenges associated with growth in a small firm.

- Growth sufficient to maintain the status quo is a goal of some entrepreneurs.
- Growing a business too quickly can be stressful for the small firm.
- A growth trap may occur when a firm's growth soaks up cash faster than it can be generated.
- Growth also puts pressure on a small firm's personnel.

2 Explain the role of innovation in a firm's growth.

- Coming up with and perfecting new products or services is often not easy.
- The risk of failure increases when innovation is the goal.
- Innovation is a means by which a firm can sustain its competitive advantage.

3 Identify stages in the product life cycle and the new product development process.

- The product life cycle portrays a product from introduction through growth and maturity to sales decline.
- The new product development process is a four-stage approach: idea accumulation, business analysis, development of the product, and product testing.

4 Describe the building of a firm's total product.

- The brand identity of a firm and/or product has an important intangible image component.
- The name is a critical component of a product; it should be easy to pronounce and remember, descriptive, eligible for legal protection, full of promotional possibilities, and suitable for use on several product lines.
- Packaging is a significant tool for increasing total product value.
- A label is an important informative tool, providing instructions on product use, care, and disposal.
- A warranty can be valuable for achieving customer satisfaction.

5 Explain product strategy and the alternatives available to small businesses.

- Product strategy describes how a product is used to achieve a firm's goals.
- There are six major product strategy alternatives which are based on the nature of the firm's product offering and the number of target markets.

6 Describe the legal environment affecting product decisions.

- Federal legislation regarding labeling and product safety was designed to protect consumers.
- The legal system provides protection for a firm's marketing assets through trademarks, patents, copyrights, and trade dress.

7 Explain the importance of supply chain management.

- Effective supply chain management can potentially lower the costs of inventory, transportation, warehousing, and packaging.
- Distribution encompasses both the physical movement of products and the establishment of relationships to guide the movement of products from producer to user.
- Intermediaries provide an efficient means of distribution if customers are widely dispersed or if special packaging and storage are needed.

8 Specify the major considerations in structuring a distribution channel.

- A distribution channel can be either direct or indirect; many firms successfully employ more than one channel of distribution.
- Costs, coverage, and control are the three main considerations in building a channel of distribution.
- Transportation, storage, materials handling, delivery terms, and inventory management are the main components of a physical distribution system.

Key TERMS

Discussion QUESTIONS

1. Discuss some of the limitations on growth in a small firm.

2. Describe the recommendations for reducing risk associated with innovation in a small business.

3. How does an understanding of the product life cycle concept help with product strategy?

4. Discuss briefly each stage of the product development process.

5. What are some of the product strategy options available to a small firm? Which ones are most likely to be used?

6. Identify and briefly describe the three ways to increase sales of an existing product once a product strategy has been implemented.

7. Select two product names, and then evaluate each with respect to the five rules for naming a product.

8. Explain how registration of a small firm's trademark would be helpful in protecting its brand.

9. Why do small firms need to consider indirect channels of distribution for their products? Why involve intermediaries in distribution at all?

10. Discuss the major considerations in structuring a channel of distribution.

You Make the CALL

SITUATION 1

Linda McMahan was getting numerous compliments on a handbag she carried to events at The University of Texas. She had purchased the handbag, which carried the UT name, at a local store but felt the quality of the bag was poor. She and her sister-in-law, Sue Craft McMahan, decided to become partners and produce and sell high-end handbags emblazoned with the college logo.

The pair designed four different types of bags—a large totebag, a smaller bag, a crescent-shaped handbag, and a "bolder" game-day bag—all marked with The University of Texas emblem. Early responses to the product line were overwhelming. They've now set their sights on other big-name schools.

Source: Nichole L. Torres, "Smells Like School Spirit," *Entrepreneur,* December 2003, p. 132.

Question 1 What problems, if any, do you see with the use of the university's brand?

Question 2 What strategy should they pursue to obtain cooperation from the university?

Question 3 What distribution options are likely to be used?

SITUATION 2

Tomboy Tools are just that—tools for women who want to do their own home improvement and repair projects. Friends Sue Wilson, Mary Tatum, and Janet Rickstrew, all of Denver, Colorado, were concerned that the tools they used for home repair projects were designed for men, not women. So, they started Tomboy Tools, whose goal is to offer "professional grade tools for women, along with the information they need to know on how to use them," says Wilson. What is most interesting is how the products are sold—exclusively at in-home workshops led by Tomboy Tools' independent sales representatives. Instead of Tupperware or cosmetics, guests see basic home repair tools in action and learn simple home repair and improvement techniques. They chose the in-home approach to market their products because of its proven success with consumers—particularly females.

Source: Susan Hirshon, *The Costco Connection,* April 2005, p. 15.

Question 1 What are the advantages and disadvantages of the in-home method of selling Tomboy Tools?

Question 2 What other channels of distribution might Tomboy Tools use?

Question 3 What do you think about the name Tomboy Tools?

SITUATION 3

Who hasn't heard of the energy drink Red Bull? It is the 900-pound gorilla in the growing energy drink market. But Hansen Natural Corporation, maker of Monster energy drink, is giving Red Bull a run for its money. The company reaches its core market of males aged 18 to

32 by flooding retailers with giant (16-ounce) cans of its various energy drink offerings, in essence super-sizing the much smaller cans sold by Red Bull. Its striking packaging and oversized cans are helping Monster make inroads in the growing energy drink market.

Source: Roben Farzad, "Who's Afraid of the Shorts? Not Monster," *Business Week,* November 28, 2006, p. 40.

Question 1 What is it about Monster's logo that makes it effective? (Hint: What tips does this textbook provide regarding logo design?)

Question 2 How can good packaging help a product?

Question 3 Why is labeling an important part of the packaging for energy drinks like Monster?

SITUATION 4

What does the Internet have to do with making ice cream? Answer: It supports the MooBella ice-cream machine. The MooBella robotic ice-cream manufactory and vending machine can custom-make and sell a cup of fresh, premium ice cream in 45 seconds. The consumer feeds the vending machine from $2.00 to $2.50 per scoop and uses the large LCD touch screen to make his or her choice of up to 12 flavors plus any of five toppings. Based on the Unix operating system, the computer that makes each cup of ice cream instantly reports via a wireless Internet connection when it needs supplies or maintenance. The MooBella machine is currently being tested in Boston.

Source: Peter Lewis, "Cream of the Crop," *Fortune*, March 6, 2006, p. 178.

Question 1 Where would be the best locations for the MooBella ice-cream vending machine?

Question 2 What are the primary advantages and disadvantages of this retailing strategy?

Experiential **EXERCISES**

1. Interview the owner or owners of a local manufacturing business to find out how they view innovation in their market. Summarize your findings.

2. Ask some owners of small firms in your area to describe their new product development processes. Report your findings to the class.

3. Visit a local retail store and observe brand names, package designs, labels, and warranties. Choose good and bad examples of each of these product components, and report back to the class.

4. Consider your most recent meaningful purchase. Compare the decision-making process you used to the four stages of the new product development process. Report your conclusions to the class.

5. Interview two different types of local retail merchants (for example, a boutique owner and a manager of a franchise) to determine how the merchandise in their stores is distributed to them. Contrast the channels of distribution used, and write a brief report on your findings.

Exploring the **WEB**

1. Visit the website of tutor2u, an online learning resource, at **http://www.tutor2u.net**. Click on "Quizzes," then "Branding," and take the "Marketing—Introduction to Brands" quiz. How did you score?

Video Case **14**

Country Supply (p. 648)

This case demonstrates how one innovative entrepreneur recognized the need to expand his customer base in order for his business to grow and describes how he met that need by utilizing available resources to expand his distribution network.

Alternative Cases for Chapter 14:

## chapter 15

Pricing and Credit Decisions

Nicole Miller
http://www.nicolemiller.com

When designer Nicole Miller and business manager Bud Konheim decided to strike out on their own, the company they both worked for gave them its blessing—and three weeks' worth of salaries for each person they had working for them. The only requirement was that Miller and Konheim clear out all existing inventory in their division before leaving the company. Surprisingly, they had no trouble at all: They just notified their existing customers that their division was changing its name to Nicole Miller.

Nicole Miller sells youthful, whimsical designs, primarily in women's wear. While Miller enjoys designing for her customers, Konheim thinks that pricing should contribute to the fun as well. That is, Konheim likes to price Miller's products so that a woman buying a Nicole Miller design will be able to enjoy her purchase without the gnawing regret that she just spent too much money. However, creating that "I-got-a-great-deal" feeling at a price that will still sustain the business is not easy.

Setting the right price for a product or service is one of the most difficult marketing activities a businessperson in any company will undertake. What makes it all the more challenging for Miller is that she is committed to manufacturing all of her clothing lines domestically, in New York's garment district, even though her competition is going offshore to reduce costs. Watch this spotlight to see how Miller and Konheim are navigating the tough challenges of pricing.

Video material provided by Hattie Bryant, Producer of Small Business School, the series on PBS Stations, Worldnet, and the Web at http://www. smallbusinessschool.org.

SmallBusinessSchool
the Series on PBS stations and the Web

Looking AHEAD

1 Discuss the role of cost and demand factors in setting a price.
2 Apply break-even analysis and markup pricing.
3 Identify specific pricing strategies.
4 Explain the benefits of credit, factors that affect credit extension, and types of credit.
5 Describe the activities involved in managing credit.

Pricing and credit decisions are vital because they influence the relationship between the business and its customers. These decisions also directly affect both revenue and cash flow. Of course, customers dislike price increases and restrictive credit policies; therefore, the entrepreneur needs to set prices and design credit policies as wisely as possible, to avoid the need for frequent changes.

Because a value must be placed on a product or service by the provider before it can be sold, pricing decisions are a critical issue in small business marketing. The price of a product or service specifies what the seller requires for giving up ownership or use of that product or service. Often, the seller must extend credit to the buyer in order to make the

price
A specification of what a seller requires in exchange for transferring ownership or use of a product or service

---

How They See It: Money Isn't Everything

Cecilia Levine

When I first started my business, I was a single mother raising three children and trying to make the business go. At a time when things were extremely tight, I received an excellent opportunity. I won a bid to make a clothing item for a large U.S. clothing firm. It would make all the difference in the world to the future of my business.

The president of this larger company asked me to come to New York and visit with him so that we could make the arrangements for the design of the plant and start producing the clothing item. I flew to New York at my own expense at a time when I had barely enough money to pay for the tickets. When I went into his office, two copies of the contract were placed on the table. As we went over the contract, I noticed that the price that I was to receive for each item was 25 cents higher than in my pro-

posal. I told him there was a mistake in the price I was to receive for my work and that it was higher than quoted in my bid. I was shocked when he said, "That's right, but I want you to add the 25 cents to your price and then take the additional money and open a personal bank account in Mexico in my name."

I can tell you that I could have used the contract. I needed the work, but not under those circumstances. I believe there are wonderful opportunities in the United States and that we don't need to do things that make it hard to sleep at night. It is a question of values for me. I stood up and thanked him and walked out of his office.

The firm I am describing is a big company, a name that you see everywhere. I have difficulty believing what happened—that someone would use that type of maneuver. I also know that someone else got that contract and, as a result, has built a big, big, big plant in Mexico. But I sleep well.

credit
An agreement between a buyer and a seller that provides for delayed payment for a product or service

exchange happen. **Credit** is simply an agreement between buyer and seller that payment for a product or service will be received at some later date. This chapter examines both the pricing decisions and the credit decisions of small firms.

Setting a Price

1 Discuss the role of cost and demand factors in setting a price.

In setting a price, the entrepreneur decides on the most appropriate value for the product or service being offered for sale. This task might seem easy, but it isn't. The first pricing lesson is to remember that total sales revenue depends on just two components—sales volume and price—and even a small change in price can drastically influence revenue. Consider the following situations, *assuming no change in demand*:

Situation A

Quantity sold × Price per unit = Gross revenue
250,000   × $3.00   = $750,000

Situation B

Quantity sold × Price per unit = Gross revenue
250,000   × $2.80   = $700,000

The price per unit is only $0.20 lower in Situation B than in Situation A. However, the total difference in revenue is $50,000! Clearly, a small business can lose significant revenues if a price is set too low.

Pricing is also important because it indirectly affects sales quantity. Setting a price too high may result in lower quantities sold, reducing total revenue. In the above example, quantity sold was assumed to be independent of price—and it very well may be for such a small change in price. However, a larger increase or decrease might substantially affect the quantity sold. Pricing, therefore, has a dual influence on total sales revenue. It is important *directly* as part of the gross revenue equation and *indirectly* through its impact on demand.

Before beginning a more detailed analysis of pricing, we should note that services are generally more difficult to price than products because of their intangible nature. However, the impact of price on revenue and profits is the same. Because estimating the cost of providing a service and the demand for that service is a more complex process, the following discussions will focus on product pricing.

Cost Determination for Pricing

For a business to be successful, its pricing must cover total cost plus some profit margin. Pricing, therefore, must be based on an understanding of the nature of costs. As illustrated

exhibit

15-1   *The Three Components of Total Cost in Determining Price*

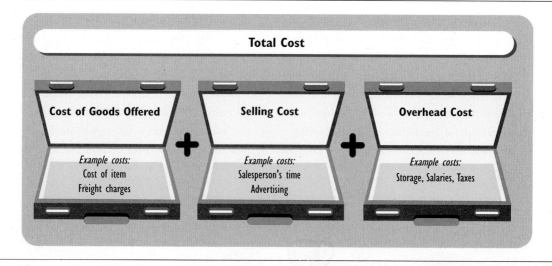

Living the Dream   entrepreneurial challenges

Fixing a Pricing Mistake

© Waddevah

Because they badly need the business, entrepreneurs often set prices really low, figuring that they can raise them later. But to some customers low price means low quality. So don't assume that all purchases are made based on price considerations.

For six years, Yvonne Shortt, 31, worked long hours for a major insurance company in New York. After deciding, in 2001, that "there is more to life than money," she resigned her position to pursue her entrepreneurial dream with her husband and children.

Shortt chose jewelry and accessories because she had made them as a hobby for years. She felt that jewelry making offered her the ability to create something that makes people happy. Also, she says, "So many individuals are losing jobs to overseas manufacturers. . . I wanted to give jobs to those in the United States." So she began advertising online and showing her products to retailers and consumers. Shortt's company, named Waddevah, now has a website where the jewelry can be purchased online.

Her initial strategy was to win sales with low wholesale and online retail prices, but Shortt soon learned that going against competitors with a low sticker price meant losing money. After visiting numerous retailers who carried her products and observing their huge markups, she decided to raise her online retail prices. For example, after making slight changes to the color and shape of her earrings, shortt now sells them for up to $30, instead of $10.

Shortt's move to higher prices coincided with a successful publicity campaign, during which photographs of her jewelry appeared in fashion magazines.

Sources: http://www.waddevah.com/vision.html, accessed March 15, 2007; and Lee Gimpel, "The High Cost of Low Prices," *MyBusiness*, August/September 2006, p. 50.

http://www.waddevah.com

---

in Exhibit 15-1, **total cost** includes three components. The first is the cost of goods offered for sale. An appliance retailer, for example, must include in the selling price the cost of the appliance and related freight charges. The second component is the selling cost, which includes the direct cost of the salesperson's time (salary plus commissions), as well as the cost of other selling activities such as advertising and sales promotion. The third component is the overhead cost applicable to the given product, which includes costs related to warehouse storage, office supplies, utilities, taxes, and employee salaries and wages. *All* of these cost classifications must be incorporated into the pricing process.

Costs respond differently as the quantity produced or sold increases or decreases. **Total variable costs** are those that increase in total as the quantity of product increases. Material costs and sales commissions are typical variable costs incurred as a product is made and sold. **Total fixed costs** are those that remain constant at different levels of quantity sold. For example, advertising campaign expenditures, factory equipment costs, and salaries of office personnel are fixed costs.

An understanding of the nature of different kinds of costs can help a seller minimize pricing mistakes. Although fixed and variable costs do not behave in the same way, small businesses often treat them identically. An approach called average pricing

total cost
The sum of cost of goods sold, selling expenses, and overhead costs

total variable costs
Costs that vary with the quantity produced or sold

total fixed costs
Costs that remain constant as the quantity produced or sold varies

exhibit

15-2   *Cost Structure of a Hypothetical Firm, 2007*

Sales revenue (25,000 units @ $8)		$200,000
Total costs:		
Fixed costs	$75,000	
Variable costs ($2 per unit)	50,000	
		125,000
Gross margin		$ 75,000

$$\text{Average cost} = \frac{\$125,000}{25,000} = \$5$$

average pricing
An approach in which total cost for a given period is divided by quantity sold in that period to set a price

exemplifies this high-risk practice. With **average pricing**, you divide the total cost (fixed costs plus variable costs) over a previous period by the quantity sold in that period to arrive at an average cost, which is then used to set the current price. For example, consider the cost structure of a firm selling 25,000 units of a product in 2007 at a sales price of $8.00 each (see Exhibit 15-2). The average unit cost would be $5.00 (that is, $125,000 ÷ 25,000). The $3.00 markup provides a profit at this sales volume (25,000 × $3 = $75,000).

However, the impact on profit will be very negative if sales in 2008 reach only 10,000 units and the selling price has been set at the same $3.00 markup, based on the average cost in 2007 (see Exhibit 15-3). At the lower sales volume (10,000 units), the average unit cost increases to $9.50 (that is, $95,000 ÷ 10,000). This increase is, of course, attributable to the need to spread fixed costs over fewer units. *Average pricing overlooks the reality of higher average costs at lower sales levels.*

On rare occasions, pricing at less than total cost can be used as a special short-term strategy. Suppose some fixed costs are ongoing even if part of the production facility is temporarily idle. In this situation, pricing should cover all marginal or incremental costs—that is, those costs incurred specifically to get additional business. In the long run, however, all costs must be covered.

How Customer Demand Affects Pricing

Cost analysis can identify a level below which a price should not be set under normal circumstances. However, it does not show how much the final price might exceed that minimum figure and still be acceptable to customers. You must consider demand factors before making this determination.

exhibit

15-3   *Cost Structure of a Hypothetical Firm, 2008*

Sales revenue (10,000 units @ $8)		$80,000
Total costs:		
Fixed costs	$75,000	
Variable costs ($2 per unit)	20,000	
		95,000
Gross margin		($15,000)

$$\text{Average cost} = \frac{\$95,000}{10,000} = \$9.50$$

ELASTICITY OF DEMAND   Customer demand for a product is often sensitive to the price level. *Elasticity* is the term used to describe this sensitivity, and the effect of a change in price on the quantity demanded is called **elasticity of demand.** A product is said to have **elastic demand** if an increase in its price *lowers* demand for the product or a decrease in its price *raises* demand. A product is said to have **inelastic demand** if an increase in its price *raises* total revenue or a decrease in its price *lowers* total revenue.

In some markets, the demand for products is very elastic. With a lower price, the amount purchased increases sharply, thus providing higher revenue. For example, in the personal computer industry, a decrease in price will frequently produce a more than proportionate increase in quantity sold, resulting in higher total revenues. For products such as salt, however, the demand is highly inelastic. Regardless of price, the quantity purchased will not change significantly, because consumers use a fixed amount of salt.

The concept of elasticity of demand is important because the degree of elasticity sets limits on or provides opportunities for higher pricing. A small firm should seek to distinguish its product or service in such a way that small price increases will incur little resistance from customers and thereby yield increasing total revenue. Entrepreneur Damon Risucci built his Synergy Fitness Club in midtown Manhattan into a successful business despite stiff competition from several chain fitness clubs. For nearly a decade, members paid only $49.99 a month. "We thought our prices had to be low," Risucci recalls. Finally, prompted by falling margins, he raised monthly fees 16 percent; no one complained, and he didn't lose a single member! [1] We can conclude from Risucci's experience that demand for his fitness club service is quite inelastic—at least through the price range presented here.

PRICING AND A FIRM'S COMPETITIVE ADVANTAGE   Several factors affect the attractiveness of a product or service to customers. One factor is the firm's competitive advantage—a concept discussed in Chapter 3. If consumers perceive the product or service as an important solution to their unsatisfied needs, they are likely to demand more.

Only rarely will competing firms offer identical products and services. In most cases, products differ in some way. Even if two products are physically similar, the accompanying services typically differ. Speed of service, credit terms offered, delivery arrangements, personal attention from a salesperson, and warranties are but a few of the factors that can be used to distinguish one product from another. A unique and attractive combination of goods and services may well justify a higher price.

A pricing tactic that often reflects competitive advantage is **prestige pricing**—setting a high price to convey an image of high quality or uniqueness. Its influence varies from market to market and product to product. Because higher-income buyers are usually less sensitive to price variations than those with lower incomes, prestige pricing typically works better in high-income markets.

When Anthony Shurman, president of Yosha Enterprises Inc. in Westfield, New Jersey, introduced Momints breath mints, he set the price high. Shurman explains, "I think when you're launching a new product or starting a new business, there are plenty of examples of businesses going after a target audience and creating a cachet for themselves by pricing a little higher and adopting an elite strategy, where you present yourself as this high-end competitor in the market." [2] Later, when he took Momints nationwide, Shurman dropped the price to be competitive with other brands in the new markets.

elasticity of demand
The degree to which a change in price affects the quantity demanded

elastic demand
Demand that changes significantly when there is a change in the price of the product

inelastic demand
Demand that does not change significantly when there is a change in the price of the product

prestige pricing
Setting a high price to convey an image of high quality or uniqueness

Applying a Pricing System

A typical entrepreneur is unprepared to evaluate a pricing system until he or she understands potential costs, revenue, and product demand for the venture. To better comprehend these factors and to determine the acceptability of various prices, the entrepreneur can use break-even analysis. An understanding of markup pricing is also valuable, as it provides the entrepreneur with an awareness of the pricing practices of intermediaries—wholesalers and retailers.

2 Apply break-even analysis and markup pricing.

Break-Even Analysis

Break-even analysis allows the entrepreneur to compare alternative cost and revenue estimates in order to determine the acceptability of each price. A comprehensive break-even analysis has two phases: (1) examining cost–revenue relationships and (2) incorporating sales forecasts into the analysis. Break-even analysis is typically presented by means of formulas or graphs; this discussion uses a graphic presentation.

EXAMINING COST AND REVENUE RELATIONSHIPS   The objective of the first phase of break-even analysis is to determine the sales volume level at which the product, at an assumed price, will generate enough revenue to start earning a profit. Exhibit 15-4(a) presents a simple break-even chart reflecting this comparison. Total fixed costs are represented by a horizontal section at the bottom of the graph, indicating that they do not change with the volume of production. The section for total variable costs is a triangle that slants upward, depicting the direct relationship of total variable costs to output. The entire area below the upward-slanting total cost line represents the combination of fixed and variable costs. The distance between the sales and total cost lines reveals the profit or loss position of the company at any level of sales. The point of intersection of these two lines is called the **break-even point**, because sales revenue equals total cost at this sales volume.

break-even point
Sales volume at which total sales revenue equals total costs

To evaluate other break-even points, the entrepreneur can plot additional sales lines for other prices on the chart. On the flexible break-even chart shown in Exhibit 15-4(b), the higher price of $18 yields a more steeply sloped sales line, resulting in an earlier break-even point. Similarly, the lower price of $7 produces a flatter revenue line, delaying the break-even point. Additional sales lines could be plotted to evaluate other proposed prices.

Because it shows the profit area growing larger and larger to the right, the break-even chart implies that quantity sold can increase continually. Obviously, *this assumption*

exhibit

15-4   *Break-Even Graphs for Pricing*

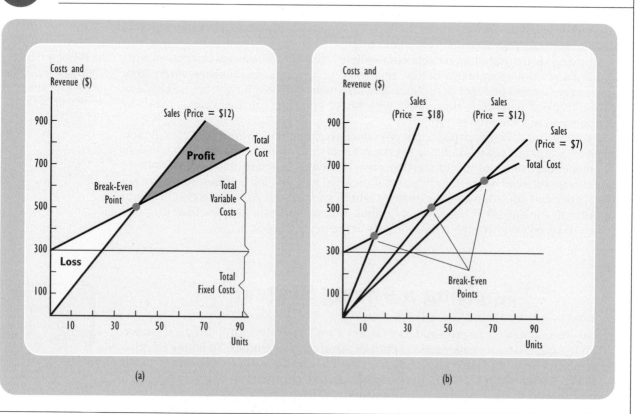

(a)

(b)

is unrealistic and should be factored in by modifying the break-even analysis with information about the way in which demand is expected to change at different price levels.

INCORPORATING SALES FORECASTS The indirect impact of price on the quantity that can be sold complicates pricing decisions. Demand for a product typically decreases as price increases. However, in certain cases, price may influence demand in the opposite direction, resulting in increased demand for a product at higher prices. Therefore, estimated demand for a product at various prices, as determined through marketing research (even if it is only an informed guess), should be incorporated into the break-even analysis.

An adjusted break-even chart that incorporates estimated demand is developed by using the initial break-even data and adding a demand curve. This graph allows a more realistic profit area to be identified. The break-even point in Exhibit 15-5 for a unit price of $18 corresponds to a quantity sold that appears impossible to reach at the assumed price (the break-even point does not fall within the sales curve), leaving $7 and $12 as feasible prices. Clearly, the preferred price is $12. The potential for profit at this price is indicated by the shaded area in the graph.

Markup Pricing

Up to this point, we have made no distinction between pricing by manufacturers and pricing by intermediaries such as wholesalers and retailers, since break-even concepts apply to all small businesses, regardless of their position in the distribution channel. Now, however, we briefly present some of the pricing formulas used by wholesalers and retailers in setting their prices. In the retailing industry, where businesses often carry many different products, **markup pricing** has emerged as a manageable pricing system. With this cost-plus approach to pricing, retailers are able to price hundreds of products much more quickly than they could using individual break-even analyses. In calculating the selling

markup pricing
Applying a percentage to a product's cost to obtain its selling price

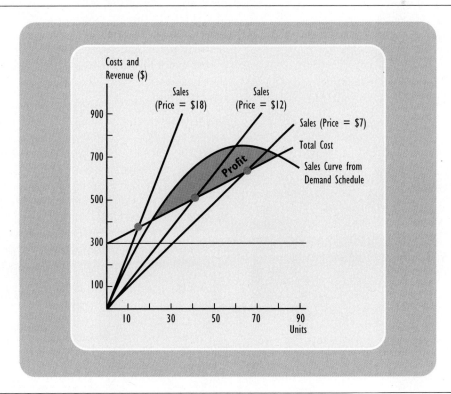

price for a particular item, a retailer adds a markup percentage (sometimes referred to as a *markup rate*) to cover the following:

- Operating expenses

- Subsequent price reductions—for example, markdowns and employee discounts

- Desired profit

It is important to have a clear understanding of markup pricing computations. Markups may be expressed as a percentage of either the *selling price* or the *cost*. For example, if an item costs $6 and sells for $10, the markup of $4 represents a 40 percent markup of the selling price [($4 markup ÷ $10 selling price) × 100] or a $66\frac{2}{3}$ percent markup of the cost [($4 markup ÷ $6 cost) × 100]. Two simple formulas are commonly used for markup calculations:

$$\frac{\text{Markup}}{\text{Selling price}} \times 100 = \text{Markup expressed as a percentage of selling price}$$

or

$$\frac{\text{Markup}}{\text{Cost}} \times 100 = \text{Markup expressed as a percentage of cost}$$

Living the Dream   entrepreneurial challenges

© R. Alcorn/SWPCO

Setting the Right Price

Doing business overseas presents many challenges for the owner of a small firm, including setting the right prices for products. Determining a foreign price by simply multiplying the U.S. price by the appropriate exchange rate may be a mistake.

Anthony Sosnick is CEO of the New York City–based company Anthony Logistics For Men, which sells a line of multi-functional, multi-benefit, natural skin care products designed for men. And the company is expanding its product offerings. For example, Sosnick recently celebrated the birth of his twin boys by launching Anthony For Little Men. Products include a baby bath wash that was endorsed by Sarah Jessica Parker after she used it for her baby son.

Taking the business into international markets, however, has presented quite a challenge for Sosnick. Arriving at prices for overseas markets "has been one of the hardest parts of doing business overseas. In each country, it's like starting from scratch," Sosnick says. For example, his Glycerin Cleansing Soap, which sells for $8 in a U.S. specialty shop, goes for $16.40 in Australia and about $11 in England. Sosnick and his team research new markets for months before pricing the skin care products, studying a market's competitive dynamics, surveying customers in stores, and traveling to visit buyers.

Pricing decisions should never be taken lightly, especially when it is easy to misread the market.

Sources: http://www.anthony.com, accessed March 15, 2007; http://www.rescu.com, accessed March 15, 2007; and Lora Kolodny, "The Price Might Be Wrong," *Inc.*, February 2005, p. 28.

http://www.anthony.com

To convert markup as a percentage of selling price to markup as a percentage of cost, use the following formula:

$$\frac{\text{Markup as a percentage of selling price}}{100\% - \text{Markup as a percentage of selling price}} \times 100 = \text{Markup expressed as a percentage of cost}$$

To convert the other way, use this formula:

$$\frac{\text{Markup as a percentage of cost}}{100\% + \text{Markup as a percentage of cost}} \times 100 = \text{Markup expressed as a percentage of selling price}$$

Selecting a Pricing Strategy

> **3** Identify specific pricing strategies.

Although techniques such as break-even analysis yield a good idea of a feasible price for a specific product, their seemingly precise nature can be very misleading. Such analyses are only one kind of tool for pricing and should not by themselves determine the final price. *Price determination must also consider market characteristics and the firm's current marketing strategy.* Pricing strategies that reflect these additional considerations include penetration pricing, skimming pricing, follow-the-leader pricing, variable pricing, price lining, and pricing at what the market will bear. [3]

Penetration Pricing

A firm that uses a penetration pricing strategy prices a product or service at less than its normal, long-range market price in order to gain more rapid market acceptance or to increase existing market share. This strategy can sometimes discourage new competitors from entering a market niche if they mistakenly view the penetration price as a long-range price. Obviously, a firm that uses this strategy sacrifices some profit margin to achieve market penetration.

penetration pricing strategy
Setting lower than normal prices to hasten market acceptance of a product or service or to increase market share

Skimming Pricing

A skimming price strategy sets prices for products or services at high levels for a limited period of time before reducing prices to lower, more competitive levels. This strategy assumes that certain customers will pay a higher price because they view a product or service as a prestige item. Use of a skimming price is most practical when there is little threat of short-term competition or when startup costs must be recovered rapidly.

skimming price strategy
Setting very high prices for a limited period before reducing them to more competitive levels

How They See It: Pricing a Service

Sally Lifland

Pricing a service is quite different from pricing a product, because services are far less interchangeable than products. As a new business trying to establish a foothold in the market, you almost have to start with a penetration pricing strategy—pricing your services below the normal long-range market price in order to motivate potential customers to give you a chance to show them what you can do.

As time goes on, though, if you routinely provide excellent service to your customers, your company will develop a reputation for getting projects done on time and on budget

and for applying the expertise needed to avert problems along the way. Once your reputation has been established, customers will be willing to pay more to ensure that their important projects are handled well. You can move gradually to a "what the market will bear" strategy—in the case of my company, working on the books that have enough market share that publishers want to make sure that they get high-quality personal attention as they work their way through the production process.

Follow-the-Leader Pricing

follow-the-leader pricing strategy
Using a particular competitor as a model in setting prices

A **follow-the-leader pricing strategy** uses a particular competitor as a model in setting a price for a product or service. The probable reaction of competitors is a critical factor in determining whether to cut prices below a prevailing level. A small business in competition with larger firms is seldom in a position to consider itself the price leader. If competitors view a small firm's pricing as relatively unimportant, they may not respond to a price differential. On the other hand, some competitors may view a smaller price-cutter as a direct threat and counter with reductions of their own. In such a case, the use of a follow-the-leader pricing strategy accomplishes very little.

Variable Pricing

variable pricing strategy
Setting more than one price for a good or service in order to offer price concessions to certain customers

Some businesses use a **variable pricing strategy** to offer price concessions to certain customers, even though they may advertise a uniform price. Lower prices are offered for various reasons, including a customer's knowledge and bargaining strength. In some fields of business, therefore, firms make two-part pricing decisions: They set a standard list price but offer a range of price concessions to particular buyers—for example, those that purchase large quantities of their product.

dynamic (personalized) pricing strategy
Charging more than the standard price when the customer's profile suggests that the higher price will be accepted

Sellers using a type of variable pricing strategy called a **dynamic (personalized) pricing strategy** charge *more* than the standard price after gauging a customer's financial means and desire for the product. The information-gathering capability of the Internet has allowed such retailers as Amazon.com to use dynamic pricing.[4]

Price Lining

price lining strategy
Setting a range of several distinct merchandise price levels

A **price lining strategy** establishes distinct price categories at which similar items of retail merchandise are offered for sale. For example, men's suits (of differing quality) might be sold at $250, $450, and $800. The amount of inventory stocked at different quality levels would depend on the income levels and buying desires of a store's customers. A price lining strategy has the advantage of simplifying the selection process for the customer and reducing the necessary minimum inventory.

Pricing at What the Market Will Bear

The strategy of pricing on the basis of what the market will bear can be used only when the seller has little or no competition. Obviously, this strategy will work only for non-standardized products. For example, a food store might offer egg roll wrappers that its competitors do not carry. Busy consumers who want to fix egg rolls but have neither the time nor the knowledge to prepare the wrappers themselves will buy them at any reasonable price.[5]

Some Final Notes on Pricing Strategies

In some situations, local, state, and federal laws must be considered in setting prices. For example, the Sherman Antitrust Act generally prohibits price fixing. At the time this book went to press, the U.S. Supreme Court was considering a case related to a manufacturer's ability to set specific minimum retail prices. The case is on appeal by Leegin Creative Leather Products of City of Industry, California, which was ordered to pay damages after it stopped shipping handbags to Kay's Kloset, a Dallas-area retailer, because Kay's repeatedly discounted Leegin's popular Brighton handbags.[6] Most federal pricing legislation is intended to benefit small firms as well as consumers by keeping large businesses from conspiring to set prices that stifle competition.

When a small business markets a line of products, some of which may compete with each other, pricing decisions must take into account the effects of a single product price on the rest of the line. For example, the introduction of a cheese-flavored chip will likely affect sales of an existing naturally flavored chip. Pricing can become extremely complex in these situations.

Continually adjusting a price to meet changing marketing conditions can be both costly to the seller and confusing to buyers. An alternative approach is to use a system of discounting designed to reflect a variety of needs. For example, a seller may offer a

Living the Dream   entrepreneurial challenges

eBusiness Pricing

Web shoppers may not always be looking for the lowest prices, as they once were. Just like other businesses, online stores are learning that they need to differentiate their businesses from the competition based on factors other than price in order to attract customers.

This is what Jeff Rhoads, president and founder of JR's Sports Collectibles (which created SportStation.com), learned. Rhoads, a graduate of Chapman University, was a restaurant manager for 13 years prior to becoming a retailer of sports collectibles and apparel. "You have to run an e-business like any other business," says Rhoads, 36, whose company had sales of $2.5 million in 2004. "You can't be one-sided with just price."

Today's more sophisticated online shoppers look for customer service, privacy and security, and product selection. Rhoads still keeps a close eye on bigger competitors, knowing that "we have to have a lower price than the goliaths." But his prices have gone up over time, and he offers fewer discounts. Rhoads competes through promotions offering free shipping and handling and a free upgrade from ground to three-day delivery. All these "freebies" cost money, and that impacts pricing.

Sources: http://www.sportstation.com, accessed March 15, 2007; and Melissa Campanelli, "Price Point," *Entrepreneur,* November 20, 2005, pp. 56–58.

http://www.jrsports.com

---

trade discount to a particular buyer (such as a wholesaler) because that buyer performs a certain marketing function for the seller (such as distribution). The stated, or list, price is unchanged, but the seller offers a lower actual price by means of a discount.

Small firms should not treat bad pricing decisions as uncorrectable mistakes. Remember, pricing is not an exact science. *If the initial price appears to be off target, make any necessary adjustments and keep on selling!*

Offering Credit

> 4 Explain the benefits of credit, factors that affect credit extension, and types of credit.

In a credit sale, the seller provides goods or services to the buyer in return for the buyer's promise to pay later. The major reason for granting credit is to make sales; credit encourages decisions to buy by providing an incentive for customers, who can buy now but would prefer to pay later. Most firms offering credit actively promote this option to potential customers. An added bonus to the seller is that it provides credit records containing customer information that can be used for sales promotions, such as direct-mail appeals to customers.

Benefits of Credit

If credit buying and selling did not benefit both parties in a transaction, their use would cease. Borrowers obviously enjoy the availability of credit, and small firms, in particular, benefit from being able to buy on credit from their suppliers. Credit provides small firms with working capital, often allowing marginal businesses to continue operations. Additional benefits of credit to borrowers are as follows:

- The ability to satisfy immediate needs and pay for them later
- Better records of purchases on credit billing statements
- Better service and greater convenience when exchanging purchased items
- Establishment of a credit history

Traditional short-term creditors include suppliers and local banks. These lenders extend credit to small businesses in order to facilitate increased sales volume and also to earn money on unpaid balances. They expect the increased revenue to more than offset the costs of extending credit, so profits will increase. Other benefits of credit to sellers are as follows:

- Closer association with customers because of implied trust
- Easier selling through telephone- and mail-order systems and over the Internet
- Smoother sales peaks and valleys, since purchasing power is always available
- Easy access to a tool with which to stay competitive

Factors That Affect Selling on Credit

An entrepreneur must decide whether to sell on credit or for cash only. In many cases, credit selling cannot be avoided, as it is standard trade practice in many types of businesses. It is important to note that in today's marketplace credit-selling competitors will almost always outsell a cash-only firm.

Although a seller always hopes to increase profits by allowing credit sales, it is not a risk-free practice. Small firms frequently shift or at least share credit risk by accepting credit cards carried by customers rather than offering their own credit. For example, the operator of a Texaco gasoline station may accept Texaco credit cards and other major credit cards, thereby avoiding the hassles of credit management. The business will pay a fee to the credit card company, but that cost may be less than the expense of managing its own independent credit system, especially when losses from bad debts are factored in. A retailer following this strategy must obtain merchant status with individual credit card companies. This is not an automatic process and can be problematic, particularly for home-based businesses.

Unfortunately, the cost of accepting major credit cards for payment over the Internet has increased. To deal with Internet fraud, small e-retailers turn to third-party firms that specialize in handling Internet credit card payments. These firms provide a degree of fraud protection for the small business. For example, PayPal (http://www.paypal.com) lets firms (and individuals) accept credit card payments. There are no set-up costs and no monthly fees. PayPal is compensated with a transaction fee of 2 to 3 percent, plus 30 cents.[7] Other credit card–processing companies include Charge.com, eCommerce Exchange, Merchant Accounts Express, and the Canadian corporation InternetSecure, Inc.

Also, if a small firm makes credit sales online, it is subject to "chargebacks" whenever buyers dispute a transaction. Some credit card companies assess fines and threaten account termination if the number of chargebacks is excessive.

For a variety of reasons, a small business may or may not decide to sell on credit. Four factors related to the entrepreneur's decision to extend credit are the type of business, credit policies of competitors, customers' income levels, and the availability of working capital.

TYPE OF BUSINESS   Retailers of durable goods typically grant credit more freely than do small grocers that sell perishables or small restaurants that serve primarily local customers. Indeed, most consumers find it necessary to buy big-ticket items on an installment basis, and such a product's life span makes installment selling feasible.

CREDIT POLICIES OF COMPETITORS   Unless a firm offers some compensating advantage, it is expected to be as generous as its competitors in extending credit. Wholesale hardware companies and retail furniture stores are examples of businesses that face stiff competition from credit sellers.

INCOME LEVEL OF CUSTOMERS   The age and income level of a retailer's customers are significant factors in determining its credit policy. For example, a drugstore adjacent to a high school might not extend credit to high school students, who are typically undesirable credit customers because of their lack of both maturity and steady income.

AVAILABILITY OF WORKING CAPITAL   There is no denying that credit sales increase the amount of working capital needed by the business doing the selling. Open-credit and installment accounts tie up money that may be needed to pay business expenses.

Types of Credit

There are two broad classes of credit: consumer credit and trade credit. **Consumer credit** is granted by retailers to final consumers who purchase for personal or family use. A small business owner can sometimes use his or her personal consumer credit to purchase supplies and equipment for use in the business. **Trade credit** is extended by nonfinancial firms, such as manufacturers and wholesalers, to business firms that are customers. Consumer credit and trade credit differ with respect to types of credit instruments, the paperwork, sources for financing receivables, and terms of sale. Another important distinction is that credit insurance is available only for trade credit.

> **consumer credit**
> Financing granted by retailers to individuals who purchase for personal or family use

> **trade credit**
> Financing provided by a supplier of inventory to a given company

A 2003 study of credit and small business, sponsored by the National Federation of Independent Business, reported extensively on credit use by small firms.[8] The survey found that 45 percent of small business owners feel that their most significant problem in the area of consumer credit is slow or late payment.

CONSUMER CREDIT   The three major kinds of consumer credit accounts are open charge accounts, installment accounts, and revolving charge accounts. Many variations of these credit accounts are also used.

Open Charge Accounts   When using an **open charge account**, a customer takes possession of goods (or services) at the time of purchase, with payment due when billed. Stated terms typically call for payment at the end of the month, but it is customary to allow a longer period than that stated. There is no finance charge for this kind of credit if the balance on the account is paid in full at the end of the billing period. Customers are not generally required to make a down payment or to pledge collateral. Small accounts at department stores are good examples of open charge accounts.

> **open charge account**
> A line of credit that allows the customer to obtain a product at the time of purchase, with payment due when billed

Installment Accounts   An **installment account** is a vehicle for long-term consumer credit. A down payment is normally required, and annual finance charges can be 20 percent or more of the purchase price. Payment periods are commonly from 12 to 36 months, although automobile dealers often offer an extended payment period of 60 months or even longer. An installment account is useful for large purchases such as that of a car, washing machine, or television.

> **installment account**
> A line of credit that requires a down payment, with the balance paid over a specified period of time

Revolving Charge Accounts   A **revolving charge account** is a variation of the installment account. A seller grants a customer a line of credit, and charged purchases may not exceed the credit limit. A specified percentage of the outstanding balance must be paid monthly, forcing the customer to budget and limiting the amount of debt that can be carried. Finance charges are computed on the unpaid balance at the end of the month. Although credit cards offer this type of account, they are discussed separately in the next section because of their widespread use.

> **revolving charge account**
> A line of credit on which the customer may charge purchases at any time, up to a preestablished limit

CREDIT CARDS   Credit cards, frequently referred to as plastic money, have become a major source of retail credit. As just mentioned, credit cards are usually based on a revolving charge account system. Depending on the issuer, we can distinguish three basic types of credit cards: bank credit cards, entertainment credit cards, and retailer credit cards.

Bank Credit Cards   The best known bank credit cards are MasterCard and VISA. Bank credit cards are widely accepted by retailers that want to offer credit but don't provide their own credit cards. Most small business retailers fit into this category. In return for a set fee (usually 2 to 5 percent of the purchase price) paid by the retailer, the bank takes the responsibility for making collections. Some banks charge annual membership fees to their cardholders. Also, cardholders are frequently able to obtain cash up to the credit limit of their card.

Entertainment Credit Cards   Well-known examples of entertainment credit cards are American Express and Diner's Club cards. While these cards have traditionally charged an annual fee, American Express recently started offering the Blue Card, which has no fee for use. Originally used for services, these cards are now widely accepted for sales of merchandise. As with bank credit cards, the collection of charges on an entertainment credit card is the responsibility of the sponsoring agency.

Retailer Credit Cards   Many companies—for example, department stores, oil companies, and telephone companies—issue their own credit cards specifically for use in their outlets or for purchasing their products or services from other outlets. Customers are usually not charged annual fees or finance charges if their balance is paid each month.

Trade Credit

Firms selling to other businesses may specify terms of sale, such as 2/10, net 30. This means that a 2 percent discount is given by the seller if the buyer pays within 10 days of the invoice date. Failure to take this discount makes the full amount of the invoice due in 30 days. For example, with these terms, a buyer paying for a $100,000 purchase within 10 days of the invoice date would save 2 percent, or $2,000.

Sales terms for trade credit depend on the product sold and the buyer's and the seller's circumstances. The credit period often varies directly with the length of the buyer's turnover period, which obviously depends on the type of product sold. The larger the order and the higher the credit rating of the buyer, the better the sales terms will be, assuming that individual terms are fixed for each buyer. The greater the financial strength and the more adequate and liquid the working capital of the seller, the more generous the seller's sales terms can be. Of course, no business can afford to allow competitors to outdo it in reasonable generosity of sales terms. In many types of business, terms are so firmly set by tradition that a unique policy is difficult, if not impossible, for a small firm to implement.

Managing the Credit Process

5 Describe the activities involved in managing credit.

Unfortunately, many small firms pay little attention to their credit management systems until bad debts become a problem. Often, this is too late. Credit management should precede the first credit sale (in the form of a thorough screening process) and then continue throughout the credit cycle.

As mentioned previously, many small firms transfer all or part of the credit function to another party. For example, a small repair shop or retail clothing store that accepts VISA or MasterCard is transferring much of the credit risk; in effect, the fee that the business pays the credit card company covers the credit management process. Nevertheless, a number of small firms want to offer their own credit to their customers and, therefore, need to understand the credit function. Let's take a look at some of the major considerations in developing and operating a comprehensive credit management program for a small business.

Evaluation of Credit Applicants

In most retail stores, the first step in credit investigation is having the customer complete an application form. The information obtained on this form is used as the basis for examining an applicant's creditworthiness. Since the most important factor in determining a customer's credit limit is her or his ability to pay the obligation when it becomes due, it is crucial to evaluate the customer's financial resources, debt position, and income level. The amount of credit requested also requires careful consideration. Drugstore customers usually need only small amounts of credit. On the other hand, business customers of wholesalers and manufacturers typically expect large credit lines. In the special case of installment selling, the amount of credit should not exceed the repossession value of the goods sold. Automobile dealers follow this rule as a general practice.

THE FOUR CREDIT QUESTIONS   In evaluating the credit status of applicants, a seller must answer the following questions:

1. Can the buyer pay as promised?

2. Will the buyer pay?

3. If so, when will the buyer pay?

4. If not, can the buyer be forced to pay?

The answers to these questions have to be based in part on the seller's estimate of the buyer's ability and willingness to pay. Such an estimate constitutes a judgment of the buyer's creditworthiness. For credit to be approved, the answers to questions 1, 2, and 4 should be "yes" and the answer to question 3 should be "on schedule."

Every applicant is creditworthy to some degree; a decision to grant credit merely recognizes the buyer's credit standing. But the seller must consider the possibility that the buyer will be unable or unwilling to pay. When evaluating an applicant's credit status, therefore, the seller must decide how much risk of nonpayment to assume.

THE TRADITIONAL FIVE C'S OF CREDIT   Ability to pay is evaluated in terms of the five C's of credit: character, capital, capacity, conditions, and collateral.

■ *Character* refers to the fundamental integrity and honesty that should underlie all human and business relationships. For business customers, character is embodied in the business policies and ethical practices of the firm. Individual customers who are granted credit must be known to be morally responsible persons.

■ *Capital* consists of the cash and other liquid assets owned by the customer. A prospective business customer should have sufficient capital to underwrite planned operations, including an appropriate amount invested by the owner.

■ *Capacity* refers to the customer's ability to conserve assets and faithfully and efficiently follow a financial plan. A business customer should utilize its invested capital wisely and capitalize to the fullest extent on business opportunities.

■ *Conditions* refer to such factors as business cycles and changes in price levels, which may be either favorable or unfavorable to the payment of debts. For example, economic recession places a burden on both businesses' and consumers' abilities to pay their debts. Other adverse factors that might limit a customer's ability to pay include fires and other natural disasters, strong new competition, and labor problems.

■ *Collateral* consists of designated security given as a pledge for fulfillment of an obligation. It is a secondary source for loan repayment in case the borrower's cash flows are insufficient for repaying a loan.

Sources of Credit Information

One of the most important, and most frequently neglected, sources of credit information is a customer's previous credit history. Properly analyzed, credit records show whether a business customer regularly takes cash discounts and, if not, whether the customer's account is typically slow. One small clothing retailer has every applicant reviewed by a Dun & Bradstreet–trained credit manager, who maintains a complete file of D&B credit reports on thousands of customers. Recent financial statements of customers are also on

Living the Dream   entrepreneurial challenges

Extend Credit Wisely

A big mistake, often made by small firms, is extending credit without having strict credit policies in place. When evaluating the credit risk of a client, you might consider following the policy of Robert Smith, 30, president of Robert Smith & Associates, a public relations firm in Rockford, Illinois.

Smith says, "Extending credit is a double-edged sword. . . . I give credit terms so more people can afford my publicity services. I also have people who still owe me money—and who will probably never pay."

After a few bad episodes, Smith implemented a reference-checking policy for his clients, most of which are small businesses: "If a customer wants to make payments, that customer has to supply three past business creditors as references. I call them and find out: Did they pay on time? Did they pay the amount they were supposed to? If they were late, did they inform in advance?"

Smith admits he has lost potential clients who think his credit qualification terms are too tough. "But I get a better quality prospect, a better lead, and a better client," he says. Establishing a well-planned credit policy can make a big difference.

Source: C. J. Prince, "Give 'Em Credit," *Entrepreneur*, April 2004, p. 59.

file. These reports, together with the retailer's own credit information, are the basis for decisions on credit sales, with heavy emphasis on the D&B credit reports. Nonretailing firms should similarly investigate credit applicants.

Manufacturers and wholesalers can frequently use a firm's financial statements as an additional source of information. Obtaining maximum value from financial statements requires a careful ratio analysis, which will reveal a firm's working-capital position, profit-making potential, and general financial health (as discussed in Chapter 23).

Pertinent data may also be obtained from outsiders. For example, arrangements may be made with other sellers to exchange credit data. Such credit information exchanges are quite useful for learning about the sales and payment experiences others have had with the seller's own customers or credit applicants.

Another source of credit information for the small firm, particularly about commercial accounts, is the customer's banker. Some bankers willingly supply credit information about their depositors, considering this to be a service that helps those firms or individuals obtain credit in amounts they can successfully handle. Other bankers believe that credit information is confidential and should not be disclosed.

trade-credit agencies
Privately owned organizations that collect credit information on businesses

Organizations that may be consulted regarding credit standings are trade-credit agencies and credit bureaus. Trade-credit agencies are privately owned and operated organizations that collect credit information on businesses only, not individual consumers. After analyzing and evaluating the data, trade-credit agencies make credit ratings available to client companies for a fee. Dun & Bradstreet, Inc. (http://www.dnb.com), a nationwide, general trade-credit agency, offers a wide array of credit reports, including the Small Business Risk New Account Score and the Payment Analysis Report. Manufacturers and wholesalers are especially interested in Dun & Bradstreet's reference book and credit reports. Available to subscribers only, the reference book covers most U.S. businesses and provides a credit rating, an evaluation of financial strength, and other key credit information on each firm.

Credit bureaus are the most common type of consumer reporting agency. These private companies maintain credit histories on individuals, based on reports from banks, mortgage companies, department stores, and other creditors. These companies make possible the exchange of credit information on persons with previous credit activity. Some credit bureaus do not require a business firm to be a member in order to get a credit report. The fee charged to nonmembers, however, is considerably higher than that charged to members. Most credit bureaus operate on one of the three online data-processing networks: Experian (formerly TRW Credit Data); Equifax, Inc.; or TransUnion Corporation.[9]

credit bureaus
Privately owned organizations that summarize a number of firms' credit experiences with particular individuals

Aging of Accounts Receivable

Many small businesses can benefit from an aging schedule, which divides accounts receivable into categories based on the length of time they have been outstanding. Typically, some accounts are current and others are past due. Regular use of an aging schedule allows troublesome collection trends to be spotted so that appropriate actions can be taken. With experience, a small firm can estimate the probabilities of collecting accounts of various ages and use them to forecast cash conversion rates.

aging schedule
A categorization of accounts receivable based on the length of time they have been outstanding

Exhibit 15-6 presents a hypothetical aging schedule for accounts receivable. According to the schedule, four customers have overdue credit, totaling $200,000. Only customer 005 is current. Customer 003 has the largest amount overdue ($80,000). In fact, the schedule shows that customer 003 is overdue on all charges and has a past record of slow payment (indicated by a credit rating of C). Immediate attention must be given to collecting from this customer. Customer 002 should also be contacted, because, among overdue accounts, this customer has the second largest amount ($110,000) in the "Not due" classification. Customer 005, however, could quickly have the largest amount overdue and should be watched closely.

Customers 001 and 004 require a special kind of analysis. Customer 001 has $10,000 more overdue than customer 004. However, customer 004's overdue credit of $40,000, which is 60 days past due, may well have a serious impact on the $100,000 not yet due ($10,000 in the beyond-discount period plus $90,000 still in the discount period). On the other hand, even though customer 001 has $50,000 of overdue credit, this customer's payment is overdue by only 15 days. Also, customer 001 has only $50,000 not yet due ($30,000 in the beyond-discount period plus $20,000 still in the discount period), compared to the $100,000 not yet due from customer 004. Both customers have an A credit rating. In conclusion, customer 001 is a better potential source of cash. Therefore, collection efforts should be focused on customer 004 rather than on customer 001, who may simply need a reminder of the overdue amount of $50,000.

exhibit 15-6 *Hypothetical Aging Schedule for Accounts Receivable*

Account Status	CUSTOMER ACCOUNT NUMBER					
	001	002	003	004	005	Total
(Days past due)						
120 days	—	—	$50,000	—	—	$ 50,000
90 days	—	$ 10,000	—	—	—	10,000
60 days	—	—	—	$40,000	—	40,000
30 days	—	20,000	20,000	—	—	40,000
15 days	$50,000	—	10,000	—	—	60,000
Total overdue	$50,000	$ 30,000	$80,000	$40,000	$ 0	$200,000
Not due (beyond discount period)	$30,000	$ 10,000	$ 0	$10,000	$130,000	$180,000
Not due (still in discount period)	$20,000	$100,000	$ 0	$90,000	$220,000	$430,000
Credit rating	A	B	C	A	A	—

Billing and Collection Procedures

Timely notification of customers regarding the status of their accounts is one of the most effective methods of keeping credit accounts current. Most credit customers pay their bills on time if the creditor provides them with information verifying their credit balance. Failure on the seller's part to send invoices delays payments.

Overdue credit accounts tie up a seller's working capital, prevent further sales to the slow-paying customer, and lead to losses from bad debts. Even if a slow-paying customer is not lost, relations with this customer are strained for a time at least.

A firm extending credit must have adequate billing records and collection procedures if it expects prompt payments. Also, a personal relationship between seller and customer must not be allowed to tempt the seller into being less than businesslike in extending further credit and collecting overdue amounts. Given the seriousness of the problem, a small firm must decide whether to collect past-due accounts directly or turn the task over to an attorney or a collection agency.

Perhaps the most effective weapon in collecting past-due accounts is reminding the debtors that their credit standing may be impaired. Impairment is certain to happen if the account is turned over to a collection agency. Delinquent customers will typically attempt to avoid damage to their credit standing, particularly when it would be known to the business community. This concern underlies and strengthens the various collection efforts of the seller.

A small firm should deal compassionately with delinquent customers. A collection technique that is too threatening not only may fail to work but also could cause the firm to lose the customer or become subject to legal action.

Many businesses have found that the most effective collection procedure consists of a series of steps, each somewhat more forceful than the preceding one. Although the procedure typically begins with a gentle written reminder, subsequent steps may include additional letters, telephone calls, registered letters, personal contacts, and referral to a collection agency or attorney. The timing of these steps should be carefully standardized so that each one automatically follows the preceding one in a specified number of days.

bad-debt ratio
The ratio of bad debts to credit sales

Various ratios can be used to monitor expenses associated with credit sales. The best known and most widely used expense ratio is the **bad-debt ratio**, which is computed by dividing the amount of bad debts by the total amount of credit sales. The bad-debt ratio reflects the efficiency of credit policies and procedures. A small firm may thus compare the effectiveness of its credit management with that of other firms. A relationship exists among bad-debt ratio, profitability, and size of the firm. Small profitable retailers have a much higher bad-debt ratio than large profitable retailers do. In general, the bad-debt losses of small firms range from a fraction of 1 percent of net sales to percentages large enough to put them out of business!

Credit Regulation

The use of credit is regulated by a variety of federal laws, as well as state laws that vary considerably from state to state. Prior to the passage of such legislation, consumers were often confused by credit agreements and were sometimes victims of credit abuse.

By far the most significant piece of credit legislation is the federal Consumer Credit Protection Act, which includes the 1968 Truth-in-Lending Act. Its two primary purposes are to ensure that consumers are informed about the terms of a credit agreement and to require creditors to specify how finance charges are computed. The act requires that a finance charge be stated as an annual percentage rate and that creditors specify their procedures for correcting billing mistakes.

Other federal legislation related to credit management includes the following:

- *The Fair Credit Billing Act* provides protection to credit customers in cases involving incorrect billing. A reasonable time period is allowed for billing errors to be corrected. The act does not cover installment credit.

- *The Fair Credit Reporting Act* gives certain rights to credit applicants regarding reports prepared by credit bureaus. Amendments such as the FACT Act, signed into law in December 2003, have strengthened privacy provisions and defined more clearly the responsibilities and liabilities of businesses that provide information to credit reporting agencies.

- *The Equal Credit Opportunity Act* ensures that all consumers are given an equal chance to obtain credit. For example, a person is not required to reveal his or her sex, race, national origin, or religion to obtain credit.

- *The Fair Debt Collection Practices Act* bans the use of intimidation and deception in collection, requiring debt collectors to treat debtors fairly.

It should be apparent by now that pricing and credit decisions are of prime importance to a small firm because of their direct impact on its financial health. *Ultimately, experience will be the entrepreneur's best teacher,* but we hope that the concepts presented in this chapter will help smooth the trip.

Looking BACK

1 Discuss the role of cost and demand factors in setting a price.

- The revenue of a firm is a direct reflection of two components: sales volume and price.
- Price must be sufficient to cover total cost plus some margin of profit.
- A firm should examine elasticity of demand—the relationship of price and quantity demanded—when setting a price.
- A product's competitive advantage is a demand factor in setting price.

2 Apply break-even analysis and markup pricing.

- Analyzing costs and revenue under different price assumptions identifies the break-even point, the quantity sold at which total costs equal total revenue.
- The usefulness of break-even analysis is enhanced by incorporating sales forecasts.
- Markup pricing is a generalized cost-plus system of pricing used by intermediaries with many products.

3 Identify specific pricing strategies.

- Penetration pricing and skimming pricing are short-term strategies used when new products are first introduced into the market.
- Follow-the-leader and variable pricing are special strategies that reflect the nature of the competition's pricing and concessions to customers.
- A price lining strategy simplifies choices for customers by offering a range of several distinct prices.

- State and federal laws must be considered in setting prices, as well as any impact that a price may have on other product line items.

4 Explain the benefits of credit, factors that affect credit extension, and types of credit.

- Credit offers potential benefits to both buyers and sellers.
- Type of business, credit policies of competitors, income level of customers, and availability of adequate working capital affect the decision to extend credit.
- The two broad classes of credit are consumer credit and trade credit.

5 Describe the activities involved in managing credit.

- Evaluating the credit status of applicants begins with the completion of an application form.
- A customer's ability to pay is evaluated through the five C's of credit: character, capital, capacity, conditions, and collateral.
- Pertinent credit data can be obtained from several outside sources, including formal trade-credit agencies such as Dun & Bradstreet.
- An accounts receivable aging schedule can be used to improve the credit collection process.
- A small firm should establish a formal procedure for billing and collecting from charge customers.
- It is important that a small firm follow all relevant credit regulations.

Key **TERMS**

price, p. 397

credit, p. 398

total cost, p. 399

total variable costs, p. 399

total fixed costs, p. 399

average pricing, p. 400

elasticity of demand, p. 401

elastic demand, p. 401

inelastic demand, p. 401

prestige pricing, p. 401

break-even point, p. 402

markup pricing, p. 403

penetration pricing strategy, p. 405

skimming price strategy, p. 405

follow-the-leader pricing strategy,
    p. 406

variable pricing strategy, p. 406

dynamic (personalized) pricing
    strategy, p. 406

price lining strategy, p. 406

consumer credit, p. 409

trade credit, p. 409

open charge account, p. 409

installment account, p. 409

revolving charge account, p. 409

trade-credit agencies, p. 412

credit bureaus, p. 413

aging schedule, p. 413

bad-debt ratio, p. 414

Discussion **QUESTIONS**

1. Why does average pricing sometimes result in a pricing mistake?

2. Explain the importance of total fixed and variable costs to the pricing decision.

3. How does the concept of elasticity of demand relate to prestige pricing? Give an example.

4. If a firm has fixed costs of $100,000 and variable costs per unit of $1, what is the break-even point in units, assuming a selling price of $5 per unit?

5. What is the difference between a penetration pricing strategy and a skimming price strategy? Under what circumstances would each be used?

6. If a small business conducts its break-even analysis properly and finds the break-even volume at a price of $10 to be 10,000 units, should it price its product at $10? Why or why not?

7. What are the major benefits of credit to buyers? What are its major benefits to sellers?

8. How does an open charge account differ from a revolving charge account?

9. What is meant by the terms 2/10, net 30? Does it pay to take discounts when they are offered?

10. What is the major purpose of aging accounts receivable? At what point in credit management should this activity be performed? Why?

You Make the CALL

SITUATION 1

Steve Jones is the 35-year-old owner of a highly competitive small business, which supplies temporary office help. Like most businesspeople, he is always looking for ways to increase profit. However, the nature of his competition makes it very difficult to raise prices for the temps' services, while reducing their wages makes recruiting difficult. Jones has, nevertheless, found an area—bad debts—in which improvement should increase profits. A friend and business consultant met with Jones to advise him on credit management policies. Jones was pleased to get this friend's advice, as bad debts were costing him about 2 percent of sales. Currently, Jones has no system for managing credit.

Question 1 What advice would you give Jones regarding the screening of new credit customers?

Question 2 What action should Jones take to encourage current credit customers to pay their debts? Be specific.

Question 3 Jones has considered eliminating credit sales. What are the possible consequences of this decision?

SITUATION 2

Tom Anderson started his records storage business in the New York metropolitan area in 1991. His differentiation strategy was to offer competitive prices while providing state-of-the-art technology, easy access to his warehouse, and, of course, great service.

After opening the business, Anderson learned that most potential customers had already signed long-term storage contracts with competitors. These contracts included a removal fee for each box permanently removed from the storage company's warehouse, making it difficult for customers to consider switching.

Anderson believes that the survival of his company hinges on his view of what the essence of his business is. In other words, is he operating a storage company or a real estate business? He is convinced that he must answer this question before making any decision regarding pricing strategy.

Question 1 What do you think Anderson means when he asks, "Is my business storage or real estate?" Why do you think he feels a need to ask this question prior to developing a pricing strategy?

Question 2 What pricing strategy would be effective in combatting the existing contractual relationships between potential customers and competitors?

Question 3 Assuming that business costs would allow Anderson to lower prices, what problems do you see with this approach?

Question 4 Do you believe his business could benefit from offering credit to customers? Why or why not?

SITUATION 3

Paul Bowlin owns and operates a tree removal, pruning, and spraying business in a metropolitan area with a population of approximately 200,000. The business started in 1975 and has grown to the point where Bowlin uses one and sometimes two crews, with four or five employees on each crew. Pricing has always been an important tool in gaining business, but Bowlin realizes that there are ways to entice customers other than quoting the lowest price. For example, he provides careful cleanup of branches and leaves, takes out stumps below ground level, and waits until a customer is completely satisfied before taking payment. At the same time, he realizes his bids for tree removal jobs must cover his costs. In this industry, Bowlin faces intense price competition from operators with more sophisticated wood-processing equipment, such as chip grinders. Therefore, he is always open to suggestions about pricing strategy.

Question 1 What would the nature of this industry suggest about the elasticity of demand affecting Bowlin's pricing?

Question 2 What types of costs should Bowlin evaluate when he is determining his break-even point?

Question 3 What pricing strategies could Bowlin adopt to further his long-term success in this market?

Question 4 How can the high quality of Bowlin's work be used to justify somewhat higher price quotes?

Experiential EXERCISES

1. Interview a small business owner regarding his or her pricing strategy. Try to ascertain whether the strategy being used reflects the total fixed and variable costs of the business. Prepare a report on your findings.

2. Interview a small business owner regarding his or her policies for evaluating credit applicants. Summarize your findings in a report.

3. Interview the credit manager of a retail store about the benefits and drawbacks of extending credit to customers. Report your findings to the class.

4. Ask several small business owners in your community who extend credit to describe the credit management procedures they use to collect bad debts. Report your findings to the class.

Exploring the WEB

1. The Marketing Teacher website maintains lessons on topics related to marketing. Go to http://www.marketingteacher.com/Lessons/ lesson_pricing.htm and read the pricing strategies lesson.

   a. After reading the lesson, draw the pricing strategies matrix on a piece of paper.

   b. Click on the "Exercise" link and complete the companion exercise on pricing, placing the six examples in the correct matrix quadrant.

2. Go to Cleveland-based KeyCorp's website at http://www.key.com. KeyCorp is the largest bank-based financial services firm in the United States. Follow the links from KeyCorp's homepage to "Small Business," then "Solutions Center," "Tools and Resources," "Offering Credit to Your Customers," and "Accepting Credit Cards." Read the short article on boosting sales through achieving merchant status with credit card companies.

   a. What kinds of fees should you expect to be assessed when accepting payment from your customers by credit card?

   b. How might you attempt to lower these fees?

Video Case **15**

NICOLE MILLER INC. (p. 650)
This case illustrates how choosing a price strategy appropriate to a firm's industry can create perceived added value to the product when it is coupled with an effective marketing campaign.

Alternative Cases for Chapter 15:

Case 13, Rodgers Chevrolet, p. 646
Case 20, Modern Postcard, p. 660

## chapter 16

Promotional Planning

In the SPOTLIGHT

Bald Guyz
http://www.baldguyz.com

If you're brave enough to start a business, you also need to be bold enough to shout about it. Whether you call it audacious advertising or guerilla, street-level, or in-your-face marketing, it's all about breaking through the clutter and getting the attention of your target consumers.

This style of "no holds barred" marketing has been embraced by Howard Brauner, 49, founder of Bald Guyz grooming products. Bald Guyz is the first line of products designed to meet the special needs of bald men. Brauner's products were created to help the "hairing-impaired" embrace, not hide, their baldness. Brauner knew that his target audience would respond favorably to an in-your-face approach to marketing, including a "Bald Is Beautiful Day" in New York City. The event featured a six-mile walk for proud bald men, at which the Bald Guyz street team, composed of attractive women, passed out product samples to walkers.

A thorough understanding of your customer is key to the success of any such marketing attempts. Knowing that his customers attend such events as the NBA All-Star game and the Super Bowl, Brauner plans to take his Bald Guyz street team to those cities during the festivities. Plans are to have the team pass out bright blue and orange shirts emblazoned with "Bald Guyz Are Sexy" and to encourage customers or their loved ones to send in to the firm's website nominations, in the form of photos, for "Bald Guy of the Week."

Brauner's bold attempts to build brand recognition appear to be working. He expects sales to reach seven figures in 2007. Bald truly is beautiful.

Source: Nichole L. Torres, "Audacious Advertising," Entrepreneur.com, http://www.entrepreneur/advertising/article173464.html, accessed February 2007.

© Larry Ford/Ford Photography

Looking AHEAD

After studying this chapter, you should be able to

1 Describe the communication process and the factors determining a promotional mix.
2 Explain methods of determining the appropriate level of promotional expenditures.
3 Describe personal selling activities.
4 Identify advertising options for a small business.
5 Discuss the use of sales promotional tools.

The old adage "Build a better mousetrap and the world will beat a path to your door" suggests that innovation is the foundation of a successful marketing strategy. Unfortunately, the narrow focus of the saying minimizes the roles of other vital marketing activities, such as promotion. Promotion informs customers about any new, improved "mousetrap" and how interested buyers can find the "door." Customers also must be persuaded that the new mousetrap is actually better than their old one. Clearly, entrepreneurs cannot rely on product innovation alone; they need to understand the promotional process in order to develop an effective marketing strategy for their particular "mousetrap."

Let's begin with a simple definition of *promotion*. **Promotion** consists of marketing communications that inform potential consumers about a firm or its product or service and try to persuade them to buy it. Small businesses use promotion in varying degrees; a given firm seldom uses all of the many promotional tools available. In order to simplify our discussion of the promotional process, we group the techniques discussed in this chapter into three traditional categories—personal selling, advertising, and sales promotional tools.

promotion
Marketing communications that inform and persuade consumers

Before examining the categories in the promotional process, let's first look at the basic process of communication that characterizes promotion. If an entrepreneur understands that promotion is just a special form of communication, she or he will be better able to grasp the entire process.

The Communication Process in Promotion

Promotion is based on communication. In fact, promotion is wasted unless it effectively communicates a firm's message.

Communication is a process with identifiable components. As shown in Exhibit 16-1, every communication involves a source, a message, a channel, and a receiver. Each of us communicates in many ways each day, and these exchanges parallel small business communications. Part (a) in Exhibit 16-1 depicts a personal communication—parents communicating with their daughter, who is away at college. Part (b) depicts a small business communication—a firm communicating with a customer.

1 Describe the communication process and the factors determining a promotional mix.

As you can see, many similarities exist between the two. The receiver of the parents' message is their daughter. The parents, the source in this example, use three different channels for their message: e-mail, a personal visit, and a special gift. The receiver of the message from the XYZ Company is the customer. The XYZ Company uses three message channels: a newspaper, a sales call, and a business gift. The parents' e-mail

exhibit

16-1   *Similarity of Personal and Small Business Communication Processes*

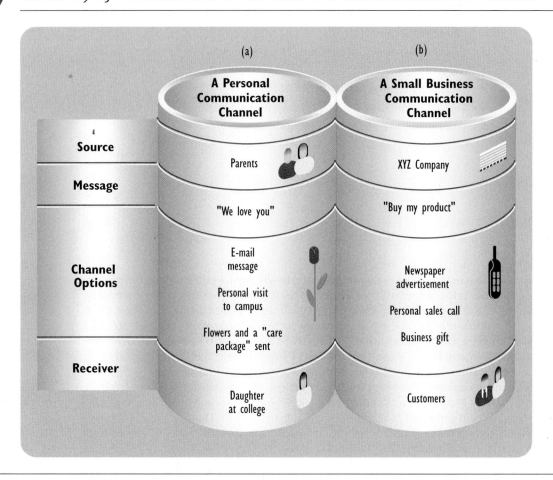

and the company's newspaper advertisement both represent nonpersonal forms of communication—there is no face-to-face contact. The parents' visit to their daughter and the sales call made by the company's representative are personal forms of communication. Finally, the flowers and care package and the business gift are both special methods of communication. Thus, the promotional efforts of the small firm, like the communication between parents and daughter, can be viewed as encompassing nonpersonal (advertising), personal (personal selling), and special (sales promotion) forms of communication.

A term commonly used to denote a particular combination of promotional methods is *promotional mix*. A **promotional mix** describes the blend of nonpersonal, personal, and special forms of communication techniques used in a promotional campaign. The particular combination of the various promotional methods—advertising, personal selling, and sales promotional tools—is determined by many factors. One important factor is the geographical nature of the market to be reached. A widely dispersed market generally requires mass coverage through advertising, in contrast to the more costly individual contacts of personal selling. On the other hand, if the market is local or if the number of customers is relatively small, personal selling may be more feasible.

Another factor is the size of the promotional budget. Small firms may not select certain forms of promotion because the costs are just too high. Television advertising, for example, is generally more expensive than radio advertising.

A third factor that heavily influences the promotional mix is the product's characteristics. If a product is of high unit value, such as a mobile home, personal selling will be a vital ingredient in the mix. Personal selling is also an effective method for promoting highly technical products, such as automobiles or street-sweeping machinery, because a customer normally has limited knowledge about such products. On the other hand, nonpersonal advertising is more effective for a relatively inexpensive item, like razor blades.

promotional mix
A blend of nonpersonal, personal, and special forms of communication aimed at a target market

There are, of course, many other considerations to be evaluated when developing a unique promotional mix. Nevertheless, promotional planning should always strive to begin with the optimum mix of techniques. The entrepreneur can then make any necessary adjustments—for example, by cutting back on the effort or seeking more funds to support the promotional plan.

Determining the Promotional Budget

2 Explain methods of determining the appropriate level of promotional expenditures.

Unfortunately, no mathematical formula can answer the question "How much should a small business spend on promotion?" There are, however, four commonsense approaches to budgeting funds for small business promotion:

1. Allocating a percentage of sales

2. Deciding how much can be spared

3. Spending as much as the competition does

4. Determining what it will take to do the job

Allocating a Percentage of Sales

Often, the simplest method of determining how much to budget for promotion is to earmark promotional dollars based on a percentage of sales. A firm's own past experiences should be evaluated to establish a promotion-to-sales ratio. If 2 percent of sales, for example, has historically been spent on promotion with good results, the firm should budget 2 percent of forecasted sales for future promotion. Secondary data on industry averages can be used for comparison. *Advertising Age* magazine is one of several sources that report what firms are doing with their advertising dollars.

A major shortcoming of this method is an inherent tendency to spend more on promotion when sales are increasing and less when they are declining. If promotion stimulates sales, then reducing promotional spending when sales are down is illogical. Unfortunately, new firms have no historical sales figures on which to base their promotional budgets.

Deciding How Much Can Be Spared

Another piecemeal approach to promotional budgeting widely used by small firms is to spend whatever is left over when all other activities have been funded. The decision about promotional spending might be made only when a media representative sells an owner on a special deal that the business can afford. Such an approach to promotional spending should be avoided because it ignores promotional goals.

Spending as Much as the Competition Does

Sometimes, a small firm builds a promotional budget based on an analysis of competitors' budgets. By duplicating the promotional efforts of close competitors, the business hopes to reach the same customers and will at least be spending as much as the competition. If the competitor is a large business, this method is clearly not feasible; however, it can be used to react to short-run promotional tactics by small competitors. Unfortunately, this approach may result in the copying of competitors' mistakes as well as their successes.

Determining What It Will Take to Do the Job

The preferred approach to estimating promotional expenditures is to decide what it will take to do the job. This method requires a comprehensive analysis of the market and the firm's goals. If these estimates are reasonably accurate, the entrepreneur can determine the total amount that needs to be spent.

In many cases, the best way for a small business to set promotional expenditures incorporates all four approaches. In other words, compare the four estimated amounts and

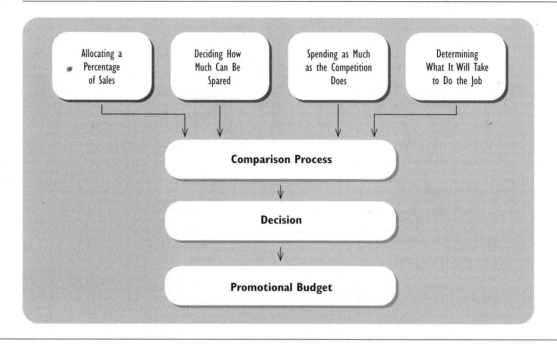

exhibit 16-2   *Four-Step Method for Determining a Promotional Budget*

set the promotional budget at a level that is somewhere between the maximum and minimum amounts (see Exhibit 16-2). After the budget has been determined, the entrepreneur must then decide how dollars will be spent on the various promotional methods. Which methods are chosen depends on a number of factors. We will now examine personal selling, a frequent choice for small firms.

Personal Selling in the Small Firm

3 Describe personal selling activities.

personal selling
A sales presentation delivered in a one-on-one manner

Many products require **personal selling**—promotion delivered in a one-on-one environment. Personal selling includes the activities of both the inside salespeople of retail, wholesale, and service establishments and the outside sales representatives who call on business customers and final consumers. Frequently, the entrepreneur is the primary salesperson for a venture.

The Importance of Product Knowledge

Effective selling is built on a foundation of product knowledge. If a salesperson is well acquainted with a product's advantages, uses, and limitations, she or he can educate customers by successfully answering their questions and countering their objections. Most customers expect a salesperson to provide knowledgeable answers—whether the product is a camera, a coat, an automobile, paint, a machine tool, or office equipment. Customers are seldom experts on the products they buy; however, they can immediately sense a salesperson's knowledge or ignorance. Personal selling degenerates into mere order-taking when a salesperson lacks product knowledge.

prospecting
A systematic process of continually looking for new customers

The Sales Presentation

The heart of personal selling is the sales presentation to a prospective customer. At this crucial point, an order is either secured or lost. A preliminary step leading to an effective sales presentation is **prospecting**, a systematic process of continually looking for new

Living the Dream
entrepreneurial challenges

All He Wanted Was a Little Respect

A key to successful selling is selling yourself. This can be a tall order when you are a young entrepreneur just starting out. "You're too young. What could someone so young know about business? Call me in a few years when you grow up." These are common refrains when a young, energetic entrepreneur meets older potential clients for the first time.

You must convince them that you're serious and capable. How can you project such an image, you ask? First, make sure you're an authority on your business and the industry it operates in. Second, be sure you look the part. Dress appropriately and act professionally. Everything, including your PowerPoint slides, business cards, and other materials, must look professional as well. If you're worried how your presentation might go, practice it before you make your pitch. Feedback from friends and trusted advisors can be helpful. Third, be confident that you have what it takes.

An air of confidence can quell concerns about your youth. Just ask Jason Smith, 24, founder of GoSMG.com, a distributor of fund-raising products and programs for schools and organizations. He felt the concerns regarding his age when he met new potential customers as a college entrepreneur, but his knowledge, preparation, and confidence quickly dispelled any concerns. Smith has built his Brea, California, company into a million-dollar business. "[People] may have misgivings about doing business with a younger person, but as soon as I talk with them face to face, they see that I know exactly what I'm doing," says Smith.

Source: Nichole L. Torres, "Getting No Respect," *Entrepreneur*, February 2005, p. 110.

http://www.gosmg.com

customers. Prospecting also includes consideration of whether a potential customer can be well-served by the company.

USING PROSPECTING TECHNIQUES   One of the most efficient prospecting techniques is obtaining *personal referrals*. Such referrals come from friends, customers, and other businesses. Initial contact with a potential customer is greatly facilitated when the salesperson is able to say, "You were referred to me by. . . ."

Another source of prospects is *impersonal referrals* from media publications, public records, and directories. Newspapers and magazines, particularly trade magazines, often identify prospects by reporting on new companies and new products. Engagement announcements in a newspaper can serve as impersonal referrals for a local bridal shop. Public records of property transactions and building permits can be impersonal referrals for a garbage pick-up service, which might find prospective customers among those planning to build houses or apartment buildings.

A high-tech variation of impersonal referrals may soon be taking place on MySpace, which was purchased for $630 million by Rupert Murdoch's News Corp in 2005.[1] MySpace ad salespeople plan to use software to sift through MySpace members' profile pages and sort the pages based on the often highly personal information posted on them. These salespeople will then create "buckets" of similar MySpace members, access to whom they will offer to interested advertisers. The mining of such information has long been a dream of marketers and could be a boon in MySpace's attempt to boost its ad revenue.

Prospects can also be identified without referrals through *marketer-initiated contacts.* Telephone calls or mail surveys, for example, help locate prospects. In a market survey conducted to identify prospects for a small business, one of the authors of this book used a mail questionnaire. The questionnaire asked technical questions about a service and then concluded with the following statement: "If you would be interested in a service of this nature, please check the appropriate space below and your name will be added to the mailing list." This prospecting approach generated a number of leads for potential selling opportunities.

Finally, prospects can be identified by recording *customer-initiated contacts.* Inquiries by a potential customer that do not lead to a sale can still create a "hot prospect." Small furniture stores often require their salespeople to fill out a card for each person visiting the store. These prospects are then systematically contacted over the telephone or by e-mail, and contact information is updated periodically. Firms with websites can similarly follow up on visitors who have made inquiries.

PRACTICING THE SALES PRESENTATION   Practicing always improves a salesperson's success rate; after all, "practice makes perfect." Prior to making a sales presentation, a salesperson should give his or her presentation in front of a spouse, friend, or mirror. Even better, he or she may want to use a camcorder to make a practice DVD that can be carefully studied to improve delivery.

The salesperson should think about possible customer objections to the product and prepare to handle them. Most objections can be categorized as relating to (1) price, (2) product, (3) timing, (4) source, (5) service, or (6) need. Although there is no substitute for actual selling experience, salespeople find training helpful in learning how to deal with customers' objections. One popular sales book suggests the following techniques for responding to customers' objections.[2] The first two responses are appropriate when a potential buyer states an objection that is factually untrue; the remaining suggestions can be used when a buyer raises a valid objection.

- *Direct denial:* Deny the prospect's objection and give facts to back up the denial.

- *Indirect denial:* Express concern about the prospect's objection and follow with a denial.

- *Boomerang technique:* Turn the valid objection into a valid reason to buy.

- *Compensation method:* Admit to agreeing with the objection and then proceed to show compensating advantages.

- *Pass-up method:* Acknowledge the concern expressed by the prospect and then move on.

MAKING THE SALES PRESENTATION   Salespeople must adapt their sales approach to meet customers' needs. A "canned" sales talk will not succeed with most buyers. For example, an individual selling personal computers must demonstrate the capacity of the equipment to fill a customer's particular needs. Similarly, a boat salesperson must understand the special interests of particular customers and speak their language. Every sales objection must be answered explicitly and adequately.

Successful selling involves a number of psychological elements. Personal enthusiasm, friendliness, and persistence are required. Approximately 20 percent of all salespeople secure as much as 80 percent of all sales made because they bring these elements to the task of selling.

Some salespeople have special sales techniques that they use with success. One automobile salesperson, for example, offered free driving lessons to people who had never taken a driver's training course or who needed a few more lessons before they felt confident enough to take the required driving test. When such customers were ready to take the driving test, this salesperson would accompany them to the examination to provide moral support. Needless to say, these special efforts were greatly appreciated by new drivers who were in the market for cars.

How you handle objections during a sales presentation is also critical. Following are some examples of how Dann Ilicic, of Wow! A Branding Company, responds to potential roadblocks to a successful sales presentation.[3]

1. "We can't afford your price."

Dann's response: *We present three price options in our proposals. If they still say we're too expensive, that means we haven't demonstrated the value of what we're doing. Nothing's expensive if it provides you a return greater than the cost.*

2. "You guys are too small."

Dann's response: *"Those guys are too big. You're a small piece of business to them; to us, you'd be huge."*

3. "We can't do it now. Come back in a year."

Dann's response: *I ask, "What would it take for you to make a decision right now?" If it's "We don't have the money," I say, "Okay, what if you could pay us in six months?" You can tell if they're just hedging.*

Customer Goodwill and Relationship Selling

A salesperson must look beyond the immediate sale to building customer goodwill and creating satisfied customers who will continue buying from the company in the future. Selling effectiveness is enhanced when a salesperson displays a good appearance, has a pleasant personality, and uses professional etiquette in all contacts with customers. A salesperson can also build goodwill by listening carefully to the customer's point of view. Courtesy, attention to details, and genuine friendliness will help gain the customer's acceptance.

Of course, high ethical standards are of primary importance in creating customer goodwill. Such standards rule out any misrepresentation of the product and require confidential treatment of a customer's plans.

Cost Control in Personal Selling

Both efficient and wasteful methods exist for achieving a given volume of sales. For example, routing traveling salespeople economically and making appointments prior to arrival can save time and transportation expenses. The cost of an outside sales call on a customer is likely to be considerable—perhaps hundreds of dollars—so efficient scheduling is crucial. Moreover, a salesperson for a manufacturing firm can contribute to cost economy by pushing certain products, thereby giving the factory a more balanced production run. Similarly, a salesperson can increase profits by emphasizing high-margin products.

How They See It: Selling Yourself

Sally Lifland

In a small service business, what you are selling basically is your own ability to provide or coordinate the provision of whatever services you specialize in. When the object of your promotion is yourself, clearly there is no substitute for personal selling—presenting yourself to the customer, one on one.

Of course, there is an element of personal selling in every contact you and your employees have with a customer, whether via telephone, e-mail, or memo, and it is important to keep that in mind when you are phrasing your various content-driven business communications. But equally important is making sure to find time on a regular basis to get together face to face with your customers in an unstructured situation; whenever possible, I like to meet over a good lunch or dinner. Though the costs of a personal visit may seem high, particularly if your customers are far-flung geographically, the benefits can be huge. An informal post mortem may give both you and your customers ideas on how to make future projects flow more smoothly, and the rapport you establish may put you first in the customer's mind when the next big project comes along. The final bonus: It's fun. I can hardly believe that I'm working when I'm traveling around the country, visiting with the company's many interesting clients over some really delicious meals.

The Compensation Program for Salespeople

Salespeople are compensated in two ways for their efforts—financially and nonfinancially. A good compensation program allows its participants to work for both forms of reward, while recognizing that a salesperson's goals may be different from the entrepreneur's goals. For example, an entrepreneur may seek nonfinancial rewards that are of less importance to salespeople.

NONFINANCIAL REWARDS   Personal recognition and the satisfaction of reaching a sales quota are examples of nonfinancial rewards that motivate many salespeople. Small retail businesses sometimes post the photograph of the top salesperson of the week or the month for all to see. Engraved plaques are also given as a more permanent record of sales achievements.

FINANCIAL REWARDS   Typically, financial compensation is the more critical factor for salespeople. Two basic plans used for financial compensation are commissions and straight salary. Each plan has specific advantages and limitations for the small firm.

Most small businesses would prefer to use commissions as compensation, because such an approach is simple and directly related to productivity. Usually, a certain percentage of the sales generated by the salesperson represents his or her commission. A commission plan thereby incorporates a strong incentive for sales effort—no sale, no commission! Also, with this type of plan, there is less drain on the firm's cash flow until a sale is made.

The straight salary form of compensation provides salespeople with more income security because their level of compensation is ensured, regardless of sales made. However, working for a straight salary can potentially reduce a salesperson's motivation, by providing income despite low performance or no sales at all.

Combining the two forms of compensation creates the most attractive plan for most small businesses. It is common practice to structure combination plans so that salary represents the larger part of compensation for a new salesperson. As the salesperson gains experience, the ratio is adjusted to provide more money from commissions and less from salary.

Advertising Practices for Small Firms

> **4** Identify advertising options for a small business.

Another significant promotional expenditure for the small firm is advertising. **Advertising** is the impersonal presentation of an idea that is identified with a business sponsor. Ideas in advertising are communicated to consumers through media such as television, radio, magazines, newspapers, billboards, and the Internet.

advertising
The impersonal presentation of a business idea through mass media

Advertising Objectives

As its primary goal, advertising seeks to sell by informing, persuading, and reminding customers of the availability or superiority of a firm's product or service. To be successful, it must rest on a foundation of positive features such as product quality and efficient service. It is important to remember that advertising can bring no more than temporary success to an otherwise second-rate product. Advertising must always be viewed as a complement to a good product and never as a replacement for a bad product.

The entrepreneur must avoid creating false expectations with advertising, as such expectations are likely to disappoint customers and leave them dissatisfied. Advertising can accentuate a trend in the sale of an item or product line, but it seldom has the power to reverse a trend. It must, consequently, be able to reflect changes in customer needs and preferences.

At times, advertising may seem to be a waste of money. It is expensive and adds little value to the product. But the primary alternative to advertising is personal selling, which is often more expensive and time-consuming.

product advertising
The presentation of a business idea designed to make potential customers aware of a specific product or service and create a desire for it

Types of Advertising

The two basic types of advertising are product advertising and institutional advertising. **Product advertising** is designed to make potential customers aware of a particular product or service and create a desire for it. **Institutional advertising**, on the other hand, conveys information about the business itself. It is intended to make the public aware of the company and enhance its image so that its product advertising will be more credible and effective. Bill Weber is continually concerned with his company's image in the community

institutional advertising
The presentation of information about a particular firm, designed to enhance the firm's image

as he attempts to sell garage door products from his Dayton, Ohio, location. In his advertising, Weber stresses that the company is locally owned, and he participates in local community events as part of his image-building efforts. "It's more than buying radio ads," says Weber, who frequently serves as the local high school football broadcaster. "Our company is connected to the town, because people feel like they know our family. Promoting the family-owned image has been good business."[4]

Most small business advertising is of the product type. Small retailers' ads often stress products exclusively, such as weekend specials at a supermarket or sportswear sold exclusively in a women's shop. It is important to note, however, that the same advertisement can convey both product and institutional themes. Furthermore, a firm may stress its product in newspaper advertisements, while using institutional advertising in the local Yellow Pages. Decisions regarding the type of advertising to be used should be based on the nature of the business, industry practice, available media, and the objectives of the firm.

Obtaining Assistance with Advertising

Most small businesses rely on others' expertise to create their promotional messages. Fortunately, there are several sources for this specialized assistance, including advertising agencies, suppliers, trade associations, and advertising media.

Advertising agencies can provide the following services:

- Furnish design, artwork, and copy for specific advertisements and/or commercials
- Evaluate and recommend the advertising media with the greatest "pulling power"
- Evaluate the effectiveness of different advertising appeals
- Advise on sales promotions and merchandise displays
- Conduct market-sampling studies to evaluate product acceptance or determine the sales potential of a specific geographic area
- Furnish mailing lists

Since advertising agencies charge fees for their services, an entrepreneur must make sure that the return from those services will be greater than the fees paid. Quality advertising assistance can best be provided by a competent agency. For example, Flowers & Partners, an agency specializing in small business clients, offers a program called Underdog Advertising to assist small firms with package design, media planning, new product development, and public relations.[5] Of course, with the high level of computer technology currently available, creating print advertising in-house is becoming increasingly common among small firms.

Other outside sources may assist in formulating and carrying out promotional programs. Suppliers often furnish display aids and even entire advertising programs to their dealers. Trade associations also provide helpful assistance. In addition, the advertising media can provide some of the same services offered by an ad agency.

Frequency of Advertising

Determining how often to advertise is an important and highly complex issue for a small business. Obviously, advertising should be done regularly, and attempts to stimulate interest in a firm's products or services should be part of an ongoing promotional program. One-shot advertisements that are not part of a well-planned promotional effort lose much of their effectiveness in a short period. Of course, some noncontinuous advertising may be justified, such as advertising to prepare consumers for acceptance of a new product. Such advertising may also be used to suggest to customers new uses for established products or to promote special sales. Deciding on the frequency of advertising involves a host of factors, both objective and subjective, and a wise entrepreneur will seek professional advice.

Where to Advertise

Most small firms restrict their advertising, either geographically or by customer type. Advertising media should reach—but not overreach—a firm's present or desired target market. From among the many media available, a small business entrepreneur must choose those that will provide the greatest return for the advertising dollar.

The most appropriate combination of advertising media depends on the type of business and its current circumstances. A real estate sales firm, for example, may rely almost exclusively on classified advertisements in the local newspaper, supplemented by institutional advertising in the Yellow Pages of the telephone directory. A transfer-and-storage firm may use a combination of radio, billboard, and Yellow Pages advertising to reach individuals planning to move household furniture. A small toy manufacturer may emphasize television advertisements and participation in trade fairs. A local retail store may concentrate on display advertisements in the local newspaper. The selection of media should be based not only on tradition but also on a careful evaluation of the various methods that are available to cover a firm's particular market.

A good way to build a media mix is to talk with representatives from each medium. A small firm will usually find these representatives willing to recommend an assortment of media, not just the ones they represent. Before meeting with these representatives, the entrepreneur should learn about the strengths and weaknesses of each medium. Exhibit 16-3 summarizes important facts about major advertising media. Study this information carefully, noting the particular advantages and disadvantages of each medium.

The newest medium discussed in Exhibit 16-3 is the Internet. Because the various options for Web advertising may be less familiar than those associated with more traditional media, Web advertising is examined separately in the next section.

exhibit

16-3   *Advantages and Disadvantages of Major Advertising Media*

Medium	Advantages	Disadvantages
Newspapers	Geographic selectivity and flexibility; short-term advertiser commitments; news value and immediacy; year-round readership; high individual market coverage; co-op and local tie-in availability; short lead time	Little demographic selectivity; limited color capabilities; low pass-along rate; may be expensive
Magazines	Good reproduction, especially for color; demographic selectivity; regional selectivity; local market selectivity; relatively long advertising life; high pass-along rate	Long-term advertiser commitments; slow audience buildup; limited demonstration capabilities; lack of urgency; long lead time
Radio	Low cost; immediacy of message; can be scheduled on short notice; relatively no seasonal change in audience; highly portable; short-term advertiser commitments; entertainment carryover	No visual treatment; short advertising life of message; high frequency required to generate comprehension and retention; distractions from background sound; commercial clutter
Television	Ability to reach a wide, diverse audience; low cost per thousand; creative opportunities for demonstration; immediacy of messages; entertainment carryover; demographic selectivity with cable stations	Short life of message; some consumer skepticism about claims; high campaign cost; little demographic selectivity with network stations; long-term advertiser commitments; long lead times required for production; commercial clutter
Outdoor Media	Repetition; moderate cost; flexibility; geographic selectivity	Short message; lack of demographic selectivity; high "noise" level distracting audience
Internet	Fastest-growing medium; ability to reach a narrow target audience; relatively short lead time required for creating Web-based advertising; moderate cost	Difficult to measure ad effectiveness and return on investment; ad exposure relies on "click-through" from banner ads; not all consumers have access to the Internet

Source: Charles W. Lamb, Jr., Joseph F. Hair, Jr., and Carl McDaniel, *Marketing,* 9th ed. (Cincinnati: South-Western, 2008), p. 475.

Web Advertising

The Internet has provided an entirely new way for small firms to advertise. With color graphics, two-way information exchanges, streaming video, and 24-hour availability, online advertising is challenging traditional media for promotional dollars. Web advertising allows advertisers to reach large numbers of global buyers in a timely manner, at less expense, and with more impact than many alternative forms of advertising.

Advertisers of all types have flocked to the Internet, hoping (with good reason) that the information superhighway will be the next great mass medium. Most large businesses have a presence on the Web, and more and more small firms are using Internet technology. The basic methods of Web advertising are (1) banner ads and pop-ups, (2) e-mail, (3) sponsorships and linkages, and (4) a corporate website.

BANNER ADS AND POP-UPS **Banner ads** are advertisements that appear across a webpage, most often as moving rectangular strips. In contrast, **pop-up ads** burst open on webpages but do not move. When viewers respond by clicking on an ad, they are automatically linked to the site providing the product or sales activity. Both banner and pop-up ads can be placed on search engine sites or on related webpages.

banner ads
Advertisements that appear across a Web page, most often as moving rectangular strips

pop-up ads
Advertisements that burst open on computer screens

These types of Web advertising are often carried out through an affiliate program. In an affiliate program, a website carries a banner ad or a link for another company in exchange for a commission on any sales generated by the traffic sent to the sponsoring website. Affiliate programs have become quite popular among Web retailers, with one of the most lucrative being eBay's program. A primary reason for the success of eBay's affiliate program is the sheer volume of visitors to its website every day. The millions of items for sale at any given time on eBay provide ample advertising opportunities for affiliates. eBay pays an affiliate a commission not only on sales generated by the users it sends, but also on each already-registered eBay user it sends back to eBay and on each bid and qualified Buy it Now transaction.

These commissions have allowed many affiliates to profit handsomely from their relationship with eBay. The top 50 of the approximately 10,000 affiliates in the eBay program generate more than $1 million annually in commissions. Affiliates can choose from an array of eBay banners, buttons, and logos to feature on their websites. A cookie identifying the affiliate is attached to anyone sent to eBay. Affiliates can also add real-time listings to their sites. For example, if your website reviews musical releases, it can provide up-to-date listings of the CDs for sale on eBay.[6]

Price comparison pop-ups are an effective way to lure surfers from competitive websites. Here's how they work: When a shopper who is browsing in an online store clicks on a specific product, comparison shopping software generates a pop-up ad that features links to other vendors selling the same item at a lower price. This software works much the same way as a bargain hunting website like Shopping.com, but it offers competitive prices wherever consumers shop on the Web. Comparison shopping software has helped Steve Hafner, founder of the travel website Kayak.com, to compete with online giants such as Expedia and Travelocity. Buying keywords on Google and putting banner ads on travel websites were not working for Hafner, but as soon as he started his comparison shopping ads, he could see the results. The ads generated a click-through rate of 8 to 10 percent, compared with 1 percent for his search engine ads. The icing on the cake was that shoppers who clicked on the new ads were 50 percent more likely to book a trip than those arriving at the website via banner ads or search engines.[7]

DIRECT E-MAIL PROMOTION **E-mail promotion**, in which electronic mail is used to deliver a firm's message, provides a low-cost way to pinpoint customers and achieve response rates higher than those for banner ads. However, as more and more businesses use e-mail for this purpose, customer inboxes are becoming cluttered. And users are reluctant to open some e-mail messages, fearing they may contain computer viruses.

e-mail promotion
Advertising delivered by means of electronic mail

Despite their limitations, e-mail promotions can be very effective. Larry and Charlene Woodward operate their book business, Dogwise, from Wenatchee, Washington. When new books are published, Dogwise sends personalized e-mails to people who have previously purchased books on similar subjects. "Customers love it, and we sell lots of books every time we send a batch of e-mails," says Larry. Before using e-mail to promote new books, the company sent postcards to its customers.[8]

Two obstacles to e-mail promotion have arisen, as the volume of unsolicited e-mails (better known as *spam*) has turned many customers against this type of advertising. First, Congress passed the Can-Spam Act of 2003, which took effect on January 1, 2004, and established standards regarding the use of commercial e-mail enforceable by the Federal Trade Commission (FTC).[9] Second, anti-spam software, which also blocks legitimate e-mails, became popular. In 2003, Bill Broadbent, co-founder and CEO of T-ShirtKing.com in Emeryville, California, was sending a weekly e-mail newsletter to more than 300,000 people who had requested the newsletter on the firm's website. Despite the customers' desire to receive the newsletter, anti-spam software directed it to their spam boxes, and it was never read by many intended recipients.[10] Anti-spam software has certainly changed the potential of e-mail campaigns.

SPONSORSHIPS AND LINKAGES   In Web sponsorship, a firm pays to be part of another organization's webpage. When the webpage includes a click-on link to the paying firm's site, a linkage has been established. Research shows that a significant number of online purchases originate from online links. Unfortunately for many firms that choose to advertise through Web sponsorship, blocking software from such companies as Web-Washer can be used to prevent ads from appearing on a viewer's webpage.[11]

CORPORATE WEBSITES   The fourth form of Web advertising involves a more serious commitment by a small firm—launching a corporate website. Numerous decisions must be made prior to launching a site. Three critical startup tasks are related to the promotional success of a corporate website: (1) creating and registering a site name, (2) building a user-friendly site, and (3) promoting the site.

Creating and Registering a Site Name   The Domain Name System (DNS) allows users to find their way around the Internet. Selecting the best domain name for a corporate website is an important promotional decision, and contrary to general opinion, plenty of website names remain available. Domain names can have up to 63 characters preceding the domain designation. The three most popular domain designations are .com, .net, and .org.[12]

Since a domain name gives a small business its online identity, it's desirable to select a descriptive and appealing name. Obviously, some of the shorter, more creative names have already been taken. But, like real estate, website names can be bought and sold. In the first month of 2007, 10 domain names sold for $35,000 or more. Tied for ninth, the domain name Frisbee.com sold for $35,000; in sixth place was Joystick.com, which sold for $65,250; and in first place, Sportsbook.mobi sold for $129,000.[13]

Once a desired name has been selected, it should be checked for availability and then registered. The Internet Corporation for Assigned Names and Numbers (ICANN) is a nonprofit corporation currently overseeing the global Internet. ICANN, however, does not register names; this must be done through a domain registration firm. InterNIC, a registered service mark of the U.S. Department of Commerce, provides an Accredited Registrar Directory that lists ICANN-accredited domain registrars, such as NameSecure. Several domain registrars allow a search of the Internet to see if a proposed name is already taken.

Building a User-Friendly Website   First impressions are important, and high-quality Web design gives a small e-commerce business the opportunity to make a good first impression on each visitor. The technical aspects of developing a website are beyond the scope of this chapter. Fortunately, there are many technical specialists available to help design and build a site. Our purpose here is simply to provide some useful tips about website design. Exhibit 16-4 shows 10 design tips for e-commerce websites.

There are many reasons why websites fail to retain customers. One of the most frequent problems is slow downloading. Online shoppers are a fickle bunch, and the slightest inconvenience sends them away. If your business is conducting a considerable amount of online business, a slow website translates into lost sales revenue. Lost revenue can be direct—missed sales if you're selling online—or indirect—loss of customer trust if you're providing Web-based solutions to clients. The more important a website is to your business, the less you can afford to have it perform slowly or, worse, experience downtime.[14]

Believe it or not, studies show that first-time visitors to your website spend as little as 10 seconds there before deciding whether or not to stay. Web entrepreneurs cannot afford to squander any of these precious seconds with slow downloads. Whenever possible, reduce the number and size of files on your webpages. The more files a page contains and the larger they are, the longer it will take to load.[15]

Web sponsorship
A type of advertising in which a firm pays another organization for the right to be part of that organization's Web page

linkage
A type of advertising agreement in which one firm pays another to include a click-on link on its site

Living the Dream

utilizing the internet

If the Shoe Fits, Wear It

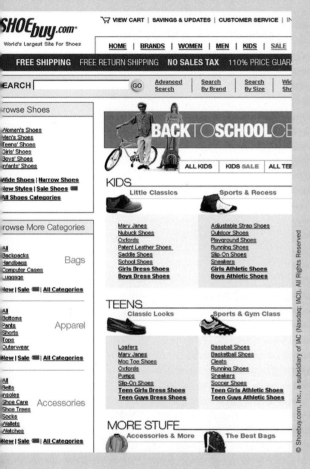

Sometimes, entrepreneurs decide to copy marketing tactics used by big businesses if they think the ideas will work well for their small firm. Scott Savitz did just that when he launched the Boston-based online footwear venture Shoebuy.com in 2000.

Amazon.com and other online marketers have experimented with offering free shipping ever since the Internet's earliest days, and it seems to work. Several major Internet research firms concur that free shipping offers by Web-based companies encourage customers to fill their shopping carts more than they would otherwise.

Savitz, the 37-year-old president, CEO, and founder of Shoebuy.com, says, "We decided we didn't want to even enter this business if we couldn't sell a product that offered free shipping, because we thought it was part of the whole value proposition." Free shipping encourages buyers to take a little more risk; in the case of Shoebuy.com, they end up buying multiple pairs of shoes since they know the merchandise will be shipped at no charge to them.

Shoebuy.com is able to make this promotional offer because it doesn't have salespeople to pay or warehouse space to maintain. It works one on one with manufacturers, which send out products directly to the customer. Other benefits promoted to shoppers by Shoebuy.com are no sales tax, free returns and exchanges, a 110-percent price guarantee, and a 100-percent sales purchase guarantee.

Currently, Shoebuy welcomes over 4,000,000 visitors to its website each month, and 60 percent of Shoeboy.com sales come from repeat purchases. Word-of-mouth is critical advertising for the company. It's the "most significant way we drive traffic to the site," says Savitz.

Shoebuy is rated as a top customer service provider on the Web and represents over 400 brands of shoes and $3 billion in accessible inventory. Free shipping and free return shipping are the company's biggest online promotions.

Sources: Personal conversation with Scott Savitz, February 2, 2007; Melissa Campanelli, "Shipping Out," *Entrepreneur,* June 2003, pp. 42–44; and http://www.shoebuy.com/sb/contact/press.jsp, accessed April 10, 2004.

http://www.shoebuy.com

Websites also will fail if they do not satisfy visitors' information needs. Frequently, this is because designers look inward to the business for Web design ideas, rather than outward to customer needs.

Promoting the Website   How do customers learn about a website? You have to tell them—and there are many ways to do this. A Web address can be promoted both to existing customers and to prospects by including the URL on print promotions, business cards, letterhead, and packaging. Special direct mail and radio campaigns can also be designed for this purpose. Additionally, a website can be promoted by placing banner advertisements on other websites, where a quick click will send users to the advertised site. The advantage of banner advertisements is that they are placed in front of thousands of visitors to other websites. Payment for banner advertising is usually based on the number of people who actually click on the banner.

exhibit

16-4   *Website Design Tips*

Tip 1: Make It Easy to Buy
This tip may seem vague and ambiguous, but it truly is the most important recommendation. Put yourself in your customer's shoes and test your designs. Isolate issues that might block users from making a successful purchase. Ask questions, such as

- How many pages and clicks does it take to make a purchase?
- How much information do users have to fill out initially, versus when they make a second-time purchase?
- Can a quick purchase be made directly from the home page?
- Does the site provide clear instructions on how to store selected items before completing a transaction?
- How well does the site communicate with a user?
- Does the site acknowledge users' actions and provide clear, concise feedback as users progress through the purchasing process?
- Can users collect multiple items before checking out?

Tip 2: Make a Strong First Impression
The e-commerce home page must make a strong first impression. This is where users are grounded to your company and persuaded to start shopping. It is first and foremost important to provide branding for your store. Next, it is important to provide a clear visual definition of your store's categories or departments. This can be accomplished with tabs or within the navigation bar.

Tip 3: Minimize Distractions: Advertising Isn't Always Necessary
You may consider not providing any advertisements on the home page or in other places throughout the purchase process. Remember that the goal of your home page is to encourage shopping and purchasing. You don't want to deter or lose users by having them click on another company's advertisement.

Tip 4: Make It Personal
Looking for a way to build a strong rapport with your shoppers? Provide personalization for the user, after the user registers as a shopper or member. Use this information to provide a personalized greeting to the home page or various department pages. *Welcome, Najia, enjoy your shopping experience.* Provide a private place that requires a password, where each user can check past orders, order status, wish lists, gift certificates, and so forth.

Tip 5: Avoid Long Instructions
If you need to include long instructions on how to use the site or make a purchase, it is time to redesign! To complete a quick purchase, a user needs minimal-to-no instructions. Most users will not read long instructions, and may turn away in confusion.

Tip 6: Provide Visual Clues to Location
For stores that have multiple departments, it is important to create a sense of varying location. This can be accomplished by changing colors on the navigation bar or the background page, and by providing different titles with text or graphics.

Tip 7: Show Off Products
If at all possible, provide photographs of individual products. Process the photos in three sizes: thumbnail, medium, and large. A thumbnail photo is best used in a list of several products. At the individual product level, provide a medium-sized image and the ability to click to view the enlarged version of the product. The larger view is not necessary but worth considering if your product has details that are not reflected in the medium-sized or thumbnail photograph.

The more details you can provide about the product the better. If you have a long page about the product, be sure to provide the option to purchase or add to your basket or cart from both the top and the bottom of the informational text.

Tip 8: Encourage Spontaneous Purchases
This can be accomplished in various ways. If a product is mentioned on the home page, place product images and details, the sale price, and a direct link to purchase the item there. In a news or feature article, include direct links to purchase products discussed within the article. Or on the side column, where advertisements for other companies traditionally would go, create intimate, focused advertisements for your products, with a direct link to purchase the items from the advertisements.

Tip 9: Alternate Background Colors in Long Lists
One good visual trick to make a long table of items easier to read is to alternate a light color background for each row or item. You can see an example of this if you search on an author's name at http://barnesandnoble.com. The search results return in alternate item background colors of gray and white.

Tip 10: Allow Users to Collect Items
Provide a shopping basket or a place for users to collect items before checking out. Never make the user fill out the lengthy payment, shipping, and other forms more than once in a transaction! At the product level, provide a link to check out and a link to add that product to the shopping cart while continuing to shop.

One item-storage feature that is currently becoming popular is called a wish list. This feature is similar to a shopping cart, but it does not provide purchasing features. Think of it as a place to store items as you are shopping. When items in your wish list go on sale, the site may notify you.

Source: Nadja Vol Ochs, "Easy-to-Buy E-Commerce Site Design Tips," http://www.microsoft.com/technet/prodtechnol/sscomm/reskit/sitedes. mspx, accessed July 13, 2007. © 1999 Microsoft Corporation. All rights reserved.

Probably the most direct approach to website promotion is making sure that the site is listed on Internet search engines. Search engines are databases, available on the Internet, that allow users to find websites based on keywords included in the site's pages. If a popular search engine does not list a firm's website, many potential visitors will undoubtedly miss it. Registering a site with a search engine is free. However, to get a position at or near the top of a search listing, you may have to pay. For example, Mark Kini, of Boston Chauffeur, spent about $60,000 in 2002 purchasing keywords and placement for his limousine service site in search engines. This seemed to be a great deal of money to promote the 18-person firm, but it has been effective. Anyone typing a phrase like "Boston limo service" into the search field would get a clickable ad for Kini's business.[16]

Search engine optimization (SEO) is the process of increasing the volume and quality of traffic to a particular website. The sooner your small business is presented in search engine results (i.e., the higher it ranks), the more visitors it will attract. An important goal is to make your website as search engine–friendly as possible.

Obviously, your website should include keywords that someone looking for that particular subject might use. Many businesses try to get to the top of a search engine's results by designing their websites to match a particular search engine's ranking index. If they don't, business can be hurt. For example, after Google adjusted how it ranked sites in its index, the Unforgettable Honeymoons website of Renee Duane, of Portland, Oregon, literally disappeared from searches. Her business, which packages honeymoon tours, felt the impact. "We used to get e-mails and calls every day from people who found us on Google. That's come to a complete stop," she says.[17] Specific content is also important; for example, including brands with descriptions can improve your placement.

There are several ways of submitting a website to search engines. A description of submission options appears in Exhibit 16-5.

exhibit 16-5   *Options for Getting Your Website Listed in Search Engines*

1. Use a Free Submission Service
Basically, free submission services offer to submit your website to as many as 500 of the top search engines for free. And while that may sound like a great deal to the inexperienced site owner, the truth is that using a free submission service will cost you traffic and sales. Every search engine has a different "rule book" that it uses to decide where your website will rank. Because they submit the same information to every single engine, free submission services are useless in achieving top-ranking positions for your firm.

2. Use a Low-Cost, Automated Submission Service
Low-cost, automated submission services offer to submit your website to as many as 900+ search engines for a minimal fee (usually between $40 and $80). Much like the free submission services, automated submission services automatically submit the same set of information to ALL of the search engines. Once again, your website is being submitted to multiple search engines without being optimized to meet their individual requirements.

3. Do It Yourself by Manually Submitting Your Website to Individual Search Engines
This is one of the best ways to submit your website to the search engines. Visit each search engine separately, and manually submit the information for each Web page you wish to have listed. On the downside, submitting your website this way can be very time consuming and labor intensive. Also, there are no professionals to help you.

4. Use a Professional Search Engine Consultant
Search engine consultants will educate you and work with you to maximize your site's exposure in each search engine. They know all of the latest tricks and techniques for securing a top spot and will show you exactly what you need to do to optimize your website for the best possible ranking.

5. Use Submission Software
Most of the software out there does exactly what the free and low-cost automated submission services do—it submits the same set of information to all of the search engines. So, your site is never optimized, and you never secure the top ranking you need.

Final Thoughts: However you decide to submit your website to the search engines, take your time. Don't rush in and make mistakes that could destroy your chances of securing a top ranking. Remember that search engines receive thousands of requests every day from people who want to make changes to their listing!

Source: Adapted from the Internet Marketing Center's website, http://www.marketingtips.com/newsletters/search-engines/search-engine-strategies.html, accessed July 13, 2007.

Sales Promotional Tools

5 Discuss the use of sales promotional tools.

sales promotion
An inclusive term for any promotional techniques other than personal selling and advertising that stimulate the purchase of a particular good or service

Sales promotion serves as an inducement to buy a certain product while typically offering value to prospective customers. Generally, **sales promotion** includes any promotional technique, other than personal selling or advertising, that stimulates the purchase of a particular good or service.

Sales promotion should seldom comprise all the promotional efforts of a small business. Typically, it should be used in combination with personal selling and advertising. Popular sales promotional tools include specialties, contests, premiums, trade show exhibits, point-of-purchase displays, free merchandise, publicity, sampling, and coupons. For example, Dan Banfe, CEO of Banfe Products, Inc., in Westville, New Jersey, a provider of soil and mulch to nurseries, uses an incentive program to promote his company's products. Banfe treats his sales staff and loyal customers to free week-long getaways in exotic locales, such as Cancun and Curacao, when they earn a certain level of points based on quantities ordered. For smaller customers, who have no hope of reaching the necessary points, Banfe holds a yearly raffle for a free trip.[18]

The scope of this textbook does not allow discussion of the wide variety of promotional tools available to small businesses. However, we will briefly examine three of the most widely used options: specialties, trade show exhibits, and publicity.

Living the Dream   entrepreneurial challenges

Experiential Marketing

Brendan Synott regularly asks potential customers "Do you want to get Bear Naked?" Such questions are designed to promote the desired brand experience for Synott and co-founder Kelly Flatley's Bear Naked line of granola and breakfast products. Bear Naked products are natural, including oats, dried fruits, nuts, and honey. There are numerous ways to eat Bear Naked—mixed with yogurt, splashed with milk, naked (straight out of the bag), or baked into muffins, cookies, or desserts.

Sampling has played an important role in Bear Naked's success. Early on, Synott and Flatley brought Bear Naked granola, along with milk and yogurt, when attempting to convince retailer Stew Leonard's to carry their product. Stew Leonard Jr. loved it so much that he ordered 50 cases on the spot. Today, sampling is still an important part of the growth strategy of Bear Naked. Synott and Flatley frequently participate in community and retailer events as a way to stay in touch with their customers and gain valuable feedback regarding their products. A photo contest focusing on customers who eat Bear Naked products on their world travels is a popular feature of their webpage.

Their approach to marketing appears to be working. Bear Naked products are sold in more than 11,000 stores across the United States, and 5,000,000 pounds of Bear Naked granola were hand-baked in 2006.

Sources: Gwen Morgan, "Be the Brand," Entrepreneur.com, February, 2007; and http://www.bearnaked.com, accessed February 2, 2007.

http:www.bearnaked.com

Specialties

The most widely used specialty item is a calendar. Other popular specialty items are pens, key chains, coffee mugs, and shirts. Almost anything can be used as a specialty promotion, as long as each item is imprinted with the firm's name or other identifying slogan.

The distinguishing characteristics of specialties are their enduring nature and tangible value. Specialties are referred to as the "lasting medium." As functional products, they are worth something to recipients. Specialties can be used to promote a product directly or to create goodwill for a firm; they are excellent reminders of a firm's existence.

Finally, specialties are personal. They are distributed directly to the customer in a personal way, they can be used personally, and they have a personal message. A small business needs to retain its unique image, and entrepreneurs often use specialties to achieve this objective. More information on specialties is available on the website of Promotional Products Association International at http://www.ppa.org.

Trade Show Exhibits

Advertising often cannot substitute for trial experiences with a product, and a customer's place of business is not always the best environment for product demonstrations. Trade show exhibits allow potential customers to get hands-on experience with a product.

Trade show exhibits are of particular value to manufacturers. The greatest benefit of these exhibits is the potential cost savings over personal selling. Trade show groups claim that the cost of an exhibit is less than one-fourth the cost of sales calls, and many small manufacturers agree that exhibits are more cost-effective than advertising. One website devoted to marketing tactics lists the following helpful tips regarding trade shows:[19]

- *Check out the trade show's history.* Does the show regularly attract large crowds? Will the show be adequately promoted to your potential customers?

- *Prepare a professional-looking display.* You do not need to have the biggest, flashiest booth on the trade show floor to attract attendees. But signs, photographs of your products, and other business-related elements used in the display should appear to be professionally prepared.

- *Have a sufficient quantity of literature on hand.* Have plenty of professionally prepared brochures or other handouts to distribute, and have them prepared well in advance of the show.

- *Make sure you have a good product.* If your product doesn't work or doesn't work properly, you'll lose more customers than you'll ever gain.

- *Do pre-show promotion.* To get the most traffic at your booth, send out mailings prior to the show inviting your customers and prospects to stop by your booth. Insert announcements in bills you send out, on your webpage, and in ads you run near the show date.

- *Have a giveaway or gimmick.* The giveaway or gimmick doesn't have to be big or elaborate. Samples of your product given away at intervals during the show are ideal. Novelty items such as keychains, pencils, and pads of paper with your company name and product name are good, too.

- *Train booth personnel.* Choose your booth staff carefully, and be sure they know how to deal with the public, especially prospective customers.

- *Follow up!* Have a plan in place for following up on leads as soon as you get home from the show.

Publicity

Of particular importance to small firms is **publicity**, which provides visibility for a business at little or no cost. Publicity can be used to promote both a product and a firm's image; it is a vital part of public relations for the small business. A good publicity program requires regular contacts with the news media.

publicity
Information about a firm and its products or services that appears as a news item, usually free of charge

Although publicity is not always free, the return on a relatively small investment can be substantial. Cypriana Porter, owner of the educational toy store The Gingerbread House, in Wolcott, New York, wanted to get the attention of the news media. To this end, she came up with the idea of Puzzleman, Defender of Creativity—a man in a superhero costume. Puzzleman visits her store to encourage creative play among its young customers. When she first introduced Puzzleman, Porter invited a local television station to the superhero's debut. The station later invited Puzzleman to be a guest on one of its shows. The local newspaper even dubbed the character "Wolcott's Own Superhero." Puzzleman has participated in programs at the local library and fire department and has appeared in town parades. The total cost of this publicity was less than $500.[20]

Other examples of publicity efforts that entail some expense include involvement with school yearbooks and youth athletic programs. While the benefits are difficult to measure, publicity is nevertheless important to a small business and should be used at every opportunity.

A high-tech spin on publicity can be found in the phenomenon of social shopping websites. A social shopping website results from the merging of a search engine, such as Google, with a social networking element, such as MySpace. Although the power of Google can't be contested, Google can't tell shoppers what is cool or what their friends or other consumers recommend. Social shopping websites like Crowdstorm, Kaboodle, StyleChic, and ThisNext do just that. A search on a typical search engine yields the most prominent brands and retailers on its first few pages. A similar search on a social shopping site displays a wider array of smaller and arguably "cooler" brands. It also includes the recommendations of the site's most fashion-conscious and influential users. Marketing on such sites must be done carefully, as they are geared toward consumers, not marketers. A forward-thinking entrepreneur, however, can post his or her own favorite products on such sites and potentially influence other users' buying decisions. After surfing the ThisNext website, Alex Klump, co-founder of Topu Ranch, an apparel manufacturer in Venice, California, posted his personal list of favorite products—which included, among others, his own Topu Ranch hooded sweatshirt. Since his initial postings, traffic to Topu Ranch's website has increased by nearly one-third and sales have risen an astonishing 165 percent.[21]

When to Use Sales Promotion

A small firm can use sales promotion to accomplish various objectives. For example, small manufacturers can use it to stimulate channel members—retailers and wholesalers—to market their product. Wholesalers can use sales promotion to induce retailers to buy inventories earlier than they normally would, and retailers, with similar promotional tools, may be able to persuade customers to make a purchase.

Consider Scott Androff and Bruce Hilsen, co-founders of TwinStar Industries in Bloomington, Minnesota. After introducing Atmos-Klear Odor Eliminator, a nontoxic biodegradable spray that gets rid of odors, they needed a low-cost promotional approach. Androff decided to use publicity. His strategy was to send a news release to magazines and newspapers, followed up by a phone call to the editors. The company also demonstrated the product at trade shows. Prior to using these two promotional tactics, sales had been slow, but they've now picked up considerably.[22]

At its core, successful promotion is all about effective communication. The source (a small business) must send out its message in such a way that intended recipients (in the target market) receive it, understand it, and are moved to respond to it. But this is no simple exercise. Many decisions must be made along the way—decisions regarding the size of the promotional budget, the promotional mix, the nature and placement of advertising, the identification of high-potential prospects, participation in trade shows, and the list goes on. You will, no doubt, make promotional errors along the way. But practice makes perfect. Learn from your mistakes, and move on. Don't give up. . . . Success awaits you!

Looking **BACK**

1 **Describe the communication process and the factors determining a promotional mix.**

· Every communication involves a source, a message, a channel, and a receiver.

· A promotional mix is a blend of nonpersonal, personal, and special forms of communication techniques.

· A promotional mix is influenced primarily by three important factors: the geographical nature of the market, the size of the promotional budget, and the product's characteristics.

2 **Explain methods of determining the appropriate level of promotional expenditures.**

· Earmarking promotional dollars based on a percentage of sales is a simple method for determining expenditures.

· Spending only what can be spared is a widely used approach to promotional budgeting.

· Spending as much as the competition does is a way to react to short-run promotional tactics of competitors.

· The preferred approach to determining promotional expenditures is to decide what it will take to do the job, while factoring in elements used in the other methods.

3 **Describe personal selling activities.**

· A sales presentation is a process involving prospecting, practicing the presentation, and then making the presentation.

· Salespeople are compensated for their efforts in two ways—financially and nonfinancially.

· The two basic plans for financial compensation are commissions and straight salary, but the most attractive plan for a small firm combines the two.

4 **Identify advertising options for a small business.**

· Common advertising media include television, radio, magazines, newspapers, billboards, and the Internet.

· Product advertising is designed to promote a product or service, while institutional advertising conveys an idea regarding the business itself.

· A small firm must decide how often to advertise, where to advertise, and what the message will be.

· A firm's Web advertising generally takes the form of banner ads and pop-ups, e-mail campaigns, sponsorships and linkages, and a corporate website.

5 **Discuss the use of sales promotional tools.**

· Sales promotion includes all promotional techniques other than personal selling and advertising.

· Typically, sales promotional tools should be used along with advertising and personal selling.

· Three widely used sales promotional tools are specialties, trade show exhibits, and publicity.

Key **TERMS**

promotion, p. 421

promotional mix, p. 422

personal selling, p. 424

prospecting, p. 424

advertising, p. 428

product advertising, p. 428

institutional advertising, p. 428

banner ads, p. 431

pop-up ads, p. 431

e-mail promotion, p. 431

Web sponsorship, p. 432

linkage, p. 432

sales promotion, p. 436

publicity, p. 437

Discussion **QUESTIONS**

1. Describe the parallel relationship that exists between a small business communication and a personal communication.

2. Discuss the advantages and disadvantages of each approach to budgeting funds for promotion.

3. Outline a system of prospecting that could be used by a small camera store. Incorporate all the techniques presented in this chapter.

4. Why are a salesperson's techniques for handling objections so important to a successful sales presentation?

5. Assume you have the opportunity to "sell" your course instructor on the idea of eliminating final examinations. Make a list of the objections you expect to hear from your instructor, and describe

how you will handle each objection, using some of the techniques listed on page 426.

6. What are some nonfinancial rewards that could be offered to salespeople?

7. What are the advantages and disadvantages of compensating salespeople by salary? By commissions? What do you think is an acceptable compromise?

8. What are some approaches to advertising on the Web?

9. Discuss some recommendations for designing an effective website.

10. How do specialties differ from trade show exhibits and publicity? Be specific.

You Make the **CALL**

SITUATION 1

The driving force behind Cannon Arp's new business was several bad experiences with his car—two speeding tickets and four minor fender-benders. Consequently, his insurance rates more than doubled, which resulted in Arp's idea to design and sell a bumper sticker that read "To Report Bad Driving, Call My Parents at. . . ." With a $200 investment, Arp printed 15,000 of the stickers, which contain space to write in the appropriate telephone number. He is now planning a promotion to support his strategy of distribution through auto parts stores.

Question 1 What role, if any, should personal selling have in Arp's total promotional plan?

Question 2 Arp is considering advertising in magazines. What do you think about this medium for promoting his product?

Question 3 Of what value might publicity be for selling Arp's stickers? Be specific.

SITUATION 2

Cheree Moore owns and operates a small business that supplies delicatessens with bulk containers of ready-made salads. When served in salad bars, the salads appear to have been freshly prepared from scratch at

the delicatessen. Moore wants additional promotional exposure for her products and is considering using her fleet of trucks as rolling billboards. If the strategy is successful, she may even attempt to lease space on other trucks. Moore is concerned about the cost-effectiveness of the idea and whether the public will even notice the advertisements. She also wonders whether the image of her salad products might be hurt by this advertising medium.

Question 1 What suggestions can you offer that would help Moore make this decision?

Question 2 How could Moore go about determining the cost-effectiveness of this strategy?

Question 3 What additional factors should Moore evaluate before advertising on trucks?

SITUATION 3

If people are willing to pay to have groceries delivered to their home, why not high-fashion clothing? This type of thinking is what led Claudine Gumbel and her husband, Brian, to develop Caravan, a boutique-on-wheels that brings the latest in high fashion to people all over New York City. Their mobile "caravan" is stocked with merchandise from the trendiest designers. "People like the convenience of a shop that comes to them," comments

Brian. "If an area doesn't work, we move on," he adds. Plans are to expand into Los Angeles and Miami soon. Sales for the NYC Caravan were expected to top $700,000 in 2006. It appears that the Gumbels' business has been given the green light.

Source: Karen Edwards, "Shop and Go," *Entrepreneur,* June 2006, p. 97.

Question 1 What might be the best ways for the Gumbels to promote their business?

Question 2 How can the Gumbels prospect for new customers?

Question 3 In what ways, if any, could the Gumbels use the Internet to promote their business?

Experiential EXERCISES

1. Interview the owners of one or more small businesses to determine how they develop their promotional budget. Classify the owners' methods into one or more of the four approaches described in this chapter. Report your findings to the class.

2. Plan a sales presentation. With a classmate role-playing a potential buyer, make the presentation in class. Ask the other students to critique your technique.

3. Locate a small business website and evaluate its promotional effectiveness.

4. Interview a media representative about advertising options for small businesses. Summarize your findings for the class.

Exploring the WEB

1. Go to the Bank of America's website at **http://www.bankofamerica.com**. Click on "Small Business," and then follow the link under "Resource Center" to "Growing Your Business." Click on the workshop called "Advertising Your Business." How might an average figure for advertising and promotion costs be calculated?

2. Return to the Bank of America's website (**http://www.bankofamerica.com**). Follow the steps outlined in Exercise 1, but once at the "Resource Center," click on the workshop entitled "Promoting Your Business."

   a. How many trade shows are held in the United States each year?

   b. What are the pros and cons of trade shows?

3. Visit *Entrepreneur* magazine's website at **http://www.entrepreneur.com/sales/presentations/article59346.html**. Read the article entitled "Nail Your Sales Presentation," in which business coach Tony Parinello offers advice on turning prospects into clients. What are some of the do's and don'ts Parinello suggests for sales presentations?

Video Case 16

Glidden Point Oyster Company, A.G.A. Correa & Son, Hardy Boat Cruises, Maine Gold (p. 652)
This case looks at four distinct businesses and their individual promotional techniques, offering suggestions and clear examples of how to market goods and services to customers outside a business's immediate customer base.

Alternative Cases for Chapter 16:

Case 1, Boston Duck Tours, p. 620

Case 20, Modern Postcard, p. 660

Global Marketing

CarAlarmsEtc
http://stores.ebay.com/CarAlarmsEtc

More than a million automobiles are stolen in the United States each year. If that statistic causes you to worry about whether you locked the doors when you left your car today, then maybe you need to talk to Jeff Nipert. As owner of CarAlarmsEtc, he tries to give customers peace of mind where auto theft is concerned. His Bonney Lake, Washington–based firm specializes in mobile electronics—specifically, car alarms, keyless entry units, remote starters, and other related accessories. CarAlarmsEtc may not always have the lowest price on a given product, but the company boldly declares that it is the value alternative when it comes to providing the equipment that can keep your car out of a chop shop. In other words, Nipert makes up any ground lost on price when it comes to installation support and customer service.

Though Nipert's company is just a small operation, the *world* is his sales floor. How is that possible? Easy . . . eBay. The online marketplace giant can help the tiniest of businesses connect with customers anywhere in the world, and getting started takes about as much time as it would to apply for a passport! And consider this: Of those who buy products on eBay, half live outside the United States—and that half of the business is growing twice as fast as the U.S. segment! Nipert says, "I felt if it wasn't costing me a dime extra for the [worldwide] exposure, I would be a fool not to take advantage of it."

Of course, taking a small business global can be challenging. Suddenly, you have to worry about communicating in a language other than English, translating payments into other currencies, and setting up international shipping. But think about it as an adventure—with partners who want you to succeed. For example, eBay offers an International Selling Toolkit (http://pages.ebay.com/globaltrade/SellingToolkit.pdf), and the U.S. government offers many resources to help you (http://www.export.gov). This chapter will also offer direction as you begin to market your product or service globally.

The important thing to realize is that you can do it, and earn a nice living while you're at it. Jeff Nipert and his car alarm business have already shown that. Still not convinced? Read on. . . .

Sources: Janelle Elms, "Go Global," *Entrepreneur*, Vol. 34, No. 9 (September 2006), pp. 130–131; http://cgi3.ebay.com/ws/eBayISAPI.dll?ViewUserPage&userid=caralarmsetc, accessed February 22, 2007; and http://www.forbesautos.com/advice/toptens/most_stolen/vehicles.html, accessed March 6, 2007.

© Jeff Nipert/www.caralarmsetc.com

Looking AHEAD

After studying this chapter, you should be able to

1   Describe the potential of small firms as global enterprises.
2   Identify the basic forces prompting small firms to engage in global expansion.
3   Identify and compare strategy options for global businesses.
4   Explain the challenges that global enterprises face.
5   Recognize the sources of assistance available to support international business efforts.

The business world is undergoing profound change. There was a time when national economies were isolated by trade and investment barriers, differences in language and culture, distinctive business practices, and various government regulations. However, these dissimilarities are fading over time as market preferences converge, trade barriers fall, and national economies integrate to form a global economic system. This process is the essence of **globalization**. Though the trend toward convergence has been developing for some time, the pace is quickening, creating global opportunities that did not exist even a few years ago. And with the astounding rate of economic growth in countries such as China and India, it would be unwise to ignore overseas opportunities.

As hindrances to globalization diminish, the commercial potential of markets abroad continues to grow. To track this trend, the Heritage Foundation and the *Wall Street Journal* publish the *Index of Economic Freedom,* an annual analysis of trade policy, wages and prices, government intervention, and other similar variables in 157 nations. According to the 2007 report, economic freedom remains high; in fact, scores for 2007 were the second highest since the first index was published in 1996. The benefits of economic liberty speak for themselves: Countries with high levels of economic freedom enjoy higher rates of long-term economic growth and substantially greater prosperity than do those with less economic freedom. For example, the per capita GDP of the countries in the top 25 percent (the most economically free countries) was nearly $28,000, whereas that measure for the 25 percent of countries at the bottom of the index was below $5,000.[1] This positive impact on prosperity translates into increased demand for products and services in international markets, fueling interest in global enterprises.

globalization
The expansion of international business, encouraged by converging market preferences, falling trade barriers, and the integration of national economies

Small Businesses as Global Enterprises

The potential of a global business is clear, but does that potential extend to small companies?[2] Research has shown that recent startups and even the smallest of businesses are internationalizing at an increasing rate. In fact, small companies in virtually all major trading countries are increasingly being launched with cross-border business activities in mind.[3] The arrangements in these companies, often called **born-global firms**,[4] sometimes can get more than a little crazy. You may be familiar with a company called Skype, which was acquired by eBay in 2005; here is its born-global startup story:

> *In 2003, [Niklas] Zennstrom, who is Swedish, and his partner Janus Friis, a Dane, launched their Internet telephony company Skype in Luxembourg, with sales offices in London. But*

1 Describe the potential of small firms as global enterprises.

born-global firms
Small companies launched with cross-border business activities in mind

they outsourced product development to Estonia, the same fertile womb that had earlier gestated their music-sharing system, Kazaa.[5]

You may be thinking, "That's fine in this case—Skype is a big company." That's true today, but in 2003, the company was just a startup, and it was clearly an international business right from the beginning. Many new ventures, as well as established small businesses, are being swept up in the wave of globalization.

As global communication systems become more efficient and trade agreements pry open national markets to foreign competition, entrepreneurs are focusing more on international business. Today's sophisticated technologies are expensive to develop and can be quickly replaced; therefore, it is important to recover research and development costs over a larger market and in less time by taking advantage of international sales. Small firms may decide to go global to expand their opportunities, or they may be forced to enter foreign markets in order to compete with those firms in their industry that have already done so. In any case, the research is clear: *Size does not necessarily limit a firm's international activity, and small companies often become global competitors in order to take advantage of their unique resources.*[6]

In 1995, near Pittsburgh, Pennsylvania, Bob Williams and Dave Ogborne launched Air Excellence International as a born-global business to renovate commercial aircraft interiors. Its first customer was a Venezuelan company that contracted for restoration work on a single jetliner. Business gradually expanded as larger airlines contracted for the company's services. Early on, the firm nearly doubled its workforce each year, and that pace of growth continued as more renovation work was scheduled. Demonstrating its commitment to international business, the company established additional locations in the United States and a facility in Shannon, Ireland, to serve European airlines. The enterprise was so successful that it attracted the attention of Triumph Group, Inc., a global supplier of aerospace systems and components, which recently acquired it.[7] Over its years of operation, Air Excellence International has proved that the global marketplace is not limited to large multinational firms.

The fact that many firms are going global does not mean that it is *easy* for small companies; the challenges small businesses face in international markets are considerable. First, a small business owner must decide whether the company is up to the task. To help entrepreneurs assess the impact of going global on their small business, the U.S. Department of Commerce publishes *A Basic Guide to Exporting*. This handbook outlines important questions entrepreneurs should consider when assessing readiness for the challenges of global business (see Exhibit 17-1).

Once small business owners decide to expand internationally, they should study the cultural, political, and economic forces in foreign markets to figure out how best to adapt the product or service to local demand or make other adjustments necessary to ensure smooth entry. A practice that is acceptable in one culture may be considered unethical or morally wrong in another. When cultural lines are crossed, even gestures as simple as a "good morning" and a handshake may be misunderstood. The entrepreneur must evaluate the proper use of names and titles and be aware of different cultural styles and business practices. The cultural challenges of doing business abroad are great.

Entrepreneurs are likely to make costly mistakes if they fail to study a foreign market carefully. For example, a U.S. mail-order concern offering products to the Japanese didn't realize that the American custom of asking for a credit card number before taking an order would be seen as an insult by customers. The misstep was corrected when a consultant explained that in Japan, where business deals may be secured with a handshake rather than a contract, this approach is interpreted as indicating a lack of trust. Such insights can go a long way in preventing blunders.

Differences in types of trading systems and import requirements can also make international trade challenging. A small manufacturer of diagnostic and surgical eye care equipment discovered that a global company must regularly modify its products to meet rigid design specifications, which vary from country to country. For example, before the firm could sell its testing device in Germany, it had to remove an on/off switch on the product's alarm. Such adjustments are an unavoidable part of conducting global business.

Trade barriers are falling in some regions of the world, as countries agree to eliminate **tariffs** (taxes charged on imported goods) and trade restrictions. In 1989, Canada and the United States signed the Free Trade Agreement (FTA), which gradually eliminated most tariffs

tariffs
Taxes charged on imported goods

exhibit 17-1   *Questions to Consider Before Going Global*

Management Objectives	• What are the company's reasons for going global? • How committed is top management to going global? • How quickly does management expect its international operations to pay off?
Management Experience and Resources	• What in-house international expertise does the firm have (international sales experience, language skills, etc.)? • Who will be responsible for the company's international operations? • How much senior management time should be allocated to the company's global efforts? • What organizational structure is required to ensure success abroad?
Production Capacity	• How is the present capacity being used? • Will international sales hurt domestic sales? • What will be the cost of additional production at home and abroad? • What product designs and packaging options are required for international markets?
Financial Capacity	• How much capital can be committed to international production and marketing? • How are the initial expenses of going global to be covered? • What other financial demands might compete with plans to internationalize? • By what date must the global effort pay for itself?

Source: Adapted from U.S. Department of Commerce, *A Basic Guide to Exporting,* cited in John B. Cullen and K. Praveen Parboteeah, *Multinational Management: A Strategic Approach,* 3rd ed. (Cincinnati, OH: South-Western College Publishing, 2005), p. 208.

and other trade restrictions between the two countries. This free trade area was extended in 1993, when the United States, Canada, and Mexico established the **North American Free Trade Agreement (NAFTA)**, which phased out tariffs over time. These agreements have promoted commerce within North America, just as the formation of the **European Union (EU)** facilitated trade among its member countries. In 1957, six Western European nations (large anchor economies in the region) were the first to join the European Community, which was later transformed into the EU. This union grew slowly, reaching 15 countries in 1995; but 2004 was a year of rapid expansion, as 10 more countries were added. Two more countries joined in 2007, and three candidate countries (Croatia, Macedonia, and Turkey) are currently waiting for approval to join. Although these agreements and others have eased formal barriers to trade among nations, cultural, technological, and economic differences (discussed later in the chapter) still pose an intimidating challenge for small companies.

North American Free Trade Agreement (NAFTA)
An agreement that encourages free trade among the United States, Canada, and Mexico by removing trade restrictions

European Union (EU)
An organization whose purpose is to facilitate free trade among member countries in Europe

The Forces Driving Global Businesses

At one time, most entrepreneurs in the United States were content to position their start-ups for the home market and look forward to the day when international sales *might* materialize. With untapped market potential at home and few overseas competitors, many small business owners used this strategy successfully. Today, more small businesses are planning from the start to penetrate all available markets, both domestic and foreign.

Given the difficulty of international business, why would any entrepreneur want to get involved? Among the reasons small firms have for going global are some that have

2 Identify the basic forces prompting small firms to engage in global expansion.

motivated international trade for centuries. Marco Polo traveled to China in 1271 to explore the trading of western goods for exotic Oriental silk and spices, which would then be sold in Europe. Clearly, the motivation to take domestic goods to foreign markets and bring foreign goods to domestic markets is as relevant today as it was in 1271. Consider the clothing designer who sells western wear in Tokyo or the independent Oriental rug dealer who scours the markets of Morocco to locate low-cost sources of high-quality Persian rugs.

Complementing these traditional reasons for going global are advantages that once were of little interest to small companies. One small business international trade expert describes the motivations to go global as follows:

> *Certainly the overall motivation is increased sales, but that is the simple answer. A more complex analysis opens the door to the real fun—the larger game. Ultimately the goal of global trade is to expand the scope and reach of your company so that the tools and resources available to fight your competition give your company an unbeatable edge—an edge that renews and transforms itself faster than the competition can keep up.*[8]

In other words, many small firms are looking to do more than simply expand a profitable market when they get involved in international business. No longer insulated from global challengers, they must consider the dynamics of the new competitive environment. The rival on the other side of the street may be a minor threat compared to an online competitor on the other side of the globe!

One way to adjust to these emerging realities is through innovation. In many industries, innovation is essential to competitiveness, giving a small company an advantage over its large-firm counterparts. Small businesses that invest heavily in research and development often outperform their large competitors. But as R&D costs rise, they often cannot be recovered from domestic sales alone. Increasing sales in international markets may be the only viable way to recover the firm's investment. In some cases, this may require identifying dynamic markets that are beginning to open around the world and locating in or near those markets.[9]

The basic forces behind global expansion can be divided into four general categories (see Exhibit 17-2): expanding markets, gaining access to resources, cutting costs, and

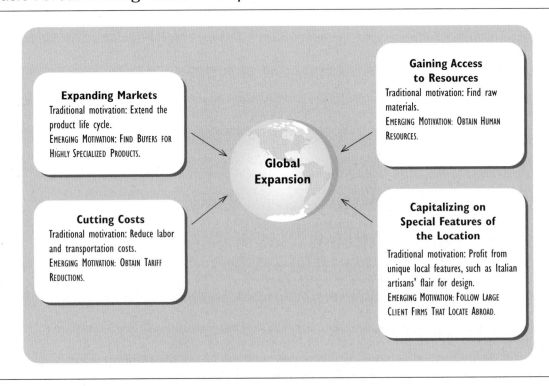

exhibit

17-2 Basic Forces Driving Global Enterprises

Expanding Markets
Traditional motivation: Extend the product life cycle.
EMERGING MOTIVATION: FIND BUYERS FOR HIGHLY SPECIALIZED PRODUCTS.

Gaining Access to Resources
Traditional motivation: Find raw materials.
EMERGING MOTIVATION: OBTAIN HUMAN RESOURCES.

Global Expansion

Cutting Costs
Traditional motivation: Reduce labor and transportation costs.
EMERGING MOTIVATION: OBTAIN TARIFF REDUCTIONS.

Capitalizing on Special Features of the Location
Traditional motivation: Profit from unique local features, such as Italian artisans' flair for design.
EMERGING MOTIVATION: FOLLOW LARGE CLIENT FIRMS THAT LOCATE ABROAD.

capitalizing on special features of location. Within each category fall some tried and true motivations, as well as some new angles that have emerged with the global economy. We discuss each of these four categories in the sections that follow.

Expanding the Market

More than 95 percent of the world's population lives outside the United States. It follows that globalization greatly increases the size of an American firm's potential market. A recent study of small companies found that their primary interest in internationalization was accessing new markets and growing their business, as opposed to seeking resources abroad, gaining access to technologies, avoiding regulatory pressures at home, etc.[10]

COUNTRIES TARGETED   Because the primary motivation for going global is to develop market opportunities outside the home country, the focus of globalization strategies tends to be on those countries with the greatest commercial potential. In the past, these were the developed countries (those with high levels of widely distributed wealth). Today, companies are paying greater attention to emerging markets, where income and buying power are growing rapidly. The U.S. Department of Commerce labeled the largest of these countries as Big Emerging Markets (see Exhibit 17-3).

Because of their immense populations and potential market demand, countries such as China and India have attracted the greatest attention from international firms. Combined, these two nations account for nearly 40 percent of the world's six billion inhabitants, thus providing fertile ground for international expansion. Small companies are among the competitors battling for position in these emerging markets.

Dahlgren & Company, Inc., a firm based in Crookston, Minnesota, specializes in the custom processing, roasting, flavoring, and packaging of sunflower seed products. Of the firm's $50 million in sales, 50 percent comes from exports to more than 30 countries around the world. In an effort to boost Dahlgren's business overseas, Tom Miller, vice president of international sales, visited China to meet with the president of a snack-food company there. The effort paid off with a $1 million contract. This is a huge deal for a small business, but it only scratches the surface of a market with a population of well over one billion people. Dahlgren & Company recognizes the potential of the Chinese market, which is why its website features pages in Chinese as well as in English.[11]

exhibit 17-3 *Big Emerging Markets*

Country	2005 Population (in millions)	2005 Wealth (GNI per capita)	2004–2005 Economic Growth (GDP growth, %)
Argentina	38.7	4,470	9.2
Brazil	186.4	3,460	2.3
China	1,304.5	1,740	9.9
India	1,094.6	720	8.5
Indonesia	220.6	1,280	5.6
Mexico	103.1	7,310	3.0
Poland	38.2	7,110	3.2
South Africa	48.2	4,960	4.9
South Korea	48.3	15,830	4.0
Turkey	72.6	4,710	7.4
World	**6,437.8**	**6,987**	**3.6**

Source: Adapted from The World Bank Group, "World Development Indicators, 2007," http://www.worldbank.org/data/countrydata-query.html, accessed February 9, 2007.

PRODUCTS PROMOTED   In the mid-1960s, international business authority Raymond Vernon observed that firms tend to introduce new products in the United States first and then sell them in less-advanced countries later, as demand in the home market declines.[12] In other words, they use international expansion to extend a product's life cycle.

Although this approach is effective under some circumstances, it has become less viable as customer preferences, income levels, and delivery systems have become more similar and product life cycles have contracted. Consider the following observations, based on the experience of two small-business practitioners:

> *The time lags between U.S. and foreign adoption have . . . disappeared. Today it is essential to roll out new products in several countries almost simultaneously. . . . No longer does the small company have the luxury of using cash flow from domestic sales to support the building of international marketing a few years later. The ever-shortening product cycle virtually dooms such a strategy. Terrific. Now, in addition to getting the product to work, setting up your new team, getting some U.S. customers, and finding money, you now have to worry about selling in six or eight additional countries, most of whom don't even speak English![13]*

Products that sell at home are now more likely to be introduced very quickly abroad, with little or no adaptation in many cases. The role of television programs, movies, and print media in shaping cultural tastes throughout the world has eased the entry of small businesses into international markets. American interests have long held a starring role in the cultural arena, inspiring widespread purchases of products such as blue jeans and fast food and generating international interest in U.S. sports and celebrities. By informing consumers about the lifestyles of others, globalization is leading the world toward common consumer preferences.

In addition to the trendy products associated with popular culture, another type of product well suited to international markets is the highly specialized product. As technology makes possible increasingly sophisticated goods, this allows markets to demand more differentiated products that satisfy their unique needs and interests. Fewer consumers in the home market are likely to be interested in a highly differentiated (and often more expensive) product, so it may become necessary to search for international markets with the same unique demand in order to increase sales enough to recover product development costs. Because small companies often follow focused business strategies (with limited domestic market potential) and aspire to grow rapidly, efforts to exploit the competitive advantage of specialized products across international markets may be even more important to them than to their larger counterparts.[14]

Martin Goodwin and Bob Henry work with a very specialized product in international markets. MSS Global, their Riverside, California, company, progressed from a basement venture to a global enterprise in just a few years. It all started in 1993, when Goodwin ran a supermarket and a few general stores owned by his family. To monitor inventories, price products, and issue purchase orders, he used a dozen separate software programs. In an effort to streamline the process, Goodwin teamed up with Henry, a computer systems specialist, to develop an integrated software package that could handle all of these functions. Goodwin and Henry created Retail, the first Windows-compatible software program of its kind for retailers. The product tracks inventory, calculates pricing, gathers customer data, and tracks cashier productivity, so sales trends can be determined with only a few computer keystrokes.

The market interest in the United States for this focused product was healthy but limited, leaving MSS Global with scant opportunity to recover development costs. To overcome this constraint, Goodwin and Henry decided to go global. Using strategic partnerships (including an alliance with Microsoft), MSS Global managed to sell nearly 25,000 licenses in 20 countries before the close of the year 2000—amazing growth for a company with only 10 employees! The expansion continues. To date, the company has sold more than 40,000 licenses and has set up international offices in Europe, Asia, South America, and Central America. With so much of its revenue coming from international markets, MSS Global can attest to the importance of going global to exploit a competitive advantage.[15]

burden for the small confectioner. To deal with this challenge, the company decided to move into Asian markets, such as Japan, Taiwan, South Korea, and China, where the cycle of holidays is different. Thanks to exports to these countries (representing 15 percent of the firm's total sales), the company is able to operate its plant full time for nine months out of the year.[32]

The rise of the Internet has fueled vigorous growth in export activity. Small firms now see the Internet as a powerful tool for increasing their international visibility, allowing them to connect with customers who were previously beyond their reach. Entertainment Earth is an Internet toy retailer, based in Los Angeles, California, that specializes in action figures, gifts, and other collectibles. Aaron and Jason Labowitz and a friend started the company in 1995, operating out of a small office in a garage in the San Fernando Valley. It wasn't long before they decided to expand their reach by selling over the Internet. They describe their motivations on the company's website:

> We admit to being selfish when we started this business. We wanted to find a simple way to personally buy all of the new action figures and toys at reasonable prices without wasting our time [driving around to shop]. Our solution was right in front of us—and it was similar to the big-box warehouse store model coupled with the old fashion mail order business placed on a website.[33]

To date, Entertainment Earth has sold collectibles to hundreds of thousands of clients all around the world. The typical customer is 32 years old, has income above $65,000 per year, and would prefer not to be seen in a toy store. Clearly, Entertainment Earth knows its globe-spanning market well, which allows it to offer the high-quality service that has earned the company extremely high marks from e-commerce rating services.[34]

Of course, selling goods to international customers is seldom a "walk in the park." Products may have to be modified to meet government standards or the unique interests of buyers abroad, language barriers and a lack of government connections can put a company at a great disadvantage in negotiations, and unfair exchange rates can make it next to impossible to offer products at competitive prices. And some countries' markets can be difficult to enter unless a company is willing to reveal the specifics of its core technologies, which are often the bedrock of its competitive advantage.[35] Nonetheless, small companies are proving that export success is within reach. For example, a recent study revealed that between 1999 and 2003 the value of goods shipped to China (a challenging market to crack) by small and medium-sized manufacturers increased by 281 percent to $9.3 billion, and 49 percent of these exporters had fewer than 20 employees.[36] What's the secret? Do your homework and figure out what products will sell (for example, find out what products Chinese companies cannot yet make for themselves), get close to the market and develop personal connections with influential decision makers, and get assistance wherever you can find it. A good place to start in your search for customers around the globe is the U.S. Commercial Service (http://www.export.gov). Or get in touch with the Washington, DC, foreign embassy community (http://www.embassy.org), select a country where you want to do business, and e-mail the country specialist for assistance. You will be surprised at the leads this can generate. Finally, check with officials from your state to see if they can provide assistance; many do. A Google search on "_____ foreign trade office," including the name of your state, should lead you where you need to go.

Importing

The flip side of exporting is **importing**, which involves selling goods from abroad in the firm's home market. When a small company finds a product abroad that has market potential at home or identifies a product that would sell at home but cannot find a domestic producer, an import strategy may be the best solution. Rich Birnbaum is the founder of ProWorth, a bare-bones operation in Englewood Cliffs, New Jersey, that also employs his brother, as well as several high school students and retirees part-time. Birnbaum sells exquisite Swiss brand-name watches and diamond jewelry through eBay, other online auction services, and the firm's website. Birnbaum decided to use eBay because the customer

importing
Selling goods produced in another country to buyers in the home country

acquisition costs are limited to the cost of a listing, which allows him to keep prices low. The venture has been very successful. Launched in January 1999, the company racked up $1 million in sales by that year's end, allowing Birnbaum to pay himself a salary of about $100,000 and still break even.[37] Not a bad start—and business at ProWorth continues to build over time.

One variation on the import theme is a global sourcing strategy, which is essentially an effort to connect with overseas suppliers that can provide the products or services a company needs to operate successfully. This sounds easy enough to do, especially in this era of Internet-enabled matching services, online communication tools (from e-mail to videoconferencing), and flexible and affordable travel options. However, finding and managing international suppliers can be challenging. Thad Hooker learned this the hard way when he and his wife, Lisa, bought a Fort Lauderdale, Florida–based high-end furniture company called Spirit of Asia in 2001. Their experiences were similar to those of many small-company owners who decide to work with international suppliers to build their businesses. "I decided to source from Southeast Asia, but I had to find out everything myself," Hooker says. "It felt like a crapshoot." That's not surprising—it's a big world, and it seems as if everyone wants to partner up and sell product. So, to sort out the situation, Hooker quickly broke the challenge down. He studied sourcing options thoroughly before venturing abroad, comparing possible sourcing countries to one another. Then he did some on-the-ground research himself, visiting the country he targeted and looking for clues that would lead him to the best sourcing partners available. Of course, a lucky break or two also helped. "On [Hooker's] initial trip to Chiang Mai, a city in northern Thailand, Hooker caught a ride with a local taxi driver who was interested in art and antiques. Hooker signed the man up, gave him a digital camera, and now employs the former driver as a furniture scout on the ground."[38]

Mission accomplished! The shop in Fort Lauderdale is profitable, and the Hookers are thinking about opening new locations to leverage their overseas sourcing power. In fact, Florida may not be big enough to satisfy their ambitions. The couple recently launched a website that will allow them to sell furniture and accessories across the United States.[39]

It's worth repeating that global sourcing presents its share of hassles, so don't expect this to be an easy option. However, it holds tremendous potential, especially if you follow a few simple guidelines:

- Learn as much as you can about the culture and business practices of the country from which you will be sourcing to avoid making deal-breaking mistakes.

- Do your research and be sure to select a source that is not a competitor or a company that hopes to learn from your operations so as to compete against you in the future.

- Protect your intellectual property so that your suppliers cannot easily take it from you. Some entrepreneurs even require their suppliers to sign a nondisclosure agreement so that they cannot patent the item in the country where the sourcing takes place.

- Don't rush the process of forming a relationship with a sourcing partner. You need time to ask difficult questions about important factors such as quality standards and capabilities, manufacturing flexibility, and time to order fulfillment.

- Work out transportation logistics ahead of time. A good freight forwarder can assist you with the mechanics of shipment, as well as help you with the confusing jumble of required documents. To get a sense of the process, review the rules and regulations on the Customs and Border Protection website at http://www.customs.ustreas.gov and see the SBA notes on importing at http://www.smallbusinessnotes.com/international/importing.html.

At times, the process may seem so complicated that you may wonder if small companies should even be attempting to source from abroad, but take heart—*others have done it, and so can you!*

Foreign Licensing

Importing and exporting are the most popular international strategies among small firms,[40] but there are also other options. Because of limited resources, many small firms are hesitant to go global. One way to deal with this constraint is to follow a licensing strategy. **Foreign licensing** allows a company in another country to purchase the rights to manufacture and sell a firm's products in overseas markets. The firm buying these rights is called the **licensee**. The licensee makes payments to the **licensor**, or the firm selling those rights, normally in the form of **royalties**—a fee paid for each unit produced.

International licensing has its drawbacks. The licensee makes all the production and marketing decisions, and the licensor must share returns from sales with the licensee. However, foreign licensing is the least expensive way to go global, since the licensee bears all the cost and risk of setting up a foreign operation.[41]

Recall that MSS Global (described on page 448) uses a foreign licensing strategy; the company has sold more than 40,000 licenses around the globe. The small company could never have achieved such rapid expansion if it had had to set up its own offices abroad, learn the culture and tax laws, and establish a market position in each country in which it did business. Licensing agreements with major computer hardware manufacturers covering the South and Central American markets have paid off. MSS Global may not have a marketing team, a direct sales staff, or even venture capital, but the company makes money every time a licensee sells its product to a foreign retailer.[42] This is the beauty of foreign licensing.

Small companies tend to think of products when they explore international licensing options, but licensing intangible assets such as proprietary technologies, copyrights, and trademarks may offer even greater potential returns. Just as Disney licenses its famous Mickey Mouse character to manufacturers around the world, a small retailer called Peace Frogs has used licensing to introduce its copyrighted designs in Spain. As Peace Frogs' founder and president, Catesby Jones, explains, "We export our Peace Frogs T-shirts directly to Japan, but in Spain per capita income is lower, competition from domestic producers is stronger, and tariffs are high, so we licensed a Barcelona–based company the rights to manufacture our product."[43] From this agreement, Peace Frogs has been able to generate additional revenue with almost no added expense.

Foreign licensing can also be used to protect against **counterfeit activity**, or the unauthorized use of intellectual property. Licensing rights to a firm in a foreign market provides a local champion to ensure that other firms do not use protected assets in an inappropriate way.

International Franchising

International franchising is a variation on the licensing theme. As outlined in Chapter 4, the franchisor offers a standard package of products, systems, and management services to the franchisee, which provides capital, market insight, and hands-on management. Though international franchising was not widely used before the 1970s, today it is the fastest-growing market-entry strategy of U.S. firms, with Canada as the dominant market (followed by Japan and the United Kingdom, in that order). This approach is especially popular with U.S. restaurant chains that want to establish a global presence. McDonald's, for example, has raised its famous golden arches in more than 121 countries around the world. But international franchising is useful to small companies as well.

Danny Benususan is the owner of Blue Note, a premier jazz club in Manhattan that opened its doors in 1981. Considered one of the top venues in the world for jazz and other forms of music, this club has attracted the attention of international businesspeople who have established franchises abroad. The Tokyo location was opened in 1988, followed by clubs in Osaka, Fukuoka, and Nagoya, Japan. The first European club, in Milan, Italy, was added to the Blue Note family in March of 2003, and that was followed by another Asian franchise in Seoul, South Korea. As a result of these international extensions, the club has successfully established itself as the world's only franchised jazz club network.[44] Blue Note has proved that there is more than one way for a small business to globalize.

---

foreign licensing
Allowing a company in another country to purchase the rights to manufacture and sell a company's products in international markets

licensee
The company buying licensing rights

licensor
The company selling licensing rights

royalties
Fees paid by the licensee to the licensor for each unit produced under a licensing contract

counterfeit activity
The unauthorized use of intellectual property

international franchising
Selling a standard package of products, systems, and management services to a company in another country

International Strategic Alliances

international strategic alliance
A combination of efforts and/or assets of companies in different countries for the sake of pooling resources and sharing the risks of an enterprise

Moving beyond licensing and franchising, some small businesses have expanded globally by joining forces with large corporations in cooperative efforts. An **international strategic alliance** allows firms to share risks and pool resources as they enter a new market, matching the local partner's understanding of the target market (culture, legal system, competitive conditions, etc.) with the technology or product knowledge of its alliance counterpart. One of the advantages of this strategy is that both partners take comfort in knowing that neither is "going it alone."[45]

There are many different ways in which strategic alliances can be used by small companies to gain advantage internationally. Tony Raimondo is CEO of Behlen Mfg. Co., a Columbus, Nebraska–based maker of agricultural grain bins, drying systems, and metal-frame buildings. At one time, the company exported products to China, but Raimondo suspended shipments when he found out that Chinese copycats were making the same products, using local advantages such as cheaper labor and an undervalued currency to undercut Behlen on cost and sell at much lower prices. For a time, it looked as if the company would no longer be able to tap into this huge market, the largest on earth! But then Raimondo hit on the idea of forming a 50/50 joint venture (a form of alliance in which two companies share equal ownership in a separate business) in Beijing. "In order for us to sustain market share," says Raimondo, "we had to be on the inside." Making product within China made it possible for Behlen to capitalize on the same advantages that Chinese factories had, and that has made all the difference. Behlen's success in China has spread to other international business initiatives. The company now does about 10 percent of its business overseas.[46]

Locating Facilities Abroad

A small business with advanced global aspirations may choose to establish a foreign presence of its own in strategic markets, especially if the firm has already developed an international customer base. Most small companies start by locating a production facility or sales office overseas, often as a way to reduce the cost of operations. Amanda Knauer, 25, wanted to start a business, but she concluded that launching a business in the United States was too expensive. On the advice of a friend, she set her sights on Argentina. After doing some research, she went to Buenos Aires in late 2004. A few months later, she was running her own business, Qara Argentina, a luxury leather goods manufacturer. "I came to Argentina looking for my opportunity," she says. "The beauty of the leather inspired me, and I saw it as an entryway into this world [of business ownership]." It hasn't been easy. Knauer has had to pick up the local Spanish dialect and learn about a new set of laws and business practices, but the work is paying off—and fast! The company had more than $1 million in sales before the end of its first year in business.[47] Locating abroad has its advantages!

Opening an overseas sales office can be a very effective strategy, but small business owners should wait until sales in the local market are great enough to justify the move. An overseas office is costly to establish, staff, manage, and finance; thus, this alternative is beyond the reach of most small companies. Furthermore, the anticipated advantages of overseas offices are sometimes difficult to achieve. Often U.S. firms locate their first international sales office in Canada, but some small companies are finding it profitable to open an office that provides access to the European region (the English-speaking United Kingdom and Ireland are popular locations).

cross-border acquisition
The purchase by a business in one country of a company located in another country

greenfield venture
A wholly owned subsidiary formed from scratch in another country

Some small firms have grand ambitions that go beyond locating a production facility or sales office overseas. Companies in this category sometimes purchase a foreign business from another firm through what is known as a **cross-border acquisition**, or they may start a **greenfield venture** by forming from scratch a new wholly owned subsidiary in another country. Such go-it-alone strategies are complex and costly. These options give firms maximum control over their foreign operations and eliminate the need to share any revenues generated; however, they force companies to bear the entire risk of these expensive undertakings. If the subsidiary is a greenfield venture, the firm may have much to learn about running an enterprise in a foreign country, managing host-country nationals, and developing an effective marketing strategy. The commercial potential of a wholly owned international subsidiary may be great, but the challenges of managing it can be even greater. This option is not for the faint of heart.

Living the Dream   entrepreneurial challenges

© R. Alcorn/SWPCO

Packaging Company's Fate Sealed

You could say that Emerald Packaging, Inc., is on top of its game. Having served the fresh produce industry for more than 40 years, the company knows what it's doing when it comes to the flexible packaging business. The firm's website provides a precise description of the company's success and capabilities:

> Emerald Packaging, Inc. has quickly become an industry leader and is one of the largest plastic bag and roll stock manufacturers on the west coast with over $40 million in annual sales. . . . With six printing presses, 28 bag lines, four slitters, eight zipper bag lines, Innolok Zipper for roll stock, macro-perforation and laser micro-perforation at our main manufacturing plant in Union City, California, we specialize in up to 8 color, high quality printing with very short lead times and are constantly striving to improve our quality and capabilities.

Emerald is doing very well, but there is always room for growth and improvement.

Emerald is run by Kevin Kelly, whose family has owned the company for many years. Very interested in expansion, Kelly had already attempted to put together two acquisition deals, but they had fallen through. This time, as he looked over the terms of the latest contract, all seemed well—a factory in Tijuana, Mexico, with the right equipment and at a fair price. But international acquisitions can be tricky—especially in Mexico—and it wasn't long before Kelly learned the deal was in trouble. Machines in disrepair, sagging sales, and potential liability for the company's difficult-to-verify debts all raised red flags. And the fact that the seller was now requesting far more money than Kelly was willing to pay didn't help.

It was really death by a thousand cuts—nothing big, just a lot of small concerns that stacked up over time. Kelly describes his experience with the owner of the factory as follows:

> Both of us had our confidence rattled by small surprises. During the late summer the [factory owner] decided, without notifying us, to stop taking new orders—essentially announcing to customers that he was closing his doors. I had counted on his $5 million in annual sales to help make the deal work. On my side, I was so distracted by the day-to-day demands of running my family's business that I often went weeks without talks with him. Those communication issues doomed the deal.

Acquisitions are always a challenge. An acquisition *by a small business* is even more difficult to pull off. And a cross-border acquisition can be next to impossible for a small firm to work out. An international acquisition program can be crucial to a small company's growth plan, but given the number of places where a good deal can run aground, it certainly calls for an extra dose of caution and care in the handling.

Sources: Kevin Kelly, "Mexican Standoff," *Fortune Small Business*, Vol. 16, No. 2 (March 2006), p. 29; and http://www.empack.com, accessed February 22, 2007.

Challenges to Global Businesses

4 Explain the challenges that global enterprises face.

Small businesses face challenges; small *global* businesses face far greater challenges. How well can a small firm do in the global marketplace? The success of enterprising entrepreneurs in international markets proves that small firms can do better than survive—they can thrive! However, success is unlikely without careful preparation. Small business owners must recognize the unique challenges facing global firms and adjust their plans accordingly. Specifically, they need to pay attention to political risks, economic risks, and managerial limitations.

Political Risk

political risk
The potential for political forces in a country to negatively affect the performance of businesses operating within its borders

The potential for a country's political forces to negatively affect the performance of business enterprises operating within its borders is referred to as **political risk**. Often, this risk is related to the instability of a nation's government, which can create difficulties for outside companies. Potential problems range from threats as trivial as new regulations restricting the content of television advertising to challenges as catastrophic as a government takeover of private assets. Political developments can threaten access to an export market, require a firm to reveal trade secrets, or even demand that work be completed in-country. Exhibit 17-5 highlights variations in political risk across nations, based on the "Country Risk Rankings" published in *Euromoney* magazine. Countries are color-coded to indicate their riskiness—green represents "go," or safe, countries; yellow, "proceed with caution" countries; and red, "stop and think very carefully" countries. Firms hoping to do business in "red" countries should make appropriate adjustments.

Economic Risk

economic risk
The probability that a government will mismanage its economy and thereby change the business environment in ways that hinder the performance of firms operating there

Economic risk is the probability that a government will mismanage its economy and change the business environment in ways that hinder the performance of firms operating there. Economic risk and political risk are therefore related. Two of the most serious problems resulting from economic mismanagement are inflation and fluctuations in exchange rates.

exhibit

17-5 *Country Risk Rankings Map*

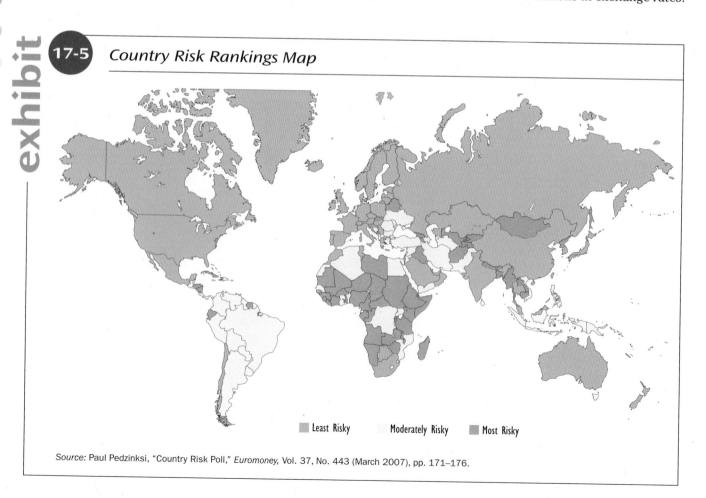

Least Risky   Moderately Risky   Most Risky

Source: Paul Pedzinksi, "Country Risk Poll," *Euromoney,* Vol. 37, No. 443 (March 2007), pp. 171–176.

While a discussion of these factors is beyond the scope of this textbook, it is important to recognize that inflation reduces the value of a country's currency on the foreign exchange market, thereby decreasing the value of cash flows the foreign firm receives from its operations in the local market.

Exchange rates represent the value of one country's currency relative to that of another country—for example, the number of Mexican pesos that can be purchased with one U.S. dollar. Sudden or unexpected changes in these rates can be a serious problem for small international firms, whether the firm exports to that market or has a local presence there.

Mary Ellen Mooney of Mooney Farms (mentioned earlier in this chapter) has kept an eye on the European market, as well as that of Mexico. She recognized the potential of exporting her sun-dried tomato products to France and came close to striking a deal with a local distributor a few years ago, but the negotiations fell through when the value of the dollar rose sharply relative to European currencies.[48] To understand her dilemma, suppose the French distributor was willing to pay 5 euros for a package of sun-dried tomatoes. If the dollar and the euro were exchanged one-to-one, Mooney could convert the 5 euros to $5.00. If $4.50 covered costs of production, transportation, insurance, and so on, then Mooney would earn a $.50 profit ($5.00–4.50) per unit. But when the dollar *increased* in value relative to the local currency, the situation changed drastically. Assume the exchange rate changed to .80 dollar per euro. Then units selling for 5 euros would yield only $4.00 each, which would result in a $.50 loss on every sale.

Mooney's experience illustrates how a good deal can quickly fall apart if exchange rates take a turn for the worse. This risk is especially serious for small companies that are just getting established in international markets. To protect against currency-related risks, such firms must take measures such as stating contracts in U.S. dollars or using currency-hedging strategies.

exchange rate
The value of one country's currency relative to that of another country

Managerial Limitations

Conducting business internationally will never be as easy as doing business at home— it is likely to stretch managerial skills and resources to the limit. Global commerce complicates every task and raises difficult questions related to every function of the firm.

- *Product Planning.* Will the product/service satisfy customer tastes? Does the foreign location have the employees we need to manufacture the products we plan to offer? Do available workers have the skills required for our operations? Will government restrictions hinder our planned product introductions?

- *Marketing.* How will we conduct marketing research? Who should be included in the target market? What sales projections are reasonable in the international market? What price should we charge for our product? How can we deal with counterfeit products manufactured locally?

- *Finance.* Can we maintain cash flow for our international operations? How will we manage currency exchange rate fluctuations? Will government policy impact capital transfers? Will local law allow us to send home profits from the foreign market? Does the host country government maintain sufficient foreign currency reserves to allow us to take profits out of the country? Will barter or other forms of countertrade be necessary to do business?

- *Management.* Will the management approaches used at home work in the international setting? How can we identify the people best suited for overseas positions with our company? How much should we pay our local employees? How should we work with labor unions in foreign locations? How can we overcome language, culture, and communication barriers? Can we develop a trusting relationship with foreign employees? What should we do when ethical standards are different in the host nation? Given that the Foreign Corrupt Practices Act prohibits U.S. firms from engaging in certain behaviors, how can we compete when our foreign rivals offer bribes to obtain preferential treatment?

- *Accounting.* What will it take to integrate accounting systems across global operations? How do we account for currency conversions that are continually changing? Can we harmonize accounting rules that vary from country to country? Does our accounting system capture the information necessary for international trading?

- *Legal Issues.* What are the IRS reporting requirements for international firms? How can we be sure that we are paying appropriate taxes in the home and host environments? What is required to comply with local government regulations? Will host country trade restrictions, including tariffs and nontariff barriers, hinder our export program? Do we have patent protections to shield our key technologies?

As you can see, international business decisions are complicated, which explains why many small firm owners choose to focus solely on their home market. However, the motivations to go global are sound, and others have already proved that it can be done. You can do it, too, if you plan carefully and take advantage of the resources available to help you achieve your global aspirations.

Assistance for Global Enterprises

5 Recognize the sources of assistance available to support international business efforts.

Help is available to small companies with international interests—you need only open your eyes to find it. Once you decide to enter the global marketplace, you will be amazed at how many resources there are to help you.

Analyzing Markets and Planning Strategy

Among the many activities required to prepare a small firm for the challenges of going global, two are especially fundamental to success abroad: finding international markets that fit the company's unique potentials and putting together a game plan for entry into the markets targeted.

A small business should begin its research of foreign markets and entry strategy options by exhausting secondary sources of information. The U.S. government offers a number of publications on how to identify and tap into global market opportunities. The Small Business Administration stands ready to help small companies expand abroad. The international programs and services of the SBA are delivered through U.S. Export Assistance Centers (USEACs).

One excellent source of information about global marketing is *Opportunities in Exporting*, which is available on the website of the Small Business Administration (http://www.sba.gov). Also available from the same source is *Breaking into the Trade Game: A Small Business Guide to Exporting*, which provides an overview of export strategy that is useful for new and experienced exporters. This nuts-and-bolts handbook is designed to guide small firms through the complexities of going global, with chapters focused specifically on identifying markets, choosing an entry strategy, managing transactions, financing trade, arranging transportation, and forming strategic alliances.

Though not focused on small businesses alone, a website maintained by the International Trade Administration of the U.S. Department of Commerce (http://trade.gov) supplies helpful insights about international expansion. Publications such as *World Trade* magazine (http://www.worldtrademag.com) can also be useful, providing timely, in-depth analyses of world trade markets and business issues. Beyond these resources, state and private organizations are excellent sources of trade information, trade leads, and company databases. One such source, TradePort (http://www.tradeport.org), offers information online to promote international trade with California-based companies.

Talking with someone who has lived in or even just visited a potential foreign market can be a valuable way to learn about it. For example, conversations with international students at a local university can be very helpful. However, the best way to study a foreign market is to visit the country personally. A representative of a small firm can do this either as an individual or as a member of an organized group.

Connecting with International Customers

A small company cannot sell abroad unless it connects with customers in targeted international markets. But, have no fear—numerous resources are available to help you connect.

17-6 A Sample of International Trade Leads on the Web

Bidmix.com	Bidmix.com provides an electronic marketplace for buying and selling worldwide. No membership is required to use the site to search for leads or post new leads. Users can also receive e-mail about new trade leads.
International Business Forum	This site provides information about opportunities in the international marketplace. It features a company directory, trade opportunities, business event listings, business education information, resources, and associations.
TradeLeads.com	Use of TradeLeads.com requires a membership. Nonmembers can post leads, but they are unable to read or search for leads.
World Bank FundLine	The World Bank's Private Sector Development Department operates this site to connect potential equity investors with enterprises. Coverage includes countries in Central and Eastern Europe and the former Soviet Union.
World Trade Markets	World Trade Markets allows firms to capture, disseminate, and search Trade Point Trade Leads throughout the world. This database is updated daily by the United Nations, Trade Points, World Trade Markets agents and research staff, and the Internet public.
WCTA Trade Opportunities Bulletin Board	If you want to buy or sell any kind of product, service, or opportunity, you can post it on this bulletin board. You can view trade opportunities with a free membership, but posting a trade opportunity requires an annual fee.
ASIA: Asian Sources On-Line	Designed for sourcing operations (volume buyers) in Asia, this site can be searched by country, product, or supplier. It also features other services, such as e-mail alerts, forums, product news, and libraries.
EUROPE: ECeurope.com	This site offers a business-to-business trading bulletin board that helps small to medium-sized companies access trade leads. Membership is required, but it is free.
Australia: Australia on Display	This site provides trade leads to thousands of Australian companies and their products or services. Users can browse by industry category or keyword.
India: Tradeindia	This website is dedicated to India and features news briefs, export-import opportunity listings, a bulletin board, and company directories.
Taiwan: Taiwan Products Online	This website allows you to search trade leads in Taiwan and China. You can use the product or supplier search option to find companies of interest. Trade information is provided, as well as other useful information for international companies.

Source: Michigan State University CIBER website, http://www.ciber.msu.edu/busres/static/trade%2Dleadsold.htm, accessed February 16, 2007.

TRADE LEADS   Trade leads are essential in identifying potential customers in target markets. Exhibit 17-6 lists a sample of trade lead sources. Accessed via the Internet, they provide an inexpensive way to establish vital links with buyers in target markets.

exhibit

17-7   *Trade Intermediaries Most Suited for Small Businesses*

Confirming Houses	If a foreign firm is interested in purchasing U.S. products, it may retain the services of a confirming house (sometimes called a *buying agent*). These finders "shop" for the lowest possible price for items requested and are paid a commission for their services. In some cases, foreign government agencies or quasi-governmental firms may serve this purpose.
Export Management Companies	An export management company (EMC) acts as the export department for one or several producers of goods or services. It solicits and transacts business in the names of the producers it represents or in its own name, in exchange for a commission, salary, or retainer plus commission. Some EMCs provide immediate payment for the producer's products by either arranging financing or directly purchasing products for resale. The best EMCs know their products and the markets they serve very well and usually have well-established networks of foreign distributors already in place. This immediate access to foreign markets is one of the principal reasons for using an EMC.
Export Trading Companies	An export trading company (ETC) facilitates the export of U.S. goods and services. Like an EMC, this type of intermediary can either act as the export department for producers or take title to the product and export for its own account. Some ETCs are set up and operated by producers. These can be organized along multiple- or single-industry lines and can also represent producers of competing products.
Export Agents, Merchants, or Remarketers	Export agents, merchants, or remarketers purchase products directly from the manufacturer, packing and marking the products according to their own specifications. They then sell these products overseas in their own names through their contacts and assume all risks for accounts. In transactions with these intermediaries, a firm gives up control over the marketing and promotion of its product. This can hinder future sales abroad if the product is underpriced or incorrectly positioned in the market or if after-sales service is neglected.
Piggyback Marketers	Piggyback marketers are manufacturers or service firms that distribute a second firm's product or service. This is commonly seen when a U.S. company has a contract with an overseas buyer to provide a wide range of products or services.

Source: U.S. Department of Commerce, *A Basic Guide to Exporting* (Washington, DC: Department of Commerce and Unz & Co., Inc.), http://www.unzco.com/basicguide/c4.html, accessed February 19, 2007.

TRADE MISSIONS Joining a trade mission is another excellent way to evaluate a foreign market and link up with overseas customers. As mentioned earlier, a trade mission is a planned visit to a potential foreign market, designed to introduce U.S. firms to prospective foreign buyers and to establish strategic alliances. These missions usually involve groups of 5 to 10 business executives and are designed to maximize international sales. Members of the group typically pay their own expenses and share in the operating costs of the mission. Foreign governments sometimes sponsor trade missions in order to promote business links with U.S. firms.

TRADE INTERMEDIARIES   Perhaps the easiest way to break into international markets is to use a **trade intermediary**, which is an agency that distributes products to international customers on a contract basis. These agencies tap their established web of contacts, as well as their local cultural and market expertise. In short, an intermediary can manage the entire export end of a business, taking care of everything except filling the orders—and the results can be outstanding. American Cedar, Inc., located in Hot Springs, Arkansas, is a producer of cedar products. With the assistance of a trade intermediary, American Cedar took in 30 percent of its sales from exporting. Company president Julian McKinney reports, "We displayed our products at a trade show, and an export management company found us. They helped alleviate the hassles of exporting directly. Our products are now being distributed throughout the European Community from a distribution point in France."[49] An export management company is only one of the many types of trade intermediaries. Exhibit 17-7 describes the trade intermediaries that can best provide the assistance small businesses need.

Financing

Arranging financing is perhaps the biggest barrier to international expansion. The more information small firms have about direct and indirect sources of financing, the more favorably they tend to view foreign markets. Sources of this information include private banks and the Small Business Administration.

PRIVATE BANKS   Commercial banks typically have a loan officer who is responsible for handling foreign transactions. Large banks may have an entire international department. Exporters use banks to issue commercial letters of credit and to perform other financial activities associated with exporting.

A **letter of credit** is an agreement to honor a draft or other demand for payment when specified conditions are met. It helps to assure a seller of prompt payment. A letter of credit may be revocable or irrevocable. An irrevocable letter of credit cannot be changed unless both the buyer and the seller agree to the change. The following steps outline the procedure typically followed when payment is made by an irrevocable letter of credit confirmed by a U.S. bank:

1. After the seller (the exporter) and the buyer (the importer) agree on the terms of sale, the buyer arranges for its local bank to open a letter of credit.

2. The buyer's bank prepares an irrevocable letter of credit, including all instructions to the seller concerning the shipment.

3. The buyer's bank sends the irrevocable letter of credit to a U.S. bank, requesting confirmation. The exporter may request that a particular U.S. bank be the confirming bank, or the buyer's bank will select one of its U.S. correspondent banks.

4. The U.S. bank prepares a letter of confirmation to forward to the exporter along with the irrevocable letter of credit.

5. The exporter carefully reviews all conditions in the letter of credit. The exporter's freight forwarder (something like a "travel agent" for cargo) is generally contacted to make sure that the shipping date can be met. If the exporter cannot comply with one or more of the conditions, the buyer should be alerted at once.

6. The exporter arranges with the freight forwarder to deliver the goods to the appropriate port or airport.

7. When the goods are loaded, the freight forwarder completes the necessary documents.

8. The exporter (or the freight forwarder) presents to the U.S. bank documents indicating full compliance.

9. The bank reviews the documents. If they are in order, the documents are forwarded to the buyer's bank for review and then transmitted to the buyer.

trade intermediary
An agency that distributes a company's products on a contract basis to customers in another country

letter of credit
An agreement issued by a bank to honor a draft or other demand for payment when specified conditions are met

10. The buyer (or agent) obtains the documents that may be needed to claim the goods.

11. A draft, which may accompany the letter of credit, is paid to the seller by the importer's bank at the time specified; if paid earlier, it may be discounted.

A guarantee from a reputable bank that the exporter will indeed be paid is critical to a small business that has stretched its resources to the limit just to enter the global game and thus cannot afford an uncollected payment. But what if the small business is on the import end of the exchange? How will its interests be protected? The letter of credit provides security for the receiving firm as well, because the exporter does not receive payment from the bank until it has released the title, or proof of ownership, of the delivered goods. Once the product has been shipped and the title transferred, the exporter receives a document called a **bill of lading** to confirm this. This document must be received before the bank will pay on the letter of credit. In brief, the letter of credit ensures that the exporter will receive payment only when the goods are delivered in-country, and it also guarantees that the exporter will be paid.

bill of lading
A document indicating that a product has been shipped and the title to that product has been transferred

SMALL BUSINESS ADMINISTRATION   The Small Business Administration (SBA) serves small U.S. firms primarily through its regional, district, and branch offices. Small businesses that are either already exporting or interested in doing so can receive valuable information from the SBA through conferences and seminars, instructional publications, and export counseling. An extended list of the financial assistance programs offered by the SBA to small firms is posted on the agency's website at http://www.sba.gov/services/financialassistance/index.html.

It is clear that a growing number of small firms are choosing to participate in international business. The reasons for this expansion include both time-honored motivations and those emerging in the new competitive landscape. To achieve their global aspirations, most small businesses follow an export strategy; however, this is not the only alternative. Small companies can also implement international strategies that involve licensing, franchising, developing strategic alliances, or establishing a presence in foreign markets. In any case, firms that enter the global arena are certain to run up against serious challenges that purely domestic firms do not have to face. This is the nature of the terrain, but assistance is available in abundance from a number of private and public agencies. With a little help and a lot of hard work, your company can succeed in the global marketplace.

Looking BACK

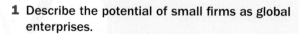

1 Describe the potential of small firms as global enterprises.

· Recent startups and even the smallest of businesses are internationalizing at an increasing rate.

· Small companies called born-global firms are increasingly being launched with cross-border business activities in mind.

· Small business owners who decide to go global must study the political, cultural, technological, and economic forces in the foreign markets to figure out how best to adapt products and ensure smooth entry.

· Trade barriers are falling in some regions of the world, making it easier for small businesses to go global.

2 Identify the basic forces prompting small firms to engage in global expansion.

· Since more than 95 percent of the world's population lives outside the United States, globalization greatly expands the size of a firm's potential market.

· The 10 Big Emerging Markets are attracting small firms that wish to tap their enormous market potential.

- Small businesses with a highly differentiated product may need an international market in order to increase sales enough to recover product development costs.

- Going global can accelerate gains from experience curve efficiencies (resulting from learning effects and economies of scale), especially for startups based on complex technologies.

- Sometimes small businesses go global to gain access to resources, including raw materials and skilled labor.

- Another reason small firms enter foreign markets is to cut their costs in such areas as labor, transportation, or tariffs.

- Small businesses may want to capitalize on special features of an international location: exploiting the unique features of a local environment, taking advantage of favorable government policies, establishing a presence within an emerging trade area, or following a large client firm.

3 Identify and compare strategy options for global businesses.

- Exporting is an international strategy commonly used by small firms. It can be facilitated by using the Internet to increase their international visibility and joining trade missions that help them make contacts abroad.

- Importing involves selling goods from abroad in the home market. It is a strategy that should be used when products manufactured abroad have market potential at home.

- Non-export strategies include foreign licensing, international franchising, international strategic alliances, and locating facilities abroad. They can be more complex than export strategies, but some (especially licensing) are actually the safest options for the small global business.

4 Explain the challenges that global enterprises face.

- Political risk is the potential for a country's political forces to negatively affect the performance of small businesses operating there. Political risk varies greatly across nations.

- Economic risk is the probability that a government will mismanage its economy and change the business environment in ways that hinder the performance of firms operating there (most notably through inflation and fluctuations in exchange rates).

- Globalization raises numerous concerns related to every function of the firm, thus stretching managerial skills and resources to the limit.

5 Recognize the sources of assistance available to support international business efforts.

- Numerous public and private organizations provide assistance to small businesses in analyzing markets and planning a strategy.

- Small businesses can connect with international customers by reviewing sources of trade leads, joining trade missions, or using the services of trade intermediaries.

- For assistance in financing its entry into a foreign market, a small firm can turn to private banks (which can issue letters of credit) and programs initiated by the Small Business Administration.

Key TERMS

globalization, p. 443

born-global firms, p. 443

tariffs, p. 444

North American Free Trade Agreement (NAFTA), p. 445

European Union (EU), p. 445

experience curve efficiencies, p. 449

learning effects, p. 449

economies of scale, p. 449

international outsourcing, p. 449

offshoring, p. 449

exporting, p. 453

trade mission, p. 454

importing, p. 455

foreign licensing, p. 457

licensee, p. 457

licensor, p. 457

royalties, p. 457

counterfeit activity, p. 457

international franchising, p. 457

international strategic alliance, p. 458

cross-border acquisition, p. 458

greenfield venture, p. 458

political risk, p. 460

economic risk, p. 460

exchange rate, p. 461

trade intermediary, p. 465

letter of credit, p. 465

bill of lading, p. 466

Discussion QUESTIONS

1. Discuss the importance of a careful cultural analysis to a small firm that wishes to enter an international market.

2. How have trade agreements helped reduce trade barriers? Do you believe these efforts will continue?

3. Do you believe that small companies should engage in international business? Why or why not?

4. Identify the four basic forces driving small businesses to enter the global business arena. Which do you think is the most influential in the globalization of small firms?

5. Give examples of some emerging motivations persuading small business owners to go global. Are any of these motivations likely to remain powerful forces ten years from now? Twenty years from now?

6. Why is exporting such a popular global strategy among small businesses? Do you think this should be the case?

7. What impact has the Internet had on the globalization of small firms? How do you think small companies will use the Internet for business in the future?

8. What non-export strategies can small businesses adopt? In view of the unique needs and capabilities of small firms, what are the advantages and disadvantages of each of these strategies?

9. What are the three main challenges small businesses face when they go global? What strategies can a small company use to deal with each of these challenges?

10. What forms of assistance are available to small global firms? Which is likely to be of greatest benefit to small companies? Why?

You Make the CALL

SITUATION 1

Bill Moss and several other small business owners joined a trade mission to China to explore market opportunities there. The group learned that China has a population of 1.3 billion and is the third-fastest-growing export market for small and medium-sized U.S. firms. Average annual income for farmers in China is approximately $413 per person; typical urban income is about $1,322, with an average of $3,442 a year in more prosperous cities like Shanghai. In any given year, the Chinese software market grows by 30 percent and the number of Internet users quadruples. Furthermore, the demand for management consulting services is increasing, especially information technology consulting. Members of the group were surprised by the number of people who had cell phones and regularly surfed the Internet, especially in large urban centers such as Beijing, Shanghai, and Guangzhou. On the downside, they found that counterfeit goods (from clothing and leather goods to software and CDs) were readily available at a fraction of the cost of legitimate merchandise and that local merchants expressed an interest in doing business only with vendors with whom they had established relationships.

Sources: Data from http://english.people.com.cn/200603/08/eng20060308_248960.html, accessed February 21, 2007; and

http://www.businessweek.com/globalbiz/content/feb2007/gb20070216_056285.htm, accessed February 21, 2007.

Question 1 What types of businesses would prosper in China? Why?

Question 2 What are the challenges and risks associated with doing business in China?

Question 3 What steps should Moss take to address these challenges and risks in order to increase his chance of success in the market?

SITUATION 2

Lynn Cooper owns and operates BFW, Inc., in Lexington, Kentucky, where she produces fiber-optic lights and headgear-mounted video cameras used for medical exams and surgery. She sees exporting as a means of increasing sales, but with just one employee, she wonders how best to handle the additional marketing and distribution tasks exporting would require.

Question 1 What sources of information would be helpful to Cooper?

Question 2 Would you recommend that she consider using an international distributor? If so, what characteristics should she look for in a distributor?

Question 3 Do you think exporting is a feasible alternative for Cooper at this time? Why or why not?

SITUATION 3

Dr. Juldiz Afgazar, a native of the Republic of Kazakhstan, had been invited to spend a semester in the United States as a visiting scholar in entrepreneurial finance. Kazakhstan gained its independence from the former Soviet Union in 1991, and only after that were laws passed allowing citizens to own private businesses. Dr. Afgazar wanted to learn more about the free market economy of the United States to determine whether such a system could be implemented in Kazakhstan.

Prior to this visit to the United States, Dr. Afgazar had not traveled extensively outside her country. Although she enjoyed many aspects of U.S. culture, she was particularly impressed by the seemingly unlimited quantity and variety of goods and foods that were readily available. After a visit to a local restaurant's pizza buffet, she became an avid fan of American-style pizza! Dr. Afgazar found the crisp yeast crust, spicy tomato sauce, melted mozzarella cheese, and assortment of toppings to be a delicious combination. Pizza was an entirely new type of food for her, since it was not available in Kazakhstan. A true entrepreneur, Dr. Afgazar began to wonder if a pizza restaurant could be successful in her country.

Source: Developed by Elisabeth J. Teal of Northern Georgia College and State University, Dahlonega, Georgia, and Aigul N. Toxanova of Kokshetau Higher College of Management and Business, Kazakhstan.

Question 1 What obstacles would an entrepreneur have to overcome to establish a pizza restaurant in a country with a developing market-based economy, such as Kazakhstan?

Question 2 Is Dr. Afgazar's idea of developing a pizza restaurant in Kazakhstan ahead of its time? That is, do you think the economy of Kazakhstan is sufficiently developed to support a pizza restaurant?

Question 3 What methods could an entrepreneur use to evaluate the likelihood of success of a pizza restaurant in Kazakhstan?

Experiential EXERCISES

1. Conduct phone interviews with 10 local small business owners to see if they engage in international business. Discuss their reasons for going global or for choosing to do business only domestically.

2. Contact a local banker to discuss the bank's involvement with small firms participating in international business. Report your findings to the class.

3. Review recent issues of *Entrepreneur, Inc.,* and other small business publications, and be prepared to discuss articles related to international business.

4. Do a Web search to find an article about a small business that first expanded internationally using an entry strategy other than exporting. From what you understand of the company's situation, suggest guidelines that could lead a firm to go global with non-export strategies.

5. Consult secondary sources to develop a political/economic risk profile for a given country. Select a small company and explain what it would have to do to manage these risks if it were to enter the market of the country profiled.

6. Speak with the owner of a small international company. Which sources of assistance did that entrepreneur use when launching the global initiative? Which sources did the entrepreneur find most helpful? Which did the entrepreneur find least helpful?

Exploring the WEB

1. Go to the Small Business Administration's website at **http://www.sba.gov**. Under SBA programs, find "International Trade." Click on the various tabs to learn about what programs and services the SBA offers. Summarize a particular program or service described there that interests you.

2. At the BuyUSA.gov website (**http://www.buyusa.gov**), maintained by the U.S. Department of Commerce, business owners can purchase a subscription that will allow them to connect with "thousands of international buyers, distributors and agents." Explain how your business could use this website.

3. Return to the SBA's Office of International Trade website at **http://www.sba.gov/gopher/Business-Development/International-Trade/Guide-To-Exporting**. This time, read Chapter 3 of the *Small Business Guide to Exporting*. What methods of foreign market entry are discussed?

Case **17**

Sunny Designs, Inc. (p. 654)

This case describes the experiences of an entrepreneur as he attempts to expand his furniture business by establishing a production facility in China.

Managing Growth in the Small Business

## chapter 18

Professional Management in the Entrepreneurial Firm

In the **VIDEO SPOTLIGHT**

Goshow Architects
http://www.goshow.com

Creating a high-performance company takes leadership. When Nancy and Eric Goshow founded their architecture firm in their living room, they probably weren't thinking as much about leadership as about the survival of their enterprise. Over time, though, as their firm grew, they needed to consider how to build and lead a team capable of developing and managing the large projects required to sustain the company in the long run.

The key to building that team has been collaboration. Eric Goshow likens the process to creating a harmonious choir with a perfect blend of male and female voices. The Goshows look for people with different yet complementary strengths so that the company can go after a broad spectrum of work. And the formula has been successful. Not only has the firm been responsible for numerous residential projects; it has also worked on the renovations of U.S. post offices throughout New York City and has landed contracts with the Port Authority of New York, the U.S. Departments of Energy and Labor, and the New York City School Construction Authority (Goshow has already renovated 44 of New York City's 1,100 schools).

Watch this video spotlight to see how the Goshows have shored up weaknesses, overcome constraints, and used solid planning to build their management team, develop their business, and ensure long-term success.

Video material provided by Hattie Bryant, Producer of Small Business School, the series on PBS Stations, Worldnet, and the Web at http://www.smallbusinessschool.org.

SmallBusinessSchool
the Series on PBS stations and the Web

After studying this chapter, you should be able to

1 Discuss the entrepreneur's leadership role.
2 Explain the distinctive features of small firm management.
3 Identify the managerial tasks of entrepreneurs.
4 Describe the problem of time pressure and suggest solutions.
5 Explain the various types of outside management assistance.

Celebrated poet William Wordsworth once observed, "The child is father of the man." This simply means that childhood experiences tend to shape a person's direction later in life. In a similar way, a startup leaves its imprint on the established company it becomes, although the two are very different. A startup's needs are unique, so adjustments will be necessary sooner or later. Unless you plan to remain a tiny one-person business, leadership and management problems are sure to come your way. When that time arrives, you must find ways to integrate the efforts of employees and give direction to the business. This is absolutely necessary if production employees, salespeople, and support service personnel are to work together effectively. Even long-established businesses need vigorous leadership if they are to avoid stagnation or failure. This chapter examines the leadership challenges facing entrepreneurs and the managerial activities required as firms mature and grow.

Entrepreneurial Leadership

Leadership roles differ greatly depending on the size of the business and its stage of development. A business that is just beginning, for example, faces problems and uncertainties unlike those of a family firm that has been functioning well over several generations. We must begin, therefore, with the recognition that leadership cannot be reduced to simple rules or processes that fit all situations.

1 Discuss the entrepreneur's leadership role.

What Is Leadership?
The question is simple, but the answer is not. Here is the response of a contemporary business leader, Richard Barton, former president and CEO of Expedia, Inc., to the question "How do you define leadership?"

> I'll tell you what it's not. It's not management.
>
> I think a lot of people—especially at large companies—get confused. You have all these people with titles that have some kind of "manager" in it, and people talking about "management." I hate the word management. Management is passive. Management is minding the store. Management is something that you have to do, that you don't necessarily enjoy doing. Leadership to me means leaning forward, looking

> *ahead, trying to improve, being fired up about what you're doing and being able to*
> *communicate that, verbally and nonverbally, to those around you.*
> *Leaders don't lean back, leaders lean forward.*[1]

Clearly, leadership is concerned with pointing the way. It is far more focused on the destination than on the details of getting there. Entrepreneurs must convey their vision of the firm's future to other participants in the business so that everyone involved can contribute most effectively to the accomplishment of the mission. Although leaders must also engage in some of the more mundane processes of management, particularly as the business grows, the first task of the entrepreneur is to create and communicate the vision.

Leadership Qualities of Founders

The entrepreneur is the trailblazer who enlists others, both team members and outsiders, to work with him or her in a creative endeavor. Others may then buy into this vision for the venture as they join their efforts with those of the entrepreneur.

In a totally new venture, the leader faces major uncertainties and unknowns. Amar V. Bhide has discussed the qualities needed by individuals who are launching "promising startups," or startups having the prospect of attaining significant size or profitability.[2] One quality that Bhide identifies is a tolerance for ambiguity—a condition almost always present in launching a new business. Because of the inherent uncertainty, another necessary quality is a capacity for adaptation, the ability to adjust to unforeseen problems and opportunities. These qualities are useful in most settings but are particularly important in business startups.

What Makes an Effective Leader?

Many people assume that a business leader must have a flashy, highly charismatic, take-charge personality to be effective, but this is not the norm and is not required. In a classic study of companies that went from "good" to "great" over a period of several years, Jim Collins and his research team discovered that the great leaders were not egocentric stars but, rather, were often described as "quiet, humble, modest, reserved, shy, gracious, mild-mannered, self-effacing."[3] Even so, these leaders exhibited a resolve and a determination to do whatever was needed to make their companies great. It seems clear, therefore, that effective leadership is based not on a larger-than-life personality but, instead, on a focus on the attainment of business goals.

In most small firms, leadership of the business is personalized. The owner-manager is not a faceless unknown, but an individual whom employees see and relate to in the course of their normal work schedules. This situation is entirely different from that of large corporations, where most employees never see the chief executive. If the employer–employee relationship is good, employees in small firms develop strong feelings of personal loyalty to their employer.

In a large corporation, the values of top-level executives must be filtered through many layers of management before they reach those who produce and sell the products. As a result, the influence of those at the top tends to be diluted by the process. In contrast, personnel in a small firm receive the leader's messages directly. This face-to-face contact facilitates their understanding of the leader's vision as well as her or his stand on integrity, customer service, and other important issues.

Leadership Styles

Leaders use many different styles of leadership, and the styles may be described in various ways. Certain leadership styles may be better suited to certain situations, and most leaders choose from a variety of approaches as they deal with different issues. Daniel Goleman has described the following six distinct leadership styles:[4]

1. *Coercive leaders* demand immediate compliance.

2. *Authoritative leaders* mobilize people toward a vision.

3. *Affiliative leaders* create emotional bonds.

4. *Democratic leaders* build consensus.

5. *Pacesetting leaders* set high standards and expect excellence.

6. *Coaching leaders* develop people.

An entrepreneur may use different styles at different times as she or he attempts to get the best out of the organization and its employees. Even coercive leadership might be necessary and expected, for example, in a genuine emergency, although it would not be appropriate in most settings.

Living the Dream   entrepreneurial challenges

© Dorling Kindersley

A Management Style That Shakes It Up!

Danny Meyer owns five of New York's best and most popular restaurants. He started his first, Union Square Cafe, in October of 1985, and the successes have rolled in over the years. But it has not always been easy. Meyer remembers a time, in his twenties, when his managers and waiters were continually testing him and pushing him to the limit. Pat Cetta, the owner of a highly celebrated steakhouse, happened to drop by for a visit and offered a few words of advice to his young friend. He had the table cleared of everything but a single saltshaker and then asked Meyer to put it right where he wanted it. Meyer put it in the center of the table, and Cetta immediately pushed it three inches off center. "Now put it back where you want it," Cetta insisted. After Meyer returned it to dead center, Cetta moved it six inches away, asking, "Now where do you want it?" Meyer sat back, ready to be mentored.

"Listen," Pat started. "Your staff and your guests are always moving your shaker off center. That's their job. It's the job of life. It's the law of entropy! Until you understand that, you're going to get [ticked] off every time someone moves the saltshaker off center. It's not your job to get upset. You just need to understand: That's what they do. Your job is to move the shaker back each time and let them know exactly what you stand for. Let them know what excellence looks like."

Meyer gets it now. In fact, he has a name for it: constant, gentle pressure. As Meyer sees it today, "It's my job, and consequently the job of every other leader in my company, to teach everyone who works for us to distinguish center from off center and always to set things right." Things are going to come up, conspiring to throw everything out of balance, but Meyer is committed to moving them back to where they should be. That's the "constant" feature of his approach. But he'll never respond in a way that robs his employees of their dignity. That's why he calls it "gentle." He's also committed to watching every table and moving every out-of-place saltshaker to its proper place, insisting on excellent performance. So that's where the "pressure" comes in. It's not easy, but it's a management style that works!

Sources: Danny Meyer, "The Saltshaker Theory," *Inc.,* Vol. 28, No. 10 (October 2006), pp. 69–70; http://www.unionsquarecafe.com/aboutusc.html, accessed March 19, 2007; and http://www.cbsnews.com/stories/2003/03/03/sunday/main542606.shtml, accessed March 8, 2007.

http://www.unionsquarecafe.com

For the large majority of entrepreneurial firms, leadership that recognizes and values individual worth is strongly recommended. Several decades ago, many managers were hard-nosed autocrats, giving orders and showing little concern for those who worked under them. Over the years, this style of leadership has given way to a gentler and more effective variety that emphasizes respect for all members of the organization and shows an appreciation both for their work and for their potential.

Progressive managers frequently seek some degree of employee participation in decisions that affect personnel and work processes. And often the focus is on important features of the business, such as superior customer service. In many cases, managers carry this leadership approach to a level called **empowerment**. The manager who uses empowerment goes beyond solicitation of employees' opinions and ideas by increasing their authority to act on their own and to make decisions about the processes they're involved with. Glenn Ross, an expert on dealing with customers, points out how small business owners can use employee empowerment to help resolve customer complaints.

> *As the immortal philosopher, Barney Fife [from "The Andy Griffith Show"], used to say, "Nip it! You've got to nip it in the bud!" Stop the complaint before it escalates into something major. The best way to do that is to see that your employees understand your vision, policies, and procedures as they relate to customer service. Empowering your employees also shows them that you trust them to do the right thing. This in turn has a positive impact on employee morale. The higher the employee morale, the better service they will provide to your customers. It's that "Circle of Life" thing.*[5]

Ross goes on to point out that empowering frontline staff to take care of customers in this way offers additional benefits, such as freeing up time for the owners and managers to take care of other pressing business challenges.

Some companies carry employee participation a step further by creating self-managed **work teams**. Each work team is assigned a given task or operation; its members manage the task or operation without direct supervision and assume responsibility for the results. When work teams function properly, the number of supervisors needed decreases sharply.

Management practices that include a high level of involvement by employees contribute to productivity and profits, according to research studies. Jeffrey Pfeffer and John F. Veiga explain the reasons for improved performance as follows:

> *Simply put, people work harder because of the increased involvement and commitment that comes from having more control and say in their work; people work smarter because they are encouraged to build skills and competence; and people work more responsibly because more responsibility is placed in hands of employees farther down in the organization. These practices work not because of some mystical process, but because they are grounded in sound social science principles that have been shown to be effective by a great deal of evidence. And, they make sense.*[6]

Leaders Shape the Culture of the Organization

Over time, an organization tends to take on a life of its own. That is, an organizational culture begins to emerge that helps employees understand what the business stands for and how to go about their work. You could think of organizational culture as the factor that determines the "feel" of a business. It tends to be the "silent teacher" that sets the tone for employee conduct, even when managers are not present.

A company's culture does not emerge overnight; it unfolds over the lifetime of the business and usually reflects the character and style of the founder. (You may recall that we discussed the founder's imprint on organizational culture in a family business in Chapter 5.) Because of its power to shape how business is conducted, the culture of the organization should not be left to chance. If a founder is honest in his or her dealings, supportive of employees, and quick to communicate, he or she will likely set a standard that others will follow. An entrepreneur can create an innovative cultural environment by setting aside his or her ego and opening up to the ideas of others, supporting experimentation through the elimination of unnecessary penalties for failure, and looking for

empowerment
Giving employees authority to make decisions or take actions on their own

work teams
Groups of employees with freedom to function without close supervision

and tapping into the unique gifts of all employees. Like empowerment, creating a culture that fosters innovation tends to draw employees into the work of the company and often provides a boost to commitment and employee morale.[7]

The above-mentioned actions are largely symbolic, focusing attention on the thrust of the business and its purpose. However, deliberate physical design efforts can also influence the culture, shaping the way people in the organization interact and what they achieve together. Joe Anthony owns New York City–based Vital Marketing, a company that brings in around $20 million a year doing multicultural and youth marketing. Anthony and his management team have taken very intentional steps to set the tone of business and generate specific results. In Anthony's words, "We group our project teams together . . . [and] create these bullpens so people will always be able to turn around and troubleshoot."[8]

Jonathan Vehar, senior partner of New & Improved, an innovation training and development company in Evanston, Illinois, offers more design suggestions. For example, he notes that an entrepreneur can spur creativity by sprinkling all work spaces with visually stimulating features, including idea-inspiring artwork, video monitors, and well-positioned windows that open up the view to other environments. It is also possible to encourage communication, for example, by positioning work spaces far away from bathroom facilities, which naturally creates occasions for employees to run into one another and start idea-generating conversations.[9] These are relatively simple concepts for setting up physical space, but they can have a profound effect on the mind-set employees assume when they come to work.

One feature that every leader should strive to incorporate into the organizational culture is a positive, "can-do" attitude. You can work on your own attitude and inspire others to follow your lead; Exhibit 18-1 offers some practical steps you can take to become more positive in your outlook. Attitude often is everything—whether an event is mentally framed as a setback or a positive life experience is entirely up to you. If all the parking

exhibit 18-1   *Steps to a Positive Attitude*

1. **Recognize accomplishments at the end of each day.** Take a moment to celebrate the day's achievements, knowing that you are one step closer to achieving your business ambitions. Don't dwell on the fact that some things remain undone—that is just the adventure left for the next day.

2. **At the close of business, take time to set goals for the next day.** Establishing priorities for the next day will increase your focus and boost your motivation. Write them down and e-mail them to yourself. Then relax, knowing that you have already gotten a head start on tomorrow's tasks.

3. **Take care of yourself.** Tend to your health. Eat nourishing food, and get appropriate exercise. Find activities that you enjoy and spend time doing them. Change up your life from time to time to avoid falling into a rut and lapsing into boredom.

4. **Spend time with friends who are upbeat.** It's difficult to maintain a positive frame of mind if everyone around you is breathing the fire of doom and gloom. Optimism is contagious. Catch it, and spread it!

5. **Imagine your way to success.** Mind-set alone will not lead the way to results, but neither will a good game plan encumbered by flagging motivation and a negative frame of mind. Envision positive outcomes, such as customers being satisfied as they use your products.

6. **Use thoughts of failure as a signal to turn your attention back to achievement.** You will have setbacks, but it's time to move on (mentally) once you have addressed the root problem. Adventure calls from the business opportunities that lie before you.

Source: Adapted from Romanus Wolter, "A Brand New Day," *Entrepreneur,* Vol. 33, No. 3 (March 2005), pp. 134–135.

spaces close to the store are full, taking one farther away can be seen as a chance to get some exercise. A new competitor can present a fresh reminder of why it is so important to serve your customers to the best of your ability. And a lost sale can show you how to improve your product or adjust your presentation so that many more sales can be generated in the future. Develop a positive mind-set, and let it shape the culture of those you have hired to work alongside you.

Distinctive Characteristics of Small Firm Management

2 Explain the distinc-
tive features of small
firm management.

professional manager
A manager who uses
systematic, analytical
methods of management

As one entrepreneur commented, "Unless you thrive on chaos, a small company can be tough." Small firm operations are not always chaotic, of course, but small business owners face challenges that differ greatly from those of corporate executives. Furthermore, small companies experience changes in their leadership and management processes as they move from startup to the point where they employ a full staff of **professional managers**, trained in the use of systematic, analytical methods.

Professional-Level Management

There is, of course, much variation in the way business firms, as well as other organizations, are managed. Between the extremes of very unskilled and highly professional types of management lies a continuum. At the less professional end of this continuum are entrepreneurs and other managers who rely largely on past experience, rules of thumb, and personal whims in giving direction to their businesses. In most cases, their ideas of motivation are based on the way they were treated in earlier business or family relationships.

Other entrepreneurs and managers display much more professionalism. They are analytical and systematic in dealing with management problems and issues. Because they emphasize getting the facts and working out logical solutions, their approach is sometimes described as scientific in nature. The challenge for small firm leaders is to develop as much professionalism as possible, while still retaining the entrepreneurial spirit of the enterprise.

Limitations of Founders as Managers

Founders of new firms are not always good organization members. As discussed in Chapter 1, they are creative, innovative, risk-taking individuals who have the courage to strike out on their own. Indeed, they are often propelled into entrepreneurship by precipitating events, sometimes involving their difficulty in fitting into conventional organizational roles. Even charismatic leaders may fail to appreciate the need for good management practices as the business grows.

Though he believes the problem may sometimes be overstated, Adam Hanft, CEO of Hanft Unlimited Inc., a New York City–based consulting, advertising, and publishing firm, points out that many experts believe it is very difficult (often impossible) for entrepreneurs to make the shift from founder to professional manager.

> *If I had a dime for every time I have heard it, I could start another business: Entrepreneurs are passionate people, great at building companies, but only to a certain level. As their enterprises reach maturity, these impatient, impetuous founders need to be replaced by "professional" managers. . . . In [venture capital] land they even have a name for the problem: founderitis.*[10]

Some entrepreneurs recognize the problem early on and make adjustments. In 2003, Elise and Rick Wetzel founded Pasadena, California–based iSold It, a franchisor of drop-off stores for those looking for someone to sell items on eBay for them. Within a year, the wild growth of the company had led the husband-and-wife team to conclude that the business was more than they could handle. Rick realized, "You have to set your ego aside...and

---

How They See It: Building a Team

Sara Blakely

Building the team was one of my toughest challenges. For someone who's never taken a business class, never managed anyone, to all of a sudden be a business owner and manager and be responsible for all of my employees' livelihoods, I was shocked and confused on how to be an effective manager. Then I realized, "It's OK if you're not good at this; hire someone who is." One of the smartest business decisions I made was to hire a CEO. It's best to let go of control in the areas that aren't your strongest and focus on the areas that are. I'm the face of SPANX, spreading the word, and involved in product development and marketing ideas. The person who starts a company from the ground up is not always the best person to grow it. I think this is the most important lesson an entrepreneur can learn.

---

say, 'This is too big for me; we need a stronger team.'" The Wetzels were able to find an experienced manager and brought him on as CEO in 2004, and now the company is running at top speed.[11] Knowing when to make the transition can have an important positive impact on company performance.

Although many entrepreneurs are professional in their approach to management and many corporate managers are entrepreneurial in the sense of being innovative and willing to take risks, a founder's less-than-professional management style has been known to act as a drag on business growth. Ideally, the founder should be able to add a measure of professional management without sacrificing the entrepreneurial spirit and basic values that have given the business a successful start.

Managerial Weakness in Small Firms

Although some large corporations experience poor management, small businesses seem particularly vulnerable to this weakness. Many small firms are marginal or unprofitable businesses, struggling to survive from day to day. At best, they earn only a meager living for their owners. They operate, but to say that they are managed would be an exaggeration.

Consider American Dixie Group, Inc., founded by Lay Cooper in 1989 in Albany, New York, to build the industrial machines used in food processing, packaging, and plastics making.[12] The business became successful, was praised for its problem-solving wizardry, and served customers like Nestlé and Campbell Soup. As long as the business remained small, with no more than two dozen employees in the shop and a half dozen or so projects in the pipeline, it apparently performed quite well. As it expanded, however, it ran into problems. Suppliers began griping about late payments, and customers became unhappy because of delayed deliveries and shoddy workmanship. In September 1998, American Dixie Group filed for bankruptcy; it had failed because it lacked professional management.

Managerial weakness of the type just described is all too typical of small firms. The good news, however, is that poor management is neither universal nor inevitable.

Constraints That Hamper Management

Managers of small firms, particularly new and growing companies, are constrained by conditions that do not trouble the average corporate executive—they must face the grim reality of small bank accounts and limited staff. A small firm often lacks the money for slick sales brochures, and it cannot afford much in the way of marketing research. The shortage of cash also makes it difficult to employ an adequate number of clerical employees. Such limitations are painfully apparent to large-firm managers who move into management positions in small firms.

A former CEO of a telecommunications company described some of the drastic differences between her experiences managing in a *Fortune* 500 firm and in a startup. In a startup situation,

> *Money doesn't come from any single source. There's no single boss to whom you make your case. In fact, the money to build the business comes from several external sources—each with slightly different agendas. . . . [T]here's no guarantee that you can survive even if you hit your milestones. In other words, there's no room for error. . . .*
> *[U]nless you also realize that you have to become a one-person version of your Fortune 500's chief financial officer, investor-relations and PR staffs, and fund-raising machine, you will be ill-prepared for the mission.*[13]

Small firms typically lack adequate specialized professional staff. Most small business managers are generalists. Lacking the support of experienced specialists in such areas as marketing research, financial analysis, advertising, and human resource management, the manager of a small firm must make decisions in these areas without the expertise that is available in a larger business. This limitation may be partially overcome by using outside management assistance. But coping with a shortage of internal professional talent is part of the reality of managing entrepreneurial firms.

Firm Growth and Managerial Practices

As a newly formed business becomes established and grows, its organizational structure and pattern of management change. To some extent, management in any organization must adapt to growth and change. However, the changes involved in the early growth stages of a new business are much more extensive than those that occur with the growth of a relatively mature business.

A number of experts have proposed models related to the growth stages of business firms.[14] These models typically describe four or five stages of growth and identify various management issues related to each stage. Exhibit 18-2 shows four stages of organizational growth characteristic of many small businesses. As firms progress from Stage 1 to Stage 4, they add layers of management and increase the formality of operations. Though some firms skip the first stage or two by starting as larger businesses, thousands of small firms make their way through each of the stages pictured in Exhibit 18-2.

exhibit 18-2 *Organizational Stages of Small Business Growth*

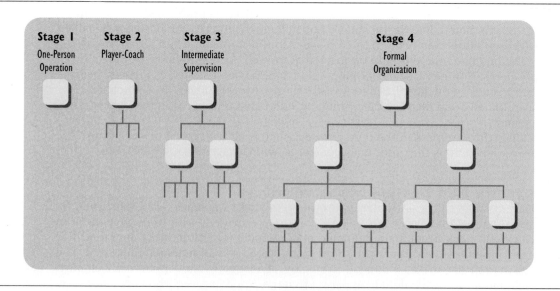

Stage 1 — One-Person Operation

Stage 2 — Player-Coach

Stage 3 — Intermediate Supervision

Stage 4 — Formal Organization

In Stage 1, the firm is simply a one-person operation. Some firms begin with a larger organization, but the one-person startup is by no means rare. Many businesses remain one-person operations indefinitely. In Stage 2, the entrepreneur becomes a player-coach, which implies continuing active participation in the operations of the business. In addition to performing the basic work—whether making the product, selling it, writing checks, or keeping records—the entrepreneur must also coordinate the efforts of others.

A major milestone is reached in Stage 3, when an intermediate level of supervision is added. In many ways, this is a turning point for a small firm, because the entrepreneur must rise above direct, hands-on management and work through an intervening layer of management. Stage 4, the stage of formal organization, involves more than increased size and multi-layered organization. The formalization of management entails adoption of written policies, preparation of plans and budgets, standardization of personnel practices, computerization of records, preparation of organizational charts and job descriptions, scheduling of training conferences, institution of control procedures, and so on. While some formal managerial practices may be adopted prior to Stage 4, the steps shown in Exhibit 18-2 outline a typical pattern of development for successful firms. Flexibility and informality may be helpful when a firm is first started, but the firm's growth requires greater formality in planning and control. Tension often develops as the traditional easy-going patterns of management become dysfunctional. Great managerial skill is required of the entrepreneur in order to preserve a "family" atmosphere while introducing professional management.

As a firm moves from Stage 1 to Stage 4, the pattern of entrepreneurial activities changes. The entrepreneur becomes less of a doer and more of a manager. Managers who have strong doing skills often have weak managing skills, and this is understandable. Most entrepreneurs build businesses on their specialized skills; for example, they may know software development inside and out, have a knack for raising money, or possess enviable selling skills. But when it comes to tasks like assessing talent in others, they often come up short. That is simply not their strong suit, and this limitation can be a serious problem.[15]

As a firm grows, the entrepreneur needs to fill key positions with individuals who have the capacity to perform well as managers. Can the best salesperson or most skilled technician be advanced to a higher level? Sometimes, but not always.

> *Erika Mangrum was a year into her business and was feeling pressured to promote a star employee to general manager. "She wanted more responsibility and more pay," says Mangrum, co-founder and president of Iatria Day Spas and Health Center, a 40-employee company in Raleigh, North Carolina. Mangrum felt a deep sense of loyalty to this employee, who had been with the company from the start, so she went ahead with the promotion. However, it wasn't long before Mangrum realized she was promoting doom and gloom.[16]*

The new manager's rudeness and inability to manage conflict created customer complaints and tension among employees. The manager left 14 months after the promotion. And unfortunately, the business also lost key employees in the turmoil.[17]

Sometimes the personal skills or brilliance of the entrepreneur can enable a business to survive while business skills are being acquired. This was the case with Ronald and Rony Delice, Haitian-born twin brothers, who are igniting fashion runways and men's clothing with their edgy designs.[18]

Their father worked as a tailor in Haiti, and their mother was a seamstress in New York City. After earning degrees in fashion merchandising from New York City's acclaimed Fashion Institute of Technology, Ronald and Rony began work as custom tailors and designers. They soon started their own business and quickly won awards for their designs. By 2003, their company, with revenues estimated at $475,000, listed such celebrities as actor Will Smith and basketball star Latrell Sprewell among its clients.

The business side of their venture, however, presented the biggest challenge. The twins found that keeping the books, paying bills, and preparing a business plan were much harder than designing clothing. As Ronald explained it, "We're more artists than businesspeople." Overcoming that challenge meant bringing in qualified people.

Small firms that hesitate to move through the various organizational stages and acquire the necessary professional management often limit their rate of growth. On the other hand, a small business may attempt to grow too quickly. If an entrepreneur's primary strength lies in product development or selling, for example, a quick move into Stage 4 may saddle the entrepreneur with managerial duties and deprive the organization of her or his valuable talents.

In his study of the origin and evolution of new businesses, Amar V. Bhide found that entrepreneurs play different roles in starting businesses than they play in building what he calls long-lived firms.[19] Likewise, the personal qualities involved in starting businesses differ from the qualities required to develop long-lived firms. This helps explain why so few ventures actually become established businesses with staying power. Growing a business requires maturation and adaptation on the part of the entrepreneur.

Managerial Tasks of Entrepreneurs

3 Identify the managerial tasks of entrepreneurs.

So far, our discussion of the management process has been very general. Now it is time to look more closely at how entrepreneurs implement their leadership in organizing and directing the firm's operations.

Planning Activities

Most small business managers plan to some degree. However, the amount of planning they do is typically less than ideal. Also, what little planning there is tends to be haphazard and focused on specific, immediate issues—for example, how much inventory to purchase, whether to buy a new piece of equipment, and other questions of this type. Circumstances affect the degree to which formal planning is needed, but most businesses can function more profitably by increasing the amount of planning done by managers and making it more systematic.

The payoff from planning comes in several ways. First, the process of thinking through the issues confronting a firm and developing a plan to deal with those issues can improve productivity. Second, planning provides a focus for a firm: Managerial decisions over the course of the year can be guided by the annual plan, and employees can work consistently toward the same goal. Third, evidence of planning increases credibility with bankers, suppliers, and other outsiders.

long-range plan (strategic plan)
A firm's overall plan for the future

short-range plan
A plan that governs a firm's operations for one year or less

budget
A document that expresses future plans in monetary terms

TYPES OF PLANS   A firm's basic path to the future is spelled out in a document called a **long-range plan**, or **strategic plan**. As noted in Chapter 3, strategy decisions concern such issues as niche markets and features that differentiate a firm from its competitors. Such planning is essential even in established businesses, in order to ensure that changes in the business environment can be addressed as they occur.

Short-range plans are action plans designed to deal with activities in production, marketing, and other areas over a period of one year or less. An important part of a short-range operating plan is the **budget**, a document that expresses future plans in monetary terms. A budget is usually prepared one year in advance, with a breakdown by quarters or months. (Budgeting is explained more fully in Chapter 22.)

PLANNING TIME   Small business managers all too often succumb to the "tyranny of the urgent." Because they are busy putting out fires, they never get around to planning. Planning is easy to postpone and, therefore, easy for managers to ignore while concentrating on more urgent issues in such areas as production and sales. And, just as quarterbacks focusing on a receiver may be blindsided by blitzing linebackers, managers who have neglected to plan may be bowled over by competitors.

Creating an Organizational Structure

While an entrepreneur may give direction through personal leadership, she or he must also define the relationships among the firm's activities and among the individuals on the firm's payroll. Without some kind of organizational structure, operations eventually become chaotic and morale suffers.

THE UNPLANNED STRUCTURE   In small companies, the organizational structure tends to evolve with little conscious planning. Certain employees begin performing particular functions when the company is new and retain those functions as it matures.

This natural evolution is not all bad. Generally, a strong element of practicality characterizes these types of organizational arrangements. The structure is forged through the experience of working and growing, rather than being derived from a textbook or another firm's organizational chart. Unplanned structures are seldom perfect, however, and growth typically creates a need for organizational change. Periodically, therefore, the entrepreneur should examine structural relationships and make adjustments as needed for effective teamwork.

THE CHAIN OF COMMAND   A chain of command implies superior–subordinate relationships with a downward flow of instructions, but it involves much more. It is also a channel for two-way communication. As a practical matter, strict adherence to the chain of command is not advisable. An organization in which the primary channel of communication is rigid will be bureaucratic and inefficient. At the same time, frequent and flagrant disregard of the chain of command quickly undermines the position of the bypassed manager.

In a **line organization**, each person has one supervisor to whom he or she reports and looks for instructions. All employees are directly engaged in the firm's work, producing, selling, or performing office or financial duties. Most very small firms—for example, those with fewer than 10 employees—use this form of organization.

A **line-and-staff organization** is similar to a line organization in that each person reports to a single supervisor. However, a line-and-staff structure also has staff specialists who perform specialized services or act as management advisors in specific areas (see Exhibit 18-3). Staff specialists may include a human resource manager, a production control technician, a quality control specialist, and an assistant to the president. The line-and-staff organization is widely used in small businesses.

chain of command
The official, vertical channel of communication in an organization

line organization
A simple organizational structure in which each person reports to one supervisor

line-and-staff organization
An organizational structure that includes staff specialists who assist management

---

exhibit 18-3   *Line-and-Staff Organization*

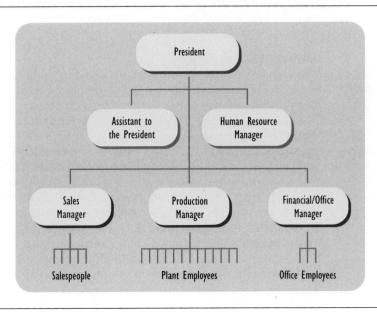

span of control
The number of subordinates supervised by one manager

SPAN OF CONTROL   The **span of control** is the number of employees who are supervised by a manager. Although some authorities have stated that six to eight people are all that one individual can supervise effectively, the optimal span of control is actually a variable that depends on a number of factors. Among these factors are the nature of the work and the manager's knowledge, energy, personality, and abilities. In addition, if the abilities of subordinates are better than average, the span of control may be broadened accordingly.

As a very small firm grows and adds employees, the entrepreneur's span of control is extended. The entrepreneur often has a tendency to stretch the span too far—to supervise not only the first five or six employees hired, but also all the employees added as time goes on. Eventually, a point is reached at which the attempted span of control exceeds the entrepreneur's reach, demanding more time and effort than she or he can devote to the business. It is at this point that the entrepreneur must establish intermediate levels of supervision and dedicate more time to management, moving beyond the role of player-coach.

Understanding Informal Groups

The types of organizational structures just discussed address the formal relationships among members of an organization. All organizations, however, also have informal groups composed of people with something in common, such as jobs, hobbies, carpools, or affiliations with civic associations.

Although informal groups are not created by management, managers should observe them and evaluate their effect on the functioning of the total organization. An informal group, for example, may foster an attitude of working hard until the very end of the working day or doing the opposite—easing up and coasting for the last half-hour. Ordinarily, no serious conflict arises between informal groups and the formal organization. Informal leaders often emerge who influence employee behavior. The wise manager understands the potentially positive contribution of informal groups and the inevitability of informal leadership.

Informal interaction among subordinates and managers can facilitate work performance and can also make life in the workplace more enjoyable for everyone. The value of compatible work groups to the individual became painfully clear to one college student working on a summer job:

> *I was employed as a forklift driver for one long, frustrating summer. Soon after being introduced to my work group, I knew I was in trouble. A clique had formed and, for some reason, resented college students. During lunch breaks and work breaks, I spent the whole time by myself. Each morning, I dreaded going to work. The job paid well, but I was miserable.*[20]

Delegating Authority

delegation of authority
Granting to subordinates the right to act or make decisions

Through **delegation of authority**, a manager grants to subordinates the right to act or to make decisions. Turning over some functions to subordinates by delegating authority frees the superior to perform more important tasks.

Although failure to delegate may be found in any organization, it is often a special problem for entrepreneurs, given their backgrounds and personalities. Because they frequently must pay for mistakes made by subordinates, owners are inclined to keep a firm hold on the reins of leadership in order to protect the business.

Inability or unwillingness to delegate authority is manifested in numerous ways. For example, employees may find it necessary to clear even the most minor decisions with the boss. At any given time, a number of subordinates may be trying to get the attention of the owner to resolve some issue that they lack the authority to settle. This keeps the owner exceptionally busy—rushing from assisting a salesperson to helping iron out a production bottleneck to setting up a new filing system. Entrepreneurs often work long hours, and those who have difficulty delegating compound the problem, imposing on themselves even longer work hours.

Russ Lewis, who operates a small bakery in Vermont with his wife, Linda, faces this problem at a very basic level. He personally bakes between 2,000 to 3,500 loaves of bread each day and finds it extremely tiring. As Linda puts it, "I don't think he loves it anymore." The bakery supplies restaurants and cafés with great bread and provides the owners with the highest income they've ever had, but it also dominates their lives.

> *They employ three other people—more in summer months when Vermont swells with tourists—but limit the workers' duties to things other than baking. So, six days a week Mr. Lewis wakes at 12:30 a.m., is in the bakery by 1 a.m., first doing croissants and then loaves of artisan bread, heading home around 2 p.m.*
>
> *When they're especially busy, "I'll just start two or three hours earlier," Mr. Lewis says. "I haven't seen prime-time television in five years. It's not natural. Your body never gets used to it."*
>
> *Ms. Lewis starts a little later and finishes a little later, handling deliveries and paperwork. [She says,] "Russ always says, 'I'm so tired of being so tired.'" Indeed, they're too tired to change the habits that make them so tired.[21]*

The business could be taken to a higher level, but Russ is finding it difficult to give up his duties or control. As he puts it, "I enjoy baking, but I like to handle everything myself." Until he can learn to delegate, Russ Lewis will be a victim of his own success.[22]

But when entrepreneurs do decide to take the "delegation plunge," they often run into unexpected problems. Joshua Schechter started Online Business Services, Inc., with his brother Jeff in 1993 to provide payroll services for San Antonio businesses. According to Joshua, he and Jeff realized that they needed to turn over more work to their employees. However, after delegating some of the work that he personally had been doing, Jeff found that some employees were not as careful as he was in meeting tax deposit deadlines for clients. This was one of several signs that managing a growing business would require new skills and managerial insights, and the Schechter brothers had no choice but to learn these "on the fly." To clear the way for effective delegation, the Schechter brothers had to shift their focus to adequate employee training and motivation.[23]

How well the delegation process works depends not just on the quantity but also on the quality of delegation. Stephen R. Covey distinguishes between what he calls "gofer" delegation and "stewardship" delegation.[24] Gofer delegation refers to work assignments in which the supervisor-delegator controls the details, telling subordinates to "go for this" or "go for that." This is not true delegation. Stewardship delegation, on the other hand, focuses on results and allows the individual receiving an assignment some latitude in carrying it out. Only stewardship delegation provides the benefits of delegation to both parties.

Controlling Operations

Despite good planning, organizations seldom function perfectly. As a result, managers must monitor operations to discover deviations from plans and to ensure that the firm is functioning as intended. Managerial activities that check on performance and correct it when necessary are part of managerial control; they serve to keep the business on course.

The control process begins with the establishment of standards. This is evidence of the connection between planning and control, for it is through planning and goal setting that control standards are established. Planners translate goals into norms (standards) by making them measurable. A goal to increase market share, for example, may be expressed as a projected dollar increase in sales volume for the coming year. Such an annual target may, in turn, be broken down into quarterly target standards so that corrective action can be taken early if performance begins to fall below the projected amount.

As Exhibit 18-4 shows, performance measurement occurs at various stages of the control process. Performance may be measured at the input stage (perhaps to determine the quality of materials purchased), during the process stage (perhaps to determine if the product being manufactured meets quality standards), and/or at the output stage (perhaps to check the quality of a completed product).

exhibit

18-4   *Stages of the Control Process*

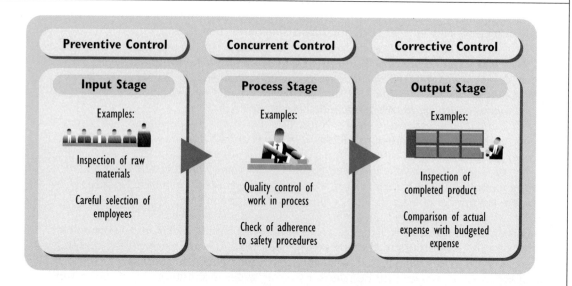

Corrective action is required when performance deviates significantly from the standard in an unfavorable direction. To prevent the deviation from recurring, such action must be followed by an analysis of the cause of the deviation. If the percentage of defective products increases, for example, a manager must determine whether the problem is caused by faulty raw materials, untrained workers, or some other factor. For a problem to be effectively controlled, corrective action must identify and deal with the true cause.

Communicating

Another key to a healthy organization is effective communication—that is, getting managers and employees to talk with one another and openly share problems and ideas. To some extent, the management hierarchy must be set aside so that personnel at all levels can speak freely with those higher up. The result is two-way communication—a far cry from the old-fashioned idea that managers give orders and employees simply carry them out. The need for good communication has been eloquently expressed as follows: "It's a no-brainer—you've got to talk, email, and kibitz with employees. The speed with which information moves through a company is critical to how well the mechanism works. Information is the oil that turns the gears."[25]

To communicate effectively, managers must tell employees where they stand, how the business is doing, and what the firm's plans are for the future. While negative feedback may be necessary at times, giving positive feedback to employees is the primary tool for establishing good human relations. Perhaps the most fundamental concept managers need to keep in mind is that employees are people, not machines. As people, they quickly detect insincerity but respond to honest efforts to treat them as mature, responsible individuals. In short, an atmosphere of trust and respect contributes greatly to good communication.

There are many practical tools and techniques that can be used to stimulate two-way communication between managers and employees, including the following:

- Periodic performance review sessions to discuss employees' ideas, questions, complaints, and job expectations

- Bulletin boards to keep employees informed about developments affecting them and/or the company

- Blogs (user-generated websites where entries are made in journal style) for internal communication, especially in companies that have open organizational cultures and truly want transparent dialogue[26]

- Suggestion boxes to solicit employees' ideas

- Wikis (websites that allows visitors to add, remove, edit, and change content) set up to bring issues to the surface and draw feedback from employees[27]

- Formal staff meetings to discuss problems and matters of general concern

- Breakfast or lunch with employees to socialize and just talk

These methods and others can be used to supplement the most basic of all channels for communication—the day-to-day interaction between each employee and his or her supervisor.

So far, the focus has been on interpersonal communication, but entrepreneurs must also make presentations to groups of people, from pitching product ideas at trade shows to selling bankers on the need for funding to offering keynote speeches at community events. And the need for public speaking skills is sure to increase as the company grows and develops. The fear of public speaking is one of the most common phobias (ranking even above the fear of dying!), and an inability to communicate in public can hold back the progress of the business. The good news is that, through practice, you can keep your stage fright under control (if that is a problem) and you can certainly improve your delivery. Exhibit 18-5 provides some tips that will help you develop confidence in your speaking and be more interesting as a presenter.

Negotiating

In operating a business, entrepreneurs and managers must personally interact with other individuals much of the time. Some contacts involve outsiders, such as suppliers, customers, bankers, realtors, and providers of business services. Typically, the interests of the parties are in conflict, to some degree at least. A supplier, for example, wants to sell a product or service for the highest possible price, and the buyer wants to purchase it for the lowest possible price. To have a successful business, a manager must be able to reach agreements that both meet the firm's requirements and contribute to good relationships over time.

Even within the business, personal relationships pit different perspectives and personal interests against one another. Subordinates, for example, frequently desire changes in their work assignments or feel that they are worth more to the company than their salary level indicates. Managers in different departments may compete for services offered by a maintenance department or a computer services unit.

The process of developing workable solutions through discussions or interactions is called **negotiation**. We are all negotiators in our daily lives, both inside and outside our family relationships. Conflicting interests, desires, and demands require that we reconcile, or negotiate, differences in order to live together peacefully.

Many people consider negotiation to be a win–lose game; that is, one party must win, and the other must lose. There is a problem, however, with this concept of negotiation. If parties feel that they have lost, they may go away with thoughts of getting even in subsequent negotiations. Clearly, such feelings do not contribute to good long-term relationships. In contrast, other negotiators advocate a win–win strategy. A win–win negotiator tries to find a solution that will satisfy at least the basic interests of both parties.

Implementing a win–win strategy in relationships involves thinking about one's own interests and also exploring the interests of the other party. After clarifying the interests of the involved parties and their needs, the negotiator can explore various alternatives to identify their overall fit, looking for a solution that will produce a plan that is workable for all. There are situations in which a win–win solution is impossible, but a positive solution should be pursued whenever possible. And, of course, a foundation for successful negotiating is created by developing strong relationships between the negotiating parties, which can facilitate cooperation.[28]

negotiation
A two-way communication process used to resolve differences in needs, goals, or ideas

exhibit

18-5   *Presentation Tips*

1. **Do your homework.** You need to know the purpose of the presentation and to whom you will be presenting. If you can find out in advance who will be attending your presentation, you will be able to adapt your comments to their needs and concerns.

2. **Know your material "spot on."** The better you know what you plan to talk about, the more you can concentrate on the delivery. And being prepared inspires confidence.

3. **Be interactive.** It's easy for listeners to be lulled into disinterest when they are not engaged. Find ways to get the audience involved in what you have to say. And don't, for example, read from your notes for extended periods of time—doing so will ensure that the communication goes in only one direction, and your audience will know it immediately.

4. **Make vivid mental connections in the minds of listeners.** Telling stories helps here, but so can other tools and techniques. For example, use props to focus attention, or employ a metaphor throughout the presentation to draw listeners back to a central theme. Humor is entertaining and can provide comic relief, but it can also be used to make a point unforgettable.

5. **Emphasize relevance.** Your listeners are busy people, so be sure to deliver information that they will find useful and worth their time.

6. **Be dynamic, but be yourself.** Let your listeners know that you are passionate about the topic by the way you invest yourself in the presentation. It is much easier for an audience to remain engaged when the presenter is energetic and uses voice, gestures, movement, and facial expressions to show it. Maintaining eye contact communicates that you want to connect with each individual in the room, which is motivating. However, if your level of energy and your use of your voice and body are less than authentic, listeners will quickly pick up on that and may write off the talk as insincere.

7. **Use PowerPoint with care.** Text-laden slides can produce the same effect as sleeping pills. If a picture paints a thousand words, then adding pictures and graphics can certainly help the audience access the ideas you want to convey (as long as they are not flashy to the point of distraction). Limit the text on each slide, and do not read from the slides you are showing. Try to imagine how you would respond to the slides if you were not particularly interested in the topic, and then make adjustments based on what you conclude.

8. **Dress appropriately.** Though your audience may be wearing more casual clothing, it is safest to dress in business-professional attire. Avoid distracting clothing (like a tie that draws attention away from what you have to say), and check to be sure your collar is straight, your blouse or shirt is tucked in, and everything else is in order before standing up to speak.

9. **Avoid food and drink that make speaking difficult for you.** Caffeinated drinks and sugary foods can make you jittery, which will only add to your nervousness. If you find that you need to clear your throat often after consuming certain foods or beverages, avoid them before speaking engagements.

10. **Practice, practice, practice.** The more presentations you give, the more you will feel confident while giving them. And one of the best ways to conquer stage fright is to spend time speaking in front of others. Recognize that your discomfort with public speaking is likely to fade with experience on the podium.

Sources: Adapted from Naomi Rockler-Gladen, "Fear of Public Speaking," January 12, 2007, http://collegeuniversity.suite101.com/article.cfm/fear_of_public_speaking, accessed March 15, 2007; "Presentation Tips for Public Speaking," A Research Guide for Students, http://www.aresearchguide.com/3tips.html, accessed March 15, 2007; and Kimberly L. McCall, "All That Jazz," *Entrepreneur,* Vol. 34, No. 1 (March 2006), p. 36.

Personal Time Management

A typical entrepreneur spends much of the working day on the front line—meeting customers, solving problems, listening to employee complaints, talking with suppliers, and the like. She or he tackles such problems with the assistance of only a small staff. As a result, the owner-manager's energies and activities are diffused, and time becomes a scarce resource.

{ 4 Describe the problem of time pressure and suggest solutions.

The Problem of Time Pressure

The hours worked by most new business owners are particularly long. Many owner-managers in small firms work from 60 to 80 hours per week. A frequent and unfortunate result of such a schedule is inefficient work performance. Owner-managers may be too busy to see sales representatives who could supply market information on new products and processes, too busy to read technical or trade literature that would tell them what others are doing and what improvements might be adapted to their own use, too busy to listen carefully to employees' opinions and grievances, and too busy to give employees the instructions they need to do their jobs correctly.

Getting away for a vacation seems impossible for some small business owners. In extremely small firms, owners may find it necessary to close the business during their absence. Even in somewhat larger businesses, owners may fear that the firm will not function properly if they are not there. Unfortunately, keeping one's nose to the grindstone in this way may cost an entrepreneur dearly in terms of personal health, family relationships, and effectiveness in business leadership.

Time Savers for Busy Managers

Part of the solution to the problem of time pressure is application of the managerial approaches discussed in the preceding section. For example, when possible, the manager should assign duties to subordinates who can work without close supervision. For such delegation to work, though, a manager must first select and train qualified employees.

The greatest time saver is the effective use of time. Little will be accomplished if an individual flits from one task to another and back again. Use of modern technology, including cell phones, e-mail, and the Internet, can be very helpful in allowing a manager to make the most of his or her time. (A note of caution is in order: Because these tools can become a distraction—for example, checking and responding at length to incoming e-mail messages throughout the day can distract from the tasks at hand—they need to be used wisely.)

The first step in time management should be to analyze how much time is normally spent on various activities. Relying on general impressions is not only unprofessional but also unscientific and likely to involve error. For a period of several days or (preferably) weeks, the manager should record the amounts of time spent on various activities during the day. An analysis of these figures will reveal a pattern, indicating which projects and tasks consume the most time and which activities are responsible for wasted time. It will also reveal chronic time wasting due to excessive socializing, work on trivial matters, coffee breaks, and so on.

If your habits are typical, you will probably find that the workplace "time-wasters" in your life are similar to the 10 most common ones revealed in a survey of employees:[29]

1. Shifting priorities

2. Telephone interruptions

3. Lack of direction/objectives

4. Attempting too much

5. Drop-in visitors

6. Ineffective delegation

7. Cluttered desk/losing things

8. Procrastination/lack of self-discipline

9. Inability to say no

10. Meetings

Knowing the distractions that others find to be time-wasters may help you pinpoint those that are creating a problem for you. Only after recognizing these distractions can you take steps to deal with them.

After eliminating practices that waste time, a manager can carefully plan his or her use of available time. A planned approach to a day's or week's work is much more effective than a haphazard do-whatever-comes-up-first style. This is true even for small firm managers whose schedules are continually interrupted in unanticipated ways.

Many time management specialists recommend the use of a daily written plan of work activities, often called a "to-do" list. A recent survey of 2,000 executives from mostly small companies found that around 95 percent of them keep a list of things to do. Those executives may have 6 to 20 items on their list at any given time, though fewer than 1 percent of them complete all listed tasks on a daily basis.[30] Many entrepreneurs use Microsoft Outlook or a day planner to create and manage these lists, but others use PDAs, note cards, or even sticky notes. Regardless of the medium you choose, the method you use should highlight priorities among listed items. By classifying duties as first-, second-, or third-level priorities, you can identify and focus attention on the most crucial tasks.

There are countless guides to time management, and they offer many valuable tips: Get a time management system and use it, try to make meetings more efficient, work passionately, unsubscribe from magazines and catalogues you never read, create a file folder for active projects, keep your desk and office organized, and so on. However, the one bit of advice that seems to show up on just about every list of suggestions is to set aside time to work undisturbed.[31] As the pace of business and the flow of information pick up speed and new technologies and media channels increasingly compete for your attention, preserving time for focused work on important projects becomes more and more difficult—but it is critical that you do so. The health and future of your company may very well depend on it!

In the final analysis, effective time management requires self-discipline. An individual may begin with good intentions but lapse into habitually attending to whatever he or she finds to do at the moment. Procrastination is a frequent thief of time—many managers delay unpleasant and difficult tasks, retreating to trivial and less threatening activities with the rationalization that they are getting those duties out of the way in order to be able to concentrate better on the more important tasks.

Outside Management Assistance

5 Explain the various types of outside management assistance.

Because entrepreneurs tend to be better doers than they are managers, they should consider the use of outside management assistance. Such outside assistance can supplement the manager's personal knowledge and the expertise of the few staff specialists on the company's payroll.

The Need for Outside Assistance

Entrepreneurs often lack opportunities to share ideas with peers, given the small staff in most new enterprises. Consequently, they may experience a sense of loneliness. Some entrepreneurs reduce their feelings of isolation by joining groups such as the Entrepreneurs' Organization (http://www.eonetwork.org) and the Young Presidents' Organization (http://www.ypo.org), which allow them to meet with peers from other firms and share problems and experiences.[32]

By obtaining help from peer groups and other sources of outside managerial assistance, entrepreneurs can overcome some of their managerial deficiencies and ease their sense of loneliness. Outsiders can bring a detached, often objective point of view and new ideas. They may also possess knowledge of methods, approaches, and solutions beyond the experience of a particular entrepreneur.

Sources of Management Assistance

Entrepreneurs seeking management assistance can turn to any number of sources, including business incubators, SBA programs, and management consultants. Other approaches the entrepreneur can take to obtain management help include consulting public and university libraries, attending evening classes at local colleges, and considering the suggestions of friends and customers.

BUSINESS INCUBATORS   As discussed in Chapter 9, a business incubator is an organization that offers both space and managerial and clerical services to new businesses. There are now more than 1,100 incubators in the United States, and the number continues to grow.[33] Most of them involve the participation of government agencies and/or universities, although some have been launched as purely private endeavors. The primary motivation in establishing incubators has been a desire to encourage entrepreneurship and thereby contribute to economic development.

Often, individuals who wish to start businesses are deficient in pertinent knowledge and lacking in appropriate experience. In many cases, they need practical guidance in marketing, record keeping, management, and preparation of business plans. Business incubators offer new entrepreneurs on-site business expertise; the services available in an incubator are shown in Exhibit 18-6.

exhibit

18-6   *Services Provided by Business Incubators to New Firms*

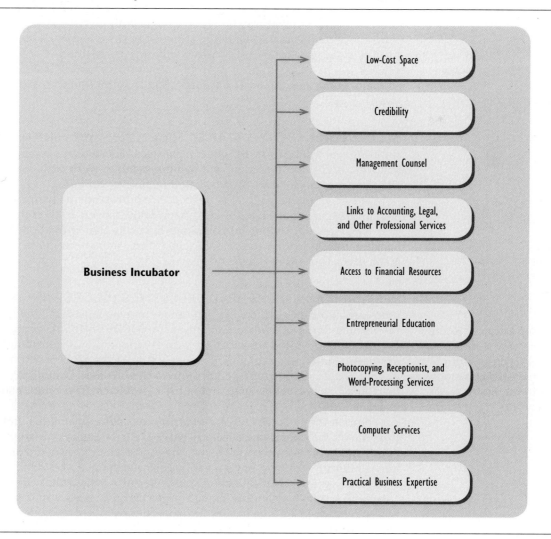

Business Incubator

- Low-Cost Space
- Credibility
- Management Counsel
- Links to Accounting, Legal, and Other Professional Services
- Access to Financial Resources
- Entrepreneurial Education
- Photocopying, Receptionist, and Word-Processing Services
- Computer Services
- Practical Business Expertise

An incubator provides a supportive atmosphere for a business during the early months of its existence, when it is most fragile and vulnerable to external dangers and internal errors. If the incubator works as it should, the fledgling business gains strength quickly and, within a year or so, leaves the incubator setting.

In 1985, when John Botti started AuthentiDate Holding Corp. to offer security software applications and other computer-related services, he wondered about the advantages of taking the company into an incubator sponsored by Rensselaer Polytechnic Institute. But looking back on the experience, he concludes, "I think there's a good chance we wouldn't be here if the incubator structure wasn't there." Getting in wasn't easy. Botti had to come up with an acceptable business plan before being accepted by the incubator, but that turned out to be a good thing. "It gave us a sense of legitimacy when we would have been just a couple of guys starting a business," Botti later realized. In other words, writing a business plan and getting accepted by the incubator provided a sense that the company was "doing something real."[34] And, of course, being "real" is key to obtaining capital, attracting high-quality managers, persuading customers to purchase from you, and otherwise positioning your company for success.

Today, some incubators in the United States are reinventing themselves as "virtual incubators"—that is, they no longer require client companies to set up shop at a single location. Instead, these organizations focus on connecting a greater number of entrepreneurs with the high-quality experts and mentors they need. Because this model is less expensive to operate, the cost savings can be passed on to the entrepreneurs. This kind of arrangement has worked out very well for entrepreneurs like Christie Stone, co-founder of Ticobeans, a New Orleans–based coffee distributor. She needed help executing her business plan, but relocating to an incubator was out of the question—she wanted an office near a warehouse where her beans could be stored. Eventually, she joined a virtual incubator called Idea Village, without having to move. The team of lawyers, accountants, and salespeople assigned to the company helped her get off to a very solid start, at very little cost. It was a win–win proposition. Ticobeans received around $30,000 worth of legal and consulting services for only $3,000, from lawyers and accountants who saw the assistance as a way to build their networks.[35] Everyone walked away happy!

STUDENT CONSULTING TEAMS   Many colleges and universities have student consulting teams willing to assist small businesses. These teams of upper-class and graduate students, under the direction of a faculty member, work with owners of small firms in analyzing and devising solutions to their business problems.

The program has mutual benefits: It provides students with a practical view of business management and supplies small firms with answers to their problems. The students who participate are typically combined in teams that provide a diversity of academic backgrounds. Individual teams, for example, may include students specializing in management, marketing, accounting, and finance.

SERVICE CORPS OF RETIRED EXECUTIVES (SCORE)   By contacting any SBA field office, small business managers can obtain free management advice from a group called the **Service Corps of Retired Executives**, or **SCORE** (http://www.score.org). SCORE is an organization of retired business executives who serve as consultants to small business managers. Functioning under the sponsorship of the SBA, SCORE provides an opportunity for retired executives to contribute to the business community and, in the process, help small business managers solve their problems. The relationship is thus mutually beneficial.

Stories abound of SCORE's successfully assisting small firms. Judson Lovering, an entrepreneur who operated a specialty bakery in New England, wished to improve his business.[36] A SCORE business counselor, who had formerly owned a small business, helped him capitalize on the bakery's most popular products and eliminate low-profit offerings. This required Lovering to decline some specialty orders that had made the business a "personal bakery" without adequate profit margins. As a result of the advice Lovering received from SCORE, the bakery has consistently shown growth.

Service Corps of Retired Executives (SCORE)
An SBA-sponsored group of retired executives who give free advice to small businesses

SMALL BUSINESS DEVELOPMENT CENTERS (SBDCs) Small business development centers (SBDCs), which are patterned after the Agricultural Extension Service, are affiliated with colleges or universities as a part of the SBA's overall program of assistance to small business. SBDCs provide direct consultation, continuing education, research assistance, and export services. One of their special priorities is to lend support to minority-owned firms. The staff typically includes faculty members, SCORE counselors, professional staff, and graduate student assistants.

MANAGEMENT CONSULTANTS Management consultants serve small businesses as well as large corporations. Types of consultants range from large global firms to one- and two-person operations. Small firm managers, however, are often reluctant to use outside advisors, for a host of reasons. For example, some believe that they can solve problems themselves, that an outsider could never truly understand the business, or that bringing in an outside advisor would simply cost too much.

But some small businesses need analysis by consultants—especially companies that have paid very little attention to their productivity. When Mario Arcari and Gregory Goldfarb started Hi-Tech Manufacturing in Schiller Park, Illinois, they were "just two guys and a shop making machine parts," as Arcari put it.[37] The business grew, but there were problems.

> Orders were processed on the fly. About 1% of all product material was left over as "scrap" and dumped or paid for out of Hi-Tech's pocket, costing thousands every year. There were no procedures to handle customer complaints. Machines went for months without maintenance checks. Imperfect parts—too long or short by fractions of an inch—were often shipped. Companies like Lockheed-Martin refused to talk to Hi-Tech until it had a quality-control program.[38]

By obtaining consulting help from the nonprofit Chicago Manufacturing Center, these entrepreneurs were able to eliminate many wasteful practices, reduce scrap, and increase customer satisfaction. The $15,000 consulting fee was easily recovered in the revenue resulting from the firm's improved performance.

To ensure client–provider satisfaction, the owner and the consultant should reach an understanding on the nature of the assistance to be provided before it begins. Any consulting fees should be specified, and the particulars of the agreement should be put in writing. Fees are often quoted on a per-day basis and might easily range from $500 to $5,000 or more. Although the cost may seem high, it must be evaluated in terms of the expertise that it buys.

Directories are available to help entrepreneurs find the right management consultant. One such directory is published by the Institute of Management Consultants USA, 2025 M Street NW, Suite 800, Washington, DC 20036-3309 (http://www.imcusa.org). The code of ethics to which institute members subscribe is an indication of their desire to foster professionalism in their work.

ENTREPRENEURIAL NETWORKS Entrepreneurs can also gain management assistance from peers through **networking**, the process of developing and engaging in mutually beneficial informal relationships. As business owners meet other business owners, they discover a commonality of interests that leads to an exchange of ideas and experiences. The settings for such meetings may be trade associations, civic clubs, fraternal organizations, or any other situation that brings businesspeople into contact with one another. Of course, the personal network of an entrepreneur is not limited to other entrepreneurs, but those individuals may be the most significant part of his or her network.

In 1998, Vaneese Johnson used $10,000 of personal savings to establish On the Move Staffing, a San Francisco–based full-service staffing firm, in her home. Johnson networked with city officials and local business leaders, and within months she landed her first deal with a major client: a $60,000 contract with Major League Baseball's San Francisco Giants for employees to run concession stands, clean the facilities, and so on. As the business grew, Johnson needed additional and more professional space in which to interview people and conduct business. Once again using networking, she found the Renaissance Entrepreneurship Center, a nonprofit organization that provides support services

small business development centers (SBDCs)
University-affiliated centers offering consulting, education, and other support to small businesses

networking
The process of developing and engaging in mutually beneficial relationships

Living the Dream

entrepreneurial challenges

A Healthy Social Life Pays Off

A fraternity or sorority can be a great place to meet people, but have you ever thought about the networking you can do there—or in any other social organization, for that matter? In 2004, Ryan Bonifacino used his Pi Kappa Alpha connections to launch a company dedicated to special event and corporate photography. Today, his New York City–based business has a new name, Bozmedia, and has expanded to offer digital media services, brand management, and Internet marketing and advertising. The company's website defines the flashy image Bonifacino and his management team hope to project: "Welcome to a place where the right and left brain work in concert. Where outside the box is a fixed position, where the words 'hopefully, maybe, try, and if' are omitted from our vocabulary and maximum success for the client is our only goal."

Bonifacino was a founding member of his fraternity at the University of Delaware, and his experience there offered a real foothold in the world of business. "Our main investor was actually one of our sponsors for a fraternity philanthropic event," says the 22-year-old entrepreneur. "He loved the plan, the fraternity, and our energy."

Harnessing a fraternity or sorority network can give a tremendous boost to the launch of a new business. For example, your fraternity brothers or sorority sisters could be used as a focus group to assess your ideas or serve as a PR team to spread news of your product or service across campus. They may even become loyal and effective business partners, if the fit is right. And if they connect you to alumni, you may find just the professionals you are looking for to take care of your legal, banking, accounting, or other needs.

Bonifacino's relationship with his fraternity has been a real help. His first gigs were at Greek events, and he estimates that he "must have given out thousands of business cards at fraternity functions alone." The results speak for themselves. Bonifacino graduated in 2005; Bozmedia's sales for 2006 were around $460,000, and the growth continues. He has already pulled together a strong nine-person management team. It seems that it sometimes pays just to hang out!

Sources: http://www.bozmedia.com/about.html, accessed March 20, 2007; Nichole L. Torres, "Family Ties," *Entrepreneur,* Vol. 34, No. 10 (September 2006), pp. 132–133; and personal communication with Ryan Bonifacino, co-founder and CEO of Bozmedia, May 2, 2007.

http://www.bozmedia.com

for microbusinesses. For $150 per month, she obtained use of 100 square feet of space, fax and copy machines, a mailbox, and a receptionist, as well as consulting services as needed. Networking not only got the business started but also helped increase revenues from $35,000 in the first year to $1.2 million just a few years later.[39]

OTHER BUSINESS AND PROFESSIONAL SERVICES   A variety of business and professional groups provide management assistance. In many cases, such assistance is part of the business relationship. Sources of management advice include bankers, certified public accountants, attorneys, insurance agents, suppliers, trade associations, and chambers of commerce.

It takes initiative to draw on the management assistance available from such groups. For example, rather than limiting his or her business relationship with a certified public accountant (CPA) to audits and financial statements, the owner-manager must think to ask the CPA to advise on a much broader range of subjects.

A good accountant can not only offer advice on tax matters, but also recommend an appropriate severance package when it comes time to fire someone. If you are thinking about opening a new branch, an accountant can tell you if your cash flow will support it. Thinking about launching an additional business? An accountant's insight will help you determine whether the margins will be adequate. Accountants can help you make informed assessments of your insurance needs, the impact of taking on a big account (as well as the downside of losing it), and the bottom-line effects of cutting expenses.

As you can see from these examples, potential management assistance often comes disguised as service from professionals and firms encountered in the normal course of business activity. By taking advantage of such opportunities, an entrepreneur can strengthen a small firm's management and improve its operations with little, if any, additional cost.

Looking BACK

1 Discuss the entrepreneur's leadership role.

- Entrepreneurs must establish and communicate a vision of the firm's future.
- Founding entrepreneurs need a tolerance for ambiguity and a capacity for adaptation.
- Entrepreneurs need resolve to make the business succeed more than they need a flashy personality.
- An entrepreneur exerts strong personal influence in a small firm.
- Progressive managers use various leadership styles, incorporating participative management, empowerment, and work teams.
- Entrepreneurs should deliberately shape the organizational culture, which can greatly influence how business is conducted in the company and how the company performs.

2 Explain the distinctive features of small firm management.

- Founders tend to be more action-oriented and less analytical than professional managers.
- A founder's less-than-professional management style can adversely affect business growth.
- Small companies are particularly vulnerable to managerial inefficiency, and even failure.

- Small firm managers face special financial and personnel constraints.
- As a new business grows, it adds layers of supervision and increases formality of management.
- A firm's growth requires the entrepreneur to become more of a manager and less of a doer.

3 Identify the managerial tasks of entrepreneurs.

- Both long-range planning and short-range planning are required, but they are often postponed or neglected.
- Managers must create an organizational structure to provide for orderly direction of operations.
- Informal groups within the organization can be encouraged to make a beneficial contribution to the firm.
- Managers who delegate authority successfully can devote more time to more important duties.
- Managers exercise control by monitoring operations in order to detect and correct deviations from plans.
- Effective two-way communication is important in building a healthy organization.
- Managers must be able to negotiate with both insiders and outsiders.

4 Describe the problem of time pressure and suggest solutions.

- Time pressure creates inefficiencies in the management of a small firm because the entrepreneur's energies are diffused.

- A manager can reduce time pressure through such practices as eliminating wasteful activities and planning work carefully, using such tools as a "to-do" list.

- The greatest time saver is the effective use of time, which requires self-discipline.

5 Explain the various types of outside management assistance.

- Outside management assistance can be used to remedy staff limitations and reduce an entrepreneur's sense of isolation, among other things.

- Business incubators provide guidance as well as space for beginning businesses.

- Three government- and/or university-sponsored sources of assistance are student consulting teams, the Service Corps of Retired Executives (SCORE), and small business development centers (SBDCs).

- Management assistance may be obtained by engaging management consultants and by networking with other entrepreneurs.

- Professionals such as bankers and CPAs can also provide valuable management assistance.

Key TERMS

empowerment, p. 476

work teams, p. 476

professional manager, p. 478

long-range plan (strategic plan), p. 482

short-range plan, p. 482

budget, p. 482

chain of command, p. 483

line organization, p. 483

line-and-staff organization, p. 483

span of control, p. 484

delegation of authority, p. 484

negotiation, p. 487

Service Corps of Retired Executives (SCORE), p. 492

small business development centers (SBDCs), p. 493

networking, p. 493

Discussion QUESTIONS

1. Would most employees of small firms welcome or resist a leadership approach that sought their ideas and involved them in meetings to let them know what was going on? Why might some employees resist such an approach?

2. Is the quality of management likely to be relatively uniform in all types of small businesses? If not, what might account for differences?

3. What are the four stages of small business growth outlined in this chapter? How do management requirements change as the firm moves through these stages?

4. Some professional football coaches have written game plans that they consult from time to time during games. If coaches need formal plans, does it follow that small business owners also need them as they engage in their particular type of competition? Why or why not?

5. What type of small firm might effectively use a line organization? When might it be necessary to change the firm's structure? To what type of structure? Why?

6. Explain the relationship between planning and control in a small business. Give an example.

7. There is a saying that goes "What you do speaks so loudly I can't hear what you say." What does this mean, and how does it apply to communication in small firms?

8. What practices can a small business manager use to conserve time?

9. What are some advantages and possible drawbacks for a startup retail firm of locating in a business incubator?

10. Are student consulting teams of greater benefit to the client firm or to the students involved?

You Make the CALL

SITUATION 1

In one small firm, the owner-manager and his management team use various methods to delegate decision making to employees at the operating level. New employees are trained thoroughly when they begin, but no supervisor monitors their work closely once they have learned their duties. Of course, help is available as needed, but no one is there on an hour-to-hour basis to make sure that employees are functioning as needed and that they are avoiding mistakes.

Occasionally, all managers and supervisors leave for a day-long meeting and allow the operating employees to run the business by themselves. Job assignments are defined rather loosely. Management expects employees to assume responsibility and to take necessary action whenever they see that something needs to be done. When employees ask for direction, they are sometimes simply told to solve the problem in whatever way they think best.

Question 1 Is such a loosely organized firm likely to be as effective as a firm that defines jobs more precisely and monitors performance more closely? What are the advantages and the limitations of the managerial style described above?

Question 2 How might such managerial methods affect morale?

Question 3 Would you like to work for this company? Why or why not?

SITUATION 2

A few years after successfully launching a new business, an entrepreneur found himself spending 16-hour days running from one appointment to another, negotiating with customers, drumming up new business, signing checks, and checking up as much as possible on his six employees. The founder realized that his own strength was in selling, but general managerial responsibilities were very time consuming and interfered with his sales efforts. He even slept in the office two nights a week.

Despite his hard work, however, he knew that employees weren't organized and that many problems existed. He lacked the time to set personnel policies or to draw up job descriptions for his six employees. One employee even took advantage of the laxity in supervision to skip work sometimes. Invoices were sent to customers late, and delivery schedules were sometimes missed. Fortunately, the business was profitable in spite of the numerous problems.

Question 1 Is this founder's problem one of time management or general managerial ability? Would it be feasible to engage a management consultant to help solve the firm's problems?

Question 2 If this founder asked you to recommend some type of outside management assistance, would you recommend a SCORE counselor, a student consulting team, a CPA firm, a management consultant, or some other type of assistance? Why?

Question 3 If you were asked to improve this firm's management system, what would be the first steps you would take? What would be your initial goal?

SITUATION 3

After a slow start in a spare bedroom in his home, an entrepreneur's business flourished. He wondered if he had the necessary talent to ensure its continued success. The business had grown to 100 employees and then to 200 employees. When the business was small, the entrepreneur could figure out the solutions to problems on a case-by-case basis, but the problems were becoming increasingly complicated.

Question 1 What kinds of practices or procedures will this entrepreneur need to adopt to enable the business to continue to operate successfully?

Question 2 What resources might this entrepreneur use to get good feedback to help him assess his competence and understand the issues his growing business is facing?

Experiential EXERCISES

1. Interview a management consultant, SCORE member, university director of student consulting teams, or representative of a CPA firm to discuss small business management weaknesses and the willingness or reluctance of small firms to use consultants. Prepare a report on your findings.

2. Diagram the organizational relationships in a small business of your choice. Report on any organizational problems that are apparent to you or that are recognized by the manager or others in the firm.

3. Prepare a report on your personal observations of leadership and delegation of authority by a supervisor in an organization where you have been an employee or volunteer. Include references to the type(s) of leadership exercised and the adequacy of authority delegation (if any), clarity of instructions, and any problems involved.

4. Select an unstructured time block of one to four hours in your schedule—that is, hours that are not regularly devoted to class attendance, sleeping, and so on. Carefully record your use of that time period for several days. Prepare a report summarizing your use of the time and outlining a plan to use it more effectively.

Exploring the WEB

1. Go to *Inc.* magazine's website at **http://www.inc.com** and follow these links: "How-To Guides," then "Leadership and Strategy."

   a. Read three articles, and make note of their titles and authors.

   b. What suggestions from these articles would you implement in your small business and why?

2. Calculate the cost of your time. Go to **http://businessknowhow.com/manage/timecalc2.htm** and answer the questions you find there. What is the cost of your time for a five-minute interruption? Do the results surprise you?

3. Two influential and informative online resources for small businesses and entrepreneurs are provided by SCORE ("Counselors to America's Small Business") and the SBDC. Explore the SCORE (**http://www.score.org/**) and SBDC (**http://www.sba.gov/sbdc/**) websites.

   a. What resources on the SCORE website do you like the most, and how would you utilize them?

   b. What SBDC resources do you like the most, and how would you utilize them?

Case **18**

Douglas Electrical Supply, Inc. (p. 656)

An outside trainer-consultant encounters quality issues that touch on leadership and integrity.

Alternative Cases for Chapter 18:

chapter 19

Managing Human Resources

In the SPOTLIGHT

Manhattan Feather Dusters Inc.

What do dancers, artists, actors, costume designers, and even a documentary film writer have in common? They all work for a commercial and residential cleaning service: Manhattan Feather Dusters Inc.

Everet H. Goldberg founded the business in 1988, and he concluded long ago that the secret to the success of his small business lies in the talents of its employees. "People in the arts make excellent cleaners," says Goldberg. "They approach everything they do with gusto, and they have a unique understanding of aesthetics and attention to detail." Not only do they bring their creativity to the job; they also tend not to break things because they recognize the value of keepsakes and valuables. Such employees really are a good fit for Manhattan Feather Dusters.

Finding the right employees for your business is critical, but keeping them is just as important. Once Goldberg figured out that entertainers made good cleaners, he had to find a way to hire them and then to keep them from quitting. Hiring them was easy because many entertainers are always looking for work. To retain these multi-talented employees, Goldberg himself had to be creative—and very flexible. It makes sense that artistic endeavors should take priority, so the company adapts to rehearsal schedules and travel commitments by allowing employees to complete their work when they can.

Every business is different, but the "people factor" cannot be ignored if success is the goal. Goldberg understands this and knows how to find the employees his company needs. After that, it's just a matter of "care and feeding" for those hired. In the big picture, it really is that simple.

© Larry Ford/Ford Photography

Sources: Laura S. Green, "Taking a Break from Creativity to Clean," *Downtown Express,* http://www.zwire.com/site/news.cfm?BRD51841&dept_id=505432&newsid=7660751&PAG=461&rfi=9, accessed April 11, 2007; and Sara Wilson, "Off Broadway," *Entrepreneur,* Vol. 34, No. 4 (April 2006), p. 89.

After studying this chapter, you should be able to

1 Explain the importance of employee recruitment and list some sources that can be useful in finding suitable applicants.
2 Identify the steps to take in evaluating job applicants.
3 Describe the roles of training and development for both managerial and nonmanagerial employees in a small business.
4 Explain the various types of compensation plans, including the use of incentive plans.
5 Discuss the human resource issues of employee leasing, legal protection, labor unions, and the formalizing of employer–employee relationships.

A recent Google search on the phrase "Our people make the difference!" generated nearly 63,000 hits! It's certainly true that good businesses require good people, but is this the way most companies think about their employees or is it just a time-worn, feel-good cliché? Any entrepreneur who wants to build a competitive business needs to think carefully about how to find and hire the best people available and then consider how to hold onto them. Honest, competent, motivated employees are a critical resource for any business; therefore, it is vital that entrepreneurs manage employees competently and efficiently.

Many of the human resource management (HRM) practices of giant corporations like Wal-Mart and General Motors will not work for small businesses. However, they can, and should, use personnel management methods that are suitable for smaller firms. Sadly, many small companies follow what is, at best, a haphazard HRM program, choosing to "shoot from the hip" on personnel management decisions, only to miss their employment targets entirely in many cases. Research has shown that, compared to large firms, small businesses are much less likely to use professional HRM practices related to recruitment, training, performance assessment, and other processes.[1] This regrettable state of affairs may be the result of a lack of knowledge; we hope to prevent it from hampering your business. The goal of this chapter is to present HRM practices that work best for entrepreneurial firms.

Recruiting Personnel

Recruitment brings applicants to a business; the goal is to obtain a pool of applicants large enough to contain a number of talented prospects. In a subsequent stage of the selection process, management decides which applicants are "keepers."

1 Explain the importance of employee recruitment and list some sources that can be useful in finding suitable applicants.

The Need for Quality Employees

In his classic study of good-to-great companies (companies that advanced from being really good to become truly great), Jim Collins found that the great companies first "got the right people on the bus."

The executives who ignited the transformations from good to great did not first figure out where to drive the bus and then get people to take it there. No, they first got the right people on the bus (and the wrong people off the bus) and then figured out where to drive it. They

How They See It: Character Trait Most Valued

Scott Salmans

I was once asked by a dear friend, "What character trait do you consider most valuable when hiring your people?" After several frustrating and difficult experiences with dishonest, untrustworthy people, I quickly answered, "Honesty." My entrepreneurial friend, in turn, stated that creativity was the character trait he most valued in a small growing business. It wasn't long after that discussion that he had to admit that the creativity trait might not have been so valuable in places of key trust, since his CEO and CFO had worked together to bilk him out of thousands of dollars over a period of years.

It is my belief that, when building a company, honesty and trustworthiness are the most important characteristics of key associates, assuming that the candidates under consideration have the basic required skill set. Using multiple interviews over time and letting the person talk in formal and informal settings is one helpful technique to better understand your potential business associate.

said, in essence, "Look, I don't really know where we should take this bus. But I know this much: If we get the right people on the bus, the right people in the right seats, and the wrong people off the bus, then we'll figure out how to take it someplace great."[2]

This reasoning is particularly relevant to personnel in key positions, as the right people in the right places provide a strong foundation for any business. In a broad sense, this concept is applicable to all employees, in view of their direct and indirect impact on business success.

Employees affect profitability in many ways. In most small firms, salespeople's attitudes and their ability to serve customer needs directly affect sales revenue. Also, payroll is one of the largest expense categories for most businesses, having a direct impact on the bottom line. By recruiting the best possible personnel, a firm can improve its return on each payroll dollar.

Recruitment and selection of employees establish a foundation for a firm's ongoing human relationships. In a sense, the quality of a firm's employees determines its potential. A solid, effective organization can be built only with a talented, ambitious workforce.

The Lure of Entrepreneurial Firms

Competing for well-qualified business talent requires small firms to identify their distinctive advantages, especially when recruiting outstanding prospects for managerial and professional positions. Fortunately, there are many good reasons to work for an entrepreneurial business. This is especially true of growing enterprises led by individuals or teams with a compelling vision of a desirable and attainable future. It is exciting to work for a company that is going somewhere!

The work itself can also attract talented prospects. The opportunity to make decisions and to obtain general management or professional experience at a significant level is appealing to many individuals. Rather than toiling in obscure, low-level, specialized positions during their early years, capable newcomers can quickly move into positions of responsibility in a well-managed small business. In such positions, they can see the fruits of their labor and how they make a difference in the success of the company.

Small firms can structure the work environment to offer professional, managerial, and technical personnel greater freedom than they would normally have in a larger business. In this type of environment, individual contributions can be recognized rather than hidden under numerous layers of bureaucracy. In addition, compensation packages can be designed to create powerful incentives. Flexibility in work scheduling and job-sharing arrangements are other potential advantages.

For a business called THQ Inc., attracting bright and capable people is the name of the game . . . literally! The company started in 1990 with several dozen employees and has proven itself a tough competitor in the video game market. THQ uses its small size as a selling point. According to CEO Brian Farrell, "We let people know, 'You'll be a big fish in a somewhat smaller pond here at THQ.'"[3] And this approach is definitely working—attracting brilliant game developers has been one of the firm's secret weapons. These high-potential employees are lured with a combination of creative freedom and financial incentives. They get to share in the firm's successes, because anyone who designs a great game at THQ is noticed and given greater responsibility. And their jobs are structured in such a way that they can avoid the drudgery of bureaucratic or otherwise unpleasant tasks they might have to endure at other businesses. Even though THQ is not the largest player in the industry, its success has not escaped the notice of competitors. When it comes to video games, THQ is definitely a force to be reckoned with.[4]

Sources of Employees

To recruit effectively, the small business manager must know where and how to find qualified applicants. Sources are numerous, and it is impossible to generalize about the best source in view of the differences in companies' personnel needs and the quality of the sources from one locality to another. The following discussion describes some sources of employees most popular among small firms.

HELP-WANTED ADVERTISING   Hanging a "Help Wanted" sign in the window is one traditional form of recruiting used by some small firms. A similar but more aggressive form of recruiting consists of advertising in the classifieds section of local newspapers. For some technical, professional, and managerial positions, firms may advertise in trade and professional journals. Although the effectiveness of help-wanted advertising has been questioned by some, many small businesses recruit in this way.

WALK-INS   A firm may receive unsolicited applications from individuals who walk into the place of business to seek employment. Walk-ins are an inexpensive source of personnel, particularly for hourly work, but the quality of applicants varies. If qualified applicants cannot be hired immediately, their applications should be kept on file for future reference. In the interest of good community relations, all applicants should be treated courteously, whether or not they are offered jobs.

SCHOOLS   Secondary schools, trade schools, colleges, and universities are desirable sources of personnel for certain positions, particularly those requiring no specific work experience. Some secondary schools and colleges have internship programs that enable students to gain practical experience in business firms. Applicants from secondary and trade schools often have useful educational backgrounds to offer a small business. Colleges and universities can supply candidates for positions in management and in various technical and professional fields. In addition, many colleges are excellent sources of part-time employees.

PUBLIC EMPLOYMENT OFFICES   At no cost to small businesses, employment offices in each state offer information on applicants who are actively seeking employment and administer the state's unemployment insurance program. These offices, located in all major cities, are for the most part a useful source of clerical workers, unskilled laborers, production workers, and technicians. They do not actively recruit but only counsel and assist those who come in. Although public employment offices can be a source of good employees, the individuals they work with are, for the most part, untrained or only marginally qualified.

PRIVATE EMPLOYMENT AGENCIES   Numerous private firms offer their services as employment agencies. In some cases, employers receive these services without cost because the applicants pay a fee to the agency; however, more often, the hiring firms are responsible for the agency fee. Private employment agencies tend to specialize in people with specific skills, such as accountants, computer operators, and managers.

EXECUTIVE SEARCH FIRMS   When filling key positions, small firms sometimes turn to executive search firms, often called **headhunters**, to locate qualified candidates. The key positions for which such firms seek applicants are those paying a minimum of $50,000

headhunter
A search firm that locates qualified candidates for executive positions

to $70,000 per year. The cost to the employer may run from 30 to 40 percent of the first year's salary. Because of the high cost, use of headhunters may seem unreasonable for small, entrepreneurial firms. At times, however, the need for a manager who can help a firm "move to the next level" justifies the use of an executive search firm. A headhunter is usually better able than the small firm to conduct a wide-ranging search for individuals who possess the right combination of talents for the available position.

EMPLOYEE REFERRALS   If current employees are good employees, their recommendations of suitable candidates may provide excellent prospects. Ordinarily, employees will hesitate to recommend applicants unless they believe in their ability to do the job. Many small business owners say that this source accounts for more new hires than any other. A few employers go so far as to offer financial rewards for employee referrals that result in the hiring of new employees.

John Boyce of Janitron, a small cleaning-service company in St. Louis, found it difficult to recruit relatively unskilled workers.[5] When he offered a $100 referral bonus to his building managers and supervisors, however, he soon found 47 entry-level employees for his 225-employee company. (The bonus is not paid unless the new employee stays for at least 90 days.)

INTERNET RECRUITING   Recruiters are increasingly seeking applicants via the Internet. A variety of websites, such as http://www.careerbuilder.com, http://www.monster.com, and http://www.hotjobs.com, allow applicants to submit their résumés and permit potential employers to search those résumés for qualified applicants. And as the Internet is becoming more and more popular as a source of applicants, many firms are posting job openings on their own websites.

TEMPORARY HELP AGENCIES   The temporary help industry, which is growing rapidly, supplies employees (or temps)—such as word processors, clerks, accountants, engineers, nurses, and sales clerks—for short periods of time. By using an agency such as Kelly Services or Manpower Inc., small firms can deal with seasonal fluctuations and absences caused by vacation or illness. For example, a temporary replacement might be obtained to fill the position of an employee who is taking leave following the birth of a child—a type of family leave now mandated by law for some employees. In addition, the use of temporary employees provides management with an introduction to individuals whose performance may justify an offer of permanent employment. Staffing with temporary employees is less practical when extensive training is required or continuity is important.

Diversity in the Workforce

Over time, the composition of the workforce has changed with respect to race, ethnicity, gender, and age. In 1990, for example, 76 percent of the workforce was White; by 2000, only 69 percent was White.[6] Much of this change can be attributed to the growing proportion of Hispanic workers. The balance is shifting rapidly toward greater **workforce diversity**, not only because of increased participation of racial minorities but also because of higher proportions of women and older workers entering the labor force.

workforce diversity
Differences among employees in such dimensions as gender, age, ethnicity, and race

The challenge for human resource management is to adapt to a more diverse pool of potential employees. To remain fully competitive, business owners need to step up recruitment of women and minorities and be open to innovative ways to access the available pool of applicants. When Dick Snow found it difficult to recruit American teenagers for summer work at his six East Coast Ben and Jerry's ice cream stores, his solution was to hire 12 British ice cream scoopers through the British Universities North American Club.[7] These workers were just what Snow needed.

Other small businesses have tapped immigrants as a source of workers. In fact, small companies are more likely to employ immigrants than larger firms. Approximately 17 percent of small company workers are immigrants (citizens and noncitizens), which works out to nearly one out of every five employees. Of the nearly 20 million immigrants employed in the United States, around two-thirds work for small companies—about 3.3 million of these in companies with fewer than 10 employees.[8] Though we strongly discourage entrepreneurs from hiring illegal or undocumented workers, it is important

Living the Dream   entrepreneurial challenges

Some Great and Some Not-Quite-So-Great Ideas for Recruitment

A company that can't recruit good employees will find it very difficult to stay in business for long, but there are many strategies for locating the people you need.

Safilo USA has been in business for more than 70 years and is a leader in the eyewear industry, an accomplishment that would be impossible without great employees. Robin Kreitner, director of human resources, says recruitment at the firm works best when current employees refer other people for jobs. To encourage this, the company offers cash bonuses—$500 if the new hire stays for six months and another $500 after a year. If $500 would be a budget-buster for your company, adjust the figure down; you are likely to end up with the same results.

To achieve its goal of delighting its customers by providing superior construction services, Kay Construction uses a team approach, which wouldn't be possible without high-quality staff. The principals of the company, Lorraine Kay and Steve Walsh, believe that it is necessary to support the local education system to "build a reservoir of appropriately trained and motivated employees." So they work with nearby colleges to fine-tune courses offered to project management, engineering, and architecture students. By hiring some of the students as interns, the company gets inexpensive part-time help for the present and the inside track on offering them full-time positions after they graduate.

Some small businesses like to use online employee recruiting services, but this can be risky. Scott Wheeler founded a diesel engine repair company in Chesapeake, Virginia. Within five years, the business had doubled in size, reaching $10 million in sales and 44 employees. Wheeler was having trouble finding qualified mechanics to add to the rowdy mix of ex-French Foreign Legionnaires, bikers "with tattoos you wouldn't believe," and others who worked on engines for the company. So when an online service told him that it had 93 résumés for "generator technicians," Wheeler couldn't resist signing up. Unfortunately, the results were disappointing—very few of the candidates were even close to qualified. Wheeler's advice? "Don't give them your credit card number based on what they tell you. Make them send some sample résumés first."

Sources: http://kayconstruction.com/company.html, accessed April 11, 2007; http://www.opticiansma.org/sponsor-safilo.htm, accessed April 11, 2007; and Mark Henricks, "Search Party," *Entrepreneur,* Vol. 35, No. 2 (February 2007), p. 83.

© Digital Vision/Getty Images

http://www.kayconstruction.com

to cast the employment net as broadly as possible to find the best people available. By developing an awareness of the potential in various parts of the talent pool, small firms can improve the effectiveness of their recruitment methods.

Adapting to diversity is important not only because the workforce is becoming more diverse but also because diversity in itself can be a good thing, through the innovation it introduces to the workplace and the positive effect it has on problem solving. Researchers at Northwestern University recently studied the value of diversity by asking 50 groups of subjects to solve a murder mystery. Groups that included individuals from different social backgrounds were more likely to solve the case; homogeneous groups were both more often wrong and more confident that they were right.[9] Venture capitalists are very much aware of this phenomenon and thus are less likely to invest in a company where the management team more closely resembles the results of a cloning experiment than a group of individuals who bring unique perspectives to bear on business challenges. Evidence suggests that various forms of diversity (based on gender and ethnicity, as well as more subtle forms of variation related to personality, sensibility, work style, and the like) are beneficial, especially when innovation is important to a firm's competitiveness.

Job Descriptions

A small business manager should analyze the activities or work to be performed to determine the number and types of jobs to be filled. Knowing the job requirements permits more intelligent selection of applicants for specific jobs.

Certainly, an owner-manager should not select personnel simply to fit rigid specifications of education, experience, or personal background. Rather, he or she must concentrate on the overall ability of an individual to fill a particular position in the business. Making this determination requires an outline, or summary, of the work to be performed.

Duties listed in such job descriptions should not be defined too narrowly. It is important that job descriptions minimize overlap but also avoid creating a "that's not my job" mentality. Technical competence is as necessary in small firms as it is in large businesses, but versatility and flexibility may be even more important. Engineers may occasionally need to make sales calls, and marketing people may need to pinch-hit in production.

In the process of examining a job, an analyst should list the knowledge, skills, abilities, and other characteristics that an individual must have to perform the job. This statement of requirements is called a **job specification** and may be a part of the job description. A job specification for the position of stock clerk, for example, might state that the individual must be able to lift 50 pounds and must have completed 10 to 12 years of schooling.

job specification
A list of skills and abilities needed to perform a specific job

Job descriptions are very important human resource management tools, but only if they are taken seriously. There are sound legal reasons for developing great—not just good—job descriptions.[10] For example, if you do not specify important aspects of the job and how it is to be done *in detail,* the Americans with Disabilities Act presumes that an employee can go about the actual job duties in any way he or she wants to, regardless of company policy or what you think is the best and proper way of doing them. Also, the precise wording of a job description will determine whether an employee in that job is eligible for overtime pay, according to the new guidelines established by the U.S. Department of Labor.[11] Getting the job description right can avert serious legal hassles, saving you money and giving you one less worry when you go to bed at night!

While job descriptions are primarily an aid in personnel recruitment, they also have other practical uses. For example, they can bring focus to the work of employees, provide direction in training, and supply a framework to guide performance reviews.

Evaluating Prospects and Selecting Employees

2 Identify the steps to take in evaluating job applicants.

Recruitment activities identify prospects for employment. Additional steps are needed to evaluate these candidates and to extend job offers. To reduce the risk of taking an uninformed gamble on applicants of unknown quality, an employer can follow the steps below.

Step 1: Using Application Forms

By using an application form, an employer can collect enough information to determine whether a prospect is minimally qualified and provide a basis for further evaluation. Typically, an application asks for the applicant's name, address, Social Security number, educational history, employment history, and references.

Although an application form need not be lengthy or elaborate, it must be carefully written to avoid legal complications. In general, a prospective employer cannot seek information about sex, race, religion, color, national origin, age, or disabilities. The information requested should be focused on helping the employer make a better job-related assessment. For example, an employer is permitted to ask whether an applicant has graduated from high school. However, a question regarding the year the applicant graduated would be considered inappropriate, because the answer would reveal the applicant's age.

Step 2: Interviewing the Applicant

An interview permits the employer to get some idea of the applicant's appearance, job knowledge, intelligence, and personality. Any of these factors may be significant to the job to be filled. Although the interview can be a useful step in the selection process, it should not be the only step. Some managers have the mistaken idea that they are infallible judges of human nature and can choose good employees on the basis of interviews alone. Even when conducted with care, an interview can lead to false impressions. Applicants who interview well have a talent for quick responses and smooth talk, but this skill set may not be helpful when it comes to managing people and technology. The interview may reveal little about how well they work under pressure or when part of a team, what motivates them, and other important issues. In fact, research has shown that the typical job interview (unstructured and unfocused) is of limited value in predicting success on the job.[12]

In light of a growing concern regarding the value of interviews as they are typically used, many companies have adopted new methods that are variations on the interview theme. For example, some companies have found **behavioral interviews** to be much more predictive of a candidate's potential for success on the job. Jeffrey Pfeffer, a highly regarded management expert at Stanford University's Graduate School of Business, describes this form of interviewing as "asking people not so much about accomplishments but how they might react to hypothetical situations, how they spend their free time, and how they embody core values."[13] Though it can be a taxing process that may come across to the applicant as a barrage of challenging questions, the behavioral interview is designed to get a sense of the applicant's past performance and likely responses in future situations. The nature of the method makes bluffing difficult, and the focus is on facts rather than feelings, leading to a more accurate impression of what a person is *capable* of doing and what he or she is *likely* to do on the job.

behavioral interview
An interview approach that assesses the suitability of job candidates based on how they would respond to hypothetical situations

Susan Heathfield is a management consultant who specializes in human resource systems and knows a great deal about behavioral interviews. The management of one company she worked with was trying to hire a sales representative and decided on a set of questions that they thought would provide them with the insights they needed to make an informed hiring decision. To give you a sense of how the interview was structured, here are a few of the questions they asked:[14]

- Tell me about a time when you obtained a new customer through networking activities.

- Give me an example of a time when you obtained a customer through cold calling and prospecting. How did you approach the customer?

- What are your three most important work related values? Please provide an example of a situation in which you demonstrated each value at work.

- Your manufacturing facility shipped the wrong order to one of your important customers. Describe how you would solve this problem both internally and externally.

- Give me an example of a time when your integrity was tested and prevailed in a selling situation.

As you can see from these questions, the focus is on patterns of performance and behaviors in past situations similar to situations that are likely to come up in the job for which the applicant is being considered. Designing this emphasis into the interview process will lead to more effective hiring decisions.

Regardless of the interview method you choose, remember that serious legal consequences can result from a poorly conceived process. Just as in application forms, it is very important to avoid asking questions that conflict with the law. Some companies believe that applicants should be interviewed by two or more individuals in order to provide a witness to all interactions and to minimize bias and errors in judgment, but this is not always possible—and it certainly makes the process more expensive. In any case, careful process planning up front can prevent serious trouble in the future from discrimination lawsuits and poor employee selection.

Time spent in interviews, as well as in other phases of the selection process, can save the company time and money in the long run. In today's litigious society, firing an employee can be quite difficult and expensive. A dismissed employee may bring suit even when an employer had justifiable reasons for the dismissal.

It's important to remember that employment interviewing is actually a two-way process. The applicant is evaluating the employer while the employer is evaluating the applicant. In order for the applicant to make an informed decision, she or he needs a clear idea of what the job entails and an opportunity to ask questions.

Step 3: Checking References and Other Background Information

Careful checking with former employers, school authorities, and other references can help an employer avoid hiring mistakes. Suppose, for example, that you hired an appliance technician who later burglarized a customer's home. If you failed to check the applicant's background and she had a criminal record, your decision might be considered a negligent hiring decision. Trying to prevent such scenarios from arising is becoming more important as time goes on, since the number of negligent hiring lawsuits is on the rise.

It is becoming increasingly difficult to obtain more than the basic facts about a person's background from previous employers because of the potential for lawsuits brought by disappointed applicants. Although reference checks on a prior employment record do not constitute infringements on privacy, third parties are often reluctant to divulge negative information, which limits the practical usefulness of reference checking.

At the same time, gathering information online about an applicant's financial, criminal, and employment history has never been easier. While some employers conduct their own background checks by accessing databases that are readily available, most outsource this function to one of hundreds of vendors that specialize in performing this service. A number of companies advertise that they will provide *free* background checks over the Internet. This certainly sounds appealing. But, given the importance of the task, we suggest that you check with the Association of Professional Background Screeners at http://www.napbs.com before selecting a company for this purpose.

A few final cautions on background checks are in order. You should keep in mind that if a prospective employer requests a credit report to establish an applicant's employment eligibility, the Fair Credit Reporting Act requires that the applicant be notified in writing that such a report is being requested. But this is good practice, in general, when it comes to background checks. Most experts suggest that you require applicants to sign a written consent (detailing how and what you plan to check) before you conduct a check, to ensure legal compliance and to give the applicant the opportunity to withdraw from further consideration. If an applicant refuses to sign the consent form, it is legal for the company to decide against hiring him or her based on that refusal.[15]

Getting access to data is critical to making an informed hiring decision; however, you may be legally prevented from using some of the insights revealed to reject an applicant. One small business expert points out some of the things you can and cannot use: "Anything recent and relevant to job duties can legally be taken into account, but even a past felony conviction may be considered irrelevant if it was more than seven years ago."[16] Use gathered information with care!

Step 4: Testing the Applicant

Many kinds of jobs lend themselves to performance testing. For example, an applicant for a secretarial or clerical position may be given a standardized keyboarding or word-processing test. With a little ingenuity, employers can improvise practical tests that are clearly related to the job in question, and these can provide extremely useful insights for selection decisions.

In 2001, Marvis Nichols took over Computer Friends, Inc., a Pittsburgh business that provides information-technology services for small companies. When the recession made it difficult to find new business, she decided to hire a sales representative. She was impressed with one prospect, a woman experienced in selling technical services. But to be sure the candidate was right for the job, Nichols retained her for a one-time project—a networking event that was intended to produce sales leads. Nichols then took the prospective sales manager with her to follow-up meetings. This trial period showed Nichols that her initial impression of the prospective hire was totally wrong. Aghast at the prospect's bizarre combination of aggression and confusion, Nichols says, "At the end of the day, I felt it was a disaster."[17] If Nichols had hired the sales representative before those meetings, she would never have known about her jarring demeanor. A practical test averted a hiring disaster!

Psychological examinations may also be used by small businesses, but the results can be misleading because of difficulty in interpreting the tests or adapting them to a particular business. In addition, the U.S. Supreme Court has upheld the Equal Employment Opportunity Commission's requirement that any test used in making employment decisions must be job-related.

To be useful, tests of any kind must meet the criteria of **validity** and **reliability**. For a test to be valid, its results must correspond well with job performance; that is, the applicants with the best test scores must generally be the best employees. For a test to be reliable, it must provide consistent results when used at different times or by various individuals.

validity
The extent to which a test assesses true job performance ability

reliability
The consistency of a test in measuring job performance ability

Step 5: Requiring Physical Examinations

A primary purpose of physical examinations is to evaluate the ability of applicants to meet the physical demands of specific jobs. However, care must be taken to avoid discriminating against those who are physically disabled. The Americans with Disabilities Act requires companies with 15 or more employees to make "reasonable" adaptations to facilitate the employment of such individuals.

Although some small businesses require medical examinations before hiring an applicant, in most cases the company must first have offered that individual a job.[18] As

---

How They See It: Finding and Keeping Good Employees

Rick Davis

In the retail service industry, employees are your product, and they represent your brand. At DAVACO, we consider recruiting the best professionals we can find as a priority. Recruiting the best people is the single most important thing DAVACO can do. Not only do I make every effort to meet all employees before they are hired, but our human resources team also takes every measure to assure that we've recruited and selected the top candidate for every position to maximize their, and the company's, success. We incorporate practices into our recruiting efforts based on position, including telephone screening, face-to-face interviews, background checks, credit checks, drug screening, personality and behavior testing, skills assessment, and motor vehicle record check.

DAVACO recruits individuals with expertise that encompasses the various retail industry segments serviced, including specialty retail, drug stores, banking/financial, department stores, and convenience stores/restaurants. In addition to industry expertise,

the company also believes that strength of character is just as, if not more, important than skills. Skills can be taught, but ethics, loyalty, and high standards are inherent qualities.

We want employees to have a great career at DAVACO and encourage retention by offering a comprehensive benefits package, opportunities for professional growth in a fast-moving company, and the chance to work for some of the best-known brands in retail. DAVACO's corporate culture encourages hard work and a balanced personal/professional life. Employees are rewarded and recognized for their efforts.

DAVACO has an outstanding management team that not only understands the challenges of retail, but also can offer best practices from their knowledge in managing retail rollouts. With over 250 combined years of retail operations and branding experience, our management team understands what is important, why it is important, and what our clients are trying to achieve.

part of the physical examination process, the law permits drug screening of applicants. The National Federation of Independent Business recently conducted a poll of small businesses and found that 35 percent check a potential employee's background for drug and/or alcohol abuse, though very few actually require drug testing. Only 8 percent had asked one or more employees to take a drug and/or alcohol test in the previous three years, and most of those were random tests or requirements for a new hire.[19]

3 Describe the roles of training and development for both managerial and nonmanagerial employees in a small business.

Training and Developing Employees

Once an employee has been recruited and added to the payroll, the process of training and development must begin. The purpose of this process is to transform a new recruit into a well-trained technician, salesperson, manager, or other employee.

Purposes of Training and Development

One obvious purpose of training is to prepare a new recruit to perform the duties for which she or he has been hired. There are very few positions for which no training is required. If an employer fails to provide training, the new employee must learn by trial and error, which frequently wastes time, materials, and money—and sometimes alienates customers.

Training to improve skills and knowledge should not be limited to new hires; the performance of current employees can often be improved through additional training. In view of the constant change in products, technology, policies, and procedures in the world of business, continual training is necessary to update knowledge and skills—in firms of all sizes. Only with such training can employees meet the changing demands being placed on them.

Both employers and employees have a stake in the advancement of qualified personnel to higher level positions. Preparation for advancement usually involves developmental efforts, possibly of a different type than those needed to sharpen skills for current duties. Because personal development and advancement are prime concerns of able employees, a small business can profit from careful attention to this phase of the personnel program. Opportunities to grow and move up in an organization not only improve the morale of current employees but also serve as an inducement for potential applicants.[20]

Orientation for New Personnel

The development process begins with an individual's first two or three days on the job. It is at this point that the new employee tends to feel lost and confused, confronted with a new physical layout, a different job title, unknown fellow employees, a different type of supervision, changed hours or work schedule, and/or a unique set of personnel policies and procedures. Any events that conflict with the newcomer's expectations are interpreted in light of his or her previous work experience, and these interpretations can either foster a strong commitment to the new employer or lead to feelings of alienation.

Recognizing the new employee's sensitivity at this point, the employer can contribute to a positive outcome through proper orientation. Taking steps to help the newcomer adjust will minimize her or his uneasiness in the new setting.

Some phases of the orientation can be accomplished by informal methods. For example, a software company in San Mateo, California, uses bagels and muffins as a means of introducing newcomers to the rest of the staff. On the first morning of work for a new employee, a tray of breakfast food is strategically placed near her or his desk. An e-mail invites everyone to come by and get acquainted.

Other phases of the orientation must be structured or formalized. In addition to explaining specific job duties, supervisors should outline the firm's policies and procedures in as much detail as possible. A clear explanation of performance criteria and the way in which an employee's work will be evaluated should be included in the discussion. The new employee should be encouraged to ask questions, and time should be taken to provide careful answers. The firm may facilitate the orientation process by providing a written list of company practices and procedures in the form of an employee handbook. The handbook may include information about work hours, paydays, breaks, lunch hours, absences, holidays, overtime policy, employee benefits, and so on. Since new employees are faced with an information overload at first, a follow-up orientation after a week or two is suggested.

Training to Improve Quality

Employee training is an integral part of comprehensive quality management programs. Although quality management is concerned with machines, materials, and measurements, it also focuses on human performance.

Training programs can be designed to promote high-quality workmanship. The connection between effective quality management programs and employee training has been supported by a study of small manufacturing firms.[21]

Christian Kar, operator of Espresso Connection, an 11-store chain of drive-through coffee bars in Everett, Washington, found he was losing customers at the same time he was advertising for new ones. In an effort to keep the customers he already had, he beefed up employee training. New hires now spend a week learning how to use the equipment and prepare drinks. Later, they undergo another 40 hours of on-the-job training at a store. By improving customer service, the business almost doubled daily store revenues and increased per-store profits by 50 percent.[22]

To a considerable extent, training for quality performance is part of the ongoing supervisory role of all managers. In addition, special classes and seminars can be used to teach employees about the importance of quality control and ways in which to produce high-quality work.

Training of Nonmanagerial Employees

If a company has job descriptions or job specifications, these may be used to identify abilities or skills required for particular jobs. To a large extent, such requirements determine the appropriate type of training.

Phenix and Phenix, Inc., a small literary publicity firm based in Austin, Texas, encourages sharing of learning among its employees.[23] Anyone attending a "learning situation"—which might be anything from a breakfast meeting to a several-day seminar—is expected to write up a summary and present it at a staff meeting or distribute it to coworkers.

For all classes of employees, more training is accomplished on the job than through any other method. However, on-the-job training may be haphazard unless it follows an effective method of teaching. One program designed to make on-the-job training effective is known as **Job Instruction Training**. The steps in this program, shown in Exhibit 19-1, are intended to help supervisors become more effective in training employees.

Job Instruction Training
A systematic step-by-step method for on-the-job training of nonmanagerial employees

Development of Managerial and Professional Employees

A small business has a particularly strong need to develop managerial and professional employees. Whether the firm has only a few key positions or many, it must ensure that the individuals who hold these positions perform effectively. Incumbents should be developed to the point where they can adequately carry out the responsibilities assigned to them. Ideally, other staff members should be trained as potential replacements in case key individuals retire or leave for other reasons. Although an entrepreneur often postpones grooming a personal replacement, this step is crucial in ensuring a smooth transition in the firm's management.

Establishing a management training program requires serious consideration of the following factors:

- *The need for training.* What vacancies are expected? Who needs to be trained? What type of training and how much training are needed to meet the demands of the job description?

- *A plan for training.* How can the individuals be trained? Do they currently have enough responsibility to permit them to learn? Can they be assigned additional duties? Should they be given temporary assignments in other areas—for example, should they be shifted from production to sales? Would additional schooling be beneficial?

exhibit **19-1** *Steps in Job Instruction Training*

PREPARE EMPLOYEES

- Put employees at ease.
- Place them in appropriate jobs.
- Find out what they know.
- Get them interested in learning.

PRESENT THE OPERATIONS

- Tell, show, and illustrate the task.
- Stress key points.
- Instruct clearly and completely.

TRY OUT PERFORMANCE

- Have employees perform the task.
- Have them tell, show, and explain.
- Ask employees questions and correct any errors.

FOLLOW UP

- Check on employees frequently.
- Tell them how to obtain help.
- Encourage questions.

- *A timetable for training.* When should training begin? How much can be accomplished in the next six months or one year?

- *Employee counseling.* Do the individuals understand their need for training? Are they aware of their prospects within the firm? Has an understanding been reached as to the nature of training? Have the employees been consulted regularly about progress in their work and the problems confronting them? Have they been given the benefit of the owner's experience and insights without having decisions made for them?

Living the Dream   entrepreneurial challenges

Photo courtesy of Headsets.com, Inc.

Right Employee . . . Wrong Position

Management development strategies sometimes work wonderfully, but they do have their limits. As a result, in many situations the best strategy for development is to be careful not to promote an employee beyond the position he or she is best suited to perform. Mike Faith, founder, CEO, and president of the online retailer Headsets.com, found this out the hard way.

> *One of my longest-standing employees—in fact my only employee in the early days—is a good example [of promoting a person beyond success]. With us now for about ten years, this guy is a genius. Really. He can see the big picture and take an idea and make it work. Because he was so good at what he did, we wanted to get him into middle management. So we moved him into a management position, and it was a disaster. My A player quickly became a B player; management became a millstone around his neck. Recognizing our mistake, we moved him out of management. Now he takes on a variety of projects and is back to being a genius.*
>
> *Lesson learned: people can be an A player in one position and a B player in another. But I believe that everyone has the potential to be an A player in the right position.*

Sources: Mike Faith, "A Systems Approach to Hiring the Right People," March 1, 2006, http://www.eventuring.org/eShip/appmanager/eVenturing/eVenturingDesktop?_nfpb=true&_pageLabel=eShip_articleDetail&_nfls=false&id=Entrepreneurship/Resource/Resource_500.htm, accessed April 11, 2007; and http://www.headsets.com, accessed April 12, 2007.

http://www.headsets.com

Compensation and Incentives for Employees

Compensation is important to all employees, and small firms must acknowledge the role of the paycheck in attracting and motivating personnel. In addition, small firms can offer several nonfinancial incentives that appeal to both managerial and nonmanagerial employees.

> 4 Explain the various types of compensation plans, including the use of incentive plans.

Wage and Salary Levels

In general, small firms must be roughly competitive in wage and salary levels in order to attract well-qualified personnel. Payments to employees either are based on increments of time—such as an hour, a day, or a month—or vary with the output of the employees. Compensation based on time is most appropriate for jobs in which performance is not easily measured. Time-based compensation is also easier to understand and used more widely than incentive systems.

Small businesses often struggle to pay their lowest-level employees even the minimum wage required by law. However, some employers, such as Borealis Breads, located in Wells, Maine, try to improve the lives of their employees by paying wages that exceed the minimum required by law. Jim Amaral, owner of Borealis Breads, started bumping up the wages of his 60 employees until, in 2001, they reached $8 an hour. It is important to note that the business benefited along with the employees. Amaral saw improvement in recruiting and retention, particularly in the baking and early-morning delivery positions. He believes that the business also gained in terms of its public image with customers and the community. You could say that Amaral earned a respectable return on his investment—and on more than one front![24]

Financial Incentives

Incentive plans are designed to motivate employees to increase their productivity. Incentive wages may constitute an employee's entire earnings or merely supplement regular wages or salary. The commission system for salespeople is one type of incentive compensation (see Chapter 16 for further discussion of this topic). In manufacturing, employees are sometimes paid according to the number of units they produce, a practice called piecework. Although most incentive plans apply to employees as individuals, such plans may also involve the use of group incentives and team awards.

General bonus or profit-sharing plans are especially important for managers and other key personnel, although they may also include lower-level employees. These plans provide employees with a "piece of the action" and may or may not involve assignment of shares of stock. Many profit-sharing plans simply entail distribution of a specified share of all profits or profits in excess of a target amount. Profit sharing serves more directly as a work-related incentive in small firms than in large firms, because the connection between individual performance and success can be more easily appreciated in a small firm.

Performance-based compensation plans must be designed carefully if they are to work successfully. Such plans should be devised with the aid of a consultant and/or public accounting firm. Some keys to developing effective bonus plans are the following:

- *Set attainable goals.* Performance-based compensation plans work best when workers believe they can meet the targets. Tying pay to broad, companywide results leaves workers feeling frustrated and helpless. Complex financial measures or jargon-heavy benchmarks should be avoided—employees are motivated only by goals that they understand.

- *Include employees in planning.* Employees should have a voice in developing performance measures and changes to work systems. Incentive plans should be phased in gradually so that employees have a chance to get used to them.

- *Keep updating goals.* Performance-based plans must be continually adjusted to meet the changing needs of workers and customers. The life expectancy of such a plan may be no more than three or four years.

Stock Incentives

In young entrepreneurial ventures, stock options are sometimes used to attract and hold key personnel. The option holders get the opportunity to share in the growing—perhaps even skyrocketing—value of the company's stock. If the business prospers sufficiently, such personnel can become millionaires.

But stock ownership need not be reserved only for executives or key personnel. Some small firms have created employee stock ownership plans (ESOPs), which give employees a share of ownership in the business.[25] These plans may be structured in a variety of ways. For example, a share of annual profits may be designated for the purchase of company stock, which is then placed in a trust for employees. When coupled with a commitment to employee participation in business operations, ESOPs can motivate employees, resulting in improvements in productivity.

ESOPs also provide a way for owners to cash out and withdraw from a business without selling the firm to outsiders. (See Chapter 12 for a discussion of this topic.)

fringe benefits
Supplements to compensation, designed to be attractive and beneficial to employees

Fringe Benefits

Fringe benefits, which include payments by the employer for such items as Social Security, vacation time, holidays, health insurance, and retirement compensation, are expensive. The cost to many firms is equal to 40 percent or more of salary and wage

Living the Dream   entrepreneurship and integrity

A Company That Knows How to Laugh Its Way to Great Performance

Richard Tait and Whit Alexander were both employees of Microsoft, the software giant. But that all changed in 1998 when they decided to launch Cranium, Inc., a Seattle-based game maker that is all about changing the rules. The company says its mission is to "create a lifestyle brand fueled by experiences that [will] lighten and enlighten people's lives." Its goal is expressed in an interesting way: "[To] bring people together through laughter, discovery, and opportunities to shine."

With official titles of Grand Poo Bah (for Tait) and Chief Noodler (for Alexander), the company clearly strays from the ordinary, but not without effect. Its original game, Cranium, quickly became the fastest-selling independent board game in history and has many passionate fans, including high-profile celebrities like Julia Roberts, Mike Myers, and Drew Barrymore. Today, the company offers 14 games, which are sold in 30 countries and 10 languages, and it is quickly moving into other product lines, including interactive books and toys—products that "celebrate the full range of everyone's natural abilities."

What's the secret of success at Cranium, Inc.? The whackiness, believe it or not, doesn't hurt, nor do the celebrity associations. But Tait and Alexander believe the happiness of their 100 workers also has a lot to do with it, and the company goes to great lengths to keep its employees *creatively* happy. Here are some of the things it does to keep the fun and creative juices flowing:

- The main office is designed to look like the original Cranium board game.
- Employees get to come up with their own job titles—as long as they fit the job.
- Every employee receives 15 free games (10 for family and friends and 5 for charity).
- All four corner offices are reserved for employees, for inspiration or just a scenery break.
- The vacation plan is generous—from three weeks after one year to five weeks after ten years.
- The company pays 100 percent of employee premiums for medical, dental, and vision care.
- Up to four weeks of paid maternity leave is available to mothers and fathers.
- Employees get to use a juice bar that is well stocked with free drinks and snacks.

The bottom line? Companies like Cranium, Inc., have learned how to use creative incentives to motivate employees, with money being only a part of the equation.

Sources: "The Cranium Story," http://www.cranium.com/rd/en/cranium_story.aspx, accessed April 11, 2007; "Cranium Continues to Change the Rules, with Shining Results," press release, February 9, 2007, http://www.cranium.com/rd/files/2007_ToyFair_Release.pdf, accessed April 11, 2007; and Bruce Horovitz, "Cranium Guys Have Their Inner Child on Speed Dial," *USA Today,* May 8, 2006, p. 7B.

exhibit

19-2 *Some Affordable Perks*

1. Give employees a paid day off on their birthday.

2. Offer employees $100 a year to use for personal enrichment, such as taking an art class, getting a massage, or attending a play—if it makes them happy, they may be more productive.

3. Bring in lunch for everyone on Fridays.

4. Have employees select a "star employee" for his or her contributions at the office, and reward that individual with an extra day of vacation, a cash prize, or some other gift.

5. Offer recruitment bonuses to those who refer potential employees who stay with your company six months or longer—one good employee can often lead to another.

6. Pass on to employees perks accrued from the use of corporate credit cards, including airline miles, tickets to fun events, and other benefits.

Sources: Rich Mintzer, "20 Low-Cost Employee Perks," *Entrepreneur,* December 8, 2006, http://www.entrepreneur.com/article/printthis/171630.html, accessed December 12, 2006; and Kathleen Landis, "Blue Sky Thinking," *MyBusiness,* June-July 2003, p. 39.

payments. Furthermore, the cost of some benefits, such as health care, continues to increase at a double-digit rate each year. In general, small companies are somewhat less generous than large firms in providing fringe benefits for their employees. Even so, the cost of such benefits is a substantial part of total labor costs for most small businesses.

Though fringe benefits are expensive, a small firm cannot ignore them if it is to compete effectively for good employees. A small but growing number of small businesses now use flexible benefit programs (or cafeteria plans), which allow employees to select the types of fringe benefits they wish to receive.[26] All employees receive a core level of coverage, such as basic health insurance, and then are allowed to choose how an employer-specified amount is to be divided among additional options—for example, child care reimbursement, dental care, pension fund contributions, and additional health insurance.

For small companies that wish to avoid the detailed paperwork associated with administering cafeteria plans, outside help is available. Many small firms—some with fewer than 25 employees—turn over the administration of their flexible benefit plans to outside consulting, payroll accounting, or insurance companies that provide such services for a monthly fee.

Providing a full range of fringe benefits may be prohibitively expensive for many small businesses. A number of firms, however, have devised relatively inexpensive fringe benefits tailored to their particular situation—benefits that make employment more attractive for their employees. Some of the more affordable benefits are shown in Exhibit 19-2.

5 Discuss the human resource issues of employee leasing, legal protection, labor unions, and the formalizing of employer–employee relationships.

Special Issues in Human Resource Management

So far, this chapter has dealt with the recruitment, selection, training, and compensation of employees. Several related issues—employee leasing, legal protection of employees, labor unions, the formalizing of employer–employee relationships, and the need for a human resource manager—are the focus of this final section.

Employee Leasing

Leasing equipment and property has long been an accepted alternative to buying them. **Employee leasing**, as surprising as it may seem, has become a common alternative to direct hiring. Today, an estimated 700 employee-leasing companies, also known as **professional employer organizations (PEOs)**, operate in all 50 states with the specific purpose of "renting" personnel to small businesses. For a fee of 1 to 5 percent of payroll, a PEO writes paychecks, pays payroll taxes, and files the necessary reports with government agencies. Although small firms using this service avoid a certain amount of paperwork, they do not usually escape the tasks of recruitment and selection. In most cases, the firm still determines who works, who gets promoted, and who gets time off.

Many employees like the leasing arrangement. It may allow small employers to provide better benefit packages, since leasing companies generally cover hundreds or thousands of employees and thus qualify for better rates. Of course, the small business must bear the cost of insurance and other benefits obtained through a leasing company, in addition to paying a basic service fee. However, this may be the only way the firm can afford to offer the fringe benefits necessary to attract and hold onto high-quality employees. The fact that the PEO also assumes the burden of managing payroll and other administrative processes makes this arrangement even more attractive.

A note of caution about selecting a leasing company is in order. When a company decides to use the services of a PEO, both are considered co-employers and share legal obligations as a result. That is, the law holds both parties responsible for payment of payroll taxes and workers' compensation insurance and compliance with government regulations—the client company cannot simply offload these obligations to the PEO and forget about its responsibilities to staff. This highlights the importance of selecting a PEO carefully to ensure that you are dealing with a responsible firm. We recommend that you follow the guidelines offered by the National Association of Professional Employer Organizations (http://www.napeo.org) when you choose a PEO, to be sure you are linking up with a service provider that is honest, dependable, and right for your company.

Another note of caution pertains to the application of government regulations to small businesses. Very small firms are often excluded from specific regulations. For example, firms with fewer than 15 employees are exempt from the Americans with Disabilities Act. When these employees officially become part of a large leasing organization, however, the small company using the leased employees becomes subject to this law. It always pays to treat your employees with care and respect, of course, but taking on added legal obligations by working with a PEO can make managing a small company more complicated.

Legal Protection of Employees

Employees are afforded protection by a number of federal and state laws.[27] One of the most far-reaching statutes is the **Civil Rights Act**, originally enacted in 1964, and its amendments. This law, which applies to any employer of 15 or more people, prohibits discrimination on the basis of race, color, religion, sex, or national origin. Other laws extend similar protection to the aged and handicapped. Any employment condition is covered, including hiring, firing, promotion, transfer, and compensation.

The Civil Rights Act includes protection against sexual harassment. Given the growing attention to sexual harassment in our society, this issue must be addressed by small firms as well as large corporations. Education and prompt response to complaints are the best tools for avoiding sexual harassment and the possibility of liability claims. The following practical action steps have been expressly recommended for small businesses:[28]

1. Establish clear policies and procedures regarding sexual harassment in the workplace.

2. Require employees to report incidents of harassment to management immediately.

3. Investigate any and all complaints of sexual harassment fairly and thoroughly.

4. Take appropriate action against violators and maintain claimant confidentiality.

5. If a lawsuit is likely to be filed, contact an attorney.

employee leasing
The "renting" of personnel from an organization that handles paperwork and administers benefits for those employees

professional employer organization (PEO)
A personnel-leasing company that places employees on its own payroll and then "rents" them to employers on a permanent basis

Civil Rights Act
Legislation prohibiting discrimination based on race, color, religion, sex, or national origin

Occupational Safety and Health Act
Legislation that regulates the safety of workplaces and work practices

Fair Labor Standards Act (FLSA)
Federal law that establishes a minimum wage and provides for overtime pay

Family and Medical Leave Act
Legislation that assures employees of unpaid leave for childbirth or other family needs

Employees' health and safety are protected by the **Occupational Safety and Health Act** of 1970. This law, which applies to business firms of any size involved in interstate commerce, created the Occupational Safety and Health Administration (OSHA) to establish and enforce necessary safety and health standards.

Compensation of employees is regulated by the minimum wage and overtime provisions of the **Fair Labor Standards Act (FLSA)**, as well as by other federal and state laws. The FLSA applies to employers involved in interstate commerce and having two or more employees; it sets the minimum wage (which is periodically increased by Congress) and specifies time-and-a-half pay for nonsupervisory employees who work more than 40 hours per week.

The **Family and Medical Leave Act** was passed and signed into law by President Clinton in February 1993. The law requires firms with 50 or more employees to allow workers as much as 12 weeks of unpaid leave for childbirth, the adoption of a child, or other specified family needs. The worker must have been employed by the firm for 12 months and have worked at least 1,250 hours. Furthermore, the employer must continue health care coverage during the leave and guarantee that the employee can return to the same job or one that is comparable.

Labor Unions

Most entrepreneurs prefer to operate independently and to avoid unionization. Indeed, most small businesses are not unionized. To some extent, this results from the predominance of small business in services, where unionization is less common than in manufacturing. Also, unions typically focus their attention on large companies.

Though uncommon, labor unions are not unknown in small firms. Many types of small business—building and electrical contractors, for example—negotiate labor contracts and employ unionized personnel. The need to work with a union formalizes and, to some extent, complicates the relationship between a small company and its employees.

If employees wish to bargain collectively—that is, to be represented in negotiations by a union—the law requires the employer to participate in such bargaining. The demand for labor union representation may arise from employees' dissatisfaction with their pay, work environment, or employment relationships. By following constructive human resource policies, a small company can minimize the likelihood of labor organization or improve the relationship between management and union.

Formalizing Employer–Employee Relationships

As explained earlier in this chapter, the management systems of small companies are typically less formal than those of larger firms. A degree of informality can be a virtue in small organizations. As personnel are added, however, the benefits of informality decline and its costs increase. Large numbers of employees cannot be managed effectively without some system for regulating employer–employee relationships. This situation can be best understood in terms of a family relationship. House rules are generally unnecessary when only two people are living in the home. But when several children are added to the mix, Mom and Dad soon start sounding like a government regulatory agency.

Growth, then, produces pressure to formalize personnel policies and procedures. Determining how much formality to introduce and how soon involves judgment. Some employee issues should be formalized from the very beginning; on the other hand, excessive regulation can become paralyzing.

One way to formalize employer–employee relationships is to prepare a personnel policy manual or employee handbook, which communicates the firm's basic ground rules to employees. It can also provide a basis for fairness and consistency in management decisions affecting employees. The content of an employee handbook may be as broad or as narrow as desired. It may include an expression of company philosophy—an overall view of what the company considers important, such as standards of excellence or quality considerations. More specifically, personnel policies usually cover such topics as recruitment, selection, training, compensation, vacations, grievances, and discipline. Such policies should be written carefully and clearly to avoid misunderstandings. In some states, an employee handbook is considered part of the employment contract.

Procedures relating to management of personnel may also be standardized. For example, a performance review system may be established and a timetable set up for reviews—perhaps an initial review after six months and subsequent reviews on an annual basis.

The Need for a Human Resource Manager

A firm with only a few employees cannot afford a full-time specialist to deal with personnel problems. Some of the more involved human resource techniques used in large corporations may be far too complicated for small businesses. As a small company grows in size, however, its personnel problems will increase in both number and complexity.

The point at which it becomes logical to hire a human resource manager cannot be precisely specified. In view of the increased overhead cost, the owner-manager of a growing business must decide whether circumstances make it profitable to employ a personnel specialist. Hiring a part-time human resource manager—a retired personnel manager, for example—is a possible first step in some instances.

Conditions such as the following favor the appointment of a human resource manager in a small business:

- There are a substantial number of employees (100 or more is suggested as a guideline).

- Employees are represented by a union.

- The labor turnover rate is high.

- The need for skilled or professional personnel creates problems in recruitment or selection.

- Supervisors or operative employees require considerable training.

- Employee morale is unsatisfactory.

- Competition for personnel is keen.

Until a human resource manager is hired, however, the owner-manager typically functions in that capacity. His or her decisions regarding employee selection and compensation, as well as other personnel issues, will have a direct impact on the operating success of the firm. As this chapter points out, the human resource management function is simple in concept, but it can be complicated to put into practice. Nonetheless, it is critical to get this part of managing a small business right. No wonder so many small companies declare, "Our people make the difference!"

 Looking **BACK**

1 Explain the importance of employee recruitment and list some sources that can be useful in finding suitable applicants.

- Recruitment of good employees contributes to customer satisfaction and to profitability.

- Small firms can attract applicants by stressing unique work features and opportunities.

- Recruitment sources include help-wanted advertising, walk-ins, schools, public and private employment agencies, executive search firms, employee referrals, the Internet, and temporary help agencies.

- The increasing diversity of the workforce requires a broadening of the scope of recruitment, but the

varied perspectives of a diverse workforce can offer advantages, such as improved decision making.

- Job descriptions outline the duties of the job; job specifications identify the skills, abilities, and other characteristics applicants need to have.

2 Identify the steps to take in evaluating job applicants.

- In the first step, application forms help the employer obtain preliminary information from applicants. (Employers must avoid questions about sex, race, religion, color, national origin, age, and disabilities.)

- Additional evaluation steps are interviewing the applicant (with *behavioral interviews* offering the best insights), checking references and other background information, and testing the applicant.

· The final evaluation step is often a physical examination, which may include drug screening.

3 Describe the roles of training and development for both managerial and nonmanagerial employees in a small business.

· Effective training enables employees to perform their jobs effectively and also prepares them for advancement.

· An orientation program helps introduce new employees to the firm and its work environment.

· Training is one component of a firm's quality management program.

· Training and development programs are appropriate for both managerial and nonmanagerial employees.

4 Explain the various types of compensation plans, including the use of incentive plans.

· Small companies must be competitive in salary and wage levels.

· Payments to employees either are based on increments of time or vary with employee output.

· Incentive systems relate compensation to various measures of performance.

· Fringe benefit costs are often equal to 40 percent or more of payroll costs.

· Employee stock ownership plans enable employees to own a share of the business.

5 Discuss the human resource issues of employee leasing, legal protection, labor unions, and the formalizing of employer–employee relationships.

· Small businesses can reduce paperwork by transferring personnel to the payroll of a leasing company, but legal obligations remain.

· All small businesses with 15 or more employees must observe laws that prohibit discrimination, protect employee health and safety, establish a minimum wage, and provide for family and medical leave.

· Some small businesses must work with labor unions.

· As small firms grow, they must adopt more formal human resource management methods.

· Employment of a human resource manager becomes necessary at some point as a company continues to add employees.

Key TERMS

headhunter, p. 503
workforce diversity, p. 504
job specification, p. 506
behavioral interview, p. 507
validity, p. 509
reliability, p. 509

Job Instruction Training, p. 511
fringe benefits, p. 514
employee leasing, p. 517
professional employer
   organization (PEO), p. 517
Civil Rights Act, p. 517

Occupational Safety and Health Act,
   p. 518
Fair Labor Standards Act (FLSA),
   p. 518
Family and Medical Leave Act,
   p. 518

Discussion QUESTIONS

1. As a customer of small businesses, you can appreciate the importance of employees to company success. Describe one experience you had in which an employee's contribution to his or her employer's success was positive and one in which it was negative.

2. What factor or factors would make you cautious about going to work for a small business? Could these reasons for hesitation be overcome? How?

3. In what ways is the workforce becoming more diverse, and how do these changes affect recruitment by small companies?

4. Based on your own experience as an interviewee, what do you think is the most serious weakness in the interviewing process? How could it be remedied?

5. What steps and/or topics would you recommend for inclusion in the orientation program of a printing firm with 65 employees?

6. Choose a small business with which you are well acquainted. Determine whether adequate provisions have been made for replacement of key management personnel when it becomes necessary. Is the firm using any form of executive development?

7. What problems are involved in using incentive plans in a small company? How would the nature of the work affect management's decision concerning the use of such a plan?

8. Is the use of a profit-sharing plan desirable in a small business? What might lessen such a plan's effectiveness in motivating employees?

9. How does employee leasing differ from using a temporary help agency? What are the greatest benefits of employee leasing?

10. Explain the impact of the Civil Rights Act and the Fair Labor Standards Act on human resource management.

You Make the CALL

SITUATION 1

The following is an account of one employee's introduction to a new job:

> It was my first job out of high school. After receiving a physical exam and a pamphlet on benefits, I was told by the manager about the dangers involved in the job. But it was the old-timers who explained what was really expected of me.
>
> The company management never told me about the work environment or the unspoken rules. The old-timers let me know when I could take breaks and which supervisors to avoid. They told me how much work I was supposed to do and which supervisor to see if I had a problem.

Question 1 To what extent should a small firm use "old-timers" to help introduce new employees to the workplace? Is it inevitable that newcomers will look to old-timers to find out how things really work?

Question 2 How would you rate this firm's orientation effort? What are its strengths and weaknesses?

Question 3 Assume that this firm has fewer than 75 employees and no human resource manager. Could it possibly provide more extensive orientation than that described here? How? What low-cost improvements, if any, would you recommend?

SITUATION 2

Technical Products, Inc., distributes 15 percent of its profits quarterly to its eight employees. This money is invested for their benefit in a retirement plan and is fully vested after five years. An employee, therefore, has a claim to the retirement fund even if he or she leaves the company after five years of service.

The employees range in age from 25 to 59 and have worked for the company from 3 to 27 years. They seem to have recognized the value of the program. However, younger employees sometimes express a preference for cash over retirement benefits.

Question 1 What are the most important reasons for structuring the profit-sharing plan as a retirement program?

Question 2 What is the likely motivational impact of this compensation system?

Question 3 How will an employee's age affect the appeal of this plan? What other factors are likely to strengthen or lessen its motivational value? Should it be changed in any way?

SITUATION 3

When Peter Mathis learned that a former employee had filed a complaint alleging that Ready Delivery, his Albuquerque-based freight hauling business, had fired her because of her race, it seemed like the right time to rethink his company's human resource management methods. The complaint was eventually dismissed, but that didn't stop Mathis from worrying about the possibility that other employee problems might arise in the future. And with 12 workers already on the payroll, he was finding that the paperwork associated with payroll preparation, government regulation, tax reporting, and other human resource management matters was beginning to consume too much of his time at the office.

A professional employer organization (PEO) approached him about taking over much of Ready Delivery's human resource management work. It would cost the company 3 percent of payroll, but the PEO could also offer additional benefits and services (at additional cost, of course) that might help the company in other ways, too. For example, joining the PEO would give Mathis's employees access to better health and dental care plans that would actually be less expensive than those the company currently offered. It could also provide affordable group life insurance benefits, making the switch even more attractive. Mathis realized that partnering with the PEO could reduce his flexibility in selecting benefit options, but he was nonetheless giving serious consideration to accepting the offer.

Question 1 How can Mathis be sure that the PEO is reputable and that his company and employees will receive real value for the money?

Question 2 How might contracting with the PEO affect employee relationships at Ready Delivery? Is there any chance that his employees' loyalty might be transferred to their new "employer"?

Question 3 What steps should Mathis take before entering into an agreement with the PEO?

Experiential EXERCISES

1.   Interview the director of the placement office for your college or university. Ask about the extent to which small companies use the office's services, and obtain the director's recommendations for improving college recruiting by small firms. Prepare a one-page summary of your findings.

2.   Examine and evaluate the help-wanted section of a local newspaper. Summarize your conclusions and formulate some generalizations about small business advertising for personnel.

3.   With another student, form an interviewer–interviewee team. Take turns posing as job applicants for a selected type of job vacancy. Critique each other's performance, using the interviewing principles outlined in this chapter.

4.   With another student, take turns playing the roles of trainer and trainee. The student-trainer should select a simple task and teach it to the student-trainee, using the Job Instruction Training method outlined in Exhibit 19-1. Jointly critique the teaching performance after each turn.

Exploring the WEB

1.   Carter McNamara, a contributor to the Free Management Library, wrote an article entitled "Employee Training and Development: Reasons and Benefits." Go to the Free Management Library website at **http://www.managementhelp.org** and follow the link to "Training and Development" and then "Reasons and Benefits for Training and Development."

   a. Read McNamara's article, and then list some common reasons for employee training and development.

   b. What are some typical topics of employee training?

2.   The U.S. Equal Employment Opportunity Commission (EEOC) publishes on its website advice and information of interest to small businesses. To learn about employment laws that the EEOC enforces, go to **http://www.eeoc.gov**, and under "Employers & EEOC" choose "Small Businesses," then "An Overview of EEOC and Small Businesses." What EEOC laws apply to small businesses?

Case **19**

Gibson Mortuary (p. 658)
This case explores the human resource problems encountered by one small family business.

Alternative Cases for Chapter 19:

## chapter 20

Managing Operations

In the VIDEO SPOTLIGHT

Modern Postcard
http://www.modernpostcard.com

Modern Postcard prides itself on being able to turn around a customer's order in two days. That means designing the postcard, printing it, and mailing it out to the addresses on the customer's mailing list. On the surface, it sounds quite simple, but these postcards are anything but. They showcase beautiful color photography and elegant, powerful design. And when you consider that the company produces 100 million postcards a year for some 150,000 customers, producing such a high-quality product in just two days is quite a feat.

The founder of Modern Postcard, Steve Hoffman, started with real-estate brochures—full-color, glossy ones with *Architectural Digest*–style photography. The costs of producing the upscale brochures were quite high, so Hoffman, in an effort to make something that people could afford, began thinking about postcards. Even though his colleagues had serious reservations about producing postcards, which they perceived as "cheap," Hoffman persisted, because he realized that providing an affordable, high-quality product would be the best way to build his business.

So how does Modern Postcard continue to produce beautifully designed postcards of superior quality in such quantities for so many customers—and for one-sixth the cost of a full-color glossy brochure? The answer lies in its operations. This video spotlight will show you how manufacturing, service, and technology can work together to create an operations process that satisfies many customers, day in and day out.

Video material provided by Hattie Bryant, Producer of Small Business School, the series on PBS Stations, Worldnet, and the Web at http://www.smallbusinessschool.org.

Small**Business**School ▣
the Series on PBS stations and the Web

Looking AHEAD

After studying this chapter, you should be able to

1   Explain the key elements of total quality management (TQM) programs.
2   Discuss the nature of the operations process for both products and services.
3   Explain how reengineering and other methods of work improvement can increase productivity and make a firm more competitive.
4   Discuss the importance of purchasing and the nature of key purchasing policies.
5   Describe ways to control inventory and minimize inventory costs.

Managing operations almost sounds like something that happens in a hospital, but you don't have to be a doctor to manage the kind of operations we discuss in this chapter. It is really all about understanding the individual activities involved in a company's creation of goods or services and the way they fit together in an orderly and effective sequence—and then managing all of these with efficiency in mind. Every business uses some type of **operations process** to create products or services for its customers. This process consists of the activities involved in creating value for customers and earning their dollars. A bakery, for example, purchases ingredients, combines and bakes them, and makes bakery products available to customers at some appropriate location. For a service business like a hair salon, the operations process includes the purchase of supplies and the shampooing, haircutting, and other procedures involved in serving its clients.

> **operations process**
> The activities that create value for customers through production of a firm's goods and services

Such operations are at the heart of any business; indeed, they are the reasons for its very existence. It should come as no surprise, then, that their design and effectiveness can determine the success of a business.

Though we initially focus on quality issues in this chapter, operations management goes well beyond this one very important feature. Later in the chapter, we explain methods of work improvement that can increase productivity and boost the performance of a company. We also address the importance of establishing suitable purchasing policies, as well as introducing ways to control inventory and minimize the cost of inputs. Simply put, the thrust of this chapter is to examine ways a business can function economically and profitably, providing a high-quality product or service that keeps customers coming back for more. Most significantly, operations management is an important means of building a firm's competitive strength in the marketplace. And for this, there is no substitute!

Quality Goals of Operations Management

> 1   Explain the key elements of total quality management (TQM) programs.

Quality must be more than a slogan. Owners of successful small firms realize that quality management is serious business and that a strong commitment to the achievement of quality goals is essential.

Quality as a Competitive Tool

Quality may be defined as the characteristics of a product or service that determine its ability to satisfy stated and implied needs. Quality obviously has many dimensions. For example, a restaurant's customers base their perceptions of its quality on the taste of

> **quality**
> The features of a product or service that enable it to satisfy customers' needs

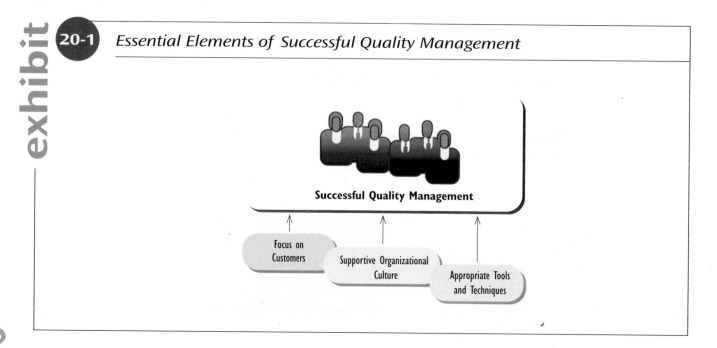

20-1   *Essential Elements of Successful Quality Management*

the food, the attractiveness of the décor, the friendliness and promptness of servers, the cleanliness of silverware, the appropriateness of background music, and many other factors. The operations process establishes a level of quality as a product is being produced or as a service is being provided. Although costs and other considerations cannot be ignored, quality must remain a primary focus of a firm's operations.

International competition is increasingly turning on quality differences. Automobile manufacturers in the United States, for example, now place greater emphasis on quality in their attempts to compete effectively with foreign producers. However, it is not solely big business that needs to make quality a major concern; the operations process of a small firm also deserves careful scrutiny. Many small firms have been slow to give adequate attention to producing high-quality goods and services. In examining the operations process, therefore, small business managers must direct special attention to achieving superior product or service quality.

The American Society for Quality (ASQ) has been the leading quality improvement organization in the United States for more than 50 years and has introduced many quality improvement methods throughout the world. Among these is an approach known as **total quality management (TQM)**, an aggressive effort by a firm to achieve superior quality. Total quality management is an all-encompassing, quality-focused management approach to providing products and services that satisfy customer requirements. Firms that implement TQM programs are making quality a major goal.

Many businesses merely give lip service to achieving excellent quality standards; others have introduced quality programs that have failed. As Exhibit 20-1 shows, the most successful quality management efforts incorporate three elements—a focus on customers, a supportive organizational culture, and the use of appropriate tools and techniques.

total quality management (TQM)
An all-encompassing management approach to providing high-quality products and services

The Customer Focus of Quality Management
A firm's quality management efforts should begin with a focus on the customers who purchase its products or services. Without such a focus, the quest for quality easily degenerates into an aimless search for some abstract, elusive ideal.

CUSTOMER EXPECTATIONS   Quality is ultimately determined by the extent to which a product or service satisfies customers' needs and expectations. Customers have expectations regarding the quality of products (durability and attractiveness, for example) and services (speed and accuracy, for example). A customer is concerned with *product quality* when purchasing a camera or a loaf of bread; a customer's primary concern is *service quality* when having an automobile repaired or a suit tailor made. Frequently, a customer expects some combination of product *and* service quality—when buying a lawnmower, a purchaser may be concerned with the performance of the lawnmower, knowledge and courtesy of the salesperson, credit terms offered, and warranty coverage.

When it comes down to it, though, what customers want is usually very simple. For example, a car owner who takes his automobile to a repair shop hopes to receive competent service (that is, a successful repair), to get a reasonable explanation of what had to be done, and to be treated with respect. Similarly, a hotel patron is looking to be provided with a clean room, to have reasonable security, and to be treated like a guest. Such uncomplicated expectations open up an avenue of opportunity. Exceeding these basic expectations can leave a lasting favorable impression on customers, which often results in repeat business and free promotion through positive word of mouth.

A *genuine* concern for customer needs and satisfaction is a powerful force that can energize the total quality management effort of a company. When a business pursues customer satisfaction merely as a way to increase profits, the effect on quality often is limited and difficult to sustain. It simply is not an honest effort, and everyone involved knows it. But if the customer becomes the focal point of honest quality efforts, real quality improvement is more likely to occur, and profits tend to grow as a result.

CUSTOMER FEEDBACK   Attentive listening to customers' opinions can provide information about their level of satisfaction. Employees having direct contact with customers can serve as the eyes and ears of the business in evaluating existing quality levels and customer needs. Unfortunately, many managers are oblivious to the often subtle feedback from customers. Preoccupied with operating details, managers may not listen carefully to, let alone solicit, customers' opinions. Employees having direct contact with customers— servers in a restaurant, for example—are seldom trained or encouraged to obtain information about customers' quality expectations. Careful management and training of servers could make them more alert to consumers' tastes and attitudes and provide a mechanism for reporting these reactions to management.

Experts now recommend that firms work hard to involve and empower customers in efforts to improve quality.[1] The marketing research methods of observation, interviews, and customer surveys, as described in Chapter 7, can be used to investigate customers' views regarding quality. Some businesses, for example, provide comment cards for their customers to use in evaluating service or product quality.

Ultimately, the most reliable customer feedback on quality comes in the most obvious form—sales. When the In-N-Out Burger chain opened an outlet in Phoenix, cars were backed up for blocks, and long lines of hamburger lovers spilled into the streets. When it debuted in San Francisco, lines of customers snaked out the doors for weeks. Why? Some people believe that In-N-Out simply makes the best burger in the world! Founded in 1948 as a tiny drive-through in a Los Angeles suburb, the business has maintained its original menu of burgers, fries, sodas, and ice cream shakes—no chicken, no salads, no desserts, and no toys for the kids, just great quality. In-N-Out has always been a family-owned firm, and it operates by a very simple business philosophy: "Give customers the freshest, highest quality foods you can buy and provide them with friendly service in a sparkling clean environment." The formula is obviously working. In-N-Out has grown to nearly 200 outlets, but it maintains its superb quality standards through tight family control and by refusing to franchise or go public. And customers have clearly responded to the high quality of its food and service.[2]

Organizational Culture and Total Quality Management

A crucial element of effective quality management is a supportive organizational culture. As described in previous chapters, the values, beliefs, and traditional practices followed by members of a business firm constitute its organizational culture. Some firms are so concerned with quality levels that they will refund money if a service or product is unsatisfactory or will schedule overtime work to avoid disappointing a customer. Quality is a primary value in such a business's organizational culture. Quality management experts believe that a quality-oriented culture is necessary if a firm is to achieve outstanding success.

Time and training are required to build a TQM program that elicits the best efforts of everyone in the organization in producing a superior-quality product or service. A small business that adopts a total quality management philosophy commits itself to the pursuit of excellence in all aspects of its operations. Dedication to quality on an organization-wide basis is sometimes described as a *cultural phenomenon*.

Total quality management goes beyond merely ensuring that existing standards are met. Its objective is **continuous quality improvement**, an ongoing effort to improve quality. For example, if a production process has been improved to a level where there is only 1 defect in 100 products, the process must then be shifted to the next level and a new goal set of no more than 1 defect in 200 or even 500 products. The ultimate goal is zero defects, a target that has been popularized by many quality improvement programs.

Continuous quality improvement efforts may include **benchmarking**, which is the process of identifying the best products, services, and practices of other businesses; carefully studying those examples; and using any insights gained to improve one's own operations. A simple type of benchmarking occurs when owner-managers eat in competitors' restaurants or shop in competitors' stores and then use what they learn to make improvements in their own businesses.

Tools and Techniques of Total Quality Management

Another element in effective quality management consists of the various tools, techniques, and procedures needed to ensure high-quality products and services. Once the focus is on the customer and the entire organization is committed to providing top-quality products and services, operating methods become important. Implementing a quality management program requires developing practical procedures for training employees, inspecting products, and measuring progress toward quality goals. We will discuss three important areas—employee participation, the inspection process, and the use of statistical methods of quality management.

EMPLOYEE PARTICIPATION   In most organizations, employee performance is a critical quality variable. Obviously, employees who work carefully produce better quality products than those who work carelessly. The admonition "Never buy a car that was produced on a Friday or a Monday!" conveys the popular notion that workers lack commitment to their work and are especially careless prior to and immediately after a weekend away from the assembly line. The vital role of personnel in producing a high-quality product or service has led managers to seek ways to involve employees in quality management efforts.

Chapter 18 discussed the implementation of work teams and empowerment of employees as approaches to building employee involvement in the workplace. Many businesses have adopted these approaches as part of their TQM programs. Japanese firms are particularly noted for their use of work teams. Many self-managed work teams, both in Japan and in the United States, monitor the quality level of their work and take any steps necessary to continue operating at the proper quality level.

The quality circle is another technique that solicits the contributions of employees in improving the quality of products and services. Originated by the Japanese, it is widely used by small companies in the United States and other parts of the world. A **quality circle** consists of a group of employees, usually a dozen or fewer. Such groups meet on company time, typically about once a week, to identify, analyze, and solve work-related problems, particularly those involving product or service quality. Quality circles can tap employees' potential to make enthusiastic and valuable contributions.

THE INSPECTION PROCESS   Management's traditional method of maintaining product quality has been **inspection**, which consists of examining a part or a product to determine whether or not it is acceptable. An inspector often uses gauges to evaluate important quality variables. For effective quality control, the inspector must be honest, objective, and capable of resisting pressure from shop personnel to pass borderline cases.

Although the inspection process is usually discussed with reference to product quality, comparable steps can be used to evaluate service quality. Follow-up calls to customers of an auto repair shop, for example, might be used to measure the quality of the firm's repair services. Customers can be asked whether recent repairs were performed in a timely and satisfactory manner.

continuous quality improvement
A constant and dedicated effort to improve quality

benchmarking
The process of studying the products, services, and practices of other firms and using the insights gained to improve quality internally

quality circle
A group of employees who meet regularly to discuss quality-related problems

inspection
The examination of a product to determine whether it meets quality standards

In manufacturing, **inspection standards** consist of design tolerances that are set for every important quality variable. These tolerances indicate, in discrete terms, the variation allowable above and below the desired level of quality. Inspection standards must satisfy customer requirements for quality in finished products. Traditionally, inspection begins in the receiving room, where the condition and quantity of materials received from suppliers are checked. If the quality of incoming materials or components is unacceptable, it is important to work with the supplier as soon as possible to correct the problem. It may also be necessary to inspect for quality at other critical processing points—for example, *before* any operation that might conceal existing defects and *after* any operation that might produce an excessive amount of defects.

Many operations management experts point out that it is critical to inspect for quality at points that precede any bottlenecks in the system. A **bottleneck** is any point in the operations process where limited capacity reduces the production capability of an entire chain of activities (for example, a bottleneck would be created by a machine that could not operate as fast as those on the rest of the assembly line). Since a bottleneck determines the efficiency of the system, it is imperative that inputs at that point in the process be defect free. If you find a problem before a bottleneck, little efficiency will be lost because the system has excess capacity at that point. However, if the defect is not recognized until after a bottleneck, the efficiency burden to the overall system is much greater.

Of course, the inspection of finished products is also important. Inspecting each item in every lot processed, called *100 percent inspection,* might seem to ensure the elimination of all bad materials and all defective products prior to shipment to customers. However, such inspection goals are seldom reached, and this method of inspection is both time-consuming and costly. Furthermore, inspectors often make honest errors in judgment, both in rejecting good items and in accepting defective items. Also, some types of inspection, such as opening a can of vegetables, destroy the product, making 100 percent inspection impractical.

In an inspection, either attributes or variables may be measured. **Attribute inspection** determines quality acceptability based on attributes that can be evaluated as being either present or absent. For example, a light bulb either lights or doesn't light; similarly, a water hose either leaks or doesn't leak.

Variable inspection, in contrast, determines quality acceptability based on where variables (such as weight) fall on a scale or continuum. For example, if a box of candy is to be sold as containing a minimum of one pound of candy, an inspector may judge the product acceptable if its weight falls within the range of 16 ounces to 16.5 ounces.

STATISTICAL METHODS OF QUALITY CONTROL   The use of statistical methods can often make controlling product and service quality easier, less expensive, and more effective. As some knowledge of quantitative methods is necessary to develop a quality control method using statistical analysis, a properly qualified employee should be available to lead this part of the process. The savings made possible by use of an efficient statistical method usually will more than justify the cost of hiring a specialist to set up and manage it.

Acceptance sampling involves taking random samples of products and measuring them against predetermined standards. Suppose, for example, that a small firm receives a shipment of 10,000 parts from a supplier. Rather than evaluate all 10,000 parts, the purchasing firm might check the acceptability of a small sample of parts and then accept or reject the entire order. The smaller the sample, the greater the risk of either accepting a defective lot or rejecting a good lot due to sampling error. A larger sample reduces this risk but increases the cost of inspection. A well-designed plan strikes a balance, simultaneously avoiding excessive inspection costs and minimizing the risk of accepting a bad lot or rejecting a good lot.

Statistical process control involves applying statistical techniques to control work processes. Items produced in a manufacturing process are not completely identical, although the variations are sometimes so small that the items seem to be exactly alike. Careful measurement, however, can pinpoint differences.

The use of statistical analysis makes it possible to establish tolerance limits that allow for inherent variation due to chance. When measurements fall outside these tolerance limits, however, the quality controller knows that a problem exists and must search for the cause. The problem might be caused by variations in raw materials, machine wear,

inspection standard
A specification of a desired quality level and allowable tolerances

bottleneck
Any point in the operations process where limited capacity reduces the production capability of an entire chain of activities

attribute inspection
The determination of product acceptability based on whether it will or will not work

variable inspection
The determination of product acceptability based on a variable such as weight or length

acceptance sampling
The use of a random, representative portion to determine the acceptability of an entire lot

statistical process control
The use of statistical methods to assess quality during the operations process

Living the Dream   entrepreneurial challenges

Garbage In, but No Garbage Allowed Out

When Ross O. Youngs finds something that doesn't work as well as it should, the inventor in him just has a way of coming out. For example, he never did like hard plastic jewel cases for CDs, so he combined a piece of soft plastic with a piece of fabric to create the Safety-sleeve, a product that serves the same purpose—only does it better.

To turn this product idea into a startup, Youngs launched Univenture Media Packaging with a $20,000 bank loan. The new product was a hit and the company had more than $1 million in sales within just a few years, but there were a few bumps on the road to success. Early on, Youngs learned about the problems a small business can run into when working with a large supplier.

> *Like an idiot, I quit my job and started advertising my product. By May 1988, I had $1,200 in orders. The next month, that number jumped to $12,000. But I still hadn't delivered a product. The manufacturer kept pushing my orders aside. I called each customer to apologize. When the manufacturer finally delivered, the quality of the product was pathetic. Every single sleeve had to be cleaned with a Post-it note on a popsicle stick.*

Of course, Youngs fixed the problem as soon as he could, but his experience shows just how important it is to inspect for quality. If a supplier fails to deliver what you need when you need it and with the quality you require, the entire operation breaks down—as does the business.

Sources: As told to Nadine Heintz, "Ross O. Youngs: The Fix It Man," *Inc. 500 Special*, Vol. 25, No. 12 (Fall 2004), pp. 28, 30; and http://www.univenture.com/company/history.html, accessed April 22, 2007.

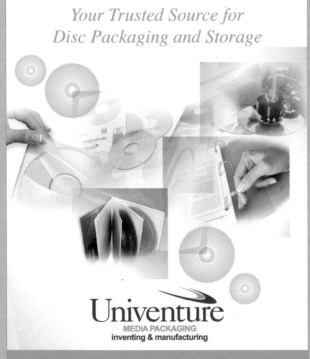

Your Trusted Source for Disc Packaging and Storage

Univenture
MEDIA PACKAGING
inventing & manufacturing

1.800.992.8262
www.univenture.com

Ad image courtesy of Univenture

http://www.univenture.com

or changes in employees' work practices. Consider, for example, a candy maker that is producing one-pound boxes of chocolates. Though the weight may vary slightly, each box must weigh at least 16 ounces. A study of the operations process has determined that the actual target weight must be 16.5 ounces, to allow for the normal variation between 16 and 17 ounces. During the production process, a box is weighed every 15 or 20 minutes. If the weight of a box falls outside the tolerance limits—below 16 or above 17 ounces—the quality controller must immediately try to find the problem and correct it.

A **control chart** graphically shows the limits for the process being controlled. As current data are entered, it is possible to tell whether a process is under control or out of control. Control charts may be used for either variable or attribute inspections. Continuing improvements in computer-based technology have advanced the use of statistical control processes in small firms.

control chart
A graphic illustration of the limits used in statistical process control

International Certification for Quality Management

A firm can obtain international recognition of its quality management program by meeting a series of standards, known as **ISO 9000**, developed by the International Organization for Standardization in Geneva, Switzerland. The certification process requires full documentation of a firm's quality management procedures, as well as an audit to ensure that

ISO 9000
The standards governing international certification of a firm's quality management procedures

the firm is operating in accordance with those procedures. In other words, the firm must show that it does what it says it does. ISO 9000 certification can give a business credibility with purchasers in other countries and thereby ease its entry into export markets. However, substantial costs are involved in obtaining certification.

ISO 9000 certification is particularly valuable for small firms, because they usually lack a global image as producers of high-quality products. Buyers in other countries, especially in Europe, view this certification as an indicator of supplier reliability. Some large U.S. corporations, such as the major automobile makers, require their domestic suppliers to conform to these standards. Small firms, therefore, may need ISO 9000 certification either to sell more easily in international markets or to meet the demands of their domestic customers.

The International Organization for Standardization also offers ISO 14001 certification. Though not always considered part of a total quality management program, ISO 14001 certification is concerned with how companies should set up and improve their operations processes in order to control the impact of vehicle and smokestack emissions, noise, and other fallout on air, water, and soil.

SWD Inc., a small metal-finishing company located in Addison, Illinois, opened for business in 1980 with just three employees in a 9,000-square-foot leased facility. Because customers, especially auto manufacturers, seek product quality certification, SWD decided to apply for environmental certification at the same time that it sought ISO 9000 certification. In 1998, it received the ISO 14001 environmental certification, and business has really taken off. One phrase in SWD's mission statement reads, "Be a leader in environment conservation." Tim Delawder, son of the founder and the firm's vice president of operations, cites some practical benefits from good environmental management: "At this point, it's more of a tool to make your organization stronger. If I produce more product with less water, energy and chemistry, I've just saved money." In other words, what is good for the environment may also be good for business.[3]

Quality Management in Service Businesses

As discussed earlier, maintaining and improving quality are no less important for service businesses—such as motels, dry cleaners, accounting firms, and automobile repair shops—than for manufacturers. In fact, many firms offer a combination of tangible products and intangible services and effectively manage quality in both areas.

According to the American Customer Satisfaction Index (published by the University of Michigan), customer satisfaction with service businesses overall has been higher in recent years,[4] but there is still room for improvement. For example, some large corporations gear the quality of the services they provide to the profitability of the customer—with better customers getting better service—and this can easily lead to dissatisfaction. But poor service (automated telephone answering systems that do not allow callers to speak to a live representative, long lines, reluctance to respond to customer problems, etc.) opens the door for small service-oriented firms. Although some services are too costly to be used as powerful competitive weapons, high-quality service may sometimes involve nothing more than simple attention to detail.

Measurement problems are always an issue in assessing the quality of a service. It is easier to measure the length of a piece of wood than the quality of motel accommodations. As noted earlier, however, methods can be devised for measuring the quality of services. For example, a motel manager might maintain a record of the number of problems with travelers' reservations, complaints about the cleanliness of rooms, and so on.

For many types of service firms, quality control constitutes management's most important responsibility. All that such firms sell is service, and their success depends on customers' perceptions of the quality of that service.

The Operations Process

The operations process is necessary to get the job done—that is, to perform the work and create the quality expected by customers. Thus far, this chapter has discussed the way quality concerns drive operations management. Let's now turn to other important aspects of business operations.

2 Discuss the nature of the operations process for both products and services.

operations management
Planning and controlling the process of converting inputs to outputs

The Nature of the Operations Process

Operations management involves the planning and control of a conversion process. It includes acquiring inputs and then overseeing their transformation into products and services desired by customers. An operations process is required whether a firm produces a tangible product, such as clothing or bread, or an intangible service, such as dry cleaning or entertainment. The production process in clothing manufacturing, the baking process in a bakery, the cleaning process in dry cleaning, and the process of producing a play for a community theater are all examples of operations processes.

Despite their differences, all operations processes are similar in that they change inputs into outputs. Inputs include money, raw materials, labor, equipment, information, and energy—all of which are combined in varying proportions, depending on the nature of the finished product or service. Outputs are the products and/or services that a business provides to its customers. Thus, the operations process may be described as a conversion process. As Exhibit 20-2 shows, the operations process converts inputs of various kinds into products, such as baked goods, or services, such as dry cleaning. A printing plant, for example, uses inputs such as paper, ink, the work of employees, printing presses, and electric power to produce printed material. Car wash facilities and motor freight firms, which are service businesses, also use operating systems to transform inputs into car-cleaning and freight-transporting services.

Managing Operations in a Service Business

The operations of firms providing services differ from those of firms producing products in a number of ways. One of the most obvious is the intangible nature of services—that is, the fact that you cannot easily see or measure them. As pointed out earlier, managers of businesses such as auto repair shops and hotels face special challenges in assuring and controlling the quality of their services, given the difficulty inherent in measuring and controlling intangibles.

exhibit

20-2   *The Operations Process*

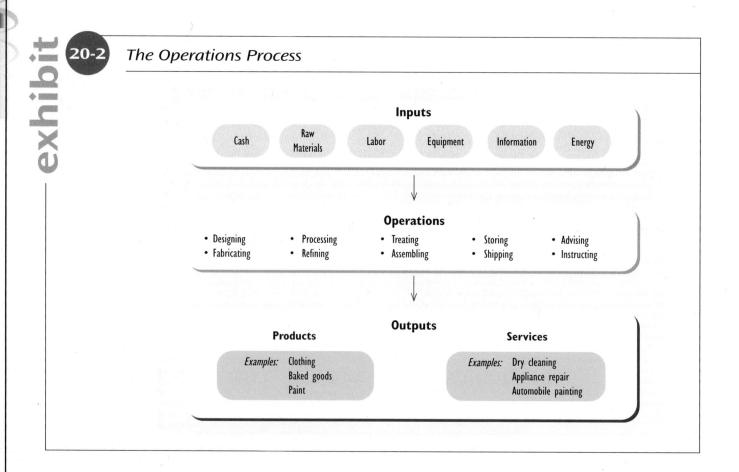

Another distinctive feature of most service businesses is the extensive personal interaction of employees with customers. In a physical fitness facility, for example, the customer is directly involved in the process and relates personally to trainers and other service personnel. In a beauty salon, the customer is a participant in the various processes of hair styling. The more extensive the relationship between customer and service provider, the more important the relationship is to customer satisfaction and the more likely employees and customers are to develop social bonds and share information.

Some service businesses have taken unique steps to understand the service provider–customer connection. Herb Kelleher, founder of Southwest Airlines, wanted top management to get close enough to customers to see what they had to say about various facets of the company.[5] To this end, each officer of the company was sent into the field each quarter to fill a customer contact position. Research into employee–customer relations had shown that greater closeness with customers enabled employees to understand and report customer sentiment more accurately.

Living the Dream   entrepreneurial challenges

© M. Spencer Green/Associated Press

Getting the Details Right Makes for Happy Customers

Operating details can make or break a business, especially in an industry such as food service. In 1971, Richard Melman, a highly successful restaurateur, started his first restaurant in Chicago—R.J. Grunt's, a low-priced burger joint. Within one month, the new eatery was already a success. However, within a few years, Melman began to turn his attention to launching other kinds of restaurants, and R.J. Grunt's started to lose its luster. Cost-conscious managers cut back on some of the ingredients and became less meticulous in food preparation. Eventually, the eatery began to lose money.

Melman considered closing the restaurant, but in 2002 he decided to turn it over to his son, R.J. (named in honor of that first restaurant), who already had experience managing one of Melman's other highly successful restaurants. Together, father and son found problems—the milk shakes weren't as good as they used to be, and neither were the hamburgers and fries.

The Melmans began tinkering with the shakes and malts, increasing the amount of ice cream used, buying better malt powder, adding flavors and better displaying them on the menu. Sales doubled to about 100 a day on weekends.

The burger was deconstructed. "How does it not fall apart?" Mr. Melman asked. Placed on top of the meat, the tomato slides off, so they tucked it underneath. Grilling instructions—"only flip once, no smashing, light salt and pepper"—were posted and enforced. They bought a new toaster for the buns.

The Melman team's hard work paid off. They were able to rescue the burger hot spot, leading R.J. Grunt's back to its best month in nine years. The business was saved by carefully attending to the details of its basic operations and correcting the weaknesses that were afflicting the system.

Sources: Jeff Bailey, "A Restaurant's Turnaround Is All in the Details," *Wall Street Journal,* May 20, 2003, p. B-3; and http://www.leye.com/company/history.htm, accessed April 20, 2007.

http://www.leye.com

For a service business, the critical importance of its relationship with customers carries implications for managing personnel. For example, those making hiring decisions must consider the employee's role in relating to the firm's clientele and select individuals capable of relating well. Employee training must emphasize the skills needed to serve customers well and encourage employees to find ways to improve customer satisfaction. Employee relationships with customers can create unique problems in scheduling work, as we will discuss later in this chapter.

The adoption of various technologies has enabled customers of many businesses to provide more of their own services. Self-service gasoline stations permit customers to pay at the pump, and many telephone systems allow customers to obtain information without speaking to a salesperson or other personnel. The extent to which such systems are satisfactory from a customer point of view depends on whether they are more convenient than traditional systems and whether they function efficiently and accurately in meeting customers' needs.[6]

Types of Manufacturing Operations

Manufacturing operations differ in the degree to which they are repetitive. Some factories produce the same product day after day and week after week. Other production facilities have great flexibility and often change the products they produce. There are four basic types of manufacturing operations—job shops, project manufacturing, repetitive manufacturing, and batch manufacturing.

job shop
A type of manufacturing operation in which short production runs are used to produce small quantities of unique items

Job shops are characterized by short production runs. Only one or a few products are produced before the general-purpose machines are shifted to a different production setup. Each job may be unique, requiring a special set of production steps to complete the finished item. Machine shops exemplify this type of operation.

project manufacturing
A type of manufacturing operation designed to produce unique but similar products, often in an outdoor setting

We tend to think of manufacturing as a factory operation, but this is not always the case. Similar in some ways to the job shop, **project manufacturing** is designed to produce unique but similar products, often (though not always) in an outdoor setting. Specialized products such as site-built homes, custom boats, and grandstands for sports facilities are all produced in this way. Like the job shop, project manufacturing leads to a customized product, and this requires a great deal of production flexibility. However, because the process is designed to make unique but similar products, a company can achieve operational efficiencies by following manufacturing methods that, in some ways, resemble those of repetitive manufacturing.

repetitive manufacturing
A type of manufacturing operation in which long production runs are used to produce a large quantity of a standardized product

Firms that produce one or relatively few standardized products use **repetitive manufacturing**, which is considered mass production as it involves long production runs. Repetitive manufacturing is associated with the assembly-line production of automobiles and other high-volume products. Highly specialized equipment can be employed, because it is used over and over again in manufacturing the same item. Few small businesses engage in repetitive manufacturing.

batch manufacturing
A type of manufacturing operation that is intermediate (between job shops and repetitive manufacturing) in volume and variety of products

An intermediate type of production is called **batch manufacturing**. Batch manufacturing involves more variety (and less volume) than repetitive manufacturing but less variety (and more volume) than job shops. In batch manufacturing, one production run of 100 standardized units may be followed by a second production run of 100 units of another type of standardized product. A bottling plant that fills bottles with several varieties of soft drinks is engaging in batch manufacturing.

Operations Planning and Scheduling

In manufacturing, production planning and scheduling procedures are designed to achieve the orderly, sequential flow of products through a plant at a rate commensurate with scheduled deliveries to customers. In order for this objective to be reached, it is essential to avoid production bottlenecks and to utilize machines and personnel efficiently. Simple, informal control procedures are often used in small plants. If a procedure is straightforward and the output small, a manager can keep things moving smoothly with a minimum of paperwork. Eventually, however, any manufacturing organization experiencing growth will have to establish formal procedures to ensure production efficiency.

Because service firms are so closely tied to their customers, they are limited in their ability to produce services and hold them in inventory for customers. An automobile repair shop must wait until a car arrives, and a beauty shop cannot function until a customer is available. A retail store can perform some of its services, such as transportation and storage, but it, too, must wait until the customer arrives to perform other services.

Part of the scheduling task for service firms relates to planning employees' working hours. Restaurants, for example, schedule the work of servers to coincide with variations in customer traffic. In a similar way, stores and medical clinics increase their staff to meet times of peak demand. Other strategies of service firms focus on scheduling customers. Appointment systems are used by many automobile repair shops and beauty shops, for example. Service firms such as dry cleaners and plumbers take requests for service and delay delivery until the work can be scheduled. Still other firms, such as banks and movie theaters, maintain a fixed schedule of services and tolerate some idle capacity. Some businesses attempt to spread out customer demand by offering incentives to use services at off-peak hours—examples include early-bird dinner specials at a restaurant and lower-price tickets for afternoon movies.

Plant Maintenance

Murphy's Law states that if anything can go wrong, it will. In operating systems that use tools and equipment, there is indeed much that can go wrong. The maintenance function is intended to correct malfunctions of equipment and, as far as possible, to prevent breakdowns from occurring.

THE ROLE OF MAINTENANCE   Effective maintenance contributes directly to product and service quality and thus to customer satisfaction. Poor maintenance often creates problems for customers. A faulty shower or a reading lamp that doesn't work, for example, makes a motel stay less enjoyable for a traveler.

Equipment malfunctions and breakdowns not only cause problems for customers but also increase costs for the producing firm. Employees may be unproductive while repairs are being made, and expensive manufacturing equipment may stand idle when it should be producing. Furthermore, improperly maintained equipment wears out more rapidly and requires early replacement, thus adding to the overall costs of operation.

The nature of maintenance work obviously depends on the type of operations process and the type of equipment being used. In an office, for example, machines that require maintenance include computers, fax machines, copiers, and related office equipment. Maintenance services are usually obtained on a contract basis—either by calling for repair personnel when a breakdown occurs and/or by scheduling periodic servicing. In manufacturing firms that use more complex and specialized equipment, plant maintenance is much more difficult and clearly requires the close attention of management. In small plants, maintenance work is often performed by regular production employees. As a firm expands its facilities, it may add specialized maintenance personnel and eventually create a maintenance department.

TYPES OF MAINTENANCE   Plant maintenance activities fall into two categories. **Preventive maintenance** consists of inspections and other activities intended to prevent machine breakdowns and damage to people and buildings. **Corrective maintenance** includes both the major and the minor repairs necessary to restore equipment or a facility to good condition.

A small firm can ill afford to neglect preventive maintenance. A machine that is highly critical to the overall operation must be inspected and serviced regularly to avoid costly breakdowns.

Major repairs, which are a part of corrective maintenance, are unpredictable as to time of occurrence, repair time required, loss of output, and cost of downtime. Because of this unpredictability, some small manufacturers contract with outside service firms for major repair work.

preventive maintenance
Activities intended to prevent machine breakdowns, injuries to people, and damage to facilities

corrective maintenance
Repairs necessary to restore equipment or a facility to good condition

3 Explain how re-
engineering and other
methods of work
improvement can
increase productivity
and make a firm more
competitive.

productivity
The efficiency with which
inputs are transformed
into outputs

Competitive Strength Through Improved Productivity

A society's standard of living depends, to some extent, on its **productivity**—the efficiency with which inputs are transformed into outputs. Similarly, the competitive strength of a particular business depends on its productivity. This section discusses approaches that can be used by small businesses to become more competitive through improved productivity.

The Importance of Improving Productivity

To remain competitive, a firm should continually try to improve its productivity. Improvement efforts vary greatly. Some involve major reorganizations or changes in technology, while others merely upgrade existing operations.

A business firm's productivity may be expressed as follows:

$$\text{Productivity} = \frac{\text{Outputs}}{\text{Inputs}} = \frac{\text{Products and/or services}}{(\text{Labor} + \text{Energy} + \text{Cash} + \text{Raw materials} + \text{Equipment} + \text{Information})}$$

A firm improves its productivity by doing more with less—increasing outputs and/or decreasing inputs. This can be accomplished in many different ways. For example, a small restaurant may improve its pastry making by sending the chef to cooking school, buying better ingredients, getting a more efficient oven, or redesigning the kitchen.

Michael Hammer argues that companies that are doing well today rely primarily not on a clever plan or hot concept but on innovation. Here's his formula for achieving a solid advantage in the marketplace:

> *It depends on how regular, mundane, basic work is carried out. If you can consistently do your work faster, cheaper, and better than the other guy, then you get to wipe the floor with him—without any accounting tricks. Relentless operational innovation is the only way to establish a lasting advantage.*[7]

At one time, productivity and quality were viewed as potentially conflicting. However, production at a high-quality level reduces scrap and rework. Therefore, quality enhancement, automation, and other improvements in operations methods can also boost productivity.

Improving productivity in the labor-intensive service sector is especially difficult, since managers have less opportunity to take advantage of automation. Nevertheless, small service firms can find ways to become more efficient. At one time, for example, customers in barber shops wasted time waiting for barbers who took them on a first-come, first-served basis. To improve the system, many shops now use an appointment schedule. A drop-in customer can still get service immediately if a barber isn't busy or else sign up for the first convenient appointment. Such a system provides continuity in the barber's work schedule and reduces delays and frustration for customers.

Reengineering for Improved Productivity

reengineering
A fundamental restructuring to improve the operations process

In the early 1990s, Michael Hammer and James Champy described a method for restructuring companies to provide better service for customers. In their best-selling book *Reengineering the Corporation*, Hammer and Champy defined **reengineering** as "the fundamental rethinking and radical redesign of business processes to achieve dramatic improvements in critical, contemporary measures of performance, such as cost, quality, service, and speed."[8]

Reengineering is concerned with improving the way in which a business operates, whether that business is large or small. Hammer and Champy concentrated their early analysis on large corporations such as Wal-Mart, Taco Bell, and Bell Atlantic (now Verizon Communications), which redesigned their rigid bureaucratic structures to become more efficient. Firms that engage in reengineering seek fundamental improvements by asking questions about why they perform certain functions the way they do. They expect to make dramatic, radical changes rather than minimal adjustments to traditional operating methods. Reengineering involves careful analysis of the basic processes followed by a firm in creating goods and services for customers.

Reengineering's emphasis on basic processes is crucial and holds the potential for substantial improvements in operations. Like effective quality control efforts, it directs attention to activities that create value for the customer. Essentially, reengineering asks how the operations process can be better managed, even if it means eliminating traditional departmental lines and specialized job descriptions.

Upgrading Information Systems

In recent years, small firms have attained extensive improvements in productivity by using computers, new software, and Internet links with suppliers and customers. Tedious, paper-based processes for tracking orders, work in progress, and inventory have been replaced by simplified and accelerated computer-based processes.

Consider Dee Electronics, Inc., a 62-employee company that operates an electronics distribution center in Cedar Rapids, Iowa.[9] In 1999, it was selling 50,000 items such as switches, fuses, and circuit breakers, with all sales documented by a huge amount of paper. By shifting to a paperless, wireless computer network, the business greatly increased its efficiency of operations. The system cost $65,000, but it cut order-processing time by 35 to 40 percent and shelving errors by 90 percent, while shipping accuracy increased to nearly 100 percent. According to its president, the company was able to recoup its $65,000 investment from cost savings in just five months.

Management information systems are in a continuous stage of reinvention and improvement. Microsoft, for example, is spending billions of dollars to offer software that will automate practically every aspect of a company's business (such as order processing and inventory management) and create a base layer of technology upon which smaller software makers can build applications.[10]

Operations Analysis

Improving productivity for an overall operation involves analyses of work flow, equipment, tooling, layout, working conditions, and individual jobs. For a specific manufacturing process, it means finding answers to questions such as these:

- Are the right machines being used?

- Can one employee operate two or more machines?

- Can automatic feeders or ejectors be used?

- Can power tools replace hand tools?

- Can the jigs and fixtures be improved?

- Is the workplace properly arranged?

- Is each operator's motion sequence effective?

Work methods can be analyzed for service or merchandising firms as well as for manufacturers. For example, a small plumbing company serving residential customers might examine its service vehicles to make sure they are equipped with the best possible assortment and arrangement of parts, tools, and supplies. In addition, the company might analyze the planning and routing of repair assignments to minimize backtracking and wasting of time.

Sometimes, in their efforts to improve highly repetitive operations, analysts examine detailed motions of individual employees. By applying **time and motion studies,** which concern work arrangement, the use of the human hands and body, and the design and use of tools, they can often make work easier and more efficient. Though this technique, which was originally used to improve bricklaying methods, is usually applied to fairly simple tasks, analyzing processes in detail with the goal of streamlining them can be helpful in many settings and work situations.

time and motion studies
Detailed analyses of work processes with the goal of increasing the efficiency of human movement and tool design

Relatively simple changes can sometimes improve productivity. Julie Northcutt founded Chicagoland Caregivers LLC in 2002 to provide in-home care for seniors who would otherwise have to move into assisted living centers or nursing homes.[11] Northcutt found that the hiring of nurse's aides and others took so much of her time that she was missing important calls from clients. She solved the problem by adding a phone line specifically for job seekers, requiring them to supply certain information. Now Northcutt can check the information when free of client work and call prospects who sound promising.

Purchasing Policies and Practices

4 Discuss the importance of purchasing and the nature of key purchasing policies.

purchasing
The process of obtaining materials, equipment, and services from outside suppliers

Although its importance varies with the type of business, **purchasing** constitutes a key part of operations management for most small businesses. Through purchasing, firms obtain materials, merchandise, equipment, and services to meet production and marketing goals. For example, manufacturing firms buy raw materials, merchandising firms purchase goods to be sold, and all types of firms obtain supplies.

The Importance of Purchasing

The quality of a finished product depends on the quality of the raw materials used. If a product must be made with great precision and close tolerances, the manufacturer must acquire high-quality materials and component parts. Then, if the manufacturer uses a well-managed production process, excellent products will result. Similarly, the acquisition of high-quality merchandise makes a retailer's sales to customers easier and reduces the number of necessary markdowns and merchandise returns.

Purchasing also contributes to profitable operations by ensuring that goods are delivered when they are needed. Failure to receive materials, parts, or equipment on schedule can cause costly interruptions in production operations. In a retail business, failure to receive merchandise on schedule may mean a loss of sales and, possibly, a permanent loss of customers who were disappointed.

Another aspect of effective purchasing is securing the best possible price. Cost savings go directly to the bottom line, and purchasing practices that seek out the best prices can have a major impact on the financial health of a business.

Note, however, that the importance of the purchasing function varies according to the type of business. In a small, labor-intensive service business—such as an accounting firm—purchases of supplies are responsible for a very small part of the total operating costs. Such businesses are more concerned with labor costs than with the cost of supplies or other materials they may require in their operations process.

Purchasing Practices and Cost Management

A small firm can increase the cost effectiveness of its purchasing activities by adopting appropriate purchasing practices. Through decisions related to making or buying, outsourcing, and other procurement options, the firm's management can maximize both present and future earnings.

make-or-buy decision
A firm's choice between producing and purchasing component parts for its products

MAKING OR BUYING   Many firms face **make-or-buy decisions**. Such decisions are especially important for small manufacturing firms that have the option of making or buying component parts for products they produce. A less obvious make-or-buy choice exists with respect to certain services—for example, purchasing janitorial or car rental services versus providing for those needs internally. Some reasons for making component parts, rather than buying them, follow:

- More complete utilization of plant capacity permits more economical production.

- Supplies are assured, with fewer delays caused by design changes or difficulties with outside suppliers.

- A secret design may be protected.

- Expenses are reduced by an amount equivalent to transportation costs and the outside supplier's selling expense and profit.

- Closer coordination and control of the total production process may facilitate operations scheduling and control.

- Products produced may be of higher quality than those available from outside suppliers.

Some reasons for buying component parts, rather than making them, follow:

- An outside supplier's part may be cheaper because of the supplier's concentration on production of the part.

- Additional space, equipment, personnel skills, and working capital are not needed.

- Less diversified managerial experience and skills are required.

- Greater flexibility is provided, especially in the manufacture of a seasonal item.

- In-plant operations can concentrate on the firm's specialty—finished products and services.

- The risk of equipment obsolescence is transferred to outsiders.

The decision to make or buy should be based on long-run cost and profit optimization, as it may be expensive to reverse. Underlying cost differences need to be analyzed carefully, since small savings from either buying or making may greatly affect profit margins.

OUTSOURCING   Buying products or services from other business firms is known as **outsourcing**. As mentioned earlier, firms can sometimes save money by buying from outside suppliers specializing in a particular type of work, especially services such as accounting, payroll, janitorial, and equipment repair services. The expertise of these outside suppliers may enable them to provide better-quality services by virtue of their specialization.

outsourcing
Purchasing products or services that are outside the firm's area of competitive advantage

When fashion stylist Natalie Chanin designed and hand-sewed a one-of-a-kind garment from a recycled T-shirt, she realized she had a product that would sell. But Chanin was unable to find a manufacturer in New York able to do the extensive handwork required to adorn and embroider the shirts with everything from flowers to roosters. The similarity of the work process to quilting inspired her to think of the quilting circles back in her native Alabama. After locating a group of women in Alabama who could provide the skilled handwork necessary to produce the uniquely decorated shirts, she outsourced the basic production process. Even though it's made from recycled T-shirts, Chanin's unique, high-fashion product is sold at prices as high as $2,000 in stores in the United States, Europe, and Asia. The shirts are featured in such stores as Barney's in New York, Brown's in London, and Maxfield's in Los Angeles. Thanks to outsourcing, the product is created by a contemporary version of the old-fashioned quilting circle.[12]

Chapter 19 explained the practice of employee leasing, through which a small firm transfers its employees to a leasing company, which then leases them back to the firm. In this case, the small business is outsourcing the payroll preparation process.

BUYING ON THE INTERNET   Increasingly, small companies are turning to buying on the Internet as an important alternative method of purchasing. Many tasks that once required telephone calls or out-of-office time can now be accomplished simply and quickly on the Web.

The purchasing environment is changing rapidly. In the past, small businesses had scant buying power and very limited access to resources and information, which put them at a serious disadvantage relative to their large firm competitors. That is all changing, thanks (mostly) to the Internet. A writer for *Fortune* magazine puts it this way:

Today's connected small-business owners can find themselves sitting happily as hundreds of suppliers, large and small, bid for their business. Instead of buying costly

Living the Dream · putting technology to work

How to Make eBay Employee of the Month, Every Month

After graduating from Columbia University, Michael Prete went to work for a major investment bank in New York City. But he soon tired of the corporate life and decided to redirect his time and energy to one of his true passions—motorcycles. He started a company called Gotham Cycles. As a Platinum Power Seller on eBay, the business sells parts for Ducati, Aprilia, MV Agusta, and other Italian motorcycles. After only a year or so in his new business, he was already bringing in $30,000 a month in income.

Not bad for a guy who insists on working alone. But the fact is, he doesn't exactly work alone. He has eBay as his one and only employee. Of course, the online auction site isn't exactly an employee—it's more like an *army* of employees (more than 12,000 strong, in fact) that can help an online company with many of its needs. Prete knows he never could have accomplished what he did all by himself; making use of eBay's rich stable of resources to automate his operation allowed him to concentrate on building his business.

Hiring eBay as your next employee may give your business exactly the boost it needs. For example, eBay offers sophisticated tools that can help with shipping, handling e-mail messages and feedback for buyers, and managing listings. It can even help you decide which tools are right for your business (see http://pages.ebay.com/sell/toolrecommendations.html).

Hiring eBay has certainly worked for Prete, who now says, "These tools have enabled me to continue to work alone while allowing my business to expand." He is living life in the fast lane . . . but riding solo.

Sources: Janelle Elms, "Automatic Transition," *Entrepreneur,* Vol. 35, No. 2 (February 2007), p. 118; and http://www.gotham-cycles.com, accessed April 20, 2007.

© Ducati/PR Newswire Photo Service

http://www.gotham-cycles.com

software packages, they can rent only the applications they need, and add more as the company grows. And they can outsource nearly any function—from business planning and human resources management to the purchase of office supplies.[13]

The Internet is a powerful tool, and small companies that fail to find new ways of using it to improve their operations are very likely to lose ground in the marketplace. Sometimes cheaper sources can be found locally, so it pays to shop around; however, small business owners who have no plan to tap into the power of the Internet will find it difficult to survive in the increasingly intense competitive environments they will face.

Even small farmers are purchasing on the Internet as a way of reducing costs. Jerry Brightbill, who farms 4,200 acres near Cotton Center, Texas, with his father and brother, visited a website called XSAg.com, looking for deals on farm supplies.[14] He found that he could buy herbicides at 20 percent or more off the list price and ended up spending $40,000 during the year at this one site. XSAg is only one of many Internet companies targeting the farm market. It seems probable that many of the nation's more than 2 million farmers, as well as millions of other small firms, will continue to increase their buying on the Internet.

DIVERSIFYING SOURCES OF SUPPLY   Small businesses often must decide whether it is better to use more than one supplier when purchasing a given item. The somewhat frustrating answer is "It all depends." For example, a business would rarely need more than one supplier when buying a few rolls of tape. However, several suppliers might be involved when a firm is buying a component part to be used in hundreds of products.

A small company might prefer to concentrate purchases with one supplier for any of the following reasons:

- A particular supplier may be superior in its product quality.

- Larger orders may qualify for quantity discounts.

- Orders may be so small that it is impractical to divide them among several suppliers.

- The purchasing firm may, as a good customer, qualify for prompt treatment of rush orders and receive management advice, market information, and flexible financial terms in times of crisis.

Also, a small company may be linked to a specific supplier by the very nature of its business—if it is a franchisee, for example. Typically, the franchise contract requires purchasing from the franchisor.

The following reasons favor diversifying rather than concentrating sources of supply:

- Shopping among suppliers allows a firm to locate the best source in terms of price, quality, and service.

- A supplier, knowing that competitors are getting some of its business, may provide better prices and service.

- Diversifying supply sources provides insurance against interruptions caused by strikes, fires, or similar problems with sole suppliers.

Some companies compromise by following a purchasing policy of concentrating enough purchases with a single supplier to justify special treatment and, at the same time, diversifying purchases sufficiently to maintain alternative sources of supply.

Relationships with Suppliers

Before choosing a supplier, a purchaser should be thoroughly familiar with the characteristics of the materials or merchandise to be purchased, including details of construction, quality and grade desired, intended use, maintenance or care required, and the importance of style features. In manufacturing, the purchaser must focus especially on how different grades and qualities of raw materials affect various manufacturing processes.

SELECTING SUPPLIERS   A number of factors are relevant in deciding which suppliers to use on a continuing basis. Perhaps the most significant are price and quality. Price differences are clearly important to a firm's bottom line, if not offset by quality issues or other factors.

Quality differences are sometimes difficult to detect. For some types of materials, statistical controls can be applied to evaluate vendors' shipments. In this way, the purchaser can obtain overall quality ratings for various suppliers. The purchaser can often work with a supplier to upgrade quality. If satisfactory quality cannot be achieved, the purchaser clearly has a reason for dropping the supplier.

Supplier location becomes especially important if a firm tries to keep inventory levels low, depending instead on rapid delivery of purchased items when they are needed. A supplier's overall reliability in providing goods and services is also significant. The purchaser must be able to depend on the supplier to meet delivery schedules and to respond promptly to emergency situations.

The services offered by a supplier must also be considered. The extension of credit by suppliers provides a major portion of the working capital of many small businesses. Some suppliers also plan sales promotions, provide merchandising aids, and offer management advice.

BUILDING GOOD RELATIONSHIPS WITH SUPPLIERS   Good relationships with suppliers are essential for firms of any size, but they are particularly important for small businesses. The small firm is only one among dozens, hundreds, or perhaps thousands buying from that supplier. And the small company's purchases are often very limited in volume and, therefore, of little concern to the supplier.

To implement a policy of fair play and to cultivate good relations with suppliers, a small business should try to observe the following purchasing practices:

- Pay bills promptly.

- Give sales representatives a prompt, courteous hearing.

- Avoid abrupt cancellation of orders merely to gain a temporary advantage.

- Avoid attempts to browbeat a supplier into special concessions and/or unusual discounts.

- Cooperate with the supplier by making suggestions for product improvements and/or cost reductions, whenever possible.

- Provide courteous, reasonable explanations when rejecting bids, and make fair adjustments in the case of disputes.

Some large corporations, such as UPS, Dell, FedEx, and Office Depot, have made special efforts to reach out to small business purchasers.[15] By offering various kinds of assistance, such suppliers can strengthen small companies, which then continue as customers. Of course, it still makes sense to shop around, but low prices can sometimes be misleading. The low bid for an air conditioning system sought by one small company was one-half the next lowest bid. It looked too good to be true—because it was. When examined closely, the low bid was found to have left out crucial items.

Hallmark Cards provides managerial help to some 4,000 independently owned small shops called Hallmark Gold Crown Stores:

> *Hallmark helped hundreds of the independents renegotiate leases last year, providing local real-estate market data and other help to keep rents lower.*
>
> *Hallmark also provides employee hiring and training programs, customer-satisfaction surveys, theft-prevention plans and a newsletter that spotlights best selling products and slow sellers, helping the retailers better plan their buying.*
>
> *An inventory management system installed in about 1,000 of the Gold Crown stores—mostly in ones whose owners operate multiple stores—has helped increase inventory turns, which lifts cash flow.*
>
> *And it helps merchants, with precise numbers, to make difficult decisions to get rid of product lines that move slowly, including collectibles, which were so hot in the 1990s but now have cooled off.[16]*

Building strong relationships with larger suppliers can clearly help small businesses become more competitive.

DEVELOPING STRATEGIC ALLIANCES   Some small firms have found it advantageous to develop strategic alliances with suppliers. This form of partnering enables the buying and selling firms to work much more closely than is customary in a simple contractual arrangement.

The strategic alliance option can be a good one, but the choice of partner can quickly determine whether the arrangement succeeds or fails—so choose carefully! Laurel Delaney is a successful entrepreneur, author, and educator with more than 20 years of experience in business. During that time, she guided her small businesses into strategic alliances with global powerhouses like Mitsui & Co., Ltd., the Japanese trading company. From those experiences, Delaney gained some important insights on selecting a strategic alliance partner. For example, she learned to begin her search by looking at companies with which she already had a relationship, such as a faithful supplier or distributor or a trading company that was struggling to keep up with demand. And she learned to look for partners that offered the right fit, were trustworthy, and had track records of true performance.[17] If a strategic alliance is well planned and executed, everyone involved comes out ahead.

Inventory Management and Operations

{ 5 Describe ways to control inventory and minimize inventory costs.

Inventory management is not glamorous, but it can make the difference between success and failure for a small firm. The larger the inventory investment, the more vital proper inventory management is. Inventory management is particularly important in small retail or wholesale companies, as inventory typically represents a major financial investment by these businesses.

Objectives of Inventory Management

Both purchasing and inventory management share the same objective: to have the right goods in the right quantities at the right time and place. As shown in Exhibit 20-3, achieving this general objective requires pursuing more specific subgoals of inventory control—ensuring continuous operations, maximizing sales, protecting assets, and minimizing inventory costs.

Ensuring continuous operations is particularly important in manufacturing, as delays caused by lack of materials or parts can be costly. Furthermore, sales can be maximized by completing production in a timely manner and by stocking an appropriate assortment of merchandise in retail stores and wholesale establishments. Protecting inventory from theft, shrinkage, and deterioration and optimizing investments likewise contribute to operational efficiency and business profits.

Inventory Cost Control

Maintaining inventory at an optimal level—the level that minimizes stockouts and eliminates excess inventory—saves money and contributes to operating profits. To determine the optimal level, managers must pay close attention to purchase quantities, because those quantities affect inventory levels. The ideal quantity of an item to purchase (at least some of which will be carried in inventory) is the number of items that minimizes total inventory costs. This number is called the **economic order quantity (EOQ)**.

economic order quantity (EOQ)
The quantity to purchase in order to minimize total inventory costs

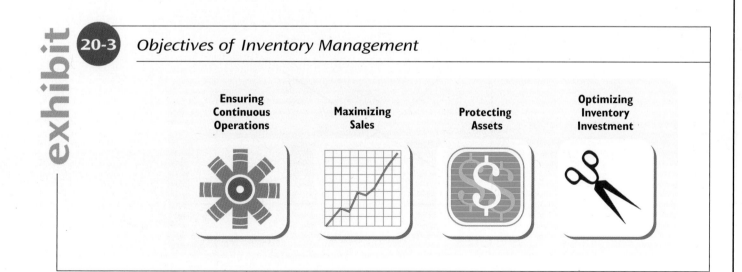

exhibit

20-3   *Objectives of Inventory Management*

| Ensuring Continuous Operations | Maximizing Sales | Protecting Assets | Optimizing Inventory Investment |

If a firm could order merchandise or raw materials and carry inventory with no expenses other than the cost of the items, there would be little concern about what quantity to order at any given time. However, inventory costs are affected by both the costs of purchasing and the costs of carrying inventory—that is,

$$\text{Total inventory costs} = \text{Total ordering costs} + \text{Total carrying costs}$$

Carrying costs include storage costs, insurance premiums, the cost of money tied up in inventory, and losses due to spoilage or obsolescence. Carrying costs go up as inventories increase in size. Ordering costs, on the other hand, include expenses associated with preparing and processing purchase orders and expenses related to receiving and inspecting the purchased items. The cost of placing an order is a fixed cost; therefore, total ordering costs increase as a firm purchases smaller quantities more frequently. Quantity discounts, if available, favor the placement of larger orders.

The point labeled EOQ in Exhibit 20-4 is the lowest point on the total costs curve; it coincides with the intersection of the carrying costs and ordering costs curves. In cases in which sufficient information on costs is available, this point can be calculated with some precision.[18] Even when the economic order quantity cannot be calculated with precision, a firm's goal must be to minimize both ordering costs and carrying costs.

ABC INVENTORY ANALYSIS   Some inventory items are more valuable or more critical to a firm's operations than others. Therefore, those items have a greater effect on costs and profits. As a general rule, managers should attend most carefully to those inventory items requiring the largest investment.

ABC method
A system of classifying items in inventory by relative value

One approach to inventory analysis, the **ABC method**, classifies inventory items into three categories based on value. The purpose of the ABC method is to focus managerial attention on the most important items. The number of categories could easily be expanded to four or more, if that seemed more appropriate for a particular firm.

In the A category are a few high-value inventory items that account for the largest percentage of total dollars or are otherwise critical in the production process and, therefore, deserve close control. They might be monitored, for example, by an inventory system that keeps a running record of receipts, withdrawals, and balances of each such item. In this way, a firm can avoid an unnecessarily heavy investment in costly inventory items.

exhibit

20-4   *Graphic Portrayal of the Economic Order Quantity*

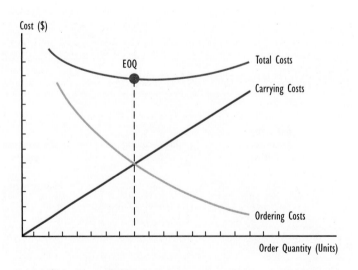

Category B items are less costly but deserve moderate managerial attention because they still make up a significant share of the firm's total inventory investment. Category C contains low-cost or noncritical items, such as paperclips in an office or nuts and bolts in a repair shop. The carrying costs of such items are not large enough to justify close control. These items might simply be checked periodically to ensure that a sufficient supply is available.

JUST-IN-TIME INVENTORY SYSTEM   The just-in-time inventory system attempts to cut inventory carrying costs by reducing inventory to an absolute minimum. First popularized by the Japanese, the just-in-time approach has led to cost reductions in many countries. New items are received, presumably, just as the last item of that type from existing inventory is placed into service. Many large U.S. firms have adopted some form of the just-in-time system for inventory management, and small businesses can also benefit from its use.

just-in-time inventory system
A method of reducing inventory levels to an absolute minimum

Adoption of a just-in-time system requires careful coordination with suppliers. Supplier locations, production schedules, and transportation schedules must be carefully considered, as they all affect a firm's ability to obtain materials quickly and in a predictable manner—a necessary condition for using a just-in-time inventory system.

The potential for failure is high in the just-in-time system. Stockout situations (which arise when delays or mistakes occur and inventory is depleted) may result in interrupted production or unhappy customers. Most firms using the just-in-time inventory system maintain some safety stock (a reserve amount for use in an emergency) to minimize difficulties of this type. Although safety stock represents a compromise of the just-in-time philosophy, it protects a firm against large or unexpected withdrawals from inventory and delays in receiving replacement items.

Inventory Record-Keeping Systems

The larger the company is, the greater the need for record keeping, but even a very small business needs a system for keeping tabs on its inventory. Because manufacturers are concerned with three broad categories of inventory (raw materials and supplies, work in process, and finished goods), their inventory records are more complex than those of wholesalers and retailers. Small firms should emphasize simplicity in their control methods. Too much control is as wasteful as it is unnecessary.

In most small businesses, inventory records are computerized. Many different software programs are available for this purpose. The manager, in consultation with the firm's accounting advisors, can select the software best suited for the particular needs of the business.

A **physical inventory system** depends on an actual count of items on hand. The counting is done in physical units such as pieces, gallons, and boxes. By using this method, a firm can create an accurate record of its inventory level at a given point in time. Some businesses have an annual shutdown to count everything—a complete physical inventory. Others use **cycle counting**, scheduling different segments of the inventory for counting at different times during the year. This simplifies the inventorying process and makes it less of an ordeal for the business as a whole.

physical inventory system
A method that provides for periodic counting of items in inventory

cycle counting
A system of counting different segments of the physical inventory at different times during the year

A **perpetual inventory system** provides an ongoing, current record of inventory items. It does not require a physical count. However, a physical count of inventory should be made periodically to ensure the accuracy of the system and to make adjustments for such factors as theft.

perpetual inventory system
A method for keeping a running record of inventory

Any part of the operations process can damage a firm's sales and profit performance if it is not done well. Therefore, careful management is needed, not only in such often-highlighted areas as quality performance and cost efficiency, but also in such mundane areas as plant maintenance and inventory control. Achieving satisfactory customer service requires a company to fine-tune its basic operations, but the financial payback from managing operations well makes this more than worth the hassle.

Looking BACK

1 Explain the key elements of total quality management (TQM) programs.

- Providing products or services of superior quality is a primary goal of the operations process.

- Quality management efforts are focused on meeting customer needs, which depends on accurate feedback from customers.

- Effective quality management requires an organizational culture that places a high value on quality.

- Quality management tools and techniques include employee involvement, quality circles, inspections, and statistical analysis.

- Small firms can obtain international recognition of quality management performance by meeting ISO 9000 standards and environmental performance by meeting ISO 14001 standards.

- Service businesses can benefit as much as manufacturers from the use of quality management programs.

2 Discuss the nature of the operations process for both products and services.

- Operations processes vary from one industry to another, but they all change inputs into outputs.

- Service and manufacturing operations typically differ in the extent of their contact with customers and the level of difficulty of establishing quality standards.

- The four types of manufacturing operations are job shops, project manufacturing, repetitive manufacturing, and batch manufacturing.

- Operations management involves planning and scheduling activities that transform inputs into products or services.

- Proper plant maintenance is necessary for efficient operations and achievement of high-quality performance.

- Preventive maintenance is needed to minimize breakdowns in machinery; corrective maintenance is used to restore equipment to good condition.

3 Explain how reengineering and other methods of work improvement can increase productivity and make a firm more competitive.

- The competitive strength of a business depends on its level of productivity.

- Reengineering involves restructuring firms by redesigning their basic work processes.

- Many small firms have improved productivity by using computers, new software, and Internet links with suppliers and customers.

- Time and motion studies can be used to make work easier and more efficient.

4 Discuss the importance of purchasing and the nature of key purchasing policies.

- Purchasing is important because it affects quality and profitability.

- A key decision for manufacturers is whether to make or buy components.

- In outsourcing, a company contracts with outside suppliers for accounting, equipment repair, or other products and services.

- Small firms are doing more purchasing on the Internet, and many are finding bargains online.

- Decisions concerning diversifying sources of supply must take into account both the advantages and the disadvantages of having multiple suppliers.

- Careful selection of suppliers will identify those offering the best price, quality, and services.

- Paying bills promptly and dealing professionally with suppliers will help build good relationships, which in turn can bring benefits, such as training provided by a supplier.

- Strategic alliances enable small companies to work closely with their suppliers.

5 Describe ways to control inventory and minimize inventory costs.

- The calculation of economic order quantities, ABC inventory analysis, and the just-in-time inventory system can all help minimize inventory costs.

- Inventory record-keeping systems include the physical inventory method and the perpetual inventory method.

Key **TERMS**

operations process, p. 525

quality, p. 525

total quality management (TQM), p. 526

continuous quality improvement, p. 528

benchmarking, p. 528

quality circle, p. 528

inspection, p. 528

inspection standard, p. 529

bottleneck, p. 529

attribute inspection, p. 529

variable inspection, p. 529

acceptance sampling, p. 529

statistical process control, p. 529

control chart, p. 530

ISO 9000, p. 530

operations management, p. 532

job shop, p. 534

project manufacturing, p. 534

repetitive manufacturing, p. 534

batch manufacturing, p. 534

preventive maintenance, p. 535

corrective maintenance, p. 535

productivity, p. 536

reengineering, p. 536

time and motion studies, p. 537

purchasing, p. 538

make-or-buy decision, p. 538

outsourcing, p. 539

strategic alliance, p. 542

economic order quantity (EOQ), p. 543

ABC method, p. 544

just-in-time inventory system, p. 545

physical inventory system, p. 545

cycle counting, p. 545

perpetual inventory system, p. 545

Discussion **QUESTIONS**

1. Why is the customer focus of quality management so important?

2. What is meant by total quality management?

3. A small manufacturer does not believe that statistical quality control charts and sampling plans are useful. Can traditional methods suffice? Can 100 percent inspection by final inspectors eliminate all defective products? Why or why not?

4. What are some distinctive features of operations processes in service firms?

5. Customer demand for services is generally not uniform during a day, week, or other period of time. What strategies can be used by service businesses to better match a company's capacity to perform services to customer demand for services?

6. Explain the purpose and nature of reengineering.

7. Doing something rapidly and doing it well can be incompatible. How might quality improvement contribute to productivity improvement?

8. What conditions make purchasing a particularly vital function in a small business? Can the owner-manager of a small firm safely delegate purchasing authority to a subordinate? Explain.

9. Under what conditions should a small manufacturer either make component parts or buy them from others?

10. Explain the basic concept underlying the calculation of an economic order quantity.

You Make the **CALL**

SITUATION 1

The owner of two pizza restaurants in a city with a population of 150,000 is studying her firm's operations to be sure the company is functioning as efficiently as possible. About 70 percent of the firm's sales represent dine-in business, and 30 percent come from deliveries. The owner has always attempted to produce a good-quality product and minimize the waiting time of customers both on- and off-premises.

A recent magazine article suggested that quality is now generally abundant and that quality differences in businesses are narrowing. The writer advocated placing emphasis on saving time for customers rather than producing a high-quality product. The owner is contemplating the implications of this article for the pizza business. Realizing that her attention should be focused, she wonders whether to concentrate primary managerial emphasis on delivery time.

Question 1 Is the writer of the article correct in believing that quality levels now are generally higher and that quality differences among businesses are minimal?

Question 2 What are the benefits and drawbacks of placing the firm's primary emphasis on minimizing customer waiting time?

Question 3 If you were advising the owner, what would you recommend?

SITUATION 2

Derek Dilworth, owner of a small manufacturing firm, is trying to deal with the firm's thin working capital situation by carefully managing payments to major suppliers. These suppliers extend credit for 30 days, and customers are expected to pay within that time period. However, the suppliers do not automatically refuse subsequent orders when a payment is a few days late. Dilworth's strategy is to delay payment of most invoices for 10 to 15 days beyond the due date. Although he is not meeting the "letter of the law," he believes that the suppliers will go along with him rather than lose future sales. This practice enables Dilworth's firm to operate with sufficient inventory, avoid costly interruptions in production, and reduce the likelihood of an overdraft at the bank.

Question 1 What are the ethical implications of Dilworth's payment practices?

Question 2 What impact, if any, might these practices have on the firm's supplier relationships? How serious would this impact be?

SITUATION 3

The owner of a small food products company was confronted with an inventory control problem involving differences of opinion among his subordinates. His accountant, with the support of his general manager, had decided to "put some teeth" into the inventory control system by deducting inventory shortages from the pay of route drivers who distributed the firm's products to stores in their respective territories. Each driver was considered responsible for the inventory on his or her truck.

When the first "short" paychecks arrived, drivers were angry. Sharing their concern, their immediate supervisor, the regional manager, first went to the general manager and then, getting no satisfaction there, appealed to the owner. The regional manager argued that there was no question about the honesty of the drivers. He said that he personally had created the inventory control system the company was using, and he admitted that the system was complicated and susceptible to clerical mistakes by the driver and by the office. He pointed out that the system had never been studied by the general manager or the accountant, and he maintained that it was ethically wrong to make deductions from the small salaries of honest drivers for simple record-keeping errors.

Question 1 What is wrong, if anything, with the general manager's approach to making sure that drivers do not steal or act carelessly? Is some method of enforcement necessary to ensure careful adherence to the inventory control system?

Question 2 Is it wrong to deduct from drivers' paychecks shortages documented by inventory records?

Question 3 How should the owner resolve this dispute?

Experiential **EXERCISES**

1. Outline the operations process involved in your present educational program. Be sure to identify inputs, operations, and outputs.

2. Outline, in as much detail as possible, your customary practices in studying for a specific

course. Evaluate the methods you use, and specify changes that might improve your productivity.

3. Using the ABC inventory analysis method, classify some of your personal possessions into the

three categories. Include at least two items in
each category.

4. Interview the manager of a bookstore about the
type of inventory control system used in the
store. Write a report in which you explain the

methods used to avoid buildup of excessive
inventory and any use made of inventory turnover
ratios (ratios that relate the dollar value of
inventory to the volume of sales).

Exploring the WEB

1. For an additional perspective on quality and the
managerial and organizational commitment necessary to achieve the highest quality standards,
find the Total Quality Management (TQM) tutorial
webpage at **http://home.att.net/~iso9k1/tqm/
tqm.html**. Choose the "Introduction" link and
read the content provided there.

    a. According to the site's content provider, TQM
    is the foundation for what activities? What are
    the principles of TQM, as discussed on this
    site?

    b. Of these TQM activities and principles, which
    seem to focus most on the customer?

2. The Automotive Service Association is a leading
organization for owners and managers of automotive services businesses. Go to the association's
website and read the article on improving inventory control by Rick Lavely. It can be found at
**http://www.asashop.org/autoinc/march/invntctr.
htm**. Lavely discusses different ways an auto
shop can determine inventory profitability.

    a. According to the article, how can an owner/
    manager determine the cost to order? What
    does cost to order imply for selling parts from
    inventory?

    b. At the end of the article, the author gives five
    basic rules for inventory control. List these
    rules. Do you agree that they are good rules
    to live by?

3. This chapter discusses how a firm can obtain international recognition of its quality improvement
programs through the International Organization
for Standardization. Go to the ISO website at
http://www.iso.org and then answer the following
questions based on information you find there.

    a. What is the ISO? You can find the answer to
    this question by choosing "Introduction" on
    the main page.

    b. Now use the site to learn more about ISO
    9000 and ISO 14001. What additional infor-
    mation did you learn about these particular
    forms of certification?

Video Case **20**

Modern Postcard (p. 660)
This case focuses on the use of new technology and
advances in operations management that can lead
to higher quality and greater efficiency, which allows
a company to respond better to customer needs and
market trends.

Alternative Cases for Chapter 20:
Case 17, Sunny Designs, Inc., p. 654

Case 18, Douglas Electrical Supply, Inc., p. 656

Case 21, Protecting Intellectual Property, p. 662

## chapter 21

Managing Risk

Crisis Management in the Eye of the Storm
http://www.leidenheimer.com

Sandy Whann is the president of family-owned-and-operated Leidenheimer Baking Company. He is the fourth generation of Leidenheimer men to run the company, which was founded in 1896 in the city of New Orleans by Whann's great-grandfather, George Leidenheimer, of Germany. The bakery produces French bread made famous by traditional local dishes like the muffaletta and po boy sandwiches that originated in the heart of the French Quarter.

As a lifetime citizen of New Orleans, Whann has experienced many evacuations and has become adept at hurricane planning through the years. When a hurricane alert was issued on August 27, 2005, Whann immediately put his family emergency plan into effect, as his wife and two children prepared to leave the city. He remained near the plant to keep a close eye on his 110-year-old company and keep production working at a minimal capacity. With his family out of the city, Whann focused on his employees and their families.

The next day, after meeting with upper management, Whann decided to shut the bakery down and secure its exterior, gas lines, and doors. He encouraged his employees to prepare their own homes and loved ones for the storm and potential evacuation. Both Whann and the Leidenheimer management team keep a list of home phone numbers and emergency evacuation contact information for all employees. After the employees had left, only Whann, his plant manager, and chief engineer—all of whom play key roles in the business's preparedness plan—remained in New Orleans and, once they had completed their assigned duties in the emergency shutdown, they left as well.

Whann's trip to Baton Rouge was unusual—a drive that normally takes one hour took seven hours. "Things were very different this time around," said Whann. "But in the gridlock, I still made the most of the little time we had before the storm hit. Having an emergency preparedness plan helps you focus your priorities and helps you know what you need to be doing with the limited time you have in any situation."

En route, Whann contacted his insurance provider, accountants, legal consultant, and customers via cell phone to keep them abreast of the situation and the effect of his shutdown on customers' supply of baked goods. His business evacuation kit played a large part in his success; it included financial and payroll records, utility contact information, updated phone lists for his

© Eric Futran/FoodPix/Jupiter Images

customers and employees, backup files and software, as well as computer hard drives. Well before the evacuation, Whann had placed the kit in a mobile waterproof/fireproof case that could be taken with him at a moment's notice. As part of his written plan, he set up a satellite office for the Leidenheimer Baking Company in Baton Rouge, where he made contact with his bank, forwarded phone calls, and was receiving forwarded mail within two days after the evacuation.

On August 29, Whann breathed a sigh of relief that his family and his company had escaped a major disaster. But once he received word of extensive flooding in New Orleans, his anxiety as a business owner really started to set in. Water in the plant was the worst problem from a business standpoint. "My first instinct was to return and help with recovery, repair damages, and get home," Whann said. "But this was impossible because Katrina's wake of devastation was so severe."

Whann was able to return to his plant within a week of the storm and found serious damage, but no flooding. Thousands of pounds of melted yeast and other ingredients had been sitting wet for weeks without refrigeration. The roof had severe damage, there was no power and no usable water, and only the National Guard was permitted back into the city. Temperatures at the plant exceeded 120 degrees and foul smells emanated from every square inch of it. All Whann could focus on was getting the plant back into production as soon as possible.

Though he cared deeply for his business, more important to Whann were his employees, and he felt fortunate that all of the company's employees were safe. "The rebuilding process included a handful of things," said Whann. "Number one is the employees. What some of our folks faced and what they are still facing in their personal lives is heart-breaking. It is important to listen to the needs of employees."

In summing up his experience, Whann said, "Katrina was severe enough to teach even us experienced hurricane survivors a few new things about our emergency planning." Since Hurricane Katrina, he has revised his business emergency plan and gained a more extensive understanding of the importance of preparation.

Source: Adapted from the United States Department of Homeland Security, "Case Studies and Testimonials," http://www.ready.gov/business/other/testimonials.html, accessed August 7, 2007.

 Looking **AHEAD**

After studying this chapter, you should be able to

1 Define risk and explain the nature of risk.
2 Classify the different types of business risk.
3 Identify the steps in the risk management process and explain how risk management can be used in small companies.
4 Explain the basic principles used in evaluating an insurance program.
5 Identify the common types of business insurance coverage.

We live in a world of uncertainty, so how we see risk is vitally important in almost all dimensions of life. Risk must certainly be considered in making any business decisions. As sixth-century Greek poet and statesman Solon wrote,

> *There is risk in everything that one does, and no one knows where he will make his landfall when his enterprise is at its beginning. One man, trying to act effectively, fails to foresee something and falls into great and grim ruination, but to another man, one who is acting ineffectively, a god gives good fortune in everything and escapes from his folly.*[1]

While Solon gave more credit than we would to Zeus for the outcomes of ventures, his insight reminds us that little is new in this world—least of all, the need to acknowledge and compensate as best we can for the risks we encounter.

Risk means different things to different people. For a student, risk might be represented by the possibility of failing an exam. For a coal miner, risk might be represented by the chance of an explosion in the mine. For a retired person, risk could mean the likelihood of not being able to live comfortably on his or her limited income. Of course, an entrepreneur's risk takes the form of the chance that a new venture will fail.

As Benjamin Franklin once said, "In this life nothing is certain except death and taxes." Entrepreneurs might extend this adage to include small business risks. Chapter 1 noted the moderate risk-taking propensities of entrepreneurs and their desire to exert some control over the risky situations in which they find themselves by seeking to minimize business risks as much as possible. This chapter outlines how this can be done. Our study of this important topic begins with a definition of risk.

What Is Risk?

1 Define risk and explain the nature of risk.

risk
The possibility of suffering harm or loss

market risk
The uncertainty associated with an investment decision

pure risk
The uncertainty associated with a situation where only loss or no loss can occur

Simply stated, **risk** is the "possibility of suffering harm or loss."[2] Applied to a business, risk translates into the possibility of losses associated with the assets and the earnings potential of the firm. Here, the term *assets* includes not only inventory and equipment but also such factors as the firm's employees, its customers, and its reputation.

Business risks can be classified into two broad categories: market risk and pure risk. **Market risk** is the uncertainty associated with an investment decision. An entrepreneur who invests in a new business hopes for a gain but realizes that the eventual outcome may be a loss. Only after identifying the investment opportunity, developing strategies, and committing resources will she or he find out whether the final result is a gain or a loss.

Pure risk describes a situation where only loss or no loss can occur—there is no potential gain. Owning property, for instance, creates the possibility of loss due to fire or severe weather; the only outcomes are loss or no loss. As a general rule, only pure risk is insurable. That is, insurance is not intended to protect investors from market risks, where the chances of both gain and loss exist.

Classifying Business Risks

2 Classify the different types of business risk.

The pure risks that any business faces can be put into the following categories: property risks, liability risks, and personnel risks. Let's take a look at these risks, related to the physical, legal, and human aspects of a business.

Property Risks

real property
Land and anything physically attached to the land, such as buildings

In the course of establishing a business, an owner acquires property that will be necessary to provide the goods and services of the company. If this property is damaged or destroyed, the business sustains a loss. In addition, the temporary loss of use of the property can add to the negative financial impact on the business. Several characteristics of business property and the risks associated with it are worthy of attention.

There are two general types of property—real property and personal property. **Real property** consists of land and anything physically attached to land, such as buildings.

Living the Dream   entrepreneurial challenges

SAMBAZON®

Get with the purple berry.

© Sambazon

Fruits of Success

"The first guy on the beach usually gets shot," says Jeremy Black, one of a pair of entrepreneurial brothers who introduced a nutrient-rich Brazilian berry called acai to the U.S. market. With $100,000 from friends and family, Jeremy and his brother, Ryan, set up an infrastructure in Brazil to harvest acai. Then, with the help initially of the Juice It Up! franchise, they began to market a smoothie under the brand name Sambazon.

But the brothers encountered a risk inherent in a successful business: Other firms wanted to cash in on their success. Coca-Cola and Pepsico added the fruit to their product lines. Sometimes, Sambazon's acai products get stocked inside the cooler for Coca-Cola's Odwalla acai juices. To make sure this doesn't happen, the brothers have had to absorb the costs associated with sending more Sambazon sales associates into the stores.

Still, the firm, which is based in San Clemente, California, has grown to 100 employees. For the year ending January 2007, Sambazon acai products accounted for 10 percent of all U.S. frozen-fruit sales in natural-food channels.

Source: Gwendolyn Bounds, "The Perils of Being First," *Wall Street Journal,* March 19, 2007, pp. R1, R4.

http://www.sambazon.com

Some business owners purchase land and buildings, while others choose to lease necessary real property. It is important to note, however, that some leases make the lessee responsible for any damage or loss to the leased premises. **Personal property** can be defined simply as any property other than real property. Personal property includes machinery, equipment (such as computers), furniture, fixtures, stock, and vehicles. While the location of real property is fixed, personal property can be moved from place to place. Among the risks to the personal property of the small firm are the security threats to their computers posed by hackers and spyware, for example. (See Exhibit 21-1.)

    Property can be valued in a number of ways. The **replacement value of property** is the cost to replace or recreate the property at today's prices. For example, a building that was constructed 10 years ago at a cost of $200,000 may have a current replacement value of $250,000 because of the rising costs of materials and labor. The **actual cash value (ACV)** of a property can be very different from its replacement value; this insurance term refers to the depreciated value of a property. Assuming a rate of depreciation of 3 percent per year for the 10-year-old building, we would find the building to have an estimated actual cash value of $175,000 [that is, $250,000 − (0.03 × 10 × $250,000)]. By common practice, commercial property insurance typically values all property loss at the actual cash value of the damaged or lost property. It also takes into account two primary features—perils (the cause) and losses (the effect).

personal property
Any property other than real property, including machinery, equipment, furniture, fixtures, stock, and vehicles

replacement value of property
The cost to replace or replicate property at today's prices

actual cash value (ACV)
An insurance term that refers to the depreciated value of a property

exhibit

21-1 *Security Threats to Computers*

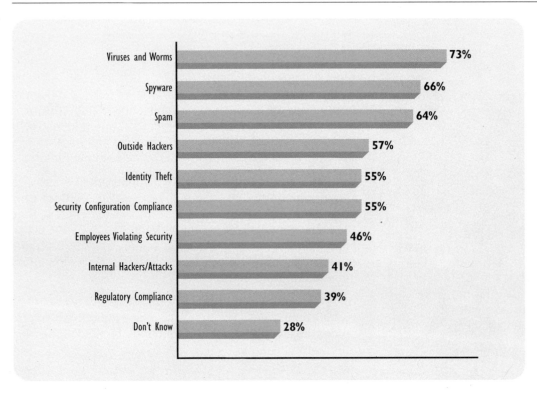

Viruses and Worms — 73%
Spyware — 66%
Spam — 64%
Outside Hackers — 57%
Identity Theft — 55%
Security Configuration Compliance — 55%
Employees Violating Security — 46%
Internal Hackers/Attacks — 41%
Regulatory Compliance — 39%
Don't Know — 28%

Source: Forrester Survey in "What We're Worrying About," *Inc.,* Vol. 29, No. 3 (March 2007), p. 36.

peril
A cause of loss, either through natural events or through the acts of people

PERILS   A **peril** is defined as a cause of loss. Some perils are naturally occurring events, such as windstorms, floods, earthquakes, and lightning. The location of property may increase the likelihood of its loss from certain perils—for example, coastal properties are more susceptible to wind damage and flooding, and properties near fault lines are more prone to damage from earthquakes.

Not all perils, however, are natural events; some are related to the actions of people. Perils such as robbery and employee dishonesty involve criminal acts performed by people against business owners. The rapid growth of electronic commerce (e-commerce) has led to new forms of dishonest acts, such as hacking, denial of access, and improper use of confidential information.

direct loss
A loss in which physical damage to property reduces its value to the property owner

indirect loss
A loss arising from inability to carry on normal operations due to a direct loss to property

LOSSES   Usually, when you think of property loss, you envision a **direct loss**, in which physical damage to property reduces its value to the property owner. The direct loss of property as a result of windstorm, fire, or explosion is obvious to everyone and has the potential to significantly hinder any business.

A less obvious type of property loss is an **indirect loss**, which arises from inability to carry on normal operations due to a direct loss. For example, if a delivery truck is damaged in an accident, the resulting loss of use can impair the ability of a business to get its goods to customers. The indirect loss component of this event may cause a reduction in revenue or an increase in expense (from having to outsource the delivery function), either of which will have an adverse impact on business income.

It should be pointed out that business income can also be reduced by events or conditions that are not related to direct losses. For example, a strike by UPS employees a few years ago created serious logistical problems for many of its business customers, which were unable to receive goods from suppliers or deliver goods to customers. The financial impact of such a labor action may be just as real to a business as physical damage to property, but the insurance protection available for indirect losses applies only when *direct* damage events trigger the loss of use. More will be said on this issue later in the chapter.

Liability Risks

A growing business risk today is the legal liability that may arise from various business activities. A society creates laws to govern interactions among its members. Individual rights and freedoms are protected by these laws. If a business or any of its agents violates these protected rights, the business can be held accountable for any resulting loss or damage to the affected party. Legal liability may arise from statutory liability, contractual liability, or tort liability.

STATUTORY LIABILITY   Some laws impose a statutory obligation on a business. For example, each state has enacted **workers' compensation legislation** that creates an absolute liability on the employer to provide certain benefits to employees when they are injured in a work-related event. This means that fault is not an issue; an employer is responsible for work-related injuries without regard to fault. While the benefits differ slightly from state to state, most workers' compensation statutes require employers to provide the following benefits to employees injured at work: coverage of medical expenses, compensation for lost wages, payment of rehabilitation expenses, and death benefits for employees' families.

> **workers' compensation legislation**
> Laws that obligate the employer to pay employees for injury or illness related to employment, regardless of fault

   This statutory liability is potentially significant for any business. The attacks on the World Trade Center provided a stark example of the magnitude of this liability, especially for companies whose employees worked in a concentrated area. Marsh, Inc., the leading insurance broker in the world, lost over 300 employees in the 9/11 disaster, creating an enormous financial obligation on the part of the employer to the families of the victims. Most businesses protect themselves from this type of financial loss through the purchase of workers' compensation insurance. Some large employers choose to self-insure (that is, they set aside part of their earnings to offset any potential future losses), but most purchase extra insurance protection to guard against catastrophic events such as the 9/11 tragedy.

CONTRACTUAL LIABILITY   Businesses often enter into contracts with other parties. These contracts could involve a lease of premises, a sales contract with a customer, or an agreement with an outsourcing firm. Nobody enjoys reading pages of legal documents, but it is important to closely examine all contracts to determine the risks assumed. For example, some lease agreements make the lessee responsible for any loss or damage to the leased premises. This usually requires the lessee to purchase some form of property insurance or lessee liability coverage.

   Insurance agents and brokers can be helpful in assessing the risk presented by contractual agreements. Be sure to include all contracts in the initial risk assessment process.

TORT LIABILITY   Civil wrongs include breach of contract and torts. **Torts** are wrongful acts or omissions for which an injured party can take legal action against the wrongdoer to seek monetary damages. Tort actions commonly include an allegation of negligence, but four elements must be present for someone to be found guilty of a negligent act.

> **torts**
> Wrongful acts or omissions for which an injured party can take legal action against the wrongdoer for monetary damages

   First, there must exist a legal duty between the parties. For example, a restaurant owner has a legal duty to provide patrons with food and drink that are fit for consumption. Likewise, an employee making a delivery for an employer has a duty to operate a vehicle safely on public roads.

   The second element of negligence is the failure to provide the appropriate standard of care. The standard of care normally used is the **reasonable (prudent person) standard**, based on what a reasonable or prudent person would have done under similar circumstances. This standard of care may be elevated, however, if a "professional" is involved. In professional liability actions, the standard of care is determined by the established standards of the profession. For example, a negligence action against a CPA would use the standards of the accounting profession as the benchmark. Expert witnesses are often used to help establish the standard and determine what clients can reasonably expect.

> **reasonable (prudent person) standard**
> The typical standard of care, based on what a reasonable or prudent person would have done under similar circumstances

The third element in establishing negligence is the presence of injury or damages. Negligence may exist, but if no injury or damage is sustained by the claimant, tort liability does not exist. Two types of damages may be awarded in a tort action: compensatory and punitive damages.

Compensatory damages are intended to make the claimant whole—that is, to compensate the claimant for any injuries or damage arising from the negligent action. Compensatory damages can be economic or noneconomic in nature. **Economic damages** relate to economic loss, such as medical expenses, loss of income, or the cost of property replacement/restoration. Economic damages are relatively easy to quantify. **Noneconomic damages** cover such losses as pain and suffering, mental anguish, and loss of physical abilities. In comparison to economic damages, noneconomic damages are difficult to express in financial terms. Civil courts usually have a hard time setting these awards, and many of today's substantial awards include a large amount for noneconomic damages.

Punitive damages are a form of punishment that goes beyond any compensatory damages. Punitive damages have a dual purpose. First, they punish wrongdoers in instances where there is gross negligence or a callous disregard for the interests of others. Second, punitive damages are intended to have a deterrent effect, sending a message to society that such conduct will not be tolerated.

The final element in a successful tort liability claim is demonstrating that the negligent act is the **proximate cause** of the loss—that is, proving that the negligence actually caused the damages sustained. There may be negligence and there may be damages, but if no link can be established between the two, there is no tort liability.

Tort liability can arise from a number of business activities. Some of the more significant sources of tort liability follow.

- *Premises liability*. People may sustain injuries while on a business's premises. Retailers have significant premises liability exposure because they have many customers entering stores to purchase goods. Some other businesses, however, have little in the way of premises liability exposure. A consulting firm or a Web-design company would not typically have clients visit its business location; therefore, its premises liability exposure would be minimal.

- *Professional liability*. Any business providing professional services to the public is potentially subject to professional liability claims. Recognizing this exposure is important, since separate liability insurance is necessary to properly protect a business from professional liability claims.

- *Employee liability*. As mentioned previously, employers have a statutory obligation to pay certain benefits to employees injured in the course of employment. Negligence on the part of the employer is not an issue; this is a statutory obligation of the employer to its employees.

- *Vehicular liability*. If a business uses vehicles for various purposes, the business has vehicular liability exposure. Even a company that does not own or lease vehicles has potential liability if employees use their personal vehicles for business purposes.

- *Product liability*. The products or services provided by a business can be a source of legal liability. Any directions or advice given by the business regarding the use of products can become a source of liability as well. For example, if a retailer assembles a product for a customer, any mistakes made in the assembly process could result in a tort claim against the seller.

- *Directors and officers liability*. An increasing concern among businesses today is the threat of suits against the directors and officers of a company. The exposure is greatest for publicly held firms, but it exists also for private firms and nonprofit organizations. For example, a business owner who accepts membership on the board of a YMCA or other nonprofit organization may possibly be sued by someone who has a claim against that organization.

compensatory damages
Economic or noneconomic damages intended to make the claimant whole, by indemnifying the claimant for any injuries or damage arising from the negligent action

economic damages
Compensatory damages that relate to economic loss, such as medical expense, loss of income, or the cost of property replacement/restoration

noneconomic damages
Compensatory damages for such losses as pain and suffering, mental anguish, and loss of physical abilities

punitive damages
A form of punishment that goes beyond compensatory damages, intending to punish wrongdoers for gross negligence or a callous disregard for the interests of others and to have a deterrent effect

proximate cause
In the area of tort liability, a negligent act with a causal link to the damages sustained

Personnel Risks

Personnel risks are risks that directly affect individual employees but may have an indirect impact on a business as well. The primary risks in this category include premature death, poor health, and insufficient retirement income.

PREMATURE DEATH   The risk associated with death is not if but when. We all expect to die; however, there is a risk that we may die early in life. This risk poses a potential financial problem for both the family of the person and his or her employer. Individuals deal with this risk by maintaining a healthy lifestyle and purchasing life insurance to protect family members who rely on their income.

Employers can be quite adversely impacted by the untimely death of an employee if that employee cannot be easily replaced. And what if a partner or owner of the business dies? Normally, such an event triggers a buyout of the interest of the deceased owner. Life insurance is often used to fund these buyout provisions.

POOR HEALTH   A more likely occurrence than death of an employee is poor health. The severity of poor health varies, ranging from a mild disorder to a more serious, disabling malady. And as with premature death, the consequences of this event may affect an employer as well as family members.

The financial consequences of poor health have two dimensions. First are medical expenses, which can range from the cost of a doctor's visit to catastrophic expenses related to surgeries and hospitalization. Second are consequences of the inability to work. Disability most often is a temporary condition, but it can be lengthy or even permanent. A worker's permanent disability can have the same financial impact on her or his family as death.

Employers often provide some form of health insurance as a benefit of employment. In some instances, the cost of the health insurance is shared by the employer and the employee; in most instances, however, the bulk of the cost is absorbed by the employer. In addition to the health insurance costs, the fact that the employer is without the services of the employee for some time period may add to the adverse financial impact on the business.

INSUFFICIENT RETIREMENT INCOME   The final category of personnel risk involves the possibility of outliving one's wealth. The goal in dealing with this risk is to defer income and accumulate sufficient wealth to provide a satisfactory level of income during the nonworking years.

There are three primary sources of retirement income: Social Security, employer-funded retirement programs, and personal savings. Social Security provides a retirement income benefit, although for most retirees this benefit is not sufficient to meet expected consumption during retirement. To supplement this income, most workers have a retirement program associated with their employment. In the past, these programs were primarily funded by employers as a form of deferred compensation. While employer-funded pension plans still exist, it is more common today to encounter employee-funded retirement plans, where the employee can elect to defer current income for retirement. Usually, these plans are partially funded by employers as an incentive for employees to participate. Finally, individual saving can be used to accumulate wealth for retirement. All of these sources should be carefully considered in the retirement income planning process.

Risk Management

Risk management consists of all efforts to preserve the assets and earning power of a business. Since risk management has grown out of insurance management, the two terms are often used interchangeably. However, risk management has a much broader meaning, covering both insurable and uninsurable risks and including non-insurance approaches to reducing all types of risk. Risk management involves more than trying to obtain the most insurance for each dollar spent; it is concerned with finding the best way possible to reduce the cost of dealing with risk. Insurance is only one of several approaches to minimizing the pure risks a firm is sure to encounter.

---

personnel risks
Risks that directly affect individual employees but may have an indirect impact on a business as well

3 Identify the steps in the risk management process and explain how risk management can be used in small companies.

risk management
Ways of coping with risk that are designed to preserve the assets and earning power of a firm

exhibit *Risks on the Road to Success*

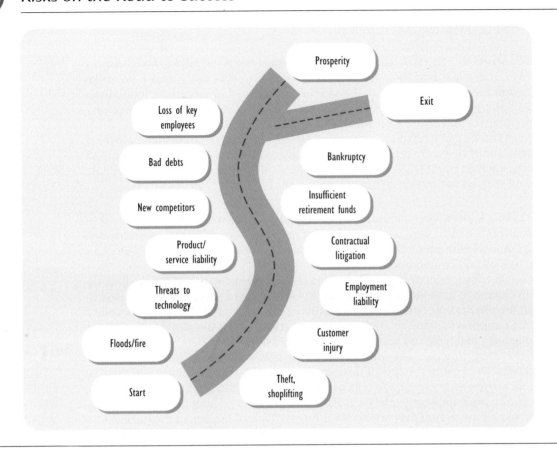

The Process of Risk Management

Five steps are required to develop and implement a risk management program.

> *Step 1: Identify and understand risks.* It is essential that a business owner be aware of the risks the firm faces on the road to success. To reduce the chance of overlooking important risks, a business should adopt a systematic approach to identifying risks. Useful identification methods include insurance policy checklists, questionnaires, analysis of financial statements, and careful analysis of a firm's operations, customers, and facilities. Exhibit 21-2 depicts just a few of the risks that a small company may encounter.

> *Step 2: Evaluate risks.* Once the various risks have been identified, they must be evaluated in terms of the potential size of each loss and the probability that it will occur. At a minimum, risks should be classified into three groups: critical (losses that could result in bankruptcy), extremely important (losses that would require investment of additional capital to continue operations), and moderately important (losses that can be covered with current income or existing assets).

> *Step 3: Select methods to manage risk.* The two approaches used in dealing with risk are risk control and risk financing, both of which will be discussed later in this chapter.

> *Step 4: Implement the decision.* Once the decision has been made to use a particular technique or techniques to manage a firm's risks, this decision must be followed by action, such as purchasing insurance and setting aside dedicated funds to cope with any risks that have been retained. Failure to act—or even simple procrastination—could be fatal.

Step 5: Evaluate and review. Evaluation and review of the chosen risk management technique are essential because conditions change—new risks arise and old ones disappear. Also, reviewing earlier decisions to use specific methods may identify mistakes made previously.

Risk Management and the Small Business

Regardless of the nature of the business, risk management is a serious issue for small companies, as well as large corporations. Too often, small businesses pay insufficient attention to analyzing potential risk. "Small companies often spend more time planning their company picnics than for an event that could put them out of business," says Katherine Heaviside, a partner in Epoch 5, a Huntington, New York, public relations firm that specializes in crisis communication.[3] To avoid being put out of business by an unexpected development, the small business owner must take an active role in managing the risks of her or his firm.

Risk management in a small business differs from that in a large firm in several ways. First, insurance companies are not always eager to insure small companies and may even turn them down in some cases. Also, in a large firm, the responsibilities of risk management are frequently assigned to a specialized staff manager. It is more difficult for a small company to cope with risk management since its risk manager is usually the owner and the owner wears so many hats. Furthermore, risk management is not something that requires immediate attention—until something happens. A prudent small business owner will take the time to identify the different types of risks faced by the firm and find ways to cope with them, through either risk control or risk financing.

RISK CONTROL **Risk control** involves minimizing loss through prevention, avoidance, and/or reduction. **Loss prevention**, as the name implies, focuses on stopping loss from happening. For example, if a mail-order business finds that goods are being damaged in the delivery process, it may switch to a more secure and reliable delivery service, thus eliminating property damage and customer dissatisfaction. **Loss avoidance** is achieved by choosing not to engage in a hazardous activity. For instance, the risk of losing critical computer records can be avoided by storing backup files at a different physical location. (Keeping backup files in the desk drawer in the same office as the computer will do little good if the desk is damaged by fire or water). **Loss reduction** addresses the potential frequency, severity, or unpredictability of loss, thereby lessening the impact of the loss on the business. Crisis planning is a form of loss reduction in that it provides a template to follow in the case of a catastrophic loss. Installing automatic sprinkler systems in a building is another good example of a loss reduction strategy. If a fire occurs in a building with an automatic sprinkler system, the sprinklers will be activated, minimizing the amount of fire damage to the building.

RISK FINANCING **Risk financing** focuses on making funds available for losses that cannot be eliminated by risk control; it involves transferring the risk or retaining the risk. **Risk transfer** is accomplished largely through buying insurance but can also be achieved by making other contractual arrangements that transfer the risk to others. Contractual arrangements, for example, can include subcontracting an activity or purchasing a fidelity bond to protect against employee fraud. **Risk retention** entails financing loss through operating revenues or retained earnings. One common form of risk retention is **self-insurance**, in which part of a firm's earnings is designated as a cushion against possible future losses. Self-insurance can take a general or a specific form. In its general form, a part of the firm's earnings is earmarked for a contingency fund against possible future losses, regardless of the source. In its specific form, a self-insurance program designates funds to individual loss categories such as property, health care, or workers' compensation. Some firms have begun to rely heavily on self-insurance, particularly in the area of medical coverage for employees. For several years now, the cost of health insurance has increased 10–15 percent annually—and much more in some cases. For instance, in 2002, Flat Rock Furniture, a manufacturing firm in Waldron, Indiana, paid $326,000 in health insurance premiums for the firm's 80 employees. The firm's owner, Van McQueen, was

risk control
Minimizing potential losses by preventing, avoiding, or reducing risk

loss prevention
Stopping loss from happening

loss avoidance
Avoiding loss by choosing not to engage in hazardous activities

loss reduction
Lessening the frequency, severity, or unpredictability of losses

risk financing
Making funds available to cover losses that could not be eliminated by risk control

risk transfer
Buying insurance or making contractual arrangements with others in order to transfer risk

risk retention
Financing loss intentionally, through operating revenues or retained earnings

self-insurance
Designating part of a firm's earnings as a cushion against possible future losses

Living the Dream   entrepreneurial challenges

© Matt Rourke/Associated Press

Eminent-Domain Risk

The federal government tries to befriend small businesses, but sometimes it is just another source of risk. One example is the 2005 Supreme Court ruling *Kelo v. City of New London*, which affirmed local governments' right to condemn and seize private property for outside private development.

Bob Blue, owner of Bernard Luggage Company, received a letter one day from his neighborhood's redevelopment agency. It informed Blue that his building, along with 30 others, was being condemned.

Blue knew that a move would be devastating for the business, as 40 to 50 percent of the company's revenue comes from foot traffic. The building that Blue owns—and in which his business has been located since 1955—sits on the posh corner of Hollywood and Vine in Hollywood, California. Customers may not remember the Bernard Luggage name, but they do remember its location.

Blue filed a lawsuit and also moved his fight into the public eye by appearing on local television news programs. Blue says that small business owners shouldn't wait for abuse to happen but instead protect their firm before the business is targeted. The threat of eminent domain is a real risk for some small firms, even though many states recently have introduced legislation restricting the abuse of this legal right.

Sources: Karen J. Bannan, "Condemnation," *MyBusiness*, June-July, 2006, pp. 31–34; and "Bernard Luggage Co. User Reviews," http://losangeles.citysearch.com/review/54595, accessed March 19, 2007.

sadly surprised when the insurance company increased the firm's premiums for 2003 to $480,000—a 47 percent increase in a single year! McQueen decided to self-fund employee health benefits—and saved $325,000 of what the firm would have paid the insurance company.[4]

It should be understood, however, that self-insurance is not suitable for every small firm. As a rule of thumb, a firm should have a net worth of at least $250,000 and 25 or more employees to be self-funded. Moreover, very few firms can practice unlimited self-insurance, especially when it comes to liability claims. Unless a small company has insurance to cover losses above a certain level, any large loss could put it out of business. In any case, self-insurance plans need to be approved and monitored to protect the interests of those covered.

In choosing the appropriate method for managing risk, the small business owner should consider the size of each potential loss, its probability of occurrence, and what resources would be available to cover the loss if it did occur. Exhibit 21-3 shows the appropriate risk management techniques for potential losses of different probabilities (low frequency and high frequency) and loss amounts (low severity and high severity).

exhibit 21-3   *Tools for Managing Risk*

	Probability of Loss	
Amount of Loss	**High Frequency**	**Low Frequency**
High Severity	• Loss prevention • Loss avoidance • Loss reduction	• Self-insurance • Contractual agreements
Low Severity	• Loss reduction • Risk retention	• Risk retention

Note: To find a listing of the risk management tools appropriate for dealing with a potential loss, see the box corresponding to the severity and frequency of the potential loss.

Basic Principles of a Sound Insurance Program

4 Explain the basic principles used in evaluating an insurance program.

What kinds of risks can be covered by insurance? What types of coverage should be purchased? How much coverage is adequate? Unfortunately, there are no clear-cut answers to these questions. A reputable insurance agent can provide valuable assistance to a small company in evaluating risks and designing proper protection plans, but an entrepreneur should become as knowledgeable as possible about what insurance is available. Three basic principles should be followed in evaluating an insurance program:

1. Identify business risks to be insured.
2. Limit coverage to major potential losses.
3. Relate premium costs to probability of loss.

IDENTIFYING INSURABLE BUSINESS RISKS   A small firm must first obtain risk coverages required by law or by contract, such as workers' compensation insurance and automobile liability insurance. Then a careful investigation should be carried out to identify risks less obvious than the common insurable risks pointed out earlier in the chapter. As part of the risk-identification process, plants and equipment should be reevaluated periodically by competent appraisers in order to ensure that adequate insurance coverage is maintained.

LIMITING COVERAGE TO MAJOR POTENTIAL LOSSES   A small company must determine the magnitude of loss that it could bear without serious financial difficulty. If the firm is financially strong, it may decide to minimize its insurance costs by covering only those losses exceeding a specified minimum amount. It is important, of course, to guard against underestimating the severity of potential losses.

RELATING PREMIUM COSTS TO PROBABILITY OF LOSS   Because insurance companies must collect enough premiums to pay for the actual losses of insured parties, the cost of insurance is proportional to the probability of occurrence of the insured event. As the loss becomes more certain, premium costs become so high that a firm may find that insurance is simply not worth the cost. Thus, insurance is most applicable and practical for *improbable* losses—that is, situations where the probability that the loss will occur is low, but the overall cost of the loss would be high.

Common Types of Business Insurance

5 Identify the common types of business insurance coverage.

It is beyond the scope of this chapter to describe all forms of business insurance. But we'll look at a few common types: business owner's policies, key-person insurance, and disability insurance.

Living the Dream   entrepreneurial challenges

Insuring Small Business Success

Annual double-digit increases in the cost of health care are a big concern for small business owners. Of the nation's estimated 46 million uninsured, 27 million are small business owners or their employees or dependents. Entrepreneur Jim Henderson, 43, feels something must be done to provide affordable health care for employees of small companies.

Henderson, owner of St. Louis–based Dynamic Sales Co., Inc., a construction and industrial supply firm with annual sales of $1.5 million, has struggled to provide insurance coverage for his seven employees for the past 17 years. He remembers when he could afford to offer a zero-deductible, 100 percent coverage plan, but those days are long gone. This past year, Henderson went to a $2,000 deductible, with his employees responsible for the first $1,000. "It's a solution, but it's not one I'm happy with," Henderson explains.

Source: J. Louise Larson, "Call a Doctor!," *Entrepreneur,* Vol. 35, No. 6 (June 2007), http://www.entrepreneur.com/magazine/entrepreneur/2007/June/17-8358.html, accessed July 27, 2007.

http://www.dynamicsalescoinc.com

BUSINESS OWNERS' POLICIES   Some business insurance policies are generic contracts containing numerous options to fit the coverage needs of individual insurance buyers. These types of policies could conceivably address the needs of a wide range of potential buyers, from small commercial enterprises to large and complex corporations.

    An alternative approach to insurance policy design is to create a policy appropriate for a certain class of insured parties. For example, a homeowner's policy is designed to meet the property and liability insurance needs of individuals who own their residences. A version of homeowner's insurance has been adapted to meet the needs of those individuals who live in leased houses or apartments.

    The **business owner's policy (BOP)** is a business version of the homeowner's policy, designed to meet the property and liability insurance needs of small business owners. The eligibility criteria for a BOP are fairly broad, with the only excluded classes being manufacturers, financial institutions, and auto repair facilities. A BOP is intended to be a comprehensive contract that needs few enhancements. A brief description of the coverage provided by a BOP follows.

business owner's policy (BOP)

A business version of a homeowner's policy, designed to meet the property and liability insurance needs of small business owners

Property Covered   A BOP can be used to cover both real property and personal property. For businesses that own buildings or other structures or are required to be responsible for property damage to non-owned real property, real property coverage can be provided.

Businesses that do not have the responsibility for real property damage can elect to insure personal property only, including furniture and fixtures, equipment, inventory, and supplies.

Perils Covered   Insurers use two approaches to define the perils covered by property insurance. With the **named-peril approach**, the specific perils covered are identified. Any loss caused by a peril not named in the policy is not covered. In contrast, with the **all-risk approach**, all direct damages to property are covered except those caused by perils specifically excluded. In other words, if a particular peril is not excluded in an all-risk policy, any loss caused by that peril is covered.

> **named-peril approach**
> Identifying, in an insurance policy, the specific perils covered

> **all-risk approach**
> Stating, in an insurance policy, that all direct damages to property are covered except those caused by perils specifically excluded

BOPs offer both named-peril and all-risk options; the choice is up to the insured. The named-peril option typically covers damage done by fire, lightning, explosion, windstorm and hail, smoke, aircraft and vehicles, riot and civil commotion, vandalism, sprinkler leakage, sinkhole collapse, and volcanic action, as well as certain transportation perils. Cyber insurance is an additional option with the named-peril approach. Greater numbers of small business owners are considering such coverage; a typical $100,000 policy costs $1,000 in yearly premiums.[5] The all-risk insurance option covers all direct physical damage and loss, except that caused by such perils as earth movement, flood, war, nuclear explosions, and intentional damage caused by the insured. The all-risk option is generally preferable for the insured, but the benefit of an enhanced scope of coverage must be evaluated in terms of the additional cost.

Valuation   A unique, attractive feature of a BOP is that both real and personal property are valued on a replacement-cost basis. This means that all property damage and loss will be reimbursed at the rate required to rebuild or replace the property. For example, if the roof of a building is damaged, the cost of repairing the damage will be covered. Likewise, damage and loss to equipment will be evaluated based on the cost of repairing or replacing the equipment.

Unlike most property insurance policies, a BOP does not contain a provision called **insurance to value**, which requires that the policy limit be at least a specified percentage of the actual value of the property. But the prevalence of insurance to value in property insurance policies requires that a small business owner be on the lookout for such a clause. The most common version is a **coinsurance provision**, which requires that the property be insured for at least 80 percent of its value; if that minimum is not carried, a penalty is applied to any covered loss. For example, if an insured building had a replacement value of $500,000, the 80 percent policy limit would require that the property be insured for at least $400,000 ($500,000 × 0.80). If the building was insured for only $300,000 and an insured loss of $100,000 occurred, the recovery would be limited to $75,000, calculated as follows:

> **insurance to value**
> A provision, common in property insurance policies, requiring that the policy be at least a specified percentage of the actual value of the property

> **coinsurance provision**
> The most common version of an insurance to value clause, requiring that property be insured for at least 80 percent of its value or else a penalty will be applied to any covered loss

$$\frac{\text{Coinsurance}}{\text{provision}} = \frac{\text{Insured value}}{\text{Policy limit \% × Replacement value}} \times \text{Property loss}$$

$$= \frac{\$300,000}{0.80 \times \$500,000} \times \$100,000$$

$$= 0.75 \times \$100,000$$

$$= \$75,000$$

Thus, insuring for less than the actual property value can be expensive, with the cost far exceeding what an entrepreneur might save in premiums. "A far better approach," explains Jerry Milton, an insurance industry consultant, "is to insure for full value with a larger deductible." Milton advises a business owner to increase coverage if the property value increases for any reason.[6]

Business Interruption   As mentioned previously, the financial loss associated with a property loss is not limited to direct damage to the property. There may be an indirect loss as well, usually associated with the loss of use of the affected property. **Business interruption coverage** provides a business with reimbursement for the loss of anticipated income, allowing the business to pay continuing expenses that otherwise could not be met because of the negative impact of the direct loss on business revenues. Preparing for the potential impact of an indirect loss is particularly important for small businesses, as they may not be able to survive financially without business interruption insurance protection.

> **business interruption coverage**
> Coverage that reimburses a business for the loss of anticipated income, allowing the business to pay continuing expenses that otherwise could not be met because of the negative impact of the direct loss on business revenues

Business interruption coverage is an integral part of a BOP. Two limits are applicable to this coverage. First, the time period is restricted to 12 months. This is generally not a

exhibit   **21-4**   *Risk-Taking Begins Early*

Source: © Harley I. Schwadron

problem, since most small businesses can be fully restarted within that period, even after sustaining substantial direct damage. Second, the dollar limit for business interruption losses is a shared limit with direct damage coverage. Thus, when setting property damage limits in a BOP, the insured must consider the potential loss due to both direct damage and business interruption.

General Liability Coverage   A BOP integrates business property coverage with the liability coverage needed by most small businesses. It contains **commercial general liability (CGL) coverage**, which provides payment for bodily injury and property damage for which the insured business is liable. The CGL coverage takes care of premises liability exposure, product liability exposure, and other potential liabilities of the business. It does not cover vehicle liability, professional liability, or employee liability, which all require a separate policy for adequate protection.

Medical Payments Coverage   BOP **medical payments coverage** provides payment for injuries sustained by customers and the general public. The unique feature of medical payments coverage is that it does not require any fault on the part of the insured. This "no fault" coverage pays the medical expenses of others up to a per-person limit described in the policy.

LIFE AND DISABILITY INSURANCE   Two types of insurance provide coverage for key individuals within a business: key-person insurance and disability insurance.

Key-Person Insurance   By carrying **key-person insurance**, a small business can protect itself against the death of key personnel. Such insurance may be written on an individual or group basis. It is purchased by a firm, with the firm as the sole beneficiary.

Most small business advisors suggest term insurance for key-person insurance policies, primarily because of lower premiums. How much key-person insurance to buy is more difficult to decide. Face values of such policies usually begin around $50,000 and may go as high as several million dollars.

Disability Insurance   One risk that small businesses often do not consider is loss due to disability of a partner or other key employee of the company. Statistics, however, show that the odds of a person being disabled are much higher than most people think.

commercial general liability (CGL) coverage
Coverage providing payment for bodily injury and property damage for which the insured business is liable

medical payments coverage
Coverage providing payment for injuries sustained by customers and the general public, with no fault required on the part of the insured

key-person insurance
Coverage that provides benefits upon the death of a firm's key personnel

---

How They See It: Managing Risk

Denny Fulk

The area of risk management as it relates to the purchase of insurance has been well covered in the text. It is a particularly challenging issue for the newer, smaller startup. My personal perspective is that you should not place your family, your employees, or others involved with you at risk by not purchasing the proper insurance. Plan for it, budget for the most essential coverage, and buy it. Income protection for your dependents in case of death or disability is a top priority. All lending institutions require the pledge of security or guarantee to repay business debt or personal borrowing, so purchasing your own insurance to cover the amount of the debt is a better alternative than purchasing the lender's "credit life" insurance.

My business partner and I agreed that purchasing whole life insurance rather than term insurance for buy-sell insurance and real estate and equipment debt provided sound protection for our young families. It proved to be an excellent investment decision for the years we operated as a regular corporation. Having the premiums paid as a business expense of the corporation resulted in each of us being charged a certain percentage of that amount as additional personal income, but this was still an advantageous situation. The resulting cash values of the policies after 32 years were a very significant asset. Over the long term, the returns realized from a quality, dividend-paying, fixed premium, whole life insurance policy from a reputable company will far outweigh the benefits of buying a term policy (with annual premiums increased for age and current health conditions). Attempting to invest any amount of premium saved from the purchase of term insurance in something that will provide a greater return is difficult, at best. Your top priority should be to focus on your company's business objectives rather than gamble with guaranteed protection for your family.

After selling the corporation, along with investing in stocks and mutual funds, I invested a significant portion of the resulting funds in a single payment annuity policy. This policy provides a selection of well-diversified mutual funds that, in the event of my death, guarantee the market value of the investments at that time but no less than the amount I originally invested. We also maintained disability policies on both partners until the sale of the company.

For example, the Social Security Administration cites studies showing that a 20-year-old worker has a 30 percent chance of being temporarily disabled before retirement age.[7]

The most common type of **disability insurance** provides for the payment of a portion (typically two-thirds) of the disabled person's normal monthly income for a period of time after the disability occurs. However, it protects only the disabled person and not the business. Alternatively, partners can purchase disability buyout insurance. This type of disability insurance protects both partners by guaranteeing that the healthy partner will have enough cash to buy out the disabled partner without draining capital from the business.

disability insurance
Coverage that provides benefits upon the disability of a firm's partner or other key employee

Another option is key-person disability insurance, which replaces revenue lost because of the disability of a key employee. For example, if a firm's top salesperson, who brings in $5,000 a month, becomes disabled, this coverage will provide up to 125 percent replacement income for a year or more, to give the firm time to recruit and train someone else.

Another type of disability insurance is designed to cover fixed overhead expenses, such as rent, utilities, employee salaries, and general office expenses, while an owner or other key employee recuperates. This type of insurance is especially well suited for a sole proprietorship, since the firm would have no income if the owner were unable to work.

There is no question that risk is a part of life, but how you manage it will affect the success of your small business. As described in this chapter, business risks can be classified into two broad categories: market risk and pure risk. Because market risk is the uncertainty associated with an investment decision, starting any new business entails a certain amount of this form of risk. Pure risk, on the other hand, includes property risks, liability risks, and personnel risks. The chapter offers a five-step risk management program to help you deal with risk. Regardless of the nature of the uncertainty, risk management is a serious issue for small businesses. That's why the basic principles of a sound insurance program are so important. They can help you deal with many of the uncertainties that you will surely encounter. In fact, you can bet on it . . . but gambling can be risky, too.

Looking BACK

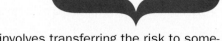

1 Define risk and explain the nature of risk.

· Risk is the possibility of suffering harm or loss.

· Business risks can be classified into two broad categories: market risk and pure risk.

· Market risk is the uncertainty associated with an investment decision.

· Pure risk exists in a situation where only loss or no loss can occur—there is no potential gain.

· In general, only pure risk is insurable.

2 Classify the different types of business risk.

· Pure risks that face any business fall into three groups: property risks, liability risks, and personnel risks.

· Property risks involve potential damage to or loss of real property (e.g., land and buildings) and personal property (e.g., equipment).

· For insurance purposes, property may be valued based on its replacement value or its actual cash value (ACV).

· A peril is defined as a cause of loss, either from naturally occurring events or from the actions of people.

· Property losses are categorized as direct losses, arising from obvious physical damage, or indirect losses, which result from inability to carry on normal operations because of a direct loss to property.

· Liability risks arise from statutory liabilities, contractual liabilities, or tort liabilities.

· Personnel risks, such as premature death, poor health, and insufficient retirement income, directly affect individuals but may indirectly impact the business as well.

3 Identify the steps in the risk management process and explain how risk management can be used in small companies.

· Risk management is concerned with protection of the assets and the earning power of a business against loss.

· The risk management process involves identifying and understanding risks, evaluating the severity of risks, selecting methods for managing risk, implementing the decision, and evaluating and reviewing prior decisions.

· The two ways to manage business risks are risk control and risk financing.

· Risk control is designed to prevent, avoid, or reduce risk.

· Risk financing involves transferring the risk to someone else or retaining the risk within the firm.

4 Explain the basic principles used in evaluating an insurance program.

· Three basic principles should be followed in evaluating an insurance program: (1) identify the business risks to be insured, (2) limit coverage to major potential losses, and (3) relate the cost of premiums to the probability of loss.

· A firm must first secure risk coverage required by law or by contract.

· Property should be revalued periodically to be certain that adequate insurance is being maintained.

· A company should determine the magnitude of loss it can sustain without serious financial difficulty.

· The cost of insurance is proportional to the probability of occurrence of the insured event.

5 Identify the common types of business insurance coverage.

· A business owner's policy (BOP) is a business version of a homeowner's policy, designed to meet the property and liability insurance needs of small business owners.

· A BOP can cover both real property and personal property; offers named-peril and all-risk options; values property on a replacement-cost basis; and includes business interruption coverage, commercial general liability (CGL) coverage, and medical payments coverage.

· Insurers use two approaches to define the perils covered by property insurance. With the named-peril approach, the specific perils covered are identified; with the all-risk approach, all direct damages to property are covered except those caused by perils specifically excluded.

· Most property insurance policies contain an insurance to value provision, which requires that the policy limit be at least a specified percentage of the actual value of the property. The most common version is a coinsurance provision, which requires that the property be insured for at least 80 percent of its value or else a penalty will be applied to any covered loss.

· Two types of insurance provide coverage for key individuals within a business: key-person insurance and disability insurance.

Key TERMS

risk, p. 552

market risk, p. 552

pure risk, p. 552

real property, p. 552

personal property, p. 553

replacement value of property,
  p. 553

actual cash value (ACV), p. 553

peril, p. 554

direct loss, p. 554

indirect loss, p. 554

workers' compensation legislation,
  p. 555

torts, p. 555

reasonable (prudent person)
  standard, p. 555

compensatory damages, p. 556

economic damages, p. 556

noneconomic damages, p. 556

punitive damages, p. 556

proximate cause, p. 556

personnel risks, p. 557

risk management, p. 557

risk control, p. 559

loss prevention, p. 559

loss avoidance, p. 559

loss reduction, p. 559

risk financing, p. 559

risk transfer, p. 559

risk retention, p. 559

self-insurance, p. 559

business owner's policy (BOP),
  p. 562

named-peril approach, p. 563

all-risk approach, p. 563

insurance to value, p. 563

coinsurance provision, p. 563

business interruption coverage,
  p. 563

commercial general liability (CGL)
  coverage, p. 564

medical payments coverage, p. 564

key-person insurance, p. 564

disability insurance, p. 565

Discussion QUESTIONS

1. Define risk, and then distinguish between pure risk and market risk.

2. What are the different types of risk that a business may encounter?

3. What are the basic ways to manage risk in a business?

4. Describe the different sources of legal liability.

5. Can a small company ever safely assume that business risks will never turn into losses sufficient to bankrupt it? Why or why not?

6. When is it logical for a small business to utilize self-insurance?

7. Why might a small business owner decide not to purchase business insurance?

8. Under what conditions would purchasing life insurance on a business executive provide little protection for a company? When is such life insurance helpful?

9. Describe a business owner's policy. List the advantages of this type of policy, and tell what types of insurance coverage are available with a BOP.

10. What is the purpose of a coinsurance provision and how does it work?

You Make the CALL

SITUATION 1

The Amigo Company manufactures motorized wheelchairs in its Bridgeport, Michigan, plant, under the supervision of Alden Thieme. Alden is the brother of the firm's founder, Allen Thieme. The company has 100 employees and does $10 million in sales a year. Like many other firms, Amigo is faced with increased liability insurance costs. Although Alden is contemplating dropping all coverage, he realizes that the users of the firm's product are individuals who have already suffered physical and emotional pain. Therefore, if an accident occurred and resulted in a liability suit, a jury might be strongly tempted to favor the plaintiff. In fact, the company is currently facing litigation. A woman in an Amigo wheelchair was killed by a car on the street. Because the driver of the car had no insurance, Amigo was sued.

Question 1 Do you agree that the type of customer to whom the Amigo Company sells should influence its decision regarding insurance?

Question 2 In what way, if any, should the outcome of the current litigation affect Amigo's decision about renewing its insurance coverage?

Question 3 What options does Amigo have if it drops all insurance coverage? What is your recommendation?

SITUATION 2

Pansy Ellen Essman is a 48-year-old grandmother who is chairperson of a company that does $5 million in sales each year. Her company, Pansy Ellen Products, Inc., based in Atlanta, Georgia, grew out of a product idea that Essman had as she was bathing her squealing, squirming granddaughter in the bathroom tub. Her idea was to produce a sponge pillow that would cradle a child in the tub, thus freeing the caretaker's hands to clean the baby. From this initial product, the company expanded its product line to include nursery lamps, baby food organizers, strollers, and hook-on baby seats. Essman has seemingly managed her product mix risk well. However, she is concerned that other

sources of business risk may have been ignored or slighted.

Question 1 What types of business risk do you think Essman might have overlooked? Be specific.

Question 2 Would a risk-retention insurance program be a good possibility for this company? Why or why not?

Question 3 What kinds of insurance coverage should this type of company carry?

SITUATION 3

H. Abbe International, owned by Herb Abbe, is a travel agency and freight forwarder located in downtown Minneapolis. When the building that housed the firm's offices suffered damage as a result of arson, the firm was forced to relocate its 2 computers and 11 employees. Moving into the offices of a client, Abbe worked from this temporary location for a month before returning to his regular offices. The disruption cost him about $70,000 in lost business and moving expenses. In addition, he had to lay off four employees.

Question 1 What are the major types of risk faced by a firm such as H. Abbe International? What kind of insurance will cover these risks?

Question 2 What kind of insurance would have helped Abbe cope with the loss resulting from arson? In purchasing this kind of insurance, what questions must be answered about the amount and terms?

Question 3 Would you have recommended that Abbe purchase insurance that would have covered the losses in this case?

Experiential **EXERCISES**

1. Log on to *Entrepreneur* magazine's website at http://www.entrepreneur.com and find two articles on new small business startups. Select one new firm that is marketing a product and another that is selling a service. Compare their situations relative to business risks. Report on your analysis to the class.

2. Contact a local small business owner and obtain his or her permission to conduct a risk analysis

of the business. Report to the class on the business's situation in regard to risk and what preventive or protective actions you would suggest.

3. Arrange to interview the owner or one of the agents of a local insurance company. Determine in the interview the various types of coverage the company offers for small businesses. Write a report on your findings.

Exploring the WEB

Go to the Small Business Administration's website at **http://www.sba.gov**. Click on "Tools," then under "Library and Resources," click on "Publications" and then on "Management and Planning Series." Read No. 17, "Small Business Risk Management Guide (MP-28)," and answer the following questions.

1. What are the major categories of loss that a business owner must address to be sure that she or he has adequate insurance coverage for the business?

2. What employee benefits are required by law? What optional benefits might you provide to employees to attract the most qualified individuals?

3. List the ways you can limit your exposure to loss. Explain at least two of these methods.

4. What services do insurance companies provide to policyholders?

5. Print and complete "Appendix A: Checklist for Insurance Needs." If you don't already have a business of your own, base your answers on a business you hope to start.

Video Case **21**

PROTECTING INTELLECTUAL PROPERTY (p. 662)

This case explores the definition of intellectual property, its importance to the small firm, and its history.

Part 6

Understanding What the Numbers Mean

## chapter 22

Managing the Firm's Assets

Home and Garden Party, Ltd.
http://www.homeandgardenparty.com

Home and Garden Party, Ltd., is a home-based party planning business featuring home decor items such as hand-turned stoneware pottery, framed prints, and brass accessories. The firm was started by Steve and Penny Carlile in 1996. Their story is very similar to those told by other entrepreneurs about the potential opportunity and the risk resulting from unexpected growth in a startup's early years.

Our first year in business was very slow. We held events in several cities, and we ran ads in newspapers explaining our business and the opportunity for individuals to be part of an independent sales force, or what we called "designers." During 1996 and the first half of 1997, we developed a strong home office staff. . . . The next 18 months were exciting, but frightening to say the least.

1998 was a very difficult year because our growth outpaced our production and fulfillment abilities. Our sales in 1997 were $1,200,000. In 1998, our sales jumped to $15,400,000, and we were overwhelmed. Our problem was compounded by the fact that we manufactured approximately 65 percent of all the products we sold. We not only had to invest in shipping and warehousing infrastructure, we also had to completely re-engineer our production facilities to keep pace with the growth. We ran out of product, refunded money, and sent gift certificates. For several months, it appeared as if we would implode. The solution to our dilemma was based on three things:

■ *We knew we had to deal directly and honestly with the problem. We needed to let our designers know that we understood we had failed them and that we were committed to fixing the problem.*

■ *We determined what areas were causing us the most pain and dealt with them immediately. System changes were implemented in every department.*

■ *We made large capital contributions to the company through equity injections, personal loans, and bank loans.*

Our company has continued to grow, but the stress of 1998 is a constant reminder that we need to work to get ahead of potential problems. Continuing to improve the process and to develop exceptional employees is the key to preparing for the challenges we face ahead.

Ours is an ever-changing market, but our goal is to provide affordable, quality products and an appealing catalog in addition to a lucrative compensation plan for our designers.

Watching our costs and improving each department of the company will always be important to us.

Source: Personal communication with Penny and Steve Carlile, August 7, 2007.

Looking AHEAD

After studying this chapter, you should be able to

1 Describe the working-capital cycle of a small business.

2 Identify the important issues in managing a firm's cash flows, including the preparation of a cash budget.

3 Explain the key issues in managing accounts receivable, inventory, and accounts payable.

4 Discuss the techniques commonly used in making capital budgeting decisions.

5 Describe the capital budgeting practices of small firms.

When a firm grows as Home and Garden Party did, the entrepreneur's dream can become a nightmare. The nightmare results in part from problems with managing the firm's assets during high-growth periods, in terms of both working capital and long-term investments, such as those for computer systems, equipment, and buildings. In this chapter, we look at what is involved in effectively managing a company's assets.

The Working-Capital Cycle

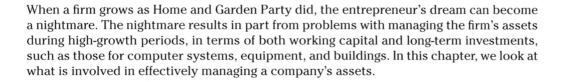

Ask the owner of a small business about financial management and you will likely hear about the joys and tribulations of managing cash, accounts receivable, inventories, and accounts payable. **Working-capital management**—managing short-term assets (current assets) and short-term sources of financing (current liabilities)—is extremely important to most small companies.[1] In fact, there may be no financial discipline that is more important, and yet more misunderstood. Good business opportunities can be irreparably damaged by ineffective management of a firm's short-term assets and liabilities.

A firm's **working-capital cycle** is the flow of resources through the company's accounts as part of its day-to-day operations. As shown in Exhibit 22-1, the steps in a firm's working-capital cycle are as follows:

Step 1. Purchase or produce inventory for sale, which increases accounts payable—assuming the purchase is a credit purchase—and increases inventories on hand.

Step 2. a. Sell the inventory for cash, which increases cash, or
b. Sell the inventory on credit, which increases accounts receivable.

Step 3. a. Pay the accounts payable, which decreases accounts payable and decreases cash.
b. Pay operating expenses and taxes, which decreases cash.

Step 4. Collect the accounts receivable when due, which decreases accounts receivable and increases cash.

Step 5. Begin the cycle again.

1 Describe the working-capital cycle of a small business.

working-capital management
The management of current assets and current liabilities

working-capital cycle
The daily flow of resources through a firm's working-capital accounts

exhibit

22-1   *Working-Capital Cycle*

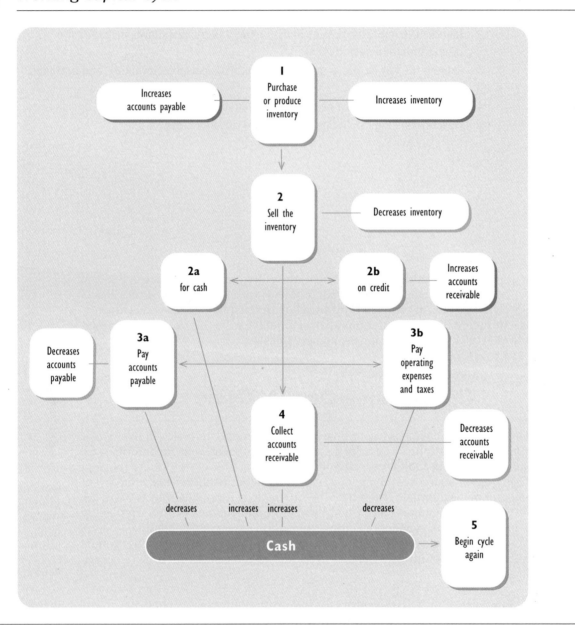

Depending on the industry, the working-capital cycle may be long or short. For example, it is only a few days in the grocery business; it is longer, most likely months, in an automobile dealership. Whatever the industry, however, management should be working continuously to shorten the cycle.

The Timing and Size of Working-Capital Investments

It is imperative that owners of small companies understand the working-capital cycle, in terms of both the timing of investments and the size of the investment required (for example, the amounts necessary to maintain inventories and accounts receivable). The owner's failure to understand these relationships underlies many of the financial problems of small companies. Too many entrepreneurs wait until a problem arises to deal with working capital.

exhibit 22-2 *Working-Capital Time Line*

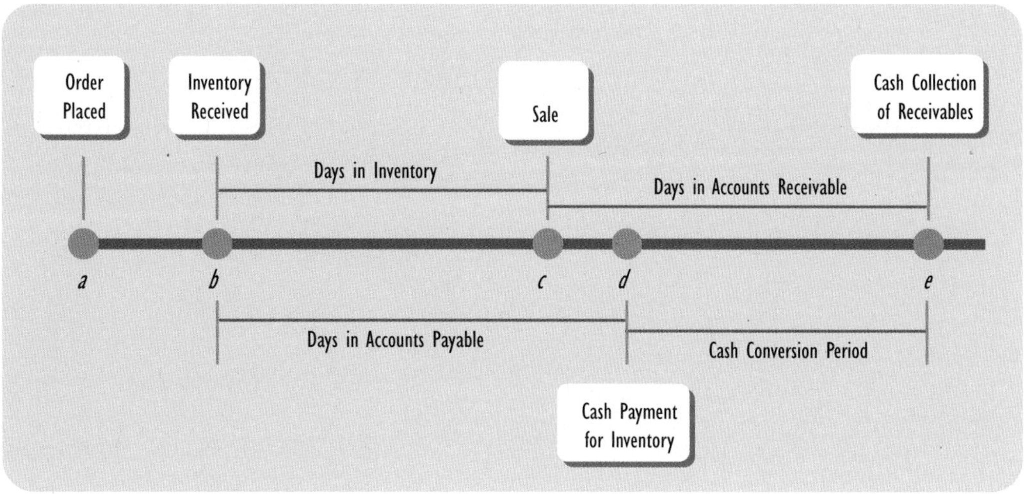

Exhibit 22-2 shows the chronological sequence of a hypothetical working-capital cycle. The time line reflects the order in which events unfold, beginning with an investment in inventory and ending with collection of accounts receivable. The key dates in the exhibit are as follows:

Day a. Inventory is ordered in anticipation of future sales.

Day b. Inventory is received.

Day c. Inventory is sold on credit.

Day d. Accounts payable come due and are paid.

Day e. Accounts receivable are collected.

The investing and financing implications of the working-capital cycle reflected in Exhibit 22-2 are as follows:

■ Money is invested in inventory from day *b* to day *c*.

■ The supplier provides financing for the inventories from day *b* to day *d*.

■ Money is invested in accounts receivable from day *c* to day *e*.

■ Financing of the firm's investment in accounts receivable must be provided from day *d* to day *e*. This time span, called the **cash conversion period**, represents the number of days required to complete the working-capital cycle, which ends with the conversion of accounts receivable into cash. During this period, the firm no longer has the benefit of supplier financing (accounts payable). The longer this period lasts, the greater the potential cash flow problems for the firm.

cash conversion period
The time required to convert paid-for inventories and accounts receivable into cash

Examples of Working-Capital Management

Exhibit 22-3 offers two examples of working-capital management by firms with contrasting working-capital cycles: Pokey, Inc., and Quick Turn Company. On August 15, both firms buy inventory that they receive on August 31, but the similarity ends there.

22-3   *Working-Capital Time Lines for Pokey, Inc., and Quick Turn Company*

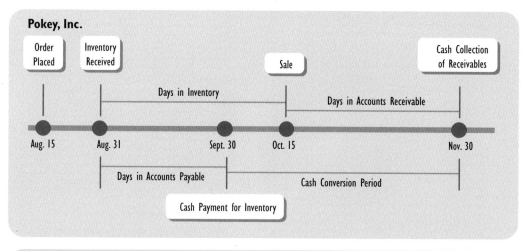

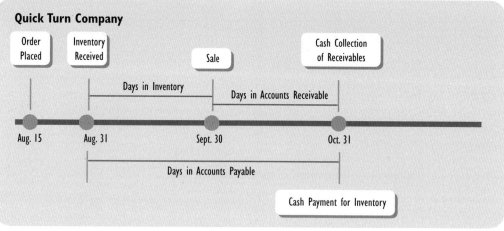

Pokey, Inc., must pay its supplier for the inventory on September 30, before eventually reselling it on October 15. It collects from its customers on November 30. As you can see, Pokey, Inc., must pay for the inventory two months prior to collecting from its customers. Its cash conversion period—the time required to convert the paid-for inventories and accounts receivable into cash—is 60 days. The firm's managers must find a way to finance this investment in inventories and accounts receivable, or else they will experience cash flow problems. Furthermore, although increased sales should produce higher profits, they will compound the cash flow problem because the company will have to finance the investment in inventory until the accounts receivable are collected 60 days later.

Now consider Quick Turn Company's working-capital cycle, shown in the bottom portion of Exhibit 22-3. Compared to Pokey, Quick Turn Company has an enviable working-capital position. By the time Quick Turn must pay for its inventory purchases (October 31), it has sold its product (September 30) and collected from its customers (October 31). Thus, there is no cash conversion period because the supplier is essentially financing Quick Turn's working-capital needs.

To gain an even better understanding of the working-capital cycle, let's see what happens to Pokey's balance sheet and income statement. To do so, we will need more information about the firm's activities. A month-by-month listing of its activities and their effects on its balance sheet follow. Pay close attention to the firm's working capital, especially its cash balances.

July: Pokey, Inc., is a new company, having started operations in July with $1,000, financed by $300 in long-term debt and $700 in common stock. At the outset, the owner purchased $600 worth of fixed assets, leaving the remaining $400 in cash. At this point, the balance sheet would appear as follows:

Cash	$ 400
Fixed assets	600
TOTAL ASSETS	$1,000
Long-term debt	$ 300
Common stock	700
TOTAL DEBT AND EQUITY	$1,000

August: On August 15, the firm's managers ordered $500 worth of inventory, which was received on August 31 (see Exhibit 22-3). The supplier allowed Pokey 30 days from the time the inventory was received to pay for the purchase; thus, inventories and accounts payable both increased by $500 when the inventory was received. As a result of these transactions, the balance sheet would appear as follows:

	July	August	Changes: July to August
Cash	$ 400	$ 400	
Inventory	0	500	+$500
Fixed assets	600	600	
TOTAL ASSETS	$1,000	$1,500	
Accounts payable	$ 0	$ 500	+$500
Long-term debt	300	300	
Common stock	700	700	
TOTAL DEBT AND EQUITY	$1,000	$1,500	

So far, so good—no cash problems yet.

September: On September 30, the firm paid for the inventory; both cash and accounts payable decreased by $500, shown as follows.

	July	August	September	Changes: August to September
Cash	$ 400	$ 400	($ 100)	−$500
Inventory	0	500	500	
Fixed assets	600	600	600	
TOTAL ASSETS	$1,000	$1,500	$1,000	
Accounts payable	$ 0	$ 500	$ 0	−$500
Long-term debt	300	300	300	
Common stock	700	700	700	
TOTAL DEBT AND EQUITY	$1,000	$1,500	$1,000	

Now Pokey, Inc., has a cash flow problem in the form of a cash deficit of $100.

October: October was a busy month for Pokey. On October 15, merchandise was sold on credit for $900; sales (in the income statement) and accounts receivable increased by that amount. The firm incurred operating expenses (selling and administrative expenses) in the amount of $250, to be paid in early November; thus, operating expenses (in the income statement) and accrued expenses (current liabilities in the balance sheet) increased by $250. (An additional $25 in accrued expenses resulted from accruing taxes that will be owed on the firm's earnings.) Finally, in October, the firm's accountants recorded $50 in depreciation expense (to be reported in the income statement), resulting in accumulated depreciation on the balance sheet of $50.

The results are as follows:

	July	August	September	October	Changes: September to October
Cash	$ 400	$ 400	($ 100)	($ 100)	
Accounts receivable	0	0	0	900	+$900
Inventory	0	500	500	0	−500
Fixed assets	600	600	600	600	
Accumulated depreciation	0	0	0	(50)	−50
TOTAL ASSETS	$1,000	$1,500	$1,000	$1,350	
Accounts payable	$ 0	$ 500	$ 0	$ 0	
Accrued operating expenses	0	0	0	250	+$250
Income tax payable	0	0	0	25	+25
Long-term debt	300	300	300	300	
Common stock	700	700	700	700	
Retained earnings	0	0	0	75	+75
TOTAL DEBT AND EQUITY	$1,000	$1,500	$1,000	$1,350	

The October balance sheet shows all the activities just described, but there is one more change in the balance sheet: It now shows $75 in retained earnings, which had been $0 in the prior balance sheets. As you will see shortly, this amount represents the firm's income. Note also that Pokey, Inc., continues to be overdrawn by $100 on its cash. None of the events in October affected the firm's cash balance. All the transactions were the result of accruals recorded by the firm's accountant, offsetting entries to the income statement. The relationship between the balance sheet and the income statement is as follows:

Change in the Balance Sheet		Effect on the Income Statement
Increase in accounts receivable of $900	→	Sales of $900
Decrease in inventories of $500	→	Cost of goods sold of $500
Increase in accrued operating expenses of $250	→	Operating expenses of $250
Increase in accumulated depreciation of $50	→	Depreciation expense of $50
Increase in accrued taxes of $25	→	Tax expense of $25

November: In November, the accrued expenses were paid, which resulted in a $250 decrease in cash along with an equal decrease in accrued expenses. At the end of November, the accounts receivable were collected, yielding a $900 increase in cash and a $900 decrease in accounts receivable. Thus, net cash increased by $650. The final series of balance sheets is as follows:

	July	August	September	October	November	Changes: October to November
Cash	$ 400	$ 400	($ 100)	($ 100)	$ 550	+$650
Accounts receivable	0	0	0	900	0	−900
Inventory	0	500	500	0	0	
Fixed assets	600	600	600	600	600	
Accumulated depreciation	0	0	0	(50)	(50)	
TOTAL ASSETS	$1,000	$1,500	$1,000	$1,350	$1,100	
Accounts payable	$ 0	$ 500	$ 0	$ 0	$ 0	
Accrued operating expenses	0	0	0	250	0	−$250
Income tax payable	0	0	0	25	25	
Long-term debt	300	300	300	300	300	
Common stock	700	700	700	700	700	
Retained earnings	0	0	0	75	75	
TOTAL DEBT AND EQUITY	$1,000	$1,500	$1,000	$1,350	$1,100	

As a result of the firm's activities, Pokey, Inc., reported $75 in profits for the period. The income statement for the period ending November 30 is as follows:

Sales revenue		$900
Cost of goods sold		500
Gross profit		$400
Operating expenses:		
Cash expense	$250	
Depreciation expense	50	
Total operating expenses		$300
Operating income		$100
Income tax (25%)		25
Net income		$ 75

The $75 in profits is reflected as retained earnings on the balance sheet to make the numbers match.

    The somewhat contrived example of Pokey, Inc., illustrates an important point that deserves repeating: An owner of a small firm must understand the working-capital cycle of his or her firm. Although the business was profitable, Pokey ran out of cash in September and October (−$100) and didn't recover until November, when the accounts receivable were collected. This 60-day cash conversion period represents a critical time when the firm must find another source of financing if it is to survive. Moreover, when sales are ongoing throughout the year, the problem can be an unending one, unless financing is found to support the firm's sales. Also, as much as possible, a firm should arrange for earlier payment by customers (preferably in advance) and negotiate longer payment schedules with suppliers (preferably over several months).

    An understanding of the working-capital cycle provides a basis for examining the primary components of working-capital management: cash flows, accounts receivable, inventory, and accounts payable.

Managing Cash Flows

It should be clear by now that the core of working-capital management is monitoring cash flows. Cash is continually moving through a business. It flows in as customers pay for products or services, and it flows out as payments are made to other businesses and individuals who provide products and services to the firm, such as employees and suppliers. The typically uneven nature of cash inflows and outflows makes it imperative that they be properly understood and managed. Keith Lowe, an experienced entrepreneur and co-founder of the Alabama Information Technology Association, expresses it this way:

> *If there's one thing that will make or break your company, especially when it's small, it's cash flow. A banker once told me that of the many companies he saw go out of business, the majority of them were profitable—they just got in a cash crunch, and that forced them to close. If you pay close attention to your cash flow and think about it every single day, you'll have an edge over almost all your competitors, and you will keep growing while other companies fall by the wayside. The amount of attention you pay to cash flow can literally mean the difference between life and death for your company.*[2]

2 Identify the important issues in managing a firm's cash flows, including the preparation of a cash budget.

The Nature of Cash Flows Revisited

A firm's net cash flow may be determined quite simply by examining its bank account. Monthly cash deposits less checks written during the same period equal a firm's net cash flow. If deposits for a month add up to $100,000 and checks total $80,000, the firm has a net positive cash flow of $20,000. The cash balance at the end of the month is $20,000 higher than it was at the beginning of the month.

    Exhibit 22-4 graphically represents the flow of cash through a business. It includes not only the cash flows that arise as part of the firm's working-capital cycle (shown in

exhibit

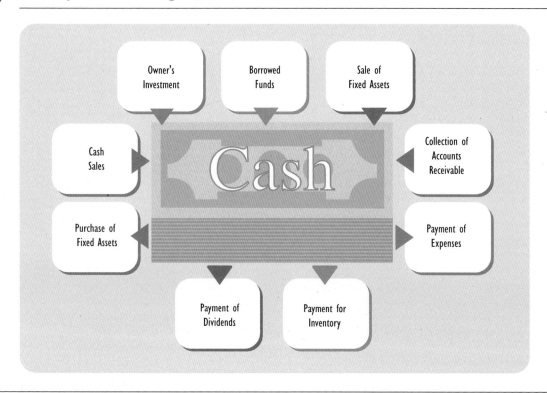

Exhibit 22-1) but other cash flows as well, such as those from purchasing fixed assets and issuing stock. More specifically, cash sales, collection of accounts receivable, payment of expenses, and payment for inventory reflect the inflows and outflows of cash that relate to the working-capital cycle, while the other items in Exhibit 22-4 represent other, longer-term cash flows.

As has been emphasized on several occasions, calculating cash flow requires that we distinguish between sales revenue and cash receipts—they are seldom the same. Revenue is recorded at the time a sale is made but does not affect cash flow at that time unless the sale is a cash sale. Cash receipts, on the other hand, are recorded when money actually flows into the firm, often a month or two after the sale. Similarly, it is necessary to distinguish between expenses and disbursements. Expenses occur when materials, labor, or other items are used. Payments (disbursements) for these expense items may be made later, when checks are issued. Depreciation, while shown as an expense, is not a cash outflow.

Given the difference between cash flows and profits, it is absolutely essential that the entrepreneur develop a cash budget to anticipate when cash will enter and leave the business. In the next section, we will describe and illustrate the cash budgeting process.

The Cash Budget

cash budget
A planning document strictly concerned with the receipt and payment of dollars

The **cash budget** is a primary tool for managing cash flows. The budget is concerned specifically with dollars received and paid out. In contrast, the income statement takes items into consideration before they affect cash—for example, expenses that have been incurred but not yet paid and income earned but not yet received.

By using a cash budget, an entrepreneur can predict and plan the cash flows of a business. *No single planning document is more important in the life of a small company, either for avoiding cash flow problems when cash runs short or for anticipating short-term investment opportunities if excess cash becomes available.*

To better understand the process of preparing a cash budget, consider the example of the Davies Corporation, a manufacturer of food storage containers. Its owner, Peggy Davies, wishes to develop a monthly cash budget for the next quarter (July through September) and has made the following forecasts.

- Historical and predicted sales:

Historical Sales		Predicted Sales	
April	$ 80,000	July	$130,000
May	100,000	August	130,000
June	120,000	September	120,000
		October	100,000

- Of the firm's sales dollars, 40 percent are collected the month of the sale, 30 percent one month after the sale, and the remaining 30 percent two months after the sale.

- Inventory is purchased one month before the sales month and is paid for in the month in which it is sold. Purchases equal 80 percent of projected sales for the next month.

- Cash expenses have been estimated for wages and salaries, rent, utilities, and tax payments, all of which are reflected in the cash budget.

- Interest on a $40,000 bank note (with the principal due in December) is payable at an 8 percent annual rate for the three-month period ending in September.

- The firm has a $20,000 line of credit with its bank at an interest rate of 12 percent annually (1 percent monthly). The interest owed is to be paid monthly.

- The firm's beginning cash balance for the budget period is $5,000. This amount should be maintained as a minimum cash balance.

Based on this information, Davies has prepared a monthly cash budget for the three-month period ending September 30. Exhibit 22-5 shows the results of her computations, which involved the following steps:

Step 1. Determine the amount of collections each month, based on the projected collection patterns.

Step 2. Estimate the amount and timing of the following cash disbursements:
   a. Inventory purchases and payments. The amount of the purchases is shown in the boxed area of the table, with payments made one month later.
   b. Rent, wages, tax payments, utilities, and interest on the long-term note
   c. Quarterly interest on a $40,000 bank note is $800 ($40,000 $\times$ 8% $\times \frac{1}{4}$ year).
   d. Interest to be paid on any outstanding short-term borrowing. For example, the table shows that for the month of July the Davies Corporation will need to borrow $10,600 to prevent the firm's cash balance from falling below the $5,000 acceptable minimum. Assume that the money will be borrowed at the end of July and that the interest will be payable at the end of August. The amount of the interest in August is $106, or 1 percent of the $10,600 cumulative short-term debt outstanding at the end of July.

Step 3. Calculate the net change in cash (cash receipts less cash disbursements).

Step 4. Determine the beginning cash balance (ending cash balance from the prior month).

Step 5. Compute the cash balance before short-term borrowing (net change in cash for the month plus the cash balance at the beginning of the month).

Step 6. Calculate the short-term borrowing or repayment (the amount borrowed if there is a cash shortfall for the month or the amount repaid on any short-term debt outstanding).

Step 7. Compute the cumulative amount of short-term debt outstanding, which also determines the amount of interest to be paid in the following month.

exhibit

22-5   *Three-Month Cash Budget for the Davies Corporation for July–September*

		May	June	July	August	September
Step 1	Monthly sales	$100,000	$120,000	$130,000	$130,000	$120,000
	Cash receipts:					
	Cash sales for month			$ 52,000	$ 52,000	$ 48,000
	1 month after sale			36,000	39,000	39,000
	2 months after sale			30,000	36,000	39,000
	Total collections			$118,000	$127,000	$126,000
	Purchases (80% of sales)		$104,000	$104,000	$ 96,000	$ 80,000
Step 2	Cash disbursements					
Step 2a	Payments on purchases			$104,000	$104,000	$ 96,000
	Rent			3,000	3,000	3,000
Step 2b	Wages and salaries			18,000	18,000	16,000
	Tax payment			1,000		
	Utilities (2% of sales)			2,600	2,600	2,400
Step 2c	Interest on long-term note					800
Step 2d	Short-term interest					
	(1% of short-term debt)				106	113
	Total cash disbursements			$128,600	$127,706	$118,313
Step 3	Net change in cash			($ 10,600)	($ 706)	$ 7,687
Step 4	Beginning cash balance			5,000	5,000	5,000
Step 5	Cash balance before borrowing			($ 5,600)	$ 4,294	$ 12,687
Step 6	Short-term borrowing (payments)			10,600	706	(7,687)
	Ending cash balance			$ 5,000	$ 5,000	$ 5,000
Step 7	Cumulative short-term debt outstanding			$ 10,600	$ 11,306	$ 3,619

As you can see in Exhibit 22-5, the firm does not achieve a positive cash flow until September. Short-term borrowing must be arranged, therefore, in both July and August. By preparing a cash budget, the Davies Corporation can anticipate these needs and avoid the nasty surprises that might otherwise occur.

A cash budget should anticipate occasions when a small business has idle funds or has generated unexpected excess funds. Taking advantage of the many short-term investment opportunities that are available, including certificates of deposit and money market accounts, can put excess cash to work for a firm.

Once a cash budget has been prepared, an entrepreneur has to decide how to use it. Entrepreneurship is about seeking opportunities, and there is a real danger that a cash budget may lead to inflexibility. A strict cost-containment strategy in order to "make the budget" can discourage managers from being creative and shifting their approach when it makes sense to do so. And inflexible budgets can lead to a "use it or lose it" mentality, where managers spend remaining budgeted money at year's end so that allocations will not be cut the following year. Such a mind-set negatively impacts the entrepreneurial process. Jeremy Hope, a former venture capitalist, describes the risk of becoming too focused on a budget: "I'm not opposed to a budget as a finance statement, but to the way it's used as an almost fixed performance contract on which employees have to deliver. The pressure to deliver on budgets drives a lot of irrational, stupid, and crazy behavior you see within businesses."[3]

Allowing the management team and employees to become focused on the budget instead of opportunities is counterproductive and should be avoided.

Managing Accounts Receivable

3 Explain the key issues in managing accounts receivable, inventory, and accounts payable.

Chapter 15 discussed the extension of credit by small firms and the managing and collecting of accounts receivable. This section considers the impact of credit decisions on working capital and particularly on cash flows. The most important factor in managing cash well within a small firm is the ability to collect accounts receivable quickly.

How Accounts Receivable Affect Cash

Granting credit to customers, although primarily a marketing decision, directly affects a firm's cash account. By selling on credit and thus allowing customers to delay payment, the selling firm delays the inflow of cash.

The total amount of customers' credit balances is carried on the balance sheet as accounts receivable—one of the firm's current assets. Of all noncash assets, accounts receivable are closest to becoming cash. Sometimes called *near cash,* or *receivables,* accounts receivable typically are collected and become cash within 30 to 60 days following a sale.

The Life Cycle of Accounts Receivable

The receivables cycle begins with a credit sale. In most businesses, an invoice is then prepared and mailed to the purchaser. When the invoice is received, the purchaser processes it, prepares a check, and mails the check in payment to the seller.

Under ideal circumstances, each of these steps is taken in a timely manner. Obviously, delays can occur at any stage of this process. For example, a shipping clerk may batch invoices before sending them to the office for processing, thus delaying the preparation and mailing of invoices to customers. Such a practice will also delay the receipt of customers' money and its deposit in the bank—money that is then used to pay bills. In other words, receivables may be past due because of problems in a company's organization, where information is not getting transferred on a timely basis among salespeople, operations departments, and accounting staff. The result: delayed payments from customers and larger investments in accounts receivable.

Credit management policies, practices, and procedures affect the life cycle of receivables and the flow of cash from them. It is important for small business owners, when establishing credit policies, to consider cash flow requirements as well as the need to stimulate sales. A key goal of every business should be to minimize the average time it takes customers to pay their bills. By streamlining administrative procedures, a firm can facilitate the task of sending out bills, thereby generating cash more quickly.

If a firm is encountering a cash flow problem, it may well have something to do with poor management of accounts receivable. Michelle Dunn, who owns M.A.D. Collections, a collections agency, says, "One thing business owners always tell me is that they never thought about [the difficulties in collecting their receivables] when they started their own business."[4]

When dealing with large corporations, small companies are especially vulnerable to problems caused by slow collections. Some large firms have a practice of taking 60 or 90 days to pay an invoice, regardless of the credit terms stated in the invoice. Many a small company has had to file bankruptcy because it could not get a large customer to pay according to the terms of the sale.

5 Stones Group, a small film production company, is "blessed" with a number of high-profile customers. According to the company's credit terms, customers are to pay one-third up front, one-third at mid-project, and the remainder on completion of the project. Mike Edwards, the firm's president, says the terms are intended to provide his company with a steady stream of cash. "Cash flow is critical," he explains. "If a client says that a payment will be made next Friday, you have to call next Friday. You have to continually track payments." Unfortunately, large clients don't always do what they say they will do. Edwards says they may quibble about when the clock began on the payment-term period or balk at some of the expenses in the bill. Edward's wife, Tiffany, who manages the company's finances, asks, "Do you go after them and be faced with not getting repeat business? Our stance so far is that we want the relationship more than the terms. We've given in."[5] In the meantime, 5 Stones has to pay its bills, and the money has to come from credit card cash advances or a bank loan. So, an entrepreneur needs to be careful about how much credit to extend—especially to industry giants.

Here are some examples of credit management practices that can have a positive effect on a firm's cash flows:

- Minimize the time between shipping, invoicing, and sending notices on billings.

- Review previous credit experiences to determine impediments to cash flows, such as continued extension of credit to slow-paying or delinquent customers.

- Provide incentives for prompt payment by granting cash discounts or charging interest on delinquent accounts.

- Age accounts receivable on a monthly or even a weekly basis to identify quickly any delinquent accounts.

- Use the most effective methods for collecting overdue accounts. For example, prompt phone calls to customers with overdue accounts can improve collections considerably.

lock box
A post office box for receiving remittances from customers

- Use a **lock box**—a post office box for receiving remittances. If the firm's bank maintains the lock box to which customers send their payments, it can empty the box frequently and immediately deposit any checks received into the company's account.

Living the Dream   entrepreneurial challenges

You Sold It; Now You Have to Collect for It

Today, when a customer asks to open a house account, Hugh McHugh, owner of Overhill Flowers Inc., in Overbrook, Pennsylvania, requests a credit card number. And those customers who had house accounts have been switched to credit card accounts.

House accounts offering credit covered almost 85 percent of McHugh's business just a few years ago. He would bill clients at the end of each month, printing and mailing the statements, then processing the checks. But many customers paid late, and 2 percent didn't pay their bills at all. "That's a significant blow to a small business with profit margins of 12 percent," McHugh says.

The change to credit card accounts keeps McHugh from worrying about making payroll while awaiting payments for holiday bouquets. Collecting debts efficiently is one of the best ways for small businesses to manage cash flows and hold on to precious capital.

Source: Paulette Thomas, "Why Debt Collection Is So Essential for Startups," *The Wall Street Journal Online,* http://www.startupjournal.com/runbusiness/billcollect/20050920-thomas.html, September 25, 2005.

http://www.overhillflowers.com

Accounts Receivable Financing

Some small businesses speed up the cash flow from accounts receivable by borrowing against them. By financing receivables, these firms can often secure the use of their money 30 to 60 days earlier than would be possible otherwise. Although this practice was once concentrated largely in the apparel industry, it has expanded to many other types of small businesses, such as manufacturers, food processors, distributors, home building suppliers, and temporary employment agencies. Such financing is provided by commercial finance companies and by some banks.

Two types of accounts receivable financing are available. The first type uses a firm's **pledged accounts receivable** as collateral for a loan. Payments received from customers are forwarded to the lending institution to pay off the loan. In the second type of financing, a business sells its accounts receivable to a finance company, a practice known as *factoring* (discussed in Chapter 11). The finance company thereby assumes the bad-debt risk associated with the receivables it buys.

The obvious advantage of accounts receivable financing is the immediate cash flow it provides for firms that have limited working capital. As a secondary benefit, the volume of borrowing can be quickly expanded proportionally in order to match a firm's growth in sales and accounts receivable.

A drawback to this type of financing is its high cost. Rates typically run several points above the prime interest rate, and factors charge a fee to compensate them for their credit investigation activities and for the risk that customers may default in payment. Another

pledged accounts receivable
Accounts receivable used as collateral for a loan

Living the Dream   entrepreneurial challenges

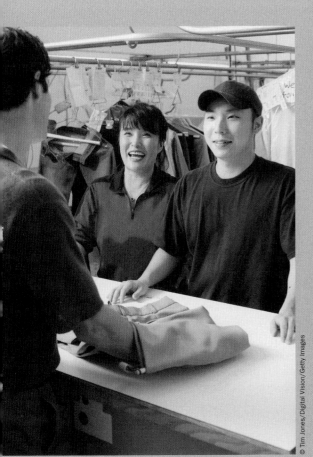

© Tim Jones/Digital Vision/Getty Images

Factoring Can Make the Difference

A reputable factor can prove invaluable to a small firm at a critical time in its life. That's how it worked out for James Choung's $6 million laundry and dry-cleaning business, Newtex.

The business was started with the help of a Korean American bank, as are many Korean enterprises. Choung had come to the United States to train as a nuclear engineer and had worked on nuclear submarines in Newport News, Virginia, until the Navy stopped building them. With a wife and four children (in private schools), he needed income, and he decided to buy a tiny dry cleaner in New York City. He soon expanded his South Bronx plant, selling laundry services to restaurants and hotels and doing laundry for hotel guests.

His books told him he was making a lot of money, but as he hired people and leased machines, he found that his cash outflow was higher than his cash inflow. The mailing of monthly bills to his customers was preceded by several weeks of expenses. (And "the monthly bill," he says, "just starts the clock.") He found that few restaurants and hotels paid in less than 30 days after the receipt of his bills—and many took more than 60 days.

Choung's primary Korean bank was unwilling to study the credit ratings of New York City restaurants and hotels or to take on faith that receivables would eventually be paid. Factoring was what kept Newtex alive. "For me," [Choung] says, "factoring is cash flow."

Choung now employs 60 people, and nearly all his $6 million in annual revenue passes through the hands of his factor. Without it, the business would not have survived.

Source: Martin Mayer, "Taking the Fear Out of Factoring," *Inc.,* Vol. 25, No. 14 (December 2003), p. 92. Copyright 2003 by Mansueto Ventures LLC. Reproduced with permission of Mansueto Ventures LLC in the format Textbook via Copyright Clearance Center.

weakness of accounts receivable financing is that pledging receivables may limit a firm's ability to borrow from a bank by removing a prime asset from its available collateral.

Managing Inventories

Inventory is a "necessary evil" in the financial management system. It is "necessary" because supply and demand cannot be managed to coincide precisely with day-to-day operations; it is an "evil" because it ties up funds that are not actively productive.

Reducing Inventory to Free Cash

Inventory is a bigger problem for some small businesses than for others. The inventory of many service companies, for example, consists of only a few supplies. A manufacturer, on the other hand, has several inventories: raw materials, work in process, and finished goods. Retailers and wholesalers—especially those with high inventory turnover rates, such as firms in grocery distribution—are continually involved in solving inventory management problems.

Chapter 20 discussed several ideas related to purchasing and inventory management that are designed to minimize inventory-carrying costs and processing costs. The emphasis in this section is on practices that will minimize average inventory levels, thereby releasing funds for other uses. The correct minimum level of inventory is the level needed to maintain desired production schedules and/or a certain level of customer service. A concerted effort to manage inventory can trim excess inventory and pay handsome dividends.

Monitoring Inventory

One of the first steps in managing inventory is to discover what's in inventory and how long it's been there. Too often, items are purchased, warehoused, and essentially forgotten. A yearly inventory for accounting purposes is inadequate for proper inventory control. Items that are slow movers may sit in a retailer's inventory beyond the time when markdowns should have been applied.

Computers can provide assistance in inventory identification and control. Although physical inventories may still be required, their use will only serve to supplement the computerized system.

Controlling Stockpiles

Small business managers tend to overbuy inventory for several reasons. First, an entrepreneur's enthusiasm may lead him or her to forecast greater demand than is realistic. Second, the personalization of the business–customer relationship may motivate a manager to stock everything customers want. Third, a price-conscious manager may be overly susceptible to a vendor's appeal to "buy now, because prices are going up."

Managers must exercise restraint when stockpiling. Improperly managed and uncontrolled stockpiling may greatly increase inventory-carrying costs and place a heavy drain on the funds of a small business.

Managing Accounts Payable

Cash flow management and accounts payable management are intertwined. As long as a payable is outstanding, the buying firm can keep cash equal to that amount in its own checking account. When payment is made, however, that firm's cash account is reduced accordingly.

Although payables are legal obligations, they can be paid at various times or even renegotiated in some cases. Therefore, financial management of accounts payable hinges on negotiation and timing.

Negotiation

Any business is subject to emergency situations and may find it necessary to ask creditors to postpone its payable obligations. Usually, creditors will cooperate in working out a solution because it's in their best interest for a client firm to succeed.

exhibit

22-6   An Accounts Payable Timetable for Terms of 3/10, Net 30

Timetable (days after invoice date)	Settlement Costs for a $20,000 Purchase
Days 1 through 10	$19,400
Days 11 through 30	$20,000
Day 31 and thereafter	$20,000 + possible late penalty + deterioration in credit rating

Timing

"Buy now, pay later" is the motto of many entrepreneurs. By buying on credit, a small business is using creditors' funds to supply short-term cash needs. The longer creditors' funds can be borrowed, the better. Payment, therefore, should be delayed as long as acceptable under the agreement.

Typically, accounts payable (trade credit) involve payment terms that include a cash discount. With trade-discount terms, paying later may be inappropriate. For example, terms of 3/10, net 30 offer a 3 percent potential discount. Exhibit 22-6 shows the possible settlement costs over the credit period of 30 days. Note that for a $20,000 purchase, a settlement of only $19,400 is required if payment is made within the first 10 days ($20,000 less the 3 percent discount of $600). Between day 11 and day 30, the full settlement of $20,000 is required. After 30 days, the settlement cost may exceed the original amount, as late-payment fees are added.

The timing question then becomes "Should the account be paid on day 10 or day 30?" There is little reason to pay $19,400 on days 1 through 9, when the same amount will settle the account on day 10. Likewise, if payment is to be made after day 10, it makes sense to wait until day 30 to pay the $20,000.

By paying on the last day of the discount period, the buyer saves the amount of the discount offered. The other alternative of paying on day 30 allows the buyer to use the seller's money for an additional 20 days by forgoing the discount. As Exhibit 22-6 shows, the buyer can use the seller's $19,400 for 20 days at a cost of $600. The percentage annual interest rate can be calculated as follows:

$$\text{Percentage annual interest rate} = \frac{\text{Days in year}}{\text{Net period} - \text{Cash discount period}} \times \frac{\text{Cash discount \%}}{100\% - \text{Cash discount \%}}$$

$$= \frac{365}{30 - 10} \times \frac{3\%}{100\% - 3\%}$$

$$= 18.25 \times 0.030928$$

$$= 0.564, \text{ or } 56.4\%$$

By failing to take a discount, a business typically pays a high rate for use of a supplier's money—56.4 percent per year in this case. Payment on day 10 appears to be the most logical choice. Recall, however, that payment also affects cash flows. If funds are extremely short, a small firm may have to wait to pay until the last possible day in order to avoid an overdraft at the bank.

We now turn from management of a firm's working capital to management of its long-term assets—equipment and plant—or what is called *capital budgeting*.

Capital Budgeting

Capital budgeting analysis helps managers make decisions about long-term investments. In order to develop a new product line, for example, a firm needs to expand its manufacturing capabilities and to buy the inventory required to make the product. That is, it makes investments today with an expectation of receiving profits or cash flows in the future, possibly over 5 or 10 years.

capital budgeting analysis
An analytical method that helps managers make decisions about long-term investments

Some capital budgeting decisions that might be made by a small firm include the following:

- Develop and introduce a new product that shows promise but requires additional study and improvement.

- Replace a firm's delivery trucks with newer models.

- Expand sales activity into a new territory.

- Construct a new building.

- Hire several additional salespersons to intensify selling in the existing market.

In a 2003 study by the National Federation of Independent Business, small business owners were asked, "In terms of dollars, what was the purpose of the largest investments made in your business over the last 12 months?" Their responses were as follows:[6]

Replacement and maintenance	45.6%
Extension of existing product or service lines	21.2
Expansion into new business areas	22.9
Safety or environmental improvement	3.5
No response	6.7

Thus, nearly half of all long-term capital investments by small companies are made for replacement and maintenance; when we add in the extension of existing product lines, we can account for two-thirds of all dollars invested by small owners. Nearly one-fourth of all dollars are invested in new product lines and businesses.

Although an in-depth discussion of capital budgeting is beyond the scope of this textbook, in the following sections we will discuss techniques used in making capital budgeting decisions and the capital budgeting practices of small companies. For a more detailed presentation, see a financial management textbook, such as *Foundations of Finance*.[7]

Capital Budgeting Techniques

4 Discuss the techniques commonly used in making capital budgeting decisions.

The three major techniques for making capital budgeting decisions are (1) the accounting return on investment technique, (2) the payback period technique, and (3) the discounted cash flow technique, using either net present value or internal rate of return. They all attempt to answer the same basic question: Do the future benefits from an investment exceed the cost of making the investment? However, each technique addresses this general question by focusing on a different specific question. The specific question each addresses can be stated as follows:

1. *Accounting return on investment*. How many dollars in average profits are generated per dollar of average investment?

2. *Payback period*. How long will it take to recover the original investment outlay?

3. *Discounted cash flows*. How does the present value of future benefits from the investment compare to the investment outlay?

Three simple rules are used in judging the merits of an investment. Although they may seem trite, the rules state in simple terms the best thinking about the attractiveness of an investment.

1. The investor prefers more cash rather than less cash.

2. The investor prefers cash sooner rather than later.

3. The investor prefers less risk rather than more risk.

With these criteria in mind, let's now look at each of the three capital budgeting techniques in detail.

ACCOUNTING RETURN ON INVESTMENT A small business invests to earn profits. The **accounting return on investment technique** compares the average annual after-tax profits a firm expects to receive with the average book value of the investment:

$$\text{Accounting return on investment} = \frac{\text{Average annual after-tax profits}}{\text{Average book value of the investment}}$$

Average annual profits can be estimated by adding the after-tax profits expected over the life of the project and then dividing that amount by the number of years the project is expected to last. The average book value of an investment is equivalent to the average of the initial outlay and the estimated final projected salvage value. In making an accept–reject decision, the owner compares the calculated return to a minimum acceptable return, which is usually determined based on past experience.

To examine the use of the accounting return on investment technique, assume that you are contemplating buying a piece of equipment for $10,000 and depreciating it over four years to a book value of zero (it will have no salvage value). Further assume that you expect the investment to generate after-tax profits each year as follows:

Year	After-Tax Profits
1	$1,000
2	2,000
3	2,500
4	3,000

The accounting return on the proposed investment is calculated as follows:

$$\text{Accounting return on investment} = \frac{\left(\dfrac{\$1,000 + \$2,000 + \$2,500 + \$3,000}{4}\right)}{\left(\dfrac{\$10,000 + \$0}{2}\right)}$$

$$= \frac{\$2,125}{\$5,000} = 0.425, \text{ or } 42.5\%$$

For most people, a 42.5 percent profit rate would seem outstanding. Assuming the calculated accounting return on investment of 42.5 percent exceeds your minimum acceptable return, you will accept the project. If not, you will reject the investment—provided, of course, that you have confidence in the technique.

Although the accounting return on investment is easy to calculate, it has two major shortcomings. First, it is based on accounting profits rather than actual cash flows received. An investor should be more interested in the future cash produced by the investment than in the reported profits. Second, this technique ignores the time value of money. Thus, although popular, the accounting return on investment technique fails to satisfy any of the three rules concerning an investor's preference for receiving more cash sooner with less risk.

PAYBACK PERIOD The **payback period technique**, as the name suggests, measures how long it will take to recover the initial cash outlay of an investment. It deals with cash flows as opposed to accounting profits. The merits of a project are judged on whether the initial investment outlay can be recovered in less time than some maximum acceptable payback period. For example, an owner may not want to invest in any project that will require more than five years to recoup the original investment.

To illustrate the payback method, let's assume that an entrepreneur is considering an investment in equipment with an expected life of 10 years. The investment outlay will be $15,000, with the cost of the equipment depreciated on a straight-line basis, at $1,500 per year. If the owner makes the investment, the annual after-tax profits have been estimated to be as follows:

Years	After-Tax Profits
1–2	$1,000
3–6	2,000
7–10	2,500

accounting return on investment technique
A capital budgeting technique that evaluates a capital expenditure based on the expected average annual after-tax profits relative to the average book value of an investment

payback period technique
A capital budgeting technique that measures the amount of time it will take to recover the cash outlay of an investment

To determine the after-tax cash flows from the investment, the owner merely adds back the depreciation of $1,500 each year to the profit. The reason for adding the depreciation to the profit is that it was deducted when the profits were calculated (as an accounting entry), even though it was not a cash outflow. The results, then, are as follows:

Years	After-Tax Cash Flows
1–2	$2,500
3–6	3,500
7–10	4,000

By the end of the second year, the owner will have recovered $5,000 of the investment outlay ($2,500 per year). By the end of the fourth year, another $7,000, or $12,000 in total, will have been recouped. The additional $3,000 can be recovered in the fifth year, when $3,500 is expected. Thus, it will take 4.86 years [4 years + ($3,000 ÷ $3,500)] to recover the investment. Since the maximum acceptable payback is less than five years, the owner will accept the investment.

Many managers and owners of companies use the payback period technique in evaluating investment decisions. Although it uses cash flows, rather than accounting profits, the payback period technique has two significant weaknesses. First, it does not consider the time value of money (cash is preferred sooner rather than later). Second, it fails to consider the cash flows received after the payback period (more cash is preferred, rather than less).

DISCOUNTED CASH FLOWS   Managers can avoid the deficiencies of the accounting return on investment and payback period techniques by using discounted cash flow analysis. Discounted cash flow techniques take into consideration the fact that cash received today is more valuable than cash received one year from now (called the time value of money). For example, interest can be earned on cash that is available for immediate investment; this is not true for cash to be received at some future date.

discounted cash flow (DCF) techniques
Capital budgeting techniques that compare the present value of future cash flows with the cost of the initial investment

net present value (NPV)
The present value of expected future cash flows less the initial investment outlay

internal rate of return (IRR)
The rate of return a firm expects to earn on a project

Discounted cash flow (DCF) techniques compare the present value of future cash flows with the investment outlay. Such an analysis may take either of two forms: net present value or internal rate of return.

The net present value (NPV) method estimates the current value of the cash that will flow into the firm from the project in the future and deducts the amount of the initial outlay. To find the present value of expected future cash flows, we discount them back to the present at the firm's cost of capital, where the cost of capital is equal to the investors' required rate of return. If the net present value of the investment is positive (that is, if the present value of future cash flows discounted at the rate of return required to satisfy the firm's investors exceeds the initial outlay), the project is acceptable.

The internal rate of return (IRR) method estimates the rate of return that can be expected from a contemplated investment. For the investment outlay to be attractive, the internal rate of return must exceed the firm's cost of capital—the rate of return required to satisfy the firm's investors.

Discounted cash flow techniques can generally be trusted to provide a more reliable basis for decisions than can the accounting return on investment or the payback period technique.

Capital Budgeting Analysis in Small Firms

5 Describe the capital budgeting practices of small firms.

Historically, few small business owners have relied on any type of quantitative analysis in making capital budgeting decisions. The decision to buy new equipment or expand facilities has been based more on intuition and instinct than on economic analysis. And those who do conduct some kind of quantitative analysis rarely use discounted cash flow techniques, neither net present value nor internal rate of return.

In the study cited earlier, the National Federation of Independent Business asked entrepreneurs to indicate the method(s) they used in analyzing capital investments. The results were encouraging:[8]

Gut feel	25.3%
Payback period technique	18.7
Accounting return on investment technique	13.6

Discounted cash flow techniques	11.9
Combination	10.5
Other	6.1
No response	4.5
Not applicable—no major investments	2.6

Interestingly, 55 percent of the small business owners indicated that they use some form of quantitative measure (payback period, accounting return on investment, discounted cash flow techniques, or some combination) to assess a capital investment; only 25 percent of the respondents said that they use their intuition (gut feel). Furthermore, 67 percent of the company owners said that they make some effort to project future cash flows.

We could conclude that the small business owners surveyed were not very sophisticated about using theoretically sound financial methods, given that only 12 percent said they use discounted cash flow analyses. However, the cause of their limited use of DCF tools probably has more to do with the nature of the small business itself than with the owners' unwillingness to learn. Several more important reasons might explain these findings, including the following:

- For many owners of small firms, the business is an extension of their lives—that is, business events affect them personally. The same is true in reverse: What happens to the owners personally affects their decisions about the firm. The firm and its owners are inseparable. We cannot fully understand decisions made about a company without being aware of the personal events in the owners' lives. Consequently, nonfinancial variables may play a significant part in owners' decisions. For example, the desire to be viewed as a respected part of the community may be more important to an owner than the present value of a business decision.

- The undercapitalization and liquidity problems of a small business can directly affect the decision-making process, and survival often becomes the top priority. Long-term planning is, therefore, not viewed by the owners as a high priority in the total scheme of things.

- The greater uncertainty of cash flows within small firms makes long-term forecasting and planning seem unappealing and even a waste of time. The owners simply have no confidence in their ability to predict cash flows beyond two or three years. Thus, calculating the cash flows for the entire life of a project is viewed as a futile effort.

- The value of a closely held firm is less easily observed than that of a publicly held firm whose securities are actively traded in the marketplace. Therefore, the owner of a small firm may consider the market-value rule of maximizing net present values irrelevant. Estimating the cost of capital is also much more difficult for a small company than for a large firm.

- The smaller size of a small firm's projects may make net present value computations less feasible in a practical sense. The time and expense required to analyze a capital investment are generally the same, whether the project is large or small. Therefore, it is relatively more costly for a small firm to conduct such a study.

- Management talent within a small firm is a scarce resource. Also, the owner-manager frequently has a technical background, as opposed to a business or finance orientation. The perspective of owners is influenced greatly by their backgrounds.

The foregoing characteristics of a small business and its owner have a significant effect on the decision-making process within the firm. The result is often a short-term mind-set, caused partly by necessity and partly by choice. However, the owner of a small firm should make every effort to use discounted cash flow techniques and to be certain that contemplated investments will, in fact, provide returns that exceed the firm's cost of capital.

Looking BACK

1 Describe the working-capital cycle of a small business.

- The working-capital cycle begins with the purchase of inventory and ends with the collection of accounts receivable.
- The cash conversion period is critical because it is the time period during which cash flow problems can arise.

2 Identify the important issues in managing a firm's cash flows, including the preparation of a cash budget.

- A firm's cash flows consist of cash flowing into a business (through sales revenue, borrowing, and so on) and cash flowing out of the business (through purchases, operating expenses, and so on).
- Profitable small companies sometimes encounter cash flow problems by failing to understand the working-capital cycle or failing to anticipate the negative consequences of growth.
- Cash inflows and outflows are reconciled in the cash budget, which involves forecasts of cash receipts and expenditures.

3 Explain the key issues in managing accounts receivable, inventory, and accounts payable.

- Granting credit to customers, primarily a marketing decision, directly affects a firm's cash account.
- A firm can improve its cash flows by speeding up collections from customers, minimizing inventories, and delaying payments to suppliers.
- Some small businesses speed up the cash flows from receivables by borrowing against them.
- A concerted effort to manage inventory can trim excess inventory and free cash for other uses.

- Accounts payable, a primary source of financing for small firms, directly affect a firm's cash flow situation.
- Financial management of accounts payable hinges on negotiation and timing.

4 Discuss the techniques commonly used in making capital budgeting decisions.

- Capital budgeting techniques attempt to determine whether future benefits from an investment will exceed the initial outlay.
- Capital budgeting techniques include the accounting return on investment, the payback period, and the discounted cash flow techniques.
- The accounting return on investment technique has two significant shortcomings: It is based on accounting profits rather than actual cash flows received, and it ignores the time value of money.
- The payback period technique also has two major weaknesses: It ignores the time value of money, and it doesn't consider cash flows received after the payback period.
- The discounted cash flow techniques—net present value and internal rate of return—provide the best accept–reject decision criteria in capital budgeting analysis.

5 Describe the capital budgeting practices of small firms.

- Few small firms use any type of discounted cash flow technique. However, the majority of small companies do use some type of formal analysis.
- The very nature of small firms may explain, to some degree, why they seldom use the conceptually richer techniques for evaluating long-term investments.

Key TERMS

working-capital management, p. 573
working-capital cycle, p. 573
cash conversion period, p. 575
cash budget, p. 580
lock box, p. 584

pledged accounts receivable, p. 585
capital budgeting analysis, p. 587
accounting return on investment technique, p. 589
payback period technique, p. 589

discounted cash flow (DCF) techniques, p. 590
net present value (NPV), p. 590
internal rate of return (IRR), p. 590

Discussion **QUESTIONS**

1. List the events in the working-capital cycle that directly affect cash and those that do not. What determines the length of a firm's cash conversion period?

2. What are some examples of cash receipts that are not sales revenue? Explain how expenses and cash disbursements during a month may be different.

3. How may a seller speed up the collection of accounts receivable? Give examples that may apply to various stages in the life cycle of receivables.

4. Suppose that a small firm could successfully shift to a just-in-time inventory system—an arrangement in which inventory is received just as it is needed. How would this affect the firm's working-capital management?

5. How do working-capital management and capital budgeting differ?

6. Compare the different techniques that can be used in capital budgeting analysis.

7. What does net present value measure?

8. Define internal rate of return.

9. a. Find the accounting return on investment for a project that costs $10,000, will have no salvage value, and has expected annual after-tax profits each year of $1,000.

   b. Determine the payback period for a capital investment that costs $40,000 and has the following after-tax profits. (The projected outlay of $40,000 will be depreciated on a straight-line basis over 7 years to a zero salvage value.)

Year	After-Tax Profits
1	$4,000
2	5,000
3	6,000
4	6,500
5	6,500
6	6,000
7	5,000

10. Why would owners of small businesses not be inclined to use the net present value or internal rate of return measurements?

You Make the **CALL**

SITUATION 1

A small company specializing in the sale and installation of swimming pools was profitable but devoted very little attention to management of its working capital. It had, for example, never prepared or used a cash budget.

To be sure that money was available for payments as needed, the firm kept a minimum of $25,000 in a checking account. At times, this account grew larger; it totaled $43,000 at one time. The owner felt that this approach to cash management worked well for the small company because it eliminated all of the paperwork associated with cash budgeting. Moreover, it enabled the firm to pay its bills in a timely manner.

Question 1 What are the advantages and weaknesses of the minimum-cash-balance practice?

Question 2 There is a saying "If it ain't broke, don't fix it." In view of the firm's present success in paying bills promptly, should it be encouraged to use a cash budget? Be prepared to support your answer.

SITUATION 2

Ruston Manufacturing Company is a small firm selling entirely on a credit basis. It has experienced successful operation and earned modest profits.

Sales are made on the basis of net payment in 30 days. Collections from customers run approximately 70 percent in 30 days, 20 percent in 60 days, 7 percent in 90 days, and 3 percent bad debts.

The owner has considered the possibility of offering a cash discount for early payment. However, the practice seems costly and possibly unnecessary. As the owner puts it, "Why should I bribe customers to pay what they legally owe?"

Question 1 Is offering a cash discount the equivalent of a bribe?

Question 2 How would a cash discount policy relate to bad debts?

Question 3 What cash discount policy, if any, would you recommend?

Question 4 What other approaches might be used to improve cash flows from receivables?

SITUATION 3

Adrian Fudge of the Fudge Corporation wants you to forecast the firm's financing needs over the fourth quarter (October through December). He has made the following observations relative to planned cash receipts and disbursements:

- Interest on a $75,000 bank note (due next March) at an 8 percent annual rate is payable in December for the three-month period just ended.
- The firm follows a policy of paying no cash dividends.
- Actual historical and future predicted sales are as follows:

Historical Sales		Predicted Sales	
August	$150,000	October	$200,000
September	175,000	November	220,000
		December	180,000
		January	200,000

- The firm has a monthly rental expense of $5,000.
- Wages and salaries for the coming months are estimated at $25,000 per month.

- Of the firm's sales, 25 percent is collected in the month of the sale, 35 percent one month after the sale, and the remaining 40 percent two months after the sale.
- Merchandise is purchased one month before the sales month and is paid for in the month it is sold. Purchases equal 75 percent of sales. The firm's cost of goods sold is also 75 percent of sales.
- Tax prepayments are made quarterly, with a prepayment of $10,000 in October based on earnings for the quarter ended September 30.
- Utility costs for the firm average 3 percent of sales and are paid in the month they are incurred.
- Depreciation expense is $20,000 annually.

Question 1 Prepare a monthly cash budget for the three-month period ending in December.

Question 2 If the firm's beginning cash balance for the budget period is $7,000, and this is its desired minimum balance, determine when and how much the firm will need to borrow during the budget period. The firm has a $50,000 line of credit with its bank, with interest (10 percent annual rate) paid monthly. For example, interest on a loan taken out at the end of September would be paid at the end of October and every month thereafter so long as the loan was outstanding.

Experiential EXERCISES

1. Interview the owner of a small company to determine the nature of the firm's working-capital time line. Try to estimate the cash conversion period.
2. Interview a small business owner or credit manager regarding the extension of credit and/or the collection of receivables in that firm. Summarize your findings in a report.
3. Identify a small business in your community that has recently expanded. Interview the owner of

the firm about the methods used in evaluating the expansion.

4. Either alone or with a classmate, approach an owner of a small company about getting data on a current problem or one the company encountered at some time in the past, to see whether you would reach the same decision as the owner did.

Exploring the WEB

1. Visit the Bank of America's Web site at **http://www.bankofamerica.com**. Click on "Small Business," then "Resource Center" and

"Managing Your Finances." Then go to "Managing Your Cash Flow." Watch the video; then click on

"Resources" and answer the following questions based on what you read there.

a. What is the purpose of a cash flow statement?

b. What should be included in the operating activities section of the cash flow statement? In the investing activities section? In the financing activities section?

c. What are the two methods of calculating cash flow? Briefly explain each method.

2. Go to **http://www.inc.com/resources** and do a search for the *Inc.* article "The 10 Absolutely Must-Follow Cash Flow Rules." Compare what the article discusses with what you learned in this chapter.

Case 22

Barton Sales and Service (p. 664)
This case looks at the financial performance of a small air conditioning and heating services company, with emphasis on its working-capital policies.

## chapter 23

Evaluating Financial Performance

In the **SPOTLIGHT**

Pro Flora

Whenever an owner tries to sell a business, prospective buyers want to know about the company. In the case of Pro Flora, a Florida-based flower wholesaler, potential buyers were probably interested to know that the company buys flowers from 30 domestic growers and resells them to more than 200 retail customers, that 40 percent of inventory is sold prior to being delivered, and that 58 percent of inventory is sold to florists who purchase directly off the truck and consider the Pro Flora truck to be a mobile floral shopping mall.

First and foremost, though, people interested in buying a business want to know how successful the company is financially. Often, the highlight of due diligence is a careful review of financial indicators, because those numbers help the seller and buyer negotiate a fair price for the business. For Pro Flora, the asking price was $2.2 million. How did the owners arrive at that figure?

Well, they figured that gross annual revenue was $4.1 million and EBITDA (earnings before interest, taxes, depreciation, and amortization) was $478,000. The net income, then, was 11.65 percent of sales. Current inventory levels were $23,000, and the value of the equipment owned by the company was $508,000. The owners also had the foresight to secure a prequalified loan for the buyers to finance 80 percent of the $2.2 million purchase price. If cash flows stay constant, the buyers should be able to cover the monthly payment of $24,000 without infusing any more capital into the business.

Business buyers are not the only people interested in this kind of information, however. Current business owners need to pay attention to it, too.

Source: Elaine Appleton Grant, "Business for Sale: Pro Flora Earnings," *Inc.,* May 2007, p. 24.

© Christine Glade/iStockphoto International, Inc.

Looking AHEAD

After studying this chapter, you should be able to

1 Identify the basic requirements for an accounting system.
2 Explain two alternative accounting options.
3 Describe the purpose of and procedures related to internal control.
4 Evaluate a firm's ability to pay its bills as they come due.
5 Assess a firm's overall profitability on its asset base.
6 Measure a firm's use of debt and equity financing.
7 Evaluate the rate of return earned on the owners' investment.

For a number of years, Dan had wanted to start his own business—an idea that had originated when he was in college. However, the time never seemed to be right. But then his long-time friend Hank approached him about starting a new company to provide sales training materials for companies with large sales staffs. Given Hank's experience in educational training and Dan's sales background, Dan believed they would make a good team.

So Dan left his sales position and began to work full time at building the new company, Sales Unlimited. Despite some stressful times, it has gone well. Early on, the partners hired technical support and two salespersons. In addition to leading the small sales staff, Dan assumed responsibility for keeping the company's accounting records—a task for which he had no education or experience. He bought QuickBooks, an accounting software package, which allowed him to keep up with the firm's accounting.

Eventually, the partners decided it would be good for Dan to devote all his time to sales, so they hired a bookkeeper to assume the accounting responsibilities. In time, this person took over all the accounting-related activities, including making deposits, paying suppliers, reconciling bank statements, writing payroll checks, and preparing monthly financial statements. Finally being free of the accounting responsibilities was like a breath of fresh air for Dan—his passion was sales.

As the firm continued to grow, Dan and Hank's banker recommended that they hire an accounting firm to oversee the accounting and finance functions of the business. After interviewing several accounting firms, Dan and Hank chose a firm that seemed to fit their needs well. After the initial review, the accountant expressed some concerns. The accountant was particularly worried about the lack of internal controls, noting, "Having one person conduct all the accounting functions is asking for trouble and needs to be changed." Dan responded, "I have known the bookkeeper for years and have total confidence in his integrity. Besides, I don't want to give the impression that I don't trust him, because I do."

Dan's concern is more about not knowing how to interpret the financial statements when he receives them. He wants help interpreting what the statements say about the company's financial performance. So, at the moment, both he and Hank are perplexed as to what they should do.

Their concerns are shared by many entrepreneurs who struggle to understand accounting matters and effectively use financial statements in managing their businesses. This chapter examines the basic elements of an effective accounting system and presents suggestions on how to use accounting data to draw conclusions about a firm's financial performance.

Accounting Activities in Small Firms

Managers must have accurate, meaningful, and timely information if they are to make good decisions. This is particularly true of financial information about a firm's operations. An inadequate accounting system is a primary factor in small business failures. Owner-managers of small companies sometimes believe that they have less need for financial information because of their personal involvement in day-to-day operations, but they are only deceiving themselves.

Rarely are small business owner-managers expert accountants—nor should they expect to be *or even want to be.* But every one of them should know enough about the accounting process, including developing and interpreting financial statements, to recognize which accounting methods are best for their company.

Basic Requirements for Accounting Systems

1 Identify the basic requirements for an accounting system.

An accounting system structures the flow of financial information to provide a complete picture of a firm's financial activities. Conceivably, a few very small firms may not require formal financial statements. Most, however, need at least monthly financial statements, which should be computer-generated. The benefits of using a computer in developing financial information are so great and the costs so low that it makes absolutely no sense to do otherwise.

Regardless of its level of sophistication, an accounting system for a small business should accomplish the following objectives:

- Provide an accurate, thorough picture of operating results

- Permit a quick comparison of current data with prior years' operating results and budgetary goals

- Offer financial statements for use by management, bankers, and prospective creditors

- Facilitate prompt filing of reports and tax returns to regulatory and tax-collecting government agencies

- Reveal employee fraud, theft, waste, and record-keeping errors

THE RECORD-KEEPING SYSTEM   An accounting system provides the framework for managerial control of a firm. Its effectiveness rests on a well-designed and well-managed record-keeping system. In addition to the financial statements intended for external use with bankers and investors (balance sheets, income statements, and cash flow statements), internal accounting records should be kept. The major types of internal accounting records are as follows:

- *Accounts receivable records.* Records of receivables are vital not only for making decisions on credit extension but also for billing accurately and maintaining good customer relations. An analysis of these records will reveal the effectiveness of a firm's credit and collection policies.

- *Accounts payable records.* Records of liabilities show what the firm owes to suppliers, facilitate the taking of cash discounts, and allow payments to be made when due.

- *Inventory records.* Adequate records are essential for the control and security of inventory items. Inventory records supply information for use in making purchases, maintaining adequate stock levels, and computing turnover ratios.

- *Payroll records.* Payroll records show the total salaries paid to employees and provide a base for computing and paying payroll taxes.

- *Cash records.* Carefully maintained records showing all receipts and disbursements are necessary to safeguard cash. They provide essential information about cash flows and cash balances.

- *Fixed asset records.* Fixed asset records show the original cost of each asset and the depreciation taken to date, along with other information such as the condition of the asset.

- *Other accounting records.* Among the other accounting records that are vital to the efficient operation of a small business are the insurance register (showing all policies in force), records of leaseholds, and records of the firm's investments outside its business.

COMPUTER SOFTWARE PACKAGES   Software packages can be used to generate the required accounting records. Most computer software packages include the following features:

- A checkbook that automatically calculates a firm's cash balance, prints checks, and reconciles the account with the bank statement at month's end

- Automatic preparation of income statements, balance sheets, and statements of cash flows

- A cash budget that compares actual expenditures with budgeted expenditures

- Preparation of subsidiary journal accounts—accounts receivable, accounts payable, and other high-activity accounts

In addition, numerous software packages fulfill specialized accounting needs such as graphing, cash flow analysis, and tax preparation.

Although the options are almost unlimited for accounting software programs appropriate for use in a small firm, there are several leaders in the entry-level category. Ranging in cost from $100 to $300, they include

- *DacEasy*
  http://www.daceasy.com

- *MYOB*
  http://www.myob.com

- *QuickBooks*
  http://www.quickbooks.com

- *Peachtree by Sage 2007*
  http://www.peachtree.com

- *Simply Accounting 2007*
  http://www.simplyaccounting.com

- *NetSuite*
  http://www.oraclesmallbusiness.com

Although all these programs have been well tested and widely used, the small business owner should carefully consider the appropriateness of computer software or hardware before purchasing it. The chance of acquiring computer equipment or programs that do not fit a firm's needs is significant.

OUTSIDE ACCOUNTING SERVICES   Instead of having an employee or a member of the owner's family keep records, a firm may have its financial records kept by a certified public accountant or by a bookkeeping firm or service bureau that caters to small businesses. Very small companies often find it convenient to have the same person or agency keep their books and prepare their financial statements and tax returns.

Numerous small public accounting firms offer complete accounting services to small businesses. Such accounting firms usually offer their services at a significantly lower cost than do larger accounting firms. Besides, larger accounting firms have recently become more focused on publicly traded companies, following passage of the Sarbanes-Oxley legislation, which was designed to reduce fraud in large firms. Cost is, of course, an important consideration in selecting an accountant, but other major factors, such as whether the accountant has experience in the particular industry in which the entrepreneur is operating, should play an important role in this decision as well.

In some areas, mobile bookkeepers also serve small companies. Bringing to a firm's premises a mobile office that includes computer equipment, they obtain the necessary data and prepare the financial statements on site. Use of mobile bookkeeping can be a fast, inexpensive, and convenient approach to filling certain accounting needs.

Living the Dream — entrepreneurial challenges

A Good Accounting System Is Essential for Good Decisions

A good accounting program will take a lot of bookkeeping drudgery off your shoulders. Just recording your transactions in a program like Peachtree creates the most important database you'll ever own—the one with your company's key financial details.

Devra Walker, co-owner of Walker Pharmacy & Gifts in Statesboro, Georgia, has an even better approach. She manages her own books with the help of in-house data-entry staff and uses an outside accountant to double-check them, file taxes, and act as a sounding board. Peachtree 2007's improved access privilege system promotes this kind of close-but-safe relationship. A CPA herself, Walker, 45, needs quick data access because she and her husband, Lindsay, 47, manage eight separate business units with combined annual sales of $8 million and a 60-employee payroll. Peachtree lets her roll up the accounts of all her units when preparing payroll or financial statements, but isolate their performance milestones when meeting with her unit managers.

Paula Gilliland, a Roswell, Georgia, accounting consultant and owner of e-commerce site PocketScope.com, uses Peachtree to orchestrate the incoming and outgoing flows of thousands of parts and assemblies for her $900,000 medical instrumentation business and one client's large inventory. Many parts are used in several different subassemblies, and if there's a failure, Gilliland, 44, has to quickly find the bad part among hundreds of similar subassemblies, see if it's under warranty, and arrange a replacement.

Of course, not every growing business faces the same challenges. But all companies need an accounting system that provides relevant and timely information in order to make sound business decisions.

Source: Mike Hogan, "Analyze This," *Entrepreneur*, July 2006, pp. 42–43.

http://www.pocketscope.com

© Jonny McCullagh/iStockphoto International, Inc.

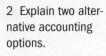

2 Explain two alternative accounting options.

Alternative Accounting Options

Accounting records can be kept in just about any form as long as they provide users with needed data to meet legal requirements. Very small companies have choices when selecting accounting methods and accounting systems. Two such options—cash versus accrual accounting and single-entry versus double-entry systems—reflect the most basic issues in an accounting system.

CASH VERSUS ACCRUAL ACCOUNTING   As discussed in Chapter 10, the major distinction between cash-basis and accrual-basis accounting is in the point at which a firm reports revenue and expenses. The cash method of accounting is easier to use; revenue and expenses are reported only when cash is received or a payment is made. In contrast, the accrual method of accounting reports revenue and expenses when they are incurred, regardless of when the cash is received or payment is made.

The cash method of accounting is sometimes selected by very small firms, as well as by firms with slow-moving receivables that want to improve their cash flows by avoiding the payment of taxes on income not yet received. However, the cash method does not ultimately provide an accurate matching of revenue and expenses. The accrual method, although it involves more record keeping, is preferable because it provides a more realistic measure of profitability within an accounting period. The accrual method of accounting matches revenue against expenses incurred in obtaining that revenue. Alternating between a cash method and an accrual method of accounting is unacceptable, because it violates the accounting principle of consistency.

SINGLE-ENTRY VERSUS DOUBLE-ENTRY SYSTEMS　A single-entry record-keeping system is occasionally still found in very small businesses. It is not, however, a system recommended for firms that are striving to grow and achieve effective financial planning. A single-entry system neither incorporates a balance sheet nor directly generates an income statement. A single-entry system is basically a checkbook system of receipts and disbursements.

Most introductory accounting textbooks provide information on setting up a **double-entry system**.[1] This type of accounting system provides a self-balancing mechanism in the form of two counterbalancing entries for each transaction recorded. It can be done

single-entry system
A checkbook system of accounting reflecting only receipts and disbursements

double-entry system
A self-balancing accounting system that requires that each transaction be recorded twice

Living the Dream　entrepreneurial challenges

© Ethan Hill/Ethan Hill Photography.

Sam and Me

Norm Brodsky, a noted columnist in *Inc.* magazine and a successful entrepreneur in his own right, always introduces his partner, Sam Kaplan, as the man who made him a millionaire. Brodsky tells how Kaplan made the difference in their company:

Sam's arrival had an immediate impact. To begin with, he took over the management of our finances, which I had been overseeing. That was a great relief to me because I could put the accounting stuff out of my mind and focus on the parts of the business I enjoyed most—sales and operations. At the same time, he introduced systems and practices that were rare in a company of our size, including some that I questioned the need for. "What do you mean, we have to have audited financial statements?" I demanded. "We're a $4 million business. It's crazy for us to spend $30,000 or $40,000 a year on that."

"You'll be sorry three years from now if you don't do it," Sam said. "The banks will insist on audited statements, and it will be much more expensive to do them retrospectively, assuming you can get them done at all. A lot of accounting firms won't do it."

So we started having audited annual statements, as well as regular monthly statements, which I hadn't insisted on before. I have my own key numbers that I track and that I thought were giving me a good sense of our financial situation. Yet I found that the monthly statements let me see things I might have missed otherwise. If a number didn't make sense to me, I'd ask for an explanation. Soon the accounting people began anticipating my questions and answering them before I asked. In the process, Sam elevated the entire business. It's easy for small companies to ignore accounting, unlike sales or operations. If you ignore either of those, you'll feel the pain immediately. But you can always tell yourself that you'll deal with accounting issues later. And then, by the time the problems become urgent, you're in serious trouble. Sam made sure that our accounting issues never became urgent.

with the record-keeping journals and ledgers found in most office supply retail stores. However, the relatively simple accounting software programs designed for small companies are preferable.

Internal Accounting Controls

3 Describe the purpose of and procedures related to internal control.

internal control
A system of checks and balances that safeguards assets and enhances the accuracy and reliability of financial statements

As already noted, an effective accounting system is vital to a firm's success. Without the information it provides, management cannot make informed decisions. However, the quality of a company's accounting system is dependent on the effectiveness of the controls that exist within the firm. **Internal control** is a system of checks and balances that plays a key role in safeguarding a firm's assets and in enhancing the accuracy and reliability of its financial statements. The importance of internal control has long been recognized in large corporations. Some owners of smaller companies, concerned about the cost or relevance of a system of internal control for their business, do not appreciate its value—but they should.

Building internal controls may be difficult within a small company, but it is no less important than within a large corporation. The absence of internal controls significantly increases the chances not only of fraud and theft but also of bad decisions based on inaccurate and untimely accounting information. Effective internal controls are also necessary for an audit by independent accountants. Certified public accountants are unwilling to express an opinion about a firm's financial statements if the firm lacks adequate internal controls.

Although a complete description of an internal control system is beyond the scope of this textbook, it is important to understand the concept. An example of an internal control is separation of employees' duties so that the individual maintaining control over an asset is not the same person recording transactions in the accounting ledgers. That is, to discourage fraud or financial mismanagement, the employee who collects cash from customers should not be allowed to reconcile the bank statement. Here are some other examples of internal control:

- Designating the types of transactions that require the owner's approval
- Requiring that checks presented for signature be accompanied by complete supporting documentation
- Limiting access to accounting records
- Sending bank statements directly to the owner
- Safeguarding blank checks
- Requiring all employees to take regular vacations so that any irregularity is likely to be revealed

The importance of developing an effective system of internal control cannot be overemphasized. Extra effort may be needed to implement internal controls in a small company, in which business procedures may be informal and segregation of duties is difficult because of the limited number of employees. Even so, it is best to try to develop such controls. An accountant may be of assistance in minimizing the problems that can result from the absence of internal controls.

Evaluating the Firm's Financial Performance

Once an effective accounting system is in place, a firm's owner must determine how to use the data it generates most productively. Mark Twain said, "He who does not read is no better off than he who cannot read." An owner who has a good accounting system but doesn't use it is similarly disadvantaged. This section provides a framework for interpreting financial statements, designed to clarify these statements for individuals with various levels of accounting knowledge and experience.

How They See It: Evaluating Performance

John Stites

The importance of evaluating one's business performance is often underestimated by the small business owner. In many cases it is because the owners may not have the knowledge base necessary to adequately and properly assess a financial statement. Often, even accountants fail to understand the negative issues a financial statement may reveal. Often, the financial statement provides too broad a view of the company to accurately assess where the problems in the company exist. The business owner must identify those processes necessary for the success of the company and measure the success and the improvement of those processes. If each of the critical success factors is protected and nurtured, the company will have a greater chance of success. The financial statement then becomes only one of the dashboard indicators of the business and retains its rightful place in business success measurements. The danger of waiting for the financial statement to act on business monetary issues is that the financial statement only portrays the past and often does little to predict the future, which is the more important view for the long-term viable life of the business.

An owner needs to understand the financial effect—positive or negative—that management decisions may have. Ultimately, the results of operating decisions appear in a firm's financial statements.

The exact methods used to interpret financial statements can vary, with the perspective of the interpreter determining which figures are emphasized. For example, if a banker and an entrepreneur were analyzing the same financial statements, they might focus on different data. But whatever perspective is taken, the most important issues are fundamentally the same and are captured in the following four questions:

1. Can the firm pay its bills as they come due? In other words, does the company have the capacity to meet its short-term (one year or less) financial commitments?

2. Is the business providing a good rate of return on its assets? There is no more important question when it comes to determining if a business is strong economically.

3. How much debt is the firm using, compared to its equity financing?

4. Are the owners getting a good rate of return on their equity investment? Here we want to know whether the combined effect on the owners of all financial decisions is positive or negative.

Answering these questions requires restating the data from the income statement and the balance sheet in relative terms, or **financial ratios**. Only in this way can comparisons be made with other firms, with industry averages, and across time. Typically, the industry averages or norms used for comparison purposes are those published by companies such as Dun & Bradstreet, Robert Morris Associates, and Standard & Poor's.[2] Exhibit 23-1 shows the industry norms for the computer and software retailing industry for 2006–2007, as reported by Robert Morris Associates, which compiles financial ratios for banks to use in their analyses of firms seeking loans. As shown in the table, the ratios are reported by firm size.

We can best demonstrate the use of financial ratios to evaluate a firm's performance by looking at the financial statements for Trimble & Associates Leasing, Inc., presented in Chapter 10. For ease of reference, the firm's income statement and balance sheets are reproduced in Exhibits 23-2 and 23-3. Using these financial statements to compute the firm's ratios and relying on industry norms selected by the firm's management, we can answer the four fundamental questions regarding Trimble's financial performance.

financial ratios
Restatements of selected income statement and balance sheet data in relative terms

23-1 *Financial Ratios for Retail Computer and Software Stores, 2006–2007*

	FIRM SIZE BY TOTAL ASSETS		
	Less than $500,000	$500,000 to $2 Million	$2 Million to $10 Million
Current ratio	1.0	1.2	1.3
Accounts receivable turnover	20.8	12.8	7.7
Inventory turnover	23.1	15.8	25.9
Return on assets	−1.34%	7.4%	18.4%
Operating profit margin	−0.2%	2.0%	5.1%
Fixed asset turnover	46.5	63.2	34.2
Total asset turnover	6.7	3.7	3.6
Debt/total assets	132.6%	74.9%	76.1%
Return on equity (before tax)	NA*	22.8%	45.5%

*Not applicable. Firms in this group have a negative equity on average, preventing computation of return on equity.
Note: RMA cautions that the Studies be regarded only as a general guideline and not as an absolute industry norm. This is due to limited samples within categories, the categorization of companies by their primary Standard Industrial Classification (SIC) number only, and different methods of operations by companies within the same industry. For these reasons, RMA recommends that the figures be used only as general guidelines in addition to other methods of financial analysis.

Source: Adapted from *RMA 2006–2007 Annual Statement Studies,* published by Robert Morris Associates, Philadelphia, Pa. Copyright Robert Morris Associates, 2007.

Can the Firm Pay Its Bills as They Come Due?

4 Evaluate a firm's ability to pay its bills as they come due.

A business—or a person, for that matter—that has enough money to pay off any debt owed is described as being highly liquid. In other words, the liquidity of a business (discussed in Chapter 10) depends on the availability to the firm of cash to meet maturing debt obligations. Measuring liquidity answers the question "Does the firm now have or will it have in the future the resources to pay creditors when debts come due?"

This question can be answered in two ways: (1) by comparing the firm's assets that are relatively liquid in nature with the debt coming due in the near term or (2) by examining the timeliness with which liquid assets, primarily accounts receivable and inventories, are being converted into cash.

23-2 *Income Statement for Trimble & Associates Leasing, Inc., for the Year Ending December 31, 2007*

Sales		$850,000
Cost of goods sold		550,000
Gross profit on sales		$300,000
Operating expenses:		
Marketing expenses	$90,000	
General and administrative expenses	80,000	
Depreciation expense	30,000	
Total operating expenses		$200,000
Operating income		$100,000
Interest expense		20,000
Earnings before taxes		$ 80,000
Income tax (25%)		20,000
Net income		$ 60,000

23-3 *Balance Sheet for Trimble & Associates Leasing, Inc., for December 31, 2007*

Assets	
Current assets:	
Cash	$ 50,000
Accounts receivable	80,000
Inventories	220,000
Total current assets	$350,000
Fixed assets:	
Gross fixed assets	$960,000
Accumulated depreciation	(390,000)
Net fixed assets	$570,000
TOTAL ASSETS	$920,000
Debt (Liabilities) and Equity	
Current liabilities:	
Accounts payable	$ 20,000
Short-term notes	80,000
Total current liabilities (debt)	$100,000
Long-term debt	200,000
Total debt	$300,000
Owner's equity:	
Common stock	$300,000
Retained earnings	320,000
Total ownership equity	$620,000
TOTAL DEBT AND EQUITY	$920,000

    The first approach to measuring liquidity is to compare cash and the assets that should be converted into cash within the year against the debt (liabilities) that is coming due and will be payable within the year. The liquid assets within a firm are its current assets, and the maturing debt consists of the current liabilities shown in the balance sheet. So, to measure liquidity, we use the current ratio, discussed in Chapter 10, and determine the current ratio for Trimble & Associates Leasing, Inc.:

$$\text{Current ratio} = \frac{\text{Current assets}}{\text{Current liabilities}} = \frac{\$350,000}{\$100,000} = 3.50$$

Based on Dun & Bradstreet data, the industry norm for the current ratio is 2.70. Thus, Trimble & Associates would appear to be more liquid than the average firm in its industry. Trimble has $3.50 in current assets for every $1 in current liabilities (debt), compared to $2.70 for a "typical" firm in the industry.

    The second view of liquidity examines a firm's ability to convert accounts receivable and inventory into cash on a timely basis. The ability to convert accounts receivable into cash may be measured by computing how quickly the firm is collecting its receivables. This can be determined by measuring the number of times that accounts receivable are "rolled over" during a year, or the **accounts receivable turnover**. The accounts receivable turnover is computed as follows:

$$\text{Accounts receivable turnover} = \frac{\text{Credit sales}}{\text{Accounts receivable}}$$

    If we assume that Trimble & Associates' sales are all credit sales, as opposed to cash sales, the accounts receivable turnover for Trimble & Associates in 2007 is 10.63 days. The computation is as follows:

$$\text{Accounts receivable turnover} = \frac{\text{Credit sales}}{\text{Accounts receivable}} = \frac{\$850,000}{\$80,000} = 10.63$$

accounts receivable turnover
The number of times accounts receivable "roll over" during a year

The industry norm for accounts receivable turnover is 10.4. Thus, we may conclude that Trimble & Associates is comparable to the average firm in the industry in terms of its collection of receivables.[3]

To gain some insight into the liquidity of Trimble's inventories, we now need to determine how many times the firm is turning over its inventories during the year. The **inventory turnover** is calculated as follows:

inventory turnover
The number of times inventories "turn over" during a year

$$\text{Inventory turnover} = \frac{\text{Cost of goods sold}}{\text{Inventory}}$$

Note that in this ratio sales are shown at the firm's cost, as opposed to the full market value when sold. Since inventory (the denominator) is at cost, it is desirable to measure sales (the numerator) on a cost basis also in order to avoid a biased answer.

The inventory turnover for Trimble & Associates is calculated as follows:

$$\text{Inventory turnover} = \frac{\text{Cost of goods sold}}{\text{Inventory}} = \frac{\$550,000}{\$220,000} = 2.50$$

The industry norm for inventory turnover is 4.0, which reveals a significant problem of Trimble & Associates. The firm is carrying excessive inventory, possibly even some obsolete inventory. It is generating only $2.50 in sales at cost for every $1 of inventory, compared to $4.00 in sales at cost for the average firm.

Is the Business Providing a Good Return on Its Assets?

A vitally important question to a firm's owners and investors is whether the company's operating profits are sufficient relative to the total amount of assets invested in the company.

5 Assess a firm's overall profitability on its asset base.

Exhibit 23-4 provides a graphical representation of the drivers of a firm's return on assets. As shown in the exhibit, a firm's assets are invested for the express purpose of producing operating profits. A comparison of operating profits to total invested assets reveals the rate of return that is being earned on all the firm's capital. For Trimble & Associates, we compute the return on assets (discussed in Chapter 11) as follows:

$$\text{Return on assets} = \frac{\text{Operating income}}{\text{Total assets}} = \frac{\$100,000}{\$920,000} = 0.1087, \text{ or } 10.87\%$$

The firm's return on assets is less than the industry norm of 13.2 percent. For some reason, Trimble & Associates is generating less operating income on each dollar of assets than are its competitors.

The owners of Trimble & Associates should not be satisfied with merely knowing that they are not earning a competitive return on the firm's assets. They should also want to know *why* the return is below average. To gain more understanding, the owners could separate the return on assets into its two components: (1) operating profit margin and (2) total asset turnover. Separating the return on assets into its two factors better isolates a firm's strengths and weaknesses when it is attempting to identify ways to earn a competitive rate of return on its total invested capital.

The equation for the return on assets can be restated as follows:

$$\text{Return on assets} = \frac{\text{Operating income}}{\text{Total assets}} = \underbrace{\frac{\text{Operating profits}}{\text{Sales}}}_{\substack{\textbf{Operating} \\ \textbf{Profit Margin}}} \times \underbrace{\frac{\text{Sales}}{\text{Total assets}}}_{\substack{\textbf{Total Asset} \\ \textbf{Turnover}}}$$

operating profit margin
The ratio of operating profits to sales, showing how well a firm manages its income statement

The first component of the expanded equation, the **operating profit margin**, shows how well a firm is managing its operations, as reflected in the income statement. There are five factors, or driving forces, that affect the operating profit margin and, in turn, the return on assets:

1. The number of units of product or service sold (volume)

2. The average selling price for each product or service unit (sales price)

3. The cost of manufacturing or acquiring the firm's product (cost of goods sold)

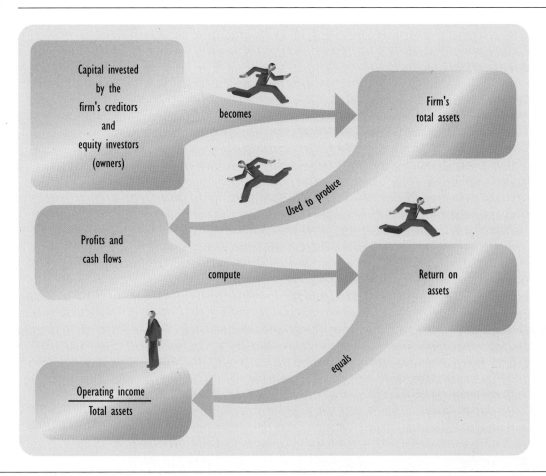

exhibit

23-4 *Return on Assets: An Overview*

4. The ability to control general and administrative expenses (operating expenses)

5. The ability to control expenses in marketing and distributing the firm's product (operating expenses)

The second component of a firm's return on assets, the **total asset turnover**, indicates how efficiently management is using the firm's assets to generate sales—that is, how well the firm is managing its balance sheet. If Company A can generate $3 in sales with $1 in assets while Company B generates $2 in sales per asset dollar, then Company A is using its assets more efficiently in generating sales. This is a major determinant in the firm's return on investment.

For Trimble & Associates, the operating profit margin and total asset turnover can be computed as follows:

total asset turnover
The ratio of sales to total assets, showing the efficiency with which a firm's assets are used to generate sales

$$\text{Operating profit margin} = \frac{\text{Operating profits}}{\text{Sales}} = \frac{\$100{,}000}{\$850{,}000} = 0.1176, \text{ or } 11.76\%$$

$$\text{Total asset turnover} = \frac{\text{Sales}}{\text{Total assets}} = \frac{\$850{,}000}{\$920{,}000} = 0.92$$

The industry norms for the two ratios are as follows:

Industry norm for operating profit margin = 11%

Industry norm for total asset turnover = 1.20

Living the Dream   entrepreneurial challenges

A Penchant for Profits

Surviving rapid top-line growth requires a bottom-line focus to keep things under control.

Revenue at software provider Avidian Technologies in Bellevue, Washington, was growing at 400 percent annually in 2003 and 2004—and 2005 promised more of the same. Co-founder and CEO James Wong knew that such growth could be dangerous, and he was doing all he could to control it carefully.

That means vigilantly watching cash flows and bottom-line profits. Wong, 33, has strong policies regarding both: Avidian never ships a product until payment is received and never lets net profits dip below 15 percent of sales. With cash on hand and profits to reinvest, Avidian fuels its growth with no significant debt and no outside investors.

Avidian now has over 7,000 registered users of its software, and sales are approaching $5 million. Still, profits are always on Wong's mind.

Source: David Worrell, "A Penchant for Profits," *Entrepreneur,* August 2005, p. 53.

http://www.avidian.com

Thus, comparing Trimble & Associates to the industry, we have

		Operating Profit Margin		Total Asset Turnover		Return on Assets
Return on assets $_{Trimble}$	=	11.76%	×	0.92	=	10.82%[4]
Return on assets $_{Industry}$	=	11.0%	×	1.20	=	13.2%

    Clearly, Trimble & Associates is competitive when it comes to managing its income statement—keeping costs and expenses in line relative to sales—as reflected by the operating profit margin. In other words, its managers are performing satisfactorily in controlling the five driving forces of the operating profit margin. However, Trimble & Associates' total asset turnover shows why the firm is not earning a good return on its assets. The firm is not using its assets efficiently; the balance sheet is not being managed well. Trimble's problem is that it generates $0.92 in sales per dollar of assets, while the competition produces $1.20 in sales from every dollar in assets.

    The analysis should not stop here, however. It is clear that Trimble's assets are not being used efficiently, but the next question should be "Which assets are the problem?" Is this firm overinvested in all assets or mainly in accounts receivable or inventory or fixed assets? To answer this question, we must examine the turnover ratio for each asset. The first two ratios—accounts receivable turnover and inventory turnover—were calculated earlier. The third ratio, **fixed asset turnover**, is found by dividing sales by net fixed assets.

fixed asset turnover
A measure of the relationship of sales to fixed assets

Thus, the three turnover ratios are as follows:

Turnover Ratios		Trimble & Associates		Industry Norm
Accounts receivable turnover $= \dfrac{\text{Credit sales}}{\text{Accounts receivable}}$	$= \dfrac{\$850,000}{\$80,000}$	$= 10.63$		10.4
Inventory turnover $= \dfrac{\text{Cost of goods sold}}{\text{Inventory}}$	$= \dfrac{\$550,000}{\$220,000}$	$= 2.50$		4.0
Fixed asset turnover $= \dfrac{\text{Sales}}{\text{Net fixed assets}}$	$= \dfrac{\$850,000}{\$570,000}$	$= 1.49$		2.5

Trimble's problems can now be better understood. The firm has excessive inventories, as was evident earlier. Also, it is too heavily invested in fixed assets for the sales being produced. It appears that these two asset categories are not being managed well. Consequently, Trimble & Associates is experiencing a lower-than-average return on assets.

We have shown how to analyze a firm's ability to earn a satisfactory rate of return on its total invested capital. To this point, we have ignored the firm's decisions as to whether to use debt or equity financing and the consequences of such decisions on the owners' return on the equity investment. So let's examine how Trimble & Associates finances its assets.

How Much Debt Is the Firm Using?

As discussed in Chapter 11, the use of debt, or **financial leverage**, can increase a firm's return on equity, but with some financial risk. Are Trimble's assets financed to a greater extent by debt or by equity? One of two ratios is generally used to answer this question (although many others could be used). The debt ratio, which is total debt divided by total assets, was discussed in Chapter 10; it tells us what percentage of the firm's assets is financed by debt—both short-term and long-term. (The remaining percentage must be financed by equity.) The *debt-equity ratio* is total debt divided by total equity, rather than total assets. Either ratio leads to the same conclusion.

> **6** Measure a firm's use of debt and equity financing.

financial leverage
The use of debt in financing a firm's assets

For Trimble & Associates in 2007, debt as a percentage of total assets is 33 percent, compared to an industry norm of 40 percent. The computation is as follows:

$$\text{Debt ratio} = \frac{\text{Total debt}}{\text{Total assets}} = \frac{\$300,000}{\$920,000} = 0.33, \text{ or } 33\%$$

Thus, Trimble & Associates uses somewhat less debt than the average firm in the industry, which means that it has less financial risk.

A second perspective on a firm's financing decisions can be gained by looking at the income statement. When a firm borrows money, it is required, at a minimum, to pay the interest on the debt. Thus, determining the amount of operating income available to pay the interest provides a firm with valuable information. Stated as a ratio, the computation shows the number of times the firm earns its interest. The **times interest earned ratio**, which is commonly used in examining a firm's debt position, is calculated as follows:

times interest earned ratio
The ratio of operating income to interest charges

$$\text{Times interest earned ratio} = \frac{\text{Operating income}}{\text{Interest expense}}$$

For Trimble & Associates, the times interest earned ratio is as follows:

$$\text{Times interest earned ratio} = \frac{\text{Operating income}}{\text{Interest expense}} = \frac{\$100,000}{\$20,000} = 5.00$$

The industry norm for the times interest earned ratio is 4.0. Thus, Trimble & Associates is better able to service its interest expense than most comparable firms. Remember, however, that interest is paid not with income but with cash. Also, the firm may be required to repay some of the debt principal, as well as the interest. Thus, the times interest earned ratio is only a crude measure of a firm's capacity to service its debt. Nevertheless, it gives a general indication of the firm's debt capacity.

How They See It: Benchmark Even If You Are Small

John Stites

It is very difficult for a small family-owned business to benchmark its progress with similar firms. Most family-owned firms are closely held businesses, and data for benchmarking is extremely difficult to come by. Larger firms, even if they are closely held family firms, have the benefit of being able to compare themselves with publicly traded firms. Often, due to a lack of data, smaller firms may think they are successful, when in reality they have a high lost-opportunity cost.

We have tried to mitigate this problem in our family business by identifying similar family businesses with which we can share detailed data. This process allows us to benchmark ourselves with companies who don't compete with us and who can speak candidly about our performance. This forum also allows us the opportunity to share "trial balloons" and prototype pro forma statements that can be reviewed critically without risk of competitors seeing a potentially successful business plan or strategy.

---

7 Evaluate the rate of return earned on the owners' investment.

Are the Owners Getting a Good Rate of Return on Their Equity Investment?

The last question looks at the accounting return on the owners' investment, or return on equity, which was discussed in Chapter 11. We must determine whether the earnings available to the firm's owners (or stockholders) are attractive when compared to the returns of owners of similar companies in the same industry. The return on equity for Trimble & Associates in 2007 is as follows:

$$\text{Return on equity} = \frac{\text{Net income}}{\text{Owner's equity}} = \frac{\$60,000}{\$620,000} = 0.097, \text{ or } 9.7\%$$

The industry norm for return on equity is 12.5 percent. Thus, it appears that the owners of Trimble & Associates are not receiving a return on their investment equivalent to that of owners of competing businesses. Why not? To answer this question, we have to understand the following:

1. The return on equity will increase as the difference between the return on assets and the interest rate paid for the use of debt financing increases; that is, as (return on assets − interest rate) increases, return on equity increases. But, if the difference between the return on assets and the interest rate decreases, then the return on equity will also decrease.

2. As a firm's debt ratio (total debt ÷ total assets) increases, return on equity will increase if the return on assets is greater than the interest rate, but return on equity will decrease if the return on assets is less than the interest rate.

It is important for an entrepreneur to understand the foregoing relationships, illustrated in Exhibit 23-5. Note how Exhibit 23-5 builds on Exhibit 23-4. Also, you are encouraged to return to the illustrations in Chapter 11 (pages 300–305) showing the effects on an owner's return on equity (net income ÷ common equity) of (1) a firm's return on assets (operating income ÷ total assets) and (2) a firm's debt ratio (total debt ÷ total assets).

In the case of Trimble & Associates, we see that the firm has a lower return on equity in part because it is not as profitable in its operation as its competitors are. (Recall that the return on assets is 10.87 percent for Trimble & Associates, compared to 13.2 percent for the industry.) Also, Trimble uses less debt than the average firm in the industry, causing its return on equity to be lower than that of other firms—provided, of course, that these firms are earning a return on their investments that exceeds the cost of debt (the interest rate). However, we should recognize that the use of less debt does reduce Trimble's risk.

exhibit 23-5 *Return on Equity: An Overview*

To conclude, a profile of the financial ratios used in evaluating the financial performance of Trimble & Associates for 2007 are presented in Exhibit 23-6. The ratios are grouped by the issue being addressed: liquidity, operating profitability, financing, and owners' return on equity. Recall that the turnover ratios for accounts receivable and

Living the Dream   entrepreneurial challenges

© Keith Brofsky/Photodisc/Getty Images

How to Make a True Profit

From almost every angle, it looked like one sweet deal.

Morgan Stanley was seeking a company to host a massive software program designed to digest stock market data. Among the candidates for the job was a little-known firm with big ambitions, Rackspace Managed Hosting, based in San Antonio.

The project promised to be a blockbuster: $20 million in revenue over two years and the chance to work for a respected giant on Wall Street, an enticing opportunity for a small company.

Not too many young companies eager to break into the big time would take a pass on such a project, but Rackspace did. After a wrenching series of meetings with his top executives, CEO Graham Weston decided against it—despite intense pressure from the sales team.

Weston took a lot of heat for his decision but held firm. "We could have made a profit on this deal, but not enough to risk our capital," he says. "We are 100 percent committed to making a true profit."

That concept, true profit, is a religion at Rackspace, and Weston preaches it with the passion of a zealot. It is based on a very basic principle: Create new wealth. Rackspace defines true profit as a company's operating profit (after taxes) minus its total annual cost of capital.

This sounds elementary, but there is a twist. The cost of capital includes not only borrowed money, which is usually relatively inexpensive, but also the far more costly capital contributed by investors and shareholders. Essentially Rackspace's magic number is 15 percent—any return on investment lower than that is unacceptable.

Today every deal—indeed, every major business decision—is tested against the principle of true profit. Weston has set the bar high, putting the cost of capital at 15 percent. That forces a strict and sometimes painful financial discipline on the company.

Weston has passed on some compelling opportunities—and pulled the plug on others—because they did not pass the true-profit test. Last year, for instance, Rackspace sold off a fast-growing, moneymaking subsidiary because the new venture did not generate enough money to clear the hurdle.

Weston's faith is reaping big rewards for Rackspace, especially compared to the scores of companies in the savagely competitive Web-hosting business that have been driven into bankruptcy or have simply disappeared since the dot-com bust of 2000.

Source: Patricia B. Gray, "How to Make a True Profit," *Fortune Small Business*, November 6, 2006.

http://www.rackspace.com

inventories are used for more than one purpose. These ratios have implications for both the firm's liquidity and its profitability; thus, they are listed in both areas. In any case, it should be apparent by now that the numbers tell a clear story about a company's health and performance. Those who know how to read that story will always have an advantage over competitors that are unable to sort this out—and that can make all the difference!

23-6 *Financial Ratio Analysis for Trimble & Associates Leasing, Inc.*

Financial Ratios	Trimble & Associates	Industry Norm
1. Firm liquidity		
Current ratio $= \dfrac{\text{Current assets}}{\text{Current liabilities}}$	$\dfrac{\$350,000}{\$100,000} = 3.50$	2.70
Accounts receivable turnover $= \dfrac{\text{Credit sales}}{\text{Accounts receivable}}$	$\dfrac{\$850,000}{\$80,000} = 10.63$	10.43
Inventory turnover $= \dfrac{\text{Cost of goods sold}}{\text{Inventory}}$	$\dfrac{\$550,000}{\$220,000} = 2.50$	4.00
2. Operating profitability		
Return on assets $= \dfrac{\text{Operating income}}{\text{Total assets}}$	$\dfrac{\$100,000}{\$920,000} = 10.87\%$	13.2%
Operating profit margin $= \dfrac{\text{Operating profits}}{\text{Sales}}$	$\dfrac{\$100,000}{\$850,000} = 11.76\%$	11.0%
Total asset turnover $= \dfrac{\text{Sales}}{\text{Total assets}}$	$\dfrac{\$850,000}{\$920,000} = 0.92$	1.20
Accounts receivable turnover $= \dfrac{\text{Credit sales}}{\text{Accounts receivable}}$	$\dfrac{\$850,000}{\$80,000} = 10.63$	10.43
Inventory turnover $= \dfrac{\text{Cost of goods sold}}{\text{Inventory}}$	$\dfrac{\$550,000}{\$220,000} = 2.50$	4.00
Fixed asset turnover $= \dfrac{\text{Sales}}{\text{Net fixed assets}}$	$\dfrac{\$850,000}{\$570,000} = 1.49$	2.50
3. Financing		
Debt ratio $= \dfrac{\text{Total debt}}{\text{Total assets}}$	$\dfrac{\$300,000}{\$920,000} = 33.00\%$	40.0%
Times interest earned ratio $= \dfrac{\text{Operating income}}{\text{Interest expense}}$	$\dfrac{\$100,000}{\$20,000} = 5.00$	4.00
4. Return on equity		
Return on equity $= \dfrac{\text{Net income}}{\text{Owner's equity}}$	$\dfrac{\$60,000}{\$620,000} = 9.70\%$	12.5%

Looking **BACK**

1 Identify the basic requirements for an accounting system.

· An accounting system structures the flow of financial information to provide a complete picture of financial activities.

· Financial reports should be computer-generated.

· The system should be accurate and thorough, allow a quick comparison of data over the years of operation, provide financial statements, facilitate filing of reports and tax returns, and reveal internal problems such as fraud and record-keeping errors.

- In addition to the balance sheet and income statement, an accounting system should provide internal records that show accounts receivable, accounts payable, inventories, payroll, cash, and fixed assets, as well as insurance policies, leaseholds, and outside investments.

2 Explain two alternative accounting options.

- Accounting systems may use either cash or accrual methods and may be structured as either single-entry or double-entry systems.

- With the cash method of accounting, transactions are recorded only when cash is received or a payment is made; the accrual method of accounting matches revenue earned against expenses associated with it.

- A single-entry system is basically a checkbook system of receipts and disbursements; a double-entry system of accounting requires that each transaction be recorded twice.

3 Describe the purpose of and procedures related to internal control.

- Internal control refers to a system of checks and balances designed to safeguard a firm's assets and enhance the accuracy and reliability of its financial statements.

- Some examples of internal control procedures are separation of employees' duties, limiting access to accounting records and computer facilities, and safeguarding blank checks.

- Building internal controls within a small business is difficult but important.

4 Evaluate a firm's ability to pay its bills as they come due.

- Liquidity is a firm's capacity to meet its short-term obligations.

- One way of measuring a firm's liquidity is to compare its liquid assets (cash, accounts receivable, and inventories) and its short-term debt, using the current ratio.

- A second way to measure liquidity is to determine the time it takes to convert accounts receivable and inventories into cash, by computing the accounts receivable turnover and the inventory turnover.

5 Assess a firm's overall profitability on its asset base.

- Operating profitability is evaluated by determining if the firm is earning a good return on its total assets, through computation of the return on assets.

- The return on assets can be separated into two components—the operating profit margin and the total asset turnover—to gain more insight into the firm's operating profitability.

- The operating profit margin is determined by dividing operating profits by sales.

- The total asset turnover is computed by dividing sales by total assets.

6 Measure a firm's use of debt and equity financing.

- The debt ratio (total debt divided by total assets) can be used to measure how much debt a firm uses in its financing mix.

- A firm's ability to cover interest charges on its debt can be measured by the times interest earned ratio (operating income divided by interest expense).

7 Evaluate the rate of return earned on the owners' investment.

- The accounting return on the owners' investment (return on equity) is measured by dividing net income by the common equity invested in the business.

- The return on equity is a function of (1) the firm's return on assets less the interest paid and (2) the amount of debt used relative to the amount of equity financing.

Key TERMS

single-entry system, p. 601

double-entry system, p. 601

internal control, p. 602

financial ratios, p. 603

accounts receivable turnover, p. 605

inventory turnover, p. 606

operating profit margin, p. 606

total asset turnover, p. 607

fixed asset turnover, p. 608

financial leverage, p. 609

times interest earned ratio, p. 609

Discussion QUESTIONS

1. Explain the accounting concept that income is realized when earned, whether or not it has been received in cash.

2. Should entrepreneurs have an outside specialist set up an accounting system for their startup or do it themselves? Why?

3. What are the primary types of records required in a sound accounting system?

4. What are the major advantages of a double-entry accounting system over a single-entry system?

5. What is liquidity? Differentiate between the two approaches given in this chapter to measure liquidity.

6. Explain the following ratios:

   a. Operating profit margin

   b. Total asset turnover

   c. Times interest earned

7. Explain the relationship among these ratios: return on assets, operating profit margin, and total asset turnover.

8. What would be the difference between using operating profit and using net income when calculating a firm's return on investment?

9. What is financial leverage? When should it be used, and when should it be avoided? Why?

10. What determines a firm's return on equity?

You Make the CALL

SITUATION 1

In 2008, Carter Dalton purchased the Baugh Company. Although the firm has consistently earned profits, little cash has been available for other than business needs. Before purchasing Baugh, Dalton thought that cash flows were generally equal to profits plus depreciation. However, this does not seem to be the case. The financial statements (in thousands) for the Baugh Company, 2007–2008, and the industry norms for the financial ratios follow.

Balance Sheet

	2007	2008
ASSETS		
Current assets:		
Cash	$ 8,000	$ 10,000
Accounts receivable	15,000	20,000
Inventory	22,000	25,000
Total current assets	$ 45,000	$ 55,000
Fixed assets:		
Gross plant and equipment	$ 50,000	$ 55,000
Accumulated depreciation	15,000	20,000
Net fixed assets	$ 35,000	$ 35,000
Other assets	12,000	10,000
TOTAL ASSETS	$ 92,000	$100,000

DEBT (LIABILITIES) AND EQUITY

	2007	2008
Current liabilities:		
Accounts payable	$ 10,000	$ 12,000
Accruals	7,000	8,000
Short-term notes	5,000	5,000
Total current liabilities	$ 22,000	$ 25,000
Long-term liabilities	15,000	15,000
Total liabilities	$ 37,000	$ 40,000
Total ownership equity	55,000	60,000
TOTAL DEBT AND EQUITY	$ 92,000	$100,000

Income Statement, 2008

Sales revenue		$175,000
Cost of goods sold		105,000
Gross profit on sales		$ 70,000
Operating expenses:		
Marketing expenses	$ 26,000	
General and administrative expenses	20,000	
Depreciation expense	5,000	
Total operating expenses		$ 51,000
Operating income		$ 19,000
Interest expense		3,000
Earnings before taxes		$ 16,000
Income tax		8,000
Net income		$ 8,000

Financial Ratios	Industry Norms
Current ratio	2.50
Average collection period	30.00
Inventory turnover	6.00
Debt ratio	50.0%
Return on assets	16.0%
Operating profit margin	8.0%
Total asset turnover	2.00
Fixed asset turnover	7.00
Times interest earned	5.00
Return on equity	14.0%

Question 1 Why doesn't Dalton have cash for personal needs? (As part of your analysis, measure cash flows, as discussed in Chapter 10.)

Question 2 Evaluate the Baugh Company's financial performance, given the financial ratios for the industry.

SITUATION 2

The following financial statements are for the Cherokee Communications Corporation. The company provides pay-phone service at many of the small convenience stores in the southwestern United States, primarily in Texas and New Mexico. The business was "meeting plan" until 2007, when a problem developed.

Balance Sheet

	2006	2007
ASSETS		
Current assets:		
Cash and cash equivalents	$ 668,778	$ 592,491
Accounts receivable	4,453,192	3,888,621
Inventories	137,036	112,699
Prepaid expenses and other current assets	411,990	407,274
Total current assets	$ 5,670,996	$ 5,001,085
Fixed assets:		
Property, plant and equipment (net)	$12,935,453	$16,466,001
Site licenses	1,941,467	3,771,571
Investments in affiliates	164,549	251,672
Total fixed assets	$15,041,469	$20,489,244
Other assets	681,754	455,488
TOTAL ASSETS	$21,394,219	$25,945,817

DEBT (LIABILITIES) AND EQUITY		
Current liabilities:		
Notes payable	$ 2,151,371	$ 3,320,197
Current portion of capital lease	1,094,381	668,826
Accounts payable	310,358	835,384
Accrued expenses	2,971,935	3,036,633
Income taxes payable	256,140	475,945
Total current liabilities	$ 6,784,185	$ 8,336,985

Long-term liabilities:		
Notes payable	$ 6,605,835	$10,030,963
Capital lease obligations	780,593	56,219
Deferred income taxes	342,359	306,021
Total long-term liabilities	$ 7,728,787	$10,393,203
Preferred stock	$ 2,400,000	$ 2,400,000
Common stockholders' equity:		
Common stock	$ 1,438,903	$ 1,438,903
Additional paid-in capital	10,630	10,630
Retained earnings	3,031,714	3,366,096
Total ownership equity	$ 4,481,247	$ 4,815,629
TOTAL DEBT AND EQUITY	$21,394,219	$25,945,817

Income Statements

	2006	2007
Sales revenue	$31,591,640	$34,910,951
Operating expenses:		
Telephone charges	$ 7,851,842	$ 9,078,851
Commissions	4,909,445	5,627,288
Telecommunications fees	1,821,930	1,519,095
Depreciation	4,298,090	5,353,797
Field personnel	2,016,935	2,988,456
Chargebacks	1,104,896	1,111,857
General and administrative expenses	5,520,405	6,435,919
Total operating expenses	$27,523,543	$32,115,263
Operating income	$ 4,068,097	$ 2,795,688
Interest expense		
Other income (expenses)	($ 1,631,416)	($ 1,816,222)
Interest income	57,278	5,069
Losses on affiliates	(34,608)	(108,556)
Unusual gains	1,160,238	27,234
Total other income (expenses)	($ 448,508)	($ 1,892,475)
Income before taxes	$ 3,619,589	$ 903,213
Income taxes	1,399,140	424,831
Net income	$ 2,220,449	$ 478,382

Question 1 Using financial ratios, compare the firm's financial performance for 2006 and 2007.

Question 2 What do you think might have happened from 2006 to 2007?

SITUATION 3

The 2002–2006 financial statements presented on the following pages are for Phillips, Inc., a masonry business located in Corsicana, Texas. The firm was started in 2002 by parents of a student of one of the authors.

Income Statement for Year Ending August 31, 2006

	2002	2003	2004	2005	2006
Sales	$848,109	$2,004,553	$1,843,012	$2,337,627	$3,633,666
Cost of goods sold	441,001	1,428,585	1,276,913	1,823,382	2,912,550
Gross profit	$407,108	$ 575,968	$ 566,099	$ 514,245	$ 721,116
Operating expense	334,091	580,444	503,050	484,917	669,617
Operating income	$ 73,017	$ (4,467)	$ 63,049	$ 29,328	$ 51,499
Interest expense	37,739	27,234	25,992	20,126	20,447
Other income/expense					
Interest income	$ 547		$ 667	$ 743	$ 1,121
Gain (loss) on asset disposals	(36,000)	31,734	(36,200)	(6,000)	19,088
Total other income/expense	$ (35,453)	$ 31,734	$ (35,533)	$ (5,257)	$ 20,209
Earnings before taxes	$ (175)	$ 24	$ 1,524	$ 3,945	$ 51,261
Federal income taxes	234	0	553	916	12,815
Net income	$ (409)	$ 24	$ 971	$ 3,029	$ 38,446

Balance Sheet for Year Ending August 31, 2006

	2002	2003	2004	2005	2006
ASSETS					
Current assets					
Cash	$148,021	$ 39,129	$ 169,187	$187,290	$ 333,016
Accounts receivable	5,817	176,231	39,546	121,186	145,632
Inventory	400,000	219,500	222,500	222,325	225,600
Prepaid federal taxes		299			
Total current assets	$553,838	$435,159	$ 431,233	$530,801	$ 704,248
Fixed assets					
Property and equipment	$371,200	$285,867	$ 248,100	$233,100	$ 233,100
Accumulated depreciation	(37,083)	(82,574)	(106,235)	(150,193)	(150,193)
Net fixed assets	$334,117	$203,293	$ 141,865	$ 82,907	$ 82,907
TOTAL ASSETS	$887,955	$638,153	$ 573,098	$613,708	$ 787,155
DEBT (LIABILITIES) AND EQUITY					
Current liabilities:					
Accounts payable		$ 41,205	$ 45,066	$142,325	$ 178,117
Accruals		29,022	29,023	24,226	42,296
Federal income tax payable	$ 234		287	633	3,000
Total current liabilities	$ 234	$ 70,227	$ 74,376	$167,184	$ 223,413
Notes payable	$787,130	467,610	$ 386,134	$330,907	$ 409,680
Total liabilities	$787,364	$537,837	$ 460,511	$498,091	$ 633,093
Equity:					
Common stock	$ 1,000	$ 1,000	$ 1,000	$ 1,000	$ 1,000
Paid in capital	100,000	100,000	111,000	111,000	111,000
Retained earnings	(409)	(384)	587	3,617	42,063
Total ownership equity	$100,591	$100,616	$ 112,587	$115,617	$ 154,063
TOTAL DEBT AND EQUITY	$887,955	$638,453	$ 573,098	$613,708	$ 787,155

Question 1 Compute the various financial ratios presented in the chapter. (An Excel spreadsheet of the financial statements is provided on the website for the text, at academic.cengage.com/management/longenecker, to save you time in your computations.)

Question 2 Compare your results across the years, and interpret your findings.

Experiential EXERCISES

1. Interview a local CPA who consults with small firms on small business accounting systems. Report to the class on the levels of accounting knowledge the CPA's clients appear to possess.

2. Contact several small businesses and explain your interest in their accounting systems. Report to the class on their level of sophistication—for example, whether they use a single-entry system, a computer, or an outside professional.

3. Find out whether your public or university library subscribes to Robert Morris Associates or Dun & Bradstreet. If the library does not subscribe to either of these financial services, ask whether it subscribes to another service that provides industry norms. Once you find a source, select an industry and bring a copy of its ratios to class for discussion.

4. Locate a small company in your community that will allow you to perform a financial ratio analysis on its financial statements. You will need to decide which industry's data to use for comparative purposes and then find the norms in the library. You may need to promise the company's owners that you will change all names on statements to provide confidentiality.

Exploring the WEB

1. At the American Express website, at **http://www133.americanexpress.com/osbn/Tool/collections/manage.asp,** choose the article "Manage Your Receivables and Collections."

   a. According to the article, what percentage of past-due accounts will never be collected?

   b. Take the quiz to test the effectiveness of your receivables policy. What areas of your receivables policy need to be improved?

   c. List 10 steps to effective collections.

   d. Read about collection laws. Jot down some laws of which you were not aware.

   e. List seven tips for avoiding overdue accounts.

2. Go to the *Inc.* magazine website at **http://www.inc.com**.

   a. Type "Forecasting" in the Search box. In the search results, locate the article entitled "Action Plan: Forecasting and Cash-Flow Budgeting." List the steps in creating a cash flow budget.

   b. Now type "Prioritizing Bills" in the Search box, and locate the article entitled "Prioritizing Bills When Money Is Short." List the items that must be paid first when your business is facing a severe cash shortage.

   c. Find the article entitled "Is Your Company at Risk? Contingency Planning." List the key questions, and note which ones deal with cash flow issues.

Video Case **23**

Understanding Financial Statements, Part 2 (p. 667)

This case examines the importance of financial statements to the business owner and offers suggestions on how to encourage ideas for growth and money management by making everyone in the business accountable for financial results.

Alternative Cases for Chapter 23:

Case 10, Understanding Financial Statements, Part 1, p. 640

Case 11, My Own Money, p. 642

Boston Duck Tours

How Perseverance and Creativity Led an Entrepreneur to Great Success

It is not uncommon for entrepreneurial ventures to meet with resistance. Even though small businesses account for more new job creation than larger established firms, many people and organizations are often reluctant to embrace entrepreneurial opportunities. Andy Wilson, founder of Boston Duck Tours, experienced this firsthand. But despite the overwhelming obstacles he faced in starting and growing his business, he persisted with a positive attitude and commitment to his idea.

After working for seven years in an investment banking firm, Wilson was no longer motivated by the suit-and-tie atmosphere of corporate America. So he left his job, bought a 90-day Greyhound Bus pass, and began touring the country. At a stop in Memphis, he was awakened by a Duck Tour being conducted outside his hotel. Intrigued, he took the tour. He didn't think any more about it until he got home to his native Boston and saw a stream of trolleys, packed with sightseers. Instantly, the Duck Tour idea came to mind.

Wilson decided to bring the Duck Tour concept to Boston and create a lively, informative, historical tour to showcase the city from both the land and the river. He invested $30,000 of his own money and then began making the rounds, seeking government permits and additional investors. He quickly encountered skepticism, and even derision, as he wended his way through a maze of nearly 100 government agencies. Because the Duck (a World War II–era amphibious vehicle) is part bus, part truck, and part boat, he had a difficult time explaining his business concept to government bureaucrats and potential investors. "The short and sweet of it is that everybody thought I was nuts because it was a new idea," said Wilson. One government official even told him that he would have better luck trying to build a skyscraper in the center of Boston Public Garden!

About to give up, Wilson decided to check out the competition before he threw in the towel. His first trolley tour, which he called "such a pathetic experience," gave him the determination to keep

Sources: http://www.bostonducktours.com; and Laura Tiffany, "Making Waves: More Than One Hundred Government Agencies Mocked Andy Wilson's Idea, but Look Who's Quacking Now," *Entrepreneur*, June 1999, p. 97.

pushing forward. He located investors to provide the $1.25 million he required to launch Boston Duck Tours, and he began the arduous task of securing the 29 permits necessary to operate his business. He researched other Duck Tour operations that had been successful in the Midwest and formed an alliance with the operator in Branson, Missouri, to get the Ducks he needed to start the business in Boston. And he began looking for employees by running newspaper ads in the Boston Globe for Coast Guard captains.

Duck drivers (called conDUCKtors) need four licenses: a captain's license from the U.S. Coast Guard, a commercial driver's license from the state of Massachusetts, a license from the Department of Public Safety, and a sightseer's license from the city of Boston. Despite these requirements, applicants responded in droves. Determined to create a different kind of tourist attraction, Wilson decided to abandon traditional interviewing techniques. Instead, he had applicants meet with a theatrical coach who put them through theatrical skill sets. Applicants then selected items from a group of props, created a character, and put together a costume. The 45 Duck captains play characters like "Captain Courageous," a World War II radio operator downed in the South Pacific, and "Penny Wise," a Southern Belle who now drives her Duck around Boston looking for her long-lost love. The cast of conDUCKtors makes Boston Duck Tours "the best show on wheels," Wilson said.

Boston Duck Tours was only open for two months its first season. The next year, it carried almost 15 times as many passengers as it had the previous year, and tours were selling out every day. By the third year, the company was a well-established part of the city's tourism industry, and those adversaries who had made things difficult at the beginning started embracing Boston Duck Tours.

Wilson used the success of his business to strengthen his presence in the community. He got involved in local environmental groups and sponsored contests in which local schoolchildren named new Ducks. He donated one million pennies to his one-millionth passenger's charity of choice, and he gave veterans free tours during the week of Veteran's Day in honor of his father, a World War II veteran who died when Wilson was young. (The company still does that every year.)

What began as a four-Duck, 15-employee business in October of 1994 has grown to a 23-Duck, 100-employee tourism powerhouse in the Boston market. Today, over 2,700 passengers a day quack at passersby from the deck of a colorfully painted Duck, captained by an equally colorful character. And Duck Tours have hatched all over, in places like Austin, Chicago, Dublin, Liverpool, London, Oahu, Seattle, Singapore, Tampa Bay, and the Wisconsin Dells. In 2000, Andy Wilson sold his stake in Boston Duck Tours to pursue other projects, but his management team took over and continues to build on his foundation.

This case study was developed in cooperation with the Small Business School, the series on PBS stations. To learn more and to see the video, go to http://www.smallbusinessschool.org.

Questions

1.   What is Andy Wilson's primary motivation for leading an entrepreneurial life?

2.   What kind of entrepreneurial venture is Boston Duck Tours?

3.   Describe the competitive advantage of Boston Duck Tours.

4.   What characteristics of successful entrepreneurs does Andy Wilson embody?

Activities

1.   Now that you are familiar with Duck Tours, do some research to determine whether there is a Duck Tour company in your city or area. If there is, make an appointment to interview the owner. Draft a set of interview questions that address the issues you learned about in Chapter 1. Here are some examples to get you started:

   • When did you get the idea for the business?

   • Why did you want to start this business?

   • What made you take the plunge into entrepreneurship?

   • What obstacles did you encounter while starting the business?

   • What competitive advantage do you have over other tourist attractions?

   Many other questions are also possible. Write a brief summary of what you learned during the interview.

2.   If you do not have a Duck Tour company in your area, think about what you would need to start one. Is your town or area suited for Duck Tours? If there isn't a body of water in your city, could you still create a business based on the Duck Tour concept? Visit the Boston Duck Tours website at http://www.bostonducktours.com to find out more about the company and what made it a business opportunity rather than just a business idea. Write a short description (no more than a couple of paragraphs) of a unique tourism company in your city.

Joseph's Lite Cookies

Integrity Creates a Strong Foundation for Growth

Recall from the video spotlight that opened Chapter 2 that Joseph Semprevivo, a diabetic and founder of Joseph's Lite Cookies, began his entrepreneurial career at the age of 12, when he created and sold gourmet sugar-free ice cream in his family's restaurant. Three years later, when his parents perfected their recipe for a sugar-free cookie for him, Semprevivo decided to expand his business and offer the cookie to diabetics around the country.

From its humble beginnings in 1986, Joseph's Lite Cookies has grown into a business that generates annual sales of over $100 million, producing over 9 billion cookies a year. Although the financial success of the business is impressive, money is not the whole story. What puts Semprevivo's business into the spotlight is the way he runs it—as a team effort, with honesty, integrity, and a commitment to his employees. For instance, when someone joins the Joseph's Lite Cookies team, Semprevivo promises, "You start with me, you can end with me. You can work with me the rest of your life until you retire."

Semprevivo's upbringing strongly influences how he runs his business, which currently employs 26 team members at its New Mexico plant, 12 team members in its Florida offices, and about 1,000 independent sales representatives nationwide. He took to heart the advice of his father, who said, "Son, always ask yourself right before you go to bed, did you give 100 percent that day? And if your answer is ever no, when you wake up the next morning, you give it 100 percent that day." Semprevivo lives out that advice every day, and he decided to make it possible for each of his team members to do the same.

As you read in Chapter 2, an employee may fail in his or her ethical obligation to do "an honest day's work" by loafing on the job or working too slowly. But Semprevivo has found that with the guarantee of

a lifetime job, his team members are happy to give 100 percent effort. He has also built in other incentives for employees to give their all, including profit sharing and matching 401(k) contributions. The company matches each dollar a team member contributes to his or her 401(k) retirement savings account with $2.19—more than any other company on record. Because team members know they will continue to share in the company's success, they have a stake in building Joseph's Lite Cookies into an efficient and profitable operation. As Semprevivo states at the end of the video, "Believe in your team members, give them great benefits, and empower them, and you know what? They'll perform."

Before you answer the questions and work the activities, you will need to watch the video case on Joseph's Lite Cookies. You may also want to review the video spotlight that introduced Chapter 2.

Questions

1. Based on what you saw in the videos, describe how Semprevivo reveals his underlying values and applies them to building a strong business.

2. Referring to the video and the text, describe the components of a business that constitute a "framework for integrity." Explain how the framework for integrity on which Joseph's Lite Cookies is built may contribute to the company's position in a competitive environment.

3. Review what you learned in Chapter 1 about building an entrepreneurial team and the advantages of doing so. Explain how this relates to the video segment in which Semprevivo says an employee will perform well if *empowered*.

Activities

1. Large corporations often have documents outlining ethical guidelines for their employees. Kellogg's, the world's leading producer of cereal and a leading

Video material provided by Hattie Bryant, Producer of Small Business School, the series on PBS Stations, Worldnet, and the Web at http://www.smallbusinessschool.org.

SmallBusinessSchool ▣
the Series on PBS stations and the Web

Sources: http://www.josephslitecookies.com; April Y. Pennington, "Making Their Mark," Entrepreneur.com, February 15, 2006; http://www.stevieawards.com; and http://www.kelloggcompany.com.

producer of cookies and convenience foods, is one such corporation. At the company's website, http://www. kelloggcompany.com, you will find Kellogg's corporate social responsibility statement and a long list of what it terms "K Values"—written very much like a mission statement. Draft a mission/values statement for Joseph's Lite Cookies that reflects what you saw in the videos. (At the time this book was published, there was no such document posted on the Joseph's Lite Cookies website.) Share your work with your classmates or study group partners.

2. Now practice writing a mission/values statement for your own business enterprise. Even if you don't currently have a business concept or plan, you can still organize your thoughts about the values that will guide your future business ventures. How detailed should you be? Dow Chemical's Code of Business Conduct is 35 pages; Nordstrom's fits on a 3 × 5 index card.

3. Once you have written down your own underlying values, consider ways in which you will act on them. You may find the following list of questions a good starting point for thinking about how your business will reflect your personal values:

- Will your business give to charities? If so, how will you select the organizations and groups that will receive donations?

- Will you be involved in the community? If so, how? If not, why not?

- How will you find employees? For example, will your recruitment efforts take into account the disabled, those with low income, minorities, and others in underrepresented groups?

- How will you manage your company's waste? If it costs more to recycle, will you still do so?

- Will you reward employees for their community involvement with non-profit organizations or civic groups? Will you encourage your employees to become active in their community?

- How will you determine pay levels?

- What kinds of benefits will you offer?

- Where will you locate?

Biolife LLC

Clearing Hurdles

When it comes to the hurdles that every startup faces, eight-year-old Biolife has already cleared a few. Its sole product—Quick Relief (QR), a patented powder that stops bleeding within seconds—is unlike anything else out there and has impressed several hard-to-impress gatekeepers, including Wal-Mart, the nation's largest retailer, and CVS Stores, the drugstore chain. Both have already given QR valuable shelf space in several thousand stores. Plus, the head athletic trainer of the Los Angeles Lakers has been seen using QR on national TV. But the hard part of CEO Doug Goodman's job is really just beginning: Now he needs to figure out the best way to convince the world to give QR a try.

It was back in 1999 that Jim Patterson and John Alf Thompson first developed QR. The two men were long-time research scientists who formed Biolife with the goal of discovering a new way to purify water. They never solved that puzzle, but one day, while working in the lab, Patterson either pricked his finger accidentally or sliced it on purpose (the story has changed several times, Goodman concedes), leading to the discovery of QR, a patented combination of resin and salt, the two components Patterson had been experimenting with at the time.

In 2002, the company sent some samples of QR to Gary Vitti, the head trainer for the Lakers. After testing it for several weeks during the off-season, Vitti used QR one day during a regular-season game, prompting the on-air announcers to wonder why Vitti was sprinkling pepper on one of his players. QR was never mentioned by name, but it was the product's first appearance on TV, and it started to create some buzz for the company, at least among sports fans. Wooing Vitti made sense, Goodman says, because the product is especially useful to the NBA, which allows only a 30-second timeout to stop a player from bleeding.

Vitti estimates that he gets around 100 requests a week from "different snake oil salesmen" hoping to get him to try out their magic potion on [Lakers players]. But there was something about QR that managed

to catch his attention. At the time, he was using another product that neither he nor the players were particularly crazy about because it stung and left dark stains on the skin. "I gave this a try, and I was really surprised," says Vitti. "This one popped out because it was so different."

In fact, Vitti liked the product so much that he now has a part-time job selling QR to other trainers at the professional and college level. Goodman estimates that as many as 75 percent of the teams in the National Hockey League and NBA use QR regularly.

Without "real missionaries" like Vitti, as well as several prominent doctors on the west coast of Florida, Biolife might not have had any sales at all. In 2002, the year QR was launched, Biolife had revenue of $150,000. In 2003, after convincing more health care providers to try QR, Biolife's sales increased tenfold. The company began by training 16 pharmacists at CVS stores in the Tampa Bay area, figuring that people often ask pharmacists for medical advice. But after an initial bump in sales, interest in the product, which costs between $5 and $10 a box and comes in four different packages designed for different uses, such as Nosebleed QR, quickly died down.

The company has experimented with its packaging in an attempt to not look like a typical medical product. On the Kids QR package, for example, Goodman's eight-year-old son, Bakie, is seen riding his bike and kicking a soccer ball. Actually, all of QR's boxes feature employees or investors. On a new package of Urgent QR, an extra-strength version of the product, Charlie Entenmann (Biolife's main financial backer), 74, is shown rappelling down a mountain.

Eventually, Goodman hopes that ordinary consumers will be as enthusiastic about QR as Vitti has been. If that ever does happen, a box of QR just might replace the box of Band-Aids that most people have in the back of their medicine chests.

Questions

1. Chapter 3 discusses three types of startup ideas: Type A, Type B, and Type C. Which of these is illustrated by Biolife's startup based on its QR product?

Source: Michelle Leder, "The Problem," *Inc.*, June 2004, pp. 44–46.

2. Most new business ideas come from personal experience, hobbies, accidental discoveries, or a deliberate search. From which of these sources did the idea for Biolife's launch come?

3. Considering what you have learned about this startup and its development, would you say that the founders followed more of an outside-in or an inside-out approach to identify this business opportunity and launch the company? Explain your answer.

4. Conduct a SWOT analysis of the company. What do you think are Biolife's most significant strengths, weaknesses, opportunities, and threats?

5. How would you characterize the strategy that Biolife is following? Is it a cost-based or differentiation-based strategy? Or is it a focus strategy centered on one of these two fundamental strategies? Be sure to identify the facts or assumptions on which you based your conclusion.

Mo's Chowder

An Entrepreneur from Within

Many people find the idea of running a restaurant appealing but lose their motivation at the prospect of creating a business plan, finding investors, navigating legal issues, and juggling the other complexities associated with new startups. For those disheartened by the prospect of such risky undertakings, buying an existing restaurant often seems like a simpler and safer alternative. Still, buying a restaurant is not for the fainthearted. According to a study conducted by H. G. Parsa, a professor in the hospitality program at Ohio State University, 25 percent of restaurants close or change ownership within their first year in business. Over three years, the number rises to 60 percent, a figure that is comparable to cross-industry failure rates cited by the Small Business Administration.

One avenue that might increase your chance of success, as well as your comfort level, is to buy a business in an industry you've worked in for a long time. Better yet, buy the actual business you've worked in for a long time, as Cindy McEntee did.

McEntee is the current owner of Mo's Chowder, a diner chain along the Pacific Northwest coast. McEntee's grandmother, Mohava Neimi, or "Mo," started a neighborhood diner in Newport, Oregon, to support her two growing boys during World War II. Mo chose the diner business because she loved to feed—and socialize with—her neighbors. For years, Mo's Chowder operated as a simple diner, where McEntee grew up working as a dishwasher, waitress, and cook. The evolution of Mo's into the business that would become an Oregon landmark didn't begin until the day McEntee asked her grandmother how much she paid for clams.

Mo confessed that she had no idea. She had been content to use whatever was in the cash register at the end of the day to buy supplies for the next day's menu. Because McEntee had worked in so many areas of the business, she was starting to see ways to improve the diner's operations. She installed accounting software and food preparation equipment to save time and money. Eventually, Mo and McEntee made plans for McEntee to formally buy the business from her grandmother over time. Mo changed the legal form of the business from a sole proprietorship to a corporation, and McEntee began buying stock in the company through payroll deductions.

Eventually, McEntee was able to buy more locations along the coast with some investment partners. Now a culinary tourist attraction, Mo's has more than 200 employees and $3.5 million in annual revenues, with six store locations and new distribution channels for its chowder. And the company recently won the Oregon Governor's Community Service Award for Restaurants and the National Restaurant Neighbor Award, given out by the National Restaurant Association.

To learn more about what it takes to buy an existing business, watch the video case for Chapter 4 and then answer the questions and work the activities below.

Questions

1. Which of the advantages of buying an existing business, as explained in the textbook, did McEntee enjoy when she bought her grandmother's diner? Explain.

2. How could an entrepreneur who does not have a stake in an existing family business re-create for himself or herself the advantages McEntee enjoyed?

3. What five features of family firms offer unique advantages? Which of these features did Mo's Chowder possess?

Video material provided by Hattie Bryant, Producer of Small Business School, the series on PBS Stations, Worldnet, and the Web at http://www.smallbusinessschool.org.

SmallBusinessSchool
the Series on PBS stations and the Web

Sources: http://www.moschowder.com; Kerry Miller, "The Restaurant-Failure Myth," *BusinessWeek* (Small Business Edition), April 16, 2007, http://www.businessweek.com/smallbiz/content/apr2007/sb20070416_296932.htm; http://www.score.org/template_gallery.html; http://www.sba.gov/sbdc; and http://www.startupjournal.com.

Activities

Imagine that you have just inherited $500,000 in business capital from an elderly relative who admired your entrepreneurial spirit. The only stipulation in the will is this: You must use the money to buy and run one of the small businesses for sale locally. Also, before the money will be released to you, you must submit a preliminary business plan to the trustees of the estate (your instructor). Finally, you must start the process of buying an existing business immediately or else the inheritance will pass to another likely entrepreneur in the family! How will you start?

1. Local businesses are often advertised for sale in the classifieds of the local paper. You can also find many listings by looking on the *Wall Street Journal*'s online center for entrepreneurs at http://www.startupjournal.com or by conducting a Web search using the key terms "business for sale." Do some preliminary research to see what's available that interests you and select one of those businesses to use in this activity.

2. Once you have identified a company that interests you, find the template "Business Plan for an Established Business" on the SCORE website, at http://www.score.org/template_gallery.html. Fill out page 5, the General Company Description, with all the information that you can gather on your target purchase.

3. When your plan is complete, make sure that you have covered everything by checking your plan against the recommendations of the Small Business Administration at http://www.sba.gov/smallbusinessplanner/start/buyabusiness/index.html.

The Brown Family Business

Defining Work Opportunities for Family Members in a Family Firm

For nearly seven decades, the Brown family has operated an agricultural products business in central Texas. As Brown Bros. has grown, family leaders have attempted to preserve family relationships while operating the business in a profitable manner. At present, five members of the second generation, three members of the third generation, and one member of the fourth generation are active in the business. Other members of the family, of course, have ownership interests and a concern about the firm even though they are pursuing other careers.

In the interest of building the business and also preserving family harmony, the family has developed policies for entry and career opportunities for family members. The human resource policies governing family members follow.

Family Philosophy Concerning Family and Work Opportunities

1. A family working together as one unit will always be stronger than individuals or divided units.

2. Family is an "umbrella" that includes all direct descendants of P. and L. Brown and their spouses.

3. The Brown family believes that a career with Brown Bros. is only for those who

   - Believe in working for their success;

   - Believe that rewards they receive should come from the work they have done;

   - Believe in working for the company versus working for a paycheck; and

   - Believe that everyone must work to provide an equal and fair contribution for the good of the whole business.

4. While work opportunities and career opportunities with the family business will be communicated to all family members, there will be no guarantee of a job in the family business for any member of the family at any time.

5. A family member working in the family business, whether in a temporary or a long-term career position, will be offered work and career counseling by a supervisor or officer/family member (depending on the job level). However, the family member/employee is not guaranteed a job or a career position. His or her job performance and qualifications must be the primary factors in determining whether the family member will be allowed continued employment.

6. While the family business is principally agriculture-related, there are many jobs that both men and women can perform equally and safely.

7. Compensation will be based on comparable positions held by other employees.

Committee on Family Employee Development

1. Review, on an annual basis, policies for entry and recommend changes.

2. Receive notices of positions available and communicate them to all family members.

3. Review, on an annual basis, evaluations of family members' performance, training provided, outside training programs attended, and goals and development plans. Offer counseling to upper management when appropriate.

4. Committee composed of three persons—one of four Brown brothers in the business; one of seven non-operating Browns; one of the spouses of the eleven Browns. The general criteria for having a career at Brown Bros. are given in Exhibit C5-1.

Questions

1. What are the key ideas embodied in the statement of philosophy concerning family and work opportunities?

2. Evaluate each of the criteria specified for a management career in the firm. Which, if any, would you change or modify?

3. Evaluate the structure and functions of the committee on family employee development.

Source: This case was prepared by Nancy B. Upton, founder of the Institute for Family Business, Baylor University.

exhibit

c5-1   *Criteria for a Career at Brown Bros.*

	Mid-Management Positions	Upper-Management Positions
Personal:		
No criminal record	Required	Required
No substance abuse	Required	Required
Education:		
High school	Required	Required
College degree (2.5 on a 4-point system)	Recommended	Required
Work experience with others:		
While completing college	Recommended	Recommended
After completing college (one to three years)	Recommended	Required

AdGrove.com, Inc.

Raising Capital for an Adfomediary

AdGrove.com, Inc., is being founded by Amy George to assist businesses in their efforts to purchase advertising. However, launching the business will require significant capital, an amount far beyond George's capabilities. To raise the needed capital, George has prepared a business plan. The executive summary is provided below. (The business plan in its entirety is available at http://www.businessplans.org/AdGrove/adgro00.html.)

ADGROVE.COM, INC., EXECUTIVE SUMMARY

Buying and creating advertising in any media is a time-intensive process reflecting hours of transactions between buyers, sellers, and creative agents. For example, if a buyer wants to advertise in the radio media, he targets a few radio stations with desired listener demographics, discusses contract options with a radio account executive, bids on an ad schedule, negotiates a price, creates ad copy, approves the final ad, and pays for the service. For a skilled buyer, this entire transaction can take up to 3 weeks to complete. For a local deli or sporting goods shop with little or no demographic information, small purchasing power, and less familiarity with radio advertising, this transaction process can take more than 3 weeks and cost the small business more money per ad than large ad agencies. For the seller, in this case the radio stations, the transaction costs of dealing with such small customers can prove to be cost ineffective. AdGrove.com is an internet advertising infomediary ("adfomediary"®) that provides a one-stop shop for demographic information, ad rates, ad campaign schedule planning, ad buys, and creative development, reducing transaction time and costs for buyers and sellers of advertising spots.

The Company

AdGrove.com, Inc. ("the Company") is a C-corporation located in Austin, Texas. The Company is located on the Internet at www.AdGrove.com and is the first adfomediary® dedicated to the needs of small businesses.

Source: http://www.businessplans.org/AdGrove/adgro00.html.

Products & Services

AdGrove's featured product will be a user-friendly Internet website that provides free and fee-based services to meet the needs of its customers—advertising buyers and sellers. AdGrove's first product line will be dedicated to reaching the highly fragmented buyers and sellers of advertising space in the radio advertising sector. Qualified buyers and sellers are invited to join AdGrove.com's community as members. Membership is free and provides users access to valuable, customized services. Selling members receive opportunity to list ads, and gain access to the buying community. Buyers receive access to up-to-the minute aggregated, radio market information, ad campaign planning tools, creative services, ad space, buying discounts, monitoring services, and account management. AdGrove.com's information-rich services reduce a buyer's time while enabling the development of a cost-effective advertising strategy. In addition, AdGrove.com buyers receive unique buying discounts, usually reserved for major ad agencies and companies, and an opportunity to participate in discounted "over-capacity" ads. Adgrove.com serves as a third sales channel for radio stations, complementing their national and local sales efforts. Unlike traditional sales methods, the Internet offers radio stations access to a national market and 24-hour selling power. AdGrove.com provides radio station members with a listing and brokerage service, access to customers, on-line web advertising, and monthly value reports. These monthly AdGrove.com value reports will include buyer profiles, competitive analysis, market analysis, and savings calculated.

Market & Opportunity

AdGrove.com represents the intersection of two growing U.S. markets: advertising and business-to-business electronic commerce. The advertising industry represents a $190 billion industry and is expected to grow at 5.7% compound annual growth. The radio advertising market is a $17.7 billion sector represented by more than 12,275 radio stations in 268 major markets. Approximately 75% of radio advertising is purchased at the local level. Although there has been consolidation in the radio industry since the Telecommunications Act of 1996, the industry is still highly fragmented and growing at an 8.5% annual rate. In addition, radio stations have generally been slow to adopt Internet strategies. Business-to-business e-commerce revenues for 1998 were $17 billion and were projected to grow to $1.7 trillion by 2003. It is projected that by the year 2002 almost one-third of all business-to-business transactions will be performed via e-commerce.

Customers: As an intermediary agent AdGrove.com has two primary customers: radio stations and small business advertisers. AdGrove.com will target the top 4,000 radio stations, which represent 80% of the industry revenues. AdGrove.com will target small, high-growth businesses as its primary market. In the U.S., there are currently 24 million small businesses with approximately 885,000 new firms each year. These businesses represent 47% of all sales in the U.S. According to research, approximately 41% of small businesses are online and one in three conducts business transactions on the Internet. Each of these firms represents an average of $3.79 million annual revenues, significantly more than the $2.72 million average.

Competitors: BuyMedia.com and AdOutlet.com are websites that have launched within the last 18 months that connect buyers and sellers of radio advertising space. However, AdGrove.com is the only website with customized services and a pricing model to meet the needs of small businesses. In so doing, AdGrove.com will expand the current advertising market.

Marketing Strategy

AdGrove.com's marketing efforts are centered on strategic partnerships, an educational advertising and public relations campaign, and a regional sales force. AdGrove.com will forge a strategic partnership with the Radio Advertising Bureau, the national association that represents 4,300 radio stations and 80% of U.S. radio advertising revenues. AdGrove.com will forge an alliance with the U.S. Chamber of Commerce, the world's largest business federation, representing nearly 3 million companies, 96% of which are small businesses. AdGrove's marketing campaign will focus on driving volume to the website and converting visitors to buyers.

The Start-Up Plan

AdGrove.com will follow a three-phase start-up plan. During the first phase, the AdGrove.com team will create a demonstration site, refine product and services mix, and alpha test among focus groups of buyers and sellers. During the second phase, AdGrove.com hopes to raise the required venture funding of $2 million to launch the site. The funds will be used to finalize the development of an integrated website, negotiate strategic alliances and radio station partnership agreements, launch a marketing and sales plan, and launch the website in Austin, Texas. To meet the objectives of the first two phases, AdGrove.com will incrementally hire 16 additional staff and outsource the initial development of the website. The third phase will include a launch in 10 cities, including San Francisco, Atlanta, Washington, Seattle, Minneapolis, Boston, New York, Chicago, and Miami.

Management

AdGrove's management team has extensive experience in the marketing, Internet, and high-tech sectors. Amy George, Chief Executive Officer, has seven years of professional experience in the field of marketing for small businesses and national clients in the telecommunication, real estate, multimedia, and education industries. Alex Krishnan, Chief Operating Officer, has five years of experience in the high-tech industry in the areas of Internet strategy, program management, software design, and development. Brink Melton, Chief Technology Officer, has three years experience as a software developer and technology consultant. He has experience launching a successful technology consulting partnership dedicated to serving the needs of small businesses in Austin, TX. He is currently pursuing his MBA at the University of Texas, concentrating in information management and entrepreneurship. AdGrove.com's team of consultants are experts in the small business, radio, advertising, high-tech, and Internet start-up fields.

Financial Overview

AdGrove's five-year financials are displayed in Exhibit C6-1. AdGrove.com derives its primary revenue from the following sources:

- Transaction fees for brokering the sale of radio advertising spots. This is the primary revenue stream and the fee collected will be 5% of each transaction.

exhibit c6-1 *Financial Summary and Operating Statistics*

Key Operating Statistics	Yr1	Yr2	Yr3	Yr4	Yr5
Employees	27	57	78	86	98
Financial Statistics					
Revenue	$ 53,700	$2,625,000	$12,770,000	$19,200,001	$26,900,000
Expenses	4,130,597	8,029,597	10,699,663	14,315,827	18,003,609
Net Income	−$4,076,897	−$5,404,597	$ 2,070,337	$ 4,884,174	$ 8,896,391

- Fees for value-added market research information provided to buyers.
- Advertisements and paid promotions.

Because of the high investment needs in year 1 and year 2, the Company does not achieve profitability until year 3. By year 5 revenues will grow to $26.9 million with net income of $8.9 million. The Company is seeking $2 million in first-round financing with a return on investment for investors of 70%.

Questions

1. Is the AdGrove.com executive summary more of a synopsis or a narrative?

2. If you were an investor, would the AdGrove.com executive summary spark your interest in the opportunity? In other words, would you continue reading the business plan for more details?

3. What do you like about this executive summary? What do you not like?

4. Would you suggest that George make any changes or additions to the executive summary? If so, what do you suggest?

eHarmony

In the Market for Marriage

You read in Chapter 7 of your textbook that successfully applying the marketing concept to a small business is a two-stage process: (1) identifying the needs of the consumer and (2) satisfying those needs. Dr. Neil Clark Warren, eHarmony's founder and a clinical psychologist for 35 years, believed that his decades of marriage counseling and research could be applied to satisfy a need. Warren explained, "Forty-three percent of all people over 18 in this country are single. . . . Most of them have never been around a single really good marriage, but do they want it? Oh my gosh . . . they are so pulling for a good marriage for themselves."

Warren was convinced that the current divorce rate is so high because many couples are ill-matched from the beginning. Compatibility, he argued, is the key to a strong, long-term relationship. Eventually, Warren and his son-in-law, Greg Forgatch, launched a series of seminars based on the principles of his best-selling book, *Finding the Love of Your Life*. By 2000, the team had transitioned their work to the Web and established the first online relationship service—eHarmony.com.

In the video, Forgatch says that finding a mate for life is something that most of us really desire, but that determining how to go about finding the perfect mate is perhaps "one of the largest unmet consumer needs" out there today. Indeed, by 2003, as many as 55 million Americans had visited dating sites on the Internet and were spending more than $300 million on Internet dating services. These numbers proved that people were using the Internet to find dates, but eHarmony was interested in creating more than just another dating service, so the team set out to come up with a means by which people could be screened for compatibility. Warren's team developed an extensive

online questionnaire that screens for "29 dimensions of compatibility" and patented the resulting Compatibility Matching System™. The team also targeted a particular market segment—single, serious relationship seekers, especially women. And unlike the myriad Internet dating services at the time, eHarmony did not allow subscribers to search its database of people. Matches and subsequent invitations to meet occur in a very careful manner, and registered users are given the power to decide if, when, and how they want to share a photograph of themselves.

Online analysts determined that many women are put off by dating services that seem to be based on looks or are poorly screened. eHarmony responded by building into its system an exhaustive questionnaire that casual daters would probably not take the time to fill out. eHarmony then uses the results of the questionnaire to determine a respondent's number of previous marriages, assess psychological health (e.g., depression), and identify other characteristics the company deems too challenging to result in relationship success. eHarmony rejects up to 20 percent of its respondents because they do not meet the criteria for participating in a successful, long-term relationship. Though the policy might seem a bit harsh, it must be working: More than 6,000 marriages are credited to eHarmony so far, and the site has more than six million registered users and 10,000 to 15,000 new users each day.

eHarmony was not an overnight success, however. During its first couple of years, Warren almost gave up. He suggested they refund the money to registered eHarmony users, because they just didn't have enough people in their database to build compatible matches. Forgatch persisted, however, and after spending upward of $10 million on radio advertising and $40 million on television ads, eHarmony began to reach millions of prospective clients. Today, eHarmony is worth approximately $165 million.

Video material provided by Hattie Bryant, Producer of Small Business School, the series on PBS Stations, Worldnet, and the Web at http://www.smallbusinessschool.org.

Small**Business**School ▶
the Series on PBS stations and the Web

Sources: http://www.eharmony.com; Neil Clark Warren and Ken Abraham; "Falling in Love for All the Right Reasons: How to Find Your Soul Mate," 2005; and http://www.startup-review.com/blog/eharmony-case-study-offline-advertising-the-key-to-scale.php.

Before answering the questions and working the activities, re-read Chapter 7 in your textbook and watch the video on eHarmony.

Questions

1. Describe eHarmony in terms of its bundle of satisfaction.

2. How does eHarmony define its market segment? What strategy or strategies does eHarmony use to target one particular segment?

3. Referring to the video, describe the four parts of eHarmony's winning ad campaign. In what way(s) do you think the ad campaign reveals components of the company's marketing plan?

Activities

What entrepreneurs create for a specific market often finds unexpected success with a completely different target market. For example, after becoming discouraged trying to fix broken marriages (his initial target market), Dr. Neil Clark Warren shifted his focus to single people who wanted to find the right person to marry in the first place (his new target market) and found great success.

For this activity, break into groups of three to four students.

1. Working as a team, identify a problem in the university system that presents an opportunity for an entrepreneur—that is, a problem that can be solved by a new product or service. For instance, a common problem in universities is night security; a business opportunity might be a volunteer escort service. Once you have identified the problem, describe the product or service that could solve the problem.

2. Identify a specific target market for your product or service. You may think that college students represent a single target market, but if you think less broadly, you will see that the group "college students" is composed of many subsets of students: international students, returning students, commuting students, part-time and full-time students, and work-study students, as well as segments identified by college attended, major field of study, social group, and so on. Using the discussion of segmentation variables from the chapter, describe your target market segment in great detail. Why did you choose this group?

3. Continue to develop your marketing plan by identifying competitors (present or future), assessing the external business environment, and outlining your distribution, pricing, and promotion plans.

4. Present your plan to the class. Consider creating visual materials to make your presentation more engaging.

Silver Zephyr Restaurant

Choosing a Form of Organization

Attorney Linda McGrath leaned back in her chair and surveyed her clients as they conducted several conversations simultaneously. The "Magnificent Seven," as the group had labeled itself, consisted of Alan Anderson, C.P.A.; Bill Barnes, M.D.; Carl Cochran, M.D.; Don Davis, president of Davis Petroleum Distributors, Inc.; Eilene Ellis, co-owner of the Collectors' Gift and Antique Shoppe, Inc.; Farrah F. Fischer, artist and widow of the former president of Northern Savings and Loan Association; and Gino Ginelli, managing partner of Wichita Falls Vending and Catering Company.

The group had retained Linda McGrath six weeks earlier to assist them in starting a restaurant in Wichita Falls, Texas. The idea of a new family-style restaurant with a distinctive motif had been developed by the group at a series of neighborhood dinner parties during the winter months. Linda could not help smiling as she recalled that Eilene Ellis and Bill Barnes had commented that they were the "chief engineers" of the railroad theme that the group favored.

Fortunately for the other members of the group, Alan Anderson had taken the initiative and seemingly done a thorough job. He had prepared pro forma financial data, determined the costs of various sites, and gathered preliminary bids from several contractors on the site work, paving, and restaurant facility. Alan and Don Davis had discussed the project with the executive vice president of commercial lending at Texoma Bank, and it was Alan who had suggested that Gino Ginelli was the logical person to operate the restaurant and should be included in the group.

According to Anderson's figures, the acquisition of land, building, and fixtures would require approximately $875,000 to $890,000. Further, Alan had estimated in the pro formas that working capital needs in the first two years would reach between $180,000 and $200,000. In addition, Eilene and Farrah Fischer believed that the unique furnishings and railroad memorabilia could be obtained for $125,000 to $150,000.

Based on a forecasted total requirement of $1,200,000, officials at Texoma Bank had suggested capitalization of $600,000 and were willing to loan the other $600,000 on a five-year note, floating at 3 percent above prime, assuming *unlimited* personal guarantees by all group members and their spouses. Although Alan and Don commented that they were surprised Texoma had not asked for their first-born children as further collateral, they told the group that there had been indications that the loan officers would be willing to extend the term to seven years and perhaps accept an initial debt-to-equity ratio of 1.5 to 1.

Individual Concerns

Whenever the group had met with Linda McGrath, all of the members had professed a strong desire to initiate the business. Gino, who had successfully managed a restaurant in Omaha before purchasing his present business in Wichita Falls, was particularly enthusiastic about getting back into the restaurant business. Eilene and Farrah had talked excitedly about collecting the furnishings needed to create the desired atmosphere, and Alan and Bill had always seemed solidly in favor of the venture. In fact, Alan and Bill had discussed the possibility of having a series of railroad restaurants and involving other investors if this venture was successful.

In private conversations with the attorney, however, several of the group members had expressed concern about their involvement in the project. Inasmuch as everyone agreed that Gino should have the controlling interest in the proposed business, Gino was somewhat apprehensive about the amount of initial capital required and its potential effect on the vending and catering business that he and his brother had developed and were expanding. Bill, on the other hand, expressed concern that opportunities to establish other locations might be foreclosed by Gino's reluctance or inability to expand beyond Wichita Falls.

Don, accompanied by his accountant, had asked several questions concerning the marketability and protection of minority interests in closely held companies and the tax consequences of his investment. Don and Carl Cochran were quite disturbed by the bank's requirement of unlimited guarantees by all investors. Indeed, Carl stated that he would rather invest in real estate than in restaurants but felt that he had given his word to his colleague Bill and would be horribly embarrassed to withdraw at this point.

Lastly, even Alan, in spite of herculean efforts on behalf of the group, admitted to Linda that he would prefer the relative safety of a limited partnership, as he was aware of the high rate of failure among restaurants.

Legal Advice

Attorney Linda McGrath quieted the group and began to speak:

I've given the restaurant venture a lot of thought this week, as I'm sure all of you have. Based on my analysis of the situation, several alternative forms of ownership appear feasible. Each of these legal forms has certain advantages and disadvantages, and I certainly want us to explore thoroughly the pros and cons of each legal form before you reach a decision. However, before we discuss the alternatives, please let me make a few observations that I believe are germane to your decision-making process.

First, the legal form you choose must be flexible enough to include seven people. To be sure, you appear to be seven of the most congenial and compatible persons I have ever encountered, let alone represented, in a business situation. On the other hand, you must be aware that you are also seven unique individuals with different circumstances, perspectives, and perhaps objectives as they relate to the restaurant. Hopefully, we can devise a vehicle which will meet the needs of everyone, but some compromise of individual positions may be necessary to ensure the initiation of the venture.

In a similar vein, I want to emphasize the long-term nature of the commitment you are about to make. Although it is far more exciting and romantic to focus on the construction phases and gala grand opening, I believe you must adjust your thinking—particularly as it pertains to the choice of an appropriate legal form—to the long and sometimes arduous days of operating the business, and even beyond, to its termination. In other words, you have selected Gino Ginelli to manage the restaurant and are agreeable to giving him control through a majority interest. This is fine. However, we must prepare for the time when he may either wish or need to terminate his interest in the venture. How will management continuity be ensured, and how will your interests be protected? Certainly these issues should be addressed in your decision.

If Gino Ginelli is able to operate the restaurant at the levels you have projected, all of you will have opportunities to profit or, perhaps, to "capital gain." Accordingly, we need to be cognizant of marketability or transferability of interests both for those who may choose to "cash out" and for those who wish to remain. In the event additional resources are required to support this restaurant or the development of other locations, you may well need the ability to add investors to secure equity capital.

I am also compelled to say that we should prepare for termination under unfavorable circumstances. Without reflection on Gino Ginelli's abilities, I must tell you that statistics indicate that more than 50 percent of new restaurants fail within two years. This means that it would be foolish to consider only the "upside" potential of the venture and not the "downside" as well. Most of you own businesses and all of you have estates, and I believe that the liability issue must be one of your foremost considerations.

Indeed, part of the responsibility that Gino Ginelli must accept for the control or authority that he would be granted in the proposed venture is unlimited liability. Gino Ginelli understands this point and has indicated his willingness to comply with this condition. However, it seems unreasonable that the rest of you, who will not have the management control and cannot achieve as large a reward as Gino Ginelli, would be willing to risk so much by agreeing to unlimited personal guarantees. It is my belief that we definitely need to reduce your potential risk or liability through the choice of a suitable legal form, with some "bare-fisted" negotiating with Texoma Bank.

Another major point is the matter of initial investment. Once again, this is going to have to be negotiated with the financial institution, but I naturally advocate as little initial capital and as much leverage, particularly long-term debt, as possible to maximize your return on investment. Of course, there is simply no substitute for managing the assets properly, but some of the legal forms offer greater advantage and return-on-investment possibilities than others.

A final consideration involves taxation of the business and tax consequences of the venture for each of you. I'm confident that Alan Anderson would concur with the statement that tax regulations are going to affect the restaurant and you from the initial choice of organization form to its hopefully profitable conclusion and beyond. With Alan's help, I can state that we will always try to minimize the adverse effects of code regulations throughout your involvement in the venture.

In summary, I submit that you should consider carefully the following issues before selecting the most desirable legal form of organization for the restaurant:

1. *Your liability as investors*
2. *Management and control continuity*
3. *Marketability or transfer of interest*
4. *Ability to secure additional equity capital*
5. *Initial capitalization and return on investment*
6. *Taxation*

And please consider these issues while recognizing your different perspectives and the long-term nature of your commitment of resources.

Linda paused and then presented the following alternative legal forms:

The first alternative would be to incorporate, with Gino Ginelli holding 50 to 52 percent of the stock and the remaining shares divided among the other investors. All stock would be issued as Section 1244 stock. Of course, the more adventuresome among you could buy more than your pro rata share of the stock issued, if you so desired.

A second possibility would be to incorporate as a Subchapter S corporation. Again, the stock would be issued as Section 1244 stock, and the ownership percentages would be the same as with the first alternative.

A third alternative would be to form a limited partnership, with Gino Ginelli as a general partner and the rest of you choosing either limited or general status.

A fourth alternative would be to establish a limited liability company, which would allow more of you to participate in management and still have favorable liability and tax treatment.

A fifth alternative, which I believe may have real merit, would involve the creation of two or more legal entities. In other words, one company with several of you as investors might own the real estate and lease it on a long-term basis to the restaurant business, which would be owned by the remaining members of the group. The lease could be secured by the personal guarantees of the stockholders in the restaurant business.

I don't know if the idea of multiple entities appeals to you, but it seems to me that you have, in essence, three companies: a restaurant, a furnishings business, and a property company with land, building, and fixtures. We did this type of thing with the warehouse, truck fleet, and operating company of Allied Van Lines in Abilene, and it may prove to be a better match of personal interests and risk-versus-return than squeezing everything into one organization.

In any event, these are five possibilities and I'm sure others exist, so let's begin to discuss things. And, once we have reached a consensus on the appropriate legal form, we will want to consider a buy/sell agreement with a method of valuation and various funding options.

Questions

1. Evaluate the simple corporation, the Subchapter S corporation, and limited partnership options. Note the advantages and disadvantages of each.

2. Explain the nature and significance of Section 1244 stock.

3. Could a limited liability company be the answer for the "Magnificent Seven"? What would be the disadvantages of this legal form of organization?

4. Explain how the multiple entities option might be worked out, and evaluate the extent to which it might be used to meet the varied interests of the group.

Le Travel Store

Moving with the Times

From the casual beachfront store to the glitzy urban shopping mall to the big-box retail model (selling more for less), Bill and Joan Keller have successfully adapted the location of their travel business, Le Travel Store, to match the expectations of their customers. Even as the location changed and the business evolved, however, the Kellers have continued to indulge their original passion for independent travel.

The Kellers started Le Travel Store in 1976 in a beachfront store near San Diego. They used $3,000 in wedding presents to rent a storefront, from which they sold charter flights, rail passes, travel books, and other items for the budget-conscious international traveler. In their first year, while Joan continued to work full-time at a bank, the couple set themselves the goal of selling 300 flights to Europe; they managed to sell 328, and the business survived. Thirty years later, Le Travel Store is in its third location.

The Kellers' decisions to change location were, in part, prompted by changes in their target market. The first customers of Le Travel Store were students, who would pull up to the store in beat-up Volkswagen bugs and vans. Over time, Bill began to notice those same customers pulling up in Volvo sedans or station wagons. These customers now had less time but more money to spend. They were taking shorter trips and staying in better hotels. The customers no longer needed—or wanted—budget travel materials (think *Europe on $20 a Day*). The Kellers decided to adapt to this changing business model and move off the beachfront property into a new development, Horton Plaza shopping center, which was part of the city's revitalization plan for the San Diego downtown area.

As exciting as the Horton Plaza location was, Joan calculated that the Kellers had paid a million dollars in rent over the 10-year term of the lease. For that kind of money, they could own a building. With an SBA loan, they purchased a 10,000-square-foot building in a historic district that soon became energized with retail ventures. Having realized the potential for growth and revenue in the new setting, the Kellers now invest their profits back into the building. Joan calls the excitement surrounding the re-growth of historic city centers as ideal places for business "the wave of the future."

Before answering the questions and working the activities, re-read Chapter 9 in your textbook and watch the video on Le Travel Store.

Questions

1. Review the five key factors in selecting a good business location. Which of those factors guided the Kellers' choice for the site of the original Le Travel Store? Explain.

2. Referring to the video, determine which factor or combination of factors the Kellers seem most excited about in their newest location. Recall how the text describes the importance of a building's "image." Describe how each of the Kellers' locations reflects the evolution of their business plan.

Activity

Many successful entrepreneurs got their start working out of their garage, basement, or home office. But part of what made those entrepreneurs successful was their ability to visualize and plan for growth. In essence, the company had to grow up and move away from home.

Video material provided by Hattie Bryant, Producer of Small Business School, the series on PBS Stations, Worldnet, and the Web at http://www. smallbusinessschool.org.

SmallBusinessSchool
the Series on PBS stations and the Web

Sources: http://www.letravelstore.com; and Karen Spaeder, "How to Find the Best Location," Entrepreneur.com, accessed June 5, 2007.

Imagine your start-up business is ready to move out of the house. (Give your business idea some shape—for example, consider what you're going to sell.) Review local or regional newspapers or real estate websites for business properties for sale. Choose two properties and analyze the advantages and disadvantages of buying each for your start-up venture. Then make your final selection.

- What were the three most important criteria you used when deciding where to locate your company? Why?

- What were the three least important criteria you used? Why?

- Write a brief paragraph about the advantages and disadvantages each location offers your business and why you ultimately selected the location you did.

Understanding Financial Statements, Part 1

Measure Your Growth in Real Numbers

As an entrepreneur, you won't know whether your business venture is economically feasible without a good understanding of financial statements. That's because your financial statements allow you to forecast your business venture's profits, its asset and financing requirements, and its cash flow—all critical elements in determining the profitability of your business.

In the video segment, you'll meet Jim Schell, business owner, author, and small business advisor. He says that if you ask an entrepreneur "How's business?" he or she invariably says, "Sales are up." He never hears the response "I made a return on sales of 10 percent." Schell's goal as an advisor is to get small business owners to measure their results in real numbers, and to know those numbers, the small business owner must know the company's financials.

After years of observing and consulting, Schell realized that the majority of small business owners do not understand how to properly use their financial statements to manage and grow their business. He says the typical small business owner thinks that his or her greatest opportunities for improvement are in the day-to-day management of the business, such as dealing with employees or marketing the product or service. Few, if any, will mention learning how to use financial statements. Bankers, CPAs, and business consultants have a different perspective: they all agree that the small business owner's number one opportunity to improve day-to-day management is to learn how to better utilize the information in the company's financial statements. Having a certain level of financial literacy allows an entrepreneur to spot potential problems in the company and work more intelligently with his or her financial advisors.

Does having money in your checking account mean your business is profitable? Do you have a clear understanding of the difference between profit and cash? Which financial statement allows you to keep an eye on the financial trends of your business? You learn in this video segment that Schell wrote a book, entitled *Understanding Your Financial Statements,* to help small business owners. In the book, Schell starts with the basics: selecting a CPA, working with your banker, using your balance sheet to determine your business's solvency, using your profit and loss statement to manage your business's direction, understanding the concept of cash flow, and so on. The exercises below are designed to help you start thinking about, and practicing, the basics of finance.

Before answering the questions and working the activities, watch the video entitled "Understanding Financial Statements, Part 1."

Questions

1. In the video, what three things does Schell say the small business owner must do to make a positive impact on his or her company's profitability? Why does Schell think that understanding the relationship among those three things is so important? How does gross margin differ from gross profit?

2. What does Schell advise Nani to do to improve her company's gross margin? Given what you learned in the text about the four variables on which net income is dependent, do you think that advice is sound? Explain.

3. What are the three parts of a financial statement? How does each part serve as a snapshot of your business in time? Create a diagram of a basic balance sheet, using the explanation and example Schell gives in the video.

Video material provided by Hattie Bryant, Producer of Small Business School, the series on PBS Stations, Worldnet, and the Web at http:// www.smallbusinessschool.org.

the Series on PBS stations and the Web

Sources: Jim Schell, "Understanding Your Financial Statements," *Visuality,* 2002, http://www.opp-knocks.org/Order_Our_Book, accessed June 12, 2007; Pam Newman, "Financial Fundamentals," April 10, 2006, Entrepreneur.com, accessed June 13, 2007; and Financial Ratio Worksheets, http://www.inc.com/tools/2000/10/20612.html, accessed June 13, 2007.

Activities

1. Imagine that you are the finance person in your small business but, unfortunately, you don't have any accounting experience. Since you are expected to fill the role of the company's accountant, you need to purchase some accounting software. An online retailer lists the following accounting software as its top-rated sellers: MYOB Premier Accounting Small Business Suite 2007, QuickBooks Simple Start 2007, Microsoft Office Accounting Express, Timeslips 2007, and Microsoft Office Accounting 2007. Which software will you choose and why? Be prepared to share your decision with the class.

2. You've just watched the video segment and are determined to start watching your company's financial trends. You decide to build a spreadsheet to help monitor changes between the most recent month's findings and the previous month's results, which will let you set monthly goals. You know the spreadsheet will also help you write your annual business plan and make strategies for the future. You can find an excellent two-page spreadsheet for download on *Inc.* magazine's website at http://www.inc.com/tools/2000/10/20612.html (free with registration at inc.com), or you can build your own spreadsheet with examples found in Chapter 10. Print out the spreadsheet, with the real or imaginary name of your company as its title.

3. Most business advisors insist that an entrepreneur acquire at least basic financial skills before starting a business. As your business grows, you may need someone, such as a CPA, with the qualifications to advise you on your business finances and to prepare your income and payroll tax returns. Visit the website of the American Institute of Certified Public Accountants to learn more about CPAs and accounting regulations (http://www.aicpa.org/MediaCenter/FAQs.htm#aicpa_answer12). Summarize the answers to the following questions in a one-page report.

    a. What are the requirements for becoming a CPA?

    b. What is the FASB?

    c. What are GAAP, and who determines them?

My Own Money

Finding Sources for Funding

Entrepreneurs often want to the know the answer to the question "Where do I find money to start or grow my business?" Initially, most depend on their own money—personal assets, earnings retained from their business, or a creative mix of the two types of personal funding. This kind of self-funding, or internal financing, is commonly called MOM, or "My Own Money." In this video segment, you'll learn that one entrepreneur sold his home and invested almost every dime from the sale back into his business, sharply cutting his living expenses. Another entrepreneur quit his job, sold his home, and lived in the Australian outback in order to take the photos that would become his sole asset. When he's asked how he started his business, he says he just "knocked on doors" until he found a buyer. A pair of entrepreneurs closed out their profit-sharing plans to invest in their start-up venture. These entrepreneurs relied heavily on investments they had made earlier in life: equity from their home and savings. Others started with even less: One entrepreneur started with nothing more than the proceeds from an insurance policy, and another worked the night shift for 10 years while running his startup during the day.

As you read in Chapters 10 and 11, bootstrap financing is a resourceful way to come up with the capital to finance a startup. Bootstrap financing is one of the most popular forms of self-financing, or using MOM. In bootstrap financing, the entrepreneur must utilize all of the company's resources to free the capital needed to meet operational needs or expand the business. By managing his or her finances better, the entrepreneur can finance the growth of the startup with its current earnings and assets, eliminating—or at least delaying—the need to go after outside sources of funding. Types of bootstrap financing mentioned in the text include trade credit and factoring.

Trade credit, or accounts payable, involves getting your supplier to extend credit to you, interest free, for 30, 60, or even 90 days. Usually a supplier won't extend credit to a new account until it proves reliable, but entrepreneurs with sound financial plans can sometimes talk suppliers into extending credit on their first orders to allow them to launch their business. Factoring is a type of asset-based loan in which you sell your accounts receivable to a buyer to raise capital. A "factor," such as a commercial finance company, buys your accounts receivable at a discount rate and becomes the creditor and collector of the receivables. Numerous other options that can be considered bootstrap financing include operating your business from home, accepting credit card payments, drop-shipping products, obtaining advance deposits and retainers from your customers, licensing your invention for royalties, aggressively controlling costs, bartering, getting extended terms from suppliers, establishing strict credit and collection policies and procedures, renting or leasing equipment instead of buying, buying used equipment instead of new, selling off excess inventory and equipment, and obtaining free publicity instead of paying for advertising.

If an entrepreneur decides to widen the net beyond using MOM, he or she may tap into OPM, or "Other People's Money." Entrepreneurs featured in this video borrowed money from parents, secured financing from a business for sale by owner, and found an established business owner who was willing to co-sign on a loan from a bank. One entrepreneur was frustrated that he couldn't secure a loan because he didn't have enough experience in the type of business he wanted to launch. Eventually, he and his partner started to work with an attorney who, as it turned out, served as a board member at a bank and was willing to put in a good word for them with the bank. Financing with OPM seems to work best when

Video material provided by Hattie Bryant, Producer of Small Business School, the series on PBS Stations, Worldnet, and the Web at http://www. smallbusinessschool.org.

Sources: Michael S. Malone, "John Doerr's Startup Manual," February 1997; and Garage Technology Ventures, "Writing a Compelling Executive Summary," http://www.garage.com/resources/writingexecsum.shtml.

entrepreneurs have the support of someone who knows them, has the means to provide financial support, and is convinced of the worth of the business plan.

Before answering the questions and working the activities, re-read Chapter 11 and watch the video entitled "My Own Money."

Questions

1. Why would an entrepreneur choose MOM over OPM, and vice versa?

2. What is bootstrap financing, and why is it popular with entrepreneurs?

3. Why do you think investors expect an entrepreneur to have some "skin in the game"? What kinds of sacrifices did the featured entrepreneurs make to fund their business ventures?

4. What evidence of networking did you see in the video segment? How were those networks established? How did networking and other relationships benefit the entrepreneurs?

Activities

1. Arrange for an interview with the owner of a start-up business in your community. Ask the following questions, and share your results with the class.

- How did you decide to start [business name], and how did you get funding to get it off the ground?

- How does [business name] make money, and where do you see your growth coming from in the future?

- What is the most important thing you've learned in the course of developing [business name]?

- What advice would you give to other entrepreneurs who want to start their own company?

- What are your thoughts on the following quote by John Doerr, a venture capitalist? *If you focus on success, you won't get there. If you focus on contribution and customer value, then you can win.*

2. Imagine you're just stepping into an elevator in the hotel that is hosting a seminar you're attending: "Funding for Continued Growth: Investors Meet One on One with Entrepreneurs." The venture capitalist whom you really, really wanted to talk to about your business venture gets in at the same time. You have about 20 seconds to make a good impression. "Thank goodness for Jay," you think. Jay, a friend who runs an animal training center, always begins business introductions by saying, "Hi, I'm Jay Doe. I help pet owners raise likeable pets. I work with people who want to avoid letting bad behaviors come between them and their friends, but don't know where to start. As a result of working with me, my clients say they enjoy their pets so much more." Jay encouraged you to plan out a 15-second introduction of yourself and your company before coming to the event. You take a semi-deep breath and start, "Hello, my name is . . . .

Write a creative elevator speech of your own to share with the class. To get started, follow the three steps below. A template has also been provided.

Step 1. Get someone's attention. Say who you are and what you can do for others (not what you do). Get the person to think, "How do you do that?"

Step 2. Tell the person about your deliverables. Explain what your product or service provides.

Step 3. Explain the benefits of your product or service.

"I'm the [occupation/line of work you're in] who [grab their attention—think up a "hook" for your line of work]. I specialize in [action verb followed by your deliverables] for the [target market]. I help [audience types] [benefits]."

3. Jay also encouraged you to have a business plan ready; yours is 30 pages. The venture capitalist you just met in the elevator gave you her business card, but she asked you to send over only your executive summary. She's going to review it and then call to arrange a time to meet and discuss how she can help you grow your business. It's a good thing you have an executive summary that is clear, concise, and compelling; you really want to make a good first impression and sell your business idea.

Search the Internet for two examples of executive summaries (use the keywords "example executive summary" to get started). Print them out, and then evaluate them on the criteria listed below. Rate each executive summary from 1 to 5 on each criterion, with 1 indicating that the summary does not incorporate that key component and 5 indicating that it contains a stellar example of that key component. Where applicable, label the portion of the executive summary with the letter of the guideline it meets.

The executive summary for [business name]:

_____ **a.** leads with a compelling statement about why the company is qualified to offer a unique solution to a big problem/opportunity.

_____ **b.** makes it clear that a problem or opportunity exists and how it plans to solve or exploit that problem or opportunity.

_____ **c.** clarifies what it has or what it does to solve or exploit the problem or opportunity.

_____ **d.** describes its market: the number of people or companies, dollars available, the growth rate, what drives its market segment.

_____ **e.** states its competitive advantage (unique benefits and advantages).

_____ **f.** specifies what levels it will reach in three to five years: how much revenue will be generated and how it will be evaluated (customers, units, margin, etc.).

_____ **g.** presents a uniquely qualified and winning team or management.

_____ **h.** outlines a believable financial projection summary.

_____ **i.** states the amount of funding expected.

Tires Plus

Determining the Best Way to Sell Your Business

As you read in Chapter 12, entrepreneurs sell their businesses for any number of reasons: They retire, the business takes an irrevocable downturn, they can't provide the necessary capital to grow the business, or they just want to cash out their investment. Tom Gegax and Don Gullett owned Tires Plus in a tightly defined partnership. Over the 24 years they owned and operated the company, they never took outside investment dollars. In fact, retained earnings powered the company's entire growth from a startup to a company with 150 stores generating $220 million in annual sales.

Neither Gegax's nor Gullett's children wanted to take over the company, which motivated the founders to prepare their business for sale. Numerous management consultants warn against taking harvest strategies too casually. Owners must think about what buyers will want. Owners also need to think about the payment terms that they will accept (cash or note or other arrangement). The management team needs to be broad enough that the business is not dependent on the owners. Buyer and seller need to think of ways to encourage key managers to stay after the sale. Companies preparing to sell must also conduct due diligence on themselves (usually an attorney can help with this) and have an accountant create a set of audited financial statements dating back at least a year. One consultant recommends having 9 to 12 months' worth of cash on the balance sheet, so as not to give the appearance of a fire sale. To help with the post-sale transition, it is helpful to have documentation on all aspects of the business, from operations to human resources to accounting systems. Entrepreneurs are notorious for rolling up their sleeves and doing things themselves, but that can be a mistake when selling a business. Harvesting is a complex process, so it is a good idea to seek council. For

example, investment bankers often help shepherd companies through the sales process, as in the case of Tires Plus.

After investigating other options, such as taking on outside investors, Gegax and Gullett decided that a complete sale was their best alternative to harvest the business. One month before Bridgestone/Firestone issued its historic tire recall, they sold Tires Plus to the Japanese-owned company, which merged it with its Morgan Tire unit, a 400-store chain based in Clearwater, Florida, operating under various trade names. At the time of the sale, Tires Plus had experienced years of record growth and profits.

What distinguished the sale of Tires Plus was Gegax and Gullett's continued commitment to their employees. The sale proceeds included up to $10 million paid out to many employees, including a couple dozen key employees who had been given equity in the company over the years. Loyalty bonuses were also paid to veteran employees, and severance payments were set aside for headquarters employees who either weren't offered jobs or declined positions elsewhere in the merged organization. Although not all sales transactions include such generous provisions for employees, the culture at Tires Plus was one of employee involvement and participation. According to Gegax, "The employees helped build the company."

This case study was developed in cooperation with Small Business School, the series on PBS stations. To learn more and to see the video, go to http://www.smallbusinessschool.org.

Questions

1. What harvest strategies did Gegax and Gullett consider before deciding to sell to Bridgestone/Firestone/Morgan Tire?

2. How did Gegax and Gullett manage the emotional transition from being owners to being non-owners?

3. Overall, how do you think Gegax feels about the sale? Why do you think so?

Sources: Neal St. Anthony, "Tires Plus Sold to Florida Company," *Star Tribune,* July 7, 2000, p. 1D; Virginia Munger Kahn, "Ripe for Selling? If You're Thinking About Selling Your Business, Now Is the Time," *BusinessWeek,* July 5, 2004, p. 74; and Constance Gustke, "Back Door Plan," *Internet World,* June 1, 2001, p. 23.

Activities

1. Tom Gegax and Don Gullett offered stock options to key employees so that the company would "have more people with skin in the game." Stock options are not the same as employee stock ownership programs (ESOPs). Research ESOPs using the Internet. Some sites of interest include the National Center for Employee Ownership (NCEO) at http://www.nceo.org and The ESOP Association at http://www.esopassociation.org. You may find other resources as well. The NCEO provides information on stock option purchase plans as well as ESOPs. Write a summary of the information you find on both types of employee ownership.

2. When you finance a car, the bank writing the loan wants to know the make, model, mileage, value, and price of the car. When you finance a home (which usually is a much larger loan), the bank wants to know the price, size of the house, its features, and the amount of land and will even send an appraiser to verify that the house is actually worth the amount (or more) that you want to mortgage. Imagine that you are looking to buy a company from an entrepreneur who wants to harvest the business. Find out what kind of information the bank will need to know about the company before agreeing to finance the purchase. (Finding out this information will help you when you want to harvest a business.)

Rodgers Chevrolet

Keep Your Customers

Recall from the video spotlight for this chapter that an average business keeps only 70 to 90 percent of its customers each year and that it costs nearly five times as much to acquire a new customer as to keep an existing one. Statistics on the auto industry further indicate that if an auto dealer can hold on to an additional 5 percent of its customers each year—increasing its retention rate from 90 to 95 percent, for example—then total lifetime profits from a typical customer will rise, on average, by 81 percent.

The president of Rodgers Chevrolet, one of the nation's first woman-owned car dealerships, knows about customer retention. Pamela Rodgers considers service to be her company's backbone. She says, "This is where our customer stability is going to be . . . providing good service to our customers. That will keep customers coming back, and the referral business coming back."

Rodgers also attributes her business success to employee satisfaction. In a recent interview, she said, "[The] client is the reason we come to work every day, [and in order] for your clients to be happy, you have to have satisfied employees." That is, she considers the employees of Rodgers Chevrolet to be her "customers" as well. She must be doing something right. In 1996, when Rodgers moved in, the dealership was selling 40 cars per month. Today, that figure has grown to more than 200, with annual sales averaging around $75 million.

How can you build customer and employee satisfaction into your business plan? One way to do so is by learning to listen. That is, to meet or exceed customer needs, the business owner must really listen to what the customer is saying. Your customer should feel listened to, valued, and important to you and your company. One study indicates that 68 percent of customers leave a business relationship because of a "perceived attitude of indifference" from the business. At Rodgers Chevrolet, Rodgers makes certain the company's service advisors speak to each and every customer. To be successful, she says, "It's important that they know their stuff . . . that they're trained properly, that they have good communication skills and good customer relation skills."

Before working the activities, re-read Chapter 13 and watch the video on Rodgers Chevrolet. You may also want to review the simplified model of consumer behavior in Chapter 13. The three interrelated aspects of the model include the consumer's decision-making process, psychological influences, and sociological influences.

Activity

Imagine that you are the customer service manager at Rodgers Chevrolet. You have begun sorting customer comments into groups based on the type of vehicle owned. After reviewing a couple of years of feedback, you discover that Corvette owners do not feel they are being served as well as their friends who own foreign sports cars. Many comments mention the service level of the Lexus brand and indicate that customers may be considering changing to a Lexus SC just to get the white-glove service. You would like to develop a way to serve

Video material provided by Hattie Bryant, Producer of Small Business School, the series on PBS Stations, Worldnet, and the Web at http://www.smallbusinessschool.org.

Sources: http://www.rodgerschevrolet.com; G. Brewer, "The Ultimate Guide to Winning Customers: The Customer Stops Here," *Sales and Marketing Management,* March 1998, p.150; C. B. Furlong, "12 Rules for Customer Retention," *Bank Marketing,* January 5, 1993; Frederick F. Reichheld and Thomas Teal, *The Loyalty Effect: The Hidden Force Behind Growth, Profits, and Lasting Value* (Cambridge: Harvard Business School Press, 2001); and Robert L. Desatnick and Denis H. Detzel, *Managing to Keep the Customer: How to Achieve and Maintain Superior Customer Service Throughout the Organization* (San Francisco: Jossey Bass Business and Management Series, 1993).

SmallBusinessSchool
the Series on PBS stations and the Web

your high-end clients better (the base price of a Corvette is $45,000, compared to $10,000 for a Chevy Aveo).

- Identify the elements of consumer behavior affecting your situation.

- Outline the criteria that car owners use to evaluate service to their vehicles. Do those criteria change as the vehicle sticker price rises? How?

- What new service offering could you provide to Corvette owners to entice them to continue to drive a Corvette and use Rodgers Chevrolet for service?

- Create an ad campaign or marketing program (a multi-media piece, poster, or brochure) that promotes your new service features and takes into account the elements influencing the behavior of your target market.

Country Supply

An Effective Distribution Strategy

Scott Mooney built his business for customers like himself. He wanted supplies for his horse, he wanted the very best price, and he wanted those supplies right away. Mooney started out selling horse tack to people in his small Iowa town, but he knew the town offered a limited customer base. For his business to grow, he needed to reach customers outside his geographic area. That meant sending out a catalog.

Catalogs are an important contributor to retail sales in the United States. In 2006, U.S. catalog purchases topped $160 billion, a figure which represents a compound annual growth rate of about 6 percent over a five-year period. Consumers accounted for a whopping $96 billion of that total.

Establishing a successful catalog, however, takes a tremendous amount of work. Unlike traditional retail, where customers visit a store to make a purchase, the catalog channel requires the additional expenses of printing and mailing the catalog and packing and shipping the products. Costs need to be lower in other areas of the business to offset the increased expenses. So Mooney sought out low-cost suppliers who offered products he knew would sell. He found a friend of the family to print the catalog for him for free until he made some money.

Printing a catalog and stocking a warehouse are useless without a mailing list of potential customers. To build his list, Mooney scoured newspapers, magazines, and phone books for names and addresses of people involved with horses; he then made mailing labels on the local library's copy machine. He scrounged packing boxes from his local supermarket to ship his supplies. The first headquarters of Country Supply was a small barn on his parents' property, where Mooney stored and managed his inventory. He shipped orders as soon as he could, to be certain

his new mail-order customers would have their purchases within a few days.

Mooney was a typical entrepreneur in that he recognized an opportunity and took some risks to build a business around that opportunity. He was atypical in that he was only 14 years old when he started his venture. Mooney started very small, appealed to a customer base of like-minded people, shoved all his profits into growing that business, and did all of the work himself. Country Supply provides a stellar example of a very lean supply chain management system.

Before you answer the questions and work the activities, watch the video on Country Supply. You may also want to review the video spotlight that introduced Chapter 14.

Questions

1. Based on what you saw in the videos, describe Country Supply's initial channel of distribution. Why do you think customers continue to choose Country Supply as an intermediary?

2. How did Mooney differentiate his distribution system so as to be successful in satisfying customer needs? How do you think that helped Mooney sustain his competitive advantage? What else do you see in the video that shows how Mooney strives to sustain competitive advantage?

Activities

1. In the video, you learned that Scott Mooney decided at a young age to sell horse supplies because those were the products he needed himself and horses were something he found endlessly interesting.

Video material provided by Hattie Bryant, Producer of Small Business School, the series on PBS Stations, Worldnet, and the Web at http://www.smallbusinessschool.org.

Sources: http://www.countrysupply.com; and http://retailindustry. about.com/library/bl/q2/bl_dma060401a.htm.

What did you find endlessly interesting at the age of 14? Go back in time and have your 14-year-old self build a business around one of your hobbies or interests. Write an outline describing which product you'd like to sell, who your customers would be, what channels you would use, etc. Share your ideas with your classmates.

2.   In the video, Mooney does not mention the Internet as one of his distribution channels. Country Supply does operate a website, however. Visit http://www.countrysupply.com and write down any examples of competitive advantage you find on the site. Then search using the keywords "horse tack" or "horse supplies" on Google or Yahoo! Visit the websites of some of Country Supply's competitors, and compare their Internet presence to that of Country Supply. What evidence of competitive advantage did you find on their sites?

Nicole Miller Inc.

The Challenges of Pricing

Bud Konheim, chief executive officer of Nicole Miller Inc., is a fourth-generation apparel producer in New York. He's been in the clothing industry for 52 years, so he's seen many changes. One unpleasant change was the United States' loss of its competitive advantage of cost-efficient production to Asia. The shift so unnerved him that he made a commitment that took him in a different direction. When most fashion houses were outsourcing the production of their clothing overseas, Konheim brought all of his company's production back to the United States.

With that decision made, Konheim turned his focus to building a business around design, instead of demographics. When Konheim and Miller decided to start their own business, after working together for years in the industry, Konheim told Miller that she should design what she herself would wear. "You make stuff that you really love to wear, and I'll find a crowd in the United States that shares your aesthetic," he said.

Focusing on design generally results in higher-priced clothing. For Konheim, however, the pricing strategy has to be "part of the fun" of shopping. So the Nicole Miller team decided to design a women's clothing line that was youthful and fun—Miller's specialty—but wasn't priced so high that women would consider the cost and worry about regretting the purchase. That is, a woman shopping for a Nicole Miller design shouldn't look at the price tag and say, "This is uncomfortable for me; it's not fun." The price and quality must be in line with the customer's expectations.

Jerry Bernstein is a renowned pricing strategy expert whose advice to entrepreneurs confirms Konheim's pricing strategy. Bernstein, founder of

Price Improvement Team in St. Louis, encourages entrepreneurs to find out how their customers "perceive, use, and apply" their product—in other words, how they "value" the product. He also urges business owners to determine what they are doing right with their profitable customers. Research helps an entrepreneur determine the value of a product or service to the marketplace. That value should be communicated in every sales and marketing promotion, and in every conversation with customers. In fact, Bernstein reveals, the price selected for the product is one of the most powerful means by which the entrepreneur communicates the value of the product.

Before answering the questions and working the activities, watch the video on Nicole Miller. Watch for the various types of pricing decisions you learned about in Chapter 15.

Questions

1. Which pricing strategy (or strategies) has Bud Konheim used to build the Nicole Miller design house? Be specific, citing examples you saw in the video clip. What evidence do you see that Konheim is using pricing to build a competitive advantage?

2. Why do you think Konheim says that price strategy has to be "part of the fun"? Do you agree or disagree with his selling philosophy? Explain.

Activities

1. Nicole Miller's core clothing collection is strong and remains a priority, but lately Miller has broadened her design portfolio. Use the Internet to research Nicole Miller's product lines. Write a brief analysis

Video material provided by Hattie Bryant, Producer of Small Business School, the series on PBS Stations, Worldnet, and the Web at http://www.smallbusinessschool.org.

Sources: http://www.nicolemiller.com; http://www.licensing.org/ intro/Introduction.cfm; Evan Clark, "The 'Sourcerer's' Apprentice," *WWD*, March 20, 2007, p. 18S; and "The Secrets to Price-Setting: Price Is the Most Important Factor in Determining Profit Yet Countless Businesses Fail to Get Their Pricing Strategy Right," *Business Week Online*, November 6, 2006.

SmallBusinessSchool
the Series on PBS stations and the Web

of Miller's new products' relationship to the existing product line. In your analysis, try to anticipate the implications of the new products on manufacturing methods, distribution channels, type of promotion, and/or manner of personal selling. How do you think Konheim determines pricing for the new product?

2. Nearly half of Nicole Miller Inc.'s $130 million in annual revenue comes from licensing Miller's designs to 15 different firms that make handbags, travel accessories, socks, and more. Visit the International Licensing Industry Merchandisers' Association website at http://www.licensing.org/intro/Introduction.cfm. Summarize the characteristics of licensing and the advantages to the licensor. What is the difference between licensing one's products and franchising?

Glidden Point Oyster Company, A.G.A. Correa & Son, Hardy Boat Cruises, Maine Gold

Promotion from a Distance

At first glance, the four companies featured in the video for this chapter seem to have little in common outside of the fact that they're all located in Maine. What can a small business that harvests oysters possibly have in common with one that offers birding cruises? What connects a business that designs nautical jewelry to one that produces maple syrup? Once you watch the video and become a little more familiar with the products each company offers, you'll realize the connection—each offers a top-quality, unique product that draws customers from a distance.

Barbara Scully takes a great deal of pride in offering the best oysters to be had anywhere. She and her husband started harvesting their oysters, by hand, in 1987. Every part of the process is demanding—even the constant water-quality monitoring they must do to assure their oysters are grown in pristine waters. The care the Glidden Point Oyster team puts into its product results in an oyster of exceptional quality, which means Scully can target a customer who can afford to buy the best. Glidden Point Oyster Company does direct mailing and has an Internet site, but Scully credits her marketing success to customer service (not easy to come by in the seafood industry) and her reputation for offering the highest-quality oyster available.

When Tony Correa was a young man, he started designing jewelry with a nautical theme, based on his love for sailing and marine hardware. Today, Correa and his son, Andy, sell the jewelry in a highly successful direct-mail catalog business. Andy Correa says the catalog they send out is beautiful, with copy that makes the customer feel confident about ordering a piece of jewelry he or she can only see in a picture. But Tony argues that their marketing success is as likely the result of their purchase of very specific mailing lists from a list broker. The jewelers mail their catalog only to a targeted group of people—customers who have a recent history of purchasing through mail order.

Hardy Boat Cruises also engages in distance marketing. Al and Stacie Crocetti started their nature cruise and ferry business with just an idea and a boat. Today, they are winners of a Gulf of Maine Visionary Award, for sustaining both their business and their community while preserving the health of the marine environment. Part of the company's promotion strategy involves mailing out brochures to names on mailing lists from birding groups. The Crocettis also rely a great deal on word-of-mouth advertising, hoping that a cruise on the Hardy Boat will be such a great experience that tourists will tell other tourists and townspeople, who in turn will recommend the cruises to even more people. Stacie is most excited, however, by the ever-expanding reach of the Web, saying that it is the number one advertising tool they couldn't do without. Type a keyword such as "Maine puffins" or "Monhegan Island" into a search on the Web and the Hardy Boat website will be in the search engine's list.

Further inland are Perry Gates and Deborah Meehan, owners of Maine Gold, a maple-product gift business. Gates and Meehan had been tapping maple trees for 30 years and knew where all the sweetest trees were located when they came across a maple syrup contest sponsored by Maine's Department of Agriculture. After winning first prize in the contest for five years running, the couple decided to try to build a business out of their talent. Today, they have about 13,000 people on their mailing list and have never bought a name or a list. Maine Gold just keeps growing, as tourists buy their products from the retail store and then send for the mail-order brochure or buy products through the company's website. Those initial customers then turn their friends

Video material provided by Hattie Bryant, Producer of Small Business School, the series on PBS Stations, Worldnet, and the Web at http://www.smallbusinessschool.org.

SmallBusinessSchool
the Series on PBS stations and the Web

Sources: http://www.oysterfarm.com; http://www.agacorrea.com; http://www.hardyboat.com; http://www.mainegold.com; and http://www.gulfofmaine.org/mediaroom/documents/2006Visionaryawards.pdf.

and relatives into customers by sending gifts of sweet maple syrup products to them. Gates and Meehan agree that their business success is built on relationships, including the connections between the customer and the Maine Gold staff and the customer and the person who is receiving their gift.

Before answering the questions and working the activities, watch the video on Glidden Point Oysters, Correa jewelers, Hardy Boat Cruises, and Maine Gold. Watch for the various types of promotion you learned about in Chapter 16.

Questions

1. Which promotional techniques has each of the companies used to build its business? Be specific. Once you have a list of ways in which they promote their business, organize the promotional techniques on your list into the categories discussed in the chapter (personal selling, advertising, and sales promotion).

2. The objectives of advertising are to inform, persuade, and remind consumers about the existence or superiority of a firm's product or service. Which function best describes the goal of each company's advertising? Explain why you think as you do. What type of advertising does each company create—product, institutional, or something else altogether?

Activities

1. Stacie Crocetti of Hardy Boat Cruises considers her website to be one of her best promotional activities. Visit http://www.hardyboat.com and write down the types of promotional strategies being used on the site. Then search using keywords "Maine puffin" or "Maine boat tours" on Google or Yahoo! Visit the websites of some of the competitors, and compare their Internet presence to that of Hardy Boat Cruises.

2. Imagine that you have recently been hired by Correa jewelers as a marketing manager. You are familiar with the company's current website, and you would like to improve it. Before you present your ideas to the company owners, however, you decide to mock up some four-color (i.e., full-color) website plans to show them. Create a full-page webpage that communicates a message consistent with the company's business philosophy but utilizes a more user-friendly or more appealing format. (See the company's website at http://www.agacorrea.com.) Use call-outs to describe the various sections on the page and explain how the elements you have chosen convey your intended message. Share your ideas with your classmates.

Sunny Designs, Inc.

An Adventure in China

To strengthen their businesses, increasing numbers of entrepreneurs are expanding into the international domain. One common motivation behind such moves is the hope of achieving gains in productivity by locating factories in countries where local conditions are favorable to these operations; however, this strategy is not without its drawbacks. Consider, for example, the case of Sunny Hwang, president of Sunny Designs, Inc., a manufacturer, importer, and wholesale distributor of wooden furniture with offices in Hayward, California. Hwang tells the story in his own words.

Cheap and good has been my motto in doing business. I started my business in a flea market as a retail vendor and then soon became a jobber, then a direct importer, and finally a manufacturer. To get better value, I delved into the original source—manufacturing in China.

China is one of the best places for the manufacturing of wooden furniture due to the cheap labor, materials, and other costs. I could hire approximately 20 workers in China for the wage of 1 in the United States. The cost of lumber is about half, and rent is about 20 percent compared to the U.S. There is also reasonable infrastructure available, such as transportation, electricity, and communication.

There are many cheap products available from Chinese factories; however, the quality is greatly lacking in many cases. Therefore, low prices alone are not sufficient justification for doing business in China. As a result, I contracted with an agent who hired several inspectors to control for the quality and delivery of our furniture products. Also, I established a partnership with a local Chinese manufacturer. However, none of these individuals were able to meet our needs.

After the partnership failed, I changed my business strategy by taking charge of my own factory. I hired my nephew, who was trained in the U.S., to oversee building a new factory and take care of purchases from other Chinese factories. Because of the different

culture and expectations, it was always a challenge to get along with government officials, who happen to hold most of the properties in China. They are eager to attract overseas investors, but primarily to increase job availability for the local people.

We located our factory in a town near a large city where we had negotiated favorable terms with the local government officials. However, after the company was launched, their attitudes changed. They began demanding what we considered to be unreasonable requests and would interfere with management decisions. Even purchasing lumber became difficult due to a lack of supply chains. Advance payments would be requested by the suppliers for security, which was risky because the lumber shipments would frequently be delayed and even sometimes never delivered. Within six months, the venture failed.

The previous experience, while a failure financially, did provide us a better understanding about doing business in China. This time we found an opportunity to move to a building twice as large as the first one and containing equipment that we could use. The total rent was only half the amount we had paid for the smaller building. This time we were very careful in negotiating strict terms with the government officials. Consequently, hiring qualified workers became much easier, without interference from the government officials and the local workers. Purchasing lumber also became much easier and cheaper by developing relationships of mutual trust with a limited number of agents. It takes time to acquire trust from the Chinese.

The final result has been a much-improved environment for doing business: we can now produce quality products more cheaply. It was a long and tedious journey, involving a lot of hard work, expense, and some tough lessons. But the adventure into China has proven to be a good one.

Sunny Hwang certainly recognizes the importance of knowing as much as possible about the challenges of doing business in a foreign country before getting involved there. An entrepreneur who is considering expanding into China—to connect with an outsourcing partner, to establish a production facility, or to reach a new market—should know the following key facts about the country:

- China's population of 1.3 billion people is the largest of any country in the world.
- China is one of the fastest-growing export markets for small and medium-size U.S. firms.
- Income disparities in China are great. Annual income in urban areas ranges from around $3442 per person in Shanghai (China's wealthiest city) to the more typical $1322 per year in other cities. Income in rural areas is much lower, with the average farmer earning a mere $413.
- The Chinese software market is growing at an annual rate of 30 percent.
- Use of the Internet is increasing dramatically.
- The demand for consulting services in China is increasing, especially those related to information technology.
- China has entered the World Trade Organization (WTO), a development that has raised concerns about intellectual property protection. Many hope that its entry into the WTO will force more vigilant protection of intellectual property rights and a crackdown on counterfeiting.
- Many Chinese consumers have cell phones and regularly surf the Internet (especially in large urban centers such as Beijing, Shanghai, and Guangzhou).
- Counterfeit goods (including clothing, leather goods, software, and CDs) are readily available in China at a fraction of the cost of brand name items.
- Chinese merchants usually do business only with vendors with whom they have established relationships.

Questions

1. What is the primary force that motivated Hwang to internationalize? Did he make a good decision when he located his manufacturing facility in China? What other countries should have been considered? Why?

2. What strategy option did Hwang select for his China-based enterprise? Did he select the right strategy?

3. Given the details of the case and the key facts about China, assess the opportunities for U.S. firms in China. What features of the country should be particularly attractive to small businesses seeking to expand internationally?

4. What challenges to doing business in China did Hwang experience? Given the key facts about China, list issues that may present distinct problems for small U.S. firms doing business there.

Douglas Electrical Supply, Inc.

A Management Consultant Examines an Entrepreneurial Firm

Jim Essinger is a management consultant and training specialist from St. Louis who specializes in continuous process improvement and total quality management. Each month, he goes to Springfield, Illinois, and provides three days of training to employees of a privately owned electrical wholesaler-distributor, Douglas Electrical Supply, Inc.

Most of the employees attending this fourth session are from the Springfield branch and have either gone back to the office or to their favorite restaurants during the lunch break. Jim has noticed that one of the class members is alone in the coffee shop of the hotel where the training sessions are conducted, and he has invited the young man to join him for lunch. The nervousness of his young companion is apparent to Jim, and he decides to ask a few questions.

Jim: Tony, you seem a little distracted; is there something wrong with your lunch?

Tony: Oh, it's not that, Jim. I . . . I'm having a problem at work, and it kind of relates to the training you are doing with us.

Jim: Really? Tell me about it.

Tony: Well, as you might know, I drive a van for the company, delivering electrical products and materials to our customers.

Jim: You work at the Quincy branch, right?

Tony: Yes. I drive about 250 miles a day, all over western Illinois, making my deliveries.

Jim: I see.

Tony: About seven weeks ago, I was making a big delivery at Western Illinois University in Macomb. A lady pulled out in front of me, and I had to brake hard and swerve to miss her!

Jim: You didn't hit her?

Tony: No! She just drove off. . . . I don't think she ever saw me. Anyway, I had a full load of boxes, pipe, conduit, and a big reel of wire. The load shifted and came crashing forward. Some of it hit me hard in the back and on the back of my head.

Source: This case was prepared by John E. Schoen of Baylor University.

Jim: Were you injured?

Tony: I'm not sure if I was ever unconscious, but I was stunned. Some people stopped and helped me get out of the van. I was really dizzy and couldn't get my bearings. Eventually, they called an ambulance. The paramedics took me to the hospital, and the doctors kept me for two days while they ran some tests.

Jim: Did you have a concussion?

Tony: Yes, I had some cuts and a slight concussion. My wife was really upset, and she made me stay home for the rest of the week. We have two little kids under four, and she wants me to quit and get a safer job.

Jim: She wants you to quit?

Tony: Yes! Sooner or later, all of the drivers get hit or have close calls. When you have a full load, those loads can shift and do a lot of damage. When I get in the van lately, especially when I have pipe or big reels of wire, I'm frightened. My wife is scared for me. I don't want to be killed or paralyzed, or something!

Jim: I can understand your concern, Tony. What can the company do to protect you? Can you put in some headache racks or heavy-gauge metal partitions in the van that would keep the load from hitting you if it shifts?

Tony: That's exactly what I was thinking! I've been talking with some of the other drivers during our TQM sessions. We've learned that we can get heavy-gauge partitions that would keep us safe built for about $350 per vehicle.

Jim: Good! Have you talked to management about making the modifications?

Tony: Yes, I had all the information and talked to my boss in Quincy, Al Riess. However, he hardly seemed to listen to me. When I pressed the issue, he said the company had nearly 30 vans, counting the ones in Chicago and northern Illinois, and that the company could not afford to spend $10,000 for headache racks, partitions, or anything else! Al finally said that I was just being paranoid, that I should drive more carefully, and that I should definitely stop talking to the other drivers if I valued my job.

Jim: You mean he threatened you?

Tony: You could say that. He said to keep my mouth shut and just drive . . . or else!

Jim: Tony, is there someone else you could talk to about this problem? It would seem to me that one injury lawsuit would certainly cost the company more than the modifications you're proposing.

Tony: Well, there's the problem! You know how expensive the TQM training is . . . and all of us "little people" were actually excited about TQM and continuous process improvement when the owners and you first talked to us. We believed management was changing and was really interested in our ideas and suggestions. We thought maybe they cared about us after all.

Jim: Well, I believe the owners do want to change the culture and improve the operations.

Tony: Maybe it's different in Chicago and northern Illinois, Jim, but the guys in Peoria and Springfield are like military types and are really into control. I think they're authoritarians—is that the right term?

Jim: Yes, authoritarians, autocrats . . . .

Tony: Al Riess, my boss, is the son-in-law of Bob Spaulding, who heads our division. As you probably know, Bob has a real bad temper and nobody crosses him twice, if you know what I mean. Bob is particularly sensitive about Al—because everyone knows Al doesn't have much ability and we're losing money at the Quincy branch.

Jim: Okay, I see your problem with going to Bob. Is there a safety officer or anyone at headquarters who could logically be brought into this situation?

Tony: I don't know! The owners seem to have a lot of confidence in Bob and give him a free hand in the management of our division. No, I don't see much hope of change. It makes the TQM training pretty hollow and kind of a crock! No offense, Jim!

Jim: No, I see what you mean, Tony.

Tony: See, I have eight years invested in this company! I used to like my job and driving the van. But, now, I'm afraid, my wife is afraid. . . .

Jim: Sure, I can understand where you're coming from! Let me ask you a question. How many van drivers are there in the entire company?

Tony: I'm not absolutely sure. There are 17 drivers in our division, and I believe 13 to 15 drivers in the north. About 30 vans and drivers would be close to the correct numbers.

Jim: Are any of the drivers in a union?

Tony: None of us in this area, but all of the truck and van drivers in the north are Teamsters.

Jim: Aha! Have any of you ever talked to those drivers about this safety issue?

Tony: Oh, I see where you're coming from. . . .

Jim: Hang on! That might be your fallback position, but you won't necessarily be protected if you're regarded as a troublemaker. Let me think about ways I might be able to intercede in a functional way.

Tony: Gee, that would be great if you could. I mean we like our jobs, but we've got to be safe and we've got to be heard when it is a matter of life and death!

Questions

1. How would you describe and evaluate the leadership style of Douglas Electrical Supply?

2. What are the apparent values and assumptions of management in this business?

3. If you were asked to predict the effectiveness of this training effort, what would you say? Explain.

4. Based on this conversation, how would you size up the communication process in this business?

5. What is the proper role of a management consultant? Should Essinger try to intervene in the management process by discussing safety and personnel issues with management?

Gibson Mortuary

Human Resource Problems in a Small Family Business

Gibson Mortuary was founded in 1929 and has become one of the best-known funeral homes in Tacoma, Washington. One of its most persistent problems over the years has been the recruitment and retention of qualified personnel.

Background of the Business

Gibson Mortuary is a family business headed by Ethel Gibson, who owns 51 percent of the stock. As an active executive in the business, Ethel is recognized as a community leader. She has served in various civic endeavors, been elected to the city council, and served one term as mayor.

The mortuary has built a reputation as one of the finest funeral homes in the state. The quality of its service over the years has been such that it continues to serve families over several generations. While large corporations have bought up many mortuaries in recent years, Gibson Mortuary continues to remain competitive as an independent family firm—a "family serving families." Funeral homes in general have recently become the target of public criticism, and books such as *The American Way of Death* reflect adversely on this type of business. Nevertheless, Gibson Mortuary has withstood this threat by its determined, consistent effort to provide the best possible customer service. In its most recent year, it conducted 375 funerals, which places it in the top 9 percent of all funeral homes in the nation when measured in terms of volume of business.

Ethel's son, Max Gibson, entered the business after completing military service and became general manager of the firm. He is a licensed funeral director and embalmer. Both mother and son are active in the day-to-day management of the firm.

Recruitment and Retention Problem

Perhaps the most difficult problem facing Gibson Mortuary is the recruitment and retention of qualified personnel. The image of the industry has made it difficult to attract the right caliber of young people as employees. Many individuals are repelled by the idea of working for an organization in which they must face the fact of death daily. In addition, the challenges raised by social critics reflect poorly on the industry and conveyed to many people the impression that funeral homes are profiting from the misery of those who are bereaved.

One source of employees is walk-in applicants. Also, Gibson Mortuary works through local sales representatives who often know of people who might be considering a change in their careers.

As a small business, Gibson Mortuary presents fewer total opportunities than a larger company or even a funeral home chain. The fact that it is a family business also suggests to prospective employees that top management will remain in the family. It is apparent to all that the two top management spots are family positions. However, Ethel and Max (who is 49 years old) are the only family members employed, so there is some hope for the future for nonfamily employees.

Training Problem

Gibson Mortuary uses two licensed embalmers—Max and another individual. The pressure of other managerial work has made it difficult for Max to devote sufficient time to this type of work.

Any individual interested in becoming a licensed embalmer has to attend mortuary college (mortuary science programs are part of some community-college programs) and serve a two-year apprenticeship. The apprenticeship can be served either prior to or after the college training. Gibson Mortuary advises most individuals to take the apprenticeship prior to the college training so that they can evaluate their own aptitude for this type of career.

Gibson Mortuary prefers its personnel to be competent in all phases of the business. The work involves not only embalming, but also making funeral arrangements with families and conducting funerals and burials. However, some part-time employees only assist in conducting funerals and do not perform preparatory work.

Source: Personal communication; names have been disguised.

Personal Qualifications for Employment

All employees who meet the public and have any part in the funeral service need to be able to interact with others in a friendly and relaxed but dignified manner. The personalities of some individuals are much better suited to this than those of others. Ethel describes one of the problem personalities she had to deal with as follows:

In the first place, he didn't really look the part for our community here. He was short and stocky, too heavy for his height. His vest was too short, and he wore a big cowboy buckle! Can't you see that going over big in a mortuary! He wanted to stand at the door and greet people as they came. We do furnish suits, so we tried to polish off some of the rough edges.

But he was still too aggressive. He became upset with me because I wouldn't get him any business cards immediately. One day I had to send him to the printer, and he came back and said, "While I was there, I just told them to make some cards for me. I'll pay for them myself." I said to him, "Willis, you go right back there and cancel that order! When you are eligible for cards, I'll have them printed for you." We couldn't have him at that point scattering his cards with our name all over town.

Another young applicant made an impressive appearance but lacked polish. His grammar was so poor that he lacked the minimal skills necessary for any significant contact with the public.

Two characteristics of employment that discourage some applicants are the irregular hours and the constant interruptions that are part of the life of a funeral director.

A funeral director might start to do one thing and then find it necessary to switch over to another, more urgent matter. Also, some night and weekend duty in the work schedule is required.

Solving the Human Resource Problems

Although Gibson Mortuary has not completely solved its need for qualified personnel, the business is working at it. While waiting for the right person to come along, Gibson Mortuary started another apprentice prior to any college training. In addition, it is following up on a former apprentice who worked during summer vacations while attending mortuary college. The business also employs a part-time minister as an extra driver. In these ways, Gibson Mortuary is getting along, but it still hopes to do a better job in personnel staffing.

Questions

1. Evaluate the human resource problems facing this firm. Which appear most serious?

2. How can Gibson Mortuary be more aggressive in recruitment? How can it make itself more attractive to prospective employees?

3. Does the fact that Gibson Mortuary is a family firm create a significant problem in recruitment? How can the firm overcome any problems that may exist in this area?

4. Assuming that you are the proper age to consider employment with Gibson Mortuary, what is the biggest question or problem you would have as a prospective employee? What, if anything, might the Gibsons do to deal with that type of question or problem?

Modern Postcard

Leveraging the Quality Process

Operations management is an important means of building any firm's competitive strength in the marketplace. You learned in Chapter 20 that quality concerns drive operations management. You also read that, to remain competitive, a firm should continually try to improve its productivity. At one time, productivity and quality were viewed as potentially conflicting. However, if a firm is able to consistently produce at a superior quality level, the company saves the high costs of scrap and rework. One expert says, "If you can consistently do your work faster, cheaper, and better than the other guy, then you get to wipe the floor with him—without any accounting tricks. Relentless operational innovation is the only way to establish a lasting advantage." Our featured entrepreneur for this video segment combined his passion for high-quality work and his technical savvy to create an efficient organization that gave him a definite competitive advantage during an economic slump and beyond.

Like many entrepreneurs, Steve Hoffman found a profitable niche market that allowed him to turn a passion into a business. In 1976, he started offering his services as a photographer to realtors who wanted to showcase their high-end real estate properties in glossy, photo-filled brochures. Eventually, Hoffman purchased printing equipment to expand his business and develop entire brochures for his clients. Then, in 1993, a business downturn affected his core market. Demand for luxury real estate dropped, and real estate agents were less interested in spending money on glossy brochures to advertise their listed properties. Hoffman and his team had to reposition the company and its product to be more affordable. Being resourceful, Hoffman

used his technological know-how to make a product that the rest of the team thought of as cheap—the postcard—into something affordable and beautiful. The resulting company, Modern Postcard, is now the industry leader in postcard products and mailing solutions.

Hoffman was one of the first in his industry to embrace technology as the means to gain advantage over his competitors. In 1993, before many companies had even implemented company-wide e-mail systems, Hoffman employed a completely digital work flow, using automated systems before anyone else in the industry. The resulting efficiencies allowed Hoffman to price his products much lower than those of competitors who still had not made the conversion to digital processes. By integrating technology throughout the organization and bringing in house functions that other companies were outsourcing, Modern Postcard grew faster and better than its competitors.

Today, Modern Postcard prints more than 1 billion postcards per year and serves over 250,000 clients from 40 unique industries. But Hoffman is still not satisfied with his system. He is constantly planning ways to keep his processes efficient—as he says, to "serve better, faster, less expensively, [and] be able to pay out larger bonuses".

Before answering the questions and working the activities, watch the video on Modern Postcard.

Questions

1. What kind of manufacturing operation is Modern Postcard?

2. In the video, Hoffman mentions using a process called the theory of constraints (ToC). What is the theory of constraints, and how does it relate to total

Video material provided by Hattie Bryant, Producer of Small Business School, the series on PBS Stations, Worldnet, and the Web at http://www.smallbusinessschool.org.

Sources: http://www.modernpostcard.com; http://www.asq.org/; Jessica Long, "Entrepreneurs Learn How to Win at All Stages of the Game: Startups and Entrenched Businesses Overcome Barriers to Beat the Odds," *San Diego Business Journal,* January 22, 2007, p. 23; and Michael Hammer, "Forward to Basics," *Fast Company,* November 2002, p. 38.

quality management (TQM), the managerial approach you learned about in Chapter 20? Do you agree with Hoffman that constraints are the "weakest link in a chain"? Explain.

3. When Hoffman decided to branch out into printing postcards, he found that the product quality was inconsistent. How did he solve the quality-control issue?

Activities

1. Total quality management (TQM) is based on having all members of an organization participate in the overall improvement of the processes, products, and services, as well as the culture in which they work. Methods for implementing TQM can be found in the teachings of Philip B. Crosby, W. Edwards Deming, Armand V. Feigenbaum, Kaoru Ishikawa, and Joseph M. Juran. Look on the Web or in the business section of the library to find works by these leaders in the field. In one paragraph or so, summarize the contribution that each man made to TQM. Be certain to include, attribute, and explain the following terms or concepts in your written report: the "hidden"

plant, "the vital few and the trivial many," the System of Profound Knowledge, DIRTFT, and quality circles.

2. a. Imagine that you are the purchasing manager for a company that buys postcards to announce additions to its product line. Your factories are in New England, Missouri, and Montana, and you have been a customer of Modern Postcard for years. Your boss recently talked to you about diversifying your supplier base for postcards. You, however, prefer to concentrate your purchases with one supplier. Use the Internet to research at least three other postcard manufacturers and find out what they offer. Write a memo to your boss listing the reasons why you are against diversifying. Include specifics about the competition, where possible.

   b. Imagine that you are now the boss in the scenario. Write a memo to your purchasing manager about why you think diversifying your supplier base is important. Compare Modern Postcard to at least two other companies.

Protecting Intellectual Property

How Innovators Can Manage Risk

Peter Drucker, the legendary management consultant, said an entrepreneur is a business leader who creates something new, something different—someone who changes or transmutes values. Entrepreneurs are innovators. This video segment focuses on the protection of innovation. Specifically, the topic under discussion is the protection of intellectual property—innovations in the world of "intangible creativity." You read in Chapter 11 that there are two types of business assets: tangible (such as inventories, equipment, and buildings) and intangible (such as goodwill, patents, copyrights, and investment in research). Intellectual property (IP) is becoming a very valuable intangible asset.

In the past, protecting against risks to IP was difficult. Until very recently, neither accountants nor bankers recognized intangible assets in financial statements or for insurance purposes. In 1997, one business journalist wrote, "How ironic that accounting is the last vestige of those who believe that things are assets and that ideas are expendable." Another journalist wrote in 1999 that the intangible assets of high-tech companies "walk out the door every night." In the video segment, you will learn that about 35 percent of software installed on PCs worldwide is pirated. How can a company protect itself against the theft of its intangible assets? Just what is the definition of loss?

Intangibles are not lost to tangible threats, such as storms, floods, or fire. The risk to intangible assets comes from intangible forces, such as increased competition, new technology, and changes in employment and overall economic conditions. Losses that threaten the value of IP include loss of royalty

earnings, invalidations, unenforceability, infringement, and loss of ownership. Arriving at the value of intangible assets has been, so far, an unreliable process. However, there is little doubt today that innovative ideas and IP have value and innovators must protect against their loss.

All businesses are vulnerable to IP theft, but small businesses are at a particular disadvantage because litigation insurance is expensive. Nevertheless, such insurance is necessary to protect a company that is trying to enforce an IP claim against a competitor or defending itself against an allegation of IP infringement. Some banks have begun accepting intangible assets as collateral, based on appraisals. New accounting standards recognize certain intangible assets, such as trademarks, Internet domain names, customer lists, advertising contracts, patented and unpatented technologies, and secret formulas.

Copyright law protects authors of original works, including literary, dramatic, musical, artistic, audiovisual, and architectural works. One of the most significant developments in copyright law in the past 20 years was the Supreme Court's ruling in *Metro-Goldwyn-Mayer Studios v. Grokster,* which protects copyright and innovation. In that online music distribution case, the Court ruled that those who offer products and services in a way that encourages others to engage in copyright infringement can be held liable for that infringement. Such a high-profile case helped raise public awareness that unauthorized file sharing of copyrighted works is illegal.

Putting the law into place also led to increasing competition for legitimate online music services—something many people in the music and movie industries were desperately hoping for. Under the *Grokster* decision, legitimate services can obtain some

Video material provided by Hattie Bryant, Producer of Small Business School, the series on PBS Stations, Worldnet, and the Web at http://www. smallbusinessschool.org.

Small**Business**School ◙
the Series on PBS stations and the Web

Sources: http://www.ladas.com/Patents/USPatentHistory.html; http://www.uspto.gov/web/offices/dcom/olia/aipa/index.htm; Jon Dudas "A Copyright Refresher," U.S. Patent and Trademark Office, http://www.uspto.gov/web/offices/dcom/olia/copyright/copyrightrefresher.htm; and http://www.quickmba.com/strategy/porter.shtml, accessed June 15, 2007.

relief from unfair competition by unlawful services that offer copyrighted works for free. Mark Litvack, a lawyer featured in the video segment who once worked for the Motion Picture Association, said that when the framers of the U.S. Constitution included copyright protections, they understood that "to encourage people to create intellectual property, you have to protect that property." Or, as Abraham Lincoln once said, you have to add "the fuel of interest to the fire of genius."

Watch the video for Chapter 21, and then answer the questions and work the activities below.

1. What do you think Mark Litvack meant when he said that the writers of the U.S. Constitution understood that "to encourage people to create intellectual property, you have to protect that property"? Before recent laws and standards were put into place to protect IP, how do you think innovators protected their innovations and the profit they could make from them? What changed that made innovators seek new laws and standards?

2. What is risk control? Based on the video, describe how businesses and individuals implement risk control in the music and video industries.

3. What is the difference between tangible and intangible assets? What are the risks to a company's intangible assets?

Activities

1. Using the Internet or your local library as your source, choose one of the following topics to summarize in a brief written report. Include examples of products or services that are protected.

    a. The constitutional basis for federal patent and copyright systems
    b. American Inventor's Protection Act of 1999
    c. First Inventor Defense of 1999
    d. Copyright law

2. Shown below is a graphical representation of Porter's Five Forces, a tool that is normally used to measure the competitive intensity of a marketplace. For this exercise, you'll use the tool to measure risk. In a group of three to four students, brainstorm the factors that contribute to business risk in the software, video gaming, music, or movie industry. Once you've filled out the risk portion of the graphic, write a summary statement explaining how the industry can protect its intellectual property. (You may also write a summary of how it does protect its intellectual property if you're familiar with the particular industry you're covering.) Be prepared to share your results with the rest of the class.

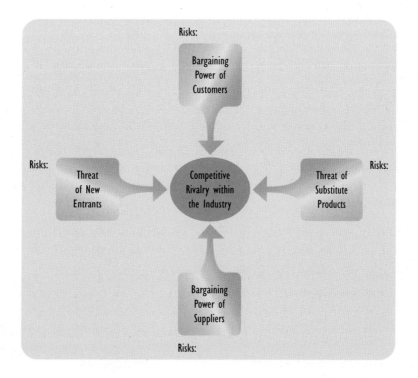

Barton Sales and Service

Managing a Firm's Working Capital

The owners of Barton Sales and Service, based in Little Rock, Arkansas, are John and Joyce Barton. John serves as general manager, and Joyce as office manager. The firm sells General Electric, Carrier, and York air-conditioning and heating systems to both commercial and residential customers and services these and other types of systems. Although the business has operated successfully since the Bartons purchased it in 1996, it continues to experience working-capital problems.

Barton's Financial Structure

The firm has been profitable under the Bartons' ownership. Profits for 2006 were the highest for any year to date. Exhibit C22-1 shows the income statement for Barton Sales and Service for that year.

The balance sheet as of December 31, 2006, for Barton Sales and Service is shown in Exhibit C22-2. Note that the firm's equity was somewhat less than its total debt. However, $10,737 of the firm's liabilities was a long-term note payable to a stockholder. This note was issued at the time the Bartons purchased the business, with payments going to the former owner.

Barton's Cash Balance

A minimum cash balance is necessary in any business because of the uneven nature of cash inflows and outflows. John explained that they need a sub-stantial amount in order to "feel comfortable." He believed that it might be possible to reduce the present balance by $5,000 to $10,000, but he stated that it gave them some "breathing room."

Barton's Accounts Receivable

The trade accounts receivable at the end of 2006 were $56,753, but at some times during the year the accounts receivable were twice this amount. These accounts were not aged, so the firm had no specific knowledge of the number of overdue accounts. However, the firm had never experienced any significant loss from bad debts. The accounts receivable were thought, therefore, to be good accounts of a relatively recent nature.

Customers were given 30 days from the date of the invoice to pay the net amount. No cash discounts were offered. If payment was not received during the first 30 days, a second statement was mailed to the customer and monthly carrying charges of 1/10 of 1 percent were added. The state usury law prohibited higher carrying charges.

On small residential jobs, the firm tried to collect from customers when work was completed. When a service representative finished repairing an air-conditioning system, for example, he or she presented a bill to the customer and attempted to obtain payment at that time. However, this was not always

c22-1 *Barton Sales and Service Income Statement for the Year Ending December 31, 2006*

Sales revenue	$727,679
Cost of goods sold	466,562
Gross profit	$261,117
Selling, general and administrative expenses (including officers' salaries)	189,031
Earnings before taxes	$ 72,086
Income tax	17,546
Net income	$ 54,540

possible. On major items such as unit changeouts—which often ran as high as $2,500—billing was almost always necessary.

On new construction projects, the firm sometimes received partial payments prior to completion, which helped to minimize the amount tied up in receivables.

Barton's Inventory
Inventory accounted for a substantial portion of the firm's working capital. It consisted of the various heating and air-conditioning units, parts, and supplies used in the business.

The Bartons had no guidelines or industry standards to use in evaluating their overall inventory levels. They believed that there *might* be some excessive inventory, but, in the absence of a standard, this was basically an opinion. When pressed to estimate the amount that might be eliminated by careful control, John pegged it at 15 percent.

The firm used an annual physical inventory that coincided with the end of its fiscal year. Since the inventory level was known for only one time in the year, the income statement could be prepared only on an annual basis. There was no way of knowing how much of the inventory had been used at other points and, thus, no way to

---

exhibit

c22-2   *Balance Sheet for Barton Sales and Service for December 31, 2006*

ASSETS

Current assets:

Cash	$ 28,789
Trade accounts receivable	56,753
Inventory	89,562
Prepaid expenses	4,415
Total current assets	$179,519
Loans to stockholders	41,832
Autos, trucks, and equipment, at cost,	
less accumulated depreciation of $36,841	24,985
Other assets: goodwill	16,500
TOTAL ASSETS	$262,836

Debt (Liabilities) and Equity

Current debt:

Current maturities of long-term notes payable*	$ 26,403
Trade accounts payable	38,585
Accrued payroll taxes	2,173
Income tax payable	13,818
Other accrued expenses	4,001
Total current debt	$ 84,980
Long-term notes payable*	51,231
Total stockholders' equity	126,625
TOTAL DEBT AND EQUITY	$262,836

*Current and long-term portions of notes payable:

	Current	Long-Term	Total
• 10% note payable, secured by pickup, due in monthly installments of $200, including interest	$ 1,827	$ 1,367	$ 3,194
• 10% note payable, secured by equipment, due in monthly installments of $180, including interest	584	0	584
• 6% note payable, secured by inventory and equipment, due in monthly installments of $678, including interest	6,392	39,127	45,519
• 9% note payable to stockholder	0	10,737	10,737
• 12% note payable to bank in 30 days	17,600	0	17,600
	$26,403	$51,231	$77,634

calculate profits. As a result, the Bartons lacked quarterly or monthly income statements to assist them in managing the business.

Barton Sales and Service was considering changing from a physical inventory to a perpetual inventory system, which would enable John to know the inventory levels of all items at all times. An inventory total could easily be computed for use in preparing statements. Shifting to a perpetual inventory system would require the purchase of proper file equipment, but the Bartons believed that that cost was not large enough to constitute a major barrier. A greater expense would be involved in the maintenance of the system—entering all incoming materials and all withdrawals. The Bartons estimated that this task would necessitate the work of one person on a half-time or three-fourths-time basis.

Barton's Note Payable to the Bank

Bank borrowing was the most costly form of credit. Barton Sales and Service paid the going rate, slightly above prime, and owed $17,600 on a 90-day renewable note. Usually, some of the principal was paid when the note was renewed. The total borrowing could probably be increased if necessary. There was no obvious pressure from the bank to reduce borrowing to zero. The amount borrowed during the year typically ranged from $10,000 to $25,000.

The Bartons had never explored the limits the bank might impose on borrowing, and there was no clearly specified line of credit. When additional funds were required, Joyce simply dropped by the bank, spoke with a bank officer, and signed a note for the appropriate amount.

Barton's Trade Accounts Payable

A significant amount of Barton's working capital came from its trade accounts payable. Although accounts payable at the end of 2006 were $38,585, the total payable varied over time and might be double this amount at another point in the year. Barton obtained from various dealers such supplies as expansion valves, copper tubing, sheet metal, electrical wire, and electrical conduit. Some suppliers offered a discount for cash (2/10, net 30), but Joyce felt that establishing credit was more important than saving a few dollars by taking a cash discount. By giving up the cash discount, the firm obtained the use of the money for 30 days. Although the Bartons could stretch the payment dates to 45 or even 60 days before being "put on C.O.D.," they found it unpleasant to delay payment more than 45 days because suppliers would begin calling and applying pressure for payment.

Their major suppliers (Carrier, General Electric, and York) used different terms of payment. Some large products could be obtained from Carrier on an arrangement known as "floor planning," meaning that the manufacturer would ship the products without requiring immediate payment. The Bartons made payment only when the product was sold. If still unsold after 90 days, the product had to be returned or paid for. (It was shipped back on a company truck, so no expense was incurred in returning unsold items.) On items that were not floor-planned but were purchased from Carrier, Barton paid the net amount by the 10th of the month or was charged 18 percent interest on late payments.

Shipments from General Electric required payment at the bank soon after receipt of the products. If cash was not available at the time, further borrowing from the bank became necessary.

Purchases from York required net payment without discount within 30 days. However, if payment was not made within 30 days, interest at 18 percent per annum was added.

Can Good Profits Become Better?

Although Barton Sales and Service had earned a good profit in 2006, the Bartons wondered whether they were realizing the *greatest possible* profit. Slowness in the construction industry was affecting their business somewhat. They wanted to be sure they were meeting the challenging times as prudently as possible.

Questions

1. Evaluate the overall performance and financial structure of Barton Sales and Service.

2. What are the strengths and weaknesses in this firm's management of accounts receivable and inventory?

3. Should the firm reduce or expand the amount of its bank borrowing?

4. Evaluate Barton's management of trade accounts payable.

5. Calculate Barton's cash conversion period. Interpret your computation.

6. How could Barton Sales and Service improve its working-capital situation?

Understanding Financial Statements, Part 2

Create a Key Indicator Report

A common problem area for many business managers is a lack of understanding of financial statements. As you learned in Chapter 10, the three major financial statements include the income statement, the balance sheet, and the cash flow statement. These three financial statements provide the structure for your planning efforts. If used properly, they act as a budgeting tool, an early warning system, a problem identifier, and a solution generator. You'll learn in this video segment that keeping track of your business's finances should be a priority for you as business owner, but it also should be the job of everyone who works with you and for you.

The best way to make that possible is to encourage everyone in your company to read, understand, and act on your monthly financial statements. Jim Schell, business consultant and the author of the book *Understanding Your Financial Statements,* says that successful business owners share their financial information with partners and employees—giving everyone accountability through what he calls "key indicators" in the company's financial statements.

Once they are made partially responsible for tracking and interpreting the firm's key indicators, a company's employees, advisors, bankers, and advocates are often inspired with ideas on how to save money and focus attention on emerging business trends and directions. Likewise, you, as the business owner and manager, will be better positioned to plan profitable strategies, make better business decisions, and set reasonable objectives for the future. In the video, Jim Schell says, "When a business owner gets to the point where his favorite day is the day his financials come out—or even better than that, his favorite day of the month is the day he can push the button on his software and out will kick a preliminary income statement—then you know you've arrived at the point where financial statements are meaningful to you. When you know that, you get it—that it's all about numbers."

Before answering the questions and working the activities, watch the video case for Chapter 23, entitled Understanding Financial Statements, Part 2.

Questions

1. Based on what you learned in the video, tell where in a company's financial statements you would find each of the 11 key indicators suggested by Jim Schell. What is the purpose of a key indicator report?

2. What are the four questions you learned in Chapter 23 that can be used to evaluate a firm's financial performance? How are these questions best answered? What relationship do you see between the answers to the questions and the key indicators you defined above?

3. What is an internal control system? How do you think a company can implement effective internal controls and also include employees and partners in the management of the company's financials?

Video material provided by Hattie Bryant, Producer of Small Business School, the series on PBS Stations, Worldnet, and the Web at http://www. smallbusinessschool.org.

Sources: http://www.microsoft.com/smallbusiness/hub.mspx, accessed June 15, 2007; Karen Berman and Joseph Knight "Unlock The Secret to a Better Banking Relationship with These 4 Strategies," Business Literacy Institute; and Pam Newman, "The Ins and Outs of Cash Flow Statements," http://www.entrepreneur.com/money/moneymanagement/financialmanagementcolumnistpamnewman/article178302.html.

Activities

1. Use the Internet or your local library to find financial statements for a real company. Based on the firm's income statement and balance sheet, evaluate the company's financial performance using the approach suggested in Chapter 23.

2. Interpret the company's cash flow statement in terms of the sources and uses of cash. (See Chapter 10 for a refresher on cash flow statements.)

3. List, and briefly describe, five techniques for improving cash flow. Visit the Small Business Help Center at Microsoft.com (http://www.microsoft.com/smallbusiness/hub.mspx), and search using the key terms "improve cash flow." Compare your results with those of two or three other students.

Sample Business Plan

Business Plan

Prepared for the Small and Medium Enterprise Development Bank of Thailand

September 2005

Table of Contents

I. Executive Summary

1.1 The Opportunity

1) Thai food is one of the fastest growing food trends in the U.S. and is rapidly moving into the mainstream[1].

2) Americans are leading a busier lifestyle and thus rely more on meals outside the home. Restaurants account for 46% of total food dollars spent[2], up from 44.6% in 1990 and 26.3% in 1960[3]. By 2010, 53% of food dollars will be spent on away-from-home sources[4].

3) Americans are demanding better quality food and are willing to pay for that quality. As a result, fast food establishments have recently added premium items to their menu. For example, Arby's has a line of "Market Fresh" items[5]; Carl's Jr. offers "The Six-Dollar Burger."[6]

The fast casual segment emerged to meet the demands for better-quality foods at a slightly higher price than that of fast food. Despite the immense popularity of Asian food, and Thai food in particular, the fast casual segment is dominated by cafés/bakeries (Panera Bread, Au Bon Pain) and Mexican (Chipotle Grill, Baja Fresh, Qdoba). In recent years, however, Asian fast casual players have begun to emerge in various regions in the U.S. Such players include Mama Fu's, Nothing but Noodles, and Pei Wei Asian Diner, but are still considered regional players.

Therefore, customers are limited in choices:

- Thai food patrons are currently limited to full-service restaurant options, requiring more time and money than fast food or fast casual options.

- Busy consumers are currently limited to hamburgers, sandwiches, pizzas, and Mexican food, when it comes to fast-served options.

1.2 The Company

- *Benjapon's* is a fast casual restaurant serving fresh Thai food, fast, at affordable prices, in a fun and friendly atmosphere. We will open our first location in February 2006, with future plans to grow through franchising.

- The restaurant will be counter-order and table-service with an average ticket price of $8.50. Store hours are from 11 am to 10 pm, seven days a week. We expect 40% of our business to come from take-out orders.

- Our target customers are urban, 18–35-year-old college students and young working professionals.

- The size of the restaurant will be approximately 1,500 square feet with 50 seats. The first location will be selected from one of the bustling neighborhood squares in the city of Somerville or Cambridge, Massachusetts, due to proximity to the target market.

1.3 The Growth Plan

Our plan is to grow via franchising after opening two company-owned stores. We plan to first saturate the Greater Boston Area, and then move towards national expansion via Area Development Agreements. According to our calculations, the city of Boston can support three to five stores, while the Greater Boston Area can support twenty stores.

---

[1] Packaged Facts, Marketresearch.com, 2003.
[2] "Restaurant Industry Report", The Freedonia Group, Inc., 2003.
[3] "Restaurant Industry Report", Standard and Poor's, 2003.
[4] National Restaurant Association.
[5] Arby's website: www.arbys.com
[6] Carl's Jr. website: www.carlsjr.com

1.4 The Team
Management Team:
Benjapon Jivasantikarn, Founder and Owner—Six years of experience in finance and business incentives at KPMG, a Big Four professional services firm. MBA, Magna Cum Laude, from Babson College. Douglass Foundation Graduate Business Plan Competition Finalist. Sorensen Award for Entrepreneurial and Academic Excellence.
Zack Noonprasith, General Manager—Six years experience in financial services. Five years experience in restaurant management.
Supranee Siriaphanot, Chef—Over 15 years experience as Thai restaurant owner and chef in the U.S.

Board of Advisors:
Rick Hagelstein—Lifelong successful entrepreneur. Founder and CEO of The Minor Group, a marketing, manufacturing, food, property, and hotel development company in Thailand and Asia Pacific. The Minor Food Group is the Thai franchisee of Burger King, Swensen's, Dairy Queen, and Sizzler, and a franchisor of The Pizza Company, which owns 75% of the pizza market in Thailand.
Steve Sabre—Co-founder of Jiffy Lube International and expert in entrepreneurship and franchising.
Hull Martin—Former venture capitalist in the restaurant industry and current advisor to start-up ventures.

1.5 The Financials
We estimate an initial required investment of $550,000. The following are our summary financials for a five-year forecast period.

	Year 1	Year 2	Year 3	Year 4	Year 5
Summary Financials ($)					
# Company-Owned Stores	1	1	2	2	2
# Franchises Sold	—	—	—	3	13
# Franchises in Operations	—	—	—	—	3
Revenue	691,200	881,280	1,977,59	22,293,859	2,874,559
Gross Profit	451,080	601,749	1,380,195	1,623,578	2,122,505
EBIT	(110,145)	74,104	129,202	363,687	525,670
EBITDA	(72,526)	111,723	204,440	430,592	592,575
Net Earnings	(138,145)	48,904	81,602	196,068	296,922
Cash	109,784	168,277	561,526	751,112	989,152
Total Equity	(28,179)	20,725	302,327	498,395	795,317
Total Debt	350,000	315,000	595,000	525,000	385,000
Profitability					
Gross Profit %	65.3%	68.3%	69.8%	70.8%	73.8%
EBIT%	−15.9%	8.4%	6.5%	15.9%	18.3%
EBITDA%	−10.5%	12.7%	10.3%	18.8%	20.6%
Net Earnings %	−20.0%	5.5%	4.1%	8.5%	10.3%
Returns					
Return on Assets	−37.1%	12.2%	8.0%	16.8%	21.8%
Return on Equity	490.2%	236.0%	27.0%	39.3%	37.3%
Return on Capital (LT Debt + Equity)	−42.9%	14.6%	9.1%	19.2%	25.2%

II. The Industry, Target Customers, and Competitors

2.1 The Restaurant Industry

- The restaurant industry has grown 4.5% per year from 1998 to 2003 and reached $385 billion in sales in 2003[7]. Restaurant sales are projected to grow at 5% per year in the next five years, reaching total sales of $491 billion in 2008, and exceed $577 billion by 2010[8].

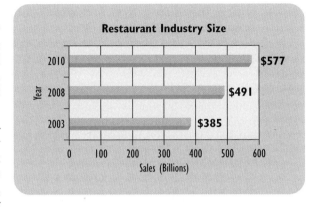

- People devote less time to preparing home-cooked meals and therefore look to faster dining options such as fast food and fast casual as a meal replacement. Restaurants account for 46% of total food dollars spent[7], up from 44.6% in 1990 and 26.3% in 1960[9]. By 2010, 53% of food dollars will be spent on away-from-home sources[9].

- A survey by the National Restaurant Association shows that 27% of Americans are not dining out or ordering out as much as they prefer due to relatively high prices of dining out, indicating an upside potential for growth in the industry, especially in the lower priced segments such as fast food and fast casual.

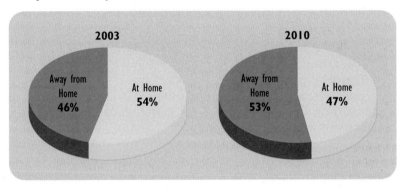

2.2 Fast Casual Segment

- The fast casual segment is positioned (according to price, quality, and experience) between fast food and casual dining. Fast casual restaurants offer higher quality menus at slightly higher prices than those of fast food, and offer a more upscale décor.

- While the restaurant industry as a whole is projected to grow at 5% per year in the next five years, the fast casual segment is projected to grow 15–20%[7]. The fast casual segment is a mere $5 billion, compared to overall industry size of $385 billion, but with vast potential for growth.

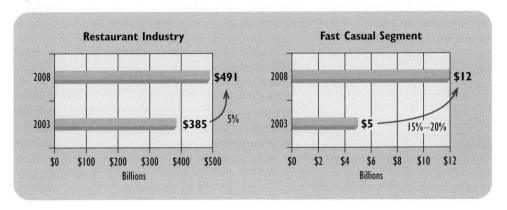

---

[7] "Restaurant Industry Report", The Freedonia Group, Inc., 2003.
[8] National Restaurant Association.
[9] "Restaurant Industry Report", Standard and Poor's, 2003.

- Ticket prices are generally between $6 and $9. Approximately 60% of fast casual customers are between the ages of 18 and 49.

- Most of the major players in this segment are bakery-café and Mexican concepts such as Panera Bread (the segment leader), Au Bon Pain, Chipotle Grill, Baja Fresh, and Qdoba. Due to the high popularity of Asian cuisine, there are currently pockets of players starting up throughout the country; the most notable is Pei Wei Asian Diner.

2.3 Asian Food

- Asian cuisine is popular amongst mainstream American consumers. Sales from these consumers totaled $837 million in 2002[10]. A study done by Packaged Facts projects that retail sales of Asian cuisine will climb from a total of $855.5 million in 2003 to $974.7 million in 2008.

- Asian food, mostly Chinese and Japanese, has long made its way into the mainstream. In the past few decades, however, Americans have expanded their tastes to the bolder flavors of Southeast Asia, with Thai food rising as one of the most popular and well-recognized cuisines. This trend is led by Generations X and Y, who tend to favor high-impact flavors with exotic appeal[10].

- According to The National Restaurant Association's Ethnic Cuisines II study, Thai and other Southeast Asian cuisines appeal primarily to "internationalists" and "urban professionals" who reside and/or work in urban environments. These people tend to be more adventurous in their food tastes and prefer the bolder, spicier flavors of Thai cuisine.

2.4 Target Customer

U.S. consumers are increasingly demanding fast, convenient food to fit their busy lifestyles; they are also demanding healthier menu selections, better quality, and more ethnic choices. These needs are reflected in the current market trends as follows:

1) Busy consumers

Many working Americans lead fast-paced lives with little time to prepare lunch or dinner. According to the Bureau of Labor Statistics, in 2003 more than 50% of U.S. families were dual-earner households. With the number of dual-income families on the rise, as well as longer working hours, eating lunch or dinner out is often the easiest and most convenient option. Restaurants account for 46% of total food dollars spent[11], up from 44.6% in 1990 and 26.3% in 1960[12]. By 2010, 53% of food dollars will be spent on away-from-home sources[12].

2) Increased emphasis on health and quality

The American culture is becoming more health-conscious. The surge in obesity lawsuits against fast food chains, coupled with the recent low-carb, low-fat, and low-calorie crazes, has contributed to Americans' demands for healthier and better quality food. Restaurants are responding to these demands by adding healthier food selections to their menus. For instance, McDonald's offers premium salads[13], and Panera Bread offers low-fat and low-carb options[14]. According to our marketing survey and focus group, Thai food is generally perceived as healthy.

3) Ethnic foods on the rise

Americans are becoming more sophisticated diners and are demanding higher variety of selections. Bold, spicy cuisines are becoming vastly popular. Many traditional restaurants are incorporating flavors from various ethnic cuisines into their menus (e.g., teriyaki, Thai peanut sauce, curry, etc.)[15]. Thai food is among the fastest growing food trends in the U.S. and is making its way into the mainstream[15].

Thai food patrons are currently limited to full-service options, as most Thai restaurants in the U.S. are full-service establishments. An opportunity exists for a Thai fast casual restaurant serving fresh fast, at affordable prices.

---

[10] Packaged Facts, Marketresearch.com, 2003.
[11] "Restaurant Industry Report", The Freedonia Group, Inc., 2003.
[12] "Restaurant Industry Report", Standard and Poor's, 2003.
[13] McDonald's website: www.mcdonalds.com
[14] Panera Bread website: www.panerabread.com
[15] Packaged Facts, Marketresearch.com, 2003.

We considered various ways of segmenting the market: demographical bases, geographical bases, behavioral bases, and psychographic bases. We segment our market by age, education level, and lifestyle, as, according to our marketing research, customers who dine at fast casual establishments and who enjoy Asian foods are of a certain age group, education level, and lifestyle.

Our marketing survey of 350 participants revealed that those most likely to become our customers are between the ages of 18 and 34 years, well educated, single or married, eat out or order take-out quite frequently regardless of income, and enjoy Asian foods and bold flavors.

Our survey reveals a strong demand, as 82% of people aged 18–34 would "definitely" or "probably" eat at *Benjapon's* and would eat there at least twice a month to more than once a week.

2.5 Competitors

Benjapon's competitors include local Thai restaurants as well as limited-service restaurants of other genres. However, we highlight the Asian fast casual players that have emerged in recent years as our benchmark companies and future potential competitors on an expansion scale. Our Asian fast casual competitors include the following:

Mama Fu's: A Pan-Asian fast casual cuisine with 10 stores and over 200 franchises sold. Founded in 2002, the first few stores are located mainly in the South and Mid-West. The average ticket price is about $7.50 for lunch and $10.50 for dinner. Mama Fu's provides counter order and table delivery.

Noodles & Co.: A global noodle fast casual concept that focuses on healthy selections of noodles, salad, and grilled items. The company currently has 58 restaurants in six states focusing on the West, Mid-West, and Atlantic regions. The company plans to franchise 240 new stores in the next four years.

Nothing But Noodles: A fast casual global noodle concept similar to Noodles & Co. The company emphasizes fresh ingredients. The company was founded in 2001 and has sold over 300 franchises, focusing on the South, Mid-West, and Northwest.

Pei Wei: A Pan-Asian fast casual sister restaurant to PF Chang's. The company has over 50 stores, all company-owned. Pei Wei is located in the West and Southwest.

2.6 Competitive Advantage

Our competitive advantage lies in our ability to consistently deliver our brand promise of flavorful, fresh, fast, fun, and friendly, through every customer touchpoint. We will develop standardized kitchen and front-end operations, which will subsequently lower costs and enable us to develop a franchising model.

III. The Company

3.1 Company Overview

- *Benjapon's* is a fast casual restaurant serving fresh Thai food, fast, at affordable prices, in a fun, friendly atmosphere.

- The restaurant will be counter-order, table-service style with an average ticket price of $8.50. Store hours will be from 11 am to 10 pm, daily. We expect 40% of our business to come from take-out orders.

- Our quality of service is a key point of differentiation. Thailand is known as "The Land of Smiles" and our hospitality is second to none. *Benjapon's* will instill a culture of superb customer service among all staff and employees, through a comprehensive staffing and training program.

- The size of the restaurant will be approximately 1,500 square feet with 40–50 seats.

3.2 The Menu

The menu offers a familiar selection of Thai foods with description of ingredients and method of preparation for each dish. In addition, each menu item will be accompanied by a picture, to facilitate the decision-making of the customer and make the experience as stress-free as possible. Therefore, the menu selections will not be extensive, but limited items that are familiar and exceptionally well-prepared. There will be a menu-board behind the ordering counter, as well as a folded paper menu for take-out.

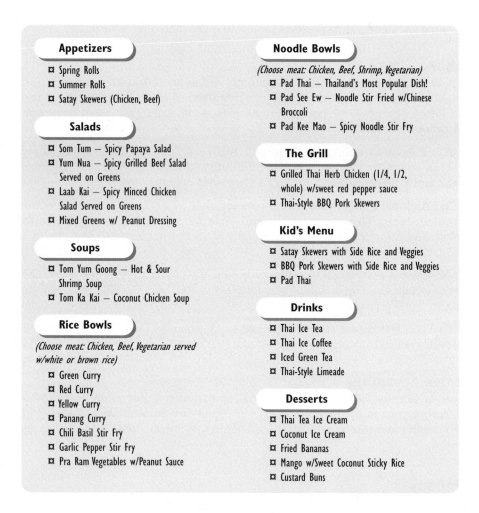

Appetizers
- Spring Rolls
- Summer Rolls
- Satay Skewers (Chicken, Beef)

Salads
- Som Tum — Spicy Papaya Salad
- Yum Nua — Spicy Grilled Beef Salad Served on Greens
- Laab Kai — Spicy Minced Chicken Salad Served on Greens
- Mixed Greens w/ Peanut Dressing

Soups
- Tom Yum Goong — Hot & Sour Shrimp Soup
- Tom Ka Kai — Coconut Chicken Soup

Rice Bowls

(Choose meat: Chicken, Beef, Vegetarian served w/white or brown rice)
- Green Curry
- Red Curry
- Yellow Curry
- Panang Curry
- Chili Basil Stir Fry
- Garlic Pepper Stir Fry
- Pra Ram Vegetables w/Peanut Sauce

Noodle Bowls

(Choose meat: Chicken, Beef, Shrimp, Vegetarian)
- Pad Thai — Thailand's Most Popular Dish!
- Pad See Ew — Noodle Stir Fried w/Chinese Broccoli
- Pad Kee Mao — Spicy Noodle Stir Fry

The Grill
- Grilled Thai Herb Chicken (1/4, 1/2, whole) w/sweet red pepper sauce
- Thai-Style BBQ Pork Skewers

Kid's Menu
- Satay Skewers with Side Rice and Veggies
- BBQ Pork Skewers with Side Rice and Veggies
- Pad Thai

Drinks
- Thai Ice Tea
- Thai Ice Coffee
- Iced Green Tea
- Thai-Style Limeade

Desserts
- Thai Tea Ice Cream
- Coconut Ice Cream
- Fried Bananas
- Mango w/Sweet Coconut Sticky Rice
- Custard Buns

3.3 The Store Layout

The store design will facilitate customer flow. There will be two main registers, or Point of Sale systems (POS), with one extra POS for peak-hour take-out orders. Customers order and pay at the counter, and the food is delivered to their tables. Take-out customers wait for their food at a designated area. Delivery will take 3–5 minutes after ordering. There will be a condiment bar for hot sauces, utensils, and napkins. Fountain drinks and coffee will be served at a separate station.

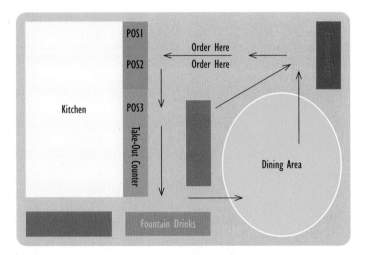

Example of Restaurant Interior

Example of Menu Board with Accompanying Pictures

IV. The Marketing Plan

4.1 Marketing Objectives

Benjapon's marketing mix will cause the target audience to:

- Come for a first visit. (Generate new customers.)
- Visit our website for information and feedback. (Build brand loyalty.)
- Spread the word. (Generate word-of-mouth buzz.)
- Become a regular customer. (Generate repeat business.)

4.2 Targeting and Positioning

4.2.1 TARGETING *Benjapon's* targets the busy student and young professional (mainly between ages 18 and 35) who are looking for a better alternative for a quick meal.

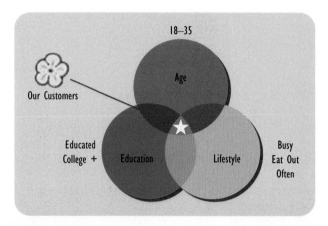

Our first location will be in the Somerville/Cambridge area, located near Tufts University, Harvard University, and MIT. Both Somerville and Cambridge are populated with relatively young demographics. The median age of Somerville residents around Davis and Porter Squares is 30 years old[16]. In addition, Somerville boasts a median family income and per capita income that are higher than national averages. The city of Cambridge also has a young demographic, with the largest group (38.6%) between 25 and 44 years old, followed by 18–24-year-olds at 21.2%. Cambridge boasts a highly educated population, with over 65% of its residents over 25 years old achieving a bachelor's degree or higher[17].

4.2.2 POSITIONING *Benjapon's* is positioned as

"A Thai fast casual restaurant that offers the busy customer a flavorful, fresh, fast, and fun dining experience."

Our marketing survey reveals a strong demand, as 82% of people aged 18–34 would "definitely" or "probably" eat at *Benjapon's*.

4.3 Market Penetration

The store will be located in an area with high visibility and heavy foot and car traffic, with cumulative attraction of nearby retailers and entertainment. We expect to generate high pre–store opening interest from local residents and students, via direct mailing of menu and coupons and postings of flyers (countdown to opening day).

Our Financial Plan in Section IX provides further details on the costs involved in our marketing budget.

---

[16] American Fact Finder.
[17] www.cambridgema.gov

4.4 Pricing Strategy

Average Ticket Price
$8.50

| Starters/Soups | Salads/Entrees | Grilled Chicken Whole **$9.99** ½ **$6.99** ¼ **$4.99** | Kid's Meal | Drinks | Dessert |
| **$4.50** | **$6.50–$7** | | **$3.99** | **$1.50-$2.50** | **$3.50** |

The $8.50 average ticket price is within the fast casual range. These price points are derived from studying Thai restaurants in the Boston area and fast casual restaurants across all genres (e.g., Pei Wei, Qdoba, Mama Fu's, Noodles & Co., Panera Bread). Through our focus groups, we realized that many women would appreciate the option of purchasing a half portion for a lower price. This gives flexibility to the customer, delivers on our customer-friendly brand promise, and makes it easier for customers to try more than one dish.

4.5 Marketing Mix

A mix of marketing vehicles will be created to convey our unique image and message. We will leverage public relations as our main vehicle for marketing communications.

1. <u>Print media:</u> Local newspapers, magazines and student publications.

2. <u>Broadcast media:</u> Local programming and radio stations.

3. <u>Local colleges:</u> Communication with local colleges.

4. <u>Direct mail:</u> Mail menu and coupons to local residential neighborhoods. See our Financial Plan in Section IX for details on mailing costs.

5. <u>Become part of community:</u> Community involvement and donations.

Our strategy is to build the *Benjapon's* brand by delivering a consistent message to our customers at every touchpoint. Everything we do will be associated with Thai food that is flavorful, fresh, fast, fun, and friendly. Our goal is to have top-of-mind awareness with customers and to build a brand that commands a loyal following.

V. The Operations Plan

5.1 Location

Our strategy is to locate in a convenient location close to our target market.

5.1.1 REAL ESTATE CRITERIA

1. **Population**

   We aim to locate near our target market of 18–35-year-old students and young working professionals who are well educated and busy and earn above average income. The following are our criteria:
   - Locate near target market. That is:
     - o Near college or university, and
     - o Near residential area populated by young working professionals, and
     - o Near local businesses.
   - High concentration of daytime population: 10,000 within a one-mile radius
   - Residential population: 15,000 within one mile or 60,000 within three miles

- Income:
    - o Median household income in the top 30% for the MSA (Metropolitan Statistical Area)
    - o Per capita income 20% greater than MSA average

2. **Traffic volume**
We favor locations with high foot traffic and, to a lesser degree, vehicle traffic. Thus we elect to locate near synergistic retailers that draw foot traffic, such as other restaurants, entertainment, daily needs shopping, as well as daytime employment.

3. **Site visibility**
The site should be easily spotted by a walking or driving target customer from both sides of the street across all seasons.

4. **Site neighbors**
    - The site should be surrounded by other synergistic businesses to draw foot traffic.
    - The site should be located near restaurants of other genres in order to attract the "food" crowd.

5. **The site**
    - High visibility site of approximately 1,500 square feet
    - Location-specific parking not required. Although we rely more on foot traffic, street parking should be reasonably available.

5.1.2 POTENTIAL LOCATION According to our criteria, we are working with realtors and specifically focusing on the various "Squares" in the cities of Somerville and Cambridge—that is, Davis Square, Porter Square, Inman Square, Union Square, Kendall Square, and Harvard Square.

5.2 Hours of Operation
The restaurant will be open for lunch and dinner, daily. Service will begin at 11:00 am and end at 10:00 pm. The restaurant will be closed for Christmas, Thanksgiving, New Year's Eve and Day, and the Fourth of July.

5.3 Employee Hiring and Training
We will develop a comprehensive hiring and training manual. Kitchen employees will be hired based on prior experience in Asian, preferably Thai, kitchens. Wiruya Pearce, former chef and owner of a Thai restaurant in Texas, and Rin Jingjit, a chef and restaurant owner in Thailand, will both join the team as chefs. They will be responsible for training kitchen staff and standardizing our processes.

5.4 The Production
The kitchen will be closed from customers' view to create a cleaner look and feel. Food production in the initial store will be headed by a chef and will be standardized and measurable, facilitating the training process for our kitchen staff. The kitchen comprises 40% of the store space and is closed from customers' view. The kitchen computer receives the information ordered from the front registers.

5.4.1 EMPLOYEES Full-Time Employees: Initially, we need three full-time employees—the founder, a store manager, and a chef.
Hourly Employees: We need four hourly employees present (plus the three full-time employees). During non-peak hours, we need one hourly employee, along with the three full-time employees.

5.5 Facilities and Equipment
Space: We will focus on leasing a space that is approximately 1,500 square feet and that was formerly a restaurant and needs only minor modifications.

Equipment: Equipment will be purchased and installed by one of the following companies:

- The Boston Showcase Company, which can also provide assistance with the restaurant design and architecture
- Seidman Brothers

5.6 Suppliers

- We will source our meat and vegetables from Sysco or Performance Food Group (PFG).

- We will purchase our cleaning supplies from Sysco or PFG. We will reorder supplies on an as-needed basis.

- We will purchase smallware from Sysco or US Foodservice.

VI. The Development Plan

We plan to launch a soft-opening/VIP party of the restaurant in January 2006 and a Grand Opening by February 2006. The following timeline sets out detailed activities planned prior to opening.

Our key milestones include securing funding in the August to October timeframe in order to complete our site selection process by November and start building out the restaurant. We also need to have our complete team in place by December in order to start the training process and get ready for our soft opening in January.

Detailed Timeline

Activity	July	August	September	October	November	December	January	February
Menu development.	▓	▓	▓					
Restaurant concept designer.	▓	▓	▓					
Look at site with real estate agents.	▓	▓	▓					
Investigate options to obtain cash.	▓	▓	▓					
Cost-out menu items.	▓	▓						
Line up funding.		▓	▓	▓				
Competitive analysis of restaurants in area, menu, & prices.		▓	▓					
Determine equipment needs.		▓	▓					
Operations manual and employee handbooks.		▓						
Get estimate from equipment supplier.				▓				
Set up name & legal entity. Obtain taxpayer ID.			▓	▓				
Select two sites.			▓	▓				
Chef and store manager.			▓	▓				
Determine staff needs, wages, benefits packages.			▓	▓				
Design procedures: cash handling, checklists, controls processes.				▓		▓		
Check w/zoning board, planning board, health commission.				▓	▓			
Floor plan finalized.					▓			
Select location & complete deal.					▓			
Schedule contractors and vendors.					▓			
Build schedule of contruction plan w/contractor.					▓			
Apply for permits.					▓	▓		
Join Chamber of Commerce and Nat'l Restaurant Assoc.						▓		
Determine office set up.					▓			
Set up office and accounting systems.					▓			
Marketing pieces designed and printed.					▓			
Meet vendors to prepare order and delivery schedule.						▓		
Order equipment, furniture, smallwares, POS.						▓		
Order food & beverage products.							▓	
Menu finalized and printed.						▓		
Arrange for credit card acceptance.						▓		
Finalize job description, policies, and procedures.						▓		
Insurance in place.						▓		
Finalize financials. Meet with bankers/advisors.						▓		
Place hiring ads. Interview. Determine start dates.						▓		
Set up utility service.						▓		
Pre-opening promotion.							▓	▓
Send VIP invitations.							▓	
Dress rehearsal with friends and family.							▓	
VIP party.							▓	
Grand opening.								▓

VII. The Growth Plan

- Our plan is to grow via franchising after opening two company-owned stores.

- The plan is to start selling franchises in the fourth year of operations. In the third year of operations, the second store is to be opened and plans are set to build an infrastructure to support the franchising strategy.

- We plan to grow nationwide via franchising after meeting our goals for the local area.

VIII. The Team

8.1 Launch Team

Founder: Benjapon Jivasantikarn is a 2005 MBA graduate (Magna Cum Laude) of Babson College, the nation's #1 program for entrepreneurship. Prior to graduate school, Benjapon worked for six years at KPMG (a Big Four professional services firm) in San Francisco in business incentives and valuations. Although her background is in finance, her passion lies in the food service industry. Throughout her undergraduate years in Texas, she worked in a Thai restaurant, gaining operations and customer service experience. She also worked at Panera Bread part-time during graduate school to gain further insight into the fast casual business. She was a finalist in the Douglass Graduate Business Plan Competition and won the Sorensen Award for Entrepreneurial and Academic Excellence.

General Manager: Zack Noonprasith has six years experience in financial services and five years experience in restaurant management. Zack will work with the founder on day-to-day operations and on developing and standardizing the system in preparation for replication and franchising.

Chef: Supranee Siriaphanot was a co-founder and chef of a Thai restaurant in Texas for over 15 years. The chef will oversee food preparation in the kitchen and develop standardized processes, as well as train part-time staff on those processes.

8.2 Board of Advisors

Rick Hagelstein

Mr. Hagelstein, a life-long successful entrepreneur, is the founder and CEO of The Minor Group, a hospitality and leisure, food service, and lifestyle company in Thailand and Asia Pacific. The Minor Group comprises two companies: Minor International and Minor Corporation. Minor International is the Thai franchisee of Burger King, Swensen's, Dairy Queen, and Sizzler. After ending a Pizza Hut franchising relationship with Yum! Brands, the Minor Food Group founded The Pizza Company, which now owns 75% of the pizza market in Thailand and is expanding to franchised locations throughout Asia.

Steve Sabre

Dr. Sabre is a franchising expert and a recognized leader in defining the field of entrepreneurship. He cofounded Jiffy Lube International and subsequently founded and served as chairman and CEO of American Oil Corporation, which he sold in 1991. As an educator, he has authored numerous business cases and coauthored the following books: *Franchising: Pathway to Wealth Creation, Business Plans for the 21st Century,* and *New Venture Creation for the 21st Century.* Dr. Sabre has consulted for major corporations such as Fidelity Investments, Intel Corporation, IBM Corporation, and Allied Domecq.

Hull Martin

Dr. Martin is Chair of the Entrepreneurship Department and holds the Edith Y. Babson Term Chair in Entrepreneurship. Martin's primary research areas include the venture capital process and entrepreneurial growth strategies. Dr. Martin actively consults with entrepreneurs and small business start-ups. He is a former venture capitalist with experience in the restaurant field.

IX. The Financial Plan

9.1 Single Store Financials

In this section, we discuss the unit economics of our first store.

9.1.1 INCOME STATEMENT

9.1.1.1 Revenue: We project to eventually serve approximately 400 customers per day on average.

Due to our initial lack of brand awareness, we assume that we will achieve 60% of this number of customers in the first year of operations.

	Year 1	Year 2	Year 3	Year 4	Year 5
Customers per Day	240	288	323	363	407

9.1.1.2 COGS: The cost of goods sold as percentage of sales per each item was derived from an estimate from interviews with restaurateurs regarding food costs. We assume that in years 1 and 2, due to portion control and waste issues, our COGS will be higher than forecasted by 15% and 5%, respectively. After the first few years, COGS is expected to be around 30.2% of sales (a decrease from 34.7% and 31.7% in years 1 and 2).

9.1.1.3 Operating Expenses:

1) Sales and Marketing: Our sales and marketing efforts for the first store consist of mainly direct mail and promotional programs.

Direct Mail: $8,400 per year.

Promotion:

Yearly Promotional Costs	Year 1	Year 2	Year 3	Year 4	Year 5
Promotional Costs per Year per Store	$9,600	$10,560	$12,672	$16,474	$23,063

2) Salaries and Wages: We will have three full-time employees: the founder, a general manager, and a chef. In addition, we will hire a part-time accountant.

Hourly Employees:

Hourly Wages Per Year	Year 1	Year 2	Year 3	Year 4	Year 5
Wage per Year per Store (360 days; 4% raise per year)	$ 95,472	99,291	103,263	107,393	111,689
# store	1	1	2	2	2
Total Hourly Wages	**$95,472**	**$99,291**	**$206,525**	**$214,786**	**$223,377**

3) Depreciation: Office equipment depreciation is three years. Equipment and leasehold improvements are depreciated at seven and ten years, respectively.

4) Rent: We estimate $55 per square foot for rental cost. Therefore, our initial needs at 1,500 square feet will result in a total of $82,500 per year. Rent deposit is estimated at $20,000. We adjust for increase in rental cost after reaching a certain level of sales.

5) Other: Repairs and maintenance costs at 2% of sales per year, insurance at 1.2%, and utility at 3% are all industry standard for independent limited service restaurants. We estimate other operating expenses at 1% to capture any other miscellaneous expenses.

9.1.2 CASH FLOWS

9.1.2.1 Working Capital: Our restaurant is a cash business, so we assume negligible accounts receivables. We will turn over inventory 52 times per year, assuming weekly delivery of goods on average. *Benjapon's* will rely on fresh ingredients and will need delivery at least once a week. We will pay employees semi-weekly.

9.1.2.2 Capital Expenditure: For each new store, we incur approximately $255,000 worth of capital expenditures: $25,000 Point-of-Sales system, $80,000 equipment, $150,000 leasehold improvements.

Benjapon's will be cash flow positive after 12 months.

9.1.3 BALANCE SHEET

9.1.3.1 Assets & Liabilities: *Benjapon's* primary asset base is fixed assets, representing 60% of total assets in year 1. As *Benjapon's* is a restaurant operation, accounts receivable will not be significant.

9.1.4 SUMMARY FINANCIALS   The following is the summary of our first store financial performance.

	Year 1	Year 2	Year 3	Year 4	Year 5
Summary Financials ($)					
# Company-Owned Stores	1	1	1	1	1
Revenue	691,200	881,280	988,796	1,109,429	1,244,780
Gross Profit	451,080	601,749	690,097	774,289	868,752
EBIT	(110,145)	74,104	143,475	178,080	232,805
EBITDA	(72,526)	111,723	181,094	207,366	262,091
Net Earnings	(116,145)	68,104	102,421	104,688	138,243
Net Cash from Operating Activities	(53,182)	112,693	139,588	131,426	171,105
Cash	137,284	249,977	379,565	500,991	662,096
Total Equity	299,321	367,425	469,847	574,535	712,778
Total Debt	50,000	50,000	40,000	30,000	20,000
Growth					
Revenue Growth Rate—CAGR:		28%	12%	12%	12%
Profitability					
Gross Profit %	65.3%	68.3%	69.8%	69.8%	69.8%
Operating Expenses %	76.1%	59.9%	55.3%	53.7%	51.1%
EBIT%	−15.9%	8.4%	14.5%	16.1%	18.7%
EBITDA%	−10.5%	12.7%	18.3%	18.7%	21.1%
Net Earnings %	−16.8%	7.7%	10.4%	9.4%	11.1%
Returns					
Return on Assets	−29.1%	14.1%	17.9%	15.5%	17.0%
Return on Equity	−38.8%	18.5%	21.8%	18.2%	19.4%
Return on Capital (LT Debt + Equity)	−33.2%	16.3%	20.1%	17.3%	18.9%

9.2 Capital Requirements

Initial funding is by private investors of $200,000 and an equipment loan of $350,000.

Our start-up costs total $330,000 and include $20,000 rent deposit, $10,000 legal costs, $25,000 office and Point-of-Sales system, $30,000 architecture cost, $80,000 equipment, $150,000 leasehold improvements, and $15,000 opening inventory.

Source of Funds		Uses of Funds	
		Rent Deposit	$ 20,000
		Legal Costs	$ 10,000
Investors	$ 200,000	Office Equipment	$ 25,000
		Architecture Cost	$ 30,000
Debt	$ 350,000	Equipment Costs	$ 80,000
		Leasehold Improvements	$ 150,000
		Opening & Misc Inventory	$ 15,000
		Funding for Working Capital	$ 202,000
		1st Year Marketing	$ 18,000
Total Sources	**$550,000**	**Total Uses**	**$550,000**

9.3 Franchising Revenues and Costs

In year 3, we raise an additional $400,000 in capital to fund growth.

We start by growing our company-owned stores to two stores in year 3 of operations. In year 4, we begin to sell franchises. We assume that the franchises sold will be up and running within one year of signing the franchise agreement. Therefore, if three franchises were sold in year 4, there will be three franchises operating by year 5.

We assume that in year 5, we are able to sell ten more franchises.

Our royalty fee is 5% and franchise fee is $25,000. This is comparable with our Asian fast casual benchmark companies.

In order to calculate our royalty revenues, we assume franchisee revenue of close to $1,000,000 per store (estimated by averaging first five year forecasted sales of franchisees, which takes into account the sales ramp up time in the initial years).

		Year 3	**Year 4**	**Year 5**
New Franchises Sold in the year			3	10
Total Franchises Sold			3	13
Total Franchises in Operations			0	3
Royalty	5%			
Revenue per Store	$1,000,000			
Franchisee Revenues		$0	$0	2,700,000
Royalty Revenue		$0	$0	$135,000
Franchise Fee	$25,000	$0	$75,000	$250,000
Total Revenue from Franchising		**$0**	**$75,000**	**$385,000**

In order to build a franchising organization, we need to create a support infrastructure. In the first year of franchising (year 4), we will invest in marketing to advertise our franchise to prospective franchisees. We will also incur legal costs associated with creating the UFOC and franchise agreements. Costs for training material and internal communications systems are based on number of franchisee stores.

In terms of staffing, we will need a franchise director by year 5, when we start to sell up to ten franchises and have plans to begin saturating the local market. We also need to hire a field agent (called a "Team Coach") to serve as a link between the company and its franchisees.

Franchise Support Staff

		Year 3	Year 4	Year 5
Total Franchises Sold		0	3	13
Total Franchises in Operations		0	0	3
Franchise Support Staff				
Field Agents				1
Total Franchise Support Staff		0	0	1
Salary per franchise support staff	$50,000			
Franchise Director				$100,000
Total Salary		$0	$0	$150,000

Other Franchisee Support Costs	Per Store	Year 3	Year 4	Year 5
Total Franchises Sold		0	3	13
Total Franchises in Operations		0	0	3
Support Costs				
Marketing Expense (sell franchises)		$100,000	$50,000	$50,000
Legal Costs		$100,000	$20,000	$20,000
Training Material	$50	$0	$150	$650
Internal Communication Network	$1,000	$0	$3,000	$13,000
Other Support Costs		$200,000	$73,150	$83,650
Estimated Costs Related to Franchising		$200,000	$73,150	$233,650

9.4 Overall Financial Performance

The following includes the income statement, balance sheet, and cash flow statement for the company, which reflects the following milestones:

- One company-owned store in years 1 and 2. Break-even of the first store after 12 months.

- Launch a second company-owned store in year 3 to prove duplicability.

- In year 3, start working with legal team to create franchising structure and agreement. Begin marketing efforts to target potential franchisees.

- Start selling franchises in year 4. We expect to sell three franchises initially. We receive the franchise fee up front, but the build-out of the three franchisee stores will likely materialize in year 5. No formal staffing infrastructure is in place in year 4.

- In year 5, we hire a franchising director and a field agent (or "team coach") as a base team for our franchise operations. We aim to sell ten franchises in year 5. The three franchises sold in year 4 should be in operation, thus resulting in royalty revenues for us.

Although our financial forecast spans the timeline of our first five years of operations, our growth strategy lies in the two stages as set out in this report, which extends beyond the five-year horizon. Since our first-stage growth allows for a total of 20 stores, we expect completion of our first stage growth in the 6- to 7-year timeframe. Our second stage of growth will see nationwide expansion, which we expect will start in years 7–10. The financials set out below are for the first five years of operations.

9.4.1 SUMMARY FINANCIALS

	Year 1	Year 2	Year 3	Year 4	Year 5
Summary Financials ($)					
# Company-Owned Stores	1	1	2	2	2
# Franchises Sold	—	—	—	3	13
# Franchises in Operations	—	—	—	—	3
Revenue	691,200	881,280	1,977,592	2,293,859	2,874,559
Gross Profit	451,080	601,749	1,380,195	1,623,578	2,122,505
EBIT	(110,145)	74,104	129,202	363,687	525,670
EBITDA	(72,526)	111,723	204,440	430,592	592,575
Net Earnings	(138,145)	48,904	81,602	196,068	296,922
Cash	109,784	168,277	561,526	751,112	989,152
Total Equity	(28,179)	20,725	302,327	498,395	795,317
Total Debt	350,000	315,000	595,000	525,000	385,000
Profitability					
Gross Profit %	65.3%	68.3%	69.8%	70.8%	73.8%
EBIT%	−15.9%	8.4%	6.5%	15.9%	18.3%
EBITDA%	−10.5%	12.7%	10.3%	18.8%	20.6%
Net Earnings %	−20.0%	5.5%	4.1%	8.5%	10.3%
Returns					
Return on Assets	−37.1%	12.2%	8.0%	16.8%	21.8%
Return on Equity	490.2%	236.0%	27.0%	39.3%	37.3%
Return on Capital (LT Debt + Equity)	−42.9%	14.6%	9.1%	19.2%	25.2%

9.4.2 BREAK-EVEN ANALYSIS

Benjapon's will break even within 12 months. The following chart shows *Benjapon's* break-even sales over the five-year period.

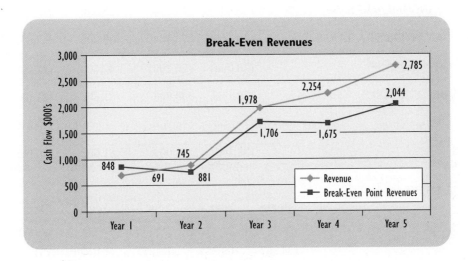

9.4.3 INCOME STATEMENT

	Year 1	Year 2	Year 3	Year 4	Year 5
# Company-Owned Stores	1	1	2	2	2
# of Franchises Sold	—	—	—	3	13
Revenue from Company Stores	691,200	881,280	1,977,592	2,218,859	2,489,559
Revenue from Franchising			—	75,000	385,000
TOTAL REVENUE	**691,200**	**881,280**	**1,977,592**	**2,293,859**	**2,874,559**
COST OF REVENUE	240,120	279,531	597,398	670,280	752,054
% of Revenues	34.7%	31.7%	30.2%	30.2%	30.2%
GROSS PROFIT	451,080	601,749	1,380,195	1,623,578	2,122,505
% of Revenues	65.3%	68.3%	69.8%	70.8%	73.8%
OPERATING EXPENSES					
Franchise-Specific Expenses			200,000	73,150	233,650
Public Relations	—	—	60,000	90,000	120,000
Direct Mail Campaign	8,400	8,400	16,800	16,800	16,800
Promotions Programs	9,600	10,560	12,672	16,474	23,063
Less: 0.8% Franchisee Marketing Contribution			—	—	(21,600)
Salaries and Benefits	294,340	303,114	570,396	690,212	710,821
Depreciation	37,619	37,619	75,238	66,905	66,905
Rent	82,500	82,500	82,500	97,193	126,228
Corporate Office	—	—	—	—	70,000
Training	44,000	22,000	66,000	44,000	44,000
Repairs and Maintenance	13,824	17,626	39,552	45,877	57,491
Insurance	8,294	10,575	23,731	27,526	34,495
Utility	20,736	26,438	59,328	68,816	86,237
Other G&A	6,912	8,813	19,776	22,939	28,746
Total Operating Expenses	526,225	527,645	1,225,993	1,259,891	1,596,835
% of Revenues	76%	60%	62%	55%	56%
EARNINGS FROM OPERATIONS	(75,145)	74,104	154,202	363,687	525,670
	−11%	8%	8%	16%	18%
EXTRAORDINARY INCOME/(EXPENSE)	(35,000)	—	(25,000)	—	—
EARNINGS BEFORE INTEREST & TAXES	(110,145)	74,104	129,202	363,687	525,670
	−16%	8%	7%	16%	18%
INTEREST INCOME/(EXPENSE)	(28,000)	(25,200)	(47,600)	(42,000)	(30,800)
NET EARNINGS BEFORE TAXES	(138,145)	48,904	81,602	321,687	494,870
TAXES	—	—	—	(125,619)	(197,948)
NET EARNINGS	(138,145)	48,904	81,602	196,068	296,922
% of Revenues	**−20.0%**	**5.5%**	**4.1%**	**8.5%**	**10.3%**

9.4.4 BALANCE SHEET

	Begin	Year 1	Year 2	Year 3	Year 4	Year 5
ASSETS						
CURRENT ASSETS						
Cash	184,967	109,784	168,277	561,526	751,112	989,152
Accounts Receivable		2,534	3,231	6,372	7,358	9,091
Inventories		17,741	22,620	44,606	51,506	63,640
Other Current Assets		4,562	5,816	11,470	26,489	32,729
Total Current Assets	184,967	134,621	199,944	623,974	836,464	1,094,612
PROPERTY & EQUIPMENT	275,000	237,381	199,762	399,524	332,619	265,714
TOTAL ASSETS	459,967	372,002	399,706	1,023,497	1,169,083	1,360,326

	Begin	**Year 1**	**Year 2**	**Year 3**	**Year 4**	**Year 5**
LIABILITIES & SHAREHOLDERS' EQUITY						
CURRENT LIABILITIES						
Short Term Debt	—	—	—	—	—	—
Accounts Payable & Accrued Expenses		45,619	58,164	114,700	132,444	163,644
Other Current Liabilities		4,562	5,816	11,470	13,244	16,364
Current Portion of Long Term Debt	—	35,000	70,000	70,000	140,000	175,000
Total Current Liabilities	—	85,181	133,981	196,170	285,688	355,009
LONG TERM DEBT (less current portion)	350,000	315,000	245,000	525,000	385,000	210,000
STOCKHOLDERS' EQUITY						
Common Stock	200,000	200,000	200,000	400,000	400,000	400,000
Preferred Stock	0	0	0	0	0	0
Retained Earnings	(90,033)	(228,179)	(179,275)	(97,673)	98,395	395,317
Total Equity	109,967	(28,179)	20,725	302,327	498,395	795,317
TOTAL LIABILITIES & EQUITY	459,967	372,002	399,706	1,023,497	1,169,083	1,360,326

9.4.5 CASH FLOW STATEMENT

	Begin	**Year 1**	**Year 2**	**Year 3**	**Year 4**	**Year 5**
OPERATING ACTIVITIES		1	1	2	2	2
Net Earnings	(90,033)	(138,145)	48,904	81,602	196,068	296,922
Depreciation	0	37,619	37,619	75,238	66,905	66,905
Working Capital Changes						
(Increase)/Decrease Accounts Receivable	0	(2,534)	(697)	(3,141)	(986)	(1,733)
(Increase)/Decrease Inventories	0	(17,741)	(4,879)	(21,986)	(6,900)	(12,134)
(Increase)/Decrease Other Current Assets	0	(4,562)	(1,255)	(5,654)	(15,019)	(6,240)
Increase/(Decrease) Accts Pay & Accrd Expenses	0	45,619	12,545	56,536	17,743	31,201
Increase/(Decrease) Other Current Liabilities	0	4,562	1,255	5,654	1,774	3,120
Net Cash Provided/ (Used) by Operating Activities	(90,033)	(75,182)	93,493	188,249	259,586	378,041
INVESTING ACTIVITIES						
Property & Equipment	(275,000)	—	—	(275,000)	—	—
Other						
Net Cash Used in Investing Activities	(275,000)	—	—	(275,000)	—	—
FINANCING ACTIVITIES						
Increase/(Decrease) Short Term Debt		—	—	—	—	—
Increase/(Decrease) Curr. Portion LTD		35,000	35,000	—	70,000	35,000
Increase/(Decrease) Long Term Debt	350,000	(35,000)	(70,000)	280,000	(140,000)	(175,000)
Increase/(Decrease) Common Stock	200,000	—	—	200,000	—	—
Increase/(Decrease) Preferred Stock	0	—	—	—	—	—
Dividends Declared		—	—	—	—	—
Net Cash Provided/(Used) by Financing	550,000	—	(35,000)	480,000	(70,000)	(140,000)
INCREASE/(DECREASE) IN CASH	184,967	(75,182)	58,493	393,249	189,586	238,041
CASH AT BEGINNING OF YEAR		184,967	109,784	168,277	561,526	751,112
CASH AT END OF YEAR	184,967	109,784	168,277	561,526	751,112	989,152

Valuing a Business

At certain times, an entrepreneur may need to determine the value of her or his business. Despite the subjective nature of assigning value to a privately held company—that is, a firm whose stock is not traded publicly—and especially a *small* privately owned firm, there are times when the value must be estimated.

THE NEED TO COMPUTE FIRM VALUE

A variety of specific situations may call for a firm valuation, including the following:

1. An entrepreneur decides to buy a business, rather than starting one from scratch. He or she needs to know the answers to two questions, which may seem the same but are not: "How much is the business worth to me?" and "What should I pay for it?"

2. An owner has decided to make an employee stock ownership plan (ESOP) part of the firm's retirement program (see Chapter 12). The stock has to be valued each year so that the appropriate number of shares can be contributed to the employees' retirement plan.

3. A firm is raising money from outside investors. The firm's value must be determined to establish the percentage of ownership the new investors will receive in the company (see Chapter 11).

4. One partner wants to buy out another partner or the interest of a deceased partner. The value of the business must be set so that a price can be agreed on.

5. An owner wants to exit (harvest) the business. Knowing the value of the company is essential if the business is to be sold or transferred to family members (see Chapter 12).

These are the most common reasons for valuing a business. Note that they are, for the most part, driven by external influences and exceptional circumstances. But it is a good idea to value a business on an ongoing basis—at least once a year. As a firm grows and becomes more profitable, the owner needs to know if the business is also increasing in value. In some situations, a profitable business may lose value over time. Therefore, being aware of its value is important in the management of a business. Knowing your firm's value provides critical insight into how the firm is performing, what options it has, and how it can improve long-term.

VALUATION METHODS

firm value (enterprise value)
The value of the entire business, regardless of how it is financed

equity value (owner's value)
The value of the firm less the debt owed by the firm

In valuing firms, it is important to distinguish between *firm value* and *owner value*. **Firm value**, or **enterprise value**, is the value of the entire business, regardless of how it is financed. It reflects the value of the underlying assets of the business. **Equity value**, or **owner's value**, on the other hand, is the total value of the firm less the amount of debt owed by the firm. That is,

$$\text{Firm value} - \text{Outstanding debt} = \text{Equity value}$$

Some approaches to determining firm value focus on the first quantity on the left side of the equation—estimating the value of the firm as an entity. The question is "Given the firm's assets and its ability to produce profits from these assets, what is the firm worth?" The equity value is then found by subtracting the outstanding debt from the total firm value.

Other approaches involve determining the value of the outstanding debt and the equity value separately. In those cases, firm value is found by summing the amount of outstanding debt and the equity value. While both processes produce similar results, we recommend finding the firm value and then subtracting the outstanding debt in order to determine the equity, or owner's, value.

There are three basic methods for valuing a business: (1) asset-based valuation, (2) valuation based on comparables, and (3) cash flow–based valuation. Each of these methods can be used as a stand-alone measure of firm value, but more often they are used in combination.

Asset-Based Valuation

An **asset-based valuation** assumes that the value of a firm can be determined by examining the value of the underlying assets of the business (the left-hand side of the balance sheet). Three variations of this approach use (1) the modified book value of assets, (2) the replacement value of assets, and (3) the liquidation value of assets.

The **modified book value method** starts with the numbers shown on a company's balance sheet. These amounts are adjusted to reflect any obvious differences between the historical cost of each asset (as given on the balance sheet) and its current market value. For instance, the market value of a firm's plant and equipment may be totally different from its depreciated historical cost or book value. The same may be true for real estate. The **replacement value method** entails estimating the cost to replace each of the firm's assets. And the **liquidation value method** involves estimating the amount of money that would be received if the firm ended its operations and liquidated its assets.

Asset-based valuation is of limited worth in valuing a business. The historical costs shown on the balance sheet may be very different from the current value of the assets. The three variations to some extent adjust for this weakness, but their estimate of value has a weak foundation, as all asset-based techniques fail to recognize the firm as an ongoing business. However, the liquidation value method yields an estimate of the value that could be realized if the assets of the business were all sold separately, which is sometimes helpful information.

Valuation Based on Comparables

A **valuation based on comparables** looks at the actual market prices of recently sold firms similar to the one being valued—either publicly traded firms (market comparables) or private firms that have been sold (transaction comparables). "Similar" means that the two firms are in the same industry and are alike in such characteristics as growth potential, risk, profit margins, assets-to-sales relationships, and levels of debt financing.

For instance, you might start by finding several recently sold companies with growth prospects and levels of risk comparable to those of the firm being valued. For each of these firms, you calculate the **earnings multiple**, or *value-to-earnings ratio*,[1]

$$\text{Earnings multiple} = \frac{\text{Value}}{\text{Earnings}}$$

Earnings may be one of the following:

1. **Earnings before interest, taxes, depreciation, and amortization**, frequently referred to as EBITDA

2. **Earnings before interest and taxes (EBIT)**, which is also a firm's operating income

3. Net income

Of these three options, earnings before interest, taxes, depreciation, and amortization is the most popular.

asset-based valuation
Determination of the value of a business by estimating the value of its assets

modified book value method
Determination of the value of a business by adjusting book value to reflect obvious differences between the historical cost and the current market value of the assets

replacement value method
Determination of the value of a business by estimating the cost of replacing the firm's assets

liquidation value method
Determination of the value of a business by estimating the money that would be available if the firm were to liquidate its assets

valuation based on comparables
Determination of the value of a business by considering the actual market prices of firms that are similar to the firm being valued

earnings multiple
A ratio determined by dividing a firm's value by its annual earnings; also called *value-to-earnings ratio*

earnings before interest, taxes, depreciation, and amortization (EBITDA)
A firm's profits after subtracting cost of goods sold and cash operating expenses, but before subtracting depreciation and amortization, interest expense, and taxes

Then, assuming that the company being valued should have an earnings multiple comparable to those of similar firms, you apply the calculated ratio to estimate the company's value. That is, you apply the multiple in the following equation:

Value = Earnings of company being valued × Earnings multiple of comparable firms

Potential buyers of one novelty manufacturer and importer in Missouri offered 4.9 times the firm's annual EBITDA of $45,000. That is, the buyer was willing to pay $220,500 for the firm (EBITDA of $45,000 × 4.9 = $220,500).[2]

The market-comparable valuation method is not as easy to use as it might seem. First, finding other firms that are comparable in every way to the firm being valued is often difficult. It is not enough simply to find a firm in the same industry, although that might provide a rough approximation. As already noted, the ideal comparable firm is one that is in the same industry, is a similar type of business, and has a similar growth rate, financial structure, asset turnover ratio (sales ÷ total assets), and profit margin (profits ÷ sales). Fortunately, considerable information is published about firm sales. For instance, a publication called *Mergerstat* reports the prices of all such sales announced in the public media. Also, some accounting firms can provide information about the selling prices of comparable businesses.

normalized earnings
Earnings that have been adjusted for unusual items, such as fire damage, and leakages, such as an excessive salary for the owner

Second, ideally **normalized earnings** should be used in this computation. Normalizing earnings involves adjusting for any unusual items, such as a one-time loss on the sale of real estate or as the consequence of a fire. In addition, normalizing earnings involves adding back any "leakages" that are occurring in the firm's income. For instance, if the owners have been paying themselves a salary above what it would take to find a similarly qualified manager, the excess should be deducted in ascertaining the firm's normalized earnings.

A variation on valuation based on comparables is simply to assign an appropriate earnings multiple. There are two fundamental drivers of a firm's earnings multiple—risk and growth. The two are related as follows:

1. The more (less) risky the business, the lower (higher) the appropriate earnings multiple and, as a consequence, the lower (higher) the firm's value.

2. The higher (lower) the projected growth rate in future earnings, the higher (lower) the appropriate earnings multiple and, therefore, the higher (lower) the firm's value.

These relationships are presented graphically in Exhibit B-1.

As already noted, earnings multiples vary with the nature of the firm. (In practice, of course, earnings multiples are also affected by conventional wisdom and the perspective

exhibit

B-1   *Risk and Growth: Key Factors Affecting the Earnings Multiple and Firm Value*

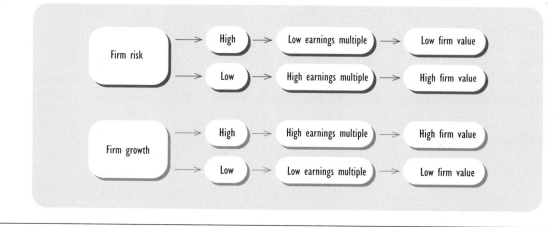

and experience of the person performing the valuation.) Following are some examples of multiples based on the type of firm:

Type of Firm	Earnings Multiple
Small, well-established firm, vulnerable to recession	7
Small firm requiring average executive ability but operating in a highly competitive environment	4
Firm that depends on the special, often unusual, skill of one individual or a small group of managers	2

Earnings multiples also vary by industry, as shown by the following average multiples in different industries:[3]

Industry	Earnings Multiple
Manufacturing	5.5 to 8.5
High-tech	6.0 to 12.0
Health-care services	5.0 to 9.0
Retail	4.5 to 7.5
Public relations, advertising, media	3.0 to 6.5
Restaurant	4.0 to 8.0

Consider a real-life example. When Robert Hall, former owner of Visador Corporation, was considering selling his firm, he received an offer based on a multiple of five times the firm's operating income plus depreciation expense.[4] The offer was presented to Hall in the following format:[5]

Company's operating income plus depreciation expense	$ 3,300,000
Earnings multiple	$\times$ 5
Firm value	$16,500,000

To determine what Hall would receive for his ownership of the business, we subtract the $750,000 of debt owed by the firm, to get $15,750,000.

Hall rejected the offer of $15.75 million but made a counter-offer of $20 million for his ownership. Hall's counter-offer was accepted, which suggests that the buyer wanted the firm more than he let on initially.

The appropriateness of using earnings to value a firm is the subject of ongoing debate. Some contend that markets value a firm based on future cash flows, not reported earnings. Moreover, they argue, there are simply too many ways (within generally accepted accounting principles) to influence a firm's reported earnings, leading to material differences in valuation estimates when there is no difference in the intrinsic value of the firm. For these individuals, a firm's value is the present value of the firm's projected future cash flows.

Cash Flow–Based Valuation

Although not popular among smaller companies, **cash flow–based valuation**, in which a company is valued based on the amount and timing of its future cash flows, makes a lot of sense. Valuations based on earnings, although used more often, present a conceptual problem. From an investor's or owner's perspective, the value of a firm should be based on future cash flows, not reported earnings—especially not reported earnings for just a single year.

Measuring the value of a firm's future cash flows for a cash flow–based valuation is a three-step process:

Step 1. Project the firm's expected future cash flows.

Step 2. Estimate the investors' and owners' required rate of return on their investment in the business.

cash flow–based valuation
Determination of the value of a business by estimating the amount and timing of its future cash flows

Step 3. Using the required rate of return as the discount rate, calculate the present value of the firm's expected future cash flows, which equals the value of the firm.

The cash flow–based approach is the most complicated of the three valuation methods discussed here; an in-depth explanation is well beyond the scope of this book. But it has one distinct advantage: A cash flow–based evaluation requires that *explicit* assumptions be made about the firm's future growth rates, its profit margins (profits to sales), how efficiently it is managing its assets (sales relative to the amount of the assets), and the appropriate discount rate (required rate of return). In contrast, a valuation based on comparables only *implicitly* considers the relationship between the multiple being used and the factors that should determine the multiple. Thus, using cash flow–based valuation requires the estimator to examine more carefully *why* the firm has value.

CHAPTER 1

1. http://www.sba.gov/idc/groups/public/documents/sba_homepage/tools_podcast_entrepreneurtran.doc, accessed June 1, 2007.

2. John J. Fernandes, "Management and Entrepreneurship Education: Looking over the Horizon," speech given at the 2006 United States Association of Small Business and Entrepreneurship/Small Business Institute Conference, Tucson, Arizona, January 15, 2006.

3. Patricia B. Gray, "Business Class," *Fortune,* April 17, 2006, http://money.cnn.com/magazines/fortune/fortune_archive/2006/04/17/8374351/index.htm, posted June 6, 2006.

4. Personal interview with Shannon Guderian, December 2006.

5. Conversation with Maggie Adams, Public Relations Coordinator of SPANX, June 1, 2007.

6. Adapted from Courtney Pahmiyer, "A Labor of Love," *UMHB Life,* Vol. 25, No. 3 (Summer 2006), pp. 14–15.

7. Arlene Weintraub, "Hot Growth Companies," *Business Week,* June 5, 2006, p. 50.

8. Nancy M. Carter, William B. Gartner, Kelly G. Shaver, and Elizabeth J. Gatewood, "The Career Reasons of Nascent Entrepreneurs," *Journal of Business Venturing,* Vol. 18 (2003), pp. 13–39.

9. For a discussion on "making meaning," see Guy Kawasaki, *The Art of the Start* (The Woodlands, TX: Portfolio, 2004), pp. 4–6.

10. Thomas J. Stanley and William D. Danko, *The Millionaire Next Door* (New York: Simon & Schuster, 1996), p. 227.

11. "Poll: Most Like Being Own Boss," *USAToday,* May 6, 1991. For a scholarly study confirming the importance of a quest for independence as a motivational factor, see Marco Virarelli, "The Birth of New Enterprises," *Small Business Economics,* Vol. 3, No. 3 (September 1991), pp. 215–223.

12. Bob Moos, "Boomers Become Self-Starters," *The Dallas Morning News,* December 20, 2006, p. A1.

13. *Ibid.*

14. Gangaram Singh and Alex DeNoble, "Early Retirees as the Next Generation of Entrepreneurs," *Entrepreneurship Theory and Practice,* Vol. 27, No. 3 (Spring 2003), pp. 218–220.

15. Moos, *op. cit.*

16. Personal conversation with Rick Davis, December 20, 2006.

17. Chris McCuan, "How I Did It: Bill Thomas, Founder and CEO, Bill's Khakis," *Inc.,* June, 2006, pp. 104–106.

18. William J. Dennis, Jr., "Success, Satisfaction and Growth," *NFIB National Small Business Poll* (Washington: National Federation of Independent Business, 2001), p. 1.

19. Amar V. Bhide, *The Origin and Evolution of New Businesses* (New York: Oxford University Press, 2000), Chapter 1.

20. Norman R. Smith, *The Entrepreneur and His Firm: The Relationship Between Type of Man and Type of Company* (East Lansing: Bureau of Business and Economic Research, Michigan State University, 1967). See also Norman R. Smith and John B. Miner, "Type of Entrepreneur, Type of Firm, and Managerial Motivation: Implications for Organizational Life Cycle Theory," *Strategic Management Journal,* Vol. 4, No. 4 (October–December 1983), pp. 325–340; Carolyn Y. Woo, Arnold C. Cooper, and William C. Dunkelberg, "The Development and Interpretation of Entrepreneurial Typologies," *Journal of Business Venturing,* Vol. 6, No. 2 (March 1991), pp. 93–114.

21. Center for Women's Business Research, http://www.cfwbr.org/national/index.php, accessed January 31, 2007.

22. U.S. Small Business Administration, "Idaho's Small Business Person of the Year," http://www.sba.gov/id/success; accessed August 6, 2003; Del E. Web School of Construction, "Elaine Martin," http://construction.asu.edu/banquet/wom_2002_bio, accessed August 6, 2003; Aliza Pilar Sherman, "Wild, Wild West," *Entrepreneur,* July 2002, p. 30.

23. Aliza Pilar Sherman, "A Man's World," *Entrepreneur,* August 2003, p. 26.

24. Personal conversation with Jim Ruschman, June 2001.

25. Jeffry A. Timmons and Stephen Spinelli, *New Venture Creation: Entrepreneurship for the 21st Century* (New York: McGraw-Hill/Irwin, 2007), p. 326.

26. Thomas L. Friedman, *The World Is Flat* (Waterville, ME: Thorndike Press, 2005).

27. Chris Pentilla, "All Shook Up," *Entrepreneur,* December 2005, pp. 112–113.

28. Steve Hamm and Ian Rowley "Speed Demons," *Business Week,* March 27, 2006, pp. 68–76.

29. Chris Penttila, "Keeping Fresh," *Entrepreneur,* Vol. 33, No. 4 (April 2005), p. 86.

30. Pete Engardio, with Michael Arndt and Dean Foust, "The Future of Offshoring," *Business Week,* January 30, 2006, p. 46.

31. Personal conversation with Lowe's Supermarkets' management, January 2007.

32. Sarah Wilson, "Learning from the Best," *Entrepreneur,* March 2006, p. 62.

33. Personal conversation with Tyler Self, November 2006.

34. Cited in Gary M. Stern, "Young Entrepreneurs Make Their Mark," *Nation's Business,* Vol. 84, No. 8 (August 1996), pp. 49–51.

35. Patricia B. Gray, "Beats Bussing Tables," *Fortune Small Business,* http://money.cnn.com/ galleries/2007/fsb/0701/gallery. entrepreneur_profiles/4.html, accessed February 16, 2007.

36. http://www.womenhomebusiness. com/success/glenfiddich.htm, February 8, 2006.

37. J. B. Rotter, "Generalized Expectancies for Internal versus External Control of Reinforcement," *Psychological Monographs,* 1966. A more recent review is given in Robert H. Brockhaus, Sr., and Pamela S. Horwitz, "The Psychology of the Entrepreneur," in Donald L. Sexton and Raymond W. Smilor (eds.), *The Art and Science of Entrepreneurship* (Cambridge, MA: Ballinger, 1986), pp. 25–48.

38. Timmons and Spinelli, *op. cit.,* pp. 249–255.

39. See Walter Kuemmerle, "A Test for the Fainthearted," *Harvard Business Review,* May 2002, pp. 4–8.

40. Roberta Maynard, "Sliding into Home," *Nation's Business,* Vol. 86, No. 1 (January 1998), p. 52.

41. Paul Rerucha, Letters, *Inc.,* Vol. 22, No. 16 (November 2000), p. 22.

42. Personal interview with Ed Bonneau, 2006.

43. *Ibid.*

44. Ilan Mochari, "What Would You Do Differently?" *Inc.,* Vol. 23, No. 3 (March 2001), p. 65.

45. Personal conversation with Bernard Rapaport, 2006.

46. Stephen R. Covey, *The Seven Habits of Highly Effective People* (New York: Simon and Schuster, 1989), pp. 106–142.

CHAPTER 2

1. Max DePree, *Leadership Is an Art* (New York: Bantam Dell, 1989), pp. xvii–xviii.

2. Leslie E. Palich, Justin G. Longenecker, Carlos W. Moore, and J. William Petty, "Integrity and Small Business: A Framework and Empirical Analysis," Proceedings of the 49th World Conference of the International Council for Small Business, Johannesburg, South Africa, June 2004.

3. Laura L. Nash, *Good Intentions Aside: A Manager's Guide to Resolving Ethical Problems* (Boston: Harvard Business School Press, 1993), p. 61.

4. Milton Friedman, *Capitalism and Freedom* (Chicago: University of Chicago Press, 1963), p. 133.

5. Jana Matthews and Jeff Dennis, *Lessons from the Edge: Survival Skills for Starting and Growing a Company* (Oxford: Oxford University Press, 2003), pp. 119–123.

6. Hattie Bryant, Producer of Small Business School, the series on PBS Stations, Worldnet, and the Web at http://smallbusinessschool.org.

7. Jodie Carter, "Rolling in Dough," *Entrepreneur,* Vol. 31, No. 6 (June 2003), p. 106; and personal conversation with Mike Jacobs, October 6, 2006.

8. David Dorsey, "Happiness Pays," *Inc.,* Vol. 26, No. 2 (February 2004), pp. 88–94.

9. Palich et al., *op. cit.*

10. Geoff Williams, "Call for Help," *Entrepreneur,* Vol. 30, No. 7 (July 2002), p. 32.

11. http://www.salesforce.com/ company/management.jsp, accessed September 29, 2006;

and "Two-Faced Capitalism," *The Economist,* January 22, 2004.

12. Michael Kinsman, "Corporate Caring," *San Diego Union-Tribune,* December 15, 1997, p. C-1.

13. Kenneth E. Aupperle, F. Bruce Simmons, III, and William Acar, "An Empirical Investigation into How Entrepreneurs View Their Social Responsibilities," paper presented at the Academy of Management Meetings, San Francisco, California, August 1990.

14. Priscilla Elsass, "The Cost of Illegal Business Practices," *Academy of Management Executive,* Vol. 12, No. 1 (February 1998), pp. 87–88.

15. "Cone Corporate Citizenship Study," http://www.coneinc. com/Pages/pr_30.html, accessed September 29, 2006.

16. William J. Dennis, Jr., "Contributions to Community," National Federation of Independent Business, quarterly research report, Vol 4, No. 6 (2004).

17. Janet Novack, "You Know Who You Are, and So Do We," *Forbes,* Vol. 153, No. 8 (April 11, 1994), pp. 88–92.

18. Eric Knopf, "One Step at a Time," in Michael McMyne and Nicole Amare (eds.), *Beyond the Lemonade Stand: 14 Undergraduate Entrepreneurs Tell Their Stories of Ethics in Business,* (St. Louis, MO: St. Louis University, 2004) pp. 47–48.

19. Paulette Thomas, "Virtual Business Plans Require Human Touch," *The Wall Street Journal,* August 2, 2005, p. B2.

20. Nadine Heintz, "For Rolling Up Her Sleeves," *Inc.,* April 2004, pp. 128–129.

21. Justin G. Longenecker, Joseph A. McKinney, and Carlos W. Moore, "Egoism and Independence: Entrepreneurial Ethics," *Organizational Dynamics,* Vol. 16, No. 3 (Winter 1988), pp. 64–72.

22. These differences were significant at the .05 level.

23. Justin G. Longenecker, Carlos W. Moore, J. William Petty, Leslie E. Palich, and Joseph A. McKinney, "Ethical Attitudes in Small

Businesses and Large Corporations: Theory and Empirical Findings from a Tracking Study Spanning Three Decades," *Journal of Small Business Management,* Vol. 44, No. 2 (2006), pp. 167–183.

24. These differences were significant at the .05 level.

25. John C. Maxwell and Jim Dornan, *Becoming a Person of Influence* (Nashville, TN: Thomas Nelson Publisher, 1997), p. 20.

26. As cited in Jeffrey L. Siglin, "Do It Right," *MBA Jungle,* November 2001, p. 69.

27. Del Jones, "Poll: More Workers Value E-Mail, Voice-Mail Privacy," *USAToday,* March 27, 2000, p. 1B.

28. David H. Freedman, "Worried That Employees Are Wasting Time on the Web? Here's Why You Shouldn't Crack Down," *Inc.,* Vol. 28, No. 8 (August 2006), pp. 77–78.

29. "2005 Electronic Monitoring & Surveillance Survey: Many Companies Monitoring, Recording, Videotaping—and Firing—Employees," American Management Association and The ePolicy Institute, May 18, 2005, http://amanet.org/press/amanews/ems05.htm, accessed October 2, 2006.

30. Pamela Mendels, "The Rise of the Chief Privacy Officer," *BusinessWeek,* http://www.businessweek.com, accessed December 14, 2000.

31. Carl M. Cannon, "Ambushed," *Forbes ASAP,* February 19, 2001, p. 50.

32. "Fake Gucci, Vuitton Bags Seized in Italy," CNNMoney.com, September 25, 2006, http://money.cnn.com/2006/09/25/news/international/counterfeit_bags.reut/index.htm?postversion=2006092518, accessed October 2, 2006.

33. Gail Edmondson, Kate Carlisle, Inka Resch, Karen Nickel Anhalt, and Heidi Dawley, "Workers in Bondage," *BusinessWeek,* No. 3709 (November 27, 2000), pp. 146–162.

34. Nicholas G. Moore, "Ethics: The Way to Do Business," speech given at the Sears Lectureship in Business Ethics, Bentley College, Waltham, MA, February 9, 1998.

35. A study by Justin G. Longenecker, Joseph A. McKinney, and Carlos W. Moore ["Religious Intensity, Evangelical Christianity, and Business Ethics: An Empirical Study," *Journal of Business Ethics,* Vol. 55, No. 2 (2004), pp. 373–386] provides evidence to support this position. The authors examined data from 1,234 business leaders responding to a national survey. They asked study participants to evaluate the ethical quality of responses described in a series of vignettes (from "never acceptable" to "always acceptable") and also to identify which of the following five broad categories best described their religious faith: Catholic, Protestant, Jewish, other religions, no religion. Study results found no difference between these general groups. However, respondents who indicated that religious interests were of high or moderate importance to them demonstrated a higher level of ethical judgment than did others in the study, as did those who considered their beliefs to be consistent with the basic tenets of Evangelical Christianity. These findings suggest that religious values play a part in ethical decision making, though *general* religious categorizations do not seem to have this same impact.

36. Moore, *op. cit.*

37. Jan Cienski, "Faith Jostles with Profits for Some Christian Businesses," *Waco Tribune-Herald,* May 24, 1997.

38. *Ibid.;* and "The Best 100 Companies to Work For," *Fortune,* Vol. 143, No. 1 (January 8, 2001), pp. 148–168.

39. Excerpt from an interview with J. C. Huizenga in "Virtuous Business and Educational Practice," *Religion & Liberty* (a publication of the Acton Institute for the Study of Religion and Liberty), Vol. 12, No. 2 (September-October 2002), p. 1.

40. Kenneth H. Blanchard and Norman Vincent Peale, *The Power of Ethical Management* (New York: Harper-Collins, 1989).

41. J. Michael Alford, "Finding Competitive Advantage in Managing Workplace Ethics," paper presented at the 2005 meeting of the United States Association for Small Business and Entrepreneurship, Indian Wells, California, January 13–16, 2005.

42. Sample codes of ethics can be obtained from the Ethics Resource Center, Inc., 1025 Connecticut Avenue, N.W., Washington, DC 22036.

43. "Resource Toolkit: The PLUS Decision Making Model," Ethics Resource Center, http://www.ethics.org/resources/plus_decisionmaking.html, accessed October 3, 2006.

44. http://www.rotary.org/aboutrotary/4way.html, October 24, 2003.

45. Brian K. Burton and Michael Goldsby ["The Golden Rule and Business Ethics: An Examination," *Journal of Business Ethics,* Vol. 56, No. 3 (2005), pp. 371–383] offer an extended discussion of the history, meaning, and problems of the Golden Rule. They document the appearance of this general principle in the writings of several major world religions and philosophers and provide examples of companies that have used the Golden Rule explicitly as a guide for decision making (e.g., JCPenney and Lincoln Electric Co.). The influence of the Golden Rule is so pervasive that Burton and Goldsby conclude that it "seems to be one of the few candidates for a universally acceptable moral principle."

46. Kant actually offered a critique of the Golden Rule, but only as a footnote to his discussion of the categorial imperative. In his opinion, the categorical imperative is a superior concept for a number of reasons, all of which are related to his expanded view of the imperative [see Immanuel Kant, *Grounding for the Metaphysics of Morals, with a Supposed Right to Lie Because of Philanthropic Concerns,* 3rd ed., trans. J.W. Ellington (Indianapolis: Hackett Publishing, 1993)].

47. This definition is offered in James Austin, Howard Stevenson, and Jane Wei-Skillern, "Social and Commercial Entrepreneurship: Same, Different, or Both?" *Entrepreneurship Theory & Practice,* Vol. 30, No. 1 (2006), pp. 1–22. However, the authors recognize that definitions of the term vary from an emphasis on nonprofit enterprises to corporate philanthropy and many other activities. Indeed, in their article, Austin, Stevenson, and Wei-Skillern identify key differences between social and commercial entrepreneurship. Using Sahlman's analytical framework [W. A. Sahlman, "Some Thoughts on Business Plans," in W. A. Sahlman, H. Stevenson, M. J. Roberts, and A. V. Bhide (eds.), *The Entrepreneurial Venture* (Boston: Harvard Business School Press, 1996), pp. 138–176], the authors compare the two forms of entrepreneurship across four factors: the *people,* the *context,* the *deal,* and the *opportunity.* They highlight substantial differences across all four factors. For example, commercial entrepreneurs tend to focus on breakthrough opportunities where new needs are emerging, whereas social entrepreneurs are concerned with opportunities based on basic, longstanding needs that can be served more effectively with innovative approaches. However, they also conclude there are notable similarities. Taken together, the authors' observations suggest that the concept of social entrepreneurship, though becoming less ambiguous, is still not defined to the satisfaction of many entrepreneurship researchers.

48. Paul Sloan, "Doughing the Right Thing," *Business 2.0,* Vol. 7, No. 7 (August 2006), p. 82.

49. Elaine Pofeldt, "Beyond the Bottom Line," *Fortune,* Vol. 150, No. 13 (December 27, 2004), p. 170[H].

50. Esther Nguonly, "Wheels of Fortune," *Entrepreneur,* Vol. 33, No. 3 (March 2005), p. 128.

51. "Greening Your Business: A Primer for Smaller Companies," http://www.greenbiz. com/toolbox/essentials_third. cfm?LinkAdvID=15205, accessed October 24, 2006.

52. http://www.epa.gov/epaoswer/ hazwaste/sqg/sqghand.htm, accessed October 20, 2006.

53. Sara Wilson, "Clean and Green," *Entrepreneur,* Vol. 33, No. 10 (October 2005), p. 20.

54. April Y. Pennington, "Making a Move," *Entrepreneur,* Vol. 33, No. 4 (April 2005), p. 118.

55. Esther Nguonly, "Garden State," *Entrepreneur,* Vol. 33, No. 4 (April 2005), p. 127.

56. Lora Kolodny, "A New Industry Dials Up Growth," *Inc.,* Vol. 27, No. 2 (February 2005), p. 22.

57. See David Worrell, "Keen on Green," *Entrepreneur,* Vol. 34, No. 9 (September 2006), pp. 67–71, for a helpful summary of trends related to "green" technologies and the investments they have attracted.

58. Karen E. Spaeder, "Think Green," *Entrepreneur,* Vol. 34, No. 3 (March 2006), pp. 52–53; Roger Sideman, "New Solar-Powered Trash Cans Put the Squeeze on Downtown Mess," October 3, 2006, http://www.santacruzsentinel.com/archive/2006/October03/local/stories/02local. htm, accessed October 23, 2006; Donald Bertrand, "BigBelly Puts the Squeeze on Garbage," *Daily News* (New York), August 14, 2006, p. 1; Matt Viser, "Solar-Power Compactors Press the Mess in Boston," *The Boston Globe,* July 26, 2006, p. A1; and "About Seahorse Power Company," http://www. seahorsepower.com/about.php, accessed October 23, 2006.

59. Bo Burlingham, "The Coolest Little Start-Up in America," *Inc.,* July 2006, pp. 78–85; Gary Wisby, "Kids Help Turn Worm Poop into a Growth Industry," *Chicago Sun-Times,* May 2, 2006, p. 20; "Early Years," http://www.terracycle.net/ history.htm, accessed October 20, 2006; and "The TerraCycle Story," http://www.terracycle.net/story. htm, accessed October 20, 2006.

60. Marc Gunter, "Tree Huggers, Soy Lovers, and Profits," *Fortune,* Vol. 147, No. 12 (June 23, 2003), pp. 99–104.

CHAPTER 3

1. To read more about an interesting framework that integrates three forms of the search process (deliberate search, industry insight guided search, and alertness to opportunities), see Robert A. Baron, "Opportunity Recognition as Pattern Recognition: How Entrepreneurs 'Connect the Dots' to Identify New Business Opportunities," *Academy of Management Perspectives,* Vol. 20, No. 1 (February 2006), pp. 104–119.

2. Israel M. Kirzner, *Competition and Entrepreneurship* (Chicago: University of Chicago Press, 1973), p. 74.

3. For an in-depth discussion of the concept and the essence of the mindset of the entrepreneur, see Jeffery S. McMullen and Dean A. Shepherd, "Entrepreneurial Action and the Role of Uncertainty in the Theory of the Entrepreneur," *Academy of Management Review,* Vol. 31, No. 1 (2006), pp. 132–152.

4. Amar Bhide, "Bootstrap Finance: The Art of Start-Ups," *Harvard Business Review,* Vol. 70, No. 6 (November-December 1992), pp. 109–117.

5. For the latest information on Branson's enterprise, visit http:// www.virgingalactic.com.

6. Quoted in Mark Henricks, "What Not to Do," *Entrepreneur,* Vol. 32, No. 2 (February 2004), pp. 84–90.

7. Quoted in April Y. Pennington, "Copy That: In Business, Imitation Is More Than a Form of Flattery," *Entrepreneur,* Vol. 34, No. 3 (March 2006), p. 22.

8. Lee Gimpel, "Idea Mining," *Entrepreneur,* Vol. 34, No. 12 (December 2006), p. 70.

9. Jim Hopkins, "Ex-GM, Pentagon Official Scoots into Own Startup," *USAToday,* May 21, 2003, p. 7B.

10. "Electric Bicycles to Be Introduced at Bicycle Industry Trade Show—Clean, Green, No Gasoline—Real Electric Transportation—Just Pennies per Charge to Operate," press release, September 26, 2005, http://www.prweb.com/releases/2005/9/prweb289689.php, accessed November 16, 2006.

11. Jada Cash, "Cure Couture," *Entrepreneur,* Vol. 34, No. 12 (December 2006), p. 128.

12. Gerry E.Hills and R. P. Singh, "Opportunity Recognition," in W. B. Gartner, K. G. Shaver, and P. D. Reynolds (eds.), *Handbook of Entrepreneurial Dynamics: The Process of Business Creation* (Thousand Oaks, CA: Sage Publications, 2004), Table 24.4, p. 268.

13. April Y. Pennington, "Snapshot," *Entrepreneur,* Vol. 31, No. 9 (September 2003), p. 23.

14. John Heilemann, "Digging Up the News," *Business 2.0,* Vol. 7, No. 3 (April 2006), pp. 42–44.

15. Nichole L. Torres, "Roamin' Holiday," *Entrepreneur,* Vol. 31, No. 9 (September 2003), p. 102.

16. http://www.totelemonde.com/aboutus.html, accessed November 16, 2006.

17. Edward Clendaniel, "Greek Hero," *Forbes ASAP,* April 2, 2001, p. 24.

18. Caryn Eve Murray, "The World in His Pocket," *Newsday,* March 2, 2003, http://www.newsday.com/news/local/longisland/ny-lfcov0302,0,1730732,print.story?coll=ny-homepage-longisland-utility, accessed November 16, 2006.

19. Peter Drucker, *Innovation and Entrepreneurship* (New York: HarperBusiness, 1993), p. 35.

20. Peter F. Drucker, "The Discipline of Innovation," *Harvard Business Review,* Vol. 76, No. 6 (November-December 1998), p. 149.

21. http://www.aimiesdinnerandmovie.com, accessed November 17, 2006.

22. Lauren Etter, "The Joys of Juggling," *Wall Street Journal,* January 30, 2006, p. R9.

23. Susan Warren, "To Scare Off Grackles, Texans Pull Out Guns and Strobe Lights," *Wall Street Journal,* January 19, 2005, p. A1.

24. Chris Pentila, "Hit or Miss," *Entrepreneur,* Vol. 32, No. 6 (June 2004), pp.108–113.

25. *Ibid.*

26. Nichole L. Torres, "New and Improved," *Entrepreneur,* Vol. 33, No. 5 (May 2005), p. 96.

27. Amanda Pennington, "Creature Comforts," *Entrepreneur,* Vol. 34, No. 7 (July 2006), pp. 120–122.

28. Kristin Ohlson, "Niche Gyms," *Entrepreneur,* Vol. 34, No. 12 (December 2006), p. 90.

29. Siri Schubert, "A Duffer's Dream," *Business 2.0,* Vol. 7, No. 10 (November 2006), p. 56.

30. Tony Manning, *Making Sense of Strategy* (New York: American Management Association, 2002), p. 17.

31. Much of the research on this subject is based on firms of all sizes, not just small businesses; however, there is no reason to rule out entirely the applicability of this research to entrepreneurial companies. Some studies present strong evidence that context is important [Suresh Kotha and Anil Nair, "Strategy and Environment as Determinants of Performance: Evidence from the Japanese Machine Tool Industry," *Strategic Management Journal,* Vol. 16, No. 7 (1995), pp. 497–518; A. M. McGahan and Michael E. Porter, "How Much Does Industry Matter, Really?" *Strategic Management Journal,* Vol. 18, Summer Special Issue (1997), pp. 15–30; R. Schmalensee, "Do Markets Differ Much?" *American Economic Review,* Vol. 75, No. 3 (1985), pp. 341–351], whereas others show that context is important but not as great a driver of firm performance as such internal factors as a company's resources [Gabriel Hawawini, Venkat Subramanian, and Paul Verdin, "Is Performance Driven by Industry- or Firm-Specific Factors? A New Look at the Evidence," *Strategic Management Journal,* Vol. 24, No. 1 (2003), pp. 1–16;

Mona Makhija, "Comparing the Resource-Based and Market-Based Views of the Firm: Empirical Evidence from Czech Privatization," *Strategic Management Journal,* Vol. 24, No. 3 (2003), pp. 433–451]. Thomas J. Douglas and Joel A. Ryman ["Understanding Competitive Advantage in the General Hospital Industry: Evaluating Strategic Competencies," *Strategic Management Journal,* Vol. 24, No. 2 (2003), pp. 333–347] interpret the results of their study to suggest that both external context and internal factors are important to the formation of competitive advantage, a conclusion that is consistent with evidence from studies of small and medium-sized enterprises, such as those conducted by Bo Eriksen and Thorbjorn Knudsen ["Industry and Firm Level Interaction: Implications for Profitability," *Journal of Business Research,* Vol. 56, No. 3 (2003), pp. 191–199], Stewart Thornhill ["Knowledge, Innovation and Firm Performance in High- and Low-Technology Regimes," *Journal of Business Venturing,* Vol. 21, No. 5 (2006), pp. 687–703], and Clement K. Wang and Bee Lian Ang ["Determinants of Venture Performance in Singapore," *Journal of Small Business Management,* Vol. 42, No. 4 (2004), pp. 347–363].

32. Logan Kugler, "Targeting the Eye in the Sky," *Business 2.0,* Vol. 7, No. 3 (April 2006), p. 26.

33. Rich Karlgard, "Schumpeter on Speed," *Forbes,* Vol. 178, No. 3 (August 14, 2006), p. 35.

34. Kelly Greene, "Still Sexy at 60?" *Wall Street Journal,* July 25, 2006, p. B1.

35 Krysten Crawford, "The Big Opportunity," *Business 2.0,* Vol. 7, No. 5 (June 2006), pp. 95–99.

36. *Ibid.*

37. Michael Porter, *Competitive Advantage* (New York: Free Press, 1985), pp. 7–29.

38. Personal communication with Bill Waugh and Burger Street management; and http://www.burgerstreet.com, accessed December 1, 2006.

39. William A. Sahlman, "How to Write a Great Business Plan," *Harvard Business Review,* Vol. 75, No. 4 (July-August 1997), pp. 103–104.

40. Paul Hansen, "Big Dog Motorcycles Encourages Riders to 'Break the Leash' in New Advertising," press release, October 24, 2006; and Karen Stevens and Dale Kurschner, "That Vroom! You Hear May Not Be a Harley," *BusinessWeek,* No. 3549 (October 20, 1997), p. 159.

41. Gary Hamel, "Strategy as Revolution," *Harvard Business Review,* Vol. 74, No. 4 (July-August 1996), p. 80.

42. For an interesting discussion of this case and others where relaxing assumptions that guide business behavior has made a significant difference in entrepreneurial efforts of businesses around the world, see C. K. Prahalad, *The Fortune at the Bottom of the Pyramid: Eradicating Poverty through Profits* (Upper Saddle River, NJ: Wharton School Publishing, 2005).

43. Hamel, *op. cit.*

44. http://www.starbucks.com, accessed December 1, 2006.

45. http://www.kens-fishfarm.com, accessed December 1, 2006; and James P. Serba, "Here's Why Asians Are All Hopped Up about Frog Farming," *Wall Street Journal,* March 17, 2001, pp. A1, A8.

46. William M. Bulkeley, "The Competitor," *Wall Street Journal,* October 28, 2002, p. R8.

47. It should be pointed out that a recent study of small businesses conducted by the National Federation of Independent Business found that 34.4 percent of all small businesses surveyed said that competing on price is a very significant feature of their strategy, which is consistent with an emphasis on controlling costs (specifically, 51 percent said that keeping overhead to a minimum is a very significant feature of their strategy). However, it is also important to note that providing better service and offering the highest quality possible were significantly important to even more firms (83.4 percent and 86.3 percent, respectively), which indicates that differentiation strategies are even more important to small businesses. See William J. Dennis, Jr. (ed.), "Competition," *National Small Business Poll,* Vol. 3, No. 8 (2003).

48. April Pennington, "Worn Well," *Entrepreneur,* Vol. 34, No. 4 (April 2006), p. 32.

49. *Ibid.*

50. http://www.ufit.com, accessed December 5, 2006.

51. Philip Kotler, *Marketing Insights from A to Z* (New York: John Wiley & Sons, 2003), p. 65.

52. Mark Halper, "Revving up the PC," *Business 2.0,* Vol. 6, No. 10 (November 2005), pp. 70–72.

53. John Naisbitt, *Global Paradox* (New York: Morrow, 1994).

54. Daniel Nasaw, "Shrinking Supply Crimps Bright Hopes for Growth," http://www.startupjournal.com/columnists/enterprise/20030828-nasaw.html, accessed December 6, 2006; and "Historic Newspapers Ltd," http://www.rsascotland.gov.uk/rsa/355.html, accessed August 29, 2007.

55. Nasaw, *op. cit.*

56. Nasaw, *op. cit.*

57. Amar Bhide, "How Entrepreneurs Craft Strategies That Work," *Harvard Business Review,* Vol. 72, No. 2 (March-April 1992), p. 154.

58. William A. Cohen, *The Art of the Strategist: 10 Essential Principles for Leading Your Company to Victory* (New York: AMACOM Books, 2004), p. 127.

59. http://www.zanescycles.com, accessed December 6, 2006; and Donna Fenn, "A Bigger Wheel," *Inc.,* Vol. 22, No. 16 (November 2000), pp. 78–88.

60. Porter, *op. cit.,* p. 5.

CHAPTER 4

1. http://www.expressfranchising.com, January 12, 2007.

2. http://www.franchiseregistry.com/partnership.asp, April 7, 2004.

3. Dianne H. B., Welsh, Ilan Alon, and Cecilia M. Falbe, "An Examination of International Retail Franchising in Emerging Markets," *Journal of Small Business Management,* Vol. 44, No. 1 (2006), pp. 130–149.

4. http://www.gaebler.com, January 12, 2007.

5. Dennis Rodkin, "Leap of Faith," *Entrepreneur,* Vol. 26, No. 2 (February 1998), pp. 150–155.

6. Peter Weaver, "New Owners Take Stock," *Business Advisor,* January–February 2001, pp. 12–15.

7. http://www.astutediligence.com, January 12, 2007.

8. *Ibid.*

CHAPTER 5

1. James Hayton, "Explaining Competitive Advantage in Family Firms: The Effectuation Paradox," paper presented at the 2006 meeting of the United States Association of Small Business and Entrepreneurship, Tucson, Arizona, January 2006.

2. These findings seem to be consistent across studies. For example, this is reported in Isabelle Le Breton-Miller and Danny Miller, "Why Do Some Family Businesses Out-Compete? Governance, Long-Term Orientations, and Sustainable Capabilities," *Entrepreneurship Theory and Practice,* Vol. 30, No. 6 (November 2006), p. 731. The article reports the specific measures tested in various studies and offers a theoretical model to explain the superior performance of family-controlled businesses. Another study that confirms these findings and offers its own theory on the topic is Jim Lee, "Family Firm Performance: Further Evidence," *Family Business Review,* Vol. 19, No. 2 (June 2006), pp. 103–115.

3. Family-owned businesses have been surprisingly well studied. In fact, the highly regarded journal *Entrepreneurship Theory and*

Practice has recently published an ongoing series of special issues exploring various theories and facets of family enterprise. A total of 38 articles have been published as part of this series, dating back to the summer of 2003 (see Vol. 27, No. 4; Vol. 28, No. 4; Vol. 29, No. 3; and Vol. 30, No. 6). These articles represent much of the cutting edge work done on the topic.

4. This is only one definition among many offered in the literature on family-owned businesses, but most definitions address three core elements: family ownership and control, family involvement in management, and the expectation of family succession [see Michael Carney, "Corporate Governance and Competitive Advantage in Family-Controlled Firms," *Entrepreneurship Theory and Practice,* Vol. 29, No. 3 (May 2005), pp. 249–266].

5. For these findings and others, see William J. Dennis, Jr. (ed.), "Families in Business," *NFIB National Small Business Poll,* Vol. 2, No. 6 (2002), p. 1.

6. *Ibid.,* p. 17.

7. This is reported in Khai Sheang Lee, Guan Hua Lim, and Wei Shi Lim, "Family Business Succession: Appropriation Risk and Choice of Successor," *Academy of Management Review,* Vol. 28, No. 4 (October 2003), pp. 657–658.

8. Jerry Haar, "Miami Business: All in the Family," *Take Five,* (January-February 2005), http://www. pinoentrepreneurshipcenter.com/view_article.asp?newsletter=39 &id83, accessed December 15, 2006; and Mary Winter, Sharon M. Danes, Sun-Kang Koh, Kelly Fredericks, and Jennifer J. Paul, "Tracking Family Businesses and Their Owners over Time: Panel Attrition, Manager Departure and Business Demise," *Journal of Business Venturing,* Vol. 19, No. 4 (2004), pp. 537.

9. Lowell J. Spirer, *The Human Factor in Starting Your Own Business* (BlueBell, PA: Lowell J. Spirer, n.d.), e-book.

10. Meg Lundstrom, "Mommy, Do You Love Your Company More than Me?" *BusinessWeek,* No. 3660 (December 20, 1999), p. 175.

11. "Self-Awareness and Family Importance," http://bases.stanford. edu/forums/viewtopic.php?t=688 &sid=a02336ac762514260cb33a6e 73e009ba, accessed December 12, 2006; John Canter, "A New Retailer Learns to Curtail Long Hours," StartupJournal.com, http://www. startupjournal.com/columnists/ entrepreneursdiary/20041110-canter.html, accessed December 13, 2006; Mark Henricks, "Parent Trap?" *Entrepreneur,* Vol. 33, No. 9 (September 2005), p. 17; and Kevin Voigt, "Tales from the Trenches: Balancing Work and Family," CareerJournal.com, http://www. careerjournal.com/myc/ workfamily/20041005-voigt.html, accessed December 13, 2006.

12. Kerry Capell, "Sweden's Answer to Sam Walton," *Business Week,* No. 3959 (November 14, 2005), pp. 96–106; "Ingvar Kamprad: Ikea Always Was a Disaster to Assemble," TimesOnline, February 13, 2005, http://www.timesonline. co.uk/article/0,,2088-1481652,00. html, accessed December 14, 2006; and http://www.ikea.com, accessed December 14, 2006.

13. Daniel L. McConaughy, "Family CEOs vs. Non-Family CEOs in the Family-Controlled Firm: An Examination of the Level and Sensitivity of Pay to Performance," *Family Business Review,* Vol. 13, No. 2 (June 2000), pp. 121–131; and Simon Bartholomeusz and George A. Tanewski, "The Relationship Between Family Firms and Corporate Governance," *Journal of Small Business Management,* Vol. 44, No. 2 (April 2006), pp. 245–267.

14. David G. Sirmon and Michael A. Hitt, "Managing Resources: Linking Unique Resources, Management, and Wealth Creation in Family Firms," *Entrepreneurship Theory and Practice,* Vol. 27, No. 4 (Summer 2003), pp. 341–344. These findings are consistent with the results of other recent

research—see, for example, Ronald C. Anderson and David M. Reeb, "Founding-Family Ownership and Firm Performance: Evidence from the S&P 500," *Journal of Finance,* Vol. 58, No. 3 (June 2003), pp. 1301–1328.

15. John L. Ward, "New Research on Family Business Culture," proceedings of the Fifth Annual Kellogg Family Business Invitational Conference, Evanston, IL, May 16–17, 2006, pp. 51–65.

16. W. Gibb Dyer and David A. Whetten, "Family Firms and Social Responsibility: Preliminary Evidence from the S&P 500," *Entrepreneurship Theory and Practice,* Vol. 30, No. 6 (November 2006), pp. 785–802.

17. "Chick-fil-A Founder and Restaurant Industry Icon Truett Cathy Celebrates 60 Years in the Restaurant Business," press release, May 17, 2006, http://www.mar-ketwire.com/mw/release_html_b1? release_id=129730, accessed December 15, 2006.

18. http://media.marketwire.com/ attachments/EZIR/112/349199_ 7CowAppreciationDayRelease.doc, accessed July 18, 2007.

19. A description of these bases of commitment and an extensive discussion of the theory and analysis that back up these conclusions can be found in Pramodita Sharma and P. Gregory Irving, "Four Bases of Family Business Successor Commitment: Antecedents and Consequences," *Entrepreneurship Theory and Practice,* Vol. 29, No. 1 (January 2005), pp. 13–33. Our discussion of these commitment bases and the quotes we use are sourced from this article.

20. *Ibid.,* pp. 25–26.

21. Quoted in Jeff D. Opdyke, "Readers' Views on Family, Feuds and Quality of Life," CareerJournal. com, April 26, 2005, http://www. careerjournal.com/myc/ workfamily/20050426-opdyke. html, accessed December 13, 2006.

22. Loretta Chao, "When Your Spouse Is Your Business Partner,"

StartupJournal.com, September 28, 2005, http://www.startupjournal. com/runbusiness/family/20050928-chao.html, accessed December 19, 2006.

23. Sue Birley, "Attitudes of Owner-Managers' Children Toward Family and Business Issues," *Entrepreneurship Theory and Practice,* Vol. 26, No. 3 (Summer 2002), pp. 5–19.

24. Jonathan Black, "How to Raise an Entrepreneur," *Inc.,* Vol. 27, No. 8 (August 2005), pp. 81–85.

25. Teo Pau Lin, "Spilling the Beans," *The Straits Times,* July 16, 2006, http://www.stomp.com.sg/ stfoodiesclub/hawkerfare/28/ index.html, accessed December 20, 2006.

26. John L. Ward, "Family Humor," proceedings of the Fifth Annual Kellogg Family Business Invitational Conference, Evanston, IL, May 16–17, 2006, p. 45.

27. *Ibid.*

28. Darren Dahl, "Was Firing Him Too Drastic?" *Inc.,* Vol. 28, No. 10 (October 2006), pp. 51–54.

29. Jeff Dennis, "Your Not-So-Silent Partner," *Profit,* Vol. 24, No. 2 (May 2005), pp. 21–22.

30. John L. Ward, quoted in Margaret Steen, "The Decision Tree of Family Business," *Stanford Business,* August 2006, http://www.gsb. stanford.edu/news/bmag/ sbsm0608/feature_familybiz.html, accessed December 22, 2006.

31. Kenneth Meeks, "Family Business," *Black Enterprise,* Vol. 34, No. 1 (August 2003), p. 91.

32. Matthew Fogel, "A More Perfect Business," *Inc.,* Vol. 25, No. 8 (August 2003), p. 44.

33. *Ibid.*

34. John L. Ward, "Family Humor," proceedings of the Fifth Annual Kellogg Family Business Invitational Conference, Evanston, IL, May 16–17, 2006, p. 46.

35. *Ibid.,* p. 47.

36. Timothy Aeppel, "A Father and Son Meld New Economy and Old, and the Business Flows," *Wall Street Journal,* May 24, 2000, pp. A1, A16.

37. For an extended discussion of various aspects of mentoring in the family firm, see Barbara Spector (ed.), *The Family Business Mentoring Handbook* (Philadelphia: Family Business Publishing Co., 2004). Only one of many resources on mentoring, this edited volume provides articles outlining a number of proven mentoring strategies as well as case examples of family companies that have used these approaches to achieve effective succession transitions. The book addresses processes and strategies as they apply specifically to family businesses.

38. This topic is explored in depth in Johan Lambrecht, "Multigenerational Transition in Family Businesses: A New Explanatory Model," *Family Business Review,* Vol. 18, No. 4 (2005), pp. 267–282. We base our model of succession in this chapter primarily on the work of Lambrecht.

39. Austin Ramirez, quoted in Margaret Steen, "The Decision Tree of Family Business," *Stanford Business,* August 2006, http://www. gsb.stanford.edu/news/bmag/ sbsm0608/feature_familybiz.html, accessed December 22, 2006.

CHAPTER 6

1. Amar Bhide, *The Origin and Evolution of New Businesses* (New York: Oxford University Press, 2000).

2. The MIT Enterprise Forum (http:// web.mit.edu/entforum) sponsors sessions across the United States in which aspiring entrepreneurs present business plans to panels of venture capitalists, bankers, marketing specialists, and other experts.

3. David E. Gumpert, *How to Really Create a Successful Business Plan,* 4th ed. (Needham, MA: Lauson Publishing Co., 2003), p. 10.

4. Several of these studies include Stephen C. Perry, "The Relationship Between Written Business Plans and the Failure of Small Business in the U.S.," *Journal of Small Business Management,* Vol. 39, No. 2 (2001), pp. 201–208; Frederic Delmar and Scott Shane, "Does Business Planning Facilitate the Development of New Ventures?" *Strategic Management Journal,* December 2003, pp. 1165–1185; Scott Shane and Frederick Delmar, "Planning for the Market: Business Planning Before Marketing and the Continuation of Organizing Efforts," *Journal of Business Venturing,* Vol. 19 (2004), pp. 767–785; Tomas Karlsson, Benson Honig, and Wilfrid Laurrier, "Business Planning Practices in New Ventures: An Institutional Perspective," presented at the Babson Conference, April 2007; and Julian E. Lange et al., "Pre-Startup Formal Business Plans and Post-Startup Performance: A Study of 116 New Ventures," forthcoming in *Venture Capital Journal.*

5. Thomas Stemberg, "What You Need to Succeed," *Inc.,* Vol. 29, No. 1 (January 2007), pp. 75–77.

6. Kelly Spors, "Do Start-Ups Really Need Formal Business Plans?" *Wall Street Journal,* January 9, 2007, p. B9.

7. Bhide, *op. cit.* p. 53.

8. Stephen Lawrence and Frank Moyes, "Writing a Successful Business Plan," copyright by the Regents of the University of Colorado at Boulder, 2005, http://leeds-faculty.colorado.edu/ moyes/html/resources.htm

9. Bhide, *op. cit.,* p. 70.

10. "Conversations with Ewing Marion Kauffman," Ewing Marion Kauffman Foundation, March 2004.

11. Peter Drucker, quoted in Brian Tracy, "7 Secrets to Success," *Entrepreneur,* Vol. 35, No. 2 (February 2007), pp. 96–103.

12. Gumpert, *op. cit.,* pp. 30–34.

13. Portions of the content in this section draw on Jeffry A. Timmons, Andrew Zacharakis, and Stephen Spinelli, *Business Plans That Work* (New York: McGraw-Hill, 2004).

14. Rhonda M. Abrams, *The Successful Business Plan: Secrets and Strategies,* 2nd ed. (Grants Pass, OR: Oasis Press, 2003).

15. http://www.inc.com/articles/ 1999/10/14877.html, accessed February 17, 2007.

16. http://www.powerhomebiz.com/ vol3/badbplan.htm, accessed November 9, 2006; http://www. bpiplans.com/Articles.htm, accessed November 9, 2006; and Robert A. Baron and Scott A. Shane, *Entrepreneurship: A Process Perspective,* 2nd ed. (Cincinnati: Thomson South-Western, 2008), p. 220.

17. Mark Stevens, "Seven Steps to a Well-Prepared Business Plan," *Executive Female,* Vol. 18, No. 2 (March 1995), p. 30.

18. Ellyn E. Spragins, "How to Write a Business Plan That Will Get You in the Door," *Inc. Guide to Small Business Management,* 2004, pp. 6–8.

19. Kenneth Blanchard and Spencer Johnson, *The One-Minute Manager* (New York: William Morrow, 1982).

20. Personal conversation with Tim Smith, March 2005.

21. For additional information on business plans, visit academic. cengage.com/management/ longenecker.

22. Jill Andresky Fraser, "Who Can Help Out with a Business Plan?" *Inc.,* Vol. 21, No. 8 (June 1999), pp. 115–117.

CHAPTER 7

1. Karen E. Spaeder, "Beyond Their Years," *Entrepreneur,* November 2003, p. 83.

2. From the business plan of Adorable Pet Photography, http:// www.bplans.com, accessed June 20, 2007.

3. J. D. Ryan and Gail P. Hiduke, *Small Business: An Entrepreneur's Business Plan,* 6th ed. (Cincinnati: South-Western, 2003), p. 354.

4. Personal conversation with Todd Stoner of Disciplined Investors, December 2006.

5. From the business plan of Fantastic Florals, Inc., http://www.bplan. com, accessed September 10, 2007.

6. Shannon Scully, "Protecting Your Good Name," *My Business,* February/March 2002, p. 14.

7. Carl McDaniel and Roger Gates, *Marketing Research,* 7th ed. (New York: John Wiley & Sons, 2007), p. 210.

8. Jim Hopkins, "Entrepreneur 101: Competition," *USAToday,* February 14, 2001, p. 6B.

9. McDaniel and Gates, *op. cit.,* pp. 94–95.

10. Isabella Trebond, "On Target," *Entrepreneur,* August 2004.

11. Michael Porter, *Competitive Advantage* (New York: Free Press, 1985), p. 5.

12. Joann S. Lublin, "Fountain Pen Fashion: Try 5,072 Diamonds or Abe Lincoln's DNA," *Wall Street Journal,* August 24, 2001, p. 81.

CHAPTER 8

1. Michael Fitzgerald, "Turning Vendors into Partners," *Inc.,* Vol. 27, No. 8 (August 2005), p. 95.

2. The exact percentage of solo start-ups is hard to pin down. Recent analyses of startups based on data from the Panel Study of Entrepreneurial Dynamics have determined that nearly one-half of all new ventures are launched by individuals [see "Teaming with Entrepreneurs: A Look at the Research of Howard Aldrich," in *Understanding Entrepreneurship: A Research Policy Report* (Kansas City, MO: Ewing Marion Kauffman Foundation, 2005), p. 40; and Paul D. Reynolds, Nancy M. Carter, William B. Gartner, Patricia G. Greene, and Larry W. Cox, *The Entrepreneur Next Door: Characteristics of Individuals Starting Companies in America* (Kansas City, MO: Ewing Marion Kauffman Foundation, 2002), p. 5]. A study of small businesses conducted by the National Federation of Independent Business found that more than 58 percent of the companies in the study sample were owned by a single individual [see "Business Structure," in William J. Dennis (ed.), *National Small Business Poll,* Vol. 4, No. 7 (Washington, DC: National Federation of Small Business, 2004), p. 10]. One recent review of studies on the topic puts the number of solo startups closer to one-third of new ventures [see Gaylen N. Chandler, "New Venture Teams," in Andrew Zacharakis and Stephen Spinelli, Jr. (eds.), *Entrepreneurship: The Engine of Growth* (Westport, CT: Praeger Perspectives, 2007), pp. 75–76]. Regardless of the percentage accepted, it is clear that many firms are started by individual entrepreneurs.

3. Chandler, *op. cit.* It also bears noting that, in many cases, one or more members of high-performing entrepreneurial teams have had prior experience with business startups. This pattern is emerging in recent studies, including those by Michael D. Ensley, Allison W. Pearson, and Allen C. Amason, "Understanding the Dynamics of New Venture Top Management Teams: Cohesion, Conflict, and New Venture Performance," *Journal of Business Venturing,* Vol. 17, No. 4 (July 2002), pp. 365–366; and Elizabeth J. Teal and Charles W. Hofer, "Key Attributes of the Founding Entrepreneurial Team of Rapidly Growing New Ventures," *Journal of Private Equity,* Vol. 4, No. 2 (Spring 2001), pp. 19–31.

4. This point is emphasized in Daniel P. Forbes, Patricia S. Borchert, Mary E. Zelmer-Bruhn, and Harry J. Sapienza, "Entrepreneurial Team Formation: An Exploration of New Member Addition," *Entrepreneurship Theory and Practice,* Vol. 30, No. 2 (March 2006), p. 226.

5. The field has evolved toward a view that sees management team members as those with financial ownership and significant decision-making responsibilities in the venture (see Chandler, *op. cit.*). Other definitions are more restrictive and emphasize factors such as being a part of the founding of the venture [see Iris Vanaelst, Bart Clarysse, Mike Wright, Andy Lockett, Nathalie Moray, and Rosette S'Jegers, "Entrepreneurial Team Development in Academic Spinouts: An Examination of Team Heterogeneity," *Entrepreneurial*

Theory and Practice, Vol. 30, No. 2 (March 2006), p. 251]. At the other end of the spectrum, some entrepreneurs consider all employees and advisors to be a part of the team. Because our discussion is focused on those who hold important leadership positions in the small business but may not share ownership in the firm, we use the broader term *management team* rather than *entrepreneurial team* to reflect this more general view.

6. For an interesting study of the addition of members to the management team, see Daniel P. Forbes, Patricia S. Borchert, Mary E. Zellmer-Bruhn, and Harry J. Sapienza, "Entrepreneurial Team Formation: An Exploration of New Member Addition," *Entrepreneurship Theory and Practice,* Vol. 30, No. 2 (March 2006), pp. 225–248.

7. Simon Stockley, "Building and Maintaining the Entrepreneurial Team—A Critical Competence for Venture Growth," in Sue Birley and Daniel F. Muzyka (eds.), *Mastering Entrepreneurship: The Complete MBA Companion in Entrepreneurship* (London: Financial Times/ Prentice-Hall, 2000), pp. 206–212.

8. This may explain why research using Panel Study of Entrepreneurial Dynamics data found that around three-fourths of *solo* entrepreneurs were starting service firms (49 percent) or retail businesses (26 percent). In other words, these types of startups tend to be less complicated than, for example, technology-based firms or manufacturing businesses, so a single founder is more likely to have the knowledge and experience necessary to get the business going. A more complex startup is likely to require the combined expertise and insight of a *team* of entrepreneurs. For a closer look at the data, see *Expected Costs of Startup Ventures,* a consulting report prepared for the SBA's Office of Advocacy by Blade Consulting Corporation, Vienna, VA, November 2003.

9. It should be noted that research has not always supported the view that functional balance leads to improved venture performance. Some studies have found that functional heterogeneity is correlated with small firm growth, while others offer no evidence to indicate a relationship with team performance (see Chandler, *op. cit.*).

10. Andy Lockett, Deniz Ucbasaran, and John Butler, "Opening Up the Investor-Investee Dyad: Syndicates, Teams, and Networks," *Entrepreneurship Theory and Practice,* Vol. 30, No. 2 (March 2006), p. 119.

11. Chandler, *op. cit.,* p. 71.

12. Howard E. Aldrich and Nancy M. Carter, "Social Networks," in William B. Gartner, Kelly G. Shaver, Nancy M. Carter, and Paul D. Reynolds (eds.), *Handbook of Entrepreneurial Dynamics: The Process of Business Creation* (Thousand Oaks, CA: Sage, 2004), p. 331.

13. Robert B. Cialdini, *Influence: Science and Practice* (Needham Heights: MA: Allyn and Bacon, 2001), p. 20.

14. The figures offered here are based on Internal Revenue Service projections of returns for the 2007 tax year. These numbers differ from those reported elsewhere, and this deserves some explanation. For example, some may choose to use PSED data, but Paul D. Reynolds, ["Nature of Business Start-ups," in William B. Gartner, Kelly G. Shaver, Nancy M. Carter and Paul D. Reynolds (eds.), Handbook of *Entrepreneurial Dynamics: The Process of Business Creation* (Thousand Oaks, CA: Sage, 2004), p. 250] points out that 52.7 percent of nascent entrepreneurs intend to operate as sole proprietorships, whereas actual tax filings put the figure at 71.9 percent. While we cannot rule out the possibility that this is a result of the PSED sampling frame, it would be reasonable to conclude that many entrepreneurial hopefuls fully anticipate incorporating or forming a partnership, but they end up moving toward the least complicated form, the sole proprietorship, when the more pressing challenges of starting and running a business take priority. On the other hand, a recent survey of small businesses from the NFIB reveals that only 20.9 percent are organized as sole proprietorships, which is far more at variance with IRS data [see "Business Structure," in William J. Dennis, Jr. (ed.), *NFIB National Small Business Poll,* Vol. 4, No. 7 (Washington, DC: NFIB Research Foundation, 2004), p. 8]. The sampling frame was drawn from the files of the Dun and Bradstreet Corporation, which may represent more mature businesses, many of which started as proprietorships but changed to more sophisticated organizational forms as a shield against liability or for other reasons. In any case, we use IRS figures here because they are based on the population of all companies submitting returns and represent the most recent data available.

15. Liability insurance and other forms of protection are discussed further in Chapter 21. However, there are many forms of liability protection, and a full discussion of these goes beyond the scope of this text. Experts and specific sources of information should be consulted when making these decisions.

16. Nancy Mann Jackson, "Dream Team or Nightmare Relationship," *MyBusiness,* April-May 2003, pp. 35–37.

17. Jana Matthews and Jeff Dennis, *Lessons from the Edge: Survival Skills for Starting and Growing a Company* (Oxford: Oxford University Press, 2003).

18. Fred S. Steingold, *Legal Guide for Starting and Running a Small Business* (Berkeley, CA: Nolo Press, 2006).

19. Marc Diener, "Friends Forever?" *Entrepreneur,* Vol. 31, No. 6 (June 2003), p. 77.

20. Karen Cheney, "Meet Your Match," http://www.quicken.com/cms/ viewers/article/small_business/ 55318, accessed January 29, 2007.

21. Karen Cheney, "The Perfect Partnership Plan," http://www. quicken.com/cms/viewers/article/ small_business/55340, accessed January 29, 2007.

22. Steingold, *Op. cit.*

23. David Gage, *The Partnership Charter: How to Start Out Right with Your New Business Partnership (or Fix the One You Have)* (New York: Basic Books, 2004).

24. Nichole L. Torres, "Left in the Lurch?" *Entrepreneur,* Vol. 34, No. 5 (May 2006), p. 108.

25. http://www.irs.gov/pub/irs-soi/histab22.xls, accessed February 5, 2007.

26. Chris Harrison, "Form Is Everything," http://www.welcomebiz.com/articlesDisplay.asp?articleID=49&deptID=4, accessed January 30, 2007.

27. For tax years beginning after 2004, the law increased the maximum number of shareholders permitted in an S corporation from 75 to 100. (Note that husband and wife count as one stockholder.) Other changes to the law may offer tax advantages to shareholders that should be considered when choosing an organizational form [see Joan Szabo, "Grab Your Opportunity," *Entrepreneur,* Vol. 33, No. 6 (June 2005), pp. 66–67].

28. The rules have been modified in recent years to allow more types of trusts to hold Subchapter S stock.

29. As stated, S corporations can own other business entities but cannot be owned by C corporations, other S corporations, many trusts, limited liability companies, or partnerships. For more information on the subject, see "Small Business Answer Handbook," *Entrepreneur,* Vol. 34, No. 10 (October 2006), pp. 41–46.

30. Kelly Spors, "Small Talk," *Wall Street Journal,* September 9, 2006, p. B8.

31. For a description of the tax advantages of the limited liability company, see Steingold, *op. cit.*

32. Nichole L. Torres, "Lofty Ideals," *Entrepreneur,* Vol. 34, No. 6 (June 2006), pp. 150–151.

33. "Strategic Alliances," *National Small Business Poll,* William J. Dennis, Jr. (ed.), Vol. 4, No. 4 (Washington, DC: NFIB Research Foundation, 2004), pp. 1–8.

34. *Ibid.,* p. 4.

35. Erik Sherman, "License to Thrive," *Inc.,* Vol. 27, No. 8 (August 2005), p. 38.

36. Shirley Leung, "The Lure—and Danger—of Big Company Jobs," *Wall Street Journal,* September 2, 2003, p. B9.

37. "Entrepreneur Being Honored by 10th Annual Eddy Awards," press release, September 29, 2005, http://www.act-1.com/media/eddyAwards10.asp, accessed February 2, 2007.

38. "Strategic Alliances," *op. cit.,* pp. 9–14.

39. Michael Fitzgerald, "Turning Vendors into Partners," *Inc.,* Vol. 27, No. 8 (August 2005) pp. 95–100.

40. Ilan Mochari, "Fishing for Big-Name Partners," *Inc.,* Vol. 22, No. 6 (May 2000), p. 163.

41. Christopher Caggiano, "Hotlinks," *Inc.,* Vol. 21, No. 14 (October 1999), pp. 72–81.

42. Mark Hendricks, "License to Thrive: How You Can Profit from Big Companies' Tech Ideas," *Entrepreneur,* Vol. 33, No.10 (October 2005), p. 22.

43. "Strategic Alliances," *op. cit.,* p. 7.

44. Jeffrey Shuman, Janice Twombly, and David Rottenberg, *Everyone Is a Customer: A Proven Method for Measuring the Value of Every Relationship in the Era of Collaborative Business* (Chicago: Dearborn Trade Publishing, 2002).

45. Carol Hymowitz, "How to Be a Good Director," *Wall Street Journal,* October 27, 2003, p. R1.

46. National Association of Corporate Directors, *Effective Entrepreneurial Boards: Findings from the 2001–2002 Entrepreneurial Boards Survey* (Washington, DC: National Association of Corporate Directors, 2002), p. 3.

47. Lynn Cowan, "The Board of Directors," *Wall Street Journal,* October 28, 2002, p. R6.

48. National Association of Corporate Directors, *op. cit.,* p. 17.

49. "Boards for Beginners," *Inc.,* Vol. 27, No. 2 (February 2005), p. 44.

50. Ronald I. Zall, *A Guide for Directors of Privately Held Companies* (Washington, DC: National Association of Corporate Directors, 2003), p. 43.

CHAPTER 9

1. Del Jones, "California Proves Too Costly for Departing Businesses," *USAToday,* October 2, 2003, p. 1B.

2. For a more comprehensive treatment of relocation issues, visit http://www.entrepreneur.com and read "Choosing a Location for Your Business," April 20, 2006.

3. J.D. Ryan and Gail P. Hiduke, *Small Business—An Entrepreneur's Business Plan,* 7th ed. (Cincinnati: Thomson-South Western, 2006).

4. http://www.hatworld.com, accessed January 30, 2007.

5. Ryan Chittum, "A New Mantra: Location, Location, Technology," *Startup Journal,* WSJ.com, accessed July 21, 2005.

6. Binaj Gurubacharya, "Linking Up Everest," *Waco Tribune-Herald,* March 7, 2003, p. 14A.

7. Wyoming Department of Revenue, http://revenue.state.wy.us, accessed December 20, 2006.

8. http://www.econ.state.or.us/enterthezones/whatare.htm, accessed December 21, 2006.

9. "Zoning In," *Entrepreneur's Start-Ups,* June 2003.

10. http://www.treehouseworkshop.com, accessed December 20, 2006; and Debra Cash, "There's No Office Like Home," *Inc. Technology,* Vol. 20, No. 4 (1998), p. 36.

11. Richard Breeden, "Small Businesses Favor Buying over Leasing," *Wall Street Journal,* February 24, 2004, p. B11.

12. Nichole L. Torres, "No Place Like Home," *Entrepreneur's Start-Ups,* Vol. 12, No. 9 (September 2000), p. 40.

13. Nichole L. Torres and April Y. Pennington, "Home Court Advantage," *Entrepreneur's Start-Ups,* May 2005.

14. Broderick Perkins, "Realize the Dream of a Home-Based Business,"

http://www.startupjournal.com, accessed April 9, 2004.

15. Susan Smith Hendrickson, "Balancing Work and Family," http://www.allbusiness.com, accessed December 18, 2006.

16. Torres and Pennington, *op. cit.*

17. Paul and Sarah Edwards, "Handling Houseguests in Your Home Office," *Entrepreneur,* August 11, 2003.

18. Michael J. McDermott, "Avoid Zoning Pitfalls When Working from Home," http://www.busop1.com/pitfall.html, accessed September 20, 2003.

19. Leigh Buchanan, "Early to Web," *Inc.,* Vol. 24, No. 13 (December 2002), p. 84.

20. http://www.witiger.com/ecommerce/benefits-limitations.htm, accessed July 10, 2007.

21. Perri Capell, "How to Make Money on eBay," *Wall Street Journal,* December 18, 2006, p. R5.

22. http://www.premium.hoovers.com, accessed December 20, 2006.

CHAPTER 10

1. Reva Berman Brown, Mark N. K. Saunders, and Richard Beresford, "You Owe It to Yourself: The Financially Literate Manager," *Accounting Forum,* Vol. 30, No. 2 (June 2006), p. 191.

2. Philip Campbell, "Are You Really Focused on Profits?" http://www.inc.com/resources/finance/articles/20060601/campbell.html, accessed February 26, 2007. Inc. Magazine, June 2006. Copyright 2006 by Mansueto Ventures LLC. Reproduced with permission of Mansueto Ventures LLC in the Format Textbook via Copyright Clearance Center.

3. Jan Norman, "You're Making Sales, but Are You Making Money?" http://www.entrepreneur.com/article/0,4621,228680,00.html, March 2004, accessed October 14, 2006.

4. For a more in-depth presentation of how to measure cash flows and the cash flow statement, see Appendixes 10A and 10B at the end of the chapter.

5. Paul A. Broni, "Persuasive Projections," *Inc.,* Vol. 22, No. 4 (April 2000), p. 38.

6. Rhonda Abrams, "How Can I Make Financial Projections in My Business Plan When I Have No Solid Numbers?" *Inc.com,* September 2000, http://www.inc.com/articles/2000/09/20226.html, accessed February 15, 2006.

7. David Worrell, "A Penchant for Profits," *Entrepreneur,* Vol. 33, No. 8 (August 2005), pp. 53–57.

8. Investors also look to financial projections to determine the sales level necessary for the firm to break even. A firm's break-even point, while important from a financial perspective, is also important to pricing its products or services. The issue of pricing is discussed in Chapter 15.

9. Personal communication with Cecilia Levine, August 13, 2004.

10. Matt Ackermann, "Many Entrepreneurs Need Better Financial Planning," *American Banker,* Vol. 168, No. 189 (October 1, 2003), p. 9.

11. Scott Bernard Nelson, "Fee Agents," *Entrepreneur,* January 2003, p. 63.

12. See Chapter 23 for further discussion of the debt ratio.

13. This percentage can be found by dividing the number of days of credit the supplier is offering (30 days, in this case) by the 365 days in a year (30/365 = 8.2%).

14. Information in this section was taken from Linda Elkins, "Real Numbers Don't Deceive," *Nation's Business,* Vol. 85, No. 3 (March 1997), pp. 51–52; and Broni, *op. cit.,* pp. 183–184.

15. Broni, *op. cit.*

CHAPTER 11

1. "Financing Patterns of Small Firms: Findings from the 1998 Survey of Small Business Finance," SBA Office of Advocacy, Washington, DC, September 2003.

2. Mike Hofman, "The Big Picture," *Inc.,* Vol. 25, No. 12 (October 2003), p. 87.

3. Ilan Mochari, "The Numbers Game," *Inc.,* Vol. 24, No. 12 (October 2002), pp. 65–66.

4. *Ibid.,* p. 64.

5. Personal conversation with Jack Griggs, Fall 2006.

6. To compute the $730 monthly payment, we can use a financial calculator or a computer spreadsheet.

PV (present value) = 50,000 (current loan)

N (number of payments) = 84 (7 years × 12 months = 84)

I/yr (interest rate/month) = 0.5% (6% interest rate per year ÷ 12 months = 0.005 = 0.5%)

FV (future value) = 0 (in 7 years)

Then solve for

PMT (payment) = $730.43

7. As discussed in Chapter 10, the ratio of current assets to current liabilities is called the *current ratio;* the ratio of total debt to total assets is called the *debt ratio.*

8. Mochari, *op. cit.,* p. 64.

9. Personal interview with Bill Bailey, former owner of Cherokee Communications, Spring 2005.

10. For an excellent source on business angels, see Frances M. Amatucci and Jeffrey E. Sohl, "Business Angels: Investment Processes, Outcomes, and Current Trends," in Andrew Zacharakis and Stephen Spinelli, Jr. (eds.), *Entrepreneurship: The Engine of Growth* (Westport, CT: Praeger, 2007), pp. 87–107.

11. Julian Lange, Benoit Leleux, and Bernard Surlemont, "Angel Network for the 21st Century," *Journal of Private Equity,* Spring 2003, p. 18.

12. Amatucci and Sohl, *op. cit.*

13. For a description of how angel networks function, see Aja Carmichael, "The Money Game: In Search of an Angel," *Wall Street Journal,* January 30, 2006, p. R4.

14. http://www.centexangels.org, accessed January 10, 2007.

15. Aja Carmichael, "VCs' Tips for Winning the Support of Investors," *Wall Street Journal Online,* http://www.startupjournal.com/financing/capital/20060202-carmichael.html?refresh=on, accessed February 2, 2006.

16. C. J. Prince, "Alternate Financing Routes," *Entrepreneur,* March 2007, pp. 66–68.

17. Jim Hopkins, "Corporate Giants Bankroll Start-Ups," *USA Today,* March 29, 2001, p. 1B.

CHAPTER 12

1. Thomas Kostigen, "Small Firms Are Cashing Out," *Wall Street Journal Online,* June 3, 2005.

2. Personal interview with Robert Hall, former CEO of Visador Corporation, May 15, 2005.

3. John Case, "The Ultimate Employee Buy-In," *Inc.,* December 2005, pp. 107–116.

4. Nancy Mann Jackson, "The ABCs of ESOPs," *MyBusiness,* February-March 2003, http://www.mybusinessmag.com/fullstory.php3?sid=903, accessed May 2004.

5. S. T. Certo, "Influencing Initial Public Offering Investors with Prestige: Signaling with Board Structure," *Academy of Management Review,* Vol. 28, No. 3 (2003), pp. 432–447.

6. Woojin Kim and Michael S. Wiesbach, "Do Firms Go Public to Raise Capital?" presented at the annual Financial Management Association Meeting, October 14, 2005.

7. Monica Zimmerman Teichel and David L. Deeds, "Entrepreneurial Exit," in Andrew Zacharakis and Stephen Spinelli, Jr. (eds.), *Entrepreneurship: The Engine of Growth,* (Westport, CT: Praeger, 2007), p. 186.

8. The source for this information is Heritage Partners, a Boston venture capital firm, which obtained a registered trademark for a process it calls the Private IPO®.

9. Richard D. Dorf and Thomas H. Byers, *Technology Ventures: From Idea to Enterprise* (New York: McGraw-Hill, 2005), p. 120.

10. The unattributed quotes in this part of the chapter are taken from personal interviews conducted as part of a research study on harvesting, sponsored by the Financial Executive Research Foundation and cited in J. William Petty, John D. Martin, and John Kensinger, *Harvesting the Value of a Privately Held Company* (Morristown, NJ: Financial Executive Research Foundation, 1999). To acquire a copy of the book, write the Financial Executive Research Foundation, Inc., P.O. Box 1938, Morristown, NJ 07962-1938, or call 973-898-4600.

11. Jeff Bailey, "Selling the Firm—and Letting Go of the Dream," *Wall Street Journal,* December 10, 2002, p. B6.

CHAPTER 13

1. G. Brewer, "The Ultimate Guide to Winning Customers: The Customer Stops Here," *Sales and Marketing Management,* Vol. 150 (March 1998), p. 30.

2. C. B. Furlong, "12 Rules for Customer Retention," *Bank Marketing,* January 5, 1993, p. 14.

3. Charles Wilamb, Joseph F. Hair, and Carl McDaniel, *Marketing,* 9th ed. (Cincinnati: Thomson-South-Western, 2008), p. 602.

4. Marjorie J. Cooper, Nancy Upton, and Samuel Seaman, "Customer Relationship Management: A Comparative Analysis of Family and Nonfamily Business Practices," *Journal of Small Business Management,* Vol. 43, No. 3 (July 2005), pp. 242–256.

5. Brian Vellmure, "Let's Start with Customer Retention," http://www.initiumtech.com/newsletter_120602.htm, September 4, 2004.

6. Amy Barrett, "True Believers," http://www.businessweek.com, accessed March 2, 2007.

7. Thomas O. Jones and W. Earl Sasser, Jr., "Why Satisfied

Customers Defect," *Harvard Business Review,* Vol. 73, No. 6 (November-December 1995), p. 90.

8. Jerry Fisher, "The Secret's Out," http://www.entrepreneur.com/mag/article/0,1539,228496.html, June 8, 2004.

9. Bruce Horovitz, "Whatever Happened to Customer Service?" *USAToday,* September 26, 2003, pp. 1A–2A.

10. Heather Larson, "Coffee Talk," *MyBusiness,* October-November 2006, p. 12.

11. Dionne Searcey, "For Better or Worse," *Wall Street Journal,* October 30, 2006, p. R5.

12. "Intimate Relationships in Bloom," http://www.sas.com/success/1800FLOWERS.html, accessed July 10, 2007.

13. Russell S. Wimer, "Customer Relationship Management: A Framework, Research Directions, and the Future," http://groups.haas.berkeley.edu/fcsuit/PDF-papers/CRM%20paper.pdf, June 8, 2004.

14. "Get to Know Your Customer Profile," http://peerspectives.org/index.peer?page=main&storyid=0035, September 4, 2004.

15. *Ibid.*

16. See, for example, Del I. Hawkings, David L. Mothersbaugh, and Roger J. Best, *Consumer Behavior: Building Marketing Strategy,* 10th ed. (New York: McGraw-Hill Irwin, 2007), Chapter 17.

CHAPTER 14

1. Debra Kahn Schofield, "Grow Your Business Slowly: A Cautionary Tale," http://www.gmarketing.com, May 14, 2004.

2. http://www.coloradowebsolutions.com/featured_merchant_current.htm, accessed February 7, 2007; and Aliza Pilar Sherman, "Parallel Universe," *Entrepreneur,* June 2004, p. 36.

3. Julie Fields, "Caught in a Candy Crunch," http://www.businessweek.com, May 20, 2004.

4. Jeffry A. Timmons and Stephen Spinelli, *New Venture Creation:*

Entrepreneurship for the 21st Century (New York: McGraw-Hill/Irwin, 2004).

5. Rebecca Quick, "As Our Reporter Said, This Apparel Web Site Was Just Way Too Hip," *Wall Street Journal,* October 25, 2000, p. B1; and "Body Scanning Kiosks May Improve Clothes' Fit," *St. Louis Post-Dispatch,* October 18, 2000, p. C1.

6. http://www.potomacswimschool.com/index.htm, accessed February 7, 2007; and Donna Boone, "Entrepreneurial Growth: Think Regional, Act Local," http://www.entreworld.com, May 20, 2004.

7. http://www.180s.com, accessed February 7, 2007; Don Debelak, "Warm Reception," *Entrepreneur,* December 2003, p. 142; and Mary E. Medland, "Keeping Warm While Looking Cool," http://www.mddailyrecord.com/innovator/2003180s/html, May 21, 2004.

8. http://www.ddssystem.com/index.html, accessed February 7, 2007; and Nanci Hollmich, "Dental Appliance Ensures That You Don't Stuff Your Face," *USAToday,* May 19, 2004, p. 1B.

9. http://www.sba.gov/va/success.html, May 21, 2004.

10. http://www.biolife.com/about-biolife.html, accessed February 7, 2007; and Margaret Ann Miille, "A Profitable Accident," http://www.heraldtribune.com, May 20, 2004.

11. http://www.munchkininc.com, accessed February 7, 2007; and Seth Lubove, "Family Affair," *Forbes,* Vol. 170, No. 11 (November 25, 2002), p. 58.

12. http://www.unclaimedbaggage.com/aboutus.html, accessed February 7, 2007; and Geoff Williams, "Salvage Operation," *Entrepreneur,* November 2003, p. 32.

13. http://www.1000ventures.com/business-guide/crosscuttings/sca, accessed January 10, 2007.

14. Mark Henricks, "Stay on Top with Fresh Products," *Entrepreneur,*

December 5, 2005, http://www.entrepreneur.com/growyourbusiness/howtoguide/article81252.html, accessed July 11, 2007.

15. http://www.etrema-usa.com, accessed February 7, 2007; and Cora Daniels, "Etrema's Magic Metal," *Fortune,* November 10, 2003, pp. 195–196.

16. Kim T. Gordon, "Test Your Product or Service First," http://www.entrepreneur.com/marketingcolumnistkimtgordon/article62938.html, July 7, 2003.

17. http://www.theparkingspot.com, accessed February 7, 2007; and Elizabeth J. Goodgold, "Dot Your Eyes," *Entrepreneur,* February 2002, http://www.entrepreneur.com/mag/article, May 25, 2004.

18. Tahl Raz, "Not Just a Pretty Typeface," *Inc.,* Vol. 24, No. 13 (December 2002), pp. 120–122.

19. *Ibid.*

20. *Ibid.*, p. 122.

CHAPTER 15

1. Nadine Heintz, "Flexing Your Pricing Muscles," *Inc.,* Vol. 26, No. 2 (February 2004), pp. 25–26.

2. Geoff Williams, "Name Your Price," *Entrepreneur*, September 2005, pp. 108–112.

3. For an excellent discussion of price setting, see Charles W. Lamb, Jr., Joseph H. Hair, Jr., and Carl McDaniel, *Marketing,* 9th ed. (Cincinnati: South-Western, 2008), Chapter 18.

4. http://www.technewsworld.com/story/31271.html, accessed March 16, 2007.

5. For more information about market-driven pricing, see John A. Boyd, "Market-Driven Pricing Strategies," Iowa Small Business Development Centers, http://www.iabusnet.org.

6. For more details, see Sarah Goldstein, "Who Gets to Say When the Price Is Right?" *Inc.,* March 2007, p. 24.

7. "Online Payment Processing," *Inc.,* June 2006, p. 86.

8. Jonathan A. Scott, William C. Dunkelberg, and William J. Dennis, Jr., *Credit, Banks and Small Business—The New Century* (Washington, DC: NFIB Research Foundation, 2003).

9. For a detailed look at the Equifax Credit Report, see https://www.econsumer.equifax.com/consumer/sitepage.ehtml?forward=cs_cpo.

CHAPTER 16

1. Peter Kafka, "Blue Sky," *Forbes,* February 12, 2007, pp. 86–92.

2. Barton A. Weitz, Stephen B. Castleberry, and John F. Tanner, Jr., *Selling: Building Partnerships* (New York: McGraw Hill/Irwin, 2007), Chapter 11.

3. Stephanie Clifford, "Putting the Performance in Sales Performance," *Inc.,* February 2007, pp. 87–95.

4. Shannon Scully, "Why Image Matters," *My Business,* December-January 2003, p. 30.

5. http://www.flowers-partners.com, accessed February 5, 2007.

6. Melissa Campanelli, "Sharing the Wealth," *Entrepreneur,* February 2005, p. 40.

7. Jennifer Gill, "Attention, Shoppers," Inc.com, accessed April 2006.

8. Shannon Scully, "Go Fetch More Money!" *My Business,* June-July 2003, p. 41.

9. http://spamlaws.com/federal/index.sutml, accessed February 2, 2007.

10. Melissa Campanelli, "Canning Spam," *Entrepreneur,* March 2004, p. 39.

11. http://www.webwasher.com, accessed February 5, 2007.

12. For more details regarding domain name rules, see http://www.register.com/domain-rules.cgi.

13. http://www.dnjournal.com/ytd.-sales-charts.htmi, accessed February 1, 2007.

14. Chris Kivelhan, "Improve Your Website's Performance," *Entrepreneur,* May 3, 2006, http://www.

entrepreneur.com/ebusiness/ operations/article159400.html, accessed July 30, 2007.

15. Corey Rudl, "4 Fatal Website Design Mistakes," http://www. entrepreneur.com, accessed January 29, 2007.

16. Ellen Neuborne, "Finding the Right Keyword," *Inc.,* Vol. 25, No. 11 (October 2003), p. 44.

17. Jefferson Graham, "For Google, Many Retailers Eagerly Jump Through Hoops," *USAToday,* February 5, 2004, p. 2A.

18. Jess McCuan, "The Ultimate Sales Incentive," *Inc.,* Vol. 26, No. 5 (May 2004), p. 32.

19. Adapted from Janet Attard, "Trade Show Dos and Don'ts," http:// www.businessknowhow.com/tips/ tradesho.htm, accessed February 5, 2007.

20. Melany Klinck, "Puzzleman to the Rescue," *MyBusiness,* December-January 2003, pp. 12–13.

21. Ryan McCarthy, "The Power of Suggestion," *Inc.,* February 2007, pp. 48–49.

22. Don Debelak, "Make Your Mark," *Entrepreneur,* May 2004, p. 146; and http://www.maryellenproducts. com, accessed February 5, 2007.

CHAPTER 17

1. Mary Anastasia O'Grady, "The Poor Get Richer," *Wall Street Journal,* January 16, 2007, p. A21.

2. Statistics have already answered this question. Data published by the International Trade Administration indicate that SMEs accounted for 97 percent of all U.S. exporters and that these firms accounted for 29.2 percent of all U.S. goods exported. These findings show that small and medium-sized companies are already actively involved in international trade. The data reflect only export activity, so the numbers would be even more striking if other forms of internationalization were included in the report. For an extensive analysis of the ITA study, see Leslie E. Palich and D. Ray Bagby, "Trade Trends in

Transatlantica: A Profile of SMEs in the United States and Europe," in Lester Lloyd-Reason and Leigh Sears (eds.), *Trading Places—SMEs in the Global Economy: A Critical Research Handbook* (Cheltenham, UK: Edward Elgar Publishing, 2007).

3. Michael V. Copeland ["The Mighty Micro-Multinational," *Business 2.0,* Vol. 7, No. 6 (July 2006), pp. 107–114] points out just how fast the number of startups with global ambitions is growing. He cites UN data to indicate that the number of startups that are global from day one doubled between 1990 and 2006, from 30,000 to 60,000. Many of these are technology-focused companies, but the phenomenon certainly extends to non-tech companies as well. But, in many cases, the emphasis is not on starting a business in the United States and selling product internationally; rather, it is on establishing operations wherever in the world it makes sense to do so. In other words, it could be a way to draw on the talents of highly trained employees or to locate near abundant resources or low-cost labor to enhance the value proposition of the new venture.

4. Terms other than *born global* are sometimes used to refer to this category of firms and others that are similar to them; other labels include *born international firms, global startups, international new ventures,* and *instant exporters.* Pat H. Dickson, "Going Global," in Andrew Zacharakis and Stephen Spinelli, Jr. (eds.), *Entrepreneurship: The Engine of Growth* (Westport, CT: Praeger Perspectives, 2007), pp. 155–161; Gary A. Knight and S. Tamar Cavusgil, "Innovation, Organizational Capabilities, and the Born-Global Firm," *Journal of International Business Studies,* Vol. 35, No. 2 (March 2004), pp. 124–141; Svante Andersson, "Internationalization in Different Industrial Contexts," *Journal of Business Venturing,* Vol. 19, No. 6 (2004), p. 856; and Erkko Autio, Harry J.

Sapienza, and James G. Almeida, "Effects of Age at Entry, Knowledge Intensity, and Imitability on International Growth," *Academy of Management Journal,* Vol. 43, No. 5 (October 2000), pp. 909–924.

5. Leigh Buchanan, "The Thinking Man's Outsourcing," *Inc.,* Vol. 28, No. 5 (May 2006), pp. 31–33.

6. *Ibid.*

7. "RSM EquiCo Capital Markets Advises Air Excellence International Inc. on Its Acquisition by Triumph Group Inc," news release, June 29, 2006, http://www.primezone.com/ newsroom/news.html?d=101455, accessed February 7, 2007.

8. James F. Foley, *The Global Entrepreneur: Taking Your Business International* (Chicago: Dearborn Financial Publishing, 1999), p. 5.

9. Svante Andersson, "Internationalization in Different Industrial Contexts," *Journal of Business Venturing,* Vol. 19, No. 6 (2004), pp. 851–875; "Don't Laugh at Gilded Butterflies," *Economist,* Vol. 371, No. 8372 (April 22, 2004), pp. 71–73; and Oliver Burgel, Andreas Fier, Georg Licht, and Gordon C. Murray, "The Effect of Internationalization on Rate of Growth of High-Tech Start-Ups—Evidence for UK and Germany," in Paul D. Reynolds et al. (eds.), *Frontiers for Entrepreneurship Research,* proceedings of the 20th Annual Entrepreneurship Research Conference, Babson College, June 2002.

10. This study focused on the expansion of American firms into Europe. It is possible that the primary motivation for involvement in other parts of the world is different. For example, it could very well be that most American small companies doing business in Asia are seeking to access low-cost component sources or to relocate business processes via outsourcing. For an extended discussion of the particular study cited, see Edmund Prater and Soumen Ghosh, "Current Operational Practices of U.S. Small and Medium-Sized Enterprises in Europe," *Journal of Small Business Management,*

Vol. 43, No. 2 (April 2005), pp. 155–169.

11. Karen E. Klein, "The Bumpy Road to Global Trade," *BusinessWeek,* No. 3702 (October 9, 2000), p. 32; and http://www.sunflowerseed. com/html/company_profile.html, accessed February 9, 2007.

12. Raymond Vernon, "International Investment and International Trade in the Product Cycle," *Quarterly Journal of Economics,* Vol. 80, No. 2 (May 1966), pp. 190–207.

13. Gordon B. Baty and Michael S. Blake, *Entrepreneurship: Back to Basics* (Washington, DC: Beard Books, 2003), p. 166.

14. Rodney C. Shrader, Benjamin M. Oviatt, and Patricia Phillips McDougall, "How New Ventures Exploit Trade-Offs Among International Risk Factors: Lessons for the Accelerated Internationalization of the 21st Century," *Academy of Management Journal,* Vol. 43, No. 6 (December 2000), pp. 1227–1247.

15. http://www.itretail.com/about/ company.php, accessed February 9, 2007.

16. This is not to suggest that small businesses no longer follow the pattern of establishing themselves first in the domestic market before stepping out into international opportunities. Pat H. Dickson *(op. cit.)* refers to firms in this category as *gradual globals* and mentions that this pattern of expansion is consistent with the well-developed and still influential Uppsala Internationalization Model. The Uppsala school suggests that firms internationalize slowly and incrementally, perhaps taking years to gain the knowledge, skills, and resources necessary to expand into international markets. Stepping out is likely to begin with low-commitment strategies first (such as sourcing abroad or exporting) and then move into more resource-intensive options (for example, forming a joint venture with an overseas partner and then moving in time to establish a wholly owned international subsidiary). The logic extends to selection of markets as well, suggesting that companies first seek to enter countries that are similar and easy to penetrate. They will expand into markets that are more and more dissimilar as they they develop the capabilities to move in that direction and find that they have tapped out the potential of the markets they are currently in. Though we now have evidence that many start-ups internationalize early on (the born-global phenomenon), many other entrepreneurs choose the gradual-global option instead.

17. Patricia P. McDougall, Rodney C. Shrader, and Benjamin M. Oviatt, "International Entrepreneurs: Risk Takers or Risk Managers?" in Sue Birley and Daniel F. Muzyka (eds.), *Mastering Entrepreneurship* (London: Financial Times/Prentice Hall, 2000), pp. 246–250.

18. Palich and Bagby, *op. cit.*

19. In the United States, this problem has been exacerbated by problems related to the War on Terror. In an attempt to prevent dangerous individuals from entering the country, the U.S. government has tightened visa and work permit restrictions, which has made it more difficult for companies to bring in the foreign talent they need. To make the situation worse, many international students from countries like China and India train in the best universities in the U.S. and then return home, hoping to use their skills to get in on the ground floor of opportunities that are emerging in their rapidly developing home countries.

20. The Boston Consulting Group/ Knowledge@Wharton, "China and the New Rules for Global Business," http://knowledge.wharton. upenn.edu/papers/download/ BCG-KWspecialreport-final.pdf, accessed February 12, 2007.

21. Timothy Appel, "Small Firms Outsource Abroad by Tapping Offshore Producers," *Wall Street Journal,* January 7, 2004, p. A2.

22. Kara Swisher, "U.S. Tech Town Rises in India," *Wall Street Journal,* January 7, 2002, p. A1.

23. Eric Wahlgren, "The Outsourcing Dilemma," *Inc.,* Vol 28, No. 4 (April 2004), pp. 41–42.

24. http://www.kirkhammotorsports. com/about/index.html, accessed February 12, 2007.

25. http://www.dubaiinternetcity. com/why_dubai_internet_city, accessed February 13, 2007; and http://uaeinteract.com/news/ default.asp?ID=134, accessed February 14, 2007.

26. Prater and Ghosh, *op. cit.,* p. 161.

27. Jan Stojaspal, "Back in the Driver's Seat," http://www.time. com/time/europe/specials/ff/ trip6/hungarybuses.html, accessed February 14, 2007; and Palich and Bagby, *op. cit.*

28. Shrader, Oviatt, and McDougall, *op. cit.*

29. SBA Office of Advocacy, Economic Statistics and Research, "Small Business Frequently Asked Questions," http://app1.sba.gov/faqs/ faqindex.cfm?areaID=24, accessed February 13, 2007.

30. James A. Wolff and Timothy L. Pett, "Internationalization of Small Firms: An Examination of Export Competitive Patterns, Firm Size, and Export Performance," *Journal of Small Business Management,* Vol. 38, No. 2 (April 2000), p. 35.

31. http://www.mooneyfarms.com/ html/about-us.htm, accessed February 14, 2007; and Klein, *op. cit.*

32. James Flanigan, "Globalization in a Nutshell," *Los Angeles Times,* May 31, 2000, p. C1.

33. http://www.entertainmentearth. com/help/aboutee.asp, accessed February 14, 2007; DIRECT, "DIRECT Listline," March 1, 2004, p. 3; http://www.mysimon.com, accessed February 14, 2007; and http://www.bizrate.com/ratings_ guide/cust_reviews__mid-484. html, accessed February 14, 2007.

34. *Ibid.*

35. For an outstanding discussion of this issue as it applies specifically to export approval for shipments to China, see Ted C. Fishman "America's Most Innovative Industries Are Being Robbed Every Day on the Floors of Chinese Factories," *Inc.,* Vol. 28, No. 6 (June 2006), pp. 98–102.

36. Ian Mount, "Right Back at You," *Fortune Small Business,* Vol. 16, No. 2 (March 2006), p. 18.

37. Melanie Warner, "Going Pro on eBay," *Fortune,* Vol. 141, No. 7 (April 3, 2000), pp. 250–252.

38. Joshua Kurlantzick, "On Foreign Soil," *Entrepreneur,* Vol. 33, No. 6 (June 2005), pp. 88–92.

39. *Ibid.*

40. A recent study of SMEs in the European Union revealed that international sourcing is used far more than exporting strategies. While 16 percent of firms in the study used exporting alone, 49 percent engaged in foreign sourcing alone. Twenty-seven percent had both foreign suppliers and exports. These findings may not generalize beyond European firms, given their unique setting within the region, but they certainly highlight the importance of these two international strategies for SMEs. For more details, see the *2003 Observatory of European SMEs: 2003/4 Internationalization of SMEs,* which can be accessed at http://ec.europa.eu/enterprise/enterprise_policy/analysis/doc/smes_observatory_2003_report4_en.pdf.

41. Michael A. Hitt, R. Duane Ireland, and Robert E. Hoskisson, *Strategic Management: Competitiveness and Globalization* (Cincinnati, OH: Thomson South-Western, 2007), p. 246.

42. http://www.itretail.com/about/company.php, accessed February 15, 2007.

43. U.S. Small Business Administration, *Breaking into the Trade Game: A Small Business Guide to Exporting,* http://www.sba.gov/gopher/Business-Development/International-Trade/Guide-To-Exporting/trad26.txt, accessed February 15, 2007.

44. http://www.bluenote.net/franchise/index.shtml, accessed February 15, 2007.

45. Space here is limited, but there is much more to know about strategic alliances and small business. For example, Dickson (*op. cit.,* pp. 162–163) reviews research showing that features of national culture can shape the formation of alliances and the use of equity ties. This source will lead to more interesting research on the topic for interested readers.

46. Elizabeth Wasserman, "Happy Birthday, WTO?" *Inc.,* Vol. 27, No. 1 (January 2005), pp. 21–23.

47. Nichole L. Torres, "Change of Scenery," *Entrepreneur,* Vol. 34, No. 8 (August 2006), p. 90.

48. http://www.mooneyfarms.com/about_us.htm, accessed June 7, 2004.

49. http://www.sba.gov/gopher/Business-Development/International-Trade/Guide-To-Exporting/trad8.txt, accessed February 19, 2007.

CHAPTER 18

1. Julie H. Case, "The Art of Leadership," *U.W.* [University of Washington] *Business,* Spring 2003, p. 17.

2. Amar V. Bhide, *The Origin and Evolution of New Businesses* (New York: Oxford University Press, 2000), Chapter 4.

3. Jim Collins, *Good to Great* (New York: HarperCollins, 2001), p. 27.

4. Daniel Goleman, "Leadership That Gets Results," *Harvard Business Review,* Vol. 78, No. 2 (March-April 2000), pp. 78–90.

5. Glenn Ross, "Employee Empowerment Contributes to the Customer Service Experience," http://www.allbusiness.sfgate.com/blog/CustomerServiceExperience/10783/006807.html, accessed March 12, 2007.

6. Jeffrey Pfeffer and John F. Veiga, "Putting People First for Organizational Success," *Academy of Management Executive,* Vol. 13, No. 2 (May 1999), p. 40.

7. For more on this topic, see Nichole Torres, "Thinking Bigger," *Entrepreneur,* Vol. 34, No. 8 (August 2006), p. 53.

8. Nichole Torres, "Setting the Mood," *Entrepreneur,* Vol. 34, No. 8 (August 2006), p. 52.

9. *Ibid.*

10. Adam Hanft, "Save the Founder," *Inc.,* Vol. 27, No. 10 (October 2005), p. 156.

11. Sara Wilson, "iSold It LLC," *Entrepreneur,* Vol. 34, No. 6 (June 2006), p. 84.

12. William W. Horne, "Machine Maker Unhinged by Sales Emphasis," *Inc.,* Vol. 21, No. 3 (March 1999), p. 25.

13. Gwen Edwards, "Going from *Fortune* 500 to Startup," March 5, 2007, http://www.businessweek.com/print/smallbiz/content/mar2007/sb20070305_965709.htm, accessed March 14, 2007.

14. One of the more recent articles on the subject is Colin Gray, "Stages of Growth and Entrepreneurial Growth Career Motivation," *International Small Business Journal,* Vol. 18, No. 3 (April-June 2000), pp. 81–84. This author condenses previous stage models into five stages that are determined by "decision points" in the life of the small business. These five stages are (1) startup, (2) survival (whether to continue in the business), (3) take-off (whether to go beyond a point of maintaining personal control), (4) professionalization (whether to introduce a more sophisticated managerial structure), and (5) transformation (the decision to make the transition from a small business to a large business). This view obviously runs parallel to what we present in this section of the chapter.

15. Alison Stein Wellner, "Hands On," *Inc.,* Vol. 26, No. 10 (October 2004), pp. 39–40.

16. Chris Penttila, "Can You Manage?" *Entrepreneur,* Vol 31, No. 7 (July 2003), pp. 74–75.

17. *Ibid.*

18. Demetria Lucas, "Twin Tailors," *Black Enterprise,* Vol. 33, No. 9 (April 2003), p. 47.

19. Bhide, *op. cit.,* p. 315.

20. Personal communication from a student of one of the authors.

21. Jeff Bailey, "Enterprise: The Long-Term Perils of Being a Control Freak," *Wall Street Journal,* March 25, 2003, p. B-6.

22. *Ibid.*

23. Jana Matthews and Jeff Dennis, *Lessons from the Edge* (New York: Oxford University Press, 2003), pp. 44–48.

24. Stephen R. Covey, *The 7 Habits of Highly Effective People* (New York: Simon & Schuster, 2004), pp. 173–179.

25. Rodes Fishburne, "More Survival Advice: Communicate," *Forbes ASAP,* April 3, 2000, p. 120.

26. The use of blogs for the expression of personal opinions online has been increasing rapidly, but applications to the business setting are expanding even faster. For example, blogs can be employed as a public relations tool or a channel to address customer complaints or to pass along product or service insights. For an interesting analysis of the use of blogs in business, see Deutsch Bank Research, "Blogs: The New Magic Formula for Corporate Communications?" in Stefan Heng (ed.), *Economics: Digital Economy and Structural Change,* No. 53 (August 22, 2005), pp. 1–8, http://www.dbresearch. com/PROD/DBR_INTERNET_ DE-PROD/PROD0000000000190745. pdf, accessed March 15, 2007.

27. For more on the use of wikis for internal communication and other purposes, see PriceWaterhouseCoopers, "View," February 2007, http:// pwc.com/Extweb/pwcpublications. nsf/docid/9C138D10508 82FC78525727400121B1D?WT. srch=1&WT.mc_id=MRK070301WS.

28. Numerous resources provide excellent background on the principles and skills of negotiation. One popular book on the subject, a national bestseller, is by Roger Fisher, William Ury, and Bruce Patton: *Getting to Yes: Negotiating Agreement Without Giving In* (New York: Random House, 2003). This book emphasizes several very important concepts, including bargaining for mutual gains, separating people from the problem and positions from interests, and agreeing on objective criteria for evaluating outcomes. With its readable style and practical orientation, this book—and others like it—would be very useful reading for any small business owner.

29. Erika Kotite, "Focus, People!" *Entrepreneur,* Vol. 34, No. 9 (September 2006), p. 34.

30. As reported in Mark Henricks, "Just 'To-Do' It," *Entrepreneur,* Vol. 32, No. 8 (August 2004), p. 71.

31. Suggestions were adapted from the following articles: Emma Johnson, "A Stress-Free Guide to Time Management," *MyBusiness,* October-November 2005, pp. 29–33; Lisa Kanarek, "Clean Sweep," *Entrepreneur,* Vol. 34, No. 6 (June 2006), pp. 43–44; Nichole L. Torres, "In Good Time," *Entrepreneur,* Vol. 33, No. 12 (December 2005), p. 38; Romanus Wolter, "A Clean Sweep," *Entrepreneur,* Vol. 32, No. 7 (July 2004), pp. 108–109; and Romanus Wolter, "Easy Does It," *Entrepreneur,* Vol. 33, No. 10 (October 2005), pp. 122–123.

32. Jeff Bailey, "Enterprise: Peer Groups Provide Expertise Firms Lack—Organizations Like YEO Bring Owners Together to Talk and Swap Advice," *Wall Street Journal,* December 17, 2002, p. B-7.

33. Darren Dahl, "Percolating Profits," *Inc.,* Vol. 27, No. 2 (February 2005), pp. 38–40.

34. Richard A. D'Errico, "Local Incubators Hatch Idea to Collaborate," *The Business Review,* March 19, 2004, http://www. albany.bizjournals.com/albany/ stories/2004/03/22/story1.html, accessed March 16, 2007.

35. Dahl, *op.cit.*

36. http://www.score.org/success_ bakers_peel.html, accessed March 16, 2007.

37. Joanne Gordon, "Calling Dr. Demetria," *Forbes,* Vol. 165, No. 14 (June 12, 2000), p. 212.

38. *Ibid.*

39. Nicole Lewis, "The Power of Networking," *Black Enterprise,* Vol. 33, No. 11 (June 2003), p. 51.

CHAPTER 19

1. For an extended discussion of small business and HRM practices, especially as applied to family firms, see Jan M. P. de Kok, Lorraine M. Uhlaner, and A. Roy Thurik, "Professional HRM Practices in Family Owned-Managed Enterprises," *Journal of Small Business Management,* Vol. 44, No. 3 (May 2006), pp. 441–460.

2. Jim Collins, *Good to Great* (New York: HarperCollins, 2001), p. 41.

3. Donna Fuscaldo, "Special Report: Small Business, The Key Employees," *Wall Street Journal,* October 28, 2002, pp. R-1, R-10.

4. *Ibid.*

5. Rifka Rosewein, "Help Still Wanted," *Inc.,* Vol. 23, No. 5 (April 2001), p. 54.

6. Robert L. Mathis and John H. Jackson, *Human Resource Management* (Cincinnati: South-Western College Publishing, 2006), p. 130.

7. Rochelle Sharpe and Felicia Morton, "Summer Help Wanted: Foreigners Please Apply," *BusinessWeek,* No. 3691 (July 24, 2000), p. 32.

8. Bruce D. Phillips, "The Future Small Business Workforce," paper presented at the national meeting of the United States Association for Small Business and Entrepreneurship, Indian Wells, CA, January 2005.

9. As reported in Dee Gill, "Dealing with Diversity," *Inc.,* Vol. 27, No. 11 (November 2005), p. 38.

10. Chris Kelleher, "Writing Great

Job Descriptions," http://www. entrepreneur.com/humanresources/ hiring/article70642.html, accessed March 23, 2007.

11. For more detail on overtime regulations as they may apply to small businesses, visit the U.S. Department of Labor's website at http:// www.dol.gov/esa/regs/ compliance/whd/fairpay/main. htm, March 23, 2007.

12. For more on this and other features of the hiring process, see Stephanie Clifford, "The Science of Hiring," *Inc.* Vol. 28, No. 8 (August 2006), pp. 90–98. The article reports that the correlation between interview-based assessments and actual performance is a mere 0.20, which is not very encouraging. However, the author offers many insights that could be used to improve the hiring process.

13. Jeffrey Pfeffer, "Why Resumes Are Just One Piece of the Puzzle," *Business 2.0,* Vol. 6, No. 11 (December 2005), p. 106.

14. © 2007 by Susan M. Heathfield, (http://humanresources.about. com/od/interviewing/ a/behavior_interv.htm). Used with permission of About, Inc., which can be found online at www. about.com. All rights reserved.

15. Beth Gaudio, "Tell Me About Yourself," *MyBusiness* (October-November 2006), p. 14.

16. Mark Henricks, "Check That Temp," *Entrepreneur,* Vol. 34, No. 4 (April 2006), pp. 91–92.

17. Paulette Thomas, "Case Study: Not Sure of a New Hire? Put Her to a Road Test," *Wall Street Journal,* January 7, 2003, p. B-7.

18. As with many governmental regulations that affect small businesses, this applies only to those companies that have at least 15 employees. In this case, crossing the 15-employee threshold means that the company is subject to federal laws against disability discrimination.

19. William J. Dennis, Jr. (ed.), "Alcohol, Drugs, Violence and Obesity in the Workplace," *NFIB National Small Business Poll,* Vol. 4, No. 3 (2004), pp. 7–8.

20. For a substantive study of reported training practices of small businesses, see William J. Dennis Jr. (ed.), "Training Employees," *NFIB National Small Business Poll,* Vol. 5, No. 1 (2005), pp. 1–39.

21. Gaylen N. Chandler and Glenn M. McEvoy, "Human Resource Management, TQM, and Firm Performance in Small and Medium-Size Enterprises," *Entrepreneurship Theory and Practice,* Vol. 25, No. 1 (Fall 2000), pp. 43–57.

22. Emily Barker, "Hi-Test Education," *Inc.,* Vol. 23, No. 10 (July 2001), pp. 81–82.

23. Shannon Scully and Lisa Waddle, "Back to School," *MyBusiness,* September-October 2001, pp. 28–29; and http://www. bookpros.com, accessed April 13, 2007.

24. Chris Penttila, "Who's Paying?" *Entrepreneur,* Vol. 29, No. 12 (December 2001), pp. 88–90.

25. Get more information about ESOPs on the website of the National Center for Employee Ownership at http://www.nceo.org.

26. George Bohlander and Scott Snell, *Managing Human Resources,* 13th ed. (Cincinnati: South-Western College Publishing, 2007), p. 473.

27. For more detailed information on laws protecting employees, see Bohlander and Snell, *op. cit.*

28. Beth Gaudio, "Stay Out of Court," *MyBusiness,* October-November 2005, p. 46.

CHAPTER 20

1. Anthony W. Ulwick, "Turn Customer Input into Innovation," *Harvard Business Review,* Vol. 8, No. 1 (January 2002), pp. 91–97.

2. Mike Steere, "A Timeless Recipe for Success," *Business 2.0,* Vol. 4, No. 8 (September 2003), pp. 47–49; and http://www.in-n-out.com/history. asp, accessed April 18, 2007.

3. Mark Henricks, "A New Standard," *Entrepreneur,* Vol. 30, No. 10 (October 2002), pp. 83–84; Lee Strouse, "Metal Finisher Forges Quality Alliance," *Finishers' Management,* February 1999; and "Company History," http:// www.swdinc.com, accessed April 20, 2007.

4. "Customer Spending Growth Likely to Remain Strong as Customer Satisfaction Hits an All-Time High," ASCI News, February 20, 2007, http://www. theasci.org/index?option=com_ content&task=view&id= 165&Itemid=161, accessed April 24, 2007.

5. S. Douglas Pugh, Joerg Dietz, Jack W. Wiley, and Scott M. Brooks, "Driving Service Effectiveness Through Employee-Customer Linkages," *Academy of Management Executive,* Vol. 16, No. 4 (November 2002), pp. 73–84.

6. For fuller discussion of this issue, see Mary Jo Bitner, Amy L. Ostrom, and Matthew L. Meuter, "Implementing Successful Self-Service Technologies," *Academy of Management Executive,* Vol. 16, No. 4 (November 2002), pp. 96–109.

7. Michael Hammer, "Forward to Basics," *Fast Company,* Vol. 3, No. 10 (November 2002), p. 38.

8. Michael Hammer and James Champy, *Reengineering the Corporation* (New York: HarperCollins, 1994), p. 32.

9. Anne Stuart, "Going Mobile," *Inc.,* Vol. 24, No. 13 (December 2002), pp. 124–125.

10. Jay Greene, "Small Biz: Microsoft's Next Big Thing," *BusinessWeek,* April 21, 2003, pp. 72–73.

11. Jeff Bailey, "Entrepreneurs Share Their Tips to Boost a Firm's Productivity," *Wall Street Journal,* July 9, 2002, p. B-4.

12. April Y. Pennington, "Snapshot: Natalie Chanin and Enrico Marone-Cinzano," *Entrepreneur,* Vol. 31, No. 2 (February 2003), p. 20; Julia Reed, "Art of the Craft: Sweet Home Alabama," *Vogue,* March 2002, pp. 280ff; and http://www. projectalabama. com, accessed April 20, 2007.

13. "Big Help for the Little Guy," *Fortune Technology Guide,* Vol. 142, No. 12 (Winter 2001), p. 208.

14. Thane Peterson, "E-I-E-I-E-Farming," *BusinessWeek,* May 1, 2000, p. 202.

15. Jeff Bailey, "Small Firms Enjoy the Courtship of Big Suppliers," *Wall Street Journal,* June 24, 2003, p. B-9.

16. Jeff Bailey, "Big Companies Can Provide Much-Needed Help," *Wall Street Journal,* November 4, 2003, p. B-9.

17. Laurel Delaney, "Howdy Partner," *Entrepreneur,* Vol. 35, No. 4 (April 2007), p. 87.

18. Most operations management textbooks offer formulas and calculations related to determining the economic order quantity. However, one exceptionally good resource for this and many other operations management computations is Wallace J. Hopp and Mark L. Spearman, *Factory Physics,* 2nd ed. (Boston: Irwin McGraw-Hill, 2001), pp. 49–53.

CHAPTER 21

1. Translated by Arthur W. H. Adkins from the Greek text of Solon's poem "Prosperity, Justice and the Hazards of Life," in M. L. West (ed.), *Iambi et Elegi Gracci ante Alexandrum Canttati,* Vol. 2 (Oxford: Clarendon Press, 1972).

2. "Risk," http://www.thefreedictionary.com/risk, accessed March 26, 2007.

3. Daniel Tynan, "In Case of Emergency," *Entrepreneur,* Vol. 3, No. 4 (April 2003), p. 60.

4. Christopher Windham, "Self-Insurance Plans Gain as Premiums Jump," *Wall Street Journal,* December 30, 2003, p. B2.

5. Dan Briody, "Full Coverage: How to Hedge Your Cyber Risk," *Inc.,* April 2007, pp. 47–49.

6. Jacquelyn Lynn, "It's a Gamble," *Entrepreneur,* Vol. 31, No. 1 (January 2003), p. 67.

7. Social Security Administration, as cited in Randy Myers, "The Fine Art of Self-Protection," *CFO,* July 1, 2006, http://www.cfo.com, accessed July 27, 2007.

CHAPTER 22

1. Accruals are not considered in terms of managing working capital. Accrued expenses, although shown on financial statements as a short-term liability, primarily result from the accountant's effort to match revenues and expenses. There is little that can be done to "manage" accruals.

2. Keith Lowe, "Managing Your Cash Flow," http://www.entrepreneur.com/article/0,4621,295043,00.html, December 3, 2001.

3. Suzanne McGee, "Breaking Free from Budgets," *Inc.,* October 2003, p. 73.

4. Paulette Thomas, "Why Debt Collection Is So Essential for Startups," *Wall Street Journal Online,* September 25, 2005, http://www.startupjournal.com/runbusiness/billcollect/20050920-thomas.html, accessed August 21, 2007.

5. Amy Feldman, "The Cash Flow Crunch," *Inc.,* December 2005, pp. 51–52.

6. William J. Dennis, Jr. (ed.), *The National Small Business Poll: Reinvesting in the Business,* Vol. 3, No. 3 (2003), NFIB Research Foundation, p. 13.

7. Arthur J. Keown, John D. Martin, J. William Petty, and David F. Scott, Jr., *Foundations of Finance: The Logic and Practice of Financial Management,* 5th ed. (Englewood Cliffs, NJ: Prentice-Hall, 2006).

8. Dennis, *op. cit.,* p. 11.

CHAPTER 23

1. See, for example, Walter T. Harrison, Charles T. Horngren, and Tom Harrison, *Financial Accounting,* 6th ed. (Englewood Cliffs, NJ: Prentice-Hall, 2006).

2. For example, Dun & Bradstreet publishes annually a set of 14 key financial ratios for 125 types of businesses. Robert Morris Associates (RMA) publishes a set of 16 key ratios for over 350 types of businesses. In both cases, the ratios are classified by industry and by firm size to provide a basis for more meaningful comparisons.

3. Instead of computing the accounts receivable turnover, we could calculate the average collection period. Simply stated, if Trimble & Associates turns its accounts receivable over 10.63 times in a year, then, on average, the firm collects its receivables every 34.3 days, determined by dividing 365 days by 10.63 (accounts receivable turnover).

4. When we computed Trimble's return on assets earlier, we found it to be 10.87 percent. Now it is 10.82 percent. The difference is the result of rounding error.

Appendix B

1. Other multiples, besides value to earnings, that are used in valuing a firm include value to sales, value to equity book value, and value to cash flows, just to mention a few.

2. http://www.buysellbiz.com/Mid%20west%20fsbos.htm, February 4, 2004.

3. Justin Martin, "What's Your Business Worth—Really?" http://money.cnn.com/magazines/fsb/fsb_archive/2006/09/01/8384898/index.htm, accessed August 28, 2007.

4. Depreciation expense was added back to operating income, since it is a non-cash expense. The resulting number is equal to the firm's cash flow from operations.

5. The numbers in this example have been changed, but they still represent the valuation process.

A

ABC method A system of classifying items in inventory by relative value

acceptance sampling The use of a random, representative portion to determine the acceptability of an entire lot

accounting return on investment technique A capital budgeting technique that evaluates a capital expenditure based on the expected average annual after-tax profits relative to the average book value of an investment

accounts payable (trade credit) Outstanding credit payable to suppliers

accounts receivable The amount of credit extended to customers that is currently outstanding

accounts receivable turnover The number of times accounts receivable "roll over" during a year

accrual-basis accounting A method of accounting that matches revenues when they are earned against the expenses associated with those revenues, no matter when they are paid

accrued expenses Short-term liabilities that have been incurred but not paid

accumulated depreciation Total depreciation expense taken over the assets' life

actual cash value (ACV) An insurance term that refers to the depreciated value of a property

adjusted income After-tax cash flow

advertising The impersonal presentation of a business idea through mass media

advisory council A group that functions like a board of directors but acts only in an advisory capacity

agency power The ability of any one partner to legally bind the other partners

agents/brokers Intermediaries that do not take title to the goods they distribute

aging schedule A categorization of accounts receivable based on the length of time they have been outstanding

all-risk approach Stating, in an insurance policy, that all direct damages to property are covered except those caused by perils specifically excluded

area developers Individuals or firms that obtain the legal right to open several franchised outlets in a given area

artisan entrepreneur A person with primarily technical skills and little business knowledge who starts a business

asset-based loan A line of credit secured by working-capital assets

asset-based valuation Determination of the value of a business by estimating the value of its assets

attitude An enduring opinion based on knowledge, feeling, and behavioral tendency

attractive small firm A small firm that provides substantial profits to its owner

attribute inspection The determination of product acceptability based on whether it will or will not work

auction sites Web-based businesses offering participants the ability to list products for bidding

average pricing An approach in which total cost for a given period is divided by quantity sold in that period to set a price

B

bad-debt ratio The ratio of bad debts to credit sales

balance sheet A financial report showing a firm's assets, liabilities, and ownership equity at a specific point in time

balloon payment A very large payment that the borrower may be required to make at a specified point about halfway through the term over which the payments were calculated, repaying the rest of the loan in full

banner ads Advertisements that appear across a Web page, most often as moving rectangular strips

batch manufacturing A type of manufacturing operation that is intermediate (between job shops and repetitive manufacturing) in volume and variety of products

behavioral interview An interview approach that assesses the suitability of job candidates based on how they would respond to hypothetical situations

benchmarking The process of studying the products, services, and practices of other firms and using the insights gained to improve quality internally

benefit variables Specific characteristics that distinguish market segments according to the benefits sought by customers

bill of lading A document indicating that a product has been shipped and the title to that product has been transferred

board of directors The governing body of a corporation, elected by the stockholders

bootstrapping Minimizing a firm's investments by using other people's resources

born-global firms Small companies launched with cross-border business activities in mind

bottleneck Any point in the operations process where limited capacity reduces the production capability of an entire chain of activities

brand A verbal and/or symbolic means of identifying a product

brand image People's overall perception of a brand

brand mark A brand that cannot be spoken

brand name A brand that can be spoken

break-even point Sales volume at which total sales revenue equals total costs

breakdown process (chain-ratio method) A forecasting method that begins with a larger-scope variable and works down to the sales forecast

brick-and-mortar store The traditional physical store from which businesses have historically operated

budget A document that expresses future plans in monetary terms

build-up LBO A leveraged buyout involving the purchase of a group of similar companies with the intent of making the firms into one larger company

buildup process A forecasting method in which all potential buyers in the various submarkets are identified and then the estimated demand is added up

business angels Private individuals who invest in others' entrepreneurial ventures

business format franchising A franchise arrangement whereby the franchisee obtains an entire marketing system geared to entrepreneurs

business incubator A facility that provides shared space, services, and management assistance to new businesses

business interruption coverage Coverage that reimburses a business for the loss of anticipated income, allowing the business to pay continuing expenses that otherwise could not be met because of the negative impact of the direct loss on business revenues

business model A group of shared characteristics, behaviors, and goals that a firm follows in a particular business situation

business owner's policy (BOP) A business version of a homeowner's policy, designed to meet the property and liability insurance needs of small business owners

business plan A document that presents the basic idea for the venture and includes descriptions of where you are now, where you want to go, and how you intend to get there

business-to-business (B2B) model A business model based on selling to business customers electronically

business-to-consumer (B2C) model A business model based on selling to final customers electronically

bust-up LBO A leveraged buyout involving the purchase of a company with the intent of selling off its assets

C

C corporation An ordinary corporation, taxed by the federal government as a separate legal entity

capabilities The integration of various organizational resources that are deployed together to the firm's advantage

capital budgeting analysis An analytical method that helps managers make decisions about long-term investments

capital gains and losses Gains and losses incurred from sales of property that is not a part of the firm's regular business operations

cash-basis accounting A method of accounting that reports transactions only when cash is received or a payment is made

cash budget A planning document strictly concerned with the receipt and payment of dollars

cash conversion period The time required to convert paid-for inventories and accounts receivable into cash

cash flow–based valuation Determination of the value of a business by estimating the amount and timing of its future cash flows

cash flow statement A financial report showing a firm's sources and uses of cash

cash flows from operations Net cash flows generated from operating a business, calculated by adding depreciation back to operating income, deducting income taxes, and subtracting changes in net working capital

Certified Development Company (CDC) 504 Loan Program SBA loan program that provides long-term financing for small businesses to acquire real estate or machinery and equipment

chain of command The official, vertical channel of communication in an organization

channel of distribution The system of relationships established to guide the movement of a product

chattel mortgage A loan for which items of inventory or other movable property serve as collateral

Civil Rights Act Legislation prohibiting discrimination based on race, color, religion, sex, or national origin

code of ethics Official standards of employee behavior formulated by a firm

cognitive dissonance The anxiety that occurs when a customer has second thoughts immediately following a purchase

coinsurance provision The most common version of an insurance to value clause, requiring that property be insured for at least 80 percent of its value or else a penalty will be applied to any covered loss

commercial general liability (CGL) coverage Coverage providing payment for bodily injury and property damage for which the insured business is liable

common carriers Transportation intermediaries available for hire to the general public

community-based financial institution A lender that uses funds from federal, state, and private sources to provide financing to small businesses in low-income communities

compensatory damages Economic or noneconomic damages intended to make the claimant whole, by indemnifying the claimant for any injuries or damage arising from the negligent action

competitive advantage A benefit that exists when a firm has a product or service that is seen by its target market as better than those of competitors

competitive environment The environment that focuses on the strength, position, and likely moves and countermoves of competitors in an industry.

comprehensive plan A full business plan that provides an in-depth analysis of the critical factors that will determine a firm's success or failure, along with all the underlying assumptions

consumer credit Financing granted by retailers to individuals who purchase for personal or family use

content/information-based model A business model in which the website provides information but not the ability to buy or sell products and services

continuous quality improvement A constant and dedicated effort to improve quality

contract carriers Transportation intermediaries that contract with individual shippers

control chart A graphic illustration of the limits used in statistical process control

copyright The exclusive right of a creator to reproduce, publish, perform, display, or sell his or her own works

core competencies Those resources and capabilities that provide a firm with a competitive advantage over its rivals

corporate charter A document that establishes a corporation's existence

corporation A business organization that exists as a legal entity and provides limited liability to its owners

corrective maintenance Repairs necessary to restore equipment or a facility to good condition

cost-based commitment Commitment based on the belief that the opportunity for gain from joining a business is too great to pass up

cost-based strategy A plan of action that requires a firm to be the lowest-cost producer within its market

cost of goods sold The cost of producing or acquiring goods or services to be sold by a firm

counterfeit activity The unauthorized use of intellectual property

credit An agreement between a buyer and a seller that provides for delayed payment for a product or service

credit bureaus Privately owned organizations that summarize a number of firms' credit experiences with particular individuals

critical risks A section of the business plan that identifies the potential risks that may be encountered by an investor

cross-border acquisition The purchase by a business in one country of a company located in another country

culture Behavioral patterns and values that characterize a group of consumers in a target market

current assets (gross working capital) Assets that can be converted into cash within a company's operating cycle

current debt (short-term liabilities) Borrowed money that must be repaid within 12 months

current ratio A measure of a company's relative liquidity, determined by dividing current assets by current liabilities

customer profile A description of potential customers in a target market

customer relationship management (CRM) A company-wide business strategy designed to optimize profitability and customer satisfaction by focusing on highly defined and precise customer groups

cycle counting A system of counting different segments of the physical inventory at different times during the year

D

debt Business financing provided by creditors

debt ratio A measure of the fraction of a firm's assets that are financed by debt, determined by dividing total debt by total assets

dehydrated plan A short form of a business plan that presents only the most important issues and projections for the business

delegation of authority Granting to subordinates the right to act or make decisions

demographic variables Specific characteristics that describe customers and their purchasing power

depreciable assets Assets whose value declines, or depreciates, over time

depreciation expense Costs related to a fixed asset, such as a building or equipment, allocated over its useful life

design patent Registered protection for the appearance of a product and its inseparable parts

desire-based commitment Commitment based on a belief in the purpose of a business and a desire to contribute to it

differentiation-based strategy A plan of action designed to provide a product or service with unique attributes that are valued by consumers

direct channel A distribution system without intermediaries

direct forecasting A forecasting method in which sales is the estimated variable

direct loss A loss in which physical damage to property reduces its value to the property owner

disability insurance Coverage that provides benefits upon the disability of a firm's partner or other key employee

disclosure document A detailed statement provided to a prospective franchisee, containing such information as the franchisor's finances, experience, size, and involvement in litigation

discounted cash flow (DCF) techniques Capital budgeting techniques that compare the present value of future cash flows with the cost of the initial investment

distribution Physically moving products and establishing intermediary relationships to support such movement

double-entry system A self-balancing accounting system that requires that each transaction be recorded twice

dual distribution A distribution system that involves more than one channel

due diligence The exercise of reasonable care in the evaluation of a business opportunity

dynamic (personalized) pricing strategy Charging more than the standard price when the customer's profile suggests that the higher price will be accepted

E

e-commerce The paperless exchange of business information via the Internet

e-mail promotion Advertising delivered by means of electronic mail

earnings before interest, taxes, depreciation, and amortization (EBITDA) A firm's profits after subtracting cost of goods sold and cash operating expenses, but before subtracting depreciation and amortization, interest expense, and taxes

earnings before taxes Earnings or profits after operating expenses and interest expenses but before taxes

earnings multiple A ratio determined by dividing a firm's value by its annual earnings; also called *value-to-earnings* ratio

economic damages Compensatory damages that relate to economic loss, such as medical expense, loss of income, or the cost of property replacement/restoration

economic order quantity (EOQ) The quantity to purchase in order to minimize total inventory costs

economic risk The probability that a government will mismanage its economy and thereby change the business environment in ways that hinder the performance of firms operating there

economies of scale Efficiencies that result from expansion of production

elastic demand Demand that changes significantly when there is a change in the price of the product

elasticity of demand The degree to which a change in price affects the quantity demanded

Electronic Customer Relationship Marketing (eCRM) An electronically based system that emphasizes customer relationships

employee leasing The "renting" of personnel from an organization that handles paperwork and administers benefits for those employees

employee stock ownership plan (ESOP) A method by which a firm is sold either in part or in total to its employees

empowerment Giving employees authority to make decisions or take actions on their own

enterprise zones State-designated areas that are established to bring jobs to economically deprived regions through regulatory and tax incentives

entrepreneur A person who starts or owns and operates an enterprise

entrepreneurial alertness Readiness to act on existing, but unnoticed, business opportunities

entrepreneurial legacy Material assets and intangible qualities passed on to both heirs and society

entrepreneurial opportunity An economically attractive and timely opportunity that creates value for interested buyers or end users

entrepreneurial team Two or more people who work together as entrepreneurs on one endeavor

environmentalism The effort to protect and preserve the environment

equipment loan An installment loan from a seller of machinery used by a business

equity value (owner's value) The value of the firm less the debt owed by the firm

ethical imperialism The belief that the ethical standards of one's own country can be applied universally

ethical issues Questions of right and wrong

ethical relativism The belief that ethical standards are subject to local interpretation

European Union (EU) An organization whose purpose is to facilitate free trade among member countries in Europe

evaluative criteria The features or characteristics of a product or service that customers use to compare brands

evoked set A group of brands that a consumer is both aware of and willing to consider as a solution to a purchase problem

exchange rate The value of one country's currency relative to that of another country

executive summary A section of the business plan that conveys a clear and concise overall picture of the proposed venture

experience curve efficiencies Per-unit savings gained from the repeated production of the same good

exporting Selling products produced in the home country to customers in another country

external equity Capital that comes from the owners' investment in a firm

external locus of control A belief that one's life is controlled more by luck or fate than by one's own efforts

F

factoring Obtaining cash by selling accounts receivable to another firm

Fair Labor Standards Act (FLSA) Federal law that establishes a minimum wage and provides for overtime pay

Family and Medical Leave Act Legislation that assures employees of unpaid leave for childbirth or other family needs

family business A company that two or more members of the same family own or operate together or in succession

family business constitution A statement of principles intended to guide a family firm through times of crisis and change

family council An organized group of family members who gather periodically to discuss family-related business issues

family retreat A gathering of family members, usually at a remote location, to discuss family business matters

financial leverage The use of debt in financing a firm's assets

financial plan A section of the business plan that projects the company's financial position based on well-substantiated assumptions and explains how the figures have been determined

financial ratios Restatements of selected income statement and balance sheet data in relative terms

financial statements (accounting statements) Reports of a firm's financial performance and resources, including an income statement, a balance sheet, and a cash flow statement

financing costs The amount of interest owed to lenders on borrowed money

firm value (enterprise value) The value of the entire business, regardless of how it is financed

fixed asset turnover A measure of the relationship of sales to fixed assets

fixed assets Relatively permanent assets intended for use in the business, such as plant and equipment

focus strategy A plan of action that isolates an enterprise from competitors and other market forces by targeting a restricted market segment

follow-the-leader pricing strategy Using a particular competitor as a model in setting prices

foreign licensing Allowing a company in another country to purchase the rights to manufacture and sell a company's products in international markets

formal venture capitalists Individuals who form limited partnerships for the purpose of raising venture capital from large institutional investors

founder An entrepreneur who brings a new firm into existence

franchise The privileges conveyed in a franchise contract

franchise contract The legal agreement between franchisor and franchisee

franchisee An entrepreneur whose power is limited by a contractual relationship with a franchisor

franchising A marketing system involving a legal agreement, whereby the franchisee conducts business according to terms specified by the franchisor

franchisor The party in a franchise contract that specifies the methods to be followed and the terms to be met by the other party

fringe benefits Supplements to compensation, designed to be attractive and beneficial to employees

G

general environment The broad environment, encompassing factors that influence most businesses in a society

general partner A partner in a limited partnership who has unlimited personal liability

general-purpose equipment Machines that serve many functions in the production process

globalization The expansion of international business, encouraged by converging market preferences, falling trade barriers, and the integration of national economies

greenfield venture A wholly owned subsidiary formed from scratch in another country

gross fixed assets Original cost of depreciable assets before any depreciation expense has been taken

gross profit Sales less the cost of goods sold

H

harvesting (exiting) The process used by entrepreneurs and investors to reap the value of a business when they leave it

headhunter A search firm that locates qualified candidates for executive positions

high-potential venture (gazelle) A small firm that has great prospects for growth

home-based business A business that maintains its primary facility in the residence of its owner

I

importing Selling goods produced in another country to buyers in the home country

income statement (profit and loss statement) A financial report showing the profit or loss from a firm's operations over a given period of time

indirect channel A distribution system with one or more intermediaries

indirect forecasting A forecasting method in which variables related to sales are used to project future sales

indirect loss A loss arising from inability to carry on normal operations due to a direct loss to property

industry environment The combined forces that directly impact a given firm and its competitors

inelastic demand Demand that does not change significantly when there is a change in the price of the product

informal venture capital Funds provided by wealthy private individuals (business angels) to high-risk ventures

initial public offering (IPO) The first sale of shares of a company's stock to the public

inspection The examination of a product to determine whether it meets quality standards

inspection standard A specification of a desired quality level and allowable tolerances

installment account A line of credit that requires a down payment, with the balance paid over a specified period of time

institutional advertising The presentation of information about a particular firm, designed to enhance the firm's image

insurance to value A provision, common in property insurance policies, requiring that the policy be at least a specified percentage of the actual value of the property

intangible resources Those organizational resources that are invisible and difficult to assess

integrity An uncompromising adherence to doing what is right and proper

intellectual property Original intellectual creations, including inventions, literary creations, and works of art, that are protected by patents or copyrights

internal control A system of checks and balances that safeguards assets and enhances the accuracy and reliability of financial statements

internal equity Capital that comes from retaining profits within a firm

internal locus of control A belief that one's success depends on one's own efforts

internal rate of return (IRR) The rate of return a firm expects to earn on a project

international franchising Selling a standard package of products, systems, and management services to a company in another country

international outsourcing A strategy that involves accessing foreign labor through contracts with independent providers

international strategic alliance A combination of efforts and/or assets of companies in different countries for the sake of pooling resources and sharing the risks of an enterprise

inventory A firm's raw materials and products held in anticipation of eventual sale

inventory turnover The number of times inventories "turn over" during a year

ISO 9000 The standards governing international certification of a firm's quality management procedures

J

Job Instruction Training A systematic step-by-step method for on-the-job training of nonmanagerial employees

job shop A type of manufacturing operation in which short production runs are used to produce small quantities of unique items

job specification A list of skills and abilities needed to perform a specific job

just-in-time inventory system A method of reducing inventory levels to an absolute minimum

K

key-person insurance Coverage that provides benefits upon the death of a firm's key personnel

L

learning effects Insights, gained from experience, that lead to improved work performance

legal entity A business organization that is recognized by the law as having a separate legal existence

letter of credit An agreement issued by a bank to honor a draft or other demand for payment when specified conditions are met

leveraged buyout (LBO) A purchase heavily financed with debt, where the future cash flow of the target company is expected to be sufficient to meet debt repayments

leveraged ESOP An employee stock ownership plan that is financed with borrowed money

LIBOR (London InterBank Offered Rate) The interest rate charged by London banks on loans to other London banks

licensee The company buying licensing rights

licensor The company selling licensing rights

lifestyle business A microbusiness that permits the owner to follow a desired pattern of living

limited liability The restriction of an owner's legal financial responsibilities to the amount invested in the business

limited liability company A form of organization in which owners have limited liability but pay personal income taxes on business profits

limited partner A partner in a limited partnership who is not active in its management and has limited personal liability

limited partnership A partnership with at least one general partner and one or more limited partners

line-and-staff organization An organizational structure that includes staff specialists who assist management

line of credit An informal agreement between a borrower and a bank as to the maximum amount of funds the bank will provide at any one time

line organization A simple organizational structure in which each person reports to one supervisor

linkage A type of advertising agreement in which one firm pays another to include a click-on link on its site

liquidation value method Determination of the value of a business by estimating the money that would be available if the firm were to liquidate its assets

liquidity The degree to which a firm has working capital available to meet maturing debt obligations

loan covenants Bank-imposed restrictions on a borrower that enhance the chances of timely repayment

lock box A post office box for receiving remittances from customers

long-range plan (strategic plan) A firm's overall plan for the future

long-term debt Loans from banks or other sources with repayment terms of more than 12 months

loss avoidance Avoiding loss by choosing not to engage in hazardous activities

loss prevention Stopping loss from happening

loss reduction Lessening the frequency, severity, or unpredictability of losses

M

make-or-buy decision A firm's choice between producing and purchasing component parts for its products

management buyout (MBO) A leveraged buyout in which the firm's top managers become significant shareholders in the acquired firm

management team Managers and other key persons who give a company its general direction; a section of the business plan that describes a new firm's organizational structure and the backgrounds of its key players

market A group of customers or potential customers who have purchasing power and unsatisfied needs

market analysis The process of locating and describing potential customers

market risk The uncertainty associated with an investment decision

market segmentation The division of a market into several smaller groups with similar needs

marketing mix The combination of product, pricing, promotion, and distribution activities

marketing plan A section of the business plan that describes the user benefits of the product or service and the type of market that exists

marketing research The gathering, processing, interpreting, and reporting of market information

markup pricing Applying a percentage to a product's cost to obtain its selling price

master licensee An independent firm or individual acting as a sales agent with the responsibility for finding new franchisees within a specified territory

matchmakers Specialized brokers that bring together buyers and sellers of businesses

medical payments coverage Coverage providing payment for injuries sustained by customers and the general public, with no fault required on the part of the insured

mentoring Guiding and supporting the work and development of a new or less-experienced organization member

merchant middlemen Intermediaries that take title to the goods they distribute

microbusiness A small firm that provides minimal profits to its owner

modified book value method Determination of the value of a business by adjusting book value to reflect obvious differences between the historical cost and the current market value of the assets

mortgage A long-term loan from a creditor for which real estate is pledged as collateral

motivations Forces that organize and give direction to the tension caused by unsatisfied needs

multiple-unit ownership Holding by a single franchisee of more than one franchise from the same company

multisegment strategy A strategy that recognizes different preferences of individual market segments and develops a unique marketing mix for each

N

named-peril approach Identifying, in an insurance policy, the specific perils covered

need-based commitment Commitment based on an individual's self-doubt and belief that he or she lacks career options outside the current business

needs The starting point for all behavior

negotiation A two-way communication process used to resolve differences in needs, goals, or ideas

net fixed assets Gross fixed assets less accumulated depreciation

net income available to owners (net income) Income that may be distributed to the owners or reinvested in the company

net present value (NPV) The present value of expected future cash flows less the initial investment outlay

net working capital The amount of current assets less current liabilities

networking The process of developing and engaging in mutually beneficial relationships

noneconomic damages Compensatory damages for such losses as pain and suffering, mental anguish, and loss of physical abilities

nonprofit corporation A form of corporation for enterprises established to serve civic, educational, charitable, or religious purposes but not for generation of profits

North American Free Trade Agreement (NAFTA) An agreement that encourages free trade among the United States, Canada, and Mexico by removing trade restrictions

normalized earnings Earnings that have been adjusted for unusual items, such as fire damage, and leakages, such as an excessive salary for the owner

O

obligation-based commitment Commitment that results from a sense of duty or expectation

Occupational Safety and Health Act Legislation that regulates the safety of workplaces and work practices

offering A section of the business plan that indicates to an investor how much money is needed and when, and how the money will be used

offshoring A strategy that involves relocating operations abroad

open charge account A line of credit that allows the customer to obtain a product at the time of purchase, with payment due when billed

operating expenses Costs related to marketing and selling a firm's product or service, general and administrative expenses, and depreciation

operating income Earnings or profits after operating expenses but before interest and taxes are paid

operating profit margin The ratio of operating profits to sales, showing how well a firm manages its income statement

operations and development plan A section of the business plan that offers information on how a product will be produced or a service provided, including descriptions of the new firm's facilities, labor, raw materials, and processing requirements

operations management Planning and controlling the process of converting inputs to outputs

operations process The activities that create value for customers through production of a firm's goods and services

opinion leader A group member who plays a key communications role

opportunistic entrepreneur A person with both sophisticated managerial skills and technical knowledge who starts a business

opportunity cost of funds The rate of return that could be earned on another investment of similar risk

opportunity recognition Identification of potential new products or services that may lead to promising businesses

ordinary income Income earned in the ordinary course of business, including any salary

organizational culture Patterns of behaviors and beliefs that characterize a particular firm

organizational test Verification of whether a nonprofit organization is staying true to its stated purpose

other assets Assets other than current assets and fixed assets, such as patents, copyrights, and goodwill

outsourcing Purchasing products or services that are outside the firm's area of competitive advantage

ownership equity Owners' investments in a company, plus profits retained in the firm

P

partnership A legal entity formed by two or more co-owners to carry on a business for profit

partnership agreement A document that states explicitly the rights and duties of partners

patent The registered, exclusive right of an inventor to make, use, or sell an invention

payback period technique A capital budgeting technique that measures the amount of time it will take to recover the cash outlay of an investment

penetration pricing strategy Setting lower than normal prices to hasten market acceptance of a product or service or to increase market share

percentage-of-sales technique A method of forecasting asset investments and financing requirements

perception The individual processes that give meaning to the stimuli confronting consumers

perceptual categorization The process of grouping similar things so as to manage huge quantities of incoming stimuli

peril A cause of loss, either through natural events or through the acts of people

perpetual inventory system A method for keeping a running record of inventory

personal property Any property other than real property, including machinery, equipment, furniture, fixtures, stock, and vehicles

personal selling A sales presentation delivered in a one-on-one manner

personnel risks Risks that directly affect individual employees but may have an indirect impact on a business as well

physical distribution (logistics) The activities of distribution involved in the physical relocation of products

physical inventory system A method that provides for periodic counting of items in inventory

piggyback franchising The operation of a retail franchise within the physical facilities of a host store

plant patent Registered protection for any distinct, new variety of living plant

pledged accounts receivable Accounts receivable used as collateral for a loan

political risk The potential for political forces in a country to negatively affect the performance of businesses operating within its borders

pop-up ads Advertisements that burst open on computer screens

pre-emptive right The right of stockholders to buy new shares of stock before they are offered to the public

precipitating event An event, such as losing a job, that moves an individual to become an entrepreneur

prestige pricing Setting a high price to convey an image of high quality or uniqueness

preventive maintenance Activities intended to prevent machine breakdowns, injuries to people, and damage to facilities

price A specification of what a seller requires in exchange for transferring ownership or use of a product or service

price lining strategy Setting a range of several distinct merchandise price levels

primary data New market information that is gathered by the firm conducting the research

prime rate The interest rate charged by commercial banks on loans to their most creditworthy customers

private carriers Lines of transport owned by the shippers

private equity Money provided by venture capitalists or private investors

private placement The sale of a firm's capital stock to selected individuals

pro forma financial statements Projections of a company's financial statements for up to five years, including balance sheets, income statements, and statements of cash flows, as well as cash budgets

product A total bundle of satisfaction—including a service, a good, or both—offered to consumers in an exchange transaction

product advertising The presentation of a business idea designed to make potential customers aware of a specific product or service and create a desire for it

product and trade name franchising A franchise agreement granting the right to use a widely recognized product or name

product item The lowest common denominator in the product mix—the individual item

product life cycle A detailed picture of what happens to a specific product's sales and profits over time

product line The sum of related individual product items

product mix The collection of a firm's total product lines

product mix consistency The similarity of product lines in a product mix

product/service plan A section of the business plan that describes the product and/or service to be provided and explains its merits

product strategy The way the product component of the marketing mix is used to achieve a firm's objectives

productivity The efficiency with which inputs are transformed into outputs

professional corporation A form of corporation that shields owners from liability and is set up for individuals in certain professional practices

professional employer organization (PEO) A personnel-leasing company that places employees on its own payroll and then "rents" them to employers on a permanent basis

professional manager A manager who uses systematic, analytical methods of management

project manufacturing A type of manufacturing operation designed to produce unique but similar products, often in an outdoor setting

promotion Marketing communications that inform and persuade consumers

promotional mix A blend of non-personal, personal, and special forms of communication aimed at a target market

prospecting A systematic process of continually looking for new customers

prospectus (offering memorandum) A document that contains all the information necessary to satisfy federal and state requirements for warning potential investors about the possible risks of the investment

proximate cause In the area of tort liability, a negligent act with a causal link to the damages sustained

publicity Information about a firm and its products or services that appears as a news item, usually free of charge

punitive damages A form of punishment that goes beyond compensatory damages, intending to punish wrongdoers for gross negligence or a callous disregard for the interests of others and to have a deterrent effect

purchasing The process of obtaining materials, equipment, and services from outside suppliers

pure risk The uncertainty associated with a situation where only loss or no loss can occur

Q

quality The features of a product or service that enable it to satisfy customers' needs

quality circle A group of employees who meet regularly to discuss quality-related problems

R

real estate mortgage A long-term loan with real property held as collateral

real property Land and anything physically attached to the land, such as buildings

reasonable (prudent person) standard The typical standard of care, based on what a reasonable or prudent person would have done under similar circumstances

reciprocation A powerful social rule based on an obligation to repay in kind what another has done for or provided to us

reengineering A fundamental restructuring to improve the operations process

reference groups Groups that an individual allows to influence his or her behavior

refugee A person who becomes an entrepreneur to escape an undesirable situation

reliability The consistency of a test in measuring job performance ability

reluctant entrepreneur A person who becomes an entrepreneur as a result of some severe hardship

repetitive manufacturing A type of manufacturing operation in which long production runs are used to produce a large quantity of a standardized product

replacement value method Determination of the value of a business by estimating the cost of replacing the firm's assets

replacement value of property The cost to replace or replicate property at today's prices

resources The basic inputs that a firm uses to conduct its business

retained earnings Profits less withdrawals (dividends) over the life of the business

return on assets Rate of return earned on a firm's total assets invested, computed as operating income divided by total assets

return on equity Rate of return earned on the owners' equity investment, computed as net income divided by owners' equity investment

revolving charge account A line of credit on which the customer may charge purchases at any time, up to a preestablished limit

revolving credit agreement A legal commitment by a bank to lend up to a maximum amount

risk The possibility of suffering harm or loss

risk control Minimizing potential losses by preventing, avoiding, or reducing risk

risk financing Making funds available to cover losses that could not be eliminated by risk control

risk management Ways of coping with risk that are designed to preserve the assets and earning power of a firm

risk retention Financing loss intentionally, through operating revenues or retained earnings

risk transfer Buying insurance or making contractual arrangements with others in order to transfer risk

royalties Fees paid by the licensee to the licensor for each unit produced under a licensing contract

S

S corporation (Subchapter S corporation) A type of corporation that offers limited liability to its owners but is taxed by the federal government as a partnership

sales forecast A prediction of how much of a product or service will be purchased within a market during a specified time period

sales promotion An inclusive term for any promotional techniques other than personal selling and advertising that stimulate the purchase of a particular good or service

secondary data Market information that has been previously compiled

Section 1244 stock Stock that offers some tax benefit to the stockholder in the case of corporate failure

segmentation variables The parameters used to distinguish one form of market behavior from another

self-insurance Designating part of a firm's earnings as a cushion against possible future losses

serendipity A gift for making desirable discoveries by accident

Service Corps of Retired Executives (SCORE) An SBA-sponsored group of retired executives who give free advice to small businesses

service mark A brand that a company has the exclusive right to use to identify a service

7(a) Loan Guaranty Program Loan program that helps small companies obtain financing through a guaranty provided by the SBA

7(m) Microloan Program SBA loan program that provides short-term loans of up to $35,000 to small businesses and not-for-profit childcare centers

short-range plan A plan that governs a firm's operations for one year or less

short-term notes Cash amounts borrowed from a bank or other lending sources that must be repaid within a short period of time

single-entry system A checkbook system of accounting reflecting only receipts and disbursements

single-segment strategy A strategy that recognizes the existence of several distinct market segments but focuses on only the most profitable segment

skimming price strategy Setting very high prices for a limited period before reducing them to more competitive levels

small business development centers (SBDCs) University-affiliated centers offering consulting, education, and other support to small businesses

Small Business Innovative Research (SBIR) program A government program that helps to finance companies that plan to transform laboratory research into marketable products

small business investment companies (SBICs) Privately owned banks, regulated by the Small Business Administration, that provide long-term loans and/or equity capital to small businesses

small business marketing Business activities that direct the creation, development, and delivery of a bundle of satisfaction from the creator to the targeted user and that satisfy the targeted user

social capital The advantage created by an individual's connections in a social network

social classes Divisions within a society having different levels of social prestige

social entrepreneurship Entrepreneurial activity whose goal is to find innovative solutions to social needs, problems, and opportunities

social network An interconnected system comprising relationships with other people

social responsibilities Ethical obligations to customers, employees, and the community

sole proprietorship A business owned by one person, who bears unlimited liability for the enterprise

span of control The number of subordinates supervised by one manager

special-purpose equipment Machines designed to serve specialized functions in the production process

spontaneous financing Short-term debts, such as accounts payable, that automatically increase in proportion to a firm's sales

stages in succession Phases in the process of transferring leadership of a family business from parent to child

stakeholders Individuals who either can affect or are affected by the performance of the company

statistical process control The use of statistical methods to assess quality during the operations process

stock certificate A document specifying the number of shares owned by a stockholder

strategic alliance An organizational relationship that links two or more independent business entities in a common endeavor

strategic decision A decision regarding the direction a firm will take in relating to its customers and competitors

strategy A plan of action that coordinates the resources and commitments of an organization to achieve superior performance

supply chain management A system of management that integrates and coordinates the means by which a firm creates or develops a product or service and delivers it to customers

sustainable competitive advantage (SCA) A value-creating position that is likely to endure over time

SWOT analysis A type of assessment that provides a concise overview of a firm's strategic situation

T

tangible resources Those organizational resources that are visible and easy to measure

tariffs Taxes charged on imported goods

term loan Money loaned for a 5- to 10-year term, corresponding to the length of time the investment will bring in profits

time and motion studies Detailed analyses of work processes with the goal of increasing the efficiency of human movement and tool design

times interest earned The ratio of operating income to interest charges

torts Wrongful acts or omissions for which an injured party can take legal action against the wrongdoer for monetary damages

total asset turnover The ratio of sales to total assets, showing the efficiency with which a firm's assets are used to generate sales

total cost The sum of cost of goods sold, selling expenses, and overhead costs

total fixed costs Costs that remain constant as the quantity produced or sold varies

total quality management (TQM) An all-encompassing management approach to providing high-quality products and services

total variable costs Costs that vary with the quantity produced or sold

trade credit Financing provided by a supplier of inventory to a given company

trade-credit agencies Privately owned organizations that collect credit information on businesses

trade dress Elements of a firm's distinctive image not protected by a trademark, patent, or copyright

trade intermediary An agency that distributes a company's products on a contract basis to customers in another country

trade mission A trip organized to help small business owners meet with potential buyers abroad and learn about cultural and regulatory obstacles in foreign markets

trademark A legal term identifying a firm's exclusive right to use a brand

transaction-based model A business model in which the website provides a mechanism for buying or selling products or services

transactional relationship An association between a business and a customer that relates to a purchase or a business deal

transfer of ownership Passing ownership of a family business to the next generation

24/7 e-tailing Electronic retailing providing round-the-clock access to products and services

Type A ideas Startup ideas centered around providing customers with an existing product not available in their market

Type B ideas Startup ideas, involving new technology, centered around providing customers with a new product

Type C ideas Startup ideas centered around providing customers with an improved product

U

underlying values Unarticulated ethical beliefs that provide a foundation for ethical behavior in a firm

Uniform Franchise Offering Circular (UFOC) A document accepted by the Federal Trade Commission as satisfying its franchise disclosure requirements

unlimited liability Liability on the part of an owner that extends beyond the owner's investment in the business

unsegmented strategy (mass marketing) A strategy that defines the total market as the target market

utility patent Registered protection for a new process or a product's function

V

validity The extent to which a test assesses true job performance ability

valuation based on comparables Determination of the value of a business by considering the actual market prices of firms that are similar to the firm being valued

variable inspection The determination of product acceptability based on a variable such as weight or length

variable pricing strategy Setting more than one price for a good or service in order to offer price concessions to certain customers

W

warranty A promise that a product will perform at a certain level or meet certain standards

Web sponsorship A type of advertising in which a firm pays another organization for the right to be part of that organization's Web page

work teams Groups of employees with freedom to function without close supervision

workers' compensation legislation Laws that obligate the employer to pay employees for injury or illness related to employment, regardless of fault

workforce diversity Differences among employees in such dimensions as gender, age, ethnicity, and race

working-capital cycle The daily flow of resources through a firm's working-capital accounts

working-capital management The management of current assets and current liabilities

Z

zoning ordinances Local laws regulating land use